THE HEAVENLY TRUMPET

Margaret M. Mitchell

The Heavenly Trumpet

John Chrysostom
and the Art of Pauline Interpretation

Westminster John Knox Press
LOUISVILLE • LONDON

Cover design by Lisa Buckley

Cover art courtesy of Leonidas Ananiades,
used with permission of the National Library, Athens.

This edition published by Westminster John Knox Press
Louisville, Kentucky

Previously published in 2000 by J.C.B. Mohr (Paul Siebeck)
P.O. Box 2040, D–7010 Tubingen.

This book is printed on acid-free paper that meets the American National Standards Institute Z39.48 standard. ∞

PRINTED IN THE UNITED STATES OF AMERICA

02 03 04 05 06 07 08 09 10 11—10 9 8 7 6 5 4 3 2 1

Cataloging-in-Publication Data is on file with the Library of Congress

ISBN 0–664–22510–1

For B.J. and Janet, in love and friendship

Table of Contents

Acknowledgements and Permissions

I have many to thank for making this study possible, and providing various forms of support and encouragement.

This book was completed in the academic year 1998–99, when I had the good fortune of receiving the incomparably generous support of the Henry Luce III Fellows in Theology Program, which has permitted me leave from my teaching responsibilities at the University of Chicago Divinity School. I would like to express my profound thanks to the Luce Foundation and ATS, and to Dean W. Clark Gilpin of the Divinity School for making this precious study time available to me. I have also greatly benefitted from the company of scholars the Luce Fellows program has created, which has been a source of invaluable and thoroughly enjoyable conversation. I am also grateful to McCormick Theological Seminary, where I taught from 1986–1998, for support for my research, especially a sabbatical leave during 1993–94, which I spent as a senior fellow in the Institute for the Advanced Study of Religion at the University of Chicago Divinity School.

In the completion of the manuscript and its movement into production I have incurred further debts of gratitude. Prof. Hans Dieter Betz, my dear friend and most provocative conversation partner, has stimulated my thinking in various ways, and offered priceless encouragement. I would especially like to thank him and the editors of Hermeneutische Untersuchungen zur Theologie, Profs. Pierre Bühler, Dietz Lange and Ingolf Dalferth, for accepting the book in this series; I am particularly pleased for it to appear here because I consider it among other things primarily a case study in biblical hermeneutics. I am also very grateful to other scholarly friends who generously read a long manuscript and offered valuable feedback, corrections, and encouragement: Robert M. Grant, Wayne A. Meeks, Paul Griffiths, Stephanie Paulsell, Kevin Madigan, and Richard A. Rosengarten. For the oversights that remain I unfortunately have only myself to thank.

Special thanks are reserved for Karl Frantz of the American Theological Library Association who out of friendship agreed once again to index one of my books. His computer wizardry, combined with scholarly sagacity, has improved the volume in countless ways. I could not possibly repay the long hours of toil this involved. My research assistants, Clare Rothschild and Jason Horn, also painstakingly worked their way through earlier drafts of the work to catch errors and infelicities. I thank Jason in particular for carefully compiling the list of abbreviations and bibliography, and for catching errant etas.

Thanks are also necessary to librarians and archivists at the University of Chicago, the Jesuit-Krauss-McCormick Library, and around the world. In particular I would like to acknowledge with gratitude the permission to reprint images from Biblioteca Ambrosiana (Milan), Biblioteca Apostolica Vaticana, the British Library, and the National Library in Athens, and thank the staff members of those libraries who were so helpful in procuring the prints. I am also grateful for an email act of kindness by Miodrag Markovic, of the Department of Art History at the University of Belgrade, who provided me with an image of the fresco from Lesnovo. Prof. Robert S. Nelson of the University of Chicago kindly provided me with a copy of his essay, "To Say and to See" in advance of its publication, for which I am also grateful.

I would like to acknowledge the University of Chicago Press, and the Johns Hopkins University Press for permission to reproduce and adapt portions of this work that appeared in earlier articles: "'The Archetypal Image': John Chrysostom's Portraits of Paul," *The Journal of Religion* 75 (1995) 15–43 (©1995 by The University of Chicago), and "'A Variable and Many-sorted Man': John Chrysostom's Treatment of Pauline Inconsistency," *Journal of Early Christian Studies* 6 (1998) 93–111 (©1998 by Johns Hopkins University).

The staff at Mohr Siebeck has done their usual expert job. I would particularly like to thank Mr. Matthias Spitzner for his remarkable competence and diligence in the publication of a complicated book, and Mr. Georg Siebeck, for the gracious and respectful way he treats his authors.

No one could ask for more encouraging friends or family than I have. Earle and Elvire Hilgert have taught me much about life, art, friendship, and the joys of conversation. From my wonderful family I would like to single out the inspiration of my Aunt, Bea Brennan, RSCJ, Mary and Dick Rosengarten, and my mother, Margaret Brennan Mitchell (of blessed memory). My husband, Rick, in addition to countless hours spent helping me to refine my argument (particularly his nettlesome question: "is this a book about Paul or a book about Chrysostom?"), and helping to bring my prose style up to the level of the eighteenth century, has been such a compelling and entertaining father to Nora and Katie that they hardly missed me in the many hours I spent behind my study door. He never (at least, as far as I know) emulated the wife of Henry Savile, who, as Philip Schaff tells it, "was so jealous of his devotion to Chrysostom that she threatened to burn his manuscript." And I want to thank Katie and Nora for patient endurance of my long hours with the book, and for stealing into my study for drawing paper (and kisses) on a regular basis. But most of all I am grateful for the sheer joy that surrounds them.

Two of my closest friends in the whole world are my brother and sister, to whom I happily dedicate this book.

Chicago, April 3, 2000   Margaret M. Mitchell

Preface

Over a decade ago I first began reading the homilies of John Chrysostom, with a very specific purpose in mind. I was then writing an exegetical study of Paul's 1 Corinthians, which I was convinced drew self-consciously upon Greco-Roman political commonplaces against factionalism, in order to persuade the tiny church community in that urbanized Greek context to end their divisiveness and pursue peace and concord in a unity centered in their existence as the body of Christ. Knowing that my own reading, even with the supporting evidence of considerable parallels from contemporary and near-contemporary Greco-Roman literature, was not self-validating, I sought verification of my thesis in the writings of Greek patristic authors, who, I judged, could be counted upon to recognize Greek political vocabulary and commonplace arguments when confronted with them. Besides the early writing, *1 Clement* (a crucially important source because it is a revision of 1 Corinthians for a later situation of church conflict), the next major Greek commentary on 1 Corinthians is that of Origen, which I found very useful, but somewhat teasingly so, because extant only in fragments. For a completely preserved, full-scale commentary on the letter in Greek one had to reach to the late fourth century, to the exegetical homilies of John Chrysostom. I immersed myself in these forty-four homilies and soon discovered that the rhetorically trained preacher from Antioch understood 1 Corinthians in very much the same way that I did, both commenting upon Paul's purpose and execution as pervasively rooted in the quest for ecclesial unity, and also even describing what Paul was doing by employing technical political terminology himself. I was thrilled and delighted to find such a compatriot reader across the centuries, one who had a far better pedigree than I in cultural literacy of late antique Greek culture in the cities of the east, and who therefore provided expert testimony for my particular thesis.

But as I read through Chrysostom's homilies on 1 Corinthians I was also aware that there was a great deal that I was "running past" (as John would chidingly put it) in my search for corroboration of a particular exegetical argument. In doing this, I was dimly conscious that I was perpetrating a crime that New Testament scholars are forever committing with patristic (and later) commentators: only engaging them on short visits which are really reconnaisance missions on our own terms, rather than conversations with these literary and oratorical giants on theirs. The image that always comes to my (guilty) mind is of being invited in to tea in good faith, and accepting ostensibly in kind, when one is really only interested in getting a single piece of information from the venerable ancient host, and once that is retrieved, packing up hurriedly and fleeing the antique, dusty drawing room leaving the host in mid-sentence. I was aware, for instance, that I tended to focus my attention on the first halves of the homilies, and to move rather quickly through the seemingly endless moralizing of their later portions, but always with a somewhat remorseful sensibility that in doing so I was evading what their author thought most important. I vowed (in my haste) to return to these texts at a later date to savor and understand them as hermeneutical products both of an insightful exegetical mind and of the very particular rhetorical, liturgical and ecclesial culture of late antiquity. I was also cognizant of the fact that this homily series on 1 Corinthians was only a fraction of an immense corpus of writings by Chrysostom who, in addition to being the most prolific commentator on Paul preserved from the early church, left extensive quantities of other exegetical homilies, treatises, panegyrics, and letters. Coming to this literary corpus from the tiny pamphlet known as the New Testament, Chrysostom's mountain of texts loomed large, enticing for its promise of a raft of fresh source material, yet frighteningly indigestible. How could one even begin to assimilate and comprehend this huge collection of texts? And how could one do it in a manner that exhibits better drawing room behavior than the impatient guest one knows oneself tempted to be?

Chrysostom himself provided my answer to these questions. One finding of my earliest readings of Chrysostom arrested my attention to such a degree that it has preoccupied me ever since, and has provided my entry-way into Chrysostom's voluminous oeuvre on Paul. In his thirteenth homily on 1 Corinthians, when Chrysostom meets the famous passage 4:16 ("be imitators of me"), he composes a portrait of the apostle Paul; in fact, what he constructs by literary artistry is a portrait within a portrait, of Paul as the artist painting his own self-portrait in imitation of Christ.[1] The graphic literalism of the passage surprised and charmed me. New Testament scholars often use the term "portrait" – to refer to the literary characterization of Paul in Acts, or in the deutero-Pauline epistles, for instance – but here I was face-to-face with an *actual* portrait of Paul from the early church. It was not the kind of (supposedly) straightforward physical description of Paul as the hermeneutically suggestive narrative passage in *Acta Pauli et Theclae*,[2] but a more complicated rhetorical and artistic product. Amazed by my discovery, I carefully translated the passage in question (observing its exact technical vocabulary from the graphic arts as I went), and posted the excerpt above my desk, alongside a few graphic images of the apostle I had collected through the years. Always instinctively aware that each Pauline interpreter is governed by a mental image of the author, I now had before me the example of an ancient exegete who was explicit

---

[1] I provide a translation and detailed analysis of this passage below, pp. 50–55, and 104–17.
[2] See the discussion of this important passage in chap. 4, n. 20.

about it, and who in the act of interpreting Paul's letters quite overtly was *composing* the author whose words (and life) he sought to understand. Next to that passage (on a rather cluttered wall) I soon placed a Chrysostomic caption: Οὐδὲν τῆς Παύλου ψυχῆς ἀγωνιστικώτερον ("nothing was more ready for combat than Paul's soul"). In the juxtaposition of these two Pauline word-portraits this study was born.

A sabbatical afforded me the possibility to join Chrysostom for an extended tea and to hear from him about the art of Pauline interpretation. I spent a year blissfully reading in Chrysostom's wide corpus, enjoying his clear Attic prose, and gaining a sense of the larger literary and historical contours of his interpretations of Paul. I found mention of Paul and his letters to be ubiquitous in John's writings, and in particular devoured his set of seven panegyrics to Paul, which are largely unknown to New Testament scholars. Subsequently, even as I encountered in Frederic Henry Chase, Chrysostomus Baur, Maurice Wiles, and a few others notice of Chrysostom's pervasive and intense interest in the person of Paul, I was greatly surprised to find that a paucity of scholarship exists on this most important patristic commentator's interpretations of Paul. In my readings in Chrysostom's writings I soon was able to articulate what is *the* interpretive key to John's exegesis: his author-centered devotion to the person of Paul. For Chrysostom, Pauline biography and exegesis of the Pauline epistles go hand in hand; they are by no means separate tasks, just as the composition of portraits of the author to assist readers in understanding the text must accompany explication and application of his words. I soon learned that my initially discovered passage of Pauline portraiture by Chrysostom was one of many in his collection of writings, and began to collect the myriad texts in which John dwelt lovingly on his hero and to seek to comprehend them as rhetorical, artistic and hermeneutical creations grounded in the quite specific historical and cultural context of the late fourth century, with its distinctive concerns: the "victory of Christianity," the rise of ecclesiastical oratory, the cult of the saints, martyrdom and forms of ascetic life.

John's portraits of his beloved Paul must be seen as part and parcel of his interpretation of the apostle's letters, for he regards Paul as alive and speaking the very words there penned. Thus, taking my cue from Chrysostom's own hermeneutical posture, in this study I have sought to read him in terms of what *he* thought most important, rather than arbitrarily imposing upon him the pressing questions or exegetical presuppositions of other, imported, contexts. That is why the present study begins with John's portraits of the apostle, for these are the starting place and the inescapable foundation of his interpretive enterprise. And they help us to understand the person and values of John himself, as he has inscribed them in his depictions of the person of his saintly author. John's portraits of Paul, as we shall see, constitute a type of creative literary mosaic. They draw upon the biblical sources of the letters and the Acts of the Apostles, but reconfigure and recast them in the forms of Greco-Roman pulpit rhetoric. Each individual portrait is crafted

to suit a given catechetical and oratorical function, just as each has its own implications for the interpretation of the epistles. This hermeneutical starting place,
with the construction of the author, also allows us to put at the forefront the issues
of personality and relationship as they apply in biblical interpretation: even as he
was composing portraits of Paul as "the archetypal image" of virtue as he knew it
(particularly embodying the monastic virtues which defined his own life), Chrysostom was making himself over in the Pauline image. Symbiotic engagement
with the author is an essential ingredient of the task of biblical interpretation as
John carried it out, to such an extent that one cannot separate John's "biographical"
interest in Paul from some imagined, distinct "exegetical" conclusions. But who
did he imagine Paul to be?

The present study, a hermeneutical essay on the nature of Pauline interpretation, is a kind of "gallery exhibition" of Chrysostom's many and varied portraits
of the apostle Paul. These portraits, including miniatures and full-scale images,
portraits of Paul's body, of his soul, and of the episodes of his life, are found
sprinkled throughout John's voluminous treatises and biblical homilies. In the
present book I have sought to bring together as many of these copious sources as
possible in one place, and analyze them as the complex rhetorical compositions
they are. Prominent on the enormous heap of source material is Chrysostom's
remarkably rich set of seven encomia to Paul, in which the apostle is portrayed in
complex and diverse hues, and deliberately varied brush strokes. These panegyrics
have unfortunately been largely overlooked in scholarship, abetted by the fact that
the only English translation of them has been long out of print (and was not
widely available in the first place).[3] Those who wished to read and study this
unique set of oratorical productions (assuming they had even heard of their existence) have had either to read them in the Greek,[4] or depend upon French or
German translations. But even in European scholarship these discourses have
never received sustained analysis in terms of their rhetorical invention and disposition, their place in the history of Pauline traditions, or their relationship to
Chrysostom's larger hermeneutical and catechetical project of Pauline personification. I shall seek to ameliorate that situation here by offering a translation of the
seven discourses, and a compositional analysis of each of those fascinating sermons
as set within their appropriate wider contexts.

In the course of this investigation of John's portraits of Paul we shall see that in
constructing his author, Paul, Chrysostom was engaging in a rhetorical art wedding literary and oral conventions, biblical sources, and authorial imagination and
ingenuity to project fresh and vivid verbal images of the apostle before the eyes and
ears of his congregations. At the same time, by idealizing Paul as the "archetypal

---

[3] Thomas Halton, *In Praise of Saint Paul by John Chrysostom* (Washington: Catholic University
of America, 1963).

[4] For which we do have a fine modern critical edition prepared by Auguste Piédagnel (*Sources
chrétiennes* 300).

image" of Christian virtue, Chrysostom's literary portraiture served as a rhetorical vehicle for social construction and replication of the Pauline model in the now-Christian society of late antiquity. These public mental images of Paul that John conjures up in the presence of his urban church audiences are the living ghost, the animating spirit hovering over the entire enterprise of biblical interpretation. They are the author come to life in saintly power to speak to auditors of the present generation and guide them to perfection by his word and example.

The present volume has a concentrated focus on John's interpretation of the *corpus Paulinum*.[5] As stated, the double entendre is intentional, for what is so conspicuous about Chrysostom as a Pauline interpreter is his fascination with both Paul's person and his letters, as coordinating and mutual influences in his exegetical enterprise. Contemporary New Testament scholars continue to differ about the importance of Pauline biography for Pauline exegesis, and though many still regard these as separate questions,[6] I would argue on principle that all exegetical projects depend upon some explicit or (more often) implicit mental image of Paul, the author.[7] In John Chrysostom we have a marvelous subject with whom to test and explore that axiom, for he quite explicitly and lovingly set about the task of portraying his cherished author before the eyes of his congregations, not merely as a diversion, but as an inescapably central part of the exegetical task. If love is the prerequisite for understanding, as John claims, then the subject to be loved must be introduced, vividly and often, as a prelude to fruitful literary conversation. Exegetical homiletics is for Chrysostom an inherently necromantic art, by which the dead come to life and breathe spiritual words to the living in order to lead them from earth to heaven. Hence in seeking to understand this most important patristic interpreter of Paul we must begin with Paul himself – that is, Paul as John knows and composes him – because that is where he begins.

---

[5] This dynamic has been nicely captured by François Bovon, "Paul comme document et Paul comme monument," in *Chrétiens en conflit: l'épître de Paul aux Galates, Dossier pour l'animation biblique*, ed. J. Allaz, *et al.* (Essais bibliques 13; Paris: Labor et Fides, 1987) 54–65.

[6] The pervasive genre of contemporary Pauline scholarship remains the commentary on a single letter, with exegetical studies in general normally separated from biographical investigations, at least in theory (see the complaints of A. E. Harvey, *Renewal Through Suffering: A Study of 2 Corinthians* [Studies of the New Testament and its World; Edinburgh: T & T Clark, 1996] 1–9). Biography as such is considered a separate genre (see Jerome Murphy-O'Connor, *Paul: A Critical Life* [Oxford: Clarendon, 1996]; Martin Hengel, *The Pre-Christian Paul* [trans. John Bowden; Philadelphia: Trinity Press International, 1991], and the earlier classic work of John Knox, *Chapters in a Life of Paul* [rev. ed.; Macon, GA: Mercer University Press, 1987]; the biographical genre was adapted recently by the novelist A. N. Wilson into a kind of historical psychological novel in *Paul: The Mind of the Apostle* [London/New York: W. W. Norton, 1997]).

[7] An easy way to see this is in treatments of Pauline consistency or inconsistency, for example, where each exegete works from presuppositions about how much self-contradiction Paul could have sustained, while remaining the person they imagine him to be (see my article, "'A Variable and Many-sorted Man': John Chrysostom's Treatment of Pauline Inconsistency," *Journal of Early Christian Studies* 6 [1998] 93–111).

In a recent essay Karlfried Froehlich has rightly maintained that the history of interpretation contains "a much more colorful palette of normative images of Paul"[8] than has been recognized or drawn upon. The present study answers the mandate implied by that remark by uncovering the range of portraits of Paul in the writings of a single author, his greatest patristic admirer. For this task Chrysostom is twice valuable, for while New Testament and patristics scholars customarily speak of "images" or "portraits" of Paul,[9] Chrysostom uses these terms with overt reference to the artistic practice and theory which underlie them. In the course of his writings Chrysostom produces a whole gallery of vivid portraits of his favorite saint. In this way he is of salutary importance, not only for the content of his portraits of Paul, fascinating literary compositions in themselves, but also for the theory of portraiture which animates them, and the rhetorical conventions which they embody. Chrysostom's writings are also valuable for their significant herme-neutical reflections upon the relationship between the author and his texts, and the role of exegesis and homiletical interpretation in bringing that author to life for the hearers. Following decades which have proclaimed "the death of the au-thor,"[10] bringing Chrysostom's interpretations of Paul to our attention at this moment − a quite literal exercise in "the project of authorial renewal"[11] − has the salutary effect of illuminating some present hermeneutical assumptions, both im-plicit and explicit, and of bringing into relief some of the ways in which the dynamic of his biblical interpretation remains present and has died out, to both our gain and our detriment. It also provides a marvelous example of the very complex interpenetration of text and image in the interpretive task, as John draws from the texts a verbal image of his author, which in turn becomes a template for the interpretation of the texts − and for the formation of the self who interprets.

The purpose of this study is to collect the abundant depictions of Paul found in Chrysostom's writings, and to analyze them both as rhetorical products of late

---

[8] "Which Paul? Observations on the Image of the Apostle in the History of Biblical Ex-egesis," *New Perspectives on Historical Theology. Essays in Memory of John Meyendorff*, ed. B. Nassif (Grand Rapids, MI: Eerdmans, 1996) 279–99, 288; cf. Bovon, "Paul comme document et Paul comme monument," 54, on the second century as "le temps de la réception polychrome des épîtres pauliniennes."

[9] Among recent titles, see, for instance, Donald Coggan, *Paul. Portrait of a Revolutionary* (London: Hodder & Stoughton, 1984); John C. Lentz, *Luke's Portrait of Paul* (SNTSMS 77; Cambridge: Cambridge University Press, 1993); Marie Eloise Rosenblatt, *Paul the Accused: his Portrait in the Acts of the Apostles* (Collegeville, MN: Liturgical Press, 1995). This metaphorical use of the concept for literary works goes largely unexamined (how does a literary "portrait" work?), though pieces of an answer to that question are treated in other generic discussions on, for instance, biography, or the rhetorical species epideictic rhetoric. My goal here is to work toward a clearer conception of what portraiture in ancient literature involved.

[10] As discussed and critiqued by Seán Burke, *The Death and Return of the Author: Criticism and Subjectivity in Barthes, Foucault and Derrida* (Edinburgh: Edinburgh University Press, 1992). We shall return to this topic in chap. 8, pp. 433–36.

[11] The phrase is Burke's (*Death and Return*, 169).

fourth-century Christian oratory, and as hermeneutical tools for biblical interpretation in that context (as well as the later contexts in which they were to become so influential). How does Chrysostom imagine the person of Paul? What are the salient and recurrent features of his portraits of the apostle? What purposes (didactic, apologetic, entertaining) propel and inform this portraiture? Who is his Paul — and for whom is he presented, and why? What aspects of the apostolic self and life seem to require a "make over"? What tensions in Paul's biography do these portraits seek to resolve, and how? Which are the most defining deeds of Paul's career — his sufferings, his miracles, his persuasive proclamation? Does the biblical picture of Paul exhibit a coherent, comprehensible personality, or not? To address these and other questions about how Chrysostom viewed Paul, once we bring together Chrysostom's varied portraits of his beloved apostle, we shall explore their content and contours, and through them the nature of author-centered biblical interpretation as John engages in it. From his example we can gain insights into the dynamics, functions, and artistry involved in these acts of composition of the author in the course of interpreting his writings.

Above all, for Chrysostom, this investigation requires that we properly situate his orations and writings within the expectations and conventions of his Greek literary-rhetorical culture. Previous scholarship on Chrysostom's portrayal of Paul has been content mostly to explain these portraits as the palpable evidence of the bishop's personal devotion to his favorite saint. This study will demonstrate how Chrysostom (like other late-fourth century Christian orators in varying ways and degrees), adopted and adapted the conventions of Greco-Roman rhetoric for verbal depiction of a person — epithets, encomia, *ekphraseis* — in order to create literary portraits by which he might lionize his favorite apostle. The purpose of Chrysostom's portraiture was to bring the saint to life in the presence of his congregational audience so that they, too, might experience the living encounter with Paul that John describes himself having when reading Paul's letters, and, most importantly, by hearing these portraits, might become like the apostle.

This study seeks to contribute to a thorough reconstruction of the overarching hermeneutical, literary, rhetorical and sociological framework within which Chrysostom, this most important of Pauline patristic commentators, operated. I seek to foster greater attention to Chrysostom's interpretation by New Testament scholars within a more thorough and contextually rich framework of understanding. And at the same time, I seek to bring contemporary Pauline scholarship to bear on Chrysostom studies, so that the discrete and intersecting questions and methods which govern each can be brought into creative and critical conversation. In particular, by employing the tools of historical rhetorical analysis[12] and concepts

---

[12] I have defined and employed this approach, which entails an examination of ancient Christian documents in the light of contemporary rhetorical conventions and possibilities as known from both actual rhetorical products and rhetorical handbooks, in *Paul and the Rhetoric of*

of Pauline "portraiture" which have arisen in work on New Testament materials,[13] I seek not to mine the writings of John Chrysostom for exegetical nuggets, but instead to understand them as meditations on Pauline texts which are themselves heavily influenced by the rhetorical expectations and religious sensibilities of Greek culture in the east in late antiquity. Chrysostom's portraits of Paul in many ways exemplify the major issues at stake in late antique Christianity and its dynamics of social creation through literary artistry, and therefore make an important contribution to those areas of study, in turn. In sum, this book is an attempt to encourage and provide resources for continuing conversation between John Chrysostom and modern interpreters who approach him from both periods of specialization. It proceeds from the recognition that Chrysostom's homilies on the Pauline epistles, and his other writings, are first order sources for the history of interpretation and the *Wirkungsgeschichte* of the Pauline corpus. But what Chrysostom's oeuvre bequeathed to later generations, including the present, is not merely a set of propositions about the meaning of Paul's words in the letters, but also a gallery of portraits of the apostle who speaks in them, which have had an equally pervasive effect on that history of reading and delectation of the Pauline corpus.

Our investigation of Chrysostom's author-based interpretation will proceed in the following manner. Chapter 1 provides an introduction to the sources upon which we shall draw in this study, both in terms of Chrysostom's oeuvre, and the rhetorical tradition which shaped and formed him, and constituted the invisible contract of expectations with the audience for whom he spoke and wrote.[14] It also positions this book within the history of scholarship pertaining to Chrysostom's

---

Reconciliation: An Exegetical Investigation of the Language and Composition of 1 Corinthians (HUT 28; Tübingen: J. C. B. Mohr [Paul Siebeck], 1991; Lousville: Westminster/John Knox, 1993) 1–19. The inescapable need for this kind of analysis in interpreting Chrysostom's writings was demonstrated most effectively by Robert L. Wilken, *John Chrysostom and the Jews: Rhetoric and Reality in the Late 4th Century* (The Transformation of the Classical Heritage 4; Berkeley: University of California Press, 1983), esp. 95–127.

[13] See, for example, Hans Dieter Betz, "Paul's 'Second Presence' in Colossians," *Texts and Contexts: Biblical Texts in Their Textual and Situational Contexts: Essays in Honor of Lars Hartman*, ed. Tord Fornberg and David Hellholm (Oslo: Scandinavian University Press, 1995) 507–18, esp. pp. 516–17, on "Paul's Literary Portrait"; *idem*, "The Portrait of Jesus in the Sermon on the Mount," *Currents in Theology and Mission* 25 (1998) 165–75; Raymond F. Collins, "The Image of Paul in the Pastorals," *LTP* 31 (1975) 147–73; M. C. de Boer, "Images of Paul in the Post-Apostolic Period," *CBQ* 43 (1980) 359–80, and further literature on portraits of Paul in the deutero-Paulines and Pastorals cited in chap. 1, n. 20.

[14] There has been debate in scholarship over the oral and literary nature of the homilies which have come down to us (see chap. 7, n. 114), but quite clearly most of the homilies, even if not all, have actual live congregations in view. More complicated is the question of *which* audiences were addressed in each homily or homily set, as demonstrated effectively by the recent work of Pauline Allen, "John Chrysostom's Homilies on I and II Thessalonians: The Preacher and His Audience," and Wendy Mayer, "John Chrysostom and His Audiences: Distinguishing Different Congregations at Antioch and Constantinople," both in *Studia Patristica*, vol. 31, ed. Elizabeth A. Livingstone (Louvain: Peeters, 1997) 3–21 and 70–75, respectively.

interpretation of Paul, and seeks to unite the fervent interests of the few past scholars who have more than briefly mentioned John's devotion to Paul with contemporary research into the role of language, literature and rhetoric in the formation of the church in late antiquity. Chapter 2 seeks to ground Chrysostom's Pauline portraiture within his own historical context by demonstrating the hermeneutical, ethical, literary, Scriptural, cultural and artistic background to the phenomenon of literary/oratorical portraiture. There we shall tackle the question of why Chrysostom constructed these verbal images of Paul in the first place, which is an essential prerequisite to an informed and rich encounter with the portraits themselves. Chapters 3 through 6 constitute the gallery itself: an exhibition of John's portraits of Paul arranged first according to size and scope, with miniatures coming first (Chapter 3), followed by full-scale portraits (Chapters 4–6), arranged according to the sub-categories of the ancient encomium: body portraits (Chapter 4), soul portraits (Chapter 5), and biographical portraits, both holistic and episodic (Chapter 6). Throughout these four chapters I shall situate Chrysostom's writings within Greco-Roman rhetorical culture in my analyses of many key compositions which demonstrate his practiced use of well-known and well-documented rhetorical techniques. Chapters 7 and 8 bring this material and the results of my analysis into dialogue with salient issues involved in the two broad areas of research it impacts: late antique Christian history specifically, and Pauline interpretation generally (Chapter 7 begins with a recapitulation of the substance of the argument in the previous chapters, so those who would like to fast-forward to the implications of this work could start there). In Chapter 7 I shall argue that Chrysostom's portraits of Paul, while defying the traditional maps of patristic biblical interpretation as fundamentally constituted by the allegory/literalism polarity, contribute significantly to recent scholarly efforts to reconceptualize and refigure patristic exegetical practice. Further, Chapter 7 asks how Chrysostom's sometimes hyperbolic praises of Paul fit with his understanding of history, and with his Christology, asking if by his concentrated and lavish attention to Paul John doesn't compromise either his Antiochene sensibility or his Nicene Christology. The answer to both questions rests to a large degree on the literary forms and social goals John seeks to wed in his Pauline portraits. In that context I propose a coherent picture of the social, ecclesial and political functions of Pauline portraiture in John's pastoral ministry and vision of the Christian society within the context of the late fourth century. Chapter 8 brings Chrysostom's enthusiastically author-centered interpretation of Paul into conversation with others in the history of interpretation who have sought to comprehend the apostle's writings, in order to see if he is unique in this regard. Through a comparison of Chrysostom with his most famous Western contemporary, Augustine, and with representatives of late twentieth-century American Pauline scholarship (my contemporaries), I shall demonstrate the extent to which Pauline exegesis is always interwoven with portraiture of the author, even if not always performed with the level of conspicuous artistry John displays. I shall close the study with a few remarks on the contributions and confusions Chrysostom's portraits of Paul may pose for the contemporary debate in literary criticism on the role of the author in interpretation.

The book has two appendices, which correspond to the literary and imagistic components of John's portraits of his beloved apostle. Appendix 1 provides my fresh translation into English of John's seven Pauline panegyrics, *de laudibus sancti Pauli*, which is the basis for the analysis of each oration found in the body of the book. I hope this translation will make these orations better known and more accessible to a wider audience. Readers unfamiliar with these discourses may wish to begin there, so as to encounter the orations as literary wholes, at first uninfluenced by my analysis, as well as to prime the pump of their curiosity about why a late antique author would concentrate his energies in such a way as John does.

Throughout my work on this project on Chrysostom's portraits of Paul I have become increasingly attuned to its synesthetic dimensions. Whereas Chrysostom was drawing portraits with words which his congregation would hear in order to "see," in turn I am depicting John's oral speech, known to me only in a written form, in words of my own, in order that my readers might be able to encounter and appreciate what this oral literary portraiture of the author-saint is intended to do, and what implications it has for the task of biblical exegesis, past and present. In grappling with these mixed media (an unavoidable part of the interpretive task) I have myself turned to graphic portraiture to accompany and inspire my text-based hermeneutical inquiry, and have incorporated various artistic images of Paul and Chrysostom into the argument in order to illustrate and (I hope) deepen some of the analysis. Appendix 2 provides a catalogue and set of bibliographic resources for the artistic images of Chrysostom and Paul from the ninth to the fourteenth century that I have collected and drawn upon in the argument of the book.

Because of the sheer quantity of Chrysostom's writings, at the outset of my book I must acknowedge that what I have written here is not exhaustive of its subject. Especially for one inclined as I am, both by temperament and by the culture of New Testament studies in my age, to track down every example on every single point, this venture into Chrysostom's plethora of texts has been both daunting and humbling. I hope that in the selections I have made in order to produce an orderly account and cogent argument, that Chrysostom's thinking and writing about Paul are adequately and accurately represented. Writing this book has been a continual battle with the dimensions of my own literary canvas, between the quests for breadth and for depth; my greatest fear is to have failed in both respects. Especially because this is part of a continuing research project into Chrysostom's interpretation of Paul, I will be most grateful for any feedback from other scholars that will assist my ability to satisfy either or both of those requirements better in the future. I would also like to highlight the fact that in the course of reading Chrysostom's works and writing this book I have formulated many more research questions than I have been able to tackle here. Some of these are mentioned in the notes in the hope that other researchers may take them up in the future.

One of the many joys of discovery in the process of writing this book has been the making of scholarly acquaintance with those long dead whose masterful and intricate work has facilitated mine in countless ways. In that spirit I would like to borrow the words with which Frederick Field in 1849 ended the preface to his critical edition of Chrysostom's *homiliae in epistulam ad Romanos: Valeas, Lector, et incepto nostro faveas.*[15]

---

[15] Frederick Field, *Sancti patris nostri Joannis Chrysostomi archiepiscopi Constantinopolitani in divi Pauli Epistolam ad Romanos* (Oxford: J. H. Parker, 1849) xiv (volume 1 of his *Interpretatio omnium epistolarum paulinarum*).

Note on Style

In this book the Greek texts of all Chrysostom's works are cited either by reference to Migne, *Patrologia graeca* (citations in brackets, followed by volume and columns), in which Chrysostom's writings span vols. 47–64, or *Sources chrétiennes* (abbreviated SC, followed by volume and page number), in which series seventeen volumes of individual works have so far appeared. For Chrysostom's homilies on the Pauline epistles, I have used the critical edition of Frederick Field, *Interpretatio omnium epistolarum paulinarum* in my research, but always cite the Migne because it will be the most accessible to readers. Where significant variants are found in the Field edition, I incorporate them and give the citation, preceded by Field, followed by volume and page number. Throughout I employ the abbreviations of Chrysostom's works used in Lampe's *Patristic Greek Lexicon*, followed by homily number (if applicable) and paragraph number (all are listed in the "Abbreviations of Ancient Works Cited"). All translations of Chrysostom's writings in this book are my own, except in the few instances indicated, as are translations of the New Testament and other patristic writers, unless stated otherwise. Classical texts are cited according to Loeb translations where available (as listed on pp. 510–13), though often altered by me, as indicated. Translations of other ancient writings are my own unless marked with an attribution. A list of all other abbreviations of ancient writers and periodicals is given below (pp. xxvii–xxxii). It largely follows the *Journal of Biblical Literature*'s "Instructions for Contributors" and *SBL Handbook of Style*, ed. Patrick H. Alexander, et al. (Peabody, MA: Hendrickson, 1999), Liddell-Scott-Jones, *Greek-English Lexicon*, Lampe's *Patristic Greek Lexicon*, and the *Oxford Classical Dictionary* (3rd edition).

Abbreviations of Ancient Works Cited

	A. Joh.	*acta Joannis*
	A. Paul. et Thecl.	*acta Pauli et Theclae*
	A. Petr. et Paul.	*acta Petri et Pauli* (Ps–Marcellus)
	mart. Apollon.	*martyrium Apollonii*
	mart. Paul.	*martyrium Pauli*
	mart. Petr.	*martyrium Petri*
	mart. Petr. et Paul.	*martyrium Petri et Pauli*
	mart. Polyc.	*martyrium Polycarpi*
Alexander	*Fig.*	*de figuris*
	Rh.	περὶ ῥητορικῶν ἀφορμῶν
Aphthonios	*Prog.*	*progymnasmata*
Aristides	*Or.*	*orationes*
	Rh.	τέχναι ῥητορικαί
Aristotle	*Eth. Nic.*	*ethica nicomachea*
	Rh.	*rhetorica*
[Aristotle]	*Phgn.*	*physiognomonica*
	Rh. Al.	*rhetorica ad Alexandrum*
Augustine	*c. ep. Pel.*	*contra duas epistulas Pelagianorum*
	c. Faust.	*contra Faustum Manicheum*
	c. Jul.	*contra Julianum*
	conf.	*confessiones*
	ep. Rom. inch.	*epistulae ad Romanos inchoata expositio*
	ex. prop. Rom.	*expositio quarundam propositionum ex epistula Apostoli ad Romanos*
	gest. Pel.	*de gestis Pelagii*
	Jo. ev. tr.	*in Johannis evangelium tractatus*
	pecc. mer.	*de peccatorum meritis et remissione et de baptismo parvulorum*
	praed. sanct.	*de praedestinatione sanctorum*
	serm.	*sermones*
	Simpl.	*ad Simplicianum*
Callistratus	*Stat.*	*statuarum descriptiones*
Cicero	*Att.*	*epistulae ad Atticum*
	De Or.	*de oratore*
	Fam.	*epistulae ad familiares*
	Inv. Rhet.	*de inventione*
	Phil.	*Philippicae*
[Cicero]	*Rhet. Her.*	*rhetorica ad Herennium*
Clement of Alexandria	*Strom.*	*stromateis*

Demosthenes	*Or.*	*orationes*
Dionysius of Halicarnassus	*Comp.*	*de compositione verborum*
	Is.	*de Isaeo*
	Isoc.	*de Isocrate*
	Lys.	*de Lysia*
[Dionysius]	*Rh.*	*rhetorica*
Doxopater	*Aphth.*	*commentarium in Aphthonii progymnasmata*
Epictetus	*Diss.*	*dissertationes*
Epiphanius	*haer.*	*panarion (= adversus lxx haereses)*
Eusebius	*h.e.*	*historia ecclesiastica*
	v. C.	*vita Constantini*
George of Alexandria	*vita Joh. Chrys.*	*de vita sancti Joannis Chrysostomi*
Gregory of Nazianzus	*Or.*	*orationes*
Gregory of Nyssa	*hom. in cant.*	*in Canticum canticorum*
	perf.	*de perfectione et qualem oporteat esse Christianum*
	Thdr.	*de Theodoro martyre*
Hermogenes	*Meth.*	περὶ μεθόδου δεινότητος
	Prog.	προγυμνάσματα
Herodian	*Fig.*	*de figuris*
Homer	*Il.*	*Iliad*
	Od.	*Odyssea*
Isidore of Pelusium	*Ep.*	*epistolarum libri quinque*
Isocrates	*Or.*	*orationes*
Jerome	*comm. in ep. ad Philem.*	*commentarius in epistulam ad Philemonem*
	vir. ill.	*de viris illustribus*
John Chrysostom	*catech.*	*catecheses ad illuminandos 1–2*
	comm. in Gal.	*commentarium in epistulam ad Galatas*
	comp.	*comparatio regis et monachi*
	compunct. 1	*ad Demetrium de compunctione (lib. 1)*
	compunct. 2	*ad Stelechium de compunctione (lib. 2)*
	cruc.	*de cruce et latrone (hom. 1–2)*
	El. et vid.	*in Heliam et viduam*
	eleem.	*de eleemosyna*
	ep. Olymp.	*epistulae ad Olympiadem (ep. 1–17)*
	Eutrop.	*in Eutropium eunuchum*
	exp. in Job	*specimen expositionis in Job*
	exp. in Ps.	*expositiones in Psalmos quosdam*
	fem. reg.	*quod regulares feminae viris cohabitare non debeant*
	fr. in Jer.	*fragmenta in Jeremiam*
	fr. Job	*fragmenta in Job*
	fragmenta in 1 Jo.	*fragmenta in primam sancti Joannis epistulam*
	fragmenta in Jac.	*fragmenta in epistulam sancti Jacobi*
	fragmenta in Petr.	*fragmenta in primam sancti Petri epistulam*

grat.	*non esse ad gratiam concionandum*
hom. div.	*homiliae diversae*
hom. in 1 Cor.	*homiliae in epistulam primam ad Corinthios (hom. 1–44)*
hom. in 1 Cor. 7:39	in illud: *mulier alligata est*
hom. in 1 Cor. 10:1	in dictum Pauli: *nolo vos ignorare*
hom. in 1 Cor. 11:19	in dictum Pauli: *oportet haereses esse*
hom. in 1 Cor. 15:28	in illud: *quando ipsi subiciet omnia*
hom. in 1 Thess.	*homiliae in epistulam primam ad Thessalonicenses (hom. 1–11)*
hom. in 1 Tim.	*homiliae in epistulam primam ad Timotheum (hom. 1–18)*
hom. in 1 Tim. 5:9	in illud: *vidua eligatur*
hom. in 2 Cor.	*homiliae in epistulam secundam ad Corinthios (hom. 1–30)*
hom. in 2 Cor. 4:13	in illud: *habentes eundem spiritum*
hom. in 2 Cor. 11:1	in illud: *utinam sustineretis modicum*
hom. in 2 Cor. 12:9	in illud: *sufficit tibi gratia mea*
hom. in 2 Tim.	*homiliae in epistulam secundam ad Timotheum (hom. 1–10)*
hom. in 2 Tim. 3:1	in illud: *hoc scitote quod in novissimis diebus*
hom. in Ac.	*homiliae in Acta apostolorum (hom. 1–55)*
hom. in Ac. 9:1	*homiliae in mutatione nominum (hom. 1–4)*
hom. in Ac. princ.	*homiliae in principium Actorum apostolorum*
hom. in Col.	*homiliae in epistulam ad Colossenses (hom. 1–12)*
hom. in Eph.	*homiliae in epistulam ad Ephesios (hom. 1–24)*
hom. in Gal. 2:11	in illud: *faciem ei restiti*
hom. in Gen.	*homiliae in Genesim (hom. 1–67)*
hom. in Heb.	*homiliae in epistulam ad Hebraeos (hom. 1–34)*
hom. in Is. 45:7	*ego dominus deus feci lumen*
hom. in Jo.	*homiliae in sanctum Joannem apostolum et evangelistam (hom. 1–88)*
hom. in Jo. 5:19	in illud: *filius ex se nihil facit*
hom. in Mt.	*homiliae in sanctum Matthaeum apostolum et evangelistam (hom. 1–90)*
hom. in Mt. 18:23	*homilia in parabolam debitoris*
hom. in Mt. 26:39	in illud: *pater, si possible est, transeat*
hom. in Phil.	*homiliae in epistulam ad Philippenses (hom. 1–15)*
hom. in Phil. 1:18	*de profectu evangelii*
hom. in Philm.	*homiliae in epistulam ad Philemonem (hom. 1–3)*

hom. in Rom.	*homiliae in epistulam ad Romanos (hom. 1–32)*
hom. in Rom. 5:3	*homilia de gloria in tribulationibus*
hom. in Rom. 8:28	in illud: *diligentibus deum omnia cooperantur in bonum*
hom. in Rom. 12:20	in illud: *si esurierit inimicus*
hom. in Rom. 16:3	in illud: *salutate Priscillam et Aquilam (hom. 1–2)*
hom. in Tit.	*homiliae in epistulam ad Titum (hom. 1–6)*
hom. prec.	*homiliae de precatione (hom. 1–2)*
incomprehens.	*de incomprehensibili dei natura (= contra Anomoeos [hom. 1–5])*
Is. interp.	*interpretatio in Isaiam prophetam*
Jud.	*adversus Judaeos (or. 1–8)*
kal.	*in kalendas*
laed.	*quod nemo laedatur nisi a se ipso*
laud. Paul.	*de laudibus sancti Pauli (hom. 1–7)*
Laz.	*de Lazaro (hom. 1–7)*
oppugn.	*adversus oppugnatores vitae monastica (lib. 1–3)*
pan. Aeg.	*laudatio martyrum Aegyptiorum*
pan. Bab. 1	*panegyricum in Babylam martyrem*
pan. Bab. 2	*panegyricum in Babylam martyrem et contra Julianum et gentes*
pan. Barl.	*laudatio Barlaam martyris*
pan. Bern.	*panegyricum in Bernicen et Prosdocen martyres*
pan. Dros.	*laudatio Drosidis martyris*
pan. Eust. Ant.	*panegyricum in Eustathium Antiochiae episcopum*
pan. Ign.	*panegyricum in Ignatium martyrem*
pan. Juln.	*panegyricum in Julianum martyrem*
pan. Lucn.	*panegyricum in Lucianum martyrem*
pan. Macc.	*panegyrica in Maccabaeos (hom. 1–2)*
pan. Macc. fr.	*fragmentum panegyrici in Maccabaeos*
pan. mart.	*panegyrica in martyres (hom. 1–3)*
pan. Rom.	*panegyrica in Romanum martyrem*
pent.	*homiliae de pentecoste (hom. 1–2)*
poenit.	*homiliae de poenitentia*
proph. obscurit.	*de prophetarum obscuritate (hom. 1–2)*
prov.	*de fato et providentia (hom. 1–6)*
res. mort.	*de resurrectione mortuorum*
sac.	*de sacerdotio (lib. 1–6)*
scand.	*ad eos qui scandalizati sunt (=de providentia dei)*
serm. in Gen.	*sermones in Genesim (serm. 1–9)*
Stag.	*adhortationes ad Stagirium a daemone vexatum*

	stat.	ad populum Antiochenum de statuis (hom. 1–21)
	subintr.	contra eos qui subintroductas habent
	Thdr.	adhortationes ad Theodorum lapsum (lib. 1–2)
	vid.	ad viduam juniorem
	virg.	de virginitate
[John Chrysostom]	hom. in Ps. 50	homiliae in Psalmum 50 (hom. 1–3)
	Petr. et Paul.	in Petrum et Paulum
Josephus	c. Ap.	contra Apionem
Julian	Ep.	epistulae
	Gal.	contra Galilaeos
Leo VI	Or.	orationes
Libanios	Arg. D.	argumenta orationum Demosthenicarum
	Decl.	declamationes
	Desc.	descriptiones
	Enc.	encomia
	Ep.	epistulae
	Or.	orationes
	Prog.	progymnasmata
Lucian	Im.	imagines
	Peregr.	de morte Peregrini
	Pr. Im.	pro imaginibus
Macarius Magnes	apocrit.	apocriticus ad Graecos
Menander	Rh.	περὶ ἐπιδεικτικῶν
Nikolaos	Prog.	progymnasmata
Palladios	v. Chrys.	dialogus de vita Joannis Chrysostomi
Philodemus	Hom.	περὶ τοῦ καθ᾽ Ὅμηρον ἀγαθοῦ βασιλέως
Plato	Resp.	respublica
	Symp.	symposium
	Tim.	Timaeus
Pliny	Ep.	epistulae
	Paneg.	panegyricus
Plutarch	Alex.	Alexander
	comp. Dem. et Cic.	comparatio Demosthenis et Ciceronis
	Mor.	moralia
Polemo	Phgn.	physiognomonica
Pseudo–Clement	Hom.	homiliae
Pseudo–Longinus	Subl.	de sublimitate
Quintilian	Inst.	institutio oratoria
Seneca	Ep.	ad Lucilium epistulae morales
Suetonius	Ner.	vita Neronis
Symeon Metaphrastes	vita s. Joh. Chrys.	de vita sancti Joannis Chrysostomi
Tertullian	praes.	de praescriptione haereticorum
Theon	Prog.	progymnasmata
Theophrastus	Char.	characteres
Tryphon	Trop.	περὶ τρόπων
Xenophon	Mem.	memorabilia

Abbreviations of Periodicals, Reference Works, and Series

AB	Anchor Bible
ABD	*Anchor Bible Dictionary*, ed. D.N. Freedman
AnBib	Analecta biblica
AusBR	*Australian Biblical Review*
BETL	Bibliotheca ephemeridum theologicarum Lovaniensium
BGBE	Beiträge zur Geschichte der biblischen Exegese
BHT	Beiträge zur historischen Theologie
BJRL	*Bulletin of the John Rylands University Library of Manchester*
BT	Bibliotheca Teubneriana
BZNW	Beihefte zur Zeitschrift für die neutestamentliche Wissenschaft
CBQ	*Catholic Biblical Quarterly*
CCSL	Corpus Christianorum, series Latina
CHR	*Catholic Historical Review*
CP	*Classical Philology*
CPG	Clavis patrum graecorum, ed. M. Geerard
CSEL	Corpus scriptorum ecclesiasticorum latinorum
EEC	*Encyclopedia of Early Christianity*, ed. E. Ferguson. 2nd ed.
EECh	*Encyclopedia of the Early Church*, ed. A. di Berardino
EstBib	*Estudios bíblicos*
FC	Fathers of the Church
FRLANT	Forschungen zur Religion und Literatur des Alten und Neuen Testaments
GCS	Die griechischen christlichen Schriftsteller
GOTR	*Greek Orthodox Theological Review*
GRBS	*Greek, Roman, and Byzantine Studies*
HTKNT	Herders theologischer Kommentar zum Neuen Testament
HTR	*Harvard Theological Review*
HUT	Hermeneutische Untersuchungen zur Theologie
JAC	Jahrbuch für Antike und Christentum
JBL	*Journal of Biblical Literature*
JECS	*Journal of Early Christian Studies*
JR	*Journal of Religion*
JSNT	*Journal for the Study of the New Testament*
JSNTSup	Journal for the Study of the New Testament Supplement Series
JTS	*Journal of Theological Studies*
KEK	Kritisch-exegetischer Kommentar über das Neue Testament (Meyer Kommentar)
LCL	Loeb Classical Library
LPGL	G. W. H. Lampe, *A Patristic Greek Lexicon*
LSJ	Liddell-Scott-Jones, *Greek-English Lexicon*
LTP	*Laval théologique et philosophique*

MScRel	*Mélanges de science religieuse*
NovT	*Novum Testamentum*
NovTSup	Novum Testamentum Supplement Series
NPNF	*Nicene and Post-Nicene Fathers*
NTAbh	Neutestamentliche Abhandlungen
NTApoc	*New Testament Apocrypha*, ed. E. Hennecke and W. Schneemelcher. Rev. ed.
NTS	New Testament Studies
OCD	*Oxford Classical Dictionary*, ed. S. Hornblower and A. Spawforth. 3rd ed.
PG	*Patrologia graeca*, ed. J.-P. Migne
PL	*Patrologia latina*, ed. J.-P. Migne
PW	*Pauly-Wissowa, Real-Encyclopädie der classischen Altertumswissenschaft*
RAC	*Reallexikon für Antike und Christentum*
RelSRev	*Religious Studies Review*
RGG⁴	*Religion in Geschichte und Gegenwart*, ed. Hans Dieter Betz, et al. (1998–). 4th ed.
RSR	Recherches de science religieuse
SBLDS	Society of Biblical Literature Dissertation Series
SBLSP	*Society of Biblical Literature Seminar Papers*
SBLTT	Society of Biblical Literature Texts and Translations Series
SC	Sources chrétiennes
SCHNT	Studia ad corpus hellenisticum Novi Testamenti
SNTSMS	Society for New Testament Studies Monograph Series
SVF	*Stoicorum veterum fragmenta*, ed. H. von Arnim
TAPA	*Transactions of the American Philological Association*
TLG	*Thesaurus Linguae Graecae*
TS	*Theological Studies*
TU	Texte und Untersuchungen zur Geschichte der altchristlichen Literatur
TynBul	*Tyndale Bulletin*
VC	*Vigiliae christianae*
WMANT	Wissenschaftliche Monographien zum Alten und Neuen Testament
WUNT	Wissenschaftliche Untersuchungen zum Neuen Testament
ZKT	*Zeitschrift für katholische Theologie*
ZNW	*Zeitschrift für die neutestamentliche Wissenschaft und die Kunde des Urchristentums (und der älteren Kirche)*
ZRGG	*Zeitschrift für Religions- und Geistesgeschichte*
ZWT	*Zeitschrift für wissenschaftliche Theologie*

List of Plates*

1. *Vatican Cod. gr. 766*, fol. 2ᵛ (with permission of the Biblioteca Apostolica Vaticana)
2. *Athen. 211*, fol. 172 (Leonidas Ananiades, used with permission of the National Library, Athens)
3. *Athen. 211*, fol. 96 (Leonidas Ananiades, used with permission of the National Library, Athens)
4. *Milan, Ambrosian A 172*, Sup., fol. 263ᵛ (property of the Biblioteca Ambrosiana. All rights reserved. Reproduction is forbidden.)
5. Fresco in the Church of the Archangel, Lesnovo, Macedonia (the legacy of Dušan and Ruzica Tasic. The Department of Art History, the Faculty of Philosophy, the University of Belgrade)
6. *British Library Add. Ms. 36636*, fol. 179ʳ (by permission of the British Library)

---

* See pp. 502–507

Chapter 1

"Of All the Saints I Love Paul the Most"

"I love all the saints, but I love most the blessed Paul,
the chosen vessel, the heavenly trumpet,
the friend of the bridegroom, Christ.
And I have said this, and brought the love
which I have for him out into the public eye
so that I might make you, too, partners in this love charm."[1]

With these words John Chrysostom (c. 349–407) freely admitted and celebrated
the special devotion to the apostle Paul and his letters which is conspicuous to any
reader of his vast corpus of writings spanning his public career as monk, deacon
and then presbyter at Antioch, and later bishop of Constantinople.[2] Chrysostom
felt an intimate relationship with the dead apostle which virtually brought him to
life in the reading and interpretation of his letters. Such a hermeneutic, a "reading
of resuscitation," meant that in his private study and in the public homilies based
thereon, Chrysostom was about the work of introducing the Paul whom he knew
so well to others.[3] And even to us, distant readers of homilies once spoken alive to
audiences of bustling, admiring, applauding, and sometimes contemptuous congregations, Chrysostom presents visions of Paul alive and speaking in the interpretation of his letters. This intense devotion to the person of Paul the saintly author
goes hand in hand in Chrysostom's writings with a characteristically Antiochene
concentration on the historical and literal interpretation of his epistles, and a
dedication to concentrated and purposeful investigation of texts in their minutest
detail. The combination of his loving attention to his author, and his overtly
described hermeneutical reflections about the letters as holy scripture, makes John
Chrysostom's interpretation of Paul and his letters a major, though still largely

---

[1] *hom. in 2 Cor. 11:1* 1 [51.301].
[2] For a contemporary biography of Chrysostom one can hardly do better than J. N. D. Kelly,
Golden Mouth: The Story of John Chrysostom-Ascetic, Preacher, Bishop (Ithaca, NY: Cornell University
Press, 1995) (see my review in *Church History* 66 [1997] 85–87), but the now dated work of C.
Baur, *John Chrysostom and His Time* (2 vols.; tr. M. Gonzaga; Westminster, MD: Newman, 1959)
remains an invaluable resource for its topical treatments and abundant citations.
[3] Resuscitation takes place through both reading and writing. As Arnaldo Momigliano observed, "The writers of biographies created a meaningful relation between the living and the
dead" (*The Development of Greek Biography* [expanded edition; Cambridge: Harvard University
Press, 1993] 104). We shall have occasion throughout this study to examine the relationship
between Chrysostom's literary portraiture and biography proper, and shall return to the question
in the final chapter.

untapped resource for contemporary historical, religious, and hermeneutical research into Paul and his writings.

The Sources

Chrysostom has left (and because of his great popularity the church has preserved)[4] a huge volume of writings,[5] which includes over two hundred and fifty homilies on the Pauline epistles, covering all fourteen of the epistles in the canon which claim Pauline authorship (including also Hebrews).[6] There are also eighteen homilies on Pauline passages which stand outside of the homily sets on each letter,[7] which were preached on various occasions outside of the liturgical cycle of *seriatim* reading and exposition, book by book. These are very interesting documents which, because they have never been translated, are largely unknown to biblical scholarship. In addition, we possess over fifty of his homilies on the Acts of the Apostles (and other occasional sermons on Acts),[8] in which Paul, as one

---

[4] We possess an enormous number of manuscripts of Chrysostom's writings, which attests to widespread admiration for him and his craft. In the early part of this century C. Baur counted c. 2500 manuscripts in the catalogues of the libraries of Europe and in Jerusalem (*S. Jean Chrysostome et ses oeuvres dans l'histoire littéraire* [Université de Louvain Recueil de Travaux 18; Louvain: Bureaux du Recueil; Paris: Fontemoing, 1907] 28–31). But that survey did not include the libraries of Russia and eastern Europe. Baur's estimate was more recently updated by Frances M. Young to three or four thousand (*From Nicaea to Chalcedon: A Guide to the Literature and its Background* [London: SCM, 1983] 157; cf. Johannes Quasten, *Patrology* [3 vols.; Westminster, MD: Newman, 1960] 3.430: "the host of Greek manuscripts is astonishing"). Baur's earlier assessment remains accurate: "les ouvrages d'aucun autre Père grec n'occupent une place égale à celle de notre Docteur" (*S. Jean Chrysostome*, 30).

[5] A full list of Chrysostom's writings may be found in Maurice Geerard, ed., *Clavis patrum Graecorum* (Corpus Christianorum; 5 vols.; Turnhout: Brepols, 1974–1987) 2.491–672; LPGL, xvii–xviii; and the invaluable overview in Quasten, *Patrology*, 3.429–70 (though the bibliographies are outdated). All of the SC volumes contain both a critical edition of the Greek text and a modern French translation. I shall note only English translations for works below.

[6] These can be most easily found in PG 60–62, but there is a superior critical edition of all the homilies on the Pauline epistles by Frederick Field, *Sancti patris nostri Joannis Chrysostomi, Interpretatio omnium epistolarum paulinarum* (7 vols.; Bibliotheca Patrum; Oxford: J. H. Parker, 1849–62). A reliable, if dated, English translation of all fourteen sets may be found in NPNF, vols. 11–13. Those translations were based upon the mid nineteenth-century Oxford Library of the Fathers of the Church series, which were revised by a team of American scholars late in the century.

[7] *hom. in Rom. 5:3* [51.155–64]; *hom. in Rom. 8:28* [51.165–72]; *hom. in Rom. 12:20* [51.171–86]; *hom. 1–2 in Rom. 16:3* [51.187–208]; *hom. in 1 Cor. 7:2* [51.207–18]; *hom. in 1 Cor. 7:39* [51.217–26]; *hom. in 1 Cor. 10:1* [51.241–52]; *hom. in 1 Cor. 11:19* [51.251–60]; *hom. in 1 Cor. 15:28* [ed. Sebastian Haidacher, "Drei unedierte Chrysostomus-Texte einer Baseler Handschrift," ZKT 31 (1907) 141–71]; *hom. 1–3 in 2 Cor. 4:13* [51.271–302]; *hom. in 2 Cor. 11:1* [51.301–10]; *hom. in Gal. 2:11* [51.371–88]; *hom. in Phil. 1:18* [51.311–20]; *hom. in 1 Tim. 5:9* [51.321–38]; *hom. in 2 Tim. 3:1* [56.271–80].

[8] *homiliae 1–55 in Ac.* [60.13–384]; *homiliae in principium Actorum Apostolorum 1–4* [51.65–112]; *hom. 1–4 in Ac. 9:1* (=*homiliae in mutatione nominum*) [51.113–56]. An English translation

might expect, plays a major role. Of most salient interest to the present inquiry are John's seven extremely important and engaging, though infrequently read homilies, *de laudibus Sancti Pauli*.[9] The sheer volume of material John wrote on Paul is astounding. But Chrysostom did not confine his comments on Paul to exegetical homilies on the letters and Acts. Because of his great admiration for the apostle he also drew upon him constantly in all of his extensive writings, which include other biblical homilies,[10] sermons preached at critical moments;[11] ascetical writ-

---

of the first may be found in NPNF, vol. 11. There is not yet a translation of the latter series, but *hom. in Ac. princ.* has now been rendered into English by Michael Bruce Compton, "Introducing the Acts of the Apostles: a Study of John Chrysostom's *On the Beginning of Acts*," Ph.D. diss., University of Virginia, 1996, Appendix 3, pp. 248–312.

[9] These are found in SC 300, edited by Auguste Piédagnel (on the out of print English translation by Thomas Halton, see Preface, n. 2). Another encomium to Paul is preserved among Chrysostom's works (*eclogae ex diversis homiliis* 36 [63.839–48]), as well as one combining praise for Paul with Peter (*in Petrum et Paulum* [59.491–96]), but because these are clearly spurious they shall not be drawn upon in this investigation. Both are largely pastiches of many of the genuine encomia we shall treat here; see the parallels laid out by J. A. de Aldama, *Repertorium pseudochrysostomicum* (Documents, études et répertoires publiés par l'Institut de recherche et d'histoire des textes 10; Paris: Centre national de la recherche scientifique, 1965), 190–91 and 133. Many encomia to Paul were later attributed to Chrysostom, a sign of his manifest status as Paul's great admirer in the church (among them CPG 4850, 4873, 4885, 4889, 4931, 4998, 5013, 5032, 5067). Since these are both textually uncertain and of dubious origin, I shall leave them aside in this study. One more homily, *in kalendas* [48.953–62], starts out as a festival oration to Paul, but Chrysostom rapidly turns it over to a castigation of those who celebrate new years and new moons.

[10] Of New Testament writings, these include homily series on the Gospels of Matthew, *homiliae 1–90 in Mt.* [57.13–58.794] and John, *homiliae 1–88 in Jo.* [59.23–482], and fragments on the Catholic Epistles (*fragmenta in Jac.* [64.1040–52]; *fragmenta in Petr.* [64.1053–61]; *fragmenta in 1 Jo.* [64.1060–68]). Translations of the two gospel commentaries may be found in NPNF, vols. 10 and 14 respectively, and the commentary on the fourth gospel has also been given a more recent English rendering by Sr. Thomas Aquinas Goggin, *Saint John Chrysostom. Commentary on Saint John the Apostle and Evangelist* (FC vols. 33 and 41; New York: Fathers of the Church, Inc., 1957–1960); the fragments remain untranslated. Also a large body of Chrysostom's homilies on Old Testament texts is extant. Genesis is the only book covered in full [53.23–54.580], which has been translated by Robert C. Hill, *St. John Chrysostom. Homilies on Genesis* (FC vols. 74, 82 and 87; Washington: Catholic University of America Press, 1986–1992). There is also a second set of homilies on Gen 1–3 [54.581–630]), which I do not believe has been rendered into English. We also possess Chrysostom's homilies on more than a third of the Psalms [55.35–528], the translation of which is now in progress (the first volume has appeared: Robert Charles Hill, *St. John Chrysostom, Commentary on the Psalms* [vol. 1; Brookline, MA: Holy Cross Orthodox Press, 1998]), on Isaiah 1–8 (critical edition and French translation in SC 304, ed. Jean Dumortier; English translation and commentary by Duane A. Garrett, *An Analysis of the Hermeneutics of John Chrysostom's Commentary on Isaiah 1–8 with an English Translation* [Studies in the Bible and Early Christianity 12; Lewiston: Mellen, 1992]), and six homilies on Is 6:1 [SC 277, ed. Jean Dumortier]. Some occasional homilies are devoted to specific Old Testament passages, and in the catenae sometimes extended fragments of other commentaries have been preserved (such as on Job [SC 346, 348, ed. Henri Sorlin]). A general introduction to Chrysostom's biblical homilies may be found in Margaret M. Mitchell, "Chrysostom, John," *Historical Handbook of Major Biblical Interpreters*, ed. Donald K. McKim (Downers Grove, IL: InterVarsity Press, 1998) 28–34.

[11] The most famous are his twenty one sermons *ad populum Antiochenum de statuis* [49.95–222], and *in Eutropium eunuchum* [52.391–414], both translated in NPNF, vol. 9.

ings,[12] apologetic texts,[13] treatises on various subjects practical and dogmatic,[14] catechetical orations,[15] and liturgical homilies,[16] including over twenty panegyrics to martyrs and renowned local figures.[17] The monasteries of Europe and the East have also preserved over two hundred of Chrysostom's letters, including a special correspondence with his friend and ascetic patron, Olympias.[18] Throughout this

[12] These include *adhortationes ad Theodorum lapsum 1–2* (SC 117, ed. Jean Dumortier); *adversus oppugnatores vitae monasticae* [47.319–386]; *comparatio regis et monachi* [47.387–92], a work long thought to be of questionable authorship, but recently claimed as authentic; *de virginitate* [SC 125, ed. Herbert Musurillo and Bernard Grillet]; *ad viduam juniorem 1–2* [SC 138, ed. Bernard Grillet]; *contra eos qui subintroductas habent* [47.495–514]; *quod regulares feminae viris cohabitare non debeant* [47.513–32]. These were circulating as an ascetical corpus by the ninth century, according to Jean Dumortier, "L'auteur présumé du corpus asceticum des S. Jean Chrysostome," *JTS* n.s. 6 (1955) 99–102. The discourses to Theodore are translated in NPNF, vol. 9. The rest of the ascetic corpus has been given good attention lately; for translations see David Hunter, *A Comparison between a King and a Monk, Against the Opponents of the Monastic Life* (Studies in the Bible and Early Christianity 13; Lewiston: Mellen, 1988), who has also mounted the campaign for their authenticity; Sally Rieger Shore, *John Chrysostom, On Virginity, Against Remarriage* (Studies in Women and Religion 9; New York: Mellen, 1983); Elizabeth A. Clark, *Jerome, Chrysostom, and Friends: Essays and Translations* (Studies in Women and Religion 2; New York/Toronto: Mellen, 1979), who provides a translation of *subintr.*

[13] These are of two types, against pagans: *panegyricum in Babylam martyrem et contra Julianum et gentes* and *panegyricum in Babylam martyrem* (SC 362, ed. Margaret A. Schatkin, Bernard Grillet and Jean-Noël Guinot; English translation by Margaret A. Schatkin and Paul W. Harkins, *Saint John Chrysostom, Apologist* [FC vol. 73; Washington: Catholic University of America Press, 1985]); and against Jews and Judaizing Christians: *adversus Judaeos 1–8* [48.843–942], trans. Paul W. Harkins, *Saint John Chrysostom, Discourses against Judaizing Christians* (FC vol. 68; Washington: Catholic University of America Press, 1979).

[14] For example, Chrysostom's most esteemed work, already in his lifetime, was a treatise in dialogue form, *de sacerdotio* [SC 272, ed. Anne-Marie Malingrey]; English translation in NPNF, vol. 9. He also wrote treatises devoted to the education and rearing of children, *de educandis liberis*, against vainglory, *de inani gloria* (SC 188, ed. Anne-Marie Malingrey), excoriating the theatre (*contra ludos et theatra* [56.263–70]), and urging almsgiving for the poor, one of his most favored topics (*de eleemosyna* [51.261–272], recently translated, along with other sermons, by Gus George Christo, *St. John Chrysostom, On Repentance and Almsgiving* [FC 96; Washington: Catholic University of America Press, 1998], and *de Lazaro 1–7* [48.963–1054], of which there is an English translation by Catharine P. Roth, *St. John Chrysostom, On Wealth and Poverty* [Crestwood, NY: St. Vladimir's Seminary Press, 1984]). On more dogmatic topics are *de incomprehensibili dei natura* (SC 28, ed. Anne-Marie Malingrey and Robert Flacelière) and *de providentia dei* [=*ad eos qui scandalizati sunt*] (SC 79, ed. Anne-Marie Malingrey).

[15] There are various manuscript traditions of these; eight such discourses may be found in SC 50, ed. Antoine Wenger.

[16] There are sermons for Christmas, Epiphany, Holy Thursday, Good Friday, Easter, Ascension, and Pentecost (for a complete listing and discussion of issues of authenticity, see Quasten, *Patrology*, 3.454–55).

[17] These range from Antiochene heroes such as the Maccabees, Ignatius, Lucian, Melitios, and Babylas, to the Roman martyrs, and martyrs in general. The Greek texts can all be found in PG 50; English translations of the panegyrics to Ignatius and Babylas (see also n. 13 above) are given in NPNF, vol. 9.

[18] The letters to Olympias may be found in SC 13 and 103, ed. Anne-Marie Malingrey, a few of which are translated in NPNF, vol. 9. There are also two historically important missives to pope Innocent [52.529–536], translated in NPNF, vol. 9, as well.

wide-ranging oeuvre the apostle Paul reappears time and time again as example, authority, conversation partner, and icon. Chrysostom is undoubtedly the most comprehensive commentator on the Pauline epistles from the patristic era.[19] He also has a strong claim to be the most ardent admirer of Paul in the early church. As such he is a force to be reckoned with by all scholars of early Christianity, and a captivating fourth-century presence as exegete, preacher, teacher, and religious and political figure.

The Historical Significance of Chrysostom as an Interpreter of Paul

Chrysostom's interpretation of Paul and his letters is of monumental importance, both for what it teaches us of trends and ideas in Pauline interpretation in the patristic age, and because of its pervasive and enduring influence on the subsequent history of interpretation. In the last twenty-five years New Testament scholars have devoted much attention to the Pauline "legacy" in the early church, especially in the first two centuries.[20] To continue this analysis of Paul's influence and

---

[19] Possible eastern rivals, such as Origen, and Chrysostom's friend Theodore of Mopsuestia, have for a range of reasons (especially heresiological censorship) not had their works preserved to the extent of Chrysostom's. Origen's exegetical corpus, including scholia, homilies and commentaries, would surely have rivaled Chrysostom's if complete, but we possess only fragments of his exegetical writings on Romans (larger portions in the Latin translation of Rufinus), 1 Corinthians and Hebrews (Berthold Altaner and Alfred Stuiber, *Patrologie: Leben, Schriften und Lehre der Kirchenväter* [7th ed.; Freiburg/Basel/Vienna: Herder, 1966] 201–203). Although we know from Ebedjesu that Theodore composed commentaries on all fourteen Pauline epistles (Quasten, *Patrology*, 3.408), not all are extant. Some Greek fragments of his commentaries on Romans, 1 and 2 Corinthians and Hebrews are found in the catenae (K. Staab, *Pauluskommentare aus der griechischen Kirche* [NTAbh 15; Münster: Aschendorff, 1933]). The Greek originals of his commentaries on the ten "minor" Pauline epistles are, regrettably, lost, although they have been preserved in a complete fifth century Latin translation (edited by H.B. Swete, *Theodori episcopi Mopsuesteni in epistolas b. Pauli commentarii* [2 vols.; Cambridge: Cambridge University Press, 1880–82]). Among Latin commentators Ambrosiaster's is the only complete set of commentaries, though Pelagius also commented on thirteen epistles, but neither are as extensive as Chrysostom's. For Augustine we have exegetical works only on Galatians and Romans (A. Di Berardino, ed., *Patrology* [tr. P. Solari; vol. 4; Westminster, MD: Christian Classics, Inc., 1986] 355), and for Jerome, only those on five of the letters are preserved (for further details, see M.G. Mara, "Paul III. Commentaries on the Pauline Epistles," *EEC* 2.658–59).

[20] Bovon, "Paul comme document et Paul comme monument"; Collins, "The Image of Paul"; de Boer, "Images of Paul"; W.S. Babcock, ed., *Paul and the Legacies of Paul* (Dallas: Southern Methodist University, 1990); E. Dassmann, *Paulus in frühchristlicher Frömmigkeit und Kunst* (Rheinisch-Westfälische Akademie der Wissenschaften – Vorträge G256; Opladen: Westdeutscher Verlag, 1982); idem, *Der Stachel im Fleisch. Paulus in der frühchristlichen Literatur bis Irenäus* (Münster: Aschendorff, 1979); P. Gorday, "Paul in Eusebius and Other Early Christian Literature," *Eusebius, Christianity, and Judaism*, ed. H.W. Attridge and G. Hata (Studia Post-Biblica 42; Leiden: Brill, 1992) 139–65; A. Lindemann, *Paulus im ältesten Christentum. Das Bild des Apostels und die Rezeption der paulinischen Theologie in der frühchristlichen Literatur bis Marcion* (BHT 58; Tübingen: J.C.B. Mohr [Paul Siebeck], 1979); D.R. MacDonald, *The Legend and the Apostle. The*

reinterpretation into the fourth century, to the towering figure of John Chrysostom, is a natural and necessary extension of that task. On the other end of the temporal spectrum, Chrysostom's homilies (often in Latin translations, which were begun almost immediately)[21] were widely available and highly influential,[22] both wholesale and as excerpted in the catenae or in the *Glossa ordinaria*, for medieval commentators such as Aquinas and Bonaventure.[23] It is most significant that John's *de laudibus sancti Pauli* were in many ways his signature piece in the centuries after his death, among his earliest works translated into Latin, listed in catalogues, and republished in different combinations into the modern period.[24] Chrysostom's

---

Battle for Paul in Story and Canon (Philadelphia: Westminster, 1983); E. Pagels, *The Gnostic Paul. Gnostic Exegesis of the Pauline Letters* (Philadelphia: Trinity Press International, 1975); D. Rensberger, "As the Apostle Teaches: The Development of the Use of Paul's Letters in Second-Century Christianity," Ph.D. diss., Yale University, 1981.

[21] Chrysostom's writings were circulating widely already within his own lifetime (as attested by his biographer, Palladios, *v. Chrys.* 12.66–68 [SC 341.236]), and the task of translating them into Latin began very soon after his death (see Baur, *S. Jean Chrysostome*, 4–5; Quasten, *Patrology*, 3.456).

[22] For a wide assessment of Chrysostom's influence in the Latin churches, see Baur, *S. Jean Chrysostome*, 60–82, who collected the range of material, including: Jerome's inclusion of Chrysostom in his catalogue *de viris illustribus*, 129 [PL 23.754], when John was still a presbyter at Antioch (392) (see *S. Jean Chrysostome*, 60, 67–68), Pelagius' citation of Chrysostom against Augustine in his lost work *de Natura* (p. 68), Augustine's counter-texts against the Pelagians culled from Chrysostom's writings (p. 68, n.5), and the highpoint of Western reception of Chrysostom – Augustine's encomium to John as a great defender of the Christian faith, sage and exalted saint in his *Contra Julianum* 22 [PL 44.654] (pp. 68–70, with a partial translation). Chrysostom was also proclaimed a martyr of the faith at the ecumenical council of Ephesus [in 431] by Leo the Great (p. 71, correcting Baur's date).

[23] Thomas is said to have remarked that he preferred Chrysostom's *hom. in Mt.* (or perhaps the *opus imperfectum in Matthaeum* attributed to Chrysostom [see Anton Naegele, "Johannes Chrysostomos und sein Verhältnis zum Hellenismus," *Byzantinische Zeitschrift* 13 (1904) 73–113]), in the Latin translation of Burgundius Pisanus (d. 1194), to the whole city of Paris (B. Smalley, *The Study of the Bible in the Middle Ages* [2nd ed.; Oxford: Blackwell, 1952] 337; see also p. 18 on Chrysostom's influence in the Middle Ages generally). Bonaventure cited Chrysostom's homilies abundantly – fully 326 times, according to Augusta Merzagora, "Giovanni Crisostomo commentatore di S. Paolo," *"Didaskaleion": studi di letteratura e storia cristiana antica* n.s. 9 (1931) 1–73 (ed. Paolo Ubaldi; Torino: Società editrice internazionale, 1931; repr. Amsterdam: John Benjamins N.V., 1969) 1–73, p. 3 n. 1.

[24] The homilies in praise of Paul were translated into Latin between 415 and 419 by the Pelagian Anianus of Celeda, who also translated Chrysostom's Matthew commentary (see Baur, *S. Jean Chrysostome*, 4–5, 61). *In laudem beati Pauli apostoli volumen egregium* figures among the works of Chrysostom in the catalogue *De viris illustribus* attributed to Gennadius, which comes from sixth-century Gaul (Baur, *S. Jean Chrysostome*, 63; on the attribution to Gennadius, and the time and place of composition, see S. Pricoco, "Gennadius of Marseille," EEC 1.342). John's Pauline panegyrics were later published in collections of Pauline interpretation, such as the ninth-century compilation by Drepanius Florus, deacon of Lyons, which was attributed to the Venerable Bede (*Divi Augusti in sacras Pauli epistolas nova et hactenus abscondita interpretatio: per Venerabile Beda ex innumeris illius codicibus … collecta* [Paris: Udalrici Gering and Bertholdi Rebolt, 1499], and *Expositio epistolarum b. Pauli apostoli, ex diversis opusculis sancti Augustini a venerabili Beda presbytero excerpta, et in unum corpus collecta* [Paris: Georgius Iosse, 1649]). For modern editions and translations, see Auguste Piédagnel, *Jean Chrysostome: Panégyriques de Saint Paul* (SC 300; Paris: Éditions du Cerf, 1982) 53–110.

homilies were prized later by the great humanist Erasmus,[25] and the influential theologians of the Reformation, Luther,[26] and especially Calvin.[27] From the fifteenth to the nineteenth centuries Chrysostom's homilies were widely published

---

[25] Erasmus translated some of Chrysostom's homilies himself between 1526 and 1527 (see Erika Rummel, *Erasmus' Annotations on the New Testament* [Toronto: University of Toronto Press, 1986] 64 for a list), and incorporated Chrysostom more with each successive edition of the *Annotations*, up to the fifth (1535), which cited Chrysostom more than any Greek father except Origen (André Godin, *Érasme. Lecteur d'Origène* [Geneva: Droz, 1982] 149–51). Erasmus insisted on the importance of reading Chrysostom in the Greek, and his letters are filled with stories of his joy on finding "a Greek Chrysostom" manuscript (first at Cambridge in 1511, according to Rummel, *Erasmus' Annotations*, 62–66). In his preface to a published edition of Chrysostom's *de sacerdotio* Erasmus called Chrysostom "the most useful teacher of Christian eloquence, who stands alone among all in combining learned piety with popular eloquence" (cited by Rummel, *Erasmus' Annotations*, 65). Among his witticisms is the saying, in the 1519 edition of the *Ratio*: "I would rather be a pious theologian with Chrysostom than an invincible one with Duns Scotus" (replacing Jerome, who was the "pious theologian" in the 1516 edition!). On these and other points, as well as the importance of Chrysostom for Erasmus generally, see the valuable study by Robert D. Sider, "'Searching the Scriptures': John Chrysostom in the New Testament Scholarship of Erasmus," *Within the Perfection of Christ. Essays on Peace and the Nature of the Church in honor of Martin H. Schrag*, ed. T. L. Brensunger and E. M. Sider (Nappanee, IN: Evangel Press, 1990) 83–105; Albert Rabil, *Erasmus and the New Testament* (San Antonio: Trinity University Press, 1972; repr. Lanham: University Press of America, 1993) 115–18, and, on interest in Chrysostom among humanists preceding Erasmus, Charles S. Singer, *The Renaissance in Rome* (Bloomington, IN: University of Indiana Press, 1985) 229–34.

[26] Luther often quoted Chrysostom with approval, especially in his lectures on Romans and Hebrews, though in the *Tischreden* he is said to have complained that Chrysostom was "nur ein Weffcher," "only a gossip!" (no. 252; text Weimar ed., trans. T. G. Tappert, *Luther's Works* [Philadelphia: Fortress, 1967], 54.34).

[27] Calvin praised Chrysostom's virtues as a preacher and expositor for the people in the preface he wrote for a published version of Chrysostom's homilies around 1540 ("Praefatio in Chrysostomi homilias," *Corpus Reformatorum: Ioannis Calvini Opera quae supersunt omnia*, vol. 37, ed. G. Baum, E. Cunitz, et al. [Braunschweig: Schwetschke, 1870] 831–38; see the analytical outline of this treatise in J. R. Walchenbach, "John Calvin as Biblical Commentator: An Investigation into Calvin's Use of John Chrysostom as an Exegetical Tutor," Ph.D. diss., University of Pittsburgh, 1974, 207–210). By virtue of the fact that they were both preachers, Calvin felt he had a "common cause" with Chrysostom [*causam habeo cum Chrysostomo coniunctam* (col. 833)], and he especially favored Chrysostom above all other ancient commentators for his refusal to contort the simple sense of the words [*ac nullam sibi licentiam sumere in simplici verborum sensu contorquendo*] (col. 835)]. Calvin's own copies of Chrysostom's writings, with his notes and underlining, have now been published: A. Ganoczy and K. Müller, *Calvins handschriftliche Annotationen zu Chrysostomus: ein Beitrag zur Hermeneutik Calvins* (Veröffentlichungen des Instituts für Europäische Geschichte Mainz 102; Wiesbaden: Steiner, 1982). Walchenback concluded that there was a basic "methodological affinity" between the two, but observed that Calvin often cites John in a "punctiliar" fashion: "A reference to Chrysostom means 'Chrysostom mentions,' and not always 'Chrysostom's interpretation is'" ("John Calvin," 199–200). A similar estimation is held by David C. Steinmetz, "Calvin and the Patristic Exegesis of Paul," ed. *idem, The Bible in the Sixteenth Century* (Durham: Duke University Press, 1990) 100–18, 231–35: "the overwhelming impression [Chrysostom's homilies on Romans 8] create is one of sound, relevant, imaginative exegesis that casts fresh light on the mind of Paul. They are remarkably shrewd in identifying the crucial problems in the Pauline text and reflect faithfully the unresolved tensions in Paul's thought about the nature of the flesh and the role of the law. It is easy to understand why Calvin admired their exegesis, even if he did not follow them in all details" (pp. 109–10). Calvin's particular esteem for

in Europe, and translated into an array of languages, thus facilitating a wide dissemination of his exegetical writings.[28] And still today, when contemporary New Testament scholars seek insights from the early church about the interpretation of the Pauline letters, particularly in regard to contested contemporary theological and ethical issues, it is most often to Chrysostom that they turn.[29] Since he is such a pivotal figure in the history of interpretation of Paul, then, Chrysostom's writings on the apostle deserve extensive attention and analysis. But no full-scale treatment of Chrysostom's interpretation of Paul exists.

Previous Scholarship

Most discussions of Chrysostom's interpretations of Paul and his letters currently available are brief treatments within larger works on John Chrysostom's life, thought and writings, such as those by Chrysostomus Baur,[30] Bruno Vandenberghe,[31] and J. N. D. Kelly.[32] Chrysostom's special love for Paul, and the signal importance of his homilies on the Pauline epistles as the most extensive such exegetical collection from the early church, are remarked upon in the standard handbooks of patristic

---

Chrysostom for his "simple, literal-historical approach to the text," was noted also by William J. Bouwsma, *John Calvin. A Sixteenth-century Portrait* (New York/Oxford: Oxford University Press, 1988) 119.

[28] Merzagora, "Giovanni Crisostomo," 4, provides a list of over ten such translations of the homilies on the Pauline epistles in particular, which she culled from the extensive catalogue in Baur, *S. Jean Chrysostome*, 82–222.

[29] Recently Chrysostom has been drawn upon by various sides in vigorous disputes in Pauline scholarship on women leaders in the Pauline churches, since he clearly regarded the famous apostle Ἰουνία in Rom 16:7 as a woman (*hom. in Rom.* 31.2 [60.670; F 1.476D]) (see Bernadette Brooten, "'Junia ... Outstanding among the Apostles' [Romans 16:7], in *Women Priests: a Catholic Commentary on the Vatican Declaration*, ed. L. Swidler [New York: Paulist, 1977] 141–44), and on Pauline teachings on the social order, including women, slaves and economic distribution (Adolf Martin Ritter, "John Chrysostom as an Interpreter of Pauline Social Ethics," *Paul and the Legacies of Paul*, ed. W.S. Babcock [Dallas: Southern Methodist University Press, 1990] 183–99, notes 360–69, with a response by Elizabeth A. Clark, "Comment: Chrysostom and Pauline Social Ethics" in the same volume, pp. 193–99). He has also been an important figure for other debates, such as on Paul's rhetorical proficiency (see, e.g., Janet Fairweather, "The Epistle to the Galatians and Classical Rhetoric," *TynBul* 45 [1994] 1–38; 213–44; cf. Reinhart Staats, "Chrysostomus über die Rhetorik des Apostels Paulus: Makarianische Kontexte zu '*de sacerdotio* IV, 5–6,'" [*VC* 46 (1992) 225–40]), and the debate about the ambiguous phrase πίστις Χριστοῦ, "faith in/of Christ" (R. A. Harrisville, "ΠΙΣΤΙΣ ΧΡΙΣΤΟΥ: Witness of the Fathers," *NovT* 36 [1994] 233–41).

[30] *John Chrysostom and His Time*, 1.290–300.

[31] B. H.Vandenberghe, *Saint Jean Chrysostome et la parole de Dieu* (Paris: Éditions du Cerf, 1961) 47–60, on Chrysostom's great love for Paul.

[32] *Golden Mouth*, e.g., 90–95, 100–103, 132–37. Because of the book's chronological order in service of biography, the homilies on the Pauline epistles are treated as historical sources pertinent to their date of composition. Unfortunately, as Kelly's book has no index of passages, these cannot easily be picked out, but his comments are always instructive.

scholarship,[33] and in Maurice Wiles' marvelous study of Pauline interpretation in the early church.[34] None of these works, however, seeks to provide a comprehensive analysis of Chrysostom's writings on Paul and how they relate specifically to his adulation for the apostle. The best full-scale work on Chrysostom's exegetical enterprise and its underpinnings for over a century has been that of Frederic Henry Chase,[35] but his treatment of the Pauline epistles unfortunately disappoints, because it engages only some exemplary passages on a few select topics (such as metaphor and other figures of thought and speech),[36] and does not inquire at all into the role of Paul the author in Chrysostom's exegetical work. Several more recent studies include Chrysostom among other patristic exegetes of selected portions of the corpus as part of a comparative study of patristic exegesis east and west,[37] but they are necessarily limited in scope, and likewise do not undertake a comprehensive investigation of how Chrysostom's interpretation of selected portions of the letters is rooted in his images of and devotion to his author.

In terms of the homilies *de laudibus sancti Pauli*, while the major handbooks and biographies mention them approvingly in passing,[38] no comprehensive study exists.[39] The major piece of scholarship to date on these discourses is the *Sources chrétiennes* critical edition of the text and introduction and notes by Auguste Piédagnel, from 1982. I have depended thoroughly and with full confidence in Piédagnel's fine edition, which has facilitated my study of these homilies greatly. His brief introduction to the orations (pp. 10–52) has targeted many of the right issues for the examination of these texts: their liturgical context, literary genre, and the portrait of Paul that emerges. But his approach is also limited in several decisive ways. First, although in the notes Piédagnel offers some largely unsupported suggestions about literary composition, this volume, in line with the series format, provides no in-depth analysis of the argumentative structure of each of the homilies, which is a

---

[33] Quasten, *Patrology*, 3.440–51; Altaner-Stuiber, *Patrologie*, 324–25.

[34] M. Wiles, *The Divine Apostle: The Interpretation of St. Paul's Epistles in the Early Church* (Cambridge: Cambridge University Press, 1967) 7, 14–25.

[35] F. H. Chase, *Chrysostom. A Study in the History of Biblical Interpretation* (Cambridge: Deighton, Bell & Co., 1887) 151–94.

[36] The study is generally less illuminating on the New than on the Old Testament.

[37] K.-H. Schelkle, *Paulus, Lehrer der Väter: Die altkirchliche Auslegung von Römer 1–11* (2nd ed.; Düsseldorf: Patmos, 1959); R. Greer, *The Captain of Our Salvation: A Study in the Patristic Exegesis of Hebrews* (BGBE 15; Tübingen: J. C. B. Mohr [Paul Siebeck], 1973), and P. Gorday, *Principles of Patristic Exegesis: Romans 9–11 in Origen, John Chrysostom, and Augustine* (New York: Mellen, 1983).

[38] Baur, *John Chrysostom*, 1.199 (but he unaccountably omits mention of them in his section on Paul [1.290–300]); Quasten, *Patrology*, 3.456–57 devotes a summarizing sentence to each of the seven and reports of the whole: "none of his encomia has won a greater reputation than the *Homiliae 7 de laudibus S. Pauli*, in which he gives enthusiastic expression to his unbounded admiration of the Apostle of the Gentiles."

[39] There is a short but important article on these homilies by Harry Hubbell, which I shall discuss later in this chapter, in the context of investigations of Chrysostom's rhetorical acumen and proficiency.

mandatory step toward understanding them. Second, in the introduction Piédagnel is far too cautious about Chrysostom's widespread employment of rhetorical conventions in these orations, asserting instead that John purposely eschews those "pagan" literary forms, a judgment based on his overly rigid view of the form of the encomium.[40] And, third, Piédagnel seeks to harmonize a singular Pauline portrait out of these multiform and complex compositions, whereas, as I shall demonstrate in this study, each has its own discreet argument line, portrait(s) and purposes which must be appreciated on its own terms. Further, it was well beyond the scope of Piédagnel's critical edition to situate these homilies within the Pauline portraits and praises found throughout Chrysostom's corpus of writings, but that is precisely where a study of them should be lodged. Seeing these panegyrics within the context of Chrysostom's larger project of Pauline portraiture yields many new insights, and demonstrates the extent to which in these panegyrics he was using shop-worn material, and at other times stretching conventional forms to construct fresh and even downright contrary versions of commonplace themes. Throughout my study I shall depend upon Piédagnel's text of *de laudibus sancti Pauli*, and debate with him on matters of interpretation, large and small, as I present a detailed analysis of each of these stimulating compositions.

When we turn from the homilies *de laudibus sancti Pauli* to Chrysostom's interpretation of Paul in general, both in the exegetical homilies and throughout his other writings, once again we find that there is a paucity of scholarship. Although no full-scale treatment of Chrysostom's interpretation of Paul exists, six articles (interestingly, none in English) have sporadically appeared on the topic during the last seventy years. Unfortunately none of these has received much attention,[41] and indeed these scholars themselves mostly worked without knowledge of or interaction with each others' work, so there has not been linear progress in research.[42] Thus it seems as though Chrysostom's interpretation of Paul was "rediscovered" in discrete European contexts (Italy, Spain, Germany, Greece) every decade or so, only to retreat once more into obscurity soon thereafter. While each of these authors has brought to the fore some of Chrysostom's writings on Paul and his letters, their articles mostly offer a simple description of the material; what analysis they provide is often based upon methodological assumptions and theological

---

[40] SC 300.21–38. As will be demonstrated later in this chapter, Piédagnel's thesis is in many ways a throwback to a consensus opinion of the last century.

[41] One can only speculate about why that is. The second world war may have played a role in the relative neglect of the earlier, pre-war studies from Germany and Italy (Merzagora and Hoffmann-Aleith; see below). It is also possible that the fact that these articles were written by women made them of less value to their contemporaries. Whether that were a factor or not, it is nonetheless interesting that this topic has attracted the interest of women scholars.

[42] In my research I am afraid that I have replicated this pattern, because it was not until fully three years into my study that I received access to the important studies of Merzagora and Di S. Maria which had preceded me, only to find that I had independently covered much of the same ground.

precommitments which are questionable. Many of these methodological difficulties are due to the state of Pauline scholarship at the time they were written, which for the earlier studies in particular focused primarily on grace and justification as the unquestioned center of Pauline theology, from which (pure) reading of Paul Chrysostom was found to diverge. The present study is written against the backdrop of the Pauline scholarship in its own day, which has witnessed the breakdown of any easy consensus about the heart and singular meaning of Paul's writings and theology. But despite the questionable assumptions upon which the earlier studies were sometimes based, they contain valuable collections of Chrysostom's utterances on Paul, and infectious enthusiasm for the importance and sheer interest of John Chrysostom's interpretation of Paul's letters. Given the inattention to those studies, and their virtually complete invisibility in English-speaking scholarship, I seek to highlight their intentions and further the examination of this rich source material with a fresh analysis of Chrysostom's writings on Paul in their historical, religious, literary, and cultural contexts. These earlier brief studies recognized the enormity of this topic and the extensive source material available for it, and implicitly called for a comprehensive treatment of Chrysostom's interpretation of Paul, the task I am pleased to take up from them.

In 1931 Augusta Merzagora published a study, "Giovanni Crisostomo commentatore di S. Paolo," which remains the most comprehensive previous treatment of the subject. The initial essay is composed of two parts, the first of which surveys ancient and modern appreciation for Chrysostom as an exegete, and the impact Paul had on Chrysostom's life and works. She insists upon the extent to which Chrysostom patterned his life on Paul, and upon the role his love for Paul played as his most noteworthy and legitimating qualification as a superior commentator on the epistles. The second part offers short, general comments on Chrysostom's homilies on the Pauline letters as samples of Antiochene exegesis, followed by select examples of Chrysostom's attention to grammatical (syntactical, etymological) and stylistic matters, and the nature of his historical method. In a follow-up essay of 1937 Merzagora set out to demonstrate that Chrysostom, in addition to his philological prowess, was also a philosophically astute interpreter of Paul (and of *his* philosophy), by treating John's expositions on reason, psychology, logic, nature, anthropology and theodicy in the Pauline epistles.[43] In this way she sought to defend Chrysostom (and perhaps Paul) against a latent charge that he was a moralizing story-teller or unsystematic thinker rather than a serious intellectual interpreter of the apostle's writings. What Merzagora hoped to accomplish – to draw scholarly attention to Chrysostom as a most excellent commentator on the Pauline epistles – has not been fully realized in the decades since her study. While

---

[43] "Giovanni Crisostomo commentatore di S. Paolo: Osservazioni su l'esegesi filosofica (I)," *Studi dedicati alla memoria di Paolo Ubaldi* (Pubblicazioni della università cattolica del sacro cuore 16; serie quinta: scienze storiche; Milan: Società editrice "vita e pensiero," 1937) 205–46.

Merzagora's strategy of defending Chrysostom's place among noteworthy Pauline interpreters on the basis of his philosophical acumen must be questioned (largely because it seeks to universalize onto both Chrysostom and Paul the model of Augustinian engagement with issues in the philosophy of religion),[44] the earlier part of her study remains of great value, because it keenly sets out the essential issue of the intimate relationship between Paul and his interpreter John which is at the heart of the exegetical enterprise. This book will take up that topic, but also add to her work an analysis of how Chrysostom's attention to the person of the apostle Paul was formulated in terms understandable in the oral-literary culture of the late fourth century, thus moving the analysis beyond a restatement of Chrysostom's expressions of attachment to Paul to an historical analysis of Chrysostom's writings on Paul as products of late fourth-century literary and ecclesiastical culture which employ rhetorical conventions for definite persuasive purposes. Furthermore, Merzagora's reading of Paul, which sees his writings as a repository of philosophical, theological or historical ideas, needs also to be moderated by more recent scholarship which insists upon seeing the Pauline letters less as systematic treatises and more as historically occasioned, situation-specific documents.

In 1939 German scholar Eva Hoffmann-Aleith followed her book surveying Pauline exegesis in the early church up to Methodius of Olympus with a short article, "Das Paulusverständnis des Johannes Chrysostomus."[45] The thesis of this tantalizingly brief piece is that while Chrysostom admired Paul very much, he often misunderstood or misconstrued his thought ("in seiner Exegese mitunter ein fremder Ton in der Klangfülle paulinischer Verkündigung aufschwirrt"), especially because of his philosophical limitations in comprehending Paul's nuances on

---

[44] Merzagora, "Osservazioni," 205 forthrightly says she does not wish to claim that Chrysostom was the equal of Augustine, but that he had his own particular mode of philosophy which was in its own way unified and coherent (see also 208 and her final praise on p. 246: "... la sua logica impeccabile, la profondità della psicologia, lo sviluppo della morale e tutti gli altri pregi del metodo per cui la sua esegesi, considerata sotto l'aspetto filosofico, non appare per nulla inferiore a quella grammaticale e storica"). But the whole endeavor presumes that an exegete's worthiness depends upon such systematic philosophical rigor, as exercised on the menu of topics that were predominant in Augustinian Pauline interpretation. Compare, for instance, the methodological approach Paula Fredriksen takes to "Augustine's Early Interpretation of Paul": "This essay examines Augustine's various interpretations of Paul's letters, particularly the Epistle to the Romans ... in so doing, it traces the themes of free will, sin, sexuality, creation, and grace as they emerge from Augustine's exegesis, and from his effort to reclaim Paul from the Manichees" (Ph.D. dissertation, Princeton University, 1979, iii). While this approach is appropriate *to Augustine*, since he was preoccupied with certain topics and points of debate, it is not for Chrysostom, whose literary form (homilies), exegetical approach (*seriatim* readings of whole books), and pastoral intention (exhortation) were very different. We shall return to this comparison of Chrysostom and Augustine in chap. 8, pp. 411–23.

[45] "Das Paulusverständnis des Johannes Chrysostomus," *ZNW* 38 (1939) 181–88. Her book, [Eva Aleith], *Paulusverständnis in der alten Kirche* (BZNW 18; Berlin: Töpelmann, 1937), contains a very broad survey of the first three centuries, but stops just before Chrysostom. To my knowledge, she never published anything else on the topic.

faith, righteousness, free will and grace.[46] This thesis of course depends upon Hoffmann-Aleith's own (undefended) assumption of what a "true reading" of Paul's theology should have been – with an appropriate emphasis on grace, sin and justification.[47] Despite the considerable problems with this approach, in her article Hoffmann-Aleith did capture nicely Chrysostom's preoccupation in his homilies with presenting portraits of Paul to his hearers, an insight which concurs with the starting point for our investigation (even as it unknowingly underscores Chrysostom's own claim that his ardor for Paul guaranteed his accuracy as his interpreter):

> Ihm ist die Gestalt des Apostels, die uns kein Bild, keine Skulptur, keine Beschreibung überliefert, lebendig und bezwingend entgegengetreten in dessen eigenen Worten, wahrhaftiger und bezeichnender als irgendein anderes nachschaffendes und widerspiegelndes Zeugnis es vermöchte, und es ist ihm gelungen, was er von seinen Hörern forderte: die Heilige Schrift so zu gebrauchen, als wäre Paulus noch leibhaftig gegenwärtig, und wir könnten mit ihm reden.[48]

What Hoffmann-Aleith did not quite realize, however, even as she uses the language, is that the very portrait, sculpture, or description of Paul which she judges lacking is actually in the very process of creation by Chrysostom in his exegetical-homiletical enterprise, as he painted word portraits of his author, his hero, Paul, in the very act of his reading of resuscitation.

---

[46] Hoffmann-Aleith, "Das Paulusverständnis des Johannes Chrysostomus," 188: "So ist die Exegese des Johannes Chrysostomus ein Beispiel von seltener Eindringlichkeit, wie ein Theologe der alten Kirche trotz echter glühender Begeisterung für den Apostel, und im Grunde unbewußt, theologisch andere Wege ging als sein verehrtes Vorbild." This is precisely the conclusion she reached in her book, also, via the same method of comparison with an assumed, although not demonstrated, standard for what Paul was really saying: "wie kaum ein zweiter Schriftsteller erfuhr er das Schicksal, mit Andacht und Verehrung fleißig gelesen, aber selten verstanden zu werden" (*Paulusverständnis in der alten Kirche*, 122). One can see here the overriding influence of Adolf von Harnack's famous saying that no one in the early church understood Paul except Marcion, who misunderstood him, and the general thrust of church history current in the late nineteenth and most of the twentieth century (though now eroded), which maintained that Paul was either ignored or misunderstood, except by heretics (for a survey of the development of these historical ideas, see Rensberger, "As The Apostle Teaches," 1–61).

[47] This discussion goes back to the early church, to the debate between free will and grace, and carries through to the modern period. Merzagora rightly resisted the standard dichotomy, as expressed by Aimé Puech (*Un réformateur de la société chrétienne au IV siècle. St. Jean Chrysostome et les moeurs de son temps* [Paris: Hachette, 1891] 327), that there were two sides of Paul, the χάρις and the *caritas*, the first of which, ironically, was captured by Augustine, and the second by John Chrysostom ("Giovanni Crisostomo," 32–33). But the negative assessment of Chrysostom along these lines has not been limited to Hoffmann-Aleith. Many generations of English readers who have been introduced to Chrysostom's writings first through the NPNF series encountered this assessment by Philip Schaff in his introductory essay, "Prolegomena: The Life and Work of St. John Chrysostom": "it cannot be said that he entered into the depths of Paul's doctrines of sin and grace, or ascended the height of his conception of freedom in Christ" (NPNF 9.19).

[48] "Paulusverständnis," 182.

This was better intuited by Melchiorre di S. Maria, whose wonderful article published in 1963, "S. Paolo nella prospettiva di S. Giovanni Crisostomo,"[49] lays out, with plentiful citations from Chrysostom's corpus of writings, the great love which Chrysostom had for Paul, and the praises which Chrysostom conferred upon the apostle for his virtues and his tremendous love for Christ. More than any other, di S. Maria's piece nicely presents the case for Chrysostom's unique role as an admirer of Paul:

> Difficilmente forse si troverà un autore che, non solo nell'età patristica ma neppure in altri tempi dell'era cristiana, abbia manifestato un amore più grande per S. Paolo e lo abbia esaltato in un modo più costante e più sublime, di quanto manifestò e fece S. Giovanni Crisostomo.[50]

Di S. Maria brings together many important statements by Chrysostom about Paul, and especially accents the love triad between Paul and Chrysostom on the one hand, and Paul and Christ on the other. The strength of his work is its well-documented catalogue of quite a few of Chrysostom's epithets and praises of Paul,[51] which makes it in many ways the best work to date on Chrysostom's special devotion to Paul. Di S. Maria has also very well understood the significance of several of the most important homilies in Chrysostom's corpus of writings which scholarship has not generally drawn upon as there is still no critical edition or translation of them.[52] The present study, like that of di S. Maria, seeks to examine Chrysostom's images of Paul and his letters, but I hope to extend his work to provide an organized and comprehensive treatment of the epithets, and, furthermore, to study this material, not only as a set of artifacts of Chrysostom's personal piety, but also as rhetorical products which are rooted in rhetorical and other cultural conventions (such as artistic and ethical theory) in the fourth century, and are produced with self-conscious catechetical goals in mind. In particular what di S. Maria's research fails to provide, because of its culling methodology, is a detailed contextual analysis of Chrysostom's compositions on Paul as literary wholes, in the light of their specific rhetorical conventions, purposes, and effects. That is our major task here.

Diametrically opposed to the thesis of Hoffmann-Aleith, but writing without apparent knowledge of her work (or any of the other authors we have surveyed),

---

[49] In *Studiorum paulinorum congressus internationalis catholicus 1961* (AnBib 18; Rome: Pontifical Biblical Institute, 1963) 491–502. This article was apparently written without knowledge of Hoffmann-Aleith's work, but was aware of Merzagora's and F. Ogara, *El Apóstol San Pablo visto a través de San Juan Crisóstomo* (Rome, 1944). Regrettably, I have been unable to locate a copy of Ogara's work.

[50] di S. Maria, "S. Paolo," 491.

[51] In this regard di S. Maria was expanding on the brief but highly suggestive section in Merzagora, "Giovanni Crisostomo," 24–26.

[52] In particular, di S. Maria draws often (as did his predecessor Merzagora) upon the occasional homilies on Paul's letters, that is, those which stand outside of the commentary or homily (see the list of these in n. 7, above).

is the 1982 article by Theodore Zese, "The Apostle Paul and John Chrysostom."[53] Whereas Hoffmann-Aleith saw Chrysostom's interpretation of Paul's writings as sadly off the mark, Zese on the contrary seeks to show that Chrysostom was the definitively accurate interpreter of Paul, both in antiquity and today. Championing the perspective of Greek Orthodoxy, Zese highlights the substantial role which Paul played in Christian history by completing the task of his forerunner, Alexander the Great, through his infusion of Greek language and culture into the Christian tradition, making possible the unity of east and west, Christianity and Hellenism, Asia and Europe.[54] Zese's next step is to spotlight John Chrysostom as Paul's most accurate and reliable interpreter, and thus to claim them both for modern Greek Orthodoxy over and against the western interpretative traditions. The basis of Zese's argument is his wide-reaching claim that, unlike in the west, in the east the image of Paul, his work and his teaching has remained truly unchanged from Ignatius of Antioch to the fall of the east to the Turks in the fifteenth century. His contention is that Orthodox Christianity has always revered and rightly interpreted Paul, and that no one exemplifies this better than John Chrysostom, as can be seen throughout Orthodox history.[55]

Despite its overall apologetic purpose, Zese's article contains some valuable observations about Chrysostom as a Pauline interpreter. In particular, aided by his Eastern Orthodox perspective, Zese is appropriately sensitive to the role of images in ethical and theological thought, something which has perhaps been less appreciated by western scholars.[56] He includes rhetorically evocative praises of the great eastern saint, John, from ancients and moderns, adding his own unequivocal endorsement of Chrysostom as "simply the most marvelous interpreter of Paul,"[57]

---

[53] Theodore N. Zese, "ΑΠΟΣΤΟΛΟΣ ΠΑΥΛΟΣ ΚΑΙ ΙΩΑΝΝΗΣ ΧΡΥΣΟΣΤΟΜΟΣ," *Kleronomia* 14 (1982) 313–23.

[54] Εἰς τὰ πλαίσια λοιπὸν τῆς θείας οἰκονομίας ἡ ἐξόρμησις τοῦ Ἀλεξάνδρου ἦτο ἡ προοδοποίησις, ἡ προετοιμασία, ἡ προδρομικὴ ἐκστρατεία τῆς ἐξορμήσεως τοῦ Παύλου ("in the framework of the divine economy, the excursion of Alexander was the advance journey, the preparatory mission, the advance expedition for the excursion of Paul" [Zese, "Apostle Paul," 314–15]).

[55] Zese cites as one example the Council of Ferrara-Florence in 1438–45, where Chrysostom's interpretation of 1 Cor 3:12–15 was produced by the eastern delegates as normative (ibid., 322).

[56] See also, for instance, the plea of Verna E. F. Harrison, "Word as Icon in Greek Patristic Theology," *Sobornost* 10 (1988) 38–49, that the study of text and image be brought together in order to understand the dynamics of "verbal iconography" that are at work in patristic literature. This viewpoint has not been entirely resisted in the west, however; see, for instance, Averil Cameron, *Christianity and the Rhetoric of Empire* (Sather Classical Lectures 55; Berkeley: University of California Press, 1991), esp. 120–54.

[57] Ὁ Χρυσόστομος δὲν εἶναι ἁπλῶς ὁ θαυμάσιος ἑρμηνευτὴς τοῦ Παύλου (Zese, "Apostle Paul," 316). See also several other expressions of high praise: ὁ Χρυσόστομος εἶναι ἡ ἐπανεμφάνισις τοῦ Παύλου ("Chrysostom is the inexpressible height of Paul," p. 317, as Paul was of Christ, p. 313), and ὁ ἀνυπέρβλητος τοῦ Παύλου ἑρμηνευτής ("the unsurpassable interpreter of Paul," p. 320). These epithets are quite similar to Chrysostom's praises of Paul (as we shall see in chap. 3).

and gives valuable attention to the legend of Paul inspiring Chrysostom and its expression in Byzantine iconography, which will occupy a very important place in my investigation.[58] Zese especially recognizes the essential role of love in the symbiosis of John and Paul: "No one loved Christ more than Paul, and no one loved Paul more than Chrysostom."[59] Most important for this study is that Zese gives a contemporary Greek affirmation of the purpose and direction of this project, for he, too, recognizes in Chrysostom a preoccupation and love "for the writer and for his writings" which binds the entire hermeneutical enterprise together.[60] This emphasis on what I term Chrysostom's "love hermeneutics" as the heart of his interpretive activity puts the focus in the right place. In the face of the exegetical riches he describes, Zese expresses his great concern that even Orthodox theologians have neglected Chrysostom's interpretations of Paul (which, if so, is indeed surprising and lamentable), and his article concludes with a clarion call (of unfortunately xenophobic bent) to his fellow Greeks that "those who teach Paul in theological and ecclesiastical schools, instead of 'foreign' commentators of doubtful worth, or even Greek ones, should appropriately make Chrysostom's commentaries the basis for their instruction."[61] Zese regards it as a special project of Orthodox theological research to fill this void and to restore "the orthodox Paul of Chrysostom."

A comparison between Hoffmann-Aleith and Zese provides a single snapshot of the ways in which scholarship on Chrysostom's interpretations of Paul has been historically caught in inter-denominational conflicts and commitments. Another justification for my study's renewed look at Chrysostom's interpretation of Paul at this moment in history is the release of tensions afforded by the ecumenical movement (at least in my own American context), and a freeing of denominational "trench warfare" in which Chrysostom and his interpretations of Paul were a pawn — sometimes explicitly, often implicitly. And this context allows one to undertake this investigation without an apologetic presupposition that Chrysostom either always understood Paul, or on the contrary misunderstood him wholesale. If many of the battles of church history that created denominational lines of self-identification were battles about Paul and Pauline interpretation, then a less

---

[58] See pp. 34–43, and Appendix 2, pp. 489–93. This iconographical tradition was also mentioned briefly, though not examined, by Baur, *S. Jean Chrysostome*, 34 and Merzagora, "Giovanni Crisostomo," 1.

[59] Οὐδεὶς ἠγάπησε τὸν Χριστὸν περισσότερον τοῦ Παύλου καὶ οὐδεὶς ἠγάπησε τὸν Παῦλον περισσότερον τοῦ Χρυσοστόμου (Zese, "Apostle Paul," 317).

[60] Δι' αὐτῶν καθορίζει ὁ Χρυσόστομος τὴν σπουδαίαν ἑρμηνευτικὴν ἀρχὴν διὰ τὴν κατανόησιν ἑνὸς κειμένου, τὴν ἀγάπην δηλαδὴ πρὸς τὸν συγγραφέα καὶ τὰ γραφόμενα, τὴν οἰκείωσιν πρὸς αὐτά ...(ibid., 319). This was also very well appreciated more recently in the careful study of Metr. Demetrios Trakatellis ("Being Transformed: Chrysostom's Exegesis of the Epistle to the Romans," *GOTR* 36 [1991] 1–24, 19: "Chrysostom's achievement, however, is even more the result of his constant focusing not only on the text but also on the author of the Epistle to the Romans. It is extremely significant that he is incessantly conversing with Paul ...").

[61] Ibid., 323. The two authors he names as exemplary of western scholarship (writing in 1982!) are Adolf Deissmann and Joseph Holzner.

prejudiced recovery to the west, as well as to the east, of the important voice of John Chrysostom in Pauline interpretation is surely a worthy task.

But Zese's explicit call for Greek Orthodoxy's proprietary claim on John Chrysostom provides us with a valuable reminder of Chrysostom's place as an eastern father, which is of undeniable importance, both for understanding him in his own setting and for appreciating his place in the history of Pauline interpretation and Christian thought and history generally. Ernst Benz's 1951 survey of medieval to modern Pauline interpretation in the east as compared with the west offers – at least potentially – a needed corrective to the one-sided evaluations of both Hoffmann-Aleith and Zese, for he argues that both western and eastern interpretations of Paul had firm grounding in the writings of the apostle. His proposal, somewhat oversimplified but still telling, is that the western exegetes' emphasis on Paul's teaching about justification was due to their concentration on Romans, and the eastern interpreters' focus on mysticism and "new creation" resulted from their preference for the Corinthian correspondence, and relative neglect of Romans.[62] Benz contends, rightly, that this diversity was rooted in Paul's own missionary attention to the cultural values and practical needs of these different churches.[63]

Much influenced by Benz is the more recent study by Ernst Dassmann,[64] who approaches the subject of Pauline interpretation in east and west from the opposite direction: from the vantage point of the early church instead of later historical theology which built upon it.[65] He provides a brief survey of Pauline interpretation from Clement of Alexandria up to Chrysostom, and notes the ways in which the eastern fathers' interpretation differed from the west, especially, apparently, in their relative disregard of Romans, and their inattention to the major Pauline themes others have found in Romans: grace and justification.[66] Dassmann, too,

---

[62] "Das Paulus-Verständnis in der morgenländischen und abendländischen Kirche," *ZRGG* 3 (1951) 289–309: "Die Verschiedenheiten des morgenländischen und des abendländischen Christentums sind zwei Seiten und Auslegungsformen derselben Sache, die in Paulus eins waren" (p. 306). In this regard it is perhaps not insignificant for my own perspective on the project, and my attraction to Chrysostom, that I have concentrated in my own Pauline research more on the Corinthian correspondence.

[63] Ibid., 308: "... viele der religiösen und theologischen Dissonanzen innerhalb der Christenheit zurückgehen auf die Unfähigkeit der Nachfahren, die ganze Polyphonie des Apostels zu begreifen."

[64] "Zum Paulusverständnis in der östlichen Kirche," *JAC* 29 (1986) 27–39, 33–38, on Chrysostom specifically.

[65] This article emanated from his extensive research on the history of Pauline interpretation, beginning in the New Testament itself (*Der Stachel im Fleisch: Paulus in der frühchristlichen Literatur bis Irenäus*), and represents his extension of those earlier studies up to the fifth century. Dassmann has also profitably studied popular images of Paul in the early church (*Paulus in frühchristlicher Frömmigkeit und Kunst*).

[66] Dassmann acknowledges his debt to Benz' article, "Das Paulus-Verständnis in der morgenländischen und abendländischen Kirche," though he also corrects some minor errors of fact in that piece (Dassmann, "Paulusverständnis," 38 n. 53), and suggests in his conclusion that the sweeping assessments Benz made need further substantiation.

recognizes that the Pauline legacy was quite complex, as manifested both in ancient and medieval readings of Paul, and in the divergent denominational perspectives of modern readers of Paul and of his interpreters. As a result Dassmann calls for a new look at the question, which, he rightly insists, requires further detailed study of the interpreters of Paul in the fourth and fifth centuries.[67]

Methodological Presuppositions of this Study

The present book seeks to meet the need Dassmann identified, assisted in that task (one hopes) by a more self-conscious awareness of the role of the assumptions interpreters bring to their work, and by a contemporary ecumenical climate which seeks less (or at the very least less overtly) to claim exclusive possession of any ancient writer for a single ecclesiastical community.[68] In a context formed by modern hermeneutics, the barrage of assaults on singular meaning of texts from a range of ahistorical methodologies for interpreting the Bible, and postmodern perspectives on pluralism, one can no longer seek to render simplified or sweeping judgments about whether or not John understood Paul "correctly." Methodologically, Dassmann's insistence on a wider lens for analysis of the Pauline legacy in the early church is well taken. Our goal here is not to attempt to compare Chrysostom's interpretations of Pauline thought or Paul's life with a single "correct" reading, as Hoffmann-Aleith sought to do,[69] but to bring Chrysostom's insights, as

---

[67] "Insgesamt bewegen sich alle diese Unterscheidungen, Zuweisungen und Interessenverteilungen auf unsicherem Boden, denn die Wirkungsgeschichte des Paulus im 4./5. Jahrhundert bedarf noch der gründlichen Erforschung. Weitere Detailuntersuchungen wären hier dringend erwünscht ..." (Dassmann, "Paulusverständnis," 39). As this quotation continues Dassmann also makes a plea for contemporary ecumenical efforts: "... und zwar nicht nur aus einem allgemeinen theologie-, exegese- und dogmengeschichtlichen Interesse, sondern auch aus ökumenischen Gründen. Paulus gehört zum neutestamentlichen Erbe aller christlichen Kirchen, seine Wirkungsgeschichte verzweigt sich zugleich in den verschiedenen Konfessionen, wobei Querverbindungen entstehen, die die sonst üblichen, geschichtlich gewordenen Verbindungen oder auch Gegensätze durchkreuzen."

[68] Indeed, Dassmann thinks that it is Paul himself who can bring about the ecumenical unity so needed now ("Darum kann Paulus, der größer ist als alle seine Ausleger, wenn man das Corpus seiner Briefe nicht zerstückelt, sondern in seiner ganzen Vielfalt zu Wort kommen läßt, helfen, die Wege wieder zusammenzuführen" ["Paulusverständnis," 39]).

[69] In this regard, Dassmann himself appears somewhat ambiguous. He begins his study of Chrysostom's interpretation of Paul's letters by asking how they compare with "Paul's intention" (ibid., 34). But he softens Hoffmann-Aleith's "skeptical reading" by saying that: "er mißversteht Paulus durchaus nicht in der groben Weise, daß er das Sollen vor das Sein setzt. Aber er akzen-tuiert doch anders als der Paulus des Römer- oder des Galaterbriefes" (p. 34, one can easily see the influence of Benz here). He does not directly address the question of whether the different accent constitutes a *misunderstanding* of Paul, but then he can say that Chrysostom "entschärft" the position of Romans, by reducing the varied behavior of God to "providence," while Paul has in view salvation and repudiation (p. 36) However, later Dassmann rightly eschews the meth-

apprehended first as much as possible on their own terms, into conversation with what contemporary Pauline scholars take him to be saying, and in particular to compare the methodological assumptions which ground each inquiry in turn, especially those about the author himself. On the other hand, my approach will differ from Dassmann's because it seems to me that, although he seeks to move away from a comparison of Pauline interpretation in the early church with a simple Lutheran reading of Paul, Dassmann's investigation, in its search for the "Grundgedanken" of Pauline thought, still too much enshrines the structural principle of that (interpretation of the) western reading associated with Augustine and Luther. Such an approach presumes that Chrysostom (or the other eastern fathers surveyed) did indeed approach Paul in search of his "main ideas," as is the predominant characterization of western exegesis, and that he wrote in such a way as to encode such a synthesis. But the reader of Chrysostom's homilies on Paul's epistles will find such a question largely unaddressed, for they are neither structured nor intended to answer this question. Therefore, such a template should not be imposed upon Chrysostom's homilies; nor should his interpretations of any text be uncharacteristically systematized, or theological "concepts" extracted from their own literary, historical, liturgical and rhetorical contexts.[70]

The "main idea" approach therefore, even if unintentionally, resonates too much with the question: "Did he get him right?" since logically there can be only one "basic" or "root idea." This kind of pursuit brings its own questions to the texts of Chrysostom, to answer them on *its* terms, rather than seeking to enter his exegetical practice on its own. It is always salutary to look into how Chrysostom deals with a particular exegetical *crux interpretum*, but I am convinced that we cannot do that well in isolation from an understanding of his general way of handling Paul and his letters. When one turns to the larger synthetic questions about Pauline thought, I am convinced that "did Chrysostom understand Paul correctly?" is not the right question to ask. And, even if it were, contemporary Pauline scholarship has produced no clear-cut baseline for comparison; indeed, it has undermined the very synthesis upon which a scholar like Hoffmann-Aleith could so confidently build.[71] Consequently, the goal of this study is neither to argue that

---

odological move of setting Chrysostom's interpretation of Romans alongside Augustine's and using it as a "whipping post" (p. 36, naming among other guilty parties Hoffmann-Aleith).

[70] This was argued effectively in terms of Chrysostom's moral teachings by Louis Meyer, "Liberté et moralisme chrétien dans la doctrine spirituelle de saint Jean Chrysostome," *RSR* 23 [1933] 283–305, 301: "On comprend donc facilement qu'on ait pu abuser de ces commentaires pour les enchâsser dans les systèmes théologiques nés depuis."

[71] The last twenty-five years has witnessed an erosion of what is for convenience sake labeled the "Augustinian-Lutheran" reading of Paul, beginning with seminal works by Krister Stendahl ("The Apostle Paul and the Introspective Conscience of the West," *Paul Among Jews and Gentiles* [Philadelphia: Fortress, 1976] 78–96), on the one hand, and E. P. Sanders (*Paul and Palestinian Judaism. A Comparison of Patterns of Religion* [Philadelphia: Fortress, 1977], on the other). We shall engage the work of these scholars in chap. 8, pp. 423–28.

Chrysostom *did* fully or always understand Paul (as he himself claimed), nor that he did not, but instead first to lay out Chrysostom's approach to Paul's letters on its own terms as much as possible, and to bring Chrysostom's work into conversation with contemporary Pauline scholarship. When one observes, as we shall repeatedly have occasion to do in this book, Chrysostom's penchant for painting portraits of Paul by selecting elements from out of the existing plethora of data within the letters and the Acts of the Apostles and recombining them in novel ways, the criterion of *the right portrait* or *the accurate portrait* of Paul is utterly elusive and ultimately useless. How could we judge such a thing? What would be the objective standard by which we would evaluate "the true portrait of Paul?" And, even more, why should we seek a *single* standard, when it is far more illuminating to see how and why John constructs varying portraits of Paul in his own liturgical and homiletical contexts? A search to nail down *the* portrait of Paul in Chrysostom's writings will end in failure, for John was not interested in doing this (though he would nonetheless claim that his portrayal of Paul is "accurate"); to the contrary, one of the reasons John loves Paul and eulogizes him so often is precisely because of his chameleonic nature.[72] And in carefully scrutinizing Chrysostom's wide array of artistic renderings of Paul, we can appreciate something of the marvelous malleability of the persona of the apostle to the Gentiles in the history of interpretation, and of Christian thought and social formations generally.

When one instead begins with the question, "*how* did Chrysostom interpret Paul?" the inquiry is different from the outset, for it includes not only the content or results of John's exegesis, but also its hermeneutical processes.[73] Then what leaps to the fore is John's own insistence upon his relationship with Paul as the inspiration and generation of all of his interpretation, and upon the inestimable importance of the apostle's example for his catechetical and ecclesial program. Consequently, in place of a wholesale judgment on Chrysostom's accuracy as an interpreter of Paul, my investigation is structured around the central issue which I perceive to be raised by Chrysostom's own Pauline interpretations: the relationship between Chrysostom's rich and imaginative depictions of the person of Paul and the way in which he understands the letters he is reading as sacred scripture. That is the focal question which structures my inquiry (one interestingly closer to di S. Maria and Zese), rather than "what is the root idea of Chrysostom's interpretation of Paul's theology?" (such as Hoffmann-Aleith and Dassmann). It is Chrysostom's oeuvre itself, which includes encomia within exegetical homilies, and full-scale festival encomia to Paul, which raises the issue of the relationship between Chrysostom's conceptions of the person of Paul (what in German scholarship is

---

[72] Which Chrysostom himself will celebrate in *laud. Paul.* 5, analyzed on pp. 330–53, below.

[73] This addresses the need identified by Charles Kannengiesser, "The Future of Patristics," *TS* 52 (1991) 128–39, 135: "Amazingly enough, the cultural and social procedures according to which the Bible functioned in given areas or periods of ancient Christian traditions are still somewhat *terra incognita* for patristic scholarship."

referred to as *Das Paulusbild*), and the way in which he interprets the apostle's letters. Consequently, my inquiry is rooted in the fundamental conviction that Chrysostom's living sense of his hero Paul is not a charming side dish to the "meat" of his interpretation of the theology in Paul's epistles, but is instead central to it, and important in its own right.[74] Therefore one cannot adequately comprehend Chrysostom's exegetical work without paying direct attention to his devotion to his subject.[75] Furthermore, my predominant concern arises primarily from my assessment of the nature and form of the material under question: John Chrysostom's actual homilies on Pauline and other texts which are addressed to specific concerns of two divergent church congregations over more than a twenty year period, during a crucial and seminal period in church history marked by burgeoning interest in saints' lives and relics, and by public oratorical forms which played crucial roles in the social construction of Christian society. This material cannot be studied in a vacuum, and, as it does not lend itself to the kind of systematic expectations some have brought to it, should not be examined primarily through that lens.[76] With this in view, the present study seeks to analyze this rich source material, Chrysostom's homilies on Paul, as compositions which are at once exegetical, liturgical and rhetorical, participating in recognized sets of expectations and functions which bound together orator and audience in the act of sermonic

---

[74] R. D. Sider, "Literary Artifice and the Figure of Paul in the Writings of Tertullian," *Paul and the Legacies of Paul*, ed. W. S. Babcock (Dallas: Southern Methodist University Press, 1990) has recognized this most effectively in the case of Tertullian: "[Tertullian] does not offer us a single sustained exposition of a well-reasoned theology in which Paul plays a precisely measurable role, but rather a varied corpus of artful compositions, individually self-contained for the most part, where both allusions to Paul the man and citations from the epistles as witness to Pauline thought play a part in the orchestration of an argument intended to be immediately persuasive. In the literary art and rhetorical design of Tertullian, the life of Paul can be as important as his thought" (p. 100). All of what Sider says here of Tertullian's interpretation of Paul applies completely to John's, with an even higher degree of effusive expression.

[75] *pace* Dassmann, "Paulusverständnis," 34: "Wichtiger noch als das Paulusbild und die panegyrischen Leistungen sind jedoch die theologischen Inhalte, die Chrysostomus aus den Paulusbriefen aufgreift, sowie das Maß an Übereinstimmung zwischen seiner Auslegung und den paulinischen Intentionen." But would Chrysostom agree with this? And why are the two questions – image of Paul and assessment of his theology – to be separated and so prioritized? Surely the former has an effect on the latter. Furthermore, an evaluation of Chrysostom's interpretations of Paul's letters should not be restricted to an evaluation of Chrysostom's grasp of Paul's theology (so Dassmann, 33: "erfaßt er die Hauptlinien der paulinischen Verkündigung?"), for there is much of interest in his exegetical enterprise which does not fit naturally under this category.

[76] Dassmann uses his recognition of this point to take John down from the "whipping post" (see n. 69 above) on which the Augustinians have put him ("Angesichts anderer Aussagen, die mit ähnlicher Deutlichkeit den Vorrang der Gnade vor allem menschlichen Tun betonen, ließe sich auch auf die Unausgewogenheit, ja Widersprüchlichkeit der Theologie des Chrysostomus hinweisen und mit den besonderen Aufgaben des Predigers, der nicht immer auf dogmatische Strigenz achten kann, verteidigen" [ibid., 36]), though this point did not lead him to reconsider the governing question of his study.

biblical interpretation.[77] When one pays attention to the inherently rhetorical quality and function of these interpretative *speeches*, the hermeneutical dimensions of biblical interpretation as a scripted encounter with the author, carried out according to the rules and expectations of the larger literary culture, come unmistakably to the fore.

Approaching Chrysostom's Rhetorical Art

Chrysostom's interpretations of the person of Paul and his letters are integrally related, and must be approached and assessed as instances of rhetorical production, because Chrysostom's predominant genre of Pauline interpretation was not the commentary (though contemporary scholars too often read them as though they were the product of a scholastic enterprise, designed to be read in that way),[78] but the homiletical discourse. In composing portraits of Paul, Chrysostom employed standard rhetorical techniques of his day for the encomium, the form used for laudably portraying an individual, which he adapted in various ways for assorted purposes, depending upon the context. He was so much at home in this métier that he exploded into it on various occasions, both predictable and entirely unanticipated, in his homilies on the letters as well as other writings not directly related to Paul. This effusion of praise for Paul needs to be investigated, not just as a quaint artifact, an instance of extreme private devotion, or a "mere rhetorical flourish," but also as a powerful vehicle for Christian meaning-making and society-formation in the late fourth century, a task well beyond the purview and aims of my predecessors in the study of Chrysostom's interpretation of Paul. Pauline interpretation as Chrysostom practices it (and no less in other contexts, including our own), is not a depersonalized, neutral endeavor in which a person (the reader) meets an object (a written text). In awakening Paul from his grave to speak to contemporary audiences and be paraded forth as an example of piety before their eyes, the orator-exegete always has a contemporary end in view.

---

[77] Again, as called for by Kannengiesser, "Future of Patristics," 136: "Can we retrace the assimilation of biblical data to the rhetorical culture of late antiquity, for instance down to Ambrose or Augustine?"

[78] The exception is the sets on Matthew and Galatians, which are traditionally given the name *commentaria*, but they, too, clearly have a live audience and liturgical context in view (with Kelly, *Golden Mouth*, 92–94 and Robert Charles Hill, *St. John Chrysostom: Commentary on the Psalms. Volume 1* [Brookline, MA: Holy Cross Orthodox Press, 1998] 14–17, against Baur, *John Chrysostom*, 1.221–23). This is the case even if one accepts Hans Lietzmann's hypothesis that the Galatians "commentary" consists of the homilies edited together, shorn of the exhortations ("Johannes Chrysostomos," PW 9/2, 1811–1828, 1818; also Max von Bonsdorff, *Zur Predigttätigkeit des Johannes Chrysostomus: Biographisch-chronologische Studien über seine Homilienserien zu neutestamentlichen Büchern* [diss. Universität Helsingfors; Helsinki, 1922] 50).

In order to appreciate the objectives Chrysostom has in mind, and the means he employs toward achieving them, one needs a measured assessment of his wider cultural context, as free as possible from the constraints of Christian apologetics which approached the issue of Christianity and rhetoric (as a subcategory of "Christianity and classical culture")[79] only in order to eschew the use of that "profane art" by the purveyors of the simple truth of the gospel. One of the most influential works of Chrysostom scholarship of the last century, Aimé Puech's book bearing the subtitle, *St Jean Chrysostome et les moeurs de son temps*, published in 1891, presented Chrysostom as completely hostile to Greek learning and rhetorical arts: "On n'a peut-être pas assez dit que Chrysostome fut, entre tous les Pères du IVe siècle, un des plus détachés de la civilisation antique et profane."[80] The great classicist Eduard Norden famously opined (on the basis of his self-confessed sparse reading in his corpus) that Chrysostom was reluctant to engage in rhetorical finery, presumably because of his predictable opposition to Hellenistic culture.[81] But the 1904 article of Anton Naegele exposed the contradictions involved in these sweeping judgments.[82] His lead was followed up in the detailed

---

[79] For the wider history of this debate, see Hans Dieter Betz, "Antike und Christentum," *RGG*[4] 1 (1998) 542–46, and *idem*, "Antiquity and Christianity," *JBL* 117 (1998) 3–22, reprinted in *idem, Antike und Christentum: Gesammelte Aufsätze IV* (Tübingen: J. C. B. Mohr [Paul Siebeck], 1998) 267–90.

[80] Puech, *Un réformateur*, 121. This general judgment is reflected also in his comment on rhetoric in particular: "Quelque différente que soit son éloquence de celle des panégyristes et des sophistes, quoiqu'il se fût même formé une rhétorique toute contraire par ses principes et sa méthode à celle de Libanius, cependant les leçons du rhéteur ne lui avaient pas été inutiles" (ibid.).

[81] Norden's comments placing both Basil and Chrysostom on a different level from Gregory of Nazianzus are found in *Die antike Kunstprosa vom VI Jahrhundert v. Chr. bis in die Zeit der Renaissance* (2 vols.; Leipzig/Berlin: Teubner, 1918, original, 1898) 569–73. In particular he remarked on "der Scheu, die Predigt ganz in die sophistische Prunkrede aufgehen zu lassen" (570, though he did acknowledge on the next page that "[Chrysostomos] mit voller Beherrschung der rhetorischen Technik schrieb"). Also influential in this regard was the remark of Edward Gibbon (who admitted that he was "almost a stranger to the voluminous sermons of Chrysostom") that in his oratory John had "the judgment to conceal the advantages which he derived from the knowledge of rhetoric and philosophy," presumably because of a derogatory assessment of those arts (*The History of the Decline and Fall of the Roman Empire*, ed. J. B. Bury [7 vols.; London: Methuen & Co., 1909] 3.396), a comment Puech repudiates because it allows for too much rhetorical skill on Chrysostom's part (*Un réformateur*, 122–23)!

[82] Anton Naegele, "Johannes Chrysostomos und sein Verhältnis zum Hellenismus," *Byzantinische Zeitschrift* 13 (1904) 73–113. He argued vigorously that Chrysostom represented in himself a deliberately worked out compromise between Hellenism and Christianity. Naegele saw this given expression also in Chrysostom's oratory: "Namentlich sind es die vielbewunderten Vergleiche, Analogien und Metaphern, in denen der Redner wie aus einem unerschöpflichen Schatze alles Schöne und Nützliche des antiken Kultur- und Geisteslebens den Zwecken der geistlichen Beredsamkeit dienstbar zu machen weiß. In diesen wie in anderen, zur Veranschaulichung, Beweisführung und Widerlegung verwandten τόποι καὶ τρόποι der Rede finden wir den Niederschlag der wesentlichen Elemente und Erscheinungen der Welt des Hellenismus, gleichviel ob nur kurz gestreift oder eingehender beleuchtet, ob unwillkürlich angenommen oder mit Absicht und entschieden abgelehnt, ob in kompromißartiger Akkommodation oder in

textual study completed by Thomas E. Ameringer in 1921,[83] which thoroughly documented the extent to which Chrysostom was at home in the milieu of Greco-Roman rhetorical techniques and conventions, especially the encomium. These two scholars demolished the apologetic and theologically motivated assessments of prior scholars who had wished to present Chrysostom as uniformly "anti-pagan" and entirely devoid of the rhetorical fancies of the external culture. Both began with the sage biographical observation that if Norden, Wilamowitz-Moellendorff[84] and other greats were right in claiming that Chrysostom completely eschewed his earlier education under the great Antiochene orator Libanios,[85] then he would have represented "a psychological phenomenon that was indeed remarkable."[86] Ameringer's detailed research into Chrysostom's prose style and argumentation provided abundant documentation of the extent to which Chrysostom's writings pervasively employ the same kinds of rhetorical figures and tropes as the predominantly epideictic compositions of the second sophistic. Unfortunately, Ameringer was still sufficiently mired in the apologetics of past scholarship that in his conclusion he sought to relegate Chrysostom's considerable exercise of rhetorical arts, of which his study had given more than ample demonstration, to acts of his "unconscious."[87] But, as we shall see throughout this study, Chrysostom

---

naturnotwendiger Verschmelzung mit den Grundlagen christlichen Denkens und Lebens" (p. 94). Among his detailed arguments Naegele demonstrated that Chrysostom did not deride, but rather justified the quotations from "pagan" authors in the Pauline letters (pp. 102–105). See also the extension of this debate about Chrysostom's supposedly negative attitude toward classical literature in Baur, *John Chrysostom*, 1.305–14.

[83] *The Stylistic Influence of the Second Sophistic On the Panegyrical Sermons of St. John Chrysostom: A Study in Greek Rhetoric* (Ph.D. Dissertation, Catholic University of America, 1921).

[84] Ameringer lumps the distinguished classicist Ulrich von Wilamowitz-Moellendorff with those who "minimize the sophistic influence on Chrysostom" (*Second Sophistic*, 102), but Ameringer has apparently misread him, because Wilamowitz actually conferred great praise on Chrysostom, as "ein beinahe puristischer Attizist" ("Die griechische Literatur des Altertums," in *Die Kultur der Gegenwart*, ed. Paul Hinneberg [Berlin: Teubner, 1924³] 1/8, pp. 295–97, 296). Perhaps Ameringer has based his negative interpretation on the somewhat barbed introduction Wilamowitz gives to his succinct treatment of Chrysostom: "Iohannes, den man leider mit dem schon bei Dion von Prusa (von dem er geborgt ist) absurden Namen Chrysostomos nennen muß" (p. 295), but what follows is quite complimentary (though critical about Chrysostom's practicality and lack of philosophical grandeur). Scholars on both sides of the debate over Chrysostom's classicism have sought to enlist Wilamowitz-Moellendorff's authority, based upon his three page discussion of Chrysostom, whom he allows he has not much read! (see Baur, *John Chrysostom*, 1.305–307).

[85] Although in the history of scholarship this fact, reported by the church historian Socrates, has been questioned, it has mostly been accepted as genuine. See the thorough and convincing discussion in David G. Hunter, "Libanius and John Chrysostom: New Thoughts on an Old Problem," *Studia Patristica* (ed. E.A. Livingstone) 22 (1989) 129–35, and the recent judgment of Kelly, *Golden Mouth*, 7.

[86] Ameringer, *Second Sophistic*, 10; also Naegele, "Johannes Chrysostomos," 101.

[87] See his conclusion, *Second Sophistic*, 102: "In fairness to [John] we must concede that, generally, he is true to his principles [Ameringer converts Chrysostom's "severely denouncing those preachers who busied themselves about the harmony and composition of their periods,

quite knowingly deployed his rhetorical skills and strategies (including those of denouncing practitioners of rhetoric and devaluing his own skill), and deliberately employed oratorical arts to enliven his arguments and entertain his audiences. The root of Ameringer's unnecessary embarrassment with Chrysostom's rhetoric can be discovered in his own predominant judgment and dismissal of this kind of rhetoric as "bad taste," and in his ascription of the more florid characteristics of Chrysostom's style, such as his heaping up of examples or metaphors, to John's "oriental" background, in contrast with (his own preference for) a more tempered and even-handed "European" approach.[88] By relegating these oratorical character-istics to Chrysostom's "unconscious," Ameringer was able to keep Chrysostom himself essentially pure of the corrupt and unseemly accoutrements of pagan rheto-ric. Hence in the final analysis the impressive array of rhetorical arts Ameringer identified in Chrysostom's corpus is regarded more as the orator's almost reluctant concession to his audience, rather than an index of his own embeddedness in his literary culture and educational background:

> In no way then do we regard it as a misfortune that Chrysostom proclaimed the simple truths of Christianity in the polished language of profane rhetoric, nor do we wish that he had rather chosen the plain and unadorned style of the first preachers of the Gospel. Such a course would have been altogether unsuited to the needs and exigencies of the times. The refined and cultured audiences of Antioch and Constantinople would have ignored a preacher whose exposition of doctrine was devoid of the graces and embellishments of language which they prized so highly.[89]

But the volume of evidence Ameringer produced attesting to Chrysostom's so-phistic-styled rhetoric incited Harry M. Hubbell in 1924 to inquire, for the first time, into the influences of classical rhetoric, not just on John's literary style, but also on his argumentation and forms of literary composition.[90] For that investigation

---

and who strove to entertain their audience by a show of eloquence" into "principles"], but that, when he violates them, *he does so unconsciously*. The mannerisms of profane rhetoric had become, as it were, his second nature, so that, while he strove to avoid the grosser excesses of the oratory of show and display, he could not altogether eradicate intellectual habits that were deep-rooted and of long standing" (emphasis added). This concession of only "unconscious" exercise of rhetoric by a Christian orator is reminiscent of recent apologetic reactions to scholarship demon-strating Paul's use of rhetorical techniques (such as Duane Litfin, *St. Paul's Theology of Proclamation: 1 Corinthians 1–4 and Greco-Roman Rhetoric* [SNTSMS 79; Cambridge: Cambridge University Press, 1994]; R. Dean Anderson, *Ancient Rhetorical Theory and Paul* [Contributions to Biblical Exegesis and Theology 17; Kampen: Kok Pharos, 1996], esp. 249–57).

[88] "… the eastern peoples, who are more imaginative than the nations of the west. Chrysos-tom was himself an Oriental, endowed with a rich and bold fancy" (Ameringer, *Second Sophistic*, 56). "The oriental peoples are of course more given to this sparkling ornament than the Euro-peans" (ibid., 68).

[89] Ibid., 103.

[90] "It has not been determined, however, I believe, how far Chrysostom's training affected what the theorists call invention and disposition, the choice of thoughts to present, and the arrangement of them in the oration" (Harry M. Hubbell, "Chrysostom and Rhetoric," *CP* 19 [1924] 261–76, 267).

Hubbell found the seven "encomia" to Paul essential sources, rightly judging them to be very much products of the explosion of Christian oratory in the fourth century, as exemplified especially by the Cappadocians. His very brief article ("a slight beginning of such an investigation") gives a concise introduction to the theory of epideictic rhetoric,[91] and a barebones analysis of each of the seven orations. It remains the only concentrated treatment of the argument of these speeches to date.[92] Hubbell concludes that while these encomia do not adhere to the chronological scheme of the classical encomium, nor its length, they can be classified as λαλιαί, talks, which "illustrate the very free use of laudatory material."[93] In many ways Hubbell presages the need for the present study, and emboldens it by the alliance with a prominent classicist of the early part of this century. And his approach – to analyze the rhetoric of actual speeches with the assistance of the considerable sources extant on ancient rhetorical theory – is indeed the right way to proceed.

But Hubbell's work also needs improvement both in scope and detail (he gave only a very cursory examination of each of the seven orations), and in methodology. His approach to Chrysostom's encomia to Paul, focusing upon arrangement, often emphasized more the occasional differences between the standard encomiastic form and Chrysostom's orations than the manifold similarities. Nor did he investigate these dissimilarities in terms of the liturgical setting of Chrysostom's orations, or the place of these seven orations within Chrysostom's considerable writings on the apostle Paul. Hubbell's major contribution was in terms of invention, where he enumerates many valuable points of similarity between Chrysostom's arguments and the rhetorical handbooks of Theon and Menander, but his guidelines for identifying contact between the two are at times too rigid. He does not often enough appreciate the extent to which, when Chrysostom quite deliberately employs rhetorical commonplaces in a way which overturns them, that is itself an *influence* of the rhetorical culture, for it is working on and with the rhetorical expectations of his audience. A more flexible approach to both rhetorical form and content will assist us in seeing how the moralizing in Chrysostom's encomia to Paul, for instance, participates in the logic that form of discourse propagates. And in seeking to comprehend how Chrysostom understood and represented Paul in a range of oratorical settings we shall focus on the varied and often deliberately ironic ways in which he adapts conventional forms of praise to fit his own hero.

The conclusions of Ameringer and Hubbell, that Chrysostom employed techniques of rhetorical style and invention, which were quite daring in their day,

---

[91] That is, the form of the encomium, which we shall describe thoroughly in chap. 4, pp. 95–100.

[92] Alongside the introduction and notes to Piédagnel's *Sources chrétiennes* volume on these discourses, which we have critiqued above.

[93] Hubbell, "Chrysostom and Rhetoric," 274.

taking on as they did the foremost classicists of the previous generations,[94] now appear largely commonplace. An index of this sea change is that in his excellent 1983 study of Chrysostom's rhetoric of invective against Jews and Judaizers, Robert Wilken no longer felt the need to contend against those who would deny outright that a Christian bishop would actually use the skills and techniques of "pagan" rhetoric.[95] And the results of his study are overwhelmingly convincing – that Chrysostom knew exactly what he was doing when he engaged his opponents using commonplace arguments, appeals and phrases from the wider rhetorical culture. In addition to Wilken's work on Chrysostom specifically, the issue of the role of biography and rhetoric in the rise of Christianity and the creation of a Christian society in the fourth century constitutes one of the most engaging areas of current scholarship in late antique historiography.[96] Scholars such as Peter Brown, Averil Cameron, and Patricia Cox, in addition to Wilken, have moved the conversation well beyond the need to justify the conclusion that the late fourth century Christian bishops employed the tools of rhetoric, to a recognized demand for full-scale examinations of this rhetorical art, its techniques and functions. What is now needed (and what this investigation seeks to contribute to) are analyses of precisely *how* rhetorical art and social construction were carried out by individual Christian writers.[97] Chrysostom's use of Paul is an ideal opportunity for such an inquiry, because his rhetorical training is sure and deep, his esteem in antiquity unques-

---

[94] But there are still hints of embarrassment or concession in Hubbell's article, also, as when he writes: "Chrysostom is full of denunciations of contemporary rhetoric and particularly of his old teacher, Libanius, but at the same time he grants that a certain amount of rhetorical artifice is justifiable in a sermon owing to the weakness of the audience" (Hubbell, "Chrysostom and Rhetoric," 267). Although this statement is true, it is not completely representative, either of passages where Chrysostom insists on the necessity for effective rhetoric (such as *sac.* 4.6–8, which we shall analyze in chap. 6), or of the self-consciousness behind Chrysostom's freely florid and playful rhetorical style. Yet Hubbell himself is able to recognize the commonplace nature of the disclaimer of rhetorical skill which perpetuates this impression for what it is (ibid., 268, in regard to *laud. Paul.* 1.1). And it is that move which most characterizes the shift from the older consensus of denial of the appropriation of "pagan rhetoric" by Christian orators to the position of the modern classicists and scholars of late antiquity whose work is listed in the following notes. (In evaluating Hubbell one should also note that he held the dubious view that the late fourth century was the moment when "rhetoric gains full control of preaching, and then the victory is sudden and decisive" [ibid., 262], holding in full confidence that "it is safe to say that the New Testament – barring possibly one exception – is untouched by current rhetorical theory" [ibid., 261]. On the apologetic force behind many such developmental theories of Christian rhetoric, including Chrysostom's own, see chap. 6, n. 203.)

[95] Wilken, *John Chrysostom and the Jews*, esp. 95–127.

[96] See Patricia Cox, *Biography in Late Antiquity: The Quest for the Holy Man* (The Transformation of the Classical Heritage 5; Berkeley: University of California Press, 1983); Averil Cameron, *Christianity and the Rhetoric of Empire*; Peter Brown, *Power and Persuasion in Late Antiquity: Towards a Christian Empire* (Madison: University of Wisconsin Press, 1992); this includes the important role of biographic and biographical literature in social construction, which is being discussed in some important publications (e.g., M. J. Edwards and Simon Swain, eds., *Portraits: Biographical Representation in the Greek and Latin Literature of the Roman Empire* [Oxford: Clarendon, 1997]).

[97] See Mark Edwards, "Epilogue," in *Portraits: Biographical Representation in the Greek and Latin*

tioned, and, perhaps most importantly, he is often quite explicit about his rhetorical purposes and strategies. Just as Wilken sought to understand the role of Chrysostomic *invective* in its own social and rhetorical culture, here I wish to investigate the flip side of that coin: how John's ubiquitous *encomia* of his champion Paul were a key force, not only in his exegetical enterprise, but also in his social and catechetical program. In the case of John's portraits of Paul we can peer into the workshop of the rhetorician as he constructs Christian piety and society by composing as its archetype his image of Paul. And one place where Chrysostom's own ambivalence about rhetoric (which, as we have seen, was so intensely reincarnated in the earlier history of scholarship) can itself be profitably explored is in his portraits of Paul as the reluctant Christian orator *par excellence*.[98] Now free from the emotionally charged dynamic of accusation and denial of the use of rhetoric that has been replayed time and again in the history of scholarship on this material, in this book we shall look unembarrassedly at Chrysostom's discourses on Paul as rhetorical compositions – i.e., literary artifacts which seek intentionally and emphatically by recognized conventions to persuade their audiences to beliefs and actions – and in so doing seek to understand something about all exegetical practice as an act of persuasive resuscitation of an author in the formation of a community of conversation for the present. We shall observe how Chrysostom's praises of Paul participate in the larger context of socio-cultural dynamics of the late fourth century, especially in terms of saints and relics and their relationship to texts, and body and self in relation to society, seen at work in a particular set of writings by one well-practiced and self-conscious in the art of rhetoric.

Contemporary Resonances with Chrysostom's Interpretation of Paul

While Chrysostom's interpretations of Paul and his letters are of interest to any age, they seem especially and strikingly relevant to current trends in Pauline interpretation. First of all, whereas earlier generations of scholars found Chrysostom's homilies on the Pauline epistles of limited value because of their lack of philosophical or systematic preoccupations, contemporary Pauline scholars more and more see Paul not as a systematic or dogmatic theologian,[99] but as a practical

---

Literature of the Roman Empire, ed. M.J. Edwards and Simon Swain (Oxford: Clarendon, 1997) 227–34: "We therefore need not only to describe the biographic, but to study it."

[98] We shall analyze Chrysostom's treatment of Paul's rhetorical training and skill at length in chap. 6, pp. 278–91.

[99] Representative of the current state of the question is the internal dialogue of C. K. Barrett, who ultimately seeks to retain the term "systematic theologian" for Paul by redefining it (*Paul: An Introduction to His Thought* [Louisville: Westminster/John Knox, 1994] 55–56): "It is important to begin the study of Paul's thought by relating it to the often contentious circumstances of his life. To fail to do this would give his theology a static quality that it did not possess ... The occasional treatment of Paul's thought is not only allowable, convenient, and interesting; it is essential. But

theologian whose letters must be read as specific responses to pastoral crises and daily-life issues affecting his churches. This was indeed how Chrysostom viewed his favorite apostle; it is likewise the setting for Chrysostom's *own* interpretations of Paul's letters, which creates a reciprocal pastoral engagement with Pauline counsel, rebuke and teaching. As such, what was formerly considered Chrysostom's liability now renders him robustly *au courant*. Chrysostom's pastoral reading of Paul,[100] which was to some degree grounded in his own pastoral identity and functions, now seems less a frustration (as it was to those who earlier found him bereft of philosophical or systematic interest),[101] than a most suitable frame of reference. It is safe to say that the prevailing portraits of Paul held by Chrysostom and by contemporary scholars are closer now than they once were, when the model of Paul was the systematic theologian of the Reformers and later dogmatically focused exegetes. Secondly, Chrysostom's interpretations of Paul's letters intersect fruitfully with two major areas of contemporary Pauline research: epistolography and rhetoric. Although for centuries the epistolary formulas of Paul's letters were largely ignored as the mere framing for his dogmatics, research in the

---

it must be supplemented by thematic treatment. It is probably better to say thematic than systematic. Whether Paul can properly be described as a systematic theologian is a question often answered in the negative. To a great extent the matter turns upon the definition of the terms used. Beyond the occasionalism of Paul's theology there is a real unity; he reacts to circumstances spontaneously but he does not react at random; he reacts in accordance with principles, seldom stated as such but detectable. He does so moreover in the light of what he knew of his environment – of a profound knowledge of Judaism and at least a smattering of Greek culture. To do this is the task of the systematic theologian, who does not need to qualify for the title by writing a large textbook of systematic theology but by his grasp of Christian principles and his ability to think them through and express them in terms of his own environment. It might be said that New Testament theology is the systematic theology of the first century, and this is pre-eminently true of Pauline theology." See also Jürgen Becker, *Paul, Apostle to the Gentiles* (trans. O. C. Dean, Jr.; Louisville: Westminster/John Knox, 1993) 373: "To begin with, we must guard against the expectation that in the end such an undertaking will lead to the derivation from Paul of a kind of standard dogmatics. The apostle's theological thought is not the early Christian counterpart of what the *loci communes* of Melanchthon provides for the Reformation period," and the methodological assumptions of the Pauline Theology Group of the SBL, which can be found throughout the publications of their work (*Pauline Theology, Volume I: Thessalonians, Philippians, Galatians, Philemon*, ed. J. M. Bassler [Philadelphia: Fortress, 1991]; *Pauline Theology, Volume II: 1 and 2 Corinthians*, ed. D. M. Hay [Philadelphia: Fortress, 1993]; *Pauline Theology, Volume III: Romans*, ed. E. E. Johnson and D. M. Hay [Philadelphia: Fortress, 1995]).

[100] See, e.g., F. M. Young, *From Nicaea to Chalcedon: A Guide to the Literature and its Background* (London: SCM, 1983) 156, on "Chrysostom's sensitive appreciation of the Pauline epistles as 'occasional' writings reflecting Paul's efforts to deal with pastoral problems," and Wiles, *Divine Apostle*, 7, who grounds this in Chrysostom's own oratorical genre and social context: "It may be indeed that the homiletic method has some advantages in the treatment of letters, whose original purpose was certainly nearer to that of homiletic than to that of theological definition." Compare recently Abraham J. Malherbe, *Paul and the Thessalonians: the Philosophic Tradition of Pastoral Care* (Philadelphia: Fortress, 1987).

[101] Such as Hoffmann-Aleith, "Paulusverständnis," 183; Quasten, *Patrology*, 3.442: "He has no leaning to theological speculation and feels more attracted by moral and ascetical questions. Thus from a theological point of view his sober Antiochene exegesis is sometimes disappointing."

twentieth century has gained important ground in the understanding of Greco-Roman epistolary forms, genres, commonplaces and mechanics.[102] Many of these findings, such as the crucial importance of the epistolary prescripts and thanksgiving formulas which Paul uses to set up the arguments and position the audience for his letters, were also appreciated by his fourth-century letter writing counterpart, John.[103] As a rhetorically trained, Greek-speaking Syrian (and student of the great "pagan" orator Libanios), Chrysostom knew intimately well the literary culture in which Paul was situated. Therefore, his abundant comments on Paul's rhetorical proficiency and crudities are of paramount importance for current research into the rhetoric of Paul's epistles. But these statements need to be subjected to a careful analysis in the light of Chrysostom's *own* rhetorical purposes and goals, something which has been insufficiently attended to in the appropriation of Chrysostom into contemporary New Testament scholarship on a range of exegetical and philological issues. Furthermore, Chrysostom's writings on Paul and his letters are of particular interest because he struggles, often openly and mostly imaginatively, with the same hermeneutical questions with which current Pauline scholars are preoccupied: determining the historical setting of each letter, adjudicating the interpretive relationship between the particularity of the letters and their universal enshrinement in the canon, and the perennial question: is Paul consistent? To all of these questions Chrysostom provides engagingly complex answers, and becomes an important conversation partner for contemporary scholarship, which too often proceeds without adequate appreciation of the degree to which it traverses ground which had already been well covered by the fourth century.[104] While this study cannot take up all these questions, it begins at the starting block with what is perhaps the most fundamental hermeneutical question, especially where the Pauline epistles, literary works in the first person voice of a unique personality, are concerned: the relationship between understanding the words of the letters and probing the mind and character of their author.

---

[102] For access to the considerable bibliography now available, see my article, "Brief I. Form und Gattung," *RGG*⁴ 1 (1998) 1757–60.

[103] Chrysostom shares with contemporary scholars the exegetical conviction that the epistolary frames of the Pauline letters should not be overlooked, but rather provide most important clues for the understanding of the letters (see, e.g., *hom. in Rom. 16:3* 1.1 [51.187], where he defends this point on both theological and literary grounds). See also Kelly *Golden Mouth*, 94: "The Pauline letters, it is worth noting, being actual letters, presented him with fewer problems; since he felt an empathy with the apostle, his explanations of them tend to be somewhat more in line with what modern critics look for." A full treatment of Chrysostom's attention to Pauline epistolography will require a study of its own.

[104] A prime example of this is Chrysostom's assessments of Pauline consistency and inconsistency, which I have analyzed in relation to contemporary scholarly debate in "A Variable and Many-sorted Man." In chap. 6 I shall discuss how Chrysostom deals with inconsistency in Pauline actions, specifically (see pp. 326–53).

Praise for Paul's Devoted Interpreter

The contemporary suitability and relevance of this study stands in a continuum, however, with exegetes throughout the history of Christian thought who have embraced and highly valued Chrysostom's exegetical writings. Within fifty years of Chrysostom's death Isidore of Pelusium remarked of him that, "if the divine Paul had taken up the Attic tongue to interpret himself, he would not have done it differently than this renowned man has done."[105] This exegetical comment was soon to be enshrined in a famous legend of Paul personally inspiring Chrysostom as he composed his homilies on the apostle's epistles, a tale which took literary form as early as the seventh century.[106] This legend, and the artistic representations of it which enshrine manuscript pages of Chrysostom's homilies as well as church walls in the east, honors Chrysostom as Paul's most authentic interpreter. The same spirit, though without the supernatural claim, has animated most assessments of Chrysostom's exegetical homilies throughout the history of interpretation,[107] such as that of Chrysostom's early twentieth-century biographer, Chrysostomus Baur: "Chrysostom's commentaries on the New Testament are considered, even in our own day, from a literary and exegetical point of view, the best and most useful that the patristic age has bequeathed to us."[108] At this end of the century,

---

[105] εἰ Παῦλος ὁ θεσπέσιος Ἀττικὴν εἴληφε γλῶτταν, ὥστε ἑαυτὸν ἑρμηνεῦσαι, οὐκ ἂν ἄλλως ἡρμήνευσεν, ἢ ὡς ὁ προειρημένος ἀοίδιμος ἀνήρ (*Ep.* 5.32, to Isidore the deacon [78.1348]). The characteristics for which he praises Chrysostom's interpretations are its adornment with "arguments, beauty, and literalness (or accuracy)" [οὕτω καὶ ἐνθυμήμασι, καὶ κάλλει, καὶ κυριολεξίᾳ κεκόσμηται ἡ ἑρμηνεία].

[106] I shall deal with this legend in depth in the next chapter, and in Appendix 2, "Artistic Images of John Chrysostom and Paul," pp. 489–93.

[107] See, e.g., Altaner-Stuiber, *Patrologie*, 324: "Kein Kirchenvater hat den heiligen Text so gründlich und zugleich so praktisch erklärt wie er, und auch heute noch liest man seine Homilien nicht nur mit Frucht und Genuß, sondern, vom exegetischen Standpunkt aus gesehen, auch oft mit voller Zustimmung, was man von den Predigten der andern Väter, Augustinus eingeschlossen, nicht immer sagen kann." Earlier Calvin had extolled Chrysostom as "the chief of all" [*Chrysostomum ex omnibus potissimum delegerim*], especially because of his outstanding gift of homiletical biblical interpretation, "a function in which all men of sound judgment agree that our writer Chrysostom excels all the ancient writers presently extant, especially when he deals with the New Testament" [*in qua Chrysostomum nostrum vetustos omnes scriptores qui hodie exstant antecedere nemo sani iudicii negaverit. Praesertim ubi novum testamentum tractat* ("Praefatio in Chrysostomi homilias," *Corpus Reformatorum*, vol. 37, col. 834; trans. John H. McIndoe, "John Calvin: Preface to the Homilies of Chrysostom," *Hartford Quarterly* 5 [1965] 19–26])].

[108] Baur, *John Chrysostom and His Time*, 1.322. The "love hermeneutic" which Chrysostom describes as facilitating and compelling his interpretation of Paul has been instantiated again in the history of interpretation of Chrysostom by this scholar. Baur, who devoted his career to the study of John Chrysostom, was a Benedictine monk who was given the sobriquet "Chrysostomus" at his entrance into the novitiate. Although in the preface to his biography Baur confidently states that he brings to his work "an entire absence of prejudice in regard to the hero of the work" (xi), he goes on to laud Chrysostom as constituting "a towering personality, which embodied a program for humanity too great and significant for his contemporaries to withhold the proper niche from him and his advocates" (xii-xiii), a judgment which is reechoed through-

J. H. W. G. Liebeschuetz has remarked on the similarities between John's homilies and contemporary scholarship in method and sensibility: "Making allowances for the pastoral bias of the author, Chrysostom's commentaries on various books of scripture are not at all unlike modern editions of literary texts annotated for use in schools. They stimulate questions why Paul, or other scriptural authors, wrote precisely what they did, in the way they did, and lay the foundation of an interest that could last a lifetime."[109] But the similarity to modern commentaries Liebeschuetz identifies might blind us to some real differences between Chrysostom's homilies and modern exegetical commentaries in underlying perspective, as well. For instance, Chrysostom often frames the questions he poses of the biblical text as direct questions to the author: "What are you saying, Paul?" [Τί λέγεις, ὦ Παῦλε;],[110] something no modern scholar would do, yet thoroughly indicative of the living conversation Chrysostom understood Paul's letters as creating. And, we must never underestimate the importance of both catechesis and entertainment in Chrysostom's interpretive work, two values largely excluded from contemporary academic commentaries.[111]

---

out the biography in tones often approaching the panegyric. In contrast, Kelly's recent biography, *Golden Mouth*, although likewise appreciating his subject's talents and accomplishments, combines that with a critical sensibility of John's faults and limitations (see my review in *Church History* 66 [1997] 85–87).

[109] *Barbarians and Bishops: Army, Church, and State in the Age of Arcadius and Chrysostom* (Oxford: Clarendon, 1990) 184. On pp. 183–85 Liebeschuetz has nicely captured the considerable pedagogical purposes of Chrysostom's homilies. Contrast Manlio Simonetti, *Biblical Interpretation in the Early Church: An Historical Introduction to Patristic Exegesis*, trans. John A. Hughes (Edinburgh: T & T Clark, 1994) 74: "His predominately ethical or exhortatory interest accounts for the fact that often the actual illustration of the text remains superficial ... The illustration of the letters of Paul is similarly [to the Gospel of John] deficient." This negative judgment is due to Simonetti's assumption that moral exhortation and exegesis are two different tasks (on which see further discussion in chap. 7, pp. 384–88).

[110] *hom. in Rom.* 16.1 [60.550]; *hom. in 1 Cor.* 36.3 [61.310], Τί λέγεις; εἰπέ μοι; *hom. in 2 Cor.* 11:1 2 [51.303]; *hom. in Phil.* 1:18 7 [51.316], and over hundreds of times in the exegetical homilies, as well as other writings (such as *ep. Olymp.* 13.3 [SC 13.340]). Significantly, elsewhere Chrysostom uses this type of direct address to an author only to refer to prophets; in the gospels he never uses it to pose a question to an evangelist, though he sometimes does directly address Peter to query him about one of his narrated speeches. However, in general it is conspicuously for Paul that John uses this form of direct speech to an author.

[111] One does not immediately consider Kelly's assessment of Antioch's embrace of homilies ("the Syrian capital was amazingly addicted to sermons") applicable to contemporary appetites for biblical commentaries (*Golden Mouth*, 57)! Chrysostom himself depicted his audience as so voracious for scriptural and moral learning that they were like baby birds peeking out of the nest, and extending their necks to their mothers for the food she would bring. He says, "also you, looking with great eagerness to the speaker, receive the discourse conveyed to you by our tongue, and before the words leap out of our mouth, your mind has snatched up what we said" (*hom. in 2 Tim.* 3:1 1 [56.271]; but on other occasions John paints more negative depictions of his audiences as talking or sleeping during his sermons, or forgetting what was said before they hit the street). But perhaps it is a premature judgment to say that this addiction to biblical scholarship is the character only of a by-gone day; see the comments of Robert Louis Wilken: "The publication of encyclopedias, commentaries, and archaeological studies, not to mention the popularity

In the chapters which follow we hope to provide a necessary first step toward the accessibility to contemporary scholars of these considerable exegetical riches, by attending to Chrysostom's interpretation of the Pauline letters within the wider context of his personal devotion to the person of Paul, the rhetorical forms in which it found expression, and his hermeneutical presuppositions, commitments, and homiletic purposes. In particular, as John described it, in the exegetical enterprise this great patristic exegete found himself face to face with his most beloved saint. This inspired and mutually influencing conversation which Chrysostom saw to be the nature of exegesis was given terse expression in a marginal notation by an eleventh-century copyist of a Greek manuscript of Chrysostom's homilies, who depicted the relationship between Paul and Chrysostom simply and poetically:

> The mouth of Christ brought forth the mouth of Paul
> and the mouth of Paul the mouth of Chrysostom.
> Χριστοῦ στόμα πέφυκε τὸ Παύλου στόμα
> στόμα δὲ Παύλου τὸ Χρυσοστόμου στόμα.[112]

More than eight hundred years after the Greek manuscript copyist penned his wise observation, a French scholar who was himself caught up in the chain of love for Chrysostom and his beloved Paul, echoed his sentiment exactly: "le plus éloquent des apôtres a formé le plus éloquent des Pères."[113] I shall seek to honor and follow my two scribal predecessors in reflection on the creative relationship between Chrysostom and the divine apostle, but I shall do so by inverting their question, to ask how the mouth of Chrysostom produced Paul, the heavenly trumpet.

> And the mouth of Chrysostom brought forth the portrait of Paul.
> στόμα δὲ Χρυσοστόμου τὸ Παύλου πρόσωπον.[114]

---

of TV programs and magazines on the Bible, make clear that the public's appetite for historical information about the Bible and its world is almost insatiable" (review of *Thinking Biblically: Exegetical and Hermeneutical Studies*, by André Lacocque and Paul Ricoeur, in *First Things* 93 [1999] 68). Whether contemporary American fascination with the historical context of the Bible is comparable to ancient Antiochenes' communal enjoyment of liturgical rhetoric remains a question; the genre of contemporary commentary, however, largely precludes the "fireworks" of a Chrysostomic oration. We shall return to the question of the genre and purpose of contemporary academic biblical scholarship in chap. 8, pp. 428–33.

[112] The manuscript is *Jerus. Sab.* 33 (s. XI) fol. 189, as cited by Baur, *S. Jean Chrysostome*, 34 (my translation).

[113] Vandenberghe, *Saint Jean Chrysostome*, 59; cf. Charles Kannengiesser, "Biblical Interpretation in the Early Church," *Historical Handbook of Major Biblical Interpreters*, ed. Donald K. McKim (Downers Grove, IL: Intervarsity Press, 1998) 1–16, 14: "in the ancient church Chrysostom is the most eloquent commentator on Paul." See also his summary comment on that page: "His exegetical homilies on both Testaments, most delivered at Antioch, are among the best Christian literature of antiquity."

[114] In composing my epigram I have deliberately chosen the ambiguous Greek term πρόσωπον, that can equally mean "face," "mask," "portrait," "character," and "person" (LSJ, 1533), to suggest the elusive connection between forms of portrayal and identity.

Chapter 2

"The Archetypal Image" (ἡ ἀρχέτυπος εἰκών)

In the course of his writings, Chrysostom not only interprets the Pauline letters, and incessantly invokes his beloved saint Paul, but he dwells upon his person, sketching adoring portraits of the apostle which he sets before his audience's eyes. Exquisite for their detail and craftmanship, these portraits exhibit his abundant preoccupation with the figure of Paul. The many and varied portraits of Paul contained within Chrysostom's writings consist of two types: miniature and full-scale, the latter including extended portraits of both Paul's body, part by part, and of his soul. But for what purposes did Chrysostom take repeated recourse to portraiture when speaking of Paul? What incited him to compose portraits and character sketches of the apostle in his homilies and other writings? Before we examine the portraits themselves in the next four chapters, we must first examine the hermeneutical framework of Chrysostom's images of the apostle Paul as simultaneously artistic and literary creations, renderings of a human person in a non-fleshly medium. Chrysostom constructed his portraits of Paul, not to preserve for posterity some memory of the exact physical details of this man, but for what he would consider higher purposes. In order to comprehend these depictions on their own terms, we shall examine the art of Christian literary portraiture in the fourth-century Greek east,[1] taking into account its hermeneutical, rhetorical, ethical and artistic dimensions.[2]

The Hermeneutical Framework of the Portraits

We shall begin this study of ancient portraiture with an actual portrait. Bound into an eleventh-century illuminated manuscript of Pseudo-Oecumenius' *commentarius*

---

[1] Christian "biographic" literature in the late fourth century should itself be seen as part of a much wider phenomenon of increased literary focus on the individual ("the literature of the Roman Empire and late antiquity displays a strong biographic turn" [p. 36]) in response to the concrete social, legal and intellectual contexts of the late empire (as argued by Simon Swain, "Biography and Biographic in the Literature of the Roman Empire," *Portraits: Biographical Representation in the Greek and Latin Literature of the Roman Empire*, ed. M. J. Edwards and Simon Swain [Oxford: Clarendon, 1997] 1–37, with discussion of the key literature on the topic of biography and the rise of the individual in late antiquity).

[2] This chapter replicates and expands upon my article, "'The Archetypal Image: John Chrysostom's Portraits of the Apostle Paul," *JR* 75 (1995) 15–28.

in epistulas Pauli (*Vatican Cod. gr. 766*, fol. 2 ᵛ)³ is an originally separate⁴ miniature portrait of Chrysostom and Paul that is the best extant example of the standard iconographical representation of the two together [see Plate 1].⁵ The highly stylized miniature depicts Chrysostom in the familiar philosophical or didactic pose, at his slanted writing desk. On the wall of his monastic cell hangs a picture of Saint Paul (easily identified for the viewer by the inscription ὁ ἅγιος Παῦλος), and yet simultaneously Paul stands, alive and embodied, peering over Chrysostom's shoulder in the pose of a muse, as he composes his homilies on the apostle's letters. The nimbi of the two saints intersect, creating a single halo which encloses the two heads. The faces of the two men are virtually indistinguishable.

This standard Byzantine portrait is based upon a legend about Chrysostom recorded by his seventh-century biographer, George of Alexandria.⁶ It tells of how Chrysostom had a picture of Paul on the wall in his bedroom in Constantinople, with which he would carry on conversation as though it were alive, by turns asking assistance in understanding from his author, and praising him for his skill.⁷ When Chrysostom was composing his homilies on Paul's letters, his secretary Proklos happened to peer in the door at the right moment (three nights running) to witness a man standing over Chrysostom's shoulder whispering exegetical hints into his right ear (in our miniature Proklos is as usual depicted as a shadowy figure in the doorway). He later identified the man for his master (who had been unaware

---

³ See Appendix 2, no. 1.

⁴ The date of this miniature is disputed; see Appendix 2, no. 1.

⁵ C. Walter, *Art and Ritual of the Byzantine Church* (Birmingham Byzantine Series 1; London: Variorum, 1982) 103; S. P. Madigan, "Athens 211 and the Illustrated Homilies of John Chrysostom" (Ph.D. diss., University of Chicago, 1984) 166–68.

⁶ *vita Joh. Chrys.* ch. 27 [François Halkin, *Douze récits byzantins sur Saint Jean Chrysostome* (Subsidia hagiographica 60; Brussels: Société des Bollandistes, 1977) 142–48, which replaces the earlier version of H. Savile, ed., *Chrysostomi opera omnia* (8 vols; Eton: Norton, 1610–12), 8.192–4. See Appendix 2 for other literary sources of this legend.

⁷ "John was in possession of a relief of the same apostle in a portrait. Sometimes he would have to stop for while because of a little bodily weakness (for he went without sleep to a degree that confounded nature). And when he was going through Paul's epistles, he used to fix his gaze on Paul's portrait and was as intent on him as if he were there alive, pronouncing blessings on Paul's power of reasoning. John would attune his whole mind to Paul, imagining that he was conversing with him via this vision" [Ἦν δὲ καὶ τὸ ἐκτύπωμα τοῦ αὐτοῦ ἀποστόλου ἔχων ἐν εἰκόνι ἔνθα ἀνεπαύετο διὰ τὴν τοῦ σώματος ἀσθένειαν βραχύ τι· ἦν γὰρ πολυάγρυπνος ὑπὲρ φύσιν. Καὶ ἡνίκα διήρχετο τὰς ἐπιστολὰς αὐτοῦ, ἐνητένιζεν αὐτῇ καὶ ὡς ἐπὶ ζῶντος αὐτοῦ οὕτως προσεῖχεν αὐτῷ, μακαρίζων αὐτοῦ τὸν λογισμόν· καὶ ὅλον αὐτοῦ τὸν νοῦν πρὸς αὐτὸν εἶχεν, φανταζόμενος διὰ τῆς θεωρίας αὐτῷ ὁμιλεῖν] (text from Halkin, *Douze récits*, 142). There is a striking parallel to this legend in one of the letters of John's teacher, Libanios, which to my knowledge has not been noticed before, and might have influenced this tradition about John: "I have the portrait of Aristides, something I have long desired, and I am almost as grateful to you as if you had resurrected the man himself and sent him to me [εἰ αὐτὸν ἡμῖν ἀναστήσας τὸν ἄνδρα ἐπεπόμφεις]. And I sit by his portrait, read some book of his and ask him whether he was the one who wrote these things [καὶ παρακάθημαί γε τῇ γραφῇ τῶν ἐκείνου τι βιβλίων ἀναγινώσκων ἐρωτῶν αὐτὸν, εἰ αὐτὸς ταῦτα]. Then I answer my question myself.'Yes, he did write them'" [εἶτ' αὐτὸς ἀποκρίνομαι ἐμαυτῷ· ναί, ταῦτά γε ἐκεῖνος] (Libanios, *Ep.* 143.1–2).

of anything unusual occurring) by pointing at the picture on the wall and exclaiming: "the man I saw speaking with you looked just like this man. Indeed, I think it is he!"[8] The legend puts into narrative form the substance of Isidore of Pelusium's earlier, famous remark (which we have quoted in the previous chapter): "if the divine Paul had taken up the Attic tongue to interpret himself, he would not have done it differently than this renowned man has done."[9] The sense is unmistakable: John interpreting Paul is as good as Paul interpreting himself.

This later manuscript illustration of John Chrysostom and Paul provides a suggestive vantage point for our inquiry into the various portraits of Paul found within Chrysostom's writings. First, Paul's dual depiction in the miniature as simultaneously a frozen icon and a living, breathing presence[10] demonstrates the genuine interpretive ambivalence Chrysostom faced and described in studying Paul's letters.[11] He was acutely aware of the absence and distance of the apostle in the present, the inability to "see" him now[12] (though that was one of the eschatological rewards for which he longingly waited),[13] yet he also felt that in touching

---

[8] ὃν εἶδον συλλαλοῦντά σοι ὅμοιός ἐστιν τούτου. Ὑπολαμβάνω, καὶ αὐτός ἐστιν (Halkin, *Douze récits*, 147), discussed in Baur, *John Chrysostom and His Time*, 1.297. On the relationship between icons and visions, see Henry Maguire, *The Icons of Their Bodies: Saints and Their Images in Byzantium* (Princeton: Princeton University Press, 1996), 12: "dreams and visions had an essential role to play, for they enabled the verisimilitude of icons to be matched against the actual appearance of long-deceased saints. There were two mechanisms for the process of checking. By the first mechanism, an icon would be verified by a subsequent vision of the saint. By the second mechanism, a vision of a saint would be verified by a subsequent viewing of his or her icon – for visions, as well as icons, might be false."

[9] *Ep.* 5.32 (to Isidore the Deacon) [78.1348].

[10] Chrysostom is at times explicit about this dynamic of the lifelessness and liveliness of graphic art. For instance, in a discussion of the phenomenon of figurative language, he remarks: "when we wish to praise a painting, we say that it speaks, that it makes utterances" [καὶ τὰς γραφομένας ὅταν θαυμάζειν βουλώμεθα, λέγομεν ὅτι λαλεῖ, ὅτι φθέγγεται] (*hom. in 2 Tim.* 8.1 [62.643]). This commonplace of artistic theory is well attested; see, for instance, Gregory of Nyssa, *Thdr.* 739M, where he describes an image in Theodore's martyrium recreating his tortured death: "all these things the painter artistically portrayed for us with colors as though in some book which could speak [πάντα ἡμῖν ὡς ἐν βιβλίῳ τινὶ γλωττοφόρῳ διὰ χρωμάτων τεχνουργησάμενος] ... for even a painting, though hanging silently on a wall, knows how to speak, and render the greatest benefit" [οἶδε γὰρ καὶ γραφὴ σιωπῶσα ἐν τοίχῳ λαλεῖν, καὶ τὰ μέγιστα ὠφελεῖν] (*Gregorii Nysseni Opera, X, 1: Sermones, pars II*, ed. Gunther Heil, *et al.* [Leiden: Brill, 1990] 63, ll. 10–14). This statement is especially rich, for it not only contrasts the animate with the inanimate, but also the artistic and the literary, both dynamics at work in Chrysostom's portraiture of Paul. And it is an interesting inversion of the widespread commonplace that a painting should be a *silent* poem (on which see n. 31 in this chapter).

[11] The portrait illustrates perfectly the point made by Sider, "Literary Artifice," 109: "... a subtle fusion on the one hand of the historical Paul imaginatively remembered and on the other hand of the portrait of the saint already become an icon."

[12] See, e.g., his tender comments on Acts 20:25 in *hom. in Ac.* 44.2 [60.310], his wistful yearning to have seen Paul give his defense speech (*hom. in Ac.* 47.1 [60.327]), or his claim that he would pay any price to be able to see Paul bound and led into prison, sitting therein, and triumphantly marching out with his fellow prisoners (*hom. in Eph.* 9.1 [62.69–70]).

[13] "Only let us make ourselves worthy of this advocacy, so that we might not only hear Paul's

the codex,[14] in hearing the apostle's words read, and in studying them carefully and preaching on them,[15] he was in constant, lively conversation with him.[16]

Continually when I hear the letters of the blessed Paul read [Συνεχῶς ἀκούων ἀναγιν-ωσκομένων τῶν ἐπιστολῶν τοῦ μακαρίου Παύλου] ... I rejoice in the pleasure of that spiritual trumpet, and am roused to attention and warmed with desire because I recognize the voice I love [χαίρω μὲν τῆς σάλπιγγος ἀπολαύων τῆς πνευματικῆς, καὶ διανίσταμαι, καὶ θερμαίνομαι τῷ πόθῳ, τὴν ἐμοὶ φίλην ἐπιγινώσκων φωνήν], and seem to imagine him all but present and see him conversing with me [μονονουχὶ παρόντα αὐτὸν δοκῶ φαντάζεσθαι, καὶ διαλεγόμενον ὁρᾶν].[17]

---

voice here [ἵνα μὴ ἐνταῦθα μόνον ἀκούσωμεν τῆς Παύλου φωνῆς], but also be found worthy to see the athlete of Christ when we go there [ἀλλὰ καὶ ἐκεῖ ἀπελθόντες ἰδεῖν καταξιωθῶμεν τὸν ἀθλητὴν τοῦ Χριστοῦ]. Indeed, if we hear him here, we shall see him completely there [μᾶλλον δὲ ἂν ἐνταῦθα ἀκούσωμεν, κἀκεῖ πάντως αὐτὸν ὀψόμεθα]" (hom. in Rom. 32.2 [60.678]; cf. laud. Paul 3.10 [SC 300.180]).

[14] In hom. in 2 Tim. 9.2 [62.652], Chrysostom describes the physical act of reading as "taking the apostle in hand" [τὸν ἀπόστολον μετὰ χεῖρας λαβών], and "examining" [περισκεψάμενος] a given passage. Here "the apostle" is used as a metonym for the codex of his letters, an ancient coalescence of author and text which in Christian literature was employed already in the New Testament of the Pentateuch (Moses) and the Psalms (David) (see Lk 16:29; 24:27; Heb 4:7). The same idea is expressed, even more poetically, in hom. in 2 Cor. 21.4 [61.546]: "let us continually have him in our hands [συνεχῶς αὐτὸν μεταχειριζώμεθα], delighting in his writings as in a meadow and garden" [ἀντὶ λειμῶνος καὶ παραδείσου τοῖς τούτου γράμμασιν ἐντρυφῶντες]. Here Chrysostom makes a deliberate word play with μεταχειρίζεσθαι, which means both to take in hand, and to pursue, as in learning or philosophy (LSJ, 1118).

[15] In one homily Chrysostom describes Paul as his συνεργός, co-worker, in the deputation he has been sent on, to plead the cause of the poor of the city to his congregation. The text for the homily is 1 Cor 16:1ff., the agency by which Paul's coworkership is activated (eleem. 1 [51.261]).

[16] See below on how letters in antiquity were viewed as a form of conversation between absent friends.

[17] hom. in Rom. Arg. 1 [60.391] (on hearing which creates seeing, a form of synesthesia, see David Chidester, Word and Light: Seeing, Hearing, and Religious Discourse [Urbana: University of Illinois Press, 1992] 14–24). That Paul is really present in the hearing of his words is a common theme in Chrysostom's writings. See also, e.g., hom. in 2 Cor. 11:1 2 [51.303]: "... as conversing with Paul himself present and with us [ὡς οὖν αὐτῷ τῷ Παύλῳ διαλεγόμενοι παρόντι καὶ συγγινομένῳ], let's hearken to the writings." Often Chrysostom describes the reading of Paul's letters as Paul discoursing [διαλέγεσθαι] in the present (hom. in Ac. 43.1 [60.303]; 54.4 [60.372]; stat. 1.1 [49.17]; hom. in 1 Cor. 10:1 1 [51.242]; hom. in 2 Tim. 4.1 [62,619]). In kal. 1 [48.953] Chrysostom says that his auditors can see Paul present when he pronounces encomia to him on his feast day: "Just now when we were praising the blessed Paul you jumped for joy as much as if you saw him present" [Πρῴην γοῦν ἡμῶν ἐγκωμιαζόντων τὸν μακάριον Παῦλον, οὕτως ἐσκιρτήσατε, ὡς αὐτὸν ὁρῶντες παρόντα]. Earlier in the same discourse he had echoed Paul's own language (1 Cor 5:3) to describe this mediation of presence despite absence: "For although he is not present in the flesh, still he is present in the spirit, and he is with us now, sitting here at home, just as also we are standing here with him" [Εἰ γὰρ καὶ μὴ τῇ σαρκὶ πάρεστιν, ἀλλὰ τῷ πνεύματι πάρεστι, καὶ νῦν μεθ' ἡμῶν ἐστιν οἴκοι καθήμενος, ὥσπερ καὶ ἡμεῖς μετ' ἐκείνου ἑστῶτες ἐνταῦθα]. In laud. Paul. 2.1 [SC 300.142] John says "Paul now stands" [καὶ νῦν ἕστηκεν] to speak in a dazzling voice against those who malign God. In hom. in Eph. 13. [62.93], Chrysostom explicitly contemporizes the Pauline voice in the letter to his congregation: "These things have not only been said to the Ephesians, but also they are being said to you right now" [Οὐ πρὸς Ἐφεσίους ταῦτα εἴρηται μόνον, ἀλλὰ καὶ πρὸς ὑμᾶς νῦν λέγεται]. Chrysostom is

Here the single word μονονουχί, "all but," neatly encapsulates both the interpretive opportunity and limitation which Paul's letters afforded Chrysostom.[18]

A second feature of our Byzantine miniature portrait, the unity of the two saints in a single nimbus and their conformity of visage, expresses pictorially Chrysostom's own fundamental hermeneutical claim: he understands the writings of the apostle so well because he loves him so much. "I love all the saints, but especially the blessed Paul."[19] This deep bond of love (which he often called a φίλτρον, "love charm") links the apostle with his most fervent interpreter and, Chrysostom believed, ensures the reliability of his interpretation.[20]

For we do not know what we know (if we do know anything) because of our clever nature or sharp mind [Οὐδὲ γὰρ ἡμεῖς ὅσαπερ ἴσμεν, εἴπερ τινὰ ἴσμεν, δι᾽ εὐφυίαν καὶ ὀξύτητα διανοίας ἐπιστάμεθα], but because we continually cleave to the man, and are so extremely well disposed toward him [ἀλλὰ διὰ τὸ συνεχῶς ἔχεσθαι τοῦ ἀνδρὸς, καὶ σφόδρα διακεῖσθαι περὶ αὐτόν].[21]

---

quite interesting on the relationship between the historical particularity of the Pauline epistles and their more universal readership. The topic is too enormous for a full discussion here; some further examples are cited in chap. 7, pp. 391–93.

[18] This is a commonplace of Greco-Roman artistic and literary theory as, e.g., in Lucian, *Imagines* 10, where Lycinus says when he reads Xenophon's literary portrait of Panthea in the *Cyropaedia*, "it makes me feel as if I saw her when I reach that place in my reading; I can almost hear her say [μονονουχὶ καὶ ἀκούω λεγούσης αὐτῆς] what she is described as saying"; and *Pr. Im.* 16: "I think I almost see her" [μονονουχὶ καὶ ὁρᾶν αὐτὴν οἴομαι]. These two important works of Lucian bear greatly on our topic and will be cited often in this study as providing salient background to Chrysostom's literary art. It is in fact possible that Chrysostom had read them himself (see J. Dumortier, "La culture profane de S. Jean Chrysostome," *MScRel* 10 [1953] 53–62, 55), though that would not have been necessary for John to be conversant with these ideas. The same *topos* about the life-like quality of prose is found in rhetorical theory, as when Theon and Hermogenes say that the appropriate style for the rhetorical form, *ekphrasis*, vivid description, "almost" [σχεδόν] renders the subject visible to the eye (for references and discussion see chap. 4, pp. 101–104). This idea is captured nicely by the artistic commonplace of statues (graphic, rather than literary depictions of persons) actually speaking. As one example, see Philostratus the Elder, *Imagines* 2.5, on the statue of Rhodogoune: "and if we wish to listen carefully, perhaps she/the statue will speak Greek" [κἂν παρακοῦσαι βουληθῶμεν, τάχα ἑλληνιεῖ].

[19] Ἅπαντας μὲν φιλῶ τοὺς ἁγίους, μάλιστα δὲ τὸν μακάριον Παῦλον (*hom. in 2 Cor. 11:1* 1 [51.301], as we had occasion to quote in the first chapter; this is a common sentiment expressed also, e.g., in *hom. in Mt.* 4.9 [57.51]). Chrysostom's special love for Paul has been noted (and applauded) by all of his biographers, ancient and modern. Symeon Metaphrastes' tenth century compendium biography includes this comment: "His love for Paul was so great that one could suitably say that for John Paul was what Christ was for Paul …" (*Vita S. Joannis Chrysostomi* 21 [114.1101]). See n. 25 below on modern commentators' assessments of Chrysostom's relationship to Paul. Although Chrysostom's devotion to Paul does not mean he entirely eclipses the other apostles, such as Peter, he does think that Paul outdid them all ("none of the apostles was his equal, but he was greater than them all" [*anom.* 8.3 [48.772]). We shall return to the relationship between Chrysostom's praise for Paul and for the other apostles in chap. 7, pp. 394–95.

[20] Cf. Lucian, *Imagines* 17, on Aeschines and Socrates as "of all craftsmen the truest copyists because they were painting with love" [μιμηλότατοι τεχνιτῶν ἁπάντων, ὅσῳ καὶ μετ᾽ ἔρωτος ἔγραφον].

[21] *hom. in Rom.* Arg. 1 [60.391]; cf. *hom. in Ac. 9:1* 1.3 [51.118]: "Paul and love for Paul compelled us to make this leap" [Παῦλος καὶ ὁ Παύλου πόθος ἠνάγκασεν ἡμᾶς πηδῆσαι τοῦτο

Chrysostom roots this hermeneutical claim in an epistemological principle, which is itself grounded in a friendship *topos*:[22] "For what belongs to those who are loved, they who love them know above all others."[23] Thus for Chrysostom the reader must embrace the sacred author for meaning to be conveyed and apprehended (not surprisingly this is also the content of his exhortation to his hearers to prepare for Scripture study).[24] His hermeneutics of love lead even to a hermeneutics of conformity, as in the interpretive conversation the two were conjoined in an unbreak-

---

τὸ πήδημα]. Chrysostom continues by urging his hearers to join him in his love hermeneutics: "Forgive me, or, rather, don't forgive me, but also you emulate this love [ζηλώσατε τὸν ἔρωτα τοῦτον]. For the one who loves a foolish lover reasonably asks forgiveness. But the one who loves such a one as this, let him boast in his love, and let him make many become partners in this desire, and fashion countless fellow-lovers of him!" [ὁ δὲ τοιοῦτον ἐρῶν, καλλωπιζέσθω τῷ πόθῳ, καὶ πολλοὺς ποιείτω κοινωνοὺς τῆς ἐπιθυμίας, καὶ συνεραστὰς αὐτοῦ κατασκευαζέτω μυρίους]. See also *hom. in Gen.* 11.5 [53.95]: Ἐκκαίομαι γὰρ εἰς τὸν τοῦ ἀνδρὸς πόθον, "For I am burning up with love for the man." In *hom. in Eph.* 8.3 [62.59] Chrysostom says he is bound even more securely by love [πόθος] for Paul than Paul was secured when placed in the stocks at Philippi (Acts 16:24). John's ardent love itself emulates Paul's chief quality. In *sac.* 4.6 [SC 272.268], in extolling Paul's self-sacrifice in Rom 9:3, Chrysostom exclaims: "Who loved Christ this much? If indeed one should call it love, and not something else greater than love" [τίς οὕτως ἐπόθησε τὸν Χριστὸν, εἴγε πόθον αὐτὸν δεῖ καλεῖν, ἀλλ᾽ οὐχ ἕτερόν τι τοῦ πόθου πλέον;].

[22] This is the universal *topos* at work here (found among the Stoics and a wide range of ancient thinkers and popular orators), not a conscious literary allusion to one text, *Phaedo* 73D, as argued by R. G. Tanner ("Chrysostom's Exegesis of Romans," *Studia Patristica* [ed. E. A. Livingstone] 17/3 [1982] 1185–97, 1186, 1190). The *Phaedo* text does, however, illuminate the phenomenon of "mental images" which are triggered by other material objects: "lovers, when they see a lyre or a cloak or something else which is customarily used by their darlings, experience this. Isn't it the case that they perceive the lyre, and receive in their mind an image of the boy [ἐν τῇ διανοίᾳ ἔλαβον τὸ εἶδος τοῦ παιδός] whose lyre it is? And this is recollection [ἀνάμνησις]" (my trans.). Later in this chapter we shall examine how oratory creates verbal artifacts for these same effects.

[23] Τὰ γὰρ τῶν φιλουμένων πρὸ τῶν ἄλλων ἁπάντων οἱ φιλοῦντες ἴσασιν (*hom. in Rom.* Arg. 1 [60.391]). On the transference of friendship conventions to the saints in the late fourth century, see Peter Brown, *The Cult of the Saints: Its Rise and Function in Latin Christianity* (Haskell Lectures on the History of Religions, n.s. 2; Chicago: University of Chicago Press, 1981) 55; note also his discussion on p. 50 of the saint as ἀόρατος φίλος, "invisible friend," or γνήσιος φίλος, "genuine friend." Chrysostom depicts Paul as a γνήσιος φίλος in *hom. in 1 Thess.* 2.4 [62.404], because he offered up his very life for others, loving with "a fiery purpose" [φιλεῖν διαθέσει πεπυρωμένῃ] (see chap. 6, pp. 354–55 on Paul's friendships).

[24] Chrysostom counsels this on his audience in several places (*hom. in 2 Cor 11:1* 2 [51.303]: "Since such is the gain for those who join with the saints, join with us in love, and let us love this saint with great abundance"; cf. *hom. in Ac. 9:1* 1.3 [51.118]). This hermeneutical principle can also work in the negative, as in his discourse on the meaning of Paul's willingness to be anathema for the sake of his people, Chrysostom laments: "but since we are far away from this love, we are not able to understand what is said" [ἀλλ᾽ ἐπειδὴ πόρρω τῆς ἀγάπης ἐσμὲν ταύτης, οὐδὲ νοῆσαι τὰ λεγόμενα δυνάμεθα] (*hom. in Rom.* 16.2 [60.551]; cf. *hom. in Rom.* 15.5 [60.546]). Elsewhere Chrysostom can formulate a general rule (in an instance where he is asserting that imprisonment for Christ, such as Paul speaks of in Eph 4:1, is the highest honor): "if someone loves [φιλεῖν] Christ, s/he knows what is said [τὸ λεγόμενον]; if someone is crazed and set on fire for the Lord [μαίνεσθαι καὶ περικαίεσθαι τοῦ Δεσπότου], s/he knows the power of the bonds" (*hom. in Eph.* 8.1 [62.55]).

able bond that was both spiritual and intellectual.[25] There is such conformity between the apostle and his readers that those who truly understand Paul, "the soul on fire," "the mind burning with desire for God," themselves receive "a mouth of fire."[26] And Paul is the appropriate anchor for this love hermeneutics, since, in Chrysostom's eyes, Paul loved Christ more than anyone else,[27] with a love that burned like fire.[28]

A third feature of the Byzantine miniature portrait which has great hermeneutical significance is its "inter-picturality." It is a study in "portraits within portraits." Likewise in his homilies Chrysostom sketches portraits of the apostle which are based on existing, fixed portraits (symbolized neatly for our analysis by the one on the wall in the manuscript illustration), such as those of Paul in the Acts of the Apostles and in the letters themselves.[29] Chrysostom paints portraits of Paul which are a collage of existing portraits and some of his own elements. The final picture bears his distinctive mark. Portraits are always, furthermore, caught in a temporal bind, for they must fix the subject in a single image, where the living one was continually in the process of motion and transformation. Added to this is the further hermeneutical challenge that all of Chrysostom's sources, and his own portraits of Paul, are word portraits, not graphic artistic renderings, though he ingeniously seeks to create a blend of the two.[30] In this undertaking John both

---

[25] "Chrysostome … s'est formé une âme à la ressemblance de Paul, enflammée comme la sienne de zèle pour le salut des âmes" (A. Wenger, SC 50.186 n. 1). For similar remarks from other Chrysostom scholars see also Baur, *John Chrysostom*, 1.290–91; Vandenberghe, *Saint Jean Chrysostome*, 59; R. C. Hill, FC 74.16; Piédagnel, *SC* 300.38 and 52: "Paul et Jean: il y avait entre ces deux hommes une sorte d'harmonie préétablie" (also p. 39: "La fréquence avec laquelle Chrysostome a parlé de S. Paul dans ses homélies prouve qu'il vivait dans une communion intime de pensée et de coeur avec lui"; cf. Dassmann, "Paulusverständnis," 34 n. 31: "er scheint wirklich ein außergewöhnliches Verhältnis zu dem Apostel gehabt zu haben").

[26] *hom. in Ac.* 55.3 [60.384]: Καθάπερ εἴ τις πυρὸς λάβοι στόμα, οὕτως ὁ Παῦλον εἰδὼς στομοῦται, "As if one should get a mouth of fire, that is the kind of mouth the person who knows Paul well will have" (on Paul see *hom. in Gen.* 34.6 [53.320]; *hom. in Ac.* 20.3; 31.1; 52.4 [60.161, 228, 364]; *hom. in Rom. 8:28* 3 [51.168]).

[27] Οὐδεὶς μᾶλλον Παύλου τὸν Χριστὸν ἀγάπησεν ("no one loved Christ more than Paul") (*sac.* 3.7 [48.645]). See the modern expansion of this sentiment by Zese, "Apostle Paul," 317: Οὐδεὶς ἠγάπησε τὸν Χριστὸν περισσότερον τοῦ Παύλου καὶ οὐδεὶς ἠγάπησε τὸν Παῦλον περισσότερον τοῦ Χρυσοστόμου ("No one loved Christ more than Paul, and no one loved Paul more than Chrysostom").

[28] *compunct.* 2 2 [47.413]: "but what is needed is that flame [φλόξ] which Christ kindled in Paul's soul. That blessed man nurtured it through this spiritual reasoning and raised it up to so great a height that, starting from below on the earth it reached even to heaven itself, and above this heaven, and again the one after that. For he himself was snatched up into a third heaven. His desire [πόθος] and his love for Christ [ἡ πρὸς τὸν Χριστὸν ἀγάπη] surpassed, not only three heavens, but all the heavens." Cf. *hom. in 1 Cor.* 22.4 [61.185]: "Have you seen [his] love, which is hotter than fire" [Εἶδες ἀγάπην πυρὸς θερμοτέραν;]?

[29] On the technique of composite portraits from existing sources, see Lucian, *Imagines* 5–6.

[30] For example, in describing his technique as a literary portraitist, Chrysostom claims that the Holy Spirit is the real painter of his portraits, and his tongue merely the stylus, as in *hom. in Ac.* 30.4 [60.227–28], quoted below, n. 82.

reflects and participates in a long-standing classical debate on the relationship between the graphic and literary arts as attempts to capture and represent living persons,[31] a discussion which had already made its way into Christian literature before him.[32] Chrysostom deals in some interesting ways with the apparent limitations of his "literary portraiture," and the opportunities it provides. In particular he regards it as the key function of *preaching* to sketch for the hearers with words the very persons of the saints.[33] His homiletic discourse, seen in this light, can be insightfully comprehended as employing a type of *ekphrasis* — an ancient rhetorical form that was designed expressly to merge the literary and graphic arts, and

---

[31] For instance, Plutarch made the analogy of portrait painting to biography (*Alex.* 1.3) and historiography (*Mor.* 346F). In the classical period Isocrates (*Or.* 9.73–75, quoted below, pp. 62–63), and in the second sophistic Lucian (*Imagines* 23), emphasized the greater endurability of literary portraits over their painted or sculpted counterparts, as well as their inspiration by the Muses. Further, in §8 Lucian refers to Homer as "the best of painters" [ὁ ἄριστος τῶν γραφέων Ὅμηρος]. This reflects the often-invoked comparison Plutarch (*Mor.* 346F) attributed to Simonides: "he called the painting a silent poem, and the poem a speaking painting" [τὴν μὲν ζωγραφίαν ποίησιν σιωπῶσαν προσαγορεύει, τὴν δὲ ποίησιν ζωγραφίαν λαλοῦσαν] (see also *Rhet. Her.* 4.28.39: *Poëma loquens pictura, pictura tacitum poëma debet esse*, and further references collected by Harry Caplan in the Loeb edition of that work, p. 327 n. c). This commonplace did not prohibit legendary stories of talking statues, however (such as Callistratus, *Statuarum descriptiones* §1 and 9). The connection between poetry and the graphic arts (as well as dance and music) as similar instances of μίμησις of course has a long history (see, e.g., Arist. *Poetica* 1.3; 2.1–7; 15.11). And not only poetry, but also oratory, was thought to be a literary form of the graphic arts. Again Callistratus (who likely wrote in the fourth century C.E.) is a good source for the concept: "Thus Scopas [of Paros, famous sculptor of the fourth century B.C.E.] fashioning creatures without life was an artificer of truth and imprinted miracles on bodies made of inanimate matter; while Demosthenes, fashioning images in words [ὁ δὲ τὰ ἐν λόγοις διαπλάττων Δημοσθένης ἀγάλματα], almost made visible a form of words by mingling the pigments of art with the creations of mind and intelligence [μικροῦ καὶ λόγων ἔδειξεν εἶδος αἰσθητὸν τοῖς νοῦ καὶ φρονήσεως γεννήμασι συγκεραννὺς τὰ τῆς τέχνης φάρμακα] (*Stat.* 2.5; text and trans. Arthur Fairbanks, LCL; cf. also Quintilian, *Inst.* 2.13.8–13). On the phenomenon in general, see the standard work of Mario Praz, *Mnemosyne: the Parallel between Literature and the Visual Arts* (A. W. Mellon Lectures in the Fine Arts 1967; Bollingen Series 35/16 [Princeton: Princeton University Press, 1970] 3–27.

[32] The language and conception of literary portraiture were already well established in Christian literature by Chrysostom's time, the conspicuous example being Eusebius' *vita Constantini*, which at the outset decries the perishability of all earthly forms of portraiture (his catalogue includes encaustic paintings, hewn statues, and inscriptions engraved on tablets or pillars), adding to this classical complaint a Christian contempt that these are only suitable when one does not hold any hope for an afterlife (*v. C.* 1.3 [text ed. Friedhelm Winkelmann, *Eusebius Werke*, GCS 1/1 (Berlin: Akademie-Verlag, 1975) 16]). Even more importantly, Eusebius explicitly calls his work of panegyric a "word portrait": "thus it is necessary to compose, in imitation of the art of mortal painting, the portrait through words, to the memory of this man so loved of God" [ὅμως ἀναγκαῖον μιμήσει τῆς θνητῆς σκιαγραφίας τὴν διὰ λόγων εἰκόνα τῇ τοῦ θεοφιλοῦς ἀναθεῖναι μνήμῃ] (*v. C.* 10.1 [text Winkelmann, GCS 1/1, 19]). On the use of imagery from the graphic arts throughout Eusebius' work, see Averil Cameron, *Christianity and the Rhetoric of Empire*, 53–56, and, further, 141–52 on the deliberate rhetorical strategy of much later fourth-century Christian oratory of incorporating and reappropriating the classical genres of encomium and βίοι to the end that lives were displayed textually as "images or verbal icons" (p. 152).

[33] See n. 82 below.

create with words a vivid, lifelike encounter between an audience and a person or work of art they were unable to see.[34] In the verbal medium of his liturgical homilies Chrysostom himself in many ways became the very medium by which Paul was displayed, in his words and the content of his discourse on Paul, and in his own demeanor, diction and disposition, which were decidedly and emphatically in the Pauline mold,[35] as the scribe quoted in the last chapter noted: "the mouth of Paul begot the mouth of Chrysostom." In Chrysostom's interpretations of Paul the identities, personalities and voices of the two men, like their faces in the miniature portrait, become conformed to one another.[36] Thus in Chrysostom's discourse on Paul we have a complex interweaving of the two persons, the two selves, of Paul and Chrysostom. This mimetic sensibility of the exegete taking on the form of the author, who is himself in some sense a product of the exegete's own construction, means that in Chrysostom's interpretation of Paul we have a

---

[34] See Pierre Hadot, "Préface" to *Philostrate: La galerie de tableaux*, trans. Auguste Bougot, revised and annotated by François Lissarrague (Paris: Les Belles Lettres, 1991) vii–xxii, on *ekphrasis* as "'peinture parlante' ... puisque les paroles y remplacement les formes et les couleurs" [these quotes are from p. xv]. We shall provide a full discussion of *ekphrasis* in chap. 4, below, when we turn to the techniques by which Chrysostom portrays Paul's body.

[35] See Merzagora, "Commentatore di S. Paolo," 14–15, on Paul's influence on Chrysostom's own homiletical style and structure ("Non ci stupisce quindi il ritrovare anche nell' eloquenza del Crisostomo le tracce di un profondo influsso paolino"). For instance, in *hom. in 1 Thess.* 5.3 [62.427] he asks his own audience, Ἀνάσχεσθε μου τι καὶ ἀκάθαρτον, in explicit imitation of 2 Cor 11:1, as also *hom. in Col.* 7.5 [62.352] he rails against silver chamber pots as the most shameful act of profligacy and contempt for the poor, by creating a parallel with Paul's 1 Cor 11:21 to express his disgust: ὁ μὲν καὶ ἐν ἀργύρῳ ἀποπατεῖ, ὁ δὲ οὐδὲ ἄρτου μετέχει ("one defecates into silver, while another does not partake even of bread"). These passages (and many others, such as *hom. in Ac.* 11.4 [60.98], and *hom. in Mt.* 85.1 [58.757]) show how Chrysostom has adopted Paul's voice.

[36] "... le proporzioni giganti di quest'anima, il cammino percorso sulle orme dell'Apostolo in uno sforzo tenace e costante di geniale imitazione e di contatto sempre più intimo" (Merzagora, "Commentatore di S. Paolo," 14). On Chrysostom's self-modeling on Paul in general see, e.g., the suggestive comment of Brown, *Cult of the Saints*, 64 about "hanging one's identity on one's hero" (and cf. Vandenberghe, *Saint Jean Chrysostome*, 59). Chrysostom's portraits of Paul, even as their main purpose is a representation of Paul, were contained within his own pulpit oratory which, like all rhetoric, was the vehicle for his own self-presentation (see the perceptive analysis of Maud W. Gleason, *Making Men: Sophists and Self-Presentation in Ancient Rome* [Princeton: Princeton University Press, 1995]), xx: "One reason these performances were so riveting was that the encounter between orator and audience was in many cases the anvil upon which the self-presentation of ambitious upper-class men was forged"). Chrysostom's self-molding in Paul's image is part of a widespread phenomenon in late fourth-century Christianity (see the insightful study of Derek Krueger, "Hagiography as an Ascetic Practice in the Early Christian East," *JR* 79 [1999] 216–232: "by representing the saints, authors hoped to resemble them"). John's own self-portraits, revealed in his homilies and letters, are often themselves a reflection of Paul, or at least of Paul's influence upon his life. One remarkable instance of this is the way in which Chrysostom interpreted the sufferings of his later years, including exile and hardships, through the lens of the Pauline epistles (see the list of key references to Paul's letters in his later writings, especially his epistles to Olympias, collected by Merzagora, "Commentatore di S. Paolo," 12–13). We shall return to this topic repeatedly throughout our study.

"Pauline" reading of Paul by one who fashioned himself in imitation of his apostolic hero.[37] Peter Brown has pointed to the significance of the suggestive comment made by Libanios (Chrysostom's teacher), that through *paideia* Greek gentlemen were taught to "install Demosthenes in their souls."[38] It would not be an exaggeration to say that Chrysostom saw himself as having installed Paul in his soul; during the two years he spent in the cave memorizing the New Testament,[39] Chrysostom downloaded a great deal of Paul into his memory and consciousness.[40] And the package of wise Pauline utterances John ingested included the prescription to imitate the apostle now held within.

"The Archetypal Image"

It is because of Chrysostom's author-centered hermeneutics that his portraits of the apostle Paul are especially important. He has utter confidence that Paul's epistles afford the reader an opportunity to "gaze into Paul's soul, just as into a certain archetypal image" [καὶ ὥσπερ εἰς ἀρχέτυπον εἰκόνα τινὰ, εἰς τὴν τούτου ψυχὴν ἐνορῶν].[41] This sensibility is rooted in three particulars, which we shall examine in turn: his overall view of Scripture, Greco-Roman epistolary theory, and ancient ethical theory of learning by imitation.

Scripture as Relic

Chrysostom's view of Scripture is that it is comprised of the "remains" or "relics" of the holy ones, the exemplars of virtue: "The grace of the Holy Spirit left us

---

[37] For the phenomenon of interpenetrated lives generally, see the similar remark of Cameron about Eusebius' Constantine: "Sacred lives functioned as ideological and literary examples. Moses is the model for Constantine: in turn, seeing Constantine as Moses enabled the audience to see Constantine more clearly" (*Christianity and the Rhetoric of Empire*, 145).

[38] ἃ δὲ τοῦ Δημοσθένους εἰς τὴν ψυχὴν ἐναπέθετο (Libanios, *Ep.* 1261.2 [Foerster 11.339], cited in *Cult of the Saints*, 7 n. 5, and again in *Power and Persuasion*, 7, 38).

[39] As reported by his biographer, Palladios, *v. Chrys.* 5.23–25 [SC 341.110], who also explains at length how John modeled his life after Paul (18.1–46 [SC 341.350–54]).

[40] Vandenberghe, *Saint Jean Chrysostome*, 47, fancifully imagines a particular and timely instantiation of Pauline infusion into John: "Le jour de son ordination à Antioche, lorsque – étendu sur les dalles de la basilique – il entendit la voix de son évêque appeler sur lui l'esprit de sagesse, de science et de sainteté, l'âme de saint Paul passa tout entière dans son âme. Il devint, depuis ce moment, le grand imitateur de ses travaux apostoliques et le puissant écho de sa parole inspirée." An 11th century wall painting in Ochrid (modern-day Macedonia) appears to depict Divine Wisdom feeding John a scroll of the Pauline epistles – but on his death bed! (see Appendix 2, no. 15).

[41] *hom. in Gen.* 11.5 [53.95]. The Greek word εἰκών can be translated with the English terms "image," "likeness," or "portrait" (LSJ, 485), a fact which is important for the argument of this chapter.

[καταλείπειν]⁴² in written form [ἀνάγραπτον] through the Holy Scriptures the lives and mode of living of all the saints" [τῶν ἁγίων ἁπάντων οἱ βίοι καὶ ἡ πολιτεία].⁴³ Therefore exegesis has as its purpose "bring[ing] the virtues of the just [τῶν δικαίων αἱ ἀρεταί] into the public eye."⁴⁴ This hermeneutic, well-entrenched in the emergent Christian piety of the late fourth century, roots religious authority in the very lives of the saints, which are mediated to later generations in a variety of ways – by their "relics."⁴⁵ Every single detail about the saints of old, even what they ate, where they slept, and what they wore, is of edificational value.⁴⁶ Chrysostom writes of the inspiration to be gained from visiting the very places where the apostle taught or was imprisoned,⁴⁷ or seeing fragments of the actual chains which bound him,⁴⁸ and confesses his deepest longing to visit Paul's funeral monument, his tomb in Rome, and kiss the very dust of his corpse.⁴⁹

---

⁴² Cf. sac. 4.7: "all this he does by those epistles which he has left to us [δι᾽ ὧν ἡμῖν κατέλιπεν ἐπιστολῶν] full of wonders and of divine wisdom" [SC 272.274]. Even Jesus "left behind" [καταλείπειν] the word of his teaching with his apostles when he went up into heaven (hom. in Gal. 2:11 9 [51.379]). This is an intriguing application of cognate terms commonly used of the bodily relics of the saints [τὰ τῶν ἁγίων λείψανα], as by Chrysostom himself elsewhere (as, e.g., pan. Bab. 2 65 and 66 [SC 362.174, 176]), to the writings or words of the saint. It is used this way also of pagan writings (see Libanios, Or. 18.303, quoted in n. 59 below).

⁴³ hom. in Gen. 11.4 [53.95].

⁴⁴ hom. in Gen. 36.8 [53.331]; cf. hom. in 1 Cor. 35.5 [61.302]: the way to train oneself in virtue is to "bring out into public view those who crushed vice underfoot, and, by looking at their image [πρὸς τὴν ἐκείνων εἰκόνα βλέπων], thus to straighten out one's own life." This purpose weds nicely with the classical rhetorical form of encomium that John adopts in his homilies. See Libanios' stereotypical description of the genre: "yet with regard to the dead, there is but one recourse for us – the praise and narration that transmit their glorious achievements to all posterity" [πρὸς δὲ τοὺς οἰχομένους ἐν ἡμῖν ὑπάρχει μόνον, εὐφημίαι τε καὶ λόγοι τὰ πεπραγμένα μετ᾽ ἀρετῆς εἰς ἅπαντα παραπέμποντες τὸν χρόνον] (Or. 18.3 [text Richard Foerster, Libanii Opera (12 vols.; Leipzig: Teubner, 1903–1923) 2.237–38]; trans. A.F. Norman, LCL).

⁴⁵ For the phenomenon, see the classic study of Brown, Cult of the Saints, which focuses on the west, but applies in large part also to what we see in the east.

⁴⁶ This is Chrysostom's defense for the place of the Epistle to Philemon in the canon (hom. in Philm. Arg. [62.702]). See also hom. in Rom. 16:3 1.3 [51.191] on Prisca and Aquila, who, by virtue of having lived with Paul for two years, were able not only to see all of his activities, but also his bed, mattress, and sandals (which, Chrysostom remarks, should have been enough to set them in a perpetual state of compunction). On Paul's clothing, see hom. in Rom. 16:3 2.1 [51.196–97], and further discussion in chap. 6, pp. 358–59.

⁴⁷ hom. in Philm. Arg. [62.702–3]; hom. in Rom. 30.4 (emphasizing how these serve as an aide-mémoire [60.666]). Chrysostom is likely referring to "the Grotto of Saint Paul," located outside the city of Antioch, on the slope of Mount Tauris, on a spot where Paul is remembered as having preached (Baur, John Chrysostom, 1.33). John's reference to "the table at which the saint ate, and the chair on which he sat, and the bed on which he reclined" in hom. in Rom. 30.4 [60.666] has been taken as a description of a contemporary shrine to Paul at Antioch [the text reads: ἔνθα ἔμεινε Παῦλος, ἔνθα ἐδέθη, ἔνθα συνεκάθισε καὶ διελέχθη] (Glanville Downey, A History of Antioch in Syria from Seleucus to the Arab Conquest [Princeton: Princeton University Press, 1961] 284, n. 47; Ernst Dassmann, "Archaeological Traces of Early Christian Veneration," Paul and the Legacies of Paul, ed. W. S. Babcock [Dallas: Southern Methodist University Press, 1990] 281–306, 284 and notes).

⁴⁸ hom. in Eph. 8.1 [62.57].

⁴⁹ hom. in Rom. 32.3 [60.678], a wish he realizes through oratory rather than physical pilgrim-

These preserved and assembled remains ensure that the love prerequisite for comprehending the writings of the now dead saints can be available to successive generations of the faithful:

For it is possible even to love a man who has gone away, and to love one who isn't seen, and especially when we see such and so great reminders of his virtue [ὑπομνήματα τῆς ἀρετῆς] every day[50] – the churches everywhere on earth, the pious behavior, the change from an evil to a better life, the deliverance from deception, the cast-down altars, the closed-up temples, the silence of the demons. For the power of Paul's tongue, inspired by the grace of God, brought down all these aforementioned things, and ignited the bright flame of piety everywhere. We have, along with these good deeds [κατορθώματα], also Paul's holy epistles, which sketch the image of that blessed soul accurately for us [τὰς ἐπιστολὰς ἐκείνου τὰς ἁγίας, αἳ τὸν χαρακτῆρα τῆς μακαρίας ἐκείνης ψυχῆς ἀκριβῶς ἡμῖν ὑπογράφουσιν].[51]

The apostolic remains or monuments which represent the deeds of the pious dead are many and concrete (including the ironic conceit that the broken down monuments of Greco-Roman paganism constitute monuments to the apostle),[52] and serve to render the saint present.[53] But pride of place among the Pauline relics belongs to Paul's literary remains, the fourteen letters, which Chrysostom in several places refers to as "pillars" or "monuments."[54] In one of his homilies on the

---

age (we shall give a comprehensive analysis of this important passage in chap. 4, pp. 121–32). In *pan. Bab. 2* 65 [SC 362.174], Chrysostom says that "the tombs of the saints occupy second place after the word in the power that they have to excite similar zeal in the souls of those who behold them" [δευτέραν ἔχουσι τάξιν οἱ τῶν ἁγίων τάφοι πρὸς τὸ διεγείρειν εἰς τὸν τῶν ἴσων ζῆλον τὰς τῶν θεωμένων αὐτοὺς ψυχάς] (trans. M. Schatkin, FC 73.112).

[50] Chrysostom reflects again on the power of mentally sketched images to mediate the presence of absent loved ones in *poenit.* 1.1 [49.277]:"But just as those who are in love with splendid bodies carry the desired image around with them wherever they go, so also we, loving the beauty of your soul, always carry around with us the lovely shape of your mind [ἀλλ' ὥσπερ οἱ τῶν λαμπρῶν ἐρῶντες σωμάτων, ὅπουπερ ἂν ἀπίωσι, μεθ' ἑαυτῶν τὴν ποθουμένην περιφέρουσιν ὄψιν, οὕτω δὴ καὶ ἡμεῖς τοῦ κάλλους τῆς ὑμετέρας ψυχῆς ἐρασθέντες, ἀεὶ μεθ' ἑαυτῶν τὴν εὐμορφίαν τῆς ὑμετέρας περιφέρομεν διανοίας] ... although not seeing you with the eyes of the flesh, I saw you with the eyes of love [καὶ οὐχ ὁρῶν ὑμᾶς τοῖς ὀφθαλμοῖς τῆς σαρκός, ἑώρων ὑμᾶς τῆς ἀγάπης τοῖς ὀφθαλμοῖς], though not present with you in body, I was present with you in disposition" [καὶ μὴ παρὼν ὑμῖν τῷ σώματι, παρήμην ὑμῖν τῇ διαθέσει] (see also the fuller context of this passage, as quoted in chap. 5, n. 3).

[51] *hom. in 2 Cor. 11:1* 2 [51.303]; cf. *hom. in Rom.* 2.2 [60.402], where conversely great love is said to be a prerequisite for keeping someone in one's memory continually. In *kal.* 1 [48.953] Chrysostom maintains that love is the power that can span distance and bind people together even beyond death, and make the deceased present:"the power of love set him [Paul] before your eyes" [ἡ τῆς ἀγάπης δύναμις πρὸ τῶν ὀφθαλμῶν αὐτὸν ἔστησε τῶν ὑμετέρων].

[52] Chrysostom regards Paul's crowning achievement to have been the complete overthrow of traditional Greek and Roman religion and philosophy (as we shall observe in detail in chap. 6, pp. 270–78).

[53] As powerfully elucidated by Brown, *Cult of the Saints*, especially p. 88. For this idea of Paul having spread his legacy around the earth, see also *anom.* 8.3 [48.772]:"the one who left memorials of his own virtue everywhere in the world" [ὁ πανταχοῦ τῆς οἰκουμένης ὑπομνήματα τῆς οἰκείας ἀρετῆς καταλιπών], and further references in di S. Maria, "S. Paolo," 496 n. 3.

[54] The role of such a monument is made clear in Chrysostom's address to Paul about his description of the Antioch incident recounted in Gal 2:"And not only did you publicly disgrace

Letter to the Romans Chrysostom explains why this is so: because of the primacy of the apostolic *word*. In assuring his fourth-century hearers that, through their shared esteem for the person of the saint, they could transcend time to be on the same, or even better, footing than Prisca, who had the opportunity to host Paul for two years and continually speak to him face-to-face, he counsels:

> If you wish, you can have him more accurately [ἀκριβέστερον] than they. For even with them the appearance of Paul [ἡ ὄψις ἡ Παύλου] was not what made them of such character, but the words of Paul [ἀλλὰ τὰ ῥήματα Παύλου]. Therefore, if you wish you may have both Paul, and Peter, and John, and the whole chorus of the prophets conversing with you [ὁμιλεῖν σοι] continually. For take the books of these blessed ones [τῶν μακαρίων τούτων αἱ βίβλοι], and continually read[55] their writings [ἐντυγχάνειν διηνεκῶς ταῖς ἐκείνων γραφαῖς], and they will be able to make you like the tent-maker's wife.[56]

The apostolic writings have the power to mediate the presence of the absent dead[57] through preservation of their word. Chrysostom sees this hermeneutical function of the letters to be rooted in Paul's own literary-epistolary intention to make himself present to churches and colleagues when separated from them.[58]

---

him [Peter], but also, as though on a monument [στήλη], you engraved the battle in words, and made the memory of it immortal, so that not only those who were present then, but also all the inhabitants of the world might learn through the epistle what happened" (*hom. in Gal.* 2:11 3 [51.374]). The same is true also of Paul's own sins, which he freely "inscribes on a stele" [στηλιτεύειν] in his letters for all – not just those alive at the time, but all who will live thereafter – to see (*hom. in 2 Cor. 11:1* 6 [51.306]; for the same idea see also *hom. in Jo.* 10.1 [59.74]; *hom. in Rom. 16:3* 1.5 [51.194]; *stat.* 1.1–2 [49.18]). One of Chrysostom's metaphorical depictions of the epistles is ὁ στῦλος καὶ τὸ ἑδραίωμα τῆς ἀληθείας, "the pillar and foundation of the truth" (*hom. in Rom. 16:3* 1.3 [51.191]). This designation extends also to the author, as Chrysostom can term Paul "the pillar of the churches" [ὁ στῦλος τῶν ἐκκλησίων] (*poenit.* 2.5 [49.291]). Interesting in this connection is Bovon, "Paul comme document et Paul comme monument," for whom Paul himself is a monument: "c'est-à-dire soit comme texte, soit comme figure" (p. 54).

55   The verb ἐντυγχάνειν could also be translated "converse with" (LSJ, 578).

56   *hom. in Rom.* 30.4 [60.665–6]. Chrysostom's obsession with this topic, and his ambivalence, can be seen in the two occasional homilies on Rom 16:3, where he contrasts Paul's physical presence with his letters, and comes down on precisely the opposite side: "For it is not only the words [τὰ ῥήματα] of the saints, nor their teachings and counsels [διδασκαλίαι καὶ παραινέσεις], but the rest of their lives [ἡ λοιπὴ τοῦ βίου], their entire behavior [πᾶσα ἀναστροφή], which may constitute a sufficient instruction in philosophy for those who pay attention to them" (*hom. in Rom. 16:3* 1.3 [51.191]). See also *hom. in Rom. 16:3* 2.1 [51.196]: "... not only the teaching, or the advice and counsel, but also the appearance [ὄψις] of the saints has great pleasure and benefit, even the very style of their garments and their type of sandals."

57   Patricia Cox Miller has nicely articulated the paradoxes about presence embodied in relics, in reference to a passage in Gregory of Nyssa's panegyric on Saint Theodore [*Thdr.* 740M]: "relics are signifiers of a person who is neither absent nor present. It was in this mediatorial gap between presence and absence, the gap expressed by Gregory's phrase 'as though he were present' [on which *topos* see n. 18 above] that the body continued to function as a magnet for expressing views of identity in an ascetic context" ("Dreaming the Body: An Aesthetics of Asceticism," *Asceticism*, ed. Vincent L. Wimbush and Richard Valantasis [New York/Oxford: Oxford University Press, 1995] 281–300, 289).

58   See *hom. in Col.* 1.1 [62.300], quoted below, p. 49, in reference to passages such as 1 Cor

And he does so through the power of his letters, which constitute verbal icons of the apostle himself.[59]

Epistolary Theory

Chrysostom's hermeneutical claim about the epistles of Paul, that they allow the reader to "gaze into Paul's soul," must also be understood as an element of ancient Greco-Roman epistolary theory, as attested, e.g., in Ps-Demetrius, *de Elocutione*: "For everyone nearly writes the image of his or her own soul in writing a letter"[60] The idea of the letter as conveying a portrait of the soul of its author[61] is related

---

5:3; 4:19 and Phil 2:12, in which Paul writes explicitly about his wish to be present with his congregations.

[59] For the concept of Scripture as "verbal icon" in patristic theology, see Harrison, "Word as Icon," 38–49 (in reference to Gregory of Nyssa and Gregory of Nazianzus). On how the image serves to mediate the presence of what is absent, with particular reference to the way this was worked out by Plotinus, see Margaret R. Miles, "Image," *Critical Terms for Religious Studies*, ed. Mark C. Taylor (Chicago: University of Chicago Press, 1998) 160–72. The application of this idea to literature is not uniquely Christian. There are contemporary oratorical uses of the commonplace close at hand to Chrysostom, such as in Libanios' funeral oration for Julian, where he muses: "We may not see him in the flesh [αὐτὸν μὲν οὐκ ἂν ἴδοιμεν], but we can see his compositions, so many in number and all of supreme art [τοὺς δὲ ἐκείνου λόγους ἐστιν ἰδεῖν τοὺς πολλοὺς καὶ πάντας σὺν τέχνῃ] ... when I take these works, I get some consolation. By means of them, his offspring [διὰ τούτων ... τῶν ἐκγόνων], you will endure your grief, for he has left them as his offspring for all eternity [παῖδας τούτους ἐκεῖνος ἀθανάτους καταλέλοιπεν], and time cannot remove them as it does the colours on his official portraits" [οὓς οὐκ ἂν ὁ χρόνος δύναιτο μετὰ τῶν ἐν ταῖς σανίσιν ἐξαλεῖψαι χρωμάτων] (*Or.* 18.303, trans. A. F Norman, LCL).

[60] σχεδὸν γὰρ εἰκόνα ἕκαστος τῆς ἑαυτοῦ ψυχῆς γράφει τὴν ἐπιστολήν (4.227). This is my translation; compare that of Doreen C. Innes in the recently revised Loeb volume: "Everyone writes a letter in the virtual image of his own soul." The reserve shown by σχεδόν in this passage matches precisely Chrysostom's μονονουχί in the text cited above (pp. 37–38) about Paul's presence in the reading of his letters – "almost, nearly."

[61] For the influence of this concept on actual letters, see also the collection of important passages referred to by Abraham J. Malherbe, *Ancient Epistolary Theorists* (Society of Biblical Literature Sources for Biblical Study 19; Atlanta: Scholars Press, 1988) 12: Cicero, *Fam.* 16.16.2: "I see you entirely in your letter" [*Te totum in litteris vidi*]; Philostratus, *De epistulis* 2.257, of Marcus Aurelius having had "his firmness of character imprinted in his letters" [τὸ ἑδραῖον τοῦ ἤθους ἐντετύπωτο τοῖς γράμμασι] (text Malherbe, p. 42); and, above all, Seneca, *Ep.* 40.1: "I thank you for writing to me so often; for you are revealing your real self to me in the only way you can [*Nam quo uno modo potes, te mihi ostendis*]. I never receive a letter from you without being in your company forthwith [*Numquam epistulam tuam accipio, ut non protinus una simus*]. If the pictures of our absent friends [*imagines nobis amicorum absentium*] are pleasing to us, though they only refresh the memory and lighten our longing by a solace that is unreal and unsubstantial [*quae memoriam renovant et desiderium falso atque inani solacio levant*], how much more pleasant is a letter, which brings us real traces, real evidences, of an absent friend! [*quanto iucundiores sunt litterae, quae vera amici absentis vestigia, veras notas adferunt*]? For that which is sweetest when we meet face to face is afforded by the impress of a friend's hand upon his letter – recognition" [*Nam quod in conspectu dulcissimum est, id amici manus epistulae inpressa praestat, agnoscere*]. The latter passage is especially suggestive for our inquiry, for it brings together the two modes of depiction of a person – the epistolary and the graphic portrait – by which Chrysostom encountered and in turn displayed

in epistolary theory to the complex dynamic of presence and absence which a letter (in its own particular way, like monuments and other relics) serves to mediate. As an epistolary handbook contemporary with Chrysostom has it: "there is holiness in honoring one's genuine friends when present, and in speaking to them when absent (through a letter)."[62] This intersects with Chrysostom's love hermeneutic, because the letter is considered the medium of communication between absent friends who desire one another's company and conversation.[63] Indeed, a letter was thought to contain the speech of its absent author.[64] Chrysostom's complete familiarity with these concepts of ancient epistolary theory is virtually guaranteed from his education in the school of Libanios, who employed these *topoi* liberally in his own correspondence, and was himself widely known as an effective practitioner of the epistolary art with its requisite grace.[65] For instance, in one of his letters Libanios recites the commonplace about a letter giving a view of the author who wrote it – the very same cliché we saw Chrysostom apply to the Pauline epistles: "But when you look at the letter, consider that you see me, all of me, in it for you" [ἀλλ' ὅταν εἰς τὰ γράμματα βλέπῃς, ἡγοῦ καὶ ἐμὲ βλέπειν ἐκεῖνον τὸν πάντα σοι].[66] However, one does not have to rely on a reconstruction of Chrysostom's schooling to ensure his full saturation in these commonplaces. Once, when explaining the concept of mystery, John turned to epistolary practice as an *exemplum*: "The inexperienced reader when taking up a letter will consider it to be papyrus and ink; but the experienced reader will both hear a voice, and

---

Paul. This commonplace of epistolary theory is well-attested from the first century B.C.E. up through the Byzantine period, and in particular in the letters of the great fourth century Christian letter writers, Basil of Caesarea, Gregory Nazianzus and Gregory of Nyssa, as demonstrated by H. Koskenniemi, *Studien zur Idee und Phraseologie des griechischen Briefes bis 400 n. Chr.* (Suomalaisen Tiedeakatemian Toimituksia, Series B, Annales Academiae Scientiarum Fennicae 102, 2; Helsinki: Suomalainen Tiedeakatemia, 1956) 40–41, 179–80.

[62] ὅσιον γὰρ ὑπάρχει τοὺς γνησίους φίλους παρόντας μὲν τιμᾶν, ἀπόντες δὲ προσερεῖν (Ps-Libanios, *Epistolimaioi characteres* 58, in the description of the "friendly" [φιλική] letter type). Compare Seneca, *Ep.* 67.2: "Whenever your letters arrive, I imagine that I am with you, and I have the feeling that I am about to speak my answer, instead of writing it" [*Si quando intervenerunt epistulae tuae, tecum esse mihi videor et sic adficior animo, tamquam tibi non rescribam, sed respondeam*].

[63] *amicorum conloquia absentium* (Cicero, *Phil.* 2.4; in practice, see *Att.* 12.53).

[64] Cicero, *Att.* 8.14.1; 9.10.1 [*tecum ut quasi loquerer*]; Seneca, *Ep.* 67.2 (Malherbe, *Epistolary Theorists*, 12).

[65] Thus the epistolary treatise *Epistolimaioi characteres* in the most popular manuscript tradition was attributed to Libanios (V. Weichert, ed., *Demetrii et Libanii qui feruntur ΤΥΠΟΙ ΕΠΙΣΤΟΛΙΚΟΙ et ΕΠΙΣΤΟΛΙΜΑΙΟΙ ΧΑΡΑΚΤΗΡΕΣ* [BT; Leipzig: Teubner, 1910]; now available in Malherbe, *Epistolary Theorists*, 66–81 (see his discussion of the authorship of the manual on pp. 4–6).

[66] *Ep.* 245.9 [Foerster 10.232]. Compare Libanios' favorite, Julian, in his epistle to Georgios: "I already saw you in your letters, and I have obtained an impression of the image of your holy soul, as though the stamp of a great character were made by a small seal. For it is possible for much to be revealed in a little thing" [ἐγὼ δέ σε καὶ εἶδον ἤδη τοῖς γράμμασι, καὶ τῆς ἱερᾶς σου ψυχῆς τὴν εἰκόνα καθάπερ ὀλίγῳ σφραγίδι μεγάλου χαρακτῆρος τύπον ἀνεμαξάμην. ἔστι γὰρ ἐν ὀλίγῳ πολλὰ δειχθῆναι] (*Ep.* 67.377A).

converse with one the one who is absent."[67] Chrysostom's comments in his own letters likewise show the liveliness of concepts of epistolary presence in his thinking and his literary practice.[68] Hence it is no surprise that when he turned to the collection of Paul's writings – which are genuine letters employing epistolary forms and commonplaces –,that these assumptions about the relationship between an epistolary author, his text, and its readers played a central role in John's hermeneutics:"Thus Paul knew his presence was everywhere a great thing, and always, though absent, he makes himself present."[69] This pervasive epistolary sensibility melds nicely with the idea of Scripture as a relic, because the concept of a letter as mediating the presence of a geographically distant author can readily accommodate an author now absent because of death.

The Ethics of Imitation

The third component of Chrysostom's author-centered hermeneutic is the ancient ethical and pedagogical theory which held that learning takes place by imitation of exemplary figures.[70] This tradition, a mainstay of Christian thought from the earliest period of Paul himself, engenders in Chrysostom the powerful sense that Paul the apostle is a supreme example of lived virtue who is to be imitated.[71] We see this explicitly in Chrysostom's statement in *hom. in Gen.* 11.5, quoted on p. 43, that the letters allow one to "gaze into Paul's soul, *just as into a certain archetypal image.*"The ἀρχέτυπος εἰκών, archetypal image or portrait, is the singularly accurate portrait from which copies are to be made.[72] In the case of Paul, he

---

[67] καὶ ἐπιστολὴν ὁ μὲν ἄπειρος λαβών, χάρτην ἡγήσεται καὶ μέλαν εἶναι· ὁ δὲ ἔμπειρος καὶ φωνῆς ἀκούσεται, καὶ διαλέξεται τῷ ἀπόντι (*hom. in 1 Cor.* 7.2 [61.56]).

[68] *ep. Olymp.* 8.13c [SC 13.216],"show us in this way the love you have for us – that when writing you a letter we have as great an influence on you as we do when present" [Δεῖξον δὴ κἂν τούτῳ τὴν ἀγάπην τὴν περὶ ἡμᾶς ὅτι καὶ μεγάλην γράφοντες ἔχομεν παρὰ σοὶ δύναμιν, καὶ τοσαύτην ὅσην παρόντες]. For the commonplace, see further the discussion by Malingrey in SC 13.40–41.

[69] Οὕτως ᾔδει μέγα ὂν τὴν παρουσίαν αὐτοῦ πανταχοῦ, καὶ ἀεὶ ἑαυτὸν καὶ ἀπόντα ἐφίστησι (*hom. in Col.* 1.1 [62.300]).

[70] See, e.g., Aristotle, *Politica* 3.4.2:"human beings learn their first lessons by imitation" [τὰς μαθήσεις ποιεῖται διὰ μιμήσεως τὰς πρώτας]. For an entry into the secondary literature on imitation in ancient education and ethics see Elizabeth A. Castelli, *Imitating Paul. A Discourse of Power* (Literary Currents in Biblical Interpretation; Louisville: Westminster/John Knox, 1991) 81–85; in ancient literary theory, see D. A. Russell, *Criticism in Antiquity* (Berkeley/Los Angeles: University of California Press, 1981) 99–113. We can see Chrysostom's familiarity with this concept by the terms in which he fashions his complaint about moral decay in his time:"No one takes it as a necessity to look after his or her own son. No one looking at the elders is incited to imitate [μιμήσασθαι] them.The archetypes [τὰ ἀρχέτυπα] are defaced.That is why the young do not become admirable in conduct, either" (*hom. in Ac.* 24.4 [60.189]).

[71] In chap. 7, pp. 396–400 we shall engage the question of whether Chrysostom's exorbitant claims for Paul compromise either his devotion to other saints or, more pointedly, his Christology.

[72] See, for example, Dionysius of Halicarnassus' distinction between an ἀρχέτυπος ("original type or model") and an ἀπόγραφον ("a copy," here a product of rhetorical skill) in *de Isaeo* 11.

is to be imitated as the perfect exemplar of ἀρετή, virtue, as Chrysostom states explicitly in his second homily *de laudibus sancti Pauli:* "I exhort you not only to marvel at, but also to imitate this archetype of virtue" [ἀλλὰ καὶ μιμεῖσθαι τὸ ἀρχέτυπον τοῦτο τῆς ἀρετῆς].[73] This plea connects seamlessly with Chrysostom's overall conception of the Scriptures:

> The Apostles therefore were a type [τύπος], and kept throughout a certain archetypal image [ἀρχέτυπός τις εἰκών]. Consider how entirely accurate their life was [πῶς αὐτοῖς ὁ βίος ἀπηκριβωμένος ἦν],[74] so that they are proposed as an archetype and example [ἀρχέτυπος καὶ παράδειγμα], and as living laws [νόμοι ἔμψυχοι].[75] The things their writings said, they manifested to all in their actions ... Take from there the type [τύπος]. You have a most excellent portrait [εἰκὼν ἀρίστη]. Proportion yourself to it.[76]

Here we see the complex blending of life and text, of image and word, and imitation and exegesis, a self-conscious dynamic which was at work in a good deal of fourth-century Christian literature,[77] but one especially pertinent to Paul,[78] since it was explicitly inaugurated and mandated in his letters themselves (μιμηταί

See also Lucian, *Imagines* 15; Cicero, *Epistulae ad Atticum* 16.3.1, of an original manuscript from which copies are to be made.

[73] *laud. Paul.* 2 [SC 300.158] (the entire discourse, which we shall analyze on pp. 152–59, is devoted to this theme); see also hom. in 1 Cor. 12.2 [61.110]). In *laud. Paul.* 6.7 [SC 300.274] Chrysostom refers to Paul as "this man, the very portrait statue of virtue" [οὗτος αὐτὸς ὁ ἀνδριὰς τῆς ἀρετῆς].

[74] The concept is applied to Paul in particular in *comm. in Gal.* 2.8 [61.646]: "Look at the accuracy of his conduct, and admire that blessed soul to the highest degree" [ὅρα τὴν ἀκρίβειαν τῆς πολιτείας, καὶ θαύμασον μεθ' ὑπερβολῆς τὴν μακαρίαν ἐκείνην ψυχήν].

[75] cf. hom. in *Mt.* 1.1 [57.15] on the apostles as "living books and laws" [βιβλία καὶ νόμοι ἔμψυχοι]; fr. in *Jer.* 31:29 [64.981], "living stelae" [ἔμψυχοι στῆλαι]. The cohesion of all this terminology can be seen in hom. in 1 *Tim.* 13.1 [62.565], where Chrysostom restates the exhortation of 4:12, "be a type for the believers" [τύπος γίνου τῶν πιστῶν]: "that is, you yourself be the archetype of life [ἀρχέτυπος τοῦ βίου], like a portrait set forth [εἰκὼν προκείμενος], like a living law" [νόμος ἔμψυχος].

[76] hom. in *Phil.* 12.3 [62.273], on 3:17. A wonderful western corollary to Chrysostom's understanding of saints as images to be copied can be found in his younger contemporary, Paulinus of Nola, who was famous for his special devotion to Martin of Tours. Paulinus was asked for a portrait of himself to be put next to that of his favorite saint, but "Paulinus had misgivings, which he voiced in Platonic terms [*Ep.* 32.2]. The divine 'person' (*homo coelestis* – the *noēton* of the Platonists) could not be copied, and the 'earthly person' (*homo terrestris*) should not be copied, he said. To prevent his image from being misunderstood or even misused next to the icon of St. Martin, Paulinus composed inscriptions reminding the beholder that Martin was an example to be imitated, and he an example to be shunned. Martin, he wrote, offered the 'perfect pattern of a proper life' (*perfecta regula vitae*), whereas he was a lesson for sinners who had to do penance" (Hans Belting, *Likeness and Presence. A History of the Image before the Era of Art*, trans. Edmund Jephcott [Chicago and London: University of Chicago Press, 1994] 93).

[77] See the astute discussion of the appropriation of biography (and its sibling encomium) by Christian authors in the fourth century by Averil Cameron, *Christianity and the Rhetoric of Empire*, 141–52 ("Lives as Image"), who examines how "sacred lives functioned as ideological and literary exemplars" (p. 145). "Through *Lives*, Christian writers could present an image not only of the perfect Christian life, but also of the life in imitation of Christ, the life that becomes an icon" (p. 143).

μου γίνεσθε in 1 Cor 4:16; 11:1; Gal 4:12, etc.). Paul as mimetic intermediary becomes increasingly important in the fourth century as Christology soars higher and higher, and the imitation of Christ seems beyond the ken of ordinary human beings, whereas imitation of Paul stands more within reach.[79] Therefore Chrysostom can exhort his audience to emulate Paul, for Paul was human just as they were.[80] But in order to cast themselves according to this Pauline model, later readers are required to formulate from the texts of the letters (and other sources as available) a portrait of the author to be imitated.[81] Creating such a portrait becomes the task for exegesis and homiletics, carried out with all the sophisticated tools of rhetoric which were in Chrysostom's employ.[82] Paul, the perfect copy of Christ, is the example for Christians to follow. Thus artistic and ethical theory merge in the conception of μίμησις.[83] This is precisely how Chrysostom ex-

---

[78] Cameron mentions Chrysostom's writing of the "life" of Paul among her examples of fourth-century rhetorics of appropriation and reproduction (*Christianity and the Rhetoric of Empire*, 145), but does not explore the extent to which Paul in many ways had textually inaugurated this pervasive strategy of Christian rhetorical social construction.

[79] "Now don't tell me, 'I am not able to imitate you, Paul, because you are a teacher, and a great one.' For the distance between me and you is not as great as that between Christ and me. But I [Paul] nonetheless imitated him [Christ]" (*hom. in 1 Cor.* 13.3 [61.110]).

[80] As the passage quoted in the previous note continues, Chrysostom stresses that Paul was made of the same material as everyone else – the same soul and body – but differed only in his extraordinary exercise of will (*hom. in 1 Cor.* 13.3 [61.110]; see the analysis of this passage in chap. 4, pp. 104–21, and many of the soul portraits in chap. 5, where Chrysostom frequently invokes this argument).

[81] This procedure is for those who did not know Paul in the flesh. In contrast, Timothy, who had been instructed by Paul not only through letters but also before them in words [οὐ διὰ γραμμάτων μόνον ... ἀλλ᾽ ἤδη καὶ διὰ ῥημάτων], had thereby received the very imprint of the Pauline image on *his* own soul, which he could pull out to contemplate and copy when needed: "In the same way as with artists [καθάπερ ἐπὶ τῶν ζωγράφων], I imprinted [ἐντυποῦσθαι] on you an image [εἰκών] of virtue, and of what seems right to God, just as if laying down a model [κανών] and archetype [ἀρχέτυπος] and standards [ὅροι] into your soul [εἰς τὴν σὴν ψυχήν]. Therefore, have these things. And if you need to take counsel about something concerning faith, or love, or moderation, take your examples [τὰ παραδείγματα] from there. You will not need to seek an image [εἰκών] from others when all reside right there" [πάντων ἐκεῖ κατακειμένων] (*hom. in 2 Tim.* 3.1 [62.613], on 2 Tim 1:13).

[82] See especially *hom. in Ac.* 30.4 [60.227–28]: "for here also we are employed in painting portraits, royal portraits [εἰκόνας γράφομεν βασιλικάς], none of any private person, employing the colors of virtue ... Moreover, our stylus is the tongue, and the artist the Holy Spirit" [γραφὶς τοίνυν ἐστὶν ἡμῖν γλῶττα, τεχνίτης δὲ τὸ πνεῦμα τὸ ἅγιον]. John's attribution of the authorship of his homilies to the Holy Spirit is a form of oratorical self-effacement meant to match that of the saints he is portraying ("In effect, the author surrendered power over the text. Turning the writer's agency into ascetic performance resolved tensions between authorship and pride" [Krueger, "Hagiography as an Ascetic Practice," 228]).

[83] On painting as imitation, see the seminal remarks of Plato, *Respublica* 10.598A-B, who regarded the painter as being three removes from the truth, for he or she copies copies. Chrysostom is clearly aware of these ideas, as he begins his exegesis of 1 Cor 4:16 with the confident assertion that Paul is the perfect archetype, though himself a copy of Christ; thus "the one who has copied the most accurate impression of the seal has copied the archetype" [ὁ γὰρ τὴν σφραγῖδα μιμησάμενος τὴν ἀπηκριβωμένην, τὸ ἀρχέτυπον ἐμιμήσατο] (*hom. in 1 Cor.* 13.3

pounds on Paul's call in 4:16 – "be imitators of me, just as I am of Christ!"[84] – in terms of the graphic arts:[85]

Let's see then how he imitated [μιμήσασθαι] Christ. For this imitation [μίμησις] needs not time and art, but only the exercise of one's free will. For if we go into a painter's [ζωγράφος] studio, we shall not be able to copy [μιμήσασθαι] the portrait [εἰκών], even if we see it ten thousand times. But it is by hearing alone that we can copy [μιμήσασθαι] him. So, do you wish us to bring the tablet into the middle here and sketch [ὑπογράφειν] for you Paul's way of life [ἡ πολιτεία τοῦ Παύλου]? Well, let it be set before you, the pictorial tablet far more illustrious than the portraits of the emperors [ὁ πίναξ πολὺ λαμπρότερος ὢν τῶν βασιλικῶν εἰκόνων]. For what underlies it is not boards glued together, nor canvas stretched out; but the work of God is what underlies it, for it is a soul and a body.[86]

In order to imitate Paul, the reader, who in the fourth-century Antiochene context was an auditor, had to work across the senses[87] and formulate a portrait to be

---

[61.110], as earlier he had exclaimed: "Profound! How great is the teacher's boldness. How accurate must the image be [πῶς ἀπηκριβωμένη ἡ εἰκών], when he exhorts even others to it!"). For the terminology of "accuracy" in portraits, compare Lucian, *Imagines* 16 [πάσαις ταῖς γραμμαῖς ἀπηκριβωμένη] and 23 [ἀκριβεστάτη εἰκών].

[84] Chrysostom's text conflates 1 Cor 4:16 and 11:1 at this point. In chap. 4, pp. 104–121 we shall thoroughly analyze this entire rhetorical composition, but for our purposes in this chapter we shall concentrate solely on its conceptualization of portraiture.

[85] Gregory of Nyssa also understood Paul's μίμησις in artistic terms, but in one place drew on the olfactory sense instead of the visual as the means of artistic inspiration: "... just as it is possible to sum up the archetypal beauty of a certain image [τινὸς εἰκόνος τὸ ἀρχέτυπον κάλλος ἀναλογίσασθαι]. This was also the case with Paul, the bride [ἡ νύμφη], the one who imitated the groom through the virtues and painted the unapproachable beauty in himself *through the sweet smell* [ὁ διὰ τῶν ἀρετῶν τὸν νυμφίον μιμούμενος καὶ ζωγραφῶν ἐν ἑαυτῷ διὰ τοῦ εὐώδους τὸ ἀπρόσιτον κάλλος] ..." (*hom. 3 in cant.* 1:12 [*Gregorii Nysseni Opera, VI: in canticum canticorum*, ed. H. Langerbeck (Leiden: Brill, 1960) 91]). See also below, pp. 63–64, for Gregory's visual rendering of the Pauline μίμησις.

[86] *hom. in 1 Cor.* 13.3 [61.110].

[87] On synesthesia as characteristic of religious discourse, see Chidester, *Word and Light*, esp. 14–24. "By defying ordinary expectations of how the senses work, literary synesthesia indicates a transcendent sensory perception that is above and beyond sense. Crossing sensory modes, synesthesia suggests the possibility of seeing beyond seeing and hearing beyond hearing ... As an antistructural, unificatory paradox, therefore, literary synesthesia provides a perceptual vocabulary that is sensory but at the same time points beyond sense to an experience that is more transcendent" (p. 19). On the precise correspondence with *ekphrasis*, the art of vivid description, see Norman Bryson, "Philostratus and the Imaginary Museum," *Art and Text in Ancient Greek Culture*, ed. Simon Goldhill and Robin Osborne (Cambridge Studies in New Art History and Criticism; Cambridge: Cambridge University Press, 1994) 255–83, 273: "What words lack (because they are only words, characters on the page, marks without light), images can fill with a presence which is based on that lack, which grows from it, and turns it into light. What images lack (because they are frozen in time, mere pigments on a surface, threads on a loom), words can supply with narration and movement. This strange, hallucinatory power of ecphrasis calls on the capacities of words and pictures to describe the world, but goes beyond their several powers into a visionary moment when 'Look!' becomes the only appropriate response. The exclamation directs the reader not towards the text, or its image, but past them both into another space where presence is alive to all the senses at once (sight, hearing, touch, taste)." We shall discuss *ekphrasis* in more detail in chap. 4, pp. 101–104, and throughout this study.

copied/imitated by hearing alone.[88] This difficulty can, however, be overcome by means of expert mediation carried out via the form of an ἔκφρασις. The preacher in interpreting the Scriptures formulates a powerful image and then represents that portrait[89] in such vivid terms that all will as much as "see" it and its brilliance which rivals the imperial portraits.[90] Even better than a customary painting on wood or cloth, this one is (or rather, was) a living body, manifested now through words. And when John paints a portrait of Paul, he is replicating a work of art which already exists, since Paul as an artist in his life composed his own self-portrait.[91] Now we are embedded, as the logic of μίμησις requires, in the complex "inter-picturality" of the portraits of Paul.

Now, let's assume our tablet is Paul's soul [ὁ πίναξ ἡμῖν ἡ ψυχὴ Παύλου]. This tablet was not long ago lying covered with soot, full of cobwebs. (For nothing is worse than blasphemy.) But when the one who refashions everything[92] came, and saw that it wasn't through carelessness and laziness that Paul was drawn this way, but through inexperience, and his not having the bright tincture [ἄνθη] of piety (for he had zeal, but the colors [χρώματα][93] were not there, because he did not have "the zeal according to knowledge" [Rom 10:2]), he

---

[88] Yet, the congregation was likely influenced also by current artistic renderings, which were becoming more and more prominent in the late fourth century (A. Grabar, *Christian Iconography. A Study of its Origins* [Bollingen Series 35/10; Princeton: Princeton University, 1968] 67–68). In fact, evidence suggests that the walls of the "Great Church" built by Constantine in Antioch, in which Chrysostom delivered most of the homilies from his Antiochene period, were covered with reliefs (Baur, *John Chrysostom*, 1.31), thus providing a multi-media experience for those in attendance. Unfortunately we do not know the content of these pictures, as the church was destroyed by an earthquake in the sixth century.

[89] See Russell's description of the role of φαντασία in this process: "... the concept of *phantasia*, the mental power that can visualize what the eye has never seen. At this point, writers like 'Longinus' and Quintilian invoke also the rhetorical precept (known to Aristotle, and indeed commonplace) that a certain degree of emotional excitement in the speaker is necessary for the adequate projection of emotion to others" (*Criticism in Antiquity*, 110–11). See n. 132 below for Chrysostom's own use of the term φαντασία to describe the psychology at work in this use of mimetic portraiture.

[90] On the rhetorical goal of transforming the listener into a viewer, see chap. 4, n. 31.

[91] On self-portraits in the epistles, see *hom. in Rom.* 5:3 4 [51.163], in reference to 2 Corinthians: "Writing in the form of a letter, [Paul] was compelled there to compose for us a portrait of his good deeds one by one" [τὸν χαρακτῆρα τῆς ἐπιστολῆς ἀπογράφων, ἀνάγκην ἔσχεν ἐντεῦθεν τῶν καθ᾽ ἑαυτὸν κατορθωμάτων συνθεῖναι ἡμῖν τὴν εἰκόνα]. Paul was a composer of other portraits also, according to Chrysostom, such as the portrait of the ideal bishop in 1 Tim 3:1–3, of which Ignatius was the perfect copy (*pan. Ign.* 1 [50.589]).

[92] On Paul's conversion making him a completely new person, see *hom. in Rom.* 8.7 [60.463]: ἡ πίστις αὐτὸν ἄλλον ἀντ᾽ ἄλλου πεποίηκεν. See also pp. 257–59 below.

[93] The idea of the colors as virtues, and Jesus as giving the believer those colors, is found already in *Acta Joannis* 28–29 (M. Bonnet, ed., *Acta Apostolorum Apocrypha* [vol. 2/1; Hildesheim: Olms, 1972] 166): "Be a good painter [ζωγράφος] for me, Lykomedes. You have colors [χρώματα] which Jesus gives you through me – Jesus, who paints us all in himself [ὁ ἑαυτῷ πάντας ἡμᾶς ζωγραφῶν Ἰησοῦς], who knows the shapes and forms and figures and conditions and types of our souls. These are the colors which I am telling you to paint with: faith in God, knowledge, piety, friendship ... [long list of virtues follows], and the whole chorus of colors which portray your soul [ὁ εἰκονογραφῶν σου τὴν ψυχήν]." See also Gregory of Nyssa, *perf.* 272M, quoted below, pp. 63–64.

gives him the bright tincture of the truth [τῆς ἀληθείας τὸ ἄνθος],[94] that is, grace. And all at once he exhibited the imperial portrait [ἡ βασιλικὴ εἰκών].[95]

Paul's self-portrait was not his handiwork alone; it was "God's work," and its full-color version was only made possible by Christ's grace bestowed in his conversion. But Paul's self-portrait was not thereby complete, for it received on-going touching up, oddly by the subject of the painting himself, and uncustomarily carried out while the portrait hung in continual public display:

For after receiving the colors [τὰ χρώματα] and learning the things of which he was ignorant, he did not wait for a long time, but immediately he appeared as an excellent artist [τεχνίτης ἄριστος]. And first he shows the imperial head, by preaching Christ. Then also he shows the rest of the body, the body of accurate conduct [τὸ τῆς πολιτείας τῆς ἀκριβοῦς]. For painters [ζωγράφοι] shut themselves up, and do all their work with great accuracy [ἀκρίβεια] and silence, not opening the doors to anyone. But Paul, setting out his tablet [πίναξ] in the midst of the world,[96] with everyone opposing him, and causing tumult and agitation, thus made this imperial portrait [οὕτω εἰργάζετο τὴν βασιλικὴν ταύτην εἰκόνα], and he was not hindered. That is why he said, "We have become a spectacle to the world" (1 Cor 4:9). In the midst of land and sea, of heaven and the whole earth, and of the cosmos, things material and spiritual, he was painting his portrait [τὴν εἰκόνα ζωγραφῶν].[97]

---

[94] The notion of colors as representing the truth figures in another of Chrysostom's homilies, in which he uses the analogy of a painter to explain the relationship between the Testaments, with the Old Testament as a σκιά or shadow of the new: "What then is the shadow [σκιά], what is the truth [ἀλήθεια]? Come, let's turn our speech to the portraits [εἰκόνες] which the artists draw. You have often seen an imperial portrait [εἰκὼν βασιλική] which is prepared on a dark background; then the artist, by drawing white lines all around it, makes an emperor, and an imperial throne, and horses standing nearby, and body guards, and bound prisoners of war lying down. Now when you see these things sketched out [σκιαγραφούμενα] you neither know everything, nor are you totally ignorant of everything, but you know that a man and a horse are drawn there, though they are indistinct. But you don't accurately [ἀκριβῶς] know what sort of emperor or what sort of prisoner it is until the truth of the colors comes [ἕως ἂν ἐλθοῦσα τῶν χρωμάτων ἡ ἀλήθεια] and makes the face distinct and clear. For just as you don't ask everything of that portrait [εἰκών] before the truth of the colors [ἡ τῶν χρωμάτων ἀλήθεια], but if you receive some indistinct knowledge of what is there, you consider the sketch [σκιαγραφία] to be sufficiently ready, in just this way consider with me the Old and the New Testaments, and don't demand from me the whole accuracy of the truth [πᾶς τῆς ἀληθείας ἡ ἀκρίβεια] in the type [τύπος]" (hom. in 1 Cor. 10:1 4 [51.247]). Chrysostom uses the same argument in his interpretation of Heb 10:1, a passage itself built upon the contrast between σκιά and εἰκών (see hom. in Heb. 17.2 [63.130]: "... 'and not itself the portrait [εἰκών] of the things.' That is, not itself the truth [ἀλήθεια]. For as in a painting, until someone draws in the colors, it is a shadowy sketch [σκιά] only. But when someone applies the bright tincture [ἄνθος], and smears on the colors [χρώματα], then it is a portrait [εἰκών]").

[95] hom. in 1 Cor. 13.3 [61.110].

[96] The main distinction among ancient portraits was between private and public works of art (Grabar, Christian Iconography, 60–61). These categories applied to the display of the portraits, not their site of production. What Chrysostom stresses here, as in other places, is the public nature of the living portrait, the Christian life.

[97] hom. in 1 Cor. 13.3 [61.110–11].

Even here in Chrysostom's description of Paul's self-portrait we see the tension between a frozen, fixed icon and a living, growing, changing presence.[98] Paul's own self-portrait was an on-going composition (a kind of "sidewalk art of the soul"), which, while continually reflecting the changing circumstances of his life, nevertheless always, after his conversion, displayed the "imperial portrait or image" of the apostle called by grace.

The Highest Artistic Standard:
The Imperial Portrait (εἰκὼν βασιλική)

The concept of "imperial portraits" [εἰκόνες βασιλικαί], recurrent in Chrysostom's writings, brings us into the practices of actual graphic artists in the fourth century. We shall look further into the conventions surrounding of the imperial portraits, for Chrysostom uses the concept extensively, not only to stress the excellence of the apostolic portrait (though he does that as well), but also in some creative metaphorical adaptations. We note initially the powerful historical irony in this positive fourth-century Christian attitude towards imperial images, given that they were uniformly treated as horrendous evils in the New Testament and early Christian literature,[99] which continued longstanding Jewish antipathy to Roman imperial images based on the first commandment.[100] For the early Christians this was hardened especially by persecution for refusal to worship (at least tacitly) those images.[101] It is therefore rather astounding from an historical perspective that within three hundred years Christians could consider "imperial images" not only tolerable, but indeed use them rhetorically in ethical exhortation.[102] Chrysostom does precisely this, both in saying

---

[98] For the oxymoronic concept, compare Clem. Alex., *Strom.* 7.9, on "living statues" [ἀγάλματα ἔμψυχα].

[99] E.g., Mk 12:16f. and pars., the many references to imperial images in Rev (13:14–15 [ἡ εἰκὼν τοῦ θηρίου]; 14:9, 11; 15:2; 16:2; 19:20; 20:4), and tales of martyrdom (*mart. Apollon.* 7).

[100] On which see, e.g., Paul Corby Finney, *The Invisible God: The Earliest Christians on Art* (New York/Oxford: Oxford University Press, 1994), 69–98, who gives a minimalist reading of the evidence in order to defuse the notion that aversion to imperial images necessarily led to Christian reticence to practice any artistic forms. But even in Finney's reading, consistent Christian fear of imperial images as symbols of possible confrontation with the powers of the empire is granted ("Under circumstances such as these it is entirely thinkable that individual Christians would have developed a strong dislike of the imperial image" [p. 82]).

[101] One need think only of Pliny's famous letter to Trajan (*Ep.* 10.96.5–6). For a narrative description of the history of relations between Christians and the Roman order within which these tensions were played out, see Robert M. Grant, *Augustus to Constantine. The Rise and Triumph of Christianity in the Roman World* (San Francisco: Harper & Row, 1970). The focus was more often on oaths by the "fortune" or "genius" of the emperor than actual worship of statues (see, e.g., *mart. Polyc.* 8–9), but the nature of the whole conflict of necessity rendered imperial images problematic for Christians.

[102] For an investigation of the common forms of cultural synthesis in the fourth century, as evident in the easy juxtaposition of "pagan" and Christian symbols in *objets d'art* and household

that Paul displayed the imperial portrait, and in exhorting his congregation to do likewise: "Let us prepare for ourselves imperial images (or portraits)."[103]

The way for imperial images to become positive symbols for Christians was opened substantially, of course, by the Christian imperium established by Constantine.[104] But artistically it had even earlier mimetic roots, for already in the second and third centuries Christian artists borrowed imperial forms for their portraits of the apostles Peter and Paul.[105] By the fourth century, imperial portraits had become the predominant models for the depictions of Christ and Mary which now began to emerge.[106] This means that Chrysostom and his audiences at Antioch and Constantinople were, from what they saw daily – including in their churches – quite inured to the coalescing of the imperial and the religious in art.

Chrysostom's metaphorical uses of imperial portraits depend upon detailed knowledge of the painter's art and technique. In the fourth century, portraits of the emperor, like those of other persons who could afford them, were usually made on wooden boards (though sometimes on canvas).[107] Chrysostom accurately describes how the artist [ζωγράφος] first made a sketch, using a white chalk capable of erasure, and then when it was perfected, finished the portrait with permanent color paints which had been carefully chosen and mixed.[108] These paints were of two types: distemper, an egg or milk-based watercolor, and encaustic, a wax paint which was burned into the panel.[109] Graphic portraits were normally of a life-

---

functional items, see Jás Elsner, *Art and the Roman Viewer: The Transformation of Art from the Pagan World to Christianity* (Cambridge: Cambridge University Press, 1995), esp. 256.

[103] βασιλικὰς εἰκόνας ἡμῖν αὐτοῖς κατασκευάζωμεν (*hom. in Ac.* 40.1 [60.288]).

[104] See Belting, *Likeness and Presence*, 103: "what [the Christians] refused to the pagan god-emperor, however, they willingly granted to the Christian representative of the state"; also A. Grabar, *L'empereur dans l'art byzantin: recherches sur l'art officiel de l'empire d'orient* (London: Variorum Reprints, 1971), and now Elsner, *Art and the Roman Viewer*, chap. 5 ("Reflections on a Roman Revolution: A Transformation in the Image and Conception of the Emperor" [pp. 159–89]).

[105] It is perhaps not insignificant in this regard that the earliest portraits of Paul, depicted face-to-face with Peter on Roman medallions from the second or third century, are identical in form to medallions depicting two emperors, or gods or heroes like the Dioskouroi. The Christian portraits depend upon the latter; "indeed, they are closer to Imperial and pagan medallions than to later images of the apostles Peter and Paul" (Grabar, *Christian Iconography*, 69).

[106] Grabar, *Christian Iconography*, 77: "The formulas for typological portraits of Christ and the Virgin do not come from the usual portraits of private persons, whether made during life or after death for funerary use. For Christ and the Virgin, the portrait formulas are derived from the official effigies of the sovereigns (*sacrae imagines*) and occasionally of the consuls. Such borrowings must have been practiced from the time of the triumph of Christianity, in the fourth century, when images of the official art of the Empire probably ceased to offend those who were formerly persecuted by the Roman state."

[107] The panel paintings (rather than statues) were especially common in the provinces because they were more portable and less likely to be confused with "pagan" images (Belting, *Likeness and Presence*, 103).

[108] *catech.* 2.3 [49.235]; *hom. in Phil.* 10.2 [62.257]; *hom. in Heb.* 17.2 [63.130]; *hom. in 1 Cor. 10:1* 4 [51.247], quoted in n. 94, above.

[109] The so-called "Fayum portraits," a term which actually refers to mummy paintings from other (primarily Egyptian) locations as well, are some of the best and most haunting examples of

sized head, often with part of the shoulders or clothing,[110] sometimes revealing a characteristic mark or badge or special ornament.[111] Chrysostom and his audiences knew these forms from infancy.[112] Imperial images, in all types of media, were ubiquitous in the fourth century: on coins, army regalia, including standards, robes of civil dignitaries, the walls of legal chambers, even on the law codes themselves.[113] The portrait of a new emperor was speedily dispatched to the cities of the empire, and the delegation bearing it would be met outside the city so that the portrait could receive an official greeting and escort inside to signify the citizenry's loyal welcome of the new sovereign.[114] Portraits of the emperor were always to be found in legal chambers so that verdicts could be pronounced in their presence. Such practices illustrate the conceptualization which lay behind the proliferation of imperial images: "the portrait of the sovereign replaced the sovereign; the emperor was, by reason of his portrait, present in the room when the judge pronounced sentence in his name."[115] That is why punishment for those who desecrated imperial images was so severe, for it was a deep afront to the emperor himself, as we know well from Chrysostom's homilies *ad populum Antiochenum de statuis*,[116] in which he dealt with a crisis in Antioch arising from a street

---

realistic ancient portraiture. They also are invaluable sources for the techniques used in ancient portraiture. The mummy portraits were primarily encaustic, but also used some water-based or tempera paints, especially in the later empire (see David L. Thompson, *Mummy Portraits in the J. Paul Getty Museum* [Malibu: J. Paul Getty Museum, 1976] 6–7; Euphrosune Doxiadis, "From *Eikon* to Icon: Continuity in Technique," *Portraits and Masks: Burial Customs in Roman Egypt*, ed. M.L. Bierbrier [London: British Museum Press, 1997] 78–80; Jean-Christophe Bailly, *L'apostrophe muette: essai sur les portraits du Fayoum* [Paris: Éditions Hazan, 1997] 29–35). For a particularly beautiful set of photographic plates of these images, see Bérénice Geoffroy-Schneiter, *Fayum Portraits*, trans. Emily Lane (London: Thames and Hudson, 1998).

[110] Imperial portraits are of course marked by the purple, and by precious gems and gold in the raiment (see *hom. in 1 Cor.* 11.4 [61.93]).

[111] Irene Weir, *The Greek Painter's Art* (Boston: Ginn, 1905) 248. These are rare in the Fayum portraits because they are limited to the head, or head and shoulders, but occasionally we find something held in the hand, or a caption that identifies the dead and his or her occupation, such as the famous Hermione γραμματική now in Girton College, Cambridge (Bailly, *L'apostrophe muette*, 17–19). For more on these emblems, and their literary analogues, see chap. 6, n. 189.

[112] In a most interesting passage in *hom. in Ac. princ.* 1.3 [51.71], Chrysostom uses such graphic portraiture as an analogy to the disposition of a literary work. He says the title of Acts functions like the structure of imperial portraits, which have the enticing image on top, and a box on the bottom with the τρόπαια of victories or good deeds.

[113] Grabar, *Christian Iconography*, 64.

[114] Belting, *Likeness and Presence*, 106.

[115] Grabar, *Christian Iconography*, 64.

[116] See, e.g., *stat.* 3.6 [PG 49.57]. Yet the limitations of the identification between the emperor and his image were also well recognized, as is illustrated by the famous story about Constantine, of which the Antiochene bishop Flavian chose to remind Theodosius at just this moment: "When his portrait once was pelted with stones, and many were inciting him to pursue the perpetrators of the insult and demand justice, saying that by stoning the image they had marred his face, the blessed Constantine is reported to have touched his face with his hand and, gently smiling, said, 'I don't see any injury on my brow. My head is sound, as is my face'" (*stat.* 21.2 [PG 49.216]).

rebellion that culminated in the destruction of some imperial images, and put the city in grave danger of unremitting imperial punishment as recompense. The indelible link between a portrait and the presence of the one represented, so obviously the case in the imperial ideology, renders the portrait a ready, living metaphor for a human life.

In Chrysostom's writings the example of imperial portraits or images serves a wide variety of rhetorical purposes. Most important for our study is that Chrysostom applies the concept to the apostle Paul, calling him "an imperial portrait" [εἰκὼν βασιλική] who replicates Christ and thus should be copied by all Christians. This metaphorical use of "imperial portraits" by Chrysostom for Paul depends upon the convergence of current artistic appreciation (because the imperial portraits are the highest standard of artistic excellence) and the Scriptural theologoumenon of Gen 1:26–27, that the human person was made in the εἰκὼν τοῦ θεοῦ, the image of the heavenly βασιλεύς.[117] This terminological overlap forms a remarkably literal instance of how late antique Christian rhetoric reappropriated the form of imperial panegyric for its own purposes (even as it now had emperors to practice on, as well).[118]

Seen against this background we can understand how Chrysostom could call Paul an εἰκὼν βασιλική, an imperial portrait, and regard him as the "archetypal image" [ὁ ἀρχέτυπος εἰκών] of perfect virtue[119] from which subsequent copies are to be made, like the official imperial portrait. As "the blessed copyist of Christ,"[120] Paul was the supreme example upon which others should mold themselves.[121]

---

[117] See *hom. in Eph.* 21.4: "For if human beings enjoy so great honor by making statues of emperors, and painting portraits [εἰκόνας γράφοντες], shall not we enjoy countless goods, since we proudly display the imperial portrait [τὴν βασιλικὴν εἰκόνα καλλωπίζοντες] (for the human being is the image/portrait of God [εἰκὼν γὰρ τοῦ θεοῦ ὁ ἄνθρωπος]), if we repay a true likeness [τὸ καθ᾿ ὁμοίωσιν ἀποδιδόντες])? For virtue is in this, the virtue of the soul [ἡ τῆς ψυχῆς ἀρετή]."

[118] With Cameron, *Christianity and the Rhetoric of Empire*, 130: "Just as the apocryphal literature of the second and third centuries had a serious evangelizing role, so too did the panegyrics and works of political theory of the fourth century and later; far from being just 'empty rhetoric,' they were essential instruments in the wider establishment of a lasting Christian political ideology." The two types of literature she discusses in that chapter (pp. 120–54), panegyrics and *Lives*, are of course very closely related in classical literature, and some works, such as the funeral orations to Basil by Gregory of Nazianzus and Gregory of Nyssa, bridge the two categories (compare pp. 135 and 143: "in Christian encomia the genres merged"). Chrysostom's portraits of Paul likewise inhabit the area of intersection formed by encomiastic and biographical purposes and conventions, as we shall see in chap. 4; see also chap. 7, pp. 404–407.

[119] The association of the emperor with virtue is another topos in imperial propaganda, even pre-dating Christian sources. See, e.g., Donald Strong, *Roman Art* (2nd ed.; London: Penguin, 1988) 264: "By his very nature [the emperor] was identified with the virtues and superhuman powers on which the survival of the State depended."

[120] *catech.* 4.22 [SC 50.193].

[121] Gregory of Nyssa expounds on the same concepts in *de perfectione* 253M: "For Paul, more than all, both accurately imitated what Christ is like and led the way by what he did in showing what is incumbent upon the person who takes on him or herself the name of Christ. So visibly was Paul imitating Christ [οὕτως ἐναργῶς αὐτὸν μιμησάμενος] that in himself he showed his own

Chrysostom could draw upon the concept of "imperial images" further to continue the cycle of imitative inter-picturality by exhorting each Christian believer in her or his living to create a full-color self-portrait,[122] in imitation of Paul and the saints, by the tincture of learned virtue. In this John is well at home in fourth-century Christian literary culture, which sought to fuse lives past, present and future through a common, authorized script: "The *Life* itself becomes an image; Christian lives of the present are interpreted in terms of their relation to sacred lives of the past, and their written forms, having taken on that shape, also acquire its evocative power."[123] The logic of imitative self-portraiture was close at hand for anyone working with the metaphors of the graphic arts, but may especially have had resonance for Chrysostom given his profound attachment to the ascetic life, which is in many ways precisely an attempt to self-sculpt the human body in relation to religious prototypes.[124] Thus John's call to his audiences to paint their self-portraits, to mold their lives in imitation of Paul and Christ, is another expression of his more general wish to inculcate a worldly asceticism, a democratized, urban form of monastic life for all Christians.[125] And his rhetoric was the vehicle used to create, sustain, and make both imaginative and plausible this chain of

---

master given shape [ἐν ἑαυτῷ δεῖξαι τὸν ἑαυτοῦ δεσπότην μεμορφωμένον], while the form of his soul was changed in the direction of the prototype through such accurate imitation that no longer did it seem to be Paul who was living and speaking, but Christ himself living in him" [διὰ τῆς ἀκριβεστάτης μιμήσεως μεταβληθέντος τοῦ τῆς ψυχῆς αὐτοῦ εἴδους πρὸς τὸ πρωτότυπον, ὡς μηκέτι Παῦλον εἶναι δοκεῖν τὸν ζῶντά τε καὶ φθεγγόμενον, ἀλλ᾽ αὐτὸν τὸν Χριστὸν ἐν αὐτῷ ζῆν] (text ed. Werner Jaeger, et al., *Gregorii Nysseni Opera, VIII, pars I: opera ascetica* [Leiden: Brill, 1952] 175, ll. 2–10).

[122] The idea of individuals as artists who form their own selves is found in Plato, *Resp.* 9.591D, for instance, but there the predominant metaphor is the musician (who creates a harmonious blend within body and soul), rather than the graphic artist. Lucian, *Peregrinus* 6 and 8, employs the *topos* of fashioning one's life as the creation of an ἄγαλμα ("portrait statue) from unshapen clay. He contrasts two masterpieces: Phidias' Zeus and "Nature's" Peregrinus Proteus (§6; cf. §10, where his early life is described as ἄπλαστος ἦν).

[123] Cameron, *Christianity and the Rhetoric of Empire*, 145–46.

[124] E.g., Krueger ("Hagiography as an Ascetic Practice," 216–232, who asked the provocative question: "If the production of an ascetic self is like the work of artistic creation, can the work of artistic creation be a form of asceticism?"), and Geoffrey Galt Harpham, *The Ascetic Imperative in Culture and Criticism* (Chicago: University of Chicago Press, 1987), xiv–v: "… the body and its desires and appetites are not, as we sometimes think, the proper subject of representation, but are in fact inimical to representation. From the ascetical point of view it is self-denial that is eminently imitable. Through discipline [Ps-Clement] suggests, the self becomes at once self-aware, structured, knowable, and valuable. Asceticism is not merely capable of assuming a multitude of forms; it is the form-producing agent itself … The ascetic body is in this sense an exemplary artifact: what the ascetics displayed to their audience was precisely their *form*."

[125] As argued especially by Peter Brown, *The Body and Society: Men, Women and Sexual Renunciation in Early Christianity* (Lectures on the History of Religions, n.s. 13; New York: Columbia University Press, 1988) 305–22. See his rendition of Chrysostom's vision: "Each married couple, down to its solemn grace for meals, was to bring into the midst of the turbulent and hard-hearted city a touch of the Christian perfection practiced by the monks in the clean, city-less air of the mountaintops" (pp. 311–12).

imitation.[126] Therefore this theme of imitative self-portraiture was a perfect one for Chrysostom's exhortations to catechumens:

> Then, as it is in the case of painters [ζωγράφοι], so let it now be the case for you. For they, after setting out their panels [σανίδες], and drawing on them with white lines, sketch out the royal images [τὰς βασιλικὰς ὑπογράφοντες εἰκόνας] before they apply the truth of the colors [τῶν χρωμάτων ἐπαγαγεῖν τὴν ἀλήθειαν]. And with full freedom they wipe out some things, and redraw other parts, and correct mistakes and change things which are not right. But when they bring in the final tempera, they no longer have the power to wipe things out or redraw them, since they will destroy the beauty of the portrait [τῷ κάλλει τῆς εἰκόνος λυμαίνονται], and the thing will be defective.[127]

In this pre-baptismal catechesis John invoked the image of imperial portraits to warn the catechumens to enact their repentance before their baptism, for while erasure and alteration are still possible in the sketching phase, they are impossible once the paint has been put on over that pencil sketch, inscribing it permanently and irremediably.[128] The direct application of this metaphor for the catechumens follows:

> Consider the soul to be your portrait [εἰκών]. So, before the true tempera of the spirit comes, wipe away the habits which have been wrongly put into it [a long list of sins follows] ... correct your habits, so that when the colors are laid upon it [τῶν χρωμάτων ἐπενεχθέντων], and the imperial portrait shines forth [λαμψάσης τῆς βασιλικῆς εἰκόνος], no longer will you wipe things out again, and damage or scar the beauty which has been given to you by God.[129]

The vehicle which facilitates the cycle of imitative inter-picturality which Chrysostom seeks to inculcate in his hearer is, as we have noted above, oratory itself.

---

[126] Averil Cameron has studied this question most effectively: "the self-conscious Christian creates his own self, and does so through the medium of texts, which in turn assume the function of models ... Written *Lives* were mimetic; real ascetic discipline in turn imitated the written *Lives*. Like visual art, early Christian discourse presented its audience with a series of images. The proclamation of the message was achieved by a technique of presenting the audience with a series of images through which it was thought possible to perceive an objective and higher truth" (*Christianity and the Rhetoric of Empire*, 57; influenced also by Harpham, *Ascetic Imperative*, 1–44). Chrysostom provides not only an exact instance of the process Cameron describes, but he even uses the precise language of the graphic arts to depict and defend it. See, e.g., his description of the mental process that leads to virtue by eradicating vice, in *hom. in 1 Cor.* 35.5 [61.302]: "by bringing out into public view [εἰς μέσον ἄγειν] those who crushed vice underfoot, and, by looking at their image [πρὸς τὴν ἐκείνων εἰκόνα βλέπειν], thus to straighten out one's own life" [τὴν ἑαυτοῦ ζωὴν κατευθύνειν].

[127] *catech.* 2.3 [49.235].

[128] The permanence of the color paints is a commonplace used also by Greco-Roman writers. See Lucian, *Imagines* 16: "[this] shall give beauty to our picture, not simply to the extent of tinting its surface [οὐκ ἄχρι τοῦ ἐπικεχρῶσθαι μόνον], but staining it all deeply with indelible colours till it will take no more" [ἀλλ' εἰς βάθος δευσοποιοῖς τισι φαρμάκοις εἰς κόρον καταβαφεῖσα].

[129] *catech.* 2.3 [49.235]. Here Chrysostom balances the paraenetical paradox of the indicative and the imperative ("you are the image of God"; "become the image of God"), by urging his converts to be good portraits who do not deface the divine portrait they bear. For other examples of this commonplace, see *hom. in Eph.* 21.4 [62.154], and *hom. in Ac.* 40.4 [60.288].

But the transference from word-portrait to copying involves also an intermediate step, whereby the homiletical image becomes imprinted in the memory of the hearer. In one passage Chrysostom describes metaphorically, in artistic terms, how he imagines this psychological and, ultimately, spiritual process, to unfold:

I wish to end my homily here, so that you will go away with the memory of that ladder[130] perfect and fresh [τῆς κλίμακος τὴν μνήμην ἀκμάζουσαν καὶ νεαρὰν ἔχοντας ὑμᾶς ἀπελθεῖν], and remember it [μεμνῆσθαι] both night and day ... Not only that ladder, but also the other punishments of the martyrs let us paint [διαγράφειν] upon the surface of our heart [ἐπὶ τὸ πλάτος τῆς καρδίας τῆς ἡμετέρας]. And just as those who make beautiful homes decorate them all over with bright colored pictures [ἀνθηρᾷ γραφῇ], thus also let us paint on the walls of our mind [ἐν τοῖς τοίχοις τῆς ἡμετέρας διανοίας ζωγραφήσωμεν] the punishments of the martyrs, because the former painting is useless, but this one has real gain. For this painting does not need money, nor expense, nor any artistic skill [τέχνη], but in place of all these it is sufficient to use willingness [προθυμία] and genuine, sober-minded reasoning [λογισμὸς γενναῖος καὶ νήφων], and by this capacity, just as by some skilled hand [χεὶρ ἀρίστη], one can draw [ὑπογράφειν] their punishments. Let us, then, paint on our souls [ζωγραφῶμεν τοίνυν ἐν τῇ ψυχῇ] those lying on frying pans, those extended over hot coals ... [a long list of tortures with various implements follows] so that, by furnishing our lovely house with the variety of this painting [τῇ ποικιλίᾳ τῆς γραφῆς ταύτης λαμπρὰν τὴν ἡμετέραν κατασκευάσαντες οἰκίαν], we might make a suitable dwelling for the king of the heavens. For if he sees such paintings in our minds [ἂν γὰρ ἴδῃ τοιαύτας ἐν τῇ διανοίᾳ τὰς γραφάς], he will come with the Father, and will make an abiding-place with us in the company of the holy spirit, and our mind will then be a royal house [βασιλικὸς ἔσται λοιπὸν οἶκος ἡ διάνοια ἡμῶν]. No absurd thought will be able to come into it while the memory of the martyrs [ἡ τῶν μαρτύρων μνήμη], like some bright-colored painting, is always stored up within us [ὥσπερ τινὸς ἀνθηρᾶς ζωγραφίας διαπαντὸς ἡμῖν ἐναποκειμένης] and releases a great shining splendor. And God, the king of all, dwells continually in us.[131]

Consequently, just as the paint of these portraits is words, the canvas upon which they are daubed and smoothed out is the memory of the individual auditor, who in the act of reception of the literary portrait recasts it synesthetically into a visual image upon his or her own heart[132] or mind,[133] where it lies in private exhibition

---

[130] This instrument of torture, described previously in the discourse, is an iron ladder on which the martyrs were suspended over hot coals.

[131] *pan. mart.* 3.3 [50.712]. Ameringer, *Second Sophistic*, 97, identifies this passage as a sophistic *ekphrasis* (the process of giving literary description of works of art, which we shall introduce fully in chap. 4, pp. 101–104). The hermeneutical process Chrysostom describes in this passage mirrors exactly the analysis of ekphrastic technique by Elsner, *Art and the Roman Viewer*, 36: "Philostratus is teaching, through his ekphrastic performance [in his *Imagines*], an hermeneutic means of relating to images [substitute "saints" for our inquiry]. This means is the viewer's narration of himself ... into the reality of the image ('the other') by assimilating the image into the framework of his own subjective consciousness, his personal context. The beholder constructs the object into his subjectivity, makes the other – which previously had no place in his experience – a constituent of that unique and intimate set of objects by which he defines his identity."

[132] For the commonplace see also, e.g., *pan. Barl.* 4 [50.680]: "let the martyr enter into each one's own house, no, heart, through the memory of what has been said" [εἰς τὴν οἰκίαν εἰσάγετω τὴν ἑαυτοῦ, μᾶλλον δὲ εἰς τὴν ἑαυτοῦ καρδίαν διὰ τῆς τῶν εἰρημένων μνήμης]. Compare Plato,

for continual viewing. And the portrait in the memory is itself supposed to bear an archetypal relationship to the body where it lies in state, for the ultimate "memorial" to the apostle is a new life which replicates his.[134]

In these concepts of literary portraiture and ethical self-sculpting Chrysostom stands in a long tradition of Greek popular philosophical reflection and rhetorical expression. To cite just one example, in his famous encomium to Evagoras, the Athenian orator Isocrates eloquently demonstrates the inherent unity of the themes we have considered in this chapter – monuments, portraits (literary and graphic) and the call for imitation of the archetypes:

For my part, Nicocles, I think that while the portraits of bodies [αἱ τῶν σωμάτων εἰκόνες] are good memorials [καλὰ μνημεῖα], it is portraits of deeds and purpose [αἱ τῶν πράξεων καὶ τῆς διανοίας], which one can see only in words composed according to artistic rules [ἃς ἐν τοῖς λόγοις ἄν τις μόνον τοῖς τεχνικῶς ἔχουσι θεωρήσειεν], that are of much greater value. And I prefer these portraits first because I know that good and worthy men do not so much pride themselves on the beauty of their body as they seek to be honored for their deeds and intention [εἰδὼς τοὺς καλοὺς κἀγαθοὺς τῶν ἀνδρῶν οὐχ οὕτως ἐπὶ τῷ κάλλει τοῦ σώματος σεμνυνομένους ὡς ἐπὶ τοῖς ἔργοις καὶ τῇ γνώμῃ φιλοτιμουμένους]. And second (I prefer literary portraits) because while the statues [οἱ τύποι] must remain only in the places where they have been erected, word portraits [οἱ λόγοι] are published [ἐξενεχθῆναι] throughout Greece. When they have been spread abroad in the assemblies of right-thinking people, they will be cherished by those whose good esteem is of more value than that of all others. And in addition to these reasons, I know that while no one can liken the nature of his body to statues or paintings which have been constructed [τοῖς μὲν πεπλασμένοις καὶ τοῖς γεγραμμένοις οὐδεὶς ἂν τὴν τοῦ σώματος φύσιν ὁμοιώσειε], it is easy (for those who desire not to be slaggardly and wish to be good) to imitate the character and purposes of one another which are contained in verbal testimony [τοὺς δὲ τρόπους τοὺς ἀλλήλων καὶ

Tim. 26C, on how memory is like an encaustic painting. Another faculty involved in this translation of the orator's image into the hearer's mind is φαντασία, the creation of an "imaginative mental picture," as Chrysostom writes in *pan. mart.* 1.2 [50.648]: "What then is it which pricks the conscience and makes streams of tears flow as freely as though from a fountain? It is the very mental image of the martyr [Αὐτὴ τοῦ μάρτυρος ἡ φαντασία], and the memory of all his virtuous deeds" [καὶ τῶν κατορθωθέντων πάντων ἡ μνήμη]. On the connection between the φαντασία of the orator and that of his audience, see Russell, *Criticism in Antiquity*, 109–10.

[133] In *hom. in 2 Tim.* 3:1 1 [56.271], Chrysostom praises his audience by saying that "before the words leap out of our mouth your mind has snatched up what we said" [πρὶν ἢ τὰ ῥήματα ἐκπηδῆσαι τοῦ στόματος ἡμῶν, ἥρπασεν ἡ διάνοια τὰ λεγόμενα].

[134] Again, compare Elsner, *Art and the Roman Viewer*, 38–39, on how *ekphrasis* accomplishes this: "We can read in Philostratus both a methodology of appropriating the image by the viewer (the contextualizing narrative) and a means ("realism") by which the image can entice its beholder. There is a reciprocity. The viewer constructs the work of art into his own world. But the reverse is also true. The work of art, by its very existence as an 'other' that demands to be assimilated, constructs the viewer *as* assimilator ... Just as the viewer constructs the object and thereby makes it other than it was, so the object constructs the viewer as assimilator and thereby makes him other than he was." This process is intensified in Chrysostom's discourse by the heightened call to move beyond "assimilation" to imitation and (ideally) full identification with the work of art, the saint's life (the latter being of course an ultimately unattainable goal, as Castelli, *Imitating Paul*, 100–17, has stressed).

τὰς διανοίας τὰς ἐν τοῖς λεγομένοις ἐνούσας ... μιμεῖσθαι]. For these reasons especially I have undertaken to write this speech ("word portrait") [ὁ λόγος οὗτος], considering it to be the most excellent encouragement to betterment [παράκλησις] for you and your children and the rest of the descendants of Evagoras, if someone might gather his virtuous deeds [ἀθροίζειν τὰς ἀρετὰς τὰς ἐκείνου] and by arranging them in a speech ("word portrait") [τῷ λόγῳ κοσμεῖν] might hand it over to you to look at [θεωρεῖν] and constantly be mindful [συνδιατρίβειν] of those virtues.[135]

The commonplaces about portraiture and imitation which are found so typically here within the classical antecedents of late antique literary culture[136] were used already by some of Chrysostom's contemporaries.[137] Gregory of Nyssa, who pre-dated Chrysostom by little more than a decade, in his treatise *de perfectione* similarly established an imitative pattern for the Christian life. Since Christians bear the name of Christ, they must likewise strive to be like Christ. In so doing they must rely on Paul, who knew Christ better than anyone else did, and who in the course of his writings produced a virtual catalogue of descriptions of Christ. Gregory puts his attention, then, not on replicating Paul, but on retrieving and resuscitating the portraits Paul painted of *Christ* in his letters. So he moves one by one through a range of Pauline Christological titles and metaphors, as he spurs his hearer (a certain Olympios, along with others) to imitate Paul by imitating Christ. When he gets to the Christological epithet εἰκὼν τοῦ θεοῦ τοῦ ἀοράτου from Col 1:15, he, like John, expounds explicitly on the theory and practice of self-portraiture in the Christian life:

Therefore, just as if we were learning the art of portrait painting [εἰ τὴν ζωγραφικὴν ἐπαιδευόμεθα τέχνην], when the teacher set before us some beautifully painted form on a

---

[135] *Or.* 9.73–75 (text L. van Hook, LCL, my trans.). See also Isocrates' *Or.* 2 (*To Nicocles*) §36: "Prefer to leave behind you as a memorial images of your virtue rather than of your body" [βούλου τὰς εἰκόνας τῆς ἀρετῆς ὑπόμνημα μᾶλλον ἢ τοῦ σώματος καταλιπεῖν]. We shall build on the distinction between somatic and psychic portraits in chaps. 4 and 5 below. See also Pericles' famous funeral oration (Thuc. 2.35–46), in which he says that the young soldiers by dying in battle "won for themselves the praise which grows not old [ὁ ἀγήρως ἔπαινος] and the most distinguished of all sepulchres [ὁ τάφος ἐπισημότατος] – not that in which they lie buried, but that in which their glory survives in everlasting remembrance [ἡ δόξα αὐτῶν αἰείμνηστος καταλείπεται], celebrated on every occasion which gives rise to word of eulogy or deed of emulation [παρὰ τῷ ἐντυχόντι αἰεὶ καὶ λόγου καὶ ἔργου καιρῷ]. For the whole world is the sepulchre of famous men, and it is not the epitaph upon monuments set up in their own land that commemorates them [οὐ στηλῶν μόνον ἐν τῇ οἰκείᾳ σημαίνει ἐπιγραφή], but also in lands not their own there abides in each breast an unwritten memorial [ἄγραφος μνήμη] of them, planted in the heart [γνώμη, 'mind'] rather than graven on stone" (2.43.2–3; text and trans. C. F. Smith, LCL).

[136] The preferability and superior endurability of writings to graphic portraits (even imperial portraits) remains as a constant Greek cultural convention down through late antiquity. See, for instance, Libanios' famous funeral oration for Julian (with which Chrysostom must have been acquainted), where he says that Julian's own writings, which provide a consolatory substitute for his missing presence, will long outlast the fading paint of his wood panel portraits [οὓς οὐκ ἂν ὁ χρόνος δύναιτο μετὰ τῶν ἐν ταῖς σανίσιν ἐξαλεῖψαι χρωμάτων] (*Or.* 18.303)

[137] See above, n. 32, on Eusebius' *vita Constantini*, and passages from Gregory of Nyssa.

panel [κεκαλλωπισμένη τις μορφή], it would be necessary for each person to copy/imitate [μιμήσασθαι] the beauty of that form completely in one's own painting [ἐπὶ τῆς ἰδίας ζωγραφίας], so that the tablets of everyone [οἱ πάντων πίνακες] be painted according to the example of beauty [τοῦ κάλλους ὑπόδειγμα] which had been set out. In the same way, since each person is a painter of one's own life [ἐπειδὴ τῆς ἰδίας ἕκαστος ζωῆς ἐστι ζωγράφος], and the power of free will [ἡ προαίρεσις] is the master crafter [τεχνίτης], and the virtues are the colors for finishing off the portrait [χρώματα δὲ πρὸς τὴν ἀπεργασίαν τῆς εἰκόνος αἱ ἀρεταί], it is no small danger that the copying/imitation [μίμησις] of the beauty of the prototype [πρωτότυπος] might alter the given shape into an ugly and misformed face, if with dirty colors they are sketching in the character of evil instead of the form of the master [ἀντὶ τοῦ δεσποτικοῦ εἴδους]. But as it is possible, one must use the clean colors of the virtues [καθαρὰ τῶν ἀρετῶν τὰ χρώματα], mixed with one another in accordance with a proper craft for such blends, so that we might become an image of the image ("a portrait of the portrait" [τῆς εἰκόνος εἰκών]), on account of this work of a sort of imitation [ὡς οἷόν τε μιμήσεως], as best as possible having created an impression of the beauty of the prototype [ἐκμαξάμενοι τὸ πρωτότυπον κάλλος], as Paul used to do, in becoming a copyist / imitator of Christ through his life lived according to virtue [ὡς ἐποίει ὁ Παῦλος μιμητὴς τοῦ Χριστοῦ διὰ τοῦ κατ' ἀρετὴν βίου γινόμενος].[138]

The ultimate goal of this literary portraiture of the saints, including Paul, is to make the hearers "living tombs," the most fitting kind of memorial to the virtuous archetypes of the past.[139]

Conclusions on the Framework of the Portraits

These identical "biographic" conventions,[140] found in Isocrates in classical Athens, and far later in Gregory of Nyssa, converge in the epideictic oratory which Chrysostom employed in composing the literary portraits of the apostle Paul which we

---

[138] *perf.* 272M [text Jaeger, *Gregorii Nysseni Opera*, 8/1, p. 195, l.14–196, l.15].

[139] See Chrysostom's use of the *topos*: "For the memorials of the saints are not coffins and urns and stelae and writings, but virtuosity in deeds, zeal in faith, and a pure conscience before God [Μνήματα γὰρ ἁγίων οὐ σοροὶ, καὶ λάρνακες, καὶ στῆλαι, καὶ γράμματα, ἀλλ' ἔργων κατορθώματα, καὶ πίστεως ζῆλος, καὶ συνειδὸς πρὸς θεὸν ὑγιές]... and each of you who is present here is a tomb of that saint [Eustathios], a living and spiritual tomb [καὶ ἕκαστος ὑμῶν τῶν παρόντων τοῦ ἁγίου τάφος ἐστὶν ἐκείνου, τάφος ἔμψυχος καὶ πνευματικός]. For if I were to unroll the conscience of each of you present here, I would find this saint dwelling inside your mind" ['Αν γὰρ ἀναπτύξω τὸ συνειδὸς ἑκάστου τῶν παρόντων ὑμῶν, εὑρίσκω τὸν ἅγιον τοῦτον ἔνδον τῆς διανοίας ὑμῶν ἐνδιαιτώμενον] (pan. *Eust. Ant.* 2 [50.600]; on Paul as a "living grave" [τάφος ἔμψυχος], see also res. *mort.* 3 [50.421], and discussion of this Gorgianic oxymoron in P. R. Coleman-Norton, "St. Chrysostom and the Greek Philosophers," *CP* 25 [1930] 305–17, 309–10).

[140] Here I am employing the useful distinction drawn by M. J. Edwards and Simon Swain between biography proper and the "biographic" element, "that which lies outside the formal genre of biography, the cuckoo which refuses to adopt a single nest" (*Portraits*, 233; see also 1–2, and 228: "whereas biography is a form of literature, the biographic is a trend in literature"). One way of describing the commonality is Cox's depiction of the role of the biographer, which is likewise suited to the encomiast: "biographers live in that mythic middle realm peopled by daemonic presences, the tropes of antiquity" (Cox, *Biography*, 147).

shall study in detail in the next three chapters. Chrysostom composed portraits of Paul with a single intention in view: to render the apostolic form visible and memorable so that it could be imitated by the next generation of hearers, who would have access to Paul through lovingly engaging his soul as engraved in his monuments, the letters. Via his reading of resuscitation, in which he heard the voice of Paul[141] and then extended it to others by composing portraits of the author in his expositions of the letters he wrote, Chrysostom midwifed a living conversation and relationship between the dead Paul and the living Christian congregation.[142] These portraits were composed along rhetorical guidelines, with full cognizance of the artistic praxis underlying the task. The use of rhetorical conventions also ensured that the audience had a clear set of expectations for praise of the subject which it was the orator's task to meet, and indeed, to surpass, by his eloquence. Such oratory of course functioned very much as a source of entertainment and communal celebration of common values in ecclesial contexts, in competition with the rivals for his congregation's attention, such as the theatre and the racetrack, which Chrysostom famously regarded with contempt. Chrysostom's age, the latter half of the fourth century, was a time of great blossoming of Christian graphic arts, including portraiture, and with it increasing veneration of the saints and their portraits.[143] While he warned his audiences against going too far

---

[141] On Chrysostom's view of all of scripture as orally spoken divine word, see Hill, *Commentary on the Psalms*, 1.31, and *idem*, "Chrysostom's terminology for the inspired Word," *EstBib* 41 (1983) 367–73.

[142] A most striking example of this is to be found in *hom. in Rom.* 32.2 [60.678]: "Who then will pray for us, since Paul has departed? These imitators of Paul" [Τίς οὖν ἄρα καὶ ἡμῖν ἐπεύξεται, ἐπειδὴ Παῦλος ἀπῆλθεν; Οἱ Παύλου ζηλωταὶ οὗτοι]. For John the mimetic chain keeps Paul alive in the Christian congregation.

[143] See Grabar, *Christian Iconography*, pp. 85–6; Cyril Mango, *The Art of the Byzantine Empire 312–1453* (Medieval Academy Reprints for Teaching; Toronto: University of Toronto Press, 1986) 21–52; Walter Elliger, *Die Stellung der alten Christen zu den Bildern in den ersten vier Jahrhunderten (nach den Angaben der zeitgenössischen kirchlichen Schriftsteller)* (Studien über christliche Denkmäler 20; ed. J. Ficker; Leipzig: Dieterich, 1930), esp. 73–76 on Chrysostom, whom he categorizes as a kind of medial figure between opposition to images and acceptance of images, but cast within his larger thesis of near-universal early Christian prohibition of art. Elliger's position (which is representative of a sturdily wide-spread consensus for most of this century, including the great art historian Ernst Kitzinger, among others), has received substantial challenges in the last decades. The seminal rebuttal was issued by Sister Charles Murray, "Art and the Early Church," *JTS* 28 (1977) 303–45, who examined the patristic literary evidence purportedly documenting this aversion to art among the Fathers, and in so doing demonstrated how Chrysostom has largely been left out of the discussion, as he didn't fit the grand hypothesis: "The Cappadocians could not on any score be made into opponents of art, nor could they be ignored as representing the official level of the Church, so they are explained away by the hypothesis as 'fleeting references' to a more positive approach ... and John Chrysostom inconveniently kept a picture of St. Paul before him, according to John Damascene. But these texts are glossed over in the standard treatments; they are omitted by Klauser, explained away by Koch and Elliger, and alluded to by Kitzinger" (pp. 324–25). Murray's argument against the old consensus has been further fortified recently by Finney, *Invisible God*.

and deifying saints,[144] he offered his own spiritual, literary brand of portraiture,[145] based upon accurate knowledge of contemporary art theory and practice, and within the structures and conventions of ancient rhetoric, which has as its single purpose the imitation of the ἀρχέτυπος εἰκών, the "archetypal image," Paul. In this way he was constructing fresh exhibitions of existing portraits and composing original images to rival attention paid both to competitors within the secular culture, and to other sources of access to the person of the saint,[146] in favor of his own mediating discourse and its ethical demands.[147] One outcome of this process, of course, is Chrysostom's implicit rhetorical claim to be the best of portrait painters, who was able to paint Paul most accurately because he loved him so much.

A Final Question: Why Paul?

While the logic and purposes of Chrysostom's portraiture of a favored saint are understandable, especially in the light of fourth-century Christian oratory and its social function of inscribing the new social reality in vibrant, enduring forms, including veneration of the saints, it remains to be answered why Paul was the hero Chrysostom singled out especially for this task. There is a confluence of reasons for this. First, as we have noted, Paul is the perfect fit for Chrysostom's mimetic program because he himself in his letters explicitly summoned his own imitation, thereby inaugurating and legitimating the entire enterprise in Scripture, Chrysostom's highest authority. Chrysostom knew this intimately, for his early Christian education at the hands of Diodore of Tarsus (who is known to have composed commentaries on Paul's letters) must have included large doses of Pauline studies.[148] Indeed, the fourth and fifth centuries were a time of unprecedented attention to

---

[144] *stat.* 1.7 [49.25]; cf. *hom. in Phil.* 7.2 [62.231].

[145] More important than the later legend of his picture of Paul (invoked by Murray, "Art and the Early Church," 324–25) for Chrysostom's legacy as regards Christian attitudes toward art and images in the period before the iconoclasm controversy are these passages we have been dealing with, which show his ready acceptance of artistic imagery and conceptions. It is possible to interpret his "spiritualizing" of the concept of early Christian art from physical media to fleshly lives as a mild polemic of graphic art, but this is not necessary (in fact, the opposite conclusion can be drawn). And, even if this is the case, it demonstrates more John's commitment to the spiritual life over the material than it does a concern with Christian art as somehow idolatrous (as the older consensus would have it).

[146] See Brown, *Cult of the Saints*, 88, on the dynamic at work here: "The carefully maintained tension between distance and proximity ensured one thing: *praesentia*, the physical presence of the holy, whether in the midst of a particular community or in the possession of particular individuals, was the greatest blessing that a late-antique Christian could enjoy."

[147] Cf. *hom. in Eph.* 8.3 [62.58], discussed below, p. 82.

[148] This receives further confirmation from the fact that Chrysostom's schoolmate Theodore of Mopsuestia likewise went on to compose commentaries on all the epistles of Paul.

the Pauline epistles in commentary form,[149] a rising tide on which Chrysostom sails. Second, John's choice of Paul as his special saint may have been further incited by the fact that Paul was regarded as a kind of "local hero" at Antioch during Chrysostom's life.[150] Third, Chrysostom's early experiences in monasticism were likely the seed-bed of his life-long private and public devotion to Paul. John expressly stated in one of his monastic treatises that what a monk (such as he was) does all day is "adorn his soul with the wisdom of Paul" [τῇ τοῦ Παύλου σοφίᾳ τὴν ψυχὴν καλλωπίζων].[151] When he lived a solitary monastic life in a cave for two years, devoting most of that time to memorizing the New Testament, Chrysostom inscribed on his brain a lot of Paul, and, at that, a lot of Paul speaking in the first person, now vocalized through his own mouth. Not only did constant rereading and memorization of these texts serve to lay the foundation for a life of Scriptural exposition, but it also oriented Chrysostom's own consciousness in a Pauline direction, because of the domination of Paul in the New Testament canon, where he is the purported author of fourteen of the twenty-seven documents, and the sung hero of two others (Acts and, in a more minor role, 2 Peter). This intense orientation to Paul would have received continual reinforcement thereafter by the liturgical life of the church, for Chrysostom says that Paul's letters appear in the lectionary every Sunday, and once even that his letters are read two to four times a week, perhaps a reference to his formal teaching in the church.[152] Consequently, as a Christian lectionary preacher Chrysostom was constantly facing Paul. Furthermore, Chrysostom also regarded Paul as a monastic, his own cherished goal from

---

[149] For the Latin church, see Peter Brown, *Augustine of Hippo* (Berkeley: University of California Press, 1967) 151; Mara, "Paul," EEC 2.658–59. Mara argues that this is due, not just to the abatement of proprietary claims to Paul by heretics in the second and third century, but to four other factors: 1) "the doctrinal maturity that the Christian community must have attained"; 2) the relevance of particularly the epistle to the Romans to contemporary issues in mutual proselytization between Jews and Christians; 3) the new questions occasioned by the Christian imperium; and, 4) "the monastic ascesis that institutionalized in the new historical situation the longing for witness of life to be borne, with emphases that varied according to the intensity with which preference was given to grace or free will, mercy or merits; all themes that found full development in Paul." It is the latter point which is especially pertinent in Chrysostom's case, as I shall argue below. In chapter 8 we shall see how Augustine fits this picture, as well.

[150] See n. 47 above on the commemorative grotto to him. However, Paul was not the only favored saint there; Peter also was claimed by Antioch (see *hom. in Ac. princ.* 2.6 [51.86–87]). But one can hear John's metropolitan pride connected particularly to Paul in the following utterance: "For truly it is for this reason that they were first called Christians in Antioch: because Paul spent so much time there" (*hom. in Ac.* 25.1 [60.192]).

[151] *comp.* 2 [47.389], trans. with Hunter, *Comparison*, 71. Although John describes monastic engagement also with other biblical books (prophets, Pentateuch, John), for none of them does he give a similarly personalized hermeneutic.

[152] *hom. in Rom.* Arg. 1 [60.391]. Marie-Louise Guillaumin has argued that some of Chrysostom's biblical homilies may have been delivered as teaching for catechumens and others, rather than strictly for eucharistic liturgies ("Bible et liturgie dans la prédication de Jean Chrysostome," *Jean Chrysostome et Augustin*, ed. Charles Kannengiesser [Théologie historique 35; Paris: Éditions Beauchesne, 1975] 161–74).

late adolescence, which was thwarted, first by his mother's wishes, and later by his poor health and by ecclesiastical demands he could not refuse. Accordingly, John saw himself in the same ambivalent position as he saw Paul: an ascetic forced by circumstances to live in the world and the church to carry out the worldly duties placed in his charge. Fourth, there was also an easy correlation between some of Chrysostom's pastoral and theological challenges and those which Paul addressed (at least, Chrysostom surely thought so). So another factor likely contributing to John's sense that Paul was his "soul-mate" was these shared vexations: inner-church conflict, Judaizing Christians, immoral behavior in the congregation, and thorny issues in the relationship between Christians and the larger social order (women, slaves, private property). This symbiosis was fostered literarily, as Chrysostom declamed first-person Pauline discourses which he deemed most pertinent to his own congregations. And especially later in his life, during his exile, Chrysostom's sense of kinship with Paul was heightened by the physical and emotional sufferings he endured which found easy resonance in the Pauline hardship catalogues. All of these factors played some role in John's special admiration for Paul and, once he began scripting his life in Pauline terms, more and more pieces fell into place, confirming and reaffirming the overall mimetic pattern.

But Chrysostom's concentration on the person of Paul has also a marked and inexplicable personal dimension. By his own explanation, John's single-minded concentration on Paul was due to the fact that he had a special love for him; this special love, Chrysostom claimed, was his unimpeachable credential as Paul's authentic interpreter and portrait painter. Chrysostom himself attributed the relationship to the live presence which visited him when he read Paul's letters. This interpretive perspective, of two living, breathing persons engaged in literary conversation across time through a text, is captured well by a medieval manuscript portrait of Paul and Chrysostom found in the earliest illustrated collection of Chrysostom's homilies [see Plate 2].[153] Two saints, Paul on the left and John on the right, facing one another with nimbi all but touching, bend their heads over a single opened codex in intense concentration. Paul and his devoted interpreter meet eye to eye over the Scriptures, two saints conversing via the book.

---

[153] The manuscript is *Athen. 211*. See Appendix 2, no. 14 for further information on this very telling iconographic image.

Chapter 3

"The Warm Lover of Christ" – Pauline Miniatures

The person of the apostle Paul looms so extraordinarily large in the writings of Chrysostom because, as he described it, the apostle would "take possession" of him when he was composing or delivering his homilies, and would move him to speak about Paul, regardless of the declared topic of his sermon. On one occasion Chrysostom rose to preach after the three lectionary passages for the day were read: the woman with the hemorrhage (one of the Synoptic versions), Paul's hardship catalogue in 2 Corinthians 11, and Isaiah 45. Although he wished to focus his sermon on the latter prophetic text, Chrysostom was hindered by a strong interference, which he described to his congregation:

But why am I troubled? Summoning great force I must flee, lest again Paul, taking possession [κατέχειν] of me, might lead me away from the text I have set forth to preach on. For you well know how repeatedly at other times, meeting me as I was going about my sermon, he took possession of me and I became diverted right in the middle of my sermon, and he so seized me that I was persuaded by him to wreck the sermon. But so that we don't experience this today, too, as though forcefully putting in a bridle here, while the sermon is being conducted, thus let's drag him[1] away, and let's go on with the prophetic saying.[2]

Indeed, in another place Chrysostom attributes his being pulled off course to being "lassoed" by Paul's chain, but he is its willing and cooperative captive:

But now Paul's chain is again dragging us away [ἀποσύρειν] from the matters at hand, and diverting us [περισπᾶν], and we cannot bear to resist [ἀντιπεσεῖν οὐχ ὑπομένομεν], but are being dragged away, and willingly [ἀλλ' ἑλόμεθα καὶ ἄκοντες], indeed by both our wish and our prayers [βουλόμενοι καὶ εὐχόμενοι]. If only it were possible always to discourse on Paul's chain! [Καὶ εἴθε ἀεὶ περὶ τῆς ἁλύσεως Παύλου διαλέγεσθαι ἦν].[3]

---

[1] Or, possibly, "it," the sermon [λόγος].
[2] hom. in Is. 45:7 3 [56.146]. It is possible that Chrysostom has in mind what happened to him in hom. in Gen. 11.7 [53.97–98], which turned into a rather detailed exegesis of 2 Cor 11:21f., for at the end of that homily he apologetically admits: "I don't know how I have fallen into discussing the wealth of good deeds of this holy man, but my tongue was swept away as though by a raging stream of water." For the phenomenon, see also hom in Ac. 9:1 1.3 [51.117]. This point about John being possessed by Paul was discussed by Baur 1.291–2; see also the note of A. Wenger in SC 50.186 n. 1: "Une simple citation de Paul au cours de ses discours suffisait bien souvent à faire perdre à Chrysostome la suite de l'exposé."
[3] hom. in Eph. 9.1 [62.69]. In the previous homily (which we shall analyze intricately in chap. 4, pp. 179–85), Chrysostom said he could not stop his discourse on Paul, just as a drunkard on a binge cannot tear himself away from liquor (hom. in Eph. 8.8 [62.66]).

Because the apostle's magnetic power prevailed more often than Chrysostom in these contests, and held sway over the homilist's imagination, mouth and pen,[4] there are many rich sources for our inquiry. This concept of apostolic possession, combined with Chrysostom's own homiletical theory that a sermon involves painting full-color portraits of the saints for the audience to imitate, led to a thorough-going preoccupation with the person of Paul in Chrysostom's homilies. This preoccupation expressed itself in portraits of his most beloved saint. The form of these portraits is, as we have noted, entirely literary, and reflects some basic tenets of Greco-Roman epistolary, rhetorical, artistic and ethical theory and practice. The compositional structure of these portraits in particular is based upon rhetorical conventions, as we shall see.[5] Chrysostom's depictions of Paul assume one of two distinguishable types, which mirror their graphic counterparts: miniature portraits and full-scale portraits, a distinction found also in ancient literary sources.[6] This chapter will treat the miniature portraits of Paul found throughout Chrysostom's homilies, and the following two will concentrate upon their full-scale counterparts.

Epithets As Portraits in Miniature

Chrysostom's miniature portraits of Paul are cast in the form of epithets. These epithets, or title-portraits, are found throughout the corpus of Chrysostom's writings, wherever he uses an introductory formula for a citation from one of the Pauline epistles.[7] Chrysostom also commonly employed epithets of Paul in his

---

[4] But, as the previous quotation shows, Chrysostom did not play a merely passive role in this relationship. In one passage, for instance, he freely admits, "therefore I continually take refuge in that holy soul for all kinds of things" [Διὰ γὰρ τοῦτο συνεχῶς ὑπὲρ ἁπάντων ἐπὶ τὴν ἁγίαν ἐκείνην καταφεύγω ψυχήν] (grat. 2 [50.656]).

[5] It is in this regard that the valuable work of di S. Maria, "S. Paolo," needs improvement, for he did not discuss the considerable rhetorical conventions at work here.

[6] In the encomiastic dialogue of Lucian, Imagines, the two men, Lycinus and Polystratus, take these two different approaches to immortalizing their subject, Panthea, an esteemed companion of the emperor Verus: a single, composite portrait, or smaller, detailed portraits of individual features: "There you have one picture [εἰκών], Lycinus, that of her exquisite speech and her singing, as it might be portrayed [εἰκάζειν] in an inadequate sort of way. And now look at the others – for I have decided not to exhibit a single picture made up, like yours, out of many [οὐ γὰρ μίαν ὥσπερ σὺ ἐκ πολλῶν συνθεὶς ἐπιδεῖξαι διέγνωκα]. That is really less artistic [ἧττον γραφικόν], to combine beauties so numerous and create, out of many, a thing of many different aspects, completely at odds with itself [συντελεσθὲν κάλλη τοσαῦτα καὶ πολυειδές τι ἐκ πολλῶν ἀποτελεῖν αὐτὸ αὑτῷ ἀνθαμιλλώμενον]. No, all the several virtues of her soul shall be portrayed each by itself in a single picture that is a true copy of the model [αἱ πᾶσαι τῆς ψυχῆς ἀρεταὶ καθ᾽ ἑκάστην εἰκὼν μία γεγράψεται πρὸς τὸ ἀρχέτυπον μεμιμημένη]" (Im. 15; text and trans. A.M. Harmon, LCL).

[7] The long lists of epithets often tend not to be in homily sets on Paul's own letters, because those are already contextualized, but rather usually serve to introduce Paul into an exegetical and

encomiastic speeches, since it was a feature of that genre, as with oratory in antiquity generally, to avoid proper names.[8] Each epithet contains in shorthand a unique miniature portrait of the apostle by reference to one of his functions or attributes, or by a metaphorical characterization. The hermeneutical sensibility informing such portraiture requires that the imagination of the hearer form a mental image which corresponds to the brief title. Chrysostom himself describes how this works:

> For truly when I hear, "Paul the apostle," I have in my mind [ἐννοῶ][9] the one in afflictions, the one in tight straights, the one in blows, the one in prisons, the one who was night and day in the depth of the sea, the one snatched up into the third heaven, the one who heard inexpressible words in paradise, the vessel of election, the leader of the bridegroom of Christ, the one who prayed to be anathema from Christ for the sake of his brothers and sisters. Just like some golden cord, the chain of his good deeds comes into the head [ἐπεισέρχεσθαι][10] of those who attend with precision along with the remembrance [μνήμη] of his name.[11]

In this passage, the mere name of Paul gives rise to a stream of epithets in the mind of the hearer. Such epithets, as Chrysostom understands and employs them, have the capacity to create, via a stunningly quick image, an immediate and vivid mental picture of the subject. In his writings, as we shall see, Chrysostom composed and employed a huge number of such epithets for Paul. The proliferation of epithets in fourth-century Christian oratory, as Chrysostom and others practiced it, performs a function remarkably similar to that in the ancient Greek cults (though the comparison would have horrified Chrysostom): "in the cult it is the task of the officiant who speaks the prayer to encircle the god as it were with epithets and to discover the just and fitting name."[12] In this case the literary form of epithet is recast from hymnic poetry to rhetorical prose, and the religious context from god-worship to saint-devotion, but still it is the task of the liturgist to name the figure for recognition and for intercession, and in so doing to make that figure come alive to the audience.[13] The repetition and succession of varying epithets has the crucial

---

homiletical context where he is unexpected. In the commentary sets, conversely, are found more large-scale portraits of Paul's soul and body (though epithets and passages more akin to these do appear in conspicuous spots, like the opening and closing homilies on Romans).

[8] See Hippolyte Delehaye, *Les passions des martyrs et les genres littéraires* (Subsidia hagiographica 13B; 2nd ed.; Brussels: Société des Bollandistes, 1966) 150–52.

[9] Translating per LSJ, 570: "have in one's thoughts."

[10] Translation according to LSJ, 615 (*s.v.*, II.2).

[11] *hom. in Ac. 9:1* 4.3 [51.149].

[12] W. Burkert, *Greek Religion*; trans. J. Raffan (Cambridge, MA: Harvard University Press, 1985) 184.

[13] "But these detached figures [the gods] are linked nonetheless to specific domains and functions in which their influence can be obtained and experienced. This link is guaranteed in two ways, by the epithets and by the personified abstractions in their retinue. Hymnic poetry, doubtless following ancient tradition, loves to heap divine epithets one upon another; epic art constructs its formulae from them ... In an established cult there will always be a fixed, well proven name, but this does not inhibit the search for further epithets. The epithets in turn are complex. Some are unintelligible and for that very reason have an aura of mystery; others result from the fusion of gods who at first were independent ... Many are formed spontaneously to

liturgical and rhetorical effect of making the dead saint come to life in the midst of the assembly in which he is invoked.

From a literary point of view, epithets are instances of the rhetorical trope ἀντονομασία, the substitution of either a title, a characteristic, or an action of a person for his or her name.[14] Logically epithets, as portraits in shorthand, often work by synecdoche, the rhetorical figure by which a whole is represented by a single part.[15] Such denotation of gods or heroes by colorful and memorable epithets is a famous characteristic of Greek and Latin literature from Homeric epic onwards.[16] Analyzed formally, we find adjectival epithets naming an attribute of the subject, such as Ὀδυσσῆος ταλασίφρονος ("stouthearted Odysseus") and γλαυκῶπις Ἀθήνη ("flashing-eyed Athena"),[17] or nouns placed in apposition.[18] These can include longer descriptive forms employing compound nouns like νεφεληγερέτα (of Zeus as "the cloud-gatherer"), or full phrases like eversor Carthaginis et Numantiae (of Scipio as "the destroyer of Carthage and Numantia") and Romanae eloquentiae princeps (of Cicero, "the prince of Roman oratory").[19] Of course, Chrysostom's use of epithets in liturgical oratory does not perform the important metrical functions

---

denote the domain in which divine intervention is hoped for; in this way each god is set about with a host of epithets which draw a complex picture of his activity" (ibid., 184).

[14] Quintilian, Inst. 8.6.29: "Antonomasia, which substitutes something else for a proper name [quae aliquid pro nomine ponit], is very common in poets: it may be done in two ways: by the substitution of an epithet as equivalent to the name which it replaces [et per epitheton, quod detracto eo, cui apponitur, valet pro nomine], such as 'Tydides' [=son of Tydeus], 'Pelides' [=son of Peleus, Achilles], or by indicating the most striking characteristics of an individual [et ex his, quae in quoque sunt praecipua], as in the phrase 'Father of gods and king of men,' or from acts clearly indicating the individual [et ex factis, quibus persona signatur], as in the phrase, 'The arms which he, the traitor, left fixed on the chamber wall'" (this third example may be a later addition to the text). See also Aristotle, Rh. 3.2.14 on disgraceful and honorable epithets [ἐπίθετοι], and further references in LSJ, 166.

[15] See Tryphon, Trop. 2.17 [L. Spengel, Rhetores Graeci (3 vols.; Leipzig: Teubner, 1853–56), 3.204], who subsumes epithets under the category of synecdoche.

[16] For an entry into the considerable research which has been done on epithets for the Greek gods and heroes, see H.J. Rose (updated by Simon Hornblower), "Epithets, Divine," OCD[3] (1996), 401–402; and Paolo Vivante, The Epithets in Homer: A Study in Poetic Values (New Haven: Yale University Press, 1982).

[17] These are used copiously throughout the Odyssea, as in 5.30 and 2.382, respectively.

[18] This accords with the definition given by William M. Sale: "an adjective, a noun in apposition, a noun-phrase in apposition (ἄναξ ἀνδρῶν), a noun in the genitive, a governing noun (as in υἷες Ἀχαιῶν), or a noun in a combination that preserves a singular sense (as in Τρῶες καὶ Τρώων ἄλοχοι)" ("The Trojans, Statistics, and Milman Parry," GRBS 30 [1989] 341–410, 350). This definition is adopted by J.H. Dee, The Epithetic Phrases for the Homeric Gods (Epitheta deorum apud Homerum): a Repertory of the Descriptive Expressions for the Divinities of the Iliad and the Odyssey (Albert Bates Lord Studies in Oral Tradition 14; New York: Garland, 1994). For the history of definitions of the ἐπίθετον/epitheton, and its grammatical and stylistic classifications (for instance, in some grammarians it means simply "adjective," as in Dionysius of Halicarnassus, Comp. 5), see L. Gondos, "Epitheton," Historisches Wörterbuch der Rhetorik, ed. G. Ueding (vol. 2, ed. G. Kalivoda, et al., Tübingen: Niemeyer, 1994) 1314–16.

[19] The latter two examples are given by Quint., Inst. 8.6.30. Quintilian remarks that these are rare in oratory, but that may largely reflect his own taste (see n. 24 below).

of the Homeric epithets, but it has in common with them the vividness of style which they effect in oral communication.[20] Chrysostom uses adjectival epithets for Paul, but even more frequently appositional substantival phrases (with a particular fondness for articular participles) to sketch Paul by brief reference to particular actions or ongoing activities of Paul which he wishes to flash before the eyes of his hearers.[21]

Chrysostom's Gallery of Miniature Portraits of Paul

In the course of his writings Chrysostom employs over sixty-five different epithets for Paul, which serve to raise the specter of Paul instantly before the eyes of his audience. All (with a few intriguing exceptions[22]) are meant to be laudatory.[23] Each epithet constitutes a self-contained miniature portrait of his beloved saint, invoked via this pithy and serviceable literary form. And these epithets are by no means exclusive, but rather complementary; thus they can be stacked up for rhetorical effect[24] with no hesitation about mixing metaphors. In fact, sometimes

---

[20] A nice description of ἐνάργεια, "vividness of style," which directly connects it with synesthesia, is supplied by Dionysius of Halicarnassus, in his treatment of Lysias: "This consists in a certain power he has of conveying the things he is describing to the senses of his audience [ὑπὸ τὰς αἰσθήσεις ἄγουσα τὰ λεγόμενα], and it arises out of his grasp of circumstantial detail. Nobody who applies his mind to the speeches of Lysias will be so obtuse, insensitive or slow-witted that he will not feel that he can see the actions which are being described going on and that he is meeting face-to-face the characters in the orator's story" [ὃς οὐχ ὑπολήψεται γινόμενα τὰ δηλούμενα ὁρᾶν καὶ ὥσπερ παροῦσιν οἷς ἂν ὁ ῥήτωρ εἰσάγῃ προσώποις ὁμιλεῖν]" (*Lys.* 7, trans. S. Usher, LCL).

[21] Though without discussing the rhetorical conventions involved here, these aspects of epithets were well appreciated by Merzagora, "Giovanni Crisostomo," 24: "Quando poi l'entusiasmo si fa più intenso e più vivo la similitudine si abbrevia nell'invocazione lirica e s'esprime in un seguito tumultuoso d'epiteti ...." She then sets before the eyes of her readers, to facilitate their imagination of how this sounded in a silent church, her own composite chain of epithets for Paul culled from a range of Chrysostom's homilies (pp. 25–26). Zese, "Apostle Paul," 317, calls these λέξεις, διὰ νὰ χαρακτηρίσῃ τὸ πρόσωπον καὶ τὸ ἔργον του, "expressions with which he characterizes Paul's person and work."

[22] For instance, Chrysostom quotes some pointedly negative epithets of Paul from outsiders: "Was he not called the pest of the world? An imposter? A subverter?" [λυμεὼν τῆς οἰκουμένης, ἀπατεών, ἀνατροπεύς] (*hom. in Heb.* 28.4 [63.197]). He also draws some arresting portraits of the pre-Christian Paul, as, e.g., "a crazed lion" (*catech.* 4.10 [SC 50.210]), and "a great fish" whom Christ hooked and landed (*hom. in Ac. 9:1* 1.4 [51.119]). He also likes to replicate the triad βλάσφημος καὶ διώκτης καὶ ὑβριστής from 1 Tim 1:13 (e.g., in *hom. in Jo.* 10.1 [59.74]; see the full discussion of Chrysostom's treatments of Paul's pre-Christian life in chap. 6, pp. 250–261).

[23] "Presque toujours, Paul est cité avec des épithètes de louange" (Wenger, SC 50.111). Therefore they constitute ἔπαινος, rather than a full ἐγκώμιον, according to the distinction made by Hermogenes, *Prog.* 7 [Spengel, 2.11]: ἐπαίνου δὲ διαφέρει τὸ ἐγκώμιον, ὅτι ὁ μὲν ἔπαινος καὶ ἐν βραχεῖ γένοιτ' ἄν, οἷον Σωκράτης σοφός, τὸ δὲ ἐγκώμιον ἐν μακροτέρᾳ διεξόδῳ.

[24] Quintilian's more conservative stylistic tastes preclude the use of a long list of epithets in oratory, an opinion he expresses with a marvelously dismissive metaphor: "while style is bare and

John delights in unexpected combinations of epithets in his live oratory as he progresses to greater heights (taking his audience along with him in the breathless train) in his praises of Paul. In this way Chrysostom seeks to depict Paul as the truly multi-form man, who excels according to all standards and on all terrains, and meets every conceivable need.

We shall begin to catalogue Chrysostom's miniature portraits of Paul with the following stunning passage, the whole of which serves to introduce a single quotation of 1 Cor 4:4:

> For Paul the apostle, the vessel of election, the temple of God, the mouth of Christ, the lyre of the spirit, the teacher of the world, the one who circumnavigated land and sea, the one who drew back the thorns of sins, the one who scattered the seeds of piety, the one who was wealthier than kings, more powerful than the rich, stronger than soldiers, wiser than philosophers, better-spoken than rhetoricians, the one who though having nothing possessed it all, the one who could destroy death by his shadow, the one who sent diseases fleeing by his clothing, the one who stopped the winds in the sea, the one who was snatched up into the third heaven and entered into paradise, the one who proclaimed Christ to be God, that one says …[25]

Although this is a rather conspicuously amplified rhetorical passage, there are quite a few like it in Chrysostom's corpus of writings.[26] Once he would get started on

---

inelegant without any epithets at all, it is overloaded when a large number are employed [*ut sine appositis nuda sit et velut incompta oratio, oneretur tamen multis*]. For when it becomes long-winded and cumbrous, in fact you might compare it to an army with as many camp-followers as soldiers, an army, that is to say, which has doubled its numbers without doubling its strength" [*Nam fit longa et impedita, ut (in quaestionibus) eam iudices similem agmini totidem lixas habenti quot milites, cui et numerus est duplex nec duplum virium*]. But then he immediately acknowledges that not only single, but multiple epithets are commonly found, though he finds the result ungraceful even in poetry (*Inst.* 8.6.41–42). Such lists are, however, common to Chrysostom's florid style, though they have earned him the scorn of some modern day Quintilians, who have found them tedious, such as Merzagora, "Giovanni Crisostomo," 24, and especially Ameringer, *Second Sophistic,* 56–57: "However, this gift of graphic representation, which constitutes one of the excellencies of his art, is likewise responsible for one of its most serious blemishes, an immoderate redundance of images. Like the quickly shifting colors of a kaleidoscope, they follow one another in rapid succession. There is no thought of selecting what is most suitable, and the main idea is often lost sight of in the long train of images that are intended to illustrate it." But here we can see where the art of oral declamation of the homilies, as opposed to reading, makes a tremendous difference in how one appreciates the literary form of the compiled list, which must have delighted live audiences who saw it as a challenge for the orator to extend the chain as far as possible. Ameringer (*Second Sophistic,* 66, 103) mentions the extent to which audiences would have been pleased by these characteristics in the oral delivery, but apparently regards that as a kind of pandering to their unsophisticated appetites.

[25] *Laz.* 6.9 [48.1041].

[26] For similar lists, see *hom. in Ac. 9:1* 4.3 [51.149]; *poenit.* 2.5 [49.290]; and *anom.* 8.3 [48.772]: "For who is better than all people? Who else than that tentmaker, the teacher of the world, the one who ran around earth and sea like a winged bird, the vessel of election, the leader of the bride of Christ, the sower of the church, the wise master-builder, the herald, the runner, the champion fighter, the soldier, the trainer, the one who left memorials of his own virtue everywhere in the world, the one who before the resurrection was snatched up into the third

a list of epithets of his beloved Paul, part of the artistry and enjoyment of this kind of oratory for the preacher and his audience was to see how long he could keep it up. Thus we often get quite extended lists, with the order sometimes clustering epithets of like type or similar reference, but equally often evincing no particular pattern. At other times we find much more abbreviated lists, which serve to conjure up larger catalogues, or even single epithets for Paul used in a range of rhetorical and liturgical contexts. In this chapter I shall provide a topical overview of the collection of Pauline miniatures by "room" in the gallery of portraits,[27] followed by an analysis of the sources of Chrysostom's epithets for Paul.

Teaching Portraits

The most frequent epithet for Paul in Chrysostom's writings[28] is ὁ διδάσκαλος τῆς οἰκουμένης, "the teacher of the world."[29] By this title Chrysostom stresses both Paul's pedagogical function and his far-flung influence. Paul's own self-designation ἐθνῶν ἀπόστολος, "apostle of the Gentiles" (Rom 11:13), which was modified by the author of the Pastorals to διδάσκαλος ἐθνῶν, "teacher of the Gentiles" (1 Tim 2:7; 2 Tim 1:11),[30] is further expanded by Chrysostom, in the direction of Col 1:23, to include "the whole world."[31] The epithet thus takes its starting point from Paul's own goal to preach the gospel to the ends of the earth, and its inferred or announced fulfillment by subsequent Christian generations (Luke-Acts, the deu-

---

heaven, the one who was taken away into paradise, the one who shared with God in the inexpressible mysteries, the one who heard and spoke such things which are not lawful for human nature to speak, the one who enjoyed more grace, and received more work?" Still another, similar example, may be found in *exp. in Ps.* 110.4 [55.284]: "Paul, that herald of the world, the one snatched up into the third heaven, the one carried off into paradise, the one who shared in the frightful mysteries, the vessel of election, the leader of the bridegroom of Christ, the one who demonstrated the angelic commonwealth, the one who came to such great virtue." Though much less frequent, Chrysostom also composed epithet lists for Peter, as in *hom. in Mt.* 18:23 3 [51.20]: "Peter, the leader of the chorus of the apostles, the mouth of the disciples, the pillar of the church, the bedrock of faith, the foundation of the profession of faith, the one who was always hot and full of boldness" (cf. also *hom. in Ac.* 6.1 [60.56]). The extremes to which the form could be brought is exemplified in an antiphonal epithet contest between Peter and Paul in the spurious work attributed to Chrysostom (*Petr. et Paul.* 1 [59.493–94]).

[27] Lycinus, in Lucian's *Imagines* 15, refers to this kind of succession of portraits of a subject as "a feast and a well-stocked banquet table" [ἑορτὴ καὶ πανδαισία].

[28] Also ubiquitous is the simple adjective μακάριος, as in ὁ μακάριος οὗτος (*hom. in Gen.* 11.7 [53.97]; *compunct.* 2 2 [47.412]; *et passim*). For other common laudatory adjectives see, e.g., *hom. in Eph.* 6.2 [62.45]: Παῦλος ὁ μέγας καὶ θαυμαστός, and *sac.* 4.6 [SC 272.266]: ὁ δίκαιος.

[29] Of many examples, see *hom. in Gen.* 25.2; 29.2; 39.2 [53.221, 264, 363]; *hom. in Philm.* 2.3 [62.712]; *hom. in Rom.* 30.3 [60.665]; *hom. in Rom. 16:3* 1.5 [51.194]; *hom. in Col.* 10.3 [62.369]; *hom. in Jo.* 10.1 [59.74]; *poenit.* 2.5 [49.290]; *Laz.* 6.9 [48.1041]; *anom.* 8.3 [48.772]; *catech.* 1.1; 4.7; 7.9 [SC 50.108, 186, 252, its frequency noted by the editor, Wenger, on p. 11]. Chrysostom's predilection for this term was observed also by Di S. Maria, "S. Paolo," 496, n. 4.

[30] *hom. in Gal. 2:11* 12 [51.382].

[31] On the historical development of this image for Paul, see de Boer, "Images of Paul," 378–9.

tero-Paulines, and 1 Clement 5:6–7), but it now includes not only the historical life of the missionary apostle, but the epistolary Paul, who teaches all people throughout all time by his letters.[32] Paul as a teacher is distinguished by his overwhelming pedagogical concern for the best interests of his students.[33] Elsewhere the content of Paul's teaching is accented, as he is called "the teacher of the heavenly dogmas,"[34] or "the one who preached that Christ was God."[35] The teaching and preaching roles of Paul are brought to life by a variety of vocal and musical epithets: Paul is "the mouth of Christ,"[36] "the voice of the gospel proclamation,"[37] "the one on whose tongue Christ sat,"[38] "the tongue which shone forth above the sun,"[39] "the spiritual rhetor,"[40] "the heavenly trumpet,"[41] and, as above, "the lyre of the Spirit."[42] Paul's verbal inspiration by Christ was of cardinal importance for Chrysostom's appreciation of him:

---

[32] sac. 4.7: "… not only to the faithful of today, but from his time to this, and even to the appearing of Christ, he has been and will be profitable, and will continue to be so as long as the human race shall last" [SC 272.272–74]. Contrast this with the perspective of 1 Clem. 5:7, where Paul's teaching activity was a thing of the past. Chrysostom is quite aware of the different types of "apostolic presence" through which Paul is active, as in laud. Paul. 3.6, where after a list of participles of Pauline activities the means are named: "through his personal presence, through letters, through words, through deeds, through disciples, through himself" [διὰ παρουσίας, διὰ γραμμάτων, διὰ ῥημάτων, διὰ πραγμάτων, διὰ μαθητῶν, δι' ἑαυτοῦ] [SC 300.172].

[33] See comm. in Gal. 6.4 [61.680], of Paul as "the one who chose both to do and to suffer all things for the sake of his disciples" [ὁ πάντα καὶ ποιεῖν καὶ πάσχειν ὑπὲρ τῶν μαθητῶν αἱρούμενος], echoed again in hom. in Eph. 8.1 [62.55]: "It is the virtue of teachers not to seek honor nor glory from those who are commencing their studies, but their salvation, and to do everything on behalf of this. This is the task of a teacher; and such a one was the blessed Paul" [Διδασκάλων ἐστὶν ἀρετὴ μὴ τιμήν, μηδὲ δόξαν ζητεῖν παρὰ τῶν ἀρχομένων, ἀλλὰ τὴν σωτηρίαν αὐτῶν, καὶ πάντα ὑπὲρ τούτου ποιεῖν … τοῦτό ἐστι διδασκάλου. τοιοῦτος ὁ μακάριος Παῦλος ἦν].

[34] ὁ τῶν οὐρανίων δογμάτων διδάσκαλος (hom. in Rom. 5:3 2 [51.158]).

[35] ὁ τὸν Χριστὸν θεὸν ἀνακηρύξας (Laz. 6.9 [48.1041]).

[36] τὸ στόμα τοῦ Χριστοῦ (Laz. 6.9 [48.1041]).

[37] ἡ φωνὴ τοῦ κηρύγματος (hom. in Ac. 25.1 [60.191]).

[38] hom. in Rom. 32.2 [60.679], although this is in sentence form [οὕτως καὶ (ἐκάθητο) ἐπὶ τῆς τοῦ Παύλου γλώττης] here, as in the previous sentence, in regard to Paul's voice: (ἡ φωνὴ τοῦ Παύλου) τὸν Χριστὸν εἶχεν ἐγκαθήμενον, so it is not, form-critically speaking, an epithet, but it is too wonderfully poetic not to be included here.

[39] hom. in Rom. Arg. 1 [60.392]. Cf. hom. in Gen. 3.5 [53.37]; hom. in Rom. 16:3 1.3 [51.191], "the tongue of the world" (a reference to the letters).

[40] ὁ ῥήτωρ ὁ πνευματικός (poenit. 2.5 [49.290]). Cf. ὁ ῥητόρων εὐγλωττότερος (Laz. 6.9 [48.1041]).

[41] ἡ σάλπιγξ ἡ οὐράνιος (hom. in 2 Cor. 11:1 1 [51.301]; hom. in Ac. 25.1 [60.191]; stat. 1.1 [49.15]; hom. in Ac. 9:1 3.4 [51.139]; cf. hom. in Rom. Arg. 1 [60.391], ἡ σάλπιγξ ἡ πνευματική, "the spiritual trumpet"). Given the inherently shorthand nature of epithets, it is unusual for Chrysostom to explain or exegete them in context, but he does do that in stat. 1.1 [49.15], the προοίμιον to the discourse, in which he explains that Paul's "heavenly trumpet" sounds for dual effect: to inspire fear in enemies and courage in compatriots. This was of course appropriate to the contentious and highly dangerous context in which Chrysostom gave the homilies de statuis.

[42] Laz. 6.9 [48.1041]; stat. 1.1 [49.15].

For it is not Paul who spoke, but Christ, who moved Paul's soul. So when you hear him shout and say:"Behold, I, Paul, tell you" (Gal 5:2), consider that only the shout is Paul's; the thought and the teaching are Christ's, who is speaking to Paul from within his heart.[43]

Paul's claim that Christ speaks in him (2 Cor 13:3) is profoundly important for Chrysostom. He often accents the inspired nature of Pauline speech by saying that "Paul spoke, or rather Christ, through Paul" [Παῦλος ἐφθέγξατο, μᾶλλον δὲ ὁ Χριστὸς διὰ Παύλου].[44] Sometimes the claim is made even more antithetically, in such a way that Paul loses place as the agent of his speech:"for Paul is not the one speaking this, but Christ, who moved his soul" [Οὐ γὰρ Παῦλός ἐστιν ὁ φθεγγόμενος, ἀλλ' ὁ κινῶν τὴν ἐκείνου ψυχὴν Χριστός].[45] Perhaps the furthest extent of this claim is reached in the impassioned portrait of Paul in *hom. in Rom.* 32 (which we shall examine in detail in the next chapter): "[Paul's] mouth ... through which Christ spoke the great and secret things, even greater than in his own person" [δι' οὗ (στόματος) τὰ μεγάλα καὶ ἀπόρρητα ὁ Χριστὸς ἐλάλησε, καὶ μείζονα ἢ δι' ἑαυτοῦ].[46]

Portraits in Flight

The widely travelled aspect of the epithet "teacher of the world" is also captured by Chrysostom with a favored likeness of Paul to "a winged bird who flew around the whole world."[47] This image of Paul as a swift bird[48] may have several roots,[49]

---

[43] *Jud.* 2.1 [48.858], trans. P. Harkins, FC 68.37 (see also *Jud.* 2.3; 3.4 [48.862, 866]).

[44] *hom. in 1 Tim.* 17.3 [62.594]. See also, e.g., *vid.* 1.68–71:"For the things Paul spoke, Christ was speaking through him" [SC 138.118]; *hom. in Heb.* 3.6; 10.1 [63.35, 83]; *hom. in 2 Tim.* 2.3 [62.610–11]; *scand.* 2.2 [SC 79.60]; *grat.* 2 [50.656]. In *hom. in Rom.* 16:3 1.3 [51.191], also in reference to 2 Cor 13:3, Chrysostom concludes: "For where Paul was, there also was Christ" ["Οπου γὰρ Παῦλος ἦν, ἐκεῖ καὶ ὁ Χριστὸς ἦν].And the passage continues:"And where Christ was, there also angels continually attended" ["Οπου δὲ Χριστὸς ἦν, ἐκεῖ καὶ ἄγγελοι συνεχῶς ἐφοίτων].

[45] *hom. in Ac. 9:1* 4.3 [51.148]. But Chrysostom in most cases takes Paul's historical authorship and intentionality as hermeneutical givens (see chap. 7, pp. 389–94).

[46] *hom. in Rom.* 32.3 [60.679].We shall directly address the theological and social implications of how Chrysostom relates Paul with Christ in chap. 7, pp. 396–400.

[47] καθάπερ ὑπόπτερος τὴν οἰκουμένην περιτρέχων ἅπαντα (*hom. in Gen.* 34.5 [53.319], in the context of several other epithets). Of many other examples, see *laud. Paul.* 1.4; 2.8 [SC 300.116, 156]; *hom. in Gen.* 23.7 [53.196]; *anom.* 8.3 [48.772]; *poenit.* 2.5 [49.290]; *Eutrop.* 2.14 [52.409]. In one place the anatomical incongruity of Paul's wide wing span is accented, as Paul is termed "the one who with a short body encircled the world" [ὁ ἐν σώματι βραχεῖ τὴν οἰκουμένην κυκλῶν] (*poenit.* 2.5 [49.290]). In *stat.* 16.5 [49.169] he says that when Paul was bound in prison his teaching itself [τοῦ κηρύγματος ὁ λόγος, ἡ διδασκαλία] sprouted wings and flew around the world.

[48] Even more exact identifications of Paul as a winged creature are made in a spurious work attributed to Chrysostom: "the restless sparrow of the church" [ἡ ἄπαυστος χελιδὼν τῆς ἐκκλησίας], and "the sparrow and cicada" [ἡ χελιδὼν καὶ τέττιξ] (*Petr. et Paul* 1 [59.493]).

[49] For instance, it was a rhetorical commonplace to construct likenesses of the Homeric gods to birds (see N.J. Richardson, *The Homeric Hymn to Demeter* [Oxford: Clarendon, 1974] 164, with references), a form which Chrysostom may be adapting for his Christian hero.

but it is especially inspired by 2 Tim 4:7, which depicts Paul as having "completed the race":

This race which Paul was running[50] upon the earth was purer than the one which he runs in heaven. How has he completed the race? He went around the whole world, beginning from Galilee and from Arabia, going to the ends of the earth (quotation of Rom 15:19 ...). And he ran through the whole world like some bird [καθάπερ τις πτηνός], but he was more zealous than even a bird. For the bird simply travels around, but he did not do so in any simple way, but with the wing of the spirit, and bursting through myriad hindrances, deaths, plots, and misfortunes. Therefore he was even swifter than a bird. If he were simply a bird, then he would have touched down and been killed. But since he was lifted up by the spirit, he was carried above all the nets, like a bird with wings of fire [ὡσανεὶ πτηνὸς πτερὰ ἔχων ἀπὸ πυρός]."[51]

Celestial Images

The aviary image has yet another distinct accent, for the bird crosses the sky from earth toward heaven.[52] Paul, winged with love,[53] flies even above heaven.[54] The ornithic portrait accents Paul's asceticism, for to Chrysostom he lived on earth as though he were in heaven.[55] Because of this, Paul was "the one who demonstrated

---

[50] See also *hom. in 2 Tim.* 2.1 [62.607]: ὁ τὴν οἰκουμένην περιδραμών. Chrysostom often depicts Paul as "running" (e.g., *scand.* 2.3 [SC 79.60]; *hom. in 1 Cor.* 13.3 [61.111]; *hom. in Rom.* 32.3 [60.679]; *laud. Paul.* 3.6 [SC 300.172]). In his view, Paul "couldn't sit still," but was constantly on the move (*hom. in Rom.* Arg. 2 [60.394]).

[51] *hom. in 2 Tim.* 9.2 [62.653].

[52] As in the text previously quoted: "This is truly a good contest, not simply entertaining, but benefitting, the spectator. And the race does not give way to nothingness, nor is it a demonstration of strength and competitive spirit, but it draws all people into heaven" (*hom. in 2 Tim.* 9.2 [62.653]).

[53] *hom. in Rom.* Arg. 2 [60.394]; see also *hom. in Ac.* 52.4 [60.364].

[54] *hom. in Mt.* 6.5 [57.68]: "soaring above the heaven, and the heaven of heaven."

[55] *hom. in Gen.* 34.5 [53.319]; cf. 4.5, he "walked on the earth, but with desire traversed the heaven" [53.44]. This is also the emphasis of the epithets, "the one simply clad in the body" [ὁ τὸ σῶμα ἁπλῶς περικείμενος] (*poenit.* 2.5 [49.290–291]; *hom. in Gen.* 4.5 [53.44]), and "the one who trampled on the necessities of nature" [ὁ πάσας καταπατήσας (for Migne's typo καπαπατήσας) τὰς ἀνάγκας τῆς φύσεως] (*proph. obscurit.* 2.4 [56.181]), and "the one who was loftier than bodily necessities" [ὁ τῶν σωματικῶν ἀναγκῶν ἀνώτερος γεγονώς] (*hom. in Gen.* 23.7 [53.196]). He was as unmoved by earthly things as the dead are unmoved by other dead. Indeed, "do you see how he stood apart from the world, how while walking on the earth he had leapt up into the very height of heaven?" [Ὁρᾷς πόσον ἀφειστήκει τῆς οἰκουμένης, πῶς ἐν τῇ γῇ βαδίζων πρὸς αὐτὴν ἀνεπεπηδήκει τοῦ οὐρανοῦ τὴν κορυφήν;] (*compunct.* 2 2 [47.413]). According to *hom. in Eph.* 1.2 [62.19], "Paul was of such a sort that even while on earth he tasted the things of heaven [ἐντεῦθεν ἤδη τῶν ἐκεῖ γεγευμένος]. Therefore he was eager and in birth pangs to leave these parts [ὥδινε τὰ ἐνθάδε ἀφεῖναι], and he continually groaned. For he saw with different eyes, having removed his entire mind to heaven [ἑτέροις γὰρ ὀφθαλμοῖς ἑώρα, πάντα τὸν νοῦν μεταστήσας ἐκεῖ]. A later homily in the series illustrates the exemplary role this image of Paul the ascetic plays in Chrysostom's oratory: "being somewhere is not a determination of position [τόπος], but of disposition [διάθεσις] ... therefore let us be in ourselves, in heaven, in the spirit" [Γενώμεθα τοίνυν ἐν ἑαυτοῖς, ἐν τῷ οὐρανῷ, ἐν τῷ πνεύματι] (*hom. in Eph.* 5.4 [62.42]). On John's picture of Paul's ascetic practice, see chap. 6, pp. 308–26.

an angelic way of life."⁵⁶ Another way Chrysostom expresses Paul's non-worldliness and the Platonic conceptions which lie behind it is with the unusual epithet ἡ οὐρανομήκης ψυχή, "the soul which reached as far as heaven."⁵⁷ This idea is codified elsewhere as ὁ οὐρανοπολίτης, "the citizen of heaven."⁵⁸ He is "the one who holds the first place in the kingdom of the heavens."⁵⁹ John can claim this because he regards Paul as having had possession of the totality of the divine secrets.⁶⁰ He was "the one who touched the very heavens, and shone so brightly with grace."⁶¹ But even this epithet is elsewhere outdone by such statements as that Paul was higher even than heaven, or any heavens above the heavens;⁶² indeed, "he was a heaven."⁶³ But Paul is not content to remain fixed in heaven; he leads

⁵⁶ ὁ ἀγγελικὴν ἐπιδειξάμενος πολιτείαν (exp. in Ps. 110.4 [55.284]). This phrase, along with ἡ τῶν οὐρανῶν πολιτεία, is very common in Chrysostom's ascetical writings, and in other contexts referring to the monastic or celibate life (fem. reg. 7 [47.527]; Thdr. 1 18 [SC 117.192]; oppugn. 3.11 and 18 [47.366, 381]; poenit. 7.7 [49.335]; cruc. 2.1 [49.407]; sac. 3.13 [SC 272.210]), as we shall discuss further in our analysis of the portrait of Paul as an ideal monk in chap. 6, pp. 308–26. Another person whom John singles out as ὁ τὴν ἀγγελικὴν ἐπιδειξάμενος πολιτείαν is John the Baptist (hom. in Mt. 36.1 [57.413]); cf. the same depiction of "all the saints" in res. mort. 7 [50.428]).

⁵⁷ hom. in Gen. 3.5; 4.5; 31.2; 41.5 [53.37, 44, 285, 381]; catech. 1.4 [SC 50.111], with Wenger's note: "une expression qui semble plus particulière à Chrysostome"; hom. in Rom. 8:28 1 [51.166]; hom. in Phil. 1:18 4 [51.314].

⁵⁸ poenit. 2.5 [49.290]. The same idea, though not in the form of an epithet, is found in hom. in Col. 10.3 [62.370]: ἐν οὐρανῷ πολιτεύεται.

⁵⁹ ὁ τὰ πρωτεῖα ἔχων ἐν τῇ βασιλείᾳ τῶν οὐρανῶν (hom. in Col. 11.3 [62.377]). There he is also termed "the one who is worthy of the world and of countless heavens" [ὁ τῆς οἰκουμένης ἀντάξιος καὶ μυρίων οὐρανῶν].

⁶⁰ Chrysostom regards Eph 3:10 as a proof of Paul's superiority even to angels and other celestial beings, because he alone was granted the knowledge of the hidden mystery of God's plan to save both Gentiles and Jews (hom. in Eph. 7.1 [62.503]).

⁶¹ ὁ τῶν οὐρανῶν αὐτῶν ἁψάμενος καὶ τοσοῦτον ἐν τῇ χάριτι λάμψας (hom. in 1 Cor. 22.2 [61.184]).

⁶² hom. in Ac. 55.3 [60.382]; hom. in Heb. 16.3 [63.126]: "I mean those such as Paul, who while on earth spent their lives in heaven. But why do I say 'in heaven'? They were higher than heaven, indeed than the other heaven, and went up to God himself." See also the extended discussion in hom. in Rom. 18.6 [60.580]: "For [Paul] has acquired a soul which is not less than heaven, able to draw in all people. For our soul is not even worthy of earth, but his soul was the equal of the heavens ... the height of his soul surpassed all the heavens, and he conversed with Christ himself" [Καὶ γὰρ ἐκέκτητο ψυχὴν τοῦ οὐρανοῦ οὐχ ἥττονα, πάντας ἐπισπάσασθαι δυναμένην. Ἡ μὲν γὰρ ἡμετέρα οὐδὲ τῆς γῆς ἀξία, ἡ δὲ ἐκείνου καὶ τῶν οὐρανῶν ἀντάξια ... τῆς ἐκείνου ψυχῆς τὸ ὕψος ἅπαντας ὑπερέβη τοὺς οὐρανούς, καὶ αὐτῷ ὁμιλεῖ τῷ Χριστῷ]. Two homilies earlier in that series, Chrysostom had said that Paul "went above heaven, and heaven's heaven, and angels and archangels, and ran around all the regions up there" (hom. in Rom. 16.2 [60.551]).

⁶³ "He was a heaven having a sun different from ours, a sun of righteousness; hence the man was better even than heaven" [καὶ οὐρανοῦ βελτίων ἀνήρ] (hom. in Ac. 55.3 [60.383]). See the narrative of Paul's creation as a sun in hom. in Phil. 4.1 [62.206]: "All the angels in unison praised you, God, when you created the stars and also when you created the sun. But not as much as when you showed Paul to us and the whole world [ἀλλ' οὐχ οὕτως, ὡς ὅτε τὸν Παῦλον ἔδειξας ἡμῖν καὶ τῇ οἰκουμένῃ πάσῃ]. Therefore the earth became brighter than heaven, and he, more radiant than the solar light, released the brightest rays and spread bright sunbeams" [φαιδρότερος οὗτος τοῦ ἡλιακοῦ φωτὸς ἀφῆκε λαμπροτέρας τὰς μαρμαρυγάς, φαιδρὰς τὰς ἀκτῖνας ἥπλωσεν].

people by the hand from earth to heaven.[64] Elsewhere he is described as a sea on which people voyage from earth to heaven.[65] Paul had the ability to make angels out of people.[66] Actually, the angels reverence Paul.[67] Elsewhere, Paul himself is "an angel come down from heaven,"[68] or "the guardian angel of the whole world."[69] Thus Paul deserves the twin oxymoronic epithets "the earthly angel" and "the heavenly human being."[70]

A Miniature Magnified: Paul as the Sun

Because these celestial epithets depict Paul in such exalted terms, Chrysostom often amplifies and embellishes them by comparing Paul with the highest heavenly competitor, the sun. Chrysostom is at his most inventive on Paul's behalf in such extended rhetorical συγκρίσεις, or comparisons, that aim to extend the epithet into a fuller composition. In one straightforward comparison Chrysostom notes that:

> While the sun, by rising and sending forth its bright rays, cheers up my sights, Paul's face illuminates my mind. For the sun enlightens things that are visible [ὄψεις], but Paul gives wings to the very vaults [ἀψῖδες] of the heavens. Indeed, he gives a complete picture[71] of the soul and the height above the sun, and above the moon. Such is the power of virtue.[72]

For such a rhetorical comparison in an epideictic speech to work, the orator must compare the one he seeks to praise with a genuine worthy, and grant the attainments and natural virtues of that figure before showing how his subject outdoes

---

[64] *hom. in Ac. 9:1* 1.3 [51.118]. In *poenit.* 2.5 [49.291] Paul is said to "make the human being into an angel, and give the soul wings into heaven" [ἄγγελον τὸν ἄνθρωπον ποιεῖ, τὴν ψυχὴν ἀναπτεροῖ εἰς τὸν οὐρανόν]. Elsewhere he is said to have "made earth into a heaven, and led all people by the hand into virtue" [οὗτος τὴν γῆν οὐρανὸν ἐποίει, καὶ πρὸς τὴν ἀρετὴν ἅπαντας ἐχειραγώγει] (*exp. in Ps.* 111.2 [55.293]; cf. *Eutrop.* 2.14 [52.409], on making earth into a heaven).

[65] *hom. in Ac.* 55.3 [60.383]. See Brown, *Cult of the Saints*, 65, on the ability of the saint to negotiate the social, even cosmic, minefields for the sake of his or her patrons.

[66] *laud. Paul.* 1.4 [SC 300.116–18], even making angels out of demons.

[67] *hom. in Eph.* 8.3 [62.59].

[68] *hom. in Rom. 16:3* 1.2 [51.190] (he was considered this because of his miracles); *hom. in Col.* 10.4 [62.371]: ἄγγελος ἐπὶ γῆς, "an angel upon the earth"; *hom. in 1 Cor.* 23.2 [61.190].

[69] *laud. Paul.* 2.8 [SC 300.156–58]. Paul possessed all the angelic virtues (*laud. Paul.* 1.1 [SC 300.114]). According to *scand.* 2.3 [SC 79.60] and *hom. in Rom. 16:3* 1.2, 5 [51.189, 194], "God put the entire world in his hands" (cf. also *Jud.* 8.3 [48.931], where this is predicated of Peter). Such claims for Paul exemplify well Brown's observation that the late fourth-century tendency to focus on human saints led to the exclusion of prior emphases on angels and other divine or semi-divine intermediaries (*Cult of the Saints*, 61).

[70] ὁ ἐπίγειος ἄγγελος, ὁ ἐπουράνιος ἄνθρωπος (*poenit.* 2.5 [49.291]), drawing upon Paul's own language for the two types in 1 Cor 15:40–49. For John the idea of Paul as an angel, as we have seen, is rooted in his asceticism. On how the ascetic is like the angel, who can uniquely mediate between heaven and earth, see Brown, *Body and Society*, 178–89 (for the cosmological roots of the idea), and 323–38 (on Syrian monasticism in Chrysostom's day and later).

[71] LSJ, 186 (*s.v.* ἀπεργάζομαι, "fill up with colour, represent in a finished picture").

[72] *poenit.* 2.5 [49.291].

the example at each point. In this passage Chrysostom has merely scratched the surface of the rhetorical possibilities of this comparison of Paul with the sun. In a homily on Romans he further embellishes the comparison by arguing successively that Paul was brighter than the sun, that he could draw all people to him, that he was higher than the sun because he talked with Christ himself, and that the creation of Paul's soul at his conversion was heralded by God himself (Acts 9:15), whereas the creation of the sun and stars was heralded only by the angels (Job 38:7). Lastly, whereas clouds may obscure the sun, Paul's soul was perpetually as undiminished as the sun at high noon.[73] When Chrysostom returns to this theme once again in a homily from his later period in Constantinople,[74] he unloads both barrels on this comparison in his saint's favor. In addition to the claim that Paul received praise from God and the angels, he adds new assertions about the superior power of Paul's rays: brighter than the sun, they nurtured the fruit of holiness (not merely pomegranates and the like), they could restore even decayed fruit (not merely promote growth in what was already healthy), and they prevailed over Satan (whereas the sun's rays give way to the night). Paul as a sun rose from the earth, filling the space not with light alone, but with joy and pleasure for the angels. Thus it is proven that Paul is greater than the sun.[75]

In yet another homily delivered in Constantinople[76] John returns to this comparison between Paul and the great orb. Discussing Col 4:3, and Paul's statement that he had been placed in chains, Chrysostom expounds on the paradox that the more Paul was bound, the more free he actually became. This leads to an exclamation about Paul's course, which John pronounces in the face of an imagined dupe:[77]

What are you doing, you stupid man? Was Paul a runner in body [σωματικὸς δρομεύς]? Did he compete in one of our stadiums [ἐν σταδίῳ τῷ παρ' ἡμῖν ἀγωνίζεται]? He is a citizen in heaven [ἐν οὐρανῷ πολιτεύεται]. Things on earth cannot bind the one who runs in heaven. You can see the sun, can't you [Οὐχ ὁρᾷς τουτονὶ τὸν ἥλιον;]? Go ahead and encircle its rays with bonds; stop its course. You will be unable. Then neither can you do it to Paul. And how much greater is Paul than the sun [καὶ πολλῷ μᾶλλον τοῦτον, ἢ ἐκεῖνον]! For he enjoys greater providence than it does, because he doesn't bring an ordinary light, but conveys the light of truth.[78]

---

[73] *hom. in Rom.* 18.6 [60.580].

[74] So Quasten, *Patrology*, 3.447–8, against Baur, *John Chrysostom*, 1.300.

[75] *hom. in Phil.* 4.1 [62.206–207]. The full text is quoted below, in chap. 6, pp. 238–39; see also n. 180 there on how this praise of Paul as the sun is likely also a polemic against the god Apollo, and consequently a barb against Julian, his faithful promoter.

[76] So Bonsdorff, *Predigttätigkeit*, 82–86; Baur, *John Chrysostom*, 2.93; Quasten, *Patrology*, 3.448.

[77] The intended figure is probably Nero, given that John had just previously contrasted the fate of the one (ostensibly) bound and that of the emperor who had bound him, just as he does in *hom. in 2 Tim.* 4.3–4 [62.621–24], which we shall analyze in chap. 6, pp. 206–12.

[78] *hom. in Col.* 10.3 [62.370].

Snapshots of Paul's Soul

In chap. 5 we shall examine some full-scale portraits John composes of Paul's ψυχή, but here we shall flip through his miniature snapshots of it. The host of epithets used by Chrysostom to depict Paul's soul includes: "a meadow of virtues and spiritual garden,"[79] "a God-loving soul,"[80] "a soul on fire,"[81] "a soul ready to encounter death,"[82] "a noble soul of steel,"[83] "a soul able to carry around everything at once,"[84] "a soul which surpassed the whole earth,"[85] "a soul ecumenical in its hospitality."[86] These myriad images of Paul's soul are also neatly captured by the following two parallel, and rather incongruous, exclamations: "Nothing was kinder, nothing sweeter, nothing more loving than that holy soul";[87] "nothing was more prepared for combat than Paul's soul."[88]

Agonistic Epithets

The last mentioned epithet for Paul's soul partakes of the biblical military image of the apostle[89] which Chrysostom also applies to him: "the noble general" [στρατηγὸς ἄριστος],[90] "the soldier" [στρατιώτης],[91] "the gladiator" [μονομάχος].[92] Chryso-

---

[79] λειμὼν ἀρετῶν καὶ παράδεισος πνευματικός (*laud. Paul.* 1.1 [SC 300.112]).

[80] ψυχὴ φιλόθεος (*hom. in Gen.* 11.5 [53.96]).

[81] ψυχὴ πεπυρωμένη (*hom. in Gen.* 34.6 [53.320]).

[82] ψυχὴ πρὸς θάνατον παρατεταγμένη (*hom. in Ac.* 31.3 [60.230]).

[83] ἡ γενναία ἐκείνη καὶ ἀδαμαντίνη ψυχή (*hom. in Ac.* 55.3 [60.384]; *laud. Paul.* 1.12; 2.7 [SC 300.132, 154]; *hom. in 1 Cor.* 3.3 [61.26]; cf. *catech.* 5.19 [SC 50.210]). Paul's spirit was adamantine, also (*hom. in Rom.* 2.4 [60.405]; cf. *hom. in Heb.* 28.4 [63.196]), and Paul himself is called ὁ ἀδαμάντινος, along with a list of associated epithets: "Paul, the one who was bold in the face of fire, the steely one, the stout one, the one who was tightly held together, the one who was nailed with the fear of God, the unflinching" [ὁ καὶ πυρὸς κατατολμῶν Παῦλος, ὁ ἀδαμάντινος, ὁ στερρός, ὁ ἀκλινής, ὁ πάντοτε συγκεκροτημένος, ὁ καθηλωμένος τῷ φόβῳ τοῦ θεοῦ, ὁ ἀκαμπής]. He is the one who contended over many adversities, "the man who laughed at the steely gates of death" [ὁ τῶν ἀδαμαντίνων τοῦ θανάτου πυλῶν καταγελῶν] (*hom. in 1 Thess.* 4.4 [62.421]).

[84] *hom. in Ac.* 55.3 [60.382], of Paul as ὁ ψυχὴν ἔχων πάντα ὁμοῦ περιλαβεῖν δυναμένην; cf. *hom. in Rom.* Arg. 2 [60.394], a soul which "carried about all people in itself" [ἐν ἑαυτῷ περιέφερεν ἅπαντας].

[85] ψυχὴ ὑπερβαίνουσα πᾶσαν τὴν γῆν (*laud. Paul.* 3.6 [SC 300.172]).

[86] *laud. Paul.* 1.11 [SC 300.130]: ἡ ψυχὴ πάσῃ τῇ οἰκουμένῃ ἥπλωτο (in sentence form).

[87] Οὐδὲν προσηνέστερον τῆς ἁγίας ἐκείνης ψυχῆς, οὐδὲν γλυκύτερον καὶ φιλοστοργότερον (*comm. in Gal.* 4.2 [61.659]).

[88] *hom. in 1 Cor.* 6.1 [61.47]: Οὐδὲν τῆς Παύλου ψυχῆς ἀγωνιστικώτερον.

[89] See, e.g., Phil 2:25; Phlm 2; 2 Cor 10:3–5; cf. 1 Cor 9:7; 1 Tim 1:18.

[90] *laud. Paul.* 3.6 [SC 300.172]; cf. *hom. in Col.* 1.1 [62.300], ἀριστεύς.

[91] "As if a single soldier [στρατιώτης εἷς], having the whole world at war with him, should go about in the midst of the ranks of the enemy, and suffer no harm. Just like this, Paul, alone among the barbarians, among the Greeks, appearing everywhere on earth, everywhere on sea, remained uncaptured" (*hom. in 2 Cor.* 25.3. [61.573]; cf. *laud. Paul.* 4.13 [SC 300.212]; *anom.* 8.3 [48.772]; *comm. in Gal.* 6.4 [61.680]). Compare the same argument in Maximus of Tyre, *Or.* 1.3 [Trapp, 8].

[92] *hom. in Ac.* 25.1 [60.192].

stom's twist on this common image is to make Paul a one-man army, a soldier who fought on all fronts, against all enemies, using all the strategic maneuvers known to military science.[93] In another place Paul the subservient general takes on all the least desirable roles in the army on behalf of his soldiers,[94] or bolsters the courage of his soldiers when they see him bleeding yet undeterred in the face of the enemy.[95] This is the same emphasis in John's athletic epithets for Paul (which are also based upon the New Testament writings):[96] Paul as "the athlete of Christ"[97] was like an ancient decathlete or modern "iron-man" who could compete and win in all sports.[98] With a range of athletic events in view Chrysostom depicts Paul as "a fighting champion," "a runner," and "a trainer."[99] Paul as ship-captain [κυβερνήτης][100] in Chrysostom becomes Paul as "all things in himself, both sailor, and pilot, and lookout, and sail, and ship."[101] All these epithets from the realm of competition can be encompassed in the single depiction of Paul as ἀκατάπληκτος, "a man not to be overcome."[102] Chrysostom also uses architectural images to

---

[93] *hom. in 2 Cor.* 25.3 [61.573]: "or like a soldier [στρατιώτης] breaching walls, fighting on foot, engaging in nautical combat, thus he pursued every form of battle. He breathed fire and was unapproachable by all. With his one body he took down the world; with his one tongue he routed them all."

[94] "Like some excellent general, he himself carried baggage, he himself was the armor carrier, himself the shield bearer, himself the man on the flank, he himself being all things for the camp" [καθάπερ τις στρατηγὸς ἄριστος, αὐτὸς σκευοφόρος, αὐτὸς ὑπασπιστής, αὐτὸς προασπιστής, αὐτὸς παραστάτης, αὐτὸς πάντα γινόμενος τῷ στρατοπέδῳ] (*laud. Paul.* 3.6 [SC 300.172]).

[95] *laud. Paul.* 7.10 [SC 300.314].

[96] See, e.g., 1 Cor 9:24–27; Phil 3:12–14; 2 Tim 4:7; Acts 20:24, and the study by V. C. Pfitzner, *Paul and the Agon Motif. Traditional Athletic Imagery in the Pauline Literature* (NovTSup 16; Leiden: Brill, 1967).

[97] *hom. in Rom.* 32.2 [60.678]; *sac.* 4.6 [48.668]; *hom. in Gen.* 11.6 [53.97]; *hom. in 2 Tim.* 3.2; 4.3 [62.614, 624], ὁ ἀθλητής; *hom. in Col.* 10.3 [62.369], ὁ ἀθλητὴς ὁ τοσοῦτος.

[98] "Like some champion [ἀθλητής] who wrestles, runs, and boxes, too" (*hom. in 2 Cor.* 25.3 [61.573]).

[99] All three (ἀγωνιστής, δρομεύς, παιδοτρίβης) are found in *anom.* 8.3 [48.772]. The last epithet shows up in expanded form in *hom. in Rom.* 5:3 2 [51.158]:ὁ τῆς οἰκουμένης παιδοτρίβης ("the trainer of the world"); cf. also *res. mort.* 3 [50.421–22]. Elsewhere Chrysostom compares Paul to an ἀριστεὺς γενναιότατος, "a most noble champion" (*sac.* 4.7 [48.670]; *hom. in Col.* 1.1 [62.300]).

[100] ὁ καλὸς κυβερνήτης Παῦλος (*hom. in Rom.* 5:3 1 [51.157]). Paul does not describe himself this way, but does include κυβέρνησις ("steerage") among the spiritual gifts in 1 Cor 12:28.

[101] *hom. in 2 Cor.* 25.3 [61.573]: "He piloted the whole world as though it were a single household or boat, pulling out out those who had gone overboard, strengthening the seasick, urging on the sailors, sitting at the rudder, overseeing the bow, tending the lines, handling an oar, stretching the sail, looking at the sky ...." Cf. also *hom. in Ac.* 53.4 [60.372]. In *poenit.* 2.5 [49.290] Paul is himself "a waveless harbor."

[102] *hom. in Ac.* 55.3 [60.383]; *res. mort.* 3 [50.423]; cf. *hom. in 2 Tim.* 3.2 [62.614]: ὁ ἄμαχος καὶ ἀκαταγώνιστος. Conversely, encountering Paul's blurting out of emotion in Gal 4:20, Chrysostom exclaims: "Look at the man who flags, the man hot with emotion, the one who is unable to endure such things!" [ὁ ἀκαρτέρητος, ὁ θερμός, ὁ οὐ δυνάμενος στέγειν τὰ τοιαῦτα] (*comm. in Gal.* 4.3 [61.660]).

depict Paul's immovability: he is "an unshakable tower"[103] and "the pillar of the churches."[104]

Traditional Titles and Roles

Among other biblical epithets, Paul himself would especially have favored Chrysostom's constant reference to him as ὁ ἀπόστολος, "the apostle,"[105] as elsewhere "the first among the apostles,"[106] and "the apostle of the world."[107] Other traditional epithets he uses for Paul are "the imitator of Christ,"[108] "the light, the illuminator of the world,"[109] "the leader of the bride of Christ (the church),"[110] "the spiritual fisherman,"[111] "the excellent ploughman,"[112] "the wise doctor of souls,"[113] "the herald,"[114] "the slave of Jesus Christ,"[115] "the prisoner of Christ,"[116]

---

[103] poenit. 2.5 [49.290]; cf. hom. in 1 Thess. 4.4 [62.421]: ὁ ἀδαμάντινος, ὁ στερρὸς, ὁ ἀκλινής.

[104] ὁ στῦλος τῶν ἐκκλησιῶν (poenit. 2.5 [49.291]; cf. proph. obscurit. 2.5 [56.181]: of Peter and Paul as πύργοι καὶ στῦλοι τῆς ἐκκλησίας).

[105] "When you say 'apostle,' immediately everyone has him in mind" [Ὅταν ἀπόστολον εἴπῃς, εὐθέως πάντες αὐτὸν ἐννοοῦσιν] (hom. in Ac. 55.3 [60.383]). Of hundreds of examples of Paul named as simply ὁ ἀπόστολος, see hom. in Ac. 27.3; 29.4 [60.208, 219]; hom. in Mt. 72.4 [58.672]; Jud. 1.4 [48.849]; hom. in Rom. 4 [51.178–79]; hom. in Ac. 9:1 4.3 [51.149]; ascens. 1 [50.443]. Paul had secured this honor already by the late second and early third centuries, in Irenaeus, Tertullian, and among the Valentinian gnostics (Pagels, The Gnostic Paul, 2, references 11 n. 10).

[106] ὁ πρῶτος τῶν ἀποστόλων (catech. 5.21 [SC 50.211]; hom. in Mt. 3.4 [57.38]; hom. in Ac. 55.3 [60.382], ὁ τὰ πρῶτα κατέχων; cf. Paul's self-reference in 1 Cor 15:9 as "the least of the apostles"). But the title "leader of the apostles" [τῶν ἀποστόλων κορυφαῖος] he usually reserves for Peter (see n. 142 below).

[107] hom. in 1 Thess. 3.1 [62.405], ἀπόστολος τῆς οἰκουμένης.

[108] ὁ τοῦ Χριστοῦ μιμητής (compunct. 1 9 [47.407]).

[109] ὁ τὴν οἰκουμένην φωτίσας (laud. Paul. 4.1 [SC 300.182]); λύχνος ἅψας κατὰ τὴν οἰκουμένην (hom. in Phil. 1:18 4 [51.314]; scand. 20.10 [SC 79.250]); also "the bright lamp" [ἡ λαμπὰς ἡ φαιδρά] (hom. in Ac. 25.1 [60.192]; cf. 31.3 [60.230]).

[110] ὁ νυμφαγωγὸς τοῦ Χριστοῦ (hom. in 2 Cor. 11:1 1 [51.301]; anom. 8.3 [48.772]; virg. 1.1 [SC 125.92]; hom. in Ac. 9:1 4.3 [51.149]; exp. in Ps. 110.4 [55.284]; catech. 4.12 [SC 50.189], and Wenger's observation: "l'expression est fréquente chez Chrysostome"; exp. in Ps. 5 [55.63]). The origin of this epithet is of course Paul's statement in 2 Cor 11:2 (perhaps with some influence of the bridegroom sayings in the gospels [e.g., Matt 9:15; 25:1; John 3:29]).

[111] ἁλιεὺς πνευματικός (hom. in Ac. princ. 4.4 [51.103]). Compare the more specific version of this: "the one who through his letters caught the world in a dragnet" [ὁ δι' ἐπιστολῶν τὴν οἰκουμένην σαγηνεύσας] (poenit. 2.5 [49.290]).

[112] ἀροτὴρ ἄριστος τὸ ἄροτρον ἔχων τῆς διδασκαλίας (Eutrop. 2.14 [52.409]); cf. hom. in Eph. 15.1; 16.2 [62.105, 113]: ὁ μακάριος οὗτος καὶ σοφὸς γεωργός, and, of all the apostles as θαυμάσιοι γεωργοί in hom. in Eph. 23.3 [62.167]).

[113] ὁ σοφὸς τῶν ψυχῶν ἰατρός (hom. in 2 Cor. 4:13 1 [51.271]).

[114] ὁ κῆρυξ (anom. 8.3 [48.772]), as he is called in the pastorals (1 Tim 2:7; 2 Tim 1:11), which is itself a natural formation of an epithet from Paul's own frequent use of the verb κηρύσσειν to describe his ministry (e.g., Rom 10:8, 14–15; 1 Cor 1:23; 9:27; 15:11; 2 Cor 4:5; 11:4; Gal 2:2; 5:11; 1 Thess 2:9). Elsewhere, Chrysostom uses the expression ὁ τῆς οἰκουμένης κῆρυξ (hom. in 1 Cor. 22.2 [61.184]; exp. in Ps. 110.4 [55.284]; hom. in 1 Thess. 3.1 [62.405]), or, even more amplified, ὁ μεγαλοφωνότατος κῆρυξ τῆς ἀληθείας, "the loudest herald of the truth" (subintr. 5 [47.501]).

and "the skilled master builder of the commonwealth of heaven."[117] Events from the autobiographical portions of Paul's letters are easily turned into epithets. The heavenly journey of "a man I know" (which Chrysostom unhesitatingly understands as a Pauline self-reference)[118] described in 2 Corinthians 12 is a favorite of Chrysostom's, which arises ubiquitously in his discussions of Paul.[119] Often he strings several epithets relating to it together: "the one who before the resurrection was snatched up into the third heaven,"[120] "the one who was taken away into paradise," "the one who shared with God in inexpressible mysteries,"[121] "the one who heard and spoke such things which are not lawful for human nature to speak."[122] Chrysostom can also transform argumentative constructs into epithets, as he does in amplifying Paul's "earthen vessel," in the light of historical and further literary development (in this case, the deutero-Pauline 2 Tim 2:20–21): "Paul was an earthen vessel, but he became a golden one."[123] Paul's mystical experiences are also encapsulated in the title "the one who shared in all the terrifying mysteries."[124] John likewise focuses on the hardship catalogues prominent in Paul's own self-

---

[115] Rom 1:1; Gal 1:10; Phil 1:1, a title Chrysostom claims is more esteemed than consul, king, or world ruler (*hom. in Eph.* 8.8 [62.67]).

[116] ὁ δέσμιος τοῦ Χριστοῦ, as in Eph 3:1; 4:1; Phlm 9. In *hom. in Eph.* 8.1 [62.55] Chrysostom engages in dueling epithets to accord praise to Paul: "Being a prisoner for Christ's sake is more magnificent than being an apostle, a teacher, or being an evangelist [Τοῦ ἀπόστολον εἶναι, τοῦ διδάσκαλον εἶναι, τοῦ εὐαγγεσλιστὴν εἶναι, τοῦτο λαμπρότερον, τὸ δέσμιον εἶναι διὰ τὸν Χριστόν]. Indeed, the dignity of this title surpasses that of both emperor and consul, and all others" [Μέγα ἀξίωμα καὶ σφοδρὸν, καὶ βασιλείας καὶ ὑπατείας καὶ πάντων μεῖζον].

[117] ὁ σοφὸς ἀρχιτέκτων τῆς οὐρανίου πολιτείας (*hom. in Rom.* 5:3 4 [51.164]; cf. *anom.* 8.3 [48.772], obviously an adaptation of 1 Cor 3:10, in combination with Phil 3:20). In *Laz.* 6.9 [48.1041] he is himself ὁ ναὸς τοῦ θεοῦ.

[118] As also in *hom. in 2 Cor.* 26.1 [61.575–76], and throughout.

[119] See chap. 6, pp. 301–302.

[120] See, e.g., *proph. obscurit.* 2.4 [56.181]: "the one snatched up into a third heaven, the one who heard inexpressible words" [ὁ εἰς τρίτον ἁρπαγεὶς οὐρανὸν, ὁ ῥήματα ἀκούσας ἄρρητα] (compare also *stat.* 1.3 [49.20], and the next note). Here this particular list is completed by two other ideas, neither of which is used elsewhere, to my knowledge: ὁ πάσας καταπατήσας τὰς ἀνάγκας τῆς φύσεως, ὁ ἐν ἀσφαλείᾳ τελείᾳ λοιπὸν ὤν ("the one who trod upon all the necessities of nature, the one who finally was in perfect security").

[121] ὁ τῶν ἀπορρήτων κοινωνός (*hom. in Rom.* 5:3 2 [51.158]; also in a much more extended form in *hom. in Gen.* 23.7 [53.196]: "The one who was found worthy to hear those inexpressible words which until this day no one else has heard" [ὁ τῶν ἀρρήτων ἐκείνων ῥημάτων ἀκοῦσαι καταξιωθείς, ὧν μέχρι τῆς σήμερον οὐδεὶς ἄλλος ἤκουσε]).

[122] All of these are found in succession in *anom.* 8.3 [48.772]. See also *hom. in Ac.* 9:1 4.3 [51.149], quoted above, p. 71, and *exp. in Ps.* 110.4 [55.284] above, n. 36. As in these examples, very often a reference to one of these epithets will generate the others; they clearly form a cluster in John's thinking.

[123] Σκεῦος ὀστράκινον ἦν ὁ Παῦλος, ἀλλ' ἐγένετο χρυσοῦν. This extended epithet is then itself further elaborated by an antithetically parallel formulation for Jesus's betrayer: "Judas was a golden vessel, but he became an earthen one" [σκεῦος χρυσοῦν ἦν ὁ Ἰούδας, ἀλλ' ἐγένετο ὀστράκινον] (*hom. in 2 Tim.* 6.1 [62.630–31]).

[124] ὁ τῶν φρικτῶν κοινωνήσας μυστηρίων (*exp. in Ps.* 110.4 [55.284]).

representation, terming him "the one who endured imprisonments, beatings and scourges,"[125] "the prisoner,"[126] "the poor man,"[127] "the one who gave himself over to death countless times,"[128] and, adjectivally, "unskilled, naked, barefoot."[129] Chrysostom retells Paul's hardships with a catalogue of his own:

> ... the one who labored greatly, the one who set up thousands of trophies against the devil, the one who walked the earth in the body, the one who ran around earth and sea and air, the one who like some bird went around the world, the one who was stoned, the one who was murdered, the one who was beaten up, the one who suffered all things for the name of God, the one who was called from above by a heavenly voice ...[130]

This passage shows how readily Chrysostom combines epithets from Paul's own letters and Acts into a composite portrait.[131] Some of these are in the form of epithets already in Acts, such as the "vessel of election,"[132] and others he forms from details in Luke's account, such as "the Cilician,"[133] "the Torah student,"[134] and "the tentmaker,"[135] or by transforming a narrative episode into an epithet,

---

[125] ὁ φυλακὰς ὑπομείνας, καὶ πληγὰς καὶ μάστιγας (*poenit.* 2.5 [49.290]).

[126] ὁ δέσμιος, ὁ δεσμώτης, or ὁ δεδεμένος (*hom. in 2 Tim.* 4.3 [62.622], and abundantly elsewhere [see n. 116 above]).

[127] ὁ πένης (as in *hom. in 2 Tim.* 4.3 [62.622], twice).

[128] ὁ μυριάκις ἑαυτὸν θανάτοις ἐκδούς (*laud. Paul.* 3.8 [SC 300.176]).

[129] ἰδιώτης, γυμνός, ἀνυπόδετος (*Eutrop.* 2.14 [52.409]). This accords with the extended description in *hom. in 2 Tim.* 4.3 [62.622]: "A man repeatedly living in famine, and going to sleep hungry, a man naked, not even having anything he might wrap himself in" [Ἄνθρωπος πολλάκις ἐν λιμῷ ζήσας, καὶ κοιμηθεὶς πεινῶν, ἄνθρωπος γυμνός, οὔτε ὅ τι περιβάλοιτο ἔχων].

[130] ὁ πολλὰ κοπιάσας, καὶ μυρία τρόπαια κατὰ τοῦ διαβόλου στήσας, ὁ ἐν σώματι τὴν οἰκουμένην πεζεύσας, ὁ γῆν καὶ θάλατταν καὶ ἀέρα περιδραμών, ὁ καθάπερ ὑπόπτερός τις τὴν οἰκουμένην περιελθών, ὁ λιθασθείς, ὁ φονευθείς, ὁ τυπτηθείς, ὁ πάντα διὰ τὸ ὄνομα τοῦ θεοῦ παθών, ὁ οὐρανίᾳ φωνῇ κληθεὶς ἄνωθεν (*poenit.* 3.4 [49.299–300]).

[131] Another, rather ungainly, epithet which owes much to the Acts narrative is "the one who was being slaughtered for this circumcision, and was slaughtering others" [ὁ γὰρ ὑπὲρ ταύτης τῆς περιτομῆς σφαττόμενος καὶ ἑτέρους ἀποσφάττων], "this is the man whom the cross persuaded to allow circumcision to be equal to non-circumcision" (*comm. in Gal.* 6.4 [61.679]).

[132] E.g., *anom.* 8.3 [48.772] and *hom. in Rom.* 30.3 [60.665], in reference to Acts 18:3 [σκηνοποιός] and 9:15 [σκεῦος ἐκλογῆς]. For the latter epithet see *poenit.* 2.5 [49.290]; *hom. in Ac. 9:1* 4.3 [51.149]; *scand.* 2 [52.482]; *exp. in Ps.* 110.4 [55.284]; *sac.* 4.8 [SC 272.278], τὸ τοῦ Χριστοῦ σκεῦος τὸ ἐκλεκτόν, and further references collected by di S. Maria, "S. Paolo," 496 n. 5, and Piédagnel, SC 300.112–13 n. 2.

[133] ὁ Κίλιξ (*hom. in 2 Tim.* 4.3 [62.622], twice, but only here among Chrysostom's writings). He never calls him ὁ Ταρσεύς (Acts 9:11; 21:39), although he does not doubt Luke's claim that this was Paul's city of origin (see the discussion in chap. 6, pp. 234–35).

[134] ὁ νομομαθής (from Acts 22:3; cf. Gal 1:14): *hom. in 1 Tim.* 3.2 [62.517]; also *hom. in 1 Cor.* 7.3 [61.58]; *hom. in Eph.* 6.2 [62.45]; *hom. in Ac.* 20.1 [60.159]; 32.2 [60.236].

[135] See how he expands Luke's brief mention that Paul was a tentmaker into three epithets: ὁ σκηνοποιός, ὁ σμίλην μεταχειριζόμενος, καὶ δέρματα ῥάπτων, "the tentmaker, the one who handled a knife and sewed skins" (*Eutrop.* 2.14 [52.409]). A similar expansion is found in *laud. Paul.* 4.10, with the addition of references to his place of employment: Ἄνθρωπος ἐπ' ἀγορᾶς ἐσχηκώς ... ὁ ἀγοραῖος, καὶ ἐπὶ ἐργαστηρίου ἑστηκώς, "a man hanging out in the market ... the market-man [or, more derogatorily, "a commoner"], one inhabiting a workshop." John can call

such as "the one who was called by a heavenly voice,"[136] "the one who raises the dead,"[137] or "the one who works thousands of signs."[138] A few other titles which Chrysostom uses for Paul are more rare, and may be his own creations:"the red-hot lover of Christ,"[139] "the foster-father of love,"[140] "the sower of the church,"[141] "the chief of all human beings,"[142] and "the one who has primacy in the kingdom of heaven."[143]

Animal Epithets

A favored class of epithets Chrysostom employs for Paul is the theriomorphic. In addition to the bird image we have already encountered, John likens Paul to other animals. These creations are well-illustrated by this last example in which Chrysostom seeks rhetorically to amplify Paul's greatness by a catalogue of different types of portrait miniatures (and an inserted aporia which accents the breathlessness of the rhetorical progression, and the inherent impossibility of the task):

... the athlete, the general, the gladiator, the lion[144] – I do not know what to say, for

---

Paul a σκυτοτόμος ("leather-cutter") and σκηνοποιός interchangeably (*hom. in 2 Tim.* 4.3 [62.622]). See the discussion of Paul as tentmaker in chap. 6, pp. 246–48.

[136] ὁ οὐρανίᾳ φωνῇ κληθείς (*poenit.* 2.5 [49.290]).

[137] ὁ νεκροὺς ἐγείρων (*hom. in 2 Tim.* 2.1 [62.607]).

[138] ὁ μυρία ἐργαζόμενος σημεῖα (*hom. in 2 Tim.* 2.1 [62.607]).

[139] ὁ διάπυρος ἐραστὴς τοῦ Χριστοῦ (*compunct.* 1 7 [47.404]); also ὁ θερμὸς ἐραστὴς τοῦ Χριστοῦ (*hom. in Gen.* 34.5 [53.319]). In *hom. in Ac.* 6.1 [60.56] John calls Peter ὁ ἐραστὴς τοῦ Χριστοῦ.

[140] ὁ τῆς ἀγάπης τροφεύς (*laud. Paul.* 3.10 [SC 300.180], translated literally "l'éleveur," full context,"qui a fait croître en lui la charité"). My translation follows LSJ and *LPGL* ("one who brings up, foster-father"). Elsewhere Chrysostom uses the similar ὁ τῆς ἀγάπης τρόφιμος (*hom. in Mt. 18:23* 1 [51.17]; *ep. Olymp.* 8.12 [SC 13.138], in connection with 1 Thess 2:17, which Malingrey renders "le noble nourisson de la charité"; also *hom. in Heb.* 3.6 [63.36]; *hom. in Mt. 18:23* 1 [51.17]).

[141] ὁ τῆς ἐκκλησίας φυτουργός (*anom.* 8.3 [48.772]); *hom. in Rom.* 11.5 [60.491]: "Learn from the good sower, who knows all such things accurately, and cultivates the spiritual vine, and tills the whole world" [Μάθε παρὰ τοῦ καλοῦ φυτουργοῦ, τοῦ τὰ τοιαῦτα ἀκριβῶς ἐπισταμένου, καὶ τὴν ἄμπελον τὴν πνευματικὴν θεραπεύοντος, καὶ τὴν οἰκουμένην γεωργοῦντος ἅπασαν] (*LPGL*, 1503 mistakenly ascribes the epithet in this passage to Christ). The source of this image is naturally Paul's own self-depiction as a planter in 1 Cor 3:6–9.

[142] ὁ κορυφαῖος τῶν ἐν ἀνθρώποις ἁπάντων (*exp. in Ps.* 110.4 [55.284]). Elsewhere Paul is chief among the friends of Christ: *hom. in Jo.* 10.1 [59.74]; cf. *hom. in Ac.* 55.3 [60.382], or τοῦ τῶν ἁγίων χοροῦ κορυφαῖος καὶ πρωτοστάτης, "chief and leader of the chorus of the saints" (*hom. in Rom.* 32.2 [60.678]). But the title τῶν ἀποστόλων κορυφαῖος, "chief of the apostles," Chrysostom normally reserves for Peter (and uses quite frequently; see, e.g., *hom. in Mt. 18:23* 3 [51.20]; *hom. in Mt. 26:39* 2 [51.34]; *hom. in Ac. princ.* 2.4 [51.83]), though he sometimes grants it to both (*hom. prec.* 2 [50.784], οἱ κορυφαῖοι τῶν ἀποστόλων, though the genuineness of this sermon is in doubt).

[143] ὁ τὰ πρωτεῖα ἔχων ἐν τῇ βασιλείᾳ τῶν οὐρανῶν (*hom. in Col.* 11.3 [62.377]).

[144] On Paul as a "spiritual lion" [πνευματικὸς λέων] see also *hom. in Rom.* 32.4 [60.680]; *stat.* 8.3 [49.100]; *hom. in 2 Cor.* 25.3 [61.573]:"as a lion roaring and darting out flame from his tongue."

whatever I say will be less than what Paul is worthy of – the hunting-dog, the lion-slayer, the strong bull, the bright lamp, the mouth sufficient for the world.[145]

Literary Analysis of the Epithets

As we have observed throughout this catalogue of epithets Chrysostom uses for Paul, they are based upon several different sources: Paul's self-designations in his own letters, the deliberate refashionings of the Pauline identity in the deutero-Pauline epistles (which Chrysostom regards without suspicion as actual self-references), the portrayal of Paul in the Acts of the Apostles,[146] earlier Christian exegetical and homiletical traditions, and his own imagination. Among these different sources it is important to see how the biblical traditions have been operative in Chrysostom's employment of Pauline epithets, and to appreciate the extent of his own innovations. But this is somewhat more complex than it might appear, for biblical sources can relate to epithets in more than one way. Following the lead of classicists who have investigated epithets of the gods, and justified in adopting their procedure since the Christian Scriptures functioned as a root text in many of the same ways as did Homeric and Hesiodic poetry for later Greek writings,[147] we may identify three general categories of epithets for Paul used by Chrysostom:

1. *"pure" biblical epithets*; i.e., those which appear exactly as they do in the biblical writings;

2. *"derived" biblical epithets*; i.e., those which go back to a biblical text, story or incident but were not couched there in the form of an epithet;

3. *"independent" epithets*; i.e., those which are not linked to a particular aspect of the biblical record. Three sub-types of these have been identified:

  a) those which depend upon an old (but not strictly biblical) tradition;

  b) those which employ everyday or colloquial speech;

  c) neologisms.[148]

---

[145] *hom. in Ac.* 25.1 [60.192]. For a tamer animal identity for Paul than those in this pericope, see *comm. in Gal.* 2.8 [61.646]: "he rendered himself docile for Christ" [εὐήνιον ἑαυτὸν τῷ Χριστῷ κατεσκεύασε].

[146] For a catalogue and analysis of the images of Paul in these sources, see especially the works of Lindemann, *Paulus im ältesten Christentum*; Dassmann, *Der Stachel im Fleisch*; and Rensberger, "As the Apostle Teaches."

[147] For just two sources documenting this point, see, on allegory, Robert Lamberton, *Homer the Theologian: Neoplatonist Allegorical Reading and the Growth of the Epic Tradition* (Berkeley: University of California Press, 1986), and on forms of literary criticism, the wise study of Robert M. Grant, *Heresy and Criticism: The Search for Authenticity in Early Christian Literature* (Louisville, KY: Westminster/John Knox, 1993), especially 15–21.

[148] Here I am adopting the model used by Anne Broger in her analysis of the Homeric and Hesiodic epithets in Sappho and Alcaeus (*Das Epitheton bei Sappho und Alkaios: eine sprachwissenschaftliche Untersuchung* [Innsbrucker Beiträge zur Sprachwissenschaft 88; Innsbruck: Institut für Sprachwissenschaft der Universität Innsbruck, 1996] 253). This overlaps to some degree with the

When applied to Chrysostom's epithets for Paul, this framework of analysis demonstrates the pervasive role of biblical precursors in Chrysostom's portraits of Paul.[149] Interestingly, among Chrysostom's many different epithets for Paul very few are "pure" biblical epithets, such as "vessel of election" (Acts 9:15), "tentmaker" (Acts 18:3, in the plural, of Paul and Aquila and Priscilla), "herald" (1 Tim 2:7; 2 Tim 1:11), "unskilled" (2 Cor 11:6), "naked" (2 Cor 11:27).[150] This is probably due to the fact that Chrysostom's predilection for copious lists of epithets for Paul quickly exhausted the resources of exact biblical epithets. Instead, most frequent among Chrysostom's epithets for Paul are the "derived" biblical epithets, which account for the majority in the collection: "*the* apostle," "the temple of God," "the teacher of the world," "the one who though having nothing possessed it all," "the one who could destroy death by his shadow," "the one who sent diseases flying by his clothing," "the one who stopped the winds in the sea," "the one who was snatched up into the third heaven and entered into paradise," "the athlete of Christ," "the soldier," "the illuminator of the world," "the skilled master-builder of the commonwealth of heaven," "the leader of the bride of Christ." All of these epithets are built either upon self-references in the letters or narrative elements in the letters or Acts, which Chrysostom transforms (sometimes transmogrifies!) into epithets. As regards "independent" or not strictly biblical sobriquets, traditional appellations might include "the spiritual rhetor" or "the heavenly trumpet," both of which are consonant with biblical tradition, but not found in it, *per se*. Quite a few of Chrysostom's embellishments for Paul have wide rhetorical currency in the Greco-Roman world, such as the animal images, and those of the ship-captain or decathlete (the latter of course having biblical roots as well),[151] and thus fit the sub-category of epithets grounded in colloquial speech. Chrysostom's neologisms include his favorite image of Paul as a bird, and his amplification of that image into complex comparisons of Paul with heaven itself. Here his rhetorical extremes, fueled by his ascetic commitments which impel him to regard Paul as having soared above the material world, lead him into new and as yet uncharted

---

content-designated categories of epithets for the Roman gods laid out by Simon Hornblower, in "epithets, divine," *OCD*³, 549: 1) "purely literary descriptions"; 2) "popular descriptions derived either from a special feature (often iconographic) of a deity ... or from a story concerning a deity"; 3) "geographical and local descriptions"; 4) "descriptions indicating association with another deity attested in archaic prayers"; 5) "epithets referring to the civic standing of a deity;" 6) most numerously, "epithets describing the function of a deity or its particular manifestation."

[149] This was also Broger's conclusion about the Lesbian lyric poets: "Dieser Befund macht den dominierenden Einfluss der homerischen Dichtersprache auf die lesbischen Lyriker deutlich" (*Das Epitheton bei Sappho und Alkaios*, 309).

[150] The latter requires a shift from the prepositional phrase, ἐν γυμνότητι, to the adjective, γυμνός.

[151] The ship-captain, for instance, is a famous and recurrent image for leadership in Greco-Roman literature and political philosophy (see Mitchell, *Paul*, 163–64), and athletic exempla are ubiquitous in Greco-Roman literature (see Pfitzner, *Paul and the Agon Motif*).

territory in Pauline onomastics.[152] Chrysostom's other inventions tend to emphasize his own preoccupation with Paul's relationship with Christ ("the warm lover of Christ") and with believers ("the foster-father of love").[153] These neologisms add a nice spice to the mix of Chrysostom's large stock of epithets, but on the whole it is clear that the central source from which Chrysostom takes or develops his epithets for the apostle is the Bible, which provided him with abundant material for these miniature portraits of his favorite saint.

A further distinction among epithets for the Homeric gods may also be useful as we complete our analysis: that between "bound" and "unbound" epithets; that is, epithets which are linked with only one figure (in this case, Paul), as opposed to epithets which are applied to several different persons.[154] This is where the distinctiveness of Chrysostom's depictions of Paul is underscored. First, although on occasion Chrysostom uses strings of epithets for other figures,[155] he gives no other figure quite the level of repeated and elaborate attention he expends on Paul. In regard to bound epithets, most of Chrysostom's derived biblical epithets fit that category, for they contain an image, function or action which already adhered to the apostle in the precursor texts of Scripture. There is some overlap in places between Paul and the other apostles, as for instance where John can refer also to Peter as the "chief of the apostles,"[156] or to all the apostles as "running around the world like a bird,"[157] but these unrestricted instances of such epithets are far less common than the bound epithets. One of Chrysostom's fresh locutions, "the soul which reached as far as heaven," is applied only to Paul among the apostles, but also, interestingly, to one other figure, Elijah.[158] This epithet is reserved by Chrysostom

---

[152] Such extreme epithets also lead to questions about whether Chrysostom's praise for Paul becomes a "Paulology" which competes in some way with his Christology. I shall take up this issue, the theological and rhetorical implications of the rhetorical excesses of Chrysostom's encomia to Paul, in chapter 7, pp. 396–400.

[153] The latter may be a reference to 1 Thess 2:7, or at least an echo of it, in which case it would be a derived epithet.

[154] A criterion usefully employed in Dee, *Epithetic Phrases*, xviii.

[155] See, e.g., *incomprehens.* 4.164–171 [SC 28.242] and *hom. in Ac. 9:1* 1.4 [51.119], of John the evangelist, and *Stag.* 3.11 [47.487], of Elijah, and n. 26 above, for lists of epithets applied to Peter.

[156] τῶν ἀποστόλων ὁ κορυφαῖος (*hom. in Ac. princ.* 2.6 [51.86–87]); compare Paul as the "first among the apostles" [ὁ πρῶτος τῶν ἀποστόλων] (see n. 106, above). Sometimes Chrysostom could attribute to Peter and Paul together the epithets he usually reserves for Paul alone, as in *exp. in Ps.* 109.6 [55.274].

[157] *hom. in Ac.* 1.1 [60.14]. Because these homilies were written late in Chrysostom's life (c. 400), and he had been using the image of a bird running around land and sea for Paul since the time of his homilies on Genesis, which are among his earliest exegetical homilies delivered in Antioch (c. 388, according to Quasten, *Patrology*, 3.434), this appears to be an extension of his normative portrait of Paul to all the apostles in Acts (where, of course, the Pauline portrait dominates).

[158] *Laz.* 3.9 [48.1004]; *Stag.* 3.1 [47.487]; *pan. Bern.* 2 [50.632]; *El. et vid.* 3 [51.340]; *ep. Olymp.* 10.3 [SC 13.158]; *hom. div.* 1.4 [63.465].

for the two persons he regarded as having risen to heaven, the one literally in his chariot, the other through his rigorous, world-denying attitudes. One other epithet is reserved by Chrysostom for these two figures: ἀκατάπληκτος, "a man not to be overcome."[159] The boundedness of these two epithets to this pair demonstrates a consistent linkage in Chrysostom's eyes between the zealous Old Testament prophet and the New Testament apostle (one likely suggested to him by Paul's own invocation of Elijah's self-portrait in Rom 11:3).

Conclusion

The sixty-five different epithets which Chrysostom uses to refer to Paul demonstrate his powerful imagination at work in constructing his subject. Chrysostom did not invent this kind of shorthand encomium – he has precursors in both Greco-Roman literature generally, and in early Christian literature specifically – but he is a highly conspicuous practitioner of this art, particularly for his favorite saint and homiletical obsession, Paul. We can see that he drew upon traditional sources – Paul's letters, the Acts of the Apostles, popular Hellenistic culture, and the work of previous Christian writers – for this undertaking. He freely mixed and matched among these sources, showing more interest in amplification than in homing in on a single, most accurate, miniature.[160] In several instances, however, the disjunction between epithets could well serve Chrysostom's rhetorical purpose: "God called him 'a vessel of election,' but he called himself 'first among sinners.'"[161] In fact it is the pluriform capacity of these epithets to incorporate the apostle Paul into a range of exegetical and homiletical contexts which makes them so useful for the preacher's art. The great variety of epithets which Chrysostom formulated for Paul constitutes a portrait gallery of the apostle who claimed to be "all things to all people" (1 Cor 9:22). The gallery of Pauline portraits[162] in mini-

---

[159] *hom. div.* 1.4 [63.465]. In *laud. Paul.* 1.14 [SC 300.134–36] Chrysostom sets Elijah and Paul in a contest for who displayed the greatest ζῆλος.

[160] The catalogue of portraits we have assembled here, from a range of sources, shows the oversimplification of Dassmann's summary of Chrysostom's image of Paul: "Hinsichtlich des Paulusbildes, das sie schildern, erheben sich einige Bedenken: es ist das Paulusbild der Apostelgeschichte, das im Vordergrund steht, das Bild des Wundertäters und geistlichen Athleten, des Dämonenbezwingers, Barbarenzähmers und Philosophenüberwinders, vermischt mit Reminiszenzen aus den echten Paulusbriefen."

[161] *grat.* 4 [50.659]. In context this serves to show that God is most merciful because he does not remember one's sins (Is 43:25). This is illustrated by the fact that God gave Paul a more flattering epithet than he gave himself (1 Cor 15:9; 1 Tim 1:15). In Eph 3:1 (and 4:1) Paul conspicuously chose the epithet ὁ δέσμιος τοῦ Χριστοῦ Ἰησοῦ instead of one stressing his religious attainments, like ὁ ῥήματα ἄρρητα ἀκούσας, thus proving the superiority of suffering for Christ to miracles in the Christian life (*hom. in Eph.* 8.1 [62.57]).

[162] The complex relationship between *ekphrasis*, interpretation, and architecture in the history of interpretation of Philostratus' *Imagines* has been most insightfully examined by Bryson,

ature has some distinct and identifiable segments, such as the agonistics room, or the aviary room, but also displays much mixing of subjects, topical referents, and sources. Chrysostom's use of epithets in each case depends upon the literary and liturgical contexts of the moment, and also upon the rhetorical interplay between preacher and audience which often leads him to entertain his congregation with long lists of epithets amplifying his point, thus literally filling the liturgical space with multi-colored mental images of the Paul whom he felt became present in the reading and exposition of his words. Therefore, Chrysostom's use of epithets for Paul is not merely an ornament of his liturgical oratory,[163] but serves a herme-neutical purpose rooted firmly in the way he understands the task of Christian preaching. He describes this most overtly in a homily in which he rebukes his congregation for applauding his sermonic skill:

> Go into a painter's study [ζωγραφεῖον], and you will observe how silent all is there. Then so ought it to be here. For here also we are employed in painting portraits, royal portraits [εἰκόνας γράφομεν βασιλικάς], none of any private person, employing the colors of virtue … Moreover, our stylus is the tongue, and the artist the Holy Spirit [γραφὶς τοίνυν ἐστὶν ἡμῖν γλῶττα, τεχνίτης δὲ τὸ πνεῦμα τὸ ἅγιον].[164]

Epithets as portraits in miniature display "the archetype of virtue" for emulation. But imitation of this many-faceted man, Paul, even as it may gain motivation from the profusion of miniature portraits via epithets, can be rendered difficult, if not logically impossible, by the sheer multiplicity of images produced. Slower-moving, more detailed portraits of Paul, which take a microscopic view of his body and his soul, such as we shall examine in the next two chapters, are required for the catechetical and social purposes of transformation to his apostolic likeness, which is the goal of Chrysostom's literary portraiture of Paul. Within Chrysostom's homiletics these epithets serve as shorthand references to the fuller narratives of

---

"Philostratus and the Imaginary Museum," 255–83. In adopting this metaphor, as well as in the way in which I have organized the material collected in this chapter, I am conscious that in a large sense I am the architect and curator of this "resurrected museum" (p. 269) of Pauline portraits. This is because in seeking to analyze Chrysostom's images of Paul and represent them verbally to a scholarly audience, I myself take on the role of the ekphrasist, who provides others with descriptions of artwork. In doing this I am in a sense replicating what Chrysostom himself did (create a unified montage from separate sources), but my purpose and methods are analytical, rather than exhortatory.

[163] It is finally this – restricting the analysis of this material to "style" – that must be respon-sible for Ameringer's impatience with Chrysostom's effluvial style: "These endless enumerations are nothing but an empty display of rhetorical skill, which, though wearisome to a modern reader, must have been highly acceptable to Chrysostom's audience" (*Second Sophistic,* 66). Though he recognizes the entertainment value of the epithet clusters, Ameringer clearly considers this technique an annoying sidelight to Chrysostom's teaching of the gospel truth for which the style should be the vehicle, but should not attract so much attention to itself. However, Ameringer never defends the criteria he uses to deem one image or construct a "turgid sophistic declama-tion" (p. 66) and another "a pastoral ecphrasis of poetical beauty" (p. 80).

[164] *hom. in Ac.* 30.4 [60.227–28].

Scripture, and the wider context formed by Chrysostom's own sermonic expositions of Paul's life, letters and thought. As a shorthand technique, the effectiveness
of the epithets depends upon sustained and continual rehearsal of the meta-narra-
tive to which they refer. These miniatures act as an aide-mémoire for the hearer-
viewer, or furnish a sound bite to stimulate further in-depth encounters with the
subject in all his multitudinous grandeur (hence as advertisements of future homiletical possibilities). Consequently, the biblical context is not the only one operative within Chrysostom's portraits of Paul. Since his homilies contain multiple
extended portraits of the apostle, as we shall see in the next three chapters, many of
which correspond with the miniatures catalogued here, Chrysostom's own oratorical context for these epithets ensured a rich reservoir of imaginative furnish-
ings for each of these shorthand portraits already stowed away in the minds of his
auditors. In other words, the "crash course" in Pauline portraiture effected by the
epithets can only be fully understood in light of the full-scale, life-size portraits of
Paul to which the shorthand verbal images make reference.

We have a precise visual counterpart to these literary epithets in the abbreviated
versions of the tale of Paul inspiring John that medieval artists managed to encapsulate into a single outsized initial kappa. In these miniatures the full legend is
compressed into one letter, formed by an upright Paul inspiring his devoted interpreter, who is seated, hunched over his writing.[165] The final stroke of this narrative
expressed in one letter, as found in the medieval Menologion, *British Library Add.
36636,* is formed by the apostle's arm, which points to heaven [see Plate 6].

---

[165] For two examples, see Appendix 2, nos. 5 and 6.

Chapter 4

"The Imperial Portrait" (εἰκὼν βασιλική) Unveiled: Portraits of Paul's Body

Full-Scale Portraits of Paul – Three Types

Chrysostom's insistent attention to the person of Paul found expression, not only in miniature renderings of Paul via epithets, but also in more extended portraits of the complete person, Paul. These do more than flash an image before the eyes of the listener; instead they dwell lovingly on the figure of Paul in careful detail, sketching piece by piece a holistic portrait. The full-scale depictions assume one of two distinct types -- somatic portraits and psychic portraits – reflecting then-current anthropology and rhetorical convention. The body portraits are composite in nature, wherein Chrysostom portrays Paul by an intricate description of individual body parts, taken up and sketched individually in attentive relation to all available evidence in biblical lore. Chrysostom's portraits of Paul's soul, on the other hand, tend not to be composite so much as separate depictions of individual virtues possessed by his uniquely endowed soul. In these respects Chrysostom's distinct portraits of Paul's body and soul correspond to ancient theories of portraiture and rhetorical composition,[1] the combination of which was thought necessary to capture accurately the mystery of a living human person.[2] Chapters 4 and 5 will be devoted to the body portraits and soul portraits, respectively. But before turning to the images of the *corpus Paulinum* which will occupy us in this chapter, we must first situate them in literary and cultural history.

---

[1] In Lucian's dialogue *Imagines*, and the companion piece, *pro Imaginibus*, we find these two types of portraiture delineated and exemplified. The same division between the topics of body and soul was made in rhetorical theory, as we shall demonstrate below.

[2] See Lucian, *Imagines* 23: "Let us put our portraits together, the statue that you modelled of her body and the pictures that I painted of her soul [ἀναμίξαντες ἤδη τὰς εἰκόνας, ἥν τε σὺ ἀνέπλασας τὴν τοῦ σώματος καὶ ἃς ἐγὼ τῆς ψυχῆς ἐγραψάμην]; let us blend them all into one [μίαν ἐξ ἁπασῶν συνθέντες], put it down in a book, and give it to all mankind to admire, not only to those now alive, but to those that shall live hereafter."

The Tools of Portrayal

Epideictic Rhetoric (the Encomium)[3]

The literary style and structure of Chrysostom's portraits of Paul's body and soul were determined by the epideictic species of rhetoric he employed.[4] With roots extending to fifth-century classical Athens, this form of rhetoric has as its central purpose the praise or vituperation of persons in public oratory that seeks to impress upon its hearers the salutary nature of the shared values the subject of the speech exemplified, and to stir them to fervent response in kind. Epideictic rhetoric, comprising encomia to persons, was literally "show rhetoric," the settings for which were highly scripted and formalized social situations: festivals, birthday celebrations, funerals, weddings, and oratorical competitions. This species of rhetoric is discussed and prescribed in all the Greco-Roman rhetorical handbooks from the fourth century B.C.E. into the Roman imperial period (Aristotle, Anaximenes, Cicero, Quintilian, Theon), and up to Chrysostom's own contemporaries (Aphthonios and, a century earlier, Menander).[5] The genre had famous prototypes which were endlessly retaught and reenacted in the progymnasmata (rhetorical exercises) of the Greco-Roman *paideia*, such as Pericles' funeral oration (Thuc. 2.34ff.) and Demosthenes ἐπιτάφιος ("funeral oration" [*Or.* 60]), which Chrysostom would

---

[3] On the relationship between encomium and biography see chap. 6, n. 17, and the summary discussion in chap. 7, 404–407.

[4] Ameringer's study (*Second Sophistic*) remains the classic on the style of Chrysostom's panegyrics, but it is lacking in treatment of the invention and arrangement of these speeches. These elements of rhetorical design were taken up by Hubbell, "Chrysostom and Rhetoric," 261–76, and Wilken, *John Chrysostom and the Jews*, 95–127. Hubbell's essay is especially important for our study because he focuses on Chrysostom's encomia to Paul. He concludes that these "illustrate a very free use of laudatory material. The comparison, the exaltation of the subject, the grouping of the events to illustrate characteristics, all are here. However, none of them conform as do the orations of Gregory of Nazianzus to the rules for the elaborate memorial addresses" (p. 274). Nevertheless, the lack of the exact rhetorical arrangement [τάξις] of an ἐπιτάφιος, "funeral oration," in Chrysostom's liturgical homilies should not lead us to overestimate his independence from the form. As we shall demonstrate, the *topoi* and, most of all, the logic of epideictic rhetoric pervade his entire enterprise of Pauline portraiture. What I hope to add to Hubbell's brief study, in addition to more detailed analyses, is fuller attention to the ways in which Chrysostom's encomia to Paul *presume* encomiastic standards which they are deliberately playing off of (rather than a too mechanical search for the precise forms themselves). The influence of classical epideictic rhetoric on late fourth-century panegyrics (the Cappadocians and Chrysostom), especially in regard to *inventio*, was established in the important study by Delehaye, *Les passions des martyrs*, 133–69, but unfortunately he did not discuss Chrysostom's encomia to Paul.

[5] For an overview of these sources, see Theodore C. Burgess, *Epideictic Literature* (The University of Chicago Studies in Classical Philology; Chicago: University of Chicago Press, 1902); D. A. Russell and N. G. Wilson, *Menander Rhetor* (Oxford: Clarendon, 1981), "Introduction: Epideictic Practice and Theory," pp. xi–xxxiv; George A. Kennedy, *Greek Rhetoric Under Christian Emperors* (Princeton: Princeton University Press, 1983) 23–27, 52–132; Mitchell, *Paul*, 213–21; still valuable is Richard Volkmann, *Die Rhetorik der Griechen und Römer in systematischer Übersicht* (repr. ed.; Hildesheim: Georg Olms, 1987 [original Leipzig: Teubner, 1885]) 314–61.

have learned in his early education, and practiced under the eye of his teacher of rhetoric, Libanios.[6] The remarkable similarities which extend across this swath of literary history indicate a well-worn but stable cultural form and social practice which was a solid backbone of Hellenistic civic and social life.

In addition to rooting Chrysostom in the classical literary tradition, his fondness for the art of epideictic rhetoric situates him within a widespread development in Christian oral and literary culture in his time. By the late fourth century Christian bishops, such as the Cappadocians (who like John shared the rhetorical education of their "pagan" contemporaries), were reputable public practitioners of the genre,[7] having adapted it to their own subject matter of Christian worthies past and present, as well as for the liturgical settings of their Christian pulpit oratory.

Nevertheless, when practised by others, the Christian oratory of the fourth century was heard. More than that, the great Christian speeches of the later part of the century, like those by Gregory of Nyssa on Bishop Meletius or on Gregory's brother Basil, gave a new meaning to public oratory. In the revived urban culture of the fourth century, Christian bishops succeeded to the place of the epideictic orators of the Second Sophistic; and their speeches were more political than the earlier ones ever could be.[8]

Chrysostom's oeuvre includes plentiful encomia to saints and holy figures, many of which were delivered on the holy days marking their commemoration in the liturgical year (such as the Maccabean martyrs, Job, Ignatius, Babylas, Diodore of Tarsus).[9] The most famous and conspicuous among these are his unparalleled *seven* such orations for Paul. But John also incorporated epideictic rhetoric (as had been done since its inception) within a variety of other host genres, launching into encomia to Paul in the midst of orations devoted to completely different subjects. This could also happen during his exegetical homilies, when an utterance in a Pauline letter or an event in Acts could spur him to utter Paul's praises as a complement to and, often, further validation of, the text.[10]

---

[6] Libanios was himself well known for his epideictic orations. Among his sixty-four orations are famous encomia: *Laudatio Constantii et Constantis* (*Or.* 49 [Foerster 4.209–96]), *Antiochicus* (*Or.* 11 [Foerster 1.437–535]), and his massive epitaphios (funeral oration) for Julian (*Or.* 18 [Foerster 2.236–71]). Nine encomia are included amoung his surviving progymnasmata (*Enc.* [Foerster 8.216–77]), proving decisively the place of this form in his pedagogical curriculum.

[7] One naturally thinks of such classics as Gregory of Nazianzus' encomium to Basil, as well as that of Gregory of Nyssa, who also composed encomia to St. Stephen, Melitios, Theodore, and Gregory Thaumatourgos. For a wider catalogue, see Burgess, *Epideictic Literature,* 240–44; Hubbell, "Chrysostom and Rhetoric," 262–67; and Kennedy, *Greek Rhetoric under Christian Emperors,* 180–264. The connection between these Christian writers and the orators of the second sophistic was stressed by Wilken, *John Chrysostom and the Jews,* 95–106.

[8] Cameron, *Christianity and the Rhetoric of Empire,* 135. For similar statements, see Brown, *Power and Persuasion,* 75–76, and earlier Delehaye, *Passions des martyrs,* 137: "C'est par ces hommes, doués d'un rare talent et pour qui la sophistique contemporaine n'avait point de secrets, que l'art profane fut adapté au service de l'Église."

[9] For a list of Chrysostom's panegyrics, see Quasten, *Patrology,* 3.456–57.

[10] It is this realization, which comes from a wider reading in Chrysostom's corpus of writings, that aids one's perspective in assessing the seven homilies *de laudibus sancti Pauli* which, despite

The genre of epideictic rhetoric is based upon anthropological and philosophical assumptions about human persons, as well as upon principles of physiognomy, on the one hand, and political theory (the macrocosm of the human person), on the other. While the conventions of epideictic rhetoric do not in themselves dictate the totality of the meaning of human existence as its practitioner understands it[11] (as is quite obvious since Platonic, Stoic, Epicurean and Christian authors were able to use the genre with equal, interchangeable ease), what they do indicate is the topics one is expected to speak about or at least select from (one always deletes topics that do not work to one's rhetorical advantage) when pronouncing an encomium on a person. The rhetorical handbooks provide a skeletal framework for how one pronounces public praise of a person. There is general agreement among the theorists and practitioners of the art that in praising a person one can assemble the material under three basic categories: praise of a person's soul, praise of his or her body, and praise of his or her "external circumstances."[12] In order to understand Chrysostom's encomiastic portraits of Paul's body and soul, we shall look at a prescriptive recipe for spoken praise from his contemporary – and perhaps schoolmate –[13] the rhetor Aphthonios:

Now this is the division of the encomium [ἐγκώμιον]. You should compose it under such topics [κεφάλαια] as these: You will introduce it by setting forth the subject [ὑπόθεσις]. Then you will put origin [γένος], which you will divide into nation [ἔθνος], fatherland [πατρίς], relatives [πρόγονοι] and parents [πατέρες]; then upbringing [ἀνατροφή], which you will divide into accomplishments [ἐπιτηδεύματα] and skills [τέχναι] and laws [νόμοι]. Then you will construct the greatest topic [τὸ μέγιστον κεφάλαιον] of the encomia – deeds [πράξεις], which you will divide into soul [ψυχή] and body [σῶμα] and chance [τύχη]. In terms of soul, treat courage [ἀνδρεία] and wisdom [φρόνησις]; of body, beauty [κάλλος] or swiftness [τάχος] or strength [ῥώμη]; of chance, power [δυναστεία] and wealth [πλοῦτος] and friends [φίλοι]. And for all of these things introduce the comparison [σύγκρισις], something great [τὸ μεῖζον] to compare with the subject of your encomium [ὁ ἐγκωμιαζόμενος]. Then a suitable conclusion [ἐπίλογος], especially with prayer [εὐχή].[14]

---

their lack of epideictic arrangement, still largely depend upon the logic and commonplaces of the form. This mitigates sharply against some of the conclusions of Piédagnel, SC 300.21–38, that Chrysostom eschewed these forms because of their "pagan" nature. I hope here to demonstrate that Chrysostom was instead creatively and deliberately drawing upon these conventions as he spoke, and that the epideictic conditioning of his congregations was an essential given, with and against which the orator played.

[11] As was recently argued Bruce J. Malina and Jerome Neyrey in *Portraits of Paul: An Archaeology of Ancient Personality* (Louisville: Westminster/John Knox, 1996). See my critique of this position in my review (*JR* 78 [1998] 611–13).

[12] *Laus igitur potest esse rerum externarum, corporis, animi* ([Cicero], *Rhet. Her.* 3.6.10). See the extensive list of ancient writers corroborating this division, who stretch from Plato and Aristotle to Apsines, that are collected by Harry Caplan in the LCL edition, p. 174 note a.

[13] He was a pupil of Libanios (Russell and Wilson, *Menander Rhetor*, xxviii n. 71), as was Chrysostom.

[14] Aphthonios, *Progymnasmata* 8 [Spengel 2.36]. Compare also Burgess, *Epideictic Literature*, 134–36, where he analyzes two imperial panegyrics by Libanios, the common teacher of John

There were, of course, some minor disputes among theoreticians and orators about both the proper arrangement [τάξις] of an encomium, and the range of topics and ladder of classifications within which they are placed.[15] But the overall structure of praise of a person's life under the topics of body, soul and circumstances was common to the rhetorical tradition. Hence it is no surprise that it was adapted and employed by Chrysostom in his many attempts to laud his favorite saint, Paul, as it correspondingly constituted the set of expectations which his audiences brought to his discourses. Because this three-fold division of praise – for body, soul, and external circumstances – is the literary model operative in Chrysostom's historical context, and in his compositions, we have arranged our analysis of his laudatory portraits of Paul accordingly. This chapter is devoted to John's images of Paul's body, chapter 5 to those of his soul, and chapter 6 to the broad array of topics concerning chance and life circumstances.[16]

When Chrysostom composed portraits of Paul's body he was not interested in Paul's historical likeness in a modern sense,[17] but confined his discussion to the legendary characteristics of the parts of Paul's body. Indeed, he did not even make use of what sources were available to him in this regard.[18] For example, Chrysostom never gives a detailed description of Paul's face,[19] nor does he make reference

---

and Aphthonios, in comparison with the rhetorical theory of Menander. The Latin treatise attributed to Cicero includes most of these same topics (Rhet. Her. 3.6.10; for the Platonic and Aristotelian roots of the schema see the long list of references in Caplan's LCL ed. of the work, p. 174, note a).

[15] For instance, Theon has three major categories: external circumstances, body, and soul, with subcategories of the latter being the virtues, and the deeds which spring from them (Prog. 8 [Spengel 2.109], quoted in chap. 6, p. 200). Even Aphthonios' long list is probably only meant to be illustrative, since he has included only two of the customary four cardinal virtues under the category of soul (missing are justice and temperance).

[16] In his valuable essay, when Hubbell compared Chrysostom's encomia to the three part division of praise advocated by Theon, he remarked: "So far there is little which would afford material for the Christian encomiast. Nobility of birth, power in the state, wealth, and even the physical virtues of health and beauty were not the ends sought by the early Church ... ("Chrysostom and Rhetoric," 264). Our investigation will demonstrate the reverse: that Chrysostom the Christian orator drew upon these divisions abundantly, just in a more paradoxical and ironic way than Hubbell quite appreciated.

[17] This accords with all contemporary panegyrics to martyrs: "[les orateurs] montrent assez qu'ils n'attachent guère d'importance à connaître et à dépeindre la physionomie exacte du saint" (Delehaye, Passions des martyrs, 168).

[18] For instance, in other places, because of 2 Cor 10:10, Chrysostom acknowledges that the presence of Paul's body was "easily despised, and not in a state of health" [εὐκαταφρόνητος καὶ οὐδὲν ἔχουσα κομψόν; note that some mss. read instead κομπόν, "something to boast about" [Field 2.444 note p.] (hom. in 1 Cor. 35.5 [61.303]), though this "fact" figures not at all in the full-scale portraits of Paul's body that we shall be examining.

[19] Once he does say of Paul's face that it was "gracious" [τὸ πρόσωπον τὸ χάριεν] (hom. in Ac. 43.2 [60.305]), and in another by inference it appears that he regards Paul as having been ἀξιοπρεπής, "becoming," along with Barnabas (hom. in Ac. 30.3 [60.224]). Chrysostom did have some mental impression of Paul's face, as he says in poenit. 2.5 [49.291] that "Paul's face enlightens my mind" [τὸ πρόσωπον Παύλου καταυγάζει μου τὴν διάνοιαν], though he does not

to the infamous features of the Pauline visage in *Acta Pauli et Theclae* – baldness, long nose and knit-eyebrows – though he knew that narrative.[20] Chrysostom's intent in these passages is thoroughly epideictic: to praise the apostle and summon his hearers to imitate him. In this quest he freelances little outside of the biblical tradition in composing and assembling these body parts, but draws upon the literary references in Paul's letters or the Acts of the Apostles, or characteristic activities of Paul inscribed there to form his descriptions.[21] These portraits are not physiognomic exercises in the strict sense (i.e., establishing a one-to-one correspondence between physical attributes and character assets and defects), but they do share with that field of ancient scientific lore a preoccupation with the question of the relationship between the physical form of the human body and its ethical character.[22] The rhetorical purpose of the portraits of Paul's body which Chrysostom composes – in common with all ancient portraiture – was not to cast the material body in isolation from the totality of the person, but ultimately, through a rendering of the body, to capture the whole of the human subject,[23] often in a narrative

---

ever offer a description of it. In contrast, Plutarch, in describing literary portraiture by analogy to painting, says that painters take up their likenesses of subjects from their faces and the shapes around the face [ἀπὸ τοῦ προσώπου καὶ τῶν περὶ τὴν ὄψιν εἰδῶν], the site where character is displayed, and pay much less attention to the other body parts (*Alex.* 1.3).

[20] He makes explicit mention of the work in *hom. in Ac.* 25.4 [60.198]. Neither does Chrysostom refer to Paul's crooked legs, another characteristic of Paul's body found in the famous passage *A. Paul. et Thecl.* 3, although, in common with that work, he apparently did think that Paul was short in stature, though he did not express it in the same language (compare *poenit.* 2.5 [49.290] and *compunct.* 2 2 [47.413]: τὸ μὲν γὰρ σῶμα βραχὺς ἦν, with *A. Paul. et Thecl.* 3: ἀνὴρ μικρὸς τῷ μεγέθει (Richard Adelbert Lipsius, ed., *Acta Apostolorum Apocryphorum* [Hildesheim: Olms, 1891, repr. 1959] 1.237)]). For important analyses of that earliest complete physical description of Paul as reflecting different ancient physiognomic types, see Robert M. Grant, "The Description of Paul in the Acts of Paul and Thecla," *VC* 36 (1982): 1–4; Abraham J. Malherbe, "A Physical Description of Paul," *Christians Among Jews and Gentiles. Essays in Honor of Krister Stendahl on His Sixty-fifth Birthday*, ed. G. W. E. Nickelsburg and G. W. MacRae (Philadelphia: Fortress, 1986) 170–75; Malina-Neyrey, *Portraits of Paul*, 100–52.

[21] "When it is impossible to model a person from life, we have the reconstructed portrait, which seeks imaginatively to do justice to the subject's characteristics on the basis of elements drawn from literary sources or tradition. It follows, however, that in this way we can create different images of the same individual" (D. Mazzoleni, "Portrait," *EEC* 2.705).

[22] See Gleason, *Making Men*, 29, on the zoological, ethnographic and dispositional theories of physiognomic speculation: "The argument on the whole depends upon the premise that there exists a certain *sympathy* between the soul and the body." Malina-Neyrey have recently made an application of ancient physiognomics to Paul (*Portraits of Paul*, 100–5), but their depiction of physiognomic determinism in antiquity as universally acknowledged needs correction (see Mitchell, "Review of Malina and Neyrey," 612).

[23] "By portrait is meant the reproduction from life of an individual's image, seen in its contingent reality. In a true portrait, imitation of physical likeness is completed by a search for psychological traits; in this way we pass from the facial, merely realistic, portrait to the more complete, physiognomical, portrait" (Mazzoleni, "Portrait," 704–5). This is generally recognized in art history; see Gisela M. A. Richter, "Greek Portraits: A Study of Their Development," *Collection Latomus* 20 (1955) 12: "A portrait as we understand it is the representation of an individual. The artist must penetrate into the characteristics of a particular person and reproduce

context which displays the person's "true blue" character.[24] As such Chrysostom does not engage directly in physiognomics, though his enterprise and his sources are permeated with some of the values and conventions underlying that discipline, as was all epideictic oratory.

Through the form of the encomium an orator praises an individual for his or her attainment of excellence as defined according to culturally established norms. We shall find that although Chrysostom's use of epideictic rhetoric echoes classical exemplars of his day and far earlier, he has of necessity adapted the values by which he forms his praise, for three reasons: the nature and life-history of his subject (to which an orator must always selectively fit the form), the material he had to work with (letters in which Paul himself stresses paradoxically his bodily weakness against his detractors),[25] and the distinct virtues he seeks to inculcate in his hearers. The customary things for which a body was expected to be praised were tidily summed up by the rhetorician Theon: health, strength, beauty and keen perception.[26] These virtues, however, are not what structure Chrysostom's portraits of Paul's body, except insofar as he is in the process (as was his subject) of redefining the standards by which a Christian ought to define and evaluate these cultural standards. And, not surprisingly, again it is Chrysostom's asceticism and Christian Stoicism which dictate what he views as genuinely important and praiseworthy in a body.

---

these in a way that sums up his individuality. To show the shape of his eyes or mouth, the form of his skull, or even the wrinkles or warts, is not enough. Something more intangible must be caught." Richter regards a pervasive fascination with the human self as typical of Greek culture, which was given expression from the early classical period in both the graphic and literary arts: "That the Greeks were able to penetrate into human nature sufficiently to reproduce a particular person, not in a photographic likeness, but in a portrait that summed up the character of a man, and to develop this art from century to century is one of their subtlest and most important achievements. It ranks with and is akin to the creation of the characters in Greek drama. Aeschylus' Clytemnestra, Sophokles' Oedipus, Euripides' Medea are the contemporary literary counterparts of the earliest Greek sculptured portraits. All spring from the same interest in that intricate phenomenon – the human individual" (ibid., 12).

[24] Chrysostom shows himself acutely aware of this as shown, for instance, in the antithetical portraits Chrysostom paints of a drunken and an abstemious woman, where in both cases the virtue or vice is imprinted on her bodily form. The woman who renounces strong drink appears "a more beautiful, well-bred woman. For the character of the soul imparts great beauty to the body [καὶ γὰρ τῷ σώματι πολὺ περιτίθησι κάλλος τῆς ψυχῆς ἡ κατάστασις]. Do not think that this beauty comes from the bodily features alone" [μὴ γὰρ δὴ νομίσῃς ἀπὸ τῶν σωματικῶν τύπων τοῦτο γίνεσθαι μόνον] (hom. in Ac. 27.2 [60.207]).

[25] Thus, for example, in laud. Paul. 6.2 [SC 300.264]: "The apparent weakness of Paul's nature is itself the greatest proof of his virtue" [Αὐτὴ γὰρ ἡ δοκοῦσα τῆς φύσεως εἶναι ἀσθένεια, αὐτὴ μέγιστον δεῖγμα τῆς ἀρετῆς ἐστι τῆς ἐκείνου].

[26] ὑγεία, ἰσχὺς, κάλλος, εὐαισθησία (Prog. 8 [Spengel 2.110]; discussion in Burgess, Epideictic Rhetoric, 121).

Ekphrasis

Rather than a thorough physiognomic work-up, or a standard encomium to bodily beauty and strength, in the portraits of Paul's body we shall consider Chrysostom adopts and ingeniously adapts a very specific rhetorical form (or sub-form), the *ekphrasis* [ἔκφρασις]. Rhetorical theorists, including Aphthonios, defined *ekphrasis* as "a descriptive discourse which visibly brings the object being manifested before one's eyes."[27] In essence, it was "a painting in words."[28] Although it was a conventional saying that poetry and oratory were word paintings of a sort,[29] ἔκφρασις focused this general insight into a specific literary form with its own rhetorical conventions and attendant expectations. The genre ἔκφρασις was not fixed, but it was recognized as having links with the related forms of *topos*, narrative and encomium, often being incorporated within the latter.[30] As expertly practiced, *ekphrasis* "almost makes the things depicted visible to the sight."[31] John

---

[27] Ἔκφρασις ἐστὶ λόγος περιηγηματικὸς ἐναργῶς ὑπ' ὄψιν ἄγων τὸ δηλούμενον (first cited by Theon, *Prog.* 11 [Spengel, 2.118], and quoted verbatim also by Hermogenes, *Prog.* 10 [Rabe 6.22]), and Aphthonios, in his *Prog.* 12 [Spengel, 2.46]). *Ekphrasis* also bears a relation to the form of characterization or portrayal (*effictio*; *Rhet. Her.* 4.49.63): "Verwandt mit der Ekphrasis und ihr in mancher Hinsicht ähnlich sind der εἰκονισμός und der χαρακτηρισμός, die auf Beschreibungen der äußeren Erscheinung des Charakters einer Person und solche von Ereignissen beschränkt sind" (Glanville Downey, "Ekphrasis," *RAC* 5 [1959] 921–44, 923; similarly R. Brändle, "Johannes Chrysostomus I," *RAC* 139/40 [1997] 448). See also Henry Maguire, *Art and Eloquence in Byzantium* (Princeton: Princeton University Press, 1981), 22–52; and the illuminating analysis of Elsner, *Art and the Roman Viewer*, 21–39.

[28] These words are Ameringer's (*Second Sophistic*, 86), reflecting the ancient cliché documented in the next note.

[29] For example, Philostratus the Younger, *Imagines* proem., states: "the art of painting is found to have a certain kinship with poetry, and common to both is imagination" [ξυγγένειάν τινα πρὸς ποιητικὴν ἔχειν ἡ τέχνη εὑρίσκεται καὶ κοινή τις ἀμφοῖν εἶναι φαντασία]. Hadot describes the ἐκφράσεις of Philostratus using this precise language: "Le discours déclamé par Philostrate est donc une 'peinture parlante' puisque les paroles y remplacent les formes et les couleurs" ("Préface," xv). See discussion and further references in chap. 2, n. 31.

[30] See Liz James and Ruth Webb, "'To Understand Ultimate Things and Enter Secret Places': Ekphrasis and Art in Byzantium," *Art History* 14 (1991) 1–17, 6: "there seems to have been some debate in antiquity as to whether ekphrasis should even be an exercise in its own right or whether it should not rather be included under the headings of narrative, commonplace or encomion. Ekphrasis was thus essentially a technique for vividly presenting a subject which could be used in various types of composition." The *ekphrasis* was particularly associated with encomium in the early handbooks because it was another of the progymnasmata, though in the fifth century C.E. Nikolaos said it could be used in any of the three species of rhetoric (*Prog.* 12 [Spengel 3.492–93]). The specific topic of ἔκφρασις of a person has a particular suitability to encomia (though it could also play a key role in accusation and defense) because of its provision for treatments of the body [σῶμα]. An important function played by an ἔκφρασις is that it gives the audience a diversion and rest from the overall argument of the speech, a lovely place to linger (as emphasized by Wilken, *John Chrysostom and the Jews*, 109–10).

[31] τοῦ σχεδὸν ὁρᾶσθαι τὰ ἀπαγγελλόμενα (Theon, *Prog.* 11 [Spengel, 2.119]; cf. Hermogenes, *Prog.* 10: δεῖ γὰρ τὴν ἑρμηνείαν διὰ τῆς ἀκοῆς σχεδὸν τὴν ὄψιν μηχανᾶσθαι, "for it is necessary that the diction through the hearing almost fashion the vision").

surely learned this form in his rhetorical education, for his writings are conspicuous for its employment[32] (as were those of his teacher, Libanios).[33] The most frequently discussed late antique *ekphraseis* are those dedicated to the literary description of works of art – paintings, statues, and architecture in particular[34] – but recent scholarship has called for a reexamination of the form as a rhetorical composition with its own discrete functions, modes and effects which go far beyond what we might term "objective description."[35] Rhetorical theory confirms this broadened perspective of the form ἔκφρασις, for it recognized a list of suitable subjects of *ekphrasis* ("paintings," interestingly enough, are not among those specifically named until the fifth century),[36] the first of which is our concern here: "persons" [πρόσωπα].[37] An ἔκφρασις of a person, or of an artistic rendering of a

---

[32] Many examples of *ekphraseis* in Chrysostom's writings have been collected by Delehaye (*Les passions des martyrs*, 154–63), and Ameringer (*Second Sophistic*, 86–100), who attributes its frequency to the predominant influence upon Chrysostom of the sophistic movement ("But the fondness for concrete and graphic representation, of which [metaphors and comparisons] are the expression, reveals itself in Chrysostom by a form of exposition which is essentially sophistic, the Ecphrasis … It is not surprising that the Christian orators of the fourth century should adopt a device so well calculated to impart life and color to their discourses and so acceptable to the public. Moreover, the topics of their sermons, such as the harrowing spectacles of martyrdom, the dramatic scenes of the Old and New Testament, the grandeur and beauty of the universe, invited and fully justified graphic portrayal" [p. 86]). Chrysostom's exceptional fondness for *ekphrasis*, even among fourth-century Christian practitioners of the art, such as the Cappadocians, was noted also by G. Downey, "Ekphrasis," *RAC* 5 (1959) 933–34, 936: "Johannes Chrysostomos, der die klassische Ekphrasis übernahm und sie für christliche Zwecke auswertete, verwendete sie verschwenderischer und in größerer Mannigfaltigkeit als irgendein Autor."

[33] In addition to extensive *ekphraseis* among his sixty-four orations (such as his famous description of the city of Antioch in *Or.* 11), there are over thirty *ekphraseis* attributed to Libanios and included among his progymnasmata (*Desc.* [Foerster 8.460–546]); while a majority are not authentic, at least the first seven are (A. F. Norman, LCL vol. 1, *Libanius, Selected Works*, xlix).

[34] Three of the most famous works are the *Imagines* by Philostratus the elder and junior (his grandson), and the *Statuarum descriptiones* of Callistratus. For full references and bibliography see Downey, "Ekphrasis," who also discusses the pre-history of this rhetorical genre from Homer (the quintessential example being the description of Achilles' shield [*Il.* 18.483f.]), to the sophists of the first to third centuries C.E., and well beyond. The form becomes especially prominent in the Byzantine period in the hands of such writers as Procopios of Gaza and Photios of Constantinople, whose *ekphraseis* of artistic monuments are often the chief sources we have for many missing artifacts and edifices (the same is true for many fourth-century shrines described by Eusebius).

[35] James-Webb, "To Understand Ultimate Things," 1–17. *Ekphraseis* must be understood as rhetorical constructions which "represent a living response to works of art, and one which is perceptual rather than objectively descriptive" (p. 3; a point made already by Arthur Fairbanks in his 1931 introduction to the LCL edition of the Philostrati and Callistratus, pp. xxi–ii: "[Philostratus] is simply trying to outdo the paintings he describes in this appeal to the emotions … we have no right to expect literal and complete descriptions by which the paintings could be reconstructed in detail."This point has been aptly underscored more recently by Elsner, *Art and the Roman Viewer*, 21–39.

[36] James-Webb, "To Understand Ultimate Things," 6.

[37] "One can compose an ekphrasis for both persons and things, seasons and places, unspeaking creatures and with them plants" [ἐκφραστέον δὲ πρόσωπά τε καὶ πράγματα, καιρούς

person, sought primarily to convey a subject's very soul and character by a recreation of his or her physical appearance.[38] Most distinctive about the ἔκφρασις was its foremost persuasive purpose: to affect the audience, by turning them from hearers to spectators, and "to recreate for the listener the effect of its subject on the viewer, who is the speaker."[39] The personal testimony of the speaker, as one who is face to face with the work of art or person described, is a major element in Chrysostom's vivid depictions of Paul, also, for he quite self-consciously speaks in the first person about his emotional responses to the Paul whom he conjures up. The essential role of the speaker indicates a further area of similarity between late antique ἐκφράσεις and Chrysostom's interpretive enterprise: both are literary texts which were used in oral performances, the scripts of one-man shows replicating and recreating absent realities and persons.[40] Consequently, it was the perfect vehicle for John's rhetorical and catechetical purpose: to orchestrate through his preaching a living encounter between Paul and his hearers which would generate the same loving response he himself felt for the apostle, which, he hoped, would lead to deeper emulation of that model of virtue.[41] Chrysostom himself brings his

---

τε καὶ τόπους, ἄλογα ζῶσα καὶ πρὸς τούτοις φυτά] (Aphthonios, *Prog.* 12 [Spengel 2.46]). Cf. Theon, *Prog.* 11 [Spengel 2.118]: γίνεται δὲ ἔκφρασις προσώπων τε καὶ πραγμάτων καὶ τόπων καὶ χρόνων. Both offer examples from Homer for *ekphraseis* for persons.

[38] See, e.g., Callistratus, *Stat.* 13, of a statue of Medea: "It was of marble and disclosed the nature of her soul [λίθος ἦν μηνύων τὸ τῆς ψυχῆς εἶδος] in that art had modelled into it the elements which constitute the soul [ἀπομαξαμένης εἰς αὐτὴν τῆς τέχνης τὰ συμπληροῦντα τὴν ψυχήν]." For the theory, compare Xenophon, *Mem.* 3.10.8: "'Therefore it is necessary,' Socrates said, 'for the sculptor to render a likeness of the works of the soul in his figurative image'" [Δεῖ ἄρα, ἔφη [Σώκρατες], τὸν ἀνδριαντοποιὸν τὰ τῆς ψυχῆς ἔργα τῷ εἴδει προσεικάζειν]."

[39] James-Webb, "To Understand Ultimate Things," 9; see also Robert S. Nelson, "To Say and To See," ed. idem, *Visuality Before and Beyond the Renaissance* (Cambridge: Cambridge University Press, forthcoming [2000]) (ms. p. 7): "In this genre [the *ekphrasis*], the author spoke to an audience about a work of art they shared in such a way as not to belabor the description of what everyone could see, but to offer personal testimony to the emotional character of the representation and thus to enhance the listeners' emphatic reactions."

[40] The orality of Philostratus' *Imagines* was nicely stressed by Hadot, "Préface," xv: "Les *Tableaux* de Philostrate, eux aussi, sont destinés à la lecture publique. Cela veut dire que ceux qui entendent sa déclamation subissent l'enchantement, non seulement des images qui évoquent les mots, mais des sonorités, du ton de la voix. Ils assistent en quelque sorte à une représentation dramatique jouée par un seul acteur, et ils ont, comme les spectateurs d'une tragédie, l'impression d'être en présence des événements mêmes qui sont 'mimés' par la parole du 'poète.'"

[41] This interpretation of John as an ekphrasist receives striking confirmation from the great humanist Erasmus, who described Chrysostom's exegetical art using this exact metaphor: "There is nothing so hidden in the depths of Sacred Literature that Chrysostom could not bring it forth with dramatic clarity and make it accessible to the common people. He draws out what is concealed, displays it, sets it before our eyes in the way those do who delay viewers with a masterpiece of art: the longer you look and the closer you come, the more there is disclosed something fresh which had escaped the eye and stimulates anew the observer. In truth Holy Scripture is like such a painting which that unmatched artist, the Spirit, has drawn for us with his celestial crayon, so that when we constantly engage in the contemplation of it, we lose sight of the weariness of this world, and sense ever some new delight from the recognition of eternal realities. But no one can be an appropriate explicator of this picture unless he himself is a

ekphrastic art and encomiastic form together for this purpose and rhetorical effect, as he directly states: "Just now when we were pronouncing an encomium on the blessed Paul, you jumped for joy as much as if you saw him present" [Πρώην γοῦν ἡμῶν ἐγκωμιαζόντων τὸν μακάριον Παῦλον, οὕτως ἐσκιρτήσατε, ὡς αὐτὸν ὁρῶντες παρόντα].[42] And the appropriateness of this description of Chrysostom's Pauline writings as ἐκφράσεις is confirmed by one of his later biographers, Symeon Metaphrastes, who wrote that John, encountering Paul in his letters, "described the mind that was in them" [καὶ τὸν νοῦν ἐκφράσαι τὸν αὐταῖς (sc. ἐπιστολαῖς)].[43]

Having introduced the contemporary rhetorical techniques which govern them, we shall now examine two extended Pauline body portraits which Chrysostom composed in his biblical homilies. What follows is a close analysis of two passages located within his homilies on 1 Corinthians and Romans, respectively, paying particular attention to each one's rhetorical structure and argumentative progression, in order to elucidate their persuasive aims and methods, and the cultural assumptions upon which they depend.

Hom. in 1 Cor. 13 – Paul as the Perfect Portrait of Christ

Introduction of Theme: Imitation as Artistic Practice

The portrait of Paul in hom. in 1 Cor. 13.3–4 begins with an exclamation about the very audacity of Paul's call to the Corinthians to imitate (copy) him, as he has Christ:[44] "Amazing! What great boldness the teacher has! How accurately composed must the portrait be [ἀπηκριβωμένη ἡ εἰκών], when he exhorts even others to copy it." John then immediately seeks to forestall the charge of arrogance that this Pauline boldness might incite, so he explains Paul's intention for making the statement (which is also his own motivation in replicating the Pauline portrait on a fuller scale here): "He does not do this to praise himself, but to show that virtue is easy" [Οὐκ ἐπαίρων δὲ ἑαυτὸν τοῦτο ποιεῖ, ἀλλὰ δεικνὺς εὔκολον οὖσαν τὴν ἀρετήν].[45] Then by ethopoiia[46] John offers his Antiochene audience Paul's first person explanation of why he takes the risk of this self-aggrandizement:

---

distinguished artist with exceptionally discerning eyes ... Who else would have seen the things Chrysostom there points out?" (the passage is from Erasmus' Ep. 1800, as translated by Sider, "'Searching the Scriptures,'" 86–87).

[42] kal. 1 [48.953].

[43] Symeon Metaphrastes, vita s. Joh. Chrys. 22 [PG 114.1101]. John also saw there depicted Paul's soul, beauty, and depth [ψυχή, κάλλος, βάθος].

[44] Chrysostom's text reads the conclusion of 1 Cor 11:1 into 4:16 (καθὼς κἀγὼ Χριστοῦ).

[45] hom. in 1 Cor. 13.2 [61.110].

[46] Another of the progymnasmata, this form involves putting speech into the mouth of a different persona than oneself (either fictional or real persons, or ghosts) to display her or his character (see Aphthonios, Prog. 11 [Spengel, 2.44]); Kennedy, Greek Rhetoric under Christian Emperors, 64).

Now don't you tell me, "I am not able to imitate you, because you are a teacher, and a great one at that." For there is not as great a distance between me and you as from Christ to me. But nevertheless, I imitated him.[47]

From this contemporizing of the epistolary words Chrysostom turns briefly to an historical and exegetical question, as to why elsewhere, in Eph 5:1, Paul did not interpose himself as a mimetic intermediary, but instead called on the Ephesians to imitate God directly. To respond to this question Chrysostom switches with ease to an historical frame of reference, explaining that it was because of the Corinthians' weakness that Paul had to invoke his own example instead of the loftier divine one. But he quickly supplements this historically particular reading with a universal one: "And, otherwise, Paul demonstrates that it is possible even thus to imitate Christ. For the one who has copied the most accurate impression of the seal has copied the archetype."[48] With this entrée into artistic language, Chrysostom has embarked on the conceit which will govern his discourse for the next ten minutes – Paul's μίμησις (imitation, or copying) of Christ.

The Portrait of Paul – Material

We have treated the next portion of the homily at length in chap. 2, but now we shall reread it in its full context, to appreciate the flow and aggregate force of the entire rhetorical composition:

Let's see then how he imitated [μιμήσασθαι] Christ. For this imitation [μίμησις] needs not time and art, but only the exercise of one's free will. For if we go into a painter's [ζωγράφος] studio, we shall not be able to copy [μιμήσασθαι] the portrait [εἰκών], even if we see it ten thousand times. But it is by hearing alone that we can copy [μιμήσασθαι] him. So, do you wish us to bring the tablet [πίναξ][49] into the middle here and sketch [ὑπογράφειν] for you Paul's way of life [ἡ πολιτεία τοῦ Παύλου]? Well, let it be set before you, the pictorial tablet far more illustrious than the portraits of the emperors [ὁ πίναξ πολὺ λαμπρότερος ὢν τῶν βασιλικῶν εἰκόνων]. For what underlies it is not boards glued together, nor canvas stretched out; but the work of God is what underlies it, for it is a soul and a body.[50]

The persuasive power and crowd-pleasing nature of this extended metaphor are proven by the fact that at this moment the audience in the church apparently broke out into applause. But John (who always had an ambivalent set of reactions to applause)[51] tells them not to applaud yet,[52] for in mentioning soul and body he had

---

[47] *hom. in 1 Cor.* 13.3 [61.110].

[48] Καὶ ἄλλως δὲ δείκνυσιν, ὅτι ἔνι καὶ οὕτω τὸν Χριστὸν μιμήσασθαι. Ὁ γὰρ τὴν σφραγῖδα μιμησάμενος τὴν ἀπηκριβωμένην, τὸ ἀρχέτυπον ἐμιμήσατο (*hom. in 1 Cor.* 13.3 [61.110]).

[49] "Tablet," "board," or "picture" (LSJ, 1405).

[50] *hom. in 1 Cor.* 13.3 [61.110].

[51] Applause constitutes an exact fault-line on the relationship between Christian and "secular" norms as they were emerging in the fourth century, for it was, after all, the very goal of the epideictic oratory which he was so grandiloquently employing. But Chrysostom is uneasy about it because it suggests to him a different cultural context than a worship service (such as the theatre

not yet brought up anything singular about his subject (and therefore had not met the task of the epideictic orator, to praise what is singularly noteworthy about his subject). The reasoning behind this is popularly philosophical:

> For the underlying material [ὕλη] belongs to all in common. Because a soul does not differ from a soul in the least, insofar as it is a soul, but the free will [προαίρεσις] is what demonstrates the difference, just as a body has no difference from another body, insofar as it is a body. Now Paul's body and that of the many are the same [ὅμοιόν ἐστι καὶ τὸ τοῦ Παύλου καὶ τῶν πολλῶν], but dangers make his body more brilliant than theirs [οἱ δὲ κίνδυνοι φαιδρότερον ἐργάζονται τοῦτο ἐκείνου]. It is the same way with the soul [οὕτω δὴ καὶ ἐπὶ ψυχῆς].[53]

Chrysostom here exploits an equivocation intrinsic to the art of the encomium about the role of the body and other "givens" in a praiseworthy life. This is in one sense to invert the encomiastic task, for he has undermined one fundamental assumption upon which it rests: that some people are better endowed, in body and in soul, than others, and consequently deserve our praise. So by reducing both to simple ὕλη, "matter," Chrysostom appears to have leveled the field of comparison. But by introducing προαίρεσις he brings in by another door what epideictic theory likewise vigorously prescribed: praise of the subject primarily for deeds which reveal the underlying character through the choices the persons made.[54] It

---

or hippodrome) and, perhaps even more agonizing for him, because it plays into complex dynamics within himself as an ascetic about honor and its evil twin, vainglory. Nonetheless, at other times he clearly relishes the applause, and works to gain it (see Wilken, *John Chrysostom and the Jews*, 105–106). For a few representative passages (of many), see *Jud.* 1.1 [48.814]: "my proof was indisputable in the end, and there was great applause, the audience was warmed up, and the assembly afire. And as for me, I rejoiced, but not because I myself was being praised, but because my Lord was being glorified" [Ἐγὼ δὲ ἔχαιρον, οὐχ ὅτι αὐτὸς ἐπηνούμην, ἀλλ᾽ ὅτι ὁ Δεσπότης ὁ ἐμὸς ἐδοξάζετο]; his complaint in *Laz.* 7.1 [48.1045] that his audience applauds him in the church, and then goes out and applauds the charioteers in the hippodrome even more; and John's expression of his preference for silent appropriation of the truth by his audience, which will accrue to their benefit, over applause and praise which merely confer esteem on him (*Laz.* 2.3 [48.985]).

[52] And, in typical fashion, he corrects himself to say that they should not just applaud later, but rather zealously put into practice what they see [ἀλλ᾽ ἐπὶ τῶν ἑξῆς καὶ τοῦ κροτῆσαι καὶ τοῦ ζηλῶσαι] (*hom. in 1 Cor.* 13.3 [61.110]).

[53] Τέως γὰρ ἡ ὕλη ὑπόκειται κοινὴ πρὸς ἅπαντας οὖσα. Ψυχὴ γὰρ ψυχῆς οὐδὲν διαφέρει, καθὸ ψυχή, ἀλλ᾽ ἡ προαίρεσις δείκνυσι τὴν διαφοράν. Ὥσπερ γὰρ σῶμα σώματος, καθό ἐστι σῶμα, οὐδὲν διενήνοχεν, ἀλλ᾽ ὅμοιόν ἐστι καὶ τὸ τοῦ Παύλου καὶ τῶν πολλῶν, οἱ δὲ κίνδυνοι φαιδρότερον ἐργάζονται τοῦτο ἐκείνου· οὕτω δὴ καὶ ἐπὶ ψυχῆς (*hom. in 1 Cor.* 13.3 [61.110]).

[54] This was argued already by Aristotle: "Since praise comes from deeds [ἐκ τῶν πράξεων ὁ ἔπαινος], and it is characteristic of the excellent person to act according to the exercise of free will [κατὰ προαίρεσιν], then we should try to show that he has acted according to this proper exercise of free will [πειρατέον δεικνύναι πράττοντα κατὰ προαίρεσιν]" (*Rh.* 1.9.32). Of hundreds of examples of this commonplace employed in actual arguments, see the classic instance of Isocrates, *Or.* 9.73–75, quoted at length in chap. 2, pp. 62–63. For the same prescription in later theory, closer to Chrysostom's time, see, for example, the Byzantine Doxopater, who argued that "deeds are a matter of free will" [αἱ πράξεις τῆς προαιρέσεώς εἰσι], but beauty and other bodily characteristics are "beyond the control of the will" [ἀπροαίρετα] (*Aphth.* 8 [Walz, *Rhetores Graeci* 2.433.15]; Burgess, 124).

was, in fact, good rhetorical technique to devalue the attributes of the physical body[55] (or pass over them entirely) when the subject of one's encomium did not possess them.[56] Hence John's hearers are alerted from the beginning that this portrait of Paul's body will not be a conventional one focused on his strength or beauty, but that it has another end in view – a graphic exhibition of Pauline προαίρεσις in action.[57] The focal point of Paul's προαίρεσις will be his endurance of dangers, a topic also recommended for encomiastic treatment by rhetorical theorists.[58] Here we see a nice confluence of epideictic possibility and preacherly preference, for Chrysostom's own ascetic value system consistently undermines the body and its desires and adornments in favor of greater, spiritual goods, even as he devotedly contemplates the Pauline corpus. In what follows we shall find him extolling Paul's soul even as he is ostensibly praising his body.

The "Moving Picture" of Paul's Body

After this introduction to his theme, Chrysostom brings his audience along with him into an imaginary exercise. "Now, let's assume our tablet is Paul's soul" [ὑποκείσθω

---

[55] See, e.g., Plutarch, *Mor.* 5D-E, in which he goes down the list of encomiastic topics, devaluing each of them in favor of his thesis that παιδεία is the most praiseworthy thing. Plutarch's treatment of bodily attributes here is representative of the internal critique within the culture of epideictic oratory about the praiseworthy attributes of the body: "Beauty [κάλλος] is highly prized, but short-lived. Health [ὑγίεια] is a valued possession, but inconstant. Strength [ἰσχύς] is much admired, but it falls an easy prey to disease and old age. And, in general, if anyone prides himself wholly upon the strength of the body [εἴ τις ἐπὶ τῇ τοῦ σώματος ῥώμῃ φρονεῖ], let him know that he is sadly mistaken in judgement. For how small is man's strength compared with the power of other living creatures! I mean, for instance, elephants and bulls and lions." A nice illustration of this commonplace employed in an *ekphrasis* is provided by Lucian, *Im.* 22: "[Panthea] deserves (the praise), because it is not in body alone [οὐ τὸ σῶμα μόνον], like Helen, that she is fair [καλή], but the soul that she harbors therein [ὑπ' αὐτῷ τὴν ψυχὴν σκέπουσα] is still more fair and lovely" [καλλίω καὶ ἐρασμιωτέραν].

[56] Quintilian regarded the topic of the body to be of less importance than character, but noted that sometimes one praises beauty and strength, and in another circumstance weakness (*Inst.* 3.7.12). On rhetorical selection and omission of material as related to the case at hand, see Burgess, *Epideictic Literature*, 116: "The encomium does not necessarily narrate, but in most cases assumes a knowledge of the facts. It presents them only so far as its chief aim – the glorification of the individual – may be best served. To this end facts may be selected at will, grouped in any order, exaggerated, idealized, understated, if detrimental points must be touched upon."

[57] This triad of the human person as σῶμα, ψυχή and προαίρεσις is illustrated nicely in a work of ἔκφρασις which dates closely to Chrysostom. Callistratus, *Stat.* 9, tells of the statue of Memnon, which, though made of stone, could talk and experience emotion. "The statue of Memnon, as it seems to me, differed from a human being only in its body [καὶ ἦν Μεμνόνιος ἡ εἰκὼν μόνῳ μὲν τοῦ ἀνθρωπίνου διαλλάττειν μοι δοκεῖ σώματι], but it was directed and guided by a kind of soul and by a will like that of a human being" [ὑπὸ δὲ ψυχῆς τινος καὶ ὁμοίας προαιρέσεως ἀγομένη κατηυθύνετο].

[58] See Theon, *Prog.* 8 [Spengel 2.110]: "therefore the punishments and dangers endured in defense of one's friends should be praised" [διόπερ ἐπαινοῦνται καὶ αἱ πρὸ τῶν φίλων τιμωρίαι καὶ κίνδυνοι].

τοίνυν ὁ πίναξ ἡμῖν ἡ ψυχὴ Παύλου].[59] Here John seeks to expound upon a double metaphor: the construction of a graphic portrait in the air, using words, of the invisible soul of the deceased person, Paul. How will this work? First, Chrysostom applies a narrative framework to the composition of this soul portrait, which corresponds to the chronological progression of Paul's life. This allows him to infuse the inherently static portrait form with the dynamic reality narrative affords, by depicting its stages of composition and not merely the final form of the artwork.[60] By setting up an episodic sequence of narrative events his portrait pictures can "move" like the frames of a film. This method is well suited to his didactic purpose, as well, for it stresses the volitional and changeable character of the human life in progress. John delineates the stages of composition of this portrait by correlating the steps in portrait production with significant events in Paul's life, as known from the letters and Acts, which Chrysostom himself paints with an ethical brush. This amounts to a series of contrasting portraits that culminates in the archetypal image he seeks to (re)construct and placard for imitation.

The first picture in the series, the initial step in the creation of the image, is the anti-portrait of Paul the blasphemer (such as is found biblically in 1 Tim 1:13): "This tablet was not long ago lying covered with soot, full of cobwebs (for nothing is worse than blasphemy)." The artistic metaphor is retained by the "soot," which corresponds to the initial charcoal sketch an artist made on the tablet, but it is rendered in a wholly negative light, especially by the poetic embellishment of the cobwebs. This initial portrait of Paul which Chrysostom produces is intentionally uncomplimentary. But of major importance is the fact that this is the temporary portrait, the initial sketch of what is to come into being, a shadowy, unattractive first step in a longer process toward the archetypal beauty. In this way Chrysostom sets up an effective then-and-now comparison which he will exploit to the fullest.

When John turns to the second step of the process, the application of the indelible color paints, the monochromed anti-portrait of Paul the blasphemer is given new detail, even as it is simultaneously effaced when the new color portrait is placed on top, forever obliterating it.

But when the one who refashions everything [ὁ πάντα μετασκευάζων] came, and saw that it wasn't through carelessness and laziness [ῥᾳθυμία καὶ βλακεία] that Paul was drawn this way, but through inexperience [ἀπειρία] and his not having the bright tincture [ἄνθη] of piety (for he had zeal, but the colors [χρώματα] were not there, because he did not have "the zeal according to knowledge"), he gives him the bright tincture of the truth [τῆς ἀληθείας τὸ ἄνθος], that is, grace. And all at once he exhibited the imperial portrait [ἡ βασιλικὴ

---

[59] *hom. in 1 Cor.* 13.3 [61.110]. The most famous examples of such tablet portraits are the mummy portraits from Fayum (see Donald Strong, *Roman Art*, rev. ed. [London: Penguin, 1982] 262–64, and note his reference to some embodying "psychological realism," along with further literature in chap. 2. n. 109).

[60] Though an actual ἔκφρασις, of course, would have to be limited to the final stage of the artwork (unless its craftsmanship were inferior!).

εἰκών]. For after receiving the colors [τὰ χρώματα], and learning the things of which he had been ignorant, he did not wait for a long time, but immediately he appeared as an excellent artist [τεχνίτης ἄριστος]. And first he shows the imperial head [ἡ κεφαλὴ βασιλική], by preaching Christ. Then also he shows the rest of the body [τὸ λοιπὸν σῶμα], the body of accurate conduct [τὸ τῆς πολιτείας τῆς ἀκριβοῦς].[61]

We see here how the decrepit, dim charcoal image of Paul the blasphemer receives quick touching up even as it is displaced. Paul the pre-Christian blasphemer was not entirely an object for unremitting scorn, for his actions are seen as the folly of youth, born of poverty of experience which encased his innate virtue of zeal in a vessel not as yet sufficiently governed by knowledge of the truth to focus it on the right object.[62] The intertextuality at work in this portrait indicates that even as he is greatly influenced by the "old master" portrait of Paul in 1 Tim 1:13 as the blaphemer from ignorance, John has also painted Paul here as a typical Jew,[63] with the special zeal [ζῆλος] of Paul's own self-portrait in Gal 1:14 and Phil 3:6 now blended with Paul's portrait of all unbelieving Israel in Rom 10:2. The result is that even in this anti-portrait Paul represents a virtue (zeal), even as he exemplifies the dangers of possessing a sole virtue untempered by its requisite attendants, such as knowledge or insight into the truth. But the process John describes here is more than an allegory of normal human progress toward or away from virtue, for the divine role in Paul's self-portraiture is paramount. Paul's transformation from black and white sketch to color portrait was only made possible by Christ, the one who "refashions everything" in his coming. From Christ alone Paul received the artist's supplies he had lacked – color paints – the visible expressions of the brilliant truth, installments of grace in encaustic form. Thus Paul's portrait was simultaneously a supernatural composition and a work of human art, the casting of a human life. Christ served as his artistic patron, equipping him to do the painting himself, which Paul undertook immediately and with enormous proficiency from the moment he took up his brush. All he had needed was correction of ignorance which, once peeled away, revealed a most excellent artist.

Now painting with the colors of virtue and truth, Paul straightaway rendered himself in a fresh form, painted a new self, a renovated and living portrait for immediate display. The composition of that new portrait involved two stages: the head first, through the preaching,[64] and then the rest of the body. The head portrait reveals Paul as the imperial image, for he has the head of the king, the royal

---

[61] *hom. in 1 Cor.* 13.1 [61.110].

[62] This kind of mild apologia for Paul the persecutor of the church is found again and again in Chrysostom's writings; see the full treatment in chap. 6, pp. 250–57.

[63] This is something conspicuously lacking in the 1 Timothy portrait, which, if read outside the wider literary context of the Paul of Acts and the letters, does not suggest in any way that Paul was Jewish, but paints him as an archetypal *Gentile* sinner awaiting redemption in Christ, and thus the perfect model for his converts (see de Boer, "Images of Paul," 370).

[64] Probably for the simple reason that the organ of preaching is in the head, but also reflecting artistic preference for the head as the most telltale part of a person.

insignia of the εἰκὼν τοῦ θεοῦ who is simultaneously the imprint of Christ (himself the εἰκὼν τοῦ θεοῦ [2 Cor 4:4]). Before doting on the portrait proper (with particular attention to the rest of the body), Chrysostom muses a bit on this image of Paul's missionary life as the composition of his metaphorical self-portrait, by noting its magnificent contradictions and victories over natural diversions and detriments to artistic achievement. He compares Paul to earthly portrait painters who shut themselves up in studios where they can concentrate, alone in the still silence which makes painstaking detail possible. But Paul, to the contrary, painted his self-portrait in the midst of the world, displaying his tablet portrait in public even as he painted it, thus defying the usual separation of studio and gallery by moving both into the streets where he engaged in his missionary activity. And unlike the quiet leisure of the artist's studio, Paul's sidewalk art was composed in the midst of opposition, tumult and agitation, none of which hindered him from rendering the very imperial image [ἡ βασιλικὴ αὐτὴ εἰκών] on the canvas of his life. By this conceit Chrysostom affords his artistic metaphorical complex a dynamism it inherently resists, for the static portrait form, when applied to Paul's life, becomes flexible, pliant and living,[65] even as simultaneously it is solidified as perfection in the "imperial image" indelibly there cast. To document this facet of Paul's career Chrysostom cites Paul's own words in 1 Cor 4:9b, that he has become a θέατρον, a "spectacle" or "dramatic representation"[66] "in the world, in the midst of land and sea, of heaven and all the earth, and of the cosmos, things material and spiritual." Out in front of this vast cosmic audience, rather than in the seclusion of a studio, Paul was painting his self portrait [τὴν εἰκόνα ζωγραφῶν] even as it was exhibited for all to see, the imperial image of God in Christ through his living, breathing apostle.

The Somatic Portrait Displayed

After this extended introduction to the portrait of Paul's body, Chrysostom launches into "the rest" of Paul's body with an ekphrastic commonplace: "Would you like to see the other parts of the portrait also, from the head down? Or would you like me to start from below and move up the body?"[67] This rhetorical question (along with the hand gestures that one can readily imagine accompanied it) makes his

---

[65] This is one of the marvelous features of the form *ekphrasis*, as analyzed by James A. W. Heffernan, "Ekphrasis and Representation," *New Literary History* 22 (1991) 297–316, 301: "... ekphrastic literature typically delivers *from* the pregnant moment of graphic art its embryonically narrative impulse, and thus makes explicit the story that graphic art tells only by implication."

[66] LSJ, 787.

[67] Βούλεσθε καὶ τὰ λοιπὰ μέρη ταύτης ἰδεῖν, τὰ ἀπὸ τῆς κεφαλῆς κάτω; ἢ βούλεσθε κάτωθεν τὸν λόγον ἀναγάγωμεν; (*hom. in 1 Cor.* 13.3 [61.111]). Compare the same use of rhetorical questions in Philostratus the Younger, *Imagines* 11: "What, now do you desire to hear about the paintings? Shall I describe the horses?" [Τί δὴ ποθεῖς τῶν γεγραμμένων; ἢ τὸ τῶν ἵππων;].

audience partners in the quest for a vivid description of Paul's body, part by part,[68] and casts them as art critics viewing a masterpiece. To some degree this move from Paul's head to the remainder of his body, which John had signalled before when he noted the two-stage process of Paul's self portrait (the head composed first, then "the rest of the body" [τὸ λοιπὸν σῶμα] in the living of his life), necessitates a shift in the artistic metaphor, since painted portraits on wood tablets were often limited in scope to the head and shoulders, and did not include the complete torso.[69] Consequently John here switches from his invented panel painting to an equally imaginary full-torso portrait statue in order to introduce into his discourse the whole Pauline body from the neck down: "Now look at the gold portrait statue [θέα τοίνυν ἀνδριάντα χρυσοῦν]! Or, rather, a statue even more precious than gold, one such as might stand in heaven."[70] In this way John has conjured up an image of an exquisite piece of Pauline statuary of the very highest possible artistic standard, in order to deliver, there in the sanctuary, an *ekphrasis* on this fictionalized piece of artwork. But just as with the panel portrait, John must tinker a bit with his artistic image to weld its static metal into a more dynamic medium. So Paul's statue "was not bound together with lead, nor affixed in one place, but it ran around from Jerusalem until Illyricum; and it even went away into Spain, and was borne like a bird everywhere throughout the world."[71] Paul, the paradoxical human (and ornithological) portrait statue was simultaneously fixed in gold yet free to roam, to traverse the whole world, a living, breathing man of metal. What does the audience see when asked to contemplate this artistic creation?

John's opening rhetorical question about the order of treatment of the members of Paul's body resonates with wider debates in rhetorical theory about the best sequence by which to describe a person. For instance, his contemporary Aphthonios recommends Chrysostom's first option: "When giving an ekphrasis of a person it is necessary to go from the first to the last, that is, from the head to the feet."[72]

---

[68] The method of drawing a composite portrait of the body, member by member, was satirized by Horace, *Ars poetica* 1–5, in his disquisition on the need for simplicity and unity in a poem. As a negative example of poor composition he offers a combined portrait concocted of a human head, the neck of a horse, feathers, etc.

[69] This is the case in the panel portraits from the first through fourth centuries found at Fayum (see chap. 2, n. 109), which were limited in size to the head and (sometimes) the bust. It was their function to be affixed to mummies to represent the living face. Full-scale paintings of persons are more often found on wall paintings, rather than panels, for they naturally afford a larger surface.

[70] *hom. in 1 Cor.* 13.3 [61.111].

[71] *hom. in 1 Cor.* 13.3 [61.111].

[72] ἐκφράζοντες δὲ δεῖ πρόσωπα μὲν ἀπὸ τῶν πρώτων ἐπὶ τὰ τελευταῖα ἰέναι, τουτέστιν ἀπὸ κεφαλῆς ἐπὶ πόδας (*Prog.* 12 [Spengel, 2.46]). The same method of treatment is recommended by Nikolaos Rhetor for artistic renderings of human persons: "beginning from the first, then we shall come to the last. Whatever sort of human image we have as the object of the description, in copper or in painting or some other sort of material, we shall go at it part by part, beginning from the head [οἷον εἰ ἄνθρωπον χαλκοῦν ἢ ἐν γραφαῖς ἢ ὁπωσοῦν ἔχομεν ἐν τῇ ἐκφράσει

This choice of order is likely rooted in a hierarchical valuation of the body parts in physiognomic theory.[73] Actual examples of *ekphraseis* also tend to move from the head down the body.[74] However, in this case, as suits his rhetorical purpose, Chrysostom opts for the less conventional second alternative, and will start from Paul's feet and move up the body,[75] treating *seriatim* Paul's feet, chest (with a minor detour to the tongue), belly, hands, and back. A noteworthy element of this *ekphrasis* is that it is largely bereft of treatment of Paul's face and head. In fact, John restricts himself to what might seem to be the hardest body parts to eulogize[76] (including a lone Pauline fingernail, which makes a surprise appearance near the end) in order both to amplify the degree of rhetorical difficulty of his encomiastic task, and to demonstrate his opening contention that it is not for the givenness of a person's body that praise should be conferred, but, au contraire, for one's laudable deeds. That is why John's portrait of Paul's body will stress its "working members," those which labored continually, expertly and indefatigably for the gospel, as empowered by the virtues in Paul's soul.

ὑποκείμενον, ἀπὸ κεφαλῆς τὴν ἀρχὴν ποιησάμενοι βαδιοῦμεν ἐπὶ τὰ κατὰ μέρος]. For thus from all directions it will be an animated discourse" [ἔμψυχος λόγος] (*Prog.* 12 [Spengel 3.492]).

[73] For instance, the pseudo-Aristotelian physiognomic treatise gives a hierarchy of body parts, ranked by their usefulness in determining character, which also moves from the head down. "The most vital place is that around the eyes and the forehead and head and face; second, the area around the chest and shoulders, then around the legs and the feet; and then least of all is that around the belly" [ἐπικαιρότατος δὲ τόπος ὁ περὶ τὰ ὄμματά τε καὶ τὸ μέτωπον καὶ κεφαλὴν καὶ πρόσωπον, δεύτερος δὲ ὁ περὶ τὰ στήθη καὶ ὤμους, ἔπειτα περὶ τὰ σκέλη τε καὶ πόδας· τὰ δὲ περὶ τὴν κοιλίαν ἥκιστα] (*Phgn.* 814B). This pecking order is based upon where the most vivid signs of intelligence may be found in the body.

[74] Good examples of this order of description in an *ekphrasis* of a human person or artistic portrait may be found in the *Imagines* of Philostratus the elder, such as 1.21 on Olympus (eye, brow, cheek, breath, hair, head in general, breast; then he says he must stop there because the painter has depicted Olympus from behind a rock, thus blocking view of the body below the waist); 1.20 on Pelops (look, hair, forehead, whiskers, buttocks, chest, noting that his garment covers up his hands and legs); 2.5 on Rhodogoune (hair, eyebrows, cheek, eyes, mouth); 2.8 description of Critheïs, who loved the river Meles (figure, cheek color, hair, veil, glance, neck, hands, fingers, forearm, breast); 2.9 of Panthea (hair, neck, cheeks, nostrils, nose, eyebrows, eyes); 2.15 of Glaucus Pontius (beard, hair, eyebrows, arm, chest, belly, stopping there because from the waist down he was a fish!).

[75] An order Polemo follows in part of his physiognomic treatise (*Phgn.* 1.198–236F; on which see the analysis of Gleason, *Making Men*, 32).

[76] In the *Imagines* of the elder Philostratus, for example, whereas the chest [τὰ στέρνα] and hands [αἱ χεῖρες] are often included (e.g., 1.21, 30; 2.5, 8, 15), the belly [ἡ γαστήρ] is only once depicted (2.15), and the back never. But all of those *ekphraseis* include extensive descriptions of facial features (cheeks, nose, nostrils, eyes, hair, beard, neck, eyebrows, mouth, forehead), which are entirely lacking here.

Paul's Feet

The mention of Paul's world-wide travels, customarily expressed in the image of Paul as an ultra-marathon runner,[77] naturally leads Chrysostom to Paul's feet.[78] These are praised for their beauty in a stock epideictic manner: "What could be more beautiful than these feet [Τί γὰρ τῶν ποδῶν τούτων ὡραιότερον γένοιτ' ἄν], which traversed the whole earth which lies under the sun!"[79] Here the approval term ὡραῖος, an encomiastic word we might expect for an adolescent or youthful somatic feature,[80] is applied to the apostolic feet in evocation of Isaiah 52:7 (which was quoted by Paul himself in Rom 10:15). This scriptural depiction of the fair feet of the one who preaches the good news which, like its later re-uses by Paul and Chrysostom, trades the literally bloody and blistered feet of the ancient traveller for a triumphal abstract portrait in exultation of a sweet mandate fulfilled, is sufficient to complete this partial portrait, so John ends with a simple rhetorical question: "Have you seen how beautiful the feet are?" [Εἶδες πῶς καλοὶ οἱ πόδες;].

Paul's Chest

John pulls his auditors' gaze up from Paul's feet with another of the rhetorical questions which punctuate this *ekphrasis*: "Do you[81] wish to see also the chest?" [Θέλεις καὶ τὸ στῆθος ἰδεῖν].[82] Having effected this transition and awakened their curiosity, he adopts the museum docent's role: "Come, I shall show this to you, too." John will depict the "brilliance" [λαμπρός] of Paul's chest by a two-fold literary σύγκρισις: "you will see how much more brilliant his chest is than these beautiful feet [λαμπρότερον τῶν ποδῶν τούτων τῶν ὡραίων], and the very chest of the ancient lawgiver." Leaving the transitional internal comparison with Paul's feet hanging in the air, John offers his proof for the external, more weighty contrast with Moses: the latter carried stone tablets on his chest, whereas Paul held Christ himself there,[83] and bore continually the imperial image. Paul's chest, understood both as the torso of his body inhabited by Christ, and as the place from which his voice emanated, proves superior not only to Moses, but to other notable ancient conduits of divine utterances: "for this reason Paul's chest was more revered [σεμνότερος] than the mercy seat and the Cherubim."[84] This is proven by means of another

---

[77] See discussion and full references in chap. 3 n. 50.
[78] Though the transition from a winged Paul to a Paul with feet is hardly smooth.
[79] *hom. in 1 Cor.* 13.3 [61.111].
[80] See LSJ, 2036 (*s.v.*, II.2; surely Chrysostom does not want to suggest, with the literal meaning of the term, that Paul's feet are "ripe"!).
[81] The verb θέλεις is singular, for immediacy (as often in Chrysostom's oratory).
[82] *hom. in 1 Cor.* 13.3 [61.111].
[83] Probably a constellation of scriptural passages lies behind this (Gal 2:20; 6:17; 2 Cor 4:10; 13:3, the latter passage suggested especially by the next turn of the discourse).
[84] Here reading Field's text (2.155) instead of Migne's (61.111).

intricate pair of comparisons: the voice which issued forth from the Cherubim was not of the same type as Paul's, for it spoke only of things that are perceptible to the senses, while the voice which sprang from Paul's tongue concerned matters higher than the heavens. And whereas the mercy seat provided oracles to the Jews alone, from Paul oracles were provided for the entire world, with the former utterances arising through the agency of inanimate things, but the latter through a virtuous soul [διὰ ψυχῆς ἐναρέτου].[85] Now the comparison becomes an identification, as Paul's chest is termed "this mercy seat" [τοῦτο τὸ ἱλαστήριον] which receives a miniature encomium of its own: "this mercy seat was more brilliant [λαμπρότερον] than the sky (literally, 'heaven'), for it did not shine with a variety of stars, nor with sunbeams, but it had the very sun of righteousness emitting its rays from there."[86] Then John spies an opening for his favored type of celestial σύγκρισις to demonstrate Paul's superiority: "whereas a cloud floating over the sky sometimes turns it gloomy, no such storm ever passed over Paul's chest." But this neat and rather obvious polarity does not quite fit some of his other building materials for this portrait statue, so Chrysostom quickly corrects himself: "or, rather, many storms repeatedly floated over his chest, yet they did not darken the light, but he shined forth this light in the midst of temptation and dangers."[87] Paul's chest is visualized as the echo chamber from which his speech originated, with a solar power of its own which through his tongue sent forth its own "rays," allowing neither fear nor danger to cloud it over. The comparison complete, Chrysostom reverts to his initial contrast with the feet, which is meant to redound to the credit of both: "perhaps his chest does seem to overtake his feet; but the latter are beautiful [καλοί] as feet, and the former as a chest."[88]

Paul's Belly

Again it is a direct inquiry of the audience which marks the transition to the next body part to be lauded for its pulchritude: "Do you wish to see also his beautiful belly?" [βούλει καὶ γαστέρα ἰδεῖν ὡραίαν;].[89] First Chrysostom allows Paul's own words to draw the portrait of the apostolic stomach, quoting in succession three sentences from the letters concerning self-restraint in eating and drinking for the sake of others (1 Cor 9:13; Rom 14:21; 1 Cor 6:13). Then in his own words John extols the very beauty of Paul's belly in an extended rhetorical question: "What could be more beautiful than this belly [Τί ταύτης τῆς γαστρὸς γένοιτ' ἂν ὡραιότερον], which was thus educated to live quietly, and taught all moderation

---

[85] *hom. in 1 Cor.* 13.3 [61.111].
[86] *hom. in 1 Cor.* 13.4 [61.111].
[87] *hom. in 1 Cor.* 13.4 [61.111].
[88] *hom. in 1 Cor.* 13.4 [61.111].
[89] *hom. in 1 Cor.* 13.4 [61.111].

[σωφροσύνη], and knew equally hungering, famishing and thirst?"[90] In an interesting twist, John then personifies Paul's belly as a horse, who exemplifies the virtues of moderation in overriding the necessities of nature by walking in a nicely-proportioned way. Paul's stomach "walked" in such a way as a well-trained horse in a golden bridle does, for the simple reason that "Christ was walking in it." Since Paul's stomach was so well perfected in the virtue of moderation, clearly all other vices were eradicated from it as well.

Paul's Hands

The rhetorical question that effects the transition to the hands introduces a novel temporal distinction: "Do you wish to see the hands he has now? Or do you wish to look upon the wickedness which they formerly had?" [βούλει καὶ χεῖρας ἰδεῖν τὰς νῦν; ἢ βούλει τὴν προτέραν αὐτῶν πρότερον κακίαν θεάσασθαι;].[91] This strategy reverts to the polar opposite portraits of Paul the blasphemer and Paul the imperial image with which this *ekphrasis* started. Chrysostom differentiates three categories of hands: animal, human, and spiritual. Once again the then-and-now comparison begins with the anti-portrait. First John conjures up a most vivid picture of the hands of Paul the persecutor which dragged believers from their houses (Acts 8:3) as not even the hands of a human, but of some savage beast [οὐχὶ ἀνδρὸς χεῖρας, ἀλλὰ θηρίου τινὸς ἔχων χαλεποῦ].[92] However, after the spiritual experience of his conversion (which John describes in the same language as he had earlier, "having received the colors of the truth") Paul's hands were transformed, but ironically were not human even then, but became spiritual entities [οὐκέτι ἀνδρὸς ἐγένοντο αἱ χεῖρες αὗται, ἀλλὰ πνευματικαί], as shown by their continual shackling for the sake of the gospel. Another praiseworthy feature of Paul's post-conversion hands is their gentleness, especially in comparison with the fiercely negative earlier portrait of Paul's persecuting hands: "they never struck anyone then, but they were stricken time and again." Then John brings a final witness as proof for the accuracy of his portrait of the hands of the converted Paul as spiritual appendages: the viper at Malta (Acts 28:3–5), which by its reverence of Paul's hands, and refusal to fix on them, showed that "they were no longer the hands of a human being" [οὐ γὰρ ἦσαν ἀνθρώπου χεῖρες λοιπόν].[93]

Paul's Back

Having profusely praised four Pauline body parts (the feet, chest, belly, and hands), John turns to Paul's back, for which he does not have to claim special prominence

---

[90] *hom. in 1 Cor.* 13.4 [61.111].
[91] *hom. in 1 Cor.* 13.4 [61.111].
[92] *hom. in 1 Cor.* 13.4 [61.111].
[93] *hom. in 1 Cor.* 13.4 [61.112].

among the rest, but rather parity with them. He expresses this with the familiar refrain: "Do you wish to see also the back, which is like the rest of the members?" [βούλει καὶ τὰ νῶτα ἰδεῖν τοῖς λοιποῖς ἐοικότα μέλεσιν;].[94] The portrait of Paul's back offered is taken from the words of Paul himself, in 2 Cor 11:24–25, from which John has selected the torments which afflicted the apostle's torso in particular: whipping, beating and stoning.

The End of the Catalogue

By extending the quotation from 2 Corinthians 11 beyond the depictions of Paul's back to his enduring night and day in the depths of the sea [ἐν τῷ βυθῷ], John has set up his next transition. "But, so that also we might not fall into a boundless deep [βυθός], and get greatly carried away by going through each of the members of his body one by one [καθ' ἕκαστον αὐτοῦ τῶν μελῶν ἐπιόντες], come, leaving off from his body [ἀποστάντες τοῦ σώματος], let's look at another beauty [ἕτερον κάλλος], that from his clothes τὸ ἀπὸ τῶν ἱματίων], which even demons reverenced." In this way John desists from his part-by-part treatment of Paul's body. These five bodily members – feet, chest, belly, hands and back – are sufficient to sketch the portrait-statue of Paul. Now he turns to its adornment.

The Clothes that Adorn the Body

Although Paul's body was not claimed by John to exemplify κάλλος, it is ironic that he can apply this traditional category of praise to its covering, Paul's apparel. As evidence Chrysostom invokes Acts 19:12, which tells of the power not only of Paul's garments, but of all the cloths and linens which, by mere contact with his skin, obtained the capacity to set demons to flight. The result was constant combat with demons whenever Paul appeared, for they would react to Paul as though he were the fighting champion of the whole world poised to annihilate them. The mere sight of a handkerchief intensely agitated the demons, stirring them to memory of Paul's battlefield prowess, and inciting their immediate departure. So Paul's garments are praised, like his body, not for their material splendor, but for their πράξεις, their deeds.

Crescendo to the Encomiastic Reversal

On his way to the final exhortation to this homily, which (as so often in the exegetical homilies) concerns almsgiving for the poor, John is moved by the mention of Paul's humble garments to contrast the resplendently adorned wealthy with the simple-living (but supernaturally effective) Paul. Now, finally, the standard

---

[94] *hom. in 1 Cor.* 13.4 [61.112].

repertoire of encomiastic topics comes to the fore, but in an inverted form. John concludes with a σύγκρισις of Paul with the wealthy, in which Paul's apparent disadvantage is shown at each turn to be his triumph – at least, that is, in the estimation of John himself, the final witness:

Where now are those who are wealthy [οἱ πλουτοῦντες], and take great pride in their possessions? Where are those who number up their dignities [οἱ τὰ ἀξιώματα ἑαυτῶν ἀριθμοῦντες],[95] and their expensive clothes? If they compare themselves in these respects, they will see that all their belongings are mud and filth. And why am I speaking about clothes and gold coins? For if someone were to give me the power to possess the whole world, I would consider Paul's fingernail [ὁ ὄνυξ] alone more powerful [ἰσχυρότερος] than all that sovereignty [πάσης τῆς βασιλείας ἐκείνης], his poverty moreso than all luxury [πάσης τρυφῆς τὴν πενίαν], his disrepute than all honor [πάσης δόξης τὴν ἀδοξίαν], his nakedness than all wealth [παντὸς πλούτου τὴν γύμνωσιν], the beating of that sacred head than all security [πάσης ἀδείας τὸν κολαφισμὸν τῆς ἱερᾶς ἐκείνης κεφαλῆς], the stones which he received than any diadem [παντὸς διαδήματος τοὺς λίθους οὓς ἐδέξατο].[96]

This denouement of Chrysostom's portrait of Paul's body accents its paradoxical nature within the form of the encomium. In the final analysis, even a lone finger-nail of Paul's is seen to be stronger than the possession of all the things the world normally accounts worthy of praise: power, wealth, honor, security, rulership.[97] So the portrait of Paul's body redounds yet again to Paul's soul and its virtue as manifested in his suffering. In the final result Paul is elevated, and his opposite, the hastily painted stock portrait of the rich whom the world regards as laudable, is lowered to the level of mire. The upside down oratory which John uses (for which Paul himself provides a literary precedent)[98] enshrines the values he wishes to impress upon his congregation – ascetic self-restraint which takes the place of the persecutions the apostle endured.[99] And by offering himself as the chief witness to these values, or, rather, chief art critic, the one who exemplifies the paradoxical preference for the excellence of the mere fingernail of the saint, John simultaneously casts himself as a Pauline look-alike before their very eyes, and calls for their own matching response.

---

[95] Of course, this is precisely the task the epideictic orator sets out to do, for others.

[96] *hom. in 1 Cor.* 13.4 [61.112].

[97] The "paradoxical encomium" itself has a long history (see the valuable treatment of Burgess, *Epideictic Literature*, 157–66).

[98] Especially 1 Cor 4:9–13, which Chrysostom had quoted previously in this discourse (*hom. in 1 Cor.* 13.3 [61.110–11]). On that passage as a "paradoxical encomium," see Mitchell, *Paul*, 213–21.

[99] "Let us desire this crown, beloved; even if there is no persecution, in the meantime let's prepare ourselves" (*hom. in 1 Cor.* 13.4 [61.112]).

Conclusion: Ekphrasis *and the Homiletical Art*

This complicated text, *hom. in 1 Cor.* 13.3–4, is an encomium to Paul constructed as an ἔχφρασις of two imaginary works of art depicting the same subject – a tablet portrait of Paul's head, and a life-size statue of his body. But those portraits are themselves metaphorical fictions which Chrysostom was in the process of creating even as he was simultaneously describing them to his hearers.[100] Both of these elements are built into the dynamics of the art of the ἔχφρασις itself, for it often was used as a "convenient fiction"[101] for reenactments of narratives that were already known to their audiences. This is an essential point, for it means that the scriptural expositor such as Chrysostom has very much the same task as the sophist undertaking an *ekphrasis* in order to describe renowned works of art to those who already know them, for both were engaged in the retelling and refashioning of sacred narratives, either Homeric (or other traditional mythologies) or biblical.[102] In both cases the common, assumed narrative places a wider frame (or gallery case) around the new composition, which is worked into and out of it, and in both instances the author's task is to recreate a vivid, fresh emotional reaction to past persons and events through a novel oral[103] restaging of them.[104] The new text, the

---

[100] Chrysostom is not unique in this; see Fairbanks, *Philostratus the Elder, Imagines*, LCL, xxvi: "Philostratus was primarily a sophist, who developed the description of paintings as a form of literary art; he would be quite consistent in describing paintings that were figments of his imagination, provided only he succeeded in preserving the illusion that he dealt with existing paintings." This is true throughout the history of *ekphrasis* as, for instance, with Keats' famous Grecian urn (see Heffernan, "Ekphrasis and Representation," 316 n. 34: "Keats *composed* his urn from a variety of sources").

[101] The phrase is applied by James-Webb, "To Understand Ultimate Things," 7, to Philostratus' *Imagines*. See also Hadot, "Préface," viii: "ceux qui écoutent Philostrate croient contempler des tableaux, alors que ces tableaux n'existent que dans leur imagination, et, qui plus est, ils oublient qu'il s'agit de tableaux, ils croient être en présence d'êtres vivants" (cf. pp. viii and xvi on "ce jeu de miroirs"). For further discussion of this important point see Elsner, *Art and the Roman Viewer*, 24–28.

[102] "Une grande partie des *Tableaux* traite effectivement de sujets empruntés à la mythologie et à l'histoire. Les peintures qu'il décrit sont donc pour la plupart des peintures narratives qui racontent des légendes et des histoires qui empruntent leurs thèmes à la tradition littéraire souvent homérique … Il faut ici insister fortement sur un point capital, l'importance de l'acte de parole dans ce processus de réactualisation du passé héroïque" (Hadot, "Préface," xiv). Though Chrysostom would be shocked and dismayed to hear of this parallel function, we can see this as another piece of his deliberate strategy of competition with and replacement of the "secular" or "pagan" institutions of the *polis* in constituting his Christian society (the latter point, to which we shall return in chap. 7, has been convincingly demonstrated by Brown, *Body and Society*, 313). But within the Great Church at Antioch John's liturgical oratory was quite intentionally seeking to kill two birds with one stone: use proven and effective rhetorical techniques from his training for public exposition of traditional texts, and to provide Christian audiences the intellectual and recreational experiences they were used to from the theatre and oratorical contests of civic life "outside."

[103] See above, n. 40, on the oral nature of *ekphraseis*.

[104] "The importance of emotion as both a constituent element and effect of vivid description is evident in *ekphraseis* of paintings from Late Antiquity on. By giving graphic accounts of

homily incorporating this *ekphrasis*, is, like all *ekphraseis*, "meant to parallel the work of art, not substitute for it,"[105] which is precisely how Chrysostom envisions the act of biblical interpretation and exposition. The interposition of a fictional painting or statue between the two texts (the biblical and the homiletical), which acts as an interpretive intermediary,[106] allows Chrysostom greater compositional freedom as he proceeds (i.e., he can range widely in the biblical canon and in his own imaginative repertoire for collage pieces),[107] and it provides him with the opportunity to create a verbal icon for his beloved Paul, one which is perfectly justified by the very text which inspired the *ekphrasis* in the first place: "Be imitators of me."[108] This

---

dramatic events and by articulating the emotion aroused by the subject of the painting, the author aimed to move the listener. Conveying the emotional response evoked by the work was more important than explaining its technical details" (James-Webb, "To Understand Ultimate Things," 9; compare Fairbanks, *Philostratus the Elder, Imagines*, LCL, xxi: "the reader must remember that he is simply trying to outdo the paintings he describes in this appeal to the emotions"). Plut., *Mor.* 347A-C gives the same purpose for vivid description [γραφικὴ ἐνάργεια] in narrative historiography, using Thucydides as his model: "Assuredly Thucydides is always striving for this vividness in his writing [ἀεὶ τῷ λόγῳ πρὸς ταύτην ἁμιλλᾶται τὴν ἐνάργειαν], since it is his desire to make the reader a spectator, as it were [οἷον θεατὴν ποιῆσαι τὸν ἀκροατήν], and to produce vividly in the minds of those who peruse his narrative the emotions of amazement and consternation which were experienced by those who beheld them" [καὶ τὰ γιγνόμενα περὶ τοὺς ὁρῶντας ἐκπληκτικὰ καὶ ταρακτικὰ πάθη τοῖς ἀναγινώσκουσιν ἐνεργάσασθαι λιχνευόμενος].

[105] Nelson, "To Say and to See," 4. Contrast Elsner, *Art and the Roman Viewer*, 24: "For the literary genre of ekphrasis, as 'description,' in the ancient world was not intended (as modern descriptions are) to go beside and to supplement the real painting or statue being described; it was intended to *replace* the sculpture or painting. The truly triumphant ekphrasis was the one which brought to mind its subject so vividly that the subject was no longer necessary. Its effects had already been achieved" (emphasis original). This debate about the relationship between the *ekphrasis* and its subject has interesting implications for Chrysostom's liturgical *ekphraseis* of Paul. Surely John does not intend his homily to replace the Scriptural text (as neither does Philostratus intend any of his *ekphraseis* to supplant the literary myth depicted in the scene), but rather to enliven it and make it accessible through his mediating, second-order discourse. But, on the other hand, Chrysostom's verbal portrait of Paul does in some sense replace the person of Paul whom he depicts, or at least lessen the requirement for a supernatural reappearance, as his portrait becomes the only required source of access to him (alongside Scripture). And, as Elsner insists, the key point for Chrysostom is that his hearers be afforded a personal encounter with Paul by means of his rhetorical portrait, which has an integrity unto itself ("[*ekphraseis*] were independent and self-sufficient works of rhetorical art in their own right" [p. 27]). Because Paul is dead (though living now in heaven) he requires an earthly double, or "replacement."

[106] "Mais l'auditeur de Philostrate est invité par lui à mettre en oeuvre son imagination pour retrouver, par l'intermédiaire du tableau, l'émotion que provoquerait la présence de la réalité elle-même. Par cette éducation de l'imagination, on apprend à percevoir l'invisible dans le visible, les états d'âme qui s'expriment dans le visage, le déroulement de l'action dans lequel s'insère l'instant choisi par le peintre, les paroles prononcées par les personnages, les odeurs et les parfums qui se dégagent des objets" (Hadot, "Préface," ix).

[107] Again a comparison with Philostratus suggests itself by this construction of a new narrative: "Plusieurs fois, en effet, il est impossible de dire si les événements successifs que décrit Philostrate sont censés être représentés simultanément sur le tableau, selon un procédé pictural qui a toujours existé, ou s'ils sont simplement imaginés par lui" (Hadot, "Préface," ix).

[108] Heffernan, "Ekphrasis and Representation," 302 suggestively refers to "the genealogical link between ekphrasis and sepulchral epigrams" in antiquity, regarding the latter as instances of

involves a hermeneutical and epistemological procedure for not just displaying the existing text, but imaginatively recreating it[109] – and its author – for contemporary delectation and deposit in the memory for on-going use and recopying in the self. So the movement is from text (Paul's first letter to the Corinthians) to body (the author, Paul), to text (the homily) to body (that of the hearers).[110] In terms of the liturgical context of Chrysostom's homilies, the ἀνάγνωσις (reading) of the scriptural passage constituted the initial rehearsal of the words of the text which in the homily Chrysostom would seek to transform textually into a public image for individual appropriation and imitation. Chrysostom's *ekphrasis* of Paul's body is an imaginative way to reassemble and recompose a Paul for public viewing who both legitimates and explicates his own text, and exemplifies the virtues Chrysostom seeks his audience to emulate. The emotional response which this *ekphrasis* seeks to generate in its audience is love for the apostolic author, which will lead (the craftsman hopes) to comprehension of his writings, and zeal to emulate his lifestyle.[111]

But Chrysostom wishes to claim even more than that he had stirred his audience; his objective is no less than to compose *the most accurate portrait* of Paul. The sources of authorization of the portrait which Chrysostom describes are twofold – it is not *his* portrait of Paul, he claims, but rather *Paul's own self-portrait*,[112] and, even that is really a divine creation, for God endowed Paul with the "raw materials," including the προαίρεσις and προθυμία that acted as the brushes for the applications of the colors, the virtues. And the real-life possibility of the choices Paul made in the living of his life is illustrated by the orator himself, who attests to the overwhelming beauty of Paul's image, which in his admiring eyes surpasses all

---

prosopopoiia, "envoicing a silent object." In the case of Chrysostom's *ekphraseis* of Paul, his letters, as though engraved on a stele (see chap. 2 n. 54), act as those epigrams do, communicating the living voice of the one represented. The relationship between the Pauline text and the created images in this instance becomes somewhat like that between title and painting which engage in mutual interpretation (ibid., 303–305). But ironically, in this case, unlike most *ekphraseis*, it is the voice which comes first, as a given in the epistles, for which a picture of the author is then sought.

[109] The same task as an *ekphrasis*, in Hadot's description: "Non seulement les sonorités du discours sont capables de faire surgir un tableau devant les yeux de l'imagination, mais elles peuvent révéler des significations qui resteraient invisibles à la simple vision et elles peuvent faire revivre par les spectateur la scène représentée en le mettant ainsi en présence de la réalité même" ("Préface," xiv).

[110] Compare Chidester, *Word and Light*, 129: "within this dialectic in the symbolic discourse of the body, perceptual metaphors are generated by the body, articulated in discourse, but always forced back again to their physiological ground in the lived experience of the body."

[111] See chap. 2, esp. pp. 49–55.

[112] This is both a statement in general (that Paul in the course of living painted his own portrait), and one with a literary warrant, given that many of Chrysostom's references are to Paul's own letters, which do contain self-portraits, both by virtue of their epistolary form (as argued in chap. 2), and their actual content (e.g., Gal 1–2). Nonetheless, Chrysostom's images do not simply replicate Paul's self-portraits, but creatively refashion them as in a palimpsest.

competitors. The medium of *ekphrasis* works perfectly to resuscitate the dead for this kind of a living encounter which is simultaneously aural and visual, and therefore tactile.[113] And, for John, the more one knows Paul, the more one can love him, which makes the cycle of love hermeneutics self-regenerating.

Hom. in Rom. 32 – Paul's Body Rejuvenated From the Dust

The portrait of Paul's body in *hom. in Rom.* 32.2–4 is one of the most rhetorically stirring in Chrysostom's corpus, and indeed has earned the reputation among some scholars as the most famous passage on Paul from the early church Fathers.[114] This excerpt constitutes the conclusion to the homily series on Romans, and follows directly upon Chrysostom's discussion of the last verse of the letter, the grace benediction of 16:24,[115] which he regarded as forming the foundation and the roof of the edifice which is the Epistle to the Romans. John regards Paul's final prayer as evidence of his nobility as a teacher whose life was spent in supplication to God on behalf of his students. But that happy reflection leads him to a mournful realization of distance from his saintly author: "Who will pray for us, since Paul has gone away?" The simple answer is that Paul's present imitators [οἱ Παύλου ζηλωταὶ οὗτοι] will perform this earthly function, but John warns that intercessory prayer [συνηγορία] must be earned by careful preparation on earth. Such cosmological dualism is then matched with a hermeneutical corollary: if here on earth we "hear Paul's voice" and prepare adequately, in heaven after we die we shall "see him completely."[116] Chrysostom embellishes this promised future heavenly vision of Paul with a few enticing details: "the athlete of God" will be visible in heaven shining brightly adjoining the royal throne, right in the midst of Cherubim glorifying God and the Seraphim in flight. John then pulls his lens out further to capture this scene in wider context: Paul will appear alongside Peter, and he will be seen to be the "chief and head of the choir of the saints."[117] This heavenly Paul will exude a love which burns even hotter than that which he displayed on earth,

---

[113] See Nelson, "To Say and To See," 12, on ancient theories of extramission: "Because the optical rays that issue forth from the eyes were thought to touch the object seen, vision was haptic, as well as optic, tactile as well as visual."

[114] Baur, *John Chrysostom*, 1.293: "In the whole of patristic literature one can scarcely find a page which glorifies Rome and St. Paul at the same time, with such power and warmth, such love and inspiration, as Chrysostom shows here. It deserves to be engraved in golden letters on the grave of the Apostle to the Gentiles" (cf. Quasten, *Patrology*, 3.443: "There is hardly a passage in the whole range of patristic literature which praises Saint Paul with such fondness and devotion").

[115] Chrysostom's text includes 16:24 (which is widely acknowledged now to be an inferior reading), but not 16:25–27.

[116] *hom. in Rom.* 32.2 [60.678].

[117] *hom. in Rom.* 32.2 [60.678]. One wonders if John may not be pointing to a heavenly enthronement scene in the church (see chap. 2, n. 88).

when he chose to remain among the living – even to the extent of renouncing the more attractive option of immediate departure to be with Christ (Phil 1:21–26).

After this quick glimpse of the portrait of Paul in heaven, John resumes his initial encomium to Rome.

> I love Rome for this ['Εγὼ καὶ τὴν 'Ρώμην διὰ τοῦτο φιλῶ], although she is due praise [ἔχων ἐπαινεῖν] for other things – for size [μέγεθος], for antiquity [ἀρχαιότης], for beauty [κάλλος], for population [πλῆθος], for power [δυναστεία], for wealth [πλοῦτος], for her successes in wars [τὰ κατορθώματα τὰ ἐν πολέμοις]. But leaving all these things aside, it is for this reason that I congratulate [μακαρίζειν] her – that when alive Paul wrote to them, and he loved them so, and when he arrived he spoke with them, and there he brought his life to an end.[118] Therefore the city is more distinguished [ἐπίσημος] for this cause than for all others.[119]

The standard epideictic topics are trotted out in force here. But these stock motifs of conventional and often repeated panegyrics to ancient cities (with particularly effusive application to the imperial city)[120] are presented here only in passing, to be trumped immediately by the real notoriety the venerable metropolis possesses, as Chrysostom tells it, from its association with the apostle Paul, both living and dead, past, present and future. Momentarily, then, it is Rome who is cast in somatic terms, in order to accent the predominant role of the apostles as her most defining physiognomic feature: "For like a great and strong body [σῶμα μέγα καὶ ἰσχυρόν], Rome has two shining eyes,"[121] the bodies [σώματα] – that is, the corpses – of Paul and Peter lying buried at Rome.[122] Rome's body is worthy of admiration for its entombment of two dead bodies which are paradoxically the very source of her vitality, her luminescence which is brighter than the rays of the sun.[123] Once more Chrysostom's discourse alternates between the earthly and heavenly, the present and the future, as he confers praise on Rome for her ultimate

---

[118] Some manuscripts add here: "and they possess his holy body" (see Field, 1.490).

[119] hom. in Rom. 32.2 [60.678].

[120] One thinks, for example, of Aelius Aristides' Roman Oration (Or. 26) (on which see the analysis of J. H. Oliver, "The Ruling Power," TAPA 43 [1953] 871–1003). The rhetorical handbook of Menander contains an extended discussion of the topics and standard arguments for praising cities, among which are all those treated in this Chrysostomic passage (Rh. 1.346–67 [Russell-Wilson, 32–75]; for further references to rhetorical theory on praise of cities see Mitchell, Paul, 215–21).

[121] cf. hom. in Gal. 2:11 2 [51.373], where the two apostles are called the eyes of the body of the church.

[122] Chrysostom was entranced by Paul's tomb at Rome, which he never had occasion to see. In hom. in 2 Tim. 4.4 [62.623–24], he depicts Paul entombed in the midst of Rome as though he were its living emperor. "Paul resides more magnificently than all the emperors in the very imperial city, the place where he was victorious, and where he set up his trophy [οὗτος δὲ πάντων βασιλέων λαμπρότερος ἐν αὐτῇ κεῖται τῇ βασιλίδι, ἔνθα καὶ ἐνίκησεν, ἔνθα καὶ τὸ τρόπαιον ἔστησεν] ... he occupies the very middle of the city, as though ruling and living there" [ὁ δὲ τὸ μέσον κατέχει τῆς πόλεως, καθάπερ βασιλεύων καὶ ζῶν].

[123] "Not so brilliant is the sky when the sun discharges its rays as the city of the Romans is when it radiates these two lights everywhere in the world" (hom. in Rom. 32.2 [60.678]).

recognition, of which she holds a present guarantee in her custody of the apostolic bodies. To do this he provides his audience with an eschatological *ekphrasis*, a verbal video of things to come:

Consider and shudder at what an incredible spectacle [θέαμα] Rome will see, when Paul in an instant rises from that grave, with Peter, and is taken up for a meeting with Christ. What sort of rose will Rome send forth for Christ, with what two crowns will the city be garlanded, with what gold chains encircled, what sort of fountains will she have! Therefore I admire [θαυμάζειν] the city for this reason: not on account of her profusion of gold, nor her columns [κίονες], nor for any prestige [φαντασία], but on account of these pillars [στῦλοι] of the church.[124]

The creative language here parades many images in succession before the eyes – flowers, diadems, chains and flowing fountains – which serve to displace the usual architectural or decorative objects of civic pride in favor of the ecclesiastical founders, the twin pillars of the church. The unevenly applied coupling of Paul with Peter in this part of the oration (Peter seems an afterthought required to complete the ophthalmic duality)[125] will now give way to a confined interest in one of the two pillars, one of the two eyes in Rome's somatic portrait. Since this involves a close-up portrait within a portrait, it requires a change in imagery and appeal.

Chrysostom ingeniously casts the portrait of Paul's body which he is about to construct in this homily as his own personal ἐγκώμιον τῆς κόνεως τοῦ Παύλου, "encomium to Paul's dust."[126] It begins with his extreme desire, expressed in a rhetorical question: "Who will allow me now to embrace Paul's body, and be nailed to the tomb, and see the dust of that body, the body which made up what is lacking in Christ (Col 1:24), that bore the marks (Gal 6:17), that scattered the seed of the gospel everywhere?"[127] In the ensuing portrait, Chrysostom will continually employ the first person refrain,[128] "I would wish to see the dust of …"

---

[124] *hom. in Rom.* 32.2 [60.678].

[125] Note, for instance, that the blessing on Rome is pronounced for Paul's fourfold relations with them (he wrote to them, loved them, spoke to them on arrival there, and died in their city), but there is no Petrine parallel. What Paul and Peter share is the last of these – that they are both buried there [Ἐκεῖθεν ἁρπαγήσεται Παῦλος, ἐκεῖθεν Πέτρος] (*hom. in Rom.* 32.2 [60.678]). Further, in the apocalyptic vision, the singular rose fits the two apostles awkwardly, whereas the two crowns deliberately refer to the pair. The same stilted attempt to incorporate Peter into this singular focus on Paul reappears at the end of the discourse (see n. 162 below).

[126] The focus on the dust of the corpse is of course hyperbolic, but also rooted in actual custom. Chrysostom's contemporary, Gregory of Nyssa, mentions the practice of collecting and revering the dust from martyrs' sepulchres as a treasured object: Εἰ δὲ καὶ κόνιν τις δοίη φέρειν τὴν ἐπικειμένην τῇ ἐπιφανείᾳ τῆς ἀναπαύσεως, ὡς δῶρον ὁ χοῦς λαμβάνεται, καὶ ὡς κειμήλιον ἡ γῆ θησαυρίζεται (*Thdr.* 740M=*Gregorii Nysseni Opera X, pars I: Sermones, pars II*, ed. G. Heil, et al. [Leiden: Brill, 1990] 63, ll. 17–19), cited by L. W. Barnard, *The Graeco-Roman and Oriental Background of the Iconoclastic Controversy* [Byzantina Neerlandica 5; Leiden: Brill, 1974] 52).

[127] *hom. in Rom.* 32.3 [60.679].

[128] In this way Chrysostom very self-consciously portrays himself as the exemplar of monastic, world-denying virtue, even as he is in the act of portraying Paul, its exemplar.

completed by a succession of discrete Pauline body parts: his mouth, heart, hands, eyes, and feet.[129] The fixation on the "dust" of Paul's body nicely captures and exploits Chrysostom's temporal engagement with his subject: a Paul who is portrayed with an eye simultaneously on the past, the present, and the future, the net effect of which is to render the present decayed corpse in a faraway city active, vibrant, and potent right there in John's sanctuary in Antioch. Even Paul's dust is the dust of a body that was in constant motion ("the body through which he ran about everywhere"), the inert though animated ashes of a hyperkinetic corpse.

Paul's Mouth

A word play on σῶμα/στόμα effects the transition from Paul's body viewed *en masse* to the composite treatment by body parts, commencing this time from the head.[130] The mouth is praised first and most extensively of all the body parts in this literary portrait, because it can function as a metonym for Paul's entire missionary career as the spokesman for the gospel, and so highlights his apostolic legitimacy. The mouth also can be given praise through a range of stand-ins, such as the voice and the tongue, each of which stands as a synecdoche for Paul's ministry of the word and words in ministry. It is Chrysostom's fervent wish to see "the dust of the mouth through which Christ spoke."[131] The portrait of Paul's mouth therefore becomes a portrait of Christ, whose speech passed through it.[132] Specifically, Paul's mouth is praised as the organ *through which*[133] extraordinary accomplishments were wrought: through Paul's mouth the light shined brighter than any star, his voice leapt forth more frightening than thunder to the demons, he spoke the blessed utterance of Rom 9:3, he addressed kings without shame. Because of Paul's mouth, and its capacity for speech "we learn of Paul, and Paul's Lord."[134] Without Paul's mouth, in other words, there would have been no apostolic career, and no witness to it (therefore also no such discourse as this in his honor!). It is only because of Paul's capacity for speech that we now have access to Paul.

Chrysostom varies his praise of Paul's mouth by switching to the voice [φωνή] which sounded forth from it, and was responsible for so many achievements. When John assembles his catalogue of the πράξεις, or accomplishments of Paul's

---

[129] We see here a flexibility in the arrangement of the body parts, which is only roughly head to toe, for the eyes break the sequence, and then after the individual body parts τὰ μέλη, "the limbs," are contemplated altogether.

[130] τὴν κόνιν ἐκείνου τοῦ σώματος, δι'οὗ πανταχοῦ διέδραμε· τὴν κόνιν τοῦ στόματος, δι'οὗ Χριστὸς ἐφθέγγετο (*hom. in Rom.* 32.3 [60.679]). The verbal exchange apparently slipped past the NPNF translators and revisers (working with the text of Savile and later Field), who translated "body" in both places.

[131] *hom. in Rom.* 32.3 [60.679].

[132] The idea is taken up from Paul's own claims in 2 Cor 13:3; Rom 15:18.

[133] The refrain δι'οὗ is used five times in the section on the mouth alone.

[134] δι'οὗ Παῦλον ἐμάθομεν, δι'οὗ τὸν Παύλου δεσπότην (*hom. in Rom.* 32.3 [60.679]).

φωνή, he puts an accent on its position in the spiritually segregated universe. Paul's exorcistic voice (which is mostly drawn from the narrative of Acts) attacked the demons, but was allied always with the divine powers. "That voice was more fearful to demons than thunder (for if they feared his garments, how much more his voice); it led demons bound, it cleaned out the world, it destroyed illnesses, cast out wickedness, elevated the truth, had Christ sitting on it, and Christ went forth with him everywhere."[135] The arresting image of Christ seated on Paul's voice leads John to a favored comparison with the heavenly Cherubim and Seraphim.[136] Substituting for the voice the fleshy tongue which projects it (and offers a more suitably solid perch), Chrysostom draws a vivid parallel between Paul's tongue, which he says served as a chair for Christ, and the Cherubim, whose backs form a seat for the Lord in the temple and in heaven.[137] The mention of the Cherubim always brings to mind their celestial cousins, so John includes them for comparison also: "For Paul's tongue became worthy of receiving Christ by speaking those things which were dear to Christ, and flying [ἵπτασθαι] like the Seraphim to an inexpressible height." So the tongue becomes a seat, which is further transformed into a bird, whose lofty speech is illustrated by a quotation from Rom 8:38–39, introduced by an epideictic commonplace: "For what could be higher [ὑψηλότερον] than that voice which said …?" The mixed metaphor continues after the Romans quotation, in dual exclamations about the microcosmic bodily form of this one Pauline body feature: "What sort of wings do you suppose this voice had? What sort of eyes?"[138] Though the logic of the intercalated metaphors is in disarray, the orator's point is clear: Paul's voice spoke the highest truths, and penetrated, searingly, into the forces of evil. John offers 2 Cor 2:11 ("for we are not ignorant of Satan's designs") as the proof text of this point, along with the historical testimony of the demons themselves, who fled, not only at the sound of his voice, but also at even a distant glimpse of his garments (Acts 19:12). But in making this point John is treading on old ground, so he reverts to his initial theme to gear up for yet another round on Paul's mouth.

"It is the dust of this mouth that I would wish to see," John repeats, and then amplifies his previous praise with even greater hyperbole: "through Paul's mouth Christ spoke great and inexpressible things, and even greater things than he spoke through his own mouth."[139] The justification John gives for this rather extraordi-

---

[135] *hom. in Rom.* 32.3 [60.679].

[136] This was employed also in the σύγκρισις of these beings with a different Pauline body part, the chest, in *hom. in 1 Cor.* 13, discussed above.

[137] "For just as he was seated upon those powers, thus also was he upon Paul's tongue" [Καθάπερ γὰρ ἐπὶ τῶν δυνάμεων ἐκείνων ἐκάθητο, οὕτω καὶ ἐπὶ τῆς τοῦ Παύλου γλώττης] (*hom. in Rom.* 32.3 [60.679]). For the scriptural allusion, see 4 Kgdms 19:15, ὁ καθήμενος ἐπὶ τῶν χερουβιν, and 2 Kgdms 6:2, τὸ ὄνομα κυρίου τῶν δυνάμεων καθημένου ἐπὶ τῶν χερουβιν.

[138] Πόσας δοκεῖ σοι πτέρυγας ἔχειν αὕτη ἡ φωνή; πόσους ὀφθαλμούς; (*hom. in Rom.* 32.3 [60.679]).

[139] *hom. in Rom.* 32.3 [60.679].

nary statement (one that exceeds even Paul's own claims!), is the promise of John 14:12, that the disciples will do even greater things than Jesus. Chrysostom takes this to apply analogically to their speech, also [ὥσπερ γὰρ εἰργάσατο μείζονα διὰ τῶν μαθητῶν, οὕτω καὶ ἐφθέγξατο]. To prop up this exalted claim further, John points both to the spiritual inspiration of Paul's speech, and to its consequently oracular character: "through Paul's voice the spirit gave the world those marvelous oracles" [οἱ θαυμαστοὶ ἐκεῖνοι χρησμοί]. Chrysostom wishes to claim for Paul's mouth the praise accorded both to word and deed, so in his last exhortation about the mouth he gives, in conventional epideictic form, an extended list of its noteworthy πράξεις.

> For what good thing did that mouth not effect [Τί γὰρ οὐκ εἰργάσατο ἐκεῖνο τὸ στόμα ἀγαθόν;]? It drove out demons, freed sins, muzzled tyrants, fenced in the tongues of philosophers, led the world to God, convinced barbarians to engage in philosophy, reformed everything on earth. And even the things in heaven he disposed of in the way that he wished, binding those whom he wished, and releasing the inhabitants there by means of the authority that had been given to him.[140]

Paul's Heart

After the lavish (and, as we have seen, somewhat serpentine) treatment of Paul's mouth, Chrysostom moves down the torso to continue his *ekphrasis* of Paul's ostensibly decomposed body. "Not only the mouth, but also the dust of that heart [καρδία] I would wish to see." Because the heart is a multi-dimensional internal organ, both the source of life pumping through the body and the seat of emotion and thought, it offers Chrysostom a range of rhetorical options. And he selects most of them. First, with litotes ("one would not be mistaken in saying …"), John depicts Paul's heart via epithets of its own: "the heart of the world," "the fountain of countless blessings," "a source and element of our life."[141] This introduces a theme which will pervade this miniature portrait of Paul's heart: it is the central bodily organ, not just for Paul's own body, but for the entire world, and specifically for the church: "for the spirit of life was provided for all from Paul's heart, and it was given to the members of Christ, not sent forth through an artery [οὐ δι' ἀρτηρίας ἐκπεμπόμενον], but through freely chosen good deeds [ἀλλὰ διὰ προαιρέσεως ἀγαθῶν]."[142] As John tells it, Paul's heart was at the center of the spiritual circulatory system of the world and the church, pumping the life force to all. And that animating spirit in this metaphorical complex is found not in the bloodstream, but in the palpable power of προαίρεσις, which Paul constantly exhibited and in some sense emitted into the very lifelines of the corporate body of the church, like platelets in a transfusion.

---

[140] *hom. in Rom.* 32.3 [60.679].

[141] *hom. in Rom.* 32.3 [60.679].

[142] *hom. in Rom.* 32.3 [60.679].

The cosmopolitan jurisdiction of Paul's heart is accented further as Chrysostom proceeds to extol Paul's heart for its virtue of "wideness" [πλατεῖα], or openness to all others. He gets the idea textually from Paul's self description in 2 Cor 6:11 – "our heart is opened wide" [ἡ καρδία ἡμῶν πεπλάτυνται] – and develops it further. Paul's heart was so wide that it took in whole cities, peoples and nations. The agent which dilated Paul's heart so it could be so commodious was his great love,[143] a love which came at the cost of oppression and affliction, as the apostle himself said in 2 Cor 2:4 (about writing a letter "from great affliction and distress of heart" [ἐκ πολλῆς θλίψεως καὶ συνοχῆς καρδίας]). This mention of the profound feelings Paul experienced in his heart engenders a like emotional response in his painter: "I would desire [ἐπεθύμουν][144] to see this broken [διαλελυμένη] heart, the heart which burned [πυρουμένη] for every single one of the lost, the heart which went into labor pains [ὠδίνουσα] a second time for the miscarried among her children (Gal 4:19), the heart which saw God [ὁρῶσα][145] ... the heart which became a sacrifice."[146] This list of verbal epithets describing the noteworthy actions of Paul's heart (which will be resumed in a minute or two) eases now into a catalogue of somewhat standard hyperbolic geophysical comparisons:

The heart higher than the heavens, wider than the world, brighter than a sunbeam, hotter than fire, harder than steel, the heart which released rivers.[147]

The last of these cola breaks out of the grammatical sequence of the string of comparatives, and provides Chrysostom with a promising theme to plumb in an excursus: water imagery and the heart. The idea that Paul's heart was the source from which rivers flowed was inspired by John 7:38,[148] which Chrysostom quotes in case anyone missed the allusion (and without feeling the need to justify the imprecise identification of heart and belly), and then he describes the aquatic vision of Paul's heart which has arisen in his mind's eye: a fountain leaping up and watering, not only the surface of the earth, but the souls of people.[149] Then John sees an opening for a connection with the tears mentioned previously: "not only did rivers come out of Paul's heart, but fountains of tears, both night and day." Reverting to the earlier scheme of naming the attributes, especially the afflictions,

[143] The same themes are found in the exposition of 2 Cor 6:11 in *hom. in 2 Cor.* 13.1 [61.491].
[144] Note the switch from the more neutral ἐβουλόμην in the other instances of this repeated refrain, here to accent John's own emotional reaction to Paul's anguished heart.
[145] A quotation from Matt 5:8 follows.
[146] *hom. in Rom.* 32.3 [60.679]. Chrysostom quotes Ps 50:19 to certify this claim.
[147] τὴν ὑψηλοτέραν τῶν οὐρανῶν, τὴν εὐρυτέραν τῆς οἰκουμένης, τὴν τῆς ἀκτῖνος φαιδροτέραν, τὴν τοῦ πυρὸς θερμοτέραν, τὴν τοῦ ἀδάμαντος στερροτέραν, τὴν τοὺς ποταμοὺς ἀφιεῖσαν (*hom. in Rom.* 32.3 [60.679–80]).
[148] "The one who believes in me, as Scripture said, rivers of living water will flow from his belly" [ὁ πιστεύων εἰς ἐμέ, καθὼς εἶπεν ἡ γραφή, ποταμοὶ ἐκ τῆς κοιλίας αὐτοῦ ῥεύσουσιν ὕδατος ζῶντος].
[149] See also *laud. Paul.* 1.1 [SC 300.112–14].

of Paul's heart which he longs to see, John says that this heart lived a new kind of life [ἡ καινὴν ζήσασα ζωήν], beyond the merely mortal, since in him Christ lived (Gal 2:20). The syllogistic conclusion that follows from this premise is predictable – Paul's heart was Christ's heart [ἄρα ἐκείνου καρδία ἦν ἡ Παύλου καρδία] – and matches the Christological focus in the previous portrait of Paul's mouth. This verbal equation engenders two more, for Chrysostom's runaway rhetoric in this homily delights in lists. The next two phrases interestingly (and intertextually)[150] describe Paul's heart as a writing, "a tablet of the holy spirit and a book of grace" [τοῦ πνεύματος τοῦ ἁγίου πλάξ, καὶ βιβλίον τῆς χάριτος].[151] But John does not dwell on these, for he extracts himself from this digression to revert to the scheme of the attributes of the apostolic heart whose dust he fervently desires to see, next focusing on that organ's disposition toward sinfulness. He does this in two parts, first showing how it trembled at the sins of others (documented by quotations from Gal 4:11; 2 Cor 11:3; 12:20), and then how the apostolic heart was by turns fearful (1 Cor 9:27) and confident (Rom 8:38) with respect to its own transgressions. This is the heart that "was found worthy of loving Christ as no one else loved him, the one which despised death and hell, and was crushed by brotherly tears[152] ... the heart which was most devoted, and did not endure being away from the Thessalonians for an hour (1 Thess 2:17)."[153] All these individual portraits of Paul's heart are available to the x-ray vision of the ekphrasist, who can, with the aid of autobiographical texts that disclose Paul's emotional state, even see inside his subject, and bring his internal organs into the light of day through his oratory.

Paul's Hands

When the discourse on the multifaceted heart finally runs out of steam, John turns to Paul's hands with the familiar refrain: "I would wish to see the dust of the hands which were in chains ...."[154] In a more streamlined treatment than he gave the mouth or the heart, John praises Paul's hands for four accomplishments: first (and most importantly), they bore the chains of imprisonment for the gospel;[155] second, when imposed on someone they conferred the Holy Spirit; third, by them Paul wrote the letters (with explicit reference to Gal 6:11 and 1 Cor 16:21), and, lastly, they are the hands from which the serpent fell (Acts 28:5). At least two things are surprising here. First, the composition of the letters is only the third thing

---

[150] There are deep resonances here with Paul's own play with tablets and hearts as writing materials in 2 Cor 3:2–3, a passage which itself contains rich echoes of the Old Testament (see Richard B. Hays, *Echoes of Scripture in the Letters of Paul* [New Haven: Yale University Press, 1989] 122–53).

[151] *hom. in Rom.* 32.3 [60.680].

[152] An inserted quotation of Acts 21:13 illustrates this.

[153] *hom. in Rom.* 32.3 [60.680].

[154] *hom. in Rom.* 32.4 [60.680].

[155] See the extended treatment of the theme of Paul's chain in chap. 5, pp. 176–85.

mentioned as an accomplishment of Paul's hands. And, furthermore, one might expect more treatment of Paul's miracles here, but consistently Chrysostom tends to downplay Paul's miracles in favor of his imprisonment and sufferings.[156]

Paul's Eyes[157]

Next in line are Paul's eyes, which are praised in a single sentence which begins with the same wistful yearning as the others: "I would wish to see the eyes ...." First, the glorious blinding of Paul's eyes and their sight recovered for the sake of the world's salvation are brought to mind. Then other praiseworthy attributes of Paul's eyes are named: they were allowed to see Christ in the body (1 Cor 9:1; 15:8); they were deserving of the paradoxical, heavenly vision described in 2 Cor 4:18, not seeing the seen, but the unseen; they didn't sleep, but were constantly watchful (2 Cor 6:5; 11:27); they did not experience what eyes normally do.[158]

Paul's Feet

Continuing the pattern of progressively shorter encomia to individual body parts, Chrysostom's longing to see the dust of Paul's feet crisply describes them with five attributive participles amounting to almost a singular portrait of the circumambulatory Paul: they ran through the whole world and didn't weary, were bound in stocks when the jail shook (Acts 16:24), travelled around to places both habitable and uninhabitable, and repeatedly set out on journeys.[159]

Paul's Limbs

As in the other body portrait Chrysostom again pulls up from the impossibility of going through each individual body part and says, "Why is it necessary to speak of

---

[156] In addition to the previous note, see *hom. in Ac.* 37.2; 54.1 [60.265, 373]. Not only does Chrysostom contrast Paul's miracles to his sufferings, but also commonly to his preaching (*hom. in Ac.* 37.1; 43.2; 55.2 [60.263–4, 304, 382]). This conforms to his catechetical motives: to insist on Paul's humanness, and, therefore, imitability. We shall give a full treatment of Chrysostom's attitudes toward Paul's miracles in chap. 6, pp. 291–95.

[157] Compare the mini-encomium to Paul's eyes (in the midst of an encomium to Paul's tears) in *hom. in Col.* 12.3 [62.384–5], where they are blessed because of the marvelous things his tears did – they emanated a spiritual beauty, saw paradise, and beheld the third heaven – but even moreso because they saw Christ. See chap. 5, pp. 186–90 for a full analysis of this passage.

[158] τῶν ὀφθαλμῶν ... τῶν οὐ πασχόντων τὰ τῶν ὀφθαλμῶν (*hom. in Rom.* 32.4 [60.680]). A variant reading deals with this uncertain reference by recasting it as "they did not suffer things from the envious" [ὀφθαλμιώντων for ὀφθαλμῶν].

[159] *hom. in Rom.* 32.4 [60.680]. This portrait of Paul's feet is similar to the previous somatic portrait from *hom. in 1 Cor.* 13, but lacks the obvious Isaiah 52:7 passage, which shows that John is starting to rush through his theme now.

each part? [Καὶ τί δεῖ κατὰ μέρος λέγειν;]."¹⁶⁰ Here Chrysostom is bowing not only to exhaustion (his and his audience's), but also to rhetorical expectation. The goal of an encomium to a person's body, as well as an *ekphrasis* of a body or work of art, is not to give an exhaustive catalogue of each single member, but to supply enough detail to achieve the desired aim: the public placarding of the virtuous or conspicuous features of a person's physical and psychic self. So Chrysostom closes the body portrait proper with a disquisition on "the rest" of the body parts via the catch-all, and Scripturally rich, category of "limbs" [μέλη]. John exclaims that he would wish to see Paul's tomb [τάφος], and the limbs [τὰ μέλη] encased there. These limbs are the weapons of righteousness (2 Cor 6:7; cf. Rom 6:13), the weapons of light (Rom 13:12), members which are now alive [τὰ μέλη τὰ νῦν ζῶντα], but were dead while he lived [νενεκρωμένα δὲ ὅτε ἔζη].¹⁶¹ Although he doesn't mention their dust, Chrysostom is claiming that Paul's limbs which are presently at Rome in a decayed state are actually more alive now than they were in their earthly sojourn. The reason for this is a seamless blend of Chrysostom's pervasive interpretation of Paul as an ascetic who was dead to the desires of the flesh and Paul's own vivid epistolary self-portraits depicting his cruciform, necrotic existence in Christ: in his limbs lived Christ (Gal 2:20), for his limbs were crucified to Christ (Gal 2:19; cf. 2 Cor 4:10). Paul's limbs were members of Christ [τὰ τοῦ Χριστοῦ μέλη] (Rom 12:15; 1 Cor 12:12–14, 27), they were clad in Christ (Rom 13:14; Gal 3:27), constituted the temple of the Holy Spirit (1 Cor 6:19; cf. 3:16), the holy building (cf. Eph 2:21), they were bound in the spirit (Acts 20:22), were nailed to the fear of God, and had the marks of Christ (Gal 6:17). The broad category of μέλη serves to conclude the inventory of Pauline body parts with this Scriptural smorgasbord of Christian anthropological concepts. The portrait of Paul's limbs which John draws is, like the apostle's own, a self-referential portrait of Christ, though drawn in an utterly impressionistic fashion, in that the portrait of Christ that it evokes remains assumed but indistinct.

Rome's Ferocious Guardian

At long last, with the reference to the "weapons" of Paul's limbs Chrysostom has found a way to return to his original subject – the city of Rome – by way of the metaphorical claim that Paul's body (oh, yes, and Peter's, too)¹⁶² is a wall which protects the city of Rome, rendering it safer than all towers or ten thousand battlements. This reversion to the panegyric on Rome recapitulates an epideictic *topos*, but here in paradoxical form: what most safeguards the imperial city is the living limbs of the saintly dead body within it, which constitutes its spiritual

---

¹⁶⁰ *hom. in Rom.* 32.4 [60.680].
¹⁶¹ *hom. in Rom.* 32.4 [60.680].
¹⁶² Note the clearly singular phrasing, which reflects the panegyric to Paul's body only: Τοῦτο τὸ σῶμα τειχίζει τὴν πόλιν ἐκείνην, ὃ παντὸς πύργου καὶ μυρίων ἐστὶ περιβόλων ἀσφαλέστερον.

bulwark against assault.[163] But a wall is a pretty tame image for one as well outfitted for spiritual combat as Paul, so John switches his slide one more time: "I would wish to see the spiritual lion [ὁ λέων ὁ πνευματικός]."[164] First he embellishes the lion image further with a simile: like a lion who breathes fire against a den of foxes, Paul struck out against the league of demons and philosophers. A second simile likens Paul to a clap of thunder crashing down on the φάλαγγες ("battle ranks") of the devil. Then John becomes captivated by the militaristic imagery, first drawing an entertaining caricature of the devil in fear and trembling at the sight of Paul, like some new recruit slunk back from the front ranks [οὐδὲ ἐκ παρατάξεως], retreating and fleeing as if he had seen a shadow or heard some unexpected noise. He documents this dramatic image from Paul's letters, interpreting 1 Cor 5:2 as indicating that the devil was distant from Paul when he "handed over" the fornicator to him, and 2 Cor 2:7 and 11 as manifesting the devil's impotence in that Paul was able "to snatch the man back up again right out of the devil's hands."[165] Chrysostom finds the same supremacy of Paul over the devil in 1 Tim 1:20, where Paul hands two heretics over to Satan.[166] The apostle is then depicted as the field general in the battle between God and the evil powers, who leads forth the men under his command to meet the enemy, rousing their spirits and soothing their anxieties. Chrysostom quotes Eph 6:12 as his proof text here, the exhortation to a non-worldly battle over a prize available only in the heavens (as a citation from 1 Cor 6:3 supports even further). "By keeping all these things in mind," John exhorts, "let us stand nobly" in this same fight.

This portrait of Paul, which forms the conclusion to the homily series on Romans, ends with a classic epideictic peroration. Customarily John heads off at the pass any proffered excuses for not imitating Paul by accenting the fact that "Paul was a human being, sharing the same nature as we, and having all other things in common, too" [Καὶ γὰρ καὶ Παῦλος ἄνθρωπος ἦν, τῆς αὐτῆς φύσεως ἡμῖν μετέχων, καὶ τὰ ἄλλα πάντα ἔχων κοινά].[167] It was his great love for Christ which

---

Then Chrysostom adds Peter as an afterthought [καὶ μετὰ τούτου τὸ Πέτρου], and immediately justifies Peter's inclusion by reference to the fact that Paul esteemed Peter when he was alive (quoting, somewhat inexactly, Gal 1:18). "This is why grace considered Peter worthy of making a common dwelling with Paul after he died" (*hom. in Rom.* 32.4 [60.680]). This attempt at parity assumes, however, that Paul has the primacy, which by argument Peter can be shown as justified to share. But of course there is nothing on Peter in the homily which is at all like the loving portrait of Paul's body, because this is a hymn to the author of the text on which John has just completed this lengthy series of expositions. We shall return to the topic of the relationship between Paul and Peter in Chrysostom's writings in chap. 7, pp. 394–95.

[163] Cf. *hom. prec.* 2 [50.784], of both as τὸ τεῖχος τῆς οἰκουμένης.

[164] *hom. in Rom.* 32.4 [60.680]. See chap 3. n. 144 for other passages where Chrysostom calls Paul a lion.

[165] *hom. in Rom.* 32.4 [60.680].

[166] *hom. in Rom.* 32.4 [60.681].

[167] *hom. in Rom.* 32.4 [60.681]; cf. *laud. Paul.* 2.1, 10; 6.2, 3; 7.3 [SC 300.144, 160, 264, 266, 298–300].

enabled Paul to ascend to heaven and stand with the angels, a virtue which any should be able to imitate [ζηλῶσαι] if they "kindle that fire in themselves."[168] And, as a final appeal, John joins archetypal image and text by pointing out that "Paul would not have cried out saying 'be imitators of me, as also I am of Christ' (1 Cor 11:1) if this were not possible."[169] The epideictic altar call follows ("therefore, let us not only marvel or be amazed at him, but also let us imitate him"), to which is conjoined a final result which forms an inclusio with the opening of this lengthy discourse on Paul's presence and body: "so that we might be worthy of *seeing him* when we go forth from here, and share in his inexpressible glory."[170] In this peroration we see clearly the intent of Chrysostom's portraiture as we have described it above: not to capture the person of Paul for posterity, but to create an image for pastoral catechesis and enrichment. The hearers are not to try to fashion their bodies cosmetically to resemble the apostle, but are to sculpt their behavior to match that exemplified by the holy man's members.

Conclusion

This living portrait of the corpse of Paul which Chrysostom composes in the last homily on Romans is thus a literary analogue to the way in which Chrysostom described the task and opportunity of Pauline exegesis in the initial *Argumentum* to the series: "Continually when I hear the letters of the blessed Paul read … I rejoice in the pleasure of that spiritual trumpet, and I am roused to attention and warmed with desire because I recognize the voice I love, and seem to imagine him all but present [καὶ μονονουχὶ παρόντα αὐτὸν δοκῶ φαντάζεσθαι] and conversing with me [διαλεγόμενον ὁρᾶν]."[171] If the goal of an *ekphrasis* is to provoke in an audience the first-hand emotional experience of something from which they are absent – a work of art, a person, or some other artifact – then one can see why it is the perfect vehicle for Chrysostom's task of biographical exegesis, for he seeks in his homilies to effect a vivid, living encounter of his congregation with the person of the apostle who springs to life for him in the reading of his letters. John wishes to recreate for others his own profound experience of Pauline presence in the act of reading and interpretation. In his portrait of Paul's body Chrysostom has overtly cast himself as the ultimate ascetic art critic – who prefers the dust of a dead saint to any earthly delight. The person of John is therefore created in the same moment as he creates Paul, placarding himself before his audience as a living image of the ascetic

---

[168] τὸ πῦρ ἐκεῖνο ἀνάψαι ἐν ἡμῖν (*hom. in Rom.* 32.4 [60.682]).
[169] *hom. in Rom.* 32.4 [60.682].
[170] *hom. in Rom.* 32.4 [60.682]; cf. 32.2 [60.678].
[171] *hom. in Rom.* Arg. 1 [60.391].

value system he lauds in Paul.[172] In these body portraits, especially the Romans homily, we encounter exegesis and exposition as necromantic acts[173] which re-vivify dead authors through their words and other sources for living encounters with new generations of readers. And this live engagement has a wider field of vision as well, for Chrysostom's mimetic logic calls for multiple and continual encounters with copies of Paul in the preacher who evokes him, in one's fellow Christians, and, above all, in the mirror of one's own soul. These portraits of Paul's body which Chrysostom ingeniously composes from bits and pieces of somatic references in the Pauline letters and Acts,[174] are intended to redound to unmatched praise for the apostle, the imitable embodiment of human virtue. Seen in this light, Paul's body is not so much flesh and bones as a canvas upon which the multiple virtues of Paul's soul were painted, as living tatoos upon the epidermis that are visible to the eye of the spectators. Even as he lovingly depicts Paul's body, Chrys-ostom's own ascetic distrust of the body requires that he spiritualize the form (rather than praise it for its usual attributes of strength, beauty, etc.). Yet the fact that he can employ the Pauline body for praise at all, and repeatedly remind his audience that they share the same φύσις and σάρξ as the apostle, is an indication that John holds out promise for the possibilities of the flesh, at least as malleable modeling clay in which a life of excellence can be shaped.[175] Chrysostom's part by

---

[172] "All asceticism has an audience, even if the audience is merely the self. Authors of hagiography not only carefully watched themselves, but, especially in their prologues and epi-logues, they invited audiences to observe them in the practice of virtue" (Krueger, "Hagiogra-phy as an Ascetic Practice," 225). As a pulpit orator, Chrysostom always had a kind of immediate visibility, but at times, such as this homily so vibrantly demonstrates, he could enhance that *ethos* even further by direct self-reference.

[173] This correlates further with Chrysostom's own ascetic logic, itself profoundly influenced by Paul's self-understanding in Gal 2:19–20, which esteems a form of "living death" in earthly existence, as seen, for instance, when he says that Paul's limbs "are living now, but while he lived were already put to death" [τὰ μέλη τὰ νῦν ζῶντα, νενεκρωμένα δὲ ὅτε ἔζη] (32.4 [60.680]). Paul's own death and resurrection logic, incorporated by Chrysostom, means that the living death of the now dead Paul is revivified for viewing.

[174] Compare Swain's description of the role of the biographer: "But it is the aim of every biographical text to gather detailed information about the individual. The individual's existence is codified and edited by the text's author, who has particular purposes and obligations in collect-ing and publishing the information. This process of documentation can often be read as exem-plifying the exercise of power on or by the individual who is the subject of the text ... When the writing of biographical texts can be identified with particular groups with particular aims, the codification of an individual's life ceases to be a simple story" ("Biography and Biographic," 2).

[175] This fits the ascetic anthropology Patricia Cox Miller (as informed by Jean-Pierre Vernant) identifies in Chrysostom's contemporaries, Gregory of Nyssa and Gregory of Nazianzus: "In this way, asceticism can be understood as an attempt to manipulate the dim body so as to drive it as close as possible toward that corporeal vitality that is the mark of its exemplar [i.e., the divine]. Asceticism, that is, attempts to control the play of the body as signifier; it attempts to reimagine how the body can be read, and what it can say" ("Dreaming the Body: An Aesthetics of Asceti-cism," 282). Chrysostom himself works at this imaginative task in his wondering aloud, "if Paul were in a bodiless nature, what could he not have said? What could he not have done" [οὗτος εἰ ἐν ἀσωμάτῳ φύσει ἦν, τί οὐκ ἂν εἶπε; τί δὲ οὐκ ἂν ἔπραξε;] (*laud. Paul.* 7.3 [SC 300.298]). Just

part portraits of Paul's body are "strong acts of visual imagination" which seek to render the divine corporeal possible before the eyes of his hearers.[176] For Chrysostom the success of the endeavor of portraiture is to be measured not solely by the immediate sensation of real encounter it provokes in the hearers (as with *ekphrasis* in general), but by its eventual replication in subsequent living. What exactly this means is (paradoxically) fleshed out even more tangibly in the portraits of Paul's soul, to which we shall turn in the following chapter.

---

prior to this passage in the same homily Chrysostom had defended the body itself: "Consequently we say that human beings are miserable, not when we see that they are clothed in flesh, but when we see them not using that flesh as they should. Since also Paul was clothed in flesh" [Ἐντεῦθεν καὶ ἀνθρώπους ἀθλίους εἶναί φαμεν, οὐχ ὅταν σάρκα περικειμένους ἴδωμεν, ἀλλ' ὅταν μὴ εἰς δέον αὐτῇ χρωμένους· ἐπεὶ καὶ ὁ Παῦλος σάρκα περιέκειτο] (*laud. Paul.* 7.3 [SC 300.298–300]).

[176] Here I am taking up a phrase from Miller, "Dreaming the Body," 282: "Since literal visual perception could not present the body of plenitude, many ascetic thinkers relied on strong acts of visual imagination to carry them from the dim body to the body from nowhere." Chrysostom's *ekphraseis* of Paul's body represent a second such strategy, alongside the dreams that are the focus of Miller's essay.

Chapter 5

"The Meadow of Virtues" (λειμὼν ἀρετῶν): Portraits of Paul's Soul

Painting a Soul

Because of Paul's status for Chrysostom as the archetype of virtue, when he lovingly portrays Paul it is his soul even more than his body that interests him. This is also to be expected, given his general Christian platonic favoring of the soul over the body.[1] Yet one would think a soul harder to paint than a body, for, being invisible, it is less susceptible to graphic depiction.[2] But this is no limitation for Chrysostom's literary art, because he regards the virtues, as we have observed earlier, as the colors with which one paints one's own self-portrait,[3] and the mind

---

[1] For one simple declaration of the soul's superiority to the body (of many in Chrysostom's writings), see *laud. Paul.* 1.11 [SC 300.128], quoted below, p. 147.

[2] The concept of painting a portrait of the soul is very old in Greek literature, given classic expression in Plato, *Resp.* 9.588B: "forming an image of the soul with words, so that the one who says those things might see what he has said" [Εἰκόνα πλάσαντες τῆς ψυχῆς λόγῳ, ἵνα εἰδῇ ὁ ἐκεῖνα λέγων οἷα ἔλεγεν]. The synesthetic dimension of the relationship between words, perception and reality is nicely marked here.

[3] Compare the discussion between Socrates and the painter Parrhasius in Xenophon, *Mem.* 3.10.3: "'Well now' [Socrates said], 'do you also reproduce the character of the soul [ἀπομιμεῖσθε τῆς ψυχῆς ἦθος], the character that is in the highest degree captivating, delightful, friendly, fascinating, lovable? Or is it impossible to imitate that [ἢ οὐδὲ μιμητόν ἐστι τοῦτο;].' 'Oh no, Socrates; for how could one imitate that which has neither shape nor colour nor any of the qualities you mentioned just now, and is not even visible?'" [Πῶς γὰρ ἄν, ἔφη, μιμητὸν εἴη, ὦ Σώκρατες, ὃ μήτε συμμετρίαν μήτε χρῶμα μήτε ὧν σὺ εἶπας ἄρτι μηδὲν ἔχει μηδὲ ὅλως ὁρατόν ἐστιν;]. In the succeeding dialogue Socrates argues that, just as emotions are expressed on human faces, so also can the painter replicate the ways in which virtuous attributes (such as τὸ μεγαλοπρεπές, ἐλευθέριον, σωφρονικόν, φρόνιμον) and vices (τὸ ταπεινὸν, ἀνελεύθερον, ὑβριστικόν, ἀπειρόκαλον) are reflected in the face, forms and movements of a human body, and consequently are artistically replicable [μιμητά]. In *poenit.* 1.1 [49.277], Chrysostom describes how he painted an image of the soul of his congregation in his mind as a consolation to him during an absence from them: "Just like painters who make pictures of bodies by mixing various colors [Καὶ καθάπερ οἱ ζωγράφοι, ποικίλα χρώματα κεραννύντες τὰς τῶν σωμάτων εἰκόνας ἐργάζονται], thus also we, just as though mixing the various colors of virtue [καθάπερ ποικίλα χρώματα ἀρετῆς κεράσαντες] – your zeal in our gatherings, your eagerness to listen, your positive disposition toward the speaker, all your other excellent deeds [τὰ ἄλλα πάντα κατορθώματα] – and sketching the character of your soul [καὶ τὸν χαρακτῆρα τῆς ψυχῆς ὑμῶν ὑπογράψαντες], placing it before the eyes of our mind [καὶ πρὸ τῶν ὀφθαλμῶν τῆς διανοίας θέντες], through this image we continually received sufficient comfort in our distance from you" [ἱκανὴν διὰ τῆς φαντασίας ταύτης ἐλαμβάνομεν τῆς ἀποδημίας παραμυθίαν].

and the imagination as their canvas. These hermeneutical assumptions about soul portraiture are laid bare in a fictional dialogue Chrysostom once engaged in with an imaginary interlocutor who resisted John's admonition to attend to the beauty of the soul, rather than to bodily beauty which leads to lust:

"But," he says, "I cannot see the beauty of a soul" ['Αλλ' οὐχ ὁρῶ, φησὶ, κάλλος ψυχῆς]" But if you wish, you will see it ['Αλλ' ἄν ἐθέλῃς, ὄψει]. Just as it is possible for a person who doesn't see absent beauties with the eyes to marvel at them in the mind [τοὺς ἀπόντας καλοὺς ἔστιν ὀφθαλμοῖς μὴ ἰδόντα τῷ νῷ θαυμάσαι], thus it is possible without eyes to see the beauty of the soul [δυνατὸν ψυχῆς κάλλος χωρὶς ὀφθαλμῶν ἰδεῖν]. Haven't you often sketched a lovely form [ὑπέγραψας … μορφὴν εὐειδῆ], and been somewhat moved by the model? Form an image now of the beauty of a soul [ἀνατύπωσον καὶ νῦν ψυχῆς κάλλος], and delight in that lovely form. He says, "but I cannot see incorporeal things" [οὐχ ὁρῶ … ἀσώματα]. Indeed we see the incorporeal, rather than the corporeal, with the mind [Καὶ μὴν τῶν σωμάτων αὐτὰ μᾶλλον ὁρῶμεν τῷ νῷ].[4]

Chrysostom sees, with his mind's eye, Paul's soul as a multi-colored tablet of enfleshed human virtue, which it is the task of his preaching to display for all to see. Using the medium of words,[5] Chrysostom paints with a dazzling palette of colors – the catalogue of virtues already well scripted in the Pauline letters and in the Acts of the Apostles.[6] He derives from those sources a mixture of characteristically Christian emphases (such as the virtue of ἀγάπη) and the modified Stoicism of the virtue catalogues found within Paul's letters[7] which provides an exact fit with Chrysostom's own ethical sensibilities as a late fourth-century Christian ascetic on whom that model had already been indelibly imprinted. The Paul who emerges from this color-sensitivity examination is a soul unendingly capacious in virtue, painted with the pure hues of a range of human virtues practiced and displayed.[8] However, this extraordinary claim – that Paul is the exemplar of all human virtues simultaneously – inevitably entails possible contradictions, such as between Paul's humility and his boasting, or his clemency and his righteous anger. Thus one of the things which generates some fire and interest in these portraits is the potential color-clash among the virtues with which Chrysostom will have to deal.[9]

---

[4] hom. in 2 Cor. 7.7 [61.453–54].

[5] Compare Plato, Resp. 9.588D: "speech is more easily molded than wax and other such media" [εὐπλαστότερον κηροῦ καὶ τῶν τοιούτων λόγος].

[6] Lentz, Luke's Portrait of Paul, for instance, has argued that Luke has portrayed Paul in such a way as to demonstrate his possession of the four cardinal virtues (σωφροσύνη, ἀνδρεία, φρόνησις, δικαιοσύνη). The influence of the standard virtues is found often in Paul's own letters.

[7] On which, see, for instance, Joachim Gnilka, Der Philipperbrief (HTKNT 10/3; Freiburg/Basel/Vienna: Herders, 1968) 221–22 (in regard to Phil 4:8); John T. Fitzgerald, "Virtue/Vice Lists," ABD 6.857–59, with extensive bibliography.

[8] See the same strategy in Lucian, Im. 15: "all the several virtues of her soul shall be portrayed each by itself in a single picture that is a true copy of the model" [αἱ πᾶσαι τῆς ψυχῆς ἀρεταὶ καθ' ἑκάστην εἰκὼν μία γεγράψεται πρὸς τὸ ἀρχέτυπον μεμιμημένη] (for the full context, see chap. 3, n. 6).

[9] An excellent example of where Chrysostom faces this fact directly is in the quasi-apologetics of laud. Paul. 5.8 [SC 300.244–46]. There he treats the diversity of virtues in support of

In this chapter we shall exhibit and analyze various portraits of Paul's soul, and then turn to a third category of portraits which focus on neither Paul's body nor his soul, *per se*, but encapsulate the entirety of the man – body and soul – in a single, personified and hypostasized attribute.

De laudibus sancti Pauli

Chrysostom sprinkles mini-encomia to individual Pauline virtues throughout his homilies and other works,[10] but the major source of his portraits of Paul's soul is his seven homilies *In Praise of St. Paul.*[11] Although they date from the same Antiochene period as the body portraits we examined in chapter 4,[12] it is no accident that these orations contain no portrait of Paul's body.[13] Chrysostom's predominant concern in these homilies is with Paul's soul,[14] as signalled by the opening line of the first homily, which now fittingly introduces the set, and serves as the master-

---

his defense of Paul's variability (for a full discussion, see chap. 6, pp. 330–53): "Therefore, when you see him fleeing dangers, marvel the same as when you see him rushing forward to meet them. For just as the latter is proof of bravery [ἀνδρεία], the former is of wisdom [σοφία]. When you see him telling his magnificent exploits, marvel the same as when you see him speaking modestly. For just as the latter shows humility [ταπεινοφροσύνη], the former indicates magnanimity of soul [μεγαλοψυχία]. When you see him boasting, marvel the same as when you see him refusing praise. For the latter shows an uninflated character [ἦθος ἄτυφον], and the former compassion and love for others [φιλόστοργον καὶ φιλάνθρωπον]."

[10] For example, *hom. in Rom.* Arg. 2 [60.394]: "That holy soul was of such a type [Τοιαύτη γὰρ ἡ ἁγία ἐκείνη ψυχή]. It encompassed the whole world, he carried all people around in himself, considering the greatest pedigree to be the godly one." Often these are in the form of brief laudatory exclamations, such as the frequent refrain, "Do you see the greatness of his soul and the height of his intelligence?" [Εἶδες ψυχῆς μέγεθος καὶ φρονήματος ὕψος] (*hom. in 1 Cor.* 25.4 [61.210]).

[11] Anianus of Celeda, who translated these seven encomia to Paul into Latin between 415 and 419 C.E., remarked that in them "the great Apostle is not only portrayed but in a certain sense awakened from the dead, so that he becomes once more a living pattern of Christian perfection" (Quasten, *Patrology*, 3.456).

[12] Piédagnel, SC 300.10–20 (around 390 C.E.).

[13] As noted already by Ernst von Dobschütz, *Der Apostel Paulus II. Seine Stellung in der Kunst* (Halle: Waisenhaus, 1928) 2–3.

[14] When we understand this to be the theme of these orations (not praise of Paul in general), the relative lack of attention to Paul's body and lesser regard to the external circumstances of his life are unsurprising. But because Chrysostom treats these extensively elsewhere in his writings (as the full investigation of chap. 6 will demonstrate), the more extreme conclusions of Piédagnel quoted below (n. 21) concerning Chrysostom's reservations about the appropriateness of epideictic rhetoric for a saint need to be tempered. This illustrates the need to understand these discourses in the light of Chrysostom's wider oeuvre, and its attention to Paul. (It also possibly undermines arguments about the date and provenance of the homilies *de laudibus sancti Pauli* which restrict themselves to these seven discourses when trying to evaluate Chrysostom's claim often to have sounded these themes to his congregation [Piédagnel, SC 300.10–13], for, as we have seen, praise of Paul was constant and ubiquitous in Chrysostom's homilies, and therefore was not restricted to this one type of festal oratory.)

portrait for the whole:"one would not be mistaken in calling Paul's soul a meadow of virtues and a spiritual paradise."[15] In the homilies which follow, individual plants in this spiritual germinator will be brought into focus for special examination and praise. These discourses are to be understood as living portraits of Paul's soul, the seat of virtue, through motion-sensitive photography of the growth and emergence of the various plants.[16] The "moving picture" quality of these soul portraits is marked by the very next sentence, for Chrysostom wishes his hearers to understand from the outset that Paul was both gifted with grace and demonstrated that the philosophical demeanor of his soul was worthy of that gift.[17] The whole collection consists of Chrysostom's reflections upon the chief traits of Paul's "physionomie spirituelle."[18] Yet, despite the fact that they share this preoccupation, the seven orations exhibit variety in form and content. Homilies 1, 2, and 3 are filled with praise for the virtues in Paul's soul, and homily 6 with defending Paul's virtue against detractors; thus they especially concern us here.[19] None of the seven follows an exact chronological schema from origins and birth to noble death, which was one ideal of encomiastic composition.[20] This is because Chrysostom's rhetorical purpose was not to compose a full life of Paul for viewing and admiration,[21] but

---

[15] laud. Paul. 1.1 [SC 300.112]: Οὐκ ἄν τις ἁμάρτοι λειμῶνα ἀρετῶν καὶ παράδεισον πνευματικὸν καλέσας τὴν Παύλου ψυχήν.

[16] The moving picture quality of these orations may also be due to the editing that has resulted in the final collection, which involves a certain progression of propositions from one oration to the next. This is a fruitful area for future research.

[17] οὕτω πολὺ μὲν ἤνθει τῇ χάριτι, ἀξίαν δὲ τῆς χάριτος ἐπεδείκνυτο τῆς ψυχῆς τὴν φιλοσοφίαν (laud. Paul. 1.1 [SC 300.112]).

[18] Piédagnel, SC 300.39; cf. Vandenberghe, Saint Jean Chrysostome, p. 51: "physionomie morale."

[19] Homilies 4, 5 and 7 are particularly concerned with the third topic of epideictic oratory, external circumstances; therefore we shall situate our analysis of those speeches in chapter 6.

[20] For discussion and references to rhetorical theory see chap. 6, pp. 200–206. As the analyses will show, each oration is structured around a central proposition, for which Paul serves as the main proof.

[21] Thus Piédagnel is correct in observing the lack of some expected commonplaces in these homilies: "Du fait même que Chrysostome n'a pas suivi le schéma traditionnel des éloges, un certain nombre de ces lieux communs disparaissaient, tels que l'éducation de Paul ou les mérites de sa ville natale" (p. 27). But he is mistaken in his conclusion that this indicates Chrysostom's "suspicion" of the rules of pagan oratory which he regards as unfit for his saintly subject ("Chrysostome, au contraire, s'est montré très indépendant et méfiant à l'égard de tels schémas qui lui semblaient réservés aux éloges d'ordre profane" [p. 27]). As we shall see in the next chapter, Chrysostom was quite willing and able to follow this schema when it suited his rhetorical purposes (as, for instance, in the comparison between Paul and Nero in hom. in 2 Tim. 4, analyzed on pp. 206–12). But in these encomia he had a different set of purposes, and that is what we seek to examine here (however, in laud. Paul. 4, as our analysis of that speech in chap. 6, pp. 212–26, will demonstrate, Chrysostom does adopt some of the very topoi Piédagnel says are lacking in the series). Piédagnel's conclusion appears to have been generated by the persuasiveness of Chrysostom's own rhetoric, which has led him to accept a wide gap between "pagan" and Christian forms of discourse ("Pourtant, en lisant ces panégyriques, on constate que Chrysostome, dans certains thèmes qu'il y introduit, abandonne quelques usages de l'éloge, et que, d'autre part, ses arguments fondamentaux y sont proprement chrétiens" [SC 300.29]).

instead to present detailed portraits of Paul's soul to placard the virtues he inculcated so that they might be imitated by others. For Chrysostom the source of praise for Paul was not a total curriculum vitae, but instead the inner cultivation and outward manifestation of a godly, virtuous soul.

The main point of the first three homilies is that Paul is the supreme example of human virtue for all time.[22] Paul is not to be praised only for excellence in one or two of the virtues, either, but indeed in his soul all the virtues are completely manifest. This makes composing encomia to him a daunting task:

For when one soul brings together all the virtues in humanity [ἅπαντα τὰ ἐν ἀνθρώποις καλά], and all of them to the highest degree – not only the human virtues, but even those of the angels – how shall we successfully render the magnitude of the praises?[23]

In making this bold assertion, Chrysostom has set a challenging proposition in front of himself. But this extravagant claim is not unparalleled in this type of rhetoric, as Lucian nicely demonstrates:

So let her be pictured as possessing all the good gifts that come from Helicon [καὶ δὴ γεγράφθω πάντα συλλήβδην τὰ ἐκ τοῦ Ἑλικῶνος ἀγαθὰ ἔχουσα]. Unlike Clio, Polymnia, Calliope, and the others, each of whom has a single accomplishment, she shall have those of all the Muses, and in addition those of Hermes and Apollo.[24]

Hence, in claiming that Paul's soul possessed all the virtues, Chrysostom was reaching for the hyperbole which epideictic rhetoric so exemplified. Yet this universal claim does not prohibit detailed dissection of individual Pauline virtues for study and praise, in analogy to the discrete members of the Pauline body portrayed in the *ekphraseis* examined in chapter. 4. Among the manifold virtues of which Paul was the perfect exemplar, particular characteristics do emerge for separate treatment in these homilies (and in other writings),[25] and they represent an amalgam of traditional virtue theory (the four cardinal virtues so customary in epideictic oratory)[26] and special Christian commitments and values.

---

[22] *laud. Paul.* 2.1 [SC 300.142]. See also the discussion in chap. 2 on Paul as the ἀρχέτυπος τῆς ἀρετῆς, and also *exp. in Job.* 9.3 [SC 346.302], on Paul, "to whom no one is equal, the farthest level of virtue" [Βούλει Παῦλον, οὗ ἴσον οὐδὲν ἂν γένοιτο; τὸ ἔσχατον τῆς ἀρετῆς μέρος]

[23] *laud. Paul.* 1.1 [SC 300.114]; cf. the conclusion to that discourse, in 1.16 [300.140]. That is also the theme of all of *laud. Paul.* 2.

[24] Lucian, *Imagines* 16.

[25] The choice of key virtues named in praise of a person may be related to the kind of principle of selection which Plutarch (*Alex.* 1.3) says he employs in his βίοι. He distinguishes a βίος from ἱστορία, saying that in the former one does not need to tell everything, but only what is most revealing of character (such as the face in painted portraits). Therefore, he says, he will concentrate on "the signs of the soul for portraying the life of each person" [τὰ τῆς ψυχῆς σημεῖα μᾶλλον ἐνδύεσθαι καὶ διὰ τούτων εἰδοποιεῖν τὸν ἑκάστου βίον], and leave to others the great exploits and battles (for he had argued earlier that sometimes a single utterance, story or joke can be more disclosive of character than long lists of victories in battle or sieges of cities).

[26] On which see Russell and Wilson, *Menander Rhetor*, xiv–xv. See also the expanded list of virtues of the soul ("the virtuous morals" [τὰ σπουδαῖα ἠθικά] and the actions which follow

Laud. Paul. 1: *Paul as the Brightest in the Biblical Portrait Gallery*

The best way to experience Chrysostom's spiritual portraiture of Paul is by a close reading and analysis of the first three homilies *de laudibus sancti Pauli*. These homilies in praise of Paul make use of two predominant motifs of the genre: proof by σύγκρισις, comparison,[27] and a call for imitation in the peroration. *laud. Paul.* 1 is a perfect example of both, as of epideictic oratory in general.[28] One of the longest, it is the most carefully crafted and developed of the three.[29] My compositional analysis of this speech (and of each of the seven homilies *de laudibus sancti Pauli*) will proceed according to the streamlined categorization of rhetorical τάξις laid out by Aristotle, which includes a προοίμιον (introduction), πρόθεσις (proposition), πίστεις (proofs of the proposition), and ἐπίλογος (conclusion and final appeal).[30]

---

from them) in Theon, *Prog.* 8 [Spengel, 2.110]), including (in adjectival form): φρόνιμος, σώφρων, ἀνδρεῖος, δίκαιος, ὅσιος, ἐλευθέριος, μεγαλόφρων, καὶ ὅσα τοιαῦτα ("wise, moderate, brave, just, holy, free, generous, and such things as these").

[27] For justification of this in rhetorical theory see, e.g., Aristotle, *Rh.* 1.9.38: "And one should compare him with illustrious persons [δεῖ δὲ πρὸς ἐνδόξους συγκρίνειν], for it affords grounds for amplification [αὔξησις] and is excellent, if he can be proved better than men of worth [καὶ καλόν, εἰ σπουδαίων βελτίων]. Amplification rightly falls among the forms of praise, for it deals with superiority, and superiority of the virtues" [πίπτει δ' εὐλόγως ἡ αὔξησις εἰς τοὺς ἐπαίνους· ἐν ὑπεροχῇ γάρ ἐστιν, ἡ δ' ὑπεροχὴ τῶν καλῶν]. Among other theorists, see Cicero, *De Or.* 2.85.348: "Moreover a splendid line to take in a panegyric is to compare the subject with all other men of high distinction" (also *Rh. Al.* 35.1441a; Quint. *Inst.* 2.4.21). Chrysostom would have practiced such rhetorical comparisons in his education under Libanios, among whose preserved school exercises (progymnasmata) are five συγκρίσεις (*Comp.* [Foerster 8.334–60]). For Chrysostom's use of comparisons in his panegyrics generally, see Ameringer, *Second Sophistic*, 68–85; Delehaye, *Passions des martyrs*, 152–54; in these orations specifically, see Hubbell, "Chrysostom and Rhetoric," 268–69; Frances M. Young, *Biblical Exegesis and the Formation of Christian Culture* (Cambridge: Cambridge University Press, 1997) 115.

[28] As Piédagnel noted, this is the most true to form of the seven encomia to Paul: "Pour le Iᵉʳ discours, si l'on examine les matériaux (τόποι) dont il est formé, on constate que c'est le seul de ces sept panégyriques qui soit encore assez proche du genre littéraire de l'ἐγκώμιον. C'est le seul, en effet, où, selon la coutume des auteurs de panégyriques, l'orateur exprime d'abord son embarras (ἀπόρησις) d'avoir à faire un tel éloge, et le seul dont le développement se compose d'une succession de comparaisons (συγκρίσεις) traditionelles dans les ἐγκώμια" (SC 300.11). In this judgment Piédagnel has downplayed the encomiastic features of the other six, however, in that he is seeking from them an exact use of the chronological structure of the ἐπιτάφιος λόγος (as I shall demonstrate in particular in chap. 6 below).

[29] Here I find myself completely at odds with Hubbell, "Chrysostom and Rhetoric," 268, who regards the first as the most rudimentary and the seventh as the most artistic. To some degree there is of course no accounting for taste in the rendering of these judgments. But Hubbell's assessment is based more on twentieth-century American literary canons than on an insider's appreciation of the rhetorical art of the encomium, which revels in αὔξησις, amplification, and ὑπερβολή, hyperbole.

[30] "Therefore the necessary parts of a speech are the proposition and the proof. These two things belong to each type of speech, and most speeches contain an introduction, proposition, proof and conclusion" ['Αναγκαῖα ἄρα μόρια πρόθεσις καὶ πίστις. ἴδια μὲν οὖν ταῦτα, τὰ δὲ πλεῖστα προοίμιον πρόθεσις πίστις ἐπίλογος] (Arist., *Rh.* 3.13.4). As in my *Paul and the Rheto-*

προοίμιον (Introduction).[31] We have already previewed the opening line of this speech, which signals its theme as praise of Paul's soul for possessing all the virtues wrapped up into one. After this direct opening,[32] Chrysostom makes the commonplace denial of his sufficiency[33] for the enormous challenge of speaking suitable praises to such a virtue-saturated soul: "What speech is sufficient to tell of his virtuous deeds? Or what sort of tongue will be able to achieve proper praises for him?"[34] After a third restatement of his proposition (that Paul's one soul contains within it all human, and even angelic virtues, to abundance),[35] Chrysostom closes his proem with another epideictic topos answering his initial, feigned lack of confidence: "for this is the greatest form of encomium, when the magnitude of the virtuous deeds overwhelmingly wins out over the skill of the speech; and our defeat is more magnificent to us than countless trophies."[36]

πρόθεσις καὶ πίστεις (Proposition and Proofs).[37] After a rhetorical question effecting a smooth transition ("Now, then, what would make a good starting point

---

ric of Reconciliation, here I employ Aristotle's terminology to describe the *partes orationis*, because it is simple and straightforward, and I find it the most concise and tidy way to analyze argumentative strategies and structures. (It is well known that later Hellenistic rhetoric delineated progressively more and more structural parts [see Harry Caplan, LCL vol. on *Rhet. Her.* p. 8, note a; p. 106 note b, etc.], but this was also decried by practitioners and critics alike.) Methodologically, I have chosen to give a full compositional analysis of each of Chrysostom's seven Pauline panegyrics because they are themselves complete literary wholes, whereas in the case of Chrysostom's other Pauline portraits which are portions of larger literary contexts, either treatises or biblical homilies, for the sake of scope I shall have to focus in on the pertinent sections (while setting the wider context in a more summary fashion).

[31] *laud. Paul.* 1.1 [SC 300.112–14].

[32] Rhetorical theorists recognized both a direct and a subtle approach in a προοίμιον/*exordium* (see *Rhet. Her.* 1.4.6; Cicero, *Inv. Rhet.* 1.15.20; Quint. *Inst.* 4.1; see also, in general, on theoretical discussion of introductions, Volkmann, *Rhetorik*, 127–48).

[33] "One of the most common features [of the προοίμιον of an ἐγκώμιον] was a profession of inadequacy before a subject so vast" (Burgess, *Epideictic Literature*, 122; for its recommendation in rhetorical theory see, e.g., Quintilian, *Inst.* 4.1.8–9). Chrysostom's use of this *topos* in the opening to *laud. Paul.* 1 was recognized also by Piédagnel, SC 300.11, and Hubbell, "Chrysostom and Rhetoric," 268, who offers an apt parallel from Libanios. This is one of many such instances of the commonplace ἀστεϊσμός in Chrysostom's writings (see also, e.g., *sac.* 4.6 [SC 272.266–68], discussed in chap. 6, n. 407) which disproves the assertion of Manlio Simonetti that Chrysostom deliberately parted company from the "pagan" orators by renouncing use of this *topos*: "Passando al Crisostomo [from examples among the Cappadocians] ci accorgiamo subito come questi nei suoi panegirici trascuri completamente il luogo topico dell'insufficienza dell'autore" ("Sulla struttura dei panegirici di S. Giovanni Crisostomo," *Rendiconti istituto Lombardo di scienze e lettere* [series 3/17] 86 [1953] 159–80, 160).

[34] Τίς οὖν ἀρκέσει λόγος τοῖς τούτου κατορθώμασιν; ἢ ποία δυνήσεται γλῶσσα ἐφικέσθαι τῶν ἐγκωμίων τῶν ἐκείνου; (1.1 [SC 300.114]).

[35] ἅπαντα τὰ ἐν ἀνθρώποις καλὰ ... καὶ πάντα μεθ' ὑπερβολῆς, οὐ μόνον δὲ τὰ ἀνθρώπων, ἀλλὰ καὶ τὰ τῶν ἀγγέλων.

[36] *laud. Paul.* 1.1 [SC 300.114].

[37] This major portion of the speech extends from 1.2–15 [SC 300.114–38]. As we have seen, Chrysostom articulated his proposition [πρόθεσις] several times already in the προοίμιον, which fits nicely Aristotle's prescription for epideictic exordia: "the speaker should say at once whatever

for our praises?"), Chrysostom proceeds to emphasize his proposition by reiterating it for the fourth time in the first few minutes of the speech,[38] and then immediately announces the plan of proof which his discourse will follow: "For if prophets or patriarchs or just ones or apostles or martyrs displayed some noble quality [τι γενναῖον], he [Paul][39] possessed all these things together to a superlative degree that none of them attained, whatever the particular virtue of each."[40] Chrysostom's homilies do not always follow a firmly set τάξις, both because they often recapture the spontaneity of live oratory and because Chrysostom liked to follow his muse (as we have noted with respect to his claimed Pauline inspirations), but they are by no means haphazard in arrangement. Each is devoted to a central proposition which the orator seeks to prove. In terms of rhetorical arrangement the first discourse is particularly clearly structured, and adheres to this plan promised at the outset. In the proof which follows, Chrysostom compares Paul with successive figures from the Old Testament[41] (culminating with one New Testament figure, John the Baptist).[42] The virtues of each man are portrayed and admitted, but in each case Paul is shown to be superior on the very ground of praise acknowledged for the noteworthy example. The Bible is the storehouse from which all these images are drawn. The ingenuity of this rhetorical design is that it embeds Paul in a gallery of carefully crafted portraits of biblical worthies, with Chrysostom in each case constructing on the facing page a portrait of Paul to match, but also exceed, that exemplar. We shall look at each "page" of this portrait gallery in turn.[43]

---

he likes, give the key-note and then attach the main subject" [ὅ τι γὰρ ἂν βούληται εὐθὺ εἰπόντα ἐνδοῦναι καὶ συνάψαι] (Rh. 3.14.1; text and trans. J. H. Freese, LCL).

[38] τοῦ δεῖξαι τὰ ἁπάντων ἔχοντα ἀγαθά: "demonstrating that he possessed the virtues of all people at once" (translation in accord with Piédagnel, "en montrant d'abord que Paul possède les vertus de tous les hommes ensemble") (1.2 [300.114]).

[39] It is conventional in encomia not to employ proper names, even of the honoree, as noted above, p. 71.

[40] laud. Paul. 1.2 [300.114].

[41] See the same argument in hom. in 1 Cor. 25.3–4 [61.209–210], where he first exemplifies the principle of seeking the advantage of the many rather than oneself (1 Cor 10:33) in Moses, David, Abraham, Jacob and Joseph (and illustrated in the negative by Lot and Jonah), but then argues that Paul excelled these [Τὸ δὲ τοῦ Παύλου πολλὴν ἔχει τὴν ὑπερβολήν] in three ways: 1) he chose to suffer alone so that others would have respite, rather than to choose to join his kin in misery; 2) they gave up their earthly goods, but Paul was willing to give up his heavenly destiny (Rom 9:3); and 3) Paul renounced himself not for those in his charge (i.e, Gentiles), but even for those outside his area of responsibility (the Jews).

[42] The σύγκρισις motif need not be confined to biblical figures (pace Piédagnel, SC 300.30: "c'est uniquement à l'Ancien et à l'Nouveau Testament qu'il emprunte les comparaisons"). In hom. in 2 Tim. 4.3–4 [62.621–24] Chrysostom contrasts Paul with Nero, and shows him on all counts superior (see the full treatment of this passage in chap. 6, pp. 206–12). On the other hand, Ameringer, Second Sophistic, 69, exaggerates in the other direction ("But in the majority of cases Chrysostom draws on profane sources for the themes of his comparisons").

[43] From a rhetorical point of view, each patriarch or other notable constitutes another discrete proof or sub-argument [πίστις] within the larger section of proofs [πίστεις].

The first page is dedicated to the patriarch Abel. Abel is rightly renowned for his sacrifice [θυσία], but Paul's sacrifice, Chrysostom contends, outdoes Abel's as much as the heavens exceed the earth. Drawing on a rich panoply of Pauline and post-Pauline self-descriptions (1 Cor 15:31; 2 Cor 4:10; 2 Tim 4:6; Phil 2:17–18; Eph 6:17), Chrysostom composes his argument for Paul's supremacy to Abel on the following logic: Abel brought one sacrifice, but Paul a daily sacrifice, and that sacrifice was of his very self. And even that daily self-sacrifice was a double offering, for it involved his own dying and his carrying around the dying of his Lord, Jesus. Then Chrysostom examines the nature of Paul's self-sacrifice: He faced extensive dangers from foes, and self-slaughter by choice, in putting to death the nature of his flesh so that he – the offering itself – was much greater than any holy priestly fare. Paul even called his own blood a σπονδή, a libation. But Paul further outdid this comparison: not content to sacrifice only himself, he sought to present the whole world as an offering. Now the portrait shifts from Paul the bloody victim to Paul the winged creature who flew around the whole world, which, faster than any magician's trick, is immediately transformed into Paul the farmer, who tends his land with the loving detail that can only come from treading it attentively on foot, plucking out thorns (of sin), and sowing the seed (of piety). From this rapid succession of images Paul once again emerges as a human being, a missionary, one who made people into angels (or, even more challenging, metamorphosed people from demons into angels). Then Paul the simultaneous priest and victim returns as one who sacrificed his own self with the sword of the spirit on an altar high above the heavens. Therefore the epideictic motif of wonder is fitting: "What could be the equal of this sacrifice?"[44] But the argument is not yet finished. For Abel also attained fame [καὶ ταύτῃ λαμπρότερος γέγονεν] for having been killed by the treachery of his brother. How can Paul compare with this? Chrysostom replies: whereas Abel was killed by one whom he had neither harmed nor helped, Paul was killed by the very people for whom he worked and suffered his whole life.[45] The futility of any comparison with Abel's meager offering is demonstrated beyond doubt.

On the next page we meet the patriarch Noah, whom Chrysostom portrays, as did the author of Genesis, as just and uniquely perfect in his generation. Chrysostom sketches Noah's great accomplishment merely in brief outline, by way of damning with faint praise: "he saved only himself with his children."[46] Though he expends no energy on the portrait of Noah (despite its legendary attraction for most artists down to the present day), John assumes the hearer can bring to mind a sufficient mental picture of Noah at work on the ark, loading it with family and animal pairs, and unloading it after the deluge, so that the comparisons that follow

---

[44] 1.3–4 [SC 300.116–18], Τί τοίνυν γένοιτ' ἂν τῆς θυσίας ταύτης ἴσον;

[45] *laud. Paul.* 1.4 [SC 300.118].

[46] *laud. Paul.* 1.5 [SC 300.118].

will make sense. Instead, Chrysostom lavishes his attention on a depiction of Paul as an ark-builder, but of a different sort, superior to Noah's comparatively minor effort in every regard. "But Paul, when a much more terrible flood seized the world, snatched not just two or three or five relatives, but the whole world from the midst of the waves when it was about to be drowned in the sea. He did this not by fastening planks [σανίδες] together and making an ark, but by composing letters to serve as planks."[47] Here Chrysostom paints a wonderful metaphorical double-image of a new sort of marine construction, the ark of Paul's letters which saves an exponentially greater number of souls from an even worse calamity than that which overtook the patriarch's generation. Having set up this conceit, Chrysostom then releases the powers of amplification in which epideictic rhetoric delights in order to develop extensively the inventive image:

The ark of Paul's letters was not such a type as to be carried about in a single place, but it reached the very ends of the world, and from that time until now he brings all people into this ark. For, having prepared his ark in proportion to the multitude of those to be saved, welcoming people who were less intelligent than animals, he made them contenders with the powers above, and with his ark proved victorious over Noah's. For Noah's ark took on board a raven and sent it out again as a raven (Gen 8:6–7); it received a wolf, yet did not alter its beastly nature. However, Paul wasn't like this, but, taking on board wolves, he made them sheep, and taking on hawks and jackdaws, he completely transformed them into doves, and, casting out all the irrationality and beastliness that belongs to human nature, in its stead he introduced the gentleness of the spirit.[48] And this ark remains sailing until now, and has not broken apart. For not even the storm of wickedness was strong enough to loosen its planks, but instead, sailing above the storm, it put an end to the tempest. With good reason! For these planks have been glued, not with asphalt and pitch, but with the holy spirit.[49]

In the course of this vivid depiction Chrysostom has entabulated no less than six different respects in which Paul's ark is superior to Noah's: construction materials, capacity for passengers, range of time and place in its sailing itinerary, treatment and conditioning of guests during the voyage, seaworthiness over the long haul, and present status. On all points Paul, through the vehicle of his letters, is hands down the superior, the savior of the whole world's population in every time and place – down to the present – through the water-fast hull of his epistles secured by the holy spirit. Here Chrysostom conjoins the graphic literary portrait of Paul with a portrait of the Pauline epistles, which are both a metonym for the apostle and, separate from him, a product of his intentions and endeavors.[50] And Noah,

---

[47] laud. Paul. 1.5 [SC 300.118–19]. This imagistic move is facilitated by a double entendre in the Greek word, σάνις, which can mean "plank or board," but also, because of its common employment for the task, "writing tablet" (see LSJ, 1583).

[48] Cf. poenit. 8.1 [49.336–37], a σύγκρισις of the ark and the church, which employs this same argument about the dispositions of the inhabitants when embarking and when later emerging.

[49] laud. Paul. 1.5 [SC 300.120].

[50] Note how in the middle of the passage just quoted Chrysostom effortlessly switches from "Paul's ark" [ἡ κιβωτός, or ἡ λάρναξ] to οὗτος, Paul himself, as the subject. Both Paul, the Noah-

caught in a single moment of bravery, is no match for all that they, together, have accomplished and still continue to achieve.

Next in turn is the patriarch Abraham, whom all people admire. "We, too, admire him for this" [Καὶ γὰρ καὶ ἡμεῖς τοῦτο θαυμάζομεν]: that he left all that he had to follow the divine summons to move to a new homeland. But being admirable does not make Abraham a match for Paul: "But what could be Paul's equal?" ['Αλλὰ τί Παύλου γένοιτ' ἂν ἴσον;].[51] Paul easily outdoes Abraham when it comes to leaving behind what he loved to follow the divine command, for he abandoned, not just homeland, house and relatives, but the very cosmos. Yet even this comparison seems paltry, so Chrysostom hikes it up two more degrees: Paul didn't just leave the world, but heaven; no, even more than that, he disdained even the heaven above the heavens for the sake of the love of Jesus (Rom 8:38–39). But, if bested there, Abraham has another claim to fame: his daring rescue of his nephew Lot in the midst of teeming dangers at the hands of the barbarians (Gen 14). "Well, Paul snatched away, not his nephew nor three or five cities, but the whole world, not from barbarians, but from the very hand of the demons, enduring countless dangers every single day, and acquiring a great measure of security for others by his own deaths."[52] Then Chrysostom brings in the coup de grâce – "the chief of good deeds and the height of philosophy" [τὸ κεφάλαιον τῶν ἀγαθῶν καὶ ἡ κορωνὶς τῆς φιλοσοφίας] – Abraham's willing sacrifice of his son Isaac. But even here Paul takes first place [τὰ πρωτεῖα] in the comparison of virtues, for he sacrificed not his offspring, but himself – and not once, but time and time again.

Beginning with Isaac the form of parallel lives, or, rather, parallel souls, takes on an even more uniform and streamlined character, as for each figure just one or two characteristic virtues are singled out, and then, with less narrative cushioning and fewer complicated cross-comparisons, Paul is found to be superior with respect to that one quality. Although Isaac possessed many other virtues [πολλὰ μὲν καὶ ἄλλα], Chrysostom chooses to concentrate especially on his ἀνεξικακία, forbearance, as illustrated in the narrative about his well-digging (Gen 26:15–33). Whereas, when he saw his foes reburying the wells he had dug, Isaac chose to move on and not contend with them face to face, Paul, when he saw his own body buried by stones, not only yielded to his opponents, but chased down the people hurling stones at him to lead them into heaven. This leads to a portrait of Paul's soul spewing forth in "rivers for endurance" [ποταμοὶ εἰς ὑπομονήν] which more than outdo Isaac's ἀνεξικακία in the meager matter of the wells.[53]

---

figure, and his letters, the ark, serve the same function: the salvation and transformation of the whole world. And, just as Noah built the ark, Paul "composed" his letters and made them water-tight, with the added seal of the holy spirit.

[51] *laud. Paul.* 1.6 [SC 300.122].
[52] *laud. Paul.* 1.6 [SC 300.122].
[53] *laud. Paul.* 1.7 [SC 300.122–24].

Jacob is taken to be the exemplar of the virtue of constancy, καρτερία, especially for his fourteen years of hired labor on behalf of his chosen wife, Rachel, for which Scripture rightly praises him. "But what sort of steely soul could demonstrate Paul's endurance" [Καὶ ποία ἀδαμαντίνη ψυχὴ τὴν Παύλου δύναιτ' ἂν ἐπιδείξασθαι ὑπομονήν;]?[54] In proof of this, Chrysostom offers the abundant evidence furnished by Paul's constant trials and tribulations in his ministry, culled especially from the peristasis catalogue of 2 Cor 11:23–29. Paul was so doggedly on task that he can be pictured momentarily in flight, "jumping over the trenches"[55] to snatch his sheep out of the throat of the devil.[56]

Joseph, ὁ σώφρων, as might be expected, is portrayed by his famous virtue of chastity in the matter of Potiphar's wife. Yet this comparison is so easy to turn to Paul's favor that Chrysostom dryly says, "I fear that it might be laughable to praise Paul for this virtue ['Αλλὰ δέδοικα μὴ γέλως ᾖ τὸν Παῦλον ἐντεῦθεν ἐγκωμιάζειν]."[57] For Paul not only was chaste; he was so untempted by attractive physical features, and all other things that he remained as unmoved by them as a corpse encountering another corpse [ὡς ἂν νεκρὸς πρὸς νεκρὸν ἀκίνητος γένοιτο]. Indeed, "So precisely did he lull to sleep the surges of nature, that he never, ever, experienced a single human passion" [Οὕτω μετὰ ἀκριβείας τῆς φύσεως τὰ σκιρτήματα[58] κατευνάζων, οὐδὲν οὐδέποτε πρὸς οὐδὲν ἀνθρώπινον πάθος ἔπαθεν]. This portrait of Paul as dead (to all human desires) therefore far excels poor Joseph, whose legendary chastity when tempted becomes in this comparison more like a piece of evidence of his lust for sexual satisfaction.

When Chrysostom turns to Job his argument assumes again a more complicated shape, for the possibilities for comparison are myriad.[59] First Chrysostom grants

---

[54] laud. Paul. 1.8 [SC 300.124].

[55] πανταχοῦ ὑπὲρ τὰ σκάμματα πηδῶν (laud. Paul. 1.8 [SC 300.124–26]). Piédagnel (SC 300.126–27) takes σκάμματα here as an athletic metaphor, for it can refer to the landing pits used by long jumpers. If so, then this is a quick glimpse at the athletic Paul. The metaphor is not uncommon in Chrysostom's writings, where it can also represent the struggle of the celibate life (see Piédagnel, SC 300.126 n. 1; LPGL, 1235; and res. mort. 3 [50.421–22]). But I have chosen the more military sense of "trenches" as more suitable to the context here (a suggestion for which I thank Clare Rothschild).

[56] laud. Paul. 1.8 [SC 300.124–26].

[57] laud. Paul. 1.9 [SC 300.126].

[58] With this term John possibly makes an intended word play (paronomasia), with σκάμματα in the previous paragraph.

[59] "Cette comparaison de Paul avec Job est composée avec beaucoup de soin" (Piédagnel, SC 300.132 n. 1). This kind of developed comparison is not much appreciated by Ameringer, although he does not defend the criteria by which he forms his judgment : "[John] frequently indulges in a heaping up of comparisons, thus giving a vain display of rhetorical pyrotechnics. His themes are largely those of the rhetorical schools. He develops them in truly sophistic fashion, with the result that many of his comparisons are exaggerated, paradoxical, far-fetched, bizarre, and puerile. Others are pursued with studied ingenuity into the minutest details" (Second Sophistic, 85). Hubbell better understood the cultural context which made arguments like these so popular: "This was the style which popular taste demanded and which rhetorical ingenuity

the elements of parity between the two, given that Job, like Paul, was a "great athlete" [μέγας ἀθλητής], whose contest with temptation showed such remarkable endurance [ὑπομονή], purity of life [ἡ τοῦ βίου καθαρότης], testimony of God [ἡ τοῦ θεοῦ μαρτυρία], and severity of battle [ἡ καρτερὰ μάχη ἐκείνη], and resulted in a marvelous victory [ἡ θαυμαστὴ νίκη ἡ μετὰ τὴν μάχην]. So this σύγκρισις becomes a contest between two portraits of legendary endurance. But Paul wins out again, of course, for his ἀγών lasted not simply a few months, but many years, and surely it was worse continually to fall into the spiritual[60] "mouth of the lion" and suffer countless trials, than to ooze pus into the dirt and sit on a dunghill. And, further, Paul was calumniated not just by three or four friends, but he was reproached, spit upon and reviled by all the unbelieving false brethren.

Next Chrysostom introduces Job's hospitality [φιλοξενία], and care for those in need [ἡ πρὸς τοὺς δεομένους κηδεμονία]. In characteristic epideictic style he grants these virtues to the Old Testament worthy, but also claims that Paul outdoes him: "We will not dispute that, either. But we shall find that his charity falls as far short of Paul as a body differs from a soul."[61] The reason for this is the type of hospitality each exercised:

For the actions Job displayed for those maimed in body, Paul performed for those mutilated in soul, correcting all those who were lame and crippled in reasoning, and clothing the naked and shameless with the cloak of philosophy.[62]

Yet even with respect to bodily concerns Paul surpassed his rival, for he helped those in need while living with them in poverty and hunger, which is far superior to doing it from one's surplus of goods.[63] Also the very nature of the hospitality each showed was different; whereas Job opened his house to anyone who approached it, Paul expanded his soul to take in the whole world (with 2 Cor 6:12), and received entire peoples. Job was willing to share his sheep and cattle in generous regard for the poor,[64] but Paul had only a single possession – his body – with which lone commodity he labored to produce revenue for the hungry and famished.

---

supplied" ("Chrysostom and Rhetoric," 269). But Hubbell doesn't like it much more than Ameringer: "in invention of comparisons, although his ingenuity rises to absurdities, he is no worse than his contemporaries."

[60] The translation of τὸ νοητόν here is somewhat difficult. While the word usually means "perceptible or intelligible," in early Christian literature it often means "spiritual," as opposed to "physical or material" or "literal," as in textual interpretation (*LPGL*, 917). Here John apparently wants to stress that when Paul uses the phrase it is a metaphor for other kinds of afflictions (*pace* Piédagnel, SC 300.129 n. 2, this is not an allusion to 1 Pet 5:8–9, but a quotation from 2 Tim 4:17).

[61] *laud. Paul.* 1.11 [SC 300.128].

[62] *laud. Paul.* 1.11 [SC 300.128].

[63] *laud. Paul.* 1.11 [SC 300.128–30].

[64] In the term φιλότιμος (meaning both "generous" and "loving distinction") Chrysostom may perhaps intend a back-handed slap at the rivalry and desire for honor that was at the heart of public benefaction in the πόλις (for further discussion of how John envisioned and championed a different form of social responsibility, see chap. 7, pp. 401–404).

But then it is back to a contest between the sufferings the two endured, reintroduced with a rhetorical question and answer: "Did the worms and the wounds produce terrible and unendurable pains for Job? Even I agree that they did." Nonetheless, when one compares with those sufferings Paul's constant afflictions, which Chrysostom admiringly documents by rehearsing the catalogues in the letters,[65] there can be no doubt who was superior in the endurance contest: "you will see how the soul that bore these things was more solid than a rock, and won out over iron and steel" [ὄψει πῶς πέτρας στερροτέρα ἦν ἡ ταῦτα φέρουσα ψυχὴ, καὶ σίδηρον καὶ ἀδάμαντα ἐνίκα].[66] In this manner Chrysostom has sketched Paul's incorporeal soul as the super-solid substance of resilience.[67] The final argument that seals the case is the reminder that Job's sufferings were only in body, whereas Paul's were in his soul as he faced, in addition to the named afflictions, the even more bitter torment of worry for his churches and those who had fallen away (Gal 4:19; cf. 2 Cor 11:28). This anxiety ate away at Paul's soul more cruelly than any worm, and rendered him a man flowing with constant tears (with Acts 20:32). In a switch to maternal imagery, John describes Paul as torn apart more keenly by the searing knife of this pain than any woman in the throes of labor pains (he cites the apostle's own words in Gal 4:19 to make the point).

After this long proof of Paul's superiority to Job, Chrysostom takes a transitional pause for breath before moving on. "With whom might one be amazed after Job? Surely Moses."[68] Now, Moses possessed other great virtues, too [μεγάλα μὲν γὰρ αὐτοῦ καὶ τὰ ἄλλα], but the chief deed and highest achievement of that holy soul [τὸ δὲ κεφάλαιον καὶ ἡ κορωνὶς τῆς ἁγίας ψυχῆς] was his voluntary self-renunciation, to the point that he was willing to have his own name struck from the Book of God for the sake of his fellow Israelites (Exod 32:32). But Paul can top this, for while Moses chose to perish along with others, Paul elected an even more tragic course: to renounce his own share of eternal glory so that others might be saved (Rom 9:3). Then John finalizes the comparison with a chain of pithy antitheses in staccato style:

> The one sparred with Pharaoh, the other with the devil, day by day. The one fought on behalf of one nation, the other on behalf of the whole world. And he was dripping, not with sweat, but in place of sweat had blood flowing from every pore, as he set straight, not just the civilized world, but also the uninhabited, not just Greece, but the barbarian land, as well.[69]

Just when his hearers might wonder if this discourse was to be interminable, given its plan of successive comparisons with the rather large inventory of biblical prec-

---

[65] Again he makes reference to 2 Cor 11:23–29, and perhaps also 6:3–10. See chap. 6, pp. 302–308 for a fuller treatment of how Chrysostom regards and depicts Paul's sufferings.

[66] *laud. Paul.* 1.12 [SC 300.132].

[67] Just as he had described Paul himself earlier (*laud. Paul.* 1.10 [SC 300.128]: πάσης πέτρας στερρότερος ἦν).

[68] *laud. Paul.* 1.13 [SC 300.132].

[69] *laud. Paul.* 1.13 [SC 300.132].

edents, Chrysostom invokes a frequent epideictic *topos*: "Now one could bring in Joshua, and Samuel, and the other prophets, but so we don't make this speech too long, let's move on to the most illustrious [οἱ κορυφαῖοι] of them; for when Paul is seen to be better than these, no dispute will remain about the others."[70] Chrysostom chooses three chief figures to complete his comparison (the hearers now have a promise that they are just three figures away from the end!): David, Elijah, and John the Baptist.[71] The portrait of David is painted with two colors. After posing the rhetorical question of which quality one should select as characteristic of David [Τί οὖν τὸ ἐξαίρετον τοῦ Δαυΐδ;], he answers: humility [ταπεινοφροσύνη] and love for God [ὁ πρὸς θεὸν ἔρως]. But despite David's excellence, the orator dispenses with this comparison by means of a simple rhetorical question, expressed with litotes: "But who isn't inferior to Paul's soul when it comes to performing both of these virtuous deeds?" [τίς δὲ οὐχ ἧττον τῆς Παύλου ψυχῆς ἀμφότερα ταῦτα κατώρθωσε].[72] Then Chrysostom quickly moves on to Elijah, again using rhetorical questions to punctuate his discourse (and keep his audience awake, no doubt). "What was so marvelous about Elijah [Τί δὲ τὸ θαυμαστὸν Ἡλίου;]?" First come some negative possibilities: was it perhaps his power to shut up heaven, cause a famine, or bring fire down from heaven? "No, I don't think it is for any of these things" [Οὐκ ἔγωγε οἶμαι]. What Chrysostom offers in place of these is Elijah's zeal [ζῆλος] and vehemence [σφοδρότης] for God. But surely no one is a match for Paul in this category. Paul's zeal exceeds Elijah's to the same degree as Elijah outshone all the other prophets, for "what could possibly be equal to those words which he spoke in zeal on behalf of the glory of the Lord: 'I would wish to be anathema for the sake of my brethren, my kin according to the flesh'" (Rom 9:3)?[73] Paul's love and zeal were so ardent and non-material that he had to make up another creation, one not yet in existence (in Rom 8:39) when he wanted to give expression to his ethereal, otherworldly desires.[74]

The portrait Chrysostom next draws of John the Baptist copies the traditional one from the Synoptics: the eater of locusts and wild honey, who thereby illustrated the virtue of frugality [εὐτέλεια]. But Paul can beat that, for he carried out his ascetic life in the midst of the world instead of in the desert, and his rations were even more meager than John the Baptist's, since in his zeal for the gospel Paul forsook even a subsistence-level diet.[75] The Baptist also had the great virtue of

---

[70] *laud. Paul.* 1.14 [SC 300.134].

[71] John argues for treating Elijah and John the Baptist together, given that both share the same title, πρόδρομος, "forerunner," Elijah of the first coming, and John the Baptist of the second (in line with Mal 3:23, as interpreted in the Synoptics, esp. Mk 9:11–13 and pars.).

[72] *laud. Paul.* 1.14 [SC 300.134].

[73] *laud. Paul.* 1.14 [SC 300.134–36].

[74] *laud. Paul.* 1.14 [SC 300.136].

[75] We see here Chrysostom's own situation rather clearly reflected ['Αλλ' οὗτος ἐν μέσῃ τῇ οἰκουμένῃ καθάπερ ἐκεῖνος ἐν τῇ ἐρήμῳ διέτριβεν] (1.14 [SC 300.136]), given that his fastidious fasting and dietary restraints were well known in his lifetime (see the full discussion of how

παρρησία, boldness, as exhibited in his daring confrontation with Herod. But Paul muzzled not one king, or two or three, but thousands, and, indeed, tyrants who were much more cruel than Herod.[76]

At the precise moment that Chrysostom appears to have completed his announced plan of proof, and the audience justifiably expects a conclusion, he embarks upon a final, provocative argument, a comparison of Paul with the angels: "Finally it remains only to compare him with the angels."[77] To facilitate this, Chrysostom beckons his audience to travel with him on an ekphrastic tour of heaven, in order to find the right vantage point for viewing the two (verbal) portraits: "So, leaving the earth behind, let's go up to the vaults of the heavens!"[78] But before they are airborne Chrysostom peremptorily wards off an expected objection: "But let no one accuse our discourse of audacity" [ἀλλὰ μηδεὶς τόλμαν καταγινωσκέτω τοῦ λόγου] for making such a comparison.[79] Since Scripture itself calls John ἄγγελος (meaning "messenger," but also "angel") in Mark 1:2 and pars., as also the priests do in one prophetic passage (Mal 2:7), then it must be appropriate to invoke such a comparison for the man who exceeds everyone (John included) in virtue. Treating them just like the mortal examples adduced above, John presents the angels by means of a portrait of their characteristic virtue – obedience [ὑπακοή] – to which David testified in Ps 102:20. Chrysostom argues that it is angelic adherence to divine ordinances, much more than their incorporeal nature, that qualifies as their most distinctive attribute.[80] But when Paul is set in contrast

---

Chrysostom depicts Paul's fasting, in relation to the monastic virtues and his own piety, in chap. 6, pp. 318–19).

[76] *laud. Paul.* 1.14 [SC 300.136].

[77] *laud. Paul.* 1.15 [SC 300.136]. This is not, however, a complete surprise, for Chrysostom had signalled this proof already in the προοίμιον (1.1 [SC 300.114], οὐ μόνον δὲ τὰ τῶν ἀνθρώπων, ἀλλὰ καὶ τὰ τῶν ἀγγέλων).

[78] *laud. Paul.* 1.15 [SC 15.136].

[79] Cf. *laud. Paul.* 2.8–9 [SC 300.156–58]. It is precisely this type of rhetorical hyperbole that occasions Panthea's complaint that Lycinus' comparison of her with the goddesses went too far: "'Such praise,' she said, 'is too high for me [ὑπὲρ ἐμὲ γάρ]; indeed, too high for human kind [μᾶλλον δὲ ὑπὲρ ἅπασαν τὴν ἀνθρωπίνην φύσιν τὰ τοιαῦτα]. For my part I did not want you to compare me [παραθεωρεῖν με] even to those great ladies, Penelope and Arete and Theano, let alone the noblest of the goddesses'" [Aphrodite and Hera] (Lucian, *pro Imaginibus* 7). Her fear was that this comparison of a mortal with the gods was "not at all reverential or pious in its allusions to the gods" [οὐ μάλα εὐσεβῶς οὐδὲ ὁσίως τὰ πρὸς τοὺς θεούς], and would make her guilty of sacrilege and a sin [ἀσέβημα καὶ πλημμέλημα] (§8). In response, Lycinus defends his extremes by appeal to rhetorical convention: "the conditions that govern us in these laudatory writings [οἱ ἐπαινετικοὶ οὗτοι λόγοι] are such that the eulogist must employ comparisons and similies [ὡς χρὴ τὸν ἐπαινοῦντα καὶ εἰκόσι καὶ ὁμοιώσεσι προσχρῆσθαι], and really the most important part of it is to make successful comparisons [εὖ εἰκάσαι]. And success would be most likely to be held attained, not if a man compares like to like [οὐκ ἦν τις τοῖς ὁμοίοις παραβάλλῃ], or if he makes his comparison with something that is inferior [οὐδ' ἦν πρὸς τὸ ὑποδεέστερον ποιῆται τὴν παράθεσιν], but if he approximates, in so far as he may, what he is praising to something that surpasses it [ἀλλ' ἦν πρὸς τὸ ὑπερέχον ὡς οἷόν τε προσβιβάζῃ τὸ ἐπαινούμενον]" (*pro Imaginibus* 19).

[80] *laud. Paul.* 1.15 [SC 300.138].

with the angels in this regard, he is shown to exceed even their virtue, in that he obeyed not only the spoken divine commands, but standards extending far and above them (as 1 Cor 9:18, Paul's vow to preach the gospel without pay, amply shows). The Psalmist tells of another quality of angels: they are like winds and fire (Ps 103:4). But Paul can match this portrait, too, for he was like wind and fire running through the whole world and cleansing the earth. In his last try at this comparison Chrysostom counters another potential objection to his comparison: the angels, after all, have attained to heaven, but Paul had not yet done so. No, Chrysostom exclaims, this is precisely the best point of comparison. For what is especially amazing about Paul is that he was able while on earth to vie with the incorporeal powers, even when clad in a mortal body.[81]

Chrysostom's proof ends with the angels, because after them there is no one left with which to compare Paul. The cumulative effect of this form of epideictic proof is the insistence, both that Paul was superior in each head to head contest, and that, being a spiritual decathlete, he outdid the whole of them in the aggregate. Through the succession of proofs in §3–15 Paul's soul has been shown to possess the virtues of self-sacrifice, steadfastness, bravery, forbearance, constancy, chastity, endurance, care for the poor, unselfishness, humility, love of God and love of enemy, zeal, frugality, obedience, and an extraterrestrial sensibility. The portrait gallery of worthies, and the portrait series of Pauls composed to better each in turn, illustrate the multifaceted excellence of the apostle, thereby confirming John's opening proposition that Paul possessed all possible qualities of excellence.

ἐπίλογος (Conclusion).[82] Chrysostom's conventional rhetorical conclusion contains a direct appeal to his congregation to imitate Paul, this paragon of virtue.[83] As throughout this speech, the final transition from proven proposition to exhortation is smooth: "Of what magnitude of blame would we not be worthy if, when one man has brought together all the virtues in himself, we are not zealous to imitate [μιμήσασθαι] him in even a tiny way? ... Let us strive to reach his zeal" [σπουδάσωμεν πρὸς τὸν ἐκείνου ζῆλον ἐλθεῖν].[84] The movement to the final doxology is made by means of Chrysostom's expressed hope that, by imitating Paul, his auditors "might be able to attain to the same goods" [ἵνα δυνηθῶμεν καὶ τῶν αὐτῶν ἀγαθῶν ἐπιτυχεῖν] as he.[85]

---

[81] *laud. Paul.* 1.15 [SC 300.138].

[82] *laud. Paul.* 1.16 [SC 300.140].

[83] Hubbell recognizes that this is true to the rhetorical form of the encomium (though he unnecessarily restricts it to an ἐπιτάφιος, proper): "It is perhaps unnecessary to find a counterpart to this exhortation in classical rhetoric. However, it may be noticed that it is the regular conclusion of that form of the encomium known as ἐπιτάφιος" ("Chrysostom and Rhetoric," 270).

[84] *laud. Paul.* 1.16 [SC 300.140]. For the customary call to imitation in the other homilies, see 2.10; 3.10; 4.21; 5.17 [SC 300.158–60, 178–80, 228, 258]; cf. *hom. in Ac.* 50.3; 55.3 [60.347–48, 384].

[85] *laud. Paul.* 1.16 [SC 300.140]. The referent here is deliberately ambiguous. The "same goods" can be either the good deeds (as in §2 [SC 300.114]), or the heavenly rewards they may

Laud. Paul. 2: *Paul as Proof of Humanity's Capacity for Virtue*

προοίμιον and πρόθεσις (Introduction and Proposition).[86] The second encomium in the series is ingeniously cast, not as an encomium to Paul *per se*, but as a philosophical argument about human nature and its capacity for virtue, in which Paul figures as Exhibit A.[87] The opening sentence names the proposition of the discourse: "What a human being is, and how great is the noble birthright of our nature, and what degree of virtue this creature is capable of showing – these things were demonstrated more by Paul than all others."[88] Paul stands here in the present [καὶ νῦν ἕστηκεν] as God's defense attorney,[89] constituting in himself the refutation of the charge (cast by Manicheans and Gnostics) that God created human beings with a functional moral defect.[90] Paul's whole life, as John tells it, demon-

---

bring (as explicitly stated in *laud. Paul.* 5.17 [SC 300.258], ἵνα καὶ αὐτοὶ τῶν αἰωνίων ἐπιτύχωμεν ἀγαθῶν). For the same double entendre see *laud. Paul.* 4.21; 7.13 [SC 300.228, 320].

[86] As we have noted in the previous analysis of *laud. Paul.* 1, it is not uncommon for Chrysostom to employ a direct opening in which the thesis statement or point at issue in the oration is articulated in the proem. This is in line with Hellenistic rhetorical theory; see *Rh. Al.* 35.1440b: "in introducing these speeches [encomia and vituperation] we must set out first the propositions" [φροιμιαστέον οὖν καὶ περὶ τούτων πρῶτον προθεμένους τὰς προθέσεις].

[87] In what follows I offer a different analysis of the homily than did Piédagnel, SC 300.142 n. 2, for whom "le thème principal de ce discours est celui de l'amour de Paul pour le Christ," which he regards as embedded in the middle of a very long exordium (§1–3) and ending (§8–9) which treat the topic of the highest virtue of Paul. It is because Piédagnel has expected the encomium to be a praise of Paul for the virtue of love (perhaps influenced by *laud. Paul.* 3), that he finds its disposition irregular ("un exorde assez long qui traite de la haute vertu de l'Apôtre") and "parfois sinueuse." But when one identifies the theme of the piece where it is to be structurally expected, its logical and rhetorical progression is actually quite neatly coherent. This is not to deny that love of Christ is a feature of this discourse (2.4, 5, 7 [SC 300.148, 156]), but that topic has its place in a more self-consciously integral design. When one attends to the rhetorical structure of the speech, it is quite evident that the dominant themes of the discourse are human nature and ardent willingness in the pursuit of the ethical life. These are predominant in both the προοίμιον and the ἐπίλογος, as expected (see nn. 97–98 below for references), whereas Paul's love of Christ appears in neither. The brief analysis of this speech by Hubbell ("Chrysostom and Rhetoric," 270), which tries to map its invention according to the technique of σύγκρισις (influenced in this by *laud. Paul.* 1), does not fully capture the rhetorical complexity of this composition, either (although he does consider the homily to be executed with "a defter touch"). In my analysis I do not seek to fit the oration into a pattern set by any of the other Pauline panegyrics, but instead attempt to follow its own, rather clear, structural pattern and markers. This composition is also more complex than Young's brief exposition suggests: "demonstrating that Paul cared for nothing except virtue … his trials and sacrifice for love of Christ are delineated by a combination of rhetorical description and allusion to Acts and the Epistles" (*Biblical Exegesis*, 115).

[88] *laud. Paul.* 2.1 [SC 300.142].

[89] The forensic terminology is Chrysostom's: πρὸς ἅπαντας τοὺς ἐγκαλοῦντας … ἀπολογούμενος ὑπὲρ τοῦ Δεσπότου (*laud. Paul.* 2.1 [SC 300.142]).

[90] Paul's behavior, both now and in the past, matches precisely *John's* intent in this speech: to counter those who calumniate human nature, and exhort all to virtue (*laud. Paul.* 2.1 [SC 300.142]). Therefore, quite self-consciously, this speech is meant to instantiate and actualize Paul's own actual work in the present [καὶ νῦν ἕστηκεν].

strates that "the gap between angels and humans is not so great, if we wish to be attentive to ourselves."[91] In justifying this assertion Chrysostom first makes a cursory trip through some customary epideictic topics:

For Paul did not obtain another nature [φύσις], nor share a different soul [ψυχή], nor inhabit another world [κόσμος], but, having been reared [τρέφεσθαι] on the same earth [γῆ], and land [χώρα], and laws [νόμοι], and customs [ἔθη], he exceeded all human beings who have existed from the time there have been human beings [πάντας ἀνθρώπους ὑπερηκόντισε τοὺς ἐξ οὗ γεγόνασιν ἄνθρωποι γενομένους].[92]

But Chrysostom is not interested in the particulars of any of these topics for his encomium, since his ironic purpose is to stress the *non-uniqueness* of Paul in these areas,[93] so that what can come into relief are the things Paul has done with what he has received, in the realm of the exercise of the virtues in his soul.

πίστεις (Proofs). Chrysostom seeks to demonstrate his proposition about the possibilities for virtue inherent in human nature through an examination of Paul's magnificent life and mission. He begins this proof with a direct citation and refutation of the counter-proposition. It becomes quickly apparent that the opposition Chrysostom really hopes to address in this discourse is neither Manichees nor Gnostics, but his own congregants, who, when they make the weary complaint that "virtue is difficult, and vice is easy" [δύσκολον ἡ ἀρετή, καὶ εὔκολον ἡ κακία],[94] may (in his judgment) be aligning themselves uncritically with the heretics who deride human nature. In refutation of their ethical truism John announces his focal theme at the end of §1: that for Paul the things which most people think are difficult were easy,[95] even as alleged afflictions are pleasures.[96] The chief reason for this is Paul's marvelous "desire" or "will to act" [προθυμία] which is indeed a

---

[91] *laud. Paul.* 2.1 [SC 300.142–44]. For other references to the theme of Paul as the perfect exemplar of moral excellence in *laud. Paul.*, see Piédagnel, SC 300.39 n. 1.

[92] *laud. Paul.* 2.1 [SC 300.144].

[93] See also *laud. Paul.* 4.21 [SC 300.228]: "For what I have repeatedly said I shall not stop saying, that the very same body was in Paul as is in us, and the same upbringing, and the same soul. But his exercise of free will was great, and his willingness to act magnificent" [Ὃ γὰρ πολλάκις εἶπον, τοῦτο λέγων οὐ παύσομαι, ὅτι καὶ σῶμα ἐν αὐτῷ τὸ αὐτὸ ἦν ἡμῖν, καὶ τροφαὶ αἱ αὐταί, καὶ ψυχὴ ἡ αὐτή· ἀλλ' ἡ προαίρεσις μεγάλη, καὶ ἡ προθυμία λαμπρά]. Some of the other topics mentioned here, such as rearing, homeland and laws, fit under the rhetorical category of τὰ ἔξωθεν, "external circumstances," with which we shall be engaged in chap. 6.

[94] *laud. Paul.* 2.1 [SC 300.144]; see also his direct confrontation of the audience in 2.9 [SC 300.158], quoted below, p. 158.

[95] The importance of this theme is demonstrated by the tie in between the προοίμιον and ἐπίλογος of δύσκολον/δυσκατόρθωτα and ἐλαφρόν/κοῦφον (*laud. Paul.* 2.1; 2.10 [SC 300.144, 160]).

[96] The noun ἡδονή and adjective ἡδύς are very frequent in this homily (2.1, 2, 6 [2x] [SC 300.144, 152], the noun found only here in the whole series; and the adjective in 2.5 [2x], 6 [SC 300.150, 152]). Language for afflictions is also ubiquitous: especially πόνος (2.2; 2.3; 2.5 [2x]; 2.6 [4x] [SC 300.144, 146, 150–52]); also κολάζεσθαι/κόλασις (2.4, 5 [2x] [SC 300.148, 150]); λύπη/λυπηρόν/λυπεῖσθαι (2.3; 2.5; 2.6 [SC 300.146, 150, 152]). A coordinated theme is the pair ἀγών and ἐπάθλον (or βραβεῖον) in 2.2; 2.5; 2.6; 2.10 [SC 300.144, 150, 152, 160]).

predominant theme of the discourse,[97] for it constitutes the necessary link Chrysostom is seeking to establish between the givenness of human nature [φύσις, the other preponderant theme][98] and the uniquely virtuous character which Paul (unlike most members of the equally endowed species) actually achieved. Προθυμία, as Chrysostom portrays it in the person of Paul, is the enzyme that activates the potential God has placed in all human persons to attain an excellence equal to that of the angels.

The proof for this attendant proposition will extend from the end of §1 through §9,[99] and it involves the establishment of an inverse table of values in which true pain and true pleasure are the reverse of conventional wisdom. Because of his profound προθυμία Paul did not feel the pains he suffered and, furthermore, unlike other people, he was not motivated by the lure of some external reward for his afflictions, because the pain itself was his reward.[100] In fact, as Paul's letters showed, he was empowered by his sufferings to do what was right, receiving fresh προθυμία from each trial and danger, so that he "flourished[101] in virtue every single day" [καθ' ἑκάστην ἤκμαζε τὴν ἡμέραν]. Chrysostom continues to draw this portrait of Paul from the hardship catalogues of the letters, notably 2 Corinthians, as he declares that Paul's virtues are his "weapons of righteousness" [ὅπλα δικαιοσύνης] (6:7), and recreates Paul's own self-portrait as one "marching in triumphal processions" [ἐν θριάμβοις ἐμπομπεύειν] (cf. 2 Cor 2:14), who sets up his continual trophies [τὰ τρόπαια] everywhere on earth.[102] Then, in a thoroughly Pauline manner Chrysostom contrasts the things Paul's ministry brought him with those "we" cherish and seek. Paul pursued discredit, insult, death, poverty, sufferings, grieving and praying for enemies (as these things accompany the gospel proclamation) with more fervent will to act than "we" chase their opposites, the normal elements of the good life: honor, life, wealth, relief, rejoicing, praying against our enemies. In adopting this standard of evaluation, as Chrysostom knows, he is placing on its head the value structure of the epideictic rhetoric he is using. For this he invokes the precedent of the apostle himself: "Paul overturned the order of things" [ἀντέστρεψε τῶν πραγμάτων τὴν τάξιν].[103] But Chrysostom (who in composing this discourse has one foot in each of these value systems) does not wish inadvertently to valorize the existing values, so he quickly corrects himself: "or, rather, it is we who have overturned it, whereas he was the one who kept to the order just as God had legislated it" [μᾶλλον δὲ ἡμεῖς ἀντεστρέψαμεν, ἐκεῖνος δέ,

---

See 2.2 [2x] and, most importantly, in the peroration at 2.9, 10 [SC 300.144, 158, 160].
[98] See *laud. Paul.* 2.1 [2x]; 2.2; 2.3; 2.8; 2.9 [2x]; 2.10 [SC 300.142, 144, 146, 156, 158, 160].
[99] I differ in my analysis of the disposition of the discourse from Piédagnel, who took the exordium to extend from §1–3 (see n. 87 above).
[100] *laud. Paul.* 2.5 [SC 300.150].
[101] Literally, "being at his prime" (LSJ, 51).
[102] *laud. Paul.* 2.3 [SC 300.146].
[103] As, for instance, in 1 Cor 4:1–13 (on this as a "paradoxical encomium" see Mitchell, *Paul,* 213–21), and elsewhere throughout his letters.

ὥσπερ ὁ θεὸς ἐνομοθέτησεν, οὕτως αὐτὴν ἐφύλαττε].[104] And the proof [ἀπόδειξις] that these virtues (and their consequences) are "in accordance with nature" [κατὰ φύσιν][105] is Paul himself who, being human, chased after the afflictions, not the prize commodities.[106] Paul considered all the attainments a panegyrist would normally praise as possessions – cities, nations, kings, legions, weapons, possessions, provinces, and power – as not even equal to a cobweb [οὐδὲ γὰρ ἀράχνην ταῦτα εἶναι ἐνόμισεν].[107] In contrast, what Paul most esteemed and valued above all else was the love of Christ, for which he happily suffered what he did, and without which all the things of this or the next world would be nothing.[108] This positive picture of Paul's scale of values is balanced by its negative corollary: what he most feared and shunned was not pain, but offending God,[109] and what would be Gehenna, chastisement, and evils uncountable to him are not earthly torments and deprivations, but a failure to gain that love of Christ.[110] Paul's vision was controlled by a completely disparate set of lenses. He viewed all visible things as one would a rotting plant, tyrants and bitter public opposition as mere gnats, death and eternal punishment as children's playthings. But when enduring these afflictions for Christ, such difficulties became no longer even tedious annoyances, but actual sources of pleasure.[111] In Paul's universe the bitter contest and the prize initially switch places, but then coalesce, as the struggle itself *becomes* the prize.[112] Paul's topsy-turvy optics become the frame within which Chrysostom's proposition that virtue is pleasurable can be laid out in its full antithetical form:

But likewise one might say that all these tribulations endured for Christ's sake were pleasure for Paul. And I, too, say that all the things which cause despondency in us produced great pleasure in him.[113]

---

[104] *laud. Paul.* 2.4 [SC 300.146].

[105] The other list, of earthly pursuits, is τοὐναντίον (*laud. Paul.* 2.3 [SC 300.146]), consequently μὴ κατὰ φύσεως.

[106] *laud. Paul.* 2.4 [SC 300.148]. Note the form of expression, which deliberately ties in with the πρόθεσις in the opening line of the speech: Τίς τούτων ἀπόδειξις; Παῦλος, ἄνθρωπος ὤν, καὶ τούτοις ἐπιτρέχων μᾶλλον ἢ ἐκείνοις.

[107] *laud. Paul.* 2.4 [SC 300.148].

[108] As far as the logic of the argument is concerned, Chrysostom is not extolling Paul's love of Christ as an independent theme (as argued by Piédagnel, SC 300.142 n. 2), but instead invoking it to explain how it was that Paul managed to find easy and pleasurable the things most people consider hard or painful.

[109] *laud. Paul.* 2.4 [SC 300.148].

[110] *laud. Paul.* 2.5 [SC 300.148]. Chrysostom says that Paul would prefer to endure the punishments of final judgment *with* Christ's love rather than without it to be placed among the elite and honored (Rom 9:3, in relation to 8:38–39, is clearly Chrysostom's biblical inspiration here, rather than, as Piédagnel suggests, 2 Cor 6:9 [SC 300.148, note g]).

[111] *laud. Paul.* 2.5 [SC 300.150].

[112] *laud. Paul.* 2.5–6 [SC 300.148–50].

[113] Ἀλλ' ἴσως εἴποι τις ἂν ὅτι πάντα ταῦτα διὰ τὸν Χριστὸν ἡδέα αὐτῷ ἦν. Τοῦτο γὰρ καὶ ἐγώ φημι, ὅτι ἅπερ ἀθυμίας ἡμῖν αἴτια, ταῦτα ἐκείνῳ μεγάλην ἔτικτεν ἡδονήν (*laud. Paul.* 2.6 [SC 300.152]).

And this includes Paul's constant weeping for the lost (such as the Jews, as in Rom 9:2–3), which, as with any grieving process, was a form of crying which actually brings with it a type of pleasure in earned consolation [καθάπερ οὖν καὶ ὁ Παῦλος, νυκτὸς καὶ ἡμέρας δακρύων, παραμυθίαν ἐλάμβανεν].[114]

The next movement of the argument takes up this portrait of Paul as the man in tears, lamenting and anxious for the fate of the whole world, and asks provocatively, "to what could one possibly compare him [τίνι ἄν τις δυνηθείη παραβαλεῖν;]? To what sort of iron? To what sort of steel?"[115] The answer to this leading rhetorical question is an extended alchemical portrait of Paul's soul as the paradigm of the inverse standard of values which Paul avidly pursued:

What might one call that soul [ψυχή]? Golden [χρυσῆ], or steely [ἀδαμαντίνη]? For it was more solid than any steel [καὶ γὰρ ἀδάμαντος ἦν παντὸς στερροτέρα], and more precious than gold and precious stones [καὶ χρυσοῦ καὶ λίθων τιμίων τιμιωτέρα]. It will outdo the former material in malleability [κἀκείνης μὲν οὖν τῆς ὕλης τὴν εὐτονίαν παρελάσει], and the latter in costliness [ταύτης δὲ τὴν πολυτέλειαν]. To what then might one compare it [Τίνι ἄν οὖν τις αὐτὴν παραβάλοι;]? To none of the things which exist; but if gold could become steel, and steel gold, then perhaps in some way his soul would attain its likeness from their combination. But why must I compare it with steel and gold? Place the whole world opposite his soul, and then you will see Paul's soul outweighing it in the balance.[116]

This is perhaps the most literal picture of Paul's soul in the homilies *de laudibus sancti Pauli*, yet it is metaphorical even as it is a σύγκρισις of Paul's soul with earthly metallic substances. A new, imaginary chemical compound amalgamating the properties of gold and steel would be needed even to provide a medium which might be appropriate to form an earthly likeness of Paul's soul. The weighing of the soul in the scales has many resonances in ancient religiosity (one naturally thinks of the vivid depictions of judgment of the heart weighed against a feather in the Egyptian Book of the Dead). Here it has been applied in such a hyperbolic fashion that this one heavily virtuous soul more than counterbalances all the matter of creation. The mental image of Paul which results from this mineral-test of the soul is of one who oxymoronically combines the qualities of softness and hardness into a singular force of compassionate zeal for the salvation of the world. Chrysostom adds to this proof that Paul's soul outweighs the world by an *a minore ad maius* inference from Heb 11:37–38: if the world was not worthy of the ancients who roamed about in animal skins and lived in caves [ὧν οὐκ ἦν ἄξιος ὁ κόσμος], then how much more is it unworthy of the very apostle who penned those words?[117] This claim receives further confirmation from a second argument of the same type centered in an appeal to the nature of the Lord who will exact the final judgment

---

[114] *laud. Paul.* 2.6 [SC 300.152].

[115] *laud. Paul.* 2.7 [SC 300.154].

[116] *laud. Paul.* 2.7 [SC 300.154].

[117] The interplay of life and text in these arguments is very interesting, for each can be used in support of the other.

according to *his* value system: as much as Paul gave greater honor to the love of Christ than to the heavenly realities, so will Christ in turn confer greater honor on Paul than on innumerable heavens, out of his divine love which is beyond expression in human words.[118]

Chrysostom next offers a range of proofs from Paul's earthly career that God testified to his worthiness [ἀξιοῦν], in order to demonstrate the ultimate reliability of the inverse table of values Paul exemplified. His string of examples includes the remarkable spiritual experiences the Lord led him through even before the final resurrection: snatched up into paradise, conducted to the third heaven, made a partner in the kind of ineffable secrets that human beings are not lawfully allowed to speak.[119] And why could Paul qualify for the superhuman status this final example seems to require? Because he behaved on earth as though consorting with angels, demonstrated angelic purity despite being bound up in a mortal body, and flew around the world like a bird or some incorporeal being [ἀσώματος], as though he had already attained heaven. This portrait of Paul hung between heaven and earth leads Chrysostom again to a σύγκρισις between Paul and the angels, an embellishment we encountered already in the initial encomium in the series. Here the point of comparison becomes guardian angels. Whereas they are given special custody of one nation (such as Michael of Israel), Paul was made the guardian angel of the whole world (later itemized to include land, sea, world, and even the uninhabited regions).[120] And it is at just this point that Chrysostom invokes a hypothetical interlocutor, as he had at the outset of the speech, this time objecting that surely "Paul was not the one managing these things" [οὐκ ἦν ὁ ταῦτα οἰκονομῶν]! Chrysostom quickly and emphatically agrees [καὶ γὰρ καὶ αὐτὸς ὁμολογῶ], for God's hand was at work here, yet he also insists in the very same breath, "that doesn't mean Paul should be excluded from the praises these acts deserve [ἀλλ' οὐδὲ οὕτως ἐκτὸς ἦν τῶν ἐπὶ τούτοις ἐπαίνων], because he had prepared himself in such a way as to be worthy of this abundant grace" [ἐπειδὴ ἑαυτὸν οὕτω κατεσκεύασεν ἄξιον τῆς τοσαύτης χάριτος].[121] So the argument has now come full circle, and Chrysostom is able to retain simultaneously his initial proposition (that Paul is the example of the virtue of which human persons are capable) and his form (praises for Paul).

A last question arises from the comparison of Paul with the angels. After an initial protestation that he does not make this contrast to insult [ὑβρίζειν] the angels, but instead to prove his opening contention that "it is possible for one who is a human being to be with the angels and to stand near them,"[122] John asks the

---

[118] *laud. Paul.* 2.7 [SC 300.156].

[119] See the full discussion in chap. 6, pp. 301–302 of how Chrysostom understands and employs these episodes from 2 Cor 12:2–4.

[120] *laud. Paul.* 2.8 [SC 300.156–58].

[121] *laud. Paul.* 2.8 [SC 300.158].

[122] δυνατὸν ἄνθρωπον ὄντα μετ' ἐκείνων εἶναι, καὶ ἐγγὺς αὐτῶν ἑστάναι (2.9 [SC 300.158]). Compare the proposition in the *prooimion*: ἀγγέλων καὶ ἀνθρώπων οὐ πολὺ τὸ μέσον (2.1 [SC 300.144]).

nettlesome theological question: why were the angels not given the same global responsibility as Paul (if this telling is accurate)? Chrysostom's answer serves his catechetical aim:"so that you might have no defense for slacking off, nor be able to take refuge in the difference between human and angelic nature for your state of ethical torpor."[123] This leads to a short paean to the marvelous accomplishments of Paul's word, the vehicle God intentionally chose to achieve his purpose:

For how is it not marvelous and incredible that a word which leapt forth from a tongue of clay [ἀπὸ γλώττης πηλίνης ἐκπηδῶν λόγος] sent death fleeing, destroyed sin, set straight an incapacitated nature,[124] and made the earth into heaven? Therefore I admire the power of God and for these things I marvel at Paul's will to act [προθυμία], since he received so great a grace due to the fact that he had prepared himself so well.[125]

ἐπίλογος (Conclusion).[126] Chrysostom's ἐπίλογος to laud. Paul. 2 skillfully combines the three functions of such a rhetorical conclusion: recapitulation, emotional appeal, and amplification.[127] As is customary in the final moments of his speeches, John not only brings together all the themes of the oration, with many resonances to the προοίμιον,[128] but trains them on the ethical imperative they mandate:"And I urge you[129] not only to marvel at, but also to imitate this archetype of virtue [μιμεῖσθαι τὸ ἀρχέτυπον τοῦτο τῆς ἀρετῆς]. For in this way we shall be able to share in the same crowns as he."[130] Then Chrysostom interrupts his own exhortation for a final argument of amplification by which he seeks yet again to dispel the incredulous objection that Paul was Paul, after all, and "ordinary folks" should not expect the same rewards he earned.This time the proof of the inductive application of Paul's fate to all who follow faithfully is offered by no less a witness than Paul himself, who, in the words of 2 Tim 4:7–8, promises that the crown reserved for him will also be extended to "all those who have loved his appearing." With that objection finally out of the way, Chrysostom returns to his paraenetic finale:

Therefore, since the same things lie in store for all, then let us all be zealous to become worthy [σπουδάζωμεν ἄξιοι γενέσθαι] of these promised goods. And let us look not only

---

[123] laud. Paul. 2.9 [SC 300.158].

[124] This phrase should be taken in reference to the moral paralysis of human nature (the very theme of this discourse), rather than more restrictively to Paul's healing of the lame man at Lystra (as Piédagnel, SC 300.158 note t takes it).

[125] laud. Paul. 2.9 [SC 300.158].

[126] laud. Paul. 2.10 [SC 300.158–60].

[127] For treatments of the ἐπίλογος in rhetorical theory, see Mitchell, Paul, 256, n. 389; 290–92, with references.

[128] These themes are: human nature's capacity for virtue, Paul's surpassing excellence in it, engagement with voiced opposition to one's ability to follow the moral life, and willingness as the key to activating the potential in human nature (the latter theme is introduced in the opening to the proof section, in laud. Paul. 2.2 [SC 300.144]).

[129] The formula καὶ ὑμᾶς παρακαλῶ marks the transition to the ἐπίλογος.

[130] laud. Paul. 2.10 [SC 300.158–60].

at the height and volume of Paul's virtuous deeds, but also at the intensity of the will to act [ὁ τόνος τῆς προθυμίας] by which he gained such great grace [δι' ἧς τοσαύτην ἐπεσπάσατο χάριν]. Let us look also at the kinship of nature which we have with him [καὶ τὸ τῆς φύσεως συγγενές], for he shared in all the same things with us [τῶν γὰρ αὐτῶν ἡμῖν ἐκοινώνησεν ἁπάντων]. And in this way the most difficult actions will seem to us easy and light [Καὶ οὕτω καὶ τὰ σφόδρα δυσκατόρθωτα, ῥᾴδια ἡμῖν φανεῖται καὶ κοῦφα] ....[131]

The argument line of this speech is, as we have seen, remarkably consistent and regular. The overarching proposition, which was signalled in the προοίμιον – that Paul in himself demonstrates the virtuous capacities of human nature [φύσις] – now is celebrated as proven, and employed as the basis for the ethical admonition for Chrysostom's church-goers to reach the same heights the apostle did. John's argument has also offered two specific minor premises which become pieces of specific advice by which his congregants can guide their emulation of the apostle: 1. eagerness of will to act [προθυμία] is the enzyme which kick-starts human nature to rev up to its full, in-built capacity; and, 2. an inverted standard of true pleasure and pain, such as Paul subscribed to, provides the greatest assurance that the life of virtue is not too difficult, but well within reach.

Laud. Paul 3: *Paul as the Embodiment of Love*

προοίμιον (Introduction).[132] At first homily 3 seems to pick up exactly where homily 2 left off, with the leitmotifs of the strength of human will to act [προθυμία], as proven by Paul, and its capacity to make people fly to heaven.[133] But then Chrysostom immediately launches into a new topic, the means which Paul used in his letters to activate "the power of the human will to act" – that is, the appeals to imitate himself, and to imitate God (in 1 Cor 11:1 and Eph 5:1–2, respectively). The question for this oration becomes: What is it that effects this "imitation" [ποιεῖ τὴν μίμησιν ταύτην]? Chrysostom's answer is love, the theme of the discourse, as introduced here in the proem and highlighted in the proof and conclusion to the speech.[134] He uses a variety of synonyms throughout the discourse to describe what this virtue of love for others[135] entails: φιλεῖν, εὐεργετεῖν, κηδεμονία, πρόνοια,

---

[131] *laud. Paul.* 2.10 [SC 300.160]. The final exhortation, as is customary for the series (and most of John's homilies), funnels into an eschatological vision and liturgical doxology.

[132] *laud. Paul.* 3.1 [SC 300.162–64].

[133] "The blessed Paul, when demonstrating the power of the human will to act, and the fact that we are able to fly to heaven itself, by-passed the angels and archangels and the other powers as examples. Instead, one time he used an appeal to himself alone when commanding them to become imitators of Christ, saying, 'Be imitators of me, just as also I am of Christ' (1 Cor 11:1). And at another time, without mentioning himself, he makes them ascend to the example of God himself, saying, 'therefore, be imitators of God, as beloved children'" (Eph 5:1) (*laud. Paul.* 3.1 [SC 300.162]).

[134] See *laud. Paul.* 3.1, 5, 9, 10 [SC 300.162, 170, 178–80].

[135] The love of which Chrysostom is speaking in this homily is not Paul's love for God or for Christ, though those themes are predominant elsewhere. For instance, in *hom. in Rom.* 16.3

σπουδή, φιλοστοργία,[136] φροντίζειν/φροντίδες. And in the proem John gives his succinct definition of love:"living for the common good, and looking toward the advantage of each" [τὸ κοινωφελῶς ζῆν καὶ πρὸς τὸ τῷ παντὶ χρήσιμον ὁρᾶν].[137] Still setting up his argument, Chrysostom first establishes his claim that love is the means of imitation of Paul, Christ and God by means of an exegetical warrant: that Paul followed both these calls to imitation with either a command to love (Eph 5:2), or a disquisition on the very topic (in 1 Cor 13). Then he proposes the more general theological axiom: "this is the virtue that makes one especially near to God."[138] The other virtues, Chrysostom argues, are inferior to love [αἰ ἄλλαι ταυτῆς καταδεέστεραι], for they are human-centered, and involve fighting off some vice (such as licentiousness, gluttony, avarice, or anger), whereas love is the divine virtue which human beings are called to share:"Loving is something common to us and to God."[139]

πρόθεσις and πίστεις (Proposition and Proofs).[140] The plan of this speech is completely straightforward. After the exordium introducing this theme – that love is the queen of the virtues – Chrysostom advances his proposition: "Therefore, knowing that this is the chief of the virtues [κεφάλαιον τῶν ἀγαθῶν], Paul demonstrated it with great precision."[141] In the proof section which follows, Chrysostom will document his thesis that Paul exhibited love in all he did by discussing Paul's love under two topical heads [κεφάλαια]: Paul's solicitation manifested in spiritual matters and in physical matters.[142] This corresponds with rhetorical theory,

---

[60.552], Paul's love for Christ is described as "a sea of love" [πέλαγος τῆς ἀγάπης], in which we can swim, and "an unspeakable flame" [φλὸξ ἄφατος] (the same image of love as fire is used later in this discourse, in §9). See also, among myriad other examples, laud. Paul. 2.4 [SC 300.148]; hom. in Rom. 32.3 [60.680]; sac. 3.7 [SC 272.156]:"no one loved Christ more than Paul" [Οὐδεὶς μᾶλλον Παύλου τὸν Χριστὸν ἠγάπησεν]. In compunct. 2 2 [47.413], Chrysostom says that it was Paul's desire and love for Christ [ὁ πόθος αὐτοῦ καὶ ἡ πρὸς τὸν Χριστὸν ἀγάπη] which surpassed not only the third, but all the heavens. A fine treatment of Paul's love for Christ can be found in Di S. Maria, "S. Paolo," 498–500, who regards this as the most striking feature of Chrysostom's depiction of Paul.

[136] Compare hom. in 2 Cor. 4.2 [61.420]: Τί ταύτης φιλοστοργότερον τῆς ψυχῆς;

[137] laud. Paul. 3.1 [SC 300.162]. In other places in Chrysostom's writings Paul is praised for his κηδεμονία, "solicitude," and φιλοστοργία, "affection" (stat. 1.3 [49.19]; hom. in Rom. 1.2 [60.402]; hom. in Eph. 8.4 [62.61]).

[138] αὕτη μάλιστα ἡ ἀρετὴ ἐγγὺς εἶναι ποιεῖ θεοῦ (laud. Paul. 3.1 [SC 300.162]).

[139] laud. Paul. 3.1 [SC 300.162–64], followed by a quotation of Mt 5:44–45.

[140] This extends from §2–9 [SC 300.164–78].

[141] 3.2 [SC 300.164]. Correspondingly, political speeches at this time, especially βασιλικοὶ λόγοι composed by men like Aristides and Themistius, accent φιλανθρωπία as the highest and most noteworthy virtue held by the emperor whom they laud (see Burgess, Epideictic Literature, 133–35, with full references).

[142] With Piédagnel, SC 300.162, n. 1:"Ce troisième panégyrique, consacré à la charité de Paul envers les hommes, présente une composition très nette, en deux parties: la charité de Paul, 1) dans l'ordre spirituel (§2–6), 2) dans l'ordre matériel (§7–8)."This disposition is not announced beforehand in a partition, but in the transition at 3.7 [SC 300.174]: "and it was not only in spiritual matters, but also in material ones that he demonstrated great forethought and great zeal."

which called first for the virtue to be named and applied to the subject, and then possession of it demonstrated through concrete incidents from the person's life.[143]

Argument One: Paul's Love in Tending to Spiritual Needs.

The first division begins with a demonstration of the sub-proposition that no one loved his enemies – those who plotted against him and afflicted him – more than Paul.[144] Paul's love was always based, not upon the merit or affiliation of those upon whom he lavished it, but on the sole criterion of a common human nature [τὸ κοινὸν τῆς φύσεως].[145] Paul treated his enemies as a father would a child who acted erratically and violently due to brain-fever – with pity and tears of compassion. Indeed the image of Paul as a father predominates in this homily,[146] because it serves for John as an explanation of the fervency with which Paul loved every single person and sought her or his salvation, as though "he himself had begotten the entire world."[147] The initial argument devises a portrait from Rom 9–11 of a Paul who mourned over his fellow Jews (Rom 9:3), always speaking gently [ἡμέρως] and compassionately [συμπαθητικῶς] about them, and acting as their protector, thwarting the efforts of those who would seek to insult them (Rom 11:20–21). Continually weeping on their behalf, and holding out hope for their salvation, Paul, like Jeremiah before him, even offers a kind of defense or excuse [ἀπολογία] for their sinfulness.

At §5 Chrysostom moves to a new set of proofs of Paul's loving care in spiritual matters by means of a rhetorical question: "And was Paul like this only to Jews, but not to outsiders?" John's answer, unsurprisingly, is "No! Paul was more gentle than all, toward both his own people and strangers."[148] As proof of this claim Chrysostom offers a chain of selective passages from the epistles which display a calm and forbearing tone, largely strung together without editorial comment, given that this mass of evidence, John assumes, speaks for itself.[149] The last Scriptural quotation, from Col 1:28, introduces a new idea: the way Paul's love was exhibited in his

---

[143] "We set out each virtue, one by one, then go through the deeds; for instance, saying first that he was prudent [σώφρων], and immediately thereafter bringing out what prudent thing he had done" [προστίθεμεν κατὰ μίαν ἑκάστην ἀρετήν, ἔπειτα τὰ ἔργα διεξιόντες, οἷον ὅτι ἦν σώφρων, προλέγειν καὶ ἐπιφέρειν εὐθὺς, τί αὐτῷ σωφρονητικὸν ἔργον πέπρακται] (Theon, *Prog.* 8 [Spengel, 2.112]).

[144] *laud. Paul.* 3.2 [SC 300.164].

[145] *laud. Paul.* 3.2 [SC 300.164].

[146] It reappears especially at the end of the proof, where Paul is said to be "a common father of the whole world" (*laud. Paul.* 3.9 [SC 300.178]).

[147] *laud. Paul.* 3.6 [SC 300.172]. It also unites Paul in the cycle of successive imitations, by presenting him in the same manner as God the Father.

[148] Ἆρ' οὖν πρὸς Ἰουδαίους μόνον τοιοῦτος, πρὸς δὲ τοὺς ἔξωθεν οὐχί; Πάντων ἡμερώτερος ἦν καὶ πρὸς τοὺς οἰκείους, καὶ πρὸς τοὺς ἀλλοτρίους (*laud. Paul.* 3.5 [SC 300.170]).

[149] The collection of passages he cites includes 2 Tim 2:24–26; 2 Cor 12:20, 21; Gal 4:19; 2 Cor 2:8; 2:4; 1 Cor 9:20–21; and Col 1:28.

missionary zeal to bring all to salvation, thus tending to their "spiritual needs." To do this Paul would go to any lengths, as a tumbling long list of all that Paul did to present every human being to God for salvation quite abundantly documents. John's catalogue of proofs of Paul's love amounts to a curriculum vitae of the apostle, a list of his disclosive πράξεις, actions, which manifest to all the character of his inner soul:

> For as though he himself had begotten the entire world, thus was he troubled, thus did he run about, thus was he zealous to lead all into the kingdom. He did so by healing, encouraging, promising, praying, supplicating, frightening the demons, driving off the corrupted, through his personal visits, through his letters, through his words, through his deeds, through his disciples, through his own self, picking up the fallen, strengthening those who were standing, raising those lying in the dirt, healing the downtrodden, goading on the slackers, casting threats at his enemies, keeping a sharp eye on his adversaries.[150]

The portrait of Paul as a father willing to try any possible means to restore his progeny then gives way to a quick and functionally parallel image of Paul as a noble general who was willing to do all forms of scut work in the camp to meet the needs of his army.

Argument Two: Paul's Love in Supplying Material Needs.

At §7 Chrysostom forges a transition into his second heading, Paul's loving concern and zeal for the physical needs of his people, by means of an explicit partition: "And it was not only in spiritual matters, but also in material ones that he demonstrated great forethought, great zeal."[151] As proofs for this sub-proposition Chrysostom brings in Paul's recommendations of support for Phoebe (Rom 16:3) and for Stephanas and his household (1 Cor 16:15–16),[152] and the Old Testament *exemplum* of the services Elisha rendered to the Shunammite woman (4 Kgdms 4:13), which included both physical and spiritual matters. Furthermore, not only did Paul write letters of recommendation for his co-workers in transit, but he also took it upon himself to exercise concern in his letters for their travelling provisions (as with Zenas and Apollos in Tit 3:13). And the crowning example of his apostolic loving oversight is that Paul wrote a whole thoughtfully intelligent and solicitous letter [πῶς συνετῶς, πῶς κηδεμονικῶς ἐπιστέλλει] on behalf of the runaway slave (and thief, no less!), Onesimus.[153] All of this shows that Paul never considered such

---

[150] *laud. Paul.* 3.6 [SC 300.172].

[151] Καὶ οὐκ ἐν τοῖς πνευματικοῖς μόνον, ἀλλὰ καὶ ἐν τοῖς σαρκικοῖς πολλὴν τὴν πρόνοιαν ἐπεδείκνυτο, πολλὴν τὴν σπουδήν (*laud. Paul.* 3.7 [SC 300.174]).

[152] From these examples Chrysostom formulates an universal rule: "giving assistance in these matters is the distinguishing feature of the tender love the saints exhibited" [τοῦτο ἴδιον τῆς φιλοστοργίας τῶν ἁγίων] (*laud. Paul.* 3.7 [SC 300.174]).

[153] *laud. Paul.* 3.8 [SC 300.174–76]. On this consistent negative characterization of Onesimus in Chrysostom's writings see Margaret M. Mitchell, "John Chrysostom on Philemon: A Second Look," *HTR* 88 (1995) 135–48.

concern for the wants of others beneath him. Only one thing did he account worthy of shame:"overlooking anything necessary for salvation" [τὸ, δέον γενέσθαι τι πρὸς σωτηρίαν, παριδεῖν]. His willingness to give of himself for others knew no bounds: "This is why he was always on the move, and didn't hesitate to expend anything on behalf of those being saved, neither words, nor money, nor body."[154] This portrait of Paul, "the total apostle," who attends to all peoples' needs, is for Chrysostom an incarnate image of the chief of the virtues – love – at work. As so often in his oratory, next Chrysostom in the blink of an eye transforms this human portrait into a material pictorial icon:

Paul was so great in love, the chief of the virtues, that he was more fervently ardent than any flame. And just as iron when it lands in fire becomes completely fire, so also Paul, ignited with the fire of love, has become completely love.[155]

But love is also, like the love of the deity, the virtue of parents. So Chrysostom can render Paul back into human form again in the very next line as he brings his proof to a neat summation:

As though a common father of the whole world, thus he served as a representative of the very human beings he had begotten. But, however, he outdid all fathers in caring for both bodily and spiritual needs, giving everything – money and words and body and soul – on behalf of those he loved.[156]

Once again the letters serve as evidence documenting this portrait of the loving soul, for John quotes four Pauline passages in succession (Rom 13:10; Col 3:14; 1 Tim 1:5; Rom 13:9) to put the final, recapitulating seal on this argument that love is "the fullness of the law, the bond of perfection, the mother of all goods, and the beginning and end of virtue."[157]

ἐπίλογος (Conclusion).[158] Once this proposition is declared proven, Chrysostom moves smoothly into his final exhortation to his audience to imitate what constitutes *the* imitable way to God: "Therefore, since love is the beginning and end and sum total of the virtues, let us zealously imitate Paul in this."[159] But the orator is not yet finished. Chrysostom then muzzles a possible objection to his satisfactory proof:"don't speak to me of the dead whom he raised (Acts 20:7–12), nor the lepers he cleansed" (Acts 19:11–12). Paul, after all, became who he was

---

[154] *laud. Paul.* 3.8 [SC 300.176].
[155] *laud. Paul.* 3.9 [SC 300.178]. One example of Paul's great love is his devotion to Timothy, praying constantly for him night and day (2 Tim 1:3), on which Chrysostom exclaims:"Do you see his boiling desire? Do you see the insanity of his love?" [ὁρᾷς ζέοντα πόθον; ὁρᾷς μανίαν ἀγάπης] (*hom. in 2 Tim.* 1.1 [62.602]).
[156] *laud. Paul.* 3.9 [SC 300.178].
[157] πλήρωμα νόμου, σύνδεσμος τελειότητος, μήτηρ τῶν ἀγαθῶν πάντων, ἀρχὴ καὶ τέλος ἀρετῆς (*laud. Paul.* 3.9 [SC 300.178]).
[158] *laud. Paul.* 3.10 [SC 300.178–80].
[159] Ἐπεὶ οὖν ἀρχὴ καὶ τέλος καὶ πάντα τὰ ἀγαθὰ ἡ ἀγάπη, καὶ ταύτῃ τὸν Παῦλον ζηλώσωμεν (3.10 [SC 300.178]).

because of this quality of love, not because of such wonders [καὶ γὰρ οὗτος ἐντεῦθεν τοιοῦτος ἐγένετο].[160] Ordinary persons need not fear that they are unable to present an acceptable dossier of accomplishments at the final judgment. Chrysostom assures his auditors that God will not demand miracles from them, and points to the only imitable route to salvation: "acquire the love of Paul and you will have a completed crown."[161] As in the ἐπίλογος to *laud. Paul.* 2, Chrysostom again brings in Paul himself as a final witness to the truth of his oratorical proposition. "Who says these things [Τίς ταῦτά φησιν;]? The very foster-father of love himself [Αὐτὸς ὁ τῆς ἀγάπης τροφεύς],[162] this man who placed love above signs and marvels and countless other things."[163] Chrysostom's words, therefore, are ultimately Paul's own. Paul's role as final authority on love is cemented by a last appeal to experience:"Since Paul succeeded in love so surpassingly, for this reason he knows precisely its·power."[164] Once again life and text intertwine in the proof and moral, as Chrysostom rounds off the sermon by calling on 1 Cor 12:31 ("I am showing[165] you a still more superlative way") to instantiate both his point, that love is the most excellent and easiest way, and his procedure, that Paul is the one who in his life displayed what that love looks like.

Other Soul Portraits

Love is not the only virtue for which Chrysostom praises Paul in these homilies, as elsewhere in his corpus of writings. Other traits which Paul is said to have exemplified include humility,[166] moderation,[167] zeal,[168] gentleness,[169] courage,[170]

---

[160] *laud. Paul.* 3.10 [SC 300.178], repeated again a few lines later:"he became such as he was from this; nothing made him so worthy as the power of love" [Ἐντεῦθεν καὶ αὐτὸς τοιοῦτος ἐγένετο, καὶ οὐδὲν οὕτως αὐτὸν ἐποίησεν ἄξιον, ὡς ἡ τῆς ἀγάπης δύναμις].

[161] *laud. Paul.* 3.10 [SC 300.178–80].

[162] On this epithet, see chap. 3, n. 140.

[163] *laud. Paul.* 3.10 [SC 300.180].

[164] Ἐπειδὴ γὰρ σφόδρα αὐτὴν κατωρθώκει, διὰ τοῦτο καὶ μετὰ ἀκριβείας αὐτῆς οἶδε τὴν ἰσχύν (*laud. Paul.* 3.10 [SC 300.180]).

[165] The present tense, δείκνυμι, is ambiguous in 1 Cor 12:31 (whether literal present or present for future), which works nicely for Chrysostom's argument here.

[166] ταπεινοφροσύνη (*laud. Paul.* 1.14; 5.9–10 [SC 300.134, 246–48]; *incomprehens.* 5.496–504 [SC 28.312]; *hom. in Rom.* 8:28 3 [51.170]); and especially the long discussion of how Paul was "truly" humble in *poenit.* 2.5 [49.290]. In particular, Chrysostom regards Paul's continual references to his former persecution of the church, and negative self-references like 1 Cor 15:8–9 and Eph 3:8, to be prime examples of an astounding level of humility on Paul's part (see, e.g., *hom. in Eph.* 7.1 [62.49]; 8.1 [62.55], and further discussion in chap. 6 on Paul's ascetic acts), as well as his lowly tentmaker's trade and his associations with commoners (*hom. in 1 Cor.* 35.5 [61.303]). For discussion and further references see di S. Maria,"S. Paolo," 497. An especially nice example is *hom. in 1 Tim.* 3.1 [62.515–16], which contains a small encomium to Paul's great humility, as manifested in the pseudepigraphical self-portrait in 1:12f. First Chrysostom begins with the proposition that humility has much profit, yet it is never easily found, though often declared. Then Chrysostom's encomium to Paul's humility begins with an ironic conceit:"But the blessed

and endurance.[171] Here we see that Chrysostom's virtue catalogue overlaps considerably with the values which govern epideictic rhetoric among non-Christian as well as Christian practitioners. The whole catalogue is required to substantiate the claim that Paul possessed all the virtues, and also to celebrate a range of ethical behaviors, the same palette of colors which Chrysostom wishes to exhort his congregants to draw upon in their self-portraiture.

Similar portraits of the virtues in Paul's soul are found outside of *de laudibus sancti Pauli*, and throughout Chrysostom's corpus of writings, of which we shall cite just one example, from one of the homily series on the Pauline epistles. The self-portrait in Eph 3:1–7 inspires Chrysostom to break into a mini-disquisition on Paul's virtues, which he uses to inveigh against the sins of his congregation at Antioch, and of his time and place generally.[172] John recognizes the literary integrity of the epistolary portrait itself by noting the inclusio formed by the self-appellation δέσμιος in 3:1 and διάκονος in 3:7, and remarking how in both cases Paul emphasizes that it is God's grace and God's power which receive the credit for his career.[173] Chrysostom next gives an exposition of Paul's success as due not solely to his own character, but to the conjunction of Pauline virtue and divine power (with 3:7, κατὰ τὴν ἐνέργειαν τῆς δυνάμεως αὐτοῦ). In laying out this argument Chrysostom first names the three virtues Paul brought to his ministry of proclamation: 1) a seething and venturesome will to act [προθυμία ζέουσα καὶ παράβολος], 2) a soul ready to endure anything whatsoever [ψυχὴ πᾶν ὁτιοῦν ὑπομεῖναι ἑτοῖμος], and, 3) combined understanding and wisdom [καὶ σύνεσις καὶ σοφία]. But Paul's venturesome will [τὸ φιλοκίνδυνον] alone, his unstoppable life, was not sufficient; it needed to be empowered by the spirit. Then Chrysostom

---

Paul so greatly pursued humility that he was everywhere looking for abundant opportunities to humble his reasoning capacity" ['Ο δὲ μακάριος οὕτως αὐτὴν μετεδίωκε Παῦλος, ὡς καὶ ἐπινοεῖν πολλὰς πανταχοῦ προφάσεις πρὸς τὸ ταπεινοῦν αὐτοῦ τὴν διάνοιαν]. This is because "those who are conscious that they have done excellent deeds, wishing to be humble, perhaps must work especially hard on themselves. So likely Paul suffered greatly in himself, swelled up by the consciousness of good as though by a rising stream." Then Paul becomes the paradigm of one who knows rightly how to give God the credit for his good deeds without altogether relinquishing his own due, thus supplying further evidence against those inclined to defend their own sloth by appeal to divine determinism of human character. Constantly in his praise for Paul's humility Chrysostom must address the counterpoint of Paul's boasting in the letters, so he has some stock ways of defusing that accusation (as here). For more in-depth discussion of how Chrysostom evaluates and treats Paul's boasting, especially in *laud. Paul.* 5, see chap. 6, pp. 339–53.

[167] μετριότης (*laud. Paul.* 5.8, 9 [SC 300.246]).

[168] ζῆλος (*laud. Paul.* 1.14; 5.3; 7.5 [SC 300.134–36, 234, 304]).

[169] ἐπιείκεια (*laud. Paul.* 6.10, 13; 7.9 [SC 300.280, 288, 312]; also *hom. in Ac.* 50.3 [60.347]).

[170] ἀνδρεία (*laud. Paul.* 5.8; 6.5, 12; 7.10 [SC 300.246, 270, 284, 312]; cf. *hom. in Gen.* 11.5 [53.95]); *hom. in Ac.* 44.1 [60.309]).

[171] ὑπομονή (*laud. Paul.* 1.7, 8 [SC 300.124, 124]; cf. *hom. in Ac.* 44.1 [60.309]).

[172] On the Antiochene provenance of these homilies, see Bonsdorff, *Predigttätigkeit*, 64–71; Quasten, *Patrology*, 3.447.

[173] *hom. in Eph.* 6.3 [62.46].

gives proofs from the Pauline letters of the blamelessness of Paul's life.[174] He concludes this introduction of Paul the exemplum by saying that a person must be unseizable [ἄληπτος], stewardly [οἰκονομικός], hurling himself into danger [ῥιψοκίνδυνος] and "ready to teach" [διδακτικός]. These virtues in Paul were the secret of his success (not his miracles).[175] Such qualities of character were what Paul "brought in" to the process of his life in mission; however, he does not give himself the honor for its resounding successes, but rather God, as befits a prudent servant. Before moving on to a condemnation of the behavior of his church members and the wider society, Chrysostom rounds off his treatment of the exemplary Paul with familiar epideictic *topoi*: the qualities of virtue which Paul embodied are not beyond our capacity to achieve, and Paul should be evoked now for imitation and for comparison with present-day slovenliness.[176]

Laud. Paul. 6: *Defacing and Replacing False Portraits*

The encomium in *laud. Paul.* 6 is cast as an *apologia* for Paul against charges by critics that he was a coward and a hothead.[177] Treatment of this theme becomes a rhetorical necessity occasioned by Chrysostom's claim that Paul possessed and exercised all virtues simultaneously, but it is also an illustration of the preacher's clever adaptation of necessity in his favor. Surely there were critics of Paul in Chrysostom's day, both from outside and within the church,[178] and of varying degrees of hostility, but Chrysostom's speech mostly fabricates or at least exaggerates the rhetorical exigency of defense for Paul in order to further specific pastoral aims.[179] For the purposes of his speech Chrysostom first rhetorically creates an

---

[174] 2 Cor 6:3; 1 Thess 2:3; Rom 12:17; 1 Cor 15:31; Rom 8:35; 2 Cor 6:4–5; 1 Cor 9:20–21; Rom 15:18; 2 Cor 12:13; 12:11.

[175] We shall discuss Chrysostom's ambiguous attitude toward Paul's miracles at length in chap. 6, pp. 291–95.

[176] *hom. in Eph.* 6.3 [62.47]. In the same series is a discussion of Paul's κηδεμονία in 16.2 [62.113].

[177] Fictional apology is a rhetorical strategy which is not unique to Chrysostom (see n. 179 below). Hubbell, "Chrysostom and Rhetoric," 272, because he is focusing on rhetorical theory alone, deems the speech more thoroughly unconventional for this than it actually is: "The sixth homily is openly in contravention of the approved rhetorical rules in that it is concerned entirely with a consideration of Paul's faults. The very first sentence shows, however, that Chrysostom is not writing an apology, but gathering together all the attacks that might be made on Paul's character in order to convert these by process of inversion into encomium."

[178] See, for example, the criticisms inveighed against Paul by the third-century Greek philosopher, perhaps Porphyry, preserved in Macarius Magnes, *apocrit.* 3 (Adolf Harnack, *Kritik des Neuen Testaments von einem griechischen Philosophen des 3. Jahrhunderts [Die im Apocriticus des Macarius Magnes enthaltene Streitschrift]*, TU 37/4 [Leipzig: Pries, 1911]), and by the emperor Julian (on which see chap. 6, n. 343, and further discussion there). These external critics of Paul also had deep veins of Christian anti-Paulinism to draw upon (see Gerd Luedemann, *Opposition to Paul in Jewish Christianity*, trans. M. Eugene Boring [Minneapolis: Fortress, 1989]).

[179] Such adoption of a fictional apology for a speech of praise is well known in Greco-

unnamed rival Pauline portraitist who engages in the twin epideictic art to his own
– the ψόγος, or speech of blame.[180] John answers this painter of atrocities, not with
independent portraits of his own, but by retouching those of the competitor
(particularly by the application of the color of προαίρεσις, "free will"),[181] in such a
way that the corrected canvas coincides brilliantly with his portrait of Paul, the
archetype of virtue.

προοίμιον and πρόθεσις (Introduction and Proposition): At the outset of the
speech, with another direct opening, Chrysostom springs a surprise on his congregation: "Would you like it, beloved, if today we left behind Paul's great and
admirable deeds and instead brought before you the things which some people
think provide 'a wrestling hold' against him?"[182] In his response to this opening
rhetorical question (and characterization of his opposition),[183] John formulates the
thesis he will seek to prove in this discourse:"For we shall see that even these things
make him no less illustrious and great than the deeds we usually praise" [καὶ γὰρ
καὶ αὐτὰ ἐκείνων ὀψόμεθα οὐκ ἔλαττον αὐτὸν ποιοῦντα λαμπρὸν καὶ μέγαν]. In
these two sentences John has neatly laid out both the proposition he will seek to
prove, and the means of its substantiation. The disposition of this speech is quite
regular, based upon the two charges of which Chrysostom attempts to exonerate
Paul – cowardice and wrathfulness. In carrying out this faux defense, Chrysostom is
in essence engaged in dueling portraits; his task is, in each case, to deface a scandalous
or unflattering portrait of Paul and replace it with one that retains many of the same
features intact, but which, to the contrary, is fully honorable and praiseworthy.

πίστεις (Proofs). The first portrait of Paul which Chrysostom seeks to take
down off the wall is a vision of the apostle, drawn from Acts 22:25 and the
narrative of the revolt and imprisonment at Philippi in Acts 16, as a fearful man.

Roman rhetoric, as, for example, in Isocrates' *Or.* 15, and Favorinus' *Corinthian Oration*, as
analyzed by Gleason, *Making Men*, 8–20.

[180] Note the prevalence of language of blame and accusation in this oration: ἔγκλημα (6.3;
6.5 [2x]; 6.13 [288], a term found only here in the seven homilies *de laudibus sancti Pauli* [SC
300.266, 270, 288]); and κατάγνωσις/καταγιγνώσκειν (6.2; 6.9 [SC 300.266, 278]). John explicitly contrasts ἐγκώμιον and ἔγκλημα in 6.5 [SC 300.270]. For the paired nature of ψόγος and
ἐγκώμιον in rhetorical theory see, e.g., Aphth. *Prog.* 9 [Spengel, 2.40]: "the speech of blame is
divided into the same heads as also the encomium, and one should cast blame on all the things
that one praises" [διαιρεῖται (ὁ ψόγος) δὲ τοῖς αὐτοῖς κεφαλαίοις, οἵπερ καὶ τὸ ἐγκώμιον, καὶ
τοσαῦτα δεῖ ψέγειν, ὅσα καὶ ἐγκωμιάζειν].

[181] The term προαίρεσις, common throughout Chrysostom writings, is extraordinarily frequent in this speech, where it occurs only nineteen times (6.3 [4x]; 6.4 [2x]; 6.5 [3x]; 6.6 [5x];
6.7 [3x]; 6.8 [2x] [SC 300.266, 268–70, 270–72, 272, 274, 276]). The word literally means one's
will in the sense of choice of actions, but as Chrysostom uses it sometimes overlaps with προθυμία,
"eagerness of will" (see Piédagnel, SC 300.265, n. 3). To ease the cumbersome quality of
translating this term over and over again, I have sometimes simply rendered it as "will."

[182] Βούλεσθε τήμερον, ἀγαπητοί, παρέντες τὰ μεγάλα Παύλου καὶ θαυμαστά, ἃ δοκεῖ
παρά τισι λαβήν τινα ἔχειν, ταῦτα εἰς μέσον ἀγάγωμεν; (*laud. Paul.* 6.1 [SC 300.260]).

[183] Those who seek to defame Paul are here cast as pugilists who grope at the man for a tight
grip or hold [λαβή] by which to pin him to the ground.

In these instances Paul is considered to have acted in order to secure his own safety and ward off similar maltreatments in the future. The negative portrait can be painted in a few simple strokes —"a body that yielded to blows and trembled before whips" [σῶμα οὕτως εἶχον πληγαῖς καὶ τρέμον μάστιγας] and a man "frightened" [δεδοικώς] – which immediately brings to mind a well-recognized ancient caricature.[184] Given the potentially damaging passages in his source material (Acts and the letters) Chrysostom cannot simply draw a rival portrait of a consistently brave Paul, but he must acknowledge some of the elements of the negative portrait, while also recasting and reframing them into a praiseworthy composition. Interestingly this is exactly the same rhetorical challenge the historical Paul faced in 2 Corinthians, so in a mimetic move Chrysostom self-consciously embraces Paul's own rhetorical approach in his grand contention that: "The apparent weakness of Paul's nature is itself the greatest proof of his virtue" [Αὐτὴ γὰρ ἡ δοκοῦσα τῆς φύσεως εἶναι ἀσθένεια, αὐτὴ μέγιστον δεῖγμα τῆς ἀρετῆς ἐστι τῆς ἐκείνου].[185] Chrysostom incessantly repeats that Paul had the same soul and the same body as everyone else, but that he also had an uncommon level of προθυμία, "eager will to act," that made him the equal of the angels. On these terms the weaknesses Paul held in common with human nature do not debase his achievement, but rather increase the degree of difficulty with which he accomplished the unthinkable. And they are part of a deliberate divine design, along with Paul's huge inventory of sufferings, to teach the rest of humanity of what it is capable.[186]

In §1.5-§9 John treats Paul's fear of physical attack under two sub-heads: fear of blows (§1.5-§3) and of death (§4-9).[187] One way he defends Paul against condemnation [κατάγνωσις] for his fear of being beaten and tortured is by comparison. In doing so Chrysostom formulates a general principle: "What is truly blameworthy is not fearing blows, but enduring something unworthy of piety because of that

---

[184] See Theophrastus, Char. 25 (περὶ δειλίας): "cowardice, of course, would seem to be a giving way of the soul in fear" ['Ἀμέλει δὲ ἡ δειλία δόξειεν ἂν εἶναι ὑπειξίς τις ψυχῆς ἐν φόβῳ] (text and trans. J. M. Edmonds, LCL). Paul himself drew upon this caricature in 1 Cor 2:3, but Chrysostom does not invoke that passage here, given that his concern is with Paul's reactions to *external* persecution.

[185] *laud. Paul.* 6.2 [SC 300.264]. John, however, will add to it a philosophical tint lacking in Paul's own writings.

[186] "Since the extreme number of dangers he faced might provide most people with this false impression, and equally make them suspect that Paul was higher than all human creatures [ἀνώτερος τῶν ἀνθρωπίνων γενόμενος], he was such a man as he was. This is why God allowed him to suffer, so that you might learn that, although one of the many where nature is concerned [εἷς τῶν πολλῶν ὢν κατὰ τὴν φύσιν], with respect to the will to act he was not only above the many, but even one of the angels [κατὰ τὴν προθυμίαν οὐ μόνον ὑπὲρ τοὺς πολλοὺς ἦν, ἀλλὰ καὶ τῶν ἀγγέλων εἷς ἦν]. This is because, endowed with such a soul and such a body [μετὰ τοιαύτης ψυχῆς καὶ τοιούτου σώματος] he continually endured countless deaths, and despised the things of the present, the things to come" (*laud. Paul.* 6.2 [SC 300.264]).

[187] This largely accords with Piédagnel's content analysis (SC 300.260, n. 3).

fear."[188] In defending his beloved saint Chrysostom changes the vantage point of the unbecoming portrait from the moment of battle itself to its aftermath:"for the man who remains uncaptured in battle to have been afraid of blows proves him more admirable [θαυμαστότερος] than the man who did not fear."[189] By switching to the later temporal perspective, Chrysostom has given the portrait of Paul's trepidation a very different shine.The anthropological syllogism John constructs in building this case is: fear is natural; what is natural cannot be worthy of condemnation [κατάγνωσις]; therefore fear itself is no cause for condemnation. It is only what one does with the fear that is potentially blameworthy.[190] And, inversely, since enduring blows without lapsing into moral failings is unnatural, given that it constitutes a victory over innate impulses,[191] the ensuing image of Paul redounds even more to his credit. So Chrysostom taunts his rival portraitist: "you are bringing these negative images before me in vain – or, rather, not in vain, but on Paul's very behalf, for by your objections you prove how great he was!"[192]

A more intense instance of Paul's anxiety is his aversion to death, which Chrysostom takes up in §4–9. Again it is the challenger who raises the curtain on this negative portrait:"But didn't he sometimes fear death, too?"[193] At first John replies to this accusation with Pauline passages in which Paul expressed his groaning agony at being alive (2 Cor 5:4; Rom 8:23), and describes Paul's procedure in terms which fit precisely what Chrysostom himself is doing in this proof:"Do you see how he introduces the power that comes from free will as a counterbalance [ἀντίρροπον] to natural weakness?"[194] Then Chrysostom offers some Christian precedents for fear in the face of death: the martyrs, and the apostle Peter. But mostly Chrysostom responds to the caricature of Paul as quaking in the face of death in a way precisely parallel to his engagement with Paul's anxiety when confronted with blows. Fear of death, Chrysostom claims, is also natural, and it

---

[188] Οὐδὲ γὰρ τὸ φοβεῖσθαι πληγὰς καταγνώσεως ἄξιον, ἀλλὰ τὸ διὰ τὸν φοβὸν τῶν πληγῶν ἀνάξιόν τι τῆς εὐσεβείας ὑπομεῖναι (*laud. Paul.* 6.3 [SC 300.266]).

[189] *laud. Paul.* 6.3 [SC 300.266].

[190] *laud. Paul.* 6.3 [SC 300.266]. Compare the statement in Aristotle, *Eth. Nic.* 2.5.3–4 that because being afraid and being angry are ἀπροαιρέτως, "not matters of choice," they cannot be a cause for either praise or blame.

[191] "While fearing blows is a matter of nature, enduring nothing unseemly on account of that fear is due to the free will correcting the weakness of nature, and proving victorious over that weakness" [τὸ μὲν γὰρ φοβηθῆναι πληγάς, τῆς φύσεως· τὸ δὲ μηδὲν διὰ τὸν φόβον τῶν πληγῶν ἀπρεπὲς ὑπομεῖναι, τῆς προαιρέσεως διορθουμένης τὸ τῆς φύσεως ἐλάττωμα, καὶ κρατούσης τῆς ἀσθενείας ἐκείνης] (*laud. Paul.* 6.3 [SC 300.266]).

[192] *laud. Paul.* 6.3 [SC 300.266]. In the process Chrysostom paints his own self-portrait, that of the verbal portraitist of Paul (a rather accurate one, at that!) – as one who is always "saying and strongly maintaining that, on the one hand, Paul was human and in no way superior to us in regard to nature, but, on the other, that he became better in regard to the exercise of his will."

[193] *laud. Paul.* 6.4 [SC 300.268].

[194] Εἶδες πῶς ἀντίρροπον τῆς φυσικῆς ἀσθενείας τὴν ἀπὸ προαιρέσεως εἰσήγαγε δύναμιν; (*laud. Paul.* 6.4 [SC 300.268]).

therefore stands in Paul's favor, since he did not act shamefully when he experienced it:"Since, what sort of blame is there in fearing death? Rather, what sort of praise isn't due for the man who, even as he fears death, endures nothing servile because of the fear."[195] This argument is based upon a philosophical premise:"For there is no blame [ἔγκλημα] in having a nature with a deficiency, but in being enslaved to those deficiencies."[196] What this amounts to is a new definition, a new portrayal of bravery that completely overturns the image of Paul as a coward:"How great and wonderful is the one who corrects the insult arising from nature by the bravery of his will!" [ὅ γε τὴν παρ' αὐτῆς ἐπήρειαν τῇ τῆς προαιρέσεως ἀνδρείᾳ διορθούμενος].[197]

In §6–7 Chrysostom engages the "nature/nurture" debate as he reckons with the anticipated objection that nature is resolutely steadfast and solid (and therefore stronger than the will). By Scriptural examples such as Abraham and the three Hebrew children of Daniel 3, and even a "pagan" proverb,[198] John argues that virtuous exercise of the will can become "second nature," indeed "first nature," given its power to overcome nature itself. His catechetical program can be summed up in a single pithy avowal:"For it is possible, yes, it *is* possible, to imitate the force of nature with the precise exercise of free will."[199] Hence Paul, "this very portrait statue of virtue" [οὗτος αὐτὸς ἀνδριὰς τῆς ἀρετῆς] is a fixed monument to the quest to make the virtues earned by the will as strong and fixed as the endowments of human nature.[200] By quoting a wide range of passages from Paul's letters, Chrysostom endeavors to show how Paul was both human in nature and possessed of a noble will.[201] In §9 Chrysostom explicitly names the challenge he faces in his role as the sculptor of Paul: to mediate between two artistic-ethical extremes, each of which would be false and dangerous: Paul's weakness must be accurately portrayed, lest the viewers think him superhuman and lose heart for their own struggle for virtue; yet Paul's great accomplishments must not be minimized in the portrait either, lest one should condemn that holy soul. This double-sided view of Paul that John constructs mirrors the duality in the letters themselves, where Paul by turns accents his weakness and his moral excellence. John

---

[195] *laud. Paul.* 6.5 [SC 300.270].

[196] *laud. Paul.* 6.5 [SC 300.270].

[197] *laud. Paul.* 6.5 [SC 300.270].

[198] "Or haven't you heard the maxim the pagans tell:'from force of habit, free will becomes second nature'" [οὐκ ἀκούεις καὶ τῆς ἔξωθεν παροιμίας λεγούσης, ὅτι δευτέρα φύσις ἡ προαίρεσις γίνεται ἐκ συνηθείας] (*laud. Paul.* 6.6 [SC 300.272]).

[199] Ἔνι γάρ, ἔνι φύσεως ἰσχὺν προαιρέσεως ἀκριβείᾳ μιμήσασθαι (*laud. Paul.* 6.7 [SC 300.274]).

[200] *laud. Paul.* 6.7 [SC 300.274].

[201] See *laud. Paul.* 6.7 [SC 300.276], where Chrysostom concludes that by turns in his writings Paul showed both τὸ ἀσθενὲς τῆς φύσεως and ἡ εὐγένεια τῆς προαιρέσεως. This rounds off the sub-argument introduced in 6.6 [SC 300.272], that προαίρεσις γενναία can become even more strongly fixed than nature [φύσις].

regards this as a deliberate and wise pastoral strategy on the apostle's part to lead others to the proper measure and mixture of all attributes.[202]

In §10–13 Chrysostom takes up a second negative portrait of Paul which one might compose and brandish about: Paul as an angry and intemperate fellow [filled with θυμός]. Expressions of this personal quality can be found in the letters and in Acts. In the epistles we have Paul's curse of Alexander (1 Tim 1:20; 2 Tim 4:15), his prayer for the punishment of his opponents in 2 Thess 1:6, his sharp treatment of the Corinthian sexual malefactor in 1 Cor 5:1–11, and his threat against the Jews in 1 Thess 2:16. But if one wants to find evidence that Paul acted in anger in those cases, then to be consistent one would have to say the same thing in the case of Elymas' blindness by Paul or Ananias and Sapphira's death at the hands of Peter. "But no one is so stupid and silly as to say that!"[203] Chrysostom's general contention is that "we find Paul both saying and doing many other things which appear to be coarse [φορτικά], and these things are what demonstrate especially his gentleness" [ἐπιείκεια].[204] Chrysostom contends that each of these Pauline utterances had a positive motivation behind it for the restoration and salvation of its hearers. From these epistolary examples he turns to instances in Acts which might support such a portrait of Paul as a hothead: his curse of the high priest (Acts 23:3), and his "provocation" [παροξυσμός] with John-Mark in Acts 15:36–41. The first event, where Paul says, "God is going to strike you down, you white-washed wall!" should be understood not as invective, but as prophecy, confirmed by the fact that it proved true (when Ananias was assassinated around 66 CE). But here Chrysostom notes that an enemy who reads with a sharply critical eye might dispute this line of defense, given that two verses later Paul himself seems to apologize for the same act on the grounds that he did not know the man was the high priest. To this Chrysostom replies that Paul said the latter words simply to enjoin the hearers to show proper respect for all rulers (thus they have no effect on the designation of the former curse as prophetic).[205] Nor, in John's telling, is the dispute over John-Mark proof that Paul was an angry man, because the would-be missionary was justly cut off [δικαίως ἐξετέμνετο]. It is essential that one who undertakes the preaching office be ready to encounter the great dangers and bloodshed that await at the front lines, and Paul wisely foreknew that John-Mark was not up to the task. Once again Chrysostom employs an argument of definition, holding that becoming provoked to anger [παροξυσμός/παροξυνθῆναι] is not in itself blameworthy [an ἔγκλημα] or terrible [χαλεπόν], but becoming so irrationally

---

[202] See the conclusion to the sub-argument: "You will find the measure and standard for all things residing with precision in Paul" [Καὶ πάντων μέτρα καὶ κανόνας εὑρήσεις παρ' αὐτῷ μετὰ ἀκριβείας κειμένους] (*laud. Paul.* 6.9 [SC 300.278]), echoing the previous discourse (*laud. Paul.* 5.16 [SC 300.256]).

[203] *laud. Paul.* 6.10 [SC 300.280].

[204] *laud. Paul.* 6.10 [SC 300.280].

[205] *laud. Paul.* 6.11 [SC 300.282]. Chrysostom brings in as a precedent for combining prophecy and respect for authority none less than Christ (with a quotation from Mt 23:2–3).

and for no just reason [ἀλόγως καὶ ἐπ' οὐδενὶ δικαίῳ] is.[206] Then, after an appeal to ontology (if anger were wrong then why would it have been given to us?),[207] Chrysostom by reference to motive turns instances of Pauline anger into Pauline praise:

> For this reason Paul, too, frequently employed this emotion [ὁ Παῦλος πολλάκις αὐτῷ ἐκέχρητο], and, though more loving than those who spoke gently, was provoked to anger [ὀργιζόμενος], because everything he did was for the sake of the gospel, in coordination with what suited the occasion. For gentleness [ἐπιείκεια] is not good in general, but is when the moment requires it; likewise, if this were not present, too, then gentleness would become sluggishness, and anger rash overconfidence.[208]

ἐπίλογος (Conclusion).[209] Having erased and replaced the defaming portraits of Paul as a coward and an angry man, in concluding Chrysostom denies he has been defending Paul here [οὐχ ὑπὲρ Παύλου ἀπολογούμενος], since Paul has no need of such defense from him, given that his praise [ἔπαινος] comes from God, not human beings.[210] This rhetorically commonplace disclaimer serves to accent Chrysostom's didactic purpose in the discourse – to instruct his hearers in the proper exercise of the emotions – of which his rehabilitated and repainted Paul has now ironically become the exemplar.[211] Even anger, paradoxically, may help the Christian to sail into "the waveless harbor" [ὁ ἀκύμαντος λιμήν] that awaits. The retouched portrait statue of Paul which emerges from this oration is of a man of timely virtue, who was willing and unafraid to use whatever actions and outbursts might be necessary for the sake of the gospel.

Holistic Depictions Through Portraits of Pauline "Accessories"

An only slightly less direct form of Pauline portraits among Chrysostom's writings is smaller encomia to various accessories of Paul or noteworthy achievements which serve rhetorically as metonyms for the apostolic person and career.[212] We

---

[206] laud. Paul. 6.13 [SC 300.288]. He bolsters this proposition by Scriptural references (Sir 1:22; Mt 5:22; Ps 4:5).

[207] John's answer to this query is not surprising: God implanted anger in us as a tool for goading sinners and slackers (laud. Paul. 6.13 [SC 300.288]). The analogy he uses is that a smelter mixes a little steel with the iron, too.

[208] laud. Paul. 6.13 [SC 300.288–89].

[209] laud. Paul. 6.14 [SC 300.290].

[210] cf. 1 Cor 4:5.

[211] laud. Paul. 6.14 [SC 300.290].

[212] I have chosen the following "accessories" according to this function; hence, even though Paul's clothing is a natural accessory, because Chrysostom never uses it to refer to the apostle and apostolic life in general, I have not included a treatment of it here. But I have discussed Paul's clothes in chap. 6, when addressing Chrysostom's portrait of Paul as a man in rags (pp. 357–60), and, differently, in discussion of Paul working miracles through the agency of his garments (pp. 291–95).

have seen an instance of this tendency already in the portrait of Paul's body in *hom. in Rom.* 32, in its employment of the conceit of praise for Paul's dust, which enables Chrysostom then to isolate the different "dusts" of various bodily parts. There the focus on the dust of Paul's now thoroughly disintegrated body emphasized Chrysostom's paradoxical and outlandish love for Paul, for by it he was able to construct arguments from the greater to the lesser, for no person, even when one looks only at the most positive attributes he or she possesses, can compare with even the lowliest parts of the great Paul. The dust of his corrupted flesh, even of his pinky fingernail, surpasses everyone in magnificence.

Elsewhere in his writings Chrysostom even more pointedly develops this rhetorical strategy of praising Paul through a detailed encomium of a stand-in double taken from a literal statement or image in Paul's letters. Most of these have as their focus some accessory of Paul's mission, or trope that encompasses it, which Chrysostom personifies (for the encomiastic form largely depends on this) so that it may receive its own speech of praise. Through this metaphorical simplification of Paul's person into a single compact image, these portraits finesse the dichotomy of soul and body and treat Paul's self, life and mission as a single, praiseworthy whole. Above all this rhetorical device of personification lends variety to a very well-worn preaching theme. It requires ingenuity from its fashioner, and attention from an audience that knows very well from experience the form of epideictic rhetoric and its expectations, but is held in some suspense about how the orator will pull off the extended encomium for an unlikely object.[213] In sum, this kind of indirection in encomia to Paul became a vehicle for original rhetorical opportunities, since the fresh focal point allowed Chrysostom to diversify his constant praise of Paul, and adapt it to different oratorical and pastoral exigencies in his ministry. We shall analyze in turn portraits of Paul's standard, Paul's chain, Paul's perfume, Paul's tears, Paul's fight, and Paul's race.

Paul's Standard

Chrysostom opens his seventh panegyric to Paul with a vivid depiction of the apostle as the standard-bearer of Christ.[214] The oration begins with a description of a magnificent imperial honor guard in full retinue entering a city carrying aloft the imperial standards,[215] with trumpets blaring and an advance guard clearing the way. The image John evokes here was well etched in his mind, and in those of his

---

[213] Praise for objects and inanimate beings is allowed in rhetorical theory, including some notorious paradoxical encomia, such as the famous duel between Dio Chrysostom and Synesius, one speaking *In Praise of Hair*, and the other *In Praise of Baldness* (see Burgess, *Epideictic Literature*, 157–66, for a full catalogue).

[214] *laud. Paul.* 7.1–2 [SC 300.292–98].

[215] These bore the portraits of the emperor, as discussed in chap. 2, pp. 55–64.

congregational audience in Antioch.[216] This most impressive display of imperial power and authority, however, is intended to be a pale competitor for John's verbal icon of Paul, the man who carries the insignia of Christ. Chrysostom invokes this picture in the proem to the speech in order to issue to his audience an invitation to respond to Paul as they would to the imperial parade – by rushing out together to view the spectacle and hear the trumpet as Paul makes his entrance on his feast day. The goal of the speech John delivers in honor of the saint is to provide his auditors with a verbal parade for their delectation, wonder, and emulation. Paul's whole ministerial life is summed up in this single accessory he carries around: the cross of Christ.

Chrysostom structures his exposition of Paul's standard as a detailed rhetorical σύγκρισις (comparison). Like the imperial cohort, Paul makes a dramatic entrance – "today" [σήμερον], in fact – only not into a city, but into the world [οὐκ εἰς πόλιν, ἀλλ᾽ εἰς τὴν οἰκουμένην]. The Pauline debut here envisioned is a cosmic epiphany rather than a local happening. Furthermore, while Paul likewise carries a "sign" [σημεῖον], his is not the emblem of "the king below" [σημεῖον ... οὐ τοῦ κάτω βασιλέως], but instead "the cross of the Christ above" [ὁ σταυρὸς τοῦ ἄνω Χριστοῦ].[217] The comparison extends also to the two advance guards: Paul's was comprised, not of human heralds, but of angels.[218] Then the σύγκρισις takes a new direction when John compares the two sets of raiment. Whereas those who are deemed worthy of the honorable post of standard-bearer are dressed in fine clothes and gold necklaces, Paul, the standard bearer of Christ, instead wore a chain. And he was not an illustrious-looking marcher, but a man persecuted, whipped, and starving.[219] At this point Chrysostom abruptly interrupts his *ekphrasis* with an admonition to the audience about how to react to what they are seeing: "do not be sad at this, beloved!"[220] Now John will provide his auditors with

---

[216] It is more likely that the speech was delivered in Antioch, probably before 390, along with the others, than at Constantinople. I do not see any reason, on the basis of the literary form or style of this speech, to separate its date of composition and delivery from the first six (with Piédagnel, SC 300.20). For the Antiochenes the image of the imperial guard was particularly unforgettable, one readily imagines, given that they had lived through tense situations like the mob riot over the statues, when they sat on tenterhooks awaiting word from the emperor, and then upon the arrival of the imperial legates swiftly ran out to greet them with full honor and respect in hopes of securing favor rather than chastisement (see Kelly, *Golden Mouth*, 2, and 72–82 on the riot and its dramatic aftereffects). As a boy Chrysostom would also have seen the emperors themselves arrive in Antioch to spend some months in the imperial palace there built by Diocletian.

[217] *laud. Paul.* 7.1 [SC 300.292].

[218] As a defense of Paul's special treatment Chrysostom offers an *a minore ad maius* argument: if God gives guardian angels to ordinary folks who have responsibility solely for their own affairs, how much more does he have "the powers above" [αἱ δυνάμεις αἱ ἄνω] accompany those to whom he has entrusted the whole world, and given such a heavy burden of gifts.

[219] It seems inconceivable that Chrysostom does not have 2 Cor 2:14 in mind here, though he does not cite the verse, nor echo it in vocabulary.

[220] Ἀλλὰ μὴ στυγνάσῃς, ἀγαπητέ (*laud. Paul.* 7.2 [SC 300.294]).

a new frame of reference by which to assess the relative merits of the two portraits. He claims that Paul's adornment [κόσμος] was far superior and more magnificent than that of the imperial standard-bearers (and then adds what is somewhat of a *non sequitur.* Paul was a friend of God).[221] What one should really marvel at is that "with bonds and whippings Paul was more magnificent than those who have the purple robe and the diadem."[222] With this move John has upped the comparison to the emperor himself, and proclaimed Paul's garments and accessories the more resplendent. And this is no mere boast [καὶ οὐ κόμπος τὰ εἰρημένα],[223] the Christian orator argues, because Paul's garments provide their own proof. In order to substantiate his case for the superiority of Paul's garments John proposes a simple empirical test: take thousands of diadems and royal robes and lay them on a single feverish man, and he will not improve one bit, whereas we know from Acts (19:12) that Paul's handkerchiefs [σιμικίνθια] alone could rout all illnesses. With an *a minore ad maius* argument Chrysostom sharpens the comparison: if the sight of an imperial standard can cause a thief to run away without a single backward glance, how much more does the sign Paul carries (the cross) send illnesses and demons flying?

But there remains one more crucial difference between Paul's standard and those of the imperial retinue, and it is by means of this argument that Chrysostom will make his transition toward the exhortatory thrust of his sermon. In the conventional wisdom of the present world, honors such as being a standard-bearer are coveted because they belong exclusively to one person and not the many, whereas when it comes to spiritual positions of prestige it is the exact opposite. And Paul is the object lesson for Chrysostom's point: "Paul bore his standard, not so that he might carry it alone, but so that he might make all people to be such as himself, and teach them to carry it."[224] Paul the standard-bearer of Christ turns out to be, not the solitary honoree of his Lord, but the man who calls all to share in the glory his position affords by becoming themselves σημειοφόροι, bearing Christ's name before Gentiles and kings.[225] In John's depiction, Paul's didactic methodology is (unsurprisingly) the same as Chrysostom's: by looking at his behavior and comportment as standard-bearer, and imitating what they see, all can share with him the honor of carrying it. Chrysostom incorporates this hermeneutic into his *ekphrasis* by means of "captions" from Phil 3:17; 4:9; 1:29, which give his verbal painting of Paul a speaking role. But John does not want to go too far in rendering the subject of his panegyric like everyone else, so he manages to slip in the fact that

---

[221] Before dropping this idea John does draw one inference from it: διὸ καὶ βαστάζων οὐκ ἔκαμνε (*laud. Paul.* 7.2 [SC 300.294]).

[222] *laud. Paul.* 7.2 [SC 300.294].

[223] *laud. Paul.* 7.2 [SC 300.296].

[224] Ἐβάσταζε δέ, οὐχ ἵνα αὐτὸς αὐτὸ φέρῃ μόνος, ἀλλ' ἵνα ἅπαντας τοιούτους ποιήσῃ καὶ διδάξῃ βαστάζειν (*laud. Paul.* 7.2 [SC 300.296]).

[225] *laud. Paul.* 7.2 [SC 300.298].

Paul carried his standard all the way to Gehenna (Rom 9:3), and hurled it high in the face of eternal punishment.[226] Paul's tell-tale insignia, the key vocational emblem in his portrait,[227] is the cross of Christ he holds aloft before the eyes of the entire world.[228]

Paul's Chain

An encomium to Paul's chain is found in one of the earliest writings from Chrysostom's career as a presbyter in Antioch, in the homilies *de statuis*, which he composed and delivered in the spring of 387.[229] This famous set of orations seeks to counsel, rebuke, and console the Antiochenes as they await in terror the reaction of the emperor Theodosius to the news that statues of himself and his wife, Flacilla, have been demolished in a spontaneous mob action. In *hom.* 16 Chrysostom's lectionary passage is the epistolary salutation from the epistle to Philemon (v. 1ff.), which (when he finally gets to his biblical passage) immediately inspires him to discourse on Paul as "the prisoner of Jesus Christ" [δέσμιος Ἰησοῦ Χριστοῦ]. The form which this takes is an encomium, in full epideictic dress, to Paul's chain. It begins, as is customary, with an effusion of praise for his subject: "Great is Paul's self-acclamation, not a name of authority and honor, but bonds and chains. Truly great!" [Μέγας ὁ τοῦ Παύλου χρηματισμός, οὐκ ἀρχῆς καὶ τιμῆς ὄνομα, ἀλλὰ δεσμὰ καὶ ἁλύσεις· ἀληθῶς μέγας].[230] Then comes an initial, striking realization by John: Paul could have mentioned any number of things in his self-designation which would have rendered him praiseworthy, especially the triad of ecstatic experiences in 2 Corinthians 12 which John loves to recall (the journey to the third heaven, the escapade to paradise, and the hearing of inexpressible words). Instead Paul deliberately designated himself a prisoner in this epistle, since "his chain was what rendered him more conspicuous and more renowned than those things" [αὕτη γὰρ αὐτὸν ἐκείνων ἐπιφανέστερον ἐποίει καὶ λαμπρότερον].[231] Then Chrysostom discovers an ingenious way to retain his comparison but not debase Paul's

---

[226] *laud. Paul.* 7.2 [SC 300.298]. But John is quick to assure his congregation that Paul did not stipulate that everyone was required to go that far.

[227] On the place of vocational implements in figurative portraiture, such as statuary contemporary to Chrysostom, see chap. 6, n. 89. What Chrysostom has offered here on the literary-oratorical level has of course been mirrored throughout the graphic iconographic traditions for Paul, though more often Paul is depicted with book and sword than with the cross (M. Lechner, "Paulus," *Lexikon der christlichen Ikonographie*, ed. W. Braunfels [Freiburg: Herder, 1974] 8.133–34). Yet, sometimes the sword Paul carries has a cruciform handle for a multivalent effect.

[228] See chap. 6, pp. 261–70 for an in-depth analysis of the rest of *laud. Paul.* 7.

[229] For general background see Kelly, *Golden Mouth*, 72–82. Paul's chain was one of Chrysostom's favorite topics; see the long list of such passages compiled by Piédagnel, SC 300.294, n. 2.

[230] *stat.* 16.3 [49.164].

[231] *stat.* 16.3 [49.165].

spiritual heights:[232] the adventures of 2 Corinthians 12 were indeed magnificent, but they were instances of divine philanthropy, whereas Paul's chains constitute an example of the devotion and endurance of a slave, which Chrysostom presumably thought particularly appropriate to the epistolary occasion and rhetorical situation of this letter.[233] The title Paul chose further demonstrates his great love for Philemon, which rendered unnecessary any need to engender adulation through an opening reminder of the apostle's own accomplishments and lofty status.

The next portion of epideictic demonstration is cast as a σύγχρισις between Paul's chain and the emperor's diadem.[234] First the comparison is set out as a proposition: "A king doesn't glory in his diadem as much as Paul showed off his bonds." But Paul's pride in his accoutrements is far more logical than an emperor's in his crown, for the practical reason that in reality the imperial crown brings only trouble. It invites sedition and betrayal, and presents such a liability in war that the emperor has to travel in disguise, whereas Paul's chain leads to none of these dangers, but instead effects the opposite: when in war its wearer need only hold up the chain, and the demons and opposing powers who assault him will be beaten off. Then Chrysostom continues the comparison between Paul's glory and that of earthly rulers by turning to consuls, who by custom are allowed to retain their title even after their term of office has expired. But as illustrious as are those titles, Paul's ignominious appellation, "a man in chains," has won the eternal adulation of both earthly and heavenly realms.[235] Next, through the assistance of an imaginary provocateur, Chrysostom engages the question of the material of this famous chain. Yes, it was iron, but an iron infused with the full-flowering of the Holy Spirit,

---

[232] This is the central tension in epideictic comparison, as we have seen: to find subjects for contrast which are exalted in themselves but which can also be shown somehow to be inferior to the one being praised. See further discussion in chap. 7.

[233] Mitchell, "John Chrysostom on Philemon," 135–48.

[234] One wonders if this comparison was not somewhat risky in Chrysostom's own historical context of insult and injury to the emperor Theodosius. Evidently Chrysostom regarded the contrast with the imperial diadem as so commonplace that it would not appear a pointed allusion to the (already provoked) emperor, but it is likely no coincidence that as he continues the comparative argument he switches from the emperor to consuls as the object of negative comparison.

[235] "Such a one is called an ex-consul, and another an ex-proconsul, but he, instead of all these, says, 'Paul, a prisoner.' And very reasonably at that. For those offices in no way constitute a demonstration of the virtue of the soul, for they are bought for money, and procured owing to the flattery of friends. But this office, that from the bonds, is a demonstration of the philosophy of the soul, and is the greatest sign of love for Christ [αὕτη δὲ ἡ ἀρχὴ ἡ ἀπὸ τῶν δεσμῶν τῆς κατὰ ψυχὴν φιλοσοφίας ἐστὶν ἔνδειγμα, καὶ τοῦ περὶ τὸν Χριστὸν πόθου τεκμήριον μέγιστον]. Those offices pass away quickly, but this office does not have a successor. For look — from that time until now, how much time has passed, and the name of this prisoner has become most illustrious. But all the consuls, whoever they have been in past times, have gone silent, and they are not even known by name to most people. But the name of this prisoner, the blessed Paul, is great here, and great in the land of the barbarians, and great among the Scythians and Indians. And if you were to go to the ends of the world, you would hear this appellation, and wherever a person might go, they would see that Paul's name is born about in the mouths of all people everywhere. And what wonder if on earth and sea, since even in the heavens Paul's name is great

since he was bound by that chain for Christ's sake. Chrysostom then points to the ironic identity shared by cross and chain: that both, machinations of the intention of persecutors to dash the faith, emerged as symbols of the salvation they offered to all. For this reason the iron of Paul's chain was far more precious than any gold [καὶ παντὸς χρυσίου τὸ σιδήριον ἐκεῖνο ἡμῖν τιμιώτερον ἦν].[236]

Chrysostom's pedagogical intentions insert themselves into the next turn of this encomium. He first poses what is to him a genuine and important exegetical and theological quandary [ζήτημα]: why is it that Paul, who celebrated his imprisonment constantly throughout his letters,[237] in his speech before Agrippa, said: "I would wish to God, in both small and large part, that not only you, but all those who hear me this day would become such as even I am, *apart from these chains*" [παρεκτὸς τῶν δεσμῶν τούτων] (Acts 26:29). Chrysostom worries that one might receive the impression that although Paul boasted in his chains everywhere else, "when he went into the tribunal he betrayed his philosophy, just when boldness was especially needed."[238] John's defense against this possible accusation is based upon an appeal to motive: it was for missionary pragmatics that Paul decided to downplay his chains in the presence of the Gentile Festus,[239] becoming "to those not under the law as though not under the law" (1 Cor 9:21), so that the potential convert might hear first the joys to be had in the gospel. Thus "Paul did this neither from agony nor from fear, but from great wisdom and spiritual intelligence."[240] In this way Chrysostom dismantles a piece of possible counter-evidence to his theme, demonstrating that "he was not begging off from the bonds themselves (No way!), but was accommodating himself to his hearer's weakness."[241] Indeed, Chrysostom demonstrates with no less than seven passages from Paul's letters that "Paul himself loved and welcomed his bonds in the same way as a woman who loves finery does her own gold jewelry."[242]

– with the angels, with the archangels and with the powers above, and the king of these, God" (*stat.* 16.3 [49.165]).

[236] *stat.* 16.3 [49.165].

[237] John cites Eph 4:1; 2 Tim 2:9; Phlm 1; Acts 28:20; Phil 1:14 in substantiation of the point.

[238] *stat.* 16.4 [49.166].

[239] John has lost sight of the fact that in the text of Acts these words are actually spoken to the Jewish king, Agrippa.

[240] *stat.* 16.4 [49.167].

[241] οὐκ αὐτὰ τὰ δέσμα παραιτούμενος, μὴ γένοιτο, ἀλλ' ἐκείνου τῇ ἀσθενείᾳ συγκαταβαίνων (*stat.* 16.4 [49.167]; see the same argument in *hom. in Eph.* 9.1 [62.69]).

[242] Interestingly Chrysostom explicitly grounds his own argument, not only by reference to Paul's words, but also his rhetorical strategy of self-comparison with his opponents in 2 Cor 10–11, where Paul "compared himself to others, and demonstrated to us his superiority in the comparison" [Καὶ ἀλλαχοῦ συγκρίνων ἑαυτὸν ἑτέροις, καὶ τὴν κατὰ σύγκρισιν ὑπεροχὴν ἡμῖν ἐνδεικνύμενος] (*stat.* 16.4 [49.167]). The idea of a martyr's chains as a beautiful adornment is already a *topos* in martyrological texts well before Chrysostom (see the letter of the churches of Lyons and Vienne in Eusebius, *h.e.* 5.1.35: ὥστε καὶ τὰ δεσμὰ κόσμον εὐπρεπῆ περικεῖσθαι αὐτοῖς, ὡς νύμφῃ κεκοσμημένῃ ἐν κροσσωτοῖς χρυσοῖς πεποικιλμένοις).

After Chrysostom demonstrates the universal attestation of Paul's boasting in his afflictions, he seems to abandon this theme to embark on a general exhortation. The slight connection is to be found in the effectiveness of apostolic suffering for the mission, which Chrysostom takes to be a paradigm of the ways of the world, both human and divine, since only imposters or cheats lure the simple-minded by profferring the goods up front (like kidnappers and hunters), but God prepares the way for the bliss of the life to come with trials on earth. Since this is a favored theme of Chrysostom's, once he embarks on it Paul's chain seems to be out of the picture, but that article reappears five minutes later or so, triggered by John's mention of womanly excesses in adornment and jewelry, which he considers an act of "self-inflicted bondage" [καταδεσμοῦσθαι]. Now Paul's chain returns triumphantly in a comparison with this female vanity in adornment, and Chrysostom recites its great deeds [πράξεις] just as one would for any subject of an encomium: unlike chains of luxury, which have been the cause of many evils, have brought wars into households, and given birth to envy, jealousy and hate, Paul's bonds "destroyed the sins of the world, and frightened demons, and caused the devil to flee." With these Paul persuaded the Philippian jailer, drew in Agrippa, and made many disciples. Now the discourse soars to its crescendo:

> Just as it is not possible to bind a sunbeam, nor shut it up in a house, thus no one can do to the word of the proclamation. However much more the teacher had been bound, the word flew about. For Paul dwelt in the prison, and the teaching, sprouting wings, was running all around the world.[243]

Another, even more detailed encomium to Paul's chain, is found in *hom. in Eph.* 8, a sermon composed after *de statuis*, and delivered to the same Antiochene audience.[244] The considerable echoes between the two homilies can be explained as Chrysostom's resumption of an earlier rhetorical strategy in a kind of short-hand, but also innovative fashion. He begins with a face-off of epithets, claiming that the title "the prisoner in the Lord" [ὁ δέσμιος ἐν κυρίῳ] (Eph 4:1, his lection-ary passage) is to be preferred to all competitors, both secular (emperor or consul) and churchly (apostle, teacher, evangelist). Then some paradoxical comparisons follow, in which Paul's chain (which is consistently singular in this discourse), made of iron, is said to be more magnificent than any gold or bejeweled diadem, and Paul's prison cell more wonderful than heaven itself. Chrysostom insists that such suffering for Christ's sake is most salutary, not because of the eternal reward which it will secure, but simply for the unification it affords with the passion of the beloved Christ. Chrysostom's own adulation for Paul comes through most fer-

---

[243] *stat.* 16.5 [49.169]. See chap. 3, pp. 77–78 for further references and discussion on Paul in ornithic guise.

[244] Bonsdorff, *Predigttätigkeit*, 64–71, dates the Ephesians homily set to 395–397. On that reckoning this homily also post-dates *hom. in Rom.* 32 (from 392, according to *Predigttätigkeit*, 39), with which it also has some affinities.

vently in this homily, as he again uses the first person to utter his paradoxical preferences for the imprisoned apostle:

If someone were to grant me anything, either heaven or that chain, I would more highly esteem the chain. If anyone were to set me above with the angels, or with Paul bound, I would choose the prison. If someone were to make me one of the powers, those in heaven, those around the throne, or such a prisoner as this, I would choose to become this prisoner … If anyone were to grant me the ability to raise the dead at this minute, I would not choose it, but the chain.[245]

The suitably encomiastic proposition that will occupy John for most of this extraordinarily long sermon is succinctly stated at the outset: "nothing is more blessed than that chain!" [οὐδὲν τῆς ἀλύσεως ἐκείνης μακαριώτερον].[246] The ensuing portrait of the chain becomes the laudatory portrait of the man who wore it, as is shown by the exact same phrasing later in the homily, transposing the two subjects: "Nothing is more blessed than that soul" [οὐδὲν τῆς ψυχῆς ἐκείνης μακαριώτερον].[247]

In a manner strikingly similar to *hom. in Rom.* 32.2–4,[248] Chrysostom expresses his intimate wish to go see Pauline relics, this time not Paul's corpse, but remnants of the actual chain which bound him. Likely John is referring to a shrine to Paul at Philippi which was in existence during his lifetime,[249] a suggestion strongly supported by his concentration later in this homily on the Philippian imprisonment narrative of Acts 16. But the fulfillment of this wish has been thwarted by John's ecclesial duties and his poor bodily health which prohibit any lengthy pilgrimage.[250] "I would wish to be in those places now (for it is said that the bonds

---

[245] *hom. in Eph.* 8.1–2 [62.56–57].

[246] *hom. in Eph.* 8.1 [62.56].

[247] *hom. in Eph.* 8.7 [62.65].

[248] See the full analysis of this passage among the body portraits in chap. 4, pp. 121–32.

[249] The earliest site for which we have documentation of veneration of Paul in the early church is in fact Philippi, making it the most probable locus for Chrysostom's unnamed reliquary shrine. A mosaic dedicatory inscription erected by Bishop Porphyry (fl. 343) indicates that a church which would have been standing in Chrysostom's lifetime was dedicated to Paul. The traditional site of the imprisonment of Paul and Silas, a converted cistern which even today provides the viewer with the place where the chains and stocks would have been set, cannot be certainly dated to Chrysostom's time. An alternate possibility is that Chrysostom is referring to a memorial to Paul's imprisonment at Ephesus, though that would be strange given that he is dealing with the letter sent *to* that church from elsewhere. One of the towers in the city wall constructed by Lysimachus in the third century B.C.E. has traditionally been assigned as the place of Paul's imprisonment at Ephesus, but there is no evidence of a shrine there before the modern period (see the valuable discussion of Ernst Dassmann, "Archeological Traces of Early Christian Veneration," in *Paul and the Legacies of Paul*, ed. William S. Babcock [Dallas: Southern Methodist University Press, 1990] 281–306, 288–95, which does not mention this passage of Chrysostom's).

[250] "If I were free from ecclesiastical worries, and robust in body, I would not beg off from making this journey just to see the chains, to see the prison where he had been bound" [εἰ τῶν ἐκκλησιαστικῶν φροντίδων ἐκτὸς ἤμην, καὶ τὸ σῶμα εὔρωστον εἶχον, οὐκ ἂν παρητησάμην ἀποδημίαν τοσαύτην ποιήσασθαι ὑπὲρ τοῦ τὰς ἀλύσεις μόνον ἰδεῖν, ὑπὲρ τοῦ τὸ δεσμωτήριον ἔνθα ἐδέδετο] (*hom. in Eph.* 8.2 [62.57]).

still remain) and to see and marvel at those men's love of Christ. I would wish to see the chains which demons feared and shivered at, but angels praised."[251] Chrysostom insists that he would rather see relics of Paul's imprisonment than of his miracles, for it is the former that impress him far more.[252]

Praise of Paul through praise of his chain is accomplished again through comparisons with other accomplishments in Paul's life:

I do not pronounce Paul so blessed because he was snatched up into paradise, as because he was thrown into prison. I do not pronounce him so blessed because he heard unspeakable words, as because he endured the bonds. I do not pronounce Paul so blessed because he was snatched up into the third heaven, as I do on account of the bonds.[253]

And to provide testimony to this, the most proper grounds for Pauline praise, Chrysostom brings in none other than Paul himself: "And that these bonds are greater than those ecstatic experiences, hear how even Paul himself knows this to be the case. For he did not say, 'I, the one who heard unspeakable words, urge you,' but what? 'I, the prisoner in the Lord, urge you.'"[254] Thus another rhetorical advantage Chrysostom gains by naming the subject of his encomium as Paul's chain is that the apostle can be enlisted as a witness on its behalf, whereas if Paul were directly its focus, he could not speak for himself without incurring the shame of self-praise.[255]

After a disquisition on the preferability of suffering for Christ to honor in him, Chrysostom returns to his comparisons with even more rhetorical amplification:

Oh, the blessed bonds, oh, the blessed hands, which that chain adorned. Paul's hands were not so honored when they raised the lame man at Lystra as when they were encircled with those bonds. If I were living at those times, I would have embraced them then and there, and put them to the very apple of my eyes.[256] I would not stop kissing the hands which were found worthy of being bound for the sake of my Lord.[257]

---

[251] *hom. in Eph.* 8.1 [62.56–57].

[252] Chrysostom frequently underplays Paul's miracles in his oratory because of their minimal utility for the mimetic cycle in which he is engaged (we shall examine this point in detail in chap. 6, pp. 291–95).

[253] *hom. in Eph.* 8.1 [62.57].

[254] *hom. in Eph.* 8.1. [62.57], an instance of Paul's own dueling epithets.

[255] On Chrysostom's anxious concern about the rhetorical propriety of Paul's boasting, and his impassioned defenses of him against the charge, see chap. 6, pp. 339–52. Chrysostom here ironically adopts Paul's own strategy of displacing the subject of the encomium (as with "the fool" or "a man I know" in 2 Cor 11:1–12:13), thus replicating his subject in approach as well as content.

[256] I am replicating the NPNF (Oxford) translation of this phrase, though the word κόρη in the phrase ἐπὶ τὰς κόρας ἔθηκα τὰς ἐμάς is odd. This translation springs from LSJ, 981, which says the noun can refer to the "pupil" because it is the "small" of the eye. Although the shift to "apple of the eye" is not so easy, clearly Chrysostom is making a high compliment here!

[257] *hom. in Eph.* 8.2 [62.57]. Perhaps Chrysostom is here influenced by Thecla's kissing of Paul's chains (*A. Paul. et Thecl.* 18 [Lipsius, *Acta* 1.247]).

After this self-testimony, Chrysostom next offers two witnesses from nature to the extraordinary quality of Paul's chain: the viper on Malta (who properly respected and feared it, as signalled by its quick departure from Paul's hand [Acts 28:4–5]), and the Mediterranean sea (for he was rescued from its grasp even while wearing the chain [Acts 27:44]). All this rhetorical attention is meant to fulfill Chrysostom's homiletical thrust – that suffering for Christ is the highest honor. He substantiates this plea with a range of biblical passages, beginning with Acts 16, which will occupy him for much of the rest of the homily, after brief treatments of Peter in jail, and of Paul's acceptance of suffering unto death in Phil 1:23–29.[258] This biblical tour impels Chrysostom once again to issue lofty personal exclamations:

What a great boast, to know that he was bound for the sake of Christ! What a great pleasure, what a great honor, what a great magnificence! I would wish always to be speaking of these things. I would wish to hold fast on the chain. I would wish, even if I am lacking in the literal deed, but to wrap his chain around my soul *by means of my discourse*, through its representation [ἐβουλόμην, εἰ καὶ τῷ πράγματι ἀπεστέρημαι, ἀλλὰ τῷ λόγῳ περιθεῖναι τὴν ἄλυσιν τῇ ψυχῇ διὰ τῆς διαθέσεως].[259]

This passage illuminates the way in which Chrysostom proposes to overcome the physical distance between himself and the relics of his beloved saint: by oratory which makes the chain come to life in his imagination and that of his hearers. This intimate desire sets in graphic terms what Chrysostom considers the rhetorical purpose and effect of his epideictic oratory: an actual physical embrace of the chosen Pauline relic of the chain, but accomplished verbally, and addressed to the soul, not the body. Therefore this encomium, ostensibly to a physical object still extant in Macedonia, actually scripts an imaginary physical encounter of two bodies, the one which wore the object and the other which desires an encounter with it. It serves as a metaphorical depiction of the soul-to-soul meeting that the verbal art form [ἐν λόγῳ] creates, sustains, and generalizes to others. Thus, despite his inability to be in the presence of the "actual chain" of Paul (the bemoaning of which he uses as a rhetorical *topos*), nonetheless Chrysostom claims later in this homily that he indeed had access to those chains, both through Scripture and through his own "love chain" to Paul:

Allow me a little more time, and give me some latitude, as I hold off from the apostolic words, and revel in the apostolic deeds, to feast on Paul's chain. Let me discourse on Paul's bonds for a bit longer. I have laid hold of that bond; no one can pull me away. I have been bound more securely now by love than Paul was by the stocks. No one frees this bond, for it comes from the love of Christ. Neither the angels nor the kingdom of heaven can free this bond (of love).[260]

---

[258] Acts 16:23, 25; 14:19; Mt 5:11; 2 Tim 4:8; Col 1:24.
[259] *hom. in Eph.* 8.3 [62.58].
[260] *hom. in Eph.* 8.3 [62.59].

Paul's love chain has become both the subject and the instigator of Chrysostom's laudatory discourse, the spirit propelling him to continue. He follows this with a narrative exegesis of Acts 16 which focuses on the character of the jailer, particularly his faith and fervency. This leads John (after a rather lengthy diversion) back to Paul, whom he praises for fervency of his own, for preaching the gospel while imprisoned and scourged. Then Chrysostom takes hold of the chain again, and personifies it into an odd and interesting mixed metaphor: "Oh blessed chain, which suffered such labor pains all that night. What children it gave birth to!"[261] Paul's chain, a stand-in for the apostle himself, but female (because the noun ἅλυσις is feminine) becomes the mother of children, as inspired by the apostle's own words in Phlm 10: "my child, whom I begot in the chains" [τοῦ ἐμοῦ τέκνου, ὃν ἐγέννησα ἐν τοῖς δεσμοῖς], which Chrysostom quotes. Then he amplifies this personification still further, astonishingly transforming Paul's chain into the perfect housewife host of a house church:

Paul's chain entered into prison, and made everything there into a church, and made all the body of Christ, and set out a spiritual table there, and bore birth pangs over which angels rejoice.[262]

In this conceit Chrysostom has invented a new way to laud Paul,[263] as he is so often fond of doing, by offering praise to Paul's chain as an extension of the apostle. The chain acts as a synecdoche of those attributes of the man who wore it that Chrysostom most wants his congregation to admire and imitate. That is why he continually engages in comparisons, for he seeks to heighten the facets of the apostolic curriculum vitae which he can insist that his congregants should likewise strive to inculcate in their own lives. But in this case, it is not really imprisonment that Chrysostom wants his audience to seek out in their quest to emulate the apostolic model. He addresses this directly near the end of the homily, when it appears that he will focus the exhortatory portion of the speech on a call for new freedom from the "bonds" of rapaciousness, a familiar theme.[264] However, somewhat unexpectedly, John signals his intention to stop his homily, and dismisses his oratorical

[261] Ὦ τῆς μακαρίας ἁλύσεως, οἵας ὤδινεν ὠδῖνας κατὰ τὴν νύκτα ἐκείνην· οἷα ἀπέτεκε παιδία (*hom. in Eph.* 8.5 [62.62]).

[262] *hom. in Eph.* 8.5 [62.62]: Εἰσῆλθεν εἰς δεσμωτήριον ἡ Παύλου ἅλυσις, καὶ ἐκκλησίαν εἰργάσατο πάντα τὰ ἐκεῖ, καὶ σῶμα Χριστοῦ πάντας ἐποίησε, καὶ τράπεζαν ἔθηκε τὴν πνευματικήν, καὶ ὠδῖνας ἔτεκεν, ἐφ' αἷς ἄγγελοι χαίρουσι.

[263] But the new can quickly become old, especially after the unusually lengthy sermon devoted to this theme. Consequently, when Chrysostom begins the next homily with not only a recapitulation, but a renewed reversion to the theme of Paul's chain, he proactively admonishes his congregation, "Don't go numb, now!" (*hom. in Eph.* 9.1 [62.69]).

[264] "But it is not necessary to be bound with a chain now. Yet there is another chain, if we wish. What sort is it? To restrain the hand from readily defrauding" (*hom. in Eph.* 8.7 [62.65–66]). He uses the same argument in the next homily: "But we are not held in bonds. Nor do I urge this on you, for now is not the time. Do not bind your hands, but do bind your mind" (*hom. in Eph.* 9.1 [62.71]).

partner, the personified subject of laudation: "giving many thanks to Paul's chain, because it has been the cause of such good things for us, let's bring our homily to a close."[265]

Despite this adieu, Chrysostom cannot relinquish his love chain so easily. First he extols the extraordinary achievements of Paul's chain. Not only did it continually display the triumph of the gospel during adversity in Paul's ministry, but it serves even now as a means by which all others can be led to heaven. The chain has now become a long rope stretching from heaven to earth, a crane with a pulley drawing those secured with it up to the celestial realm.[266] Then, what should have been a recapitulating peek at his beloved Paul in prison ("for look at this blessed man"), leads Chrysostom into further reflection on saintly prisoners in general, which takes him to the three Hebrew children of Daniel 3. So he exhorts his congregation to take a deep breath, pretend that the homily is just beginning, and leap into this new topic with him.[267] Again he claims that he is under the spell of an irresistible power; like one on a drinking binge, he simply cannot stop himself.[268] But, after all, since Paul did not keep silent in prison, nor did the Hebrew children even in the midst of the furnace, Chrysostom surely must not pass by this exemplum, so he dives in for another sounding, this time a detailed comparison of the Philippian imprisonment of Paul and Silas with the attempted immolation of the Hebrew children in their furnace prison[269] at the hands of the malevolent king. John's inventiveness in improvisational speech is illustrated nicely here. Though he begins with some expressed rhetorical bewilderment at the new theme he has belatedly taken up (which offers us a slight glimpse into his extemporaneous homi-

---

[265] hom. in Eph. 8.7 [62.65].

[266] "Paul's chain has become very long, and held us very tightly fast. For it is indeed long, and more beautiful than any gold cord. This chain pulls those who are bound with it to heaven as though it were a crane. Just like a secured gold cord, Paul's chain pulls them up to heaven itself" [Μακρὰ ἡ τοῦ Παύλου γέγονεν ἄλυσις, καὶ ἐπὶ πολὺ κατέσχεν ἡμᾶς· καὶ γάρ ἐστιν ὄντως μακρά, καὶ πάσης σειρᾶς χρυσῆς κοσμιωτέρα. Αὕτη τοὺς δεδεμένους καθάπερ διά τινος μηχανῆς ἕλκει πρὸς τὸν οὐρανόν, καὶ ὥσπερ χρυσῆ σειρὰ ἐξαρτηθεῖσα, ἀνέλκει πρὸς αὐτὸν τὸν οὐρανόν] (hom. in Eph. 8.8 [62.66]).

[267] "But our homily has done well, and has led us to other bonds and another prison [εἰς ἑτέρους δεσμοὺς καὶ δεσμωτήριον ἕτερον]. What is happening to me? I wish to be silent, but I am not able. I have found another prison even more wonderful and amazing than the former [ἕτερον δεσμωτήριον ... ἐκείνου πολλῷ θαυμαστικώτερον καὶ ἐκπληκτικώτερον]. But wake up for me [διανάστητε], as though I were just now beginning my homily, and approach with completely sharp minds" [ἀκμαζούσαις προσέλθετε ταῖς διανοίαις] (hom. in Eph. 8.8 [62.66]).

[268] "I wish to break off the homily, and I cannot bear to do so. Just as though someone in the midst of drinking would not bear to break off from it, even if another were to promise him all kinds of things, thus I too have taken hold of this marvelous cup of the prison of those bound for the sake of Christ [ἡ κύλιξ τῆς θαυμαστῆς τοῦ δεσμωτηρίου τῶν διὰ Χριστὸν δεδεμένων], and I am not able to stop, I am not able to be silent" (hom. in Eph. 8.8 [62.66]).

[269] With some effort John forces this example to fit his theme by arguing that the three were sent to prison, not death, in the flames: "For they were thrown in there in bonds, which shows from the outset that they weren't going to be burned up, but to enter into a prison. For why do you bind those who are about to be incinerated?" (hom. in Eph. 8.8 [62.66]).

letical method),[270] Chrysostom carries off the comparison by finding, on the spot, no less than six studied similarities among the two cases: holy ones bound by violence, singing (despite their torment) led to their release, they emerged from the prison only when commanded to by their captors, they were called servants of God or Christ (Dan 3:93 LXX; Rom 1:1), their examples caused Gentiles to confess the faith, and their courageous fortitude led to miraculous escapes. The latter segment of this extended homily switches to a wider encomiastic proposition: the paradoxical power of bonds,[271] which opens up far too many rhetorical possibilities worthy of exploration (Jeremiah, John the Baptist, Christ himself). But Paul's chain makes a final reappearance, as Chrysostom tries to hold it responsible for the disparate contents of his own long and contorted homily: "Thanks for Paul's chain. For how many prisons did it open up for our homily?" [Χάρις τῇ Παύλου ἀλύσει· πόσα ἀνέῳξε τῷ λόγῳ δεσμωτήρια;].[272] Hence the physical chain, which became the subject of the encomium, is revealed at the last to have been also its muse (as well as the fall-guy who takes the blame for Chrysostom's rhetorical excesses!).

Via his own rhetorical invention of Paul's chain (which was not even mentioned in his Scripture portion, *per se*) functioning as a metonym for the apostle, Chrysostom gives expression to his view of Paul as mediator between the heavenly and human realms, and simultaneously validates his own ethical exhortation to the voluntary constraints involved in self-sacrifice for Christ.[273] Paul is praised in the person of the chain that encircled his limbs, which was depicted in this convoluted homily with no less than four different portraits of its own – chain as forged metal (iron or gold), chain as mother, chain as housewife, and chain as heavenly monorail cable. Most saliently of all, Paul's chain is the contemporary homiletic agent, the inspiration and instigator of Chrysostom's own discourse of praise to itself and to its bearer, Paul.

---

[270] "Yet, many ideas are surrounding me. I do not know which I should say first, and which second. Therefore I beg that no one demand an orderly disposition [τάξις] from me. For the kinship of these matters is great" (*hom. in Eph.* 8.8 [62.66–67]). Given the late start on this theme, Chrysostom actually carries it out in a rather logical fashion, but he does not, for instance, enumerate his points of similarity between the two stories, evidence that he is doing this extemporaneously.

[271] Ὁρᾶτε πόση τῶν δεσμῶν ἡ δύναμις; (*hom. in Eph.* 8.9 [62.68]), and the final recapitulation (of many!), right before the concluding benediction, Ὁρᾶς ὅσον ἀγαθὸν ὁ δέσμος; (8.9 [62.70])

[272] *hom. in Eph.* 8.9 [62.69].

[273] This is accented in the restatement of the thesis of *hom. in Eph.* 8 at the very start of *hom. in Eph.* 9: "The great strength of Paul's chain, and its magnificence superior to miracles has been demonstrated" [ἀπεδείχθη τῆς ἀλύσεως μεγάλη ἡ ἰσχὺς τοῦ Παύλου, καὶ σημείων λαμπροτέρα] (*hom. in Eph.* 9.1 [62.69]).

Paul's Tears

The exhortation proper of *hom. in Col.* 12 begins with an encomium to Paul's chains, but in a second movement (of several, in a loosely structured homily) turns into an encomium to Paul's tears.[274] Chrysostom arrives at this second topic by a textual juxtaposition of his creation, which likely occurred to him in the course of delivering the homily. His lectionary passage is the distinctive closing phrase of Col 4:18:"Remember my chains!" [μνημονεύετέ μου τῶν δεσμῶν], which Chrysostom incorporates as a refrain to punctuate a set of rhetorical questions to his congregation about their behavior to others and their patterns of consumption. He exhorts his audience to stop before acting on their desires, and instead to bring to life in their minds a vivid portrait of Paul imprisoned[275] which will clarify in an instant their true values. One attribute he reminds them of is Paul's tears, referring to Paul's farewell speech to the Ephesians (Acts 20:31), in which the departing apostle insists that he had not stopped crying on their behalf for three years, night and day.[276] With this mental picture before him Chrysostom urges his congregation, instead of daubing on makeup and face paint, to adorn themselves with Paul's own tears as though they were a cosmetic: "beautify your cheek with this adornment. These tears [ταῦτα τὰ δάκρυα] will make it splendid."[277] From there, by the catch word of "remembering" [μνημονεύειν] common to the two passages, Chrysostom merges the Acts 20:31 passage[278] with Col 4:18 to form a pithy new locution: "Remember my tears!" [μνημονεύετέ μου τῶν δακρύων].[279] This reformulation launches John on an encomium to Paul's tears, which he considers the adornment that confers the greatest beauty. This time Chrysostom begins with paraenesis, even before the heart of the encomium. One should imitate Paul's crying, he says, through tears for one's own sins, especially those against people in lower positions. Here Chrysostom gives an impassioned plea worthy of any con-

---

[274] For other passages extolling Paul's tears, see, e.g., *laud. Paul.* 2.6–7 [SC 300.150–56]; *exp. in Job* 1.21, 23 [SC 346.136, 140], and further references collected by Piédagnel, SC 300.153 n. 3.

[275] One can see the first movements toward this rhetorical and catechetical appeal in the earlier *stat.* 16.5 [49.169].

[276] Chrysostom has no difficulty in turning the tables elsewhere in his writings, when it suits his rhetorical purpose, and stressing that Paul was constantly in a state of rejoicing (e.g., *hom. in 2 Cor.* 12.4 [61.487], Καθ᾽ ἑκάστην ἡμέραν ἀπέθνησκε Παῦλος, καὶ οὐκ ἔκλαιεν, ἀλλὰ καὶ ἔχαιρε], and further references in Piédagnel, SC 300.50–52).

[277] Presumably Chrysostom does not mean that Paul's own tears were available, but that in crying for the same causes and the same reasons as Paul, the Christian, as his copyist, would be in essence crying Paul's own tears.

[278] "... remembering that for three years night and day I did not stop admonishing each one of you with tears" [μνημονεύοντες ὅτι τριετίαν νύκτα καὶ ἡμέραν οὐκ ἐπαυσάμην μετὰ δακρύων νουθετῶν ἕνα ἕκαστον].

[279] *hom. in Col.* 12.2 [62.383]. Though he does not say so here, he likely also has 2 Tim 1:4 in mind [μεμνημένος σου τῶν δακρύων].

temporary liberation theologian: "remember that we are of the bound, not those who do the binding, of those whose heart has been crushed, not the crushers."[280]

The ensuing praise of Paul's tears includes standard epideictic motifs of σύγκρισις. First come some audacious comparisons:

> What sort of fountain could one compare with these tears? The fountain in paradise which watered the whole earth? No, you will not name anything the equal of this fountain, for although the fount of paradise did water the whole earth, the fountain of tears flowing from Paul's eyes watered souls, not earth.[281]

The next comparison sets the specter of Paul weeping against two earthly delights: a chorus adorned with brilliant crowns, and an exquisite young girl in the prime of life. In setting up the latter exemplum for comparison Chrysostom composes a quite extended *ekphrasis* of an ideally lovely young woman, providing breathtakingly exact detail about the beauty of her face, eyelids and lashes, and the exact color of her cheeks, all of which is artfully portrayed by the ascetic preacher only so that, when he reaches the very height of this magnificent portrait of youthful radiance, he can vow that he would rather look upon Paul in tears than upon her, for it is spiritual beauty [κάλλος πνευματικόν], and not merely physical, which shines forth from the apostle's eyes.[282] Of course from this Chrysostom the moralist cannot resist swiftly drawing ethical consequences: unlike the eyes of the young woman that incite burning passion in young men, the tears that fell from Paul's eyes, which have now been completely personified, beautify the eyes of the soul by leading his followers to a restrained appetite, love of wisdom, and great sympathy. His praise of the apostle's tears includes a thick catalogue of some πράξεις, "deeds," from their curriculum vitae: they watered the church, planted souls, and extinguished fires – even the burning arrows of the evil one.

Chrysostom extends his proof that tears are worthy of praise to include Scriptural evidence, first from Jesus himself in the Beatitudes,[283] then from the prophets Isaiah and Jeremiah (Is 22:4; Jer 9:1). He next weaves back to another typically antithetical epideictic formulation: "Nothing is sweeter than these tears; they are sweeter than any laughter" [οὐδὲν τῶν δακρύων τούτων ἥδιον· παντὸς γέλωτος ταῦτα ἡδύτερα].[284] Then John makes a faltering attempt to bring the twin objects of praise together by saying that the tears also fell on the chains,[285] but moves

---

[280] *hom. in Col.* 12.2 [62.383].

[281] *hom. in Col.* 12.3 [62.384].

[282] *hom. in Col.* 12.3 [62.384]. In this way John the preacher paints a portrait, not only of the lovely girl and of Paul, but also of himself, as the skilled ascetic eye trained upon the beauty which really matters.

[283] Interestingly, Chrysostom quotes both the parallel passages, Mt 5:4 and Lk 6:21.

[284] *hom. in Col.* 12.3 [62.384].

[285] τούτων μνημονεύωμεν τῶν δακρύων, τούτων τῶν δεσμῶν. Ἆρα καὶ ἐπὶ τῶν δεσμῶν δάκρυα κατέβαινεν (*hom. in Col.* 12.3 [62.384]). Note how at first he stutters over the object of the cohortative, momentarily confused between Paul's text and his own recasting of it.

quickly on from this feeble link to a more promising line of laudation in how Paul, in imitation of his master Jesus, cried while in bonds for the sake of his captors (quoting Lk 23:28).

Once again in this rather serpentine homily Chrysostom returns to the πράξεις, "deeds" or "accomplishments," this time not of Paul's tears, but of the eyes from which they oozed and dripped. Here he repeats many of the attributes we have seen in the body portraits: these eyes saw paradise, they saw the third heaven, and it was through the tears (though this is not mentioned in any of the biblical texts) that Paul saw the risen Christ (citing 1 Cor 9:1). This last was of course most worthy of praise, but in the present context Chrysostom exclaims that even the Christ-vision pales in comparison with the crying which those eyes did.[286] The first proof for this (at least on the surface) astonishing claim depends upon the privilege of scarcity: since many people shared the experience of a resurrection appearance of Christ, Paul's uncommon tears were a greater honor to the apostle (a statement which John supports with Jn 20:29:"blessed are they who, though not seeing, have believed"). This contention – that Paul's eyes were more blessed for their tears than for their sighting of the Lord Jesus – receives a proof based on logic and textual evidence using a succession of two *a minore ad maius* arguments. The first invokes Phil 1:23–24, which Paul himself cast this way:"if to remain here for Christ's sake is more necessary than to depart and be with Christ on account of the salvation of others, then how much more is it necessary to cry and groan on their behalf than to see Christ." The second proof presses another Pauline declaration (Rom 9:3) into this same form:"if it is more desirous to be in hell than to be with him, and it is more desirous to be separated from him than to be with him, then how much moreso is it desirous to cry for his sake." This elaborate proof for a sub-claim is demanded by the epideictic genre, for its structure of proof by comparison depends upon finding the most illustrious examples possible with which to compare one's subject, and stressing its superiority to them. The satisfaction of this type of oratory comes from the resolution of what seems at first sight to be an impossible claim for superiority, as here.

But Chrysostom's restlessness with his topic is shown by the rapid movement among claims in this homily. Next he forms an argument based upon motivation, in order to differentiate types of tears. Paul's tears, he maintains, were praiseworthy because they were not due to fear, but to compassion for the diseased he sought to help; in this he is consistent with Jesus' own example.[287] Then John exhorts his

---

[286] "But to cry thus is even more blessed" [ἀλλὰ μακαριώτερον τὸ δακρῦσαι οὕτως] (*hom. in Col.* 12.3 [62.384]).

[287] "This also Jesus did, so that they might have respect for tears, too. Was he a terrible sinner? Jesus gave him a rebuke. Did the man who was rebuked spit on him, and run away? He wept, so that even thus he might draw him to himself" (*hom. in Col.* 12.3 [62.385]). Is this a reference to an incident in an apocryphal gospel or agraphon? It hardly seems to fit Jn 11:35, which would be the obvious canonical referent to Jesus' tears.

congregation to weep for the right reason: when they see their daughters and sons doing evil. All, in pleasure or pain, should constantly remember Paul's tears. Those mourning their dead should exchange their tears for those of Paul, for he did not weep over the dead, but rather over those who were perishing while still alive.[288]

Now the preacher takes a breather and with a rhetorical question ostensibly seeks his audience's permission to go on (perhaps using the brief pause to plan mentally where he will go next): "Shall I speak also of other tears?" [Εἴπω καὶ ἕτερα δάκρυα;].[289] Then he embarks upon a short excursus on tears in the Bible, with Timothy as the leading example (by reference to 2 Tim 1:4, where Paul remembers *his* tears),[290] followed by the psalmist (whom Chrysostom terms a "prophet"). The latter example spills over into yet another theme, the utility of tears in different circumstances, for, John argues, praiseworthy tears are those shed in prayers and in exhortation, whereas crying over such trivial matters as poverty, bodily illness or death is useless.[291] The former receive enhanced honor from two definitional distinctions: between "the tears of philosophy" [Ταῦτα φιλοσοφίας τὰ δάκρυα] and tears shed for unworthy causes [οὐ δακρύων ἄξια];[292] and between timely and untimely weeping [ἀκαίρως αὐτὰ μεταχειρίζοντες]. Then John brings this theme to a close with a recapitulation:

Nothing is sweeter than eyes that are drenched with tears [Οὐδὲν ἥδιον ὀφθαλμῶν δεδακρυμένων], for the eye is the most noble and beautiful part of our body, and belongs to the soul [τὸ γὰρ εὐγενέστερον ἐν ἡμῖν μέλος καὶ ὡραιότερον καὶ τῆς ψυχῆς τοῦτό ἐστιν]. Therefore we are as moved with pity (by eyes brimming with tears) as if we saw the soul itself in open lament [Ἄτε οὖν ὡς αὐτὴν τὴν ψυχὴν ὁρῶντες ἀποδυρομένην, οὕτω καμπτόμεθα].[293]

So Paul's tears constitute, as it were, a hologram of his soul.

Then John veers off this poetic theme to a very specific pastoral engagement with one of his pet peeves, which appears to be a complete *non sequitur.* "I have not said these things superficially, but so that you might not attend weddings, dances, and satanic festivals."[294] He makes a brief and superficial attempt at a rhetorical transition to this theme a bit later, by means of the key term δεσμοί, because

---

[288] ὅσοι ἐν πένθει, ἀλλάττεσθε δάκρυα δακρύων. Οὐ τοὺς τεθνεῶτας ἐκεῖνος ἐπένθει, ἀλλὰ τοὺς ἀπολλυμένους καὶ ζῶντας (*hom. in Col.* 12.4 [62.385]).

[289] *hom. in Col.* 12.4 [62.385].

[290] Timothy was a copy of his teacher in this regard [μαθητὴς γὰρ ἦν τούτου], as Chrysostom tells it.

[291] In other contexts John can point to the value of tears in providing catharsis on the way toward consolation (*laud. Paul.* 2.6 [SC 300.152], in reference to Paul's tears in Acts 20:31).

[292] These include poverty, sickness, and death (the Stoic influence here is evident).

[293] *hom. in Col.* 12.4 [62.386].

[294] Ταῦτα ὑμῖν οὐχ ἁπλῶς εἴρηται, ἀλλ᾽ ὥστε ὑμᾶς μὴ γάμοις, μὴ ὀρχήμασι, μὴ χοροῖς παραγίνεσθαι σατανικοῖς (*hom. in Col.* 12.4 [62.386]). The connection (if one can be found) appears to be in the overturning of the value systems of contemporary society, which Paul's tears also did.

marriage, Chrysostom says, is also a δεσμός, a "bond." But what follows is an extended treatment of improprieties at wedding receptions. So much for Paul's tears.

In another exegetical homily Chrysostom gives a similar, though much briefer excursus on Paul's tears. His theme, taken from the blessing in 1 Thess 3:11–13, is the firm, resolute quality of genuine love. To demonstrate his point John presents a series of biblical examples beginning with the patriarchs, and then arrives at Paul, whom he describes, with no less than seven epithets, as a man of steel, steadfast and immovable.[295] This portrait of Paul the unmoved receives confirmation from the apostle's words of Rom 8:35: "Who will separate us from the love of Christ?" But even this steely character, who stood so unbending in the face of massive opposition, was once softened and broken by the tears of his beloved co-workers and the believers of Caesarea who mourned at hearing the prophecy of Agabos about Paul's impending arrest (Acts 21:10–14). Confronted by this image of Paul that shatters the portrait he has just so carefully composed, Chrysostom interrogates his subject directly:

Since this man saw the tears of some of his beloved, he was so broken and anguished – this man of steel [ὁ ἀδάμας] – that he could not hide his emotion, but immediately said, "What are you doing weeping and breaking my heart?" (Acts 21:13) What are you saying? Tell me! Was a tear strong enough to crush that steely soul? "Yes," he says. "For I stand firm against all things, except love. Because love prevails over me and wins out." This seems to be due to divine action. The primeval watery deep did not crush him, and yet tiny tears crushed him [Ἄβυσσος αὐτὸν οὐ συνέτριψεν ὑδάτων, καὶ μικρὰ δάκρυα συνέτριψε].[296]

Once Chrysostom commences this counter-portrait of Paul in tears he invokes two other examples of Paul weeping: Acts 20:31 and 2 Cor 2:4. But this testimony, introduced rhetorically as possible counter-evidence to the initial portrait of Paul as the adamantine man, actually works in its favor, because it testifies to Paul's great love for his churches. Even displays of emotion will not diminish his portrait of Paul as having had a granite-like constitution; rather they deepen it into an even more complete figure for, John maintains, the man of steel could be softened only by love, not by any other enemy or adversity – even the steely gates of death. The linkage between the two is formed by a characteristically neat paradox: these minute drops of water (the tears of his friends) were able to do what the ocean depths could not: bring the strong man to his knees, at least momentarily. Love was the only power that could conquer him, but in that victory the champion emerges as even more praiseworthy – the Goliath with a heart of gold.

---

[295] These epithets are inventoried in chap. 3, n. 103.
[296] hom. in 1 Thess. 4.4 [62.421].

Paul's Perfume

In *hom. in 1 Tim.* 2.3 an exhortation to pursue the true glory of heaven and not transient earthly pleasures turns into a brief encomium to Paul's "scent" or "perfume," inspired especially by Paul's own olfactory self-portrait in 2 Cor 2:15–16. Chrysostom begins with a condemnation of silk garments from India (which, after all, are just the effluence of worms), and then turns to the other renowned exotic export from the east – spices and perfumes. "What can one say about the precious spices from India, from Arabia, from Persia, the dry ones and the moist ones, the perfumes, the incenses, which all have a great price and no utility?" Then John trains his censure on an imaginary woman, the usual object of his excoriations against what he deems extravagance in adornment: "Why do you perfume your body when on the inside it is full of filth?" In place of this derided custom, Chrysostom pitches his advertisement for a far better perfume, the perfume of the soul, the apostolic essence of which Paul spoke in 2 Corinthians, and which that saint, and the rest of the apostles, emanated during their lives.

There is a perfume [μύρος], there is a sweet scent [ἄρωμα], with which you can anoint your soul [χρῖσαι τὴν ψυχήν], if you wish. It is not from Arabia nor from Ethiopia or Persia, but it is borne from heaven, not bought with gold, but with a good exercise of free-will, and an unhypocritical faith [πωλούμενον ... προαιρέσεως ἀγαθῆς καὶ πίστεως ἀνυποκρίτου]. Buy this perfume [τοῦτο ἀγόρασαι τὸ μύρον], whose scent can fill the whole world![297]

Chrysostom hawks his exotic commodity, shipped from a far-away place, as most advertisers do, by parading in view the notables who are associated with the product. In this instance, the apostles [οἱ ἀπόστολοι] both wore and manufactured this delicious fragrance, which they constantly emanated [τούτου ἀπόπνειν]. He anchors this claim with a paraphrase of 2 Cor 2:16 (which Paul had conveniently expressed in the plural, thus allowing Chrysostom to include all the apostles in a group portrait of Pauline proportions), with its complex notion of opposite reactions to the same smell depending upon the disposition of the sniffer ("for we are a scent of sweet perfume, to some for death, and to others for life"). The puzzling notion of a fragrance simultaneously vivifying and deadly demands explanation ("what is this?"), which it receives in the form of a comic proverb: "because it is said that even a pig is suffocated [ἀποπνίγεσθαι] by the sweet scent" [εὐωδία].[298]

This "spiritual perfume" [τὸ μύρον τὸ πνευματικόν] not only radiated from the bodies of the apostles, but also from their garments. John invokes here Acts 19:12, where Paul's clothing of its own power successfully drove out demons. The superiority of Paul's scent is accented by a few short comparisons, first of natural attribute, then of boundless accomplishment: "In comparison with what sort of plant, or what cassia, or what myrrh is Paul's perfume not both sweeter and more

---

[297] *hom. in 1 Tim.* 2.3 [62.513].
[298] *hom. in 1 Tim.* 2.3 [62.513].

useful? [Ποίου φύλλου, ποίας κασίας, ποίας σμύρνης οὐχὶ καὶ ἡδίων καὶ χρησίμη αὕτη ἡ εὐωδία;]. For if it drove off demons, then what else could it not do?"[299] Next Chrysostom intersperses his demonstration with exhortation, first by a double entendre: τοῦτο κατασκευάζωμεν τὸ μύρον ("Let's demonstrate/furnish this perfume!"). Subsequently he registers a clear connection between the Pauline image and the application to his audience by previewing his paraenesis: "spiritual grace furnishes this perfume through almsgiving" [κατασκευάζει δὲ αὐτὸ δι᾽ ἐλεημοσύνης ἡ πνευματικὴ χάρις].[300] Still pressing this type of perfume on his audience, John assures them that they will indeed attain it: "When we go off to heaven we are going to emanate this perfume" [Τούτου καὶ ἐκεῖ ἀπελθόντες μέλλομεν ἀποπνεῖν].[301] He develops this idea still further with a fantastic futuristic narrative of the parallel social impact of perfumes on earth and in heaven.

Just as on earth those who wear perfume turn the heads of everyone, and if a woman, so scented, goes into a bath or an assembly or some other heavily populated place, all hang upon her and all turn their attention to her, so also in that heavenly world, when souls enter smelling of the spiritual perfume [τῶν ἀποπνεουσῶν ψυχῶν τῆς πνευματικῆς εὐωδίας εἰσιουσῶν] all will rise and make room for them.[302]

The didactic point could not be more clear: perfume gets you noticed, and spiritual perfume gets you noticed where it really counts – in heaven. But John wants also to claim an earthly benefit for the perfume he hawks: "And even here [Καὶ ἐνταῦθα] demons and all forms of evil do not dare to approach it, nor can they endure it, for they are suffocated [ἀποπνίγεσθαι] by it."[303] This perfume is a prophylaxis, even more, a spiritual pepper-spray that repels the forces of darkness. The exhortation which follows recapitulates that found early in this disquisition: "Let's put on that spiritual perfume" [Ἐκεῖνο τοίνυν τὸ ἄρωμα περιθώμεθα]. But the formation of this inclusio does not keep Chrysostom from adding a few concluding comparisons:

Earthly perfume confers on us a reputation for sloth [βλακείας δόξα], but [the scent which Paul gave off] bestows manliness [ἀνδρεία] and true admiration [θαῦμα ὄντως], and gives us great confidence [παρρησία]. It is not a plant sprouting from the earth, but virtue gives birth to it [ἀρετὴ τίκτει]. It does not dry out, but blooms. It makes honorable those who possess it.[304]

---

[299] hom. in 1 Tim. 2.3 [62.513].

[300] hom. in 1 Tim. 2.3 [62.513].

[301] hom. in 1 Tim. 2.3 [62.514].

[302] hom. in 1 Tim. 2.3 [62.514].

[303] hom. in 1 Tim. 2.3 [62.514]. This is a deliberate reminder of the pigs who were said to "suffocate" (as quoted on the previous page).

[304] hom. in 1 Tim. 2.3 [62.514]. That the martyrs emanate the perfume of Christ is already a topos (see the letter of the churches of Vienne and Lyons, apud Eusebius, h.e. 5.1.35: τὴν εὐωδίαν ὀδωδότες ἅμα τὴν Χριστοῦ).

Unlike the cloying fragrances of the women's perfumes Chrysostom castigated at the outset of this homily, Paul's "essence" is a manly aftershave which will turn heads for the right reasons, since it is testimony, not of indolence, effeminacy, or corrupt wealth, but of inner virtue, the only currency by which this precious aromatic can be acquired. This final σύγχρισις of Paul's perfume with the earthly cheap stuff moves directly into exhortation via mention of the baptismal chrism (a kind of marketing sample of the new product) which so wonderfully emanates from the catechumens on the night of their baptism, but can only be kept fresh and unspoiled by constant zeal, to ward off contaminants. From this point on Chrysostom's exhortation shifts to a contemplation and amplification of the counter-proposition: "Nothing is more foul-smelling than sin!" [Τῆς δὲ ἁμαρτίας οὐδέν ἐστι δυσωδέστερον].[305]

The portrait of Paul that emerges here, through this depiction of his very scent, is of a manly exponent of virtue who emits a delightful supernatural odor that endows the apostle and permeates his clothes with tremendous power. In the double meaning of scent/perfume Chrysostom has found a deft vehicle for capturing the complex and mystifying relationship between the interior and exterior realities of the human self. Paul's personal "smell" conveys to the outsiders (that is, those with trained noses)[306] the true virtuous nature which lies within his body. But just as a perfume is an external agent applied to the body, Paul's virtuous life depended upon continual doses from a spiritual, heavenly aspirator which gave him a foretaste (or, rather, a "foresmell") of heavenly sensory realities in his own flesh. And Paul in turn allows his devotees to share in that glimpse by catching his scent.

Paul's Contest

Chrysostom takes up the metonym of the ἀγών ("fight" or "contest") for Paul's life-work, which had been crafted by the pseudonymous author of 2 Timothy (2:5; 4:7),[307] and expounds on it in a mini-encomium designed to entice his congregation leaders to enter the contest that Paul so valiantly endured and won. This argument is consistent with Chrysostom's constant denigration of athletic and gladiatorial games, and horse-racing, which he tried (apparently largely unsuccessfully, for the exhortations never die out) to forbid his parishioners from attending.[308] Here Chrysostom begins with a question: How can one term Paul's

---

[305] *hom. in 1 Tim.* 2.3 [62.514].

[306] The point upon which Paul himself insists in 2 Cor 2:15–16.

[307] The ubiquitous classical metaphor of life as an athletic contest was applied already by Paul to his ministry (1 Cor 9:24–27), which the pseudepigraphical author picked up and recast here (see Pfitzner, *Paul and the Agon Motif*, 182–85).

[308] These are found in an oration devoted to the theme (*contra ludos et theatra* [56.236–270]), and within a broad array of other compositions, such as *Laz.* 1.1 [48.978], and *hom. in Rom.* 16:3

life a "good" or fair fight, when it was replete with chains, bonds and death at every turn? "Is this a good fight? 'Yes,' he says, 'for these things were endured for Christ's sake, and this contest offers mighty crowns as its reward.'"[309] Then Chrysostom gives an epideictic expansion on the theme by means of a typical comparison with contemporary athletic contests and their rewards:

> Nothing is better than this contest [Οὐδὲν τούτου βέλτιον τοῦ ἀγῶνος]. This crown does not have an end. This crown is not from olive leaves, nor does the contest have a human referee, nor human spectators. The audience is filled with angels. In a usual contest they labor and endure hardship for many days, and in a single hour they receive the crown, and immediately the pleasure flies fleetingly away. But here it is not like that, but always the contest goes on in splendor, in glory, in honor. So one should rejoice. For "I am coming into rest, I am coming out of the race."[310]

Here Chrysostom extols the Pauline career in very Pauline terms, such that at the end he unhesitatingly personifies Paul himself with his ἀγών, in imitation of the deutero-Pauline author, and announces Paul's struggle and victory complete.

Paul's Race

Immediately thereafter in the same homily Chrysostom faces the second crystalization of the Pauline missionary career in 2 Tim 4:7, as a race [δρόμος] which Paul has completed. First Chrysostom demonstrates the superiority of Paul's race, in that, unlike usual athletic contests, it produced a positive benefit: "For truly the contest [ἀγών] is good, not by simply giving pleasure to the spectator, but by doing them some benefit. And Paul's race [δρόμος] did not give way to nothing, nor is it a mere show of strength or competitive spirit, but it draws all people into heaven."[311] Now follows one of those outlandish comparisons which so mark Chrysostom's praises of Paul: "this race which Paul ran on the earth was more pure than the sun, or even the race he is now running in heaven."[312] Then the discourse comes quickly down to earth, as John asks exactly how Paul did complete his race, and answers with the Mediterranean itinerary of Rom 15:19. But after the brief history lesson Chrysostom quickly reverts to his metaphorical heights with a disquisition on his favored image of Paul as a bird completing his "course" across the world:

> Just like some bird, or rather even more robust than a bird, he was passing over the earth. For the bird simply passes over, but he did not merely do that, but had the wing of the spirit,

---

1.1 [51.188], where John complains that Christians know every detail about the performers, but not even the number or name of the cities to which Paul wrote.

[309] hom. in 2 Tim. 9.2 [62.652].

[310] hom. in 2 Tim. 9.2 [62.652].

[311] hom. in 2 Tim. 9.2 [62.653].

[312] Οὗτος ὁ δρόμος τοῦ ἡλίου καθαρώτερος, ὃν ὁ Παῦλος ἔτρεχεν ἐπὶ τῆς γῆς, ἢ ὃν ἐκεῖνος τρέχει ἐπὶ τοῦ οὐρανοῦ.

and cut through countless impediments, deaths, attacks, misfortunes. Therefore he was even faster than a bird. If he had been a bird, he would have been lured to earth and killed. But since he was made light by the spirit, he had the advantage over all nets, like a bird having wings of fire.[313]

This discourse provides a nice example of how one portrait can immediately suggest another. In this case the image of the race suggests both a course (of a heavenly body such as the sun), and the chief talent it tests, swiftness, which leads John to a bird. With the aviary Pauline portrait Chrysostom is able simultaneously to stress Paul's extensive influence (over the whole world), his scarlet pimpernel-like powers of evading threats from enemies, and his spiritual empowerment. The running race is thus trumped as a metaphor, replaced by a space-age equivalent – the flight of a lone bird with flaming wings who ranges beyond even the confines of the earth.

Chrysostom's encomia to Paul, because so frequent, required fresh avenues of approach. The Pauline accessories of his standard, chain, perfume, tears, fight and race provide John with such novelty in portrayal.[314] The first four, though ostensibly things that adorn or accompany the body, are rhetorically transformed into verbal holograms, or metonyms, of Paul's whole self and life. The latter two, Paul's fight and race, encapsulate in a single image the path Paul trod, in body and soul, in his missionary career. All six objects become stand-in doubles for the saint himself, and give occasion for his loving admirer, John, to evoke the presence of the absent one by the visionary recall of one of his material possessions that immediately stirs the mind of admirers to remembrance and recognition. These portraits of Pauline accessories take their place in the gallery alongside the verbal pictures of Paul's body and Paul's soul, as an intricate fusion of the two.

Full-Scale Portraits of Paul: Conclusions

Through the construction of all of these portraits – of body, soul, and accessories – Chrysostom the Christian orator has facilitated his congregation's imitation of Paul the saintly author by bringing him back to life, piece by piece (body part by body part, virtue by virtue, accessory by accessory). By composing such vivid life-size mosaics from a host of biblical allusions and other creative adaptations, Chrysostom revivifies Paul and brings him into the sanctuary for contemplation and, most importantly, reduplication. The homilies, delivered in a liturgical setting including ritual performances and lections from Scripture, relate to those funda-

---

[313] *hom. in 2 Tim.* 9.2 [62.653].

[314] These appear to be especially frequent in the homily series devoted to the Pauline letters themselves, where the subject of Paul is already ubiquitous. And also often they seem to be extemporaneous inspirations, as we might expect.

mental root texts in an ambiguous manner. On the one hand, Scripture provides both the sources and the justification for Chrysostom's portraits of Paul, and so serves as a kind of ultimate authority. On the other hand, that ultimate authority was parcelled out liturgically only in snippets, whereas the homilies contained long, imaginative and elegantly styled disquisitions that must have, in the impression of the hearers, overshadowed the biblical text to some degree, and relegated it to a secondary position, by "air time" alone, at least. The difference would also have been reflected in the elevated and sophisticated Greek style of the preacher's homilies as compared with the simpler diction of the biblical passages liturgically pronounced by the ἀναγνώστης.[315] Though he would have blanched at the thought, Chrysostom's homilies (including his portraits of Paul), as fresh rhetorical compositions seeking to mediate religious truth to the audience, as much as they were based upon it, also in some sense competed with the biblical text.[316] In part, this is natural, because, to an extent easily underestimated by moderns, rhetoric was an agonistic, as well as a didactic and entertaining art, in Greco-Roman culture.[317] Chrysostom's homilies were also (to continue the metaphor) "live radio," commanding the attention of the listeners by their latent unpredictability, whereas the Bible was fixed, static, familiar. But the extent of variability and spontaneity Chrysostom the orator exercised in his homiletics was always a matter of careful negotiation between himself and his audience, based upon the relatively fixed expectations and conventions of the rhetorical forms he employed, and the context provided by the accumulation of his sermons over time, since what is fresh once is familiar the next time around. Yet there was no simple competition between text and homily, since the scriptures were completely constituent of and entangled in Chrysostom's portraits of Paul. Certainly Chrysostom as a teacher intended his rhetoric to be an enticement to his listeners to read more deeply and seriously in the biblical texts. And, ultimately, in Chrysostom's eyes, the goals of both his homilies and the

---

[315] See, for example, *hom. in 1 Cor.* 36.6 [61.314–15], where Chrysostom irritably quotes an exponent of ὁ τῶν πολλῶν λόγος to the effect that he cannot understand what is said [οὐδὲ οἶδα τίνα ἐστὶ τὰ λεγόμενα] in the bishop's homilies. Chrysostom has several retorts to this: first, if they stopped talking amongst themselves they would understand, and, second, he says, the preacher deliberately speaks in a mixture of clear and unclear [οὔτε σαφῆ πάντα ἐστὶν ... οὔτε ἀσαφῆ] so that they must strive to attend carefully, but not become discouraged when they do not comprehend it all.

[316] So Elsner, *Art and the Roman Viewer*, 27, on *ekphrasis*: "Their descriptions were not simply parasitic on pictures; rather, they competed with the pictures."

[317] This is demonstrated overwhelmingly in the career of Chrysostom's teacher, Libanios, as a sophist, which he recounts in his *Autobiography* (*Or.* 1). On the agonistic rhetorical culture in his day, see Paul Petit's study (*Les Étudiants de Libanius* [Paris: Nouvelles Éditions Latines, 1957] 98). Chrysostom himself describes rhetorical facility, which he regards as absolutely necessary for priests, as a skill for οἱ τῆς ἀληθείας ἀγῶνες (*sac.* 5.1 [SC 272. 280]). In the previous chapter he speaks of the devastating effect on congregations of the "defeat" [ἥττη] of their pastor in debate and disputation with heretical opponents [ὅταν δὲ ὑπὲρ δογμάτων ἀγὼν κινῆται καὶ πάντες ἀπὸ τῶν αὐτῶν μάχωνται γραφῶν] (*sac.* 4.9 [SC 272.278–280]). Chrysostom's attitudes toward rhetoric are also enshrined in his treatments of Paul's rhetorical facility, as we shall see in chap. 6, pp. 278–91.

biblical texts were identical: to convey a portrait of Paul's soul for faithful Christians to contemplate and emulate. But new discourses were required alongside the biblical authority, both because the latter does not contain a continuous or unified portrait, and because what John's age required was a portrait of Paul in contemporary hues.

The sheer ubiquity of Pauline portraits in Chrysostom's oratory must be seen as both revealing the inner devotional life of the preacher who was obsessed with his favored saint, and as itself part of a rhetorical strategy of saturation of consciousness toward ethical and even political change.[318] In these homilies one senses deep echoes of a familiar strain in Greek epideictic literature: that the truest monuments to the great figures of the past are the fleshly selves of the living who consciously mold their bodies, souls and lives to conform to the pattern of their illustrious example. John claims many of the same virtues for his hero – the Christian saint – as the classical prototypes (wisdom, courage, justice, temperance), but he ratcheted them up to a new degree of emphasis on humility and self-control, in line with his ascetic program. These portraits go well beyond any single human person, however, for Paul has become a cipher for the archetype of the urban Christian piety that Chrysostom himself exemplifies, and which he in turn urges on his congregants. But the challenge and test of Chrysostom's art is that he sought to do that in complete fidelity to the scriptural traditions about Paul, so that his Pauline portraits are not simple fabrications,[319] but sophisticated collages of minute mosaic detail culled from the literary and rhetorical traditions. In composing and displaying in such detail Paul, the imperial portrait, the supreme copyist of Christ, Chrysostom invited his generation to become such living memorials to the dead saint, who had exemplified virtue in every member of his body and every pore of his soul. By his constructions of Paul, John sought to prove the excellent capacities of the human race by stretching the category to its furthest limit, indeed to the breaking point.[320]

---

[318] "The *Lives* presented ideals of behavior for Christians to follow. The theoretical implied the moral and the practical. Without suggesting that all, or even many, Christians actually tried to put into practice in their own lives the precepts implied in Christian *Lives* or preached in Christian sermons, they were nevertheless at the receiving end of models of behavior that were all the more powerful for being often repeated" (Cameron, *Christianity and the Rhetoric of Empire*, 147).

[319] As Cox has observed for late antique biography in general: "The persistent feature of biography from Hellenistic to Graeco-Roman times was a literary process, the dynamic interaction of fantasy and historical reality whose intent was to capture the ideals suggested by the life of the hero" (*Biography*, 65).

[320] In fact, Chrysostom sometimes contradicted himself, by referring to Paul as "the man who surpassed human nature" [ὁ τὴν ἀνθρωπίνην φύσιν ὑπερβάς] (*Stag.* 1.3 [47.429]), whereas more often he wants to accent Paul's commonality with the rest of humanity, even as through his depiction of Paul he raises the bar for the human condition extremely high. "For when we bring the best of all human beings into the middle, and show him to be crowned by him, what pretense will you have left? Now, who is the best of all human beings [Τίς οὖν ἁπάντων ἀνθρώπων

As with the somatic portraits of Paul, in his soul portraits Chrysostom's own rhetorical excesses pose some potential difficulties for his call to imitate Paul (though he does not address them directly here). After all, if Paul is greater than the angels, then how can any mere human being hope to imitate him? Indeed, why should Paul be praised for his virtues, when they were gifts from God? We have observed that Chrysostom stresses repeatedly that Paul was no more than a human being: he had the same body, the same rearing and the same soul as "we" have.[321] Yet he also maintains that Paul's actions did not come about by his own power, but through God's grace.[322] The portraits of Paul's soul throughout the series of encomia to Paul thus become occasions for reflection on the relationship between divine gift and human initiative in the cultivation of virtue. Chrysostom resolves the contradiction to his satisfaction by appeal to Paul's particular virtues of προαίρεσις and προθυμία, "free will and desire to act" that are the predominant colors of all John's Pauline portraits.[323] God's grace was offered, but only through Paul's willing acceptance and fervent devotion were his mission fulfilled, and his soul enriched with virtue. Thus Paul's virtue is truly his own, while simultaneously enabled through God's grace: "he had both kinds of qualities to the highest degree, both those which God infused into him, and those which he attained by his own free will."[324] Therefore Paul is worthy of praise, and one has no excuse but to seek to

---

ἀμείνων;]? Who other than the tentmaker [Τίς δὲ ἕτερος ἀλλ' ἢ ὁ σκηνοποιός], the teacher of the world ..." (anom. 8.3 [48.772]). Again the parallel with Cox's work on biographies of holy men is instructive: "the myth of the holy man is here considered to be an imaginal 'place between' where the history of a man's life and his biographer's vision of human divinity meet and mingle" (Biography, xii).

[321] Of many passages, see laud. Paul. 4.21 [SC 300.228]; hom. in 1 Cor. 13.3 [61.110]. The stress on the humanity of a saint was an essential part of fourth–century piety, as Brown, Cult of the Saints, 62, has argued.

[322] laud. Paul. 2.4 [SC 300.156–58].

[323] laud. Paul. 1.3; 2.10; 4.21; 5.3 [SC 300.116, 160, 228, 234], which is by no means an exhaustive list (see Piédagnel's index of terms, SC 300.363–64, counting twenty-three instances of προαίρεσις, and twenty-four of προθυμία). On this tension in Chrysostom's writings on Paul, see Piédagnel, SC 300.47–50, and 271 n. 3 on the Stoic context of some of these debates. The emphasis on προαίρεσις accounts for the popularity of these discourses among the Pelagians (see p. 6 n. 24, and Baur, S. Jean Chrysostome, 61), a topic to which we shall return in our comparison between Chrysostom's and Augustine's portraits of Paul (chap. 8, pp. 411–23).

[324] Μεθ' ὑπερβολῆς γὰρ ἑκάτερα, καὶ τὰ τοῦ θεοῦ ἔπνευσεν αὐτῷ, καὶ τὰ τῆς οἰκείας προαιρέσεως ὑπῆρξε (laud. Paul. 5.3 [SC 300.234]; also 7.3 [300.300]). Chrysostom makes the same claim in hom. in 1 Tim. 3.1–2 [62.515–18], arguing that in 1 Tim 1:12–13 Paul very carefully and deliberately mixes praise to God for his accomplishments with acknowledgement of his own part in them, in order to annihilate any possibility for people to raise the objection of divine determinism, by which to obviate the need for their own volition in ethical behavior ['Ορᾷς πῶς πανταχοῦ τὸ ἑαυτοῦ κατόρθωμα κρύπτει, καὶ τὸ πᾶν ἀνατίθησι τῷ θεῷ, ἐπὶ τοσοῦτον ἐφ' ὅσον τὸ αὐτεξούσιον μὴ λυμήνασθαι;] (3.1 [62.515]). In stressing the combination in Paul of divine gift and human cooperation Chrysostom was rooted theologically, but also rhetorically, for this was a major theme the rhetoricians also shared with philosophical discourse, because it was built into the very structure of epideictic rhetoric in the treatment of τύχη and πράξεις, "chance" and "deeds" (the third category of an encomium, to which we shall turn in the next chapter).

imitate him.[325] But to do so, one must have the portrait of Paul's soul displayed before one's eyes for delectation and deposit in the memory for constant consultation. Chrysostom's engagement with Paul's moral physiognomy is precisely that vehicle. And in the process of sculpting Paul's soul, John asserted his own authoritative position as Paul's sculptor and interpreter *par excellence*.

But the image of Paul is not exhaustively captured in corporeal and psychic images. Portraits such as these, of Paul's body and soul and accessories, fasten upon and fix Paul momentarily in time, freezing him in a single moment for posterity. Yet the Paul whom Chrysostom met in his Bible and his meditations was a vibrant being whose life story included remarkable shifts and unprecedented feats. Not all that is Paul can be encapsulated in a single snapshot; hence next we shall look at how Chrysostom understands Paul biographically, i.e., how he regards Paul's life-history, and how it provides him with more fodder (as well as some innate difficulties) for his catechetical purposes.

---

[325] This theme appears very commonly elsewhere among Chrysostom's writings: *stat.* 1.6 [49.24]; *hom. in Mt.* 6.5 [57.68], "for what more than you did Paul have, that you should say that emulation of him [ὁ πρὸς ἐκεῖνον ζῆλος] is impossible for you?"

Chapter 6

"Obviously By Some Divine and Ineffable Power": Biographical Portraits of Paul

Now since there are three types of particularly good things worthy of praise, and among these goods are 1) things concerning the soul and character, 2) things concerning the body, and 3) the external things which belong to us [τὰ ἔξωθεν ἡμῖν ὑπάρχει], clearly from these three things, whatever they might be, we shall best compose an encomium (Theon, *Prog.* 8).[1]

"External Circumstances" (τὰ ἔξωθεν)

In the previous two chapters we have examined Chrysostom's encomiastic portraits of Paul's body and his soul; now we shall turn to the third category of topics comprising the encomium – "the externals" – to see how he uses it to create further portraits of Paul. In rhetorical theory a wide range of subjects and *topoi* was subsumed under this third category, which largely deals with what we would term the biographical elements of a person: family and birth, upbringing and education, trade, and, most importantly, deeds.[2] Theon lists as among the "external attributes" first noble birth, then city, nation and citizenship, parents and other relatives, and, finally, educational training, friendship, good reputation, rulership, wealth, the blessing of children, and a good death.[3]

The structure and purpose of this division of epideictic rhetoric were determined by an innately philosophical and sociological question: what is the relationship between nature and nurture, between the "givens" of each human existence,

---

[1] ἐπεὶ δὲ τὰ ἀγαθὰ μάλιστα ἐπαινεῖται, τῶν δὲ ἀγαθῶν τὰ μὲν περὶ ψυχήν τε καὶ ἦθος, τὰ δὲ περὶ σῶμα, τὰ δὲ ἔξωθεν ἡμῖν ὑπάρχει, δῆλον ὅτι τὰ τρία ἂν εἴη ταῦτα, ἐξ ὧν εὐπορήσομεν ἐγκωμιάζειν [Spengel, 2.109–110]. In Roman rhetoric see also [Cicero], *Rhet. Her.* 3.6.10 [*Laus igitur potest esse rerum externarum, corporis, animi*; Quint. *Inst.* 3.7.12: "Indeed, the praise of a man himself should be sought from his soul and his body and external circumstances [*Ipsius vero laus hominis ex animo et corpore et extra positis peti debet*]." For the long history of this division, back to Plato and Aristotle, and forward into Christian sources, see the extensive list of references in Caplan, LCL vol. on *Rhet. Her.*, 174, note a.

[2] Following the synthesis of Burgess, *Epideictic Literature*, 120–21. There is overlap between the categories in regard to where body and soul properly figure in relation to πράξεις (see n. 228 below).

[3] ἔστι δὲ τῶν ἔξωθεν πρῶτον μὲν εὐγένεια ἀγαθόν, διττὴ δὲ ἡ μὲν πόλεως καὶ ἔθνους καὶ πολιτείας ἀγαθῆς, ἡ δὲ γονέων καὶ τῶν ἄλλων οἰκείων. ἔπειτα δὲ παιδεία, φιλία, δόξα, ἀρχή, πλοῦτος, εὐτεκνία, εὐθανασία (*Prog.* 8 [Spengel 2.109–10]).

and what is done with them, to form and sculpt a unique life, one which is in the
final analysis deemed worthy of praise or vituperation? The logic behind this is, as
Cicero put it, that it is not enough to be given good attributes at birth from the gods,
but one must put those benefits to good use in one's actions.[4] Thus the question
which preoccupies the genre of encomium is unsurprisingly the same issue upon
which Chrysostom expounds so often in his moralizing exhortations: the relationship of determinism and free-will in human existence, between ἀπροαίρετα and
προαιρετικά.[5] This is particularly the case when he treats Paul's external circumstances, where he constantly has in view, whether he states it or not, what his
treatment of Paul will imply for the actual living of Christians in his own time.
And here John dances lightly on a narrow wire, for he wishes both to insist, as the
title of this chapter indicates,[6] that in his life Paul was continually and constantly
empowered by God and none other (and thus Paul was simultaneously manifesting
God's power in the world), *and* that Paul was himself responsible for his own
praiseworthy deeds, which are, therefore, perfectly emulable by later generations of
Christian believers if they exercise their free will as he did.[7] Hence, in these
portraits, biography is thoroughly wedded to rhetorical purpose.

In the conventions of the encomium John finds the appropriate vehicle to stress
that from very humble origins, by means of both divine assistance and his own
laudable exercise of free will, Paul was able to produce deeds worthy of the highest
reward of praise. This rhetorical tactic is itself recommended in rhetorical theory.
The same teacher of rhetoric with whom we began, Theon, recommended the use
of arguments showing how "virtue shone forth especially in the midst of

---

[4] "Moreover, in praise and censure it will be necessary to observe not so much what the
subject of the speech possessed in bodily endowment or in extraneous goods as what use he made
of them" [*Videre autem in laudando et in vituperando oportebit non tam, quae in corpore aut in extraneis
rebus habuerit is de quo agetur, quam quo pacto his rebus usus sit*] (*de Inventione* 2.59.178). For the
commonplace, see also Quintilian, *Inst.* 3.7.13: "Moreover the praise awarded to external and
accidental advantages is given, not to their possession, but to their honourable employment" [*Sed
omnia, quae extra nos bona sunt quaeque hominibus forte obtigerunt, non ideo laudantur, quod habuerit quis
ea, sed quod iis honeste sit usus*].

[5] The philosophical distinction received classic form by Aristotle in *Eth. Nic.* 2.5.4, αἱ δ'
ἀρεταὶ προαιρέσεις τινὲς ἢ οὐκ ἄνευ προαιρέσεως; see also Epictetus (Arrian), *Diss.* 2.10.8 on τὰ
ἀπροαίρετα, τὰ προαιρετικά. For the use of this concept and terminology in epideictic rhetoric
specifically, see Arist., *Rh.* 1.9.32 (quoted below, p. 249); on Chrysostom's usage as set within
classical and patristic sources, see Edward Nowak, *Le chrétien devant la souffrance: Étude sur la pensée
de Jean Chrysostome* (Théologie historique 19; Paris: Éditions Beauchesne, 1972) 57–63; an
illustration of the centrality of the concept in Chrysostom's exegesis is given by Trakatellis, "Being
Transformed," 5–8.

[6] The title is a quotation from *laud. Paul.* 4.13 [SC 300.210], an oration which will receive a
detailed analysis below in this chapter (pp. 212–26).

[7] The balance between human freedom and divine assistance was *the* major question of
Chrysostom's moral theology (as argued by Meyer, "Liberté," esp. 304: "... l'enseignement
pratique de Chrysostome sur toute cette question: collaboration des efforts humains et de la grâce
divine, et leur apport respectif dans l'oeuvre de notre perfection").

misfortunes," that is, in the lives of those lacking in esteemed "external circumstances."[8] This encomiastic commonplace will be replicated many times over in Chrysostom's writings on Paul, who becomes both the example to imitate and Exhibit A in his larger apologetic proof for the divine inspiration and propagation of the Christian faith, because, John asserts, only God's power could have engendered such greatness from such lowly origins. In these writings John is not interested in the "facts" of Paul's life so much as with what those facts indicate about the ways of God in the world. In so doing Chrysostom works with the sources he has at hand, most of which tend to his favor in this endeavor, for the apostle whom he imitates had made the same argument about himself (chiefly 1 Cor 1:18–2:5 and 2 Cor 11:6). His admirer John's rhetorical strategy amounts to an ingenious splitting of the two encomiastic topics of ἐπιτηδεύματα ("training" or "profession")[9] and πράξεις ("deeds"), to show that without the normally requisite *paideia*, which was the standard currency of social attainment throughout the Greco-Roman world, the apostle to the Gentiles achieved what all others (including the most celebrated and admired figures from the classical past) could not – universal victory and unanimous allegiance to his message of truth.[10]

We shall demonstrate that, as with the epithets and the portraits of Paul's body and soul, Chrysostom's discussions of Paul's external circumstances are based upon a pastiche of elements from Acts, from the letters, and from his own imaginative

---

[8] μάλιστα γὰρ ἐν τοῖς ἀτυχήμασιν ἐκλάμπει ἡ ἀρετή (*Prog.* 8 [Spengel, 2.112]). For the commonplace, see also Quintilian *Inst.* 3.7.10: "With regard to things preceding a man's birth, there are his country, his parents and his ancestors [*Ante hominem patria ac parentes maioresque erunt*], a theme which may be handled in two ways. For either it will be creditable to the objects of our praise not to have fallen short of the fair fame of their country and of their sires or to have ennobled a humble origin by the glory of their achievements" [*aut enim respondisse nobilitati pulchrum erit aut humilius genus illustrasse factis*].

[9] The term is used in varied senses. At times it is a synonym for πράξεις, as in Menander Rhetor, for whom it means "deeds implying choice and so revealing character apart from πράξεις ἀγωνιστικαί." But in the exercises called the προγυμνάσματα, for example, it often means more restrictively vocation or profession, with an emphasis on the choice involved (Burgess, *Epideictic Literature*, 122–23). Chrysostom mostly, and frequently, uses the term in the latter sense, and places it with ease in the structure of encomiastic topics. See, for instance, *hom. in 1 Cor.* 6.2, on 2:4–5: "how is it that [the apostles] having nothing attractive of their own [οἴκοθεν], not effective speech [λόγος], nor celebrity [περιφάνεια], nor wealth [πλοῦτος], nor city of note [πόλις], nor nation [ἔθνος], nor people [γένος], nor profession [ἐπιτήδευμα], nor reputation [δόξα], nor any other of such things, but having all the opposites – lack of skill [ἰδιωτεία], shabbiness [εὐτέλεια], poverty [πενία], hatred [μῖσος], enmity [ἀπέχθεια], and standing against whole peoples, proclaiming such a message, how were they able to persuade?" [61.50].

[10] The more conventional employment of the *topos* is in a then-and-now argument which contrasts one's humble beginnings with the progress one made through *paideia* to achieve great deeds. A classic example is Favorinus, in the Corinthian Oration ([Dio Chrysostom] *Or.* 37.25–28), as insightfully interpreted by Gleason, *Making Men*, 16–17. Favorinus claimed that his own meteoric rise from his birthplace in Gaul to acclaimed sophist provided the Greeks of Hellas with an example "that education can produce the same results as birth" [ὡς οὐδὲν τὸ παιδευθῆναι τοῦ φῦναι πρὸς τὸ δοκεῖν διαφέρει] (Gleason's trans.). Such an idea was conventional wisdom in Chrysostom's day, as *oppugn.* 3.5 [47.357], a quote from a typical father, shows.

retelling of the story of Paul's life. Through consideration of these topics, not always within a full-scale encomium, but in a variety of contexts, Chrysostom was in yet another way composing his author, Paul. Past influential studies have argued that Chrysostom did not make serious use of the form of epideictic rhetoric because in his encomia he does not follow the standard τάξις, which moved in a chronological fashion from the birth and family of the subject up to his death, attributing this apparent lack to his disapproval of the "pagan form."[11] This pre-

---

[11] The most important here is Piédagnel, in his authoritative introduction to the critical text of *de laudibus sancti Pauli* [SC 300.26–27]: "D'autre part, aucun de ces discours ne présente un déroulement de la vie de S. Paul fondé sur une classification de vertus variées et sur la succession chronologique des événements qui lui donnent peu à peu sa richesse … Chrysostome, au contraire, s'est montré très indépendant et méfiant à l'égard de tels schémas qui lui semblaient réservés aux éloges d'ordre profane." Piédagnel's conclusion accords completely with that argued earlier by Simonetti, "Sulla struttura dei panegirici di S. Giovanni Crisostomo," though Piédagnel does not cite the article specifically. Simonetti compared Chrysostom's panegyrics with those of the Cappadocians in regard to the *loci communes* of epideictic rhetoric, and concluded: "Se si accetta questa nostra ipotesi, si può spiegare come conseguenza del valore paradigmatico, che soprattutto il Crisostomo annette ai suoi panegirici, anche il già rilevato disinteresse quasi assoluto nei riguardi dei luoghi (topici nell' elogio pagano) della famiglia, della patria, dell'educazione del personaggio celebrato: possiamo infatti pensare che egli di regola abbia introdutto nelle sue orazioni solo quei particolari della vita dei santi che potevano servire per i fedeli di edificazione e di incitamento all'esercizio delle virtù" (p. 179). Simonetti's conclusion was repeated also by Kennedy, *Greek Rhetoric under Christian Emperors*, 249, n. 107: "although [John] uses the stylistic artifices of the sophists in these works [his encomia], sometimes even to excess, he does not seek to imitate their structural forms and topics." But this thesis requires reassessment and correction. In reaction to the classic study of Delehaye, *Les passions des martyrs*, 133–69, which effectively demonstrated the pervasive influence of classical rhetoric on the encomia composed by the Cappadocians, Simonetti had argued for a linear development in Christian panegyrics leading progressively away from the strictures of "pagan" rhetorical conventions. He placed Gregory of Nazianzus at the beginning of this spectrum, and Chrysostom at the end, as the one who "liberated" his panegyrics (and therefore Christian literary culture) from those corrupt outside influences ("Sulla struttura dei panegirici di S. Giovanni Crisostomo," 175). But that argument is patently apologetic, an attempt to purge Christian sources of the "pagan" influences. A further methodological difficulty with Simonetti's analysis which our study throws into relief is that he confined himself almost exclusively to Chrysostom's panegyrics on martyrs, but did not include any of the seven panegyrics to Paul. Despite this limitation in focus, however, Simonetti formulated his conclusion in such a broad fashion as to apply to all of Chrysostom's panegyrics (and that is how those who depend upon Simonetti, such as Kennedy, take his conclusions). In my judgment Delehaye's investigation remains the reliable standard, and I seek here to take up the challenge he issued on p. 146: "Ce serait un intéressant sujet d'étudier par la même méthode les panégyriques de Jean Chrysostome." Delehaye recognized well Chrysostom's creative adaptations of rhetorical conventions ("Chez lui le flot de l'éloquence franchit plus aisément les digues de la convention et l'adaptation est plus entière et plus géniale" [*Les passions des martyrs*, 146–47]), but, in contrast to Simonetti, rightly recognized these as imaginative recastings by a skilled practitioner, rather than outright repudiations of the art of rhetoric. Delehaye's better acquaintance with classical epideictic literature allows him to recognize the great irony that: "A quel point nos panégyristes sont tributaires de la discipline littéraire alors régnante, on le reconnaît là même où ils affectent de s'en dégager" (*Les passions des martyrs*, 138). Also, what Simonetti claims as distinctive of Chrysostom's panegyrics – the call to imitate the object of praise – is in fact a central part of epideictic rhetoric itself, not a Christian departure from it (see n. 16 below).

vailing conclusion will be overturned completely by the findings to be presented in this chapter. The lack of the precise, complete compositional *form* of the biographical encomium[12] should not blind us to Chrysostom's frequent and deft treatment of the *topoi*, the *content*, and the *logic* of that aspect of the encomium treating "external circumstances." And, indeed, we do not have merely to postulate Chrysostom's knowledge of this scheme, for he uses it himself on several occasions.[13] Chrysostom composed extended arguments whose rhetorical and catechetical effect depend entirely upon his adaptations, and, above all, the hearers' expectations, of these very epideictic conventions that are supposedly absent from his homilies.[14] In other words, even though the entire structural form is not present, its spirit animates and permeates these texts, and awareness of that fact is

---

[12] Even Quintilian recognizes that the biographical τάξις is only one option; for instance, one may also arrange the proof according to the different virtues, depending upon what seems suitable to the subject. He also notes the problem with the chronological approach: it leaves the audience waiting for the truly unique and noteworthy deeds of the individual (*Inst.* 3.7.15–16). Chrysostom more often leads with deeds when speaking of Paul, rather than giving a complete biographical narrative, as we shall demonstrate.

[13] See τὰ περὶ ψυχήν, τὰ περὶ σῶμα, τὰ ἐκτός in *hom. in 1 Tim.* 1.1 [62.505], and Chrysostom's list of the things of which the false apostles of 2 Cor 10–13 boast, which he rightly terms τὰ ἔξωθεν, including εὐγένεια, πλοῦτος, σοφία, τοῦ περιτομὴν ἔχειν (=γένος), πρόγονοι, and δόξα (*hom. in 2 Cor.* 24.2 [61.565]; of many other examples, compare the list of *topoi* in *oppugn.* 2.5 [47.339–40], including πλοῦτος, γένος, τρυφή, δύναμις λόγων, ῥώμη σώματος, εὐγένεια, καὶ οἱ ἄλλοι). We can also document that Chrysostom was taught this set of common topics in school, because they are abundantly evident in the *Progymnasmata*, or rhetorical school exercises, of his teacher, Libanios. For example, the sample encomium of Diomedes includes the following: πατρίς, πάτερες, μήτηρ, πάππος, all adding up to εὐγένεια (*Prog.* 8.1.1–4 [Foerster, 8.216–17]); τῆς ψυχῆς ἀρεταὶ καὶ ... τοῦ σώματος (8.1.4 [Foerster, 8.217]); deeds of war (8.5f. [Foerster, 8.218f.]), which showed his usefulness, χρήσιμος τοῖς πράγμασι (8.1.6 [Foerster, 8.218]); specific virtues, such as ἐγκράτεια (8.1.10 [Foerster, 8.221]) and ἀνδρεία (8.1.11 [Foerster, 8.221]), followed by σύγκρισις (8.1.16 [Foerster, 8.224]). The progymnasmatic panegyric to Odysseus contains the full panoply of topics: γένος, πρόγονοι, πατρίς (8.2.2–3 [Foerster, 8.226]), τροφή and παιδεία (8.2.3 [Foerster, 8.226]); introduction of full treatment of deeds (8.2.5 [Foerster, 8.227]) in war as well as rhetorical skill (8.2.7 [Foerster, 8.225]), and consideration of consistency in word and deed (8.2.9 [Foerster, 8.229]); attributes of σῶμα, including κάλλος, ῥώμη, and ταχυτής (8.2.12 [Foerster, 8.230]); various συγκρίσεις (8.2.19, 24 [Foerster, 8.232–3, 234–5]); and εὐθανασία (8.2.25 [Foerster, 8.235]). But the conventionality of topics is always proven most strikingly in their employment in satire. Here Libanios' paradoxical encomium to the cow is most instructive, for it too follows the encomiastic schema: φιλία (8.8.1 [Foerster, 8.267], of cows as the friends of the gods); τροφή (8.8.3 [Foerster, 8.268]); κάλλος (8.8.4–5 [Foerster, 8.269]); ἰσχύς, πραότης, θυμός (8.8.8 [Foerster, 8.270–71]); καλὸς καὶ ἀγαθός (8.8.9 [Foerster, 8.271]); σύγκρισις (8.8.10–13 [Foerster, 8.271–72], with ὁ ἵππος); and εὐθανασία (8.8.15 [Foerster, 8.273], perhaps the most ironic topic, as Libanios shows the cow to be useful to human beings in death as food, and especially honored in that καὶ ἔστιν ἡ τελευτὴ τοῦ βοὸς μελίττης γένεσις!). Libanios used these *topoi* in his own encomiastic orations, as well (such as Or. 12, 13 and 18, on Julian).

[14] There is no indication that this is a grudging concession to a distrusted, pagan form, as Bovon, echoing Piédagnel, suggests ("Même si Chrysostome, qui se méfie du caractère profane des panégyriques, bouscule le genre littéraire, il se doit de respecter certaines règles du genre" ["Paul comme document et Paul comme monument," 54]). Rather, John seems to revel quite naturally in this art.

essential to comprehending the rhetorical strategy and import of these arguments, even as it also introduces us to a broad new collection of Pauline "biographical portraits."We shall see that Chrysostom applied the full menu of epideictic topics to his hero, Paul. John was employing the epideictic form even as he rewrote the table of values upon which it was based, and upset its expectations; but even that strategy was commonplace in ancient "pagan" encomia.[15] Furthermore, to place Chrysostom's encomia in a separate category because of their "paradigmatic" function[16] is not in the least justified, for the purpose of all epideictic oratory is to provide a vehicle for public celebration of shared social values, and renewed commitment by the hearers to their inculcation of them, which is solicited by calls to imitate the exemplar. John was hardly eschewing the rhetorical arts in these writings; instead he was practicing them to their fullest, doing what everyone who praises must: singling out and emphasizing the elements of the celebrand's life which most redound to his praise. And, most importantly for our inquiry, in using this "biographic" rhetorical form which verged so close to biography proper,[17] Chrysostom found yet another way to portray his beloved Paul for viewing and copying.

The abundant material on our topic will be arranged and presented in the following manner in this chapter. First we shall provide an analysis of two com-

---

[15] See, e.g., Chrysostom's discussion of Paul's lowly trade, which fits precisely one of the unexpected examples Theon suggests, of a tentmaker become a philosopher (this is quoted below, p. 217).

[16] As was argued by Simonetti, "Sulla struttura dei panegirici," 159: "D'altra parte, nei panegirici di Giovanni Crisostomo l'unico elemento veramente nuovo rispetto alle composizioni pagane viene individuato nella loro funzione paradigmatica, nell'intento pratico, che loro si annetteva, di spingere i fedeli all'imitazione dei santi celebrati e all'esercizio delle virtù" (see also 177–80). But compare Burgess, *Epideictic Literature*, 126: "[the ἐπίλογος of an epideictic speech] is often a brief summing up of the results of the life under discussion and an appeal to others to imitate his virtues" (also Hubbell, "Chrysostom and Rhetoric," 270, in his analysis of this same form in *laud. Paul.* 1.16). In actual speeches, see Isocrates, *Evag.* (= *Or.* 9) 75–81; and compare Arist. *Rh.* 1.9.35–36 on the connection between praising and exhorting. Furthermore we can see the wide currency of the call to imitation in John's own particular rhetorical context, in the school exercises by which Chrysostom would have been taught. In Libanios, *Prog.* 9.1.2 [Foerster, 8.282], a speech vilifying Achilles (a ψόγος, the precise opposite of an ἐγκώμιον, which uses the same topics in reverse fashion), the oration begins with the common complaint: βλέπων εἰς πατέρων ἀρετὰς ἐπὶ τὴν κακίαν ὥρμησε καὶ καλῶν αὐτῷ παραδειγμάτων ἑστηκότων οὐκ ἠβουλήθη μιμήσασθαι ("looking into the virtues of the fathers one rushes to look at the wickedness and does not wish to imitate the good examples standing before him"). Libanios also employs the rhetoric of imitation in his orations, though its usage is not exclusively in encomia (see, e.g., *Or.* 35.13, τούτους τοίνυν ὑμεῖς μακαρίζετε, ζηλοῦτε, μιμεῖσθαι; 31.43, ζηλῶμεν δὴ τοὺς προγόνους, ὦ ἄνδρες, καὶ μιμώμεθα; 32.21; 64.62 [Foerster, 3.217, 144, 158, 459]).

[17] Again here I am employing the terminology of Edwards and Swain, *Portraits*, 1–2 ; for the relation between encomium and biography in general, see Burgess, *Epideictic Literature*, 117; in a specific, most provocative case, see Averil Cameron, "Eusebius' *Vita Constantini* and the Construction of Constantine," in *Portraits: Biographical Representation in the Greek and Latin Literature of the Roman Empire*, ed. M. J. Edwards and Simon Swain (Oxford: Clarendon, 1997) 145–74; Cox, *Biography*, xiv (and further discussion in chap. 8, pp. 404–407).

plete arguments which largely depend upon the epideictic *topoi* of "external circumstances." This will allow us both to examine the portraits of Paul Chrysostom
composes through creative adaptation of these κεφάλαια ("rhetorical heads"), and
to demonstrate Chrysostom's full proficiency in their use on a large scale. Then,
having established his certain acquaintance with these *topoi* by their employment
in extended discourses, we shall collect and analyze Chrysostom's treatments of
Paul in regard to each of the biographical *topoi* that in rhetorical theory are subsumed under the category "external circumstances." In this way we shall piece
together the various jigsaw puzzle pieces of Paul's biographical portrait within
Chrysostom's oeuvre, and investigate their coherence and fundamental tensions, as
Chrysostom composes his author in yet another way with an eye to his own
rhetorical and catechetical purposes.

Large-Scale Portraits of Paul's Life Circumstances

Hom. in 2 Tim. 4.3–4: Σύγκρισις of Paul and Nero

The first passage we shall treat is from one of John's homilies on 2 Timothy, in
which Paul's "external circumstances" and what he made of himself in his life
through his deeds are given extensive expression. The passage is an encomium to
Paul through an ingenious use of an extended σύγκρισις[18] with an illustrious
counter-example who, on the surface, would appear to have had all the advantages
which Paul lacked, and, indeed, commanded the authority to order his execution.[19] In *hom. in 2 Tim.* 4.3–4 we see the full panoply of conventions for a
βασιλικὸς λόγος, "speech in honor of the emperor,"[20] employed to a tee, in order

---

[18] See Burgess, *Epideictic Literature*, 125–26, on partial and holistic forms of comparison
(quoted, with further references, in Mitchell, *Paul*, 219, n. 178).

[19] The contest and comparison between Paul and Nero comes up somewhat frequently in
Chrysostom's writings, from early on in his writing career, as evidenced in *oppugn.* 1.3–4 [47.323–
324], composed either when he was living as a monk, c. 372–78, or c. 378–86 in Antioch, before
he was ordained (see Hunter, *Comparison* 39–41). Chrysostom's references to Nero, including
these passages, have been analyzed by J. Rougé, "Néron à la fin du IVᵉ et au début du Vᵉ siècle,"
Latomus 37 (1978) 79–87, who rightly observes that Chrysostom's constant reference to Nero
was due to his love for Paul: "Contrairement à Augustin, Jean est revenue à plusieurs reprises sur
le personnage de Néron; c'est en quelque sorte son paulinisme, cette admiration pour l'apôtre si
caractéristique de son oeuvre, qui l'amené à trouver plusieurs fois sur sa route notre empereur"
(p. 80).

[20] See the full treatment of the βασιλικὸς λόγος in Menander, *Rh.* 2.368–78 (Russell-Wilson,
76–95), recommending the following list of topics, which are well in evidence in Chrysostom's
adaptation of the genre: amplified proem, origin (native country and city, family), birth, natural
endowments, rearing and education, accomplishments (which display character), actions which
display the four cardinal virtues (divided into those carried out in peace and those in war, and
introduced with comparisons to others), fortune, a complete comparison with others, and epilogue.

to delight the hearers with a topsy-turvy world,[21] for it is not the Roman emperor who is found worthy of praise here, but instead the lowly tentmaker beheaded on his order who far excels him. In its homiletical context (reflections on Paul's account of his sufferings in 2 Tim 2:9–10), this rhetorical comparison of Nero and Paul constitutes Chrysostom's proof for the proposition that true glory is not the glory of this world, but the glory of heaven, for "dishonor is glory, and glory dishonor" [ἡ ἀτιμία δόξα ἐστίν, ἡ δὲ δόξα ἀτιμία]. Therefore, if anyone wishes true honor, it can only be attained through dishonor. "So come, let's test this proposition [τοῦτο ἐξετάσωμεν] by treating of two persons, of Nero and of Paul," the first of whom possessed worldly glory, and the other dishonor.[22] This head-to-head comparison, we should duly note, has a special bite in the context of the homily series on 2 Timothy, since Chrysostom assumes (and has already alerted his audience to the fact) that this epistle was written during Paul's imprisonment at Rome under this very emperor.[23]

The rhetorical comparison begins first with a portrait of Nero, whose adult achievements Chrysostom seeks to list and accent as universally deserving of praise: "he was a sovereign, he had success in many things, raised up trophies, had wealth streaming to him from every direction, countless legions, the greater part of the world subject to him, the imperial city under submission, the entire Senate, the palace itself prostrating themselves to him."[24] These would appear to be the very acme of the external praiseworthy attributes called for by the epideictic species of rhetoric. Supplementing these, Chrysostom turns also to the imperial regalia, for it will form a key point in his comparison with his beloved apostle: "Nero went out in magnificent clothing; when armed for battle, he embarked in gold and precious stones, when leading a quiet life in peace, dressed in purple." In addition to the prodigious retinue which Chrysostom catalogues, he itemizes the epithets which were applied to Nero: "master of land and sea, all powerful, Augustus, Caesar, emperor, and many other such names" [γῆς καὶ θαλάττης δεσπότης ...

---

[21] For some time before, but especially in the fourth century, Christian authors had diverted the epideictic form from imperial propaganda to use for martyrs and saints. Then from the establishment of the Christian imperium onwards the genre was devoted once again to its original use, the most famous example of course being Eusebius' *Vita Constantini* (for the debate on its title and genre see Cameron, "Eusebius' *Vita Constantini*"; Quasten, *Patrology*, 3.320). The tremendous power of this rhetorical reappropriation in the late fourth century especially has been investigated insightfully by Cameron, *Christianity and the Rhetoric of Empire*, and Brown, *Persuasion*. See, e.g., Cameron, 135: "In the revived urban culture of the fourth century, Christian bishops succeeded to the place of the epideictic orators of the Second Sophistic; and their speeches were more political than the earlier ones ever could be."

[22] *hom. in 2 Tim.* 4.3 [62.621].

[23] *hom. in 2 Tim.* 1.1 [62.601].

[24] τύραννος ἦν ἐκεῖνος, πολλὰ κατωρθωκώς, τρόπαια στήσας, πλοῦτον ἔχων ἐπιρρέοντα, πανταχόθεν στρατόπεδα ἄπειρα, τὸ πλέον τῆς οἰκουμένης μέρος ὑποτεταγμένον, τὴν βασιλίδα πόλιν ὑποτεταγμένην, τὴν σύγκλητον ἅπασαν ὑποκύπτουσαν, τὰ βασίλεια αὐτά (*hom. in 2 Tim.* 4.3 [62.622]).

αὐτοκράτωρ, Αὔγουστος, Καῖσαρ, βασιλεύς, καὶ πολλὰ ἕτερα ὀνόματα τοιαῦτα].[25]
As proof of Nero's might, and of his violent and savage personality, in his lifetime
many wise and powerful men stood in terrible fear of him. And, the very zenith of
established status, he even wished to be a god! Thus accomplishing his "proof" for
Nero's laudability, Chrysostom exclaims: "What is greater than this glory" [Τί
ταύτης τῆς δόξης κρεῖττον;]? But Chrysostom cannot quite sustain the impartiality
he feigns in setting up this rhetorical comparison, so he follows this sure claim with
the reflex editorial remark, "Or rather, what worse dishonor" [μᾶλλον δὲ τί τῆς
ἀτιμίας χεῖρον;]? Then John retreats to a quick aporial self-defense for his outburst
before returning to his fair-minded comparative exercise: "But I do not know how
– by the truth – my mouth has run ahead, and cast its verdict before the judgment."[26]
From the outset the orator's impartiality (like the audience's) is displayed as an ironic
fiction, a mask which can be lifted to allow for editorial commentary.

After this mock self-castigation which whets the audience's appetite for the
forthcoming coup de grâce, Chrysostom reverts to his original plan, to construct
a fair comparison between the two men, making it initially on the grounds of the
customary systems of valuation (which are precisely what he is seeking here to
unseat), in order to prove his proposition about true honor: "But for a while let us
demonstrate the matter according to the opinion of the many, according to that of
unbelievers, according to flattery." On that basis, one can only conclude in Nero's
favor: "Indeed he lacked not a thing in terms of human glory, but was worshipped
by all as a God."[27] In this way, remarkably, Chrysostom has produced a portrait of
Nero which largely excludes mention of his famous acts of debauchery and wickedness, including his role in the burning of Rome[28] and persecution of Christians[29] (though part of the entertainment value of the discourse rests upon the
assumption that his audience is aware of legends and reports of Nero's infamous
deeds). But this is because John wishes to compare "Nero at his best" with "Paul
at his worst" as a means of amplification of his encomium. With this conclusion

---

[25]   hom. in 2 Tim. 4.3 [62.622].

[26]   Ἀλλ᾽ οὐκ οἶδα πῶς ὑπὸ τῆς ἀληθείας προὔδραμε τὸ στόμα, καὶ πρὸ τῆς κρίσεως τὴν
ψῆφον ἤνεγκε (hom. in 2 Tim. 4.3 [62.622]).

[27]   Οὐδὲν τοίνυν ἔλιπεν αὐτῷ εἰς δόξαν τὴν ἀνθρωπίνην, ἀλλ᾽ ὡς θεὸς παρὰ πάντων
ἐθεραπεύετο (hom. in 2 Tim. 4.3 [62.623]). But, of course, any late antique audience would
supply a ready knowledge of Nero's ignominy to supplement this supposedly neutral assessment
in Nero's favor.

[28]   Rougé, "Néron," 87, notes that Chrysostom does not explicitly connect the persecution of
Christians with the fire.

[29]   Even in the places where Chrysostom accents Nero's venal behavior (such as hom. in Phil.
1:18 4 [51.314], and depicts him as a robber and burglar who "despoiled marriages, overturned
households and displayed every form of evil"), the stereotypical nature of his portrait frustrates
Rougé in his quest for historiographical information about Nero traditions in the late fourth
century ("[Néron] est un symbole de vices et de barbarie. Ce portrait est d'une imprécision
totale; Néron est présenté comme un monstre, d'accord, mais rien ne vient étayer cette accusation" ["Néron," 81]).

in hand, Chrysostom moves on to the second leg of his comparison: "But, if it seems all right, let's bring Paul against him [ἀντεπεξάγειν]."

Here John begins, as the form normally requires, with the birthplace [πατρίς] of Paul: "The man was a Cilician – and everyone knows how great the difference is between Cilicia and Rome!" Then he turns, in point for point comparison with his previous exposition of Nero,[30] to Paul's training, trade, and education [ἐπιτηδεύματα, τέχνη, παιδεία], by listing several epithets for the lowly apostle: "a leathercutter, a poor man, inexperienced in external wisdom, knowing only the Hebrew language."[31] The latter point receives some regional embellishment from the Antiochene orator,[32] for he wishes to show that the Hebrew language was the most maligned of all, especially by Italians; indeed, Syriac (to which it is a close cousin) is more disparaged than any language, even more than the barbarian or Greek tongue (as marvelous and beautiful as the latter – Chrysostom's native language – is). Turning from language to wealth and possessions [πλοῦτος], John insists that Paul repeatedly lived in famine and nakedness (as proven by a citation from 2 Cor 11:27), and, even worse, was continually imprisoned. Thus Paul's retinue of friends and associates, in comparison with Nero's, was the prison population with whom he mingled: pirates, frauds, grave robbers, and murderers. "So, which of these two men is more magnificent?" Well, a simple test shows Paul to be the winner, for today "the majority do not even know Nero's name, but Greeks and barbarians and Scythians, and those who dwell at the ends of the earth all praise Paul every single day."[33] So the paradoxical encomium awards victory to the unlikely contender (except, of course, in this Christian oratory, where the reversal

---

[30] The τάξις (rhetorical disposition) Chrysostom has chosen, to provide first a full encomiastic schema of Nero, and then the same for Paul, intertwined, involves a series of συγκρίσεις μερικαί, or partial comparisons on different points (origin, language, etc.) (on which see Menander *Rh.* 2.377 [Russell-Wilson, 92]; Burgess, *Epideictic Literature*, 125). Menander Rhetor prescribes the use of σύγκρισις as follows: "Add also a comparison to each of the main heads, comparing nature with nature, upbringing with upbringing, education with education, and so on, looking out (? [as marked by Russell-Wilson; why not "discovering"?]) also examples of Roman emperors or generals or the most famous of the Greeks" [τίθει δὲ καὶ σύγκρισιν ἐφ' ἑκάστῳ τῶν κεφαλαίων τούτων, ἀεὶ συγκρίνων φύσιν φύσει καὶ ἀνατροφὴν ἀνατροφῇ καὶ παιδείαν παιδείᾳ καὶ τὰ τοιαῦτα, ἀνευρὼν καὶ παραδείγματα, οἷον Ῥωμαίων βασιλέων καὶ στρατηγῶν καὶ Ἑλλήνων ἐνδοξοτάτων] (2.372 [text and trans. Russell-Wilson, 84–85]).

[31] σκυτοτόμος, πένης, τῆς ἔξωθεν σοφίας ἄπειρος, Ἑβραϊστὶ μόνον εἰδὼς (4.3 [62.622]). How the latter can be squared with the Greek language of Paul's letters is something Chrysostom apparently never addresses. Clearly he gets the idea of Paul speaking Hebrew from Acts 22:2 (but even in that context Paul speaks also Greek! [21:37]). One must conclude that the Hebrew tongue is part of Chrysostom's overall hyperbolic image of Paul and the rest of the apostles as unlettered, uneducated men (according to Acts 4:13), through whom God's divine wisdom was spread world-wide (see the full discussion of Chrysostom's evaluation of Paul's rhetorical education below, pp. 241–45).

[32] On language as an encomiastic topic (both Latin and Greek), see Ps-Dionysius, *Rh.* 5.3 [Hermann Usener and Ludwig Radermacher, *Dionysii Halicarnasei quae exstant* (BT; Stuttgart: Teubner, 1965) vol. 6, pp. 274–75].

[33] *hom. in 2 Tim.* 4.3 [62.622].

has become the anticipated outcome). But the entire logic of Chrysostom's case rests upon the concept of time, which is how he will structure the rest of this encomium to Paul to prove his point about genuine glory.

This encomium turns into a play in three acts, the past, the present, and the future, in each of which the two men — Paul and Nero — face off in a contest for glory based on their πράξεις. This disposition of the argument is due to the fact that Chrysostom is not content to argue simply that Paul won out in the long run, but wishes Paul to be awarded the triple crown of honor at each of the chronological intervals ("But not yet the present comparison, let us examine the events of the past").[34] So Chrysostom asks the encomiastic question afresh: "Who was more magnificent, and who more glorious? The one wrapped in a chain, and dragged, bound, from the prison, or the one wrapped in the purple, and coming out from the palace?" The answer? "No question!"

Surely the one who was bound. How? Because the latter, though having an army, and setting forth in magnificent clothing, was not able to accomplish what he wished, whereas the prisoner and so-called evil-doer, clad in worthless garments, did all that he wished authoritatively. How and in what way? Nero said, "do not disseminate the word of piety"; but Paul stated, "I cannot bear it, for the word of God has not been bound." And the Cilician, the prisoner, the tentmaker, the poor man, the one who lived in famine [ὁ Κίλιξ, ὁ δεσμώτης, ὁ σκηνοποιός, ὁ πένης, ὁ ἐν λίμῳ ζῶν], spit on the Roman, the rich man, the emperor, the one ruling over all, the one who provides countless thousands with an array of goods [ὁ ἀπὸ τῆς Ῥώμης, ὁ πλούσιος, ὁ βασιλεύων, ὁ πάντων κρατῶν, ὁ μυρίοις μυρία παρέχων].[35]

Chrysostom here scripts a face-to-face encounter between his two subjects,[36] from which Paul emerges as victorious, since he defied the imperial edict. John dramatically depicts this past defiance in several memorable ways:

Who then was magnificent? Who was dignified? The one who was victorious in chains, or the one who was vanquished in purple?[37] The one standing below and attacking, or the one sitting above and being attacked? The one who commanded and was despised, or the one being commanded and taking no account of the commands issued? The one who though alone prevailed, or the one who, with countless soldiers, was bested?[38] The emperor thus went off, his prisoner having raised up the trophy against him.[39]

---

[34] hom. in 2 Tim. 4.3 [62.622].

[35] hom. in 2 Tim. 4.3 [62.622].

[36] An encounter based upon traditions in the apocryphal Acts, as Rougé, "Néron," 83, has shown.

[37] Compare laud. Paul. 2.5 [SC 300.150], on how Paul gloried more in his chain than Nero's diadem; and hom. in Mt. 33.4 [57.393], on Paul's victory over Nero, who had outdone all rivals in the competition for wickedness [ὁ Παῦλος ἐνίκησε ... τὸν κακίᾳ νικήσαντα πάντας ἀνθρώπους Νέρωνα].

[38] Chrysostom does not make as much here as he might of the sustained comparison in the account of Paul's martyrdom in Acta Pauli (Richard A. Lipsius, Acta 1.104–17) between the two soldieries, those of Christ (whom Paul "recruited throughout the whole world, including among the imperial cohort"), and those of the emperor. But he does mention this tradition elsewhere, as in hom. in 2 Cor. 25.3 [61.573], quoted below in this chapter, p. 276.

[39] hom. in 2 Tim. 4.3 [62.623]; compare oppugn. 1.3 [47.323–24]: "What then has been the

To establish the verdict for Scene One of the epic comparison between Nero and Paul, Chrysostom calls on his own audience, asking them which of the two men they would wish to side with (restricting their judgment for the moment to the original, historical scene of encounter between the emperor and his prisoner). Of course, viewed from the standpoint of faith Paul would win, but Chrysostom wishes to demonstrate the more difficult proposition that even by worldly standards Paul should win, given the simple principle that the victor is always granted more glory than the loser. And the conquest in this case is further embellished by the comparison of the respective accoutrements of the men: Paul's chain vanquished Nero's diadem since all who saw the two together in their encounter fixed their gaze on the image of Paul in his filthy rags, and cast their eyes away from the crowned and purple-robed emperor to feast on the vision of the victorious prisoner who accosted the ruler with an astonishing height of boldness [παρρησία].[40]

Scene Two takes place in the present,[41] when the contest between Nero and Paul is no longer face-to-face, but is held in the remote arenas of public memory and mortuary. Nero is hardly remembered, and when brought to mind is assigned blame, even by his own relatives, in particular for his legendary licentiousness. On the contrary, Paul's memory is always held in good repute, not only among Christians, but even among his enemies who, even if they do not marvel at his faith as believers do, still are amazed by his courage and boldness. "So Paul is proclaimed as crowned by the mouths of all people everywhere every single day, while Nero is castigated with blame and accusations."[42] And in terms of their respective tombs, Nero's grave is unmarked;[43] he was cast somewhere outside of the city of Rome. But Paul's tomb, more magnificently than all the emperors, stands in the very middle of the imperial city, at the exact spot where he had achieved victory and raised up his trophy. Lying in state in his tomb at Rome, Paul even now (in Chrysostom's day) resides as though alive and ruling.[44] "The tentmaker is more

---

harm to the one who suffered by the wickedness? And what the gain for the one who acted with wickedness? What gain was there not for the one who then was killed, Paul? What harm was there not for the one who killed him, Nero?" [Τί οὖν ἀπὸ τούτου γέγονε βλάβος τῷ παθόντι κακῶς; τί δὲ ὄφελος τῷ δράσαντι κακῶς; τί μὲν οὐκ ὄφελος τῷ τότε ἀναιρεθέντι Παύλῳ; τί δὲ οὐ βλάβος τῷ ἀνελόντι Νέρωνι;].

[40] τοῦτο δὲ ξένον καὶ παράδοξον, δεσμώτην ὁρᾶν μετὰ τοσαύτης παρρησίας βασιλεῖ διαλεγόμενον (*hom. in 2 Tim.* 4.4 [62.623]).

[41] John uses the same rhetorical strategy in the much briefer, earlier passage *oppugn.* 1.3 [47.324]: "Is not Paul praised as an angel everywhere on earth (for I shall speak now of the present), whereas Nero is calumniated to all as the destroyer and wild demon that he truly was?" [οὐχ ὁ μὲν ὥσπερ ἄγγελος πανταχοῦ τῆς οἰκουμένης ᾄδεται (τὰ γὰρ παρόντα τέως ἐρῶ)· ὁ δὲ, ὥσπερ ὄντως λυμεὼν καὶ δαίμων ἄγριος πρὸς πάντας διαβέβληται;].

[42] *hom. in 2 Tim.* 4.4 [62.623].

[43] This reflects an old tradition (which contradicts Suetonius), reflected in *Sib. Or.* and later Christian historians (see Rougé, "Néron," 84–85).

[44] ἀλλ' ὁ μὲν βασιλεὺς ἐρριμμένος ἔξω που κεῖται, ὁ δὲ τὸ μέσον κατέχει τῆς πόλεως, καθάπερ βασιλεύων καὶ ζῶν (*hom. in 2 Tim.* 4.4 [62.624]).

magnificent than the emperor, more honored than the emperor. No one who has been emperor of Rome has enjoyed such great honor!"[45]

But Paul will best Nero on all three stages of this oratorical contest which Chrysostom has set up, for in Scene Three, in the future, at the resurrection Paul will come with magnificent vestments, while Nero will stand by, dejected and gloomy. Thus Paul's complete biography, which is the basis for the epideictic art, has yet to reach its final chapter, because in that last event, not yet consummated, Paul will enjoy "countless good things" and will finally receive his justly deserved crown of glory.[46] The temporal comparison which Chrysostom has carefully constructed has at least two functions: first, a catechetical objective, to convince his hearers from three different angles of vision of the transience of mere earthly glory, and, second, a specifically rhetorical purpose, to accrue even more glory to his beloved Paul, whose future splendor, which will exceed even his prior greatness, is beyond the telling: "If he was so magnificent when he was a tentmaker, what will he be like when he comes rivaling the very rays of the sun in brilliance?"[47] The exhortatory purpose receives additional confirmation from the insight that "if in this life things happened so beyond the natural order [τὰ ὑπὲρ φύσιν], how much more so will this be the case in the future?"[48] What is contrary to nature, contrary to the expectations of life so celebrated in an encomium, is that Paul's πράξεις, "deeds," have completely overturned the expectations of his ancestry, birth, and training. Hence in concluding, after a formulaic peroration,[49] Chrysostom can urge his congregational audience forward: "let us, as beloved children, become imitators of Paul [Παύλου μιμηταὶ ... γενώμεθα], not only in faith, but also in his life [ἀλλὰ καὶ κατὰ τὸν βίον], so that we might attain to heavenly glory, and trample underfoot what is accounted glory here" [καταπατεῖν τὴν ἐνταῦθα δόξαν].[50]

Laud. Paul. 4: *Paul's Power and Divine Providence*

Homily four *de laudibus sancti Pauli*, if not located in the series, might perhaps not be formally classified as an encomium,[51] but we shall demonstrate that the oration can only be understood as a creative adaptation and reversal of encomiastic topics.

[45] Λαμπρότερος τοῦ βασιλέως ὁ σκηνοποιός, ἐντιμότερος τοῦ βασιλέως· οὐδεὶς βασιλεὺς τῆς Ῥώμης γενόμενος, τοσαύτης ἀπέλαυσε τιμῆς (*hom. in 2 Tim.* 4.4 [62.624]).

[46] Λέγω ὅτι ἥξει Παῦλος μετὰ τοῦ βασιλέως τῶν οὐρανῶν, ὅτε ἀνάστασις ἔσται, ὅτι μυρίων ἀπολαύσει τῶν ἀγαθῶν (*hom. in 2 Tim.* 4.4 [62.624]).

[47] Εἰ ὅπου σκηνοποιὸς ἦν, οὕτως ἐγένετο λαμπρός, ὅταν ἔλθῃ ἀντιλάμπων ταῖς ἡλιακαῖς ἀκτῖσι, τί ἔσται; (*hom. in 2 Tim.* 4.4 [62.624]).

[48] Ibid.

[49] "We have given testimony to you about it all, and have left out none of the things that should have been said" [ἅπαντα γὰρ ὑμῖν διεμαρτυράμεθα, καὶ οὐδὲν ἐνελίπομεν τῶν ὀφειλόντων λεχθῆναι] (*hom. in 2 Tim.* 4.4 [62.624]).

[50] *hom. in 2 Tim.* 4.4 [62.624].

[51] As argued by Hubbell, "Chrysostom and Rhetoric," 271: "In this homily the resemblances to the formal encomium are few, being confined to the comparison, and that is not done

The speech does begin with Paul as its subject,[52] and it explicitly addresses a congregation assembled on the saint's feast day ['Ο μακάριος Παῦλος, ὁ τήμερον ἡμᾶς συναγαγών].[53] Apparently the lectionary passage for the liturgy was Acts 9, since Chrysostom begins, even more directly than usual, almost in mid-paragraph, with a meditation on Paul's call and the way that its ensuing blindness provided a foretaste of the upside-down ways of God's providential power which were to mark his entire ministry. The liturgical setting of the oration on Paul's feast day further ensures that it is socially situated within the realm of a panegyric, and not some other occasional discourse that Paul simply figures in. However, it is a more complicated argument than a conventional encomium might ordinarily contain.

προοίμιον (Introduction). John formulates at the outset the paradox which the discourse will develop: the one who enlightened the world [ὁ τὴν οἰκουμένην φωτίσας][54] began his saving work in the darkness of blindness. "But his blinding has become the illumination of the world" [ἀλλ᾽ ἡ πήρωσις ἐκείνου φωτισμὸς γέγονε τῆς οἰκουμένης].[55] The proem (§1) introduces the central theme of the discourse: the demonstration of the power of God [τῆς ἑαυτοῦ δυνάμεως ἀπόδειξις],[56] and the appropriate human response to that power modeled by Paul above all others, with enormous consequences for the whole world.

πρόθεσις and πίστεις (Proposition and Proofs).[57] Chrysostom's opening reflection on Paul's call leads him to formulate a counter-proposition in the form of an admonitory imperative: "But let no one on hearing these things think that this call was a matter of compulsion" ['Αλλὰ μηδεὶς ταῦτα ἀκούων ἠναγκασμένην νομίζετω εἶναι ταύτην τὴν κλῆσιν].[58] John's initial thesis (restated, with some of the exact same words, in §4) is that "God does not compel, but allows people to be masters of their own choices even after the call."[59] Unsurprisingly, it is Paul whom Chry-

---

systematically, but, as it were, incidentally. In fact the piece does not live up to its title. It is not an encomium on Paul but an apology for Christianity, and a proof of its divine origin, using the greatness of Paul as one of the proofs." I do not quite agree with this analysis of the thesis of the speech, as I shall show below.

[52] Not the rise of Christianity, *pace* Hubbell.

[53] *laud. Paul.* 4.1 [SC 300.182].

[54] Images of light frame the discourse, returning at the end in *laud. Paul.* 4.18 [SC 300.222], where Paul is likened to the sun, and is the bearer of "the shining flame of the truth," being as he was the man in whom "grace shined profusely" (4.20 [SC 300.226]).

[55] *laud. Paul.* 4.1 [SC 300.182].

[56] *laud. Paul.* 4.1 [SC 300.182]. The lexical evidence alone shows the preponderance of the theme, as it is punctuated again and again throughout the discourse by the terms ἰσχύς (4.7; 4.10 [SC 300.198, 202]); ἰσχύειν (4.10; 4.11; 4.13; 4.14 [2x]; 4.17; 4.18; 4.19 [2x] [SC 300.202, 206, 212, 214, 220, 224, 226]); and δύναμις (4.2; 4.7; 4.9; 4.10 [2x]; 4.13; 4.14 [2x]; 4.15 [SC 300.184, 196, 200, 202, 210, 212, 214]).

[57] The proof section extends from §2–19 [SC 300.182–226].

[58] *laud. Paul.* 4.2 [SC 300.184]. This is a favorite theme; see also *hom. in Ac. 9:1* 3.5 [51.141–42].

[59] οὐδὲ γὰρ ἀναγκάζει ὁ θεός, ἀλλ᾽ ἀφίησι κυρίους εἶναι προαιρέσεων καὶ μετὰ τὴν κλῆσιν (*laud. Paul.* 4.4 [SC 300.188]). Just before this Chrysostom had repeated the warning from §4,

sostom will offer as the example of the proper use of free will in response to divine initiative, but the argument will also demonstrate that thesis from counter-examples, given the fact that "many, after seeing other, greater marvels, turned back again" [Πολλοὶ γοῦν ἕτερα μείζονα θαύματα ἰδόντες, ὑπέστρεψαν πάλιν]. The proof for this contention will occupy the whole proof section of the discourse, which is arranged according to topical heads [κεφάλαια]: examples from the Old and New Testament (including Paul) in §2–5, examples from recent history in §6, and, preponderantly, from the present [τὰ παρόντα] in §7–20,[60] the period witnessing the overwhelming and incredible success of the gospel proclamation.

Chrysostom first promises examples from both the Old and the New Testament to establish his claim that people are not compelled to respond to God's call with faithfulness and obedience. He brings forth a host of cases where the divine voice came from heaven (as it did with Saul on the road to Damascus), and evoked mixed responses from its human auditors. On the positive side are Rahab, Job's Ninevite audience, and the good thief, and on the negative are the Israelites at Sinai making the golden calf, Jews in general, and those who crucified Jesus.[61] Then Chrysostom introduces a new set of exempla, events in his part of the world: "But what about incidents nearer to us" [Τί δὲ ἐφ' ἡμῶν;]? In a passage of signal importance for late antique history, Chrysostom proceeds to list nine events still fresh in living memory (most from the infamous reign of Julian) that he regards as expressions of the divine voice in warning or punishment that went unheeded.[62] The divine hand at work in these events was further confirmed, Chrysostom avers, when conditions reversed themselves just as piety was restored.

At §7 John moves to a new set of παραδείγματα with a rhetorical question: "But what about present events, are they not even more marvelous than these" [Τὰ δὲ παρόντα οὐ πολλῷ τούτων θαυμαστότερα;]? His answer is that there is another manifestation of God's power which is more marvelous, more clear, than even the

---

"Now when you hear these things, don't think that the call was compulsory" [Σὺ δὲ ἀκούων ταῦτα, μὴ ἀναγκαστὴν τὴν κλῆσιν εἶναι νόμιζε].

[60] My analysis differs somewhat from that of Piédagnel: §1–4 Call of Paul; §5–6 Responses to the Call of God; §7–14 The Extraordinary Power of the Cross; §15–17 No Obstacle to the Gospel; §18–20 Peroration; §21 Final Exhortation (SC 300.182–229, as laid out in his notes).

[61] *laud. Paul.* 4.5 [SC 300.190].

[62] *laud. Paul.* 4.6 [SC 300.190–96]. Piédagnel, SC 300.196, n. 2, counts seven, but the enumeration is not really important. These are all from recent history, in the reign of Julian: the fire that attacked those attempting to rebuild the Temple in Jerusalem; lightning striking the temple of Apollo; the forced transposition of the body of saint Babylas by order of the oracle of Apollo; the death of Julian's uncle as punishment for desecrating sacred vessels (described by Chrysostom borrowing the language of the death of Herod Agrippa in Acts 12:23); the death of an imperial treasurer who had defrauded the church (in language reminiscent of the death of Judas in Acts 1:18); the drying up of streams when Julian offered sacrifices and libations to the gods; the worldwide famine that coincided with Julian's reign; his death in Persia; and the miraculous escape of his soldiers when cut off and surrounded by Persian forces.

previous examples of "that voice borne from heaven,"[63] which is the rampant and total success of Christianity in his day, in which Chrysostom triumphantly exults: "Who has so prevailed over the whole world in a short time?"[64] And how did Christ win out over all the earthly dominions and authories when they all stood in opposition to the gospel? Indeed their counter-movements actually served the course of the gospel: "our cause nevertheless was not diminished by these hindrances, but indeed became even more magnificent."[65] That this victory must be due to a tremendous power is certain; but where does it come from [Πόθεν οὖν, εἴπατέ μοι, ἡ τοσαύτη ἰσχύς;]?[66] John's answer is a second proposition: the origin of this great power at work in the gospel is divine. To prove this thesis Chrysostom begins with the power [ἰσχὺς/δύναμις] of Christ. In §8–10 he supports his thesis with an argument from contraries, first refuting the accusation that Jesus' power was that of a magician. No, Chrysostom counters, in Christ we see evidence of ἡ τοῦ σταυρωθέντος δύναμις, "the power of the one who was crucified."[67] Magicians, such as Apollonios of Tyana, are swiftly snuffed out, and spawn no permanent legacy; but Jesus was quite different. Further proof of Christ's power is given in the terror demons evinced before him, an unaccountable reaction to either a charlatan or any other poor victim of crucifixion.

At §10 Chrysostom makes a smooth transition within his proof that divine force is at work in the gospel from Christ back to his main exemplum, Paul. First he concludes the argument about the power of Christ (§7–9) with a nice recapitulation: "From all this it is clear that it was not because he was a magician, nor because he was a swindler [Ὅθεν δῆλον ὅτι οὐκ ἐπειδὴ μάγος ἦν, οὐδὲ ὅτι πλάνος ἦν], but because he was a reformer of these things [ἀλλ' ἐπειδὴ τούτων διορθωτής], and a divine and unconquerable power [θεία δύναμίς τις καὶ ἄμαχος] – that is why he prevailed over all" [διὰ τοῦτο καὶ αὐτὸς πάντων περιεγένετο]. With the theme of power as his link, in the continuation of this long sentence John forges the connection between Christ and Paul: "and into this tentmaker Christ breathed such a large measure of this power as the facts themselves testify" [καὶ τῷ σκηνοποιῷ τούτῳ τοσαύτην ἐνέπνευσε δύναμιν, ὅσην αὐτὰ τὰ πράγματα μαρτυρεῖ].[68] From the "power" of Christ John has moved back to his original subject, Paul, "the man who became so powerful" [τοσοῦτον ἴσχυσεν] that he led the entire human race to the truth.[69]

---

[63] Ταῦτα οὖν οὐ δοκεῖ τῆς δυνάμεως αὐτοῦ σαφεστέραν ἔχειν ἀπόδειξιν τῆς φωνῆς ἐκείνης τῆς ἐξ οὐρανοῦ κατενεχθείσης; Note that at the end of the discourse it is Paul himself who is described as "bearing good things for us from heaven" [ὧν ἐκ τοῦ οὐρανοῦ φέρων ἦλθεν ἡμῖν ἀγαθῶν] (4.20 [SC 300.226]), thus virtually taking over the role of the heavenly voice.

[64] *laud. Paul.* 4.7 [SC 300. 196–98].

[65] καὶ τὰ ἡμέτερα ὅμως οὐκ ἠλαττοῦτο, ἀλλὰ καὶ μᾶλλον λαμπρότερα ἐγίνετο (*laud. Paul.* 4.7 [SC 300.198]).

[66] "From where then, tell me, does such great power come?" (*laud. Paul.* 4.7 [SC 300.198]).

[67] *laud. Paul.* 4.9 [SC 300.200], a phrase repeated twice again in 4.14 [SC 300.212, 214].

[68] *laud. Paul.* 4.10 [SC 300.202].

[69] *laud. Paul.* 4.10 [SC 300.202].

The rest of the proof section (§10–20) in this long discourse is devoted to Chrysostom's argument that the power at work in Paul was this same supernatural power of God in Christ, the divine agency which alone can account for the way in which the lowly have conquered the world. Of chief interest to our concern in this chapter is the extent to which this part of the proof (§10–20) depends upon encomiastic *topoi* about "external circumstances," and involves the composition of intricate portraits of Paul by reference to elements of his birth, education and life. These encomiastic topics are what Chrysostom refers to with the phrase "the facts themselves" [αὐτὰ τὰ πράγματα], the details of Paul's life and personal history. John introduces his biographical portrait of Paul in the very formulation of the proposition of this sub-argument:

> Because a man standing in the marketplace, having a trade in skins [Ἄνθρωπος ἐπ' ἀγορᾶς ἑστηκώς, περὶ δέρματα τὴν τέχνην ἔχων], became so powerful [τοσοῦτον ἴσχυσεν] that he led the entire human race – Romans, Persians, Indians, Scythians, Ethiopians, Sauromatians, Parthians, Medes and Saracenes – singly to the truth; and in less than thirty years, at that![70]

Chrysostom has here nicely amplified his point about the power of the gospel by including a lengthy list of the nations of the world to which it spread, and adding the increase in degree of difficulty of the task lent by the brief timeline within which it was accomplished. In the next breath he amplifies the argument further by repetition,[71] this time using a rhetorical question:

> From where was it, then, tell me, that the man who hung about the market [ἀγοραῖος],[72] and stood in a workshop [ἐπὶ ἐργαστηρίου ἑστηκώς], and took in hand a knife [σμίλην μεταχειρίζων], himself came to teach and practice such a great philosophy [αὐτὸς τοιαῦτα ἐφιλοσόφει], and persuaded the others [τοὺς ἄλλους ἔπεισε], even nations, both cities and countryside, despite the fact that he did not demonstrate the power of eloquence [οὐ λόγων ἰσχὺν ἐπιδεικνύμενος], but, to the utter contrary [ἀλλὰ καὶ τοὐναντίον ἅπαν], was unlearned, to the lowest degree of poor learning [τὴν ἐσχάτην ἀμαθίαν ἀμαθὴς ὤν]?[73]

Essential to this argument are the encomiastic topics of trade [τέχνη], training or vocation [ἐπιτηδεύματα],[74] and education [παιδεία]. Luke's description of Paul as a σκηνοποιός, a tentmaker (Acts 18:3), corroborated by references in the Pauline letters to manual labor (1 Cor 4:12; cf. 1 Thess 2:9), is embellished by Chrysostom

---

[70]   *laud. Paul.* 4.10 [SC 300.202].

[71]   Amplification [αὔξησις] is the chief means of epideictic proof; see Aristotle, *Rh.* 1.9.40: "Speaking generally, of the topics common to all rhetorical arguments, amplification is most suitable for epideictic speakers [ἡ μὲν αὔξησις ἐπιτηδειοτάτη τοῖς ἐπιδεικτικοῖς], whose subject is actions which are not disputed [τὰς γὰρ πράξεις ὁμολογουμένας λαμβάνουσιν], so that all that remains to be done is to attribute importance and beauty [μέγεθος περιθεῖναι καὶ κάλλος] to them" (for further references in rhetorical theory, see Burgess, *Epideictic Literature*, 105 n. 3).

[72]   Or, "was a commoner" (LSJ, 13).

[73]   *laud. Paul.* 4.10 [SC 300.202–204].

[74]   Burgess. *Epideictic Literature*, 123. See Chrysostom's exact language a few lines later: οὐδὲ ἐξ ἐπιτηδεύματος λαμπρὸς ἦν, "he was not illustrious on account of his vocation, either."

with three degrading synonyms so as to render it a despicable position, the most unlikely launching pad for the herald of the gospel. This humble trade, and the meager education [ἀμαθία] it reflects, is to be contrasted with the extraordinary deeds [πράξεις] the man came to accomplish, which culminated in his winning over the inhabitants of the entire world to the true philosophy. Chrysostom's invocation of the rhetorical triumph of the unlettered philosopher itself reflects rhetorical conventions. The rhetorical teacher Theon, employing an astonishingly similar example, observed that:

> It is admirable when the man who rises from a servile trade or bad fortune is able to accomplish something good [ἄξιον δὲ ἄγασθαι καὶ τὸν ἐκ βαναύσου τέχνης ἢ πονηρᾶς τύχης ἀγαθὸν δυνηθέντα τι ἐργάσασθαι]. For example, they say that Hero, the leather-worker [σκυτοτόμος], on the one hand, and Leontion, the courtesan [ἑταίρα], on the other, became philosophers [φιλοσοφῆσαι].[75]

Consequently, Chrysostom's rhetorical strategy of contrasting Paul's immense accomplishments with his very humble origins is misunderstood if claimed to be a distinctively Christian brand of humility.[76] While it is true that Chrysostom inherits and draws upon virtues especially prized among Christians,[77] his parading of Paul's low pedigree and possible faults is itself a rhetorical choice made from within the customary boundaries of the encomiastic art, as recommended by theorists − not a repudiation of the form, but a full-fledged use of it. The portrait of Paul as a man of poor circumstances, exemplified in his tent-making trade, can be embellished with even more detail, as Chrysostom proceeds: "Neither was he distinguished by great ancestors [Οὐκ ἀπὸ προγόνων ἐπίσημος]. For how could he be, having such a trade? [πῶς γάρ, τοιοῦτον ἐπιτήδευμα ἔχων;]. Nor was he distinguished by his native country [Οὐκ ἀπὸ πατρίδος], nor his people [οὐκ ἀπὸ ἔθνους]."[78] In the cultural context of the late fourth century (no less than the first),

---

[75] Theon, *Prog.* 8 [Spengel, 2.111–12]). This precise word, σκυτοτόμος, "tentmaker," is one of several synonyms Chrysostom uses to embellish Luke's σκηνοποιός (see, e.g., *hom. in Mt.* 61.3 [58.592]; *hom. in 2 Tim.* 4.3 [62.622]).

[76] *pace* Piédagnel, SC 300.30: "On peut remarquer d'abord que, refusant parfois une généralisation excessive, plutôt que de prêter à Paul le prestige de l'érudition et de l'éloquence, il a tendance, au contraire, à minimiser ses connaissances humaines, notamment sa culture profane ... En effet, plus que la recherche d'actions éclatantes ou l'illustration de hautes fonctions qui étaient souvent la matière des éloges profanes, plus même que les vertus de chasteté, de pauvreté volontaire ou de fermeté devant l'épreuve, c'est avant tout, explique Chrysostome, le charité de Paul qui a fait sa grandeur. C'est là un développement proprement chrétien." Better here is Hubbell, "Chrysostom and Rhetoric," 271, who (at least tentatively) recognized the rhetorical strategy at work: "It might be possible to subsume part of [this discourse] under the idea of praising one for rising above his circumstances" (with reference to Theon for the *topos* in general, but he did not remark upon the precise parallel quoted above about the "leatherworker-become-philosopher").

[77] Those which conduce especially to his monastic ideal, as we shall discuss further in this chapter, esp. pp. 308–26.

[78] *laud. Paul.* 4.10 [SC 300.204]. The degree to which Chrysostom is deliberately selecting from among the biblical biographical material at his disposal is nicely illustrated by this passage,

in which peoples' origin and destiny were thought thoroughly and predictably to line up, Paul's trade as a leather-worker is sufficient proof of his mean descent. But encomiastic rhetoric revels in the overturning of the expectations of conventional wisdom. And Paul's deeds break every mold:

But nevertheless, when he came into the public eye, and simply appeared [ἐλθὼν εἰς μέσον, καὶ φανεὶς μόνον], he threw everything pertaining to his adversaries into confusion, he encompassed all things, and, like a fire falling into stubble and grass, he thus incinerated the demonic powers and changed everything into whatever he wished [εἰς ἅπερ ἐβούλετο, πάντα μετέστησε].[79]

All these miraculous deeds of Paul's were accomplished without training or the earthly *curriculum vitae* which might make for success in adulthood. In fact, merely by appearing Paul destroyed the realm of the demonic, and forever changed the world.[80]

The degree of difficulty for Paul's seemingly impossible achievement, the transformation of the world, was further compounded by the lowliness of those to whom he brought the new philosophy, the gospel. Again epideictic *topoi* of "external circumstances" provide the language and structure for Chrysostom's argument:

And not only is it marvelous [θαυμαστόν] that he, being as he was [αὐτὸς τοιοῦτος ὤν], had such great powers [τοσαῦτα ἴσχυσεν], but also that the majority of those he was instructing were poor [πένητες], unskilled [ἰδιῶται], uneducated [ἀπαίδευτοι], living in famine [λιμῷ συζῶντες], undistinguished folk born of undistinguished stock [ἄσημοι καὶ ἐξ ἀσήμων].[81]

John finds sufficient proof of these contentions in the apostle's own declarative and unembarrassed words: the notice about the collection to relieve the hunger of the saints in Jerusalem (Rom 15:25), and the depiction of the lowly background of the Corinthian converts (1 Cor 1:26–28).

As he did in the case of Christ, next Chrysostom will use anticipation to discount other, false explanations for the success of Paul's gospel preaching. Was he, perhaps, though unskilled and untrained [ἰδιώτης καὶ ἀπαίδευτος], somehow a naturally-endowed persuasive speaker [πιθανὸς ὁπωσοῦν εἰπεῖν]?[82] No, this was not the case, as Paul himself testified in 1 Cor 2:1–4. Was it, instead, that the gospel message was so intrinsically attractive that it quite expectedly drew in its

---

since he contradicts the apostle's own words in Acts 21:39 (itself a collection of introductory epideictic *topoi*) that he was "a citizen of no undistinguished city" [οὐκ ἀσήμου πόλεως πολίτης].

[79] *laud. Paul.* 4.10 [SC 300.206]. We shall give a full treatment of this image of Paul as the victor over Greco-Roman paganism below, pp. 270–78.

[80] This means that, paradoxically, Paul's deeds are not deeds, per se, but outbreaks of the divine power at work in him. But, as we shall see below, Chrysostom will argue that it is the assent to divine power in the call and subsequent to it, by one's own free will, that is essential to virtuous, laudable behavior.

[81] *laud. Paul.* 4.11 [SC 300.206].

[82] *laud. Paul.* 4.11 [SC 300.206–208].

hearers? Hardly, for the gospel was an impossible medicine for both Jews and Greeks to swallow, as another reference to the initial two chapters of 1 Corinthians demonstrates (1:22–23). Nor was the success due to a secure climate, favorable and unthreatening to the gospel proclamation, for from the beginning both Paul and his disciples were beset by persecutions, as the letters frequently indicate.[83] Then, in a nice rhetorical recapitulation, Chrysostom brings together the improbabilities on all sides of the communicative transaction, all of which were surmounted by the success of the gospel:

> Therefore, when the one preaching is unskilled and poor and undistinguished [ἰδιώτης καὶ πένης καὶ ἄσημος], and the message preached not alluring [τὸ κηρυττόμενον οὐκ ἐπαγωγόν], but even scandalous, and the ones hearing it poor and weak and nobodies [πένητες καὶ ἀσθενεῖς καὶ οὐδένες], and the dangers continuous and unremitting for both teachers and disciples, and the one being proclaimed a victim of crucifixion, what caused it to conquer [τί τὸ ποιῆσαν κρατήσειν;]? Is it not clear that it was some divine and ineffable power [Οὐκ εὔδηλον ὅτι θεία τις καὶ ἀπόρρητος δύναμις]?[84] I suppose it is clear to every one.[85]

Nonetheless, despite this claim to have proven his thesis sufficiently, Chrysostom continues to buttress the case, next with an argument from contraries based, once again, on the epideictic commonplaces of "external circumstances." Chrysostom provides a point by point σύγκρισις between the attributes of the gospel's pro-claimers and those of its fierce and ubiquitous adversaries. Rival pagan religion had everything going for it at once: wealth [πλοῦτος], noble birth [εὐγένεια], greatness of fatherland [πατρίδος μέγεθος], the forcefulness of rhetoric [ῥητορείας δεινότης], security [ἄδεια], and wide-spread cultic service to the gods [θεραπεία πολλή]. Pagan religion also had the power routinely to snuff out religious novelties the moment they arose [εὐθέως σβεσθέντα τὰ καινοτομηθέντα].[86] Notwithstanding all this, the Christians (with Paul as their figurehead), possessed of the opposite qualities [τὰ ἐναντία],[87] prevailed over them.[88] Yet again John punctuates his point with a rhetorical question: "What is the cause of this? Tell me!" From the grand-scale comparison of the two groups, Chrysostom focuses in on Paul's singular role in the great drama of success. In a parabolic simile he casts Paul as a poor, naked and solitary man [πτωχός τις γυμνὸς καὶ μόνος], who, without so much as a javelin in his hand[89] or a garment covering his body, had the strength to conquer

---

[83] John makes reference to 1 Cor 2:3; Heb 10:32–34; 1 Thess 2:14–15; 2 Cor 1:5, 7; Gal 3:4.

[84] This deliberately echoes what Chrysostom had said about Christ in §10: θεία δύναμίς τις καὶ ἄμαχος (*laud. Paul.* 4.10 [SC 300.202]), emphasizing that it is the same power at work in both.

[85] *laud. Paul.* 4.13 [SC 300.210].

[86] *laud. Paul.* 4.13 [SC 300.210–12].

[87] In this passage Chrysostom is punning on the two possible referents of ἐναντία/ἐναντίοι: "opposite qualities" and "opponents."

[88] See the same argument in *laud. Paul.* 5.1 [SC 300.232].

[89] The phrase μηδὲ ἀκόντιον μεταχειρίζων is meant to invoke the earlier image of Paul as ὁ σμίλην μεταχειρίζων (4.10 [SC 300.202]). This is the literary counterpart to the vocational

the barbarians [κρατῆσαι τῶν βαρβάρων], a task that had previously proved impossible even for the emperor with his full military forces and armaments.[90] After a brief exhortation to the hearer to cast a daily vote of confidence in this topsy-turvy scheme, and "worship the power of the one who was crucified,"[91] a second telling of the military parable follows. A general who carefully lays siege to a city but fails to take it is compared with Paul who, alone, naked, and using only his hands, conquered not one, two or twenty cities, but tens of thousands throughout the whole world, and took captive every single one of their inhabitants.[92] As in the parable, no one would attribute the triumph of the gospel to a human power [ἀνθρωπίνη δύναμις], because there are obvious signs of God's careful forethought in the events of salvation. First, since two others were crucified with Jesus, it is clear that it is not the cross itself which inspires great fright in the demons, but "the power of the one who was crucified" [τοῦ σταυρωθέντος ἡ ἰσχύς].[93] And God has always deliberately allowed false messiahs (like Theudas and Judas mentioned in Acts 5:36–37), false prophets, and even false apostles to emerge, so as to demonstrate by comparison [ἀπὸ συγκρίσεως] the superiority of the truth, and the divine, rather than circumstantial, source of its triumph.

At §15 Chrysostom says he will approach the same, unifying theme of the oration, "the marvelous and incredible power of the gospel" [δύναμις κηρύγματος θαυμαστὴ καὶ παράδοξος], from a new direction [ἑτέρωθεν].[94] The fresh angle is furnished by the proposition already introduced in the case of Christ,[95] that "Paul[96]

---

emblem sometimes found in funerary art, such as the monuments at Palmyra in Syria (for examples, see Anna Sadurska and Adnan Bounni, *Les sculptures funéraires de palmyre* [Rivista di archeologia, supplementi 13; Rome: Bretschneider, 1994], figs. 4, 139 [woman with spindle, very common]; 13, 14, 19, 78, 79, 81, 83, 88 [men or boys with codexes, swords, priestly vessels, braided whips, and the ubiquitous, and somewhat enigmatic, *schedula*]; for their function, see Malcolm A. R. Colledge, *The Art of Palmyra* [London: Thames & Hudson, Ltd., 1976] 154: "These objects are presented surely to indicate the earthly employment of the deceased"). This same convention was of course carried over into Byzantine iconography: "the image should be sufficiently well-defined to enable them to identify the holy figure represented, from a range of signs that included the clothing, the attributes, the portrait type, and the inscription" (Maguire, *Icons of their Bodies*, 16). For the use of the corresponding literary commonplace in encomia, compare Libanios, *Or.* 18.72, of Julian: "For he always had in his hands either books or weapons [ἀεὶ γὰρ εἶχεν ἐν χεροῖν ἢ βίβλους ἢ ὅπλα], since he considered warfare to be greatly helped by philosophy …."

[90] *laud. Paul.* 4.13 [SC 300.212].

[91] *laud. Paul.* 4.14 [SC 300.212].

[92] *laud. Paul.* 4.14 [SC 300.212].

[93] *laud. Paul.* 4.14 [SC 300.214], and earlier in that same paragraph, τοῦ σταυρωθέντος ἡ δύναμις, as also in 4.9 [SC 300.200]). Note here the reversion to the earlier theme of the power the cross has over demons, which was developed in 4.9 [SC 300.200–202]).

[94] *laud. Paul.* 4.15 [SC 300.214].

[95] The main proposition is the divine power active in Paul's ministry; this minor proposition focuses in on the *means* by which that power was manifested: in the surprising fact that all hindrances actually worked in its favor. That theme was introduced in *laud. Paul.* 4.7 [SC 300.198], quoted above.

[96] In agreement with Piédagnel, SC 300.215, n. 4 about the antecedent of the pronoun αὐτόν.

was raised up and increased even by those who battled against him."The proof for this contention will occupy virtually the rest of the speech (§15–20). The first example John offers is from Paul's Epistle to the Philippians, which he assumes was composed at Rome during the time of Neronian hostility. In a long quotation he reproduces Paul's unusually conciliatory phrases about rival preachers in Phil 1:12–18 to demonstrate the reality of this serendipitous outcome: "nevertheless, he triumphed even through the opponents."[97] From these internal threats to the Pauline mission, Chrysostom moves next to the considerable opposition it faced externally at the hands of those who from either evil-mindedness or ignorance slandered the Christians as treasonous adherents of a rival king whose reign threatened both the commonwealth and the private home. Yet the false accusation turns out surprisingly to be a completely accurate description of Paul's adept military strategy in engaging his enemy on two fronts: a "variable and many-sorted war"[98] on the existing world order that combined house-to-house guerilla combat with revolutionary overthrow of municipal legislatures, law courts, ancestral customs, and the traditional feasts and cults of the pagan gods. And, lest one receive the impression that all the outside opponents were pagans, John quickly adds (though with little elaboration) that alongside them stood the considerable menace to the infant church from Jews.[99] All these lists of Paul's πράξεις, the unlikely deeds of the simple tentmaker, add up to a single portrait of Paul as the hero of the rise of Christianity who overcame all odds, and vanquished all enemies or competitors.

This heroic portrait of Paul as conquerer continues with a reversion to the earlier theme of Paul (and the gospel with which he is identified)[100] as a raging fire.[101] All the theaters of war Chrysostom has enumerated, and additional others (houses, cities, fields, desert, antagonism from Greeks, Jews, rulers, subjects, relatives, from the land, the sea, from the emperors) were fireplaces [πάντοθεν τῆς πυρᾶς ἀναπτομένης], he says, and Paul was so courageous that he leapt right into these multiple furnaces [εἰς τοσαύτας καμίνους ἐμπηδῶν]. But in the midst of these copious crucibles, despite assaults from all directions, Paul not only was not overwhelmed, but even led them all to the truth [ἀλλὰ καὶ πάντας αὐτοὺς εἰς τὴν

---

[97] Ἀλλ᾽ ὅμως καὶ διὰ τῶν ἐναντίων ἐκράτει (*laud. Paul.* 4.15 [SC 300.216]; cf. *laud. Paul.* 7.10–12 [SC 300.312–20]).

[98] ποικίλος τις ἦν ὁ πόλεμος οὗτος καὶ παντοδαπός, applying to Paul's "war" the precise same phrase used for apostle himself in *laud. Paul.* 5.4, 6 [SC 300.238, 242], ποικίλος τις ἦν καὶ παντοδαπός, on which see Mitchell, "'A Variable and Many-Sorted Man,'" and the analysis of that oration below in this chapter, pp. 330–53.

[99] *laud. Paul.* 4.16 [SC 300.218–20], quoting Acts 6:13 as though it referred to Paul instead of Stephen; cf. Acts 21:28 (Piédagnel, SC 300.220, n. 1).

[100] The two become completely intertwined in this oration, so that often where there are no explicit subjects or objects it is not possible to differentiate whether John is referring to Paul or the gospel. But this is not a problem for him (and is likely a deliberate ambiguity), as his point is that Paul completely represents the spread of the gospel, and vice versa.

[101] *laud. Paul.* 4.10 [SC 300.206]; cf. 15 [300.216]; for the same theme, see *laud. Paul.* 7.11 [SC 300.316–18].

ἀλήθειαν μετήγαγεν]. And there was yet another battleground even more fierce than all the rest: Paul's bitter disputes with the false apostles and, what grieved him most of all, the corruption that threatened the weak among his congregations (2 Cor 11:29). However, Chrysostom says simply, "he was sufficient to overcome even this." The orientation of this mini-epic of Paul's triumph toward the central thesis of the speech is then punctuated: "from whence and from what sort of power" [Πόθεν καὶ ἐκ ποίας ἰσχύος;] was Paul able to do all this?[102] A quotation from Paul's military self-portrait in 2 Cor 10:4–5 seals the case ("our weapons are not fleshly, but powerful for God's sake …"), and allows John to repeat confidently his shorthand encapsulation of the extraordinary Pauline πράξεις: "he was changing and refashioning everything, all at once" [πάντα μετεβάλλετο, καὶ μετερρυθμίζετο ἀθρόον].[103]

As this lengthy discourse continues, John develops further these images of light and fire, constructing an analogy between Paul's gospel proclamation and a conflagration. Just as when a fire starts, once it ignites the thorns they yield and eventually give way to the flame to such a degree that it clears the fields, thus also, when Paul's tongue spoke and attacked everything more violently than fire [τῆς Παύλου γλώττης φθεγγομένης, καὶ πάντα πυρὸς σφοδρότερον ἐπιούσης][104] all gave way to it – demonic cults, feasts, festivals, ancestral customs, corrupt laws, popular anger, tyrannical threats, plots from his own people, and the malefactions of false apostles. These many foes retreated in the face of the Pauline gospel in the same way that all manner of human malefactors retreat to the shelter of dark caverns when the sun rises and its rays promise to illuminate their misdeeds. "Well, in the same way, once the gospel had appeared and Paul was scattering its seed everywhere, deception was driven off, and the truth returned."[105] In the face of the ascendency of the truth like a sunrise, the many features of pagan religion (smoke of sacrifices, cymbals, drums, drunken bouts, orgies, acts of sexual misconduct and adultery, rites performed in the temples of idols) retreated and were destroyed, like wax before fire and chaff before a flame. Hence Chrysostom's minor premise is proven: "the radiant flame of the truth ascended … raised up by those hindering it, and increased by those obstructing it."[106]

---

[102] laud. Paul. 4.17 [SC 300.220].

[103] laud. Paul. 4.17 [SC 300.220].

[104] Cf. hom. in 2 Cor. 21.3 [61.545]: Καὶ γὰρ ἐφθέγγετο μόνον, καὶ παντὸς πυρὸς σφοδρότερον τοῖς πολεμίοις αἱ ῥήσεις ἐνέπιπτον.

[105] οὕτω δὴ καὶ τότε τοῦ κηρύγματος φανέντος, καὶ τοῦ Παύλου πανταχοῦ τοῦτο διασπείροντος, ἠλαύνετο μὲν ἡ πλάνη, ἐπανῄει δὲ ἡ ἀλήθεια (laud. Paul. 4.18 [SC 300.222]).

[106] ἡ δὲ λαμπρὰ τῆς ἀληθείας φλὸξ ἀνῄει … ὑπ' αὐτῶν τῶν κωλυόντων αἰρομένη, καὶ διὰ τῶν ἐμποδιζόντων αὐξανομένη (laud. Paul. 4.18 [SC 300.222]; see the exact same language in the introduction of the sub-proposition in 4.15 [SC 300.214]: δείξω σοι καὶ διὰ τῶν πολεμούντων αἰρόμενον αὐτὸν καὶ αὐξανόμενον).

An ethnographic slight about contemporary Greeks (as being apt to change heart at the slightest hint of a trivial monetary loss)[107] leads Chrysostom to an even more worthy target of comparison with Paul's achievements. With the off-hand gibe that "modern" Greeks are cheap and despicable, he calls for a σύγκρισις with the marvelous Greeks of old [οἱ θαυμαστοί], the celebrated philosophers [οἱ ἐπὶ φιλοσοφίᾳ βεβοημένοι] – such as Plato, Diagoras, and Anaxagoras of Clazomenae – in order to demonstrate the power of the gospel [τοῦ κηρύγματος ἡ ἰσχύς]. First, as is well-known, among the followers of Socrates some fled to Megara after his death, while the others were deprived of native land and freedom, and had only one convert to their credit, a woman, at that.[108] Zeno of Citium, the father of Stoicism, having left his πολιτεία behind in his writings, met his end (and that was the end of that). John amplifies this comparison even further by returning once again to the encomiastic *topoi* about external advantages that have been so central to this discourse. In the case of the Greek philosophers there was nothing to hinder them: no danger, no lack of rhetorical training [οὐκ ἰδιωτεία], for indeed, they were proficient speakers [ἀλλὰ καὶ δεινοὶ λέγειν ἦσαν], they were rich in possessions [χρημάτων εὐπόρουν], and had the fortune to belong to the native land of Greece that is universally celebrated [τῆς παρὰ πᾶσι βοωμένης πατρίδος ἐτύγχανον ὄντες].[109] But did all these gifts of fate guarantee their success? Not at all, for they had no power at all [ἀλλ' οὐδὲν ἴσχυσαν].[110] The contrasting fates are explained by John with a pair of antithetical maxims: "Such is the case with deception that even when no one troubles it, it falls in ruins; such with the truth that, even when many battle against it, it is promoted."[111] With the lofty example of the Greek philosophers sealing the case, and this pithy formulation celebrating his thesis, John has at last come to the end of his proofs.

ἀνακεφαλαίωσις (Recapitulation).[112] The concluding portion of this oration is quite regular, made up of two parts, an amplified declaration of the successful proof of the thesis, and an exhortation to the audience to emulate this man who

---

[107] This is as compared with the constancy of the Christians, who "all" are massacred and slaughtered (*laud. Paul.* 4.19 [SC 300.224]).

[108] Perhaps this is a reference to the Diotima of the *Symposium* (Piédagnel, SC 300.226, n. 1).

[109] *laud. Paul.* 4.19 [SC 300.226].

[110] The phrase also means, "they had no influence at all," but I have accented the literal sense of ἰσχύειν because of its importance in connection with the major theme of the oration, God's power (see n. 56, above).

[111] Τοιοῦτον γὰρ ἡ πλάνη, καὶ μηδενὸς ἐνοχλοῦντος, καταρρεῖ· τοιοῦτον ἡ ἀλήθεια, καὶ πολλῶν πολεμούντων, διεγείρεται (*laud. Paul.* 4.19 [SC 300.226]).

[112] *laud. Paul.* 4.20 [SC 300.226]. Here I demur from Piédagnel, who takes §18–20 as "Péroraison" in two parts (1. "L'Évangile, feu irrésistable [§18]; 2. "Paul et les philosophes païens" [§19–20]), and then §21 to be "Exhortation finale." The problem with this (in addition to the obvious fact that the peroration he identifies is not at the end of the speech!) is that §18–19 are clearly still arguments in the proof. Nor does §20 fit this narrower topic of "Paul and the pagan philosophers" (it gets mostly left out of his analysis). What we have here (as also in *laud. Paul.* 5, for instance), is a summation of the proof, followed by a corresponding exhortation.

formed its chief proof. To recapitulate this long argument (§20), Chrysostom invokes once again his star witness – the truth of these matters itself [αὐτὴ ἡ τῶν πραγμάτων ἀλήθεια] – whom he had introduced back in 4.10 when he began his extensive proof for the premise that it was divine power that was at work in Paul's ministry.[113] τὰ πράγματα in both cases refers to the astonishing story of the success of Paul's evangelizing mission, in defiance of all expectation based on his "external circumstances." As a synonym for πράξεις, it summarizes the astounding achievements of his career which verify all three of the propositions of this speech: God's call does not subvert human free will, God's power is at work in the gospel, and, Paul (and the gospel) thrived not only despite considerable obstacles, but actually because of them. Because τὰ πράγματα Παύλου themselves proclaim the truth of these premises, Chrysostom exults, "there is no need of speeches, nor words [οὐδὲν δεῖ λόγων, οὐδὲ ῥημάτων], because the world has given voice to it from all directions." This is a clever inversion of the orator's customary rhetorical disclaimer of worthiness to the task, transformed here into a claim that the entire speech his audience has just endured is unnecessary, given that the whole geosphere serves as an indisputable public witness to the truth of his propositions. But how did Paul accomplish all these incredible results? First John introduces the two agents of these wonders in tandem, saying that the marvelous overthrow of the old world order was accomplished "through Paul's tongue, through the grace put into him" [διὰ τῆς Παύλου γλώττης, διὰ τῆς χάριτος τῆς ἐντεθείσης αὐτῷ]. Then he carefully explains the synergistic relationship between these two forces: "For since Paul provided a will to action worthy of the gift [ἀξία τῆς δωρεᾶς προθυμία], grace shined forth profusely [δαψιλὴς ἡ χάρις ἐξέλαμψε], and the mass of achievements we have mentioned here were successfully accomplished through his tongue."[114] By returning to this ethical formula in his conclusion, Chrysostom has come full circle to the opening picture of Paul the converted, who exercised the correct form of choice in reacting to the divine power that revealed itself to him.

ἐπίλογος (Conclusion).[115] Having proven that Paul was "the cause of such wonderful deeds of virtue" [τοσούτων κατορθωμάτων αἴτιος][116] through that magical

---

[113] ὅσην (δύναμιν) αὐτὰ τὰ πράγματα μαρτυρεῖ (*laud. Paul.* 4.10 [SC 300.202]).

[114] *laud. Paul.* 4.20 [SC 300.226].

[115] *laud. Paul.* 4.21 [SC 300.228].

[116] κατορθώματα is another synonym for πράξεις, a Stoic term (see Piédagnel, SC 300.114 n. 2), which was now in quite popular parlance, and taken up widely by Christian writers (see Hunter, *Comparison,* 84. n. 15, who cites the definition preserved in H. F. A. von Arnim, *Stoicorum veterum fragmenta* [Leipzig: Teubner, 1905–24] 3.134, κατορθώματα δ' εἶναι κατ' ἀρετὴν ἐνεργήματα). The word and concept were also incorporated into rhetorical theory (as, e.g., in Theon, *Prog.* 8 [Spengel, 2.112]: μετὰ δὲ ταῦτα τὰς πράξεις καὶ τὰ κατορθώματα παραληψόμεθα οὐκ ἐφεξῆς διηγούμενοι). Plutarch cites Chrysippus' definition of a κατόρθωμα as "something done according to self-control, or careful devotion or forethought or courage" [Τὸ δέ γε κατ' ἐγκράτειαν ἢ καρτερίαν ἢ φρόνησιν ἢ ἀνδρείαν πραττόμενον κατόρθωμά ἐστιν] (*Mor.* 1041A=*SVF* 3.73), with which Chrysostom would agree without hesitation.

and mandatory combination of divine χάρις and human προθυμία, John issues his familiar appeal to imitate[117] the example of virtue who has been lauded in this encomium through detailed examination of his "external circumstances" and the destiny he met which quite exceeded the expectations naturally arising from them. Invoking this other customary rhetorical synonym for πράξεις, κατορθώματα, Chrysostom's sums up his argument: "The mass of achievements we have mentioned here was successfully accomplished through his tongue" [τὰ πλείονα τῶν εἰρημένων διὰ τῆς τούτου κατωρθώθη γλώττης]. Then proleptically John warns the audience, as he often does, not to consider emulation of Paul impossible. In doing so he makes explicit reference to the three-fold plan of encomiastic proof which has been woven into this entire discourse:

For what I have repeatedly said, I shall not stop saying: that the same body [σῶμα] was in him as is in us, the same rearing [τροφαί], and the same soul [ψυχή].[118]

This appeal, in a sense counter-intuitive to encomiastic logic, which is supposed to stress the *uniqueness* of the subject – opens the door to Chrysostom's usual claim for what is truly admirable in Paul. Not body, soul, nor chance circumstances of his progression from infancy to adulthood, but προαίρεσις and προθυμία were what made Paul what he was [καὶ τοῦτο ἐκεῖνον τοιοῦτον ἐποίησε].[119] His free will and desire to do God's work led to deeds which far excelled his innate capacities. And, lest he go too far out on a Pelagian limb, Chrysostom attributes this (as in the previous paragraph) to God's grace [χάρις], given the fact that it was God, after all, who fashioned the Pauline original [καὶ ἐκεῖνον αὐτὸς ἔπλασε], and who likewise created the rest of humanity from the same mold [καὶ σὲ αὐτὸς παρήγαγε]. Because God does not show partiality (Rom 2:11; Acts 10:34),[120] then all can be assured that God wishes to crown them as much as he did Paul, and therefore will extend his grace to them as profusely as he did to Paul.

In this extended discourse, *laud. Paul.* 4, Paul has been depicted in a range of portraits. The initial images of Paul as poor, unskilled, and uneducated are entirely lost from view by the end of the speech, painted over to the point of obliteration by the portrayal of Paul as the agent of the triumph of Christianity, the μονομάχος who utterly vanquished all his enemies. This portrait of Paul is fused with the image of the gospel itself; its triumph over Greco-Roman paganism is his victory, for he was the "cause" [αἴτιος] of that splendid success.[121] And within the *corpus*

---

[117] Here quite emphatically phrased with three synonyms: ζηλώσωμεν, μιμησώμεθα, σπουδάσωμεν γενέσθαι κατ᾽ ἐκεῖνον καὶ ἡμεῖς (4.21 [SC 300.228]).

[118] *laud. Paul.* 4.21 [SC 300.228].

[119] *laud. Paul.* 4.21 [SC 300.228].

[120] *laud. Paul.* 4.21 [SC 300.228].

[121] This is the point obscured by Hubbell's dichotomy: "It is not an encomium on Paul but an apology for Christianity, and a proof of its divine origin, using the greatness of Paul as one of the proofs" ("Chrysostom and Rhetoric," 271). See also below, chap. 6, pp. 270–78 for further discussion of Paul's depiction as the conquerer of paganism.

of Paul himself there is one member which serves as a synecdoche of the whole man and his career; his tongue (as moved by the power of the deity) was the agent of the sensational victory won by the gospel. And all three – Paul, gospel and tongue – are subsumed in the prevailing image of the discourse – fire – the fire that has overcome and utterly transformed the world.[122]

The analysis of these two extended discourses, *hom. in 2 Tim.* 4.3–4 and *laud. Paul.* 4, has demonstrated that Chrysostom employs the encomiastic topics of τὰ ἔξωθεν self-consciously and pointedly to praise his hero, Paul.[123] In the course of these extended arguments various portraits of Paul emerge, usually in pairs of paradoxically contrasting portraits: the uneducated tentmaker/the one who persuaded the whole world to follow the gospel; the unarmed, poor, solitary man/the conquerer of the Empire; the man executed on imperial order/the corpse that now rules Rome. The juxtaposition of the two portraits – images on facing pages of Paul lowly and exalted – confers far more praise on Paul than would the lofty portrait alone, and forces the spectator to contemplate the causality that links the two. Chrysostom the ekphrasist/narrator allows only one possible explanation of the transformation from one image to the other: direct divine intervention.

Partial Portraits of Paul's "External Circumstances"

In the encomia we have treated, as is expected in the form, the various *topoi* under the umbrella of "external circumstances" are clustered and treated together in a roughly biographical frame (even if they do not follow through Paul's entire life in a chronological schema), because that is especially suitable to sustained comparisons. Analysis of those passages allowed us to see how John at times ingeniously played with the material at his disposal to create these amalgamated portraits of the Pauline *curriculum vitae*. But Chrysostom's comments and constructions on these biographical topics were not restricted to such extended encomiastic passages. As one would expect, given his unceasing devotion to Paul and recourse to him as the

---

[122] Associated with fire is of course light, as in the προοίμιον: "Paul's blinding has become the enlightenment [φωτισμός] of the world" (*laud. Paul.* 4.1 [SC 300.182]).

[123] *pace* Piédagnel, SC 300.25: "les panégyriques de Chrysostome ... ne présentent pour ainsi dire aucune trace de tels schémas." Unfortunately this mistake, of willfully denying Chrysostom's ubiquitous use of rhetorical techniques, continues to be reproduced as, most recently, by Philip H. Kern, *Rhetoric and Galatians: Assessing an Approach to Paul's epistle* (SNTSMS 101; Cambridge: Cambridge University Press, 1998) 176–77, depending upon Kennedy, *Greek Rhetoric Under Christian Emperors*, 249, who himself merely repeated the conclusion of Simonetti, "Sulla struttura dei panegirici di S. Giovanni Crisostomo" (see n. 11 above). One hopes that the present analysis will interrupt the chain of repetition of this error, and demonstrate its genealogical weakness, and the proper remedy: a less mechanistic set of expectations for rhetorical design which allows one to see the pervasive influence and play on the form of encomium at work here, without which one does not sufficiently comprehend these arguments, either as Pauline portraits or as persuasive vehicles for Chrysostom's own goals in his pastoral ministry.

archetype to be emulated, depictions of Paul's nationality, ancestry, rearing, training, education, trade, deeds, and death are found throughout his corpus of writings.
This is due also to his mode of treatment of the biblical passages in the letters and
Acts, on a passage by passage basis, which puts him face-to-face with individual
events and utterances directly concerning all these topics. Since we have
demonstrated from the encomia that John is well aware of the place of these *topoi*
in the full encomiastic project (as we should expect, both because of his own
rhetorical training, and because in his scriptures Chrysostom finds the schema used
already in the self-representation of Paul himself in Acts 21:39–22:21),[124] we can
readily recognize each treatment of one of these topics, in whatever literary
context, as a fragmentary portrait of Paul that fits within a wider biographic framework. Our task here is to provide a survey of some of the customary features of each
of these snapshots of the Pauline career that Chrysostom draws upon in his oratory.[125] Our inventory will be arranged according to the largely chronological, biographical order of epideictic speeches in praise of persons, following the traditional
set of topics as laid out by Chrysostom's contemporary, and possibly schoolmate,
Aphthonios.[126] We shall treat in order Chrysostom's remarks on Paul's ancestry
[γένος], including the somewhat thorny issue (for Chrysostom) of his Jewishness; his
rearing and education [ἀνατροφή, παιδεία], with particular attention to the
question of proficiencies in both Jewish learning and Greco-Roman rhetorical arts;
and then a collection of topics under the umbrella category of "deeds" [πράξεις].
The latter category is the largest κεφάλαιον, which includes actions in both Paul's
pre-Christian life, such as persecuting Christians and undergoing conversion, and
his later Christian life, encompassing world-wide victory, rhetorical prowess, miracles, prophetic powers, ecstatic experiences, sufferings, and ascetic discipline. We
shall also have occasion to examine how Chrysostom deals with the question of

---

[124] The order of topics is ἔθνος, πόλις, ἀνατροφή, παιδεία, νόμος, πράξεις (the formulaic
nature of which was articulated already by W. C. van Unnik, *Tarsus or Jerusalem: The City of Paul's
Youth* [London: Epworth, 1962] 17–45). Indeed, Chrysostom refers to these verses as Paul's "great
encomia about himself" [μεγάλα περὶ αὐτοῦ ἐγκώμια εἶπε] (*hom. in Ac.* 47.1 [60.328]). John's
own easy association of these epideictic topics with one another is seen, for instance, in his
excoriation of the "celebrity hounds" of his day who can recount in an instant all the significant
social data of their favorite actors and dancing girls: καὶ γένος αὐτῶν, καὶ πατρίδα, καὶ
ἀνατροφὴν, καὶ τὰ ἄλλα πάντα καταλέγοντες (*hom. in Rom. 16:3* 1 [51.188]), and his expressed
appreciation of the uniqueness of the prologue to the Fourth Gospel, for the evangelist did *not*
proceed with the expected topics of γένος, πατρίς and ἀνατροφή (*hom. in Jo.* 2.1 [59.29]). As we
have noted, John himself refers appropriately to the three categories τὰ περὶ ψυχήν, τὰ περὶ
σῶμα, τὰ ἐκτός in *hom. in 1 Tim.* 1.1 [62.505] (see n. 13 above, for further references).
[125] Of course, an exhaustive investigation of each of these topics would require a book in itself,
but here we shall give representative examples of the material and its most typical treatments, as
a spur to further in-depth investigations.
[126] Aphth. *Prog.* 8 [Spengel 2.36]; Burgess, *Epideictic Literature*, 129. The chronological, geographical, and even personal proximity of Aphthonios to Chrysostom gives us a rare and secure
assurance of the relevance of his theoretical work to Chrysostom's actual choices in oratorial
practice.

whether Paul left behind a record of consistency in deeds, or was an impossibly variable man. Then we shall investigate a few topical categories from Theon's list of τὰ ἔξωθεν, "external circumstances" which serve to dissect further and specify particular elements of the encomiastic subject's biography: friendship, glory/reputation, rule, wealth, children, and noble death. In assembling Chrysostom's fragmentary portraits of Paul's biography we are in a sense replicating Chrysostom's own rhetorical strategy in the body portraits: from mosaic bits of corporate members composing a holistic image of the subject. Where our approach differs from that of the rhetorical artist Chrysostom is in our self-conscious attention to the ways in which the amalgamated portrait thus produced is disharmonious or uneven, in that some of the images cohere only with great difficulty with one another. Such cases are especially intriguing, and in their very tensions provide valuable evidence of the functions to which John puts these portraits he composes of his beloved saint against assorted backdrops and in varied poses. Furthermore, the goal of the present analysis is not primarily to compose a new Pauline portrait (though in essence we shall do so), but to analyze these oratorical products with attention to their literary structure and logic, and to the proximate rhetorical constraints on each of Chrysostom's fragmentary portraits of Paul. From this template of epideictic topics we shall see John's biographical images of Paul emerge.

γένος (Ancestry)

Under the category γένος, "descent," Aphthonios lists four sub-categories: ἔθνος, πατρίς, πρόγονοι, and πατέρες.[127] He gives no definitions for these categories, among which there is considerable overlap, both conceptually and in rhetorical practice. But nonetheless we shall arrange Chrysostom's material on this skeleton to provide as orderly a treatment as possible, and shape a biographical portrait ourselves out of John's fragments, paying particular attention to the rhetorical purposes for which Chrysostom drew these sketches of the apostle.

ἔθνος (Race/Nation)

Chrysostom recognizes Paul's Jewish roots (as Acts and the letters affirm), but that fact occasionally sends him into some rhetorical contortions, especially given his own (infamous) anti-Judaistic views, to which at times he gave free and virulent rhetorical expression.[128] He often refers to the Jews with vituperative epithets common in ψόγοι, speeches of blame,[129] such as "wretched and miserable" [ἄθλιοι

---

[127] Aphth. *Prog.* 8 [Spengel, 2.36].

[128] See the classic study of Wilken, *John Chrysostom and the Jews*, 116–27.

[129] The sibling rhetorical form to the encomium, in which all the same topics are used in opposite fashion.

καὶ ταλαίπωροι] or "ignorant and stupid" [ἀγνώμονες καὶ ἀναίσθητοι],[130] and, along with those denigrations, propagates insults of a particularly Christian cast, such as "the killers of Christ."[131] These negative characterizations of Jews and Judaism are also at work in Chrysostom's homilies on the Pauline epistles as, for instance, in his interpretation of 1 Tim 1:8–10, which he regards as teaching that the Torah was given to the Jews because they were "murderers, patricides and matricides, impious, unholy, and godless," offering as corroborating evidence the attempted stoning of Moses and the prophetic denunciations of the people Israel.[132] But this was Paul's ἔθνος, was it not?

In dealing with Paul's ἔθνος, on the one hand, when looking at the rhetoric of Phil 3:2–6, Chrysostom calls attention to Paul's Jewishness as a crucial facet of the argument the apostle makes for differentiating spiritual circumcision from the fleshly mutilation which goes by that name:

> For if, as a Gentile [ἐξ ἐθνῶν ὤν], he were condemning circumcision … it would appear that he was running it down because he himself lacked the noble birthright of Judaism [ὡς ἀπεστερημένος τῆς τοῦ Ἰουδαϊσμοῦ εὐγενείας], because he didn't know the holy rites [οὐκ εἰδὼς τὰ σεμνά], nor share in them [οὐδὲ μετεσχηκὼς αὐτῶν]. But, now, the one who shares in those rites *and* condemns them [ὁ μετασχὼν καὶ κατηγορῶν], does not do so because he doesn't have a share in them, but because he has formed a judgment, not from ignorance, but especially from keen insight [ἀλλ' ὡς κατεγνωκώς, οὐ δι' ἄγνοιαν, ἀλλὰ δι' ἐπίγνωσιν μάλιστα].[133]

Here John apparently assumes Paul's rightful share in the εὐγένεια of Israel, though it is perhaps noteworthy that he prefers the circumlocution about "sharing in the holy rites" to saying outright that Paul was a Jew. Likewise, in reading Paul's forthright declaration of ethnic identity in 2 Cor 11:22,[134] which begins with the proclamation of his claim to the designation "Hebrew," followed by "Israelite," John champions this as an indication of Paul's εὐγένεια, since Ammonites and Moabites are Hebrews, too, but not of the more prestigious branch, the Israelites.[135] At least through this comparative lens Chrysostom can regard Paul's γένος as being noble. This is even more the case when he turns to Phil 3:4–6, the passage in which Paul lays out his own Jewish pedigree with extended detail under the introductory claim

---

[130] *hom. in Gen.* 39.5 [53.367].

[131] See Wilken, *John Chrysostom and the Jews*, 121–27 (including references in *adversus Judaeos*), who identifies this combination of conventional and uniquely Christian invective in John's discourses on Jews and Judaizers.

[132] *hom. in 1 Tim.* 2.2 [62.512].

[133] *hom. in Phil.* 10.2 [62.257–58]. See also *Jud.* 2.2; 3.3 [48.838–39, 864]: μὴ γὰρ ἐξ' ἐθνῶν ἦλθον;

[134] A passage which Chrysostom regards as Paul's encomium to himself [τὰ οἰκεῖα ἐγκώμια], thus confirming his sense of these as traditional topics (*hom. in 2 Cor. 11:1* 5 [51.305]; *hom. in Gen.* 11.5 [53.96]).

[135] *hom. in 2 Cor.* 25.1 [61.569]. But times have changed from the Ancient Near Eastern context upon which this national pecking order was based; hence this is not his typical view, as we shall see below.

that he will show himself to be superior to his opposition [ἐγὼ μᾶλλον].[136] In assessing each of the five elements of γένος that follow in Paul's self-description, John employs the terminology of epideictic theory, as he differentiates the first four categories (circumcision, nation, tribe, ancestors) from the last (being a Pharisee), on the grounds that the former are ἀπροαίρετα, "matters of birth, not choice," whereas being a Pharisee was a conscious choice of the adult Paul [ἔρχεται λοιπὸν εἰς τὰ τῆς αὐτοῦ προαιρέσεως]. The first four criteria all demonstrate that Paul was from select, superior stock. His circumcision on the eighth day and his being ἐκ γένους Ἰσραὴλ both demonstrate that he was not a proselyte, nor descended from proselytes. Membership in the tribe of Benjamin shows that Paul was from the most esteemed group [ὥστε τοῦ δοκιμωτέρου μέρους], not one of the run of the mill eleven, but a member of the tribe whose lot was the priestly service [τὰ γὰρ τῶν ἱερέων ἐν τῷ κλήρῳ ταύτης ἦν τῆς φυλῆς]. Being a "Hebrew of Hebrews" again documents Paul's εὐγένεια, as a descendent, from far back, of distinguished Jews [ἄνωθεν τῶν εὐδοκίμων Ἰουδαίων], thus setting him apart from newcomers, and perhaps those who couldn't speak the Hebrew language because they mixed so much with Gentiles. Consequently, even though many Jews had these qualifications, Paul is proved to be eminent among them, given that "in not being a proselyte, and in being from the most distinguished tribe, and from an ancestral line going far back" he had a pedigree that few could claim [ἅπερ οὐ πολλοὶ εἶχον]. But even though Paul deserved praise for these "givens" of life, in John's eyes and catechetical program he was due even more praise for the deeds of his choice, especially his zealous life as a Pharisee, something dependent not upon divine gift, but human initiative and zeal.[137] Hence Paul is shown to have been superior on all counts, not only εὐγένεια, but also προθυμία, τρόπος and βίος. With this list of *topoi* Chrysostom completes the encomiastic package, in order to paint his pre-Christian Paul as a man of total accomplishment. But once again the portrait is painted to serve another rhetorical function (as was also the case in its source, Paul's argument in Philippians 3): to demonstrate the overwhelming superiority of the life in Christ which led Paul to reject and overturn all those earlier forms of worldly attainment.[138] In this portrait Paul's Jewish γένος is laid out resplendently, listing τὰ σεμνά, its multiple distinguishing marks. But these are all facets of the life Paul left behind; hence Paul's Jewish εὐγένεια serves for Chrysostom to make him a more valuable witness *against* the Jewish faith.

---

[136] *hom. in Phil.* 10.2 [62.257–58].

[137] For "it is possible to be a Pharisee and not to be fervently a zealot" [ἔστι γὰρ καὶ Φαρισαῖον εἶναι, καὶ μὴ σφόδρα ζηλωτήν] (*hom. in Phil.* 10.2 [62.258]).

[138] *hom. in Phil.* 10.2 [62.258]: "If indeed due to noble birth, fervent desire, manners, and form of living he was superior to all, then for what reason did he give up those grand things, he says, except that he found that the things pertaining to Christ were better, and indeed so much better" [Εἰ τοίνυν καὶ εὐγενείας ἕνεκεν, καὶ προθυμίας, καὶ τρόπου, καὶ βίου πάντων ἐκράτουν, τίνος ἕνεκεν τὰ σεμνὰ ἐκεῖνα εἴασα, φησίν, ἀλλ' ἢ διὰ τὸ μείζονα εὑρεῖν τὰ τοῦ Χριστοῦ, καὶ πολλῷ μείζονα;].

Yet despite this conspicuous example highlighting Paul's Jewish γένος, John does not always unambiguously represent Paul as a Jew. A crucial moment in his delineation of Paul's ethnic identity comes when Chrysostom reads the opening of Paul's speech in Acts 21:39: ἐγὼ ἄνθρωπος μέν εἰμι Ἰουδαῖος, at which point the fourth-century Christian orator experiences dissonance with the ethnic labels of his own historical context:

He says, "I am a Jew." By saying this he leads the chiliarch away from this suspicion [that he was "the Egyptian"] (Acts 21:37–38). And yet, so that you might not think that he was a Jew with respect to his people [ἔθνος], he is speaking with respect to religion [θρησκεία].[139] For elsewhere even he calls himself "one in the law of Christ" (1 Cor 9:21). What is this? Does Paul lie? Perish the thought! What then, was he not denying it? No way. For he was a Jew and a Christian [Ἰουδαῖος γὰρ ἦν καὶ Χριστιανός],[140] observing the things which were necessary [ὅσα ἔδει φυλάττων]; since he himself was obedient to the law more than all, while believing in Christ [ἐπεὶ καὶ τῷ νόμῳ μάλιστα πάντων αὐτὸς ἐπείθετο, τῷ Χριστῷ πιστεύων] ....[141]

Chrysostom deals with his difficulty in imagining Paul as a member of a different ἔθνος from himself by bifurcating the apostle's γένος, thereby separating national from religious allegiance.[142] By reference to this firm but nonetheless vague distinction, Paul was not a Jew in terms of ἔθνος, "people" or "nation." But, on the other hand, in terms of cultic practice [θρησκεία] – and that alone – he can be called a Jew (or, what is more to John's point, he can call himself a Jew without prevarication),[143] because he was observant of the Law. All of this clears the way for the designation of Paul's *true* γένος, as Χριστιανός. Furthermore, John argues, Paul's bold self-appellations as a Jew can be explained contextually and rhetorically.

---

[139] I.e., "cultic observance." The full text reads: Εἶτα ἵνα μὴ νομισθῇ τὸ ἔθνος Ἰουδαῖος, λέγει τὴν θρησκείαν.

[140] Contemporary scholars continue to debate Paul's identity, and the terminology and consistency with which he expressed it in the letters, as well as the contemporary labels by which we should try to explain that identity (complexified by the knowledge – not apparently recognized by John – that Paul himself did not have access to the term Χριστιανός). See most recently on the topic James D. G. Dunn, "Paul: Apostate or Apostle of Israel?" *ZNW* 89 (1998) 256–71.

[141] *hom in Ac.* 47.1 [60.325–26].

[142] Interestingly, this is the same position some contemporary scholars take on Paul and the law: that Paul wanted to maintain its "religious" but not "nationalistic," "ethnic" or "racial" aspects (James D. G. Dunn, *Jesus, Paul, and the Law: Studies in Mark and Galatians* [Louisville: Westminster/John Knox, 1990] 183–264; Frank Thielman, *From Plight to Solution: A Jewish Framework for Understanding Paul's View of the Law in Galatians and Romans* [NovTSup 61; Leiden: Brill, 1989], especially his claim that what Paul rejected was not the law itself, but "the particularly Jewish aspects of the law" [pp. 119–2-]). However, when it comes to Paul the person, most contemporary scholars, including Dunn and Thielman, would reverse Chrysostom's dichotomy to say Paul *was* a Jew with respect to ἔθνος, but *not* in terms of θρησκεία (because of his opposition to circumcision and food laws). A major source of this divergence is the fact that contemporary scholars do not feel constrained to account for the Pauline actions of Acts 16:3; 21:26, as Chrysostom did.

[143] The Greek philosopher who calumniated Christianity pointed to Acts 22:25, 27 and 22:3 as evidence that Paul was a liar: ὁ γὰρ ὑποκρινόμενος καὶ λέγων ὅπερ οὐκ ἦν (Macarius Magnes,

Paul called himself a Jew to the chiliarch to protect himself against being mistaken for the Egyptian insurgent, just as he used the term for himself again in the following speech to the assembled Jews (Acts 22:3) because he wished to accent his commonality with that audience by saying "what they desire to hear above all else" [ὃ μάλιστα πάντων ἐπόθουν ἀκοῦσαι], and making sure that, when they hear that he was born in Tarsus of Cilicia, they not suppose that he belonged to "another people" [ἵνα μὴ πάλιν νομίσωσι τὸ ἔθνος ἄλλο].[144]

This somewhat hairsplitting reasoning around Paul's Jewishness is not Chrysostom's only approach to the issue. In another context John flatly denied that Paul, after his conversion, was a Jew:

Not only did he circumcize Timothy, but also he shaved himself and offered sacrifice (Acts 18:18; 21:24), but doubtless for this reason we do not say he is a Jew [καὶ οὐ δήπου διὰ τοῦτο αὐτὸν Ἰουδαῖόν φαμεν εἶναι], but for this very reason even more do we consider him to be removed from Judaism [ἀπηλλάχθαι Ἰουδαϊσμοῦ], and cleansed, and a genuine worshipper of Christ [γνήσιος τοῦ Χριστοῦ θεραπευτής].[145]

The assertion that Paul was not a Jew appears so obvious to John that he can even cite the counter evidence to it without embarrassment, as though it corroborated his reading. Furthermore, the impression that Paul was completely estranged from Judaism is sealed completely in Chrysostom's fascination with Rom 9:3, where Paul says "I could wish to be anathema from Christ for the sake of my brothers, my relatives according to the flesh" [ὑπὲρ τῶν ἀδελφῶν μου τῶν συγγενῶν μου κατὰ σάρκα]. John returns again and again to this verse as the example of the highest self-sacrifice imaginable, in that Paul was willing to forego the love of his Lord, and the eschatological salvation which he (if anyone did) richly deserved, for the sake of the Jews, *his enemies*.[146]

Chrysostom assumes at a deep level that Paul could not *really* be a Jew, because he projects back onto Paul the social and religious labels of his own day, which

---

apocrit. 3.31 [Harnack, TU 37/4, p. 60]). His summary judgment is that Paul was ψεύστης οὖν καὶ τοῦ ψεύδους ἐκ τοῦ φανεροῦ σύντροφος.

[144] *hom. in Ac.* 47.1 [60.327]; the passage continues: "he brought in his religion" [τὴν θρησκείαν ἐπήγαγεν]."

[145] *hom. in Rom.* 16.1 [60.549]. In the next line John repeats the thought by calling Paul ἀλλότριος Ἰουδαϊσμοῦ, "estranged from Judaism."

[146] Of many passages see, e.g, *hom. in Eph.* 7.4 [62.54–56]; *laud. Paul.* 3.2–3; 5.3, where John applies to Jews Luke's description of the pre-Christian Paul, that "breathing murder, they desire to taste Paul's blood" [SC 300.164–68, 236]; *hom. in Ac.* 43.3 [60.306], *oppugn.* 1.4 [47.325]; but compare also *hom. in Rom.* 17.1 [60.563–64], where John insists that in Rom 10:1 Paul addresses the Jews "not from an intention marked by enmity" [οὐκ ἀπὸ διανοίας ἐχθρᾶς] but in "goodwill" [εὔνοια]. On this important question see the material collected by Piédagnel in his appendix, "Le problème du salut des Juifs" [SC 300.330–334, and p. 133 n. 2] who works hard to minimize John's negative views of Jews by trying to harmonize the different utterances. But since John was not consistent or systematic in his utterances on the Jews, one cannot completely temper his negative views by just counter-balancing them with the more positive statements, or use them to cancel out the impact of the former.

John himself vehemently and notoriously defended against boundary blurring of any kind, in a context where Christians in Antioch were manifestly attracted to the synagogue and Jewish festivals.[147] Because he regards Paul's γένος as manifestly Christian, the law of contradictions would seem to require logically that he not be anything else at the same time (though as we have noted, in one instance Chrysostom does say that Paul was a Jew *and* a Christian). John is of course aware, from thousands of pastoral experiences, that individual Christians partake of a whole set of overlapping social designations, but his catechetical and rhetorical project as preacher is to subsume all these to the identity of being a Christian. A most telling passage in this regard is found in his panegyric to the martyr Lucian, in which he recounts a legend about the saint's trial, and then gives his own interpretation of it.

Lucian [at his trial], answered each inquiry by saying only, "I am a Christian." And when the judge said: "of what fatherland [πατρίς] are you?" he said, "I am a Christian." "What vocation" [ἐπιτήδευμα]? "I am a Christian." "Who were your ancestors" [πρόγονοι]? "I am a Christian." ... For the one who says, "I am a Christian," makes clear everything – fatherland, nation, and trade [πατρὶς, καὶ γένος, καὶ ἐπιτήδευμα, καὶ πάντα δηλοῦν]. I

---

[147] This is the purpose of the famous discourses against Jews and Judaizing Christians (see Wilken, *John Chrysostom and the Jews*, 66–94, 116–27). Significantly (and not surprisingly), Paul is the major authority against Jewish practices whom Chrysostom draws upon repeatedly throughout these discourses. He stresses that one need only listen to Paul's words to fall back into the net of true Christian salvation (*Jud.* 2.1 [48.857–58]), and urges his audience to repeat Paul's words to one another to keep them from straying toward synagogal observances (2.3 [48.862]). But Paul functions here as even more than an external authority against Jews and Judaizing; he is an authorial agent of these discourses, as John invokes him: "I do not pronounce the curse on them, but Paul does, or rather, not even Paul, but Christ who speaks through him" [τούτους οὐκ ἐγὼ ἀνεθεμάτισα, ἀλλὰ Παῦλος· μᾶλλον δὲ οὐδὲ Παῦλος, ἀλλ' ὁ Χριστὸς, ὁ δι' ἐκείνου λαλῶν]. Paul is also the one, John stipulates, who *commands* the kind of severe treatment Chrysostom gives to Jews and Christian Judaizers, according to Titus 1:13 (2.3 [48.862]). Chrysostom regards his discourses against Judaizers as fulfilling Paul's mission, as may be seen concretely in the pronouncement he makes of his own oratorical victory, cast in Pauline terms taken from 2 Cor 10:4–5 (*Jud.* 6.1 [48.903]; see also 3.3 [48.864], Καὶ ὅπερ ὁ Παῦλος πρὸς Γαλάτας ἔλεγε, τοῦτο καὶ ἐγὼ ὑμῖν λέγω, then quoting Gal 4:12). In this way Paul is presented as the unambiguous foe of the Jews, even as Chrysostom, who claims the inspiration of his spirit, is their declared enemy. The fascinating role of Paul in the discourses *adversus Judaeos* deserves a separate investigation, including the ways in which here especially Chrysostom manages the relative authoritative weight between Paul and Jesus, and their attitudes toward Law observance. For instance, Chrysostom attempts throughout to harmonize Jesus and Paul, and when he cannot do so easily, frequently repeats that Paul's words are really those of Christ, who spoke through him. Thus, while Jesus in Mt 15:26 referred to the Gentiles as "dogs," later on the order was reversed [ἀντεστράφη μετὰ ταῦτα ἡ τάξις] in Phil 3:2, where Paul clarified that the Jews are the dogs (1.2 [48.845]). To cite another example, John acknowledges that Jesus did eat the Passover meal, but only as a prefiguration of what was to come, and insists he did not command his followers to do likewise. Then he invokes Paul's injunction against keeping feasts in Gal 4:10 as bearing the authority of Christ himself (hence even where they differ they do not, for Paul functions as a kind of "second Jesus"). These are just some issues which should be addressed in an investigation of the role of Paul in these discourses. For the purpose of the present argument, these examples suffice to demonstrate that Chrysostom understands Paul as the oratorical adversary of Jews and Judaizers *par excellence*, whose person and voice he seeks to emulate.

shall explain how this is the case. For the Christian does not have a city [πόλις] upon the earth, but the Jerusalem above (quotes Gal 4:26) ... The Christian does not have an earthly vocation [γήϊνον ἐπιτήδευμα], but acts for the commonwealth above [ἡ ἄνω πολιτεία] (Phil 3:20) .. the Christian has the saints as relatives and fellow citizens [συγγενεῖς καὶ συμπολῖται] (Eph 2:19) ... Therefore in one word Lucian accurately indicated who he was, from where, of whom, and what work he customarily performed ["Ωστε ἐνὶ ῥήματι, καὶ τίς εἴη, καὶ πόθεν, καὶ τίνων, καὶ τί πράττων διατελοίη, μετὰ ἀκριβείας ἐδίδαξε].[148]

This idealistic picture mounts a putatively wholesale corrective to the social structure of late antiquity by replacing all forms of ethnic and group identification with the single patrimony, Christian. But we are dealing with a legend which dares to imagine an overturned social order through the enthusiastic vision of a single martyr. Taken literally this passage would seem to vitiate entirely the customary employment of encomiastic topoi of external circumstance, but John of course still uses them, abundantly, in other rhetorical contexts when suitable, even as they define the very logic of the critical Christian commonplace he echoes here.[149]

πατρίς (Native Land)

Despite the claim on Paul's lips in Acts 21:39 that he was a citizen of Tarsus, "no undistinguished city" [οὐκ ἀσήμου πόλεως πολίτης], Chrysostom never grants him notoriety for this. In fact, Chrysostom on no occasion refers to him as ὁ Ταρσεύς, or Παῦλος ἀπὸ Ταρσοῦ,[150] though he acknowledges the city to be Paul's οἰκεῖα πατρίς.[151] A clue to the motivation for Chrysostom's lack of praise for Paul's native city is found in his commentary on Acts 11:25–26, where Barnabas goes to Tarsus, finds Paul, and takes him to Antioch. The reason for this decision (which is the work of the Spirit) is that Antioch is a greater city than Tarsus, with a larger population.[152] Hence, Chrysostom likely did not praise Paul for his Tarsan

---

[148] pan. Lucn. 3 [50.524–25]. This recreation of a trial scene is a longstanding topos in early Christian martyrological texts (see, e.g., the trial of Sanctus, as told in the letter of the churches of Vienne and Lyons, apud Eusebius, h.e. 5.1.20).

[149] Simonetti, "Sulla struttura dei panegirici," 167–68, cites this passage as though a wholesale repudiation of epideictic rhetoric on John's part, but he does not sufficiently appreciate the irony at work in this self-conscious employment of the rhetorical topoi about γένος.

[150] The pseudo-Chrysostomic work Petr. et Paul. stands out in this regard, calling him ὁ μακάριος Παῦλος ἀπὸ Ταρσοῦ τῆς Κιλικίας, who is now entombed at Rome (2 [59.495]). Menander Rhetor recommends that if the subject of one's praise came from a home city that was not distinguished, the orator should pass over the topic quickly (2.370 [Russell-Wilson, 78]; Delehaye, Les passions des martyrs, 143–47, with patristic examples).

[151] For this reason, Chrysostom infers, it was a relatively safe place for Paul to preach soon after his call (as in Acts 9:30; see hom. in Ac. 21.1 [60.164]). There is no evidence that Chrysostom was acquainted with the tradition, attested in his contemporary Jerome, that Paul's family was from Gischala in Galilee (comm. in ep. ad Philem. vv. 23–24 [PL 26.617]; vir. ill. 129 [PL 23.754]; see the discussion and evaluation of this tradition in Jerome Murphy-O'Connor, Paul: A Critical Life [Oxford: Oxford University Press, 1997] 36–39).

[152] μείζων ἡ πόλις, καὶ πολὺ τὸ πλῆθος (hom. in Ac. 25.2 [60.194]).

πατρίς because from his Antiochene perspective he did not consider it an esteemed city (nor did he expect his Antiochene or Constantinopolitan audiences to think so, either). The same is true to an even higher degree for the entire province of Cilicia, which John treats as a hillbilly backwater (we noted above in the comparison between Paul and Nero that Cilicia versus Rome was presented as a laughable contest).[153] In one passage where Chrysostom is customarily undermining the earthly values of "wealth, illustrious hopes and proud names," he draws in the apostle as his counter-example by invoking that gentilic[154] in the the context of other negative images: "let's bring into the middle here the one who has said these words, the tentmaker, the Cilician, the one whose father is not even known."[155]

Another factor at work in Chrysostom's inattention to and denigration of Paul's historical homeland in Cilicia is likely Chrysostom's lofty evaluation of Paul's ascetic heights, which renders Paul an οὐρανοπολίτης,[156] one who demonstrated the ἀγγελικὴ πολιτεία.[157] Taking his departure from the apostle's own words in Phil 3:20, John maintains that Paul's "commonwealth" was in heaven.[158] As such, Paul's earthly πατρίς is hardly worth comment – except when rhetorically useful – to present the lowly origins of the one who was later to earn great fame, an incorporation of a commonplace of the epideictic genre.[159]

---

[153] *hom. in 2 Tim.* 4.3 [62.622]: Κίλιξ ὁ ἄνθρωπος ἦν· ὅσον δὲ Κιλικίας καὶ Ῥώμης τὸ μέσον, πάντες ἴσασι. See also *pan. Bab.* 2 18 [SC 362.114].

[154] See also the reference to Cilicia as the province of origin of the martyr Julian, in the panegyric in his honor, immediately after a customary denigration of the insignificance and impermanence of earthly honors and miseries: "Then the nation of the Cilicians produced this saint, the same which also produced Paul. For he was a fellow citizen of Paul, and both were put forward as ministers of the church for us from there" ['Ήνεγκε μὲν οὖν τὸν ἅγιον τοῦτον τὸ τῶν Κιλίκων ἔθνος, ὃ καὶ τὸν Παῦλον ἤνεγκε· συμπολίτης γὰρ ἦν ἐκείνου, καὶ ἀμφότεροι ὑπουργοὶ τῆς ἐκκλησίας ἐκεῖθεν ἡμῖν προεβλήθησαν] (*pan. Juln.* 2 [50.668]). In this passage Paul functions as the city's claim to fame, to add prestige to Julian which his origin would otherwise surely not confer. In other words, Cilicia is honored by Paul, but not Paul by association with it.

[155] αὐτὸν τὸν ταῦτα εἰρηκότα, τὸν σκηνοποιόν, τὸν Κιλίκα, τὸν οὐδὲ τίνος ἦν πατρὸς δῆλον, παραγάγωμεν εἰς μέσον (*hom. in 1 Cor.* 15.5 [61.128]). This is followed by the same rhetorical question operative in *laud. Paul* 4 (analyzed above in this chapter): Καὶ πῶς δυνατὸν ... γενέσθαι τοιοῦτον; Paul's renunciatory form of life, testified to by his own words (such as 2 Cor 11:27; 6:10) shows the way. The full reversal claims Paul's voice to be unsurpassed in σεμνότης, μακαριότης and εὐπορία (15.6 [61.128]).

[156] *poenit.* 2.5 [49.290]. I have discussed these and the following passages above, in chap. 3, pp. 78–80.

[157] *exp. in Ps.* 110.4 [55.284]. See below, n. 511 on this as an epithet of the monastic life.

[158] *hom. in Col.* 10.3 [62.370]: ἐν οὐρανῷ πολιτεύεται.

[159] Chrysostom's argument bears some resemblance to Menander Rhetor's advice on imperial λόγοι: "If [his family] is humble or without prestige [ἐὰν δὲ ἄδοξον ᾖ ἢ εὐτελές], omit it likewise, and start with the emperor himself ... Alternatively, you can say something about the family on these lines [ἢ ἄλλως τοιαῦτα ἄττα περὶ τοῦ γένους ἐρεῖς]: ... 'Many seem to be of human stock, but in truth are sent down from God, and are verily an emanation of the higher power [πολλοὶ τῷ μὲν δοκεῖν ἐξ ἀνθρώπων εἰσί, τῇ δ' ἀληθείᾳ παρὰ τοῦ θεοῦ καταπέμπονται καί εἰσιν ἀπόρροιαι ὄντως τοῦ κρείττονος]. Heracles was believed to be the son of Amphitryon, but in reality he was the son of Zeus. So our emperor is by repute of human origin, but in reality

πρόγονοι (Ancestors)

The operative biblical passage on Pauline ancestry is Phil 3:5, where Paul calls himself "a Hebrew born of Hebrews."[160] Chrysostom recognizes the implication inherent in the assertion:"for those who are this from their ancestors and beyond [οἱ ἐκ προγόνων καὶ ἄνωθεν τοῦτο ὄντες] have something more [τι πλέον] than those who are [mere] proselytes."[161] Paul's claim to this status in Acts 23:6 [ἐγὼ Φαρισαῖός εἰμι, υἱὸς Φαρισαίων] is completely well founded, in John's eyes: "nor does he lie here in saying he was a Pharisee, for he was a Pharisee from his ancestors" [ἐκ προγόνων].[162] As such, Paul comes from "distinguished Jewish ancestors" [ἄνωθεν τῶν εὐδοκίμων Ἰουδαίων].[163] But this claim is contravened by a different rhetorical purpose in laud. Paul. 4, where Chrysostom forthrightly declared that Paul's ancestors were not distinguished [Οὐκ ἀπὸ προγόνων ἐπίσημος], as is quite clear from his tentmaking trade, which Chrysostom assumes Paul inherited from his family.[164] The ambivalence Chrysostom has about the esteem of Paul's pedigree is due both to the varied persuasive purposes for which he invokes Paul, and to the reevaluation he thought the category had undergone at the apostle's hands: "Paul considered the greatest family tree to be the godly one" [συγγένειαν μεγίστην τὴν κατὰ θεὸν εἶναι νομίζων].[165] Paul's vision was for a new type of εὐγένεια, "the noble birthright of faith" [ἡ τῆς πίστεως εὐγένεια], in which "there is no barbarian, no Greek, no stranger, no citizen, but all rise up into a single preeminence of rank."[166]

πατέρες (Parentage)

Chrysostom draws a simple and conventional conclusion from the lack of any tradition preserving the name of Paul's father – that he was not illustrious – for if

---

he has his begetting from heaven [οὕτω καὶ βασιλεὺς ὁ ἡμέτερος τῷ μὲν δοκεῖν ἐξ ἀνθρώπων, τῇ δ' ἀληθείᾳ τὴν καταβολὴν οὐρανόθεν ἔχει]; for he would not have won such a prize and such honour, except in virtue of being superior to those of this world'" [οὐ γὰρ ἂν τοσούτου κτήματος καὶ τοσαύτης ἀξίας ἔτυχε, μὴ οὐχὶ ὡς κρείττων γεγονὼς τῶν τῇδε] (2.370 [text and trans. Russell-Wilson, 80–81]; compare the succinct restatement of this advice a few lines later: ὥσπερ ἐπὶ τοῦ γένους εἰρήκαμεν ὅτι, ἐὰν μὴ ὑπάρχῃ τοῦτο ἔνδοξον, ἐρεῖς αὐτὸν ἐκ θεῶν γενέσθαι).

[160] Neither that passage nor 2 Cor 11:22 is a favorite of Chrysostom's, appearing mostly where he encounters it in its literary context (the Philippians passage a mere three times in his vast corpus of writings, the 2 Corinthians four, according to Robert A. Krupp, St. John Chrysostom: A Scripture Index [Lanham: University Press of America, 1984], though I should note that I have not always found this index to be complete).

[161] exp. in Ps. 115.5 [55.326]; he expresses the same sentiment in hom. in Phil. 10.2 [62.258].

[162] hom. in Ac. 49.1 [60.337].

[163] hom. in Phil. 10.2 [62.258].

[164] laud. Paul. 4.10 [SC 300.204], in line with general practice in antiquity (see Ronald F. Hock, The Social Context of Paul's Ministry: Tentmaking and Apostleship [Philadelphia: Fortress, 1980] 22–25).

[165] hom. in Rom. Arg. 2 [60.394].

[166] Ὅπου γὰρ ἡ τῆς πίστεως εὐγένεια, οὐδεὶς βάρβαρος, οὐδεὶς Ἕλλην, οὐδεὶς ξένος, οὐδεὶς πολίτης, ἀλλ' εἰς μίαν ἅπαντες ἀξιώματος ἀναβαίνουσιν ὑπεροχήν (hom. in Rom. 2.5 [60.406]).

he were, that fact would surely have been remembered, and paraded about.[167] Because of Paul's truthful claim[168] in Acts 22:27–28 that he possessed Roman citizenship, acquired by birth, John matter-of-factly notes: "then also he had a Roman father,"[169] but that is the extent of his curiosity. This lack of interest in Paul's father is exceeded in the case of Paul's mother,[170] whom Chrysostom only acknowledges in passing when he quotes Gal 1:15, with its reference to Paul's life *in utero*; but her role in Paul's generation and birth are for all intents and purposes usurped by the deity.[171] To some degree Chrysostom's almost complete inattention to Paul's parents represents the state of Pauline lore in the patristic period generally, which spent little time or energy on these questions (with the exception of anti-Paulinists' invectives).[172] In marked contrast to his death, no early Christian legends have been preserved about Paul's birth.[173] Probably this is the case because the Paul of the New Testament and later literature looms as an *adult* figure,[174] and what is of

---

[167] ὁ οὐδὲ τίνος ἦν πατρὸς δῆλον (*hom. in 1 Cor.* 15.5 [61.128]).

[168] John emphasizes the veracity of the claim, more as a defense of Paul and his despicable treatment than out of a particular biographical interest in Paul's citizenship: "Paul did not lie (God forbid!) in calling himself a Roman. For he was a Roman" [Οὐκ ἐψεύσατο Παῦλος, μὴ γένοιτο, Ῥωμαῖον ἑαυτὸν εἰπών· Ῥωμαῖος γὰρ ἦν] (*hom. in Ac.* 48.1 [60.333]).

[169] Ἄρα καὶ πατρὸς ἦν Ῥωμαίου (*hom in Ac.* 48.1 [60.334]).

[170] He does not think, as some commentators have, that Rufus's mother whom Paul says is "his" also (Rom 16:13), was Paul's real mother, but understands the phrase as testimony to the woman's great virtue (*hom. in Rom.* 31.3 [60.671]).

[171] See *fr. in Jer.* 1:5 [64.748]: "I am the one who formed you from the womb. It is not the work of nature, nor of birth pangs. I am the cause of all things; therefore you should justly obey me, the one who provided you with existence" [Ἐγώ ὁ πλάσας σε ἐκ κοιλίας. Οὐ τῆς φύσεως τὸ ἔργον ἐστίν, οὐ τῶν ὠδίνων· Ἐγώ πάντων αἴτιος. Ὥστε δικαίως ἂν ὑπακούσῃς ἐμοί, καὶ τῷ εἶναι παρασχόντι] (in context this refers to both Jeremiah and Paul).

[172] In polemic against Paul we do find some attacks on his ancestry. According to Epiphanius, the Ebionites said that, because Paul was from Tarsus, he was of Greek ancestry (i.e., a Gentile), the son of a Greek mother and a Greek father [Εἶτα φάσκουσιν αὐτὸν εἶναι Ἕλληνα, καὶ Ἑλληνίδος μητρός καὶ Ἕλληνος πατρὸς παῖδα]. They maintain that Paul had only become a Jew as a proselyte because he wanted to marry the daughter of the priest (*haer.* 1.30.16 [PG 41.433]). The anti-Pauline pseudo-Clementines, which associate Paul with Simon Magus (Acts 8), give a fuller pedigree for the Samaritan Simon, naming his father Antonios and his mother Rachel, and declaring his γένος to be Samaritan, his village Gittha (Ps-Clem, *Hom.* 2.22 [GCS, ed. Bernhard Rehm and Georg Strecker, *Die Pseudoklementinen I* (Berlin: Akademie Verlag, 1992), 44]). But the romance weaves Pauline associations with Simon in and out of the Acts account and later traditions of Simon as magician and gnostic, so it is uncertain in each case how far a distinctly *Pauline* referent may be inferred. Chrysostom does not appear to engage either of these "heretical" scenarios about Paul's parents in his writings.

[173] For instance, the extensive article on Paul and Pauline traditions throughout Christian history by Angelo Penna, *et al.* ("Paolo, apostolo," *Bibliotheca sanctorum* [Rome: Pontifica Università Lateranense, 1968] 10.164–228) begins with Paul's adolescence. On the traditions of Paul's death see below, pp. 363–74.

[174] The most frequent genre used, *Acta*, to some degree dictates this. But Paul himself did write of his youth and infancy in Gal 1:14–15.

greatest interest about him is his conversion and ministerial career, both of which take place outside of the orbit of his family.[175]

But Chrysostom's lack of inquisitiveness about Paul's parents is also due to his more pointed interest in Paul's heavenly origins and destination. Consequently, what takes the place of a Pauline birth narrative in Chrysostom's writings is an imaginary scene of Paul's ἐπιφάνεια, the proclamatory "debut" and manifestation of Paul as an apostolic emissary, which is depicted as an act of creation within the cosmos:

"Who will tell of your mighty acts, oh Lord" (Ps 105:2 LXX), because you did not allow Paul to escape notice [Παῦλον οὐκ ἀφῆκας λαθεῖν], but you showed such a man to the world [ἔδειξας τῇ οἰκουμένῃ τοιοῦτον ἄνδρα]? All the angels praised you with a single voice when you made the stars (Job 38:7), and then also when you made the sun, but not as much as when you showed Paul to us and to the whole world [ἀλλ' οὐχ οὕτως, ὡς ὅτε τὸν Παῦλον ἔδειξας ἡμῖν καὶ τῇ οἰκουμένῃ πάσῃ]. On account of this, earth has become more brilliant than heaven, for this man, brighter than the light of the sun, sent out beams that sparkled, spread out rays that were resplendent.[176] How great was the fruit this one[177] produced, not by fattening the corn, nor tending the pomegranates, but by bearing the fruit of piety, and by continually retrieving and leading to ripeness the fruit that was rotting. And with good reason! For this sun will not at all be able to fix the limbs of trees once torn apart, but Paul has called back from their sins people who had many putrefactions. And while this sun gives way to the night, that one (Paul) prevailed over the devil. Nothing overtook him; nothing overpowered him. That sun, born from above, sends down its rays; but he, rising up from below [αὐτὸς δὲ κάτωθεν ἀνατέλλων], didn't fill the region between heaven and earth with light, but at the moment he opened his mouth, filled up the angels with great joy [ἀλλὰ ἅμα τὸ στόμα ἀνέῳξε, καὶ τοὺς ἀγγέλους ἐνέπλησε πολλῆς τῆς ἡδονῆς]! How? For if there is joy in the heavens when one sinner repents (Lk 15:7), and he from his first public speech captured many [αὐτὸς δὲ ἐκ πρώτης δημηγορίας πολλοὺς ἐθήρευσε], how will he not fill the powers above with joy? So what am I saying? It was sufficient for Paul simply to speak, and the heavens leaped for delight and rejoiced over him [ἁπλῶς ἀρκεῖ Παῦλον φθέγγεσθαι, καὶ τοὺς οὐρανοὺς ἐπὶ τούτῳ σκιρτᾶν καὶ εὐφραίνεσθαι]. For if, when the Israelites went out from Egypt the mountains leaped with delight like rams (Ps 113:4 LXX), how great do

---

[175] Paul greets several persons as συγγενεῖς in Rom 16:7, 11 and 21, but Chrysostom does not evince much interest in them. He does not mention the term at all in the first two instances, though in treating the third passage he identifies Jason with the man of that name in Acts 17:6, whom Luke commends for his bravery. Then comes a general observation: "for Paul wouldn't just simply mention relatives, unless they were like him with respect to piety" (hom. in Rom. 32.2 [60.677]). Chrysostom also displays no personal interest in Paul's sister and nephew mentioned in Acts 23:16.

[176] This is not far from the kind of hyperbole Menander Rhetor recommends for depicting the nature with which the emperor was endowed from his γένεσις: "After 'birth,' you must say something about 'nature,' e.g.: 'Straight from the labour of his mother's womb, he shone forth radiant in beauty, dazzling the visible universe, rivalling the fairest star in the sky'" [μετὰ τὴν γένεσιν ἐρεῖς τι καὶ περὶ φύσεως, οἷον ὅτι ἐξέλαμψεν ἐξ ὠδίνων εὐειδὴς τῷ κάλλει καταλάμπων τὸ φαινόμενον ἀστέρι καλλίστῳ τῶν κατ' οὐρανὸν ἐφάμιλλος] (Rh. 2.371 [text and trans. Russell-Wilson, 82–83]).

[177] οὗτος, in reference here either to "man" or "sun" (both signifying Paul).

you suppose the joy was when people transferred from earth to heaven [ὅτε ἀπὸ γῆς εἰς οὐρανὸν μετέστησαν ἄνθρωποι, πόσην οἴει εἶναι χαράν]?[178]

Paul's "birth" is his "epiphany" before the eyes of the entire cosmos. God, the proud orchestrator of the event, "showed" [ἔδειξας] him to the world at the moment of his very first utterance of the gospel. That occasion was greeted with a celestial joy surpassing that at the creation of the stars and the sun,[179] for it marked the emergence of a new and more powerful sun that vanquishes Apollo (and his adherents!) completely.[180] He was endowed with powers – to promote the abundant growth of fruit and to repel the forces of darkness – far greater than the solar normal. The *Paulus natus* here is fully an adult;[181] the event of his parturition

---

[178] *hom. in Phil.* 4.1–2 [62.206–207]. What incites Chrysostom's praise here is 1:22–26, Paul's astounding willingness to forsake immediate unification with Christ in order to do Christ's work here on earth.

[179] See also the account of the heavenly reaction to Paul's call in *hom. in Ac. 9:1* 1.3 [51.118]: the angels jumped for joy when they saw Paul bound and led (and foresaw how many of the imprisoned he would free), led by the hand into Damascus (as he will lead many from earth into heaven), and blinded (as he would lead many out from darkness). Compare Libanios' encomium to Julian: "the gods exulted at your conversion" [θεοὶ δέ σε τῆς μεταβολῆς ἀγασθέντες], (*Or.* 13.16).

[180] There is likely an implied triumph over the pagan sun gods (Apollo, Mithras, Helios) here, and their most infamous devotée in recent memory, Julian. Chrysostom's well-known discourse *panegyricum in Babylam martyrem et contra Julianum et gentes* relates the theomachy in Daphne between Apollo (whose temple and cult were promoted and frequented by Julian) and the remains of the martyr, saint Babylas, which ended in the destruction of Apollo's temple by fire ignited from a lightning strike. In his discourse celebrating that victory over fifteen years later, John taunts Apollo worshipers: "Where now are those who insult the sun, the good creation of God made for our service, and ascribe that celestial orb to the demon [Apollo], and say that it is he" [Ποῦ νῦν εἰσιν οἱ τὸ καλὸν τοῦ θεοῦ δημιούργημα καὶ πρὸς ὑπηρεσίαν ἡμετέραν γεγονὸς τὸν ἥλιον ἐνυβρίζοντες καὶ τῷ δαίμονι τὸ ἄστρον ἐπιφημίζοντες καὶ τοῦτο ἐκεῖνον εἶναι λέγοντες;]? (*pan. Bab. 2* 83 [SC 362.204]). Julian's devotion to Apollo and a constellation of sun-gods (Mithras/Helios) was well known; he wrote a hymn "To King Helios," which begins with the triumphal confession, "I am a follower of King Helios" [εἰμι τοῦ βασιλέως ὀπαδὸς Ἡλίου] (*Or.* 4.130C). Schatkin concludes that in Chrysostom's oration *pan. Bab. 2*: "the argument is specifically directed against Julian and contains an attack upon the emperor's sun worship" (*Saint John Chrysostom, Apologist*, trans. Margaret A. Schatkin and Paul W. Harkins [FC 73; Washington: Catholic University of America Press, 1985] 38). Specifically in regard to our passage, whereas Julian argued that the sun was the master-creator [ἡ δημιουργική] of all else (*Or.* 4.141B), Chrysostom stresses that the sun is God's creation [δημιούργημα]. Given this wider religious context, it is quite reasonable that when Chrysostom lauds Paul above the sun his hyperbolic praise has a polemical, anti-Julianic edge. This is not the only place where John paints Paul as Julian's antitype, as we shall see when we turn to "Paul's Master Deed" later in this chapter (pp. 270–78).

[181] In a sense the inattention to Paul's infancy is due to the fact that he becomes of real interest to Chrysostom only in his conversion (though this does not preclude some hindsight-colored pictures of Paul the persecutor). This can be seen in the places where Chrysostom refers to the onset of Paul's ministry as the moment he burst "from the starting-gate" [ἀπὸ βαλβῖδος] (*laud. Paul.* 5.3 [SC 300.234]; *hom. in 2 Cor.* 25.3 [61.574]; *hom. in Ac.* 20.4 [60.162], ἀπὸ προοιμίων καὶ ἀπὸ βαλβῖδος; *laud. Paul.* 7.4 [SC 300.300], ἐξ ἀρχῆς ... καὶ ἀπ' αὐτῶν τῶν προοιμίων). Similarly, Chrysostom describes Paul as "entering into the world at the right moment for us"

is the moment of his first public declamation [δημηγορία], when he first opened his mouth [ἅμα τὸ στόμα ἀνέῳξε].[182] In this portrait Paul was not born, but created, a man who rose from earth into the sky to become a sun that eclipsed the light of the great orb created on the fourth day.[183] Paul's new birth in his ascension to the preaching ministry, illustrating as it does his excellence, creates a retrospective γένος for the man from Tarsus as one really born from heaven.

ἀνατροφή (Rearing)

The autobiographical opening to Paul's speech in Acts 22:3 moves directly from his γένεσις to his ἀνατροφή, as Paul says to the Jerusalemites that he was ἀνατεθραμμένος ἐν τῇ πόλει ταύτῃ, "raised in this city." Chrysostom has much to say about Paul's rearing throughout his writings. We shall follow the order of traditional topics concerned with upbringing as Aphthonios has tabulated them: ἐπιτηδεύματα, τέχνη, and νόμοι.[184]

ἐπιτηδεύματα and τέχνη (Vocation and Trade)

Paul's vocation, like that of any person in Greco-Roman antiquity, was deemed by John a consistent reflection of his education and his family of origin. The interpenetration of these elements in the classical *cursus honorum* can be seen in the

---

[Εὐκαίρως δὲ ἡμῖν ὁ μακάριος ἐπεισῆλθεν οὗτος], intentionally after the other apostles, to perform his special work of dispelling all listlessness and grief (*Stag.* 3.11 [47.487]). In *laud. Paul.* 7.1 [SC 300.292] John's language suggests a recreation of Paul's initial epiphany on the saint's feast day: "today he comes, not into a city, but into the world" [εἰσέρχεται σήμερον, οὐκ εἰς πόλιν, ἀλλ' εἰς τὴν οἰκουμένην].

[182] The fitting birth of a rhetor! We shall have occasion throughout this chapter to engage Chrysostom's ambivalence about Paul's rhetorical acumen (see pp. 278–91), but this "birth narrative" is surely telling in this regard.

[183] A very interesting contrast is provided by the Pseudo-Clementine *Homiliae*, a work of Syrian provenance to which Chrysostom might easily have had access. In that composition, drawing upon the theory of syzygies – that the deity created in pairs, with the weaker or more evil member preceding the stronger or more virtuous one – Peter disparages "Simon" [a cipher for Paul] as the first created, from the left hand of the divine [Satan]: "The person who follows this order would be able to comprehend to whom Simon belongs, the man who came first before me to the Gentiles, and to whom I happen to belong, I who have come after him, and followed him as light does darkness, as knowledge ignorance, as healing sickness" [ταύτῃ τῇ τάξει ἀκολουθοῦντα δυνατὸν ἦν νοεῖν τίνος ἐστὶν Σίμων, ὁ πρὸ ἐμοῦ εἰς τὰ ἔθνη πρῶτος ἐλθών, καὶ τίνος ὢν τυγχάνω, ὁ μετ' ἐκεῖνον ἐληλυθὼς καὶ ἐπελθὼν ὡς σκότῳ φῶς, ὡς ἀγνοίᾳ γνῶσις, ὡς νόσῳ ἴασις] (Ps-Clem., *Hom.* 2.17 [GCS, ed. Rehm and Strecker, 42]; for the identification of "Simon" with Paul in this passage and elsewhere in the Pseudo-clementine literature, see Georg Strecker, *Das Judenchristentum in den Pseudoklementinen*, 2nd ed. [Berlin: Akademie-Verlag, 1981] 188–91, and his article in *NTApoc* 2.490–91). Could Chrysostom's cosmological hymn of Pauline "origins" be countering such a Syrian anti-Pauline tradition by turning it on its head and proclaiming Paul as the great "light," whose creation was lauded by the heavenly beings?

[184] Aphth. *Prog.* 8 [Spengel 2.36].

pivotal position of Paul's humble trade in John's portraiture. Just as Paul's being a tentmaker proves that his family was not illustrious,[185] likewise his trade as a leather-worker demonstrates that he did not have the elite παιδεία, and therefore opens the question, with which Chrysostom was frequently preoccupied, of where he received the educational training sufficient to account for the utterances in his letters.[186] Consequently, in another context Chrysostom can claim that it was through "being apprenticed by the Holy Spirit" that the tentmaker became a rhetorician.[187] Because of this inseparable connection between trade and education, the latter topic requires detailed attention in its own right.

παιδεία (Education)[188]

Chrysostom presumes the account in Acts of Paul's education under Gamaliel,[189] with its stress on the "accuracy" of that instruction [κατὰ ἀκρίβειαν τοῦ πατρῴου νόμου].[190] He finds the Lukan phrase "educated at the feet of Gamaliel" [παρὰ τοὺς πόδας Γαμαλιήλου παιδευόμενος] most significant, and evocative of even more vivid pictures of Paul the ardent student: "Therefore he says, 'at the feet of Gamaliel,' and not simply 'by Gamaliel,' but 'at his feet,' showing his perseverance, his assiduity, his zeal for the hearing, and his great respect for the man."[191] That picture of Paul the devoted student of Torah, which coheres fully with Paul's self-portrait in Gal 1:14 of his youthful studious zeal,[192] can be conveniently encapsulated by John in the epithet νομομαθής ("Torah-trained"), which he often applied to Paul.[193]

---

[185] *laud. Paul.* 4.10 [SC 300.204].

[186] *hom. in Heb.* 1.2 [63.15–16], quoted on pp. 246–47.

[187] *pent.* 2.1 [52.807]: φλὸξ σοφιστεύειν τοὺς ἁλιέας διδάσκουσα, καὶ ῥήτορα τὸν σκυτοτόμον ἀπαρτίζουσα.

[188] Aphthonios does not include this as a discrete category, but I have added it from Theon's list (*Prog.* 8 [Spengel 2.110]), quoted at the beginning of this chapter, on p. 200.

[189] *hom. in 1 Tim.* 3.2 [62.517], in reference to Acts 22:3. Chrysostom makes no attempt, such as is found in *mart. Petr. et Paul.* 44, to claim that *Jesus* was Paul's teacher (Lipsius, *Acta*, 1.156; Σίμων εἶπεν· Οὐκ ἐγένετο τοῦ Παύλου διδάσκαλος ὁ Χριστός; Παῦλος εἶπεν· Ναί, δι' ἀποκαλύψεως κἀμὲ ἐπαίδευσεν), though in principle he probably would not have objected to the idea.

[190] E.g., *hom. in Gen.* 40.5 [53.367]; *hom. in Gal.* 2:11 10 [51.380].

[191] τὴν καρτερίαν, τὴν προσεδρείαν, τὴν σπουδὴν τὴν περὶ τὴν ἀκρόασιν, τὴν πολλὴν πρὸς τὸν ἄνδρα αἰδῶ δεικνύς (*hom. in Ac.* 47.1 [60.327]). Compare the advice of Menander Rhetor: "Then you must speak of his love of learning, his quickness, his enthusiasm for study, his easy grasp of what is taught him" [ἐρεῖς τὴν φιλομάθειαν, τὴν ὀξύτητα, τὴν περὶ τὰ μαθήματα σπουδὴν, τὴν ῥαδίαν κατάληψιν τῶν διδασκομένων] (*Rh.* 2.371 [Russell-Wilson, 82–83]).

[192] Paul's self-description, καὶ προέκοπτον ἐν τῷ Ἰουδαϊσμῷ ὑπὲρ πολλοὺς συνηλικιώτας ἐν τῷ γένει μου is itself echoed in rhetorical theory, as by Menander Rhetor, in recommending how to praise the emperor under the κεφάλαιον of παιδεία: ἐν οἷς ἐπαιδεύετο διαφέρων τῶν ἡλίκων ἐφαίνετο (*Rh.* 2.372 [Russell-Wilson, 82]).

[193] *hom. in 1 Tim.* 3.2 [62.517]; also *hom. in 1 Cor.* 7.3 [61.58]; *hom. in Eph.* 6.2 [62.45]; *hom. in Ac.* 20.1 [60.159]; 32.2 [60.236].

In contrast with an education in Torah, classical *paideia* constituted instruction in grammatics and rhetoric,[194] the kind of education that John himself had received. Such *paideia* – training in proper speech and in the literary classics – was limited in the Imperial period to small numbers of elites and those they supported. Its attainment maintained from generation to generation an upper social class who would know one another on sight, anywhere in the empire, just as those without paideia would give themselves away the moment they opened their mouths.[195] Access to this educational system, including the geographical mobility associated with it, provided the major opportunity for what limited social advancement existed in late antiquity.[196] Furthermore, this training was thought not only to provide necessary skills for political life, but also to secure the capacity for ἀρετή, virtue.[197] When discussing Paul's rhetorical acumen as an encomiastic topic, Chrysostom always takes the ploy familiar in early Christian literature from the time of the apologists,[198] indeed, from the New Testament writings themselves: Paul was ἰδιώτης τῷ λόγῳ (2 Cor 11:6, "unskilled in eloquence"). Chrysostom unremittingly propounds this view of Paul's education because he finds it in the biblical record (2 Cor 11:6; Acts 4:13),[199] to be sure, but also because it accords so

---

[194] See H. I. Marrou, *A History of Education in Antiquity*, trans. George Lamb (New York: Sheed and Ward, 1956) esp. 160–226, 274–98; Robert A. Kaster, *Guardians of Language: the Grammarian and Society in Late Antiquity* (Berkeley: University of California Press, 1988) 11–95.

[195] Brown, *Power and Persuasion*, 35–70; Kaster, *Guardians of Language*, 15–31.

[196] Kaster, *Guardians of Language*, 22–23. Chrysostom was well aware of this, as he disparagingly quotes (in *oppugn*. 3.5 [47.357]) parents who exhort their children to study rhetoric on the following grounds: "A certain man who was humble and from humble parents [ταπεινὸς καὶ ἐκ ταπεινῶν], acquiring power from rhetoric [τὴν ἀπὸ τῶν λόγων κτησάμενος δύναμιν], took over high rulership positions, acquired great wealth, married a well-provided for wife, built a magnificent house, and is feared and reputable in the eyes of all" [ἦρξε μεγίστας ἀρχὰς, πλοῦτον ἐκτήσατο πολὺν, γυναῖκα ἔλαβον εὔπορον, οἰκίαν ᾠκοδόμησε λαμπρὰν, φοβερός ἐστιν ἅπασι καὶ ἐπίδοξος]. On these latter *topoi* of rule, wealth, good marriage and honor, see below in this chapter.

[197] Kaster, *Guardians of Language*, 27 ("the literary culture in itself guaranteed virtue").

[198] "Following a long tradition that reached back to the apologists of the second and third centuries, Christian writers insisted that the miraculous character of their religion was proved by the manner in which it had been spread throughout the Roman world by humble men, without *paideia*" (Brown, *Power and Persuasion*, 73). Chrysostom's own awareness of pagan critiques of Christianity as founded by illiterate men who fabricated stories, and his engagement in apologetics, are well known from such writings as *pan. Bab.* 2 (see discussion and references in Schatkin-Harkins, FS 73.15–70). This historical context and rhetorical purpose of Chrysostom's treatment of Paul's rhetorical acumen or lack thereof must be given due account in any attempt by New Testament scholars to seek in Chrysostom either confirmation or repudiation of recent investigations into Paul's "rhetoric" (such as Janet Fairweather, "The Epistle to the Galatians and Classical Rhetoric: Parts 1 and 2, Part 3," *TynBul* 45 [1994] 1–338, 213–43, and especially Kern, *Rhetoric and Galatians*, 176–81). The proper perspective was set already by the steady judgment of Chase, *Chrysostom*, 151: "At first it must be admitted that Chrysostom takes an altogether exaggerated view of St. Paul's want of literary culture." I have taken up this important topic in a forthcoming essay, "Reading Rhetoric with Ancient Exegetes: John Chrysostom on Galatians."

[199] That Chrysostom easily melds the Acts passage about "the twelve" with Paul shows that he accords all the same dignity as apostles, and all the same illiteracy. 2 Cor 11:6 allows him to see

well with his own rhetorical purposes. As we have often seen in the extended passages treated above in this chapter, it is to Chrysostom's advantage always to stress Paul's humble origins, including lack of education, when speaking *biographically*, since that will serve to amplify the magnitude of Paul's later achievement in persuading the whole world to the gospel message.[200] In this way Chrysostom refutes the only socially "natural" explanation for Paul's success as an orator: that it came from his extraordinary skills as a student, combined with diligent training.[201] However, most tellingly, in an extremely important passage, Chrysostom himself admits that his own adoption of this argument is part of a *deliberate rhetorical strategy*, one that he exhorts all others to follow.

So, prove to me this – that Peter and Paul were eloquent [λόγιος]. But you cannot. For they were "unskilled," and "unlettered" [ἰδιῶται γὰρ ἦσαν, καὶ ἀγράμματοι] (Acts 4:13) ... Therefore when Greeks accuse the disciples of being unskilled, we should accuse them [i.e., the apostles] of it even more ["Οταν οὖν "Ελληνες κατηγορήσωσι τῶν μαθητῶν ὡς ἰδιωτῶν, πλέον ἡμεῖς ἐκείνων κατηγορῶμεν αὐτῶν]. Don't let anyone say that Paul was wise [σοφός], but instead let's exalt for wisdom the famous men among the Greeks, and marvel at their facility in speech [εὐγλωττία], but let's say that all the Christian figures were unskilled [τοὺς παρ' ἡμῖν ἄπαντας λέγωμεν ἰδιώτας γεγονέναι]. For in this respect we shall overthrow them in no small way; for thus the victories will be magnificent! Now the reason I have said these things is that I once heard a Christian debating in a ridiculous fashion with a Greek, and both of them were demolishing their own case in the battle against the other. For the Greek was saying the things the Christian should have said; and the Christian was proposing the things the Greek customarily should have said. For the dispute was about Paul and Plato, with the Greek trying to prove that Paul was uneducated and unskilled [ὁ Παῦλος ἦν ἀμαθὴς καὶ ἰδιώτης], while the Christian, due to simplicity, was zealously making the case that Paul was more eloquent than Plato [Πλάτωνος λογιώτερος ἦν ὁ Παῦλος]. Thus the victory belonged to the Greek, as this argument prevailed [τοῦ "Ελληνος ἐγίνετο τὰ νικητήρια, τούτου κρατοῦντος τοῦ λόγου]. For if Paul were more eloquent than Plato, likely many would argue back that it was not by grace, but by persuasive speech that he prevailed [Εἰ γὰρ Πλάτωνος ἐλλογιμώτερος ἦν ὁ Παῦλος, πολλοὺς εἰκὸς ἀντιλέγειν, ὅτι οὐ τῇ χάριτι, ἀλλὰ τῇ εὐγλωττίᾳ περιεγένετο]. Therefore what the Christian said worked to the advantage of the Greek; and what the Greek was saying to that of the· Christian. For if Paul were uneducated [ἀπαίδευτος], but he prevailed over Plato, as I was saying, the victory was magnificent [λαμπρὰ γέγονεν ἡ νίκη]. For the uneducated man [Paul], taking Plato's disciples, persuaded them all and led them to himself [Τοὺς γὰρ ἐκείνου μαθητὰς λαβὼν ὁ ἀμαθὴς ἄπαντας ἔπεισε, καὶ πρὸς ἑαυτὸν ἤγαγεν]. Whence it is clear that it was not by human wisdom that the gospel prevailed, but by the grace of God. Therefore so that we might not

---

Paul in concert with "the chorus of apostles" in this respect, in order to formulate a general rule about the leaders of the early church and their astonishing success.

[200] "Yet all such disparagement of Paul's literary abilities [by Chrysostom, Jerome, Theodore of Mopsuestia and Origen] served only to enhance the grace of God, which could use so unskilled a writer to so great effect" (Wiles, *Divine Apostle* 16–17). See also Kennedy, *Greek Rhetoric under Christian Emperors*, 252: "John here has in mind what develops as a Christian commonplace, found also in Gregory of Nazianzus (*Or.* 23.12) in the form, 'not like an Aristotelian, but like a fisherman.'"

[201] On *paideia* and the "self-made man" see Gleason, *Making Men*, xx–xxix, and *passim*.

suffer these things, nor be ridiculed when we are debating with Greeks, since Paul was the one who led them to us, let's accuse the apostles of being uneducated [κατηγορῶμεν τῶν ἀποστόλων ὡς ἀμαθῶν]. For this accusation is an encomium [ἡ γὰρ κατηγορία αὕτη ἐγκώμιον].[202]

In this rhetorical strategy of deliberately diminishing the rhetorical competence of Paul (like all the apostles), John is squarely in line with the other orator-bishops of the late-fourth century with their inherently self-contradictory stance toward rhetoric: "John Chrysostom's sermons proclaim the triumph of fishermen over philosophers, even while the speaker drew on a solid traditional education himself."[203] And here John has shown his hand as to the purpose of this reversal of the encomiastic *topoi* by insisting that Paul was ἀπαίδευτος, for it leaves only one possible cause for his success: divine intervention. But this biographical treatment of Paul's rhetorical skill is not John's only type of engagement with the question, for he comes to some quite different conclusions when addressing the letters themselves as literary and rhetorical products. The contradictions between his ubiquitous statements of approval, insight and amazement at Paul's logical and rhetorical acumen when discoursing on the texts of the letters with these biographical arguments we have been analyzing here are considerable.[204] Rhetorical

---

[202] *hom. in 1 Cor.* 3.4 [61.27].

[203] Cameron, *Later Roman Empire*, 155. See also p. 139 on the increasingly problematic nature of these traditional arguments by the late fourth century: "The many – often agonized – contemporary Christian discussions of the relation of classical to Christian learning should be read as necessary attempts to defend the extent to which Christians had in fact endorsed an educational system that could be represented as contrary to their professed beliefs. Taking the longer view, it was essential, if the growing influence of the institutional church was to be maintained and increased, to control the educational system, either by drastic change or by adaptation and justification; on the whole at this stage, it was the latter course that was chosen. The old formulation of the process in terms of the relation, or supposed conflict, between Christianity and classical culture can thus now give way to a theory of discourse in modern terms as a means to power." See also Kaster, *Guardians of Language*, 72: "When directed outward, across boundaries that could simultaneously distinguish non-Christian from Christian, and liberally educated from layman, those straightforward claims (of "the powerful model of the illiterate or ill-educated apostle as charismatic teacher, whose truth owed nothing to the conventions and institutions of men" [p. 71]) might provide comfort and reassurance, a sense of old battles fought and won once more ... But when, from the late third century onward, those boundaries became ever less distinct, and when more Christian voices came to speak with that tongue, answers to old questions became less clearcut, less easily generalized." Chrysostom himself offers a kind of developmental model of Christian appropriation of rhetoric in *oppugn.* 3.12 [47.368], identifying three stages: first were men ignorant of both letters and rhetoric (the disciples of Jesus), then those who were literate but still unpracticed in rhetoric [ἐμπειρία δὲ λόγων οὐδέπω] (such as Paul), and finally those who had both (including himself, presumably!). But even with this schema in mind John avows that "nevertheless, in the very matters in which the power of rhetoric [ἡ τῶν λόγων ἰσχύς] appeared to be especially needed, they so far surpassed those who were skilled in it as to make them appear worse than uneducated children." Chrysostom's modes of Pauline portraiture are a major means by which he deals with this tension, as we shall see below, pp. 278–91.

[204] Full documentation of this point would of course require a separate study, but a few examples may indicate the different tone of Chrysostom's appreciation of Paul's rhetorical skill in the letters themselves. See, for instance, Chrysostom's admiration at how Paul accomplishes

prowess constitutes a fault line under John's merging but not identical conceptions of Paul as author and the words of his letters, even as in his depictions of Paul's rhetorical acumen John is working out his ambivalence about his own rhetorical powers.[205] To cite one simple example of the patent contradiction at work in Chrysostom's treatments of Paul's rhetorical acumen, once when seeking to amplify Paul's lack of παιδεία, John even goes to the extent of asserting that Paul knew only Hebrew [Ἑβραϊστὶ μόνον εἰδώς].[206] This statement demonstrates unequivocally the extent to which John's evaluation of Paul's oratorical skill is itself a rhetorical statement about Paul's *person*, not a literary evaluation of his letters, which John, as well as anyone, knows were written in Greek, because that is the only language *he* reads! And, ultimately, this portrait of Paul is not really about Paul's person as much as it is about the ways of God in the world. However, when Chrysostom reads Paul's letters and expounds upon them for his congregations, a rather different portrait of Paul's rhetorical dexterity emerges: of one well-skilled in argumentation, the man more facile in speech than rhetoricians [ὁ ῥητόρων εὐγλωττότερος],[207] who composed his epistles with deliberate care and profundity of expression, setting just the right tone for maximum persuasive effect.[208]

"the most difficult" of rhetorical feats – managing to praise himself without inciting the enmity that usually results from περιαυτολογία (*hom. in 2 Cor.* 22.1 [61.547]: εἰς ἀνάγκην ἐμπέσων μεγάλην τοῦ ἐπᾶραι ἑαυτὸν, ἀμφότερα ἐργάζεται, τοῦτο τε αὐτὸ, καὶ τὸ μὴ δοκεῖν ἐπαχθῆς εἶναι τοῖς πολλοῖς διὰ τὴν περιαυτολογίαν ταύτην ... ὅπερ τῶν σφόδρα ἐστὶ δυσκολωτάτων, καὶ πολλῆς δεομένων συνέσεως; on the rhetorical terminology Chrysostom has unflinchingly applied to Paul's activities here, see below, pp. 339–52, under πράξεις ἐναντίαι). Another fine example is provided by Chrysostom's treatise, *de virginitate*, in which he repeatedly praises Paul's rhetorical acumen in the argument of 1 Cor 7 (see n. 385 below for references). Chrysostom also reacts to Paul's rhetoric often with such expressions as Βάθαι, or ὅρα τὴν σύνεσιν τοῦ ἀποστόλου, both ways he registers his mighty approval of a Pauline argument or locution (he uses the latter expression fully twenty times in his homilies on 1 Corinthians alone). Elsewhere Chrysostom praises Paul's rhetorical arrangement [τάξις], as in *hom. in Eph.* 3.2 [62.26], and *oppugn.* 3.1 [47.350], on which see Hunter's observation: "This sort of rhetorical analysis is typical of Chrysostom's exegesis and in some ways anticipates certain modern critical approaches" (*Comparison*, 125 n. 8). But the best way to demonstrate Chrysostom's prevailing high estimate of the rhetorical skill exhibited in the Pauline letters is by a sustained and careful analysis of an entire homily set, such as Galatians, on which he is equally sensitive to the argument line of the letter and Paul's deliberate alternations in tone and appeals (on which see Mitchell, "Reading Rhetoric"), or Philemon, where John throughout expresses his amazement at the fine rhetorical lines Paul draws in his persuasive appeals to Philemon.

[205] This was well appreciated by Naegele, "Johannes Chrysostomos," 105–106: "So hat er [Johannes] mit der jedesmaligen Apologie des apostolischen Verfahrens sein eigenes inneres Verhältnis zur hellenischen Kultur und Literatur zeichnen und intra muros et extra verteidigen wollen, demgemäß er, wie sein hochgepriesenes Vorbild, trotz aller Polemik die Blüten griechischen Geisteslebens überall pflückte, wo immer er sie der christlichen Religion dienstbar machen konnte."

[206] *hom. in 2 Tim.* 4.3 [62.622]. See also *comm. in Gal.* 6.3 [61.678], on the "sort of letters" Paul wrote his name in – Chrysostom thinks they are poorly formed (rather than being especially large), because he didn't know well how to write the Greek alphabet.

[207] *Laz.* 6.9 [48.1041]; cf. *poenit.* 2.5 [49.290]: ὁ ῥήτωρ ὁ πνευματικός.

[208] We shall return to the issue of Paul's rhetorical skill below, in regard to the means by which he accomplished his πράξεις (see pp. 278–91).

ὁ σκηνοποιός　(The Tentmaker)

Paul's manual labor is a very important element in Chrysostom's portraits of Paul,[209] one that he enjoys embellishing because it serves as a vivid snapshot, a vocational synecdoche by which he can economically depict the anomalies of the Pauline career. Rarely will he mention Paul as "that tentmaker" [ὁ σκηνοποιός] without expanding with graphic synonyms the simple dignity of one who of his own free will chose a trade that was seemingly beneath him ("the man with the knife in his hand," "the one who worked with skins," "the man who hung about the market-place and lived in a workshop"). All of these slightly different images of Paul at his work depend upon the same social evaluation: "What could be more debased than a tentmaker?" [τί δὲ σκηνορράφου εὐτελέστερον;].[210] This image of Paul also serves to link him with the rest of the early apostles in a single group-portrait of simple truth-tellers.[211] Another reason John likes the tentmaker image is that he regards it as the very opposite of the orator. The tentmaker works with his hands, not his mouth; indeed, he is ἄστομος, "mouthless, voiceless."[212] When faced with the anomaly that this tentmaker composed the elegantly phrased and philosophi-cally suggestive opening period to Hebrews, John exclaims:

Oh, the depth of the apostolic intelligence [Βαθαὶ τῆς συνέσεως τῆς ἀποστολικῆς]! Or, rather, it is not the intelligence of Paul but the grace of the spirit which should be admired here [μᾶλλον δὲ οὐ τὴν τοῦ Παύλου σύνεσιν, ἀλλὰ τὴν τοῦ Πνεύματός ἐστι θαυμάσαι χάριν ἐνταῦθα]. For he did not say these things from his own mind [ἐξ οἰκείας διανοίας], nor did he find such great wisdom in himself [οὐδὲ τοσαύτην σοφίαν ἐξ ἑαυτοῦ εὗρεν]. Then from where [πόθεν γάρ]? For did it come from the knife and the skins, or from the

---

[209] Compare the contemporary work of Hock, *Social Context*, the goal of which is: "the construction of a clear and detailed portrait of Paul the tentmaker" (p. 16). Hock's method combines the biblical evidence with social-historical data about work and artisanship from the wider Mediterranean world, which Chrysostom accessed immediately through his own Antio-chene context, yet viewed through the lens of his own social location (I shall return to this important point in the conclusion to this chapter, pp. 374–77).

[210] *scand.* 20.10 [SC 79.248]. In *hom. in 2 Tim.* 5.2 [62.626], John speculates that many were ashamed of Paul for being a tentmaker [Ἐπειδὴ εἰκὸς ἦν πολλοὺς ἐπαισχύνεσθαι καὶ τὸν Παῦλον αὐτόν, ἅτε σκηνοποιὸν ὄντα].

[211] Chase, *Chrysostom*, 152: "he overlooks the great distance in culture and social position between Saul of Tarsus and the Lord's personal followers." This was because of Chrysostom's rhetorical intent in these passages: to present all of Christianity in the person of the men de-scribed by Luke in Acts 4:13, over against the whole rest of the world. Elsewhere Chrysostom recognizes the varied social ranks represented by Paul and Jesus' disciples, while still maintaining Paul's place in this sorry lot: "If someone should hear Peter and Paul's trades, s/he will see that there was nothing great or dignified about them [οὐδὲν μέγα ἔχειν καὶ σεμνόν]. While the tentmaker is more honorable than the fisherman, he is more debased than the other handworking trades" [τοῦ μὲν γὰρ ἁλιέως ὁ σκηνοποιὸς τιμιώτερος, τῶν δὲ ἄλλων χειροτεχνῶν εὐτελέστερος] (pan. Bab. 2 3 [50.538]).

[212] See the parallelism in *Eutrop.* 2.14 [52.409]: ὁ σκηνοποιὸς δαιμόνων ἰσχυρότερος, ὁ ἄστομος φιλοσόφων φιλοσοφώτερος ("the tentmaker was stronger than demons, the voiceless man more astute at philosophizing than the philosophers").

workshop [ἀπὸ τῆς σμίλης γὰρ καὶ τῶν δερμάτων, ἢ τοῦ ἐργαστηρίου;]? But speaking like this was from divine activity [ἀλλὰ θείας ἐνεργείας ἦν τὸ οὕτως εἰπεῖν]. For his mind did not give birth to these thoughts, since it was then so humble and lowly that it was not better than the rest of those who hung about in the marketplace [Οὐ γὰρ αὐτοῦ ταῦτα τὰ νοήματα ἔτικτεν ἡ διάνοια, τότε μὲν οὕτω ταπεινὴ καὶ εὐτελὴς οὖσα, ὡς τῶν ἀγοραίων μηδὲν ἔχειν πλέον]. For how could it be, when it was entirely spent on preoccupations with deals and skins [πῶς γὰρ ἡ περὶ συμβόλαια καὶ δέρματα καταναλωθεῖσα;]? But it was from the grace of the spirit, which demonstrates its power through whomever it wishes [ἀλλ' ἡ τοῦ Πνεύματος χάρις, ἢ δι' ὧν ἂν ἐθέλῃ τὴν ἰσχὺν αὐτῆς ἐπιδείκνυται].[213]

The commonplace demonstrates, from the sheer impossibility of oratorical skill in a man ἀπαίδευτος, that it was divine grace, divine activity, at work in Paul's writing. But elsewhere John will insist, with no hint of contradiction, that Paul's *will* was the central reason for his accomplishments:"Do you see the loftiness of thought? Do you see what the tentmaker became, because he willed it [ἐπειδὴ ἠθέλησεν], the man who spent his entire life in the marketplace?"[214]

The denigration of Paul's tentmaking, even thusly amplified, serves John's rhetorical purpose. But in other contexts Chrysostom can, without hesitation or sense of contradiction, laud Paul's tentmaking itself for its inherent virtues. First, Paul's tentmaking models the preferability of good, honest work over a life of idleness.[215] Second, Paul's work displays his humility, for his writings show that not only was Paul not ashamed of ἑαυτοῦ τὸ ἐπιτήδευμα, but he placarded it proudly,[216] carrying on in the same trade he had learned from his youth even after he underwent the extraordinary ecstatic experiences related in 2 Corinthians 12.[217] This humility extends to his ranking of others as well, in that Paul singled out Prisca and Aquila, tentmakers like himself, for special attention in Rom 16:3, instead of people who were rich, famous, or with distinguished roots.[218] Third, despite the

---

[213] *hom. in Heb.* 1.2 [63.15].

[214] Εἶδες ὕψος διανοίας; εἶδες ὁ σκηνοποιὸς οἷος ἐγένετο ἐπειδὴ ἠθέλησεν, ὁ ἐπ' ἀγορᾶς τὸν ἅπαντα βίον διαγαγών; (*hom. in Heb.* 16.4 [63.127]). Chrysostom argues for the infinite possibility provided by the human will: Οὐδὲν γάρ ἐστι κώλυμα, οὐκ ἔστι, πάντας ὑπερβαλέσθαι, εἴ γε βουλοίμεθα. But, John continues, just as with the trades of daily life, you cannot get into heaven just by saying you want it, you must work for it.

[215] *hom. in Rom. 16:3* 1.5 [51.194]:"Work acts for human nature like a bit does in the mouth of a horse" ["Οπερ γάρ ἐστιν ὁ χαλινὸς τῷ ἵππῳ, τοῦτο τὸ ἔργον τῇ φύσει τῇ ἡμετέρᾳ], to keep it on the straight and narrow path toward virtue.

[216] Καὶ οὐ μόνον οὐκ ἐπῃσχύνετο ταῦτα ποιῶν, ἀλλὰ καὶ καθάπερ ἐν στήλῃ χαλκῇ ταῖς ἐπιστολαῖς ἐξεπόμπευσεν ἑαυτοῦ τὸ ἐπιτήδευμα ("And not only was he not ashamed of doing this work, but he even paraded his trade publicly in his letters, as though on a copper stele"; *hom. in Rom. 16:3* 5 [51.194]). Below we shall see how Chrysostom handled the obvious objection that Paul should not be given kudos for lack of shame for his trade, if indeed it were the trade into which he was born (see pp. 374–77).

[217] "Οπερ οὖν ἐξ ἀρχῆς ἔμαθε καὶ μετὰ ταῦτα αὐτὸ μετεχείριζε, καὶ τότε μετὰ τὸ εἰς οὐρανὸν τρίτον ἁρπαγῆναι, μετὰ τὸ εἰς παράδεισον ἀπενεχθῆναι, μετὰ τὸ κοινωνῆσαι ῥημάτων ἀπορρήτων τῷ θεῷ (*hom. in Rom. 16:3* 5 [51.194–95]).

[218] Οὐκ εἶπε τοὺς πλουσίους, τοὺς περιφανεῖς, τοὺς εὐπάτριδας (*hom. in Rom. 16:3* 3 [51.191]). In *hom. in Rom.* 2.5 [60.407] Chrysostom imagines Paul preaching the gospel while

social expectations accompanying *paideia* and its absence, Paul's tentmaking was never for him any hindrance to virtue.[219] Fourth, Paul is to be praised for working with his hands because of its philanthropy: he *chose* to work in order to make money for the needs of others, laboring night and day without sleep for their sakes (1 Thess 2:9; 2 Cor 11:27; Acts 20:34).[220] Fifth, this manual labor was itself a rugged ascetic discipline, a check against the human tendency to indolence.[221] Thus Paul's work can be seen as part of his abundant ἀκτημοσύνη, life of "voluntary poverty," the normal monastic requirements of which he even exceeds.[222] These five inherent goods of tentmaking render it a useful ploy in John's exhortations to his congregation to cultivate virtue, self-effacement, and dedication to what truly matters in this life. Hence this facet of Paul's "rearing," his family trade as tentmaker, could be used both to depict in a single stroke the meager preparation the apostle had had for the astounding feats he was later to accomplish, and in parallel contexts to serve as the complete example of virtuous behavior for Christian congregations to imitate.

νόμοι (Laws)

Aphthonios does not detail what he means by this topic, but in the sample encomium he provides he praises Thucydides for being well reared in his commonwealth and laws [τρέφεται μὲν πολιτείᾳ καὶ νόμοις]. This topic is quite naturally not applied by Chrysostom to Paul's foundational training in the laws of the πόλις, but what fits it precisely is Paul's training in ὁ πατρῷος νόμος (Acts 22:3), the Scriptures of Israel. Chrysostom deems Paul's education as a νομομαθής (which we have mentioned above) an essential part of his ἀνατροφή, because his early education, with its process of saturation in the Scriptures, constituted an invaluable preparation for his later ministry.

---

at his workbench sewing his skins. But this did not cause offense to his hearers, John muses, even those descended from consuls [καὶ οὐδὲ τοῦτο ἐσκανδάλισε τοὺς ἐξ ὑπάτων], for what should really be despised are not certain trades and vocations [οὐ αἱ τέχναι καὶ τὰ ἐπιτηδεύματα], but lies and false teachings.

[219] *Eutrop.* 2.14 [52.409]: καὶ αὕτη ἡ τέχνη κώλυμα τῇ ἀρετῇ οὐκ ἐγένετο; also *hom. in Mt.* 61.3 [58.592].

[220] *hom. in Mt.* 8.5 [57.88]; *hom. in Gen.* 11.7 [53.98]; *laud. Paul.* 1.11 [SC 300.130, and Piédagnel's n. 1]. In *hom. in 1 Thess.* 3.1 [62.405–6] John notes that Paul does not refer to αἱ εὐεργεσίαι αἱ παρ᾽ ἐμοῦ, "the benefactions you received from me" (though that would be the accurate term), instead calling it more diplomatically "our work and labor" [ὁ κόπος ἡμῶν καὶ ὁ μόχθος] (1 Thess 2:9), so as not to draw attention to himself as the Thessalonians' benefactor. This is accompanied by a proof from Paul's attitude toward his labor: "he did not simply work, but did so with abundant zeal" [Καὶ οὐχ ἁπλῶς εἰργάζετο, ἀλλὰ μετὰ πολλῆς τῆς σπουδῆς].

[221] *hom. in Ac.* 39.2 [60.277].

[222] *hom. in Ac.* 45.2 [60.316], discussed below, p. 318, in connection with Paul's πενία, "poverty." On Paul's ἀκτημοσύνη see pp. 308–26, in the discussion of Paul's ascetic acts.

And more than all things Paul was doing this [reading], when he was studying the ancestral Law at the feet of Gamaliel, so that even after that he was likely devoting himself to reading … Indeed, don't you see him continually employing the testimonies of the prophets and looking at the things in them ['Ορᾷς γοῦν αὐτὸν συνεχῶς ταῖς τῶν προφητῶν κεχρημένον μαρτυρίαις, καὶ θεωροῦντα τὰ ἐν αὐταῖς]? Then, indeed, Paul is devoted to reading [Εἶτα Παῦλος μὲν προσέχει τῇ ἀναγνώσει].[223]

This yields a portrait of Paul the Scripture scholar, focused intently and continually on the sacred Scriptures, a model for all who search the scriptures, including now his own epistles.[224]

πράξεις (Deeds)

Since praise is awarded from deeds [αἱ πράξεις], and it is characteristic of the excellent person to act according to free will [κατὰ προαίρεσιν], then one must try to show that the person has acted according to this. And it is useful if one can be shown to have acted in this way repeatedly.[225]

The reason πράξεις are the "most important topic-heading" [τὸ μέγιστον κεφάλαιον] of an encomium[226] is because they give the most important testimony to the subject's virtues.[227] Aphthonios separates those virtues into the three categories of a human life with which we have been working in this study: τὰς πράξεις ἃς

---

[223] *hom. in 1 Tim.* 13.1 [62.565–66], on the exhortation to reading in 1 Tim 4:13.

[224] One does not require very much imagination to see John himself in this description. But Paul even supercedes John as, for instance, although John is confounded by the origin of the famous "scriptural" quotation at 1 Cor 2:9, and can only conjecture that it came from a lost book, he says confidently that "Paul, given that he was learned in the law [νομομαθὴς ὤν], and spoke in the spirit, probably knew all things accurately" [εἰκὸς εἰδέναι πάντα μετὰ ἀκριβείας] (*hom. in 1 Cor.* 7.3 [61.58]).

[225] Aristotle, *Rh.* 1.9.32: Ἐπεὶ δ' ἐκ τῶν πράξεων ὁ ἔπαινος, ἴδιον δὲ τοῦ σπουδαίου τὸ κατὰ προαίρεσιν, πειρατέον δεικνύναι πράττοντα κατὰ προαίρεσιν. χρήσιμον δὲ τὸ πολλάκις φαίνεσθαι πεπραχότα. Note how Aristotle argued for the superiority of deeds over the other topics: "the encomium is concerned with deeds [τὸ δ' ἐγκώμιον τῶν ἔργων ἐστίν]; the attendant things [τὰ κύκλῳ], like noble birth and education [εὐγένεια καὶ παιδεία] work for persuasion [εἰς πίστιν], given that it is likely that good people are descended from such, and that one who has been brought up in that way will turn out so [εἰκὸς γὰρ ἐξ ἀγαθῶν ἀγαθοὺς καὶ τὸν οὕτω τραφέντα τοιοῦτον εἶναι]. Therefore we pronounce an encomium on those who have accomplished deeds" [διὸ καὶ ἐγκωμιάζομεν πράξαντας] (*Rh.* 1.9.33, my trans.).

[226] Aphthonios, *Prog.* 8 [Spengel 2.36].

[227] As Chrysostom himself recognizes in his interpretation of Eph 4:25: "because apart from actions a human being cannot be shown" ["Οτι χωρὶς ἐνεργείας οὐκ ἂν δειχθείη ἄνθρωπος] (*hom. in Eph.* 13.2 [62.96]). Here the encomium shows also its connection with biography, as described by Cox: "the recitation of events, the *praxeis* of the hero, is crucial to the structure of biographies of holy men. We have just seen that chronology does not provide the structural referent for the narration of the holy man's life … The acts provide the only real structure in the biographies. Each act, whether it is an actual physical deed or a verbal act (a speech, a list of treatises), is a star in the hero's personal constellation; it illumines an aspect of the ideal that his life represents in the biography" (*Biography*, 57).

διαιρέσεις εἰς ψυχὴν καὶ σῶμα καὶ τυχήν.[228] Having investigated Chrysostom's portraits of Paul's body and his soul and the virtues residing there in chapters 4 and 5, we shall devote this next part of our investigation to a more topical approach to Pauline πράξεις, arranging under this broad umbrella a selection of recurrent categories of Pauline actions and accomplishments which receive characteristic forms of treatment by Chrysostom. At the outset we should call attention again to the tension in the treatment of πράξεις for Chrysostom, as also for the rhetorical theorists and other practitioners of the art. The deeds which are most praiseworthy are those which come from the "free will" [προαίρεσις] of the subject, since compulsory or accidental achievements are not necessarily signs of inner character. Hence repeatedly John stresses that the engine driving Paul's many virtuous acts was his profound προαίρεσις. But even as Chrysostom enthusiastically appropriates the logic of this form, with its emphasis upon the surprising deeds of the man who overcame lowly beginnings by a fantastic will to virtue, he works within another boundary: not wishing to go so far as to suggest that Paul was a "self-made man." For, as he concludes in laud. Paul. 4: "God made him what he was" [καὶ τοῦτο ἐκεῖνον τοιοῦτον ἐποίησε].[229] Yet, as we shall see, Chrysostom often strays very close to this limit in his discourses, in effusively praising the Pauline πράξεις (or κατορθώματα, "virtuous deeds")[230] so that he can exhort his auditors to imitate Paul. As he seeks deftly to negotiate these boundaries, John will treat specific classes of Pauline deeds in some telltale ways, establishing distinct, if somewhat blurred, action portraits.

Pre-Christian πράξεις

Persecution of Christians

Most of the Pauline πράξεις which concern Chrysostom are those which took place after his conversion, with the single exception (made also by Paul himself) of Paul's pre-Christian persecution of the followers of Jesus. John energetically sketches this potentially devastating image of Paul's "former life" [ὁ πρότερος Παύλου βίος],[231] portraying it in both ominous and complimentary colors. In some ways this is an exemplary instance of how Chrysostom was virtually incapable of painting a completely negative, unflattering portrait of his beloved Paul. He

---

[228] Aphthonios, Prog. 8 [Spengel 2.36]. Here we have an overlap between two ways of formulating the invention of an encomiastic argument: either all topoi arranged under the three categories of soul, body and chance are instances of πράξεις (Aphthonios' scheme), or the categories of body and chance are regarded as the givens, with the soul's characteristics being the province of deeds, since they alone are willed, and therefore instances of virtue (for an overview, with the important sources, see Burgess, Epideictic Literature, 119–25).

[229] laud. Paul. 4.21 [SC 300.228].

[230] See above, n. 116, on this term.

[231] hom. in Ac. 9:1 1.6 [51.122].

recognizes the inherently shameful nature of those terrible acts, but also the abundant rhetorical and catechetical possibilities they offer.[232] For instance, when he wishes to construct a then-and-now argument to accent the magnificent, divinely-inspired turnabout made by Paul, John even heightens the viciousness of the famous, vivid Lukan picture of Paul "breathing threats and murder" [ἐμπνέων ἀπειλῆς καὶ φόνου].[233] In these portraits Paul the persecutor of Christians was a madman, one in the grip of an ungovernable insanity,[234] a crazed lion running about,[235] a murderer with thousands of malefacting hands.[236] The then-and-now contrast moves to the predictable result, as the meteoric metamorphosis of Paul's conversion recast him as gentle as a lamb,[237] or, in an equally uncanny reversal, the wolf become a shepherd.[238] But even in this raging portrait of Paul the executioner of Christians we see the seeds of a defense by appeal to insanity. Just as already the authors of the deutero-Pauline letters, even as they invoked the stereotypical portrait of Paul the persecutor for its power and rhetorical utility, painted in some apologetic tones for their hero,[239] so Chrysostom, drawing heavily upon them, emphasizes that Paul acted out of "temporary insanity,"[240] and, especially, "ignorance" (1 Tim 1:13).

The marvelous turnabout Paul made allows Chrysostom to use the saint's conversion as an exemplum in his moralizing exhortations. For this rhetorical purpose, also, it suited John to play up the grisly and ferocious qualities of Paul the persecutor,[241]

---

[232] "But let no one be ashamed when they hear these things about Paul; for these are not accusations against him, but a proposition for encomia" ['Αλλὰ μηδεὶς αἰσχυνέσθω περὶ Παύλου ταῦτα ἀκούων· οὐ γάρ ἐστιν αὐτοῦ κατηγορήματα, ἀλλ' ἐγκωμίων ὑπόθεσις] (*hom. in Ac. 9:1* 1.4 [51.119]).

[233] Acts 9:1. In *hom. in Ac. 9:1* 1.6 [51.122] Chrysostom shows his appreciation for the detail and emphasis of the portrait-master Luke's account of these matters [τὰ πρότερα ἡμῖν μετ' ἀκριβείας διηγήσατο, καὶ πολλῆς ἐμφάσεως].

[234] This portrait is found in attenuated form on the lips of Paul himself in Acts 26:11: ἐμμαινόμενος αὐτοῖς ἐδίωκον.

[235] See *scand.* 20.10 [SC 79.248]; *catech.* 4.7 [SC 50.186]; 4.10 [SC 50.187]; 5.19 [SC 50.210].

[236] In *hom. in Ac.* 18.2 [60.142] Paul is said to have "cast thousands of murderous hands" at Stephen.

[237] ἀθρόον εἰς ἡμερότητα προβάτου μεταβαλλόμενος (*catech.* 4.10 [SC 50.187]).

[238] Ὁ λύκος ἐγένετο ποιμήν (*hom. in Ac. 9:1* 1.5 [51.120]).

[239] See de Boer, "Images of Paul," 370, on "Paul, the Redeemed Persecutor": "The contrast between Paul the persecutor and Paul the apostle, between 'then' and 'now,' is exploited by Ephesians, Acts, and the Pastorals." But for Chrysostom, of course, these texts are undifferentiatedly Pauline autobiographical portraits.

[240] An insanity which Chrysostom can term (when referring to the Jews who later persecuted Paul), ἡ τῶν Ἰουδαίων μανία (*catech.* 4.10 [SC 50.188]).

[241] "And indeed, no one was held fast by so great a wicked madness as that with which he engaged the battle against the church" [καίτοι γε οὐδεὶς οὕτω μετὰ τοσαύτης μανίας ἔχεται κακίας, μεθ' ὅσης ἐκεῖνος τοῦ πολέμου τοῦ κατὰ τῆς ἐκκλησίας]. In this retelling, Paul actually grieved because he didn't have thousands of hands with which to beat Stephen (*hom. in 1 Cor.* 22.4 [61.185], cf. n. 236, above), and acted like a "beast" [θηρίον] hunting down and tearing apart the Christians.

so that he can say to his congregants that, no matter how terrible their former lives and sins, they need pose no hindrance to virtue: "Consider that Paul was a blasphemer and a persecutor and a violent man, and the first of sinners,[242] but suddenly he rose up to the very height of virtue, and his former life [τὰ πρότερα] presented him with no hindrance."[243] For this reason Paul's pre-Christian period, though marked by deeds that were the very opposite of love, allows future generations to learn "that the deed comes from one's free will, and everything is easy for those who want it" [προαιρέσεως τὸ ἔργον, καὶ βουλομένοις ἅπαντα εὔκολα].[244]

But at other times, in what is perhaps a less expected rhetorical move, John seeks to show Paul worthy of praise, not because he later turned his life around,[245] but even *in the midst of* his persecuting activities. For example, Chrysostom attributes Paul's plot to persecute Christians in Damascus to careful forethought of such proportion that it almost amounts to a prophetic insight: Paul tried to nip the new movement in the bud because he perceived its rampant success, and foresaw that the gospel might be distributed everywhere.[246] But the major piece of the logic which makes a rhetorical possibility for praise out of Paul's hunting down of Christians as his enemies is supplied by Chrysostom's pervasive anti-Judaistic persuasions. With consistent, if pernicious, logic, Chrysostom insists that even at this moment of greatest ignominy Paul's actions as persecutor showed him superior to his fellow Jews,[247] who routinely acted on their φιλαρχία, "lust for rule," whereas he was motivated by ζῆλος, "zeal."[248] Furthermore, Paul deserves added praise for

---

[242] Παῦλος βλάσφημος ἦν καὶ διώκτης καὶ ὑβριστής, καὶ τῶν ἁμαρτωλῶν πρῶτος (1 Tim 1:13, 15).

[243] *hom. in 1 Cor.* 22.4 [61.185].

[244] Ibid.

[245] A classic instance of this common argument is afforded by *hom. in Ac. 9:1* 1.4 [51.120]: "These things are encomia to Paul [Ἐγκώμια Παύλου ταῦτά ἐστιν], not because he razed the church, but because he himself built it back up again; not because he laid waste the word, but because, after laying it waste, he himself caused it to increase again; not because he made war on the apostles, not because he tore apart the group, but because, after tearing it asunder, later he himself welded it together."

[246] *hom. in 1 Tim.* 3.2 [62.517].

[247] This rhetorical move is also found prefigured in the biblical materials. As de Boer has pointed out, the deutero-Pauline portraits of Paul the persecutor conveniently leave out Paul's Jewishness: "a striking aspect of the portrayal of Paul, the redeemed persecutor [is]: there is no mention here of Paul's past ... Paul's role as a persecutor has, therefore, been generalized, and it is never specified of what he had been a persecutor ... Paul seems in fact to be, in the author's view, the prototypical Gentile sinner!" ("Images of Paul," 371).

[248] *hom. in 1 Tim.* 3.2 [62.517], stressing the statement of 1 Tim 1:13, that Paul acted "in ignorance" [ἀγνοῶν], and surely influenced also by Phil 3:6. "The Jews," on the other hand, did not act in ignorance, but vainglory [κενοδοξία], as John attempts to prove with serial quotations from John 12:42–43; 5:44; 9:22; 12:19 and Luke 5:21 [Ὅτι οὐκ ἐξ ἀγνοίας, ἀλλὰ καὶ εἰδότες καὶ σφόδρα ἐπιστάμενοι ἔπραττον ἅπερ ἔπραττον]. In *hom. in 2 Tim.* 1.1 [62.602] and *comm. in Gal.* 1.9 [61.627], Chrysostom insists that even when persecuting Christians Paul did nothing for a human reason [δι' ἀνθρωπίνην αἰτίαν], nor was his persecuting a matter of κολακεία, "flattery." In the latter passage and *hom. in Ac. 9:1* 3.4 [51.138] Chrysostom maintains that Paul

his great self-effacement and humility in continually referring to these past evil deeds in his letters, long after they had been forgiven and forgotten.[249]

There is no strict division between these negative and positive characterizations of Paul ὁ διώκτης in Chrysostom's oratory. More often he weaves the two together, seeking to heap praise on Paul's head from both directions. This approach is exemplified to the highest degree in Chrysostom's consideration of the small word ἔτι, "still," in Acts 9:1:

> What does "still" mean? For what did he do before this that he says "still?" "Still" is said about a man who had done many evil things before this [Ἔτι, περὶ ἀνθρώπου πολλὰ κακὰ πεποιηκότος ἔμπροσθεν λέγεται]. Then what did he do? Well, tell me, what evil didn't he do [Τί γὰρ οὐκ ἐποίησεν, εἰπέ μοι, κακόν;]? He filled Jerusalem with blood, exterminating the believers, he was laying the church waste, he was persecuting the apostles, he slaughtered Stephen, he didn't spare men or women. Indeed, hear what his disciple [Luke] says of him: "Saul was destroying the church, going into the houses one by one, and dragging out men and women" (Acts 8:3). For not even the public market sufficed for him, but he even plunged into houses (he says, "going into the houses one by one"). And he didn't say, "leading out," nor "drawing forth" men and women, but "dragging men and women," as though said about an animal, dragging out men and women. And not men only, but also women. For he had neither respect for nature nor mercy on that sex, nor was he broken up before their weakness.[250]

This portrait of Paul as a ferocious predator[251] accents all the details in the Lukan narrative to emphasize the tremendous extremes to which Paul went in his persecution of the early Christian converts. Nonetheless, John does not leave the portrait to dry with this vicious visage, but continues with an explanation and defense brief for his hero, based not upon his later change of heart, but on the motivation from which he conducted these very heinous acts:

> For it was by zeal, not by wrath, that he was doing these things [Ζήλῳ γὰρ, οὐχὶ θυμῷ ταῦτα ἐποίει]. For this reason, the Jews who do the same things are worthy of condemnation; but he, for doing the same things, of pardon [Διὰ τοῦτο οἱ μὲν Ἰουδαῖοι τὰ αὐτὰ ποιοῦντες, ἄξιοι κατηγορίας· οὗτος δὲ τὰ αὐτὰ ποιῶν, ἄξιος συγγνώμης].[252] For from the things they were doing it is clear that they did them to receive honor and glory from the many, whereas this was not so in his case, but he was acting in zeal for God, even if not according to knowledge [Καὶ γὰρ ἀπ' αὐτῶν ὧν ἐποίουν δῆλοι ἦσαν, ὅτι ἐκεῖνοι μὲν τιμῆς ἕνεκεν καὶ δόξης τῆς παρὰ τῶν πολλῶν ταῦτα ἔπραττον· οὗτος δὲ οὐχ οὕτως, ἀλλὰ τῷ Θεῷ ζηλῶν, εἰ

---

acted from zeal, not anger (see also Wenger's n.1 in SC 50.187). And he connects Paul's zeal with the demands of the law which he was seeking to fulfil, as in *hom. in Ac.* 18.2 [60.143]: οὕτω τὴν ψυχὴν αὐτοῦ ἔδωκεν ὑπὲρ τοῦ νόμου, and 19.2 [60.152]: ὅρα τὸν πόθον καὶ τὴν σφοδρότητα, πῶς νομικῶς ἔπραττεν.

[249] *hom. in Gen.* 31.2 [53.285]; *hom. in 1 Cor.* 38.5 [61.328]; *hom. in Phil.* 10.2 [62.258]; further discussion and references in di S. Maria, "S. Paolo," 497.

[250] *hom. in Ac. 9:1* 3.4 [51.138]. Compare *hom. in Ac.* 18.2 [60.143]: Ὅρα καὶ τὴν παρρησίαν, καὶ τὴν ὕβριν, καὶ τὴν μανίαν.

[251] *hom. in Ac.* 18.2 [60.143] stresses that Paul acted alone.

[252] Also, "forbearance."

καὶ μὴ κατ' ἐπίγνωσιν].That is why they let the women go, but waged war on the men,[253] since they were looking at those Christians with an eye to the honor which would redound to them; but Paul, in his contending, stood up against all.[254]

In this ironic reversal some of the gory details of Pauline persecution which filled in the portrait of Paul as a wild animal ravaging the early Christians have become the basis for his defense. This Paul is an anti-portrait of Chrysostom's stereotypically negative image of "the Jews." Depicted against this background, Paul is shown to have been superior to his fellow Jews because he was more effective in his persecutorial practices than they.[255] Furthermore, the very uncompromisability and impartiality of his murderous targeting of *all* Christians (regardless of gender) indicates the motive behind it – zeal for God[256] – which renders it, although functionally the same action as his fellow Jews, worthy of excuse [συγγνώμη], whereas they, who acted in vainglory (as they always do, in Chrysostom's consistently deleterious portrayal, which owes much to John 12:43) deserve only condemnation [κατηγορία] for it.[257] The Jews' comparative leniency in not hunting down the Christian women is thereby converted into a proof of their ἀρέσκεια, whereas the "beast" Paul turns out to be a religious man fired by praiseworthy zeal for his god, though unfortunately lacking in the "knowledge" that will tame it. The irony within the irony here, of course, is that the very portrait of Paul as having ζῆλος but not acting κατ' ἐπίγνωσιν[258] comes from Paul's own psychological portrait of disbelieving Israel in Rom 10:3, which Chrysostom has applied solely to the apostle, and flatly denied to its original referents, the Jews.

From this plea for exoneration John turns and paints an even more vividly negative portrayal of Paul the bloodthirsty hunter:

Therefore, knowing these things, and seeing that Saul was not yet satisfied, Luke said: "Saul was still breathing threats and murder against the disciples of the Lord." The murder of

---

[253] Chrysostom makes the same claim about the other "Jews" who persecuted Christians in *hom. in Ac.* 47.1 [60.328].

[254] *hom. in Ac. 9:1* 3.4 [51.138].

[255] Hence Chrysostom can claim Paul victorious over the Jews both before and after his conversion, as in *catech.* 4.7: "The one who before this excelled the Jews in all he did and in laying waste the church, immediately was confounding the Jews dwelling in Damascus by preaching that he who has been crucified is the son of God" [ὁ πρὸ τούτου ὑπὲρ Ἰουδαίων ἅπαντα πράττων καὶ πορθῶν τὴν ἐκκλησίαν, εὐθέως συνέχυνε τοὺς Ἰουδαίους τοὺς κατοικοῦντας ἐν Δαμασκῷ κηρύσσων ὅτι ὁ ἐσταυρωμένος αὐτός ἐστιν ὁ υἱὸς τοῦ θεοῦ].

[256] *hom. in Ac. 9:1* 1.6 [51.122]: ἀλλὰ ζήλῳ πεπυρωμένος, οὐκ ὀρθῷ μὲν, ζήλῳ δὲ ὅμως.

[257] The same argument appears, with different "evidence" in *hom. in Ac.* 19.2 [60.152]: "Hence Paul in doing this was not like Jews. No way! For it is clear that he acted from zeal by the fact that he went off to outside cities, but they were not even concerned about Christians in Jerusalem, but were conscious of only one thing, how to enjoy honor" [Οὗτος μὲν οὖν οὕτως ἐποίει, οὐχ ὡς Ἰουδαῖοι· μὴ γένοιτο. Ὅτι γὰρ ζήλῳ ἐποίει, δῆλον ἐκ τοῦ καὶ εἰς τὰς ἔξω πόλεις ἀπιέναι. Ἐκεῖνοι δὲ οὔτε κἂν τῶν ἐν Ἱεροσολύμοις ἐφρόντισαν, ἀλλ' ἑνὸς ἐγένοντο μόνου, τοῦ τιμῆς ἀπολαύειν]. See also *hom. in Ac. 9:1* 1.6 [51.122].

[258] This is a common description of the pre-Christian Paul for Chrysostom. See also, e.g., *hom. in Ac. 9:1* 1.3 [51.117].

Stephen did not satiate him, nor did the persecution of the church fill up his desire, but he went even further, and didn't stop at all from his madness [οὐδαμοῦ ἵστατο τῆς μανίας]. For it was zeal [ζῆλος γὰρ ἦν]. But now getting up from the murder of Stephen, he was persecuting the apostles. He was doing the same thing as a wild wolf who, springing upon a flock of sheep, and, after snatching a lamb from there, and tearing it to pieces with his own mouth, became even more bold by the attack. Thus also Paul sprang upon the chorus of the apostles, snatched from there the lamb of Christ, tore Stephen to pieces, finally becoming more bold by this murder.[259] That is why he says, "still."[260]

Given the ferocity of this portrait of Paul the savage beast with mouth dripping blood, the prevailing question is how this lupine Paul could possibly have been changed into one more gentle than a lamb. Chrysostom takes his first explanation from the narrative of Acts, asking who could not have been mollified and charmed by those last, forgiving words of Stephen (Acts 7:60)? That prayer for leniency for his executioners was indeed responsible for Paul's almost immediate transformation, he thinks, though not because it swayed Paul. What was decisive was that God hearkened to it. Because God held Stephen worthy to be listened to, and because of the virtue which Paul will have in the future (which God alone could foresee), he heeded Stephen's plea for mercy for his assailants.[261] Now the embellished portrait of Paul the mad marauder serves yet a new purpose, not to exculpate him, but to point to the divine source of his transformation, for only a divine power could have stopped this murderous tornado at its height, and turned the persecutor into an evangelist [ὁ διώκτης εὐαγγελιστὴς γέγονεν].

The word "still" signifies that Christ drew Paul to himself when he was still crazed, still acting as a wild beast, still at the very height of his wrath, still boiling with murder [ἔτι μαινόμενον, ἔτι ἀγριαίνοντα, ἔτι ἐν ἀκμῇ τοῦ θυμοῦ ὄντα, ἔτι τῷ φόνῳ ζέοντα ἐπεσπάσατο ὁ Χριστός]. Christ did not wait for the malady [τὸ νόσημα] to cease, and the passion [τὸ πάθος] to be extinguished, and the wild animal to become more docile [πραότερον γενέσθαι τὸν ἄγριον], thus to draw him over; but at the very height of madness [ἐν αὐτῇ τῇ ἀκμῇ τῆς μανίας] he took Saul captive, so that he might show his own power, that in the midst of that past mad frenzy [ἐν μέσῃ τῇ βακχείᾳ τότε ἐκείνῃ], when he was boiling with wrath [ζέοντος ἔτι τοῦ θυμοῦ], Christ defeated and overcame the persecutor [κρατεῖ καὶ περιγίνεται τοῦ διώκτου].[262]

---

[259] Chrysostom propounds the same view of the catalytic role of the death of Stephen in Paul's development as a murderer in *hom. in Ac.* 18.2 [60.143]: "He set upon all who fell into his hands with countless evil acts, inasmuch as he had become more bold from this murder" [Τοὺς ἐμπίπτοντας ἅπαντας μυρίοις διετίθει κακοῖς, ἅτε ἀπὸ τῆς σφαγῆς ταύτης θρασύτερος γεγονώς].

[260] *hom. in Ac. 9:1* 3.4 [51.138–39].

[261] Καὶ γὰρ ἄξιος ἦν ἀκούεσθαι Στέφανος καὶ διὰ τὴν ἀρετὴν Παύλου τὴν ἐσομένην, καὶ διὰ οἰκείαν ὁμολογίαν (quoting Acts 7:60) (*hom. in Ac. 9:1* 3.4 [51.139]).

[262] *hom. in Ac. 9:1* 3.4 [51.139]; very similar is the later *hom. in Ac.* 19.2 [60.152]: "Luke fittingly inserts mention of Paul's zeal, in order to show that he was drawn to Christ in the midst of zeal" [Εὐκαίρως παρενέβαλε τὰ περὶ τοῦ ζήλου τοῦ Παύλου, ἵνα δείξῃ, ὅτι ἐν μέσῳ τῷ ζήλῳ ἕλκεται].

Christ the tamer of wild beasts intervened, just when things appeared most dire and irreversible, to transform the bloodthirsty wolf into a lamb, the persecutor into the evangelist. Since the root of Paul's insane persecution of Christians was a "malady," only Christ's emergency medicine could have overturned it:

For we admire doctors especially when they are able to bring down and completely suppress a fever which is rising and the flame of an illness when at a severe height, which is also what happened in Paul's case. For when he was at the height of the flame, like some dew born down from above, the voice of the Lord set him completely free from the illness.[263]

The result of this miraculous move from anti-type to type, from Dr. Jekyll to Mr. Hyde,[264] was that the divine purpose was even more richly fulfilled. Hence the Christian orator must speak the unspeakable, and placard portraits of the pre-Christian Paul (as Paul did himself),[265] because they testify to the love and power of God, who both wished to save such an evil wretch, and was able to do it.[266] By

---

[263] Ἐν ἀκμῇ γὰρ αὐτὸν ὄντα τῆς φλογός, ὥσπερ τις δρόσος ἄνωθεν κατενεχθεῖσα, ἡ φωνὴ τοῦ κυρίου τοῦ νοσήματος ἀπήλλαξε παντελῶς (hom. in Ac. 9:1 3.4 [51.139]).

[264] This is especially amplified in hom. in Ps. 50 1 [55.530] (a Chrysostomic pseudepigraphon): "And then he was a wolf, but now a sheep; then he was a persecutor, now an evangelist; then he was a weed, now grain; then he was a pirate and drowner, but now the ship-pilot of the people; then he was laying waste the church, now he is entrusted with it; then he was cutting off the vineyards, now he has become a vine-dresser; then he was lead, now he has become gold" [Καὶ ὁ ποτε λύκος, νῦν πρόβατον· ὁ ποτε διώκτης, νῦν εὐαγγελιστής· ὁ ποτε ζιζάνιον, νῦν σῖτος· ὁ ποτε πειρατὴς καὶ καταποντιστής, νῦν κυβερνήτης λαοῦ· ὁ ποτε πορθῶν τὴν Ἐκκλησίαν, νῦν πιστευόμενος αὐτήν· ὁ ποτε τὰς ἀμπέλους ἐκκόπτων, νῦν φυτουργὸς γενόμενος· ὁ ποτε μόλυβδος, νῦν χρυσὸς γενόμενος].

[265] "... and he was not ashamed, but, as though recording on a pillar the things he formerly dared to do, he showed them to all, thinking it was better that his former life be placarded before all people than, by hesitating to parade his own error, to overshadow God's ineffable and inde-scribable beneficence" [καὶ οὐκ ᾐσχύνετο, ἀλλὰ καὶ ὥσπερ ἐν στήλῃ τοῖς γράμμασι τὰ πρότερον αὐτῷ τολμηθέντα καταθέμενος, ἅπασιν ἐπεδείκνυ, βέλτιον εἶναι νομίζων τὸν πρότερον αὐτοῦ παρὰ πάντων στηλιτεύεσθαι βίον ἐπὶ τὸ φανῆναι τὸ μέγεθος τῆς τοῦ Θεοῦ δωρεᾶς, ἢ συσκιάσαι τὴν ἄφατον αὐτοῦ καὶ ἀνεκδιήγητον φιλανθρωπίαν, ὀκνοῦντα τὴν οἰκείαν ἅπασιν ἐκπομπεῦσαι πλάνην] (hom. in Jo. 10.1 [59.74]). The theme of Paul τὸν πρότερον ἑαυτοῦ βίον στηλιτεύειν is a favored one of John's (see also hom. in Ac. 20.3 [60.161]; hom. in 2 Cor. 22.2 [61.550]). The result of Paul's deliberate publicizing of his sins in writing is that they are publicly known, not only by people of his own day, but by all in the future: "For he parades his sins, when there was no necessity to do so, every single day in all his letters, placarding them and making them known, not only to the people alive then, but also to all those who will live afterwards" [Τὰ μὲν οὖν ἁμαρτήματα, καὶ μηδεμιᾶς οὔσης ἀνάγκης, ἐκπομπεύει καθ᾽ ἑκάστην ἡμέραν ἐν ταῖς ἐπιστολαῖς αὐτοῦ πάσαις, στηλιτεύων καὶ δῆλα ποιῶν οὐχὶ τοῖς τότε μόνον ἀνθρώποις, ἀλλὰ καὶ τοῖς μετὰ ταῦτα ἐσομένοις πᾶσι] (hom. in 2 Cor. 11:1 6 [51.306]). Chrysostom takes this as an indication of Paul's extreme humility.

[266] "For this reason it was necessary for him to speak of his former life; for he demonstrates to us God's compassion for humanity and power: the compassion for humanity, in that he wished to save the man who had performed such great acts of evil and draw him to himself; the power in that, having so desired, he was strong enough to accomplish it" [Διὰ τοῦτο ἀναγκαῖον καὶ τὸν πρότερον βίον αὐτοῦ εἰπεῖν· καὶ γὰρ τὴν τοῦ θεοῦ δείκνυσιν ἡμῖν φιλανθρωπίαν καὶ δύναμιν· φιλανθρωπίαν μέν, ὅτι ἐβουλήθη τὸν τοσαῦτα κακὰ ἐργασάμενον σῶσαι, καὶ πρὸς ἑαυτὸν ἐπισπάσασθαι· δύναμιν δέ, ὅτι βουληθεὶς ἴσχυσε] (hom. in Ac. 9:1 1.6 [51.122]).

reframing the portrait of Paul the vicious Christian-killer within the larger context, not only of his whole βίος,[267] but also of divine salvation history, Chrysostom is able to alter both its dimensions and its final, lasting effect on the hearer/spectator. To celebrate the ultimate, fantastic results of the psychodrama thus rehearsed, Chrysostom switches to entirely new metaphors: "When the single fountain of Stephen was stopped shut, then another opened up, releasing thousands of rivers. When the mouth of Stephen went silent, immediately the trumpet of Paul [ἡ σάλπιγξ τοῦ Παύλου] sounded forth!"[268]

Conversion

Paul's conversion marks the definitive turning point in the Pauline πράξεις in Chrysostom's eyes, because it was solely up to this point that Paul was guilty of any sins; after his baptism (three days after the conversion)[269] he lived so purely that he was conscious of no infractions (as 1 Cor 4:4 attests), and had no misdeeds to bemoan. Henceforth, all Pauline deeds are unambiguous signs of his impeccable virtue, and consequently all Pauline repentance, such as in 1 Cor 15:9, is directed toward the misguided behavior of his unenlightened pre-Christian period.[270] Although one would not expect conversion to be a regular category in encomia (and it is not) it is not unprecedented. Libanios, in eulogizing Julian, likewise treats his conversion after his γένος and παιδεία as a special deed testifying to his character, marking him with divine approval and prefiguring the great acts to come.[271]

Naturally Chrysostom takes the Acts 9 account as fully historical. And, as in Luke's narrative, Chrysostom's portrait of Paul's conversion is dependent upon his depiction of Paul the persecutor. For instance, in one homily John admires the divine foresight in striking Paul blind first, since the man was ἀπρόσιτος, "unapproachable," due to his maniacal zeal for destroying the church. The blindness, therefore, served as a severe bit in the mouth of this wild horse, who otherwise would be led only by his frenzy, and thus be ill-disposed to listen to the divine address. By striking him in this way the Lord "calmed the waves of his ferocious wrath" so that then he could speak with Paul in his anesthetized state. This strategic

---

[267] What Chrysostom terms in one place τὰ κατὰ τὸν μακάριον Παῦλον ἅπαντα (*hom. in Jo.* 10.1 [59.74]).

[268] Ἐνεφράττετο μία πηγὴ ἡ τοῦ Στεφάνου, καὶ ἠνοίγετο ἑτέρα μυρίους ἀφιεῖσα ποταμούς. Ἐπειδὴ γὰρ ἐσίγησε τὸ στόμα Στεφάνου, ἤχησεν εὐθέως ἡ σάλπιγξ τοῦ Παύλου (*hom. in Ac. 9:1* 3.4 [51.139]).

[269] This is according to Acts 9:9. Chrysostom regards the three days as a period of purification and preparation (*hom. in Ac.* 1.6 [60.22]), akin to the catechumenate of his own day.

[270] *compunct.* 2 6 [47.421], and *hom. in Gen.* 31.2 [53.285], discussed further below in the treatment of Paul's ascetic acts (pp. 319–20).

[271] *Or.* 13.16; 18.18: "throwing out all that earlier nonsense, in its place he brought the beauty of the truth into his soul" [πάντα τὸν ἔμπροσθεν ἐκβαλὼν ὖθλον ἀντεισήγαγεν εἰς τὴν ψυχὴν τὸ τῆς ἀληθείας κάλλος].

move has the further result of demonstrating God's own unapproachability in wisdom [τῆς σοφίας αὐτοῦ τὸ ἀπρόσιτον] and superiority in knowledge.[272] The divine force blinded Paul, not by darkness, but by an irresistible light that cast him into darkness.

The extent to which pictures of Paul the persecutor are the negative images underlying portraits of Paul the converted is illustrated perfectly by the theriomorphic sketches of Paul as wolf and lion, that have their obvious tamed counterpart in the post-conversion Paul as gentler than a lamb. This depiction process can also work in reverse order, so that Chrysostom fashions an ingenious picture of the converted Paul which contains within it the counter-image of the persecutor he used to be. In the following homiletic passage Chrysostom takes the pose of a would-be ekphrasist, who by pining for a vision he can only imagine evokes it for others:

I desire to see this big fish caught, the fish that had roiled up the entire sea, and raised countless waves against the church. I desire to see him caught, not with a fishhook, but by a word of the Lord. For just as a fisherman sitting on a high rock, holding up his rod, lets his hook down from above into the sea, thus also our Lord, who demonstrated the spiritual fishing technique, as though sitting on the high rock of the heavens, let down this call from above, like an anchor: "Saul, Saul, why are you persecuting me?" And thus he caught this big fish.[273]

Any narrative depiction, such as this one, involves not only a portrait of Paul, but also of all supporting characters, in this case a remarkable image of Christ "angling" for Paul from heaven.[274] Once this vivid portrait has been produced, Chrysostom gives it literary embellishment in two ways. First he compares this memorable catch with Peter's aquatic tax-collection at Jesus' command (Mt 17:24–27). Paul the landed fish also had a coin in his mouth, but it was a counterfeit coin, an emblem of a personal character tuned to a false note; "for he had zeal, but not according to knowledge" [εἶχε μὲν γὰρ ζῆλον, οὐ κατ᾽ ἐπίγνωσιν δέ]. This situation was immediately remedied by God, who by giving Paul the knowledge thereby

---

[272] *laud. Paul.* 4.2 [SC 300.184–86]: "Since, therefore, Paul was so zealous and unapproachable, he stood in need of a bit that was more strong, lest, led by the strength of his will, he might misunderstand the things that were said. It is for this reason, to forestall Paul's insanity, that Christ first calms the waves of his ferocious wrath through blinding him, and then he speaks to him. In this way he demonstrates the unapproachability of his wisdom, and the superiority of his knowledge" ['Επεὶ οὖν οὕτω σφοδρὸς ἦν καὶ ἀπρόσιτος, σφοδροτέρου ἐδεῖτο χαλινοῦ, ἵνα μὴ τῇ ῥύμῃ τῆς προθυμίας ἀγόμενος, καὶ παρακούσῃ τῶν λεγομένων. Διὰ δὴ τοῦτο καταστέλλων αὐτοῦ τὴν μανίαν ἐκείνην, πρῶτον κατευνάζει τὰ κύματα τῆς ῥαγδαίας ὀργῆς ἐκείνης διὰ τῆς πηρώσεως, καὶ τότε αὐτῷ διαλέγεται, δεικνὺς τῆς σοφίας αὐτοῦ τὸ ἀπρόσιτον, καὶ τὸ τῆς γνώσεως ὑπερέχον].

[273] *hom. in Ac. 9:1* 1.3 [51.117]. Ameringer, *Second Sophistic,* 83, says this comparison "amuses by its grotesqueness"!

[274] One can only speculate about what graphic images of Paul's conversion were known to Chrysostom, that might have influenced this visual tableau, but this literary portrait seems to be a rather original creation.

made his coin genuine. Here Chrysostom has given a legendary form to his apologetic argument about Paul's motivation for persecuting the church. Next he returns to the tale of Acts 9 in order to insist that, just as fish yanked out of water are rendered blind, so Paul, "the moment he bit the hook, and immediately after being hauled up, was blinded." Then, lest we be left with the mental picture of the apostle as a beached fish, blinded and flopping around on the dock, John adds one of his favorite themes to move the comparison well beyond the everyday: Paul's blindness made the whole world see again.[275]

Name Change

Normally a person's name would not fall among one's adult "deeds," but would be included in his or her γένος.[276] However, like the adoptive *filii Caesaris*,[277] Saul's transformed adult identity was signalled by a new appellation, Paul. Chrysostom's fascination with the topic of Paul's name change is manifested by the fact that he devoted fully four discourses to it (*hom. in Ac. 9:1* 1–4),[278] in addition to consideration of it in other contexts. The change in Paul's name [προσηγορία], which one can see when comparing Acts 9:1 [Σαῦλος] with all the epistles [Παῦλος], and attending to the stuttered reference at Acts 13:9 [Σαῦλος ὁ καὶ Παῦλος], was effected by the Holy Spirit as a symbol of Paul's new master, following the everyday practice of slaves who are ransomed from captivity.[279] Chrysostom knows of a tradition explaining the significance of the two names etymologically – Σαῦλος from σαλεύειν, "shaking up" the church, and Παῦλος from παύεσθαι, "ceasing" the persecution – but he warns his hearers against being deceived by this old-fashioned, unsupported interpretation.[280] John's first counter-argument to this

---

[275] *hom. in Ac. 9:1* 1.3 [51.117].

[276] Chrysostom well recognizes the great importance of names ἐν τοῖς βιωτικοῖς, "in matters of everyday life," including how names can reveal an unrecognized συγγένεια, and how they confer social recognition (*hom. in Ac. 9:1* 2.3 [51.128]).

[277] See, for example, the βασιλικὸς λόγος of Pliny, *Paneg.* 9–10, where he mentions in passing Trajan's biological γένος (omitting reference to his undistinguished πατρίς in Spain), but then celebrates at length the new identity and status he received by the conferral first of the name *Germanicus*, and then, at his inaugural, the additions of *Caesar* and *Imperator*. Rhetorically Chrysostom and Pliny are in somewhat the same position, in that they both seek to praise a subject on the basis of the new identity he received in adulthood. For Pliny this results in the oddness of the adult Trajan's dutiful and obedient "sonship" to Nerva; for Chrysostom in Paul's "birth" at his conversion. For both speakers their subject's origin cannot really be a cause for praise, for it has been usurped by a later windfall that upset the "natural" order it set in motion.

[278] Though these four discourses stray widely from this theme, as well.

[279] *hom. in Ac. 9:1* 3.3 [51.137].

[280] ἀλλ᾽ ἕωλος οὗτος ὁ λόγος καὶ οὐκ ἀληθής, καὶ διὰ τοῦτο αὐτὸν τέθεικα εἰς μέσον, ἵνα μὴ παρακρούησθε ταῖς ψιλαῖς αἰτιολογίαις (*hom. in Ac. 9:1* 2.2 [51.127]). The encomiastic technique of giving etymological explanations or embellishments on names was well established in rhetorical education. The most common example was the play on Demosthenes as τοῦ δήμου σθένος, "the strength of the people" (Theon, *Prog.* 8 [Spengel 2.111]).

poetic reading is simply historical: the man was given the name Saul by his parents, who (despite Chrysostom's general disinterest in them) assuredly were not prophets able to foretell the future.[281] And, secondly, if this etymology were true, then why wasn't Paul's name changed the minute he was converted and left off his persecuting activity?[282] But it was not until Acts 13:9 that the new name was bestowed, on Chrysostom's reading. So, in order to answer his preoccupation with the anomalous timing of Paul's name change, Chrysostom turns to Gal 1:22–23. Since Paul says that he was "unknown by face" to the Palestinian Christians, he presumably was known by name, given that they came to recognize the monumental shift in the one person: "the one persecuting us is now preaching the faith." The reason Saul's face was not known was because his visage, as often sketched so vividly by Chrysostom, was so terrifying that the Christians in Judea had never dared to look upon it. Therefore only by keeping his original name for some time afterwards would the continuity of the personhood of Paul have been broadcast; otherwise he would have emerged, like a runaway slave who had adopted a new identity, as Paul the Christian, and no one would have known of his miraculous metamorphosis from persecutor.[283] Hence the name change from Saul to Paul functions epideictically as a crucial "deed" in the sense that, as a divine moniker, it indicates Paul's true character and destiny. Then as the signifier of the persecutor-turned-evangelist, the name Παῦλος will function as a metonym for his entire career, and its fame will attest to grand, universal praise:

For look – from that time until now, how much time has passed, and the name of this prisoner has become most illustrious [λαμπρότερον τὸ ὄνομα τοῦ δεσμίου γέγονε τούτου]. But all the consuls, whoever they have been in past times, have gone silent, and they are not even known by name to most people. Yet the name of this prisoner, the blessed Paul, is great here [τὸ δὲ τοῦ δεσμίου τούτου ὄνομα τοῦ μακαρίου Παύλου πολὺ μὲν ἐνταῦθα], and great in the land of the barbarians, and great among the Scythians and Indians. And if you were to go to the ends of the world, you would hear this appellation [ταύτης ἀκούσῃ τῆς προσηγορίας], and wherever a person might go, they would see that Paul's name is born about in the mouths of all people everywhere [Παῦλον πανταχοῦ ἐν τοῖς ἁπάντων στόματι περιφερόμενον εἴσεται]. And what wonder, if on earth and sea, since even in the heavens Paul's name is great [καὶ ἐν τοῖς οὐρανοῖς πολὺ τὸ ὄνομα Παύλου], with the angels, with the archangels and with the powers above, and the king of these, God.[284]

---

[281] οἱ γονεῖς αὐτῷ τοῦτο τεθείκασι τοὔνομα οὐχὶ προφῆταί τινες ὄντες, καὶ τὸ μέλλον προορῶντες (hom. in Ac. 9:1 2.2 [51.127]).

[282] Ibid.

[283] hom. in Ac. 9:1 3.4 [51.137–38].

[284] stat. 16.3 [49.165]; see the full analysis of this passage in chap. 5, in discussion of Paul's chain (pp. 176–79). Paul's name is also responsible for particular actions in the present; according to hom. in Ac. 55.3 [60.382], "to those who know his name it is alone sufficient to arouse their souls to wakefulness, and shake off any sleep" [οὗ τοῖς εἰδόσι καὶ τὸ ὄνομα μόνον ἀρκεῖ πρὸς διέγερσιν ψυχῆς πρὸς νῆψιν, πρὸς τὸ πάντα ὕπνον ἀποτινάξασθαι].

And, along with the proper name, Παῦλος, the man was to earn the right to primary possession of the coveted title ἀπόστολος.[285] Paul's adult name and title signal and encapsulate his illustrious career in a single locution.

The πράξεις of Paul's Christian Life

Naturally the deeds which are most noteworthy in Chrysostom's encomia to Paul are those he accomplished after his conversion, in the course of his ministerial career. These are assembled nicely *seriatim* in one passage from *de providentia dei*:

> Now who has been wiser than Paul? Tell me, was this man not the vessel of election? Did he not draw to himself the great and indescribable grace of the spirit? Did he not have Christ speaking in him? Did he not share in the inexpressible words of God? Did not he alone hear the things which no human being was allowed to speak? Was he not snatched up into paradise? Was he not borne up into the third heaven? Did he not run around land and sea? Did he not persuade barbarians to pursue philosophy [οὐ βαρβάρους φιλοσοφεῖν ἔπεισεν]? Did he not have many and various activities of the spirit [πολλαὶ καὶ ποικίλαι τοῦ πνεύματος ἐνέργειαι]? Did he not correct whole peoples and cities? Did not God place the entire world into his hands [οὐ τὴν οἰκουμένην ἅπασαν εἰς χεῖρας αὐτῷ φέρων ἔθηκεν ὁ θεός]?[286]

This rich catalogue of Paul's grand accomplishments names most of the major categories of extraordinary deeds for which Paul deserves unqualified praise: powers of persuasion, ecstatic experiences, varied spiritual endowments. The only set of deeds not represented here (because Chrysostom's point in this passage is Paul's spiritual knowledge) is Paul's sufferings for the gospel, which are also very important in Chrysostom's imaginings of his idol. But this passage is more than a laundry list of disparate actions performed by the apostle over the years. With each jigsaw puzzle piece in place, a holistic image of Pauline deeds is evoked – as the man who by all these varied means took possession of the whole world.

Laud. Paul. 7: *The Deeds of Christ's Copyist*

Although all of Chrysostom's panegyrics to Paul in some way engage the deeds the apostle accomplished, the last of the seven is explicitly structured around the encomiastic topic of πράξεις, so an analysis of it is most fitting here.[287]

---

[285] "When you say, 'apostle,' everyone has him in mind immediately" [Ὅταν ἀπόστολον εἴπῃς, εὐθέως πάντες αὐτὸν ἐννοοῦσιν] (*hom. in Ac.* 55.3 [60.383]).

[286] *scand.* 2.3 [SC 79.60].

[287] Hubbell, "Chrysostom and Rhetoric," 273, regards the seventh homily *de laudibus sancti Pauli* as "the most artistically constructed of the whole series," a judgment in which he is followed by Piédagnel, SC 300.33. I find this evaluation rather surprising, given that this discourse is in many ways like a compilation of themes and appeals found in the others, and, *contra* Hubbell, its plan is not really more (or very) artistic. Hubbell is himself somewhat inconsistent in his assessment of what constitutes artistry, once saying the discourse possesses "artistic independence," and elsewhere giving evidence, including handbook testimony, of how it follows

προοίμιον (Introduction).[288] The discourse gets off to a rousing start, with its "majestic"[289] comparison between the imperial standard-bearers and Paul the bearer of the cross of Christ. By means of this arresting and epic verbal portrait of Paul carrying the sign of the cross, Chrysostom has encapsulated the Pauline career in a single hologram.[290] And at the very heart of this portrait that he draws of Paul's life in ministry is the call to imitation, which Chrysostom highlights with three captions of Pauline exhortations from Philippians alone (3:17; 4:9; 1:29).[291] By heeding these apostolic invitations to follow in his footsteps, John hopes others might share in the fount of spiritual blessings the apostle earned. Chrysostom brandishes his claims for Paul on his feast day with five rhetorical questions in customary epideictic fashion, crafted into his own brand of Christian hyperbole:

> Do you see what great virtue our nature is capable of? How nothing is more honorable than a human being, even if he remains mortal? For what could you tell me is greater than this man, Paul? What is his equal? Of how many angels and archangels is the man who said this thing (Rom 9:3) not worthy?[292]

Having introduced the second comparison – with the angels and archangels – Chrysostom briefly addresses the encomiastic topic of σῶμα in order to argue the case that the body is not a hindrance to virtue, even as bodilessness is no guarantee of it (as the notorious counter-example of Satan attests). John allows himself a moment of public wonder about what pinnacles a bodiless Paul could conceivably have reached, in both word and deed,[293] but desists from that thought and directs his attention to the point he wishes to make: that Paul displayed his extraordinary virtue (in word and deed) *while clothed in flesh* [ἐπεὶ καὶ ὁ Παῦλος σάρκα περιέκειτο]. The theme of the oration then arises in his articulation of an ethical principle: what makes a human being miserable is not the possession of a fleshy body, but improper us of that body. Manifestly, therefore, Paul's body will not be the focus of special praise in this encomium (for what John wishes to stress is its sameness, not its

---

conventions (compare pp. 268 and 273). Even Piédagnel [SC 300.33], who tends to downplay the influence of the form of the ἐγκώμιον on the panegyrics, recognizes the frequent antitheses of this speech as being true to the rhetorical form (as did Hubbell himself: "quite in the encomiastic manner" [p. 273]). In reality, what Hubbell and Piédagnel appear to favor about this oration is its relative lack of hyperbole, and more "solemn" tone (the term Piédagnel repeatedly uses to describe the homily, though what he means by this is not self-evident [see SC 300.14, 20, 33]).

[288] The προοίμιον extends from 7.1–3 [SC 300.300]. As Hubbell noted, "the introduction leads over smoothly, almost imperceptibly, to the main portion of the encomium" ("Chrysostom and Rhetoric," 273).

[289] To borrow Piédagnel's phrasing: "on est frappé, il est vrai, dès de début de ce discours, par son tonalité particulière majestueuse" (SC 300.13). But the proposition is clearly demarcated in §4, as I shall demonstrate.

[290] I shall not repeat here the full discussion of *laud. Paul.* 7.1–2 [SC 300.292–98] given in chap. 5, pp. 173–76.

[291] These quotations are oratorical or literary analogues to the inscriptional rolls containing Pauline verses that are often used in graphic portraiture (see Lechner, "Paulus," 134–35).

[292] *laud. Paul.* 7.3 [SC 300.298].

superiority to others), but rather the superb deeds he was able to accomplish while endowed with this ordinary body. Because Paul is the perfect model of coordination and cooperation between the ethical urges of one's own nature and the divine inspiration that guides it, he is the unsurpassed model for emulation. Unlike the Lord, his complete copyist Paul is fully akin to the rest of humanity, a "fellow slave" [σύνδουλος/ὁμόδουλος] each Christian should be able to imitate with ease.[294] The anticipated theme of this discourse, therefore, is a familiar one – imitation of Paul, the acme of virtue – as is clear not only from the exordium, but also from Chrysostom's return to the refrain in the final exhortation, thus wrapping his oration in an inclusio.[295]

πρόθεσις (Proposition). While throughout his writings John incessantly claims that Paul was Christ's imitator, in this panegyric he does more than that; he explicitly sets out to *prove* that Paul did indeed imitate his master. Chrysostom introduces the rhetorical proposition of this speech in §4 as an answer to a hypothetical question:"'And how did he imitate him?'" someone says. Well, look at how this was the case from the outset and from his very beginnings as a Christian" [Καὶ πῶς αὐτὸν ἐμιμήσατο, φησί; Τοῦτο ἐξ ἀρχῆς σκόπει καὶ ἀπ᾽ αὐτῶν τῶν προοιμίων].[296]

πίστεις (Proofs).[297] An imperative ("Look!") introduces the proof section of this oration, which consists of the catalogue of evidence Chrysostom offers that *in his deeds* Paul imitated Christ from the very moment of his conversion.[298] While the proof does not, as one might have expected, give a set of correlations between Christ's behavior and Paul's, John takes his proposition to be proven if he can

---

[293] "If this man had been in a bodiless nature, what would he not have said? What would he not have done?" [οὗτος εἰ ἐν ἀσωμάτῳ φύσει ἦν, τί οὐκ ἂν εἶπε; τί δὲ οὐκ ἂν ἔπραξε] (*laud. Paul.* 7.3 [SC 300.298]).

[294] *laud. Paul.* 7.3 [SC 300.300].

[295] *laud. Paul.* 7.13 [SC 300.320]: "Let us pronounce a blessing on Paul, that man through whom these things took place, and let us pray that we too might attain the same good things" [μακαρίσωμεν τὸν Παῦλον, δι᾽ οὗ ταῦτα γέγονεν, εὐξώμεθα καὶ αὐτοὶ τῶν αὐτῶν ἐπιτυχεῖν ἀγαθῶν].

[296] *laud. Paul.* 7.4 [SC 300.300].

[297] The proof section extends from 7.4, line 27, to the end of 7.12 [SC 300.300–320]. This is roughly in accord with Piédagnel's notes [SC 300.301, 310, 314] in terms of content, but he does not offer an analysis of the structural logic of the argument, *per se*, and his sketchy comments are not always on target. For example, the first set of arguments does not consist of illustrations of Paul's apostolate, as he puts it, but confirmation of John's insistence that Paul was Christ's most fervent imitator *from the outset*.

[298] The emphasis on deeds in this speech may be seen in the repetition of the verb ποιεῖν: 7.4, τὰ ὑπὲρ τὴν ἀξίαν ἐποίει (in an analogy from Paul's pre-Christian deeds), and καλῶς ἐποίησε; 7.6, πάντα ἔπραττε ... πάντα ἐποίει ... ἐπραγματεύετο; 7.8, Τίνος οὖν ἕνεκεν τοῦτο ἐποίει; 7.9, Τοῦτο δὲ ἐποίει; and on the self-confounding deeds of Paul's enemies in 7.11, ὅπερ ἂν ἐποίησαν φίλοι καὶ συντεταγμένοι, τοῦτο ἐποίουν οἱ πολέμιοι [SC 300.302, 302, 306, 310, 312, 318]; cf. πράττειν in 7.3, τί δὲ οὐκ ἂν ἔπραξε; and πρᾶγμα in 7.5, 6, 11 [SC 300.298, 304, 306, 318].

display Paul's virtue under several categories, since this is how he conceives of Paul's imitation of Christ.[299] Because of the temporal element inherent to the proposition itself, in the proof Chrysostom begins with a roughly chronological sketch, one which at least broadly replicates the narrative of Acts,[300] as he recounts the apostle's deeds in his Christian life from Damascus to Rome.[301] But John's purpose is to demonstrate that these actions, from their very debut, were manifestations of a host of virtues, thus to secure his contention that Paul imitated Christ always. Yet deeds are not in themselves unambiguous indices of virtue. Thus, as he introduces each of the Pauline πράξεις, Chrysostom must also seek to demonstrate how the conduct in question was the manifestation of a particular virtue, rather than a vice.

The first deed Chrysostom offers in support of his thesis that Paul imitated Christ "from his very beginnnings" (§4–6) is Paul's behavior immediately after his conversion (or, hyperbolically stated, even as he rose from the baptismal font), when he began to preach the gospel and confound the Jews in Damascus with its

---

[299] I demur from Hubbell, here, who thinks that "Chrysostom then takes up no longer the idea of the imitation of Christ, but gives various incidents of Paul's life, grouped so as to exhibit certain qualities" ("Chrysostom and Rhetoric," 273), because for John the way in which Paul constituted the chief imitator of Christ was not in some specific points of correspondence with the life of Jesus as told in the Synoptics, for instance, but rather in his own inculcation of all the virtues which Chrysostom assumes Christ, as Son of God, maximally possessed.

[300] Piédagnel [SC 300.301, 309] identifies clusters of events from two periods of Paul's life: his time in Damascus immediately after his conversion (§4–7), and his journey and period of house arrest at Rome (§8–12). But this division works only in a cursory way since, while John follows a generally chronological order, he also develops treatments of particular virtues along the way, for which he incorporates events from other periods (such as the appending of two later events of submission to advice into the "Damascus" section in §7, and the invocation of the Philippian jailer in Piédagnel's "Voyage to Rome" section [§11]). The type of compositional τάξις Chrysostom employs in this oration was recommended in rhetorical theory: "Always divide the actions of those you are going to praise into the virtues (there are four virtues: courage, justice, temperance, and wisdom), and see to what virtues the actions belong" [διαίρει γὰρ ἀπανταχοῦ τὰς πράξεις ὧν ἂν μέλλης ἐγκωμιάζειν εἰς τὰς ἀρετάς (ἀρεταὶ δὲ τέσσαρές εἰσιν, ἀνδρεία, δικαιοσύνη, σωφροσύνη, φρόνησις) καὶ ὅρα τίνων ἀρετῶν εἰσιν αἱ πράξεις] (Menander, Rh. 2.373 [text and trans. Russell-Wilson, 84–85]). That this was the compositional principle at work in this speech was rightly recognized by Hubbell ("Chrysostom and Rhetoric," 272): "[he] gives various incidents of Paul's life, grouped so as to exhibit certain qualities." In support of this point Hubbell cited Theon, Prog. 8 [Spengel, 2.112]: "After these considerations we shall take up the deeds and acts of virtue, but not recounting them in succession. For when speaking of these other things, we compound them according to each single virtue. Then, going through the deeds, inasmuch as he was temperate, for instance, we say that first, and then immediately add what deed he has done which showed this temperance. And we do likewise with the other virtues" [μετὰ δὲ ταῦτα τὰς πράξεις καὶ τὰ κατορθώματα παραληψόμεθα οὐκ ἐφεξῆς διηγούμενοι· λέγοντες γὰρ ἄλλα προστίθεμεν κατὰ μίαν ἑκάστην ἀρετήν, ἔπειτα τὰ ἔργα διεξιόντες, οἷον ὅτι ἦν σώφρων, προλέγειν καὶ ἐπιφέρειν εὐθύς, τί αὐτῷ σωφρονητικὸν ἔργον πέπρακται, ὁμοίως ἐπὶ τῶν ἄλλων ἀρετῶν].

[301] He even peeks at the voyage to Spain, but does not develop that part of the narrative, probably because he has so few sources to depend upon where that segment of Paul's life is concerned (laud. Paul. 7.9 [SC 300.312]).

teaching.[302] By a simple fusion of Acts 9:20–22 and Gal 1:17 John paints a picture of the early Paul as so ardent, so filled with the fire of zeal that he acted in ἐπιπήδησις,[303] "great haste," to assume leadership [προστασία/προεδρία] in the church, without waiting for teacher, mentor or installment in an office. Chrysostom argues that Paul's ἐπιπήδησις was due to the fire kindled within him, the virtue of προθυμία,[304] "fervent will to act," by which he simply seethed in passion for the gospel. With two visually discordant but parallel images of Paul as enflamed,[305] and as the raging torrent of a swollen stream[306] Chrysostom casts the newly baptised Paul as the self-appointed messenger of the gospel who laid seige to the city, and swept away all objections Jews might have to his message. But John also recognizes that one could interpret this same Pauline behavior as a sign of presumption or, even worse, vainglorious love of rule [προεδρίας ἔρως].[307] So he embarks on a defense of Paul against that possible accusation (one which John concedes would indeed be blame-worthy if true)[308] by appeal to historical precedents, beginning with Moses. Like Paul, Moses in Egypt did not wait for appointment, but stepped in when the occasion arose to avenge the maltreatment of his Hebrew compatriots. In this claim for Moses Chrysostom lays bare the encomiastic logic about πράξεις:"These actions are proof of a noble soul and a free intent" [Ταῦτα γὰρ ψυχῆς γενναίας ἀπόδειξις καὶ γνώμης ἐλευθέρας].[309] Actions are central to an encomium because they provide proofs of the true nature of the invisible soul that dwells within. Paul, just like Moses, acted "justly" and "well"[310] in grabbing the reins of power for the sake of the salvation of others. But because internal motivations are by their very nature uncer-tain and elusive, Chrysostom offers as an even more reliable proof the external validation each man received by subsequent divine appointment.[311] Furthermore,

---

[302] *laud. Paul.* 7.4–6 [SC 300.300–306].

[303] The verb ἐπιπηδᾶν is used fully six times in the discourse (*laud. Paul.* 7.4 and 5 [SC 300.302–304].

[304] προθυμία is a leitmotif of the discourse, repeated six times (7.4, 5 [2x], 7, 10 [2x] [SC 300.302, 304, 308, 314]); cf. ζῆλος in 7.5 [SC 300.304]).

[305] Fire is an important element of this speech, to which Chrysostom will return in *laud. Paul.* 7.11 [SC 300.316–18]. John particularly likes to create oxymorons with fire and water; see 7.4, Ἐπειδὴ γὰρ ἀπὸ τῶν θείων ναμάτων τοσοῦτον πῦρ ἔχων ἀνῆλθεν, and 7.6, Διὰ τοῦτο οὐδεμίαν ἀνέμεινεν ἡμέραν ἡσυχάζων ὁ πυρὸς οὗτος σφοδρότερος, ἀλλ᾽ ὁμοῦ τε ἀνέβη ἀπὸ τῆς ἱερᾶς τῶν ὑδάτων πηγῆς, καὶ πολλὴν ἀνῆψεν ἑαυτῷ τὴν φλόγα [SC 300.300–302, 306].

[306] μετὰ πολλῆς ἐνέπιπτε τῆς ῥύμης, ὥσπερ τις χειμάρρους (*laud. Paul.* 7.6 [SC 300.306]).

[307] *laud. Paul.* 7.5 [SC 300.304].

[308] "Now if they had been hastening to do these things for the sake of honor and preeminence, then they would with reason be accused of playing court to them" [Εἰ μὲν γὰρ τιμῆς ἕνεκεν καὶ προεδρίας ἐπεπήδων τοῖς πράγμασι, καὶ τῆς αὐτῶν θεραπείας εἰκότως ἂν ἐνεκλήθησαν] (*laud. Paul.* 7.5 [SC 300.304]).

[309] *laud. Paul.* 7.4 [SC 300.302].

[310] Of Moses John says: δικαίως ἐπεπήδησε τῇ προστασίᾳ, and of Paul: καλῶς ἐποίησε τοῦ λόγου ἀψάμενος τότε καὶ τῆς διδασκαλίας (*laud. Paul.* 7.4 [SC 300.302]).

[311] "By later appointing Moses, God demonstrated that he had justly hastened to the leader-ship, which is what God has done also in the case of Paul. For God showed that Paul had done

the divine approbation of Paul's apparently self-appointed actions can also ·be verified by what did *not* happen subsequently. Chrysostom lists four biblical instances where God brought a severe punishment on those who too swiftly arrogated to themselves pretensions to authority: the people in the tower of Shechem, Korah and his associates, King Uzziah, and Simon Magus.[312] This collection of negative *exempla* chronicles biblical men who "hastened to rule and preeminence, but died." In complete contrast, "Paul acted in haste as well, but he was crowned."[313] God rewarded Paul's haste, whereas he chastised the others for theirs. The lesson learned is that one cannot judge on the basis of the act alone, for, at least on the surface, Paul and the usurpers both "hastened to rule." But the divine approval is what substantiates Chrysostom's claim that Paul's actions were due to his ζῆλος and προθυμία for Christ; that is why "his praise is proclaimed and [it is clear that] he was magnificent from the beginning" [ἀνακηρύττεται καὶ λαμπρὸς ἐκ προοιμίων ἦν].[314] Even further proof of the contention that in his initial evangelizing Paul exemplified virtue is to be found in the dangers he faced for the sake of the gospel and the salvation of the lost, throwing himself into this battle with a complete lack of concern for bodily injury or social ostracism.[315] He was a man on fire.

With this proof of Paul's προθυμία secure, Chrysostom turns next (§7) to a seemingly opposite virtue: obedience and compliance [πειθήνιος ἦν καὶ εὐήνιος].[316] An excess of προθυμία such as Chrysostom has described Paul as possessing could have rendered him an intractable man, one who always acted as a lone ranger in ministry, confident only in his own opinions.[317] But, John argues, in his ensuing missionary work Paul amazingly combined great daring and impetuosity with appropriate humility and docility to the counsel of others who sought to instruct and guide him. Paul's manifold capacity for this virtue, too, is demonstrated by a list of four incidents in which Paul yielded to the advice of others: leaving Jerusalem for Caesarea and Tarsus (Acts 9:30); being lowered down the city wall in Damascus (Acts 9:23–25; 2 Cor 11:32–33); shaving himself (Acts 21:23–25); and refraining from entering into the theatre at Ephesus (Acts 19:29–

---

well by engaging in the word and the teaching at that moment, and quickly brought him to the dignified status of the company of teachers" (*laud. Paul.* 7.4 [SC 300.302]).

[312] Judg 9:46–49; Num 16:31–32; 2 Chr 26:16–21; Acts 8:18–24.

[313] *laud. Paul.* 7.5 [SC 300.304].

[314] *laud. Paul.* 7.5 [SC 300.306]; note the triumphant declaration that the proposition (as articulated in 7.4: τοῦτο [sc. Παῦλον μιμεῖσθαι τὸν Χριστὸν] ἐξ ἀρχῆς ... καὶ ἀπ᾽ αὐτῶν τῶν προοιμίων; cf. 7.2 [SC 300.300, 294–96]: ὅτι γὰρ λαμπρότερος) is successfully proven.

[315] *laud. Paul.* 7.5–6 [SC 300.304–306].

[316] *laud. Paul.* 7.7 [SC 300.308].

[317] "Despite the fact that he was so daring and impetuous and breathing fire, yet again he was obedient and docile toward the those who gave him instructions, so that the abundant force of his ardent will did not bring him into conflict with them" [Καὶ ὅμως οὕτω τολμητὴς ὢν καὶ ὁρμητίας καὶ πῦρ πνέων, οὕτω πάλιν πειθήνιος ἦν καὶ εὐήνιος τοῖς διδασκάλοις ὥστε μὴ ἐν τοσαύτῃ ῥύμῃ προθυμίας αὐτοῖς ἀντιπεσεῖν] (*laud. Paul.* 7.7 [SC 300.308]).

30).³¹⁸ Paul's agile combination of zeal and submission demonstrates his consistent motivation, which was to do whatever would benefit the common advantage of the faithful, with an eye toward the successful propagation of the gospel.

This picture of Paul's deeds as always motivated by his zeal to be like Christ in service of the gospel coheres completely, John avers, with the rest of his ministry (§8–12). The transition from Paul's enthusiastic honeymoon period in Damascus to his journey to Rome is made rhetorically by Chrysostom's anticipatory denial of any suggestion that Paul acted in cowardice [μὴ νομίσῃς ἀνανδρείας εἶναι τὰ ῥήματα] in sending his nephew to the chiliarch (Acts 23:16–18), or in calling upon the name of Caesar (Acts 25:10–11). In this way John can at once claim the virtue of bravery for Paul,³¹⁹ and insist that it was Paul's deliberate intention to "continue to proclaim the gospel" [ἵνα ἐνδιατρίψῃ τῷ κηρύγματι]³²⁰ by remaining alive (even though he would much more have desired to die and be with Christ [Phil 1:21–26]),³²¹ and by arranging things precisely so that he would be imprisoned and sent to the great city, the imperial capital. This Paul was no victim of circumstance, but rather a deliberate, purposeful agent who set out on a mission to accomplish nothing less than "setting straight the city of Rome."³²² And *en route* Paul was able to perform even more remarkable deeds by bolstering his fellow passengers and "looking out for them" (i.e., both in prophecy and more mundane solicitation),³²³ sure proofs of his virtue given that "he did everything so that not one would be lost."³²⁴ Paul's foreknowledge on shipboard gives Chrysostom another occasion to defend Paul against any hint of spinelessness, because, he claims, Paul engaged in prophecy for his sailing companions, "although he was fully

---

³¹⁸ This list of episodes extends beyond Paul's Damascene period, because John's principle of arrangement is not just chronological, but also by individual virtue, in this case, obedience (as discussed in n. 300, above).

³¹⁹ Menander Rhetor says that one should treat ἀνδρεία first among the virtues: "Actions of courage should come into consideration first in such subjects: courage reveals an emperor more than do other virtues" [δεῖ γὰρ τὰς τῆς ἀνδρείας πράξεις πρώτας παραλαμβάνειν ἐπὶ τῶν τοιούτων ὑποθέσεων εἰς ἐξέτασιν· γνωρίζει γὰρ βασιλέα πλέον ἡ ἀνδρεία] (*Rh.* 2.372; Russell-Wilson, 84–85). The theme of bravery is found throughout Chrysostom's speech: already in the proem it is the ἀνδρεία of the standard-bearers that the spectators rush out to see (*laud. Paul.* 7.1 [SC 300.292]), and later in the discourse Paul's disciples were said to have been encouraged at seeing Paul becoming even braver [ἀνδρειότερος] when beset by revilers (7.10 [SC 300.312]).

³²⁰ *laud. Paul.* 7.8 [SC 300.310].

³²¹ As John sketches it, Paul was motivated by a different kind of fear: "For he was afraid lest he might depart from here poor and impoverished when it came to the salvation of the many" (*laud. Paul.* 7.8 [SC 300.310]).

³²² Καὶ γὰρ οὐδὲ μικρὸς ἆθλος αὐτῷ τῆς Ῥωμαίων πόλεως ἡ διόρθωσις προὔκειτο (*laud. Paul.* 7.9 [SC 300.310]). As Chrysostom reads the Acts narrative, Paul's motive is accurately represented in Agrippa's statement of regret to Festus (Acts 26:32) that if Paul had not called upon the name of Caesar, he would have been released. In John's telling, Paul called upon the name of Caesar *so that* he would not be freed, and could thereby carry the gospel to Rome.

³²³ προνοεῖν here is a *double entendre*, since it can mean both "care for" and "foretell" (*LPGL*, 1157). See the full discussion of Paul's prophetic acts below, pp. 295–301.

³²⁴ *laud. Paul.* 7.9 [SC 300.312]: ὅπως μηδεὶς ἀπόλοιτο πάντα ἔπραττεν.

confident on his own behalf, and knew that he was safe" [καίτοι γε ὑπὲρ αὐτοῦ θαρρῶν καὶ εἰδὼς ὡς ἐν ἀσφαλείᾳ ἦν].[325] Paul's actions during the sea voyage (regardless of whether the sailors obeyed or disobeyed his counsel) therefore serve as a proof of God's grace at work in Paul [διὰ πάντων δειχθῇ ἡ Παύλου χάρις], even as they exemplify the proper care and consideration he had for others, including lowly prisoners, whom he cherished with as great solicitude as if they were his own children. When Paul arrived in Rome his actions there in evangelizing demonstrated ἐπιείκεια and ἐλευθερία, "gentleness and freedom."[326]

In the final segment of proof in this discourse (§10–12), Chrysostom reflects upon the relationship between actions and results [πράξεις καὶ τὰ συμβάντα] in Paul's career. He contends that, in addition to being amazingly augmented by Paul's deeds, the gospel was promoted also by the actions of the people around him whom he inspired. Chrysostom argues first that Paul's distinguished deeds led to their emulation by his disciples, to the greater increase in his followers of the same virtues which characterized Paul's proclamation of the gospel: προθυμία, παρρησία, τόλμα, θράσος, ἀνδρεία, γενναιότης. By becoming bolder as he encountered more dangers, Paul generated a mimetic cycle such that his own disciples, on seeing his courage under fire, were themselves incited to be like him and thus to spread the gospel even further. Inspired by Phil 1:14, Chrysostom explains the centripetal effect of Paul's deeds that so captivates him: just *looking* at Paul leads to *being* like him. To illustrate this point Chrysostom takes up the ekphrasist's role and constructs an analogy with the impact on foot-soldiers of seeing their commander-in-chief handle adversity with absolute self-assurance.

For when they see their general damp with blood and carrying about his wounded body, and not even thus giving way to his enemies, but standing nobly [γενναίως], shaking his spear, attacking his enemies, and not giving in to his miseries, they, too, draw themselves up for battle with a more ardent will to act [προθυμία]. And this is precisely what happened in Paul's case. For upon seeing him bound and yet preaching in the prison, scourged and yet subduing the scourgers, they received a greater share of boldness [παρρησία].[327]

Because the feedback loop causes the disciples' increased daring in turn to elevate Paul's, his initial actions can be credited with instigating a chain reaction of power all surging toward the propagation of the gospel. This was especially true of the persecutions Paul endured, circumstances designed to halt the spread of the word which surprisingly brought about instead more and more boldness and confidence.[328] It is a favorite Chrysostomic proposition (in line with early Christian apologetics generally) that the attempts of its enemies to thwart the gospel were

---

[325] *laud. Paul.* 7.9 [SC 300.310].

[326] *laud. Paul.* 7.9 [SC 300.312]; earlier John had insisted that Moses' deeds gave evidence of "a free intent" [γνώμη ἐλευθέρα] (7.4 [SC 300.302]).

[327] *laud. Paul.* 7.10 [SC 300.314].

[328] Διὸ καὶ τοῦτο δηλῶν, οὐχ ἁπλῶς Πεποιθότας εἶπεν, ἀλλὰ προστίθησι· Περισσοτέρως τολμᾶν ἀφόβως τὸν λόγον λαλεῖν (Phil 4:14) (*laud. Paul.* 7.10 [SC 300.314]).

unwittingly the very means by which it spread.[329] Via this ironic *topos* Chrysostom can introduce in favor of Paul's praise, then, not just the apostle's own deeds, but the very πράξεις of his opponents, for these actions, contrary to their guiding purposes, facilitated the gospel's success. By the examples of Paul's conversion of his Philippian jailer, and Agrippa's memorable comment that Paul had almost convinced him to become a Christian (Acts 26:28), John celebrates the inversion Paul effected: "the judges became disciples, the opponents subjects" of the gospel.[330] Chrysostom explains the physics involved in this whirlpool effect of Paul's proclamation by reverting to his earlier image of Paul as one enflamed:

> Just as fire spreads more when it sets upon different materials, and receives an increase from the flammable matter lying underneath, so also Paul's tongue converted to his own cause the people with whom it came into contact. Those who were fighting against him, taken captive by his words, swiftly became fuel for this spiritual fire. And through them the gospel was raised up again, and advanced continually toward others.[331]

Paul's fiery tongue created a condition such that all actions, no matter their intent, became funneled toward the same result, his *own* intended goal – the dissemination of the gospel. Even though the antagonists set Paul to flight as an act of persecution [τὸ μὲν πρᾶγμα δίωξις ἦν], the effective result of their deed [τὸ δὲ συμβαῖνον] was, nonetheless, the apostolate of teachers [ἀποστολὴ διδασκάλων] spreading the word. The marvelous consequence is that Paul's enemies wound up doing the deeds that his friends and associates would have done.[332] In exiling and binding Paul and his disciples, they inadvertently "circulated this physician everywhere,"[333] bringing the message of salvation to the whole world. And during his punishments Paul accomplished specific paradoxical feats: binding the jailer who was supposed to bind him, finding converts among the prisoners with whom he was to be confined, enduring dangers and miseries meant to extinguish the gospel that instead fanned its flames. Even a shipwreck brought the unexpected result [τὸ συμβάν] of a teaching opportunity [διδασκαλίας ὑπόθεσις]. Through Paul's agency of action the deeds of Christianity's adversaries brought about the opposite ends [τοὐναντίον συνέβη]; their intended κωλύματα ("hindrances") wound up being βοηθήματα τοῦ κηρύγματος ("acts of assistance to the gospel").[334] Therefore, the

---

[329] See also especially *laud. Paul.* 4.15–20 [SC 300.214–28].

[330] γεγόνασιν οἱ δικασταὶ μαθηταί, οἱ ἀντίδικοι ὑπήκοοι (*laud. Paul.* 7.11 [SC 300.316]).

[331] Καὶ καθάπερ πῦρ ἐμπεσὸν εἰς διαφόρους ὕλας μᾶλλον αὔξεται, καὶ προσθήκην λαμβάνει τὴν ὑποκειμένην ὕλην· οὕτω καὶ ἡ γλῶσσα Παύλου, ὅσοις ἂν συνεγένετο, πρὸς ἑαυτὸν αὐτοὺς μεθίστη, καὶ οἱ πολεμοῦντες αὐτῷ τοῖς ἐκείνου λόγοις ἁλόντες τροφὴ ταχέως ἐγίγνοντο τῷ πνευματικῷ τούτῳ πυρί, καὶ δι' αὐτῶν πάλιν ὁ λόγος ᾔρετο, καὶ ἐφ' ἑτέρους προῄει (*laud. Paul.* 7.11 [SC 300.316–318]; Paul's tongue as a vanquishing fire is a major theme also in *laud. Paul.* 4.18–20 [SC 300.220–26]).

[332] Καὶ ὅπερ ἂν ἐποίησαν φίλοι καὶ συντεταγμένοι, τοῦτο ἐποίουν οἱ πολέμιοι (*laud. Paul.* 7.11 [SC 300.318]).

[333] πανταχοῦ περιάγοντες τὸν ἰατρόν (*laud. Paul.* 7.11 [SC 300.318]).

[334] *laud. Paul.* 7.12 [SC 300.320].

succession of deeds in Paul's career, which are summed up in the preaching of the gospel, led inexorably to a single result: an increase in the word, and its elevation to an indescribable height.[335]

ἐπίλογος (Conclusion). In the concluding liturgical exhortation (§13), Chrysostom urges his congregation to give thanks to the ingenious God [ὁ εὐμήχανος θεός] who caused all these benefits to accrue from unlikely places, and to bless Paul through whom they all happened [μακαρίσωμεν τὸν Παῦλον, δι' οὗ ταῦτα γέγονεν]. The Pauline πράξεις, arising from that delicate combination of divine inspiration and his own προθυμία, deserve the highest praise for pulling off the most magnificent feat imaginable.

The Summary Deed: Victory over the Entire World

Not only in *laud. Paul.* 7, but throughout his oeuvre, Chrysostom combines Paul's many actions into one great achievement,[336] in the most prominent arena from which one first garners praise, according to rhetorical theory: military conquest.[337] Paul did the impossible, and accomplished what no religious leader or philosopher was ever able to do: he taught all the inhabitants of the world – Greeks and barbarians – [338] to philosophize, by persuading all to believe in the gospel, thereby completely overturning in one blow Greco-Roman philosophy and paganism.[339] This astounding victory, the most praiseworthy πράξις conceivable, is savored and

---

[335] οὕτω καὶ Παύλου κηρύττοντος, ἅπερ ἐπῆγον ἐκεῖνοι τὸν λόγον ἐκκόπτοντες, ταῦτα αὐτὸν ηὔξησε, καὶ εἰς ὕψος ἐπῆρεν ἄφατον (*laud. Paul.* 7.12 [SC 300.320]).

[336] Again here Chrysostom engages in a task typical of the biographic: "In these biographies, the holy philosopher was depicted not as a passive figure but as a man with a mission. Whatever his historical mission might have been, in the biographies the mission was to a great extent dictated by the biographer himself" (Cox, *Biography*, 145).

[337] Rhetorical theorists often prescribed that deeds should be divided into two categories: those of war and those of peace, treated in that order (see Burgess, *Epideictic Literature*, 123–24). See Menander, *Rh.* 2.372: τὰς τοιαύτας τοίνυν πράξεις διαιρήσεις δίχα εἴς τε τὰ κατ' εἰρήνην καὶ τὰ κατὰ πόλεμον. καὶ προθήσεις τὰς κατὰ τὸν πόλεμον, ἐὰν ἐν ταύταις λαμπρὸς ὁ ἐπαινούμενος φαίνηται (Russell-Wilson, 84).

[338] οὐχὶ τὴν οἰκουμένην μόνον, ἀλλὰ καὶ τὴν ἀοίκητον διορθούμενος, οὐχὶ τὴν Ἑλλάδα μόνον, ἀλλὰ καὶ τὴν βάρβαρον (*laud. Paul.* 1.13 [SC 300.132]). See also *hom. in Rom.* 2.5 [60.407]: Τὴν Ἑλλάδα, τὴν βάρβαρον πᾶσαν ὁ σκηνοποιὸς ἐπέστρεψεν.

[339] See, e.g., *hom. in Rom.* 32.3 [60.679], where the subject is Paul's mouth, depicted as the agent of the whole Pauline career: "For what good work didn't that mouth do [Τί γὰρ οὐκ εἰργάσατο ἐκεῖνο τὸ στόμα ἀγαθόν;]? It drove off demons, it released sins, muzzled the mouths of tyrants [τυράννους ἐπεστόμισε], stopped up the tongues of philosophers [φιλοσόφων γλώττας ἐνέφραξε], led the world to God [τὴν οἰκουμένην τῷ θεῷ προσήγαγε], persuaded barbarians to philosophize [βαρβάρους φιλοσοφεῖν ἔπεισε], reformed everything on earth [πάντα μετερρύθμιζε τὰ ἐν τῇ γῇ]; and even the things in heaven he disposed of in the way he wished, binding and freeing those there whom he wished, according to the power that had been given to him" [καὶ τὰ ἐν οὐρανοῖς δὲ, ὃν ἐβούλετο, διετίθει τρόπον, δεσμῶν οὓς ἐβούλετο, καὶ λύων ἐκεῖ κατὰ τὴν δεδομένην ἐξουσίαν αὐτῷ]. Paul, the excellent general, "arrayed himself for battle against the whole world as though it were a single army, never standing still, but doing everything

enjoyed by a thorough catalogue of the multitudinous expressions of Greco-Roman paganism that Paul single-handedly demolished:

At that time there was a dirge [Τότε ἦν θρῆνος], then everywhere were altars, everywhere smoke, everywhere the smell of burnt offerings, everywhere acts of prostitution, everywhere initiations into the mysteries, everywhere sacrifices, everywhere demons in bacchic revelry, everywhere an acropolis of the devil, everywhere fornication crowned [τότε πανταχοῦ βωμοί, πανταχοῦ καπνός, πανταχοῦ κνῖσαι, πανταχοῦ πορνεῖαι, πανταχοῦ τελεταί, πανταχοῦ θυσίαι, πανταχοῦ δαίμονες βακχεύοντες, πανταχοῦ ἀκρόπολις τοῦ διαβόλου, πανταχοῦ πορνεία στεφανουμένη]. And Paul was one single person [καὶ εἷς ἦν ὁ Παῦλος]. How was he not swallowed up? How was he not torn in two? How did he open his mouth?"[340]

Significantly, this passage appears to have been modeled on Libanios' recounting, in the same terms, of Julian's reconstitution and restoration of traditional worship a few decades earlier.[341] But even if one is not persuaded by the argument for

---

as though with wings" [ὁ δὲ καθάπερ ἐνὶ στρατοπέδῳ, τῇ οἰκουμένῃ παρατεταττόμενος, οὐδαμοῦ ἵστατο, ἀλλ' ὥσπερ τις ὑπόπτερος ὤν, πάντα ἐποίει] (*hom. in 2 Cor.* 21.3 [61.545]).

[340] *Eutrop.* 2.14 [52.409].

[341] Compare the strikingly similar celebratory catalogue in Libanios, *Or.* 18.126: "First of all then, as I have said, he brought back piety [ἡ εὐσέβεια], which had fled, by building some temples, and furnishing others by bringing in statues ... Everywhere there were altars, and fire, and blood, and the smell of burnt offerings, and smoke, and initiations into the mysteries [πανταχοῦ βωμοὶ καὶ πῦρ καὶ αἷμα καὶ κνίσσα καὶ καπνὸς καὶ τελεταί], and diviners [μάντες] released from fear, and on mountain tops there were flutes [αὐλοί] and processions [πρόσοδοι], and the same ox served as worship for gods and dinner for humans" [βοῦς ὁ αὐτὸς ἀποχρῶν θεραπείᾳ τε εἶναι θεῶν καὶ δεῖπνον ἀνθρώποις] (my trans.). While it is possible that this is simply a traditional list, there are compelling arguments that there is a direct literary allusion in this case. First is Chrysostom's own biographical connection with the events of Julian's revival during his adolescence, including Julian's residence in Antioch, which surely left a life-long impression upon him. The sting of Julian's desecration of the grave of St. Babylas in order to restore the oracle of Apollo at Daphne was long remembered, and the emperor's *contra Galilaeos*, composed at Antioch, continued to circulate there, and be attacked especially by Antiochenes, Chrysostom among them (in *pan. Bab.* 2, as argued by Schatkin and Harkins, FC 73.28–29). Chrysostom's firm knowledge of the writings of Libanios, his teacher, overwhelmingly likely in principle, has been established for some documents, including quite possibly the work in question here, *Or.* 18, Libanios' famous panegyric to the dead emperor (Chrysostom may allude to 18.308 in the last line of *pan. Bab.* 2 127 [SC 362.274], as suggested by Schatkin and Harkins, FC 73.35). Moreover, the likelihood of direct adaptation of Libanios' passage here is greatly increased by the fact that Chrysostom quite consciously drew upon phrases in Libanios' orations in other works, such as his *comparatio regis et monachi* (Hunter, *Comparison*, 25–36; the literary dependence indicated by these passages was noted already by Cajus Fabricius, *Zu den Jugendschriften des Johannes Chrysostomos: Untersuchungen zum Klassizismus des vierten Jahrhunderts* [Lund: Gleerup, 1962] 120). Furthermore, and most important for this case, the allusions in that early monastic writing are all to phrases Libanios had used *for Julian*, also, thus evidencing the same rhetorical strategy at work here, of indirect castigation of Julian by reappropriating his praises to Christian figures (as Hunter has convincingly argued: "The presence of these quotations will reveal that Chrysostom's early monastic treatise is engaged in an apologetic endeavor against his former teacher, Libanios, and, beyond him, against the emperor Julian" [26]). In the earlier works it is the monks who exemplify the virtues Libanios accords to Julian; in this later oration John credits

literary dependence in this case, the precise antithesis Chrysostom constructs between Paul and Julian is nonetheless patently clear. By painting the apostle in exact counterpoint to the well-known laudatory portrait of the paganizing emperor,[342] John has portrayed the battle for true religion throughout the entire world as a contest between these two giant figures. The fact that the two men, emperor and apostle, lived three hundred years apart does not interfere with their poetic duel, for the chronological difficulty is ameliorated literarily: the Pauline epistles, his vehicle of combat, are at work in the world even now, and until eternity.[343] The inference would have been unmistakable for Chrysostom's audience: Paul was responsible for the vindication of Christianity against all competing cults, which the fire of his truthful proclamation melted like wax, and burned like chaff.[344] Hence in this portrait Paul becomes a metonym for the church of the late fourth century,[345] and correspondingly the antonym of its most dangerous assailant in

---

the apostle Paul (who also embodies the monastic virtues *par excellence*, as we shall demonstrate on pp. 308–26) with definitively overturning the pagan rites Julian had sought to reinstate. In addition, from a literary-critical point of view it is easy to see how Chrysostom has edited Libanios' list. He retained the original structure, with πανταχοῦ βωμοί heading up the list (adding, of course, τότε), and accents the initial πανταχοῦ by anaphoric repetition for each item to follow. Then Chrysostom retained three other terms from Libanios' list intact [κνῖσαι, καπνός, τελεταί], while interspersing into the list Christian derogatory terms or translations for the other rites named (such as "the acropolis of the devil" for Libanios' description of mountain-top rituals, and his characteristic Christian emphasis upon πορνεία as the accompaniment of εἰδωλολατρία). Most telling is the fact that each one of the interpositions into the list bears the overt marks of such Christian polemic. To carry forward this investigation one should compare also the list of pagan primeval rites in *hom. in Jo.* 5:19 3 [56.251], among other passages.

[342] Elsewhere in turn Chrysostom reverses the portrait of Julian as victor: ὁ πάντας ἀσεβείᾳ νικήσας Ἰουλιανός (*pan. Bab.* 1 3 [SC 362.298]).

[343] As Chrysostom argued already in his older work on the priesthood: "... the excellence of his letters [ἡ τῶν ἐπιστολῶν ἀρετή], through which, not only to the believers of his time, but even to those who have lived until this very day, and those who will live in the future up until the coming of Christ [οὐ τοὺς τότε μόνον πιστούς, ἀλλὰ καὶ τοὺς ἐξ ἐκείνου μέχρι τῆς σήμερον γενομένους, καὶ τοὺς μέλλοντας δὲ ἔσεσθαι μέχρι τῆς τοῦ Χριστοῦ παρουσίας], he has extended and will extend great benefits [ὠφέλησέ τε καὶ ὠφελήσει]. And he will not stop doing this as long as the human race persists" [καὶ οὐ παύσεται τοῦτο ποιῶν ἕως ἂν τὸ τῶν ἀνθρώπων διαμένῃ γένος] (*sac.* 4.7 [SC 272.272–74]). As Chrysostom depicts him, with the tinge of Rom 8:38, Paul is victorious in all time-frames: "Paul ... victor and triumphant over all things, those below, those above, those present, those future, those which exist, and things which do not" [Παῦλος ... ἅπαντα νικῶν καὶ ὑπερβαίνων, τὰ κάτω, τὰ ἄνω, τὰ παρόντα, τὰ μέλλοντα, τὰ ὄντα, τὰ οὐκ ὄντα] (*hom. in Mt.* 6.5 [57.68]; see also *hom. in Mt.* 1.6 [57.20], of all the apostles living and fighting for all time [διὰ παντὸς ζῶντες]). The idea of an altercation between Julian and the Pauline letters is not solely a poetic fantasy for Chrysostom, either, but is rooted in fact. Julian's *contra Galilaeos*, a work likely known to Chrysostom, charges that Paul "changes his teachings about God to suit circumstances, like the centipede changes its colors to match the rocks, at one time maintaining that the Jews alone were God's inheritance, but when seeking to persuade the Gentiles to join him he says, 'Is God only of Jews, but not also of Gentiles? Yes, also of Gentiles' (Rom 3:29)" (*Gal.* 106B).

[344] *laud. Paul.* 4.18 [SC 300.222].

[345] See also *laud. Paul.* 4.19–20 [SC 300.224–26];

recent memory, Julian.[346] Furthermore, Chrysostom is at pains to point out for his
hero what he wishes also to claim for Christianity: that his success was not due to
rhetorical skill, but to divine power at work in and through him. Again, the contrast
with Libanios is instructive, for Antioch's most famous orator had quite pointedly
assigned the credit for the triumphs of Julian's restoration program to the emperor's
rhetorical prowess: "for now the inhabitants of the world are being transformed
from mere swine into human beings. The cause of all this is eloquence."[347]
Although Chrysostom makes the exact same claim to world-wide dominion for
Paul that Libanios makes for the marvelous achievements of his favored emperor
(including the shared hyperbolic claim that they made human beings out of
beasts),[348] he nevertheless seeks to eschew the expected αἴτιον – rhetorical
prowess – in favor of the attribution to divine intervention and inspiration.[349] This
summary portrait of Paul as religious champion of the entire world must be
understood in light of the presupposed portraits of those he vanquished, since
Chrysostom, following wider trends in late antique literature, made his biographical portraits the arena of combat.[350] This Paul is a Julianic anti-type, a fitting late
fourth-century image of *Paulus victor*[351] who is simultaneously *ecclesia victrix*,
standing erect over the charred remnants of Greco-Roman polytheistic worship,

---

[346] Just as Julian served as the embodiment of pagan philosophy and cult for Libanios (Hunter,
Comparison, 62: "Libanius took the emperor himself as a symbol of the moral benefits of Greek
culture and its specifically pagan character").

[347] νῦν γὰρ δὴ τὸ τὴν γῆν οἰκοῦν ἀπὸ συῶν ἀτεχνῶς εἰς ἀνθρώπους μεταπλάττεται. τούτων
δὲ ἁπάντων αἴτιον οἱ λόγοι (Libanios, *Or.* 12.91–92).

[348] On Paul making human beings out of animals, see *laud. Paul.* 1.5 [SC 300.120]. For his
victory over the entire world, a recurrent theme of Chrysostom's see, e.g., *scand.* 20.10 [SC
79.250]: "But see how, after these doings this persecutor outdid everyone, and his behavior shined
brighter than the sun, and he took possession of the whole world" ['Αλλὰ ὅρα πῶς μετὰ ταῦτα
οὗτός τε ὁ διώκτης πάντας ὑπερηκόντισε καὶ τὸ πρᾶγμα ὑπὲρ τὸν ἥλιον διέλαμψε καὶ πᾶσαν
κατέσχε τὴν οἰκουμένην]. Whereas Julian worshipped the sun (Apollo/Helios/Mithras), Paul
even outdid the sun in glory (the anti-Julianic polemic edge of this argument was argued for
above, p. 239, esp. n. 180).

[349] This can therefore be seen as another instance of what Hunter identified in the early
monastic works: "an indirect response to Libanius' own exaltation of rhetoric" (*Comparison*, 35).

[350] See Cox, *Biography*, 135–45, on how the heroes of the writers of biographies of holy men
"had become emblems in a holy war" between Christians and pagans, as also within different
philosophical schools and Christian groups.

[351] There are many such portraits of Paul in Chrysostom's corpus of writings. Another fine
example is *hom. in 2 Cor.* 21.3 [61.544–5], which picks up on Paul's own military imagery in
2 Cor 10:1–6, where Paul is depicted as being in constant battle against the foes of the gospel,
running from one place to another to win more trophies, and lead more people into the army of
Christ (see the quotation in n. 433 below). In this regard Paul's victory over the tyrant who wields
the power of persecution is depicted in the same way as the ultimate vindication of martyrs, so
prevalently lauded in Christian literature in Chrysostom's day, including his own homilies. See,
e.g., Delehaye, *Les passions des martyrs*, 168: "sur ce fond se détache le martyr, un héros accompli,
éclairé dès ici-bas de l'auréole de son triomphe" (as, e.g., in *hom. in 2 Tim.* 4.3 [62.623], quoted
above, p. 210; *hom. in 2 Cor.* 21.3 [61.544–5], as quoted below, n. 433).

proclaiming the permanence (which, despite our hindsight view, was not as yet assured) of the victory.[352]

In Chrysostom's eyes pagan worship went hand in hand with Greek philosophy to constitute a unified opposition to Christianity, because he considered the philosophers to have provided the logic and justification for the worship of idols.[353] Hence the portrait of Paul the world conquerer, victor over paganism, is also an anti-type of Plato. It casts Paul as the true philosopher-rhetor who both possessed the truth and was able to convince all – Greeks and barbarians – to follow the way of life and worship he outlined.[354] As with Julian, Chrysostom paints this victory as a face-off – a *philosophomachia* – between two colossal figures. In Chrysostom's writings it is Plato who often serves as a metonym for all of Greek philosophy and learning.[355] As its most celebrated figure [Πλάτων ὁ δοκῶν εἶναι τῶν ἄλλων σεμνότερος],[356] Plato's defeat at Paul's hands means the dissolution of the entire enterprise.[357] So Chrysostom hammers home the σύγκρισις: despite three trips,

---

[352] Chrysostom resists the idea that the victory of Christianity was due to the emperors, instead of to God: "the current security of the church does not come from the peace of the emperors, but from the power of God" [ἡ νῦν ἀσφάλεια αὐτῆς οὐκ ἀπὸ τῆς τῶν βασιλέων εἰρήνης, ἀλλ' ἀπὸ τῆς τοῦ θεοῦ δυνάμεως γίνεται] (Jud. 5.2 [48.886]).

[353] hom. in Rom. 3.3 [60.414], citing among other examples Socrates' parting command that his disciples sacrifice a cock to Asklepios (Phaedo 118). See discussion in Baur, John Chrysostom, 1.309–11.

[354] "Don't you see that Paul turned around the whole world, and proved stronger even than Plato and all the others?" [οὐχ ὁρᾷς Παῦλον τρεψάμενον τὴν οἰκουμένην ἅπασαν, καὶ μειζόνως ἰσχύσαντα καὶ Πλάτωνος, καὶ τῶν ἄλλων ἁπάντων;] (hom. in Tit. 2.2 [62.673]). The choice of Plato is likely due to the fact that Plato (in the words of Josephus) "was most admired by Greeks as distinguished by his dignity of lifestyle, and surpassing all those who engaged in philosophy in the power of his words and persuasive speech" [Πλάτων δὲ θαυμαζόμενος παρὰ τοῖς Ἕλλησιν ὡς καὶ σεμνότητι βίου διενεγκὼν καὶ δυνάμει λόγων καὶ πειθοῖ πάντας ὑπεράρας τοὺς ἐν φιλοσοφίᾳ γεγονότας] (c. Ap. 2.223).

[355] See Joannes Bezdeki, "Chrysostom et Plato," Ephemeris Dacoromana 1 (1923) 291–337, esp. 316–37; P. R. Coleman-Norton, "Saint John Chrysostom and the Greek Philosophers," CP 25 (1930) 305–17, 310–313; Baur, John Chrysostom, 1.306, on Chrysostom's treatment of Plato generally. Chrysostom can also extol Socrates as the greatest of the Greek philosophers [ὁ μέγας δὲ Σωκράτης καὶ πάντων τῶν παρ' αὐτοῖς φιλοσοφίᾳ κρατῶν] (hom. in 1 Cor. 4.5 [61.37]). This may constitute a deliberate engagement with his teacher Libanios' rhetorical use of Socrates as the zenith and metonym of Greek culture against Christians, as was argued by Michael Crosby and William M. Calder III, "Libanius, On the Silence of Socrates: A First Translation and an Interpretation," GRBS 3 (1960) 185–202, 200: "Socrates is not meant to be the historical figure, but a symbol of pagan intellectual paideia," and followed by Hunter, Comparison, 28.

[356] hom. in Rom. 3.3 [60.414]; also ὁ κορυφαῖος αὐτῶν (ibid; also hom. in Tit. 5.4 [62.694]); ὁ παρ' αὐτοῖς ἀγόμενος καὶ περιφερόμενος Πλάτων (hom. in Rom. 2.5 [60.407]). Elsewhere Chrysostom derides him as ὁ πολλὰ ληρήσας Πλάτων, "the very silly Plato," who was rendered silent by the work of Peter and the others (hom. in Ac. 4.3 [60.47]).

[357] Although his focus is undeniably on Plato, Chrysostom also mentions other philosophers in these comparisons: Socrates (laud. Paul. 4.19 [SC 300.224]; hom. in Col. 10.4 [62.370]; Jud. 5.3 [48.886]); Pythagoras (ibid., hom. in Ac. 4.4 [60.47]; hom. in Jo. 63.3 [59.352]); Diagoras (Jud. 5.3 [48.886]; laud. Paul. 4.19 [SC 30.224]); Anaxagoras of Clazomenae (laud. Paul. 4.19 [SC 300.224]); Zeno (laud. Paul. 4.19 [SC 300.226]; Jud. 5.3 [48.886]); Apollonios of Tyana (Jud. 5.3

Plato was unable to make a convert of even the lone tyrant of Sicily, Dionysius, but Paul overran, not just Sicily or even Italy, but the whole world with the truth of his gospel, and thereby converted everyone.[358] Paul was victorious over Plato, a victory even more glorious if one maintains on his behalf that he bested the great philosopher while lacking his advanced formal education.[359] But even there Chrysostom recognizes that, despite his lack of learning, the persuasive effect of Paul's oratory and epistles was what proved decisive in the victory over philosophy: by those means "he led all people to the truth" [πάντας αὐτοὺς εἰς τὴν ἀλήθειαν μετήγαγεν].[360] Thus Paul managed to unite in himself the warring strands of classical rhetoric and philosophy, and defeat competitors from both sides by the captivating truth of his gospel.[361]

But Paul's great deed, this world-wide victory, was not only against human opposition. In his quest to conquer the whole world Paul also contended with the powers of the devil.

For this is the shining victory, this is the trophy of the church, [Αὕτη ἡ λαμπρὰ νίκη, τοῦτο τῆς ἐκκλησίας τὸ τρόπαιον]: that the devil is cast down when we suffer wickedness. For when we suffer, he is taken captive and suffers terribly, when he wishes to make us suffer so. Which also happened in the case of Paul. As much as the devil brought more dangers

---

[48.886]; laud. Paul. 4.8 [SC 300.198]); "the whole crowd of philosophers rotting away in the Academy and the Walkways" [φιλοσόφων πλῆθος τῶν κατασαπέντων ἐν Ἀκαδημίᾳ καὶ Περιπάτοις] (hom. in Ac. 4.3 [60.47]). See Baur, John Chrysostom, 1.306, on Chrysostom and the philosophers in general. On a few occasions John sets up a typological comparison between Paul and Socrates, proceeding from their common fate in being imprisoned; but whereas Socrates' disciples fled to Megara immediately after his death, not believing what he had said about immortality, Paul's disciples carried on bravely after his demise (hom. in Col. 10.4 [62.370–71]; laud. Paul. 4.19 [SC 300.224]).

[358] Τὴν Ἑλλάδα, τὴν βάρβαρον πᾶσαν ὁ σκηνοποιὸς ἐπέστρεψεν ... Ὁ δὲ σκηνοποιὸς οὗτος οὐ Σικελίαν μόνον οὐδὲ Ἰταλίαν, ἀλλὰ πᾶσαν ἐπέδραμε τὴν οἰκουμένην (hom. in Rom. 2.5 [60.407]).

[359] hom. in 1 Cor. 3.4 [61.27]: Εἰ γὰρ Παῦλος ἀπαίδευτος ἦν, ἐκράτησε δὲ Πλάτωνος, ὅπερ ἔλεγον, λαμπρὰ γέγονεν ἡ νίκη.

[360] laud. Paul. 4.17 [SC 300.220]; hom. in Rom. 32.3 [60.679], predicated of Paul's voice [ἀλήθειαν ἐπανήγαγε], also that it "cleansed the world" [τὴν οἰκουμένην ἐξεκάθηρεν]; exp. in Ps. 111.2 [55.293]: καὶ πρὸς τὴν ἀρετὴν ἅπαντας ἐχειραγώγει.

[361] "Nothing was more unlearned than Peter, nothing more unskilled than Paul ... but nevertheless this unskilled man and that unlearned one were victorious over myriad philosophers, closed the mouths of myriad rhetoricians, doing it all from their desire and the grace of God" [Οὐδὲν ἀμαθέστερον Πέτρου, οὐδὲν ἰδιωτικώτερον Παύλου ... Ἀλλ' ὅμως ὁ ἰδιώτης οὗτος καὶ ὁ ἀμαθὴς ἐκεῖνος μυρίους ἐνίκησεν φιλοσόφους, μυρίους ἐπεστόμισαν ῥήτορας, ἀπὸ τῆς αὐτῶν προθυμίας καὶ τῆς τοῦ θεοῦ χάριτος τὸ πᾶν ἐργασάμενοι] (hom. in Rom. Arg. 2 [60.394]). The parallelism of Peter with Paul here serves as a reminder that Paul was not the only figure whom Chrysostom painted in these broad strokes, though Paul was by far the most conspicuous (see the full discussion in chap. 7, pp. 394–95). hom. in Ac. 4.3–4 [60.46–50] is a marvelously imagistic paean to Peter and the fishermen as Plato's conquerers (they were so superior to the Greek rhetoricians and philosophers that they left them as dumb as fishes on the dock). In hom. in Jo. 2.2 [59.31] the evangelist John's humble background is contrasted with his literary achievement, the gospel which persuades all its hearers for all time because of its divine inspiration, and silences Pythagoras and Plato.

against him, so much more was he defeated [καὶ ὅσῳ μεῖζον ἐπῆγε τοὺς κινδύνους, τοσούτῳ μᾶλλον ἡττᾶτο]. For the devil didn't only concoct a single form of trials, but varied and diverse … yet Paul was nevertheless victorious in all [ἀλλ' ὅμως ἐν πᾶσιν ἐκράτει].[362]

The devil was Paul's most wily and ubiquitous opponent,[363] for he propounded limitless machinations and obstacles to the Pauline mission, including, naturally, pagan cult and philosophy, those massive tools of deception. Since the devil's warfare was multi-faceted, so also Paul in combat had to be proficient in a wide range of military techniques for engaging his enemy in all the places he would appear. Hence the portrait of Paul as world-conquerer can be drawn in the familiar guises of those stock combatants in Greek culture: the soldier, the athlete and the ship-captain.

As though a single soldier[364] with the whole world battling against him [στρατιώτης εἰς τὴν οἰκουμένην πολεμοῦσαν ἔχων ἅπασαν] roamed about in the midst of the ranks of his enemies and suffered no harm … As though he himself were an athlete [τις ἀθλητὴς αὐτός], wrestling, running, boxing; or a soldier breaching walls, fighting on foot, engaging in naval combat. Thus he pursued every form of combat [πᾶν εἶδος μετῄει μάχης], and breathed fire, and was unapproachable, with one body overtaking the world [ἑνὶ σώματι καταλαμβάνων τὴν οἰκουμένην], with one tongue defeating all [μιᾷ γλώττῃ πάντας τρεπόμενος]. The trumpets which fell upon the stones of Jericho and destroyed them cannot match the way his voice, sounding against the devil's fortresses, threw them to the ground [ἡ τούτου φωνὴ ἠχοῦσα τὰ ὀχυρώματα τὰ διαβολικὰ καὶ ἔρριπτε χαμαί], and transformed those who opposed him [καὶ τοὺς ἐναντίους πρὸς αὐτὸν μεθίστη]. And when he had gathered a cohort of captives, he armed them and again made his own squadron, and through them he conquered [καὶ ἡνίκα συνέλεξεν αἰχμαλώτων πλῆθος, αὐτοὺς τούτους ὁπλίσας, οἰκεῖον στρατόπεδον πάλιν ἐποίει, καὶ δι' αὐτῶν ἐκράτει].[365]

---

[362]   hom. in 2 Cor. 25.3 [61.573].

[363]   With a rhetorical flourish Chrysostom can elsewhere reject the thought that the devil posed any real threat to Paul, as in hom. in Eph. 22.4–5 [62.160–62], where he denies that Paul actually wrestled or contended with the devil, given that "the one who wrestles has not conquered, but the one who has conquered no longer wrestles. Paul subjected the devil, took him captive … therefore, never did the devil have power over Paul" [ὁ γὰρ πλαίων οὐδέπω ἐνίκησεν, ὁ δὲ νικήσας οὐκέτι παλαίει. ὑπέταξεν αὐτόν, ἐξηχμαλώτισε … Ὥστε οὐδαμοῦ ἐκράτησε τοῦ Παύλου]. But elsewhere John can just as easily describe Paul's shrewd battle techniques as due to the fact that "he knew the demons who were sparring with him" [ᾔδει τοὺς πυκτεύοντας αὐτῷ δαίμονας] (hom. in 2 Cor. 25.3 [61.574]).

[364]   This heroic image of Paul as a μονομάχος partakes of the same rhetorical device as Libanios uses in praise of Odysseus in Prog. 8.2.13 [Foerster, 8.230]: μὴ κοινὸν ἡγείσθω τῶν Ἑλλήνων τὸ ἔργον, ἀλλ' ἑνὸς ἀνδρὸς Ὀδυσσέως καὶ τῆς ἐκείνου διανοίας τε καὶ τόλμης ("let the deed not be thought to have been a joint work of the Greeks, but of one man, Odysseus, born of his mind and daring"). This corresponds with Theon's recommendation: ἐπαινεταὶ δέ εἰσιν αἱ πράξεις … εἰ μόνος ἔπραξέ τις (Prog. 8 [Spengel, 2.110]).

[365]   hom. in 2 Cor. 25.3 [61.573]. As the passage continues Chrysostom compares Paul to David, using some extremely vivid imagery: "For Paul did not bring down Goliath by throwing a stone, but by speaking alone he destroyed the entire fighting ranks of the devil [Οὗτος γὰρ οὐ λίθον ῥίπτων κατέφερε τὸν Γολιάθ, ἀλλὰ φθεγγόμενος μόνον ἅπασαν τοῦ διαβόλου κατέλυε τὴν φάλαγγα], like a lion gnashing his teeth and emitting flame from his tongue, thus was he irresistible, and running everywhere continually. He ran against some, he came to confront some

Paul was a one man complete assault-unit who vanquished the devil at every turn. The stamp of Chrysostom's own identity can be detected in this portrait of Paul the military decathlete, for it corresponds exactly with his vision of the ideal priest who contends against the enemies of the church, from outside and within, using all forms of martial arts.[366] But Paul also had powers beyond what ordinary mortals can claim: as the letters testify, the devil yielded to Paul's single commands (such as 1 Cor 5:5).[367]

This portrait of *Paulus victor* − over pagan cult, philosophy and the devil − implicitly poses the question, what were the weapons with which Paul won these contests for the souls of the entire world?[368] Chrysostom at times describes the contest in military terms, and when he does, stresses that Paul was solitary,[369] unarmed, even naked,[370] in the face of his formidable, state-sponsored foe, paganism. Yet the biblical record, especially Acts, provides Chrysostom with two sets of Pauline tools, two types of πράξεις which were operative in various ways in his success: eloquence and miracles. But Chrysostom has an ambiguous stance toward both these Pauline activities. On the one hand he seeks to eschew the claim that rhetoric was the key to Paul's success, both because it might call into question Paul's commitment to the truth, and because it would thereby give the credit for the propagation of the gospel to human prowess, because John assumes, as does his culture generally, that rhetorical acumen is the direct result of παιδεία, and therefore human striving. But, on the other hand, while John wishes to argue that Paul's accomplishments were due to divine providence and inspiration, he also down-

---

others, he turned about to some, he sped away to others, attacking more swiftly than the wind. He piloted the whole world as though it were a single household or boat" [καὶ καθάπερ μίαν οἰκίαν, ἢ πλοῖον ἕν, τὴν οἰκουμένην ἅπασαν κυβερνῶν].

[366] *sac.* 4.3 [SC 272.252]: "it is necessary for the man who is going to engage in battle against all the tactics of all [the enemies of the church] to know how, in the same person, to be an archer and a sling-shot and squadron-leader and trooper and captain and foot soldier and cavalier and fighting seaman and wall-stormer." As in the case of Paul, it is because of the wiles of the devil, who introduces continually new and different adversaries, that the priest must be practiced in all military arts.

[367] αὐτὸς ὁ διάβολος ἐπιτάγματι μόνον εἶκεν αὐτῷ τῷ Παύλῳ (*hom. in 2 Cor.* 26.2 [61.577]). This is why Chrysostom must argue to ordinary priests in *sac.* 4.3 [SC 272.250] that, although Paul had a power they do not have (to perform miracles), Paul still practiced rhetoric, a skill they *can* develop, if they are not lazy.

[368] As already in the Pauline epistles (2 Cor 6:7; 10:4–5).

[369] *hom. in 2 Cor.* 25.3 [61.573], "just like a single soldier having the entire world as his opponent … thus also Paul was alone among barbarians, among Greeks, appearing everywhere on land and sea, he remained unconquered" [καθάπερ στρατιώτης εἰς τὴν οἰκουμένην πολεμοῦσαν ἔχων ἅπασαν … οὕτω καὶ Παῦλος μόνος ἐν βαρβάροις, ἐν Ἕλλησι, πανταχοῦ γῆς, πανταχοῦ θαλάττης φαινόμενος, ἀχείρωτος ἔμενε]. In this homily Chrysostom repeatedly emphasizes that this great victory was won by "a single body," "a single soul," "a single tongue" (25.3 [61.573–74]).

[370] See, e.g., *laud. Paul.* 4.13–14 [SC 300.212]; *hom. in 2 Cor.* 21.3 [61.545], "going into the battle with nothing but a short tunic" [ἀπὸ γὰρ χιτωνίσκου μόνου εἰς τὴν παράταξιν εἰσελθών]; 25.2 [61.571], "the combatant of the whole world went into the contest naked" [ὁ τῆς οἰκουμένης ἀγωνιστὴς γυμνὸς ἠγωνίζετο]; cf. *hom. in Ac.* 4.3 [60.47], of Peter and all the apostles.

plays the force of Paul's miracles, for he wants to hold the apostle up as an example of the capacity *all* Christians have for fervency in the life of faith, as illustrated by one who acted virtuously with no more divine assistance than any common lay person could expect to receive. This theological tension between Chrysostom's salvation history and his ethics as they meet in Pauline anthropology is inscribed in the very fabric of the portraits of Paul as rhetorician and as miracle worker, rendering them virtual palimpsests of constant bold stroke followed by erasure, as John seeks both to affirm and to deny the power of these Pauline πράξεις.

Persuasive Oratory

As we have previously discussed, Paul's lack of παιδεία is for Chrysostom an assured biographical fact, which ensures that Paul could in no way have been a "rhetorician" in worldly terms. Paul's lack of formal rhetorical education weds nicely with the long-standing Christian appropriation of the classical debate between rhetoric and philosophy (given perhaps its most famous exposition in Plato's *Gorgias*), and places Paul securely on the philosophy side, as unquestionably a spokesman of the truth.[371] In following the stock argument of Christian apologetics, Chrysostom situates Paul within a group portrait of all the apostles, modeled upon Acts 4:13, and attributes to him illiteracy by association.[372] But Chrysostom has difficulty in sustaining this idealistic image of Paul as ignorant, because in depicting the apostle as the world's greatest philosopher he placards one who not only held true beliefs and lived by them, but managed to *persuade* all the people in the world of the truth of his teaching. Once that word, πείθειν, has entered into the discussion, Chrysostom has to deal with the means of Paul's persuasion. And if the apostle is situated in the arena of public oratory – a field marked by the most intense and bitter competition in antiquity[373] – then Chrysostom must proclaim him premiere there, as everywhere else, which is just what he does: "the man more philosophical than philosophers, more sweet-voiced than rhetoricians" [ὁ φιλοσόφων φιλοσοφώτερος, ὁ ῥητόρων εὐγλωττότερος].[374] One

---

[371] Chrysostom would naturally place himself, and his mentor, Paul, with philosophy, given that he views Christianity in general, and the ascetic life in particular, as φιλοσοφεῖν (see Ivo auf der Maur, *Mönchtum und Glaubensverkündigung in den Schriften des hl. Johannes Chrysostomus* [Paradosis 14; Freiburg: Universitätsverlag Freiburg Schweiz, 1959] 87–92).

[372] This portrait harmonizes Paul with the rest of the apostles, whereas in most other places Chrysostom seeks to set Paul apart, as the one who outdid them all (per 1 Cor 15:10).

[373] Chrysostom remarks on this in *oppugn.* 3.13, 19 [47.371, 382], in his effort to persuade parents that their children have hardly a chance of reaching the pinnacle of this most contentious of careers. Chrysostom would have experienced the competitive nature of Greek rhetorical culture himself, as well as through the life and writings of his teacher, Libanios, which provide the most graphic and palpable evidence of the brutal all-out war constantly carried out by rhetors in the late fourth century (see chap. 5, n. 317, above).

[374] *Laz.* 6.9 [48.1041]. Compare *Eutrop.* 2.14 [52.409]: "the tentmaker was stronger than demons, the voiceless more philosophical than philosophers" [ὁ σκηνοποιὸς δαιμόνων ἰσχυρότερος, ὁ ἄστομος φιλοσόφων φιλοσοφώτερος].

way he sustains this tension is by fresh locutions which attempt to redeem the category; thus Paul is ὁ ῥήτωρ ὁ πνευματικός, "the spiritual rhetor,"[375] whose σύνεσις, "intelligence," is apparent throughout his writings.[376] Although Chrysostom doesn't provide a systematic depiction of what such rhetoric entails, a few details emerge: it is a rhetoric that defies the elitism of ancient *paideia* (as did its proponents), for it is accessible to all manner of people because it bases its appeal, not on deductive arguments [συλλογισμοί], but on faith [πίστις].[377] Moreover, this overwhelming task of converting the world could only have been accomplished by divine initiative, given that "this power of persuading the world [τὸ πεῖσαι τὴν οἰκουμένην] was greater than that required for creating the heavens."[378]

But however named, what Chrysostom is speaking about is Paul's powers of persuasive speech to reach various audiences with his gospel proclamation and stir them to conversion. When moving on this trajectory, of accenting the effectiveness of Paul's λόγος for bringing people to the truth, Chrysostom can unabashedly and enthusiastically praise Paul's rhetorical skill as demonstrated in the letters and in his speeches in Acts, for both serve to show the power of the spirit at work in the propagation of the gospel. This of course stands in rather direct contradiction with Chrysostom's insistence, when dealing with Paul's educational background, that he was entirely an ἰδιώτης, an "unskilled person."[379] But he does it anyway, in triumphal revelry. Thus Chrysostom begins his most famous homily set on Paul's epistles, that to the Romans, with a hymn to Paul's persuasive powers of speech, as concentrated in his tongue:

Paul's tongue shone above the sun, and he exceeded all others in the eloquence of his teaching [τῶν ἄλλων ἁπάντων ἐπλεονέκτησε τῷ τῆς διδασκαλίας λόγῳ]. Since he labored more than they, he drew to himself abundant grace of the spirit. And I affirm this not from the epistles alone, but also from the Acts [Καὶ τοῦτο οὐκ ἀπὸ τῶν ἐπιστολῶν διισχυρίζομαι

---

[375] *poenit.* 2.5 [49.290].

[376] See Adele Monaci Castagno, "Paideia classica ed esercizio pastorale nel IV secolo: il concetto di 'synesis' nell'opera di Giovanni Crisostomo," *Rivista di storia e letteratura religiosa* 26 (1990) 429–59, 442–50.

[377] "For this reason the Athenians themselves now laugh at those philosophers of old, whereas even the barbarians and ignorant and untrained [βάρβαροι ... καὶ ἀνόητοι καὶ ἰδιῶται] attend to Paul. For his preaching is laid out common to all. He recognizes no difference in status [ἀξιώματος διαφορά], nor superiority of any nation [ἔθνους ὑπεροχή], or any other such thing. For it requires faith alone, not syllogisms [πίστεως γὰρ δεῖται μόνης, οὐ συλλογισμῶν]. Hence this proclamation is especially worthy of admiration, not only because of its utility and salvific power, but because it is simple and easy, and readily grasped by all [εὔκολον καὶ ῥᾷστον, καὶ τοῖς πᾶσιν εὐληπτον], which is especially a work of God's providence [τῆς τοῦ θεοῦ προνοίας ἔργον ἐστί], for he lays out all his gifts in common to all" (*hom. in Rom.* 2.5 [60.407]). For the contrast between faith and syllogisms, see also *hom. in Jo.* 63.3 [59.352]: whereas the philosophers failed to convert the world with their syllogisms, the fishermen and tentmakers accomplished it by faith [ἆρ' οὐχ ὅτι ἐκεῖνοι μὲν λογισμοῖς, οὗτοι δὲ πίστει τὸ πᾶν ἐπέστρεψαν;].

[378] Οὕτω τοῦ ποιῆσαι τὸν οὐρανὸν μείζων δύναμις αὕτη ἦν, τὸ πεῖσαι τὴν οἰκουμένην (*hom. in 2 Tim.* 2.1 [62.608]).

[379] See the argument above in this chapter, pp. 241–45.

μόνον, ἀλλὰ καὶ ἀπὸ τῶν πράξεων].[380] For if somewhere an opportunity for public oratory arose, people from all over would yield to him [Εἰ γάρ που δημηγορίας ἦν καιρὸς, αὐτῷ πανταχοῦ παρεχώρουν]. That is why he was thought to be Hermes by the unbelievers at Lystra (Acts 14:11) – because he was sovereign over the power of speech [διὰ τὸ τοῦ λόγου κατάρχειν].[381]

In this context and others[382] Chrysostom lauds Paul's rhetorical powers for the persuasion they effected. An advantage of John's use of synecdoche in this passage, whereby he encapsulates Paul's person in his tongue, is that it adumbrates any discussion of Paul's *paideia*, and thus allows for unbridled praise of him via that (naturally, untutored) member.[383]

Literarily Chrysostom treats the Pauline letters as mostly sophisticated, carefully reasoned and, at times, even sublimely expressed texts.[384] It is interesting, though hardly surprising, that this does not lead him to revise his biographical portrait, for the simple reason that that image has its own function in his oratory, by which Chrysostom makes the familiar contrast between humble origins and subsequent great deeds. And attributing rhetorical skill to *Paul the person*, rather than to *the Pauline letters*, would run afoul of Chrysostom's theological assumption and prevailing point: that it was *God* who was at work in these utterances. But what is

---

[380] See, for instance, John's approval of how Paul came ready to present his ἀπολογία in Acts 22: "a man well-prepared" [τεταγμένος ἀνήρ] (*hom. in Ac.* 47.1 [60. 326–27]). He also admires Paul's wisdom in using proofs suitable to his different audiences, as indicated in Acts 17, where Paul does not argue from scripture or the gospel, as he does with synagogue audiences, but from the pagan altar, as fitting for his Athenian audience (*Jud.* 5.3 [48.886]). Chrysostom can also register some negative evaluations, as on Acts 26:28, where Paul misunderstands Agrippa's phrase ἐν ὀλίγῳ, John explains, because οὕτως ἰδιώτης ἦν (*hom. in Ac.* 52.4 [60.363]). A comprehensive study of how Chrysostom, despite his general devaluation of Paul's rhetoric skill, positively interprets the substance and conduct of his speeches in Acts, is unfortunately beyond our scope here, but is well worth pursuing. Those speeches provide an especially interesting opportunity to explore how Chrysostom can maintain the tension between his biographical denial of Paul's rhetorical skill and his literary and theological approval of Paul's argumentation.

[381] *hom. in Rom.* Arg. 1 [60.392].

[382] This is one of many such passages; see also, e.g., *hom. in Rom.* 32.3 [60.679]: "For [Paul's voice] had Christ sitting on it, and it sallied forth with him everywhere, and as high as the Cherubim are – there was Paul's voice. For just as he [Christ] was seated upon those powers, so also was he upon Paul's tongue. For Paul was worthy to receive Christ, because he uttered only those things which were pleasing to Christ [Καὶ γὰρ ἀξία τοῦ δέξασθαι τὸν Χριστὸν ἐγένετο, ἐκεῖνα φθεγγομένη μόνον, ἃ τῷ Χριστῷ φίλα ἦν], and flew to an indescribable height [καὶ πρὸς ὕψος ἄφατον ἱπταμένη], just like the Seraphim. For what could be loftier than that voice [Τί γὰρ ὑψηλότερον τῆς φωνῆς ἐκείνης] which said … [John quotes Rom 8:38–39]"; also *hom. in 1 Thess.* 4.2 [62.418]: "who now will be able to break forth in such voice [Τίς δυνήσεται ταύτην ῥῆξαι τὴν φωνὴν νῦν;]? Or, rather, who will ever be able to think like this?" [μᾶλλον δὲ τίς δυνήσεται οὕτω φρονῆσαί ποτε;].

[383] Of many other examples, see *hom. in 2 Cor.* 25.3 [61.573], ἑνὶ σώματι καταλαμβάνων τὴν οἰκουμένην, μιᾷ γλώττῃ πάντας τρεπόμενος; *laud. Paul.* 4.18, 20 [SC 300.220–224, 226]; 7.11 [SC 300.316–18].

[384] See n. 204 above for documentation of this point. He does not fault the letters' argumentation, but does remark upon their lack of elegant prose style (on which see below).

denied by the front door is allowed to enter from the back, since the Holy Spirit, or Christ himself, who is *speaking* in Paul is capable of quite soaring heights of truth and argumentation. Such praise for Paul's rhetorical skill extends also to his writings to Christian converts, such as his first letter to the Corinthians, which Chrysostom interprets line by line in his treatise *de virginitate*, with repeatedly laudatory comments about Paul's rhetorical skill.[385] In commenting upon 1 Cor 7:32 he asks:

Why does he use this form of appeal [Τίνος οὖν ἕνεκεν τούτῳ τῆς παρακλήσεως κέχρηται τῷ τρόπῳ]? Not because of ignorance [Οὐ δι' ἄγνοιαν], nor because he does not know how to win over and persuade the hearer [οὐδὲ διὰ τὸ μὴ εἰδέναι πῶς ἄν τις ἐπαγάγοιτο καὶ πείσειε τὸν ἀκροατήν], but because he has been more successful in this art than all people – the art, I mean, of persuasion [ἀλλὰ καὶ διὰ τὸ μάλιστα πάντων ἀνθρώπων ταύτην κατωρθωκέναι τὴν ἀρετήν, τὴν τοῦ πείθειν λέγω].[386]

Here the "proof of the pudding" of Paul's rhetorical virtuosity is his texts themselves, which, in their careful, sophisticated argumentation, demonstrate that the apostle was an accomplished, indeed, *the most* accomplished, practitioner of the rhetorical craft.

However, since others could claim that Paul won converts, not because of his tongue and the truth it proclaimed, but because of the miracles he performed, Chrysostom must confront the relative weight (and rhetorical usefulness) of these two Pauline tools of conversion.[387] John frequently insists that it was the clear truth of Paul's proclamation that was responsible for its ready acceptance, not miracle working. One argument he offers in favor of this assertion is a simple literary and historical observation: when one reads through the Acts of the Apostles, one finds many narratives chronicling the success of Paul's preaching that precede any account of his miracle working, thus demonstrating that people did not believe Paul just because they saw him perform marvels.[388] Indeed, persuading people without miracles is a greater miracle than any of the marvels that might have caused be-

---

[385] See, for instance, *virg.* 13.1; 27.3–4; 35.1, on how Paul wrote οὐχ ἁπλῶς οὐδὲ ὡς ἔτυχεν; also 41.5, 7–9; 42.3; 47.4; 76.2 [SC 125.132–34, 180–82, 208, 240–44, 248, 268, 366]). Such statements stand comfortably alongside Chrysostom's repeated reminders that Paul had Christ speaking in him (2.2; 8.2; 12.1, 2; 37.4 [SC 125.100, 116, 128–30, 222]), though the two concepts are not explicitly combined.

[386] *virg.* 49.3 [SC 125.276–78].

[387] One way this comes to expression is in Chrysostom's debate with himself over which was more effective in scaring off demons, Paul's voice or his garments. See his ambiguity in *hom. in Rom.* 32.3 [60.679], where at first he says, "for if Paul's garments set them ashiver, how much more his voice" [Εἰ γὰρ τὰ ἱμάτια αὐτοῦ ἔφριττον, πολλῷ μᾶλλον τὴν φωνήν]! But less than a minute later he takes the opposite tack: "this is why the demons fled, not only because they heard him speaking, but also because they saw his garment, even when he was far off" [διὰ τοῦτο ἔφευγον δαίμονες, οὐχὶ φθεγγομένου μόνον ἀκούοντες, ἀλλὰ καὶ πόρρωθεν ὄντος ἱμάτιον ὁρῶντες].

[388] "'But,' someone will say, '[he convinced people] by the miracles.' It was not from the miracles alone. For if you go through the Acts of the Apostles, everywhere you will find him winning by the teaching – even before the miracles" ['Αλλ' ἀπὸ τῶν σημείων, φησίν. Οὐκ ἀπὸ τῶν σημείων μόνον· εἰ γὰρ ἐπέλθοις τὰς Πράξεις τῶν 'Αποστόλων, πολλαχοῦ αὐτὸν εὑρήσεις ἀπὸ τῆς διδασκαλίας κρατοῦντα καὶ πρὸ τῶν σημείων] (*hom. in Tit.* 2.2 [62.673]).

lief!³⁸⁹ The Lystra legend in Acts 14 provides Chrysostom with a second, apt proof of this contention, for it brings Paul's miracle working together with his effective speech in such a way as to accent the latter. The crowd praised both Paul and Barnabas because they healed the lame man, but Paul they singled out as Hermes, "since he was the master of the word" [ἐπειδὴ αὐτὸς ἦν ὁ ἡγούμενος τοῦ λόγου].³⁹⁰ When set in relation to his miracles, therefore, Chrysostom wishes to accent the superior force of Paul's λόγος (despite his wish to devalue Paul's capacity for λόγος elsewhere in order to insist upon the divine source of the gospel's success). The gospel spread because of Paul's magnificent powers of speech. "See how everywhere we see him doing everything through words, not miracles."³⁹¹

de sacerdotio, Book 4
Manifestly Chrysostom's treatments of Paul's rhetorical proficiency bear the traces of his own ambivalence about the role of rhetoric in his life and priestly ministry. This comes to most remarkable expression in the fourth book of *de sacerdotio*. Single excerpted passages from this argument have been presented by some scholars as determinative evidence about Chrysostom's supposedly negative attitude toward Paul's rhetorical acumen, but because this is a very complex and inverted argument, which combines within itself the very tensions about the rhetorical arts of which we have been speaking, no single part of it should be interpreted in isolation, or presented as the sum total of Chrysostom's views on Paul's rhetorical proficiency.³⁹² In order to do justice to this complex issue, we shall supply a full rhetorical analysis of this crucial and fascinating composition.³⁹³

---

³⁸⁹ *hom. in Col.* 10.4 [62.370–71].This, too, proves the divine origin of the gospel proclamation.

³⁹⁰ Chrysostom made this argument in an extended form in *sac.* 4.7 [SC 272.270–72], quoted in full below, p. 288.

³⁹¹ Ὅρα πανταχοῦ διὰ λόγων τὸ πᾶν κατορθοῦντα, οὐ διὰ σημείων (*hom. in Ac.* 43.2 [60.304]).

³⁹² A recent example is afforded by Kern, *Rhetoric and Galatians*, 178, who quotes an excerpt in support of his claim that Chrysostom distanced Paul from Greco-Roman oratory, but does not even finish the grammatical sentence he cites, leaving off the positive evaluation of rhetoric at its end. Nor does Kern even mention the whole battery of positive statements about Paul's rhetorical abilities that follow in the wider argument.

³⁹³ This analysis is grounded my judgment that the argument can be easily understood without an appeal to some focused opposition among an Antiochene Messalian circle, as was recently argued by Reinhart Staats, "Chrysostomus über die Rhetorik des Apostels Paulus." A major difficulty with his case is that Staats atomizes this argument too much from its wider context in Book Four (he treats only §5 and 6, without justification). Further, the rhetoric of 4.5 [SC 272.260], using the term οἱ οἰκεῖοι, is better understood generically and logically to refer to "orthodox" Christian priests of "today" (and their defenders) who are "lazy," in John's eyes, because they do not want to labor for the oratorical skill required to combat the opponents, both insiders and outsiders, whom Chrysostom has just previously discussed (see 4.6, compared with 4.3–4 [SC 272.270, 252–60]). In particular, Staats' claim, that Basil here is a fictional name representing the viewpoint of a larger social group ("... dessen fiktiver Name 'Basilius' steht auch für die Anschauung einer größeren sozialen Gruppe" [p. 226]), raises difficulties, given that Basil is a consistent protagonist in the treatise. Is Staats suggesting that Basil's identity changes with each question throughout the work? Surely the entire work does not have such a narrow

One of Chrysostom's most famous discourses, renowned already in his life-time,[394] *de sacerdotio* was composed relatively early in his ordained ministry at Antioch.[395] In the course of this fictional dialogue with his companion, Basil, on the priestly office, Chrysostom winds up on the topic of Paul's rhetorical skill. The larger context is Book Four of the treatise, which considers the general topic of the worthiness of men to be priests. Chrysostom advances the claim that a priest, these days, must have powers of eloquence and argumentation in order effectively to refute opponents (that is, outsiders and, perhaps even more pressing, Christian heretics). His position is straightforwardly expressed: a priest should do all that he can to acquire ἡ τοῦ λόγου βοήθεια, "the assistance of effective speech/rheto-ric."[396] At this point his protagonist Basil interrupts with a potentially devastating counter-example; if this were truly the case, then,

> why wasn't Paul zealous to achieve excellence in this art [οὐκ ἐσπούδασε ταύτην οἱ κατορθωθῆναι τὴν ἀρετήν]? But instead, he did not hide his poverty of speech [ἡ τοῦ λόγου πενία], but even explicitly admitted that he was unskilled in speech [ἰδιώτης τῷ λόγῳ], and that in a letter to the Corinthians, of all people, who most admired and esteemed eloquent speech! [οἱ ἀπὸ τοῦ λέγειν θαυμαζόμενοι καὶ μέγα ἐπὶ τοῦτο φρονοῦντες].[397]

In response to this objection (which Chrysostom takes as representing a wide-spread point of view) Chrysostom constructs proofs for two major theses. After first exco-riating the manner of thinking underly the question (as exhibiting a kind of ἀμαθία utterly at variance with Paul, based as it is on an inability or unwillingness to exam-ine the apostolic mind and the intention of his words), John pulls himself away from that tempting point and, with a rhetorical question, articulates his initial proposition: "Let's suppose (for the sake of argument) that Paul *was* an ἰδιώτης, in this matter (rhetorical skill), as they wish him to be, what does that mean for men today, anyway?"[398] The "they" to whom Chrysostom refers here and throughout the next two chapters are apparently priests, or would-be priests, who appeal to Paul's lack of rhetorical skill to excuse their own poor education and unwillingness to learn.[399]

---

focus on the Messalians, so it is hard to see why Basil's identity should be so strongly determined in *this* instance. Of even more difficulty for his thesis is the fact that most of the appeals Staats makes to particular parallels with the homilies of Makarios-Symeon deal with words or concepts that are quite pervasive and general in referent, such as the accusation of περιεργάζεσθαι, which is a favored Chrysostomic taunt against those who try to know too much (see, for instance, its very frequent use in the treatise *de incomprehensibili dei natura*). And what the present investigation demonstrates is the extent to which the debate over Paul's rhetorical skill was Chrysostom's *own* preoccupation, apart from any such narrowly defined set of opponents as Staats has postulated.

[394] Already in 392 it is mentioned by Jerome in his catalogue (*vir. ill.* 129), who says he has read it.

[395] The date is disputed, but likely c. 390 C.E. (Anne-Marie Malingrey, SC 272.10–13).

[396] *sac.* 4.5 [SC 272.262].

[397] *sac.* 4.6, ll. 2–8 [SC 272.262].

[398] Θῶμεν αὐτὸν εἶναι ἰδιώτην τοῦτο τὸ μέρος ὅπερ οὗτοι βούλονται, τί οὖν τοῦτο πρὸς τοὺς ἄνδρας τοὺς νῦν; (*sac.* 4.6, ll. 17–18 [SC 272.264]).

[399] See especially *sac.* 4.6, l. 77, and 4.8, ll. 21–22, where he first characterizes their position

First Proof – Paul's Incomparability.[400] Based upon this diagnosis of his interlocutor's objection, John's initial response is a rhetorical move which serves simultaneously to shift the argument from defense to encomium, and to slander the opposition, for his main thesis is that Paul is simply incomparable to people of today; hence he cannot be drawn upon in the way "they" suppose, even if their contention about Paul (i.e., that Paul was as unskilled an orator "as they wish him to be") were true. Only after demolishing the underlying logic of their appeal, by proving Paul to be completely superior to them on all accounts, will John return to the premise that he initially granted for the sake of argument, to demonstrate in turn that Paul was in fact *not* an ἰδιώτης in the way that they think.[401] In what is for him an uncharacteristic move, Chrysostom wishes to place Paul on an entirely different level from contemporary people and thus to eschew comparison with him entirely. To make this point John begins with the Pauline activities he repeatedly downplays in most of his encomia, the miracles. "Paul had a power much greater than that of eloquent speech and more able to accomplish good deeds" [Ἐκεῖνος μὲν γὰρ εἶχεν ἰσχὺν πολλῷ τοῦ λόγου μείζονα καὶ πλείονα δυναμένην κατορθοῦν].[402] The apostle was able to effect great miracles [θαυματουργεῖν] in wordless silence, for his appearance alone scared off demons (Acts 19:12), whereas people today [οἱ δὲ νῦν πάντες], even when they raise their voices in thousands of prayers and tearful supplications, cannot summon the power that Paul's hankies alone possessed. This power was abundantly attested: Paul raised the dead (Acts 20:10), did such wonders as to be reckoned a god (Acts 14:12), and had heavenly visitations (2 Cor 12). The *a maiore ad minus* argument comes to its sure conclusion with a threat: people today should shiver with fear [φρίττειν] at the prospect of comparing themselves with such a great man [ἀνδρὶ τηλικούτῳ παραβάλλοντες ἑαυτούς].[403]

But Chrysostom's usual instinct against allowing Paul's miracles to dominate in a portrait of the apostolic career takes over, and next he seeks to broaden his proof

---

as "welcoming lack of training" [τὴν ἰδιωτείαν ἀσπάζεσθαι], and then castigates them directly: "these arguments are speculations, pretenses for sloth and pretexts for hesitation" [Σκήψεις ταῦτα καὶ προφάσεις καὶ ῥαθυμίας καὶ ὄκνου προσχήματα] [SC 272.276]. This harsh approach to adversaries is mitigated once, with a good dose of dissimulation, when he interrupts himself in the midst of a threat to "the people of today" who should shiver with fear at daring to compare themselves with Paul, to remark, "but I cannot say anything harsh or stern; for I am now saying even these things not to trample on them, but because I am amazed ..." [ἀλλ' οὐδὲν δύναμαι δυσχερὲς εἰπεῖν οὐδὲ βαρύ· καὶ γὰρ καὶ ταῦτα οὐκ ἐπεμβαίνων αὐτοῖς λέγω νῦν, ἀλλὰ θαυμάζων] (sac. 4.6, ll. 29–30 [SC 272.266], reminiscent of Paul's disclaimer in 1 Cor 4:14).

[400] This spans sac. 4.6, ll. 17–60 [SC 272.264–68])

[401] As announced in sac. 4.6, ll. 61–62 [SC 272.268].

[402] sac. 4.6, ll. 19–21 [SC 272.264]. Already in 4.3 [272.250] Chrysostom had invoked the Pauline example against the hypothetical argument that, if people today had miraculous powers by which they could stop up the mouths of the opposition, even still "the help of rhetoric" [ἡ ἀπὸ τοῦ λόγου βοήθεια] would be required: "For the blessed Paul practiced rhetoric, even though he was marveled at everywhere because of his miracles" [Καὶ γὰρ ὁ μακάριος Παῦλος αὐτὸν μετεχείρισε, καίτοι γε ἀπὸ τῶν σημείων πανταχοῦ θαυμαζόμενος].

[403] sac. 4.6, ll. 28–31 [SC 272.266].

for the incomparability of Paul's deeds to the rest of humankind. The transition is straightforward:"For if we leave off from his miracles, and come into the life of this blessed man, and investigate his angelic form of behavior, in this even more than in the signs shall we see the athlete of Christ victorious."[404] To document the point Chrysostom emits a jumbled list of Pauline virtues and actions, all to show Paul's complete victory and possession of trophies for all arenas of possible competition among human beings: zeal, gentleness, dangers, cares, anxieties for his churches, compassion for the weak, persecutions, daily deaths. These many accomplishments of Paul's are proven by his worldwide acclaim, with all regions of the geosphere offering testimony: "For what place in the world, what continent, what sea is ignorant of the contests this just man engaged in?" [τίς γὰρ τόπος τῆς οἰκουμένης, ποία ἤπειρος, ποία θάλαττα τοῦ δικαίου τοὺς ἄθλους ἠγνόησεν;].[405] Indeed, even the uninhabited territories [ἡ ἀοίκητος] knew Paul, since he endured dangers there often. The summation confidently asserts Paul's unblemished record of competitive success: "He endured every form of treachery, won every type of victory [πάντα τρόπον ἐπῆλθε νίκης], and never ceased fighting nor being crowned" [οὔτε ἀγωνιζόμενος οὔτε στεφανούμενος διέλιπέ ποτε].[406]

But just when the praise of Paul reaches such hyperbolic heights John takes it one step further by a surprise self-accusation, a vehement, involuted incorporation of the typical rhetorical disclaimer of sufficient skill to utter praises to the subject: "Yet I do not know how, but I have been induced to insult [ὑβρίζειν] the man! For all his good deeds [κατορθώματα] surpassed [ὑπερβαίνειν] the power of speech [λόγος] – that is, my speech – to the same degree as those who know how to speak eloquently [οἱ λέγειν εἰδότες] surpass me."[407] This exclamation of a task abysmally failed (for insult is of course the precise opposite of praise) amplifies the

---

[404] Εἰ γὰρ καὶ τὰ θαύματα ἀφέντες, ἐπὶ τὸν βίον ἔλθοιμεν τοῦ μακαρίου καὶ τὴν πολιτείαν ἐξετάσαιμεν αὐτοῦ τὴν ἀγγελικὴν καὶ ἐν ταύτῃ μᾶλλον ἢ ἐν τοῖς σημείοις, ὄψει νικῶντα τὸν ἀθλητὴν τοῦ Χριστοῦ (*sac.* 4.6, ll. 32–35 [SC 272.266]).

[405] *sac.* 4.6, ll. 39–41 [SC 272.266].

[406] *sac.* 4.6, ll. 42–44 [SC 272.266].

[407] This is the precise oratorical equivalent of the narrative strategy Krueger describes in "Hagiography as an Ascetic Practice," 216:"In narratives that call the readers to a life of sanctity, the language of authorial self-denigration constitutes an aesthetic choice bearing moral value. Preparing to narrate the obvious goodness of the saint, the author's own humble gesture subtly models a Christian virtue." Of course it is an epideictic commonplace to claim that one is not equal to the magnitude of one's subject (*Rhet. Her.* 3.6.11; Isoc. *Or.* 4.13, and the great exemplar Demosthenes [*Or.* 6.11]; see Caplan's note in the LCL vol. of [Cicero] *Rhet. Her.*, p. 176, note b). The rhetorical term for this affectation not to be a powerful speaker is ἀστεϊσμός, one of the four types of irony (see Alexander, *Fig.* 18 [Spengel, 3.23]; cf. Tryphon, *Trop.* 2.24 [Spengel, 3.98]; Herodian, *Fig.* 601 [Spengel, 3.98]; and the discussion of this figure in relation to Paul by E. A. Judge, "Paul's Boasting in Relation to Contemporary Professional Practice," *AusBR* 16 [1968] 37–50). Due to the wide and thorough attestation of this rhetorical commonplace, it is difficult to claim this emphasis on humility as distinctively Christian (to demur somewhat from Krueger, 217), although the extent or manner in which the commonplace is drawn upon may in some ways be.

encomium given to Paul's indescribable good deeds, and ironically draws attention to the very pressing need for adept Christian rhetoric that Chrysostom is here championing! Furthermore, like all such rhetorical disclaimers, it is meant to highlight the reverse of its ostensible meaning – the very eloquence of the orator, who by it seeks to earn even more points of honor for his humility. But Chrysostom professes not to be working according to human standards (his obvious use of the encomiastic form notwithstanding), "for Paul (i.e., not the audience, as in most epideictic oratory) will judge us, not from the outcome of our speech [οὐδὲ ἀπὸ τῆς ἐκβάσεως], but from the free will behind it" [ἀλλ' ἀπὸ τῆς προαιρέσεως].[408] This riveting anacolouthon supposedly frees Chrysostom from "normal" rhetorical expectations, but at the same time it ironically invokes a principle at odds with the epideictic rhetoric he is employing, the whole point of which is to allocate praise for outcomes, for noble actions in human life (not for good intentions). But the principle instantiating the standards of Pauline judgment does accord with the anthropology upon which Chrysostom insists: that human virtue depends upon the integration of divine grace and human free will.[409] Despite his earlier failure to laud the apostle suitably, Chrysostom avers that he will not break off his attempt until he has spoken about the matter which is as greater than all the previous things he has mentioned as Paul is greater than all people.

So what is this thing? After such great good deeds [κατορθώματα], after the myriad crowns [στέφανοι], he prayed to go off to Gehenna and be delivered into eternal punishment, in order that the Jews, who repeatedly stoned and sought in whatever way they could to destroy him, might be saved and come to Christ.[410]

In Chrysostom's eyes Rom 9:3 represents the acme of Pauline virtue, for he not only won every single crown, but he was willing to forsake all the eschatological favor he had earned to bring about the salvation of his foes. Such love for Christ (if one can even call it by that simple name, he says) puts Paul in a category by himself. Hence John seals the first proof with two recapitulating rhetorical questions: "Shall we still, then, compare ourselves to that man [Ἔτι οὖν ἑαυτοὺς ἐκείνῳ παραβαλοῦμεν], after he received such great grace [χάρις] from above [ἄνωθεν], after he displayed such great virtue [ἀρετή] from within [οἴκοθεν]? What could be more presumptuous than this [καὶ τί τούτου γένοιτ' ἂν τολμηρότερον;]?"

Second Proof – Paul's Rhetorical Skill.[411] Having dispensed with the logic of his interlocutor's comparison with Paul's rhetorical skill in the first place, Chrysostom will bring it back in again, this time to his own advantage. In the first proof he had allowed the disputed premise – that Paul was an ἰδιώτης. Now he reengages the

---

[408] *sac.* 4.6, ll. 48–49 [SC 272.268].

[409] He will return to this distinction in the recapitulation to this proof, quoted below.

[410] *sac.* 4.6, ll. 51–56 [SC 272.268].

[411] This proof extends from *sac.* 4.6, l. 61–4.7, l. 59 [SC 272.268–74].

point, and formulates his second proposition:"That Paul was not even unskilled, as they consider him to be, I shall at last attempt to prove" ["Ὅτι δὲ οὐδὲ οὗτος ἦν ἰδιώτης, ὡς οὗτοι νομίζουσι, καὶ τοῦτο λοιπὸν ἀποδεῖξαι πειράσομαι].[412] The first argument Chrysostom makes for this revisionary proposition is rooted in definition. Somewhat surprisingly, he decides to adopt the one held by his opponents, who call an ἰδιώτης not only "the person not practiced in the pedantries of pagan words" [ὁ οὐκ ἠσκημένος τὴν τῶν ἔξωθεν λόγων τερθρείαν], but also "the one who does not know how to fight for true doctrines" [ὁ οὐκ εἰδὼς μάχεσθαι ὑπὲρ τῶν τῆς ἀληθείας δογμάτων]. John agrees with the distinction which his adversaries make [καλῶς νομίζουσιν], but not their application of it to Paul, for, he points out, the apostle himself secured that very distinction by making a precise separation between skill τῷ λόγῳ and τῇ γνώσει, and emphatically *not* claiming to be an ἰδιώτης of the second sort. Chrysostom concedes that Paul was an ἰδιώτης of the first category (as the apostle himself admitted), one lacking in elegant prose style and a flair for diction. To be sure, John admits, if I were demanding here that priests have the smoothness [λειότης] of Isocrates,[413] the weightiness [ὄγκος] of Demosthenes, the dignity [σεμνότης] of Thucydides, or the sublimity [ὕψος] of Plato, then one would rightly bring Paul as counter-testimony against me. But that is not the type of rhetorical skills Chrysostom stipulates that he is urging on priests in this treatise. He states that he will gladly leave off from discussing all these stylistic virtues of the old masters, "the meddlesome ornamentalism of pagan speech" [ὁ περίεργος τῶν ἔξωθεν καλλωπισμός], for neither expression [φράσις] nor delivery [ἀπαγγελία] concern him. In a passage whose style stands in a vividly ironic relationship to its sense, John offers his rule for priestly proficiency:

> But let it be allowed for one to be poor in style and for the arrangement of words to be simple and plain, only in knowledge and in accuracy of doctrines do not let him be unskilled.[414]

After this utterance which says one thing and demonstrates its opposite, John returns to the adversaries with some invective, for in his view they invoke Paul's ἰδιωτεία to excuse their own idleness, and thereby "rob that blessed man of the greatest of his virtues and the chief source of his praises" [μηδὲ ... τὸν μακάριον ἐκεῖνον ἀφαιρείσθω τὸ μέγιστον τῶν ἀγαθῶν καὶ τὸ τῶν ἐγκωμίων κεφάλαιον].[415]

Now that Chrysostom has signalled his intent to praise Paul for his greatest achievement – the power of his words for instructing in knowledge and accuracy

---

[412] *sac.* 4.6, ll. 61–62 [SC 272.268].

[413] His traditional virtue; see Dion. Hal. *Isoc.* 13 (LSJ, 1035).

[414] Ἀλλ' ἐξέστω καὶ τῇ λέξει πτωχεύειν καὶ τὴν συνθήκην τῶν ὀνομάτων ἁπλῆν τινα εἶναι καὶ ἀφελῆ, μόνον μὴ τῇ γνώσει τις καὶ τῇ τῶν δογμάτων ἀκριβείᾳ ἰδιώτης ἔστω (*sac.* 4.6 [SC 272.270, ll. 74–77]). What the Greek reader of the treatise is meant to appreciate, of course, is that the orator has articulated his allowance for stylistic simplicity with technical rhetorical vocabulary, and expressed it in a well crafted Greek sentence filled with rhetorical figures, such as chiasm, hyperbaton and paronomasia!

[415] *sac.* 4.6, ll. 78–79 [SC 272.270].

– he begins summoning as proof the actions Paul accomplished through his oratorical gifts. John intentionally chooses to start with a collection drawn from Acts 9, because that chapter chronologically precedes any account of a Pauline miracle, thus isolating the Pauline λόγος as the singly responsible agent. The examples include: confounding the Jews in Damascus (9:22); throwing over the Hellenists (9:29); and being sent to Tarsus (9:30) because he was so victorious with speech that he spurred his adversaries to murderous reactions when they could not bear the defeat at this hands.[416] Repeating the reminder that all these successes preceded any miracles ['Ενταῦθα γὰρ οὐδέπω τοῦ θαυματουργεῖν ἤρξατο], Chrysostom insists that the Pauline λόγος had no accomplice or assistance in achieving these feats of persuasion, either from a reputation for marvels or some favorable "conventional take" on the man. "For all that while he was prevailing by speaking alone" [τέως γὰρ ἀπὸ τοῦ λέγειν μόνον ἐκράτει]. Further examples of the amazing powers of Paul's oratory, even after the onset of his wonderworking, follow: his engagement with those who tried to Judaize in Antioch (Gal 2); his winning over of Dionysius the Areopagite and his wife (Acts 17:34); the prolonged engrossment of Eutychus by ὁ τῆς διδασκαλίας αὐτοῦ λόγος (Acts 20:9);[417] the days and nights spent interpreting the Scriptures in Thessalonica, Corinth, Ephesus, and Rome; and his discourses against Epicureans and Stoics (Acts 17:18). As the list mounts the orator takes the familiar epideictic recourse: "If I wished to recount all of these things at length, my speech would run to an extraordinary length."[418]

These proofs should be more than sufficient to convince anyone of Paul's proficiency in rhetoric:

When both before the miracles and in the midst of them [καὶ πρὸ τῶν σημείων καὶ ἐν μέσοις αὐτοῖς][419] he appears to have used rhetoric to such a great extent [φαίνηται πολλῷ κεχρημένος τῷ λόγῳ], how will they still dare to call him an ἰδιώτης, a man who was marveled at by everyone especially for his capacity to argue and discourse [ἀπὸ τοῦ διαλέγεσθαι καὶ δημηγορεῖν]?[420]

Chrysostom then makes a finessed appeal to the Lycaonians of Acts 14:11–12, whose judgment that Paul and Barnabas were gods may have been due to miracles, but their appellation of Paul as Hermes was manifestly based instead upon his rhetorical power [οὐκέτι ἀπ' ἐκείνων (sc. σημείων), ἀλλ' ἀπὸ τοῦ λόγου].[421]

---

[416] Chrysostom embellishes here the brief notice in the text of Acts 9:23.

[417] Chrysostom walks right by the other implication of the story, that Paul had bored at least one hearer!

[418] sac. 4.7, ll. 23–24 [SC 272.272].

[419] See also n. 402 above, on how Chrysostom argues that miracle-working and rhetoric co-existed in Paul's arsenal of weaponry.

[420] sac. 4.7 [SC 272.272].

[421] Although he does not quote the passage, Chrysostom must have in mind 14:12b: ἐπειδὴ αὐτὸς ἦν ὁ ἡγούμενος τοῦ λόγου.

Following these lengthy appeals to events in the narrative of Acts as evidence of Paul's persuasive oratory, Chrysostom moves to his last and greatest proof: the rhetorical power of Paul's letters. John effects this transition, as he often does, with rhetorical questions.

> In what did this blessed man surpass even the other apostles? Why is it that throughout the whole world he is so much on the lips of everyone? And why is it that not only among us Christians, but even with Jews and Greeks he is admired most of all? Is it not from the excellence of his letters [ἀπὸ τῆς τῶν ἐπιστολῶν ἀρετῆς], through which, not only to the believers of his time, but even to those who have lived until this very day, and those who will live in the future up until the coming of Christ, he has extended and will extend great benefits [ὠφέλησέ τε καὶ ὠφελήσει;]? And he will not stop doing this as long as the human race persists.[422]

In an argument stressing πράξεις, deeds, one can hardly do better than this. Through his letters Paul is the eternal source of benefit to the whole human race. John continues from this point with some marvelous metaphorical disquisitions on the Pauline epistles that build upon the apostle's own self-images in 2 Cor 10:4–5: "taking captive every thought for the obedience of Christ, destroying reasonings and every lofty idea raised up against the knowledge of God" [κατὰ τῆς γνώσεως τοῦ Θεοῦ]. The latter phrase was perhaps responsible for this depiction here, given that Chrysostom's main thesis is that Paul most emphatically *is not* an ἰδιώτης τῇ γνώσει, another quotation from this same portion of 2 Corinthians (11:6). Now the very text in dispute, widened to its larger literary context, becomes a piece of evidence supporting Chrysostom's reading, because he claims that Paul's letters themselves, in their bombastic persuasive effects, are the proof of the apostle's eloquence and its rhetorical effects: "He does all these things through those epistles he left to us, which are full of marvels and divine wisdom" [Ταῦτα δὲ πάντα ἐργάζεται δι' ὧν ἡμῖν κατέλιπεν ἐπιστολῶν τῶν θαυμασίων ἐκείνων καὶ τῆς θείας πεπληρωμένων σοφίας].[423] Then in a pointed inversion John mentions present day church leaders, who still use Paul's letters to weed true from false teaching, and to instruct the church in good living. The letters even give them the power to rout illness out of the church (imagined here as the "chaste virgin" of 2 Cor 11:2), thus qualifying those writings for the title φάρμακα, "medicines." And in the final analysis the effective power of these medicines is known best by those who dose themselves frequently with them. This ironic conclusion points both to the faulty judgment of those who claim Paul bereft of rhetorical skill, and its cause: "The ἰδιώτης' left us such medicines as these, that have so great a power, the experience[424] of which is known well to those who use them continually."[425] With this

---

[422] *sac.* 4.7 [SC 272.272–74].

[423] *sac.* 4.7, ll. 46–48 [SC 272.274].

[424] Or "proof," πεῖρα (LSJ, 1354).

[425] Τοιαῦτα ἡμῖν ὁ ἰδιώτης κατέλιπε φάρμακα, τοσαύτην ἔχοντα δύναμιν ὧν ἴσασι τὴν πεῖραν καλῶς οἱ χρώμενοι συνεχῶς (*sac.* 4.7, ll. 56–58 [SC 272.274]).

swipe at promoters of an "unlearned clergy," Chrysostom proclaims his second thesis fully demonstrated: "from these things it is clear that Paul himself exerted great zeal for this very capacity of rhetoric."[426]

Having reclaimed the rhetorical potency of the Pauline epistles by this proof, in the next two chapters of *de sacerdotio* (4.8–9) Chrysostom quotes many didactic passages from them to prod priests to learning and to cultivate talent in expression in order to refute the church's adversaries. John finds particularly good fodder for his argument in the Pastoral Epistles,[427] which are an especially good fit since they, like his present discourse, are concerned with the qualifications of church leaders.[428] No longer is Paul himself the subject of the discourse, but his letters have taken his place, and are shown to provide unqualified support for John's contention that "the man who has the lot of teaching others most of all must be practiced in such verbal contests" [μάλιστα πάντων ἔμπειρον εἶναι δεῖ τῶν τοιούτων ἀγώνων τὸν διδάσκειν τοὺς ἄλλους λαχόντα].[429] This is because, while one can teach with the personal example of one's life [βίος], that alone is not sufficient for good instruction; words also are needed (as the examples of Jesus' words in Mt 5:19 and Paul's in Acts 20:31 amply demonstrate). Above all this is because, in the competitive rhetorical culture of the fourth century, if priests are unable to respond effectively to their opponents, their flocks will go astray, for they will not be able to tell that the "defeat" [ἧττα] was due to the inexperience of the priest, rather than to the falsity of the doctrines, and will apostasize and leave their fate on the consciences of these priests who were so ill-equipped for the apologetic task.[430]

In this book of the treatise *de sacerdotio* Chrysostom has sought to refute the potential counter-example of Paul as an ἰδιώτης which was brought against his injunction for priests to be rhetorically skillful, first by saying Paul is incomparable anyway, and then by arguing down the other side of the same street by holding up Paul, the effective orator and letter-writer, as a model for the power of persuasive speech in ministry. The coup de grâce is having those (supposedly unskilled) compositions, the Pauline letters, themselves speak for John's recommendation, by issuing imperatives for priests to learn, to study and to employ words to combat adversaries. Satisfied with this double-barreled proof, Chrysostom can confidently conclude: "We have sufficiently demonstrated how much experience the teacher

---

[426] Καὶ ὅτι μὲν πολλὴν αὐτὸς ἐποιεῖτο τοῦ μέρους τούτου σπουδήν, ἐκ τούτων δῆλον (*sac.* 4.7, ll. 58–59 [SC 272.274]). τὸ μέρος here forms an inclusio with the initial concession of *sac.* 4.6, l. 18 [SC 272.264].

[427] 1 Tim 4:13; 4:16; 5:17; 2 Tim 2:24; 3:14–15; 3:16; Tit 1:7–9; also Col 3:16; 4:16; 1 Thess 5:11.

[428] See the exchange with an imaginary opponent: "'But,' he says, 'these things [Titus 1:7–9, and other passages previously quoted] are commanded to the priests.' Well, our present discourse is also about priests!" (*sac.* 4.8, ll. 2 3–24 [SC 272.276]).

[429] *sac.* 4.9, ll. 13–15 [SC 272.280].

[430] *sac.* 4.9, ll. 15–33 [SC 272.280].

must have for verbal contests on behalf of the truth."⁴³¹ The portrait of Paul as the supremely effective orator serves to justify Chrysostom's own rhetorical practice, and his injunctions to others to imitate it themselves.

Many and Various Activities of the Spirit
(Πολλαὶ καὶ ποικίλαι ἐνέργειαι τοῦ πνεύματος)

Paul's deeds were not limited to speech acts. Chrysostom depicts him as a man whose πράξεις include spiritual actions and accomplishments which exceed normal human capabilities. We shall examine these under three broad categories: miracles, prophesy, and ecstatic experiences.

Miracles: The Paul of Acts was not only a preacher but also a miracle worker with supernatural powers of healing, even long-distance, through emanations of his power from linen cloths that have touched his skin: Δυνάμεις τε οὐ τὰς τυχούσας ὁ θεὸς ἐποίει διὰ τῶν χειρῶν Παύλου (Acts 19:11; a portrait suggested also in the letters: Gal 3:5; 2 Cor 12:12; Rom 15:19). Chrysostom is well-aware of the wonders attributed to Paul, and manifestly regards him as a man of extraordinary powers, for which he was greatly admired already in his lifetime.⁴³² This portrait of Paul as a man of marvels defines him over and against a different opponent than the rhetorician Paul who battled Julian and the philosophers for the cultic and philosophical allegiance of pagans and barbarians. This Paul is cast as the foe of demons and the devil, a thaumaturgic wonder machine who sent Satan packing time and time again, effortlessly, as he faced him and his legions down in exorcisms, healings, and resuscitations.⁴³³ These opponents are not human, but are "the bodiless powers" [αἱ ἀσώματοι δυνάμεις] of the universe.⁴³⁴ However, one should not

---

⁴³¹ Ὅσης μὲν ἐμπειρίας τῷ διδασκάλῳ δεῖ πρὸς τοὺς ὑπὲρ τῆς ἀληθείας ἀγῶνας, ἱκανῶς ἡμῖν ἀποδέδεικται (*sac.* 5.1, ll. 1–4 [SC 272.280]).

⁴³² *sac.* 4.3 [272.250]: ἀπὸ τῶν σημείων πανταχοῦ θαυμαζόμενος.

⁴³³ See the catalogues of deeds of Paul, the tentmaker who was "stronger than demons" [δαιμόνων ἰσχυρότερος] in *Eutrop.* 2.13–14 [52.408–9], including stopping the mouth of the devil and strangling demons, and *exp. in Ps.* 111.2 [55.293]: making demons run away [δραπετεύειν ποιῶν δαίμονας]. Another nice example is afforded by *hom. in 2 Cor.* 21.3 [61.544–5]: "For not by fighting did he accomplish such deeds, but as though coming to a victory which was already prepared and at hand, he raised up the trophies [τὰ τρόπαια ἵστη], demolishing, destroying, decimating the devil's fortresses and the demons' devices [κατασκάπτων, καθαιρῶν, καταβάλλων τοῦ διαβόλου τὰ ὀχυρώματα καὶ τῶν δαιμόνων τὰ μηχανήματα], and led the entire booty thus won into the army of Christ [καὶ τὴν λείαν μετῆγεν ἅπασαν ἐπὶ τὸ τοῦ Χριστοῦ στρατόπεδον]. And he did not even take a small breather, but from these battles went on to others, and again from those speeding on to still others, like an excellent general [τις στρατηγὸς ἄριστος] raising up trophies every single day, or, rather, every single hour."

⁴³⁴ *hom. in Gen.* 4.5 [53.44]; *hom. in Eph.* 10.1 [62.76]; *hom. in Mt.* 1.6 [57.20], an idea inscribed in Pauline literature (Eph 6:12). Not coincidentally, these are the very powers with which ascetics constantly must do battle through temptations (*ep. Olymp.* 8.6, 46 [SC 13.182]; *virg.* 27.2 [SC 125.178]). Ironically, the same term refers to the heavenly or angelic beings on

292 *Chap. 6: "Obviously By Some Divine and Ineffable Power": Biographical Portraits of Paul*

press this distinction in adversaries too far, as Chrysostom would readily agree that demons, philosophers and pagan cults were all in conspiratorial league with one another. As part of his quest to be champion over the entire world, Paul had to contend with demonic forces spreading death, disease and delusion, and he was empowered by the divine to annihilate them all. This portrait receives its predominant hue from Acts 19:12 (an important color in Chrysostom's palette), as well as from narratives of specific miraculous events (such as the Philippian jail break of Acts 16). Furthermore, Chrysostom considers 2 Cor 12:12 to be Paul's characteristically humble shorthand reference to these σημεῖα, τέρατα and δυνάμεις.[435]

For the man who commanded demons, and raised the dead, and by a single command was able both to incapacitate and to heal the incapacitated, whose garments and shadows[436] destroyed every form of illness – it is manifestly clear that he wasn't even considered a human being, but some angel come down from heaven.[437]

Surely one who could do all these things was no ordinary mortal.

The astounding nature of these deeds had provided John with a means whereby to reverse his usual practice and praise Paul's miracles above his speech in *de sacerdotio* (as we have just had occasion to observe), when it was useful for combatting those who claimed Paul, allegedly bereft of rhetorical skill, as their excuse for not honing their own powers of oratory. There Chrysostom crowed in the face of those who calumniated Paul's rhetorical skill by declaring that Paul was endowed with a mightier power than speech, anyway, because he was able to heal the sick wordlessly through the agency of his clothing. Paul's mere clothing was able to accomplish things that those slanderers couldn't do,[438] even with thousands of prayers and tears: raise the dead, and perform other signs sufficiently marvelous to convince outsiders that he was a God (Acts 14:11–13). And, as opposed to ordinary

---

whom the ascetics are to model their lives (e.g., *virg.* 49.1 [SC 125.274]; *fem. reg.* 6 [47.525]) (for the two uses of the term see *LPGL*, 255).

[435] *hom. in 2 Cor.* 27.1 [61.584–85]. Since Paul did not do it, John himself elongates the list by mentioning numerous resuscitations of the dead, healings of the blind, cleansings of lepers, and expulsions of demons.

[436] Here Chrysostom harmonizes the Acts portraits of Paul and Peter, by applying Acts 5:15 to Paul, as he does also in *hom. in 1 Cor.* 6.1 [61.48] (though he keeps them distinct in *hom. in 2 Cor.* 7.5 [61.449]).

[437] Ὁ γὰρ δαίμοσιν ἐπιτάττων, καὶ νεκροὺς ἐγείρων, καὶ ἐξ ἐπιτάγματος καὶ πηρῶσαι, καὶ θεραπεῦσαι τοὺς πεπηρωμένους δυνάμενος, οὗ τὰ ἱμάτια καὶ αἱ σκιαὶ ἅπαν νοσημάτων εἶδος ἔλυον, εὔδηλον ὅτι οὐδὲ ἄνθρωπος λοιπὸν εἶναι ἐνομίζετο, ἀλλ' ἄγγελός τις ἐξ οὐρανοῦ καταβάς (*hom. in Rom. 16:3* 1.2 [51.190]).

[438] This is a common theme for rhetorical embellishment; see also, e.g., *hom. in Ac. princ.* 3.4 [51.93]: "Do you wish to learn how Paul had gifts of healing, also? But perhaps this needs no demonstration in words, when we see not only the apostles but even their garments possessing gifts of healing" [ὅταν ἴδωμεν οὐ μόνον τοὺς ἀποστόλους, ἀλλὰ καὶ τὰ ἱμάτια αὐτῶν χαρίσματα ἰαμάτων ἔχοντα]; and *pan. Bab.* 2 9 [SC 362.102]: "Nothing more than Paul's garments was needed by many of the crazed persons for relief from the demon who was agitating them" [πολλοῖς δὲ τῶν μαινομένων τῶν ἱματίων Παύλου οὐδὲν πλέον ἐδέησε πρὸς τὴν τοῦ κινοῦντος αὐτοὺς δαίμονος ἀπαλλαγήν].

magicians or the like, Paul did not even have to open his mouth to make all this happen – just the sight of his garments struck fear into the heart of the demons. Such a man surely defies comparison with mere mortals.

But this is precisely what renders the portrait of Paul as miracle worker problematic for most of Chrysostom's catechetical concerns.[439] So, as we observed, taking out the oratorical eraser further along in this same treatise (*sac.* 4.6), John quickly reverted to the more imitable elements of the Pauline πράξεις: his life and his "angelic conduct," claiming that in those one can see better than in the miracles the source of Paul's victory as the athlete of Christ.[440] The list that follows is predominated by Paul's sufferings of body and mind for the sake of the gospel, and his many virtues.[441] When one adds these contests to the accomplishments won by the miracles, Paul is shown to be the ultra-champion, the victor in every Olympic event [πάντα τρόπον ἐπῆλθε νίκης].[442] In this way the miracles are retained, but in the final tally are made to take a back-seat among the Pauline πράξεις.

Chrysostom's ambiguous attitude toward Paul's miracles, as exemplified in this passage, is due to the theological difficulties they raise (and have always raised) for Christian theology.[443] Chrysostom fears that if people turned to the gospel out of awe at seeing thaumaturgic acts, then faith would be rendered inconsequential. With this in mind he offers a portrait of Paul as the man of restraint, who repeatedly held back from performing the marvelous signs of which he was capable, preferring instead to lead people to the truth of Christ through his discourse, with its patient proofs from the Law and the Prophets that Jesus is the Messiah (Acts 28:23). The apostle always could perform miracles, but only chose to do so in cases of serious need.[444] This Paul is the ultimate ascetic who includes in his renunciatory portfolio his miraculous abilities, which he forgoes for the sake of the greater

---

[439] See also, e.g., *laud. Paul.* 3.10 [SC 300.178–80]: "Let's imitate Paul in love. For it is from love that he became such as he was. So don't tell me about the dead whom he raised, or the lepers he cleansed [Μὴ γάρ μοι τοὺς νεκροὺς εἴπῃς οὓς ἀνέστησε, μηδὲ τοὺς λεπροὺς οὓς ἐκάθηρεν] (Acts 20:7–12; 19:11–12). God doesn't seek any of these feats from you. Acquire the love of Paul and you will have the perfect crown. And who is saying these things? The foster-father of love himself, this man who set love above signs and marvels and countless other things (1 Cor 13)."

[440] "For if, leaving aside the miracles, we come to the life of this blessed man, and examine his angelic conduct, in this rather than in the signs will you see the athlete of Christ victorious" [Εἰ γὰρ καὶ τὰ θαύματα ἀφέντες, ἐπὶ τὸν βίον ἔλθοιμεν τοῦ μακαρίου καὶ τὴν πολιτείαν ἐξετάσαιμεν αὐτοῦ τὴν ἀγγελικὴν καὶ ἐν ταύτῃ μᾶλλον ἢ ἐν τοῖς σημείοις, ὄψει νικῶντα τὸν ἀθλητὴν τοῦ Χριστοῦ] (*sac.* 4.6 [SC 272.266]).

[441] "For they became faithful not because of his miracles. For the signs didn't bring that about." What brought Paul's converts to faith was his virtues: "the majority of his success was done by these" (a long list of virtues). If these were in place, there would be no need of signs [εἰ ταῦτα ἦν, οὐδὲν ἔδει σημείων]" (*hom. in Eph.* 6.3 [62.46–47]).

[442] Ibid.

[443] The relationship between faith and miracles, complex already in the Gospel of Mark, receives sustained treatment in the Fourth Gospel, a favorite of Chrysostom's.

[444] *hom. in Ac.* 54.1 [60.373]: ῞Ορα αὐτὸν ἐνεργοῦντα, καὶ οὐδαμοῦ θαυματουργοῦντα ἁπλῶς, ἀλλ᾽ ἀπὸ χρείας.

good, the salvation of the whole world. And the achievement he gains from this strategic choice – convincing people to believe in the gospel from arguments rather than signs – is, paradoxically, the greatest sign of all.

> You see how again (Acts 28:23) he closes their mouths, not with signs, but with appeals to the Law and Prophets, and everywhere he does this – although he could have done signs, as well, but finally it would not be a matter of faith. For this is the great sign: to persuade people from the Law and the Prophets.[445]

In this way Chrysostom collapses the two problematic Pauline weapons into one: rhetoric and healings are all "signs" – of divine activity in the world. Pauline restraint in employing his miraculous powers is matched by divine restraint: God distributes these supernatural acts in limited proportion according to a providential desire,[446] as attested also by the precedent of Christ.[447] The many reasons why miracles are not provided to right every wrong and heal every ill are laid out by Chrysostom in a theodicy lesson evoked by an unlikely Pauline verse: 1 Tim 5:23, the injunction to drink a little wine. Timothy's gastrointestinal problems incite Chrysostom to wonder why Paul, or even saint Timothy himself (whose relics were renowned at Chrysostom's time for their healing powers), didn't just zap away his infirmity. Chrysostom proposes eight different justifications for this restraint on both the human and the divine part in not seeking miracles too readily: to keep the saints from being puffed up by their miraculous powers; to ensure that other people do not deify the saints for these actions; to uphold the divine intent that the world receive the word via weak messengers; to increase the saints' capacity for patient endurance of miseries; to spur the faithful to reflect on the reality of a post-mortem existence as needed to satisfy the requirements of justice; to console by these examples believers who experience sufferings; to deny the faithful the excuse that they cannot imitate the saints because they were endowed with unique miraculous powers; and, to learn what true blessing and cursing look like.[448] For all these reasons Paul, who had unlimited supernatural powers, did not exercise them continually, but only when divine providence so instructed. And it was the Lord's purposeful design that the gospel should be spread by word, spoken by those without formal rhetorical training, so that its truthfulness and divine

---

[445] Ὅρα πάλιν οὐκ ἀπὸ σημείων, ἀλλ᾽ ἀπὸ νόμου καὶ προφητῶν ἐπιστομίζοντα αὐτοὺς, καὶ πανταχοῦ τοῦτο ποιοῦντα· καίτοι γε ἐνῆν καὶ σημεῖα ποιῆσαι, ἀλλὰ λοιπὸν οὐκ ἔτι πιστὸν τὸ πρᾶγμα ἦν· μέγα γὰρ τοῦτο σημεῖον, τὸ ἀπὸ νόμου καὶ τῶν προφητῶν διαλέγεσθαι (*hom. in Ac.* 55.2 [60.382]).

[446] *hom. in Ac.* 37.2 [60.265]:"God did not always wish them to do signs. For it is no less a sign that the persecuted prevailed without signs than the doing of signs itself. Therefore, just as now God conquers without signs, then, too, he always wished to conquer in this way" [Οὐκ ἀεὶ ἐβούλετο τούτους σημεῖα ποιεῖν θεός· τοῦ γὰρ σημεῖα ποιεῖν οὐχ ἧττον σημεῖον τὸ διωκομένους περιγενέσθαι χωρὶς σημείων. Ὥστε καθάπερ νῦν χωρὶς σημείων κρατεῖ, οὕτω καὶ τότε πολλαχοῦ ἐβούλετο κρατεῖν].

[447] *hom. in Ac.* 37.1 [60.263–64].

[448] *stat.* 1.6 [49.23–24].

origin might be always manifest.[449] This theological response to the ambiguity of miracles as a vehicle for the propagation and success of the gospel therefore deliberately inscribes libertarian preferences to God and ascetic practices to the human actors in the divine drama who carry out his wishes. Chrysostom's Pauline portraits are indelibly marked by the fact that the apostle's miracles are endlessly useful in expounding upon the limitlessness of divine power, but are far less helpful for the purposes of moral exhortation since "they were not *his* virtuous deeds."[450]

Prophecy: Another of Paul's multiple spiritual activities is the gift of prophecy.[451] Working with a simple definition of prophecy – the ability to discern the future – Chrysostom finds Paul to have exercised that power repeatedly in both the letters and in Acts. In the epistles this is especially the case where Paul foretells what will happen in the eschaton. When commenting upon 1 Tim 4:1–3 Chrysostom exclaims: "marvel with me at Paul's prophecy[452] [τοῦ Παύλου ἡ προφητεία]! For before the times at which things were going to happen he made known the exact time."[453] In 2 Tim 3:1–9 Paul exhibits the capacity to make such prophesies, not

---

[449] Once Chrysostom deliberately juxtaposed Paul's omnipotence in resuscitation and healing with his profession to lack of verbal skill 1 Cor 2:1–5, in order to ask, if Paul were so competent in things beyond any human training [τὸ δὲ πᾶσαν ὑπερβαίνει τέχνην], then why could he not attain rhetorical proficiency, given that it is just a skill acquired through learning [τὸ μὲν γὰρ ἐστι μαθητῶν]? Chrysostom's answer is that surely Paul could have picked up such training if he had wished ['Ότι γὰρ ἦν δυνατὸν καὶ τοῦτο αὐτὸν ἔχειν, δῆλον], but Christ did not allow it ['Αλλ' οὐκ ἀφῆκεν ὁ Χριστός] (*hom. in 1 Cor.* 6.1 [61.48])

[450] ἅπερ οὐκ ἦν αὐτοῦ κατορθώματα (*hom. in 2 Cor.* 27.1 [61.584]). Compare the analysis of the bases of John's moral theology by Meyer, "Liberté," 303: "Une 'action' est bien différente d'un miracle. Celui-ci est un pur don de Dieu, ayant un seul principe dans la grâce de Dieu et s'accomplissant par la seule opération divine." Compton, "Introducing Acts," has convincingly demonstrated how this dynamic is at work in Chrysostom's interpretation of Luke's work, in which he consistently downplays the miracles of the apostles, including (and most notably) Paul.

[451] Related to prophecy, but distinct (for both Paul and John who follows him) is the capacity for speaking in tongues [γλῶσσαι], another of the spiritual gifts [χαρίσματα]. On the basis of 1 Cor 14:18 John recognizes that Paul has this gift more than other people do. However, he does not consider tongues prophetic or ecstatic speech, but spontaneous multilinguality, such as the apostles experienced at Pentecost – the ability to understand in a single instant, untutored, Persian, Indian, Scythian or other such foreign languages. "For, the man who knew one language by nature was speaking in varied and different languages by grace" ['Ο γὰρ μίαν γλῶσσαν ἔχων ἀπὸ τῆς φύσεως, ποικίλαις ἐλάλει γλώσσαις καὶ διαφόροις ἀπὸ τῆς χάριτος] (*hom. in Ac. princ.* 3.4 [51.92]). In connecting the phenomenology of glossolalia with Acts 2 this way, Chrysostom is in line with many early church commentators (Gerhard Dautzenberg, "Glossolalie," *RAC* 11 [1981] 225–46, 244).

[452] Or, "gift of prophecy" more generally (for both lexical possibilities, see LSJ, 1539).

[453] Σὺ δέ μοι θαύμασον τοῦ Παύλου τὴν προφητείαν· πρὸ γὰρ τῶν χρόνων, ὧν ἔμελλεν ἔσεσθαι, ἐδήλου καὶ τὸν χρόνον αὐτόν (*hom. in 1 Tim.* 12.1 [62.558]). The same criterion is at work in identifying prophecy in this text and also in the related passage 2 Tim 3:1 in *hom. in Ac. princ.* 3.4 [51.93]: ὅτι δὲ τὰ ἐν ὑστέροις καιροῖς λέγειν, προφητεία ἐστί, παντί που δῆλον, as well as 1 Cor 7:16: Δι' ὃ καὶ ὁ μακάριος Παῦλος, ὁ τῆς οἰκουμένης διδάσκαλος, ταῦτα πάντα προορῶν ἐβόα (*hom. in Gen.* 17.9 [53.145]).

only in visions of the future, but also from readings of the past, such as Paul's divining from the Jannes and Jambres incident[454] detailed warnings about future deceptions waiting to pounce upon the unsuspecting community of faith in a later, weak moment. In discussing Paul's vivid scenario of the παρουσία of Jesus in 1 Thess 4:13–17, John raises the question of how the literary form of Pauline prophecy compares with that of the biblical prophets of Israel. He observes that Paul does not preface his oracles with the customary introductory oracular formulas used by Isaiah and Jeremiah, such as "the vision which Isaiah saw" or "the word of the Lord which came to Jeremiah," or even the ubiquitous "thus says the Lord." The reason for the disparity lies in the different mechanics of divine inspiration: whereas the prophets saw God external to themselves, sitting aloft, for instance, as in the case of Isaiah 6, Paul "had Christ speaking in himself" (2 Cor 13:3; cf. 7:40), so the prophetic mediation thus effected was so immediate as not to require an introductory attribution. Since he was Christ's mouthpiece, Paul did not have to preface his statements to accent their divine authorship, "for the apostle utters the statements of the one who sent him."[455] Paul's prophetic knowledge extended even to the encyclopedic command of exegetical detail he displayed in his writings, which he possessed by the power of the spirit.[456]

Chrysostom finds this picture of Paul the prophet both confirmed and further amplified by narrative detail in the Acts of the Apostles.[457] For instance, John argues that Paul's imprecation against the high priest Ananias in Acts 23:3 was morally acceptable since it was not mere insult, but prophecy, as shown by the fact that it later came true.[458] And above all the tale of the shipwreck in Acts 27 presents

---

[454] Exod 7:11, 22. See n. 456 below on Chrysostom's treatment of the extra-biblical development of this tradition.

[455] ὁ γὰρ ἀπόστολος τὰ τοῦ ἀποστείλαντος φθέγγεται (*hom. in 1 Thess.* 8.1 [62.439]).

[456] See, e.g., *hom. in 1 Cor.* 7.3 [61.58]:"Paul, inasmuch as he was learned in the Law and spoke by the power of the spirit, likely knew all things (including the source of the mystery quotation in 1 Cor 2:9) accurately" [τὸν δὲ Παῦλον ἅτε νομομαθῆ ὄντα καὶ πνεύματι φθεγγόμενον εἰκὸς εἰδέναι πάντα μετὰ ἀκριβείας], and *hom. in 2 Tim.* 8.2 [62.644]: Paul knew ἀπὸ τοῦ πνεύματος the names of the anonymous magicians of Egypt who contended with Moses – Jannes and Jambres (2 Tim 3:8).

[457] This is so most obviously in the seafaring narrative of Acts 27, but also throughout the entire work, as is generally recognized by contemporary scholars (e.g., Luke Timothy Johnson, *The Acts of the Apostles* [Sacra Pagina 5; Collegeville, MN: Glazier, 1992] 459; Charles H. Talbert, *Reading Acts: A Literary and Theological Commentary on the Acts of the Apostles* [New York: Crossroad, 1997] 215–25). Paul's acts of prophecy (including that of his own death, in Acts 20:25, 38), are set within the broad landscape of the "narrative of fulfillment" which is Luke-Acts (Talbert, *Reading Acts*, 3).

[458] Chrysostom quotes the opinion of some, whom he does not condemn, as follows: "Some, defending Paul [for this abusive utterance] say that what he said was a prophecy. And I do not accuse them for this; for this happened, and thus Ananias died." In saying this "Paul foretold what was going to happen" [τὸ μέλλον ἔσεσθαι προανεφώνησεν] (*laud. Paul.* 6.11 [SC 300.282]). This contention must deal with a rather conspicuous piece of counter-evidence, however, which also casts a shadow of doubt on this portrait of Paul the prophet: the fact that in 23:5 Paul answers the rebuke of the bystanders for insulting the high priest by insisting that he did not know the man

John with many examples of Paul's prophetic powers and prudent modes of communication of his supernatural knowledge to the human characters around him. John fervently insists that throughout the episode Paul does not engage in mere "guesswork" [στοχασμός] but "foretells" [προλέγειν] accurately what is going to happen.[459] Nor did Paul himself seek some prophetic word to calm his own heart, for he already knew he was safe, but he wished to comfort his fellow passengers with what he had learned on their behalf.[460] Nevertheless, in his supreme sagacity Paul chose to couch some of his prophecies *as though they were* conjectures or simple observation, such as 27:10 [θεωρῶ ...], because he knew all too well that the sailors would have rejected his prophetic words outright.[461] John worries for a moment that Paul's prophecy that all would be saved from the shipwreck might be thought not to cohere with his own overriding definition of prophecy as foreknowledge of the future, given that in this case the time elapsed between word and fulfillment was rather short. But Chrysostom counters this with the (somewhat irrelevant) response that it was prophecy nonetheless, for Paul's promise of rescue from a watery death, offered at the right moment, gave hope when all was given up for lost.[462] This constitutes a great victory over the devil, who had tried without success to thwart the realization of Paul's prophetic assurance of deliverance.[463] This portrait of Paul as a man of limitless prophetic powers hangs in the air at the end of the homily series on Acts, as John exclaims, "You see how that holy and

---

was the high priest! Chrysostom's answer? Paul feigned this ignorance in order to serve as a model for others that one should honor the office of high priest, and not voice slander against it.

[459] *hom. in Ac.* 53.1 [60.368], τὰ μέλλοντα προλέγει; 53.2 [60.368], ὅπερ οὐκ ἦν στοχασμοῦ, ἀλλὰ προφητείας; cf. *laud. Paul.* 7.9 [SC 300.310–12], προενόει; διηγησάμενος τὴν αὐτῷ φανεῖσαν ὄψιν.

[460] "... but he even took foresight for all his fellow passengers, although he was fully confident on his own behalf, and knew that he was safe" [ἀλλὰ καὶ προενόει πάντων τῶν συμπλεόντων, καίτοι γε ὑπὲρ αὐτοῦ θαρρῶν καὶ εἰδὼς ὡς ἐν ἀσφαλείᾳ ἦν]. Note the word play in this passage: προνοεῖν can mean both "provide for" (c. Gen.) and "foresee" (LSJ, 1490 and *LPGL*, 1157; my translation tries to keep a hint of both; cf. later in the same passage: ἀλλὰ πάλιν ὡς παίδων πατὴρ προενόει) (*laud. Paul.* 7.9 [SC 300.310–12]). But prophesy is clearly intended here, as John explicitly says that to calm them "he told them the vision which had appeared to him" [διηγησάμενος τὴν αὐτῷ φανεῖσαν ὄψιν] (7.9 [SC 300.312]).

[461] *hom. in Ac.* 53.3 [60.370]: "So that he might not appear to prophecy, but to speak from conjecture, he says, 'I see' [ἵνα μὴ δόξῃ προφητεύειν, ἀλλ' ὡς ἀπὸ στοχασμοῦ λέγειν, θεωρῶ, φησίν]. For they would not have accepted it if he had immediately said this. For indeed formerly [actually later, in 27:23] he prophesied [προφητεύει], and said, 'the God whom I serve,' in an effort to persuade them."

[462] *hom. in Ac.* 53.4 [60.371]: "And the prophecy came to receive its fulfillment, even if it was not so notable in length of time. For he did not foretell it many years before, but he was following the nature of the events. For all was lost, and through their own salvation they would learn who Paul was" [καὶ προφητεία τέλος ἐλάμβανεν, εἰ καὶ μὴ τῷ χρόνῳ σεμνή τις οὖσα· οὐ γὰρ πρὸ πολλῶν ἐτῶν αὐτὴν προεῖπεν, ἀλλὰ τῇ φύσει τῶν πραγμάτων ἑπόμενος· ἀνέλπιστα γὰρ ἦν πάντα, καὶ διὰ τῆς οἰκείας σωτηρίας ἐμάνθανον τίς ὁ Παῦλος ἦν].

[463] *hom. in Ac.* 53.3 [60.369]: Πάλιν πειρᾶται ὁ διάβολος ἐμποδίσαι τῇ προφητείᾳ.

divine head foreknew everything" ['Ορᾷς πῶς πάντα προεώρα ἡ ἁγία καὶ θεία κεφαλή];[464]

But in a different context Chrysostom shows that he is aware of what he terms "a matter of dispute which is debated by many" [ζήτημα παρὰ πολλῶν ζητούμενον] about the limits of Paul's foreknowledge. This is manifested in various ways in the letters and in Acts as, for instance, in 1 Thess 3:5, where Paul tells the Thessalonians that the suspense he felt in Athens, born of ignorance about their situation, was so intense that he could not bear it, so he sent Timothy to apprise him of the goings-on. First, John acknowledges the anomaly[465] by a direct confrontation with his author about the perplexity posed by this apparent curtailing of his extraordinary abilities:

> What are you saying [Τί λέγεις]? The man who knew such great things, the one who heard inexpressible words, the one who went up as high as the third heaven, this man does not know, because he was (at a distance) in Athens? ... What then can one say? That the saints did not know everything?"[466]

John roots his answer to the dilemma this time in deliberate divine design and precedent. First he states the universal rule within which he will place Paul: "One can learn from everywhere, from the earliest events as well as those that followed, that the saints did not know everything."[467] As examples John brings the fact that Elisha recognized that the Lord hid some things from him about the Shunammite woman (4 Kgdms 4:27), Elijah wrongly thought he was the only one left of the worshippers of the Lord, when there were seven thousand (3 Kgdms 19:10, 18), and Samuel had to wade through the different sons of Jesse looking for the anointee, because he could not himself discern which the Lord had chosen (1 Kgdms 16:1–13). This was no accident, nor, consequently, was it unusual to Paul, but "this happened according to God's great loving care."[468]

But how and in what way did God do this? John answers with several arguments for why God did not vest the saints, including Paul, with complete prescience. Unsurprisingly, these arguments overlap a great deal with those Chrysostom uses for the related question of the limitations of Paul's miraculous powers (discussed

---

[464] hom. in Ac. 55.3 [60.382]. George B. Stevens, the editor of the NPNF translation, adds a negative here [NPNF, 11.326 n. 4]. But this is unjustified, both because it has no manuscript support, and because of the context, in which a list of Paul's celestial epithets follows, clearly accenting Paul's miraculous powers. But, as the present argument will demonstrate, Chrysostom is capable of making both these statements.

[465] With Wiles, Divine Apostle, 24: "a limitation of knowledge [on Paul's part] is admitted with some reluctance."

[466] Τί λέγεις; ὁ τοσαῦτα εἰδώς, ὁ ἀπόρρητα ἀκούσας ῥήματα, ὁ μέχρι τρίτου ἀνελθὼν οὐρανοῦ, οὗτος οὐκ οἶδε, καὶ ἐν 'Αθήναις ὤν; ... Τί οὖν ἄν τις εἴποι; ὅτι οὐ πάντα ᾔδεισαν οἱ ἅγιοι; (hom. in 1 Thess. 4.1 [62.415]).

[467] Καὶ ὅτι οὐκ ᾔδεισαν, πολλαχόθεν ἄν τις μάθοι, ἀπό τε τῶν πρώτων, ἀπό τε τῶν μετὰ ταῦτα (hom. in 1 Thess. 4.1 [62.415]).

[468] Τοῦτο δὲ γίνεται κατὰ πολλὴν τοῦ θεοῦ κηδεμονίαν (hom. in 1 Thess. 4.1 [62.415]).

above), because the same dynamic of access to and restriction of spiritual powers is at work in both instances. First, God did so for the sake of both the saints themselves and those who would revere them.[469] This can be shown to be consistent divine policy, since God allows his holy ones to be ignorant for the same reason he allows them to suffer persecutions: to keep them down to size [ἵνα καταστέλλωνται]. As proof of this Chrysostom invokes 2 Cor 12:7, and Paul's explanation for the thorn in the flesh, "so that I might not have an exalted sense of myself" [ἵνα μὴ ὑπεραίρωμαι]. The correlate to this objective is that others in turn not think too highly of the saints, which they surely would if these notables had had constant and infallible knowledge of the future. This danger is once again conveniently exemplified for John by the narrative of Acts 14:8–18, which stands as a warning against the pervasive propensity people have for deifying those who possess super-natural powers.[470] Hence God did not give Paul and the rest of the saints such an unlimited power that it would harm both them and those to whom they were sent. The last reason Chrysostom offers is the pastor's personal favorite: if the saints had had continual access to such divine δύναμις, then later Christians could say that the virtuous accomplishments of these venerables were not human achievements, but rested entirely upon a form of divine assistance to which they, mere mortals, could not lay claim. As always Chrysostom seeks to head off at the pass any such excuses for side-stepping one's emulation of the virtuous example of the saints.[471]

Next Chrysostom generalizes from this case to another, always tricky area of conspicuous Pauline epistemological limitation, his travel plans:[472] "It is for this reason that he was ignorant [ἀγνοεῖ], for this reason also that often after proposing a visit he does not come, so that they might learn that he did not know many things" [ἵνα μάθωσιν ὅτι πολλὰ οὐκ οἶδε]. The pastoral costs of Pauline omniscience were simply too great, so God deliberately fostered Paul's ignorance of many matters, such as his itinerary, so that he might serve as a catechetical example. Hence even Paul's limitation in knowledge served the common good ("from this much gain came"),[473] and as a result it is a source more of praise than blame for the saint. Elsewhere Chrysostom explains Paul's indeterminacy about his travel plans by appeal to the spirit that conducted his every move, in such a way that Paul's lack

---

[469] This is a favored argument; see also *hom. in 2 Tim.* 10.3 [62.659]: καὶ πολλὰ δὲ καὶ ἄλλα [ὁρῶμεν αὐτὸν] ἀγνοοῦντα συμφερόντως καὶ αὐτῷ καὶ τοῖς μαθητευομένοις.

[470] *hom. in 1 Thess.* 4.1 [62.416], along with an invocation of Paul's deliberate strategy expressed in 2 Cor 12:6b.

[471] "God allows this [ignorance] for another reason, also – so that no one might say that it was not as human beings that they did the virtuous deeds they accomplished [λέγειν ὅτι οὐχὶ ἄνθρωποι ὄντες κατώρθωσαν ἅπερ κατώρθωσαν], and thus all be indolent. This is why God demonstrates that even these great ones were weak, so that he might cut off any pretence for shamelessness for those who wish to act contumaciously" (*hom. in 1 Thess.* 4.1 [62.416]).

[472] We shall have occasion to note later in this chapter (pp. 326–30) that Paul's travel plans posed also another problem for Chrysostom, in that they appear to demonstrate inconsistency on his part.

[473] Πολὺ οὖν ἐκ τούτου τὸ κέρδος ἦν (*hom. in 1 Thess.* 4.1 [62.416]).

of foreknowledge serves paradoxically as proof of his spiritual endowment, rather than an apparent compromise of it.[474]

This divine reserve in allocating the power of miraculous foreknowledge was matched by Paul's own prudence in his exercise of the gift. Chrysostom addresses this issue when he grapples with the lack of specificity given in the depiction of the opponents in 1 Tim 4:1–5 who attend to deceptive spirits and teaching of demons, words which Paul explicitly invokes as prophecy [τὸ δὲ πνεῦμα ῥητῶς λέγει]. Why didn't Paul point more directly at the Manicheans, Encratites, Marcionites and others? In reply John offers two reasons. First, Paul knew precisely who these people would be in the end times, but deliberately decided to "hint" [αἰνίττεσθαι] rather than narrate about them. This choice was rooted in Paul's prudent pastoral instincts, for he knew that if he mentioned in detail the heretical practices and beliefs that would arise in the end time but had not yet come to light, then he might unwittingly foster new forms of aberrant behavior by "sowing ideas into people's souls."[475] Hence, though knowing it all, he chose to reveal only what was most salutary for his readers. But elsewhere John shows some reservation about omniscience itself (as he often does in setting limits on proper Christian curiosity about divine secrets),[476] and calls upon Paul as an example of one who, though he had access to the full complement of divine knowledge, in humility and sagacity chose not to snoop around in it, and only sought to learn what he needed to know to carry out his ministry.[477] Once again, therefore, Paul is portrayed as having had the

---

[474] This is how Chrysostom explains 1 Tim 3:14–15: "Do not be amazed if, though foreseeing everything by means of the spirit [εἰ πνεύματι πάντα προορῶν], he was ignorant of this [ἠγνόει τοῦτο], saying, 'I hope to come, but if I am delayed,' given that such statements are made by one who does not know [τοῦτο γὰρ ἀγνοοῦντός ἐστιν]. For since he was continually led by the spirit, and he did not do what he did by force of his own resolve, likely he was ignorant of this, too" ['Ἐπειδὴ γὰρ πνεύματι ἤγετο, καὶ οὐκ οἰκείᾳ γνώμῃ ἔπραττεν ἅπερ ἔπραττεν, καὶ τοῦτο εἰκότως ἠγνόει] (hom. in 1 Tim. 11.1 [62.554]). But in another place Chrysostom can invert this very claim, saying "again Paul speaks in a human fashion [in Acts 23:6–8], and he does not always enjoy the power of grace, but is allowed also to introduce something from himself" [Πάλιν ἀνθρωπίνως διαλέγεται, καὶ οὐ πανταχοῦ τῆς χάριτος ἀπολαύει, ἀλλὰ καὶ παρ' ἑαυτοῦ τι συγχωρεῖται εἰσφέρειν] (hom. in Ac. 49.1 [60.337]).

[475] hom. in 1 Tim. 12.1 [62.558].

[476] See, for example, scand. 2.1 [SC 79.60]: "What, then, is the cause of such great illness? An overly curious and busy-bodyish mind, and one's wishing to know all the causes of all the things which have happened, and contending after the incomprehensible and indescribable providence of God, and impudently snooping and being meddlesomely curious about what is infinite and untraceable" [Τίς οὖν ἡ αἰτία τῆς ἀρρωστίας τῆς τοσαύτης ἐστίν; Ἡ πολυπράγμων καὶ περίεργος γνώμη, καὶ τὸ βούλεσθαι πάντων τῶν γινομένων εἰδέναι τὰς αἰτίας ἁπάσας, καὶ φιλονεικεῖν τὴν ἀκατάληπτον καὶ ἄρρητον τοῦ Θεοῦ πρόνοιαν, τὴν ἀπέραντον καὶ ἀνεξιχνίαστον περιεργάζεσθαι ἀναισχύντως καὶ πολυπραγμονεῖν]. To illustrate this point, Chrysostom immediately invokes Paul, in the language quoted in the following note. For other places where Chrysostom tells his congregation to restrain their excessive inquisitiveness about the secrets of God, see, e.g., hom. in Eph. 19.3 [62.132]; hom. in 1 Tim. 1.2 [62.506]; hom. in 2 Tim. 8.4 [62.647]; laud. Paul. 4.3 [SC 300.186].

[477] "Now, who has been wiser than Paul? Tell me, was this man not the vessel of election? Did

full abundance of this spiritual gift of foreknowledge; and where a saying or narrative appears to compromise his possession of that ability, John can use it to proclaim another virtue: noble human restraint matching that of the divine when it comes to the exercise of supernatural endowments.

Ecstatic Experiences: One of Chrysostom's most favorite and frequently cited Pauline deeds is the trio of heavenly experiences narrated of "the man I know" in 2 Cor 12:2–5. Chrysostom rightly recognizes Paul's adoption of a "mask" [προσωπεῖον] here,[478] and hence attributes these most laudable deeds to the apostle's credit, despite Paul's humble and satirically flavored deflection of them to "someone" of his acquaintance.[479] These three events are already in their Pauline form quite suited to Chrysostom's style, since they can be rhetorically separated or combined, and amplified in various ways. Sometimes Chrysostom largely repeats Paul's own words, sometimes names just one or two, but quite often takes them as a catalogue, embellishing them along such lines as the following:

> The one who *before the resurrection* was snatched up into the third heaven, the one who was born away into paradise, the one who shared with God in the indescribable mysteries, the one who heard *and spoke* such things as it is not fitting for human nature to speak.[480]

---

he not draw to himself the great and indescribable grace of the spirit? Did he not have Christ speaking in him? Did he not share in the inexpressible words of God? Did not he alone hear the things which no human being was allowed to speak? Was he not snatched up into paradise? Was he not borne up into the third heaven? Did he not run around land and sea? Did he not persuade barbarians to pursue philosophy? Did he not have many and various activities of the spirit? Did he not correct whole peoples and cities? Did not God place the entire world into his hands? But nevertheless, the man so great and so wonderful, the man so wise and powerful and spiritual, the one who enjoyed such great benefits, when he had the opportunity to scrutinize the providence of God (and not even the providence entire, but only a part of it), hear how he was amazed, how his head was spinning, how he quickly ran away, giving ground to the incomprehensible" ['Αλλ' ὅμως ὁ τοσοῦτος καὶ τηλικοῦτος, ὁ σοφὸς οὕτω καὶ δυνατὸς καὶ πνευματικὸς ἀνήρ, ὁ τοσούτων ἀπολελαυκώς, ὅταν εἰς τὴν ἐξέτασιν τῆς τοῦ Θεοῦ προνοίας ἐμπέσῃ καὶ οὐδὲ ὁλοκλήρου προνοίας, ἀλλὰ μόνον εἰς μέρος αὐτῆς, ἄκουσον πῶς ἐκπλήττεται, πῶς ἰλιγγιᾷ, πῶς ἀποπηδᾷ ταχέως τῷ ἀκαταλήπτῳ παραχωρῶν] (*scand.* 2.2–3 [SC 79.60–62]). In the following paragraph Chrysostom gives a long list of both heavenly and earthly secrets Paul did *not* snoop into during his celestial journey, and maintains that Paul only learned the one thing his mission required: the top-secret divine providential plan about the salvation of Jews and Gentiles (with the crucial crescendo at Rom 11:33); John makes the same argument in *stat.* 1.1 [48.843].

[478] *laud. Paul.* 5.15 [SC 300.256]; *hom. in 2 Cor.* 26.1 [61.575–76].

[479] Paul's diffidence in presenting these deeds makes them simultaneously acts of humility and self-effacement, both in the way Paul deferred the praise to another, and in Chrysostom's supposition that it was only because of the Corinthian situation that he broke fourteen years of silence about these miraculous deeds (*hom. in 2 Cor.* 26.1 [61.575–76]; *laud. Paul.* 5.9–15 [SC 300.246–56]; see the further discussion of Paul's boasting and humility below in this chapter under "Contradictory Deeds?" on pp. 339–52).

[480] *anom.* 8.3 [48.772]: ὁ πρὸ τῆς ἀναστάσεως εἰς τρίτον ἁρπαγεὶς οὐρανὸν, ὁ εἰς παράδεισον ἀπενεχθείς, ὁ ἀπορρήτων κοινωνήσας τῷ Θεῷ μυστηρίων, ὁ τοιαῦτα ἀκούσας καὶ λαλήσας, ἃ ἀνθρωπίνη φύσει λαλῆσαι οὐκ ἔνι. In the translation I have highlighted Chrysostom's additions to the text. For a sample of other references, see, e.g.: to one of the three (*hom. in Gen.* 23.7

These deeds especially accrue to Paul's glory and praise because he was found worthy to cross the divinely patrolled temporal boundary between now and the eschaton, and the geographical boundary from earth to heaven, and was welcomed to join in God's mysterious ῥήματα. Especially interesting in John's recasting of Paul's account is the fact that he restores speech to the apostle who, as he himself had described it, was rendered requisitely speechless by the event, confronted as he was by the ineffable. In saying that Paul both heard *and spoke* the unspeakable, Chrysostom implicitly includes all of Paul's written utterances among the possible packet of revelation received from the divine, thereby granting Paul and his words even more authority than they might already have. In another place John does the same thing, but biographically. He explains why Paul was snatched up into heaven in the first place by intuiting the divine design in this fashion: God did this so that Paul might not appear to be inferior to the rest of the apostles, since they had associated with Christ on earth, whereas Paul had not.[481] Furthermore, Chrysostom (like Paul, in 2 Cor 12:1) does not limit Paul's intense spiritual experiences to these famous instances. In fact, Paul's ongoing life of spiritual congress places him in a category all by himself: "Paul had so many and such continual moments of converse with God as were shared by none of the prophets or apostles."[482]

However, despite Chrysostom's intense interest in this triad of Pauline spiritual experiences, even the portrait of Paul the ecstatic in the end must take a back seat to another:

I do not pronounce Paul so blessed because he was snatched up into paradise, as because he was thrown into prison. I do not pronounce him so blessed because he heard unspeakable words, as because he endured the bonds. I do not pronounce Paul so blessed because he was snatched up into the third heaven as I do on account of his bonds.[483]

Sufferings

We have already seen how Chrysostom qualifies Paul's miraculous deeds and spiritual powers by assigning due weight also to his rhetorical proficiency in speaking the truth of the gospel. Now we spy the same strategy at work in his treatment of Paul's sufferings, which he sets in deliberate counterpoint to the miracles and the ecstatic experiences. This key element of Paul's biography, which the apostle

---

[53.196]), to two (*proph. obscurit.* 2.4 [56.181]; *hom. in Gen.* 30.6 [53.282]; *sac.* 3.7 [272.156]), or all three (*stat.* 1.3 [49.20]; *Laz.* 6.9 [48.1041]; *hom. in 2 Cor.* 26.1 [61.576]; *exp. in Ps.* 110.4 [55.284]; *hom. in Ac. 9:1* 4.3 [51.149]; *pan. Rom.* 1.1 [50.607]).

[481] *hom. in 2 Cor.* 26.2 [61.577].

[482] *laud. Paul.* 5.10 [SC 300.248].

[483] Οὐχ οὕτω μακαρίζω Παῦλον, ὅτι εἰς παράδεισον ἡρπάγη, ὡς ὅτι εἰς τὸ δεσμωτήριον ἐνεβλήθη. Οὐχ οὕτως αὐτὸν μακαρίζω, ὅτι ἤκουσεν ἄρρητα ῥήματα, ὡς ὅτι ὑπέμεινε τὰ δεσμά· οὐχ οὕτως αὐτὸν μακαρίζω, ὅτι ἡρπάγη εἰς τρίτον οὐρανὸν, ὡς μακαρίζω διὰ τὰ δεσμά (*hom. in Eph.* 8.1 [62.56–57]).

himself made an ineluctable facet of his ministerial identity, stands always in a potentially contrastive relationship with his thaumaturgic abilities, given the emblematic irony that Paul possessed the power to alleviate those same sufferings in others.[484] Chrysostom addresses this tension in a manner characteristic of Christian theology since his hero, Paul, penned his Corinthian correspondence. He holds up Paul's sufferings as of greater importance than the powerful works and wonders by redefining them as effective signs of an even greater proportion. In so doing John also through his first-person testimony authorized the ascetic values of renunciation and mortification, thereby setting the standard of evaluation in a thoroughly Pauline mode, via his own voice:

> Although there are many signs everywhere of his wonders [τῶν θαυμάτων αὐτοῦ πολλὰ πανταχοῦ σημεῖα τυγχάνει], they aren't as desirable as those of his battle scars [στίγματα]. In the Scriptures he does not gladden me so much when he works miracles as when he suffers cruelly, being whipped, dragged about [Καὶ ἐν ταῖς γραφαῖς δὲ οὐχ οὕτω με εὐφραίνει θαύματα ἐργαζόμενος, ὡς πάσχων κακῶς, μαστιζόμενος, συρόμενος]. For the handkerchiefs and linen cloths that touched his skin truly did amazing and astounding things [θαυμαστὰ καὶ παράδοξα] (Acts 19:12). But not as great as his sufferings [ἀλλ' οὐ τοιαῦτα οἷα ἐκεῖνα].[485]

For Chrysostom the collation of Pauline miseries is an easy task, given that the apostle had already provided the material in that very form, in his many *peristasis* catalogues.[486] This does not prevent John from constructing his own lists on this model, which largely parallel or replicate Paul's, as often suits his oratorical preferences for extended (and hyperbolic) catalogues and examples.[487] The *peristasis* catalogue, appropriated by John from Paul in terms of both content and form, stands in explicit contrast with Paul's mode of reference to his miracles and other virtuous deeds, which John regards as mere "shorthand" or "passing references" to innumerable and indescribably great feats.[488] Whereas Paul was sparing in his

---

[484] This is given expression in 2 Cor 11–12, but it is even more heightened when one reads the Pauline epistles, as Chrysostom does, against the tableau of Acts, where the portrait of Paul as miracle worker is so pronounced.

[485] *hom. in Eph.* 8.1 [62.57].

[486] 1 Cor 4:9–13; 2 Cor 4:8–9; 6:4–10; 11:21–33, as carefully studied by John T. Fitzgerald, *Cracks in an Earthen Vessel: An Examination of the Catalogues of Hardships in the Corinthian Correspondence* (SBLDS 99; Atlanta: Scholars Press, 1988), with further literature.

[487] Of many examples, see *laud. Paul.* 1.12 [SC 300.128]; *hom. in Ac. 9:1* 4.3 [51.149]; *hom. in Heb.* 28.3–4 [63.195–97]; *stat.* 1.11 [49.32]; *hom. in Is. 45:7* 3 [56.146]; *hom. in Gen.* 11.6–7 [53.97–98]; *compunct. 1* 7 [47.404]; *laed.* 11 [SC 103–112–14]; *res. mort.* 3 [50.423]; further references in di S. Maria, "S. Paolo," 496 n. 1. Once, after providing such a list in his own words, John turns to Paul's own writings to complete the task: Ἀλλὰ γὰρ τί δεῖ λογισμῶν ἡμῖν, παρὸν ἀκοῦσαι τῶν ῥημάτων αὐτῶν; (*Stag.* 3.11 [47.487]).

[488] Chrysostom then claims that even the *peristasis* catalogue of 11:24–29 is a meager "quick run through" of Pauline deeds [ταχέως ἅπαντα παρέδραμε], whereas the apostle could have filled thousands of books if he had wished to explain each of the things mentioned in its own right [καίτοι γε μυρίας βίβλους ἐνέπλησεν ἄν, εἰ τῶν εἰρημένων ἕκαστον ἐξαπλῶσαι ἠβούλετο]. The notice about filling many books of course reminds Christian readers of Jn 21:25, but similar

words about his miracles, he was unashamed to bring forward and recount the many pains and humiliations he endured for the sake of the gospel.[489] But even those lengthy catalogues are no match for the countless books which *could* have been written to narrate the full extent of Paul's sufferings, if described one by one: concerns for his churches, the imprisonments and virtuous acts accomplished in them, and all the other critical events and assaults.[490] John especially resonates, as one would expect given his own pastoral circumstances, with cares and worries for his churches (2 Cor 11:26, 28).

"The care for all the churches" (2 Cor 11:28). This was the chief [κεφάλαιον] of them all, that both Paul's soul was torn apart and his mind cut in two [καὶ ἡ ψυχὴ διεσπᾶτο, καὶ ἡ διάνοια διετέμνετο]. For even if none of the outside troubles attacked him, this internal war was sufficient [Εἰ γὰρ καὶ μηδὲν ἔξωθεν προσέβαλεν, ἱκανὸς ὁ ἔνδον πόλεμος], the waves upon waves, the blizzards of cares, the war of reasonings. For if one has care for a single household, having slaves and overseers and stewards, he often cannot even stop to breathe because of the cares, even when no one is giving him trouble. But as for the man who has the care, not of a single household, but of cities and peoples and nations and the entire world [ὁ οὐκ οἰκίας μιᾶς, ἀλλὰ καὶ πόλεων καὶ δήμων καὶ ἐθνῶν καὶ ὁλοκλήρου τῆς οἰκουμένης τὴν φροντίδα ἔχων], and does so with regard to much more important matters, and even when spitefully opposed, being, after all, a single person, and suffering so many things [καὶ μόνος ὤν, καὶ τοσαῦτα πάσχων], and being as tenderly concerned as a father for his children – consider what he endured![491]

Chrysostom's portrait of the foremost suffering Paul endured – his overwhelming care and responsibility for the churches in the whole world – corresponds, one can readily imagine, with the fourth-century bishop's own life and vision of the pastoral ministry. John knowingly ruminates about his hero that surely a man who burned at the stumbling of each parishioner (2 Cor 11:29) was ever on fire.[492]

Although here John termed care for his churches Paul's "chief misery,"[493] another Pauline passage perhaps has a stronger claim to that honor: 2 Cor 12:7,

---

commonplaces are widely found in epideictic oratory, as well (see Aphth. *Prog.* 8 [Spengel 2.38], in a sample encomium to Thucydides: πολλὰ ἦν ἕτερα περὶ Θουκυδίδου διεξελθεῖν, εἰ μὴ τὸ πάντα ἐρεῖν τὸ τῶν ἐπαίνων παρείλετο πλῆθος).

[489] See *hom. in 2 Cor.* 26.1 [61.575]: Τὰ μὲν γὰρ μεγάλα καυχήματα ταῦτα, ἅπερ ἀπηριθμήσατο, τὰ τῶν πειρασμῶν.

[490] John takes the claim to have worked "the signs of the apostle in signs and wonders and miracles" in 2 Cor 12:12 as a kind of shorthand reference [ἐν ὀλίγοις ῥήμασι παρέδραμε, and ἐν βραχεῖ, διὰ μιᾶς λέξεως] to "a huge sea of virtuous actions" [πηλίκον πέλαγος κατορθωμάτων] (*hom. in 2 Cor.* 25.3; 27.1 [61.574]). See also *hom. in 2 Cor.* 25.2: Πλείονα τὰ παραλειφθέντα τῶν ἀπαριθμηθέντων· μᾶλλον δὲ οὐδὲ αὐτὰ τὰ ἀπαριθμηθέντα ὅσα, ἔστιν εἰπεῖν; 27.1 [61.571, 584]; cf. *hom. in Gen.* 11.6–7 [53.97–98]; *laed.* 5 [SC 103.84]: Τί δὲ ὁ Παῦλος; οὐ τοσαῦτα ἔπαθε δεινά, ἃ μηδὲ καταλέξαι ῥάδιον;.

[491] *hom. in 2 Cor.* 25.2 [61.571]; compare also *laud. Paul.* 1.12 [SC 300.132].

[492] *Stag.* 3.11 [47.488]: Εἰ τοίνυν καθ' ἕκαστον τῶν σκανδαλιζομένων αὐτὸς ἐπυροῦτο, οὐκ ἐνῆν σβεσθῆναι τὴν πύρωσιν ταύτην ἀπὸ τῆς ἐκείνου ψυχῆς.

[493] In *laud. Paul.* 1.12 [SC 300.130] the pastor terms it the affliction "more bitter than the others" [τὰ τούτων πικρότερα].

where Paul mentions his famous "thorn in the flesh." But the exact referent of this metaphor for Paul's intense sorrows is elusive. In answering the riddle, Chrysostom projected his own experiences of affliction into his portraits of Paul's singularly painful "thorn." From his earliest writings Chrysostom consistently denied the prevalent interpretation that "the thorn in the flesh" referred to a bodily affliction, like headache,[494] insisting instead that it referred to the pervasive opposition Paul faced. But, significantly, while in his earlier period John described these enemies, "the angels of Satan" (2 Cor 12:7) as unbelievers, tyrants, and Greeks,[495] less than a decade later it is foes and false friends from *inside* the church, battering the apostle like waves, who are now identified with Paul's "thorn in the flesh."[496] Then in John's last year of life, while on forced march in exile in Armenia, when writing to his friend Olympias he represents Paul's "thorn in the flesh" as the torments of imprisonment, proddings and whippings at the hands of "public executioners."[497] We can see quite clearly that Paul's literary thorn in the flesh became a sort of mirror of Chrysostom's own lived imaginings of the worst possible agony, with no pain more vivid than that which John was currently experiencing. Yet these different portraits are not free authorial self-portraits or mere counterfeits, either, for each of the types of sorrows Chrysostom identifies in the three different periods of his life (external opposition, internal foes, and official imprisonment) actually is contained

---

[494] Τινὲς μὲν οὖν κεφαλαλγίαν τινὰ ἔφασαν αὐτὸν λέγειν ὑπὸ τοῦ διαβόλου γινομένην· ἀλλὰ μὴ γένοιτο (*hom. in 2 Cor.* 26.2 [61.577], also 26.3 [61.578]). A further argument supporting the inauthenticity of *hom. in 2 Cor. 12:9*, in addition to its composite nature and rougher style, is that the author of that homily, unlike Chrysostom, accepts that Paul's thorn in the flesh *was* headaches (2 [59.510]: καὶ κεφαλαλγίαν αὐτῷ ἐνέβαλεν ὁ διάβολος).

[495] *stat.* 1.6 [49.24]: ἀγγέλους δὲ τοῦ σατανᾶ οὐχὶ δαίμονας λέγει τινάς, ἀλλὰ ἀνθρώπους τοὺς ὑπηρετουμένους τῷ διαβόλῳ, τοὺς ἀπίστους, τοὺς τυράννους, τοὺς Ἕλληνας, οἳ συνεχῶς αὐτὸν ἔθλιβον, καὶ συνεχῶς ἤλαυνον (this discourse is securely dated in 387 [Quasten, *Patrology*, 3.457–58; Kelly, *Golden Mouth*, 72]). This insistence on the tyrannical outside opposition surely suits the tense and anxious situation in Antioch while awaiting the emperor's response to the desecration of his images.

[496] *hom. in 2 Cor.* 26.2–3 [61.577–78], again refuting those who think it is "headaches" [κεφαλαλγία], but this time arguing that it refers to Paul's antagonists Alexander, Hymenaios and Philetos (who are rebuked in 1 Tim 1:20; 2 Tim 2:17; 4:14). The date of the homilies on 2 Corinthians is not certain, but, if they are not from John's period in Constantinople (thus post-398; it depends upon whether one translates ἐνταῦθα in 26.5 [61.582] as "here" or "there"), an accepted Antiochene date is 393 (Bonsdorff, *Predigttätigkeit*, 50). More neutral is the Antiochene oration, *pan. Eust. Ant.* 3 [50.603], which insists, based upon the Hebrew meaning of the word satan, that it refers to (unnamed) "opponents": "And I know that some think it is a bodily infirmity. This is not it, it isn't! But he calls the men who oppose him 'an angel of Satan'" [καὶ οἶδα μὲν ὅτι τινὲς ἀσθένειαν εἶναι νομίζουσι σωματικήν· οὐκ ἔστι δὲ τοῦτο, οὐκ ἔστιν· ἀλλ' ἄγγελον Σατᾶν τοὺς ἀντικειμένους ἀνθρώπους καλεῖ].

[497] *ep. Olymp.* 17.3 [SC 13.212]: "'For,' he said, 'a thorn in the flesh was given to me, an angel of Satan, so that he might slap me around,' speaking of the blows, the bonds, the chains, the prisons, being led around, torn apart, pulled back and forth with whips repeatedly by public executioners" [τὰς πληγὰς λέγων, τὰ δεσμά, τὰς ἁλύσεις, τὰ δεσμωτήρια, τὸ ἄγεσθαι, σπαράττεσθαι, κατατείνεσθαι, προτείνεσθαι μάστιξιν ὑπὸ δημίων πολλάκις] (*ep. Olymp.* 8.11d [SC 13.204]).

within Paul's own catalogues of woes. What Chrysostom has done in each instance is choose from the catalogue as one would from a box of pastels, in each instance highlighting by dramatic color the image of suffering he knows best.

Chrysostom's treatment of Paul's thorn in the flesh is a vivid illustration of how a portrait of Paul as a man of sorrows and torment, especially because of the voluminous material provided in the *peristasis* catalogues of the letters, among which most miseries imaginable find a place, can become a composite portrait of Christian suffering itself:[498] "the very things all the saints suffered in so many bodies Paul bore in one body."[499] This Paul is an impossibly wracked and riven human body, beset by opposition at every turn. But this larger portrayal must also be tempered by a close-up of Paul's face in the midst of such torments: rejoicing rather than grieving at the many afflictions he underwent.[500] And one can delve even deeper into the portrait of Paul the sufferer. The accompanying x-ray portrait of Paul's soul while enduring countless tribulations reveals that it was unbending, unyielding to these onslaughts: "the soul which bore these things was harder than any rock, and proved victorious over iron and steel."[501] Paul was like a spark of unquenchable fire tossed into the sea, which despite the buffeting of cascades of waves rose again to the surface even more brilliant than before.[502]

Yet as Chrysostom paints him Paul was able to do more than simply endure[503] these arrows of the devil and rise again to the surface; indeed he profited from

---

[498] See, e.g., *hom. in Heb.* 34.3 [63.236]: "What terrible thing did he not suffer? What did he not endure?" [Τί μὲν οὐκ ἔπαθε δεινόν, τί δὲ οὐχ ὑπέστη;]. The same can be said, of course, for Christ's crucifixion (which was itself the model for Paul's own self-understanding about suffering, as in Gal 2:19; 6:14).

[499] ἅπερ ἅπαντες ἐν τοσούτοις σώμασιν οἱ ἅγιοι ἔπαθον, ταῦτα αὐτὸς ἐν ἑνὶ πάντα ἤνεγκε (*hom. in 2 Cor.* 25.3 [61.574].

[500] *compunct.* 1 7 [47.404]; *hom. in 2 Cor.* 26.3 [61.579]; *hom. in Phil.* 14.1 [62.283]; cf. *laud. Paul.* 2.7 [SC 300.152]; *Stag.* 3.11 [47.487]: Paul even derived pleasure [ἡδονή] from these miseries. Indeed, John could depict Paul as continuously laughing in the face of his tribulations and tormenters (*res. mort.* 3 [50.423]). But elsewhere Chrysostom amplifies Paul's afflictions by portraying him as crying night and day (*laud. Paul.* 1.12 [SC 300.132], drawing upon Acts 20:31 and 2 Cor 2:4). But even when Paul grieved it was not for his own sufferings, but for those of others (*laud. Paul.* 2.6 [SC 300.152]), and when he was torn apart, it was by worry for his churches as severe as the labor pains of a woman giving birth (*laud. Paul.* 1.12 [SC 300.132]).

[501] *laud. Paul.* 1.12 [SC 300.132]. See also *hom. in 2 Cor.* 25.3 [61.574]: "in one body and with one soul he endured as many dangers as would be sufficient to trouble even a soul of iron"; and the demolition of the anti-portrait of Paul as a man of fears in *laud. Paul* 6, analyzed in chap. 5 (pp. 166–72). The general impression of Paul's endurance in the face of tribulations is succinctly stated in *hom. in Heb.* 34.3 [63.239]: ἀλλὰ ταῦτα ἔφερε γενναίως.

[502] *hom. in 2 Cor.* 25.2–3 [61.572–3].

[503] As, e.g., in *hom. in 2 Tim.* 9.2 [62.653]: Ἀλλὰ πρὸς ἅπαντα ἔστη. Πῶς; Νήφων καὶ ἐγρηγορώς. On this as a special attribute of Luke's portrait of Paul's sufferings, see Victor Paul Furnish, "Paul the ΜΑΡΤΥΣ," *Witness and Existence: Essays in Honor of Schubert M. Ogden*, ed. Philip E. Devenish and George L. Goodwin (Chicago: University of Chicago Press, 1989) 73–88, 82: "Here, as throughout Acts, Paul's sufferings are part of a larger, heroic portrait, shadows added to the canvas in order to accentuate the bold, strong features of God's 'chosen instrument'" (Furnish also points to the importance of Paul's endurance of sufferings in 2 Timothy, on p. 83).

them. As we have noted in the analysis of *laud. Paul.* 4 given previously in this chapter, Chrysostom delightedly exclaims that opposition to the gospel, rather than hindering it, actually worked toward its success.[504] In John's eyes the benefits that resulted from Paul's sufferings extend well beyond his own character formation to the benefits the apostle thereby earned for the whole world. In his exegetical homily which expounds on the *peristasis* catalogue of 2 Cor 11:23–29, John rather artfully shows how each one of Paul's trials wrought a corresponding gain for others:

He endured shipwreck, so that he might halt the shipwreck of the world; he spent night and day in the briny deep, so that he might draw (the world) up from the depth of deception; he experienced weariness, so that he might give rest to the weary; he endured beatings, so that he might heal those beaten up by the devil; he spent time in prisons, so that he might lead those sitting in prison and in darkness into the light; he was at death's door repeatedly, so that he might set them free from worse deaths; five times he received the forty lashes minus one, so that he might free the very ones who inflict this punishment from the scourge of the devil; he was beaten with rods, so that he might lead them under the rod and staff of Christ; he was stoned, so that he might free them from insensate stones [idols]; he was in the desert, so that he might take them out of the desert; in journeys, so that he might stop those who are wandering and open the way that leads into heaven; he was endangered in cities, so that he might demonstrate the city above; in hunger and thirst, so that he might take them away from a worse hunger; in nakedness, so that he might clothe the unseemly with the robe of Christ; in mob attacks, so that he might lead them away from the nasty whacks of demons; he was burned, so that he might extinguish the burning arrows of the devil; he was lowered from the wall through a window, so that from below he might send up those who had been cast down to the ground.[505]

This inventive and rather exhaustive rewriting of Paul's catalogue of sufferings expresses John's theology of Pauline *peristasis*: all that Paul suffered he suffered for

---

[504] See above, pp. 268–70, and a typical expression in *laed.* 11 [SC 103.112]: "Did not Paul receive countless storms of trials? How then was he harmed by them? Was he not from them even more crowned?" [Οὐχὶ μυρίας ἐδέξατο πειρασμῶν νιφάδας; τί οὖν ἐντεῦθεν ἐβλάβη; οὐκ ἐντεῦθεν μὲν οὖν καὶ μειζόνως ἐστεφανοῦτο;].

[505] *hom. in 2 Cor.* 25.3 [61.573–74]. I quote the lengthy Greek passage so that the word plays, which I have tried to replicate in translation, can be appreciated: Ὑπέστη ναυάγιον, ἵνα τὸ ναυάγιον παύσῃ τῆς οἰκουμένης· νυχθήμερον ἐν τῷ βυθῷ πεποίηκεν, ἵνα τοῦ βυθοῦ τῆς πλάνης ἀνιμήσηται· ἐν κόπῳ γέγονεν, ἵνα τοὺς κοπιῶντας ἀναπαύσῃ· πληγὰς ὑπέμεινεν, ἵνα τοὺς ὑπὸ τοῦ διαβόλου πληγέντας ἰάσηται· ἐν φυλακαῖς διέτριψεν, ἵνα τοὺς ἐν φυλακῇ καὶ σκότῳ καθημένους εἰς φῶς ἐξαγάγῃ· ἐν θανάτοις πολλάκις, ἵνα θανάτων ἀπαλλάξῃ χαλεπῶν· πεντάκις τεσσαράκοντα παρὰ μίαν ἔλαβεν, ἵνα αὐτοὺς τοὺς ταῦτα ποιοῦντας ἐλευθερώσῃ τῆς τοῦ διαβόλου μάστιγος· ἐρραβδίσθη, ἵνα ὑπὸ τὴν ῥάβδον καὶ τὴν βακτηρίαν ἀγάγῃ τοῦ Χριστοῦ· ἐλιθάσθη, ἵνα ἀπαλλάξῃ τῶν ἀναισθήτων λίθων· ἐν ἐρημίᾳ γέγονεν, ἵνα τῆς ἐρημίας ἐξέληται· ἐν ὁδοιπορίαις, ἵνα στήσῃ πλανωμένους, καὶ τὴν εἰς τὸν οὐρανὸν φέρουσαν ὁδὸν ἀνοίξῃ· ἐν πόλεσιν ἐκινδύνευσεν, ἵνα τὴν ἄνω πόλιν ὑποδείξῃ· ἐν λιμῷ καὶ δίψει, ἵνα ἀφέληται τοῦ χαλεπωτέρου λιμοῦ· ἐν γυμνότητι, ἵνα ἀσχημονοῦντας ἐνδύσῃ τὴν στολὴν τοῦ Χριστοῦ· ἐν ἐπιστασίᾳ ὄχλου, ἵνα τῆς περιστάσεως τῶν δαιμόνων ἀπαγάγῃ· ἐπυρώθη, ἵνα σβέσῃ τὰ πεπυρωμένα βέλη τοῦ διαβόλου· διὰ θυρίδος ἀπὸ τείχους ἐχαλάσθη, ἵνα κάτωθεν ἄνω διαπέμψῃ τοὺς ἐρριμμένους χαμαί.

the sake of the salvation of the world, for which God rewarded him with a successful mission. It is on this basis that narration of Paul's afflictions properly becomes an encomium, in accord with the way the form itself was customarily employed, "because the punishments and dangers endured for friends are to be praised" [διόπερ ἐπαινοῦνται καὶ αἱ πρὸ τῶν φίλων τιμωρίαι καὶ κίνδυνοι].[506]

Ascetic Acts

Some of Paul's most notable deeds in Chrysostom's eyes are in one sense non-deeds, the abstentions of the renunciatory lifestyle associated with monks and philosophers.[507] But John, his twin ascetic, emphatically does not consider these acts of self-denial mere moments of omission, because his ethical assumptions hold that forbearing from evil alone does not constitute virtue; virtue must be won by actively pursuing the good.[508] Moments of ascetic self-denial are regarded as episodes in the Christian life viewed as a continual "mud-wrestling bout with the devil,"[509] who time and again tries to lure people in by playing on their passions for pleasure and excess. It is within this overall conception of the pious life as an ἀγών that Chrysostom portrayed Paul as having quintessentially embodied ascetic piety through his practice of all the monastic virtues and disciplines – celibacy, voluntary poverty, compunction – to the highest degree. Like the monks, the

---

[506] Theon, *Prog.* 8 [Spengel 2.110]. In Chrysostom's eyes Paul could have avoided this suffering, but willingly undertook it for the sake of others (2 Tim 2:10): "'I do not endure these things,' he says, 'for my salvation, but for yours. It was possible for me to live without danger; it was possible for me to suffer none of this, if I were looking to my own interests. But why do I suffer these things? On behalf of the good of others, so that others might attain eternal life'" (*hom. in 2 Tim.* 4.2 [62.621]).

[507] Catalogues of ascetic deeds were already well established conventions in biographies of philosophers; see Cox, *Biography*, 30: "These [ascetic] traits came together in biographies to form a pattern, a blueprint for the type of the divine philosopher. It is an ideal type, a picture of perfection, and it is difficult, if not impossible, to discern either the extent to which the biographers have molded their heroes to fit the type or the extent to which the heroes themselves actually imitated the ideal." Chrysostom regards monks as the quintessential philosophers (see n. 512 below).

[508] "For praise and admiration belong to those who accomplish virtuous deeds, not those who flee from evil" [τὸ γὰρ ἐπαινεῖσθαι καὶ θαυμάζεσθαι τῶν τὰ ἀγαθὰ κατορθούντων οὐ τῶν τὰ κακὰ φευγόντων ἐστίν] (*virg.* 1.2 [SC 125.94]; cf. 8.4 [SC 125.118]).

[509] *hom. in Ac.* 7.4 [60.68]. The homiletical context of this marvelous image is an excoriation of the rich for their luxurious garments, which are hardly the right uniform, John says, for the contest. For another vivid image, see *virg.* 38.2 [SC 125.226], where the virgin takes on the devil in mortal combat in the public arena, and *oppugn.* 1.7 [47.328–29], which depicts the demons attacking the souls of the faithful, clothing them in wickedness, biting and poisoning them, all to conform them to their own likeness, or separate them from their bodies.

[510] Chrysostom often refers to Paul as μόνος or μονομάχος (see chap. 3, n. 92; chap. 6, p. 219). One should note that virtually all of Chrysostom's portraits of Paul treat him as a man set apart, a lone ranger (the only exception being a group portrait of the heavenly chorus of all the assembled apostles). The work of New Testament scholarship in the last few decades to place Paul more firmly within the context of his fellow workers and churches (e.g., Wolf-Henning

solitary Paul[510] lived the "angelic life" while on earth,[511] carrying out the "philosophical" pursuits himself, and, even more, leading others to pursue the philosophical life by his example and teaching.[512]

This portrait of Paul the man of ascetic deeds mirrors John's frequent depictions of monks and monastic life in his homilies and writings, which are themselves colored in such Pauline hues that it is impossible to assign priority to either of these mutually influencing portraits[513] (particularly given the fact that the portraitist, John, was himself a monk).[514] Paul is consistently offered as example and

---

Ollrog, *Paulus und seine Mitarbeiter: Untersuchungen zu Theorie und Praxis der paulinischen Mission* [WMANT 50; Neukirchen-Vluyn, 1979]; Victor Paul Furnish, "Fellow Workers in God's Service," *JBL* 80 [1961] 364–70) would have been lost on him.

[511] For references to Paul as an angel, see chap. 3, nn. 68–70. On monks living the angelic life, see (among literally hundreds of references): *hom. in Mt.* 55.6 [58.548], οἱ τῆς ἐρήμου πολῖται· μᾶλλον δὲ οἱ τῶν οὐρανῶν πολῖται; *comp.* 3 [47.389], ἀγγέλοις συμβιοτεύων, θεῷ συλλαλῶν, τῶν οὐρανίων ἀγαθῶν ἀπολαύων; *oppugn.* 2.8; 3.11, καὶ γὰρ πολιτείαν οὐρανῷ πρέπουσαν εἵλοντο, καὶ ἀγγέλων οὐδὲν χεῖρον διάκεινται; 3.18, ὡς ἄγγελοι τοῖς ἐπὶ γῆς ἀνθρώποις συμπεριπολῶσιν; 3.20–21 [47.344, 366, 381, 384]; *virg.* 10.3–11.2; 27.2 [SC 125.124–128, 178]. This is a commonplace in ascetic texts generally (see Brown, *Body and Society*, chap. 16, "These Are Our Angels"; Giulia Sfameni Gasparro, "Asceticism and Anthropology: *Enkrateia* and 'Double Creation' in Early Christianity," in *Asceticism*, ed. Vincent L. Wimbush and Richard Valantasis [New York/Oxford: Oxford University Press, 1995] 127–46, 134–36, with references to further literature). And Chrysostom employs it richly (Elizabeth A. Clark, "Introduction," *John Chrysostom – On Virginity, and Against Remarriage*, trans. Sally Rieger Shore [Studies in Women and Religion 9; New York: Mellen, 1983] vii–xlii, xiv; Hunter, *Comparison*, 147 n. 51, and his conclusion on p. 13: "What stands out most in Chrysostom's descriptions of the monastic life, however, is the idea that the monk lived on earth the life of heaven"). As expressed in *virg.* 10.3 [SC 125.125], the angels are the true monastics, since they do not marry (the key inspiration here is Mk 12:25 and parallels), are not burdened with a body, spend no time on earth, nor must they endure the trouble caused by desires, or food or drink. Hence, Chrysostom portrays both the monks and Paul in images of flight, as though on wings traversing the space between earth and heaven (for monks and virgins, see *oppugn.* 2.7; 3.18, 21 [47.342, 380, 385]; *virg.* 17.1–2; 80.2 [SC 125.150, 380]; for Paul as "winged," see chap. 3, pp. 77–78).

[512] We have discussed Chrysostom's portrait of Paul as a philosopher at length above (pp. 270–78), in analyzing his "Summary Deed." It was characteristic of contemporary Christian literature to speak of monks as philosophers or those engaged in the philosophical life, which Chrysostom does ubiquitously (see auf der Maur, *Mönchtum*, 87–92, with further bibliography on p. 87, n. 7; Clark, *Jerome, Chrysostom, and Friends*, 16–18). Hunter, *Comparison*, 29, n. 66 notes that: "'Philosophy' is Chrysostom's usual term in the *Comparatio* and *Oppugnatores* for the monastic life" (see, e.g., *comp.* 1 [47.387]; *oppugn.* 1.2 [47.320], and *passim*).

[513] For instance, one can compare the σύγκρισις motif with the emperor, which Chrysostom uses for both the monks and for Paul (*comp.* 1 [47.388] and *passim*; cf. *hom. in 2 Tim.* 4.3–4, analyzed above, pp. 206–12). Given that Chrysostom's ascetical writings tend to be among his earliest, a careful comparison of the *topoi* common to his treatment of monks and of Paul might provide useful data for the dating of some of these writings, and the development of Chrysostom's Pauline images over time (which would require its own study).

[514] As Kelly reminds us: "when he left his cave and resumed city life he did not conceive of himself as ceasing to be a monk" (*Golden Mouth*, 35).

authority to the monks in all of Chrysostom's ascetical treatises,[515] even as the monks themselves are presented as moral paradigms for the rest of humanity because they best live up to the ethical program Paul exemplified.[516] Not only Paul's life, but also his words in the letters are regarded as explaining ascetic virtues and exhorting his contemporary readers to pursue them. John regards Paul as having knowingly set up procedures for the monastic life, by putting teachers of virtue over the young to set them on the right path early on,[517] and by giving intricate and wise instructions for virgins and others in the life of the church (1 Cor 7 and 1 Tim 5 being particularly essential passages).[518] So the image of Paul and the face of monasticism were already reflexively mixed in complex ways by Chrysostom's time, to which he adds further admixtures, both by portraying monks as carrying out Paul's campaign to the tee, and portraying Paul as having all the features of an excellent monk (a fact John's audience would have recognized immediately).

Yet the image of Paul as a monk does not place him simply on a par with the monks of John's time; rather, Chrysostom depicts Paul as the "super-monk" who by his superiority to them at every turn acts as a corrective and enhancement to living monks to aspire toward more brilliant and finely-tuned self-portraits in ascetic accomplishment. At the same time, in his constructions of Paul the monk Chrysostom is also working out his own ambivalence about the monastic lifestyle and its relationship to Christian piety *en masse*. And the Pauline example has also a wider referent, given that Chrysostom's pervasive goal is to challenge all claims that laypeople have any less responsibilities for leading a pious and virtuous life than monks.[519] Paul as super-monk is yet another incarnation of Paul as ὁ ἀρχέτυπος τῆς ἀρετῆς — for all Christians, indeed, the whole world. Furthermore, given that Chrysostom's depictions of Christian monastic life in general often had an apologetic intent, to demonstrate to "pagans" that the monks were far superior to any

---

[515] *adhortationes ad Theodorum lapsum 1 and 2, adversus oppugnatores vitae monasticae, comparatio regis et monachi, de compunctione ad Demetrium, de compunctione ad Stelechium, de virginitate, ad viduam juniorem 1–2; contra eos qui subintroductas habent* (see chap. 1, n. 12 for complete bibliography).

[516] See *oppugn.* 3.11,19 [47.366,382]; *comp.* 4 [47.392], further discussion and references in auf der Maur, *Mönchtum*, 142, 150–51, 154: "Paulus ist darum das zweckdienlichste Gefäß am Leibe Christi, größer als die Propheten des Alten Bundes; darum muß man ihn besonders bewundern."

[517] *oppugn.* 3.18 [47.381].

[518] The treatise *de virginitate* is largely an exposition of Paul's intentions in 1 Corinthians 7, which John consciously brings up to date for his own context by allowing for Paul's moderation in only slowly introducing the requirement of celibacy at the beginning of the church (as well as by interpreting Paul's eschatological injunctions in a more philosophically informed fashion, as Clark, "Introduction," has argued). See, e.g., *virg.* 11.1 [SC 125.126]: "Paul has removed the virgins from all these cares so that they might be diligent and undistracted (1 Cor 7:35)." Here Paul is the patron of virgins who protects and fosters their way of life against detractors; this is given graphic depictions in *virg.* 34.1 and 3 [SC 125.198–200], cited below, p. 324.

[519] See *oppugn.* 3.14 [47.372–75]. The only difference is the renunciation of marriage [47.372].

luminaries of virtue in Greek philosophy and history,[520] portraits of Paul as monk-exemplar should be seen as performing that same external function, as well.[521]

The root of monastic virtue is to be found in some fundamental internal dispositions. Paul, like the monks, exemplified the quality of ἀναισθησία, "detachment,"[522] or, more strongly, καταφρόνησις, "contempt,"[523] toward the things of this life. This is shown very clearly, for Chrysostom, in the internal dialogue of Phil 1:21–26, especially v. 23, where Paul wishes to depart life and be with Christ, which John regards as most typical of Paul's contempt or disdain [ὑπεροψία][524] for present, earthly realities. It is this attitude of "considering matters of the present to be nothing" that allows one to "trample the devil underfoot."[525] Another crucially defining passage, both for the portrait of Paul as a monk, and for Chrysostom's theology of monasticism, is Gal 6:14, which encapsulates Paul's "double detachment." Not only has "the world been crucified to him," in the sense that he pays its allures no mind, but, even more than that, *he* has been crucified to the world:

For the virtue of the soul is so great [Τοσαύτη γὰρ τῆς ψυχῆς ἡ ἀρετή], that it is easy for the one who wills to abide on the earth, but, as though sitting in heaven [ὡς εἶναι ῥᾴδιον τῷ βουλομένῳ διατρίβειν μὲν ἐπὶ τῆς γῆς, ὥσπερ δὲ ἐν οὐρανῷ καθημένῳ], to be conscious of none of the things happening on the earth [μηδενὸς ἐπαισθάνεσθαι τῶν γινομένων ἐπὶ τῆς γῆς]. For such a person was the blessed Paul [Τοιοῦτος ὁ μακάριος Παῦλος ἦν] who, while going about in the middle of cities [ἐν μέσαις στρεφόμενος πόλεσιν] stood apart from all present things [ἀφειστήκει τῶν παρόντων ἀπάντων] to the same degree as we stand aloof from dead bodies. For when he says, "The world has been crucified to me," he is speaking of this detachment [ἀναισθησία]. Or, rather, not this detachment alone, but another detachment, like the twin of the one just mentioned [μᾶλλον δὲ οὐ ταύτην μόνην, ἀλλὰ καὶ ἑτέραν τοιαύτην, ὡς εἶναι τὴν προειρημένην διπλῆν]. For he did not say only, "The world has been crucified to me," and then remain silent, but through what comes next he made clear that there is another type, by saying, "And I to the world." Therefore, while it is great philosophy to consider the world to be dead [Μεγάλη μὲν οὖν φιλοσοφία καὶ τὸ νομίζειν νεκρὸν εἶναι τὸν κόσμον], it is more than this, far more, for him to consider himself

---

[520] See the intricate and convincing argument by Hunter, *Comparison*, 25–36, 43–66, that Chrysostom is deliberately responding to Libanios and Julian in these treatises.

[521] As we have discussed above, the presentation of Paul as the "true philosopher" is part of this Christian apologetic project.

[522] See *compunct.* 2 1–2 [47.412], quoted below on this page. Another common expression is that Paul "stood apart" from this world, as in *compunct.* 2 2 [47.413]: Ὁρᾷς πόσον ἀφειστήκει τῆς οἰκουμένης, πῶς ἐν τῇ γῇ βαδίζων πρὸς αὐτὴν ἀνεπεπηδήκει τοῦ οὐρανοῦ τὴν κορυφήν;

[523] For monastic καταφρόνησις see, e.g., *oppugn.* 2.4, 5: καὶ τῆς γῆς καταφρονεῖ, πόλιν ἔχων τὸν οὐρανόν, and 9 [47.337, 337–338, 344]. For Paul's worldly contempt, of many examples, see *compunct.* 1 7 [47.405]; *laud. Paul.* 2.8 [SC 300.156].

[524] This is often named as a characteristic of the monks; see *comp.* 4 [47.391–92], ὁ γὰρ ὑπερορῶν πλούτου καὶ ἡδονῆς καὶ τρυφῆς; also *oppugn.* 2.8; 3.10, 11 [47.343, 365, 366]. ὑπεροψία is related to the proper theory of optics at work in monastic thinking; on which, see below, n. 540.

[525] *hom. in Eph.* 22.5 [62.162]: Τὸ ἐκ περιουσίας καταπατεῖν αὐτόν, οἷον ὁ Παῦλος ἐποίει, οὐδὲν ἡγούμενος εἶναι τὰ παρόντα πράγματα.

disposed to the world as if he were already dead [πλείων δὲ ταύτης καὶ πολλῷ μείζων τὸ καὶ αὐτὸν ὡς τεθνηκότα διακεῖσθαι πρὸς ἐκεῖνον].[526]

This depiction of Paul's ascetic disposition toward things of this world presents him as having a double portion of the world-denying vaccination. Cast in this way (largely a replica of the apostle's own verbal self-portrait, but now in a changed circumstance of ascetic options), the portrait of Paul the monk is the picture of a living corpse, one who was "dying every day" (1 Cor 15:31),[527] for only in this way can one explain how Paul was utterly immune to the passions affecting all living bodies.[528] The mimetic sensibility at work between Chrysostom's visions of Paul and of monks (to say nothing of that involved in Paul's original statement about the crucifixion of Christ) is reflected in the fact that, based on this Pauline passage, Chrysostom calls monks οἱ ἐσταυρωμένοι and the monastic life ὁ ἐσταυρωμένος βίος.[529]

Paul the corpse was entirely "unmoved" [ἀκίνητος] by earthly desires. The disposition of ἀταραξία, "impassibility," or ἀπάθεια, lies at the heart of monastic discipline.[530] The life of the flesh is a life of ταραχή and θόρυβος, as graphically demonstrated by the trembling lack of control which accompanies orgasm in sexual intercourse.[531] Yet another source of constant human ταραχή is the fear of death. In contrast, the monk lives a life "far from upset and turmoil," as symbolized often by the image of the calm harbor where the virgin lives, well removed

---

[526] compunct. 2 1–2 [47.412–13].

[527] Just like the monk in oppugn. 2.8 [47.343], ἑαυτὸν δείξει καθ' ἑκάστην ἡμέραν ἐν τῷ σώματι μελετῶντα τὴν τελευτήν. Cf. also subintr. 5 [47.501], and virg. 3.16 [47.376], where the monks are said to hurry to depart this life, and "groan" while in the body (with Phil 1:23; 2 Cor 5:2, 4). In laud. Paul. 1.3 [SC 300.116] Chrysostom, inspired by 2 Tim 4:6, paints Paul as a priest who sacrificed himself every day, to the degree that he "put to death his fleshly nature in such a way that he was affected not less than the slaughtered sacrificial victims, but, indeed, much more" [καὶ τῆς σαρκὸς τὴν φύσιν οὕτως ἐνέκρωσεν, ὡς τῶν σφαγιαζομένων ἱερείων μηδὲν ἔλλατον διακεῖσθαι, ἀλλὰ καὶ πολλῷ πλέον]. In res. mort. 3 [50.421] Chrysostom says, on the basis of 2 Cor 4:8–9, that Paul was like "the living dead" [ἔμψυχοι νεκροί].

[528] "However, I fear it might be laughable to praise Paul for this virtue, the man who crucified himself to the world, and regarded not only the attractive features of human bodies, but all things, as we do dust and ashes. He was as unmoved by them as a corpse encountering another corpse [ὡς ἂν νεκρὸς πρὸς νεκρὸν ἀκίνητος γένοιτο]. So precisely did he lull to sleep the surges of nature, that he never, ever, experienced a single human passion" [Οὕτω μετὰ ἀκριβείας τῆς φύσεως τὰ σκιρτήματα κατευνάζων, οὐδὲν οὐδέποτε πρὸς οὐδὲν ἀνθρώπινον πάθος ἔπαθεν] (laud. Paul. 1.9 [SC 300.126]).

[529] As in hom. in 1 Tim. 11.2 [62.556]; virg. 75.1 [SC 125.358]; see also the plentiful material collected by auf der Maur, Mönchtum, 82–83.

[530] See the list of τὰ τοῖς μοναχοῖς προσόντα ἀγαθά in sac. 6.8 [SC 272.330], which includes καθαρότης, ἀταραξία, ἁγιωσύνη, καρτερία, and νῆψις. On ἀταραξία as a monastic discipline for Chrysostom, see auf der Maur, Mönchtum, 102. ἀπάθεια (the old Stoic concept reappropriated) is characteristic of the angels, and therefore should be emulated by Christians (hom. in Mt. 19.5 [57.280]; ep. Olymp. 8.5, 7, 11, as it was by Paul [SC 13.176, 186, 204]; auf der Maur, Mönchtum, 83–85).

[531] oppugn. 2.10 [47.347].

from the storms of demonic passions.[532] The monk is unafraid of death; indeed, he welcomes it.[533] And the monastery itself is a calm harbor whose example, like a beacon, beckons people to come in out of the turbulent seas and be saved from shipwreck.[534] John views Paul as likewise living above the fray, unmoved by passions and fears, and going to meet his own death with pure equanimity. But, rather than living in a harbor, for Chrysostom Paul *was* a harbor, the very embodiment of monastic sensibility, who furthermore had the ability to lead others to that same place of calm repose.

He[535] is a sea, not conducting those who sail on it from city to city, but from earth to heaven [θάλασσά ἐστιν, οὐκ ἀπὸ πόλεως εἰς πόλιν ἄγουσα τοὺς ἐμπλέοντας, ἀλλ' ἀπὸ γῆς εἰς οὐρανόν]. And if someone sails on this sea, s/he will sail with prosperity. On this sea there are no winds, but in place of winds the divine Holy Spirit escorts those who sail upon it. There are no waves there, no promontories, no beasts. Everything is calm [πάντα γαληνά]. He is a sea which is calmer than a harbor [θάλασσά ἐστι λιμένος γαληνοτέρα], and more secure.[536]

Other monastic dispositions, such as "boldness" [παρρησία],[537] "purity" [καθαρότης],[538] "big-heartedness" [μεγαλοψυχία],[539] and purity of vision[540] likewise find their most true expression in Paul.

---

[532] "But the virgin endures none of these things [which most women do], but her home is free from upset [ἀπήλλακται ταραχῆς τὸ δωμάτιον], and every cry has been driven far off. Just as in a calm harbor [εὔδιος λιμήν] silence possesses everything inside and another calm detachment [ἀταραξία] greater than silence possesses her soul, because it doesn't undertake any human thing, but always speaks to God and looks directly at him" (*virg.* 68.1 [SC 125.338]; also 34.1 [SC 125.198, and Bernard Grillet's n. 3, on how the port in the storm is a Stoic *topos*]; cf. *oppugn.* 1.7 [47.328]).

[533] *oppugn.* 2.5, 7 [47.338, 342].

[534] *hom. in 1 Tim.* 14.3 [62.575]: "There [sc. τὰ μοναστήρια] is a calm harbor [Λιμήν ἐστιν εὔδιος], like beacons shining from a high spot upon sailors coming from afar, stationed there at the harbor, and drawing all to their calm spot [καὶ πρὸς γαλήνην τὴν αὐτῶν ἅπαντας ἕλκοντες], not allowing those who look on them to be shipwrecked, not allowing those who keep sight of them to travel in darkness."

[535] Or, his heart, or his words (all three of which are at work, interchangeably, in the context).

[536] *hom. in Ac.* 55.3 [60.583]. The spurious work *Petr. et Paul.* turns this into an epithet for Paul: Παῦλε, εὔδιος λιμὴν τῶν χειμαζομένων (1 [59.494]).

[537] On παρρησία as characteristic of the monastic outlook, see the material collected by auf der Maur, *Mönchtum*, 102, n. 2. Paul's παρρησία is amply attested in self-testimonies in his letters and in Acts (2 Cor 3:12; 7:4; Eph 3:12; 6:19; Phil 1:20; Acts 28:31), which Chrysostom heartily applauds, and sometimes defends against the possible objection that he is too harsh (e.g., *hom. in Col.* 10.3 [62.369]; *hom. in Phil.* 2.2 [62.192]; *hom. in 1 Cor.* 13.2 [61.110]; *hom. in 2 Cor.* 13.1; 14.1; 15.2; 23.1 [61.491, 498, 505, 554]). Chrysostom understands παρρησία to be the disposition with which the angels stand before God in heaven (*hom. in 2 Cor.* 16.3; 24.1 [61.518, 563]); on earth it is one of the χαρίσματα (*scand.* 2.12 [SC 79.66]).

[538] *oppugn.* 2.5 [47.338]; *virg.* 5.2 [SC 125.108]; 21.1; 63.2 [SC 125.160, 326–27], of purity of sight.

[539] Of the monks, see *oppugn.* 2.6 [47.340], and Hunter, *Comparison*, 109, n. 36. For Paul, see *stat.* 21.2 [49.213]; *laud. Paul.* 5.8 [SC 300.246].

[540] In Chrysostom's ascetical writings an important manifestation of a holy internal disposi-

There are three chief monastic πράξεις – chastity, voluntary poverty (with which we shall include fasting) and compunction[541] – and Paul excelled in each. Chastity [ἐγκράτεια] is a major characteristic of the monastic life, a life of self-control of all human passions. In the sexual arena virginity [παρθενία], or voluntary renunciation of marriage [ἀγαμία] is the one deed Chrysostom allows as separating monks from the rest of humanity.[542] He does not have to look very far to find evidence that Paul was chaste, for the apostle himself offered his life as exemplary to the Corinthians: "I wish that all might be as I am" (1 Cor 7:7–8; cf. 1 Cor 9:5). Paul's own broadcasting of his chastity raises a question for John, however, because it could be a sign of a very unascetic breach of humility in pursuit of glory through bragging or self-promotion.[543] John offers three reasons to reject such an interpretation and demonstrate that Paul has presented himself as an example of sexual self-denial for only the most laudable of motives. First, "he knew that students are especially led to zeal for virtue when they have examples from their teachers."[544] This is explained by the pedagogical commonplace that one who tries to inculcate philosophy by words only, with no deeds, does not benefit the student at all. Second, and paradoxically, John maintains that by bringing himself forward Paul has given proof of his own lack of envy or inflated ego, because he wished his students to share in the choice for chastity which he had

---

tion is proper sight. The virgin's eye, rather than being the locus of a licentious come-on, is "so beautiful and lovely that it has as a lover the incorporeal powers and their master, instead of human men. Her eye is so pure and clear than instead of bodily things it is able to look upon incorporeal beauties, so gentle and calm that it is not even angry at those who act unjustly and continually make annoyance, but stands aloof from all, and looks upon all such people in a sweet and kind manner" (*virg.* 63.2 [SC 125.326–28]; also 27.1: her eyes never sleep [SC 125.178], and 31.1 [SC 125.192], on the need to "divert the eyes of the mind" [τοὺς τῆς διανοίας ἀναρριπίζων ὀφθαλμούς]) (see also 68.1–2 [SC 125.338–40]). With this compare the description of Paul's eyes in *hom. in Rom.* 32.4 [60.680]: "those eyes, which saw the things of earth and yet didn't see them, those which beheld the things unseen, didn't know sleep, were wide awake in the middle of the night, did not experience the things most eyes do" [οἱ ὁρῶντες τὰ γήϊνα καὶ οὐχ ὁρῶντες, οἱ βλέποντες τὰ μὴ βλεπόμενα, οἱ μὴ εἰδότες ὕπνον, οἱ ἐν μέσαις ταῖς νυξὶν ἀγρυπνοῦντες, οἱ οὐ πάσχοντες τὰ τῶν ὀφθαλμιώντων]. John even describes the narrative process of Paul's change in vision: "For once he had turned the eyes of his soul to heaven [Καθάπαξ γὰρ τοὺς ὀφθαλμοὺς τῆς ψυχῆς στρέψας εἰς τὸν οὐρανόν], and been struck with amazement at the beauty there, he would not allow them to return to earth again" (*compunct. 1* 7 [47.405]). This corresponds for Chrysostom with the highest attainment of Paul's eyes – they were deemed worthy of seeing Christ even while in the body [οἱ καὶ ἐν σώματι Χριστὸν ἰδεῖν καταξιωθέντες], which is what the monastic fervently awaits after death.

[541] Following Jean-Marie Leroux, "Monachisme et communauté chrétienne d'après Saint Jean Chrysostom," *Théologie de la Vie Monastique* (Théologie 49; Paris: Aubier, 1961) 143–90, 154. Compare Chrysostom's list of τὰ ὑψηλά in *hom. in Mt.* 1.5 [57.19], including παρθενεία, ἀκτημοσύνη, and νηστεία.

[542] *oppugn.* 3.14 [47.372]; auf der Maur, *Mönchtum*, 97, with many references.

[543] περιαυτολογία, or ἐπαίρων ἑαυτόν (*virg.* 35.1 [SC 125.208]). We shall discuss the topic of Paul's boasting at length below in this chapter, in regard to "Contradictory Deeds" (see pp. 339–52).

[544] *virg.* 35.1 [SC 125.208].

made, not seeking to hoard this attainment to himself, but wanting them to become his equals.[545] And, third, by displaying himself before their eyes Paul hoped to show his readers that chastity is not impossible, but is easy, so they would embark with confidence on the same path upon which he is leading them.[546] The latter point presents one side of a genuine tension in Chrysostom's portrait of Paul as chaste, for while here Paul is the proof that chastity is easy (because he was utterly dead to all passion), elsewhere it is precisely because Paul knows how hard it is that he can be an authoritative and appropriately sensitive resource for others in this spiritual quest for purity through self-control. Here Chrysostom scripts Paul's personified voice (as formulated, no doubt, from his own ordeals):

> The experience and first-hand knowledge I already have of this battle [for chastity] makes me hesitant to advise others to it. I know the force of the matter, I know the intensity of these contests, I know the weight of the war. It requires a soul contentious and forceful and desperately disposed against the desires. For it requires treading over coals and not being burned,[547] walking over swords and not being cut. For the power of desire is as great as that of fire and iron. And if a soul has not yet been prepared to turn away from its own pains it will quickly destroy itself.[548]

Part of Chrysostom's evident dilemma is that his other portrait of Paul as the man completely unmoved by human passions does not function very well for moral exhortation. His solution involves rotating portraits, with John using the one (Paul the man of shared struggles, or Paul the unperturbed) which best suits his particular argumentative context. Hence when writing to dissuade his friend Olympias from despondency [ἀθυμία] in the monastic life during his absence, Chrysostom produces an alternate image of a thoroughly impassive Paul:

> For this man, Paul, the one who took off the flesh, and put away his body, going around the world in almost a naked soul, and banishing every passion from his mind, and imitating the impassibility of the incorporeal powers, and inhabiting the earth as though it were heaven ....[549]

---

[545] *virg.* 35.1 [SC 125.208].

[546] "Therefore, wishing to demonstrate that it is easy, he sets the man who has accomplished it before them, so that they might not think it exceedingly painful, but by looking at the man who leads the way, with confidence they too might embark on the same path" [Βουλόμενος οὖν αὐτὸ δεῖξαι ῥᾷστον, τὸν ἠνυκότα εἰς μέσον τίθησιν, ἵνα μὴ σφόδρα ἐπίπονον εἶναι αὐτὸ νομίζωσιν ἀλλὰ πρὸς τὸν ἡγησάμενον ἰδόντες μετὰ τοῦ θαρρεῖν καὶ αὐτοὶ τῆς αὐτῆς ἐπιβαίνωσιν ὁδοῦ] (*virg.* 35.2 [SC 125.210]).

[547] Cf. *virg.* 34.4 [SC 125.202], where virginity is likened to trying to carry a burning coal in one's pocket.

[548] *virg.* 27.1 [SC 125.176–78].

[549] Οὗτος γὰρ ὁ Παῦλος ὁ τὴν σάρκα ἀποδυσάμενος καὶ τὸ σῶμα ἀποθέμενος καὶ γυμνῇ σχεδὸν τὴν οἰκουμένην περιιὼν τῇ ψυχῇ καὶ πᾶν πάθος ἐξορίσας τῆς διανοίας καὶ τῶν ἀσωμάτων δυνάμεων τὴν ἀπάθειαν μιμούμενος καὶ τὴν γῆν ὡς τὸν οὐρανὸν οἰκῶν ... (*ep. Olymp.* 8.11d [SC 13.204]). The passage continues: "and standing with the Cherubim above, and sharing in that mystical melody with them, he bore all the other things easily, as though experiencing them with another body – the prisons and chains, and forced marches and whips and threats and death and

But John himself recognizes the pastoral need for an experienced leader to vary his depictions of the austerity of spiritual disciplines for the sake of the weak, a sagacity he attributes also to his mentor, Paul.[550]

Chrysostom faces one further interesting difficulty in his depiction of Paul as a man of chastity. While Paul's ἐγκράτεια is unquestionable, he apparently was not (perpetually) a virgin [παρθένος]. This is Chrysostom's conclusion from the fact that in 1 Corinthians 7, while Paul draws upon himself as the foremost example when speaking in the early part of the chapter about ἐγκράτεια, he does not do so in the latter part of the chapter (7:25f.) when discussing virgins, παρθένοι. The only explanation Chrysostom can summon for this anomaly is that Paul does not give a command about virgins because "he had not successfully accomplished this."[551] Here Chrysostom is being true to the literal sense of the text, though his conundrum is due to a terminological precision in his historical context that was not matched in Paul's. He has a fixed notion of παρθενία as more than ἀγαμία, entailing a deliberate decision for perpetual virginity accompanied by a vow. John makes these concessions briefly in passing, and they seem not to tarnish Paul's ἐγκράτεια in his eyes.[552]

Characteristic of monastic piety also is ἀκτημοσύνη, lack of possessions, which "makes one near to heaven."[553] Poverty [πενία] is "a calm harbor, a wrestling-school and gymnasium for philosophy, an imitation of the angelic life" [λιμὴν εὔδιος, παλαίστρα καὶ γυμνάσιον φιλοσοφίας, ἀγγελικοῦ βίου μίμημα].[554] Paul's own letters give ample testimony of his frugal and abstemious lifestyle. In 2 Cor 6:10 Paul described himself as having met Chrysostom's monastic ideal: ὡς πτωχοὶ

---

stonings to death and drownings, and every form of torment" [καὶ μετὰ τῶν Χερουβὶμ ἑστὼς ἄνω καὶ τῆς μυστικῆς ἐκείνης μελῳδίας αὐτοῖς κοινωνῶν, τὰ μὲν ἄλλα πάντα ῥαδίως ἔφερεν, ὡς ἐν ἀλλοτρίῳ πάσχων σώματι, καὶ δεσμωτήρια καὶ ἁλύσεις καὶ ἀπαγωγὰς καὶ μάστιγας καὶ ἀπειλὰς καὶ θάνατον καὶ τὸ καταλεύεσθαι καὶ τὸ καταποντίζεσθαι καὶ πᾶν κολάσεως εἶδος] [SC 13.204–206]).

[550] "The one who varies his argument and presents a mix of appeals, with more stress on the easy than the difficult, hides the encumbrance of the matter, and by giving the hearer some rest, thus persuades and influences the hearer even more, which is just what the blessed Paul did" (virg. 27.3 [SC 125.180]).

[551] οὐ γὰρ αὐτῷ τὸ πρᾶγμα κατώρθωτο (virg. 41.6 [SC 125.242]; see also 41.9 [SC 125.244]: διὰ τὸ τῆς ἀρετῆς ταύτης γεγονέναι ἐκτός, and the note by Bernard Grillet on p. 242, n. 3 on traditions in the early church that Paul was a widow, which Chrysostom does not appear to follow [see also below, pp. 361–62 on the topic εὐτεκνία]). Chrysostom places Peter in the same category as Paul (both exemplars of ἐγκράτεια), whereas John the Baptist, Elijah, Elisha and, interestingly, John the evangelist, are virgins, lovers of παρθενία (virg. 79.1; 82.1 [SC 125.376, 382]).

[552] Another reason is, of course, that the noun παρθένος is mostly used for women; male "virgins" are called solitaries, μοναχοί or ἀσκηταί/ἀσκητικοί. But Chrysostom can call Elijah and John the Baptist παρθένοι (virg. 82.1 [SC 125.382]; in 79.1 they were called οὗτοι οἱ γνήσιοι τῆς παρθενίας ἐρασταί [SC 125.376]).

[553] ἀκτημοσύνη δὲ ἐγγὺς εἶναι ποιεῖ τῶν οὐρανῶν (virg. 80.2 [SC 125.380]). For general discussion of this monastic practice, with further references, see auf der Maur, Mönchtum, 95–97.

[554] hom. in Mt. 90.1 [58.791].

πολλοὺς δὲ πλουτίζοντες, ὡς μηδὲν ἔχοντες καὶ πάντα κατέχοντες.[555] Such "divine paradoxes" [τοῦ θεοῦ παράδοξα] about wealth — that the rich person is most poor and the poor person most rich — which Paul applied to Christian ministry in 2 Corinthians, become incessant mantras in Chrysostom's exhortations.[556] And Paul was himself such a poor man, as John describes him.[557] He had no material goods [τὰ βιωτικά], but possessed all the spiritual blessings [τὰ πνευματικά], such as the unspeakable words of 2 Cor 12:4 that he received on his heavenly journey.[558] He gave away all that he owned, and even some things which were not his![559] His sole possession was his body, which he used to provide revenue for those in need through his labors.[560] And Paul himself was a teacher of simple financial self-sufficiency (Phil 4:11–12; 1 Tim 6:6), and warnings about the lure of wealth to others.[561] Chrysostom is famous for his fervent denunciations of wealth and championing of the poor, which appear more frequently than any other theme in his exhortations.[562] He constantly extols the monks for living a simple and un-

---

[555] This is such a key facet of Paul's identity for Chrysostom that he turns it into an epithet: ὁ μηδὲν ἔχων καὶ πάντα κεκτησμένος (*Laz.* 6.9 [48.1041]). For the use of this descriptive phrase for monks and virgins, see, e.g., *oppugn.* 2.7 [47.342], τὸ μηδὲν ἔχειν, and *virg.* 81 [SC 125.380]: ὁ γὰρ μηδὲν ἔχων ὡς πάντα κατέχων.

[556] ὁ δὲ μηδὲν ἔχων, τὰ πάντα κέκτηται (*hom. in 2 Cor.* 12.4 [61.486], preceded by its opposite, ὁ γὰρ πολλὰ κατέχων, οὐδὲν ἔχει). See also, for example, *hom. in 1 Tim.* 11.2 [62.555–56]; *hom. in Phil.* 2.1 [62.196]: Οὐκ ἔστιν, οὐκ ἔστι πένης ὁ μηδὲν ἔχων, ἀλλ' ὁ πολλῶν ἐπιθυμῶν· οὐκ ἔστι πλούσιος ὁ πολλὰ κεκτημένος, ἀλλ' ὁ μηδενὸς δεόμενος.

[557] He was πτωχός (*hom. in 1 Cor.* 11.1 [61.89]; *laud. Paul.* 4.13 [SC 300.212]), or πένης (*stat.* 5.2 [49.71]; *laud. Paul.* 4.13; 5.1 [SC 300.210, 230]; *hom. in 2 Tim.* 4.3 [62.622]). In *compunct.* 1 7 [47.405], John stresses that Paul κατεφρόνει τῆς ἐνθάδε πενίας. See the further discussion of Paul's poverty below, pp. 357–60.

[558] *hom. in 2 Cor.* 12.4 [61.486].

[559] Like the list of things in Rom 8:38–39, including "things present, and things to come, and the height and the depth and another creation" (*laud. Paul.* 7.3 [SC 300.298]).

[560] *laud. Paul.* 1.11 [SC 300.130].

[561] 1 Thess 2:9; 4:11–12; 1 Cor 4:12; 9:4–18; Phil 4:11–12; and esp. 1 Tim 6:6–19; cf. Acts 20:34. Chrysostom quotes the Stoic *topos* of 1 Tim 6:7 to his friend Theodore (*Thdr.* 2 5 [SC 117.68]).

[562] I have discussed this important topic in a forthcoming essay, "Silver Chamber Pots and Other Goods Which are Not Good: John Chrysostom's Discourse on Wealth and Possessions." The literature on Chrysostom's understanding of wealth and poverty is quite extensive. See Barry Gordon, "The Problem of Scarcity and the Christian Fathers: John Chrysostom and Some Contemporaries," *Studia Patristica* 22, ed. E. A. Livingstone (Louvain: Peeters, 1989) 108–20; Dolores Greeley, R.S.M., "St. John Chrysostom, Prophet of Social Justice," *Studia Patristica* 17/3, ed. E. A. Livingstone (Oxford/New York: Pergamon Press, 1982) 1163–68; Manfred Kertsch, *Exempla Chrysostomica: Zu Exegese, Stil und Bildersprache bei Johannes Chrysostomos* (Grazer Theologische Studien 18; Graz: Institut für ökumenische Theologie und Patrologie an der Universität Graz, 1995), esp. ch. 2: "Johannes Chrysostomus und die 'Nichtigkeit irdischer Wertvorstellungen'"; Blake Leyerle, "John Chrysostom on Almsgiving and the Use of Money," *HTR* 87 (1994) 29–47; Otto Plassmann, *Das Almosen bei Johannes Chrysostomus* (Münster: Aschendorff, 1961); Adolf Martin Ritter, "John Chrysostom as an Interpreter of Pauline Social Ethics," *Paul and the Legacies of Paul*, ed. W.S. Babcock (Dallas: Southern Methodist University Press, 1990) 183–99, with notes on pp. 360–69; idem, "Between 'Theocracy' and 'Simple Life': Dio Chry-

luxurious lifestyle, which is to be recommended not only for its saintly inattention to the allures of this world, but also for its solidarity with the poor,[563] and he often includes as further incentive to a simple lifestyle some practical arguments for its positive impact on health.[564] John regards Paul has having both lived and taught this monastic discipline consistently throughout his life, even as in all his letters he exhibited the concern for the poor characteristic of his commitment for the poor in Jerusalem (Gal 2:10). Consequently, John portrayed Paul as simultaneously a destitute man *and* the patron and caregiver of the poor.[565]

But once again Chrysostom argued that Paul even exceeded the ἀκτημοσύνη of the monks in his attitude and actions toward worldly goods. When discussing Paul's speech to the Ephesians in Acts 20:33–35, John argues that Paul's refusal to accept his rightful pay brings him to the highest level of excellence with regard to property.

> For this is greater than voluntary poverty [τοῦτο δὲ καὶ ἀκτημοσύνης μεῖζον]. For if in the gospel Jesus says, "sell your belongings, if you wish to be perfect" (Mt 19:21), when Paul, while receiving nothing, even nourishes others, what is the equal of that? It is one degree [of virtue] to dispense one's belongings, a second sufficiently to supply one's own needs, a third, to supply others', and a fourth for the one who preaches and has the authority to receive payment not to receive it (1 Cor 9). Therefore Paul was much better than those without possessions [ὥστε πολὺ τῶν ἀκτημόνων οὗτος βελτίων ἦν].[566]

Paul's abject poverty extended even to constant hunger, as elements of the *peristasis* catalogues also show (2 Cor 6:5; 11:27). Paul's famishing can serve two different functions: either to prove the depth of Paul's indigence to the point of starvation,[567] or to demonstrate his extreme monastic piety as expressed in voluntary fasting (the fact that 2 Cor 11:27 includes both ἐν λιμῷ καὶ δίψει and ἐν νηστείαις πολλάκις allows nicely for both interpretations, as does the mention of Paul and Barnabas fasting in Acts 14:23). Paul's fasting even outdid John the Baptist's severe desert menu, not even providing the apostle with necessary daily nourishment;[568] he did not fast, but starve.[569] Chrysostom was himself an inveterate faster, from his

---

sostom, John Chrysostom and the Problem of Humanizing Society," *Studia Patristica* 22, ed. E. A. Livingstone (Louvain: Peeters, 1989) 170–80; Arnold Stötzel, *Kirche als "neue Gesellschaft": Die humanisierende Wirkung des Christentums nach Johannes Chrysostomus* (Münster: Aschendorff, 1984).

[563] In *oppugn.* 2.5 [47.338] Chrysostom reshuffles the social deck, as he is wont to do, employing the famous "Stoic paradoxes," such as that derided by Plutarch in *Mor.* 1068B, of calling the rich poor and the poor rich.

[564] See, e.g., *virg.* 69.1–2; 70.1–2 [SC 125.342–46]. This is a ubiquitous theme in Chrysostom's writings. He loves to describe at length the results of over-indulgence in flabbiness, flatulence and loss of vigor to the body.

[565] ὁ ἀληθῶς προστάτης καὶ κηδεμὼν τῶν ἐν πενίᾳ ζώντων Παῦλος (*eleem.* 1 [51.261]).

[566] *hom. in Ac.* 45.2 [60.316].

[567] *hom. in Mt.* 90.4 [58.792]; *laud. Paul.* 1.12 [SC 300.130], ὁ λιμὸς ὁ διηνεκής.

[568] *laud. Paul.* 1.14 [SC 300.136]: οὐδὲ τῆς ἀναγκαίας εὐπορῶν τροφῆς. Paul exceeded John in the virtue of εὐτέλεια, "thriftiness of economy" (LSJ, 734).

[569] οὐχὶ νηστεύων, ἀλλὰ καὶ λιμώττων (*laud. Paul.* 5.9 [SC 300.248]).

days in monastic retreat to his lifestyle in cosmopolitan Constantinople, where he insisted upon eating alone.[570] And he viewed the biblical saints as having likewise practiced that discipline (for instance, he thinks extreme fasting was the cause of Timothy's stomach problems in 1 Tim 5:23).[571] The art of religious fasting is to go to the farthest possible extremes without incapacitating oneself entirely. Chrysostom was well aware of the dangerous boundary here, as he had wrecked his own health, contracting life-long kidney trouble by enduring frigid temperatures and only minimally eating and sleeping during his two years in the cave. In Paul he found one who was able to go beyond even the usual bodily deprivations to achieve the monastic nirvana: eating almost nothing and still remaining alive. Chrysostom expounds poetically on this paradox at one point by imploringly questioning his monastic mentor:

How then do you live, blessed Paul [Πῶς οὖν ζῇς, ὦ μακάριε Παῦλε;]? Do you not see the sun? Do you not breathe the common air? Are you not nourished by the same food as everyone else [οὐχὶ ταύταις ταῖς ἁπάντων τρέφῃ τροφαῖς;]? Don't you walk on the earth, like we do? Don't you need sleep [οὐχὶ ὕπνου δέῃ;]? Or clothes? Or sandals? … What are you saying, "I do not live" [οὐ ζῶ] (Gal 2:20)? How do you not live [Πῶς οὐ ζῇς]? … For the one who does not desire the present life, how does he live it [ὁ μὴ ἐπιθυμῶν τῆς παρούσης ζωῆς, πῶς ταύτην ζῇ]? The one who hastens to another [ὁ πρὸς ἑτέραν σπεύδων], how does he live it? The one who has contempt for death [ὁ θανάτου καταφρονῶν], how does he live it? The one who desires nothing here [ὁ μηδενὸς τῶν ἐνταῦθα ἐπιθυμῶν], how does he live it? … The one who to such a degree does nothing for daily food [Οὕτως ὁ μηδὲν διὰ τροφὴν ποιῶν], nothing for clothing, nothing for any present matter, how does he live? He doesn't even live the natural life [Οὗτος οὐδὲ τὴν φυσικὴν ζωὴν ζῇ]. The one who has not even a single care for worldly things does not live [ὁ μηδενὸς φροντίζων τῶν βιωτικῶν, οὐ ζῇ].[572]

Perhaps partly what is given expression here is Chrysostom's own sense of inferiority in ascetic discipline before the incomparably self-denying Pauline portrait he has drawn, with the help of Gal 2:20.[573] Paul is a monk, but a monk on spiritual steroids, so to speak, in John's eyes, a man so divorced from consumption of earthly commodities as to be virtually dead.

The same can be said of the spiritual discipline of κατάνυξις, compunction, whereby one in a spirit of humility and repentance takes stock of one's actions and attitudes, makes a commitment for renewal and change, and prays for divine assistance.[574] Compunction is necessary because the requirements of the Christian life

---

[570] As reported by Chrysostom's biographer, Palladios, who mentions this in order to refute suspicions and accusations which have arisen against John because of it (*v. Chrys.* 12.1–352 [SC 341.230–60]). Palladios invokes in John's defense the example of Paul (12.270–302 [SC 341.254–56]). For Chrysostom's attitude toward fasting, see *serm. in Gen.* 6.1 [54.604]: φιλῶ μὲν τὴν νηστείαν, ὅτι μήτηρ σωφροσύνης ἐστιν, καὶ πηγὴ φιλοσοφίας.

[571] *hom. in 1 Tim.* 16.1 [62.587]; also *stat.* 1.3 [49.19].

[572] *hom. in Phil.* 3.2 [62.200–201].

[573] And other passages, such as Gal 6:14; Rom 6:11, 13; 8:10; Phil 1:23; Col 3:5.

[574] "Cette dernière vertu ne se confond pas avec la pénitence, qui n'en est qu'un des aspects. C'est la prise de conscience de la déficience due au péché et donc de la nécessité de pratiquer une

for ethical acts *and* dispositions, as called for in the Sermon on the Mount, for instance, are so demanding that one is constantly in a state of imperfection with regard to one or more of them.[575] But the virtue of κατάνυξις is so mighty that not even a heap of foolish desires can withstand it. Paul was himself possessed by the very good desire of compunction.[576] However, in claiming Paul's excellence in this monastic discipline, Chrysostom has also posed for himself a somewhat awkward problem, given his assumption that Paul committed no post-baptismal sins for which penitence and recompense were necessary. But once again Chrysostom makes a virtue of rhetorical necessity, by depicting Paul as thoroughly and abundantly self-humbling – though always in relation to his *pre-Christian sins* of persecuting the church. Paul always brings forward these egregious faults freely, without regard for his status or reputation, thereby trumpeting his failures in a completely self-castigating way.

> For since he had washed away all his former sins through his baptism, and after that lived so purely that he was not conscious of any infraction in himself, and he did not have sins to groan about, he makes mention of the pre-baptismal sins that had been completely erased.[577]

Verses such as 1 Tim 1:12–16; Gal 1:13; and 1 Cor 15:9 provide John with a ready bulk of material to establish Paul's contrition, self-searching, and humble demeanor, and still retain his spotless post-baptismal record. Consequently, in both respects Paul proves far superior to all earthly competitors in the quest for genuine contrition. John also regards Paul as both a human example and a wise guide concerning the interrelatedness of these ascetic disciplines in the life of faithfulness: virginity can "wither the root" of avarice; fasting and sleepless nights aid continence;[578] compunction ward off the lure of luxury.[579] In addition to these are some constant preoccupations of the monastic routine, such as manual labor, scripture study, and constant prayer,[580] which, according to John, were all distinguishing marks of Paul's life, as well.[581]

---

ascèse indispensable pour demeurer ferme dans la lutte, associée à une vie de prière intense pour bénéficier du secours d'En-Haut" (Leroux, "Monachisme," 154).

[575] Chrysostom develops this theme in relation to the antitheses of the Sermon on the Mount and the Lord's Prayer in *compunct. 1* 2–5 [47.395–402].

[576] *compunct. 1* 7 [47.404]: αὐτὸς ὁ κατασχεθεὶς τῇ ἐπιθυμίᾳ ταύτῃ τῇ καλῇ (sc. κατανύξει).

[577] *compunct. 2* 6 [47.421]: Ἐπειδὴ γὰρ τὰ πρότερα ἀπενίψατο πάντα διὰ τοῦ βαπτίσματος, καὶ μετὰ ταῦτα ἐβίου καθαρῶς, οὕτως ὡς μηδὲν ἑαυτῷ συνειδέναι, καὶ οὐκ εἶχεν ὑπὲρ ὧν στενάξειεν ἁμαρτημάτων, τῶν πρὸ τοῦ βαπτίσματος ἐξηλειμμένων ἐμέμνητο. See also *hom. in Gen.* 31.2 [53.285]: "do you see the contrite soul which always carries around a remembrance of the sins he committed before his baptism?"

[578] *virg.* 27.2; 81.1 [SC 125.178, 380–82].

[579] They are as incompatible as fire and water (*compunct. 1* 7 [47.404]).

[580] See the description of a monk's life in *comp.* 1–3 [47.387–390].

[581] On these elements of the monastic life, see Leroux, "Monachisme," 156–57. For Paul, see the treatment above in this chapter on his work (pp. 246–48). In terms of Scripture study as characteristic of Paul's life, see *hom. in 1 Tim.* 13.1 [62.565–66], quoted above in relation to Laws

We have seen that, as John draws him, Paul outdid the monks in relation to all three major monastic practices: chastity, voluntary poverty, and compunction. But where the σύγκρισις between the lifestyles of Paul and the monks comes into its most stark contrast is in the arena where the apostle chose to carry out his calling. Here the symbiosis at work in John's images of Paul comes most overtly into play, for Chrysostom understood the fundamental choice of his own life – in entering solitary life but then leaving it to return to minister in the city[582] – in a thoroughly Pauline mode. He resonated deeply with the Pauline internal dialogue of Phil 1:21–26, a tight encapsulation of the tension between πόλις and ἔρημος, or κόσμος and οὐρανός, as the fitting venue for the life of piety. Chrysostom viewed himself as having reluctantly reentered the world to carry out the tasks the gospel set before him, just as Paul had not remained in Arabia, but set out to bring the kerygma to all the urban centers of the empire.

Do you see how much he stood apart from the world, how though walking on the earth he rushed up to the very height of heaven? For don't talk to me about mountaintop pinnacles, nor glens, nor ravines, nor the inaccessible desert. For these things [types of monastic

---

(p. 249). Paul's constant devotion to prayer, for his churches (Rom 1:10; 1 Thess 1:2; 2 Cor 13:7, 9; Eph 6:18; Phil 1:9), for his enemies (those who persecuted him [1 Cor 4:12], including the Jews [Rom 10:1]), and contemplative prayer of communion with the Lord, is a major part of Chrysostom's imaginings of his beloved Paul. This is illustrated amply in the homilies *laud. Paul.* alone, where it is a constant refrain (see 2.6; 3.3; 5.10; 6.10 [SC 300.152, 166, 248, 282]; see also the place of εὐχόμενος and ἱκετεύων in John's list of Pauline πράξεις in 3.6 [SC 300.172]; also *hom. in Eph.* 3.1 [62.23]).

[582] The reasons for Chrysostom's decision continue to be debated. His biographer Palladios attributed his return to the city after spending two years in the cave to John's ravaged health (regarded by Palladios as an instrument of Christ's providence for the good of the church), which should not be doubted (*v. Chrys.* 5.25–34 [SC 341.110]). But this traditional interpretation need not exclude other factors involved in the decision as well, both in terms of the ecclesiastical politics of Antioch, and John's own spiritual life and development. There is good reason to believe that John left the hermitage both to serve his bishop Melitios, who had recently been restored to his see from exile (with Kelly, *Golden Mouth*, 32–38), and to carry out his ministerial calling as he understood it, where he might have the greatest effect for the salvation of others (Leroux, "Monachisme," 152; Hunter, *Comparison*, 15–17). Kelly, *Golden Mouth*, 34–35, vigorously opposes the latter motivation when interpreted as a repudiation of the monastic life on John's part, on which he is clearly correct. But that fact is not intrinsically incompatible with Chrysostom's having decided that his own calling was elsewhere. John continued to praise monks throughout his career, but did express reservations about the monastic life when it seemed to him too self-absorbed, rather than directed toward others (see also my article, "John Chrysostom," in *The Encyclopedia of Monasticism*, forthcoming). Leroux's conclusion, therefore, in its readiness to bring various motives into play, seems to me the most sensible resolution to this historical quandary: "Jean Chrysostome avait pris conscience de son propre idéal et de la nécessité qui lui incombait d'associer la vie apostolique à la recherche de la perfection personnelle pour réaliser la plénitude de l'idéal évangélique" ("Monachisme," 152). It is quite possible that the example of Paul was crucial to Chrysostom in this regard, though precisely dating his attitudes from later written sources is as precarious as separating motivation from later rationalization (a good instance of this is *compunct.* 2 2 [47.413], quoted below on this page – does it represent John's frame of mind upon reentering the city, or later, or both?).

retreats] are not even sufficient to eradicate a single trouble of the soul. But what is necessary is that flame which Christ lit in the soul of Paul [ἀλλὰ δεῖ τῆς φλογὸς ἐκείνης, ἣν ἀνῆψε μὲν ὁ Χριστὸς ἐν τῇ τοῦ Παύλου ψυχῇ], which that blessed man for his part tended through this spiritual reasoning, and raised to such a great height that, beginning from down below on the earth, it attained to heaven itself, and to the heaven above this, and the one after that. For he was snatched up to the third heaven.[583]

As seen here, Paul's life, though imbued with ascetic disciplines, proved superior to that of monastic recluses; not only did he not retreat from the world,[584] Paul journeyed far and wide. And his involvement in the world paradoxically is what enabled him to travel as far as heaven itself. In his treatise de sacerdotio Chrysostom gives expression to the vocational choice he faced in his own life between the monastic and priestly ministry, and avows, "if someone were to offer me a choice of where I would prefer to shine, either in leadership in the church, or the life of the monks, I would vote for the former a thousand times over."[585] And in that book it is precisely a portrait of Paul as priest that further legitimizes Chrysostom's choice.[586]

Therefore, John sketches Paul as a priest who, like himself, combines all the monastic virtues with a lively engagement with people and the wider world. This model of the "worldly ascetic,"[587] in addition to being a fitting mirror-image of John's own ministerial self-consciousness, is also correspondingly the very model of the Christian piety that John throughout his ministry sought to inculcate among his congregants in Antioch and Constantinople.[588] At the same time, by sculpting

---

[583] compunct. 2 2 [47.413]. The manifest connection between this passage and John's own return to the city from his hermitage was convincingly demonstrated by Hunter, Comparison, 15–17. See also John's argument in sac. 6.2 [SC 272.306] for the superiority of priests over monks, where the latter are depicted as hiding out in the security of the desert instead of carrying out their ministry in the bustle of cities and marketplaces.

[584] This is given expression also in Chrysostom's σύγκρισις of Paul and John the Baptist in laud. Paul. 1.14 [SC 300.136]: Ἀλλ' οὗτος ἐν μέσῃ τῇ οἰκουμένῃ καθάπερ ἐκεῖνος ἐν τῇ ἐρήμῳ διέτριβεν.

[585] εἴ τις αἵρεσίν μοι προὐτίθει, ποῦ μᾶλλον βουλοίμην εὐδοκιμεῖν, ἐν τῇ τῆς Ἐκκλησίας προστασίᾳ ἢ κατὰ τὸν τῶν μοναχῶν βίον, μυρίαις ἂν ψήφοις τὸ πρότερον ἐδεξάμην ἔγωγε (sac. 6.7 [SC 272.326]).

[586] "The blessed Paul has filled out for us the portrait of the excellent priest" [ἡμῖν ὁ μακάριος Παῦλος τὴν τοῦ ἀρίστου ἱερέως ἀνεπλήρωσεν εἰκόνα] (sac. 6.5 [SC 272.322]). This passage is part of an extensive comparison between monks and priests, to the overwhelming favor of the latter, in sac. 6.2–7 [SC 272.306–330]. For example, drawing upon imagery we have been discussing, in sac. 6.6 [SC 272.324], Chrysostom says that the monk just sits in his calm harbor, whereas the priest really tests his metal and challenges his ἀνδρεία, for he takes his boat out onto the high seas.

[587] To borrow a phrase from the title of Vincent L. Wimbush's book on 1 Corinthians 7 (Paul the Worldly Ascetic: Response to the World and Self-Understanding according to 1 Corinthians 7 [Macon, GA: Mercer University Press, 1987]).

[588] Brown, Body and Society, 303–322. We shall return to this issue, of the role of Pauline portraits in Chrysostom's wider social program, in chap. 7, pp. 401–404. My emphasis here on how Chrysostom's "ascetical exegesis" involved "reading Paul" (i.e., his person, as a quintessential

Paul John is also seeking to fashion monasticism in his own day. Paul becomes for him the model both for the life of the Christian pious in the cities, and for a style of "apostolic" monasticism that is concerned not solely with retreat for self-perfection, but equally with spreading the gospel to the world.[589] In that sense, contemporary monks should imitate Paul not only in disposition and lifestyle, but also in their purpose and mission, and carry his work to completion. The successful and famous precedent of Paul, painted in such vivid verbal terms, allows Chrysostom to claim a large measure of "verisimilitude"[590] for the programs of monastic and lay lifestyle he seeks to inculcate.

But John's portraits of Paul as a monk are not solely depictions of a past ancient worthy whose spiritual athleticism is remembered and admired. Paul's monastic persona extends even beyond the grave, since the canonical Paul, by virtue of his constant epistolary advice for continence and virtue, serves even now as an abbot, a counselor for those seeking to live a life marked by ascetic practices.[591] Throughout the treatise *de virginitate* Chrysostom describes Paul as the most sensitive, knowing and careful of spiritual advisers, who offers those who approach him the most salient advice for attaining the height of virtue, which he always offers with tremendous wisdom, tact, and insight into human nature. Here the epistolary Paul of 1 Corinthians 7 is a man alive, speaking directly to people of John's day[592] who are prayerfully struggling with their sexual urges and life-choices in light of the gospel; he is the "guide" upon whom they can gaze and to whose words they can attend.[593]

---

monk), complements Elizabeth Clark's important study of how patristic authors were "reading Paul" (i.e., the letters) in such a way as to support their ascetical program (*Reading Renunciation: Asceticism and Scripture in Early Christianity* [Princeton: Princeton University Press, 1999] 257–370).

[589] auf der Maur, *Mönchtum*, 105–79 has demonstrated Chrysostom's commitment to uniting monasticism and missionary work, both in terms of this theological framework, and in terms of the programmatic ways in which he employed monks as missionaries in his leadership as bishop (also Leroux, "Monachisme," 182–89). But neither auf der Maur nor Leroux focused on the role of Paul specifically (and not just the apostles in general) in influencing Chrysostom's thinking and expressions of this ideal.

[590] Here I am employing the language Richard Valantasis has used to describe how the practices of a solitary become the world view of the many: "In their repetition, these acts take on the appearance of verisimilitude, they become natural activities for the monk as perceived within the ascetic culture. The verisimilitude points toward the successful creation of a larger frame of reference and of meaning that supports the ascetic manner of living" ("A Theory of the Social Function of Asceticism," in *Asceticism*, ed. Vincent L. Wimbush and Richard Valantasis [New York/ Oxford: Oxford University Press, 1995] 548).

[591] A glimpse of this may be found in *laud. Paul.* 4.20 [SC 300.226]. As Chrysostom is developing a rhetorical hyperbole about Paul's fame being proclaimed by the whole earth, he takes pains to include the desert: "He did not even leave the desert bereft of his benefactions, but filled it especially with the good things he came to bring us from heaven" (on this as an allusion to the monastic life, see Piédagnel, SC 300.227, n. 3).

[592] Yet also to the Corinthians; Chrysostom moves back and forth from historical to contemporary contexts here, as throughout his homilies on Pauline letters (see chap. 7, pp. 389–94 for discussion of this key element of Chrysostom's hermeneutical approach to the Pauline epistles).

[593] See *virg.* 35.2 [SC 125.210], πρὸς τὸν ἡγησάμενον ἰδόντες.

This Paul is not simply a lawgiver of carved-in-stone requirements, but a tender counselor who even now seeks the most palatable and persuasive means to lead Christians to virtue. In *de virginitate* 34 Chrysostom paints with a few strokes two different images for this Paul, the patron and spiritual counselor to today's continent married women and virgins. Each portrait in different ways gives Paul a crucial role within the nexus of the contemporary spiritual life as an ἀγών. First, John depicts Paul as a harbor master who doesn't let the neophyte sailors venture out too far. Paul the seasoned mariner knows the depth and treachery of the ocean waters, so he advises the married women who have temporarily separated themselves from their husbands to "turn around when they get tired and return to the married state."[594] In this vision Paul is the monitor also of marriage, for it is the calm harbor within which those who cannot renounce sex may keep their sexual self-control largely intact and secure from the devil, who roams the high seas like a pirate, waiting to attack women who are all alone, without any companions on their dinghy-journey to continence. Such women are the virgins who by their vow of chastity have given up the right to drop anchor or put into port.[595] While Paul the harbor master can provide refuge for the married woman in the port of her marriage-bed, the virgin requires a different kind of spiritual assistance, which John describes with a completely different metaphor. For her, Paul is not the harbor master, but the gate-keeper of martial law who does not allow the virgin to re-enter the fortification once she has gone out to do battle with the devil, no matter how violent the struggle between him and the virgin becomes.[596] The gates are forever closed to her, and the battle in which she is locked with the devil will have no cessation. As the commander of the outpost, the apostle sends out each virgin as his "noble soldier" [στρατιώτης γενναῖος] for the common war with the devil, protecting the woman by walling her off from the marital state that would defile her vow. This Paul, more than a monk himself, is the monitor of all human monastics for each generation, ready to offer consolation and legislation, by turns, as necessary.[597]

The final point at which the portraits of Paul and the monks and virgins converge is in the consequences, both negative and positive, which result from their

---

[594] Οὐδὲ γὰρ ἀφίησιν αὐτοὺς ὁ μακάριος Παῦλος πορρωτέρω πλεῖν ἀλλ᾽ ὑποστρέφειν ἡνίκα ἂν κάμωσι καὶ παραινεῖ ἐπιτρέπων ἐπὶ τὸ αὐτὸ συνέρχεσθαι (*virg.* 34.1 [SC 125.198–200]), in reference to 1 Cor 7:5).

[595] *virg.* 34.1–2 [SC 125.198–200].

[596] *virg.* 34.1, 3–5 [SC 125.198–202]. This image is in service of Chrysostom's argument that those who choose the married life have taken on themselves a far easier part; but Paul does not allow one to think of the two states as comparable, John insists, by appeal to 1 Cor 7:32.

[597] Chrysostom's unified vision of Paul as monk and monastic advisor through his letters therefore self-consciously is intended to undercut the fact that, already in the earliest Christian generations of the deutero-Paulines, each side of debates about Christian sexual lifestyle "used the apostle Paul to support and justify its claims" (Gasparro, "Asceticism and Anthropology," 127, pp. 131–34 on contrary appeals to 1 Cor 7 in the early church; as proven with much detail by Clark, *Reading Renunciation*, 259–370).

pious lifestyles. In addition to the pain and discomfort of the life of self-negation, "dying daily," Chrysostom knew in his own context that monks could be persecuted for their way of life. In the treatise *adversus oppugnatores vitae monasticae*, written in an early period when his own monastic retreat was fresh in his memory, John directly combatted those who gave trouble to the monks by dragging them into court, attacking them, beating them, and inflicting upon them all types of other punishments.[598] Most interesting for our investigation is the fact that in this context John overtly claims that Paul was persecuted *for the very same charges* as are the monks of his day.

> For this Nero accused the blessed Paul of the very things of which you accuse these holy men [οὗτος ὁ Νέρων τὸν μακάριον Παῦλον … τοιαῦτα ἐγκαλῶν, οἷάπερ ὑμεῖς τοῖς ἁγίοις τούτοις ἀνδράσι] … He accused him of being a spoiler [λυμεών], a deceiver [πλάνος], and the very same things which you are saying [καὶ τὰ αὐτὰ, ἅπερ ὑμεῖς φθέγγεσθε].[599]

United in the same persecution, on the same charges, Paul and the monks share the same earthly fate: imprisonment, binding, death. But these things only appear to be harmful, for Paul and the monks also will share the same eschatological fate: abundant glory in heaven.

Having renounced the cheap, paltry things which this world falsely thinks earn honor,[600] the monks, already shining with their own glory,[601] in the next world will be recompensed ὑπὲρ δόξης.[602] Paul's superiority even to the monks, whose fate he foreshadows, is manifest also in this final respect, since he will become, not just an angel, but a being superior even to them:

> The blessed Paul will stand with great boldness before the very throne of the king, shining brightly, and will be clothed in such glory that it will be inferior to none of the angels and the archangels [καὶ δόξαν ἠμφιεσμένος τοσαύτην, ὡς μηδὲν τῶν ἀγγέλων καὶ τῶν ἀρχαγγέλων ἀποδεῖν], and he will receive the very great reward which is fittingly given to a man who has given over his body and his soul for the things pleasing to God [καὶ τοσοῦτον λήψεται τὸν μισθὸν, ὅσον εἰκὸς ἄνθρωπον σῶμα καὶ τὴν ψυχὴν τῶν τῷ θεῷ δοκούντων ἕνεκεν ἐπιδόντα].[603]

---

[598] *oppugn.* 1.3 [47.325].

[599] *oppugn.* 1.3 [47.323]. For an analysis of this tradition about Paul's death under Nero, see below, pp. 363–74.

[600] auf der Maur, *Mönchtum*, 95.

[601] Chrysostom can, though somewhat rarely, promote the monastic life on the grounds that a monk is even given honors on earthly terms. For instance, when a monk goes into the town people confer respect on him upon seeing his telltale robe (*oppugn.* 2.6, 8 [47.340, 343]). In the monasteries there is one glory, the true glory [μία δόξα ἡ ὄντως δόξα] (*oppugn.* 3.11 [47.366]). But the ultimate glory the monk will receive is in heaven.

[602] See *oppugn.* 2.5 [47.538–39], comparing royal honors in this life with the ultimate heavenly glory to be gained by the solitary life, and *virg.* 49.1; 73.1 [SC 125.274, 350] of the heavenly glories the virgin will inherit.

[603] *oppugn.* 1.4 [47.324].

As the super-monk who excels in all the dispositions and disciplines of the monastic "angelic way of life," Paul serves as both the quintessential model and the source of hope for monks on earth (including his fervent imitator and sculptor, John) that they, too, will share his celestial and eternal reward. And, given that Chrysostom's ultimate goal is the inculcation of monastic virtues in the laity, the same Paul (as well as the monks who stand in his lineage and image) presages the glory which all Christians may one day share.[604]

Πράξεις ἐναντίαι (Contradictory Deeds)?

All encomiasts wish to stress that their subjects were consistent in their deeds, leaving behind a dependable trail of incontrovertible indices of their virtue. This consistency should also include a complete conformity of words and deeds,[605] in order to evidence a sincere heart and a stable, well-integrated (and therefore dependable) personality. In this respect the encomiastic form bears the imprint of the longstanding Greek cultural preoccupation with the concept of variability and its limits, which was famously focused, for instance, on the character of Odysseus, that ἀνὴρ πολύτροπος.[606] Because our focus here is on Chrysostom's portraits of the person of Paul, we shall not delve into the very important and rich topic of how Chrysostom deals exegetically with the consistency or inconsistency of particular Pauline utterances in and among the letters.[607] For the present investigation

---

[604] "For if imitating that saint were impossible, he would not have cried out, saying, 'Be imitators of me, just as also I am of Christ.' Hence, let us not only admire him, nor just be amazed at him, but let us also imitate him, so that after we depart from this life we might be found worthy to see him, and share in his indescribable glory" [Οὐδὲ γὰρ ἄν, εἴπερ ἀδύνατον ἦν τοῦτο (sc. ζηλῶσαι τὸν ἅγιον ἐκεῖνον), ἐβόα λέγων· Μιμηταί μου γίνεσθε, καθὼς κἀγὼ Χριστοῦ. Μὴ τοίνυν θαυμάζωμεν αὐτὸν μόνον, μηδὲ ἐκπληττώμεθα μόνον, ἀλλὰ καὶ μιμώμεθα, ἵνα καταξιωθῶμεν καὶ ἐντεῦθεν ἀπελθόντες αὐτὸν ἰδεῖν, καὶ τῆς ἀπορρήτου δόξης μετασχεῖν] (hom. in Rom. 32.4 [60.682]).

[605] On the λόγος/ἔργον topos see Hans Dieter Betz, "The Problem of Rhetoric and Theology according to the Apostle Paul," L'Apôtre Paul: personnalité, style et conception du ministère, ed. A. Vanhoye (BETL 73 [1986] 16–48, reprinted in idem, Paulinische Studien: Gesammelte Aufsätze III (Tübingen: J.C.B. Mohr [Paul Siebeck], 1994) 126–62. Chrysostom thought that Paul handed on his "traditions" (per 1 Thess 4:1, for instance) in both words and deeds [Τὸ παρελάβετε, οὐχὶ ῥήματος ἐστι μόνον, ἀλλὰ καὶ πραγμάτων] (hom. in 1 Thess. 5.1 [62.423]). The commonplace nature of this rhetorical appeal is demonstrated by Libanios, Prog. 8.2.9 [Foerster, 8.229], where in an encomium to Odysseus he introduces this rhetorical heading as follows: Ἆρ' οὖν λέγειν μὲν ἱκανός, πράττειν δὲ οὐ τοιοῦτος;

[606] See W. B. Stanford, The Ulysses Theme: A Study in the Adaptability of a Traditional Hero (2nd ed.; Oxford: Blackwell, 1963); Abraham J. Malherbe, "Antisthenes and Odysseus, and Paul at War," HTR 76 (1983) 143–73; and Clarence E. Glad, Paul and Philodemus: Adaptability in Epicurean and Early Christian Psychagogy (NovTSup 81; Leiden: Brill, 1995), esp. 15–52.

[607] I have discussed a few examples in Mitchell, "'A Variable and Many-sorted Man,'" 97–104, but a complete treatment of this important topic is beyond our scope here. Nor can we engage the equally interesting topic of how Chrysostom deals with instances where Pauline statements appear to contradict words of Christ (as, e.g., hom. in Phil. 14.1 [62.281–83]; hom. in Eph. 18.1 [62.122]; hom. in 1 Tim. 8.1 [62.539]).

into how Chrysostom depicts Pauline πράξεις, it will suffice to mention a few cases where Chrysostom encounters variable *deeds* of Paul's, or a variance between a deed and a statement, to show how John defuses possible negative portraits of his hero as having been impossibly inconsistent in his actions. Then we shall see how John once structured an entire, rather ingenious discourse around this conventional topic.

General Treatments

Because consistency in deeds is such a key facet of earned praise, Chrysostom employs a range of apologetic maneuvers in his homilies to exonerate Paul of the charge of inconsistency in regard to such things as: his attitude towards the Mosaic Law (arguing against it but also practicing it), changes in travel plans, and his diverse financial arrangements with different churches (given that he accepted money from the Philippians but refused it from the Corinthians). In such cases John seeks to demonstrate the falsity of the derogatory inference that Paul *was* inconsistent, by using customary rhetorical proofs for defense – including proposing exculpatory historical exigencies for the acts, appealing to Paul's praiseworthy motives, and shifting the blame – all means of preserving the record of Pauline blamelessness.[608] John overtly explains the methodology he employs, which is an exact description of an assumptive defense proof on the grounds of circumstance:[609] "in all such cases, by bringing together the cause [αἰτία], and intention [γνώμη] and time [καιρός] and all the things which speak in defense of what happened [πάντα τὰ ὑπὲρ τῶν γινομένων ἀπολογούμενα], thus let us examine the cases" [τὰ πράγματα ἐξετάζωμεν].[610] By such methods as these Chrysostom protects Paul's laudability against real and imagined attack, both from "pagans" and probably some Christians as well,[611] thus safeguarding the apostle's reputation as a man of sure and sincere purpose. The portrait of Paul as a man of supreme integrity hangs, inde-

---

[608] For the basis of these apologetic strategies in rhetorical theory, see Mitchell, "'A Variable and Many-sorted Man,'" 98–99. The discussion which follows here replicates some parts of that article, pp. 97–104.

[609] See Mitchell, "'A Variable and Many-sorted Man,'" 99, and n. 23 for references to this strategy in rhetorical theory.

[610] *hom. in Rom.* 16.1 [60.549].

[611] Chrysostom surely knew of pagan attacks on Paul's inconsistency. The historically closest would have been Julian's *contra Galilaeos* 106B, which was composed at Antioch (see n. 341) and perhaps the arguments of Manicheans (that they regarded Paul as hopelessly inconsistent can be inferred from Augustine's testimony in *conf.* 7.21.27). The charge that the Scriptures reveal myriad inconsistencies was earlier made by Porphyry, whose *adversus Christianos* was possibly drawn upon by Julian (Schatkin-Harkins, FC 73.18). If Porphyry's work is indeed the source quoted by Macarius Magnes, *apocriticus*, he singled out Paul for detailed excoriation as an impossibly inconsistent, feverish thinker and double-dealing person, one who "waged such a gigantic battle of words with himself" [αὐτὸς καθ᾽ ἑαυτοῦ τοιαύτην γιγαντομαχίαν λόγων καθοπλίσας] (Macarius Magnes, *apocrit.* 3.35 and 36 [text Harnack, TU 37/4, pp. 66, 68]; see Mitchell, "'Variable and Many-sorted Man,'" 93).

structible, over this entire enterprise, as John continually finds ways to keep the anti-portraits of Paul the vacillator or the chameleon from being mounted on the wall, or registered in the memory.

The most difficult case of Pauline πράξεις ἐναντίαι Chrysostom, along with other patristic authors,[612] had to face, was Paul's circumcision of Timothy in Acts 16:3, which appears rather patently to contradict the apostle's teachings in his letters against the circumcision of Gentile converts. In Chrysostom's commentary on Galatians, when he arrives at 5:11, where Paul denies that he preaches circumcision (by arguing that if he were then he would not still be persecuted), John addresses the potential blight on the character of his beloved Paul posed by this piece of damnable counter-evidence in the following way:

> What is this? Did he not preach circumcision? Did he not circumcize Timothy? Yes, he did circumcize him. Well how, then, does he say "I do not preach it?" Now here learn his accurate phrasing [Καὶ ἐνταῦθα αὐτοῦ μάθε τὴν ἀκρίβειαν]. For he did not say, "I do not perform circumcision," but "I do not preach" it [Οὐ γὰρ εἶπεν, ὅτι περιτομὴν οὐκ ἐργάζομαι, ἀλλὰ οὐ κηρύσσω]. That is, I do not command people to believe it. So do not take this as a confirmation for legal precepts. "For I circumcized, but I did not *preach* circumcision" [περιέτεμον μὲν γὰρ, οὐκ ἐκήρυξα δὲ περιτομήν].[613]

In a somewhat similarly exegetically strained manner, Chrysostom constructs several different arguments to account for Paul's apparent change in travel plans to Achaia, as reported in 2 Corinthians 1–2. One way John exonerates Paul of capricious oscillation is by a somewhat contrived textual appeal, which is founded upon his own argument of redefinition of the realm of truly blameworthy inconsistency from words to desires:

> "I was wishing to come …" (2 Cor 1:15). And indeed he promised the opposite [τοὐναντίον] formerly when he said, "And I shall come to you when I pass through Macedonia. For I am going to pass through Macedonia" (1 Cor 16:5). How therefore does he say contradictory things here [Πῶς οὖν ἐνταῦθα τἀναντία φησίν;]? He does not say contradictory things [Οὐ τὰ ἐναντία φησίν]. Certainly not [ἄπαγε]! For these things are contradictory *to what he wrote*, but they are not contradictory *to what he wished* [ταῦτα γὰρ ἐναντία μὲν ἔστιν οἷς

---

[612] For discussion and references see Margaret M. Mitchell, "Pauline Accommodation and 'Condescension' [συγκατάβασις]: 1 Cor 9:19–23 and the History of Influence" (forthcoming), and in Chrysostom's writings especially also *hom. in Ac. princ.* 4.4 [51.102]. One reason this perceived contradiction received sustained treatment is that opponents of Christianity were able to make much of it. See the derisive reaction of the Greek philosophical critic (likely Porphyry) cited by Macarius Magnes: "How then when calling circumcision mutilation (Phil 3:2) does he himself circumcize someone in Lystra, Timothy, as the Acts of the Apostles teaches (16:3)? Look at the extreme stupidity of these words [εὖ γε τῆς ὄντως ὧδε βλακείας τῶν ῥημάτων]! Theatrical productions depict such a scene as a laughable contrivance; such a thing is truly a stage trick of magicians!" [τοιοῦτον θαυματοποιούντων ὄντως τὸ παραπαίγιον] (*apocrit.* 3.30 [Harnack, TU 37/4, p. 58]). Surprisingly, Julian did not invoke Paul's circumcision of Timothy, though it would have served his argument in *Gal.* 351A–356C.

[613] *comm. in Gal.* 5.3 [61.667].

ἔγραψεν, οὐκ ἐναντία δὲ οἷς ἐβούλετο].That is why he did not say here, "I wrote to you that I am going into Macedonia," but "I wished."[614]

As clever as is this line of defense, it does not completely free the apostle of the charge of calumny, for it still calls into question the stability of the man who so readily changed his "will." Anticipating this inference, Chrysostom himself names the shameful consequence of such behavior if it can be proved uncategorically true: that Paul was "airheaded and fickle" [κοῦφος καὶ εὐρίπιστος].[615] But John immediately refutes this negative characterization by claiming that the last-minute change in itinerary was due not to Paul's mercurial will, but to his obedience to divine authority. He says (in the personified voice of Paul himself): "I am not independent of the piloting of the Spirit, nor do I have the authority to go where I wish."[616] By shifting the blame for the alteration in plans to the (irreproachable) Holy Spirit, Chrysostom has in a single stroke rescued Paul from slander and portrayed him as a man faithfully submissive to the Lord's plans.[617]

In the next homily in this exegetical series, however, Chrysostom must deal with the rather different reason Paul himself gave in 2 Cor 1:23 for not coming to Corinth: that he deliberately stayed away because he wished to spare the Corinthians. Noting the discrepancy in that now it is Paul himself who seems to be the agent of the shift in plans,[618] John queries his author directly: "What are you saying, blessed Paul? You didn't come to Corinth because you were sparing them? Then aren't you leading us into something of a contradiction [ἐναντιολογία] here?"[619] By way of his own reply to this question on Paul's behalf, Chrysostom proposes two possible solutions to the dilemma: either the Holy Spirit acted on Paul in such a way as to bring about the change in Paul's will by urging him to be mindful of the need to spare the Corinthians, or (the option Chrysostom favors), the problem can be resolved by the introduction of an historical exigency which allows John to retain both positions: there were *two* visits which were postponed – the first blocked by the Spirit, and the second delayed by Paul's attitude of

---

[614] *hom. in 2 Cor.* 3.2 [61.408].

[615] *hom. in 2 Cor.* 3.3 [61.408].

[616] καὶ οὐκ εἰμὶ τῆς τοῦ Πνεύματος ἐκτὸς κυβερνήσεως, οὐδὲ ἐξουσίαν ἔχω βαδίζειν ὅπου βούλομαι (*hom. in 2 Cor.* 3.3 [61.408]).

[617] In his homily on 2 Cor 11:8–9 Chrysostom explains Paul's inconsistency in accepting financial support from the Macedonian churches, but refusing it from the Corinthians, with a similar two-pronged defense strategy – an appeal to motive, and a shifting of the blame. "Therefore he was doing contradictory things out of love, when he both was receiving support and was not receiving it ["Ὥστε ἐναντία ἐποίει ἀπὸ τοῦ φιλεῖν, καὶ ἐλάμβανε, καὶ οὐκ ἐλάμβανεν]. But the contradiction was due to the disposition of the givers" [ἡ δὲ ἐναντιότης παρὰ τὴν τῶν διδόντων ἕξιν] (*hom. in 2 Cor.* 23.5 [61.559]). By these means John seeks once again to transform a possibly negative portrayal of Paul into a laudatory image of the man governed only by love for his converts.

[618] ἐνταῦθα δὲ σὸν φὴς εἶναι τὸ μὴ ἐλθεῖν, οὐκέτι τῆς τοῦ πνεύματος ἐξουσίας (*hom. in 2 Cor.* 4.1 [61.417]).

[619] *hom. in 2 Cor.* 4.1 [61.417].

clemency toward his wayward church.[620] As he escapes this rhetorical difficulty Chrysostom applauds Paul's genius in doing precisely what the orator has just done on his behalf: "commending himself on account of contradictory deeds."[621]

Laud. Paul. 5: *Praise for Paul as "A Variable and Many-sorted Man"*

John's suggestive observation expressed in the homily series on 2 Corinthians about Paul's own rhetorical strategy of coping with apparently contradictory acts by turning them to his advantage inspires him on one occasion, an oration on Paul's feast day to an audience of believers, to drop his normal defensive strategies, and himself exploit the rhetorical potential of the theme of inconsistency in Pauline πράξεις to address his audience's catechetical and hortatory needs. Because this fascinating speech, the fifth of the festival panegyrics to Paul, is based completely upon presuppositions about the role of *deeds* in evaluating the character of an individual, I have reserved consideration of it for here.

προοίμιον (Introduction). The opening line of the oration casts Chrysostom as a would-be pugilist issuing a challenge to his foes. These adversaries do battle by wielding an ethical excuse: "Where now are those who accuse death, and say that this passible and corruptible body is for them an impediment to virtue?" Chrysostom summons them to attend to his speech which will refute their error: "Let them listen to Paul's virtuous acts and cease from this wicked slander."[622] Once again Chrysostom has found a relatively novel way to inaugurate his speech in praise of Paul by invoking this hypothetical duel over anthropology. But the melody line of the speech is a conglomerate of strains quite familiar from our investigation to this point, as announced in the opening sentences and then made the subject of an extended exordium:[623] Paul's virtuous deeds [κατορθώματα][624] offer the surest

---

[620] *hom. in 2 Cor.* 4.1 [61.417].

[621] "Perceive here again how he has made mention of himself – about which I shall not stop continually speaking! – in order to commend himself on account of contradictory deeds" [Σὺ δέ μοι σκόπει πῶς πάλιν ἑαυτοῦ μέμνηται, ὃ συνεχῶς λέγειν οὐ παύσομαι, ἀπὸ τῶν ἐναντίων ἑαυτῷ συνιστάμενος] (*hom. in 2 Cor.* 4.1 [61.417]).

[622] *laud. Paul.* 5.1 [SC 300.230].

[623] The exordium of the speech appears to extend from 5.1 to the end of 5.3. In this judgment I am in slight disagreement with Piédagnel, SC 300.25 n. 6, who says the introduction ends at 5.3, line 13, but that oddly posits a structural break in the middle of a continuous grammatical construction formed by a relative clause. Piédagnel argues that the theme of this discourse is οἰκονομία, but that term doesn't appear prominently in either the προοίμιον or ἐπίλογος to the speech. The concept is important, however, as it constitutes the steady motivation lying behind all the divine and Pauline πράξεις: accommodation to exigencies for the salvation of all (see *laud. Paul.* 5.5 [SC 300.240, of God]; and 5.3; 5.8 [SC 300.236, 246, of Paul]). Although not the central theme of the oration itself, it is an important motif in the argument.

[624] Ἀκουσάτωσαν τῶν Παύλου κατορθωμάτων (*laud. Paul.* 5.1 [SC 300.230]; also in 5.10 and 5.15 [250, 254]). This is an exact description of what one expects in a panegyric – a recital of "virtuous deeds."

proof that for human beings there exists no insurmountable obstacle to virtue [ἀρετή].⁶²⁵ Paul suffered no hindrance [κωλῦον]⁶²⁶ to virtuous living; in fact, he demonstrated by his remarkable deeds that where there is a zealous will to act [προθυμία, ζῆλος]⁶²⁷ and the proper exercise of free will [προαίρεσις],⁶²⁸ unlimited virtue is possible.

Before entering into the full proof for this oft-repeated assertion, Chrysostom first seeks to dismantle two possible counter-contentions, in the quest of which he sharpens this conventional thesis in a novel direction.⁶²⁹ First, he attempts to refute all proposals his congregation might offer for things that do indeed obstruct people's exercise of virtue. Against those who complain that a finite nature prohibits good behavior, John emphasizes that Paul, too, was mortal [θνητός], and possessed of a body with its usual needs. Furthermore, instead of thwarting his goodness, Paul's mortality made it possible for him all the more to speak and to act out the daily dying for Christ (as a citation of 1 Cor 15:31 verifies). This is the first appearance of a key theme of the discourse: the relationship between deeds [ἔργα, πράξεις, κατορθώματα] and words [λόγοι]. In this man they stand in such perfect coordination that Paul "was able to demonstrate what he said through his deeds" [ἐπιδείξασθαι ἐδυνήθη ὃ διὰ τῶν ἔργων εἶπεν].⁶³⁰ A second hindrance to virtue one might propose comes from the "conventional wisdom" enshrined in the encomiastic form. Surely a lack of advantages in external circumstances, such as trade, wealth, family, or power can act as a detriment to the cultivation of virtue, can it not? To this objection Chrysostom responds with two exempla, one positive and the other negative. Not surprisingly, Paul is John's choice for the former: the apostle was not in the least hindered by being "unskilled, poor and earning his bread from daily labor" [ἰδιώτης, πένης, ἐκ τῆς καθ᾽ ἑκάστην ἡμέραν ἐργασίας ποιούμενος τὴν τροφήν]. This lack of influence of external circumstances has a correlate also among non-Christians [οἱ ἔξωθεν] who, though possessing the "opposite qualities" [τὰ ἐναντία] – rhetorical skill [λόγων δεινότης], abundant riches [χρημάτων πλῆθος], renowned ancestry [περιφάνεια γένους], fine reputation [δόξης μέγεθος], and being in a position of power [τὸ ἐν δυναστείᾳ εἶναι] – have received no benefit from any of these procurements when it comes to what matters most: virtue.⁶³¹ Once these counter-options have been refuted, only one alternative

---

⁶²⁵ This is a favored theme of John's; see also, e.g., *hom. in Mt.* 8.5; 61.3 [57.90, 592].

⁶²⁶ Words from this stem [κωλυ-] abound in the discourse (*laud. Paul.* 5.1, lines 12, 16, 20; 5.2; 5.16 [SC 300.230–32; 232; 256]).

⁶²⁷ The terms alternate freely with one another in this speech, but προθυμία is the most frequent (*laud. Paul.* 5.1; 5.3, lines 2, 3, 17 [SC 300.230, 234]). ζῆλος substitutes for προθυμία (as a stylistic variation) in 5.3 [SC 300.234].

⁶²⁸ *laud. Paul.* 5.3 [SC 300.234].

⁶²⁹ Up to this point the discourse has sounded like a repeat of *laud. Paul.* 2 (analyzed in chap. 5, pp. 152–59), but in §4 a new focus will emerge from the early examples Chrysostom has chosen.

⁶³⁰ *laud. Paul.* 5.1 [SC 300.230].

⁶³¹ *laud. Paul.* 5.1 [SC 300.230–32]; cf. *laud. Paul.* 4.13, 19 [SC 300.210–12, 224–26].

remains, as Chrysostom states with conviction: "this alone is a hindrance to virtue – wickedness of soul and weakness of purpose" [Τοῦτο γὰρ γίνεται κώλυμα μόνον πρὸς ἀρετήν, κακία ψυχῆς καὶ μαλακία γνώμης]. After a brief hyperbolic trip to heaven (in which he shows that even the non-corporeal nature of super terrestrial beings doesn't elevate them above Paul and the requirements of virtue), Chrysostom repeats his strict governing dichotomy: there is only one thing to mourn over, and that is evil [κακία], only one thing in which to rejoice, virtue [ἀρετή]. "If we are zealous for virtue, there is nothing to hinder us from becoming like Paul" [Ἐὰν ταύτην ζηλώσωμεν, οὐδὲν τὸ κωλῦον γενέσθαι κατὰ Παῦλον].[632]

But to this optimistic scenario as well there is a counter-argument that must be addressed, one we have seen preoccupying Chrysostom before: didn't Paul receive his power for good deeds from God, in which case not having that power would surely be a hindrance to all the rest who are trying to emulate Paul? John addresses this objection, already on everyone's mind, with a direct rebuttal: "For he did not become such as he was from grace alone, but also from his own fervent will" [Ἐκεῖνος γὰρ οὐχὶ ἀπὸ τῆς χάριτος μόνον τοιοῦτος ἐγένετο, ἀλλὰ καὶ ἀπὸ τῆς οἰκείας προθυμίας].[633] Chrysostom's exhortatory purpose influences his theology here, as he insinuates that God's grace was also responsible for Paul's extraordinary desire to do what is right.[634] But mostly John insists on balanced excellence from two independent sources: "He had both sets of qualities abundantly, the things of God [τὰ τοῦ θεοῦ] breathed into him, *and* those he possessed from his own free will [τὰ τῆς οἰκείας προαιρέσεως]."[635] When hearing "the things of God," what immediately comes to mind is the miraculous power of Paul's garments to frighten demons (Acts 19:12), but Chrysostom argues that even more marvelous is the fact that *before* this gift of grace [πρὸ τῆς χάριτος], indeed "from the starting gate" [ἀπὸ βαλβῖδος], Paul displayed tremendous zeal for Christ. This zeal, applied in vigorous evangelizing proclamation, provoked such opposition that Paul was forced go over the wall in flight from Damascus (2 Cor 11:31–33; cf. Acts 9:24–25); but even this close call instilled in him neither cowardice nor fear, but instead only magnified his προθυμία.[636] Paul's intensity even in the face of horrifying danger

---

[632]   *laud. Paul.* 5.2 [SC 300.232].

[633]   *laud. Paul.* 5.3 [SC 300.234].

[634]   That Chrysostom believes χάρις is in some sense implicated in προθυμία is suggested by the next sentence: "And this is why it was from grace, since it was also from his will" [καὶ διὰ τοῦτο ἀπὸ τῆς χάριτος, ἐπειδὴ καὶ ἀπὸ τῆς προθυμίας], but he does not engage the issue in any systematic way. He says virtually the same thing in parallel form in *laud. Paul.* 7.3 [SC 300.300]: "From what source, therefore, was he such as he was? Both from his own nature and from God; and for this reason it was from God, since it was from his own nature" [Πόθεν οὖν τοιοῦτος ἦν; Καὶ οἴκοθεν, καὶ παρὰ θεοῦ, καὶ διὰ τοῦτο παρὰ θεοῦ, ἐπειδὴ οἴκοθεν]; compare the translation of Piédagnel, SC 300.301: "et si elle venait de Dieu, c'est en même temps parce qu'elle venait de lui." In suggestive lines like these one can see why the Pelagians so quickly became enamored of these discourses (see chap. 1, n. 24, and further discussion in chap. 8, pp. 421–23).

[635]   *laud. Paul.* 5.3 [SC 300.234].

[636]   *laud. Paul.* 5.3 [SC 300.234]; cf. 7.4–7 [SC 300.300–308].

("the Jews … desired to taste of his very flesh") was exemplified in the fact that his zeal in loving life for its potential gains matched his active disdain for it.[637] But how can the same man hold two such contradictory positions? Pauline προθυμία has led Chrysostom to a crux about Pauline πράξεις.

πρόθεσις (Proposition). John responds to this quandary with a bold, entirely un-anticipated exclamation that will be the focal point of the entire proof: "As I always say about him, and never shall stop saying, no one falling into contradictory actions has practiced both so accurately" [οὐδεὶς οὕτως εἰς ἐναντία πράγματα ἐμπεσών, ἑκάτερα πρὸς ἀκρίβειαν ἤσκησεν].[638] With the introduction of this proposition, the discourse takes a fresh tack, and departs from a rather well-worn path, for now Chrysostom will seek to secure praise for Paul in what both encomiastic conven-tion and current psychology considered a cause for immediate condemnation – serial inconsistency.[639] One can imagine that Chrysostom woke a few members of his audience from their commonplace-induced sleep with this unexpected turn, especially given the self-parody of its introduction [ὅπερ γὰρ ἀεὶ λέγω περὶ αὐτοῦ], from the man who more often than not was in the business of demonstrating against detractors that Paul was *not* inconsistent![640] So now orator and audience are poised, waiting to see Chrysostom accomplish the impossible: confer praise upon Paul for being "a variable and many-sorted man" [ποικίλος τις ἦν καὶ παντοδαπός].[641]

---

[637] This is John's reflection on Paul's ruminations in Phil 1:21–26, a passage to which he turns quite frequently.

[638] *laud. Paul.* 5.4 [SC 300.236].

[639] Hubbell, "Chrysostom and Rhetoric," 271 is on the right track, but has missed the funda-mental irony at work here: "The main part of the encomium is taken up with an explanation of certain inconsistencies in Paul's career. It is one of the principles insisted on by all rhetoricians that faults should not be mentioned in an encomium, or if they must be mentioned, it should be done without calling attention to them, in order that the encomium may not be turned into an apology. *Following this principle* Chrysostom expands the idea of Paul's zeal for the salvation of the world, leading from that to the thought that in order to accomplish his purpose it was necessary for him to be inconsistent" (emphasis added). Surely Chrysostom is here not "following the principle" of leaving faults to the side and not calling attention to them! Instead, he intentionally brings these faults, especially the general practice of inconsistency in deeds, right into the middle, and dares himself and his congregation to find a way to praise Paul precisely *for* them. Hence the rhetorical strategy at work here is more complex, especially in its relations to rhetorical expectations, than Hubbell has described it.

[640] See Mitchell, "'Variable and Many-sorted Man,'" 97–104. To cite a particularly apt exam-ple, note the precisely inverse proposition Chrysostom defends in *hom. in 2 Cor.* 21.4 [61.545]: Οὐ γὰρ ποικίλος τις ἦν. Here again we note the interwoven identities of John and Paul – even as he defends Paul against unscrupulous inconsistency John ironically argues for *his own consistency* in his representations of the apostle.

[641] *laud. Paul.* 5.4 [SC 300.238].

πίστεις (Proofs). The proof section of this oration falls into roughly two parts: 1) an explication of a range of Pauline ἐναντία πράγματα ("inconsistent acts") as justified through the use of two extended συγκρίσεις; and 2) an amplified defense of two of Paul's actions which appear contradictory to other behaviors, as well as seemingly inherently wrong – boasting in oneself and insulting others.[642]

Proof #1: Paul's Contradictory Actions are Proof of his Virtue.[643] Since Chrysostom phrased his proposition in such a way as to elevate Paul over all contenders in his variability, he continues in this manner as he invokes a classic instance of Pauline inconsistency: no one desired the present life as much as he, and no one so thoroughly disdained it (Phil 1:21–26). Each contention itself receives substantiation from a comparison: he loved life even more than those with a passionate love for their lives; he despised it even more than those dying the worst death. Hence, once Paul thought living to be more of a necessity than dying and being with Christ (Phil 1:24), but at another time he described living as arduous and burdensome, and groaned to be released from it (Phil 1:23; 2 Cor 5:4).[644] But in all cases Paul's desire [ἐπιθυμία][645] was uniform: "he desired only those things that would bring him godly gain, even if they happened to be contradictory to what he had done before" [Ἐκείνων γὰρ ἐπιθυμεῖ μόνον, τῶν κατὰ θεὸν κέρδος αὐτῷ φερόντων, εἰ καὶ ἐναντία ταῦτα εἶναι συνέβαινε τοῖς προτέροις].[646] Consequently, Paul's variability was a principled one, because of its unified and praiseworthy motive: "he became all things [πάντα γινόμενος][647] that were required for the needs of the gospel and the salvation of humanity." This philanthropic motive refutes any charge that Paul's contradictory behavior constituted hypocrisy [οὐχ ὑποκρινόμενος, μὴ γένοιτο]. He was "a variable and many-sorted man" [ποικίλος τις ἦν καὶ παντοδαπός], but surely no hypocrite.[648]

By a very smooth transition at the end of this argument, Chrysostom presents his first of two laudatory precedents who will serve as exonerating exempla for Paul's behavior: "And in doing this he was imitating his own Lord."[649] Chrysostom

---

[642] The proof section extends from *laud. Paul.* 5.4, line 3 to §16, line 10 [300.246–58]. The sub-arguments flow very smoothly from one to the other, with effective transitional verses.

[643] This proof runs from 5.4, line 3, to the end of 5.8 [SC 300.236–46].

[644] *laud. Paul.* 5.4 [SC 300.236–38].

[645] Chrysostom plays on the term, and cognate verb, in this passage in two ways, since he also wants to make his ascetic point that Paul was "free of desire" [πάσης ἐπιθυμίας καθαρὸς ἦν ἐκεῖνος], i.e., earthly desires, instead training his desire to suit God's will.

[646] *laud. Paul.* 5.4 [SC 300.238]. This is meant to confer added praise on Paul, since he did not act on appearances.

[647] Cf. 1 Cor 9:22.

[648] This is a perfect example of an argument of definition (see Mitchell, "'A Variable and Many-sorted Man," 99, 100–101, 105–6). Paul was accused of living in hypocrisy [ἐν ὑποκρίσει, ὑποκρινόμενος] by the Greek philosopher quoted in Macarius Magnes, *apocrit.* 3.22, 31 (Harnack, TU 37/4, pp. 58, 60), so the question likely had actual apologetic urgency for Chrysostom.

[649] *laud. Paul.* 5.4 [SC 300.238].

offers no less a precedent for Paul's changeability than God: in the biblical record God appeared in many diverse theophanies – in fire, as a foot-soldier, an old man, a cool breeze, a traveller, in the incarnation and death of Jesus, on a throne, and seated on the Cherubim.[650] Via this entertaining *a maiore ad minus* argument, John claims that Paul, like the God of Israel, adapted his behavior with only a single goal in mind: "to do everything with a view to his underlying providential designs" [Πάντα δὲ ταῦτα πρὸς τὰς ὑποκειμένας οἰκονομίας ἔπραττε].[651] Indeed, God had explained this *modus operandi* himself in the prophetic utterance of Hosea 12:11: "I have multiplied visions, and have been given likenesses by the hands of the prophets."[652] Having set forth this august (and even self-verified) precedent of commendable divine behavior, the application to Paul follows, with Chrysostom now summoning as many examples of like variability as he can muster to place Paul in the divine company:

Therefore Paul should not be condemned if, in imitation of his own Lord, at one time he was as a Jew, and at another as one not under the Law; now was keeping the Law, then despising it; at one time was cleaving to the present life, at another condemning it; now was demanding money, then rejecting what was offered; sometimes he was sacrificing and shaving his head, and other times anathematizing those who did such things; once he circumcized, at another time he cast out circumcision.[653]

This list of six pairs of Pauline πράξεις ἐναντίαι, embedded in such a topsy-turvy argument, becomes a source for extravagant praise, offered as proof of Paul's divine likeness, rather than its expected disastrous rhetorical repercussion: excoriation and censure for capricious behavior. Chrysostom anchors his paradoxical praise further with some sophisticated anthropological diagnostics:

For the deeds were contradictory [Καὶ τὰ μὲν γινόμενα ἐναντία ἦν], but the mind and intention [γνώμη καὶ διάνοια] from which they arose were very much in agreement and united with one another [σφόδρα ἀκόλουθος καὶ ἑαυτῇ συνημμένη] ... Not only in what he was doing, but also in what he was saying [Οὐ γὰρ δὴ μόνον ἐν οἷς ἔπραττεν, ἀλλὰ καὶ

---

[650] Elsewhere Chrysostom claims Paul was imitating Christ by variable behavior, as in his alternation of gentle and harsh tones in the Epistle to the Galatians, "following in the footsteps" of Jesus, who once rebuked Peter and at another time praised him (*comm. in Gal.* 1.1 [61.612]).

[651] The very important term οἰκονομία I take to refer here to the divine providential plan for salvation; but it also has a second meaning that is likewise particularly apt in this context, "accommodation" (*LPGL*, 940–43; cf. the use of the term earlier in this discourse, at *laud. Paul.* 5.3 [SC 300.236]). Likely Chrysostom intends the reader to pick up both nuances here.

[652] On the LXX translation of this verse that renders it suitable for this argument, see Piédagnel's note in SC 300.240, n. 2.

[653] Οὕτω καὶ Παῦλος τὸν ἑαυτοῦ μιμούμενος Δεσπότην οὐκ ἂν κατεγνώσθη, νῦν μὲν ὡς Ἰουδαῖος γινόμενος, νῦν δὲ ὡς ἄνομος· καὶ νῦν μὲν νόμον ἐφύλαττε, νῦν δὲ ὑπερεώρα νόμου· καὶ ποτὲ μὲν ἀντείχετο τῆς παρούσης ζωῆς, ποτὲ δὲ κατεφρόνει αὐτῆς· καὶ νῦν μὲν ᾔτει χρήματα, νῦν δὲ καὶ διδόμενα διεκρούετο· καὶ ἔθυε καὶ ἐξυρᾶτο, καὶ πάλιν ἀνεθεμάτιζε τοὺς ποιοῦντας· καὶ νῦν μὲν περιέτεμε, νῦν δὲ περιτομὴν ἐξέβαλε (*laud. Paul.* 5.6 [SC 300.240]). John repeats this emphasis on the Law a few moments later: "at one time he exalts the Law and at another destroys it" [νῦν μὲν ἐπαίρει νόμον, νῦν δὲ αὐτὸν καθαιρεῖ].

ἐν οἷς ἔλεγε], he was variable and many-sorted [ποικίλος ἦν καὶ παντοδαπός]. However, he did not change his mind [οὐχὶ μεταβαλλόμενος τὴν γνώμην], nor become someone else [οὐδὲ ἕτερος ἐξ ἑτέρου γινόμενος], but he remained the very man that he was [ἀλλὰ μένων ὅπερ ἦν], and made use of each of the courses of action I mentioned for the present need [πρὸς τὴν παροῦσαν χρείαν].[654]

In treating Paul's deeds as (laudably) contradictory, Chrysostom must walk a fine line with respect to the other two areas from which an encomiast draws arguments – soul and body. Here we observe him maintaining the integrity of Paul's ψυχή in the face of the potentially devastating evidence of his vacillating actions, by the direct claim that Paul remained who he was, the same dependable, united personality. Any hope for an encomium would fly out the window if the subject could be convicted of διψυχία, a schizophrenic disintegration of the self which acts without any guiding reason,[655] a sure litmus test of a nature dominated by vice.[656] Chrysostom argues for the unity of Paul's mental purpose in a single-minded, all-consuming motivation which, like the behavior ensuing from it, mirrors that of the divine: "For he continually sought one thing [Ἓν γὰρ ἐζήτει] – the salvation of those hearing his words and seeing his actions" [τῶν ταῦτα ἀκουόντων καὶ ὁρώντων τὴν σωτηρίαν].[657] In this way John prepares the way for an ironic use of the λόγος καὶ ἔργα topos by saying that Paul's inconsistency was consistently manifested in both arenas: "Not only in what he did, but also in what he said [Οὐ γὰρ δὴ μόνον ἐν οἷς ἔπραττεν, ἀλλὰ καὶ ἐν οἷς ἔλεγε], he was variable and many-sorted [ποικίλος ἦν καὶ παντοδαπός]!" Now follows the predictable (if outlandish) conclusion to be drawn from this appeal to divine precedent: "Therefore don't reproach him for these things, but for them all the more proclaim his praises and crown him."[658]

---

[654]   laud. Paul. 5.6 [SC 300.242].

[655]   In another context Chrysostom argued against the charge of "doublemindedness" also in the case of the doctor who does contradictory things: "These practices are contradictory, but the mind [or intention] from which they arise is harmonious and single. For he looks to a single goal – the health of the one who is sick" [καὶ τὰ μὲν γινόμενα ἐναντία, ἡ γνώμη δέ, ἀφ' ἧς ταῦτα γίνεται, σύμφωνος καὶ μία. πρὸς γὰρ ἓν τέλος βλέπει, τὴν τοῦ κάμνοντος ὑγίειαν] (hom. in 2 Cor. 4:13 2.2 [51.283]). For the negative caricature in action, see the charge the pagan philosopher wages against Paul for his self-designation in 1 Cor 9:19: "These are not the principles of a healthy soul [οὐκ ἔνι ταῦτα ψυχῆς ὑγιαινούσης τὰ δόγματα], nor the report of free reasonings [οὐκ ἔνι λογισμῶν ἐλευθέρων ἀφήγησις], but the proposal of these words belongs to a man feverish of brain and weak in reasoning" [ὑποπύρου δὲ τὰς φρένας καὶ τὸν λογισμὸν ἀρρωστοῦντος ἡ τῶν λόγων ὑπόθεσις] (Macarius Magnes, apocrit. 3.30 [text Harnack, TU 37/4, p. 60]). Chrysostom also would have known the biblical sanctions against διψυχία in Jas 1:8 and 4:8.

[656]   See the same argument in hom. in 1 Cor. 22.3 [61.184], on 9:20: "for his mind did not change, since that would have been wicked, but it was a case of love acting in an accommodating way" [οὐ τῆς γνώμης αὐτῷ μεταβαλλομένης, ἐπεὶ κακία τὸ πρᾶγμα ἦν. ἀλλὰ τῆς ἀγάπης συγκαταβαινούσης].

[657]   laud. Paul. 5.6 [SC 300.242].

[658]   Μὴ τοίνυν διὰ ταῦτα αὐτὸν κακίσῃς, ἀλλὰ δι' αὐτὰ μὲν οὖν ταῦτα μάλιστα ἀνακήρυξον καὶ στεφάνωσεν (laud. Paul. 5.6 [SC 300.242]).

The second exemplum Chrysostom offers to prove that inconsistency in deeds can be acceptable, even commendable, is the traditional commonplace of the physician[659] who administers a wide range of treatments for different illnesses and states of disease:

Take the case of a physician. When you see him at one time cauterizing, at another feeding, now using an iron implement, then giving a medicinal remedy, once withholding food and drink, and another time providing the sick their fill of these things, sometimes completely covering up a person with a fever, and at other times ordering him to drink a full cup of cold water, you do not condemn his variability [μεταβολή], nor his constant changing [ἡ συνεχὴς μετάστασις]. But instead you praise his craft especially when you see that it introduces with confidence treatments which seem contradictory and harmful to us [τὰ δοκοῦντα ἡμῖν ἐναντία εἶναι καὶ βλαβερά], and guarantees that they are safe. For this is a man who is an expert [τεχνικός. If we accept a physician who does these contradictory things [τὰ ἐναντία ταῦτα ποιεῖν], how much more should we proclaim the praises of Paul's soul [ἡ Παύλου ψυχή], which in the same way attends to the sick?[660]

This time the relationship between the example and the subject is a marked *a minore ad maius* argument, from the everyday physician of bodies to the doctor of souls, Paul.[661] Picking up from his mention of Paul's soul [ψυχή], Chrysostom anchors his use of the medical exemplum with a transference in the realm of concern from the body to the soul as the object of Pauline medicinal care: "For those who are sick in their souls have no less need of concoction and treatment than those who are are ill in the body."[662] In both cases, Chrysostom avers, "straightfor-wardly consistent measures" [ἐξ εὐθείας] may do more harm than good.

John rounds out the proof for his first sub-argument by combining the two *exempla* of God and doctor into one. He now casts God as the adaptable physician par excellence, through another *a minore ad maius* argument. If human beings have figured out the effectiveness of less direct measures, how much more has the all-powerful God, who freely adopted this medical principle and consequently "doesn't always deal with us in a straightforward fashion."[663] In order to preserve human free will and not make people virtuous by compulsion (thereby destroying the gift of freedom he had bestowed on them), God has used "many forms of approach" [μέθοδοι πόλλοι], though Chrysostom is quick to point out that this was not because of any limitation in God, but rather was due to human weakness. Then

---

[659] On the ubiquity of this example in Greco-Roman discussions of variability see Glad, *Paul and Philodemus*, 20, 72–77 (and many further references in his Index under "Physician[s]").

[660] *laud. Paul.* 5.7 [SC 300.242–244].

[661] Chrysostom's personal investment in this image of Paul can be seen in *sac.* 6.4 [SC 272.314], where he depicts the ideal priest as ποικίλος ("variable"), like a doctor administering varied cures, but οὐχ ὕπουλος, οὐ κόλαξ, οὐχ ὑποκριτής ("not fallacious, nor a flatterer, nor a hypo-crite").

[662] *laud. Paul.* 5.7 [SC 300.244].

[663] ὅπου ὁ θεός, ὁ πάντα δυνάμενος, τούτῳ κέχρηται τῆς ἰατρείας τῷ νόμῳ, καὶ οὐ πάντοτε ἡμῖν ἐξ εὐθείας ὁμιλεῖ (*laud. Paul.* 5.8 [SC 300.244]).

the orator concludes the topic of praise for Paul's changeability with a recapitulation of his proposition:"I have not said these things to you frivolously, but to show the variability and cleverness of the blessed Paul" [τὸ ποικίλον τοῦ μακαρίου Παύλου καὶ σοφόν].⁶⁶⁴ Chrysostom follows this up immediately with a short list of some of Paul's particular πράξεις ἐναντίαι here being celebrated, except now he lauds the deeds in question not just for the adaptability to circumstance they exhibit, but for the very virtues exemplified by each member of the contrasting pair:

> Therefore, when you see him fleeing dangers, marvel the same as when you see him rushing forward to meet them. For just as the latter is proof of bravery [ἀνδρεία], the former is of wisdom [σοφία]. When you see him telling his magnificent exploits [μεγάλα φθεγγόμενος], marvel the same as when you see him speaking modestly [μετριάζων]. For just as the latter shows humility [ταπεινοφροσύνη], the former indicates magnanimity of soul [μεγαλοψυχία]. When you see him boasting [καυχώμενος], marvel the same as when you see him refusing praise [διακρουόμενος ἐγκώμιον]. For the latter shows an uninflated character [ἦθος ἄτυφον], and the former compassion and love for others [φιλόστοργος καὶ φιλάνθρωπος]. This is because he was doing all these things to administer the salvation of the many [τὴν γὰρ τῶν πολλῶν οἰκονομῶν σωτηρίαν, ταῦτα ἔπραττε].⁶⁶⁵

Here for the first time Chrysostom has pinned his praise for Paul as "a variable and many-sorted man" onto a scaffolding of virtue theory. Paul's variability is now heralded as praiseworthy, not only as a general conciliatory principle, but also in the exhibition of the full spectrum of virtues it affords. Whichever behavioral pole the changeable Paul exhibits, it is to be praised, for it constitutes proof of one virtue or another. The implication is that in order to be the archetype of ethical behavior Paul must have exhibited the full range of virtues of which the human soul is capable, even as they may stand in logical tension with one another. Hence this whimsical proof that Paul was variable in the end issues forth in three pairs of opposing virtues he possessed. The first example names an incontestable, traditional pair of virtues: bravery and wisdom (in the sense of "prudence").⁶⁶⁶ The second and third pairs are virtual synonyms for the contrast between boastfulness and humility. Here Chrysostom has broken with any conventional pairs of virtues, for it is hardly self-evident why self-commendation or boasting should be considered laudatory behavior at all, let alone how it could be an obvious demonstration of compassion and love for others.⁶⁶⁷ In invoking this example Chrysostom has managed to step into what is for him a perennially sensitive and tricky topic (especially because of his rhetorical training): the suitability of Paul's boasting and

---

⁶⁶⁴ *laud. Paul.* 5.8 [SC 300.244].

⁶⁶⁵ *laud. Paul.* 5.8 [SC 300.244–46].

⁶⁶⁶ For the traditional nature of this pairing, see Aphthonios, *Prog.* 8 [Spengel 2.36]: (αἱ πράξεις) ψυχὴν μὲν ὡς ἀνδρείαν ἢ φρόνησιν; Menander, *Rh.* 2.373 [Russell-Wilson, 84], οὐκοῦν ἐν ταῖς πράξεσι τοῦ πολέμου τὰ κατὰ τὴν ἀνδρείαν ἐρεῖς καὶ τὰ τῆς φρονήσεως.

⁶⁶⁷ The oddness of this couple in the list is also signalled by the assignment of the double virtues of φιλοστοργία καὶ φιλανθρωπία, which destroys the tidy parallelism of the previous pairs.

self-recommendation. And once he has mentioned the matter, Chrysostom is forced to contend with winds of suspicion against Paul as a braggart which have a history as far back as his own Corinthian converts. But yet again John has taken a knowingly calculated rhetorical risk, for if he can succeed in conferring praise on Paul for this action which was so vigorously repudiated in Greco-Roman culture, then he will have met his encomiastic goal with highest marks for both universality of praise and ingenuity of invention.

Proof #2: Paul's Boasting a Proof of His Love.[668] Chrysostom knows that conventional wisdom regards boasting[669] as an execrable, offensive act.[670] There are several reasons it was regarded as "offensive" [ἐπαχθές],[671] principally that such περιαυτολογία[672]

---

[668] This proof extends from *laud. Paul.* 5.9 until 5.15 [SC 300.246–56].

[669] Which Chrysostom terms variously "telling one's own virtuous deeds" [ἐξειπεῖν οἰκεῖα κατορθώματα] (*laud. Paul.* 5.14 [SC 300.254]); "speaking of one's own great actions" [τὰ ἑαυτοῦ διηγεῖσθαι, περὶ ἑαυτοῦ τι μέγα εἰπεῖν, μεγάλα περὶ ἑαυτοῦ λέγειν] (*laud. Paul.* 5.10, 12, 13 [SC 300.248, 252]; *hom. in Ac.* 44.1 [60.309]); "parading" [ἐκπομπεύειν] the things one has done (*hom. in Gen.* 11.6 [53.96]); "embarking on encomia to oneself" [εἰς τὰ ἐγκώμια ἐμβαίνειν] (*laud. Paul.* 5.12 [SC 300.250]; *hom. in 2 Tim.* 1.1 [62.602]; cf. εἰς διήγησιν τῶν οἰκείων ἐγκωμίων ἐμπεσεῖν, and διηγήσασθαι πάντα αὐτοῦ τὰ ἐγκώμια in *hom. in 2 Cor.* 11:1 3 and 4 [51.303–305]); and "adorning oneself with encomia" [καλλωπίζεσθαι τοῖς ἐγκωμίοις] (*laud. Paul.* 5.13 [SC 300.254]).

[670] At one point in this speech Chrysostom alludes to it as "doing what is forbidden" [τὰ ἀπαγορευμένα ποιεῖν] (*laud. Paul.* 5.10 [SC 300.248]). "Nothing so offends many hearers as for someone to praise himself" [Οὐδὲν γὰρ οὕτω προσίσταται τοῖς πολλοῖς τῶν ἀκροατῶν, ὡς τὸ ἑαυτόν τινα ἐγκωμιάζειν] (*hom. in 2 Cor.* 22.1 [61.548]). In the next homily in that same series he says "the noble man not only should not boast in things he doesn't have, but not even in what he does possess" (*hom. in 2 Cor.* 23.5 [61.560]). And one homily later he condemns it also for a theological reason (based upon 2 Cor 11:17), that boasting is not speaking κατὰ κύριον (*hom. in 2 Cor.* 24.1 [61.565]).

[671] Plutarch, *Mor.* 547D: "no other form of speech is so offensive or burdensome" [λόγος ἄλλος οὐδεὶς οὕτως ἐπαχθὴς οὐδὲ βαρύς]; also 539A, and throughout the treatise (see Hans Dieter Betz, "de laude ipsius," ed. *idem, Plutarch's Ethical Writings and Early Christian Literature* [SCHNT 4; Leiden: Brill, 1978] 367–93, 383). The traditional title of Plutarch's treatise uses the antonym ἀνεπιφθόνως; compare Hermogenes, *Meth.* 25 [Spengel 2.446], περὶ τοῦ ἀνεπαχθῶς ἑαυτὸν ἐπαινεῖν. For Chrysostom's description of περιαυτολογία as ἐπαχθές, see the next note.

[672] "Speaking of oneself," the term used in rhetorical theory (Alexander, *Rh.* [Spengel, 3.4]; Philodemus, *Hom.* col. 21 [Alexander Olivieri, ed., *Philodemi* ΠΕΡΙ ΤΟΥ ΚΑΘ ΟΜΗΡΟΝ ΑΓΑΘΟΥ ΒΑΣΙΛΕΩΣ *Libellus* (BT; Leipzig: Teubner, 1909) 60], and wider discussion on the theme of boasting (Plut. *Mor.* 539C, 546B [μέγα γὰρ ἡ περιαυτολογία τὴν φιλαυτίαν ὁρμητήριον ἔχουσα], *Mor.* 546C, F). Although Chrysostom does not use the term περιαυτολογία in this discourse, all three of the times it is found in his wide-ranging corpus of writings it refers to Paul, always to absolve Paul of the charge that he engaged in invidious self-praise: "The one saying something great about others [ὁ μὲν περὶ ἄλλων τι μέγα λέγων] speaks happily and boldly, but the one who is compelled to praise himself [ὁ δὲ ἑαυτὸν ἀναγκαζόμενος ἐπαινεῖν], especially when he calls himself as a witness, does so with a blushing sense of shame. It is for this very reason that this blessed man first calls himself miserable (1 Cor 15:8–9), and then speaks of that great deed (15:10, 'I labored more than all of them'). He does this to forestall the offense of self-praise [τό τε ἐπαχθὲς τῆς περιαυτολογίας ὑποτεμνόμενος], and to make the things he will say thereafter more credible" (*hom. in 1 Cor.* 38.4 [61.327–28]; compare the penultimate phrase with

looks like an expression of "self love" [φιλαυτία],[673] "vainglory" [κενοδοξία],[674] and "madness" [ἀπόνοια],[675] the act of a foolish braggart.[676] Far more preferable, as Paul himself knew, was to have someone else praise you (1 Cor 4:5).[677] Yet John was acutely aware of passages in the Pauline letters, especially 2 Corinthians 10–13,[678] wherein Paul self-consciously and overtly engaged in what even he himself termed

Plutarch, Mor. 539C: τὴν ἀηδίαν τῆς περιαυτολογίας ἀφαιροῦντες). In virg. 35 [SC 125.208], John understands the rhetorical force of 1 Cor 7:7 to be based on Paul's sensitivity to the offense resulting from περιαυτολογία. That is why Paul quickly followed up his public wish "that all be as I am" with the concession, "but each has his or her own gift": "so that he might flee from self-praise" [τὴν περιαυτολογίαν ἐξέφυγεν ἄν]. The third instance is on 2 Corinthians 10, quoted above in n. 204 (hom. in 2 Cor. 22.1 [61.547]: τὸ μὴ δοκεῖν ἐπαχθῆς εἶναι τοῖς πολλοῖς διὰ τὴν περιαυτολογίαν ταύτην ["in order not to appear offensive to the many on account of this self-praise"].

673 On φιλαυτία see hom. in Gen. 11.6 [53.96].

674 The theme of the vainglorious person, κενόδοξος, is a favorite one of Chrysostom's (throughout the corpus, and especially in his treatise, de inani gloria et de educandis liberis), and he is nervously aware that passages such as 2 Corinthians 10–13 could be read as exhibiting that character flaw in Paul. For example, in hom. in 2 Cor. 22.2 [61.550], John vehemently denies that Paul was vainglorious, ever: Κενοδοξίας γὰρ μάλιστα καθαρὸς ἦν· καὶ τοῦτο αὐτοῦ δείκνυσιν ἅπας ὁ βίος, καὶ ὁ πρότερος καὶ ὁ μετὰ ταῦτα. In the present discourse, laud. Paul. 5, he contrasts the synonym φιλότιμος with the term of his thesis, φιλάνθρωπος, in 5.14 [SC 300.256]: "to draw out his speech further would have been the act of a vainglorious man and braggadocio [φιλοτίμου καὶ ἀλαζόνος], whereas to say the very things which would be necessary for the present need is the part of one who loves humanity and looks to the advantage of the many" [φιλανθρώπου καὶ τὸ τῶν πολλῶν συμφέρον ὁρῶντος]. This refrain is repeated often in the biblical homilies (hom. in 2 Cor. 21.2 [61.542]: Εἶδες πῶς οὐκ ἦν φιλότιμος, οὐδὲ πρὸς ἐπίδειξίν τι ἐποίει). That this is a commonplace in the rhetoric of boasting is confirmed by Plutarch, Mor. 540A: "Therefore praise is vain [κένος] when those praising themselves just wish to seem laudable, and it is especially contemptible when it appears to be done for love of honor and an untimely pursuit of glory" [καὶ καταφρονεῖται μάλιστα, φιλοτιμίας ἕνεκα γίνεσθαι καὶ δόξης ἀκαίρου φαινόμενος] (see also Mor. 540A on φιλοδοξία, and the negative model afforded by Cicero's lack of self-control when it came to fame [δόξα], in comp. Dem. et Cic. 2.1 and Mor. 541A). In the same vein Chrysostom in laud. Paul. 5.10 [SC 300.248] argues that Paul did not mention all his good deeds ἵνα μὴ δόξαν ἑαυτῷ περιθῇ μεγάλην. Compare Plut. Mor. 539E, on how the politician might take the risk of engaging in "so-called περιαυτολογία, not for his own glory or pleasure [πρὸς οὐδεμίαν αὐτοῦ δόξαν ἢ χάριν] ...," and, in the conclusion to the work: "invective from others always follows upon praise for oneself, and the end of this vainglory is lost glory" [τοῖς ἰδίοις ἐπαίνοις ἀλλότριος ἔπεται ψόγος ἀεὶ καὶ γίνεται τέλος ἀδοξία τῆς κενοδοξίας ταύτης] (Mor. 547E-F, my trans.).

675 ἀπόνοια (laud. Paul. 5.9 [SC 300.246]), ἄνοια (laud. Paul. 5.13 [SC 300.252]; hom. in 2 Cor. 11:1 5 [51.310]), παραπληξία (laud. Paul. 5.13 [SC 300.254]). In Plutarch's treatise the theme occurs in the quote from Pindar near the beginning: "to boast in an untimely way is to play in harmony with madness" [καὶ τὸ καυχᾶσθαι παρὰ καιρὸν μανίαις ὑποκρέκειν] (Mor. 539C). Cf. 2 Cor 11:23, and the entire related theme of foolishness which unites Paul's discourse in 2 Corinthians 10–13.

676 See laud. Paul. 5.9 [οὔτε ἄλλος τις οὕτω καθαρὸς ἀλαζονείας] and 14 [SC 300.246, 256]. Again we find the same language in Plutarch: ἀλαζονεία, κενότης, φιλοτιμία (Mor. 540D).

677 Plutarch Mor. 539D (boasters deprive others of their right to praise them); Quintilian, Inst. 11.1.22; discussion in Mitchell, Paul, 91–95.

678 Actually, Chrysostom regards all of 2 Corinthians as a Pauline self-encomium [Καὶ οὐκ ἂν τις ἁμάρτοι, τὴν ἐπιστολὴν ταύτην ἐγκώμιον Παύλου προσειπών]. (hom. in 2 Cor. 21.1 [61.541]).

boasting. The proposition John will seek to prove here – that Paul's boasting was an instance of φιλανθρωπία, "love for others" – is intentionally formulated in counter-point to the accustomed despicable motive for speaking about one's own accomplishments: φιλαυτία. Because the rhetorical and ethical problem of Paul's boasting so troubled Chrysostom, not only here, but throughout his writings, he had constructed some customary defenses of the apostle's self-praise based upon the precise grounds of motive and circumstance recommended by Plutarch in *de laude ipsius* (themselves reflecting a long history of discussion in Greco-Roman rhetorical and other writings),[679] which he expressed in strikingly similar terms.[680] Indeed, the many parallels between Plutarch's famous treatise and John's handling of Paul's boasting in 2 Corinthians 10–13 strongly suggest that Chrysostom had read Plutarch.[681] But even if he had not met these commonplaces in that particular Plutarchean treatise, John would certainly have encountered and discussed the theme of proper and improper boasting in the course of his education, given that his teacher Libanios' favorite orator was Demosthenes,[682] whose *de corona* was the major impetus for much of the discussion of boasting in ancient rhetorical theory and literary criticism.[683] This line of inquiry provides a most interesting point of

---

[679] See the analysis of this work and further literature in L. Radermacher, "Studien zur Geschichte der griechischen Rhetorik, II: Plutarchs Schrift *de se ipso citra invidiam laudando*," *Rheinisches Museum für Philologie* n.s. 52 (1897) 419–24; Hans Dieter Betz, *Der Apostel Paulus und die sokratische Tradition: Eine exegetische Untersuchung zu seiner "Apologie" 2 Korinther 10–13* (BHT 45; Tübingen: J.C.B. Mohr [Paul Siebeck], 1972) 75–77; *idem*, "*de laude ipsius*," 367–93; and other references in Christopher Forbes, "Comparison, Self-Praise and Irony: Paul's Boasting and the Conventions of Hellenistic Rhetoric," *NTS* 32 (1986) 1–30, 8–10.

[680] As documented in nn. 698–701, 704, 706, 723, 727, 732, below.

[681] Baur is tentative on direct influence in general: "He has many sympathies with Plutarch, although actual utilization of him cannot be proved" (*John Chrysostom* 1.306). But several parallel passages are listed by Dumortier, "La culture profane de S. Chrysostome," 57, 61; and Max Pohlenz, "Philosophische Nachklänge in altchristlichen Predigten," *ZWT* 48 [1905] 72–95, 91–94 (all echoes of Plutarch's treatise, περὶ εὐθυμίας). Pohlenz concludes: "Alle diese Punkte würden für sich vielleicht noch nicht entscheidende Bedeutung beanspruchen können. Da aber bei Basilius die Benutzung von Plutarch's Schrift zweifellos ist, so werden wir sie wohl ruhig auch bei Chrysostomos annehmen dürfen" (p. 94). To my knowledge, Chrysostom's treatment of Paul's boasting has not previously been brought to bear on the question of his acquaintance with Plutarch's writings, but, as we shall see, it is a valuable source for the investigation of this question.

[682] Libanios wrote ὑποθέσεις to all the orations of Demosthenes, preceded by a short βίος of the famous Athenian who was a classic source for all Greek παιδεία (Foerster 8.600–81; Dumortier, "La culture de S. Chrysostome," 53). Demosthenes serves as the model for Plutarch's prescriptions for properly speaking about oneself "inoffensively" (see Plut. *comp. Dem. et Cic.* 2.1: ὁ μὲν ἐμμελῶς καὶ ἀνεπαχθῶς τῶν εἰς αὐτὸν ἁπτόμενος ἐγκωμίων, in contrast to Cicero, who was conspicuous for his "immoderate self-praise" [ἡ δὲ Κικέρωνος ἐν τοῖς λόγοις ἀμετρία τῆς περιαυτολογίας]).

[683] Radermacher, "Plutarchs Schrift," 420; F.C. Babbitt, *Plutarch's Moralia*, LCL vol. 4, p. 110 note a; Robert Klaerr and Yvonne Vernière, *Plutarque, Oeuvres Morales*, vol. 7, part 2 (Paris: Société d'Édition "Les Belles Lettres," 1974) 61: "De plus l'abondance, dans notre traité, des renvois au discours *Sur la couronne*, où Démosthène est obligé de 'parler de lui-même', peut faire

correspondence between Chrysostom and contemporary Pauline scholarship, given the significant attention paid recently to the question of Paul's practice of boasting (especially in 2 Corinthians 10–13), its rhetorical forms and purposes, and how it would have been received by his contemporaries.[684] In our present context of investigation into how Chrysostom treats the encomiastic topic of Paul's πράξεις, the topic of boasting is especially pertinent, for it raises the question of how a person's deeds can become known in order for those exploits to be drawn upon by others who seek to offer praise (especially in contexts where, if the subject does not narrate them, they will remain hidden).

Returning to the oration itself, the second section of proof (§9–15) supports the proposition introduced at the end of §8, that Paul's boasting was proof of his virtuous nature as φιλόστοργος καὶ φιλάνθρωπος. Repeatedly Chrysostom will insist that Paul only engaged in boasting "in conjunction with a just and reasonable cause" [μετὰ αἰτίας δικαίας καὶ εὐλόγου].[685] The seriousness of Chrysostom's attention to substantiating this thesis, both by positive arguments and by rebuttals of negative evaluations of Paul's self-praise, is shown by the fact that in closing off this sub-argument in §15 he employs a brief summation of the argument [a rhetorical ἀνακεφαλαίωσις or παλιλλογία], in this case by an enumeration [ἀπολογίζεσθαι][686] of the five different ways in which Paul, in the course of his boasting, was instructing his readers not to take up boasting themselves lightly

---

croire que c'est ce discours précisément qui a servi de modèle traditionnel de l'éloge de soi et qui a fourni à Plutarque les premiers mots de son traité, qui en sont aussi le thème."

[684] The recent movement in this direction began with E. A. Judge, "Paul's Boasting in Relation to Contemporary Professional Practice," *AusBR* 16 (1968) 37–50; Betz, *Apostel Paulus*, followed by Forbes, "Paul's Boasting and Hellenistic Rhetoric"; J. Paul Sampley, "Paul, His Opponents in 2 Corinthians 10–13, and the Rhetorical Handbooks," *The Social World of Formative Christianity and Judaism*, ed. Jacob Neusner, et al. (Philadelphia: Fortress, 1988) 162–77; and Frederick W. Danker, "Paul's Debt to the *De Corona* of Demosthenes: A Study of Rhetorical Techniques in Second Corinthians," *Persuasive Artistry: Studies in New Testament Rhetoric in Honor of George A. Kennedy*, ed. Duane F. Watson (JSNTSup 50; Sheffield: Sheffield Academic Press, 1991) 262–80. But the modern roots of this inquiry extend back much further; as Betz notes, Hans Windisch had already pointed the way in his 1924 commentary (*Der zweite Korintherbrief* [KEK, 9th ed., 1924; ed. G. Strecker; Göttingen: Vandenhoeck & Ruprecht, 1970] 345), by offering an impressive list of parallels between the Plutarchean treatise and Paul's "Fool's Speech," reaching the following summary conclusion: "P[aulus] teilt durchaus die Anschauungen Plutarchs und des Griechentums, in dessen Namen Plut[arch] spricht." Despite this proliferation of treatment, to my knowledge no one has previously brought the important testimony of John Chrysostom into the discussion of Paul's boasting and its rhetorical propriety. But Chrysostom's careful engagement with the topic gives us a rare opportunity to test the modern historical-literary analyses with the interpretations of an ancient, rhetorically trained reader.

[685] *laud. Paul.* 5.10 [SC 300.248]; cf. Plut. *Mor.* 540F: τῇ περιαυτολογίᾳ παρρησίαν συγγνώμονα τῆς αἰτίας διδούσης.

[686] Here I am using the Greek terminology of *Rh. Al.* 20.1433b (who notes that a παλιλλογία may be used both at the end of individual parts of the speech, as here, or at the end of the whole [δεῖ δ' αὐτῇ χρῆσθαι καὶ παρὰ τῶν μερῶν καὶ τῶν ὅλων λόγων τὰς τελευτάς]). The corresponding Latin terms are *conclusio, complexio*, and *enumeratio* (*Rhet. Her.* 2.18.28; 19.30).

[ἁπλῶς].[687] Such a formal enumeration of proofs is somewhat uncommon in the
seven panegyrics to Paul, which are generally not so analytically structured,[688] so
its presence here suggests both the pressing nature of the point, for which John
wants to summon an impressive volume of evidence, and equally, perhaps, the
commonality of the theme in Chrysostom's writings, such that he could marshal
a host of pre-formed arguments once he had embarked upon the theme yet again.[689]
Because in the recapitulation Chrysostom gives an orderly account of his invention of arguments, we shall begin there and work backwards to see how he has
carried out that plan in what preceded.

Do you see how many means he employed to instruct his hearer not to boast frivolously
['Ορᾷς δι' ὅσων ἐπαίδευσε τὸν ἀκροατὴν μὴ ἁπλῶς καυχᾶσθαι]? First, by showing that he
did this from necessity [ἀνάγκῃ τοῦτο ἐποίησε]. Second, by calling himself a fool [ὡς ἄφρονα
ἑαυτὸν καλέσαι], and repeatedly begging off from engaging in it [πολλαῖς χρήσασθαι
παραιτήσεσι].[690] Third, by not telling everything [μὴ πάντα εἰπεῖν], but hiding his greater
deeds [ἀλλὰ τὰ μείζονα ἀποκρύψασθαι] – and this was when there *was* a necessity [καὶ
ταῦτα ἀνάγκης οὔσης]. Fourth, by assuming another persona [προσωπεῖον ἕτερον
ὑπελθεῖν] and saying "I know a man" (2 Cor 12:2). Fifth, by not publicizing every other
virtue [μὴ καὶ τὴν ἄλλην ἀρετὴν ἅπασαν εἰς μέσον ἀγαγεῖν], but only that portion for
which the present time had special need [ἀλλ' ἐκεῖνο τὸ μέρος οὗ μάλιστα ὁ παρὼν ἐδεῖτο
καιρός].[691]

The logic of this proof is that Paul's boasting was a clear instance of his φιλανθρωπία
because it was done solely for the instruction,[692] the correction,[693] the salvation,[694]
of his hearers. This kind of didactic, humanitarian motivation for self-praise was

---

[687] Even as he seeks to prove that in his boasting Paul did not speak ἁπλῶς ("frivolously")
[Οὐδὲν γὰρ ἁπλῶς ἐκεῖνος ἐποίει] (5.10 [SC 300.248]), John insists that Paul taught others to
take the same attitude [μηδὲ παρασκευάσαι ἁπλῶς ἑαυτοὺς ἐγκωμιάζειν] (*laud. Paul.* 5.11, 15
[SC 300.250, 256]). Hence it is not accidental that John earlier in the discourse described *himself*
as adhering to this principle as well: Ταῦτα δὲ ἡμῖν οὐχ ἁπλῶς εἴρηται (5.8 [SC 300.244]).

[688] See the conclusion to this chapter (pp. 377–80), where I shall argue, in agreement with
Hubbell, "Chrysostom and Rhetoric," that this is an indication that these orations are λαλιαί,
more informal talks. But in this oration we have the most formalized τάξις of the seven.

[689] In particular, in his exegetical homilies on 2 Corinthians 10–13 Chrysostom employs all
of the same themes as are found here. One could likely make a valuable contribution to the
relative dating of both works through a detailed comparison of these *topoi* on Paul's boasting
(though that issue lies beyond our scope here).

[690] See below, pp. 346–47, on the translation of this phrase.

[691] *laud. Paul.* 5.15 [SC 300.256].

[692] "... he was also teaching the others, so that when the time befell them, they would neither
flee from the practice entirely, nor again pursue it at the wrong moment" [ἀλλὰ καὶ τοὺς ἄλλους
παιδεύων, ὥστε ἐμπεσόντος καιροῦ μὴ φεύγειν τὸ τοιοῦτον, μήτε ἀκαίρως αὐτὸ μετιέναι πάλιν]
(*laud. Paul.* 5.13 [SC 300.252]). See also the introductory formulation: ἡμᾶς ἐδίδασκε πῶς
ἕκαστον τούτων μετιέναι δεῖ and, in the homilies on 2 Corinthians 10–13 (*hom. in 2 Cor.* 25.1;
26.1; 27.1 [61.569, 575, 583]).

[693] See the example of David's διορθῶσαι in *laud. Paul.* 5.14 [SC 300.256].

[694] *laud. Paul.* 5.8 [SC 300.246].

also allowed for by Plutarch.[695] But establishing motives from actions is no easy business. To do so John offers fully five aspects of Paul's boasting technique which he regards as proof of the apostle's altruistic designs. Although the proof itself was not arranged according to the strict order of these five points (mostly because in execution the numerically impressive five appeals actually are very much intertwined), it does correspond precisely in content.

Proofs that Paul Boasted for Pedagogical Purposes

1. Necessity. The difficult argumentative pursuit John has taken on is to establish that Paul, even in the act of boasting, illustrated the very proposition by which he would appear to be condemned: "it is a great evil to tell something great and marvelous about oneself."[696] But Paul is not guilty of this, John seeks to show, even if his actions seem at cross-purposes in this regard,[697] because his goal in praising himself was to teach his hearers what the proper constraints and limits on boasting should be. To establish that more extravagant claim, Chrysostom first employs the conventional arguments justifying the act of self-praise itself, when performed in certain carefully demarcated circumstances. More than ten times in this short proof Chrysostom works from the commonplace premise, well documented in Plutarch,[698] that boasting is acceptable if one is forced into it [ἀνάγκη/ ἀναγκάζεσθαι] by another person or circumstantial need [χρεία].[699] In making

---

[695] ... οὐκ ἐπαινεῖσθαι βουλόμενος, ἀλλ᾽ ἐπαινεῖν ὡς χρὴ διδάσκων (Mor. 543B; cf. 546B).

[696] κακὸν μέγα τὸ περὶ ἑαυτοῦ λέγειν μέγα τι καὶ θαυμαστόν (laud. Paul. 5.13 [SC 300.252]). John had cited the maxim in inverted form earlier in the speech: "it is a great good not to boast [literally, "say something great"] about oneself" [μέγα ἀγαθὸν τὸ μηδὲν μέγα περὶ ἑαυτοῦ λέγειν] (5.10 [SC 300.248]).

[697] The theme of πράξεις ἐναντίαι makes a brief reappearance to mark the irony: "he pursued contradictory actions with such great wisdom as to attain the same praises everywhere!" [καὶ μετὰ τοσαύτης σοφίας μετῄει τὰ ἐναντία πράγματα, ὡς τῶν αὐτῶν πανταχοῦ τυγχάνειν ἐπαίνων] (laud. Paul. 5.10 [SC 300.248]).

[698] See, for instance, his castigation of Cicero for violating this standard, "for he employed self-praises not from necessity, but for glory" [ὁ μὲν γὰρ οὐκ ἀναγκαίως ἀλλ᾽ ὑπὲρ δόξης ἐχρῆτο τοῖς ἐπαίνοις] (Mor. 541A; comp. Dem. et Cic. 2.1); also οἱ ἀναγκασθέντες ἐπαινεῖν αὐτούς (Mor. 542E; the parallel with 2 Cor 12:11 was noted by Windisch, Der zweite Korintherbrief, 345; Betz, "de laude ipsius," 390; Victor Paul Furnish, II Corinthians [AB 32A; Garden City, NY: Doubleday, 1984] 552), and his extolling of Demosthenes for speaking of himself "when there was need of it for some other important end" [ὅτε τούτου δεῆσαι πρὸς ἕτερόν τι μεῖζον] (comp. Dem. et Cic. 2.1). The language about necessity itself came from Demosthenes: πολλάκις λέγειν ἀναγκασθήσομαι περὶ ἐμαυτοῦ (Or. 18.4), a line which was the often-cited precedent drawn upon in rhetorical theory (Hermogenes, Meth. 25 [Spengel 2.446–7], who recommends that one of the three means for inoffensive self praise is ἀνάγκης προσποίησις, "a pretense of necessity"; cf. Aristides, Rh. 1.12 [Spengel 2.506], ὡς συναναγκασθείς).

[699] ἀνάγκη/(κατ)ἀναγκάζεσθαι is the recurrent theme of John's proof in laud. Paul. 5: ἔχειν τοσαύτας ἀνάγκας (5.9 [SC 300.246]); τοσαύτης ἐπικειμένας ἀνάγκης (5.12 [252]); μόνου καιροῦ καταναγκάζοντος (5.12 [252]); ἀπολογίαν κατασκευάζων ἀπὸ τῆς τῶν καιρῶν ἀνάγκης (5.13 [252]); μηδεμιᾶς ἀνάγκης ἐπικειμένης, καὶ ἀνάγκης βιαίας (5.13 [254]); ἀνάγκης ἐμπεσούσης (5.13, twice [254]); ἀνάγκης οὔσης (5.13 [254]); ἀνάγκη τοίνυν ἦν (5.14 [256]); ἀνάγκη τοῦτο

this appeal John unites the words of the apostle himself (2 Cor 12:11, ὑμεῖς με ἠναγκάσατε) with the dispensation of classical rhetorical and ethical theory. It is frequently necessary to boast, John and Plutarch agree, when one is falsely accused. Then it is legitimate and, indeed, mandatory, to talk about oneself and one's good deeds to clear one's name.[700] This is how Chrysostom regards the pressing need for self-defense [ἀπολογία] forced on Paul by the vituperations of the "false apostles" at Corinth.[701] In addition to the language of necessity, Chrysostom often expresses this argument from circumstance by invoking the contrast between εὐκαιρία and ἀκαιρία, "timely and untimely" self-praise.[702] Paul's self-praise, because it was offered at the crucial moment [εὐκαίρως ἐποίει] when the false apostles threatened to

---

ἐποίησε (5.15 [256]); ἀνάγκης οὔσης (5.15 [256]). On χρεία see 5.11 [τῆς χρείας καλούσης]; 5.14 [εἶπεν … ἃ πρὸς τὴν παροῦσαν ἔμελλεν χρείαν ἀναγκαῖα εἶναι] (SC 300. 250, 256; cf. earlier in the homily at 5.4, 6 [238, 242]). Other instances of the *topos* are far too numerous to mention, but see *hom. in 2 Cor.* 26.1 [61.575]: οὐδὲν γὰρ ἔχει τὸ πρᾶγμα (sc. καυχᾶσθαι) ἀλλὰ καὶ βλάβην, πλὴν ἐὰν μὴ ἀναγκαία τις ᾖ πρόφασις καὶ ὠφέλιμος ἡ εἰς τοῦτο ἐνάγουσα; also 3.1 [61.406]; *hom. in Gen.* 11.5 [53.96]; *hom. in 1 Cor.* 35.5 [61.303]; *hom. in 2 Cor.* 22.1; 23.1; 25.1; 27.1 [61.547, 553, 569, 583]; *hom. in 2 Cor. 11:1* 5 [51.310].

[700] "… when time and topic require that something of the truth about oneself be told, as it would be about another" [καιροῦ καὶ πράξεως ἀπαιτούσης ὡς περὶ ἄλλου τι λεχθῆναι καὶ περὶ αὐτοῦ τῶν ἀληθῶν] (Plut. *Mor.* 539E).

[701] See *laud. Paul.* 5.13 [SC 300.252]: "Not only was he defending himself by taking recourse to the necessity of the times …" [οὐχ ἑαυτῷ μόνον ἀπολογίαν κατασκευάζων ἀπὸ τῆς τῶν καιρῶν ἀνάγκης …]; also 5.14 [SC 300.256]. This theme pervades the homilies on 2 Corinthians; see *hom. in 2 Cor.* 23.1, 3; 24.1; 25.1 [61.553, 557–558, 569]. For the acceptability of self-praise in self-defense, see Plutarch, *Mor.* 540C: "first, one can blamelessly praise oneself if doing it by way of defense against slander or accusation" [Αὐτὸν δὲ ἐπαινεῖν ἀμέμπτως ἐστὶ πρῶτον μὲν ἂν ἀπολογούμενος τοῦτο ποιῇς πρὸς διαβολὴν ἢ κατηγορίαν] (again in 541E; see also 542A, where he extols Demosthenes' argument in *de corona* for its use of self-praise to respond point by point to the charges of his enemies [this is precisely how Demosthenes himself explains his rhetorical purpose in *Or.* 18.4]). The parallel with Paul's 2 Corinthians 10–13 was noted by Betz, "*de laude ipsius*," 386, 389.

[702] For the explicit contrast see, in addition to the passages cited in the text, *laud. Paul.* 5.11 [SC 300.250], where it is applied to the physician παράδειγμα (trouble results when amateurs try to apply in an untimely fashion [ἀκαίρως] a remedy devised by a doctor μετὰ καιροῦ), and 5.13 [SC 300.252]: ἐμπεσόντος καιροῦ μὴ φεύγειν τὸ τοιοῦτον, μήτε ἀκαίρως αὐτὸ μετιέναι πάλιν. The appeals to timeliness and necessity are brought together explicitly in 5.12 [μόνου καιροῦ καταναγκάζοντος] and 5.13 [ἀπὸ τῆς τῶν καιρῶν ἀνάγκης] [SC 300.252]. The *topos* appears also in the form of a maxim in *hom. in 2 Cor.* 22.2 [61.550]: "For one can do harm by speaking modestly at the wrong time, and do benefit by saying something wonderful about oneself at the right moment" [Ἔστι γὰρ καὶ μετριάζοντα ἀκαίρως, βλάψαι, καὶ λέγοντά τι περὶ ἑαυτοῦ θαυμαστὸν εὐκαίρως, ὠφελῆσαι]. A nice example of the principle in action is afforded by Libanios' declamation, *Demosthenis apologia*: "for once embarked upon a speech about the consti-tution I shall be compelled to mention many things in an untimely fashion [πολλῶν ἀκαίρως μνημονεύειν ἀναγκασθήσομαι], but if in hesitation I keep silent [εἰ δὲ τοῦτο ὀκνήσας σιωπήσομαι], then I shall again leave untold the things which formerly it was good for me to cease from mentioning. Therefore I shall try, as best as possible, to do nothing to cause you grief. But if when now I speak of myself [ἐμαυτῷ λέγων] I appear to be in some way worse than my former custom, I should have your forbearance. For I have been silent for a long time" (*Decl.* 23.4 [Foerster, 6.376]).

destroy the church, was actually, in John's assessment, more praiseworthy than it would have been for Paul to have remained silent.[703] Indeed, turning the tables, Chrysostom asserts that if Paul had *not* praised himself at that time, he would have been more deserving of blame [κατηγορηθῆναι] than those who offer praise for others, but "at the wrong time" [οἱ ἀκαίρως ἐγκωμιάζοντες]. This is because, if he had not praised himself, Paul would have "opened the mouths of the false apostles" and "advanced the cause of his enemies."[704] Paul's wisdom is shown in the fact that he knew just when boasting should be done [Οὕτως οἶδε τῷ καιρῷ πανταχοῦ κεχρῆσθαι], and how it should be carried out. As these comparisons escalate, John exclaims that Paul was "more esteemed in the moment of boasting than anyone else would be when hiding his or her good deeds; for no one has done such good deeds in concealing his actions as Paul has done in proclaiming his."[705] Here again the words–deeds dynamic is put to good effect: Paul's boasting words, rather than in some way staining or nullifying the virtuous deeds they narrate (by bringing to light the character flaw of vainglory), instead are superior even to the good deed of humility that is exemplified by others who modestly hold their tongues.

2. *With Self-denigration, Hesitation, and Apology.* Plutarch had admiringly observed that "some, by not offering their own praises of themselves as perfectly and unadulteratedly illustrious, but throwing in some defects or failures or trivial errors, do away with the offence and indignation" boasting can cause.[706] With this principle in mind, Chrysostom praises Paul for having called himself a fool,[707] and having "employed many excuses" [πολλαῖς χρήσασθαι παραιτήσεσι] in doing so. The term used, παραίτησις/παραιτεῖσθαι, could mean either anticipatory apologies

---

[703] ὁ δὲ οὕτως αὐτὸ εὐκαίρως ἐποίει, ὡς εἰπὼν μᾶλλον ἢ σιγήσας ἐπαινεθῆναι (*laud. Paul.* 5.10 [SC 300.248]).

[704] *laud. Paul.* 5.10 [SC 300.248]. In this rhetorical move Chrysostom mirrors the advice Plutarch offered: "... the use of contrast has a certain grace to it, when one shows that doing the opposite [τοὐναντίον] of what one is accused would have been shameful and ignoble" (*Mor.* 541F). The tactic itself is used by Dio Chrysostom in his defense of Nestor against the charge of ἀλαζονεία: "Or is it not the province of a foolish person to be ashamed to praise himself when it will bring the greatest benefits [ἢ οὐκ ἀνοήτου ἀνθρώπου ἐστὶν αἰσχύνεσθαι αὐτὸν ἐπαινεῖν μέλλοντα τὰ μέγιστα ὀνήσειν], just as in the opposite case, I suppose, when one repeatedly exalts and praises himself when danger or harm are at hand?" [ὥσπερ, οἶμαι, καὶ τοὐναντίον, σεμνύνεσθαι καὶ λέγειν ὑπὲρ αὑτοῦ πολλάκις, εἰ κίνδυνός τις ἢ βλάβη προσείη;]? (*Or.* 57.4–5).

[705] Μᾶλλον γὰρ Παῦλος καυχώμενος τότε εὐδοκίμησεν, ἢ ἕτερός τις κρύπτων τὰ ἑαυτοῦ κατορθώματα· οὐδεὶς γὰρ τοσαῦτα εἰργάσατο ἀγαθὰ ἀποκρύπτων τὰ ἑαυτοῦ, ὅσα ἐκεῖνος ἐξειπὼν τὰ ἑαυτοῦ (*laud. Paul.* 5.10 [SC 300.248–50]).

[706] ἔνιοι τοὺς αὑτῶν ἐπαίνους μὴ παντελῶς λαμπροὺς μηδὲ ἀκράτους προσφέροντες, ἀλλά τινας ἐλλείψεις ἢ ἀποτεύξις ἢ ἁμαρτίας ἐλαφρὰς ἐμβάλλοντες ἀφαιροῦσι τὸ ἐπαχθὲς αὐτῶν καὶ νεμεσητόν (*Mor.* 543F; cf. 544B). The connection between this described rhetorical technique and Paul's strategy of focusing on his weaknesses in 2 Corinthians 11–12, noted by Betz, "*de laude ipsius*," 379 and 392, and Furnish, *II Corinthians*, 547, receives further confirmation here from Chrysostom's early evaluation of Paul's argumentation on these same terms.

[707] *laud. Paul.* 5.11, 15 [SC 300.250, 256]; cf. *hom. in 2 Cor.* 27.1 [61.583]; *hom. in Gen.* 11.6 [53.96].

for doing it, or the act of begging off from having to engage in self-praise in the first place.[708] Elsewhere John says Paul honorably "deflected" or "evaded" the praise.[709] Despite the fact that Paul's boasting was justified, since it was in answer to a pressing need, even under those conditions he carried it out in this self-deprecating way so as to thwart the possibility that others, seeing him rightfully boasting, might wrongly think it justified their adoption of the practice of boasting in any circumstance.[710] Chrysostom first proved Paul's reticence to praise himself exegetically, citing as instances 2 Cor 11:1, 17, 21, as well as his invocation of "the man he knows" in 12:2, and the complaint that the Corinthians "compelled" him [ὑμεῖς με ἠναγκάσατε] to do it, in 12:11. Surely only someone foolish and extremely stupid would fail to notice how Paul here "hesitated and shrank away from boasting" [ὀκνῶν καὶ ἀναδυόμενος περὶ ἑαυτοῦ τι μέγα εἶπειν].[711] Furthermore, the very example Paul brings forth, the ecstatic vision obliquely described in 2 Cor 12:2, takes him back fully fourteen years, to an event he had kept silent about in the long interval since it occurred. Also, Chrysostom reasons, in that ample duration Paul would have accrued progressively more impressive feats, any one of which he might have chosen to mention here, but did not.[712] He encapsulates this image of Paul the reluctant boaster with a memorable animal portrait: Paul in boasting was like a horse continually rearing back when it approaches a precipice.[713] Paul did not flee the deed when circumstance required it, nor did he engage in it without being compelled to do so.[714] And his honorable resistance, combined with his shrewd "anticipatory correction,"[715] shows that it was not vainglory that prompted him to boast.

3. *Hiding the Greater Deeds.* A third proof that the motivation behind Paul's boasting was the edification of his hearers is offered by the moderation he employed in naming his good deeds, for Paul "didn't tell everything, but hid his

---

[708] See also *laud. Paul.* 5.13 [SC 300.254]: "For Paul spoke all these things, and more besides that he begged off from telling, to everyone when necessity befell him" [Ταῦτα γὰρ ἅπαντα καὶ πλείονα τούτων, δι' ὧν παρῃτήσατο καὶ ἀνάγκης ἐμπεσούσης, εἶπε πρὸς ἅπαντας]; *hom. in 2 Cor.* 24.1; 25.1 [61.564–65, 569].

[709] *laud. Paul.* 5.6 [SC 300.246]: ὅταν ἴδῃς διακρουόμενον ἐγκώμιον; also *hom. in 2 Cor.* 23.1 [61.553].

[710] *laud. Paul.* 5.11 [SC 300.250]: "the others, seeing him do it, would likely take up the practice by his example, yet do it frivolously and in vain" [ἁπλῶς καὶ εἰκῇ].

[711] *laud. Paul.* 5.12 [SC 300.250–52]; the same sentiment is frequent in the homilies on 2 Corinthians (*hom. in 2 Cor.* 22.2; 24.1; 25.1 [61.550, 564, 569]).

[712] "He had so many and such continual moments of converse with God as were shared by none of the prophets or apostles" [ὁμιλίαι τοσαῦται καὶ οὕτω συνεχεῖς πρὸς τὸν θεὸν ἦσαν αὐτῷ γεγενημέναι, ὅσαι μήτε προφητῶν, μήτε ἀποστόλων ἐγένοντο μηδενί] (*laud. Paul.* 5.10 [SC 300.248]; also *hom. in 2 Cor.* 22.2; 26.1 [61.550, 575–76]). For the rhetorical strategy, compare the quotation from Libanios in n. 702, above.

[713] John obviously enjoyed the image, as he used it for the same purpose also in *hom. in 2 Cor. 11:1* 4 [51.304–5].

[714] *laud. Paul.* 5.12 [SC 300.252].

[715] προδιόρθωσις (*laud. Paul.* 5.12 [SC 300.250]), a rhetorical term (see LSJ, 1475).

greatest accomplishments" [μὴ πάντα εἰπεῖν, ἀλλὰ τὰ μείζονα ἀποκρύψασθαι].[716]
This is sure proof that Paul was not motivated by vainglory, for if he were, he could
have summoned any number of marvelous deeds to add to his case and maximize
the effect.[717] Again John accents the voluntary nature of Paul's self-restraint in
boasting, given the fact that he *was* justified to praise himself because of the dire
circumstances. "But even more than this, not even when necessity befell him did he
continually pour out all his virtuous deeds in public, but he hid the most and the
best of them."[718] On this interpretation Paul's self-disclosure of deeds in the letters
is more to be evaluated on the grounds of what it conceals than what it placards.[719]
In this way Chrysostom attempts to neutralize the obvious counter-evidence
which started the argument in the first place: the letters themselves, which rather·
frequently show Paul talking about himself and his accomplishments. Because he
has to address the question of why these things were written down in the first
place,[720] Chrysostom reiterates his view that, because the letters represent only a
paltry selection from among Paul's myriad virtuous acts, they are sure proof of the
apostle's magnificent virtue, for they demonstrate that he knew how to walk the
fine line between telling too much and too little, in his wisdom discerning just how
far he should go in boasting.[721] By so carefully choosing his words, Paul, far from
being a "foolish braggadocio" [ἀλαζών],[722] was an exemplar of the commendable

---

[716]   *laud. Paul.* 5.15 [SC 300.256]. See also *comm. in Gal.* 1.11 [61.633]; *hom. in 2 Cor.* 26.1
[61.575]; *hom. in 2 Cor. 11:1* 5 [51.310]; *hom. in Ac.* 44.1 [60.309].

[717]   "For he hid the majority of them, and didn't tell all, lest he not confer great glory on himself"
[τὰς γὰρ πλείους ἀπέκρυψε, οὔτε πάσας εἶπεν, ἵνα μὴ δόξαν ἑαυτῷ περιθῇ μεγάλην] (*laud. Paul.*
5.10 [SC 300.248]).

[718]   Τὸ δὲ τούτου μεῖζον, ὅτι οὐδὲ ἀνάγκης ἐμπεσούσης, πάντα ἐξέχεεν εἰς μέσον, ἀλλὰ τὰ
πλείονα ἀπεκρύψατο καὶ τὰ μείζονα (*laud. Paul.* 5.13 [SC 300.254]). Chrysostom's exegetical
defense of this assertion is the conjunction he makes between 2 Cor 12:1, where Paul seemingly
begins to talk about his ecstatic visions and revelations of the Lord, and 12:6b, which Chrysostom
takes as Paul's renunciation of a full listing of them, for fear it might lead the Corinthians to an
inflated evaluation of his person on account of his extraordinary actions.

[719]   See n. 490 above, on Chrysostom's analogous interpretation of Paul's use of shorthand
when talking about his miracles, and longhand when cataloguing his weakness and sufferings.

[720]   Chrysostom addresses a hypothetical objector at *laud. Paul.* 5.10 [SC 300.248]: "Now don't
tell me that these things were written down in the letters" [Μὴ γάρ μοι ταύτας εἴπῃς τὰς
ἀναγεγραμμένας], and, once again, in a more convoluted dialogue, in *hom. in 2 Cor.* 26.1 [61.575]:
"Now indeed someone might say, 'if he wished to hide his good deeds completely, then he should
not have hinted [δοῦναι αἴνιγμα] at them, nor said any such thing (as 12:1–10); but if he wished
to tell of these things, then he should have done so clearly' [σαφῶς εἰπεῖν]. Therefore, why was
it that he neither spoke clearly of these things nor kept silent [Τίνος οὖν ἕνεκεν οὔτε σαφῶς εἶπεν,
οὔτε ἐσίγησεν;]? So that he might show also here that he entered into the act of boasting
unwillingly" [ἄκων].

[721]   ἔγνω μέχρι ποῦ προσελθεῖν ἔδει (*laud. Paul.* 5.11 [SC 300.250]).

[722]   See John's reverse claim: καθαρὸς ἀλαζονείας ἦν, and the negative characterization of one
who does not recognize the proper limits of self-praise as φιλότιμος καὶ ἀλαζών (*laud. Paul.* 5.14
[SC 300.256]; cf. *hom. in 2 Cor.* 22.2 [61.548], where John says Paul showed that his
opponents, who boasted in themselves, were ἀλαζόνες). This is the term Dio Chrysostom seeks

classical virtue of μετριότης, "moderation" or "modesty," as John repeatedly emphasizes.[723] This type of even-handed modesty is also manifested by the actuality that Paul didn't just withhold laudable deeds, but also freely combined his self-praise with self-humiliation (as noted in point #2),[724] not only in the praise of his weakness and suffering in 2 Cor 11–12,[725] but also in the shocking self-confessions of 1 Cor 15:9, Eph 3:8, and 1 Tim 1:12.[726] And yet there was another form of μετριάζειν that Paul practiced even in the midst of boasting: the deferral of the credit for his praiseworthy acts from himself to God.[727]

4. *Prosopopoiia.* Not only does Paul hide the majority of his praiseworthy deeds, but he even tries to hide his own self when compelled to tell of his marvelous

to deflect from Nestor (*Or.* 57.2–3). Although Paul uses a similar word, ἄφρων, "fool," in 2 Cor 11:16; 12:6 and 11, instead of ἀλαζών, see Rom 1:30; cf. 2 Tim 3:2.

[723] *laud. Paul.* 5.9 [SC 300.246]: ἀλλ' ὅμως αὐτὸν οὐκ ἐπῆρεν, ἀλλὰ καὶ ἐν αὐτῷ τούτῳ μετριάζει; 5.11 [SC 300.250]: οὐ ... ἀμέτρως πάλιν τῷ πράγματι ἐχρήσατο. The verb μετριάζειν is the opposite of μεγάλα φθεγγόμενος in 5.8 [SC 300.246], and of ἐπαίρων ἑαυτόν in the summation of 5.16 [SC 300.258]. See also earlier in that paragraph: Καὶ πάντων μέτρα ἐστὶ παρ' αὐτῷ κείμενα. The concept of moderation figures largely also in Chrysostom's homilies on 2 Corinthians (see, e.g., *hom. in 2 Cor.* 23.4; 24.1; 27.1 [61.558, 565, 584]). It is the antithesis of Plutarch's disparaging description of Cicero's ἀμετρία τῆς περιαυτολογίας (*comp. Dem. et Cic.* 2.1; cf. *Mor.* 543E, advancing the following recommendation: τι τοιοῦτο περὶ αὐτῶν ἀνεπίφθονον καὶ μέτριον λέγουσιν). Once again the precedent and characteristic terminology for this appeal were established by Demosthenes, *Or.* 18.4: πολλάκις λέγειν ἀναγκασθήσομαι περὶ ἐμαυτοῦ. πειράσομαι μὲν οὖν ὡς μετριώτατα τοῦτο ποιεῖν.

[724] καὶ μᾶλλον ἐταπεινοῦτο διὰ ταῦτα (*laud. Paul.* 5.10 [SC 300.248]). See also, e.g., *hom. in 1 Cor.* 38.4 [61.327–8], in reference to 1 Cor 15:8–10: "For that is why here, too, he is modest [καὶ ἐνταῦθα μετριάζει] ... for first he moderates and heaps up many accusations against himself, and then he offers his own praises" [Πρότερον γὰρ μετριάσας καὶ κατηγορίας ἑαυτοῦ συμφορήσας πολλάς, τότε τὰ καθ' ἑαυτόν σεμνύνει], and *hom. in 2 Cor.* 22.1 [61.547], in reference to Galatians: καὶ μετριάζει, καὶ περὶ ἑαυτοῦ μέγα τι λέγει. Yet another form of μετριάζειν which John attributes to Paul is that, even as he tells of his magnificent heavenly journey, he mingles with the testimony notes of his own ignorance ("whether in the body, or out of the body, *I do not know*" [2 Cor 12:2–3]) (*hom. in 2 Cor.* 26.1 [61.576]).

[725] *pan. Bab.* 2 61 [SC 362.170], "imitating the blessed Paul, who turned things upside down by boasting in his wounds, his bonds, his chain, and exalting himself over things of which others are ashamed" [τὸν μακάριον Παῦλον μιμούμενος ὃς ἄνω καὶ κάτω τὰ στίγματα, τὰ δεσμά, τὴν ἅλυσιν ἔστρεφε καυχώμενος καὶ μέγα φρονῶν ἐφ' οἷς ᾐσχύνοντο ἕτεροι].

[726] All three of these examples of "modesty" are brought together in *hom. in Eph.* 7.1 [62.49], with this evaluation: "To exhibit modesty in speech in the present after accomplishing so many virtuous deeds, and to call himself 'the least of all,' is an instance of great and surpassing modesty" [τὸ δὲ μετὰ τοσαῦτα κατορθώματα καὶ ἐπὶ τοῦ παρόντος μετριάζειν, καὶ πάντων ἑαυτὸν λέγειν ἐλαχιστότερον, πολλῆς καὶ ὑπερβαλλούσης ἐστὶ μετριότητος].

[727] Chrysostom does not summon this supporting argument here, but he does so in the exegetical homilies, such as *hom. in 1 Cor.* 8.3 [61.72]: Ὅρα γοῦν πῶς μετριάζει ... ἀλλ' ὅλον ἑαυτὸν πρότερον ἀναθεὶς τῷ θεῷ; *hom. in 2 Cor.* 5.2 [61.430]: πάλιν μετριάζει, τῷ θεῷ πάντα ἀνατιθείς; 22.1, 2 [61.548, 549]; *hom. in 1 Thess.* 1.1 [62.393]: Διδάσκει δὲ αὐτοὺς καὶ μετριάζειν, μονονουχὶ λέγων, ὅτι τῆς τοῦ θεοῦ δυνάμεώς ἐστι τὸ πᾶν, a strategem recommended also by Plutarch: "those who are compelled to praise themselves are made more tolerable if they do not give themselves all the credit for everything [τὸ μὴ πάντα προσποιεῖν ἑαυτοῖς], but, as though shaking off a heavy burden of glory, deflect some to chance and some to god" [τὸ μὲν εἰς τὴν τύχην τὸ δὲ εἰς τὸν θεὸν ἀποτίθεσθαι] (*Mor.* 542E).

accomplishments. Here John points to the famous circumlocution of 2 Cor 12:2–5, where Paul brings in the testimony of "a man whom he knows," and applies to Paul's strategy the accurate (if somewhat periphrastic) rhetorical terminology: "assuming another persona" [προσωπεῖον ἕτερον ὑπελθεῖν].[728] By an ironically inverse προσωποποιία Paul does not so much take on the persona of another as he takes off that of himself, and speaks as "the fool" looking upon the apostle as though distinct from himself.[729] He does not speak the words of his new character so much as he denies that his own words, allegedly spoken about another, are really about himself. Chrysostom considers this displacement a sure sign that Paul was not trying to gain honor for himself, since "when about to embark on encomia, he hides himself [κρύπτει ἑαυτόν] saying, 'I know a man.'"[730]

5. *Telling Only What is Presently Useful.* The fifth proof of Paul's magnanimity in the midst of boasting is a version of the third (that Paul was selective in the deeds

---

[728] Or "mask" (LSJ, 1533). Chrysostom does not use this rhetorical term when he treats the passage in his *hom. in 2 Cor.* 26.1 [61.575–576], but describes what Paul is doing with other rhetorical language:"Paul is not showing that it was someone else who was snatched up. But since he conceded to do so, and was able both to speak and to evade speaking openly about himself, he put his language figuratively in this way. For what sort of logical connection would there be, if, when speaking about himself, he brought in someone else?" [οὐ τοῦτο δηλῶν, ὅτι ἕτερός τις ἦν ὁ ἁρπαγείς· ἀλλ' ὡς ἐνεχώρει καὶ δυνατὸν ἦν καὶ εἰπεῖν, καὶ διακρούσασθαι τὸ περὶ ἑαυτοῦ εἰπεῖν φανερῶς, οὕτω σχηματίζει τὸν λόγον. Ποία γὰρ ἀκολουθία ἦν, περὶ ἑαυτοῦ διαλεγόμενον, ἄλλον παράγειν εἰς μέσον;]. Several times John insists that in 2 Corinthians 12, περὶ ἑαυτοῦ πᾶς ὁ λόγος ἦν, even though Paul deliberately "obscures" [συσκιάζειν] the fact (26.2 [576, 577]). This is reminiscent of Chrysostom's well-known interpretation of Paul's admission of μετασχηματίζειν in 1 Cor 4:6 – that it refers to his having "put masks" over the faces of the real Corinthian schismatics by naming the factions in relation to himself, Cephas and Apollos in 1:12 and 3:4, which he now removes (τότε ἀπαμφιάσας αὐτό, καὶ τὸ προσωπεῖον ἀπάρας, ἔδειξε τὰ κρυπτόμενα πρόσωπα ἐν τῇ τοῦ Παύλου καὶ Ἀπολλὼ προσηγορίᾳ [*hom. in 1 Cor.* 12.1 (61.95)]). John applies the term προσωποποιεῖν itself accurately (and fully three times) to what Paul does with the cosmos in Romans 8 (*hom. in Rom.* 14.5 [60.529–30], interestingly, arguing that Paul was imitating the prophets of Israel in so doing).That John accurately recognized the rhetorical figure προσωποποιία is supported by his interpretation of Isaiah, whom he credited with using the technique [προσωποποιεῖν/προσωποποιία] in 3:10 (of the chests which mourn) and 5:14 (of "Hades' soul") (*Is. interp.* 3.10; 5.5 [56.54, 63]). Even Jesus used the figure, προσωποποιεῖται τὸν καιρὸν (in Mt 6:34), κατὰ τὴν τῶν πολλῶν συνήθειαν φθεγγόμενος (*hom. in Mt.* 22.4 [57.304]). In virtually all these instances where Chrysostom identifies biblical personification, he notes that it is done to make the utterance "more expressive" or "vivid" [ἐμφαντικώτερον]. On προσωποποιία in Hellenistic rhetorical theory, see especially Theon, *Prog.* 10 [Spengel 2.115–16], and, with particular attention to Paul's use of the trope in Romans, Stanley K. Stowers, *A Rereading of Romans: Justice, Jews, and Gentiles* (New Haven:Yale University Press, 1994) 16–21, and *idem*, "Romans 7.7–25 as a Speech-in-Character (προσωποποιία)," *Paul in His Hellenistic Context*, ed.Troels Engberg-Pedersen (Minneapolis: Fortress, 1995) 180–202.

[729] In the context of 2 Corinthians 10–13 Paul has already "put on" another persona, that of the fool (11:1; cf. 12:11). Chrysostom has a rhetorically sensitive appreciation of Paul's argumentation here; note how he demarcates the key elements of the robing and disrobing of the fool persona by quoting *seriatim* 11:1, 17, 21; 12:2, 5, 11 (*laud. Paul.* 5.12 [SC 300.250–52]).

[730] *laud. Paul.* 5.12 [SC 300.250]: ἀλλὰ πάλιν μέλλων εἰς τὰ ἐγκώμια ἐμβαίνειν κρύπτει ἑαυτόν λέγων· Οἶδα ἄνθρωπον.

he chose to mention), but with a most important new ingredient: Paul chose to tell only deeds exemplifying the virtue most needed by his auditors in the present circumstance. The accent here is on the *usefulness or advantage* [χρήσιμα, συμφέρον] of the boasting for the hearers (as opposed to the teller),[731] which is a dominant criterion of acceptable praise for Plutarch, as well.[732] Next Chrysostom exemplifies the general principle of selective self-praise by reference to two biblical notables: Samuel and David.[733] Whereas Samuel could have spoken of any number of his virtues (σωφροσύνη, ταπεινοφροσύνη, μὴ μνησικακεῖν), he chose to speak only of his δικαιοσύνη, in not stealing from anyone, taking bribes in his leadership, or lording over the people Israel unfairly (1 Kgdms 12:1–5). This was because the present king, Saul, needed to learn about justice and about keeping one's hands free of bribes.[734] David, too, only boasted of the select virtues that could set his hearer on the right path.[735] That is why in his self-recommendation to Saul, when begging for the chance to fight Goliath, David mentioned no other virtuous act [ἀρετή] but his defeat of the bear and the lion (1 Kgdms 17:34–37). By this self-restraint David modeled the principle from which Chrysostom confers praise on Paul as φιλάνθρωπος:

For to draw out his speech further would have been the act of a vainglorious man and a braggadocio [φιλοτίμου καὶ ἀλαζόνος], whereas to say the very things which would be necessary for the present need [τὸ δὲ εἰπεῖν ταῦτα ἃ πρὸς τὴν παροῦσαν ἔμελλε χρείαν

---

[731] ποιεῖν ... οὕτω χρησίμως (*laud. Paul.* 5.10 [SC 300.248]); ὅσα τοῖς ἀκούουσι χρήσιμα (5.13 [SC 300.254]); ἃ τοῖς ἀκούουσι συνέφερεν (5.14 [SC 300.254]). Note also, in the latter text, εἰς γὰρ ὠφέλειαν ἡμῶν καὶ τὰ ἐγκώμια γίνεται (cf. *hom. in 2 Cor.* 23.3 [61.557], Ἤιδει γὰρ τοῦτο μάλιστα ὠφελῆσον τοὺς μαθητάς).

[732] "... not only should self-praise be ungrievesome and inoffensive [οὐ ... ἀλύπως καὶ ἀνεπιφθόνως], but also useful and advantageous" [χρησίμως καὶ ὠφελίμως] (*Mor.* 544E; cf. 545F, ἐπαινῶν ἑαυτὸν ὠφελεῖ τὸν ἀκούοντα). "Such praise is good and useful, and teaches one to admire and love what is useful and advantageous, rather than things that are empty and superfluous" (*Mor.* 546B; cf. 539E, and the final line of the treatise, "we shall desist from speaking about ourselves, unless we are going to confer great benefits on either ourselves, or the hearers [ἀφεξόμεθα τοῦ λέγειν περὶ αὑτῶν, ἂν μή τι μεγάλα μέλλωμεν ὠφελεῖν ἑαυτοὺς ἢ τοὺς ἀκούοντας]"). This is praise which "bears good fruit" [καλὸν γὰρ ὁ τοιοῦτος ἔπαινος ἐκφέρει καρπόν], the opposite of which is, naturally, "vain" or "empty" praise [κενὸς ἔπαινος] (*Mor.* 539E–540A), an idea shared by Chrysostom [πάντα ἡμῖν κενοῖ τὸν μισθὸν μετὰ τοὺς πολλοὺς ἱδρῶτας καὶ πόνους] (5.13 [SC 300.254]; cf. 5.11 on the danger of boasting εἰκῇ [SC 300.250]). This is the same criterion Betz found operative in Paul's boasting in 2 Corinthians 10–13: "Bei allem, was er vorbringt, kann auch nicht der leiseste Verdacht der 'φιλαυτία' aufkommen; im Gegenteil, sein Beweggrund ist die Liebe zu den Korinthern ... Hier liegt denn auch der Gesichtspunkt des 'Nutzens', der ihn veranlaßt, sich auf das Selbstlob überhaupt einzulassen" (*Apostel Paulus*, 78).

[733] He draws upon these same two examples, as well as the prophet Amos, in *hom. in 2 Cor.* 25.3 [61.567–68]. But there he provides an extended σύγκρισις of David and Paul, characterizing the former's win over Goliath as mere "child's play" [παιδὸς ἔργον] compared with Paul's victory over the entire ranks of the devil, by the power of utterance alone.

[734] *laud. Paul.* 5.14 [SC 300.254].

[735] Here I am adopting Piédagnel's translation of the term διορθῶσαι (SC 300.257).

ἀναγκαῖα εἶναι] is the part of one who loves humanity and looks to the advantage of the many [φιλανθρώπου καὶ τὸ τῶν πολλῶν συμφέρον ὁρῶντος]. Which is precisely what Paul did.[736]

When forced to defend himself against charges that he was not a genuine apostle [ὡς οὐκ ὢν ἀπόστολος δόκιμος] and had no power [οὐδὲ ἔχων τινὰ ἰσχύν], Paul proved his dignified position [αὐτοῦ ἀξίωμα] by boasting in this loving, self-abnegating manner. Thus is the proposition proven, as the ensuing five-fold enumeration (with which we began our analysis of the proof) recounts.

Proof #3: Pauline Insults Worthy of Praise. Before closing the proof section of this long speech, Chrysostom ventures a very brief, parenthetical argument about a second controversial Pauline behavior which might appear a hindrance to his virtue and praise: his ὑβρίζειν, "insulting others."[737] Likely this abbreviated defense of Paul's castigation of others was inserted here because it lies at hand as another piece of potentially damaging counter-evidence to the benevolent portrait John has just so carefully painted of Paul as φιλόστοργος καὶ φιλάνθρωπος. And, like boasting, verbal attacks are a form of speech that constitutes a πρᾶξις. As with all the πράξεις ἐναντίαι for which Paul is praised in this speech, Paul's insults of his brothers are justified, as Chrysostom tells it, because Paul employed them with a sensitive eye on the present circumstances [τούτῳ δεόντως ἐχρήσατο πάλιν]. Consequently, he is more deserving of praise for his propitious maltreatment than are those who pronounce encomia.[738] The bitter Pauline invectives of Gal 3:1, 3 and Titus 1:12 should not, therefore, be regarded as counter-evidence to Paul's magnanimity, but proof of his laudability, given that he both acted on and taught the rule and standard for properly harsh speech toward those who are neglectful of their religious duties. In a final irony, the apostle of polar opposite deeds is at last proclaimed to be the mean: "the proper measure of all things resides in him" [Καὶ πάντων μέτρα ἐστὶ παρ' αὐτῷ κείμενα].[739]

ἀνακεφαλαίωσις *(Recapitulation)*.[740] As a quite regular feature of his rhetorical art, Chrysostom closes his proof with a recapitulation that summarizes its main propositions and arguments. In this oration we find, as we did with the partition in the proof, an especially close correspondence between the recapitulation and the rest of the oration. In antithetical pairings John summarizes in chiastic order

---

[736] *laud. Paul.* 5.14 [SC 300.256].

[737] Chrysostom engages Paul's harsh behavior also in *laud. Paul.* 6.10–13 [SC 300.278–90]. With this theme one notes another concurrence with John's own life, given that one of the accusations against the bishop was that in his dealings with other clergy in the church, as well as with laity and even the imperial family, he engaged in ὑβρίζειν. Palladios seeks to defend Chrysostom against this charge in *v. Chrys.* 19.93–117 [SC 341.384–86]).

[738] *laud. Paul.* 5.16 [SC 300.256].

[739] *laud. Paul.* 5.16 [SC 300.258]; cf. 6.9 [SC 300.278].

[740] This short recapitulation extends from *laud. Paul.* 5.16, lines 10–16 [SC 300.258].

the paradoxical proofs he has offered that Paul is to be praised no matter which of two contradictory actions he engaged in.

Indeed, for this reason Paul is highly esteemed in everything he does and says [πάντα ποιῶν καὶ λέγων εὐδοκίμει], both insulting and praising [ὑβρίζων καὶ ἐπαινῶν], abandoning and soliciting [ἀποστρεφόμενος καὶ θεραπεύων], exalting himself and speaking modestly [ἐπαίρων ἑαυτὸν καὶ μετριάζων], boasting and lowering himself [καυχώμενος καὶ ταλανίζων].⁷⁴¹

Here John proclaims his backwards encomium totally successful: Paul, the man of contrary behavior – in both word and deed – earns *by it* (and not just despite it) praise rather than excoriation. Reflecting the somewhat madcap spirit of this inverted encomium, John ends with a blanket appeal to the precedent of the Scriptures, Old and New Testaments, in which, he blithely maintains, insults, reviling, even murder, deception and guile are held in esteem. Leaving this controversial assertion suggestively in the air (perhaps for fear of opening yet another Pandora's box), Chrysostom moves at last to his concluding exhortation.

ἐπίλογος *(Conclusion)*. This liturgical homily ends (rather abruptly) with the customary epideictic exhortation to admire and imitate the illustrious example in order to receive the same reward – in this case, eternal blessings.⁷⁴² What justifies the entire enterprise of this speech is the stated need to "study all these things accurately" [ταῦτα ἅπαντα μετὰ ἀκριβείας ἐξετάσαντες]. The oration is meant to make available all the Pauline πράξεις, and not just those which are manifestly laudatory, for contemplation and emulation, as long as one has observed in him not just the isolated deeds, but the principles of moderation and concern for the welfare of others which stand behind his acts. Hence, once again Paul's "deeds" are regarded as a source of instruction in enacted virtue, material manifestations of the truthful word he proclaimed.

Other Encomiastic Topics

Among Theon's full list of epideictic topoi of "external circumstances" which we cited at the outset of this chapter are more specific elements of a person's life, such as education (which we have already treated), friendship, glory, rule, wealth, child-rearing, and noble death,⁷⁴³ that are not included in Aphthonios' more general set

---

⁷⁴¹ *laud. Paul.* 5.16 [SC 300.258].

⁷⁴² "Let us marvel at Paul, let us glorify God, and let us deal with him in such a way that also we ourselves might attain the eternal goods" [Παῦλον θαυμάσωμεν, καὶ τὸν θεὸν δοξάσωμεν, καὶ ἡμεῖς οὕτως αὐτὸν μεταχειρισώμεθα, ἵνα καὶ αὐτοὶ τῶν αἰωνίων ἐπιτύχωμεν ἀγαθῶν] (*laud. Paul.* 5.17 [SC 300.258]).

⁷⁴³ παιδεία, φιλία, δόξα, ἀρχή, πλοῦτος, εὐτεκνία, εὐθανασία (Theon, *Prog.* 8 [Spengel 2.110]). Aphthonios includes among αἱ πράξεις κατὰ τυχήν: δυναστεία, πλοῦτος, φίλοι (*Prog.* 8 [Spengel 2.36]). These traditional topics are of course well known to Chrysostom both individually and as a set; see, e.g., *comp.* 1 [47.387], where he names among the things that people love πλοῦτος, δυναστεία, ἀρχή and δόξα.

of categories. Because Chrysostom portrays Paul in relation to these topics, also, in some interesting and telling ways, we shall take a glimpse at each of these portraits briefly in turn, to fill out John's biographical picture of Paul.

φιλία (Friendship)

One way to praise a person is to stress that they had many loyal friends, whose friendship in itself constitutes a testimony to the virtue and kindness of the subject who could inspire such love from others.[744] In Chrysostom's view, Paul was such a person. He had some very good friends, such as Barnabas, who sought Paul out in Tarsus when everyone else was afraid of the persecutor-turned-evangelist.[745] But, even more than this, Paul had friends in high places. John proclaims that at the moment of his conversion Christ immediately enrolled Paul on the list of his friends, even among the chief of them.[746] In Christian circles this is perhaps the highest criterion of praise – closeness to the master. And Paul was also, to be sure, a friend of God.[747]

Chrysostom also views Paul as a wonderful friend to others. John was so impressed by Paul's friendly association with Prisca and Aquila that he wrote two homilies devoted just to Paul's greeting of the pair in Rom 16:3.[748] He especially admires Paul's openness to friendship with his social inferiors, such as the tent-making couple must have been, in his eyes.[749] Paul's words in 1 Thess 2:8 about giving his very soul for his beloved young Macedonian converts inspire Chrysostom to deliver a discourse in praise of "genuine" friendship [φίλος γνήσιος].[750] Invoking biblical aphorisms[751] alongside well-known classical teachings about friends,[752] and New Testament examples,[753] Chrysostom paints a picture of the necessity and great treasure of a true friend. Against this tableau, precipitated by

---

[744] On friendship as an encomiastic topic, see also [Cicero], Rhet. Her. 3.7.14. On the use of this κεφάλαιον in actual speeches see, e.g., Libanios, Or. 18.20.

[745] hom. in Ac. 21.1 [60.164].

[746] εἰς τοὺς φίλους αὐτὸν εὐθέως καὶ τὰ πρωτεῖα ἔχοντας κατέλεξε (sc. Χριστός) (hom. in Jo. 10.1 [59.74]).

[747] laud. Paul. 7.2 [SC 300.294]: θεῷ φίλος. In this same homily, Chrysostom argues that, by an incredible inversion of motivation, Paul's enemies unwittingly performed the acts of a friend and furthered the gospel [Καὶ ὅπερ ἂν ἐποίησαν φίλοι καὶ συντεταγμένοι, τοῦτο ἐποίουν οἱ πολέμιοι] (7.11 [SC 300.318]).

[748] hom. 1–2 in Rom. 16:3. These stand independent of the homily series, hom. in Rom.

[749] hom. in Rom. 16:3 1.2 [51.189]. See the full discussion of this passage, and its inherent ironies, on pp. 374–77 below. John makes the same argument about Paul's openness to friendship with those of low class in laud. Paul. 7.9 [SC 300.310–12], where he stresses that Paul was not ashamed to be associated with his fellow prisoners on the sea-voyage to Rome.

[750] hom. in 1 Thess. 2.3–4 [62.403–406].

[751] "A faithful friend is a medicine of life" and "a faithful friend is a mighty protection" (Sir 6:16, 14).

[752] Including: friends have all possessions in common; they share a single soul; one can live in darkness with friends but not without them in the sun.

[753] Such as the concordant Jerusalem community in Acts 4:32–35.

Paul's declaration of love for the Thessalonians, Chrysostom declares that Paul was such a friend, a spiritual friend, who valued nothing more than friendship, a man who, unbidden, gladly gave himself for his friends,[754] even to the extent of willingly falling into Gehenna for the sake of others (Rom 9:3). He is the perfect example of how one must "love with a fiery purpose" [οὕτω χρὴ φιλεῖν διαθέσει πεπυρωμένῃ].[755]

δόξα (Glory/Reputation)

John depicts Paul as having been possessed of the very greatest sort of glory, that which stands in direct contrast to worldly repute. This was the proposition of *hom. in 2 Tim.* 4.3–4, which we analyzed at the outset of this chapter,[756] where Paul's glory was proved to have outshone Nero's a thousandfold and more. In that argument Chrysostom very self-consciously sought to demonstrate that Paul exceeded Nero's glory, not just on Christian standards, but even by the worldly measurements of glory and celebrity themselves.[757] Hence the *topos* on δόξα presented the Christian orator with a temptation to "have his cake and eat it too," i.e., both to repudiate worldly standards and to claim them, when desirable. Chrysostom's earliest σύγκρισις between Paul and Nero was a part of his larger argument in *adversus oppugnatores vitae monasticae* against those who were reviling and punishing Christian monks. That comparison ends with a brief, triumphant depiction of Paul in glory – in heaven:

> The blessed Paul will stand with great boldness before the very throne of the King, shining brilliantly, and clothed in a glory so great that it lacks nothing possessed by the angels and archangels [καὶ δόξαν ἠμφιεσμένος τοσαύτην, ὡς μηδὲν τῶν ἀγγέλων καὶ τῶν ἀρχαγγέλων ἀποδεῖν], and he will receive the reward which is fitting for a man who gives over his body and his soul for the things pleasing to God.[758]

As John tells it, Paul's glory, especially when seen within a larger temporal and cosmic frame of reference, utterly burst the bounds of earthly measurement or comparison (even an emperor is useless at these heights), and must be registered on a celestial scale, in comparison with the glory of the highest angels in heaven. This is a context in which the δόξα of the πόλις intersects with the δόξα of the Greek Bible, in such a way that Chrysostom can use the latter to trump the former, for at the heavenly court Paul will earn his share of the divine δόξα surrounding the thronal retinue.

---

[754] See above, n. 506, on suffering for one's friends.

[755] *hom. in 1 Thess.* 2.4 [62.404].

[756] Pp. 206–12.

[757] *hom. in 2 Tim.* 4.3 [62.623]: "I am not speaking according to the discourse of faith (when I say Paul prevailed); for that is of course clear. But I am speaking according to the discourse of glory and dignity and celebrity" [οὐ λέγω κατὰ τὸν τῆς πίστεως λόγον· τοῦτο γὰρ δῆλον· ἀλλὰ κατὰ τὸν τῆς δόξης καὶ τῆς σεμνότητος καὶ τῆς λαμπρότητος].

[758] *oppugn.* 1.4 [47.324].

ἀρχή (Rule)

Rule is one of the things of this world, alongside power and wealth, which the believer is to eschew.[759] But in a characteristically paradoxical Christian sense, as we have often had occasion to note, John regards Paul as having possessed the height of rulership. This is made manifest in his constant comparisons between Paul and emperors, such as Nero, to their debasement, as it is in the summary deed of Paul as world champion. And given that godly inspiration lay behind Paul's victory, Pauline rule lays claim to being divine ordination: "Did not God present him with the whole world, placing it into his hands?"[760] In a single passage, *hom. in 2 Cor.* 25.3, John uses a variety of images for Paul the champion of the whole world. One of these, the ship-captain, is a most ubiquitous ancient *topos* for rulership.[761] Paul as sea-pilot "governed the whole world as though it were a single house or a single ship."[762] But Paul is an unconventional ruler. As Chrysostom develops the image, Paul as ship-captain was not only the pilot, but took on all the roles [πάντα αὐτὸς ὤν], as sailor, steersman, ship and sail, and performed all the tasks, from assisting the seasick to pulling an oar, to watching the sky for changes in the weather. Likewise Paul the general, as Chrysostom paints him, did not stand on protocol, but himself took on the most undesirable scuttle work for his battalion.[763] Paul was a ruler perfectly willing to lead by self-sacrifice, even self-abasement.[764] This apostolic leader, who holds the number one spot in the pecking order of the Christian community (1 Cor 12:29),[765] as a spiritual ruler,[766] had a loving and appropriate awe, even fear, of the enormous responsibility which had been conferred upon him, and he never abused his authority.[767] By this portrait

---

[759] E.g., *comp.* 1 [47.387]; *compunct.* 2 3 [47.414].

[760] οὐ τὴν οἰκουμένην ἅπασαν εἰς χεῖρας αὐτῷ φέρων ἔθηκεν ὁ θεός; (*scand.* 2 [SC 79.60]; cf. *laud. Paul.* 7.1 [SC 300.294]). The connection of this Pauline portrait with Chrysostom's own self-image is shown in *sac.* 6.4 [SC 272.314] where John says the priest is "like one who has been entrusted with the whole world" [ὥσπερ τὸν ἅπαντα κόσμον πεπιστευμένος].

[761] For literature and references, see Mitchell, *Paul*, 163–64.

[762] καθάπερ μίαν οἰκίαν, ἢ πλοῖον ἕν, τὴν οἰκουμένην ἅπασαν κυβερνῶν (*hom. in 2 Cor.* 25.3 [61.573]).

[763] *laud. Paul.* 3.6 [SC 300.172]), quoted in chap. 3, n. 94.

[764] This is the way Paul presents himself, for instance, in 1 Cor 4:9–13; 9:19–23; 2 Cor 11:7.

[765] In *hom. in Ac. princ.* 3.3 [51.92] John seeks to demonstrate that the apostolate is not only the highest position of rulership, but it confers all the rest of the spiritual gifts in Paul's list, as well (in the next paragraph employing Paul as his example).

[766] See the σύγκρισις between the apostles, termed "spiritual rulers" [ἄρχοντες πνευματικοί], and "everyday rulers" [οἱ βιωτικοὶ ἄρχοντες] in *hom. in Ac. princ.* 3.4 [51.93–94]: "For the apostles were rulers hand-picked by God, rulers who did not take charge of discrete nations and cities, but were all in common entrusted with the whole world" ['Άρχοντες γάρ εἰσιν ὑπὸ θεοῦ χειροτονηθέντες οἱ ἀπόστολοι· ἄρχοντες, οὐκ ἔθνη καὶ πόλεις διαφόρους λαμβάνοντες, ἀλλὰ πάντες κοινῇ τὴν οἰκουμένην ἐμπιστευθέντες]. The governing sphere of the apostles extends to heaven, for they have the same power as an earthly tyrant, to decide who is bound and who free, who stays and who goes (by appeal to Mt 18:18, applied to all the apostles).

[767] See *sac.* 3.7 [SC 272.156–58]: "but nevertheless, even with such advantages, he was still

Paul is the archetype of beneficent governance for all time, to be emulated by priests in the church and kings at court, for he "never seeks his own advantage, but that of the governed; he was always in this way fearful when surveying the enormity of his rule."[768] And, since Chrysostom depicts Paul's earthly rule as not ending with his death, but continuing thereafter (since he rules over the city of Rome itself from the confines of his tomb in its center),[769] Paul's governance even now relativizes any existing temporal powers.

πλοῦτος (Wealth)

As we have had occasion to observe in our treatment of Paul's voluntary poverty within the context of his ascetic acts, John's image of Paul's economic condition is drawn completely from Paul's own oxymoronic self-representation in 2 Cor 6:10, "as poor yet enriching many, as having nothing yet possessing everything" [ὡς πτωχοὶ πολλοὺς δὲ πλουτίζοντες, ὡς μηδὲν ἔχοντες καὶ πάντα κατέχοντες]. By means of this inversion Paul is simultaneously rich and poor: rich in spiritual realities, but pitifully poor in the things of this world.[770] He gave away all his belongings,[771] indeed, he even surrendered things that did not belong to him.[772] This was a constant fact of life for Paul, who "was so poor [πένης], that he often

---

afraid and trembled over this rule and those ruled by him [δέδοικεν ἔτι καὶ τρέμει περὶ ταύτης τῆς ἀρχῆς καὶ τῶν ἀρχομένων ὑπ' αὐτοῦ] ... (John cites 2 Cor 11:3; 1 Cor 2:3), a man who was snatched up into heaven and joined in unspeakable words with God, and endured as many deaths as the days he lived after he came to believe, a man who wished not to have to use the authority given him from Christ [ἄνθρωπος μηδὲ τῇ δοθείσῃ παρὰ Χριστοῦ χρήσασθαι ἐξουσίᾳ βουληθείς], lest any of the believers might be caused to stumble."The philosophy of leadership at work here is certainly based on 2 Cor 10:8 and 13:10.

[768] μηδαμοῦ τὸ ἑαυτοῦ ζητῶν, ἀλλὰ τὸ τῶν ἀρχομένων, οὕτως ἔμφοβος ἦν ἀεὶ πρὸς τὸ τῆς ἀρχῆς μέγεθος ἀφορῶν (*sac.* 3.7 [SC 272.156]). On these as political commonplaces see Mitchell, *Paul*, 142–47. Chrysostom here is picking up on the way Paul describes himself, particularly in 1 Corinthians (e.g., 9:19–23; 10:33).

[769] ὁ δὲ τὸ μέσον κατέχει τῆς πόλεως, καθάπερ βασιλεύων καὶ ζῶν (*hom. in 2 Tim.* 4.4 [62.624]). One can see hints of this in *laud. Paul.* 7.9 [SC 300.310], where Paul when journeying to Rome is depicted as "rejoicing as though sent forth to take an important official assignment [ἔχαιρεν ὡς ἐπὶ μεγίστην ἀρχὴν προπεμπόμενος]. And, indeed, it was no small task that was awaiting him – setting straight the city of Rome" [καὶ γὰρ οὐδὲ μικρὸς ἆθλος αὐτῷ τῆς Ῥωμαίων πόλεως ἡ διόρθωσις προύκειτο].

[770] In *laud. Paul.* 7.8 [SC 300.310] John admits there was one type of poverty Paul did fear: leaving this world "poor and impoverished when it came to the salvation of the many" [πτωχὸς καὶ πένης τῆς τῶν πολλῶν σωτηρίας].

[771] According to *laud. Paul.* 1.11 [SC 300.130], Paul had only a single possession, his own body [οὐδὲν πλέον κεκτημένος τοῦ σώματος]. He used that one commodity to do physical labor so that he might provide for the needs of the poor.

[772] "[He] gave up everything which he owned for Christ, and, more than that, things he didn't own [πάντα ὑπὲρ τοῦ Χριστοῦ προδούς, ὧν κύριος ἦν, μᾶλλον δὲ ὧν οὐκ ἦν] – for he gave up even the things present and things future, and height and depth and another creation (Rom 8:38–39)" (*laud. Paul.* 7.3 [SC 300.298]).

was hungry, and lacking in necessary provisions."[773] But Paul's poverty was never a hindrance to a life of virtue;[774] indeed, as with the rest of the poor, that condition of life was actually most conducive to the philosophical life, as Chrysostom himself would want to attest, by the happy convergence of his monastic experience with a generally Stoic outlook.[775] Unlike encomiasts who routinely invoke the poverty of their subject for the sake of a "rags to riches" narrative surprise, Chrysostom's Paul is poor throughout his life ("rich in rags"),[776] drawn in with fresh imaginative detail from Chrysostom's own encounters with the urban poor in Antioch and Constantinople.[777] A vivid feature of this portrait is the filthy rags in which this impoverished man met the world, and by which his poverty would have been instantly apparent.[778] Strikingly characteristic of this portrait of Paul the

---

[773] hom. in Ac. 20.4 [60.162]; also laud. Paul. 4.10 [SC 300.204]. Chrysostom regards all the apostles as having lived perpetually in hunger [λιμῷ διηνεκεῖ συνζῆν] (hom. in 1 Cor. 35.4 [61.301–302]).

[774] laud. Paul. 5.1 [SC 300.230].

[775] For Chrysostom's thoroughly romanticized notion of the poor as true philosophers because they cannot be distracted by the material things they do not own, see, e.g., hom. in 1 Cor. 34.5 [61.292]; kal. 4 [48.958]. The inverse is also true; it is the duty of a philosopher to despise both riches and glory. "Such a person is the philosopher, such is the rich person: she or he has everything, and has nothing ... the true philosopher [is] the one who has need of nothing" (hom. in Eph. 21.4 [62.153–54]). The latter is, of course, a Stoic commonplace, which Plutarch, at least, regarded as a deliberately contrary proposition: "But they want to say something paradoxical and excessive and original. Say that the wise person has need of nothing, nor asks for anything" [λέγε τὸν σοφὸν μηδενὸς ἔχειν χρείαν μηδὲ δεῖσθαί τινος] (Mor. 1068B, De communibus notitiis adversus Stoicos).

[776] Paul "lived in hunger" [ὁ ἐν λιμῷ ζῶν, ἄνθρωπος πολλάκις ἐν λιμῷ ζήσας], often going to bed hungry [κοιμηθεὶς πεινῶν] (hom. in 2 Tim. 4.3 [62.622]; hom. in Rom. 1.4 [60.400]: ὁ Παῦλος ἐν λιμῷ ζῶν τῷ διηνεκεῖ καὶ γυμνότητι; laud. Paul. 1.8 [SC 300.124]: λιμῷ διηνεκεῖ ἡμέρας καὶ νυκτός). Compare his picture of a poor man: λιμῷ παλαίει διηνεκεῖ (serm. in Gen. 5.4 [54.603]).

[777] In one of his most famous expositions on the poor, eleem. 1 [51.261], Chrysostom says that he has come before his congregation as though embarking on an embassy on behalf of the poor who dwell in the city, commissioned, as it were, not by speeches or votes or legislative decision, but by the very images of misery and bitter poverty which assaulted him on the way to church that morning [ἀλλὰ διὰ τῶν θεαμάτων τῶν ἐλεεινῶν καὶ πικροτάτων]. These are the visual material of John's portraits of Paul's poverty, just as they are for his ubiquitous exhortations to his congregants to support the poor by almsgiving and other acts of compassion (see also Kelly, Golden Mouth, 97–99 on Chrysostom's "heart-rending" descriptions of impoverished outcasts).

[778] See hom. in 2 Tim. 4.3 [62.622]: ἐν εὐτελεῖ σχήματι; 4.4 [62.623]: "filthy rags covered the unwashed man [ῥάκια περιέκειτο αὐχμῶντα] such as are worn in prison." The amplification of this image of Paul's begrimed clothes is due also to the commonplace σύγκρισις with the imperial robes (hom. in 2 Tim. 4.3–4 [62.622–23]). But it also evokes comparison with that most famous man of déshabillé, the Cynic philosopher Diogenes, who complicates the simple picture of Paul in tattered dress. Although in oppugn. 2.5 [47.339], when set against most pagans, Chrysostom rates Diogenes as superior, elsewhere when comparing Diogenes with Paul Chrysostom dresses his man more handsomely, "not just like that man of Sinope who was dressed in rags [ὁ ῥάκια περιβεβλημένος] and lived in a wine cask ... but Paul did none of these things, for he did not look toward vainglory [φιλοτιμία], but he wore clothes with all propriety [ἀλλὰ καὶ ἱμάτια περιβέβλητο μετὰ εὐσχημοσύνης ἁπάσης], and always lived in a house" (hom. in 1 Cor. 35.4

man of poverty is that it brings into sharp relief the hermeneutical role of the angle of vision of its beholder. If one has the paradoxical lens of the reversal of worldly expectations of wealth and poverty fastened on one's eyes like 3-D glasses or, better, x-ray lenses,[779] then one can view this portrait of Paul as an indigent for what it is – a thing of most exquisite beauty.[780] From that vantage point each detail of Paul's decrepitude redounds further to his renown. And here John the ekphrasist serves also as art critic, who tells his audience how to view the painting he is bringing before their minds – Paul abjectly poor, but stunningly glorious.[781]

Naturally, Chrysostom's portrait of Paul the poor man is painted in hues derived from his own conception of the poor as he knows and thinks about them.[782] This is an especially important insight given the fact that, in common with other fourth-century Christian writers, Chrysostom was engaged in a redefinition and new perspective on "the poor." Whereas in classical antiquity civic euergetism was understood as the responsibility of wealthy citizens to provide benefactions for the commonwealth, which was socially stratified in a range of recognizable ways, late antique Christian charity took its foundation from an innovative delineation of "the poor" as a distinct group, the proper object of *philanthropia*.[783] Peter Brown

---

[61.302]; for further discussion of Chrysostom's estimation of Diogenes, see Coleman-Norton, "St. Chrysostom," 308–309). Still another portrait of Paul's clothes is generated by Acts 19:12, and the extraordinary powers they commanded, a passage Chrysostom loves to evoke (see the section on miracles, pp. 291–95 above). On the other hand, Chrysostom can also often apply instead the more extreme commonplace that Paul did not have anything with which to clothe himself [οὐδὲ ἱμάτιον περιβαλέσθαι εἶχεν] (*laud. Paul.* 4.10,13 [SC 300.204,212]; *hom. in 2 Tim.* 4.3 [62.622]), and was virtually naked (*laud. Paul.* 1.12; 4.10, 13 [SC 300.130,204,212], πτωχός τις γυμνὸς; *hom. in 2 Tim.* 4.3 [62.622], ἄνθρωπος γυμνός).

[779] For true judgment, one must be able to move beyond sight of the externals into the soul. Chrysostom likes to contrast the external clothing with the genuine "clothing" of the soul, as in *hom. in Rom.* 4.4 [60.422]: "For don't look at their outer garments, but unveil their soul, and spy out if it isn't full of wounds, and dressed in rags [ῥάκια περιβέβληται] and barren and unguided. What is the benefit of this mania for the externals? For it is much better to live in virtue, though poor, than to be a king who lives with wickedness [Καὶ γὰρ πολλῷ βέλτιον πένητα εἶναι ἐν ἀρετῇ ζῶντα, ἢ βασιλέα ὄντα μετὰ πονηρίας]. For the poor person enjoys in him/herself great luxury in the soul, and isn't even conscious of external poverty because of internal wealth" ['Ο μὲν γὰρ πένης παρ' ἑαυτῷ ἀπολαύει πάσης τῆς κατὰ ψυχὴν τρυφῆς, καὶ οὐδὲ τῆς ἔξωθεν αἰσθάνεται πενίας διὰ τὸν ἔνδον πλοῦτον].

[780] In the midst of his famine Paul enjoyed more luxury than any kings ever have (*hom. in Rom.* 1.4 [60.400]).

[781] See *laud. Paul.* 7.2 [SC 300.294], μὴ στυγνάσῃς, ἀγαπητέ.

[782] See the stock descriptions of the poor, which use the identical language of πενία, αὐχμεῖν, ῥάκια περιβέβλησθαι/περικεῖσθαι, in *hom. in 2 Cor. 4:3* 3.11 [51.300]; *hom. in Jo.* 60.5 [59.333]; *serm. in Gen.* 5.4 [54.604]: οὗτος ὑμῖν ὁ πένης ἐπιστὰς, ῥυπῶν ῥάκια περιβεβλημένος.

[783] Brown, *Power and Persuasion*, 71–117; Cameron, *Later Roman Empire*, 126–127; J. H. W. G. Liebeschuetz, *Barbarians and Bishops: Army, Church, and State in the Age of Arcadius and Chrysostom* (Oxford: Clarendon, 1990) 187: "But Christian giving was different from the traditional munificence expected from the wealthy inhabitants of cities. Christian charity was not directed towards fellow citizens or political supporters but towards the poor, whoever they might be. It was given to them precisely because they were poor or sick, and because God wants Christians to look after

has argued that, by building upon the Old Testament and ancient Near Eastern concept of "the poor" (which was never a sociological category of the *polis*), Christian bishops in the late fourth century created a new social category that cut across the old political forms of the polis.[784] This stemmed from a distinctly new theological position: that the poor should be objects of concern because they share the same human body as the givers.[785] What we may add to Brown's adept picture of this transformation in social attitudes by Chrysostom is the important place played by portraits of Paul in his social program.[786] Since Paul was poor, and of the same nature as all humanity, then those who wish to align themselves with the apostolic favor must also align themselves with the poor of their own day, whose condition he shared. And because Paul called himself πτωχός, he provides a link between the Old Testament elevation of the עניים and the social geography of the late antique city that John is seeking to change. And what John praises in Paul – his true spiritual richness – he also claims for the poor.[787] Hence, the poor are dignified along with praise of Paul as poor, even as their cause is furthered by John's appeal to the apostle's constant "remembrance of the poor" [τῶν πτωχῶν μνημονεύειν], which he showed, John insists, not just in Gal 2:10, but in every single letter.[788] Consequently, Paul serves both as exemplar of the noble poor (the true philosophers), and as their generous benefactor [ὁ ἀληθῶς προστάτης καὶ κηδεμὼν τῶν ἐν πενίᾳ ζώντων Παῦλος],[789] and thus is a dual asset for Chrysostom's social project.[790]

---

those in need. In fact this was one way in which men might atone for the sins with which they were inevitably contaminated. The idea that the poor and the sick and the old ought to be helped because they were there, and were God's creatures, is not classical."

[784] See Brown, *Power and Persuasion*, 91, on the "singling out for particular concern of a category of persons that had no place in the traditional model of the urban community"; and Cameron, *Later Roman Empire*, 127: "Between these and the charitable foundations of the early empire the fundamental difference lay in their purpose and in the identification of the beneficiaries, specifically designated as the poor and needy in contrast to those of the early imperial foundations, which were often restricted to those of higher social class."

[785] Brown, *Body and Society*, 316. We shall return to this crucial topic in chap. 7, pp. 401–404.

[786] For example, one can see the larger revisioning of civic euergetism in John's comparison of Job and Paul: Job was φιλότιμος, generous out of love for the social honor such giving produces for wealthy benefactors, whereas Paul generated πρόσοδος, "revenue," for the destitute from his own physical labor (*laud. Paul.* 1.11 [SC 300.130]).

[787] "Chrysostom sketched an alternative economic system in which the rich had to acknowledge their indebtedness precisely to those who were poor and insignificant in the eyes of the world. His message was one of mutuality. He obtained this mutuality by investing the very poor, who had previously been excluded from patron-client relations because they had nothing to contribute, with a valuable commodity, namely, special access to God" (Leyerle, "John Chrysostom on Almsgiving," 41). No one better exemplifies the "special access to God" than Paul, which adds substantial weight to John's having self-consciously connected Paul and the poor of his day.

[788] *eleem.* 1 [51.261–62].

[789] Ibid. Paul champions their cause οἶδε γὰρ, οἶδεν ὅση τοῦ πράγματος ἰσχύς ("for he knew, he *knew* how mighty a matter it is"). See also the discussion above, pp. 316–18.

[790] Chrysostom unites the two facets of Paul's identity in his assumptions about private philanthropy, which arise in a comparison between the beneficence of Paul and of Job: "it is

εὐτεκνία (Children) and γάμος (Marriage)

These traditional topics get overturned by Chrysostom's ascetic value system, for John is certainly not interested in conferring praise on Paul for having married well or born an abundance of offspring. Even in the epideictic conventions proper, however, marriage is – significantly – not one of the encomiastic topics, though εὐτεκνία is,[791] reflecting the cultural values of Greco-Roman patriarchy. But we shall incorporate the issue of marriage here, since it was a prerequisite for child-bearing (at least in Chrysostom's eyes), and look first at how Chrysostom portrays Paul's marital status, before turning to the issue of Paul's progeny.

In general, as with Paul's natal family, Chrysostom had no interest in the question of whether or not Paul ever married. If he had been married, it would surely not have been a source of praise, unless in some celebrated way, like Thecla's canceling of her engagement, the tale illustrated the power of Paul's later commitment to celibacy. Chrysostom is aware of a tradition identifying σύζυγε in Phil 4:3 with Paul's wife, but rejects it.[792] In treatments of 1 Cor 7:7–8 and 9:5 John assumes that Paul was unmarried, living ἐν ἐγκρατείᾳ, but generally he does not care to speculate about the details concerning whether this was always the case or if the apostle had been widowed.[793] However, because Paul does not offer himself as the example of παρθενία, virginity, in 1 Cor 7:25f., as he had done in the first part of that chapter for ἐγκράτεια, John concedes that Paul was not a virgin.[794] But that does not render Paul any less useful as an example of ἐγκράτεια; his celibate lifestyle is for Chrysostom simply a given which does not require further analysis or embellishment. Paul was an asexual being (like the angels), as unmoved by lust as a corpse is unmoved by other corpses.[795] Therefore the thought that Paul sired biological children from an act of sexual intercourse is completely out of the question.

There are some conventional ways for dealing rhetorically with ἀπαιδία in an encomium, as for instance in Libanios' treatment of Julian: "childlessness for himself he judged to be of less importance than any harm done to the empire."[796] Chrysostom would analogously insist that Paul's concerns were for his churches

---

much better to help those in need when living with them in poverty and famine than it is to do so from one's surplus of goods" [ὅσῳ πολλῷ μεῖζον τὸ πενίᾳ συζῶντα καὶ λιμῷ βοηθεῖν τοῖς δεομένοις τοῦ ἐκ περιουσίας τοῦτο ποιεῖν] (*laud. Paul.* 1.11 [SC 300.128–30]).

[791] Theon, *Prog.* 8 [Spengel 2.110].

[792] At first he conjectures that the term must refer to some other woman or man, but then settles in on his preference: that it refers to an "illustrious man," likely either husband or brother to one of the women, "the head of the church there" [τὸ κεφάλαιον τῆς ἐκκλησίας τῆς ἐκεῖ], in whose charge Paul has placed these unruly women (*hom. in Phil.* 13.3 [62.279–80]).

[793] *hom. in 1 Cor.* 19.2; 21.2 [61.153, 171–72].

[794] *virg.* 41.6, 9 [SC 125.242–44], with Bernard Grillet's footnote 3 on p. 242. These passages are quoted above in n. 551.

[795] *laud. Paul.* 1.9 [SC 300.126].

[796] οὕτω τὴν ἀπαιδίαν τὴν αὑτοῦ τῆς εἰς τὰς πόλεις λύμης κουφότερον ἔκρινεν (*Or.* 18.181).

(with 2 Cor 11:28) and for the salvation of the entire world, rather than a few offspring. But he does not apply to Paul the other poetic claim that Libanios makes for Julian: that his writings are his "children,"[797] perhaps because he conceives of the relationship between Paul and his letters in other ways.[798]

However, if not a biological father, John does regard Paul as a spiritual father to all his converts,[799] the "foster-father of love" [ὁ τῆς ἀγάπης τρόφιμος].[800] This was especially the case with Timothy, whom Paul calls his "genuine child" in 1 Tim 1:2 (cf. Phil 2:19–24). Chrysostom regards Timothy as Paul's true son and adoptive heir, who was more in the mold of his spiritual father by imitation than are most biological sons by heredity.[801] What Paul's family life may historically have been is of no concern to Chrysostom. It has been replaced by the fictive – though utterly real – kinship of the Christian community. But now at the end of the fourth century, when Chrysostom, along with other Christian orators, proclaims the total victory of Christianity, Paul as father to converts has become like "a common father of the whole world" [κοινὸς πατὴρ τῆς οἰκουμένης ἁπάσης],[802] a man immeasurably blessed by innumerable children who look and act like him,[803] and in turn are the recipients of his loving solicitation. Not surprisingly, this is how John describes his own vocation as a priest, as well.[804] In this refashioned portrait of the single Paul, the ascetic asexual man has become the father of all, for all time, through the agency of his gospel.

---

[797] Or. 18.303.

[798] Chrysostom employs a rich set of metaphorical complexes to describe Paul and his letters including, e.g., ark builder and ark (laud. Paul. 1.5 [SC 300.118–20]); fighting champion and fortress (sac. 4.7 [SC 272.274]); doctor and medicines (sac. 4.7 [SC 272.274]); wrestling coach and megaphone (hom. in Rom. 12:20 5 [51.180]).

[799] With 1 Thess 2:11; 1 Cor 4:15; Phlm 10 (see pan. Bab. 2 58 [SC 362.166]: ὁ πατὴρ ὁ πνευματικός; hom. in 1 Cor. 12.2 [61.109–10]; hom. in Ac. 9:1 4.5 [51.151]; hom. in Philm. 2.2 [62.710]), of Onesimus, τέκνον Παύλου γέγονεν; cf. Gal 4:19, of Paul as mother, which Chrysostom immediately switches to father language (comm. in Gal. 4.2 [61.660]: εἶδες σπλάγχνα πατρικά;).

[800] For references see chap. 3, n. 140.

[801] stat. 1.3 [49.20]; hom. in 1 Tim. 1.1 [62.504–505]: Ἀλλ᾽ ἰδοὺ καὶ τέκνον, καὶ γνήσιον τέκνον, καὶ οὐδαμοῦ τῆς αὐτῆς ἐστιν οὐσίας. This is especially pointed when we remember that Chrysostom regards children as "living images" [εἰκόνες ἔμψυχοι] of their dead parents (sac. 1.2 [SC 272.68]; fr. Job 2:9 [64.560]).

[802] laud. Paul. 3.9 [SC 300.178]; also 3.6 [SC 300.172]: ὥσπερ τὴν οἰκουμένην ἅπασαν γεννήσας αὐτός. This patrimony extends not only to Christians, but also to unbelievers, whom Paul regards with the same kind of loving forbearance for their sick mania as a father extends to a deranged child (laud. Paul. 3.2 [SC 300.164]).

[803] As in the continuation of laud. Paul. 3.9 [SC 300.178]: "thus he served as a representative of the very human beings he had begotten" [οὕτω τοὺς γεγεννηκότας αὐτοὺς ἐμιμεῖτο] (my translation of the last word is in accordance with LPGL, s.v. 3, p. 871).

[804] sac. 6.4 [SC 272.314]: καὶ αὐτὸς ὢν ἁπάντων πατήρ.

εὐθανασία (Noble Death).[805]

Chrysostom accepts the "normative" scenario of Paul's latter days, based on the biblical evidence of Acts, Romans and 2 Timothy, and attested already in *1 Clement* 5, that Paul successfully accomplished his intended trip to Spain (Rom 15:24),[806] and then was imprisoned at Rome under Nero. In his homilies on 2 Timothy Chrysostom interprets that letter as Paul's last, written in the final stages of Paul's trials (2 Tim 4:16), and reflecting his calm, confident, and determined demeanor in the face of impending death. As Paul "speaks of his own death"[807] in that epistle, especially in 2 Tim 4:6–8, he has on his mind not his own situation, but the comfort and consolation [παραμυθία] of his beloved protegé, Timothy. Via that letter Paul passes on his legacy, his last will and testament,[808] and provides the

---

[805] This topic I have also added, from Theon. See the array of possible rhetorical approaches to the death of the subject in Hermogenes, *Prog.* 7 [Spengel, 2.12–13]: "Still also [you shall praise a person] from the manner of his death [ἀπὸ τρόπου τῆς τελευτῆς], such as if he died fighting for the fatherland [ἀπέθανεν ὑπὲρ τῆς πατρίδος μαχόμενος], and if there was anything remarkable [παράδοξον] in the event, such as with Callimachus, that when dead he remained standing; and you will praise him from the one who killed him [ἀπὸ τοῦ ἀποκτείναντος αὐτὸν ἐπαινέσεις], such as that Achilles was killed by the God Apollo."

[806] *hom. in Mt.* 75.2 [58.689]; *hom. in 2 Tim.* 10.3 [62.382]; *hom. in Heb.* Arg. 1 [63.11]; *laud. Paul.* 7.9 [300.312].

[807] περὶ τῆς τελευτῆς ἑαυτοῦ διαλέγεται (*hom. in 2 Tim.* 9.1 [62.649]).

[808] "The entire epistle is full of consolation, and is like a testament" [καὶ πᾶσα δὲ ἡ ἐπιστολὴ παραμυθίας ἐστὶ πλήρης, καὶ ὡσανεὶ διαθήκη τίς ἐστι] (*hom. in 2 Tim.* 9.2 [62.652]). In referring to 2 Timothy as a testament Chrysostom anticipates and corroborates a viewpoint held by many contemporary scholars (see, e.g., Michael Wolter, *Die Pastoralbriefe als Paulustradition* [FRLANT 146; Göttingen:Vandenhoeck & Ruprecht, 1988] 222–41 [for the parallels] and 140–41 for a comprehensive list of scholars who adopt the view that 2 Timothy is a testament, or contains elements of testamentary literature, which Wolter traces as far back as Luther's *Septembertestament* in 1522; Jerome D. Quinn, "Timothy and Titus, Epistles to," ABD 6.662; Jouette M. Bassler, *1 Timothy, 2 Timothy, Titus* [Abingdon New Testament Commentaries; Nashville: Abingdon, 1996] 22–23; Seán Charles Martin, *Pauli Testamentum: 2 Timothy and the Last Words of Moses* [Tesi Gregoriana, Serie Teologia 18; Rome: Pontifical Gregorian University, 1997]). However, as far as I know, Chrysostom's associated idea that the function of the piece is consolation has not been much engaged in contemporary scholarship. The form of a testament and the function of consolation are of course a perfect match in Greco-Roman literary culture. Earlier in the homily set Chrysostom had sketched precisely the rhetorical situation presupposed in a testament for 2 Timothy: "Just as if some father, with his son sitting by him, and not able to bear becoming an orphan, should console him, saying: 'My child, do not cry. We lived well, and now, after coming to old age, we are leaving you. Our life is slipping away. We are going away with a good reputation. And you, too, can be admired for the deeds we have done'" ['Ὥσπερ ἂν εἴ τις πατὴρ παιδίον αὐτῷ παρακαθήμενον, καὶ τὴν ὀρφανίαν οὐ φέρον παραμυθοῖτο λέγων· Τέκνον, μὴ κλαῖε, ἐζήσαμεν καλῶς, εἰς γῆρας ἐλθόντες καταλιμπάνομέν σε· ἄληπτος ἡμῶν ὁ βίος γέγονε, μετὰ δόξης ἀπερχόμεθα· ἔχεις καὶ σὺ θαυμάζεσθαι ἀπὸ τῶν ἡμῖν πεπραγμένων] (*hom. in 2 Tim.* 9.2 [62.652]). This emphasis on 2 Timothy as a piece of consolation literature is found consistently throughout the homily series. There are no less than six statements where Chrysostom applies the term to the whole epistle (1.1 [62.600, 601, twice]; 9.1 [62.649, three times]; 9.2 [62.652]); and nine other places where he describes the effect of single verses or appeals as παραμυθία (1.1 [62.601]; 4.2 [62.620]; 8.2 [62.645]). The often synonymous παράκλησις/

Scriptures (including his own letters) as a replacement for himself after death.[809] Paul is presented here in the familiar depiction of the death-bed testamentary, crafted (by the author of 2 Timothy as also by Chrysostom who replicates his portrait handiwork) as a typical biblical patriarch, like Abraham or one of the twelve sons of Jacob, who in his last moments guides future descendants in the ways of wisdom and fidelity to the received traditions. The death-bed portrait accents the ἀταραξία of the accused before his fate, and places the auditor/spectator in the position of bed-side receptor of the sage's precious deposit of faith, delivered in labored final breaths.

Although Chrysostom is strongly attached to these canonical images of Paul en route to his death, and replicates them in his oratory, he only modestly employs the apocryphal traditions[810] about Paul's martyrdom at Rome and Nero's motivations in executing him, though he is apparently aware of these in some form.[811] Where Chrysostom is most affected by the apocryphal traditions is in his portrayal of the death of Paul as part of a bitter battle between the raging Nero and the holy apostle, seen as a "titanic, cosmic struggle."[812] But when we turn to the specifics of the passion of Paul in John's writings, Chrysostom's use of details from the apocryphal stories is uneven. He refers in shorthand to the legend of Nero's cupbearer, Patroclus (whom he terms simply ὁ οἰνοχόος αὐτοῦ),[813] which is well

---

παρακαλεῖν are also used by John to describe the literary quality of 2 Timothy (2.1 [62.608]; 4.1, 2 [62.617, 620]; 8.2 [62.645]; 9.1, 2 [62.650, 651, twice]; 10.1 [62.656, twice]).

[809] 2 Tim 3:15–16, with Chrysostom's comment: "In place of me, he says, you have the scriptures ['Ἀντ' ἐμοῦ, φησί, τὰς γραφὰς ἔχεις]; if you wish to learn anything, you will be able to do it from there" (hom. in 2 Tim. 9.1 [62.649]). Although the text is not precisely clear, it is likely that Chrysostom includes the Pauline letters themselves in the claim of all Scripture to divine inspiration, thereby regarding Paul's testamentary as a reflexive action which serves to validate this very letter (along with the others) as Paul's authentic legacy.

[810] Paul's death by the specific means of beheading is also attested in Tertullian, praes. 36, and Eusebius, h.e. 2.21.1–2; 25.5–8 (and could therefore have been available to Chrysostom more generally).

[811] The question is rendered particularly complicated by the various works and recensions of works treating the acts and passion of Paul (both alone and with Peter). For the question, see the study of Richard Adelbert Lipsius, Die apokryphen Apostelgeschichten und Apostellegenden: Ein Beitrag zur altchristlichen Literaturgeschichte (Braunschweig: Schwetschke, 1887) vol. 2/1.246–49, who argues that "Chrysostomos die πράξεις Παύλου nicht unmittelbar vor sich gehabt, sondern bereits eine katholische Bearbeitung derselben benutzt hat." But the issue is rendered even more difficult to determine because Chrysostom himself is likely quite deliberately adapting the traditions he takes up, so peeling tradition (written and oral) from embellishment is a precarious task.

[812] Harry W. Tajra, The Martyrdom of St. Paul: Historical and Judicial Context, Traditions, and Legends (WUNT 2/67; Tübingen: J.C.B. Mohr [Paul Siebeck], 1994) 186.

[813] See hom. in 2 Tim. 10.2 [62.657]: "Already he had appeared before Nero, and had escaped. But when he catechized his cupbearer, then he beheaded him" [Παρέστη ἤδη τῷ Νέρωνι, καὶ διέφυγεν· ἐπειδὴ δὲ τὸν οἰνοχόον αὐτοῦ κατήχησε, τότε αὐτὸν ἀπέτεμεν]. This identification of the cupbearer with Patroclus (despite the lack of a name) is unmistakable (with Léon Vouaux, Les actes de Paul et ses lettres apocryphes [Paris: Letouzey et Ané, 1913] 39, against Lipsius, Die apokryphen Apostelgeschichten 2/1.246, who unnecessarily complicates matters).

[814] See mart. Paul. 1–2=pass. Paul. frag. 1–2, in Lipsius, Acta, 1.105–109.

known from *Acta Pauli*,[814] when he insists that Paul's conversion of this esteemed servant was a cause for Nero's decision to kill him. But John supplies none of the details of Patroclus' Eutychean adventure[815] or speech of confession to Nero. However, the direct causal connection between the conversion of Patroclus and Nero's decision to execute Paul is not nearly as sharply made in *Acta Pauli* as Chrysostom renders it in his writings, as part of his consistent aim at personalizing the conflict between Paul and the emperor. Elsewhere John supplies a second Neronic motive for condemning Paul to death: in his treatise *Adversus oppugnatores vitae monasticae* John asserts as a piece of common lore that Nero killed Paul because the apostle had persuaded Nero's beloved concubine [παλλακίς] to believe in the gospel, and concomitantly to refrain from her "impure intercourse" [ἀκάθαρτος συνουσία] with the emperor.[816] Chrysostom's "concubine theory" is, however, unmatched by extant literary sources.[817] *Acta Petri et Pauli* 31 recounts a tradition about *Peter* having converted Nero's *wife*, Livia, as well as Agrippina, the wife of Agrippa, with the result that "they stripped themselves away from the sides of their own husbands" [ὥστε καὶ περιελεῖν ἑαυτὰς ἀπὸ τῆς τῶν ἰδίων ἀνδρῶν πλευρᾶς].[818] But that coup is attributed to Peter, in the first place, and, secondly, the event is not represented as the cause of Nero's death sentence for either apostle in that work, for the narrative quite explicitly supplies other capital charges.[819] Also similar, but not identical, to Chrysostom's story about Paul, is *martyrium Petri* 4, which recounts

---

[815] The narrative in *mart. Paul.* 1 (Lipsius, *Acta*, 1.104–106) is obviously patterned on Acts 20:7–12. Perhaps this is another instance in which Chrysostom deliberately tones down Paul's miracles.

[816] παλλακίδα γὰρ αὐτοῦ σφόδρα ἐπέραστον πείσας τὸν περὶ τῆς πίστεως δέξασθαι λόγον, ἔπειθεν ὁμοῦ καὶ τῆς ἀκαθάρτου συνουσίας ἀπαλλαγῆναι ἐκείνης (*oppugn.* 1.3 [47.323]). A period of imprisonment is envisioned, during which Nero tried his own persuasion against Paul, which did not deter the apostle from his abstinential advice to the young woman convert [ἔδησεν, ὡς δὲ οὐκ ἔπειθε τῆς πρὸς τὴν κόρην ἀποσχέσθαι συμβουλῆς, τέλος ἀπέκτεινε]. In another place John combines these two Neronic grudge motives into one: "It is said that Paul welcomed both the cupbearer and the concubine of Nero's" [Λέγεται Νέρωνος καὶ οἰνοχόον καὶ παλλακίδα ἀσπάσαι] (this brief reference to the narrative, as usual, includes no details). John goes on to defend Paul against "guilt by association" through his insistence that Paul did not consort with these imperial associates as a sign of acceptance of their licentious ways, or in order to join them in evil deeds, but to lead them to a reformed life [Εἰ μὲν γὰρ ἐπὶ ἀσελγείᾳ ἠσπάσατο, ἢ ἐπὶ πονηροῖς πράγμασιν, εἰκότως (one should find fault with him)· εἰ δὲ ἐπὶ βίῳ ὀρθῷ, τίνος ἕνεκεν;] (*hom. in Ac.* 46.3 [60.325]; see also *hom. in* 2 *Tim.* 3.1 [62.614]: προσέκρουσε γὰρ τότε τῷ Νέρωνι, τινὰ τῶν ἀνακειμένων αὐτῷ οἰκειωσάμενος).

[817] An historical connection with Nero's concubine, the loyal freedwoman, *Claudia Acte*, known from Suetonius, *Ner.* 28 and 50, is quite tenuous (see discussion in Rougé, "Néron," 83).

[818] Lipsius, *Acta*, 1.192–93.

[819] Peter was condemned for the death of Simon Magus, and Paul for impiety towards the gods (*A. Petr. et Paul.* 79 [Lipsius, *Acta*, 1.213]), as contained in Agrippa's advice to Nero about proper sentencing: "It appears to me that it is just for Paul to be beheaded, since he is refusing to worship, and for Peter to he killed on a cross, since he brought about a murder" [Ὡς ἐμοὶ καταφαίνεται, δίκαιόν ἐστιν, Παῦλον ὡς ἀθρήσκευτον ὄντα τὴν κεφαλὴν ἀποτμηθῆναι, τὸν δὲ Πέτρον διὰ τὸ καὶ φόνον ἀνύσαι, ἐπὶ σταυροῦ ἀρθῆναι].

Peter's conversion to the faith of the four concubines [παλλακίδες] of the prefect Agrippa, and their subsequent renunciation of sexual relations with their master.[820] This time the spoiled concubinage *is*, in the course of the narrative, directly responsible for the catechist's death sentence.[821] But once again the characters do not fit John's abbreviated tale: the protagonist is Peter, not Paul, and the cuckolded-by-Christ figure is Agrippa, not Nero. Hence, from where Chrysostom took up his rendition – that it was Paul's encouraging celibacy on Nero's beloved concubine that got him killed – remains an open question.[822] Although it is not at all impossible that John has just mistakenly appropriated this conglomerated Petrine legend to Paul,[823] it is perhaps more likely that he deliberately attributed a Petrine story to Paul in order to align the accusations against Paul with those currently being made against the Christian monks whom he is defending in this treatise.[824] Even if Chrysostom had inherited a tradition recounting Paul's

---

[820] "And the concubines of the prefect Agrippa were gathered to Peter, four of them, Agrippina, Nikaria, Euphemia and Doris. Hearing the teaching about holiness and all the sayings of the Lord, they were struck to their very souls, and, conspiring with one another to remain pure of Agrippa's bed, they were being continually harassed by him" [συνήγοντο δὲ καὶ αἱ παλλακίδες τοῦ πραιφέκτου Ἀγρίππα πρὸς τὸν Πέτρον, τέσσαρες οὖσαι, Ἀγριππῖνα καὶ Νικαρία καὶ Εὐφημία καὶ Δῶρις. ἀκούουσαι τὸν τῆς ἁγνείας λόγον καὶ πάντα τὰ τοῦ κυρίου λόγια, ἐπλήγησαν τὰς ψυχάς, καὶ συνθέμεναι ἀλλήλαις ἁγναὶ τῆς Ἀγρίππα κοίτης διαμεῖναι ἠνοχλοῦντο ὑπ' αὐτοῦ] (Lipsius, *Acta*, 1.84).

[821] Agrippa, beset with rage, himself sentences Peter to death; Nero is displeased because Peter's crucifixion took place without his judgment [μὴ μετὰ γνώμης αὐτοῦ ἀνῃρέθη] for he had wanted to inflict on him an even more vicious form of execution (*mart. Petr.* 12 [Lipsius, *Acta*, 1.100]).

[822] See Lipsius, *Die apocryphen Apostelgeschichten*, 2/1.247: "Sonach setzt die Erzählung des Chrysostomus jedenfalls einen von den uns bekannten Recensionen der passio Pauli stark abweichenden Text voraus ... Ebenso wenig vermögen wir endlich über die von Chrysostomos wiederholt erwähnte Concubine des Nero etwas Sicheres auszumitteln." Lipsius himself postulates that this story has developed from a "catholic" editing of the earlier "gnostic Acts of Paul": "So bleibt die Möglichkeit stehen, dass ein katholischer Bearbeiter umgekehrt die Frau des Kaisers in eine Concubine verwandelt und ihre Bekehrung statt dem Petrus vielmehr dem Paulus zugeschrieben hat." See n. 824 below for a critique of Lipsius' position.

[823] Perhaps that error was abetted by the narrative later in *mart. Petr.* 84, which tells of the secret conveyance of Christian teachings to Nero's wife by her own sister, Potentiana, who was inspired with Pauline ideas and lore by Paul's disciple Perpetua after the apostle's death, when the two women inhabited the same prison cell (Lipsius, *Acta*, 1.218–19). This same confusion could also have already existed in the traditions Chrysostom himself received, but that is less likely, given that we have no other direct literary reference to such a combined legend.

[824] Lipsius, *Die apokryphen Apostelgeschichten*, 2/1.246–47, does not examine the literary and rhetorical contexts of Chrysostom's references to Paul's martyrdom, which are a significant factor in the assessment of these traditions (for example, Lipsius' identification of the Agrippa whom Paul "drew to himself" with the city prefect in the Pseudo-Linus *passio Pauli* is completely unnecessary when one sees that the passage in question, Chrysostom's *hom. in Ac.* 46.3 [60.325], is set within a much longer discussion of Paul's dialogue with King Agrippa in Acts 26:28). Here I side with Vouaux, *Les actes de Paul*, 39, in his conclusion that "il ne nous reste ainsi aucune raison de croire ici à une rédaction du martyre autre que celle qui nous est conservée," but find less persuasive Vouaux's hypothesis that this was due merely to "confusion" on John's part based upon

inroads into the imperial house (stemming from Phil 4:22), one can easily see how John gave the event this moralistic bent, with its outrage against "debauchery,"[825] resulting in a most useful portrait of Paul as one falsely accused by opponents of chastity.[826]

In regard to the manner of Paul's death, Chrysostom refers to it sometimes in generic[827] or euphemistic terms,[828] but uses the precise terminology for decapitation enough times to confirm his knowledge of the narrative known from *Acta Pauli*[829] of Paul's death sentence by Nero and its actualization by his soldiers at Rome.[830] Nonetheless, despite these few brief references to Paul's beheading (and to the cupbearer and the concubine), on the whole Chrysostom chose not to avail himself of the full repertoire of legends concerning Paul's death, of which he surely had some knowledge from *Acta Pauli* or other sources, such as the milk

---

his having read these *Acta* back-to-back and erroneously harmonized them. Like Lipsius, Vouaux also has not paid sufficient attention to Chrysostom's own rhetorical goals in the homilies where these references occur. Surely when one takes into account John's purpose in defending the monks against charges that they are corrupting youth by taking them away from their families to a life of celibacy, the "concubine" theory of Pauline demise is far more fitting to the case than the cupbearer (*pace* Vouaux's dismissal of the importance: "elle ne paraît pas si singulière dans un discours où il importe peu que ce soit l'échanson ou la concubine qui ait amené la mort de Paul" [*Les actes de Paul*, 39]). Surely the cupbearer would not have helped Chrysostom's argument here in the same way as the chaste concubine (for the sake of whose virtue the preacher/monk risks life and limb)! We should also observe in this context that this is not the only case where Chrysostom attributes deeds of Peter to Paul (see n. 436 above in this chapter on the miracles in Acts).

[825] Hence Chrysostom's need to defend Paul for associating with such people, in their ἀσελγεία and πονηρὰ πράγματα, in *hom. in Ac.* 46.3 [60.325].

[826] Just as the monks of John's day are accused by the parents and relatives of the boys they persuade to take up the monastic life; see the emphasis in *oppugn.* 1.3 [47.323]: "For Nero was making the very kinds of accusations you are uttering, that Paul was a corrupter and deceiver, and the like" [τοιαῦτα γοῦν ἐγκαλῶν ἐκεῖνος (sc. Νέρων), καὶ λυμεῶνα καὶ πλάνον καὶ τὰ αὐτά, ἅπερ ὑμεῖς φθέγγεσθε]. Paul is more useful than Peter for this comparison, not only because of John's overwhelming preference for Paul (see chap. 7, pp. 394–95), but also because his writings, especially 1 Corinthians 7, are in many ways the charter documents of the ascetic life, just as he personally lived ἐν ἐγκρατείᾳ, unlike Peter (according to the witness of 1 Cor 9:5).

[827] *laud. Paul.* 1.4 [SC 300.118], ἀνῃρεῖτο; *oppugn.* 1.3 [47.323], ἀπέκτεινε; *hom. in Heb.* Arg. 1 [63.11], ἀνῃρέθη; 9.5 [63.82], ἐτελεύτησε; *hom. in Rom.* 32.2 [60.678], τὸν βίον κατέλυσε (as also in *hom. in Ac.* 55.3 [60.383]).

[828] "Going away" [ἀποδημία, ἀπιέναι] (*hom. in 2 Tim.* 9.1 [62.649]; *laud. Paul.* 1.4 [SC 300.118]); "being perfected" [ἐτελειώθη] (*hom. in Ac.* 55.3 [60.383]); "a change for the better" [μετάστασις πρὸς τὰ κρείττω] (*hom. in 2 Tim.* 9.1 [62.649]).

[829] This is the title covering *Acta Pauli et Theclae, martyrium Pauli*, and the apocryphal correspondence between Paul and the Corinthians.

[830] *hom. in 2 Tim.* 5.2, ἔμελλεν ἀποκεφαλίζεσθαι; 10.2 [62.626, 657], αὐτὸν ἀπέτεμεν (compare Eusebius, *h.e.* 2.25.5, τὴν κεφαλὴν ἀποτμηθῆναι). John does not use the more exact term found in *mart. Paul.* 4–5 (Lipsius, *Acta*, 1.112–15), τραχηλοκοπηθῆναι. There is a possible ironic allusion to Paul's decapitation in *laud. Paul.* 1.4 [SC 300.118], where Paul is said to have been the minister of his own sacrifice "which he slew after drawing the sword of the spirit" [ἣν τὴν μάχαιραν τοῦ Πνεύματος σπασάμενος ἔθυεν].

spurting out of Paul's severed neck onto the garments of his slayer, his resurrection appearance to Nero,[831] the June 29 date of his death (along with Peter),[832] or the Ostian Way as the site of his demise.[833] In contrast to this wealth of entertaining detail, Chrysostom's accounts of Paul's death are mostly unlegendary, and rather journalistic in their sparseness. For one as fond as Chrysostom of the art of αὔξησις, particularly in his panegyrics to martyrs, this departure from usual practice is worthy of note, and requires some explanation. John paints Paul as a martyr, but not in the usual way via a painstaking recounting of the grueling hours that led up to his death.

One reason Chrysostom does not embellish the death of Paul is that the writings of the canon which form the basis of his homiletical expositions do not narrate Paul's death. When Chrysostom treats Paul's final testament in 2 Timothy, he preserves the narrative tension of the original with its vague and metaphorical prolepsis of what is to come [Ἐγὼ γὰρ ἤδη σπένδομαι, καὶ ὁ καιρὸς τῆς ἀναλύσεώς μου ἐφέστηκεν],[834] and its deliberate focus on the character of Paul, rather than the events of his pending execution. The biblical silence about Paul's death itself is nicely engaged in Chrysostom's final homily on the Acts of the Apostles, a work which ends, famously, with Paul preaching unhindered under house arrest at Rome, his passion unnarrated, but hanging palpably and prophetically in the air (Acts 28:30–31; cf. 21:10–14).[835] When preaching on the ending of Acts John finds

---

[831] Both these legends are recounted in mart. Paul. 5–6 (Lipsius, Acta, 1.115–16).

[832] The traditional date of Paul's death and the effusion of milk are mentioned in the Ps-Chrysostomic work, Petr. et Paul. 2 [59.494–496], yet another place where that work stands out from Chrysostom's usual treatments of Paul.

[833] This tradition was attested by the presbyter Gaius (early third century) in writing, apud Eusebius, h.e. 2.25.6–7; see also A. Petr. et Paul. 59 (Lipsius, Acta, 1.170). Other legends which Chrysostom may have known (though their dating is uncertain) but does not cite, are the tale of Perpetua's kerchief (as found in A. Petr. et Paul. 80 [Lipsius, Acta, 1.213–14], dated by Aurelio de Santos Otero in NTApoc, 2.426 to around the time of the Decretum Gelasianum, likely early sixth century, though the antiquity of its sources remains a question), and the Tre Fontane marking the spots where Paul's severed head bounced. Although it is tempting to connect John's allusion to Paul and Peter as "fountains" [πηγαί] adorning the imperial city, with an early version of that legend (hom. in Rom. 32.2 [60.678]), because that tradition is securely attested only in the sixth century (see Tajra, Martyrdom of St. Paul, 25–26), it is unlikely. Although Chrysostom always places Paul's death in Rome, he is no more specific than that.

[834] 2 Tim 4:6.

[835] Among contemporary scholars, see Richard I. Pervo, Luke's Story of Paul (Minneapolis: Fortress, 1990) 72–74, on how Paul's farewell speech in Acts 20:17–35 "foreshadows and presumes Paul's death," and on the three "passion predictions" of 20:23–25; 21:4, 11–13. This is part of the well-recognized parallelism between Jesus in the gospels and Paul in Acts (neatly entabulated by Talbert, Reading Acts, 11–12). Chrysostom himself considered the narrative caesura before Paul's death (Acts 28) an intentional authorial strategy: "the author stops his narrative at this point, and leaves the hearer thirsting, so that s/he must reckon the rest for her/himself" [Μέχρι τούτων τὸν λόγον ἵστησιν ὁ συγγραφεύς, καὶ ἀφίησι διψῶντα τὸν ἀκροατήν, ὥστε τὸ λοιπὸν ἀφ ἑαυτοῦ συλλογίζεσθαι]. The pagan authors do this, also [Τοῦτο καὶ οἱ ἔξω ποιοῦσι]. For to know everything makes the reader sluggish and released [from responsibility]" (hom. in Ac. 55.2 [60.382]).

much to embellish when he imaginatively retells Paul's "triumphal entry" into Rome. Paul arose from the sea, from shipwreck, like a king after a naval victory, and strode into the imperial city to receive his crown.[836] In an effort to coordinate the evidence of Romans, 2 Timothy and Acts about Paul's final itinerary, Chrysostom explains to his audience that there were two Roman visits, one before the trip to Spain and the second after it, during which Paul lost his life [κατέλυσεν οὕτω τὸν βίον]. Now Chrysostom feels pushed by a common expectation (incited by the persuasive impact of Luke's narrative art) that he will tell how it all came to pass: "Why do you want to learn of the things that happened after this" [Τί ἐβούλου μαθεῖν τὰ μετὰ ταῦτα]? John complies with what one anticipates will be, true to form, a list of the tortures Paul endured, such as we customarily find in his pane-gyrics to martyrs. Yet the catalogue he produces is nothing new,[837] for it constitutes the same Pauline curriculum vitae of *peristaseis* as he endured throughout his life, not a fresh encounter with the gory details of his demise, such as we find in the panegyrics to the martyrs.[838] John will tell no more than this about the manner of Paul's death. He chose to stop here in his description of Paul's last moments, going no further than did his author, Luke; but, unlike him, John offers a hermeneutical justification for this limitation:

You see this small part of him [Εἶδες αὐτοῦ μικρὸν μέρος;]? Consider that the rest is also such as this [Τοιοῦτον νόει καὶ τὸ λοιπόν]. For just as with the sky, as much of it as you see, such also is every other part [ὅσον ἂν ἴδῃς αὐτοῦ, τοσοῦτόν ἐστι καὶ τὸ ἄλλο]. For if you look at one part of the sky, wherever you go, you will see the rest to be just like this. Or just as with the sun, if you look at a portion of its rays, from these you can guess at what the sun is; it is the same way with Paul. You have seen his deeds in part; all of them are the same as these, filled with dangers [τὰς πράξεις εἶδες ἐκ μέρους αὐτοῦ, πᾶσαι τοιαῦται τυγχάνουσι, κινδύνων γέμουσαι].[839]

Here Chrysostom explains in one breath both the gap in his canonical text and that in his own oratory when it comes to narrating Paul's death. He will not give a description of Paul's final πράξεις, he says, because of the epistemological presup-position that the part that is known sufficiently illumines the part that is unknown. Therefore one does not need to know the elongated tale of Paul's death, he argues,

---

[836] *hom. in Ac.* 55.3 [60.382–83]: "For just like a king who fought a nautical battle and won, he landed at that imperial city [Καθάπερ γάρ τις βασιλεὺς ναυμαχήσας καὶ νικήσας, ἐπέβαινε τῆς βασιλικωτάτης ἐκείνης πόλεως] … Rome received him bound, and saw him crowned and heralded" [ἐδέξατο αὐτὸν ἡ Ῥώμη δεδεμένον, καὶ εἶδε στεφανωθέντα καὶ ἀνακηρυχθέντα].

[837] "Such things as these: bonds, torments, battles, imprisonments, plots, informers, daily deaths" [Τοιαῦτά ἐστι κἀκεῖνα· δεσμὰ, βάσανοι, μάχαι, φυλακαί, ἐπιβουλαί, συκοφαντίαι, θάνατοι καθημερινοί] (*hom. in Ac.* 55.3 [60.383]).

[838] To cite just one example, *pan. Barl.* 3 [50.680]: "the one who gave his hand [for a burning cinder to be placed in it], this man also gave over his head, and set forth his sides, to fire and to beasts and to the sea and the cliff and the cross and the wheel, and withstood all the punishments then heard of."

[839] *hom. in Ac.* 55.3 [60.383].

because the actions of his life tell us all we need to know of what is beyond our ken. In this way John quite deliberately harmonizes Paul's death with the rest of his life and ministry, refusing it pride of place as a special act that reveals the character of his subject, Paul. According to this passage it was on philosophical grounds that Chrysostom did not embellish Paul's death narrative with episodes from the apocryphal traditions, or from his own, vivid imagination, as he does with other martyrs. Partly this is a hermeneutical decision forced by the limits of the canon in telling this story, but there may be further reasons why John chooses to retain the lacuna of the biblical narrative.

One reason John does not replicate and amplify upon the martyrological traditions about Paul's death (alongside the fact that John probably did not consider the apocryphal traditions on a par with canonical witness), is that even they do not provide very long, excruciating scenes of Paul's terminal agony. This is quite simply because beheading, being a rather swift form of death, affords far less narrative suspense and opportunity for dialogue and delayed denouements than more prolonged executionary possibilities like crucifixion and burning at the stake. Thus in the apocryphal *Acta* and *Passiones* of Paul and Peter (and the two together) the account of Peter's upside down crucifixion is always far longer than that of Paul's single sword blow to the neck.[840] But even more than this, in Chrysostom's late fourth-century context, with martyrological accounts becoming more and more gruesome,[841] beheading appears a rather tame way to exit this life. Chrysostom knew well the genre of the detailed death account, and was himself a fond practitioner of the art in his many panegyrics to martyrs,[842] but in those same orations we find evidence that, in relative terms, he did not consider beheading such a terrible option among the forms of death available to murderous tyrants. In fact, John uses beheading as a foil in several of the panegyrics to martyrs, seemingly referring to it as the easy way out.[843] Hence, another reason Chrysostom seems not

---

[840] For instance, compare the length of the depictions of Paul's beheading and Peter's crucifixion in *A. Petr. et Paul.* 59–62 (Lipsius, *Acta*, 1.170–72). While on the cross Peter is able to give speeches (like Jesus in the gospels), whereas Paul exits the scene, by simple description, very quickly (ὁ μὲν Παῦλος ἀπετμήθη τὴν κεφαλήν).

[841] See Delehaye, *Les passions de martyrs*, esp. 147–50 ("Abus de l'hyperbole") and 152–63.

[842] Multiple examples are provided by Ameringer, *Second Sophistic*, 68–85, 96–98 ("Descriptions of scenes of martyrdom: These are very numerous in the Christian orators and writers. It was natural that, in extolling the heroism of these valiant champions of the faith, they would dwell on the details of their agonizing struggles. Chrysostom is particularly fond of such descriptions" [96]); and Delehaye, *Les passions des martyrs*, esp. 154–63. Chrysostom likely was immersed in these from his youth, because the cult of the Maccabean martyrs was centered at Antioch (he has left two orations, *pan. Macc.*, and fragments of another, *pan. Macc. fr.*), and the Maccabean literature in many ways constituted the formative text, in terms of genre, vocabulary, and commonplaces, for early Christian martyrologies. For representative passages see, in addition to n. 838 above, chap. 2, p. 61.

[843] For example, in *pan. Juln.* 2 [50.668] Chrysostom says of the martyr Julian that his tormenter "hearing his case, did not cut off his head on one day, so that he might not make his course easier by the shortness of the punishment [Οὐ γὰρ ἐν μιᾷ ἡμέρᾳ ἀκούσας ἀπέτεμεν αὐτοῦ

to have amplified the means of Paul's death was that it did not afford the rhetorical possibilities of other forms of execution and, indeed, when set in contrast with them, could not compete with immolations, suspension on iron ladders over pyres, flailings, being dipped in boiling oil, and all the other demonic μηχαναί enacted in death technology carried out by their willing minions, unnamed but lethal human tyrants.[844]

When compared with the other panegyrics of martyrs, Chrysostom's *de laudibus sancti Pauli* in particular stand out for their paucity of detailed attention to Paul's death.[845] But the limitation of beheading for amplification is not the only factor at work here. Chrysostom's concept of *how* Paul was a martyr is, simply, larger than his death. Here again John is largely influenced by the narrative theology of 2 Timothy,[846] and passages in other letters, especially the Corinthian correspondence, in which Paul's whole life of suffering in virtue is regarded as the means by which he earned his martyr's stripes, a viewpoint given particular expression in Paul's own voiced internal debate on the preferability of death over life in Phil 1:21–26.[847]

τὴν κεφαλήν, ἵνα μὴ τὸ σύντομον τῆς τιμωρίας εὐκολώτερον αὐτῷ ποιήσῃ τὸν δρόμον], but every single day led him in, led him out, applied means of persuasion, threatened countless tortures, enticed him with flattering words, by every technique attempting to move that unshakable foundation to fall apart." (Interestingly, just prior to this passage Chrysostom had invoked Paul, because he and Julian shared the same native city of Tarsus; it is not clear, however, that Chrysostom deliberately intends *Paul* as the foil here, given that it would be rather unlike him to denigrate Paul directly, though the contrast nonetheless stands in the text.) The exact same comparison of executionary means is given in *pan. Dros.* 4 [50.688] "... the tyrant had lit the fire. For he neither led her to the pit, nor cut off her head, so that he might not make the contest easier for her by the shortness of the punishment [οὐδὲ γὰρ ἐπὶ βάραθρον αὐτὴν ἤγαγεν, οὐδὲ τὴν κεφαλὴν ἀπέτεμεν, ἵνα μὴ τὸ σύντομον τῆς τιμωρίας εὐκολώτερον αὐτῇ ποιήσῃ τὸν ἆθλον], but, wishing to confound her mind, and to master her unenslaved soul by the sight of the fire, threw her into the midst of it." *pan. Rom.* 1.2 [50.609] applies a slightly different, developmental view. The devil (in the form of the tyrant) did not cut off the Roman martyr's head, since time had taught him that in the long run decapitation was not effective in stopping the gospel; instead, he cut off his tongue (but the martyr's mouth spoke even without it!). The devil asks himself: "Should I cut off his head?" ['Ἀποτέμω τὴν κεφαλὴν αὐτοῦ;]. But the answer had already been given: "He did not cut off his head; for the passing time had taught him that all these things are useless and in vain" [οὐκ ἀπέτεμεν αὐτοῦ τὴν κεφαλήν· ἐδίδαξε γὰρ αὐτὸν ὁ παρελθὼν χρόνος, ὅτι πάντα ταῦτα εἰκῇ καὶ μάτην ἐγίνετο].

[844] On the rhetorical convention of not naming the official, see Delehaye, *Les passions des martyrs*, 150–52, which is exploited by Chrysostom (and others) to merge the agency of the devil with the civic authority.

[845] Here we can only give some of the contours of similarities and differences between Chrysostom's depictions of martyrs and of Paul, a topic worthy of further detailed investigation.

[846] This is the constant refrain of the letter, along with the call for Timothy to imitate Paul in his suffering (see, e.g., 2 Tim 1:12; 2:3, 9–13; 3:10–13; 4:6–8, 16–18).

[847] Chrysostom quotes this passage dozens of times in his writings, and regards it as the manifesto for the value of "living death" over simple death in the cost-benefit ratio of Christian eschatological anthropology. Accordingly in his own final days Chrysostom wrote to Olympias counseling against desiring death as a cessation to the torments of this life. Quoting Phil 1:23–24, he recasts the wages of martyrdom from death into life: "for as long as the afflictions are extended,

When this context is the canvas on which he is painted, Paul becomes a long-term martyr regardless of his quick death. The actual execution narrative of one who "died daily" is of small significance in the total verbal depiction of his life of sufferings: "For Paul became truly a witness [μάρτυς] to Christ,[848] and a witness as it should be, both through what he did and through what he said."[849] In fact, John uses this precise language himself in *laud. Paul.* 1. In contrast to the martyrs, Paul's death was not a single event [Οὐδὲ γὰρ μία μόνον ἐστί], for he sacrificed himself every day [Καὶ γὰρ ἑαυτὸν καθ' ἑκάστην κατέθυεν ἡμέραν]. And as if that were not enough, even Paul's daily self-slaughter had a double-barrelled quality, for it consisted both in dying every day (1 Cor 15:31), and in carrying around the dying of Jesus in the body (2 Cor 4:10).[850] Viewed from this angle, Paul's true death far outshines his last day on earth; and the slaying hand belongs, not to one of Nero's soliders, but to Paul himself: "He did not offer a cow or sheep, but it was himself he slaughtered, twice over, every single day."[851] Surely Paul's death-day narrative, of a single sword stroke, pales in comparison with this.

A final reason Chrysostom does not give an extensive account of the death of Paul is that for him Paul is still alive, still preaching, still about his work, something John would not claim about other martyrs in the same way.[852] Hence, when Chrysostom encounters Paul's claim in Rom 1:5–6 that his apostleship extends to all the nations, he confidently retorts that this was not a lie, since "after his death he did not stop preaching everywhere throughout the world."[853] The Paul whom

---

so much more will the crowning rewards also be increased; as much as the gold is refined by fire, so much more pure will it be; as long as the merchant sails on the sea, so much more cargo will he gather" (*ep. Olymp.* 17.3 [SC 13.378]).

[848] See Furnish, "Paul the ΜΑΡΤΥΣ," for an insightful treatment of the development of this concept in the deutero-Paulines, Acts, and the Pastorals, which were so influential on Chrysostom in this regard (since he of course considers them all of equal historical weight).

[849] *hom. in Ac.* 47.3 [60.330]: Μάρτυς γὰρ ὄντως αὐτοῦ γέγονε, καὶ μάρτυς ὡς χρή, καὶ δι' ὧν ἔπραξε, καὶ δι' ὧν εἶπε. This is of course a tension in the encomia to martyrs as well, who are lauded not just for their endurance at the end, but for a life of virtue brought to its fitting and logical conclusion. The catechetical benefits of this version of Pauline martyrdom as a daily ordeal are far superior to single, gruesome deaths (though these do have their uses in Chrysostom's oratory), since this is the kind of martyrdom to which the preacher can call every single member of his congregation [Τοιούτους καὶ ἡμᾶς εἶναι χρὴ μάρτυρας] (ibid.). But, of course, the panegyrics to the martyrs also customarily contain similar exhortations to emulate the virtues they practiced while alive (see, *pan. Barl.* 4 [50.680]; *pan. Aeg.* 2 [50.698]).

[850] Cf. *res. mort.* 3 [50.421]: καθάπερ ἔμψυχοι νεκροὶ περιῄεσαν εἰς θάνατον παραδιδόμενοι καθ' ἡμέραν.

[851] Οὐδὲ γὰρ βοῦς καὶ πρόβατα προσέφερεν, ἀλλ' ἑαυτὸν διπλῇ καθ' ἑκάστην ἐσφαγίαζε τὴν ἡμέραν (*laud. Paul.* 1.3 [SC 300.116]). Chrysostom cites as confirmation of this portrait 2 Tim 4:6, in which Paul "calls his own blood a libation" [σπονδὴν ἑαυτοῦ τὸ αἷμα καλέσας].

[852] Though Chrysostom can talk of the potential τάφοι ἔμψυχοι καὶ πνευματικοί ("living and spiritual tombs") to the martyrs that his auditors could become (see Coleman-Norton, "St. Chrysostom," 309, and above, chap. 2, n. 139 for citations).

[853] μετὰ τελευτὴν οὐ παύεται πανταχοῦ τῆς οἰκουμένης κηρύττων (*hom. in Rom.* 1.3 [60.398].

John encountered in the words of his writings was not a dead man, but a living voice (despite the dusty remnants of his corpse in Rome that John could conjure up).[854]

Perhaps it is for the same reason that Chrysostom does not relate the fantastic tale of Paul's resurrection appearance to Nero; his Paul is alive in even more spectacular, and less episodic, forms. When Chrysostom did exercise his ekphrastic art he trained it, not on the agonizingly slow last minutes of Paul on earth, nor on the phantasmal retributive visit to Nero, but on contemplation of Paul's future resurrection from Rome, the site of his death and present guardian of his numinous body:

From there (Rome) Paul will be snatched up, from there Peter. Consider and shudder at what a spectacle Rome will see! Paul suddenly raised from that tomb with Peter, and borne up for a meeting with the Lord. What a rose Rome will send forth to Christ! What two crowns the city will be encircled in, what gold chains will gird her, what fountains she will have![855]

And with the customarily elusive temporal logic of Christian eschatology, Chrysostom can in almost the same breath speak delightedly and at length of Paul's life in heaven *at this very moment* surrounding the throne of glory.[856]

Paul's "good death" rightly earns him praise because, regardless of its circumstances, it was a death suffered for the sake of others. This Greek cultural commonplace (echoed already by Paul in Rom 5:7 about the salvific death of Christ), is given a Pauline corollary by Chrysostom in *laud. Paul.* 1, when he compares Paul's sacrifice with the primordial offering of Abel. Abel was slain by his own brother who had previously neither been harmed nor benefitted by him, but Paul is superior to Abel because he was killed by the very people whom he was trying to extrapolate from countless evils, those for whom he suffered all that he suffered [καὶ δι' οὓς πάντα ἔπασχεν ἅπερ ἔπαθεν].[857]

It was customary encomiastic fare to point not just to a noble death, but also to an illustrious entombment as a sign of status and therefore cause for praise.[858] John often finds occasion to praise Paul's resting place in Rome, and to envision him not merely lying there, but active and ruling in the midst of the imperial city.[859] But as we have seen, Paul's tomb is of prime importance as a launching pad from which the apostle to the Gentiles will rise in glory for final vindication over his execu-

---

[854] In *hom. in Rom.* 32, as analyzed in chap. 4, pp. 121–32.

[855] *hom. in Rom.* 32.2 [60.678].

[856] See, e.g., *hom. in Rom. 12:20* 5 [51.180].

[857] *laud. Paul.* 1.4 [SC 300.118].

[858] For instance, Libanios complains that Julian, whose grave was located in an undistinguished spot outside Tarsus of Cilicia, should have been buried next to Plato in the Academy (*Or.* 18.306).

[859] Because of his less illustrious burial place, Libanios draws an antithesis between Julian's grave and his actual sphere of influence: "oh, one possessing a small plot of earth in burial, but the whole world in admiration!" [ὦ μικρὸν μὲν τῆς γῆς μέρος κατέχων διὰ τοῦ τάφου, πᾶσαν δὲ τῷ θαύματι τὴν οἰκουμένην] (*Or.* 18.308).

tioners. In the same cruciform logic Paul so loved, John sees in Paul's death the ultimate sign of resurrection:

For this reason both Peter and Paul, and Ignatius after them, were sacrificed at Rome. This was so that they might cleanse the polluted city from the blood of idols by their own blood; this was so that through their deeds they might provide a demonstration of the resurrection of the crucified Christ.[860]

Paul the living is a portrait of Paul the dead, crucified daily; Paul the dead is a mirror reflecting Christ resurrected. In these framing portraits of the totality of the apostle's existence, John has captured and replicated the apostolic image in a thoroughly Pauline mode.

A Final Portrait: Paul as Assailant of "External Circumstances"

In this chapter we have demonstrated that Chrysostom employs the characteristic *topoi* of "external circumstances" both positively and negatively in his portrayals of his beloved Paul. More often than not Chrysostom seeks to demonstrate, through emphasis on Paul's humble origins in the first two categories, γένος and ἀνατροφή, the apostle's even greater excellence in the most important κεφάλαιον of epideictic rhetoric, πράξεις. But in other places Chrysostom wishes to employ the rhetoric of εὐγένεια to his own advantage, thus to claim that Paul possessed genuine excellence in all these categories, once properly understood according to his redefinitions. In these portraits we have also had occasion to remark upon Chrysostom's exclusive focus on *the adult Paul*, who for him had a kind of new birth, or cosmic debut, after his conversion and call to the role of apostolic emissary. This is the man he celebrates. John's portraits of the pre-Christian Paul are on the whole intentionally cast in predominantly negative hues[861] to render the most effective contrast with the later, dazzling apostolic career, the picture he wishes to leave with his audience.

The paradoxes involved in the appropriation of the form of epideictic rhetoric reach their culmination in the person of Paul himself, who, Chrysostom claims, recognizing the illusionary character of the table of values of Greco-Roman society, invented a new standard of social hierarchy. Such a portrait of Paul is quite consonant with his own paradoxical rhetoric of wisdom and foolishness, strength and weakness. This image is given expression in many places in Chrysostom's corpus of writings, but perhaps nowhere as vehemently as in one of his two occasional homilies on Romans 16:3, where Paul greets his friends Prisca and

---

[860] *pan. Ign.* 5 [50.593].

[861] Although, as we have shown, at times Chrysostom tries to put a positive slant on the negative portrait, usually in service of his anti-Judaistic sentiments, in order to show Paul superior to the rest of the Jews of his day in his zeal for persecution (see pp. 250–57).

Aquila, tentmakers like himself (Acts 18:3), a passage from which will form a fitting conclusion to our investigation in this chapter. First John reminds his audience of the "social facts" of the case:

> Then were Prisca and Aquila high class [ὕπατοι],[862] and soldiers, and viceroys, who had acquired some notoriety, or were endowed with great wealth, among the leaders of the city [ἄλλην τινὰ περιφάνειαν κεκτημένοι, ἢ πλοῦτον πολὺν περιβεβλημένοι, καὶ τῶν τὴν πόλιν ἀγόνωτν;]? One cannot claim any of these things, but rather the complete opposite [τοὐναντίον ἅπαν]: they were poor and impoverished, and lived from the work of their hands [πτωχοὶ καὶ πένητες, καὶ ἐκ τῆς τῶν χειρῶν ἐργασίας ζῶντες]. For they were, Luke says, tentmakers by craft (Acts 18:3). And Paul was not ashamed [οὐκ ἠσχύνετο ὁ Παῦλος], nor did he consider it some insult to the imperial city and its proud people [οὐδὲ ὄνειδος εἶναι ἐνόμιζε βασιλικωτάτῃ πόλει καὶ δήμῳ μέγα φρονοῦντι] to command them to greet those two who worked with their hands; nor did he consider it a matter of humiliation for them to join in friendship with Prisca and Aquila. Thus he had instructed all at that time to live philosophically [οὕτως ἦν ἅπαντας πεπαιδευκὼς τότε φιλοσοφεῖν]. Although we often have relatives who are somewhat poor [συγγενεῖς πενεστέροι ὀλίγῳ], we estrange ourselves from our relation to them [τῆς πρὸς αὐτοὺς οἰκειότητος ἀλλοτριούμεθα], and consider it an insult if we be unmasked as belonging to them. Yet Paul was not like this, but he even took pride in the matter, and made it clear, not only to Prisca and Aquila at that time, but afterwards also to all, that those tentmakers rated among his very top friends [ὅτι εἰς τοὺς πρώτους αὐτῷ τὴν φιλίαν ἐτέλουν ἐκεῖνοι οἱ σκηνοποιοί].[863]

Paul did not stand on social norms in his selection of associates. He was not haughty, but displayed the properties of a good friend, as a philosopher would know them. Chrysostom's perception of Pauline virtue in thus lowering himself to the humble level of Prisca and Aquila indisputably depends upon his own tacit acceptance of the conventional standards of social status, as well as an inherent presumption about Paul's duly higher position in the social order. But just those assumptions lead Chrysostom perilously close to a contradiction,[864] which he now seeks to avert:

> Now, let no one say to me, "How is it great and marvelous that he, who was from the same trade, wasn't ashamed of his fellow workers" [Καὶ μὴ μοι λεγέτω τις, Καὶ τί γὰρ μέγα καὶ θαυμαστὸν, καὶ αὐτὸν, ἀπὸ τῆς αὐτῆς ὄντα τέχνης, μὴ ἐπαισχύνεσθαι τοῖς ὁμοτέχνοις]? For this itself is indeed great and marvelous. For people who can claim some notoriety of ancestors are not as ashamed of their inferiors as those who were once of the same mean estate and have suddenly risen to some distinction and notoriety [Οὐ γὰρ οὕτως οἱ προγόνων

---

862 Or "consuls" (LSJ, 1854).

863 hom. in Rom. 16:3 1.2 [51.189].

864 Chrysostom's rhetorical strategy of stressing the surprising reversal of social determinism logically breaks down somewhat, in that he arrives at cross-purposes by wishing both to laud Paul for having "made it" (with divine assistance) up the ladder from his rough-hewn start, and also to praise him for the humility he exemplified in living by the work of his hands (though it doesn't take humility to occupy the status into which one was born!). In this Chrysostom is stuck with a tension inherent in Paul's own rhetoric about his manual labor: that it would appear to be praiseworthy only if it were a matter of choice and not of inherited social position (see Hock, *Social Context*, 50–65, on Paul's voluntary choice to maintain his trade).

ἔχοντες εἰπεῖν περιφάνειαν ἐπαισχύνονται τοῖς καταδεεστέροις, ὡς οἱ γενόμενοί ποτε ἐπὶ τῆς αὐτῆς εὐτελείας, εἶτα ἀθρόον εἰς λαμπρότητά τινα καὶ περιφάνειαν ἀναβάντες]. Now, everywhere it is clear that nothing was more illustrious or renowned than Paul [Παύλου λαμπρότερον οὐδὲν ἦν, οὐδὲ περιφανέστερον], but he was more distinguished [ἐπισημότερος] than the emperors themselves. For giving orders to demons, and raising the dead, and at a command both disabling and able to heal the disabled, he whose garments and shadows could destroy every form of illnesses – it is clear indeed that he was not considered to be human, but some angel come down from heaven [εὔδηλον ὅτι οὐδὲ ἄνθρωπος λοιπὸν εἶναι ἐνομίζετο, ἀλλ' ἄγγελός τις ἐξ οὐρανοῦ καταβάς]. But notwithstanding the fact that he enjoyed such a fine reputation, and was admired everywhere, and turned heads wherever he appeared ['Αλλ' ὅμως τοσαύτης ἀπολαύων δόξης, καὶ πανταχοῦ θαυμαζόμενος, καὶ ὅπουπερ ἂν φανείη πάντας ἐπιστρέφων], he was not ashamed of the tentmaker [οὐκ ἐπῃσχύνετο τὸν σκηνοποιόν], nor did he consider those in such a station to be inferior [οὐδὲ ἐλαττοῦσθαι ἐνομίζετο τοὺς ἐν τοσούτοις ἀξιώμασιν ὄντας].[865]

Here we glimpse the whole of Chrysostom's engagement with Paul's "external circumstances" in a nutshell. Paul's illustrious status is proven, both by conventional social observation[866] and by the acclaim which he earned from his incredible deeds, to the point that one is forced to reconsider and indeed rewrite the customary narratives about his γένος, offering the alternative tale that he was of celestial origin, an angel. Thus scripted, Paul was an elite, an aristocrat, who modeled the proper concern for his inferiors that Chrysostom, himself of high estate from birth and position, urges on his congregants. This portrait of Paul casts him as a shrewd and knowing social being, a philosopher with a keen radar for the hypocrisy holding up the social order, and the right prescription for living as a man of honor within this structure:

For he knew, he knew clearly [Ἤιδει γάρ, ἤδει σαφῶς], that customarily notoriety of wealth doesn't make nobility of birth, nor acquisition of possessions, but it is gentleness of manners which does [εὐγένειαν οὐ πλούτου περιφάνεια, οὐδὲ χρημάτων περιουσία, ἀλλὰ τρόπων ἐπιείκεια ποιεῖν εἴωθεν]. But those who are lacking in the latter, while taking great pride in the glory derived from their ancestors in these things, are preening themselves over the bare name, but not the fact, of noble birth [ὀνόματι μόνον εὐγενείας ψιλῷ, ἀλλ' οὐχὶ πράγματι καλλωπίζονται]. Yet often it can be detected from the name itself whether someone has arisen from ancestors going back deep into the past who were of noble birth [εἴ τις ἐπὶ τοὺς ἀνωτέρω προγόνους τῶν εὐγενῶν ἀναβαίη τούτων]. For if you carefully scrutinize someone who says he has notoriety and distinction, an illustrious father and grandfather, often you will find that he has some poor and unknown great, great grandfather [Τὸν γὰρ περιφανῆ καὶ λαμπρόν, καὶ πατέρα ἔχοντα ἐπίσημον εἰπεῖν καὶ πάππον, ἂν μετὰ ἀκριβείας ἐξετάσῃς, πολλάκις εὑρήσεις ἐπίπαππον εὐτελῆ τινα καὶ ἀνώνυμον ἐσχηκότα]. Likewise if we will investigate, by going back a little, the entire family tree of those who are thought to be poor, we shall often find that their ancestors far back were prefects and soldiers, just as easily as one might find them born into a family of horse and pig tenders [καθάπερ τῶν εὐτελῶν εἶναι δοκούντων ἂν τὸ γένος ἅπαν ἀναβαίνοντες κατὰ μικρὸν

---

[865] *hom. in Rom.* 16:3 1.2 [51.190].

[866] That as a rule it is the "nouveaux riches" who are more likely to look down on the poor than the old nobility (a commonplace which cements even further Paul's high status!).

διερευνησώμεθα, ὑπάρχους καὶ στρατηγοὺς εὑρήσομεν αὐτῶν πολλάκις τοὺς ἀνωτέρω προγόνους, καὶ εἰς ἱπποφορβοὺς καὶ συοφορβοὺς εὕροι τις ἂν γεγενημένους]. So, therefore, Paul, knowing all these things [ἅπαντα Παῦλος εἰδώς], did not take great account of them [τούτων μὲν οὐ πολὺν ἐποιεῖτο λόγον], but he sought "the noble birth of the soul" [ψυχῆς δὲ εὐγένειαν ἐζήτει] and taught others to admire this, too [καὶ τοὺς ἄλλους ταύτην θαυμάζειν ἐπαίδευσεν]. Therefore we can gain not a small amount of fruit from this: not to be ashamed of anyone who is poor, but to seek the virtue of the soul [ψυχῆς ἀρετὴν ἐπιζητεῖν], and to consider all the "external circumstances" with which we are invested [πάντα τὰ ἔξωθεν ἡμῖν περικείμενα] superfluous and unprofitable [περιττὰ καὶ ἀνόνητα].[867]

Most ironically of all, while he lauds Paul in this passage for disregarding τὰ ἔξωθεν, John depicts him as not at all "counter-cultural," but as one who is particularly knowledgeable[868] and astute in the ways of the world that they reflect, and the customary criticisms to which they were subjected throughout Greco-Roman antiquity. Consequently, Chrysostom depicts Paul in *his own* social likeness: as one who can criticize the prevailing social norms – and break them by associating with the poor and destitute – because he was not a social climber himself, but had a secure, recognized position in the *polis* and in the ecclesial structures which by the late fourth century mimicked it, even if he had in principle renounced the benefits of that position.[869] But the use of the encomiastic form is itself a telling emblem of John's (and his audience's) continuing embeddedness in the existing social order and its slate of values. Consequently, in this, the final portrait of our consideration, Paul becomes the ultimate social critic of the very encomiastic form in which he is being so vividly and variously portrayed.

Conclusions on the Biographical Portraits

In this chapter we have viewed a range of portraits of Paul via the rhetorical topics of "external circumstances." Each of these rhetorical heads – birth, ancestry, education, trade, deeds, wealth, friendship, death – situates the subject Paul within

---

[867] *hom. in Rom.* 16:3 1.2 [51.190]. This passage, like so many others cited above in this chapter, should serve to refute the sure conclusion of Simonetti, "Sulla struttura dei panegirici," 167: "Nei panegirici del Crisostomo le cose stanno ben diversamente: possiamo infatti affermare che di regola il nostro oratore non solo trascura questi luoghi canonici, ma non vi accenna neppure polemicamente, magari per intrecciarvi altre variazioni retoriche, come abbiamo visto fare a Basilio e al Nisseno."

[868] Note the repetition of "he knew" (three times), which frames the passage.

[869] See Kelly's general assessment: "There can be no doubt that John's family, if not of the foremost rank, was well placed socially, and also very comfortably off" (*Golden Mouth*, 4). Chrysostom mixed freely and untimidly with aristocrats at court, especially in Constantinople, and his main associates, especially the women, were wealthy, of even higher status than himself (Clark, *Jerome, Chrysostom and Friends*, 67–70). On Paul's voluntary self-lowering, see Hock, *Social Context*, 59–64; Antoinette Clark Wire, *The Corinthian Women Prophets: A Reconstruction through Paul's Rhetoric* (Minneapolis: Fortress, 1990) 66–71; Dale B. Martin, *Slavery as Salvation: The Metaphor of Slavery in Pauline Christianity* [New Haven: Yale University Press, 1990], esp. 117–35.

both a narrative context in his own life, and within a carefully circumscribed social universe. Chrysostom uses these biographical *topoi* in some paradoxical ways, but nonetheless his portraits of Paul are quite clearly and completely bound up in the rhetorical structure of epideictic rhetoric and the social values it inculcates. This interpretation of Chrysostom's deft treatments of Paul's "external circumstances" refutes the rather apologetic contention that John almost completely eschewed the "pagan" encomiastic structure in favor of his Christian catechetical guidance. A more supple and nuanced appreciation of the encomiastic art shows that, despite not following a rigid panegyrical structure, many of Chrysostom's Pauline portraits are manifestly creative adaptations and reappropriations of that genre. Here it is useful to recall Hubbell's conclusion that on the basis of structure these panegyrics are closer to informal λαλιαί than to full-scale encomia such as those of Gregory of Nazianzus.[870] The λαλιά, or "informal talk," which could be epideictic or deliberative, was a ubiquitous rhetorical form of the third and fourth-centuries, and was thus readily at hand for Chrysostom to use.[871] What distinguishes λαλιαί from other types of epideictic speeches is its lack of prescribed rhetorical disposition – precisely the quality found less in evidence in Chrysostom's panegyrics to Paul.

It is also to be noted, as a general principle, that a "talk" does not aim to preserve a regular order as other speeches do, but allows the treatment of the subject to be disorderly [λαλιὰ τάξιν μὲν οὐδεμίαν θέλει σώζειν καθάπερ οἱ λοιποὶ τῶν λόγων, ἀλλα ἄτακτον ἐπιδέχεται τὴν ἐργασίαν τῶν λεγομένων]. You can put anything you please in first or second place. The best arrangement in a "talk" is to avoid proceeding always on the same track, but to display continuous disorder [ἔστιν ἀρίστη τάξις τῆς λαλιᾶς τὸ μὴ κατὰ τῶν αὐτῶν βαδίζειν συνεχῶς, ἀλλ' ἀτακτεῖν ἀεί]. One moment, you may praise [ἐγκωμιάζειν] the subject on the basis of origin [ἀπὸ τοῦ γένους], the next on intention [ἀπὸ τοῦ προαιρέσεως], the next from recent events that have affected him [ἀπὸ τῶν χθές]; sometimes again on the basis of fortune [ἀπὸ τύχης], sometimes on a single action [ἀπὸ πράξεως μιᾶς].[872]

This description aptly fits Chrysostom's interest in novelty and in a more open form of construction of his proofs in praise of Paul.[873] But one must emphasize that the category λαλιά, as this excerpt from Menander shows, was no less a rhetorical composition than a full-blown βασιλικὸς λόγος or other epideictic

---

[870] Hubbell, "Chrysostom and Rhetoric," 274. Note that Hubbell was followed by Baur: "Also his eulogies of St. Paul and other saints breathe the spirit of the classic Greek encomiums" (*John Chrysostom*, 1.211).

[871] See Russell-Wilson, xxx–xxxi. The form of λαλιά may not extend back into the Hellenistic period, but Menander in the third century C.E. describes it as being of inestimable utility for all orators (*Rh.* 2.388–94 [Russell-Wilson, 114–26]).

[872] Menander, *Rh.* 2.391 [Russell-Wilson, 120–21]. Note that what they translate as "intention" is Chrysostom's favored word προαίρεσις, which we have usually rendered as the proper exercise of "free will."

[873] This corresponds exactly with what Wilken observed in Chrysostom's use of the inverse form, ψόγος: "In the strict sense, John's homilies on the Judaizers do not follow the formal requirements of the fixed speeches of the rhetorical tradition" (*John Chrysostom and the Jews*, 116).

composition,[874] and, like them, could partake of all the strategies common to the epideictic species. Therefore, Hubbell's designation of these orations as λαλιαί receives further confirmation from our documentation of the ubiquity of epideictic *topoi* in these homilies, and, the more discursive structure of the homilies *de laudibus sancti Pauli*,[875] in particular, can be understood as appropriate to liturgical oratory for Paul's feast day. But where Hubbell's analysis falls short is in his lack of acknowledgement of the deliberate playfulness and inventiveness within epideictic conventions that Chrysostom is engaged in here. A full appreciation of the creative ways John played with these very rhetorical conventions yields a far richer and more complex picture of Chrysostom's place in his wider literary culture, and provides us with a more nuanced awareness of how he was in ingenious ways manipulating the common topics his audience would have expected, in order to compose a series of flashcards of Paul's life which could be rearranged, restacked, and represented according to his own rhetorical and pastoral exigencies.

In these snapshot portraits of Paul's life, no less than those of his body and his soul, Chrysostom takes on the role of the ekphrasist who uses words to describe a person or work of art so powerfully that the hearer is induced to feel the same as if she or he were directly in the presence of the subject. As Chrysostom retells the "facts" and stories of Paul's life, he seeks to make Paul come to life before the eyes of his congregations so that Paul, in all his glory, can be the ethical archetype for them to copy in their own lives: "Beloved children, let us become imitators of Paul, not only according to faith, but according to life."[876] Like all ekphrasists, Chrysostom's episodic Pauline portraits are rooted in larger narratives which are known to the audience. John's artistic contribution is in recasting and reframing those well-known biographical tales to accent and interpret the element of the Pauline career which is most needed for each particular rhetorical and catechetical context. As we have seen, this oratorical work often involves "dueling portraits" from within the same Pauline career, as Chrysostom seeks, through a balanced presentation of alternate images, to temper the dangers of a reduction of the many-faceted Pauline career to a single dimension, especially any dimension that would give all the credit for his victory either to his own personal prowess (in rhetoric, for instance) or to divine inspiration (in miraculous deeds). And, indeed, each of the episodes of Paul's life contains within it inherent tensions, both in terms of the biblical record,[877] and

---

[874] For instance, as one of his examples of a λαλιά Menander Rhetor invokes one of the most famous of Attic orations, the *Panegyricus* of Isocrates (*Rh.* 2.391 [Russell-Wilson, 118]).

[875] We have provided a detailed compositional analysis of each of these seven orations in the course of this study. A comparison of the seven shows that each follows its own discrete argument line for a given occasion and homiletical purpose.

[876] Ἡμεῖς δὲ ὦ τέκνα ἀγαπητά, Παύλου μιμηταὶ μὴ κατὰ τὴν πίστιν μόνον, ἀλλὰ καὶ κατὰ τὸν βίον γενώμεθα (*hom. in 2 Tim.* 4.4 [62.624]).

[877] One might think that Chrysostom's ambiguity results from his absolute confidence in the historical accuracy of Acts, and his need, like that of all pre-modern scholars, to harmonize Luke's account, with its emphasis on Paul as miracle worker and prophet, with what we find in

in regard to its appropriateness for Chrysostom's own theological, rhetorical, and catechetical goals. Another decisive influence on Chrysostom's Pauline portraiture, as we have repeatedly demonstrated, is the vivid anti-portraits – of the Jews, of Julian, of Plato – against which John has drawn his Paul. These are polemical portraits which, when set in reverse, produce Pauline images in which he stands for Christianity *en masse*, an apostolic metonym of the morally superior and victorious philosophy. Still another factor dictating these "duels" is the extremes of Chrysostom's own rhetoric, which require him to qualify and fine-tune some portraits in relation to exaggerated claims he himself has made elsewhere. The Paul who emerges from the aggregate of these selected and redistributed portraits is a somewhat contradictory figure, but one whose inherent biographical and psychological tensions are resolved completely (in John the painter's eyes) by the ascetic varnish and harmonized hue of vigilant προθυμία common to them all.

---

the letters. But even the Paul of the letters lays claim to these powers, if not in as predominant a way as in Acts (Gal 3:5; 2 Cor 12:12; 1 Cor 14:18; 1 Thess 4:13f.; 1 Tim 4:1, etc.), while at the same time speaking as a naturally limited human being. Paul is also himself inconsistent about his use of rhetoric and the effectiveness of his oral and written λόγος, as the Corinthian correspondence especially highlights (1 Cor 1:18–2:16; 2 Cor 1:13; 10:9–11; 11:5–6; 13:3–4). So these tensions are rooted autobiographically and literarily in Paul of Tarsus and his epistolary legacy.

Chapter 7

"The Soul Which Reached as Far as Heaven:" Historiographical Issues in Chrysostom's Pauline Interpretation

Recapitulation of Chrysostom's Pauline Portraiture

The previous four chapters have demonstrated how Chrysostom's keen interest in the person of Paul pervades his writings. The portraits of Paul which he sketches – miniature and life-size, somatic and psychic, direct and indirect, snapshots and episodically textured – were composed in conformity with contemporary rhetorical and artistic practice, which offered techniques to meet the acute challenge of rendering a human person in non-fleshly media. Like all other relics, including Paul's own letters, Chrysostom's literary portraits of the apostle are intended to make the dead saint alive in the present.[1] For Chrysostom, portrait production goes hand in hand with reading Paul's letters, which themselves sketch the image of their writer's soul. Yet the portraits of Paul must also be redrawn through preaching and exegesis so that the hearers can have the model displayed before their eyes for imitation.[2] The lifeless image must always be kick-started into animation to stimulate new portrait updates by successive generations of artistic aspirants to the Christian emulative life. Because the Pauline epistles contain the genuine first-person voice of Paul, they both generate portraits of the soul of the author and in turn require a portrait of the soul of their author, drawn with love by the homiletical artist, for them to be adequately understood.[3]

Our investigation shows that Chrysostom's Pauline portraits were defined in relation to the encomiastic form of late antique rhetorical culture and its requirements, which John has manipulated according to his own theological, rhetorical

---

[1] This is therefore an extention of the pseudepigrapher's task, as Betz has identified it in Colossians: "Far from calling on its addressees merely to remember a dead martyr, the letter to the Colossians points beyond itself by facilitating the living interaction between the apostle and his future readers and listeners" ("Paul's 'Second Presence' in Colossians," 517).

[2] Chrysostom would likely resonate with Harrison's twentieth-century Orthodox contention: "The theological writer and the iconographer are thus engaged in the same task, only they work in different media" ("Word as Icon," 38).

[3] Chrysostom's homiletical art, therefore, perfectly illustrates Schleiermacher's "hermeneutical circle": "Man muß den Menschen schon kennen um die Rede zu verstehen und doch soll man ihn erst aus der Rede kennen lernen" ("Die Aphorismen von 1805 bis 1809," §11, in F. D. E. Schleiermacher, *Hermeneutik*, ed. Heinz Kimmerle [Heidelberg: Winter, 1959] 44).

and pastoral presuppositions and purposes. The form is biographic but the intention is typical, paradigmatic, and theologically providential.[4] Rhetoric is the medium with which Chrysostom scripts his relationship with Paul, and extends an invitation to others to join him in union with his hero, just as the recurrent rhetorical conventions at work in these portraits – epithets, encomia, and *ekphraseis* – constitute the set of operative expectations that govern the relationship between the orator and his audience. Chrysostom directly engages the biographic in the well-worn form of the encomium – of Paul's body, Paul's soul, and Paul's life circumstances – because for him it is a fundamentally important resource, not a mere diversion. Since Paul was a saint, everything about him is of potential enrichment and enlightenment, and everything about him is in some way significant and, for John, inherently interesting, and therefore worthy of detailed attention. The figure of Paul so engages John that he avidly seeks any available insights into his hero. Consequently, Chrysostom spends a great deal of time discussing, for instance, Paul's travel plans as outlined in the letters, not only to reconstruct the chronology of Paul's career and the placement of the letters within it, as contemporary scholars do (something Chrysostom, in common with them, also considers a crucial step in interpretation),[5] but moreover to penetrate and understand the *character* of Paul exhibited therein.

In many ways, however, Paul's letters not only contained a portrait of the soul of their author, but also served as a mirror in which Chrysostom as reader saw a portrait of himself in Paul. The Pauls whom Chrysostom paints bear striking resemblances to John himself, even as John was quite self-consciously pushing that process along by his living mimetic engagement with his beloved Paul. The love hermeneutics John practiced were inseparably linked with a hermeneutic of conformity through reading, exposition and self-sculpting. Hence the Paul he viewed as a powerful but ambivalent rhetorician served as a model for John, the Christian orator; Paul the man of sufferings and sorrows yet beloved of God a template of his own life struggles; Paul the urban pastoral ascetic the precise paradigm of his own vocation: "The blessed Paul filled out for us the portrait of the excellent priest" [ἡμῖν ὁ μακάριος Παῦλος τὴν τοῦ ἀρίστου ἱερέως ἀνεπλήρωσεν εἰκόνα].[6]

But John's investigations into Paul's character were not solely for his own vocational or devotional interest, nor were they carried out in a vacuum, in the privacy of his monastic cell. His oratory was a robustly public matter, a form of discourse aimed at particular effects. His portraits of Paul were often deliberately painted as

---

[4] Simonetti's study, "Sulla struttura dei panegyrici di S. Giovanni Crisostomo," constructs a false dichotomy between Chrysostom's paradigmatic purposes in his encomia and the "pagan" epideictic conventions. The two are in fact not opposed, but precisely complementary (see chap. 6, n. 16).

[5] He articulates the general principle in *hom. in Rom.* Arg. 1 [60.392]: "when about to enter into this epistle, we must first speak about the time in which it was written" [Μέλλοντας δὲ εἰς τὴν Ἐπιστολὴν κατιέναι ταύτην, ἀναγκαῖον καὶ τὸν χρόνον εἰπεῖν, καθ᾽ ὃν ἐγράφη].

[6] *sac.* 6.5 [272.322].

reverse or negative-images of those he cast as the notorious enemies of the church: Jews, Julian, Plato, Socrates, Pythagoras and other Greek philosophers, and satanic forces. In this bellicose artistry Paul's opponents are the same as Chrysostom's opponents, and Paul victorious represents the church victorious. John's discourse is intended to make real the victory he proclaims before the eyes of his auditors in the image of a single man: Paul, the herald of the gospel, who represents its battles, and above all its stunning and wholly unlikely ascension to power. Chrysostom's Paul is the quintessential figure incarnating the victory of Christianity in the late fourth century; he is the champion of the world – over Greek and barbarian.

These portraits of Paul in the writings of John Chrysostom, once we have put them on display and analyzed them according to form and content, raise many questions for further investigation. In Chrysostom the hermeneutical issue of the relationship between author and text in the promulgation of meaning is extremely complex. While there is no doubt that Chrysostom's hermeneutical sensibility is exuberantly author-centered, no simple or single correspondence between Chrysostom's image of Paul and his exegesis of his letters can be drawn, because of the multiplicity of portraits Chrysostom paints.[7] Although several emphases do emerge, both by volume and extent – such as Paul the prisoner for the gospel, Paul the teacher of the world, or Paul the man of sufferings – Chrysostom's rhetorical extremes, which fit completely into the expectations generated by the epideictic rhetoric he employs, lead to such a myriad of portraits of Paul as to make real Paul's own claim (1 Cor 9:22): "I have become all things to all people." Hence, Chrysostom's portraits of Paul do not constitute a single composite portrait, nor a search for *the single most accurate portrait*, but rather an extensive portrait series. But this is also precisely what makes them so valuable for Chrysostom's own oratorical purposes – Paul is a flexible cipher that he can mold for new purposes. Yet Paul is never cast *de novo* by Chrysostom, but always again creatively sculpted in the clay of the letters and Acts, which provide a range of attributes, epithets and features which can be reshaped into new homiletical-exegetical art. Furthermore, the multiplicity of Pauline portraits, as it must, reflects also the multi-faceted identities of the portraitist himself.[8] This is illustrated in an especially graphic fashion in John's varying identifications of Paul's "thorn in the flesh," which mirror the most salient worry of each stage of Chrysostom's life and ministry – from pagan opposition, to intra-Christian disputes, to imprisonment and forced march on order of

---

[7] Although it would exceed the bounds of this study, I believe it can be shown that particular Pauline portraits (such as the ones predominant within the Pauline epistle itself) often dominate the homily set on one letter, and largely affect its interpretation.

[8] As Miller concludes with respect to the dreams of Gregory of Nazianzus and Gregory of Nyssa: "What they found in their explorations was not a unitary, epistemologically certifiable self, but something more unsettling that only an imaginative act of visual perception could articulate" ("Dreaming the Body," 296).

imperial authorities.[9] The biblical figure of Paul was firm enough to model his life upon, yet malleable enough to change along with him in the course of it.

Chrysostom's portraits of Paul have a significant bearing upon many larger questions, especially about the relationship between these discourses and prevailing currents in the wider Christian world of late antiquity. In this chapter we shall investigate some of the vital implications – hermeneutical, historical, socio-cultural, and theological – of Chrysostom's catalogue of Pauline originals for broader issues in late fourth-century historiography. Specifically, we shall ask: what do Chrysostom's rhetorical depictions of the apostle to the Gentiles mean for his conception of the flesh and blood human being, Paul of Tarsus, and his overall perspective on history? For the relative status of Paul and other saints in Chrysostom's oratory? For the connection between Chrysostom's Pauline portraits and his Christology? For the social constitution of Christianity in the eastern urban environments of the Christian imperium? For the understanding of ancient biographic literature and its genres? And, finally, what does John's Pauline portraiture as such contribute to the larger scholarly project of surveying the landscape of patristic biblical interpretation? We shall begin with the last question as a backdrop for our subsequent engagement with the former ones.

Pauline Portraits and Patristic Exegesis

Chrysostom's portraits of Paul, we have argued, are not sideshows to the "main event" of the interpretation of the apostle's letters, but are themselves central to his exegetical art. Exegesis of Paul, as Chrysostom practices it, is exegesis of the author as well as of the words enshrined in his writings. The force of the present study is to argue that the fact that these constructions of the author Paul have specific rhetorical and catechetical goals makes them no less "exegesis" than other forms of biblical commentary, for they are an essential part of the reader's encounter with the text and its web of meanings (as Chrysostom himself expounds them). Such a claim goes against the grain of traditional ways of mapping the terrain of patristic exegesis. For example, in his much-read introduction to *Biblical Interpretation in the Early Church*, Manlio Simonetti devotes less than a page to Chrysostom, on the grounds that:

[John] is of less interest to us from the specifically exegetical standpoint, since the primary objective of his rhetorical output was to draw out of the sacred text a lesson to educate, warn, or edify his listeners, rather than to illustrate the text for its own sake.[10]

---

[9] See chap. 6, pp. 304–306. There is also a remarkable and uncoincidental similarity in the offenses for which John defends Paul and those with which he was confronted by his own adversaries (variability, excess fasting due to vainglory, harshness), as evidenced in Palladios, *v. Chrys.*

[10] Simonetti, *Biblical Interpretation*, 74.

But this dichotomy between exhortatory purpose and exegesis is a false one for much patristic exegesis. Ancient biblical interpretation consisted of a much wider set of practices than Simonetti has confined it to here. Moreover, his own definition is predicated upon a non-existent ideal, for no ancient Christian interpreters illustrated the text "for its own sake" (a claim of modern historical-critical exegesis that has itself been buffeted severely in the last half century). Chrysostom's vivid exegetical moralizing may be more extensive or artful than many others, but that does not remove his homilies from the realm of biblical interpretation. Rather than leaving this rich material out of account, what is needed is a better model of ancient biblical interpretation.

Precisely that desideratum has been addressed in recent scholarship, as marked by the pivotal work of such scholars as Frances Young (*Biblical Exegesis and the Formation of Christian Culture*) and Elizabeth Clark (*Reading Renunciation: Asceticism and Scripture in Early Christianity*),[11] who have problematized the old distinction between Alexandrian allegory and Antiochene literalism, not only for its rigidity (which had long been massaged by discussion of border concepts, such as Antiochene typology, and Alexandrine use of θεωρία),[12] but also for the many types of interpretive approaches falling outside the lines of this map. Young's stunning work demonstrates both the problematic of the old allegory/literalism distinction, and the value of liberation from it, in generating a fresh perspective on the similarities of technique and purpose between Antiochenes and Alexandrines, while still appreciating their social-historical and intellectual differences. Specifically, she argues that the two schools had roots in different educational milieux (the Alexandrines in the philosophical schools, and the Antiochenes in the rhetorical schools, as had been argued by Christoph Schäublin earlier),[13] which led to two different ways of viewing the text's mimetic role, either as "symbol" of true realities (Alexandrine hermeneutics) or as "ikon" of moral and dogmatic teachings (Antiochene). Young's map of patristic exegesis usefully complicates the conventional straitjacket of allegorical vs. literal readings, or even the plural "senses" of scripture, by including six categories of "reading strategies": paraenetic reading, oracular

[11] See also Clark, *Reading Renunciation*, 70–78 for a survey of previous scholars who have worked toward the erosion of the old consensus. Cameron's important work, *Christianity and the Rhetoric of Empire,* is another important contribution to this productive line of contemporary scholarship, which I shall discuss later in this chapter (pp. 397 and 404–407).

[12] As does Simonetti, *Biblical Interpretation*, 67–68, who then is assured that "having safely established the status of generalising outlines, it remains to be seen how they were put into practice ...."

[13] Christoph Schäublin, *Untersuchungen zu Methode und Herkunft der antiochenischen Exegese* (Theophania 23; Köln/Bonn: Peter Hanstein, 1974), who concluded, on the basis of his study of the Old Testament interpretation of Diodore of Tarsus and Theodore of Mopsuestia, that: "die antiochenische Exegese von der paganen Grammatik herkommt" (p. 173); Frances M. Young, "The Rhetorical Schools and Their Influence on Patristic Exegesis," *The Making of Orthodoxy: Essays in Honour of Henry Chadwick* (Cambridge: Cambridge University Press, 1989) 182–99, an argument which was expanded in *Biblical Exegesis*, 169–85.

exegesis, lexical analysis, explanatory comment, deductive expansion, and mimetic reading (consisting of four divisions: exemplary paraenesis, prophetic types, ikonic, and symbolical readings).[14] Chrysostom's homilies figure largely in Young's study,[15] especially in the designations of paraenetic exegesis and mimetic exegesis, whereas they did not find a place on Simonetti's map. Indeed, Young even gives a brief treatment of Chrysostom's *de laudibus sancti Pauli*,[16] among other fourth-century panegyrical works,[17] and reaches a conclusion fully harmonious with our findings:

> Such use of the Bible [in panegyrics] reflects an understanding of the text quite different from that presupposed by the usual categories of literal, typological, or allegorical. The text is authoritative yet far from binding. Here is an intertextuality of imaginative and creative play, far removed from the historicism of modern interpretation whether critical or fundamentalist, yet not lacking attention to the specificity of the biblical text, or its ability to lend weight to the forging of distinctive Christian values in a particular cultural dress. Maybe here there are principles worth noting, even if panegyrical practices are utterly foreign and currently unthinkable.[18]

Although in the next chapter I shall question whether Young is correct in assuming a complete divide between ancient "panegyrical exegesis" and contemporary

---

[14] Young, *Biblical Exegesis*, 212.

[15] For instance, he is the major example she treats of "paraenetic exegesis" (*Biblical Exegesis*, 203, 248–57).

[16] Young's purpose is to examine the "use of the Bible" in these compositions, as well as other panegyrics by the Cappadocians. This approach makes sense in light of the overall argument of her book (in this section she is demonstrating how in Christian discourse the biblical text comes to take the same role the Greek classics such as the Homeric epics and hymns had occupied in Greco-Roman culture), but it does not quite do justice to the seven discourses in their own right. For example, she concludes that "there is more retelling in Chrysostom's own words than direct quotation. Occasional allusions to other parts of the biblical material are woven in, but the elaborate collages found in the Cappadocian material are largely absent from these panegyrics on Paul" (*Biblical Exegesis*, 116), a judgment which contrasts rather starkly with our analysis of the seven homilies in this study, which has found them to be intricate mosaics of biblical and non-biblical material. These variant conclusions are perhaps due to the fact that Young's purpose is to examine the *formal* ways in which scripture is invoked in these discourses, with the possible options being direct quotation, allusion, proof-text, and collage, whereas our analysis has emphasized that the whole rhetorically styled enterprise is itself an act of biblical interpretation (and not just a medium for particular types of biblical invocation). We have also examined the phenomenon of allusion itself in terms of the rhetorical theory and practice of the encomium and the epithet, rather than as a less direct form of biblical "use" than quotation.

[17] But Young deliberately leapfrogs over the passage which has been in many ways the center of this study, because she (somewhat uncharacteristically) considers it beyond the bounds of "strict exegesis": "A rhetorical portrait of Paul becomes the point at which strict exegesis is abandoned, and the exhortation grows out of this exemplary servant of God, the great athlete struggling against the powers of evil through his ascetic hardships" (*Biblical Exegesis*, 256–57). However, for Chrysostom 1 Corinthians is not just a set of words to be understood, but also a person to be encountered, portrayed, and explicated (esp. 4:16; 11:1); hence for him the Pauline portrait in *hom. in 1 Cor.* 13.3–4 is "exegesis," indeed!

[18] Young, *Biblical Exegesis*, 116.

Pauline scholarship, her basic thesis is further substantiated by the present study, which attempts to show the extent to which Chrysostom's "paraenetic exegesis" runs throughout his oeuvre, and always has, either explicitly or implicitly, the goal of ikonic imitation of Paul, the archetype of virtue. As analyzed here, Chrysostom's εἰκόνες of Paul constitute an ideal graphic illustration of Young's valuable proposal of Antiochene "ikonic" mimetic reading. In addition, the documentation amassed in our investigation of Chrysostom's use of specific rhetorical techniques as outlined in the late antique handbooks and exercises (especially his own local contemporaries, Libanios and Aphthonios) provides further evidence that the firm foundation of Antiochene exegetical practice was the *paideia* of the rhetorical schools. Moreover, Young's hermeneutical insight that Chrysostom employed a form of "audience-oriented criticism,"[19] is a useful advance, which can be further enhanced by our emphasis upon his "author-centered" interpretation, and the hermeneutic of love which unites the two in the orator's exegetical work.[20] Even as Chrysostom's portraits of Paul so aptly illustrate her thesis, they also might challenge Young's analytical list of "reading strategies" in some respects, for they consistently combine what her categorization separates, such as paraenetic and mimetic readings.[21] A second area where the present study critically engages Young's proposal is in regard to the role of "history" in paraenetic exegesis, a point to which we shall return below (pp. 389–94).

Elizabeth Clark's expert study of patristic reading strategies for fostering ascetic practices and teachings demonstrates that the same interpreter, when faced with different texts and diverse socio-historical contexts of meaning, can employ a vary-

---

[19] *Biblical Exegesis*, 173.

[20] See above, pp. 38–40, on how John sought to create in his auditors the love for the author Paul which is required for the proper interpretation of his writings, and for the imitation of the exemplar in their own practice.

[21] For example, the charts in *Biblical Exegesis*, 212–13 differentiate 1) Paraenetic reading and 6) Mimetic reading, and list among subcategories of the latter a) "mimetic reading for exemplary paraenesis" and c) "mimetic reading to see how the text mirrors reality 'ikonically.'" But surely these categories overlap both in principle, and in the specific example we are treating here, where paraenetic and mimetic strategies are integrally related and combined in John's depictions of his hero Paul. One might also ask whether or how Young's "reading strategies" 2–5 (oracular exegesis, lexical analysis, explanatory comment, and deductive expansion) are operations of the same type or category as paraenetic and mimetic reading, which yet appear so similar to one another. Indeed, in places Young's own argument leaves the impression that "paraenetic reading" is not simply one approach standing alongside the five others. She speaks of "the primacy of this way of reading scripture" (*Biblical Exegesis*, 204), and later, in discussion of Chrysostom's homilies on 1 Corinthians: "the whole process of exegesis is paraenetical" (p. 249). See also statements such as the following, which generalize paraenesis across different reading strategies or methods: "such 'mimetic' use of literary heroes reinforced the paraenetic use of scripture with which we began, and provided 'types'" (p. 209), and "To that list I now suggest we should add figural allegory, noting its essentially paraenetic character" (p. 263). Such comments (and the present study) suggest that "paraenetic exegesis" may more usefully be an umbrella category that circumscribes the entire exegetical enterprise, rather than one strategy alongside the others.

ing set of "figurative" exegetical techniques to reach predetermined goals of interpretation for lived praxis.[22] Chrysostom's interpretations of Paul demonstrate this
principle repeatedly, as we have seen, particularly in his ability, even propensity, for
interpreting the same text or another piece of evidence about his hero in various
ways depending upon his rhetorical and catechetical purpose. Further, this study
specifically supplements the third part of Clark's book, a section tantalizingly entitled "Reading Paul," by devoting attention, not, as Clark has so thoroughly done, to
how Chrysostom and other interpreters dealt with key passages in the Pauline and
deutero-Pauline epistles, but to the other side of what it means to "read Paul," i.e.,
the man himself, and how depictions of him functioned in the politics of ascetic
discourse. We have demonstrated that Chrysostom exegeted not solely the text of
the Pauline letters, but the very script of the apostle's body and life (which he was
composing even as he was interpreting it) in his pursuit and advocacy of the
monastic ideal.[23] In this respect, Chrysostom's portraits of Paul provide a textbook
case for Clark's main thesis (the full explication of which will no doubt comprise an
agenda for the decades ahead) that patristic exegetes were both readers *and* writers,
a notion expressed perfectly by John's rhetorical art as practiced on the subject/
author Paul, whom he constructs as he reads. With this in view, Clark's hermeneutical conclusion, that "it is the present readers, not the original authors, who provide
meaning,"[24] needs perhaps to be widened to include in the interpretive equation
the role of the *persona* of the author, not just as an historical given [i.e., the "original"
author] but as a productive construct of the act of reading itself, which can provide
certain constraints on boundless interpretive options.

   Hence, the present study coordinates with the recent efforts of Young, Clark, and
others to refashion the map of patristic exegesis by attention to "the mechanics
employed to extract meaning,"[25] by providing a corroborating test-case in patristic
hermeneutics focused on a single interpreter and his exegetical-homiletical preoccupation with his author. John's portraits of Paul both illustrate the inadequacy of
the traditional model, and point toward some new directions to be pursued further
in the emerging new typologies of "figurative" patristic exegesis: the construction of
authors and other biblical personalities as part of exegetical practice; the creative
appropriation of ἔκφρασις as a hermeneutical technique; attention not only to
biblical interpretation *in* Christian art (which remains so valuable), but also the ways
patristic exegetes conceived of their practice *as* art; and the public contexts and
rhetorical purposes of many acts of ancient biblical interpretation.[26]

----

[22] Clark, *Reading Renunciation*.

[23] See especially John's portrait of Paul as the ideal monk, as elucidated above in chap. 6,
pp. 308–26.

[24] Clark, *Reading Renunciation*, 371–372.

[25] Young, *Biblical Exegesis*, 202.

[26] The case for this point has been made most effectively by Cameron, *Christianity and the
Rhetoric of Empire*, but it remains to be explicated by more detailed studies of individual authors
and works.

The "Historical Paul" and Chrysostom's Hermeneutics

Traditionally the Antiochene school of interpretation has been deemed "historical," in contrast with the allegorizing or spiritualizing of the Alexandrines Clement and Origen. This simple naming of the difference has always been accompanied by much discussion about what kind of "history" the Antiochenes practiced, and how it relates to modern notions and practices of historiography.[27] With the dismantling of the older dichotomy between allegorical and literal exegesis, what happens to the "historical" emphasis formerly attributed to the Antiochene school? Chrysostom's interpretations of Paul can be illuminating for this question. The heart of the matter may be expressed as follows: what is the relationship between Chrysostom's portraits of Paul and "the historical Paul"? Chrysostom's verbal images of Paul draw richly upon a wide range of New Testament literature about the apostle, which he felt great freedom in combining with other sources (either from Christian traditions or "pagan" conventions) and arranging into fresh compositions. The content, form and function of the portraits of Paul which Chrysostom produced demonstrate abundantly that he did not depict Paul simply out of antiquarian interest in this worthy man of the past, but for the higher purpose (as he would judge it) of moral exhortation. Virtue, rather than verisimilitude, was the standard of his portraiture.[28] In this respect Chrysostom is in complete accord with late antique panegyric and biographic literature in general: "Celle que nous fournissent les grands évêques orientaux est assez abondante pour permettre de caractériser un genre bien traché, intermédiaire entre l'histoire et l'invention pure, la poésie, si l'on veut."[29] Are Chrysostom's Pauline portraits, as rhetorical compositions, a kind of non-historical poetry? What kind of a historian, then, was Chrysostom, and how "historical" were his hermeneutics?

As we have mentioned above, Schäublin and Young have cogently argued that the differences between these two main strands of early Christian exegesis represent the long-standing divergence in the arts of textual interpretation practiced by rhetorical schools on the one hand, and philosophical schools on the other. The type of literary criticism taught in the former concentrated upon the careful details of textual-criticism, philological and stylistic analysis, and elucidation of subject matter, with particular interest in drawing moralizing conclusions from the text, whereas that of the philosophical schools emphasized the derivation, by allegory,

---

[27] See D. S. Wallace-Hadrill, *Christian Antioch: A Study of Early Christian Thought* (Cambridge: Cambridge University Press, 1982) 27–51; and important comments in the survey of scholarship on the origins of Antiochene hermeneutics in Schäublin, *Untersuchungen*, 25–42.

[28] Compare Cox on Eusebius' life of Origen: "But Eusebius' task was not a quest for the historical Origen. Like that of other biographers, his goal was to create a convincing portrait of a magnificent man by capturing in prose the ideals which that man represented" (*Biography*, 101).

[29] Delehaye, *Passions des martyrs*, 135; see also p. 147: "… la place du panégyrique dans la littérature, entre le document historique et l'oeuvre d'imagination."

of abstract truths: "Where philosophy found abstract doctrines or virtues through verbal allegory, rhetoric looked for concrete ethical examples in a narrative."[30] This pedagogical distinction has led Young to minimize the vaunted historical interest of the Antiochenes (she refers to "the anhistorical character of Chrysostom's exegesis"), which she regards as subservient to their pervasive moralizing intent: "expounding the *historia* is important, though not because it is historical, but because it becomes exemplary."[31]

Young's thesis nicely accounts for the stylized nature of Chrysostom's portraits of Paul, their rhetorical forms, and consequent hyperbolic expressions about their subject which move well beyond the warrants of his historical sources, at least as acts of exegesis of the plain sense of the biblical text. And she is right that Chrysostom is surely not engaged in the task of replicating, as if by photo-journalism, the historical Paul of Tarsus. However, John's portraits of Paul and doting attention to his subject exceed the "gossipy biographical interest, but no true historical sense"[32] that Young ascribes to the rhetorical schools, chiefly because, as we have seen, Chrysostom regards the Pauline biography – down to its particulars about dress, food and lifestyle – as entirely evocative of saintly existence, thus moving beyond a merely paparazzo interest in celebrities to what John fervently regarded as a demonstration of the capacities of a human person for a virtuous existence.[33] For this reason, Paul's historical rootedness in real human existence – which, as we have seen, John insists upon again and again[34] – must be recognized as a crucial factor in his moral reasoning and his exegetical paraenesis. Consequently Young's dichotomy between the "historical" and the "exemplary"[35] should be slightly reformulated to account for the fact that the exemplum usually gains its very power *from* its historical enactment. Hence it is not quite accurate in the case of Chrysostom's approach to Paul to say that "the difference between ancient and modern exegesis lies in the massive shift in what is found to be problematical. We have had problems about historical coherence; they had problems about doctrinal coherence,"[36] for Chrysostom's biographical exegesis of the Pauline corpus has a

---

[30] Young, "Rhetorical Schools," 188; see also p. 192: "Chrysostom sees morality in terms of exemplary deeds not abstract virtues and, whether it is Paul or Abraham, it is to their exemplary character and practice which he draws attention."

[31] Ibid., 192.

[32] Young, "Rhetorical Schools," 186–87.

[33] See, e.g., *laud. Paul.* 2, analyzed in chap. 5, pp. 152–59.

[34] E.g., *hom. in 1 Cor.* 13.3 [61.110]; *laud. Paul.* 4.21 [SC 300.228]: ὃ γὰρ πολλάκις εἶπον, τοῦτο λέγων οὐ παύσομαι, ὅτι καὶ σῶμα ἐν αὐτῷ τὸ αὐτὸ ἦν ἡμῖν, καὶ τροφαὶ αἱ αὐταί, καὶ ψυχὴ ἡ αὐτή; *hom. in Rom.* 32.4 [60.681]; see discussion above, pp. 133, 198–99.

[35] This dichotomy emerges in a different form in *Biblical Exegesis*, 201, where Young, adapting Michael Fishbane's categories of inner-biblical typology (from *Biblical Interpretation in Ancient Israel* [Oxford: Clarendon, 1985] 350–79), differentiates "exemplary (or biographical – potentially 'universal')," from "prophetic (or 'historical' – narrative prefiguration)" typologies, which again could be taken as separating the exemplary from the historical.

[36] Young, *Biblical Exegesis*, 207.

very high investment in the historical coherence and integrity of the subject, precisely *because* of his exemplary function.[37]

Nonetheless, the ahistorical features of some of Chrysostom's portraits of Paul, especially their hyperbole[38] ("Paul was a heaven"), are remarkable, and do serve to stretch the credulity of his own attendant claim to the historical rootedness of the personage. So our categorizations of Antiochene historiography must somehow also reckon with the innate paradox that often John wished to stress the very earth and time-boundedness of his flesh and blood human example, even as he depicted Paul as a citizen of heaven. That claim — simultaneously historical and exemplary — even as it clashes for modern exegetes with "the historical Paul," was nonetheless a real one for John. How did he hold the two together?

Perhaps what most characterizes (and, for the modern reader, confounds) Chrysostom's historiography when it comes to Paul is its temporal fluidity, for to John's mind the Paul he seeks to portray to his congregation is equally a figure of the past to be remembered, and a being fully alive in the here and now (both on earth and in heaven)[39] to be encountered in the reading of his letters and in the lives of those who attend to him. Both these hermeneutical approaches to his author co-exist in John, and he is capable of turning from one to the other readily, though he demonstrates that he is conscious of a turn in frame of reference when he does so — from the historically particular moment of composition of a Pauline letter to its perduring words for a universal readership.[40] For example, in his homilies on the

---

[37] As we have seen particularly in chap. 6, pp. 326–53.

[38] See Wilken, *John Chrysostom and the Jews*, 107, on hyperbole in general as a constituent element of John's oratory: "Passages such as these are not lonely flights of rhetorical enthusiasm sprinkled here and there throughout his sermons; they are the very stuff of his preaching, and they fill page after page, frequently overshadowing the presumed topic of the speech." Delehaye, *Passions des martyrs*, 147–50, rightly attributed the "abus de l'hyperbole" of late fourth-century panegyrists to rhetorical influence (but this does not, of course, sideline its importance).

[39] See chap. 2, nn. 13–18 for references. This is quite close to what Cox maintains for the biographers she studies, Porphyry and Eusebius: "By discussing biographies as vehicles for the social and political concerns of the biographers, we might ourselves be guilty of suggesting that Plotinus and Origen were mere toys in the hands of their biographers. In order to avoid the idea that an author's impulse to write is a conscious manipulation of his material merely for objective, sociopolitical ends, we will look at an author's intent not only as a way of imagining his work's context, but also as a reflection of the author's deep sense of himself. With this perspective, we need not think of biographers as manipulative puppeteers. For puppets are lifeless and opaque things, whereas Plotinus and Origen were translucent presences who lived, not in the misty past, but in the creative moment of their biographers' imaginations. In that creative moment, it is not only the depths of cultural situations that are sounded, but also the soulful depths of the author" (*Biography*, 135–36). This eloquent description fits John's Pauline portraits exactly, except that we must add, in Paul's case, the mediating power of his *writings* (as living spoken words) in effecting the living encounter.

[40] An adequate treatment of this topic would require its own study, but here I can cite a few examples where Chrysostom addresses this hermeneutical question directly. In *hom. in Col.* 10.1 [62.365] Chrysostom asks a question which is for him simultaneously historical and pastoral: why didn't Paul include a household code in each of his letters? His answer is that at the time Paul

Pastorals, when faced with texts ostensibly addressed several hundred years before to a single person, long dead, Chrysostom carefully differentiates the levels of readership addressed by 1 Timothy: Timothy himself, other contemporaries with Timothy, and later readers down to the present. Then he claims overtly that it is *through* Timothy that Paul speaks to all people:[41] "these things *have been said* [εἴρηται] to Timothy, but they *are being said* [λέγεται] to every teacher and disciple *through him*" [δι' ἐκείνου].[42] The very fact that Chrysostom makes this as a deliberate and overt hermeneutical assertion shows that John does not merely "collapse the time-gap" between the historical origin of the text and the present,[43] but fully recognizes and explicitly *bridges* it, when he wishes, via his acute sense of authorial presence in the act of liturgical reading and exposition of the letters. We have insisted throughout this study that the power of love is what (according to Chrysostom) forms the conduit between the past and the present.[44] Chrysostom never lost sight of the fact that Paul was an authorial voice rooted in a by-gone period, who spoke directly to concrete past people and situations,[45] even as he also knew him as a saint still alive

---

wrote there were three types of churches, one kind which was ready and willing to receive such precious teaching, and the other two who were lacking one of these attributes. He is able to categorize all the letters according to this historical reconstruction. But after all that work, John can still authorize the teachings of the *Haustafel* he so likes by saying: "But rather the things he says to them he says to all" [Μᾶλλον δὲ ἃ πρὸς τούτους λέγει, πρὸς πάντας λέγει]. This is a good example of a customary, overt hermeneutical change of lens on John's part. See also, e.g., *hom. in 2 Cor. 11:1 2* [51.303]: "Let's learn what it is then that he was crying out today, saying ..." [μάθωμεν τί ποτέ ἐστιν ὅπερ σήμερον ἐβόα λέγων] and *sac.* 4.7: "the virtue of his letters has benefitted and will benefit not only the faithful of that time, but also those from that time up until [the final] coming of Christ" [οὐ τοὺς τότε μόνον πιστούς, ἀλλὰ καὶ τοὺς ἐξ ἐκείνου μέχρι τῆς [ἐσχάτης] τοῦ Χριστοῦ παρουσίας ὠφέλησέ τι καὶ ὠφελήσει (sc. ἡ τῶν ἐπιστολῶν ἀρετή)].

[41] *hom. in 1 Tim.* 13.2 [62.566]; *hom. in 2 Tim.* 2.1; 8.1 [62.607, 644].

[42] *hom. in 1 Tim.* 4.1 [62.619; Field 6.193]; cf. *hom. in Eph.* 13.1 [62.93]: "Not to the Ephesians alone have these words been said, but they are being said now to you [Οὐ πρὸς Ἐφεσίους ταῦτα εἴρηται μόνον, ἀλλὰ καὶ πρὸς ὑμᾶς νῦν λέγεται], and not from us, but even from Paul, or rather, not from us nor from Paul but from the grace of the spirit" [καὶ οὐ παρ' ἡμῶν, ἀλλὰ καὶ παρὰ Παύλου, μᾶλλον δὲ οὔτε παρ' ἡμῶν, οὔτε παρὰ Παύλου, ἀλλὰ παρὰ τῆς τοῦ Πνεύματος χάριτος].

[43] As argued by Young, "Rhetorical Schools," 192; also *Biblical Exegesis*, 253, "implicit conflation."

[44] This thesis fits completely with Young's formulation that the homiletical hermeneutic works through the "empathy of Chrysostom the pastor with Paul the pastor" (Frances M. Young, "John Chrysostom on I and II Corinthians," *Studia Patristica* 18/1, ed. Elizabeth A. Livingstone [Louvain: Peeters, 1986] 349–52, 351; and *eadem, Biblical Exegesis*, 253–54). In both cases Young documents this by means of a very insightful discussion of the different forms of address Chrysostom uses in the homilies, switching from first to second to third, in reference to all three of the reading partners – Paul, himself, and his congregation. This is an extremely important feature of John's orchestration of the conversation between his Paul and his congregation.

[45] Chrysostom almost always refers to Paul's letters by reference to their addressees ("as Paul wrote to the Ephesians"), and situates each epistle historically, usually in the ὑπόθεσις or *Argumentum* section that prefaces the homily sets, by discussing who those people were, and why Paul wrote to them at that time. To cite only two examples, John argues that the reason the epistle to the Ephesians contains the most lofty thoughts and doctrines is that that city was renowned for

and available in those now collected texts,[46] with their "accuracy" [ἀκρίβεια] of detail.[47] But what makes him different from a modern historian is the direction of time-travel – it is not his own trek back in time, but Paul's movement forward that creates his encounter with the Paul he knows. The reason John does not hunt down a "historical Paul" as moderns understand that quest is that he does not experience *the same kind* of historical distance from his subject they do.[48]

But Chrysostom does insist upon the *historical* Paul (as a flesh and bones character), even in the midst of his hyperbole, as can be seen in his constant emphasis upon Paul having had a body, and having been mortal, just like everyone else. Body and mortality ineluctably situate the apostle in a limited historical time-frame. Yet Chrysostom's fond image of Paul as a bird, even as it visualizes Paul spanning the cosmological space from earth to heaven, also symbolizes his simultaneous corporeality and ability to exceed the constraints of the body, and hence incipient immortality and timelessness. The reason these two historical positionings of his author do not trouble Chrysostom (in addition to his fondness for paradox) is that they were apparently seamlessly united in his own experience of reading. Yet it was not the temporality that most captivated his interest, but the personality.

Furthermore, Paul's temporal fluidity entailed also a concomitant, and most useful, personal variability. If John's construal of the task of an encomium to a saint is that it should emphasize, not what is particular to that individual, but the universal virtues of which he is an emblem,[49] then the man who was "all things to all people" easily becomes the omni-referential paradigm, the exemplar of all virtues

---

its philosophers (*hom. in Eph.* Arg. [62.10]), and explains that Paul did not emphasize Christ's divinity in Galatians because what that audience needed was to learn about the powerful effects of the cross and resurrection (*comm. in Gal.* 1.2 [61.615]). See Schäublin, *Untersuchungen,* 41–42: "Eine solche grammatische Arbeit aber ruft – folgerichtig durchgehalten – nach einer ebenso klaren und nüchternen, vorerst historischen Prüfung der Aussage, die ja einem Menschen, einem 'Autor', verdankt wird, der in einer bestimmten Zeit und für eine bestimmte Zeit geschrieben hat, wie sehr auch durch ihn der Geist Gottes redet"; a point with which Young can also concur: "Yet Chrysostom is not unaware that the text belongs to another 'narrative' from that to which he and his congregation belong" (*Biblical Exegesis,* 253).

[46] This coheres with where Wallace-Hadrill (*Christian Antioch,* 51) places Chrysostom in the historiographical spectrum of Antiochene writers, from the "rigid historicism" of Theodore, to the more relaxed majority: "or adopting a moderate position without appearing to see the need to argue the matter at all, as with John Chrysostom." But, as we have seen above, Chrysostom *does* at times "argue the matter."

[47] On the importance of ἀκρίβεια in Chrysostom's approach to the text, see R. Hill, "*Akribeia:* A Principle of Chrysostom's Exegesis," *Colloquium* 14 (1981) 32–36.

[48] While Young rightly combats the tendency to turn the Antiochenes into modern historical critics, her judgement that they "had *no sense* of anachronism or historical distance" (Young, *Biblical Exegesis,* 253, emphasis added) appears to go too far.

[49] With Delehaye, *Passions des martyrs,* 168: "La méthode du développement par les lieux communs est la substitution de l'universel au particulier, et il y a la même différence entre le héros du panégyrique et celui du doucement historique qu'entre le portrait authentique pris sur le vivant et l'image hiératique où tous les détails sont idéalisés."

and roles simultaneously. Therefore the test of an "accurate" portrait of Paul, in John's estimate, is not merely correspondence with various pieces of evidence in the historical record, but also with the catechetical needs that called it forth in the first place. And ultimately the medium in which Paul is to be recreated is the pliant, fleshy clay of the lives of the orator and his audience, whom he calls to emulate him in the task of ascetic practices which will form them all into portraits of their archetypal hero. When providing *ekphraseis* in his Pauline portraits it is repeatedly Chrysostom's voice of valuation that we hear: his choice, his preference, for Paul spoken and paraded before his congregation in his favored guises and poses – Paul the prisoner, Paul the abjectly poor, Paul the ascetic, Paul the man in tears. Chrysostom as the speaker-artist played the essential role of chief compositor of Paul for the community, both in his homilies and in his own life. An adaptable, many-faced Paul, which the (for him unquestionably) historical sources of the epistles and Acts themselves contain, provided John with a perfect rhetorical vehicle for his vision of the Christian life.

Paul and Peter

How do Chrysostom's portraits of Paul compare with his treatments of the other apostles? Having trained our attention exclusively on Paul in this study, we must ask if Chrysostom's attention to Paul was truly unique, or was merely part of an overall love for the saints, so characteristic of late fourth-century piety generally. Among the apostles as a group, Paul's only possible competition for John's attention would be Peter. But even in that footrace the winner is quite clear – Paul held sole pride of place in Chrysostom's oratory. While there are seven encomia devoted to Paul among Chrysostom's writings, there are none to Peter, nor to any other of the apostles.[50] The extended encomium to Paul in the famous *hom. in Rom.* 32.2–4, although it begins with both Peter and Paul as the two shining eyes entombed at Rome, quickly veers off into a single-minded concentration on Paul, and completely obscures Peter, who only reappears, almost as an afterthought, near the homily's end.[51] Baur estimated (conservatively) that in his corpus of writings Chry-

---

[50] The complete absence of Peter in the seven discourses *de laudibus sancti Pauli* renders unthinkable even the slight chance that they could have been delivered at a joint feast of Paul and Peter on December 28 [as Piédagnel holds out the possibility for in SC 300.18]. It seems clear from these compositions that there was a sole feast day for Paul at Antioch in this time period. That would not preclude another joint feast day for Peter and Paul, but we have no homilies from Chrysostom which reflect such an occasion.

[51] "[Paul's] body forms the wall of that city, which is more secure than any tower or any thousand fortifying walls, and Peter is with him, because he used to honor him in life. For 'I went up to visit Peter.' Therefore grace considered Peter worthy to share a dwelling with Paul after he died" (*hom. in Rom.* 32.4 [60.680]). The argument that ensues is predicated on the assumption that the preacher needs to show Peter worthy of Paul, not vice versa.

sostom spoke of Paul three times more often than Peter.[52] Chrysostom did compose some smaller encomia to Peter,[53] he repeatedly called him "the chief of the
apostles" [τῶν ἀποστόλων ὁ κορυφαῖος],[54] and sometimes could attribute to Peter
and Paul together the epithets he usually reserved for Paul alone.[55] But, despite
these few ways in which Chrysostom appears to place Peter and Paul on an equal
footing, his overwhelming preference for Paul is evident, especially in passages
which compare the two, always to Paul's advantage.[56] Often he forthrightly claims
Paul's superiority: "none of the apostles was his equal; he was greater than them
all."[57] In general, Chrysostom agrees with Paul (1 Cor 15:10): "the former persecutor outdid everyone."[58] This judgment receives grounding in a general principle
which consistently works to Paul's favor: that the signs accomplished *after* the cross
were greater than those that preceded it. Hence in a series of *a minore ad maius*
examples Chrysostom sets up the dichotomy: "for while Christ was alive Peter
denied him, but after he died Paul confessed him."[59] This lack of parity between
Peter and Paul in Chrysostom's writings comes into even greater relief when one
compares his treatments with the spurious Chrysostomic work, *in Petrum et Paulum*,
which alternates between one and the other, with equal, carefully parallel praises for
each.[60] This is precisely what we do *not* find in Chrysostom's genuine writings. The
reasons for this are multiple and largely intertwined, and likely stretch back to John's
youth: the heavy toehold Paul has in the Scriptural tradition John had learned from
Diodore of Tarsus, memorized in the cave, and met daily in the lectionary; Paul's
status as a local hero in Antioch; Paul's parallels with Chrysostom's own life in
monastic discipline and in ecclesiastical challenges from insiders and Judaizers. Also
not to be underestimated here is the Pauline call to imitation of himself which is the
root-text and methodology for Chrysostom's ethical exhortations. Through these
many factors, and the ineffable variable of the intense personal encounter he experienced, John singled out Paul as his special hero. Paul, "the heavenly trumpet," has
an undeniably unique status in John's oratory.[61]

---

[52] *John Chrysostom and His Time*, 1.291.

[53] See, e.g., *hom. in Ac.* 4.3 [60.47–48]; *comm. in Gal.* 2.4 [61.640].

[54] *hom. in Ac. princ.* 2.6 [51.86–87]. For further references, see chap. 3, n. 142.

[55] As in *exp. in Ps.* 109.6 [55.274]: "For what is brighter than Paul? Or what more renowned
than Peter? Than they who ran around the world, shining above the sun, throwing down the
seeds of piety? For they were unapproachable, like angels come down from heaven."

[56] E.g., *hom. in Heb.* Arg. 1 [63.11]; *hom. in Ac. 9:1* 1.5 [51.120–21].

[57] τῶν δὲ ἀποστόλων ἴσος οὐδεὶς γέγονεν, οὗτος δὲ κἀκείνων μείζων (*anom.* 8.3 [48.772]).

[58] *scand.* 20.10 [*SC* 79.250]; *sac.* 4.7 [*SC* 272.272]: it was by means of his rhetorical skills
enshrined in his epistles that Paul surpassed the other apostles [Τίνι δὲ καὶ τῶν ἄλλων ἀποστόλων
ἐπλεονέκτησεν ὁ μακάριος οὗτος;].

[59] Ζῶντα μὲν γὰρ αὐτὸν καὶ ὁ Πέτρος ἠρνήσατο, ἀποθανόντα δὲ ὁ Παῦλος ὡμολόγησε (*hom.
in Ac. 9:1* 1.5 [51.120]).

[60] For that reason, as well as the more crude level of style and composition, it is clearly not
a genuine work, although it likely depends on some of Chrysostom's own writings.

[61] The same conclusion holds when one compares Chrysostom's encomia to the martyrs and

Paul and Christ

The heights to which Chrysostom soars in his praise of Paul ("through his mouth Christ uttered greater things than in his own person")[62] raise insistent questions, not just about his larger vision of Christian worthies, but also about how Paul fits within Chrysostom's theology. For instance, in the concluding crescendo of one of his panegyrics to Paul as having exhibited love more than any other human being, John promises his congregation a future eschatological vision – of Paul! But he quickly corrects himself to insist that, "or, rather, we shall see Paul's Lord."[63] How can we account for the theological elevation to which Chrysostom raises Paul? In particular, does it compromise, or in some sense displace, Christ?

We have repeatedly seen that, in addition to their considerable entertainment value,[64] Chrysostom's portraits of Paul had a predominantly catechetical and exhortatory purpose. Paul, "the perfect copy of Christ," served for John as the archetypal image for those who follow because, having been a human being, Paul could be set forth as an imitable example, even more so than Christ. While Christ is the master, Paul is a "fellow slave" to the rest of humanity.[65] That is why, though he rose to almost unimaginable heights in his praise of Paul, Chrysostom's Pauline portraits ultimately did not eclipse Christ.[66] Without the Christ-infusion which Paul claimed to have continually experienced (2 Cor 13:3: "… Christ is speaking in me"), the Pauline portraits would themselves have been of no interest. Thus the portraits of Paul in John's eyes are portraits of Christ, portraits of what a human being who has Christ speaking in him looks like.[67] As Chrysostom himself put it: "For where Paul was, there also was Christ."[68] Despite appearances, Christ and Paul cannot compete, since that would entail Christ boxing against himself. This portrait of Paul as having Christ sitting on his tongue, as John once put it, is

---

other figures, such as the evangelist John (*hom. in Jo.* 1 [59.25–26]), discussed in Ameringer, *Second Sophistic*, 98–99. Although such passages share some of these same features, they cannot compare in ubiquity or intensity of expression.

[62] *hom. in Rom.* 32.3 [60.679].

[63] "So now, let us also continually walk the walk of love, so that we might see Paul, or, rather, Paul's master [ἵνα καὶ Παῦλον ἴδωμεν, μᾶλλον δὲ τὸν Παύλου Δεσπότην], and attain to undefiled crowns" (*laud. Paul.* 3.10 [SC 300.180]).

[64] This was rightly stressed also by Hubbell, "Chrysostom and Rhetoric," 262–63.

[65] This is the language of Chrysostom's exhortation in *laud. Paul.* 7.3 [SC 300.300]: Ἐκεῖνος τοῦ Χριστοῦ γέγονε μιμητής, σὺ δὲ οὐδὲ τοῦ συνδούλου; ἐκεῖνος Δεσπότην ἐζήλωσε, σὺ δὲ οὐδὲ τὸν ὁμόδουλον;

[66] But the heavy emphasis in later interpretive traditions on Paul's being the sole source of John's wisdom might do so. Hence later iconographers add Christ or the Holy Spirit to the set scene of John being privately inspired by Paul (see Appendix 2, nos. 9, 10 and 11, and discussion in chap. 8, pp. 437–38).

[67] "Did he not have Christ continually speaking in him?" [οὐ τὸν Χριστὸν εἶχεν ἐν ἑαυτῷ λαλοῦντα;] (*scand.* 2 [52.482]).

[68] Ὅπου γὰρ Παῦλος ἦν, ἐκεῖ καὶ ὁ Χριστὸς ἦν (*hom. in Rom. 16:3* 1.3 [51.191]).

especially deployed by Chrysostom in instances where he wishes to emphasize and insist upon the weighty authority of a Pauline statement on contested issues, such as virginity and Judaizing.[69] Paul and Christ are not rivals for Chrysostom, but mutually reinforcing exponents of a uniform truth.[70]

Though Chrysostom's ethereal portraits of Paul may often appear to stretch the logic of his cosmological and theological system, they can be comprehended as a fusion of the two aspects of late fourth-century Christian rhetoric which Averil Cameron identified as playing a key role in scripting the Christian imperium: 1) accommodation and appropriation of rhetorical conventions of praise and biography; and 2) the language of paradox which kept the former from becoming indistinguishable from any other type of discourse.[71] Chrysostom's discourses about Paul provide an ideal illustration of these two literary strategies simultaneously, for he praises and sketches the apostle with a paradoxical paint box of clashing hues, as we have seen abundantly in chapters 4, 5 and 6. Paradoxical language is precisely the vehicle capable of rendering Chrysostom's Paul less than Christ and Christ-like at the same time, and it is such language which most soars in the epideictic form with which it is wedded in these portraits, for the Christian orator thereby scripts a universe of values which is a complex mix of the conventional and the inverted, contained and expressed within the contours of widely accepted cultural standards.[72] And it is the very nature of epideictic oratory to push the boundaries, to strive for excess and, when found, to revel unapologetically in it.[73] The bounda-

---

[69] Hence, for instance, in *de virginitate*, which is largely an exposition of Paul's 1 Cor 7, John insists over and over again that the words of Paul are the words of Christ, since Christ was speaking in his apostle. In this way John insists on the harmony of Paul and Christ, even as he claims an authority for Pauline statements commensurate to that of Christ. What is particularly ironic is that John does this with precisely the Pauline argument in which, more than any other in the *corpus*, Paul is at pains to *distinguish* between teachings that come from Christ and those which come from himself (7:8, 10, 12, 25). Another crucial instance is the homilies *adversus Judaeos*, in which Paul becomes not only Chrysostom's scriptural warrant, but his co-adjurer in hurling excoriations against Judaizing Christians (see the discussion and set of references in chap. 6, nn. 147 and 385).

[70] See chap. 6, n. 607 for references to passages that show how Chrysostom always swiftly moves to resolve any apparent inconsistency between Paul and Christ.

[71] *Christianity and the Rhetoric of Empire*, 120–88. Sometimes Cameron's separation of these two modes is surprising (e.g., p. 180: "The learned writings of the fourth century … also contributed to the spead of that essentially paradoxical and figurative trait in Christian discourse which could not find easy expression in the kind of writing discussed in the last chapter" [i.e., panegyric and *Lives*]. But in fact paradox could play a central role in the Christianized versions of those genres in the fourth century, of which Chrysostom's works give ample evidence).

[72] Therefore, Chrysostom's devoted portraits of Paul provide precisely the type of illustration of Cameron's thesis which Robert D. Sider called for in his review of *Christianity and the Rhetoric of Empire*: "would the enormous number of texts devoted to the exposition of the Bible in commentary, homily, and paraphrase develop further the portrait of early Christian discourse given here?" (*Catholic Historical Review* 78 [1992] 435–436, 435).

[73] Chrysostom at times anticipates this reaction to his speech as, for instance, in *laud. Paul.* 1.15 [SC 300.136–38], when, after a long succession of biblical worthies, he begins to compare Paul with the angels and exclaims prophylactically: "But let no one accuse our discourse of

ries of suitable comparison, when stretched, would naturally lead Christian orators, as they had pagan practitioners of the epideictic art, to the divine.[74] This is
because the genre requires the trumping of the most supreme competitors as a
means of praise for one's subject (hence the repeated refrain, "what could be the
equal of …"),[75] even if it means the relative suppression or denigration of the
others. But if that humiliation goes too far,[76] then it renders the comparison
useless for the panegyric, and, in the words of Menander Rhetor, is simply "bad
form."[77] Hence, while Chrysostom will set Paul alongside angels and heavenly
luminaries, he never constructs a rhetorical comparison with Christ. Thus it was
a fine line that a fourth-century orator trod, and Chrysostom was willing to stretch

audacity for this" [μηδεὶς τόλμαν καταγινωσκέτω τοῦ λόγου]." Ameringer, *Second Sophistic*, 40–
41 vehemently objected to such tactics: "It is hardly necessary to call attention to the bad taste
and artificiality of the instances of the paradox and hyperbole [in this passage] … Both the
oxymoron and the hyperbole are not the exact expression of an extraordinary situation, or of
moderate sentiment; on the contrary, their tendency is to distort the just proportions of the facts
exposed. Together they form one of the most objectionable and unartistic traits of sophistic
rhetoric."

[74] See, for example, Chrysostom's mocked conventional encomium to Nero (*hom. in 2 Tim.*
4.3–4, analyzed in chap. 6, pp. 206–26), which reaches its crescendo at his being universally
worshipped as a god [ἀλλ' ὡς θεὸς παρὰ πάντων ἐθεραπεύετο]. Although there are many Christian examples of hyperbolic lauds to set alongside some of Chrysostom's audacious claims for
Paul (see Cameron, *Christianity and the Rhetoric of Empire*, 168, on some of the praises to the
Virgin Mary in the fourth century: "at times they seem to go too far"), the topic had already long
been a pagan preoccupation. As evidence of this we have the dialogue on excesses in praising
human beings by comparing them with the gods in Lucian, *Pr. Im.* 7–29 (introduced and quoted
in chap. 5, n. 79, above). Most important for the present point is Lycinus' defense of his portrait
(which compared his mortal subject, Panthea, to Aphrodite and Hera), on the grounds of
rhetorical convention and necessity (§19): "Do not wonder then, that I myself, desiring to make
comparisons [εἰκάσαι βουλόμενος], as one who sought to praise was bound to do [ὅπερ ἦν τῷ
ἐπαινοῦντι ἀναγκαῖον], used an exalted counterfoil [ὑψηλοτέρῳ ἐχρησάμην τῷ παραδείγματι],
since my theme demanded it" [τοῦτο ὑποβαλόντος τοῦ λόγου]. He discusses the limits of hyperbole by summoning a stock distinction between one who utters true praise and a shameless
flatterer: "flatterers use hyperbole to the full extent of their powers, while those who really praise
are discreet in precisely that particular and remain within their bounds" [οἱ μὲν κόλακες, ἐφ' ὅσον
οἷόν τε αὐτοῖς, χρῶνται ταῖς ὑπερβολαῖς, οἱ ἐπαινοῦντες δὲ καὶ ἐν αὐταῖς ταύταις σωφρονοῦσιν
καὶ ἐντὸς τῶν ὅρων μένουσιν]. Lycinus points out, with many examples, that in comparing
humans to the divine he stands in a long line of predecessors, most notably Homer (§24–26).

[75] E.g., *hom. in 1 Thess.* 4.2 [62.418]: Τί Παύλου ἴσον γένοιτ' ἄν;

[76] Chrysostom sometimes addresses this point directly as, for instance, in *laud. Paul.* 2.9 [SC
300.158] where, after demonstrating Paul to be superior to the angels since he is the guardian
angel, not just of one nation, but of them all, he remarks, "Now I am not saying these things to
insult the angels (perish the thought!)" [Καὶ ταῦτα οὐκ ἀγγέλους ὑβρίζων λέγω, μὴ γένοιτο].
The only person set up in comparison to Paul who gets utterly humiliated is Nero (see chap. 6,
pp. 206–26), but that is a safe move rhetorically, given Nero's profoundly negative legacy among
Christians in the fourth century (see Rougé, "Néron," 79–87).

[77] "You should then proceed to the most complete comparison [ἡ τελειοτάτη σύγκρισις],
examining [ἀντεξετάζων] his reign in comparison with preceding reigns, not disparaging them
[καθαιρῶν ἐκείνας] (that is bad craftsmanship [ἄτεχνον γάρ]) but admiring them [θαυμάζων
ἐκείνας] while granting perfection to the present" [τὸ δὲ τέλειον ἀποδιδοὺς τῇ παρούσῃ] (Menander, *Rh.* 2.376–77 [text and trans Russell-Wilson, 92–93]).

further down that line for his beloved Paul than for any other saint, because his Paul, "in a real sense a rhetorical construction,"[78] was the precise vehicle for his vision of Christian perfection.[79]

In addition to this recognizable social function, Chrysostom's choice of Paul as *the* archetype of virtue must also be understood as a reflection of his broader theological commitments. Given that the Nicene orthodoxy Chrysostom confessed, embraced, and defended held that Christ's body and soul partake of the same substance as the Father, Christ could only with difficulty play the role of human moral exemplar in Chrysostom's catechetical program.[80] This is the clue to the relationship between Chrysostom's Christology and his portraits of Paul, which are in the final analysis not so conflicted as first might appear. Indeed, rather than being logically compromised by the lofty praises accorded to Paul, John's Christology was one of the engines pulling the train of extreme Pauline praise, as Maurice Wiles has wisely put it:

---

[78] Borrowing the words Cameron, *Christianity and the Rhetoric of Empire*, 169, applies to the Virgin Mary in late antique Christian texts.

[79] "The holy men of these *Lives* inhabited a world several stages removed from realism, and are described in language evocative of that extra dimension; but real or not, they worked out in their lives both the model presented by the life of Christ and the contemporary ideals of asceticism and, in so doing, brought home the possibilities for every Christian individual. This was a period when a variety of Christian roles, including that of bishop, were evolving, and when Christian writing played an important part in defining ideals for lay as well as clerical audiences; these ideals, embodying the extremes of religious paradox, had an effect on society just as powerful as the public rhetoric in which Christianity took on an apparently more imperial and familiar guise" (Cameron, *Christinianity and the Rhetoric of Empire*, 185).

[80] On Chrysostom's Christology see Baur, *John Chrysostom*, 1.356–59; Kelly, *Golden Mouth*, 11–12, 36–37. He was a student of Diodore and Flavian who "openly proclaimed the equality of the Son and the Spirit with the Father," and a partisan of Bishop Melitios, who held to the newer "three hypostaseis" form of Christology (Kelly, *Golden Mouth*, 11–12). This can be seen especially in his homilies on the fourth gospel, in which he constantly proclaims the doctrine of ὁμοούσιος against the Anomoeans (Quasten, *Patrology*, 3.439), as, for instance in *hom. in Jo.* 26.1; 52.3; 54.2; 69.1; 74.1 [59.154, 290, 298, 378, 401]. Later John was appointed patriarch at Constantinople in 398 to uphold the Nicene orthodoxy of the imperial family (in the form of the "Homoean compromise" from the Council of Constantinople in 381), which he began to do immediately (see, e.g., *Eutrop.* 2.8 [52.403]). He delivered homilies against the Anomoeans [Eunomians], in both Antioch and Constantinople, series entitled *incomprehens.* 1–5 (published together by Jean Daniélou in SC 28, 2nd ed., Anne-Marie Malingrey and Robert Flacelière, 1970), and *anom* 7–12, respectively; on Chrysostom's position vis à vis the Anomoeans, see Daniélou's discussion in SC 28.9–14). In *sac.* 4.4 [SC 272.258–60] he contended against the Arians using the terms οὐσία, ἡ ἐν τοῖς προσώποις διαφορά, αἱ τρεῖς ὑποστάσεις]. The critical distance Christ's consubstantiality with the Father left between him and the rest of the humanity is made patently clear in *incomprehens.* 7.2 [48.758], where Chrysostom refutes the "shameless" inference that all human beings are ὁμοούσιοι with God: "For if he is consubstantial with the Father since he is called 'son,' then we, too, shall be able to be consubstantial, for we too are called 'sons'" [εἰ γὰρ, ἐπειδὴ Υἱὸς λέγεται, ὁμοούσιός ἐστι τῷ Πατρὶ, δυνησόμεθα καὶ ἡμεῖς ὁμοούσιοι εἶναι· καὶ γὰρ καὶ ἡμεῖς υἱοὶ λεγόμεθα]. He replies that Christ was μονογενής in this regard (cf. also *hom. in Jo.* 26.1 [59.154]). Nor could Mary function as an exemplar of human moral possibility for John; he (rather infamously) treated Mary somewhat harshly (see Baur, *John Chrysostom*, 1.358–59).

Paul in fact represents for Chrysostom the supreme example of the moral and spiritual potentialities of human life ... There is, it may well be claimed, a remarkable similarity between Chrysostom's picture of Paul and the Jesus of liberal scholarship and piety. No moral failing must be admitted in the drawing of the picture; a limitation of knowledge is admitted with some reluctance; other human limitations are more gladly accepted as emphasizing both a oneness with ordinary men and the wonder of the life that shines through them. Perhaps the exalted Christology of the period even at Antioch tended to destroy the sense of Christ's solidarity with us and the force of his life as a human example, thus leaving a gap in popular piety which this stress on the achievements of Paul may have helped to fill. This extreme development was a characteristic of Eastern Christianity. The West was far more guarded and restrained in its evaluation of the apostles.[81]

In elevating Paul to the position of archetype of virtue, therefore, Chrysostom did not so much encroach upon his Christology as he dallied on the theological boundary to Pelagianism[82] by promoting Paul as the supreme example of humanity's boundless capacity for virtue. That is why it is not surprising that Chrysostom's *de laudibus sancti Pauli* were so popular among the Pelagians, who began translating them into Latin within decades of his death.[83] Indeed, several passages carrying the authority of Chrysostom's name were invoked in Augustine's battle with Pelagius.[84] Chrysostom's tendency to emphasize human ethical perfectionism was noted by the Reformers as well, such as Calvin, who, though praising Chrysostom, warned that he went rather overboard *in praedicando hominis libero arbitrio*.[85] As we have seen over and over again, it is portraits of Paul that are often the vehicle Chrysostom employs in promoting this theological agenda. What is of greatest importance in John's selective appropriation and representation of Paul is the fact that in this quest Paul is always more than one saint among the others, given that he himself claimed to be Christ's copyist, thus dissolving any competition between the two in the harmony of mimetic symbiosis.[86]

---

[81] *Divine Apostle*, 24.

[82] See the discussion of Chrysostom, Augustine and Pelagianism in the next chapter (pp. 411–23).

[83] See chap. 1, n. 24.

[84] See Baur, *S. Jean Chrysostome*, 68.

[85] "Praefatio in Chrysostomi Homilias," *Corpus Reformatorum*, vol. 37, col. 835. In general, Calvin finds Chrysostom wanting when it comes to *dogmata*, though he praises him for other reasons (see chap. 1, n. 27).

[86] These themes are beautifully coordinated in a single representative passage in *laud. Paul.* 7.3 [SC 300.300], that bears repeating in this context: "From what source therefore was Paul such as he was? Both from his own nature and from God, and for this reason it was from God, since it was from his own nature. For God does not play favorites. Now if you say, 'How is it possible to imitate such people,' listen to what he says, 'Be imitators of me, as also I am of Christ.' Paul has become the imitator of Christ, and you cannot even imitate the fellow slave? He emulated the Lord, and you cannot even emulate one who is a slave like yourself? And what sort of self-defense will you have?"

The Social Functions of Chrysostom's Rhetorical Art

Chrysostom's encomia to Paul represent an exact amalgam of religious paradox and public epideictic rhetoric which aims at promoting a particular view of the Christian life, and the social order it should embrace. In the case of John and Paul it was the model of the "worldly ascetic"[87] (both of whom were also conspicuously "wordy ascetics"!) which was paraded as the highest value.[88] That is why Paul was especially chosen by Chrysostom, in his oratory, but also long before, when he took up the monastic life, when he memorized the Pauline letters in the cave, when his own countenance was preformed in some Pauline way.[89] John's own ascetic life of self-molding later sought duplication in his democratic vision for an urban Christian "worldly asceticism,"[90] for which his literary portraiture of Paul was a prominent vehicle.[91] Therefore it is not surprising that Chrysostom depicts his archetype, Paul, as a citizen of heaven, one who demonstrated the heavenly πολιτεία,[92] rather than the most excellent citizen of the polis, the originally intended object of the epideictic rhetoric he employs, from its roots in classical Athens down through the Roman imperium. In fact, in sketching his Paul, Chrysostom was fashioning in words his ideal πολιτεία, through a vision of its ideal citizen, by contemplation of which one could fashion a life in its accord. Hence in essence Chrysostom was undertaking in many ways the project of Plato in the *Respublica*,[93] though he decried many of the specifics of that πολιτεία on

---

[87] See chap. 6, n. 587.

[88] See the perceptive comment of Piédagnel, SC 300.40–41, on how Chrysostom modeled his ministry on Paul's: "Cette activité inlassable de Paul plaisait à Chrysostome. Non qu'il ait lui-même traversé aussi souvent la mer et parcouru autant de continents. Mais lorsqu'il prit la décision d'abandonner le genre de vie des solitaires, c'est bien parce qu'un tel idéal et une telle ardeur apostolique l'attiraient. S. Paul fut son modèle dans le travail débordant qui fut aussi le sien."

[89] The larger phenomenon is illuminated by Brown, *Cult of the Saints*, 57: "It is not surprising perhaps, that the cult of the patron saint spread most quickly in ascetic circles: for an identity placed at a nadir of uncertainty by the ascetic's deep sense of sin cried out for some intimate thread of stability."

[90] With Brown, *Body and Society*, 305–22. See the discussion of *compunct. 2* 2 [47.412–13] in chap. 6, pp. 321–22.

[91] On the relationship between asceticism and art, see the words of Geoffrey Galt Harpham, "Asceticism and the Compensations of Art," in *Asceticism*, ed. Vincent L. Wimbush and Richard Valantasis (New York/Oxford: Oxford University Press, 1995) 357: "Within those ascetic practices, the task of converting oneself from the flawed, fallible, failing, and flailing thing that one is, to the rigid monument to the Way that one would like to be, requires a practice of framing, planning, and construction – a practice that fulfills the requirements for what we have, since Kant, learned to call aesthetic creation."

[92] See chap. 3, pp. 78–79.

[93] "'I understand,' he said, 'you are speaking of the city in which we have now come to set up our dwelling, the city which is established in words [πόλει ... τῇ ἐν λόγοις κειμένῃ], since I do not suppose it exists anywhere on earth' [ἐπεὶ γῆς γε οὐδαμοῦ οἶμαι αὐτὴν εἶναι]. 'But,' I said, 'perhaps a pattern of it is laid up in heaven for the person who wishes to look at it, and by

moral grounds (such as common wives), and was happy to celebrate its demise.[94] Consequently, the very purpose of this oratory remained for Chrysostom, as it was for all its practitioners, to ensure the maintenance and transference to the next generation of the social values which upheld the civic order. But in his case the very values he sought to inscribe through these means were such as to compromise the existing social order, undermine the institutions upon which it stood, and create as a rhetorical, ethical, and even political possibility a Christian city-state. The comprehensiveness of Chrysostom's overarching social vision has been powerfully explicated by Peter Brown:

> John elevated the Christian household so as to eclipse the ancient city. He refused to see Antioch as a traditional civic community, bound together by a common civic patriotism, expressed by shared rhythms of collective festivity. He made no secret of the fact that he wished the theatre, the hippodrome, even the busy agora, to fall silent forever. The Antioch of his dearest hopes was to be no more than a conglomeration of believing households, joined by a common meeting-place within the spacious courtyards of the Great Church.[95]

Oratory, unmoored from civic assemblies and transferred to ecclesial ones, was the principal tool by which John sought to effect this transformation of Antioch, and then Constantinople, toward this social program. Within that oratorical spadework, the apostle Paul played a crucial role. Chrysostom's Paul is a corporeal angel who despised the things of earth and yearned only for the life of heaven:

> For while walking on the earth he continually did everything as though he were going about with angels. Although bound up with a mortal body he exhibited the purity of the angels, and even when subject to such great constraints, he made it his fervent ambition to appear in no way inferior to the powers above. For he ran around the world like a bird, and like an incorporeal being disdained sufferings and dangers. He had contempt for earthly things as though he had already attained heaven; he was as continually vigilant as if he were dwelling with the incorporeal powers themselves.[96]

In this context we can see how Chrysostom's favorite image of Paul as a bird is more than poetic license (though it is certainly that), for it is a way to place Paul somehow between earth and heaven, because he is at once the ethereal mystic monastic and the very conduit between the human and divine abodes. The heavenly trumpet plays on earth, but like the Pied Piper can draw people upwards to the heavenly life. Yet there is an exquisite paradox in this depiction, for Paul, the long-dead saint, can be praised by Chrysostom in essence for having been dead

---

gazing upon it to settle him or herself there'" [ἐν οὐρανῷ ἴσως παράδειγμα ἀνάκειται τῷ βουλομένῳ ὁρᾶν καὶ ὁρῶντι ἑαυτὸν κατοικίζειν] (*Resp.* 9.592B). Like Socrates in this dialogue, through words Chrysostom sought to depict the heavenly republic, through a loving representation of its archetypal citizen, Paul.

[94] For discussion and references, see Coleman-Norton, "St. Chrysostom," 312, and above, pp. 270–78.

[95] Brown, *Body and Society*, 313.

[96] *laud. Paul.* 2.8 [SC 300.156].

during his lifetime, dead, that is, to the desires and passions of earthly existence.[97] That is why praise of Paul as living and as dead finally coalesce, for the portrait is what has taken his place, a kind of oratorical but mummified picture of Dorian Gray which encapsulates the fullest extremes of ascetic earthly piety in multiple guises. And this is at the heart of the art of portraiture itself, in which "les vivants sont les morts et les morts les vivants."[98]

To comprehend this paradox we must remember that it was Chrysostom, the Christian ekphrasist, who brought forward this model of Paul and championed him as the perfect paradigm of Christian life, faith, and citizenship. One of the most important ingredients of John's rhetorical portraiture, as we have often had occasion to note, is his own self as both painter and art critic of the Pauline persona he summons up.[99] After all, what John offered his audiences in these guises of Paul was dictated by his own theological tastes, his own monastic "ekphrastic gaze," which considered attractive bodies and all material things as dust and ashes.[100] With Chrysostom as the Pauline painter, the audience was in the hands of an artist who was admittedly governed by ὑπεροψία, "disdain" or "contempt" for the realities of this world, and was in turn providing a verbal portrait of a man who had despised all visible realities as much as if they were "a rotten plant."[101] Just as Chrysostom proclaimed that at baptism the apostle Paul received "another pair of eyes, the eyes of love,"[102] so also was he attempting by his own homiletical art to foster this kind of new vision of love that turns the tables on the world's standard of values. In this we find the centrality of Chrysostom's "love hermeneutics," which amounts, first and foremost, to a new form of oratorical optical allusion that becomes transplanted in the minds and memories of the auditors. Even as he sketched Paul before their ears, John was instructing his hearers in Christian ethical aesthetics. Hence, after lovingly depicting Paul the scourged prisoner in contrast to the brilliant imperial guard he counsels his audience: "But do not be sad at this, beloved."[103] The portrait series of Paul that John offers is meant to be a kind of training course in Christian monastic sensibilities, by which one is given images of

---

[97] See, e.g., *laud. Paul.* 1.9 [SC 300.126]: "He was as unmoved by them as a corpse encountering another corpse. So precisely did he lull to sleep the surges of nature, that he never, ever, experienced a single human passion" [ὡς ἂν νεκρὸς πρὸς νεκρὸν ἀκίνητος γένοιτο. Οὕτω μετὰ ἀκριβείας τῆς φύσεως τὰ σκιρτήματα κατευνάζων, οὐδὲν οὐδέποτε πρὸς οὐδὲν ἀνθρώπινον πάθος ἔπαθεν].

[98] These words were used by Bailly, *L'apostrophe muette*, 16, in his reflections on the Fayum mummy portraits.

[99] See below, pp. 404–407 on the central role of live oratory in effecting this.

[100] In imitation of Paul; see *laud. Paul.* 1.9 [SC 300.126]: Paul "regarded not only the attractive features of human bodies, but all things, as we do dust and ashes" (and further discussion of monastic "contempt" in chap. 6, pp. 311–12).

[101] *laud. Paul.* 2.5 [SC 300.150].

[102] *laud. Paul.* 7.6 [SC 300.306].

[103] *laud. Paul.* 7.2 [SC 300.294]

the saint to emblazon on one's mind for imitation, and also the emotive clues for the proper response to the works of art that constitute human lives.

Despite these exalted purposes, Chrysostom's portraits of Paul were not entirely abstract, but often very human and, indeed *body-centered* (as we saw particularly in chapter 4). Peter Brown has persuasively argued that the root of Chrysostom's intended social revolution was a novel philosophical-theological principle: that the bodies of all human persons, from the top to the lowest among the socially stratified levels of a late imperial city such as Antioch, were held in common.[104]

By preaching incessantly on such themes, John wished to create in Antioch a new, more all-embracing sense of community, based on a sense of solidarity with a shared human nature. As a result, his exhortations came to place a quite unusual weight on the human body. For the body was the most vocal spokesman of all, in its manifest vulnerability, of the common descent of all human beings from Adam. John preached a brotherhood of bodies at risk.[105]

Our study of Chrysostom's portraits of Paul provides a clear window into one of the central vehicles by which John promoted this new theological sensitivity: Paul functioned for Chrysostom as his rhetorical "poster child" of the human body – his Pauline portraits were an essential means by which he defined what human life in the body *truly* is, or should be. Chrysostom maintained repeatedly that Paul, in the example afforded by his life, taught the exalted height of virtue of which human nature, in the body, is capable, but only if one can overcome the passions [τὰ πάθη] by προθυμία and προαίρεσις. Chrysostom was enough of a Platonist that his body portraits were actually vehicles for images of its superior partner, the soul. The "brotherhood of bodies at risk" is enlivened and activated, in Chrysostom's eyes, by the "meadow of human virtues" in the soul, which Paul, better than anyone, exemplified in untold ways.

Oral and Written Forms of the Biographic

It is worth asking why, despite living in an age of flourishing Christian biography and hagiography, Chrysostom's reflections on Paul took the form that they did – *encomia* rather than *vitae*. It is true that the two genres of encomium and biography were by no means utterly distinct in the fourth century,[106] nor earlier.[107] That is

---

[104] Brown, *Body and Society*, 303–322.

[105] Ibid., 316.

[106] Cox, *Biography*, xiv, aptly described biography as a "halfway house" between history and oratory (panegyric). For the topic, see also the literature in chap. 6, n. 17.

[107] "The connection between the encomium and biography is still more intimate. Biography is an essential part of history, but when made a separate composition it partakes of the nature of both history and the encomium. A portrayal of character is the main aim in each, so events may be treated in summary fashion; but the encomium gives more room for choice, idealization, omission. The encomium may be more or less fully biographical as the subject is well known or not" (Burgess, *Epideictic Literature*, 117).

why Averil Cameron, for instance, can refer to Chrysostom's writings on Paul in the same breath as Gregory of Nyssa's *de vita Mosis*.[108] But they are not identical, and in particular Chrysostom's writings on Paul, even the most expansively developed ones, never follow a strict chronological order. Although it is important, for instance, to place Paul's pre-Christian life as a persecutor in the right place, beyond that Chrysostom is more concerned with cumulative portraits of Paul, rather than a continuous chronicle. But this does not place Chrysostom outside the realm of "biographic"[109] work, either, for even βίοι proper do not necessarily adhere to that structure.[110] What he shares with those works is the intense interest in deeds as revelatory of character.

A significant distinction between encomia and biographies, at least in theory, is that between oral and literary works. This difference is not absolute, of course, given that reading of literature in antiquity involved recitation and oral performance, and orations, such as *de laudibus sancti Pauli*, were published in written form and received by audiences far from their original auditors within years of their oral delivery. But, at least as far as the initial occasion of those speeches is concerned, there are some subtle yet significant distinctions between the encomium and literary biography. Recent scholarship has stressed the extent to which all ancient biographers depicted themselves in the act of composing their subject,[111] an insight that is equally applicable to Chrysostom's encomia, as works of ascetic practice:

In the hands of hagiographers, writing, like fasting or prayer, became a technology for attaining the goal of their own ascetic profession: a reconstituted ascetic self, displaying the virtues exemplified by the saints about whom they narrated. Authors strove to emulate their subjects through representation, configuring themselves through the production of texts.[112]

When we transfer this insight to the realm of public oratory, we can view Chrysostom the preacher as having been in the act of creatively fashioning Paul in his image and himself in Paul's image simultaneously, with the requisite rhetorical latitude provided by the multiple possibilities on both sides that could accommodate different liturgical and historical exigencies. But Chrysostom's live oratorical homilies on Paul (which amount to a kind of "in your face" hagiography) entail

---

[108] "Other Christian *Lives*, whether of holy men like Antony, public figures like Basil, characters from the Christian or Christianized past, like Paul or Moses, whose lives were written by John Chrysostom and Gregory of Nyssa, operated in a similar way, showing how the Christian life was to be lived" (*Christianity and the Rhetoric of Empire*, 145). Chrysostom's oratorical portraits of Paul are indeed hagiographic, even if they do not take the form of sustained narrative compositions (see, for instance, the abundant similarities between Chrysostom's images of Paul and the hagiographical sources treated by Krueger, "Hagiography as an Ascetic Practice").

[109] With Edwards and Swain, *Portraits* (see chap. 2, n. 1).

[110] As observed by Cox, *Biography*, 57: "chronology does not provide the structural referent for the narration of the holy man's life."

[111] This is a major theme of Cox's important study: "A biography's holy man images would be the author's own faces" (ibid., 146).

[112] Krueger, "Hagiography as an Ascetic Practice," 232.

an even more direct mode of interaction between audience, author, and subject. Because he was engaged in performative oratory, John was of necessity presenting himself directly, face-to-face, as Paul's portraitist/representative before the eyes of his congregation. This is a type of authorial voice similar to the biographer, but magnified – for even though his portraits of Paul *per se* were literary, his portrait of Paul as enfleshed in himself was more than that, and John apparently used this to the greatest effect. His *ekphraseis* consisted in words encountered within the multimedia presentation of his voice, demeanor, and self.[113] Yet his orations, preserved by some combination of authorial editing and stenographic record,[114] were also able to make the transition easily into the literary culture, where in subsequent centuries readers could encounter the voices and images of *two* dead saints brought to life – Paul and his most fervent admirer and portraitist locked in the embrace of their love hermeneutics.

Naturally the choice of the genre encomium was also due to John's own literary gifts and, especially, the requirements and opportunities of his ecclesiastical role. Chrysostom's extensive collection of writings does not contain a single *vita*, but dozens of panegyrics. The simplest reason for this is that Chrysostom was first and foremost a preacher, and the homily is not a genre for a *vita*,[115] though it conveniently can incorporate encomia for both expositional and exhortatory purposes, as we have seen repeatedly in our study.[116] The liturgical calendar, and other ecclesiastical events, played a major role in shaping Chrysostom's oratory and published writings, and the form they were to take. But there is also a hermeneutical reason why Chrysostom did not compose a life of Paul: quite simply, he regarded the Acts of the Apostles, the Pauline letters (and, less so, the *Acta Pauli*), as having already

---

[113] See Young, *Biblical Exegesis*, 248–57, on some of the ways that John takes up Paul's rhetorical demeanor in his homilies.

[114] A full discussion of this important point is beyond our scope here. Baur, *John Chrysostom*, 1.222, contended that not all of Chrysostom's biblical homilies were actually delivered, but many were purely literary creations. His judgment has recently been effectively challenged by Kelly (*Golden Mouth*, 92–94) and Hill (*Commentary on the Psalms*, 14–17), who argue that signs of spontaneity or direct allusions to happenings in the church at the moment of the homily cannot be the sole mark of oral delivery. Blake Goodall's important study on two of the series on Pauline texts has shown that we have received some sermons purely from stenographic notes, and others as reedited for publication (*The Homilies of St. John Chrysostom on the Letters of St. Paul to Titus and Philemon* [Berkeley: University of California Press, 1979]). This accords well with the reading experience of these texts, which reflect at times both the spontaneity of oral performance and stylistic polish of a literary nature.

[115] See Sider's similar conclusion about Tertullian, two centuries earlier: "Given the nature of Tertullian's art, we should not expect an architectonic biography to emerge, a consistent interpretation of a life where action and thought are seen to cohere. Instead we have kaleidoscopic allusions, phrases, sentences, and passages employed with a rhetorician's gift for the telling *exemplum* …" ("Literary Artifice," 100).

[116] Chrysostom's writings on Paul thus reflect his own approach to the Scriptures, as primarily hagiographical documents (on which see Hill, *St. John Chrysostom, Commentary on the Psalms*, 1.22).

done that.[117] And, perhaps this was yet another aspect of his emulation of Paul – that his predominant communicative vehicle was the sermon and, especially later, the letter. John was not so much interested in the sequentiality of Paul's life as he was in its trans-temporal totality as the prototypical witness to Christ. But that totality could be found even in the most minute, particular mosaic pieces of the Pauline biography, career, and utterances. Therefore, what Chrysostom deemed needed was not a life of Paul, but something even more pressing: a vehicle for introducing the Paul whom he encountered in existing sacred literary sources to his congregations, who were only minimally ready (in his eyes) for the encounter. Consequently, he saw himself quite self-consciously as electrifying the existing life of Paul lying, as active potential, in the texts which he read, studied, and proclaimed,[118] to be displayed and emulated in the next generation of Christian lives.[119] His task was to script his living Paul creatively so that he spoke in exciting and relevant ways to contemporary audiences who, Chrysostom believed, desperately needed to hear his voice – the embodied voice of Christ's closest copyist.[120] And those very words were proclaimed by the anagnost via liturgical reading in the sanctuary at each eucharistic service. At the heart of Chrysostom's homiletical portraiture is a simple insight – that to understand Paul's words, one must know him well, and knowing him well leads to emulation of him, and therefore ever heightened and deepened comprehension of his writings from the inside.[121] "A la vérité, on ne comprend vraiment saint Paul que si on lui ressemble un peu."[122]

---

[117] As did his contemporary, Jerome, for instance (*vir. ill.* 5 [PL 23.646]).

[118] See the perceptive comments of Frances Young on how Chrysostom in his homilies employed the strategy of reading "between the lines to bring out the tone of Paul's voice and his use of tactics to win over his hearers. The preacher makes Paul address his own congregation as he elucidates what response he wished to draw out of his readers" ("Rhetorical Schools," 192).

[119] One must also take into account here Chrysostom's own sense of his place in a perduring literary culture. Epideictic oratory is in itself an attempt to "cheat time" or "confound death" through the continuing life of discourse and the memory it sustains. See the comments of Russell and Wilson on this point: "In epideictic, on the other hand, the poet and the orator are much more on a level: both may be summoned to commemorate an occasion, both hope to leave behind them something which will endure" (*Menander Rhetor*, xxxii).

[120] This involves some ventriloquism on John's part, as he shifts his forms of address to create this living encounter – sometimes speaking *to* Paul directly [τί λέγεις, ὦ Παῦλε;], sometimes *for* Paul, either through quotation, paraphrase, or personification, sometimes *to* his audience in second person, at other times *from among* them as an auditor of Pauline directives.

[121] See, e.g., *hom. in Ac.* 55.3 [60.383–84]. The inverted principle is no less true: ignorance of the apostle and of his writings go hand in hand (*hom. in Rom.* Arg. 1 [60.391]).

[122] Vandenberghe, *Saint Jean Chrysostome*, 59. Tellingly, in the English edition and translation of that book, prepared by the author himself, the "little" is gone: "One really understands Paul when one resembles him" (*John of the Golden Mouth* [Westminster, MD: Newman, 1958] 76).

Conclusion: Hung upon the Ring of Paul

Chrysostom's mimetic portraiture is generated by a magnetic force that keeps the wheel of his "love hermeneutics" with Paul turning. This perspective has much in common with the hermeneutics of inspiration set out long before him by Plato in *Ion*:

This is not an art in you [ἔστι γὰρ τοῦτο τέχνη μὲν οὐκ ὂν παρὰ σοι], whereby you speak well on Homer, but a divine power [θεία δὲ δύναμις], which moves you [ἥ σε κινεῖ] like that in the stone which Euripides named a magnet [Μαγνῆτις], but most people call "Heraclea stone" ['Ηράκλεια]. For this stone not only attracts iron rings, but also imparts to them a power whereby they in turn are able to do the very same thing as the stone, and attract other rings; so that sometimes there is formed quite a long chain of bits of iron and rings, suspended one from another [ὥστ' ἐνίοτε ὁρμαθὸς μακρὸς πάνυ σιδηρίων καὶ δακτυλίων ἐξ ἀλλήλων ἤρτηται]; and they all depend for this power on that one stone [πᾶσι δὲ τούτοις ἐξ ἐκείνης τῆς λίθου ἡ δύναμις ἀνήρτηται]. In the same manner also the Muse inspires men herself, and then by means of these inspired persons the inspiration spreads to others, and holds them in a connected chain [οὕτω δὲ καὶ ἡ Μοῦσα ἐνθέους μὲν ποιεῖ αὐτή, διὰ δὲ τῶν ἐνθέων τούτων ἄλλων ἐνθουσιαζόντων ὁρμαθὸς ἐξαρτᾶται].[123]

The chain of inspiration described here is precisely what Chrysostom says he seeks to create in his oratory – readers linked to the blessed apostle across time and space by the commanding force of love. As the dialogue of the *Ion* progresses, Socrates propounds the view that "one poet is suspended from one Muse, another from another: the word we use for it is 'possessed,' but it is much the same thing, for he is *held*."[124] Paul was Chrysostom's muse, just as the medieval artists represented him in their author portraits of John that depicted Paul poised over his shoulder whispering in his ear.[125] But Socrates in this passage conjures up a different visual image: of the inspired one "suspended" from his muse. And this hermeneutical model also fits: Chrysostom was undoubtedly hung upon the ring of Paul – as he himself even expressed it: he was "possessed" by Paul,[126] drawn about by his chain.[127] This alternative poetics of inspiration has also found expression in the history of iconography of Chrysostom and Paul. One Byzantine artist rendered this powerfully [see Plate 3] by literally weaving Paul and John together in a manuscript illumination headlining the opening of a homily. A continuous, swirling border ribbon links medallion portraits of Paul on top and John on the bottom with one another as they together frame the words that unite them in that space, and conjoin them in the interpretive enterprise.[128]

---

[123] Plato, *Ion* 533D.

[124] καὶ ὁ μὲν τῶν ποιητῶν ἐξ ἄλλης Μούσης, ὁ δὲ ἐξ ἄλλης ἐξήρτηται· ὀνομάζομεν δὲ αὐτὸ κατέχεται· τὸ δέ ἐστι παραπλήσιον· ἔχεται γάρ (ibid.).

[125] See Appendix 2, nos. 1–8.

[126] See especially *hom. in Is. 45*:7 3 [56.146], quoted in chap. 3, p. 69, and further references in n. 2.

[127] See the extensive discussion of Paul's chain in chap. 5, pp. 176–85.

[128] The manuscript is *Athen. 211*, fol. 96 (see Appendix 2, no. 13).

Chapter 8

"Partners in This Love Charm"
The Art of Pauline Interpretation

Exegesis as Portraiture

We have focused intently in this study on John Chrysostom's obsession with Paul, and observed close up the careful craftsmanship he exercised in the construction of the apostle's image throughout his oratory and writings. Yet a simple question remains – is John unique in this? In terms of the degree of intensity and the artistry of his Pauline depictions we can conclude that Chrysostom was indeed outstanding, but I would like to argue that he is nonetheless not unparalleled in the practice of portraiture in exegesis itself. This is where Chrysostom's portraits of Paul can make a significant contribution, not only to the study of the salient dynamics of late antique Christian rhetoric and society, but also to Pauline studies generally, because they highlight the extent to which exegesis is inherently interwoven with portraiture. All interpreters of Paul, past and present, have not loved Paul in the way Chrysostom claimed to, yet I submit that each reader of Paul's letters, to the present day, formulates a portrait of the soul of the author of these letters in the act of his or her reading,[1] even if not so artistically or imagistically as John. Quite often the bricolage from which these mental images have been formed is unexamined,[2] and represents not only the biblical sources in a range of configurations, but also contacts with Christian art, hymnody, popular traditions and media forms. And these images can vary, not surprisingly, from letter to letter (for instance, I am always struck that my students often remark that the Paul of Philippians "sounds old"), even as they also experience change within the life span of the

---

[1] This is stated also, for instance, by Anthony C. Thiselton, in his discussion of "Romanticist" hermeneutics: "we interpret this or that utterance against the background of a broader understanding of the speaker" (*New Horizons in Hermeneutics: The Theory and Practice of Transforming Biblical Reading* [Grand Rapids, MI: Zondervan, 1992] 237). Thiselton roots biblical interpretation in this mode in Schleiermacher's hermeneutics of understanding, but also gives some more contemporary examples of the principle at work in Pauline interpretation on pp. 237–71.

[2] Rarely does one find the kind of directness and candor exemplified by Norman R. Petersen: "For myself, I wanted to find a social being named Paul whom I had lost behind the veils of theological criticism and comparative studies ... It is always nice to find what one is looking for, and I think I have found it. But having found what I was looking for, I must also now share the worry that I may have created the object I have found, not rediscovered the object I had lost" (*Rediscovering Paul: Philemon and the Sociology of Paul's Narrative World* [Philadelphia: Fortress, 1985] 302).

interpreter. Many disputes in contemporary Pauline scholarship (such as the πίστις Ἰησοῦ battle currently raging,[3] or the debate over Paul's Hellenism or Judaism, or Paul and the Law) rest upon different images of the apostolic author. In the former case, it depends upon the level and hue of "Jewish" tint in the televideo portrait of Paul: more the man reared on Torah observance and obligatory sacrifice, or the Maccabean-minded quester for the suffering, obedient righteous man?[4] In the latter two the same issue is at stake, but the various solutions depend upon the larger impressionistic landscape of cultural realities in the ancient Mediterranean.[5] Each portrait of Paul, despite its artificial isolation in the service of a particular exegetical argument, nonetheless builds upon an assumed tableau of "background" realities, as well as detailed portrayals of confrères, conversation partners and enemies. Every commentary on a Pauline letter relies also upon an assumed portrait of the church body which Paul is addressing; the most notorious example of this is perhaps the Corinthian community, whose unruly group personality has greatly exercised the imaginations of readers of the Corinthian correspondence from the earliest days of the church (*1 Clement* 47) to the present,[6] but it is no less true of all the letters. This fact of exegesis is given marvelous graphic illustration in medieval illuminated manuscripts, where in the historiated initial P of *Paulus* in the incipit of the Epistle to the Romans, for instance, one can see by the style of hats on the audience that Paul is imagined as addressing a mixed audience of Jews and Gentiles.[7] What

---

[3] The long-ranging debate over the phrase πίστις Ἰησοῦ ("faith in/of Jesus") has reached a decisive phase in the last twenty years, with more and more scholars questioning the old consensus (see, e.g., Luke T. Johnson, "Romans 3:21–26 and the Faith of Jesus," *CBQ* 44 [1982] 77–90; Richard B. Hays, *The Faith of Jesus Christ: An Investigation of the Narrative Substructure of Galatians 3:1–4:11* [SBLDS 56; Chico: Scholars Press, 1983], esp. 139–91, with a list of other scholars who take the genitive as subjective in n. 105 on p. 186). But others have sought to defend the traditional objective translation and meaning, such as James D. G. Dunn ("Once More, ΠΙΣΤΙΣ ΧΡΙΣΤΟΥ," *SBLSP* 1991 [ed. Eugene H. Lovering, Jr.] 730–44, and exchange with Richard B. Hays, "ΠΙΣΤΙΣ and Pauline Theology: What Is at Stake?" ibid., 714–29). A full account of the debate may be found in J. Louis Martyn, *Galatians* (AB 33A; New York: Doubleday, 1997) 263–75, who himself takes the "faith *of* Jesus" side.

[4] The biographical nature of the question is revealed in Dunn's conclusion: "I remain wholly convinced that Paul intended his audiences to hear that phrase in the sense 'faith in Christ'" ("Once More, ΠΙΣΤΙΣ ΧΡΙΣΤΟΥ," 744).

[5] The spectrum of options vis à vis Judaism and Hellenism are readily seen in the portrait of "Paul: An Anomalous Diaspora Jew," by John M. G. Barclay, *Jews in the Mediterranean Diaspora from Alexander to Trajan [323 BCE-117 CE]* (Edinburgh: T & T Clark, 1996) 381–95.

[6] One thinks of the wild gnostics of several decades ago (such as those brought forward by Walter Schmithals, *Gnosticism in Corinth*, trans. J. E. Steely [Nashville: Abingdon, 1971]), to the most recent, more gendered and intellectual portrait of Wire, *Corinthian Women Prophets*, who casts the Corinthians as quite sophisticated theologians in dialogue with Paul.

[7] E.g., the Romans *incipit* in *Oxford Bodleian Libr. Ms. Auct. D.I. 13*, fol. I[r], a mid-twelfth century English glossed Epistles of St. Paul (Christopher DeHamel, *A History of Illuminated Manuscripts* [Boston: Grodine, 1986] pl. 98). Compare the portraits of a wholly Jewish audience at Rome in the *incipit* of Romans in other medieval manuscripts collected by Luba Eleen (*The Illustration of the Pauline Epistles of the Twelfth and Thirteenth Centuries* [Oxford: Clarendon, 1982] pl. 245–47).

the medieval artist here adds as an aid to readers, in the deftly economical technique of miniature manuscript illumination, takes literary form in virtually all Pauline commentaries (including those of Chrysostom),[8] which begin with this delineation of the *dramatis personae*, and character sketches of each. The Pauline texts, even as epistles, are embedded in a narrative structure; and compelling narratives require well-drawn and intriguing characters.[9] Exegesis and portraiture, therefore, always go hand in hand. In this chapter we shall illustrate the workings of this axiom in the history of Pauline scholarship through an examination of Pauline portraiture in the two essential contexts that frame the current inquiry: late antique interpretation, as practiced by Chrysostom's contemporary Western counterpart, Augustine, and late twentieth-century Pauline scholarship in the United States.

Pauline Portraiture in Late Antiquity: Augustine and Chrysostom

Chrysostom was not alone in his age in the biographical emphasis of his Pauline interpretation. His great Latin-speaking contemporary, Augustine, was likewise preoccupied with the person of Paul throughout the various shifts and vicissitudes of his life and career. It is well known that in many ways Augustine's theological evolution was rooted in his progressive reading and autobiographical engagement with the Pauline letters.[10] But comparison of Augustine with Chrysostom brings into relief the extent to which these developments were rooted in and resulted in differing *portraits* of Paul – from his Manichean period, in which Augustine found Paul a hopelessly inconsistent thinker, to his early Christian period in which he viewed Paul as a fellow Platonist who hymned the ascent of the soul, to his anti-Pelagian view of Paul, largely based on Romans 7, as one who exemplified in his very existence the struggle between the body and its concupiscence, even when under the disposition of grace.[11] Although Augustine did not write encomia to Paul, nor dote on the apostle endlessly or with the height of emotional fervor

---

[8] This is a main purpose of the ὑπόθεσις sections that preface most of Chrysostom's homiletical series on the Pauline epistles.

[9] This has been particularly well argued by Petersen, *Rediscovering Paul*, 43–88.

[10] See Fredriksen, "Augustine's Early Interpretation of Paul," 280: "Ultimately, the most lasting result of his lifetime of meditation on Paul's letters, especially Romans, was not his specific interpretations, nor necessarily the doctrinal conclusions he teased from them. Rather, it was his mode of reading Romans, applying the words of the apostle autobiographically to the experience of the individual believer, that had the most lasting effect."

[11] This viewpoint is evident (although without explicit language of portraiture) in Peter Brown's commentary on Augustine's turn to Paul in Carthage: "Augustine did not 'discover' Paul at this time [in 394]. He merely read him differently. Previously, he had interpreted Paul as a Platonist: he had seen him as the exponent of a spiritual ascent, of the renewal of the 'inner' man, the decay of the 'outer'; and, after his baptism, he had shared in Paul's sense of triumph: 'Behold, all things have become new.' The idea of the spiritual life as a vertical ascent, as a progress towards a final, highest stage to be reached in this life, had fascinated Augustine in previous years. Now, he

Chrysostom displays, nonetheless the person of Paul (and not merely the words of his letters) played an essential role in his thinking and writings. Paula Fredriksen has pointed to this in her suggestion that it was the *person* Saul of Tarsus, as known from Acts, who continually confronted Augustine with the inadequacy of "the essentially classical model of self-improvement," and impelled his movement to the less optimistic anthropology that characterized his later writings.[12] Naturally, a thorough comparison of Chrysostom's personal relationship with Paul and Augustine's,[13] the impact of those relationships on the life, thought and theological development of each, and the forms of literary depictions of Paul each used, far exceeds our scope here, but we can offer a beginning to that investigation in this context by describing a few striking similarities and differences. In simplest terms, both men – Augustine and Chrysostom – enmeshed their personal identities in a construct (or series of constructs) of Paul's identity. Each patterned himself after Paul, yet both found the figure of Paul expansive and variable enough to grow and change with him, even as each sought to conform himself to a version of the apostle's likeness. Both Chrysostom and Augustine in their lives and writings engaged in a complex and elaborately choreographed mimetic dance with Paul.[14]

---

will see in Paul nothing but a single, unresolved tension between 'flesh' and 'spirit'" (*Augustine of Hippo: A Biography* [Berkeley: University of California Press, 1967], 151).

[12] "The Paul whom Augustine would have been most familiar with and most interested in back in Milan, both as an ex-Manichee and as a philosophically-inclined Catholic, would have been the Paul of the epistles ... But as he works through the Pauline corpus in the first half of the 390s, once back in Africa, Augustine is driven to consider the pre-Christian Paul as Paul presents himself in Galatians, and as tradition presents him in the deutero-Pauline epistles: the persecutor and blasphemer (1 Tim 1:13), the foolish, impious, and hateful man enslaved to various pleasures (Titus 3:3). And Augustine has before him, of course, Luke's narrative in Acts ... The essentially classical model of self-improvement and moral freedom, even in the extremely attenuated form in which it survived into Augustine's early Pauline commentaries, could not withstand Augustine's repeated encounters with Paul the sinner and, most particularly, the persecutor. Hence Augustine's conclusion to his exhausting exercise in scriptural exegesis and dialectical reasoning. Abruptly, dramatically, he closes the first book of his answers to Simplicianus by again invoking Paul – *not his theology, but his biography* ... The zealous Pharisee turned apostle obdurately defied any such model" (Paula Fredriksen, "Beyond the body/soul dichotomy: Augustine on Paul against the Manichees and the Pelagians," *Recherches Augustiniennes* 23 [1988] 87–114, 102–103, emphasis added). This most important insight deserves a thorough testing and documentation throughout Augustine's immense corpus of writings.

[13] A comparison between these two authors always beckons, for they were contemporaries, and both major figures, one in the East and the other in the West, who had lively personalities, and left prodigious literary remains. See, for instance, the older study of Philip Schaff, *Saint Chrysostom and Saint Augustine* (New York: Whittaker, 1891), which for the most part is merely "parallel lives," and, more recently, the symposium volume edited by Charles Kannengiesser, *Jean Chrysostome et Augustin* (Théologie Historique 35; Paris: Éditions Beauchesne, 1975), which unfortunately contains no essay on their respective treatments of Paul.

[14] To continue with the metaphor, one might heuristically ask who took the "lead" in each of these dance pairs. In Chrysostom's case it was clearly Paul, but in Augustine's perhaps it was the North African. Although this is probably overly simplistic, there is a general biographical difference in the primary direction of the mimetic arrow of each: John lived out from his reading

But there were differences in the style and steps each took, even to the point of contrariety, which merit exploration.

In the famous passage in the *Confessiones* where Augustine avidly delves into the Pauline epistles just before his conversion, it is interesting that he twice says he found there "a face" [*facies, vultus*] that brought together for him the truths of the Platonists with a human being's humble longing for God. While it is perhaps not solely Paul's face that Augustine describes in that passage (his Scriptural quotations range from the Psalms to Revelation and suggest a depiction of the whole canon), his composite image of the Scriptures contains key elements of a Paul he now views differently – no longer as the hopelessly inconsistent writer he had earlier encountered,[15] but instead a coherent thinker, consonant with Platonist philosophy.[16] Subsequent to his conversion, in which, as is well known, Rom 13:13–14 played a decisive role (*conf.* 8.22.29), Augustine's interpretations of the Pauline epistles evolved over the course of his life as believer and bishop, particularly in response to the successive controversies in which he found himself absorbed.[17] We shall peer at a few Augustinian Pauline portraits from the earlier part of his career to see how he depicted his life-long conversation partner at that time, and then focus in on his later anti-Pelagian Pauline portrait, because it is the most striking counterpart, in both form and content, to Chrysostom's images of the apostle.

---

of Paul in the formative years in the cave, whereas Augustine lived *into* his reading of Paul in his post-conversion years and successive controversies.

[15] Augustine gives a sustained defense of Paul's consistency in his 397 reply to the Manichean Faustus, who had likewise denied that Paul is inconsistent [*non equidem crediderim apostolum dei contraria sibi scribere potuisse*], but on that basis had deduced that either Rom 1:3 is inauthentic, or stands corrected by Paul's later judgment in 2 Cor 5:16 (*c. Faust.* 11.1 [text CSEL 26/6, pt. 1, ed. Joseph Zycha (Leipzig: Freytag, 1891) 313–28]). But, although Augustine maintains vigorously that Paul did not change his mind [*in hoc autem Paulum aliquando errasse et proficiendo mutasse sententiam, absit ut dicamus*] (*c. Faust.* 11.4; CSEL 25/6, pt. 1, 320), his proof is not really biographical, but exegetical, and based upon an appeal to the guaranteed authenticity of canonical Scripture.

[16] "With avid intensity I seized the sacred writings of your Spirit and especially the apostle Paul. Where at one time I used to think he contradicted himself and the text of his words disagreed with the testimonies of the law and the prophets, the problems simply vanished. The holy oracles now presented to me a simple face ... None of this is in the Platonist books. Those pages do not contain the face of this devotion, tears of confession, your sacrifice, a troubled spirit, a contrite and humble spirit, the salvation of your people, the espoused city, the guarantee of your Holy Spirit, the cup of our redemption" [*Itaque auidissime arripui uenerabilem stilum spiritus tui et prae ceteris apostolum Paulum, et perierunt illae quaestiones, in quibus mihi aliquando uisus est aduersari sibi et non congruere testimoniis legis et prophetarum textus sermonis eius, et apparuit mihi una facies eloquiorum castorum ... Hoc illae litterae non habent. Non habent illae paginae uultum pietatis huius, lacrimas confessionis, sacrificium tuum, spiritum contribulatum, cor contritum et humiliatum, populi salutem, sponsam ciuitatem, arram spiritus sancti, poculum pretii nostri*] (*conf.* 7.21.27; text CCSL 27, ed. Lucas Verheijen [Turnhout: Brepols, 1981] 110–111; trans. Henry Chadwick, *Saint Augustine, Confessions* [Oxford: Oxford University Press, 1991] 130–31).

[17] See the valuable study of Fredriksen, "Augustine's Early Interpretation of Paul."

Although Augustine's earliest writings on Paul, his propositional commentaries on Romans from 394, devote very little interest to the author of the epistle,[18] a sermon from soon thereafter (likely 399) on Mt 8:8 contains a little gem of a Pauline portrait. Augustine constructs an allegory on Christ being crushed by the crowds but touched by a lone woman in Mk 5:30–31, in which the one being crushed but touched in faith by a select few is the church, the Body of Christ. In exhorting his congregation to "be the body of Christ" and not those crushing the body of Christ, Augustine extends the metaphor in a novel way:

> You have the hem of the garment there for you to touch, in order to be cured of the issue of blood, that is of the flux of carnal pleasures [*id est, carnalium voluptatum fluxu sanemini*]. You have, I repeat, the hem of the garment there for you to touch. Imagine the apostles to be the tunic [*Vestem putate Apostolos*], the seamless robe of unity, clinging to the sides of Christ. Among these apostles there was, as the hem, the least and latest of them, Paul [*In his Apostolis erat tanquam fimbria minimus et novissimus Paulus*]; as he says of himself, "I am the least of the apostles" (1 Cor 15:9). The last and the least thing in a tunic is the hem. The hem is given a look of contempt, but it gives a touch of salvation [*Fimbria cum contemptu aspicitur: sed cum salute tangitur*] ... Touch it, if you are suffering from an issue of blood, power will go out from him whose tunic it is, and heal you [*Tange, si fluxum sanguinis pateris: exiet virtus de illo cujus vestis est, et sanabit te*]. The hem was just now held out to you to touch, when we had the reading from the same apostle [*Fimbria modo tangenda proponebatur, quando ex eodem apostolo legebatur*].[19]

Augustine creates this ingenious portrayal of Paul to form a poetic link between gospel and epistle lections, but it is also a self-contained image that conveys a sense of Paul's sheer importance (paradoxically by his very contemptibility), and his role as a conduit of Christ's power. This evocative picture of Paul as the hem of the garment of apostles clothing the body of Christ is in that sense reminiscent of some of Chrysostom's portraits of Paul and his epistles as the ark in which all humanity may sail to salvation, or the sea leading from earth to heaven.[20] Metaphorical images of Paul such as these are not nearly so common in Augustine's writings as in Chrysostom's, but this passage shows that on occasion Augustine could embrace the art of metaphorical portraiture, even if he did not as frequently pursue it.[21]

---

[18] *Expositio quarundam propositionum ex epistula Apostoli ad Romanos* and *Epistulae ad Romanos inchoata expositio* (see the edition and translation by Paula Fredriksen Landes, *Augustine on Romans* [SBLTT 23; Chico, CA: Scholars Press, 1982]). In these writings Augustine's concern is to run through the epistle verse by verse, clarifying what Paul means and teaches.

[19] *serm.* 62 [text PL 38.417; trans. Edmund Hill, *The Works of Saint Augustine, A Translation for the 21st Century, Sermons III/3 (51–94) on the New Testament* (Brooklyn: New City Press, 1991) 159]; a quotation of the lectionary passage from 1 Cor 8:10–11 follows directly on this selection.

[20] *laud. Paul.* 1.5 [SC 300.120]; *hom. in Ac.* 53.4 [60.383–84].

[21] See also, e.g., *c. Faust.* 22.70, where with a neat double word play he describes Saul the persecutor of Christians as being "like a crop of weeds showing great signs of productiveness" [*tamquam siluestre erat uitium, sed magnae feracitatis indicium*] (text CSEL 26/6, pt. 1, ed. Joseph Zycha [1891] 667; trans. Richard Stothert, NPNF 4.299).

In the *Confessiones* themselves, which also date from this period (397), is a portrait of Paul that verges closest to some of Chrysostom's in its shared celebration of Paul's holiness:

What then is the reason for your rejoicing (Phil 4:10), great Paul [*o Paule magne*]? Why your joy? Where do you find your nourishment? You are a man "renewed in the knowledge of God after the image of him who created you" (Col 3:10), a "living soul" of great continence, a tongue which flies like the birds as it proclaims mysteries [*homo renouate in agnitione dei secundum imaginem eius, qui creauit te, et anima uiua tanta continentia et lingua uolatilis loquens mysteria*].[22]

Here Augustine addresses his praises directly to Paul, the man of joys, for his ascetic prowess and for the soaring heights of his tongue, themes quite familiar from John's images of Paul (including the striking, shared metaphor of the bird). But in the same book thirteen of the *Confessiones* Augustine pencils a rather contrary portrait of Paul with a selection of apostolic quotations that color him as a man weighed down, groaning and thirsting for the completeness and deliverance that only the next world can provide:

In this life even he who says, "I could not speak to you as spiritual but as carnal" (1 Cor 3:1), does not think that he himself has comprehended. He "forgets the things behind and stretches out to those things which lie ahead" (Phil 3:13). Weighed down he groans (2 Cor 5:4) ....[23]

Most tellingly, as this lamenting confession continues, the persona and voice of Paul meld over into Augustine:

I also say [*Et ego dico*]: My God, where are you? I see you are there, but I sigh for you a little [*"Deus meus ubi es?" Ecce ubi es. Respiro in te paululum*] ... Yet still my soul is sad because it slips back and becomes a "deep", or rather feels itself still a deep [*Et adhuc tristis est, quia relabitur et fit abyssus, uel potius sentit adhuc se esse abyssum*].[24]

In this quite different portrait, Paul mirrors Augustine's sorrows and apocalyptic incompleteness even as Augustine mirrors Paul's. The suffering Paul also had a

---

[22] *conf.* 13.26.40 [text Verheijen, CCSL 27.266; trans. Chadwick, *Confessions*, 297–98]. See also the broader contours of the immediate context: "But how Paul grieved over some trees which did not render the fruit they owed him! (quoting 2 Tim 4:16, with comment) ... These fruits are owed to those who minister spiritual teaching through their interpretations of the divine mysteries, and the debt is owed to them as men. But the debt is also owed to them as 'the living soul.' For they offer themselves as a model for imitation in ascetic restraint of all kinds. Moreover, it is owed to them as 'flying birds' because of the blessings pronounced upon them which are multiplied upon the earth" [*Debetur eis autem sicut animae uiuae praebentibus se ad imitandum in omni continentia. Item debetur eis tamquam uolatilibus propter benedictiones eorum, quae multiplicantur super terram (conf.* 13.25.38 [text Verheijen, CCSL 27.265; trans. Chadwick, *Confessions*, 297])].

[23] *conf.* 13.13.14 [trans. Chadwick, *Confessions*, 281]. The passage continues at some length, with a pastiche of biblical verses, including 2 Cor 5:2; Rom 12:2: 1 Cor 14:20; Gal 3:1.

[24] *conf.* 13.14.15 [text Verheijen, CCSL 27.250; trans. Chadwick, *Confessions*, 281]. The Scriptural reference is to Job 32:20.

conspicuous place in Chrysostom's gallery of apostolic portraits, but the apostolic afflictions Chrysostom has in mind are not those of internal angst and existential turmoil, but of the earthly troubles of the ministry and its adversaries, which, as we have noted, John changes to fit with the predominant threats of his own current situation. This vision of Paul as embodying the innate *tristesse* of the human condition in the *Confessiones* is a harbinger of what is to follow in Augustine's later career.

The contrast between Augustine and Chrysostom reaches its height, as we might expect, in the North African's later writings against the Pelagians. Whereas Chrysostom's Paul represented the Christian version of classical virtue theory – that one can attain even angelic virtue if one sets one's προαίρεσις correctly – it was just this view, at least in its extreme formulation, for which Augustine attacked the Pelagians.[25] To be sure, John most often corrected his own extreme emphasis in this direction by including the role of the holy spirit, or grace,[26] in Paul's manifold achievements. But his strong exhortatory emphasis on Paul as the paradigmatically virtuous man who proved that there was no hindrance to human moral perfection was the counterpoint to Augustine's eventual picture of Paul as the emblematic man of perpetual moral struggle in the midst of this sinful existence.[27]

The starting point of Augustine's anti-Pelagian portraits of Paul is a decision at once exegetical and autobiographical, a self-conscious corrective to his earlier position, in now maintaining that the *ego* in Romans 7 who sees another law at work in his members, and does what he does not wish to do (7:14–25), is Paul himself.[28] Reading his own experience into and from this text, Augustine's portraits of Paul and of himself become inseparably enmeshed[29] (as did John's with

---

[25] The sharp comparison between the two bishops in this regard was noted by Schaff, *Saint Chrysostom and Saint Augustine*, 46–47: "[Chrysostom's] anthropology forms a wholesome contrast and supplement to the anthropology of his younger contemporary, the great Bishop of Hippo, the champion of the slavery of the human will and the sovereignty of divine grace."

[26] See Meyer, "Liberté et moralisme chrétien," for documentation of this point in Chrysostom's moral thought generally.

[27] Brown explicitly invokes our contrast: "One, Anianus of Celeda, shows the state of mind of a cultured Pelagian cleric. Depressed and shocked by the modern mystique of human incapacity, he had set himself to translate into Latin the homilies of S. John Chrysostom. Here were very different sermons from those of Augustine: they spoke of the moral achievements of S. Paul; they castigated all thoughts of a fatality of evil, and had upheld, in this darkening world, the nobility of man, and the capacity of his nature to fulfil the perfect message of the Gospels" (*Augustine of Hippo*, 371). It is surely no accident that among the very first of Chrysostom's works to be translated for Latin readers (by Anianus) were the seven homilies *de laudibus sancti Pauli*.

[28] See *serm.* 154.2; *c. ep. Pel.* 1.8.3–11.24; *praed. sanct.* 1.4.8, correcting the view expressed in *ex. prop. Rom.* 44–46 (see Fredriksen Landes, *Augustine on Romans*, 16–18), and *Simpl.* 1.1.9 (for discussion, bibliography, and further references see Fredriksen, "Body/Soul Dichotomy," 110–111; Schelkle, *Paulus*, 247–48).

[29] "Augustine's reading of Paul was autobiographical in another sense: he applied what he took to be Paul's self-description to his own personal experience. For, despite the reception of

Paul). And, like Chrysostom, Augustine's individual Pauline portraits also had a public life in oratory and exposition, where the person of Paul as a literary construct performed important theological, rhetorical and exhortatory functions. Because we can attribute some of the divergences between Augustine's and Chrysostom's portraiture of Paul to the different genres in which they worked,[30] perhaps we shall gain the most insightful comparison of the two by looking at Augustine's sermons, also.[31] *Sermo* 154, dated in the midst of the Pelagian controversy (October 14, 419), provides a most interesting counterpart to John's oratorical images of the apostle. The polemical context is set out in each homily of this series on Romans 7–8 (*serm.* 151–156), as Augustine warns his audience in the exordium to each sermon how "difficult and perilous" these texts are, and insists that one must read such passages with great care in order not to be misled. In this instance Augustine is confronted by the competing possibilities of meaning of the words in 7:14–15 (*non enim quod volo hoc ago sed quod odi illud facio*, "I do not do that which I want, but I do what I hate") if read as Paul's autobiographical self-portrait. The entire sermon is an exercise in defacing and replacing false portraits of Paul – in this case, working against two at the same time – the same operation we earlier observed John engaged in, but with different portraits in play.[32] Augustine begins with the first of two polar opposite, equally fraudulent, anti-portraits of Paul he seeks to repudiate:

How are we to understand this, my dear brothers and sisters? Does it mean that the apostle Paul did not want, for example, to commit adultery, and did commit adultery [*Itane Apostolus Paulus nolebat, verbi gratia, facere adulterium, et faciebat adulterium*]? That he didn't want to be a miser, and was a miser [*nolebat esse avarus, et erat avarus*]? Is there any of us who would

grace which he felt had enabled him to convert to Catholic Christianity, Augustine had continued to feel himself burdened by his 'former mistresses,' the appetites of his own body ... Augustine's interpretation of Paul, especially against the Pelagians, rests fundamentally upon his personal identification with the inner struggle he sees Paul describing in Romans" (Fredriksen, "Augustine's Early Interpretation of Paul," 278–79).

[30] Augustine never wrote a full set of commentaries on the Pauline epistles (although he planned to do so, but never completed it [Brown, *Augustine of Hippo*, 151]) or any encomia to the apostle; Chrysostom never wrote an autobiography. But Chrysostom's autobiography is etched in his Pauline portraits, even as Augustine's Pauline portraits and praises are embedded in his *Confessiones* and other writings. In addition to his biblical homilies, Chrysostom wrote treatises, but they were generally more exhortatory and practical than dogmatic, and, to be sure, far less philosophical. A full study comparing the two must attend to the role of genre and audience in the generation of their respective portraits of Paul. In this connection it is not insignificant that the very same distinction in literary form held between Pelagius and Augustine, the former having "perfected an art ideally suited to communicating his ideas, the difficult art of writing formal letters of exhortation" (Brown, *Augustine of Hippo*, 342), whereas a large portion of Augustine's scriptural commentary was worked out and expressed in propositions and treatises.

[31] Augustine's ways of depicting Paul in his wide ranging sermons would of course be a massive study. I have here chosen to analyze one particularly apt sermon as an entrée into the topic.

[32] In *laud. Paul.* 5 and 6 (as analyzed above, pp. 330–53, and 166–72) Chrysostom rebuts charges of specific moral failings against Paul – such as capriciousness, cowardice, boastfulness or harsh behavior – not general claims about Paul's human disposition.

have the nerve to take responsibility for such a slander, as to have that sort of opinion of the apostle [*Quis autem nostrum audeat se induere tali blasphemia, ut de Apostolo hoc sentiat*]?[33]

Augustine dismisses this image of Paul as an uncontrolled sinner (one which the Pelagians claimed was his own handiwork) by the charge of blasphemy.[34] Then immediately he unveils his own alternative portrait of Paul by a simple, first-person recasting of Paul's confession: "I want not to lust and yet I do lust" [*Volo non concupiscere, et concupisco*].[35] But even as he provides a glimpse at this, his accurate portrait of the author, in the next moment Augustine introduces a quick sketch of the other anti-portrait he must deface:

I'm telling your graces, if we believe the apostle had absolutely no weakness of lust he had to struggle against [*si crediderimus Apostolum nullam prorsus habuisse infirmitatem concupiscentiae cui reluctaretur*], then we are believing something splendid about him [*multum credimus de illo*]; and if only it were so [*atque utinam ita sit*]! It's not for us, after all, to be jealous of the apostles, but to imitate them [*Non enim invidere nos oportet Apostolis, sed Apostolos imitari*]. However, my dear friends, I can hear the apostle himself confessing that he had not yet arrived at such a perfection of justice as we believe the angels enjoy [*Verumtamen, charissimi, audio ipsum Apostolum confitentem, nondum eum ad tantam perfectionem justitiae pervenisse, quantam in Angelis esse credimus*].[36]

Augustine seeks to repudiate both these extreme Pauline portraits – the man of lust and the man of angelic purity – and replace them with his own portrait of Paul as a warrior, not, like Chrysostom, against the external and internal foes of Christian orthodoxy, but against the lusting forces of his own nature. Augustine assumes

---

[33] *serm.* 154.3 [text PL 38.834; trans. Edmund Hill, *The Works of Saint Augustine, A Translation for the 21st Century, Sermons III/5 (148–183) on the New Testament* (Brooklyn: New City Press, 1992) 69].

[34] This portrait of Paul the man of ungovernable lusts was Pelagius' (scandalously wrong, in his eyes) version of Augustine's own portrait of Paul that he hurled back at him and his partisans, according to *c. ep. Pel.* 1.8.13: "[Pelagius] says, 'They say that even the Apostle Paul, even all the apostles, were always polluted by immoderate lust'" [*Apostolum etiam Paulum, inquit, uel omnes apostolos dicunt semper inmoderata libidine fuisse pollutos*] [text CSEL 60, ed. Karl Vrba and Joseph Zycha (Leipzig: Freytag, 1913) 433; trans. Robert Ernest Wallis, NPNF 5.381].

[35] *serm.* 154.3 [PL 38.834; text Hill, *Sermons III/5*, 70]. Further embellishing detail on this portrait is provided in Augustine's instant defense of it against the incredulous: "So what are we saying, my dear brothers and sisters? That the apostle had no lust in his flesh, which he would much rather not have, but which he didn't consent to, though it arose, tickled his fancy, gave him ideas, drew him on, boiled up, tempted him" [*Quid ergo dicimus, fratres mei? Non habebat ullam concupiscentiam Apostolus in carne sua, quam habere nollet; cui tamen existenti, titillanti, suggerenti, sollicitanti, aestuanti, tentanti non consentiret*]?

[36] *serm.* 154.3 [PL 38.834; trans. Hill, *Sermons III/5*, 70]. At other times Augustine could say that Paul did attain to other, more limited forms of perfection, as in *Tract. Ev. Jo.* 122.3: "Unless any one have the boldness to imagine or to affirm, that the Apostle Paul attained not to the perfection of those who left all and followed Christ" [*Nisi forte quispiam putare audebit aut dicere, apostolum Paulum non pertinuisse ad eorum perfectionem qui relictis omnibus Christum secuti sunt*] [text CCSL 36, ed. D. R. Willems (Turnhout: Brepols, 1954) 669; trans. John Gibb and James Innes, NPNF 7.440].

his audience remembers the full-color vision of this Paul that he had placarded before their eyes just days earlier:

So it is not what he wants to that the apostle does; because he wants not to lust or covet, and yet he does so; that's why he does what he doesn't want to [*Non ergo quod vult agit Apostolus; quia vult non concupiscere, et tamen concupiscit; ideo non quod vult agit*]. Did that evil covetousness or lust subdue the apostle and drag him into fornication and adulteries? [*Numquid illa concupiscentia mala trahebat Apostolum subjugatum ad fornicationem et adulteria?*]. Perish the thought [*Absit*]. Such ideas must never enter our heads [*Non ascendant tales cogitationes in cor nostrum*]. He was struggling, he was not subdued [*Luctabatur, non subjugabatur*] ... But he set out his own struggle before your eyes, so that you wouldn't be afraid of yours [*Sed constituit tibi ante oculos pugnam suam, ne timeres tuam*] ... Observe the apostle engaged in combat, and don't let yourself grow desperate [*Vide Apostolum pugnantem, et noli te facere desperantem*].[37]

Taking a shade from each of the anti-portraits, Augustine's Paul was "struggling" (like the man of lust), "but not subdued" (like the angels). And this image, set before all Christians, is intended as an inducement to courage in followers who must endure the same struggle.[38]

But portraits are not self-validating. Augustine confronts a protagonist who questions the authority that stands behind his image of the apostle: "And how do *you* know [*Et tu unde scis*] that Paul the apostle did not yet have the justice and perfection of an angel?"[39] In reply Augustine summons the testimony of his subject himself, and claims that his portrait of Paul is identical with the apostle's self-portrait:

I'm not doing the apostle an injustice, I'm only believing the apostle himself, I'm not calling any other witness; I don't listen to suspicions, I don't care about excessive praise [*Non facio injuriam Apostolo, non credo nisi Apostolo, alium testem non quaero; suspicantem non audio, nimium laudantem non curo*]. Tell me, holy apostle, about yourself, where nobody can doubt that you

---

[37] *serm.* 151.6 [PL 38.817–18; trans. Hill, *Sermons III/5*, 44].

[38] This is reminiscent of *laud. Paul.* 7.10 [SC 300.314], among other passages, where Chrysostom likewise accents the exhortatory benefits of being able to *view* Paul's ἀγών. But the battles Augustine and Chrysostom have in mind are not the same – fighting the lustfulness of nature for the former, and waging war against legion opposition to win the world for the gospel, for the latter.

[39] This is of course not only a hypothetical objection. A most telling set of dueling Pauline portraits is found in *gest. Pel.* 14.32–47 [text CSEL 42, ed. Karl Vrba and Joseph Zycha (Leipzig: Freytag, 1902) 86–95; trans. Peter Holmes, NPNF 5.197–200], on the eleventh charge against Pelagius. There Pelagius champions Paul as the paragon of one to whom God had given all the graces, since he was proven worthy of them [*dicimus donare deum ei qui fuerit dignus accipere omnes gratias, sicut Paulo apostolo donauit*], a point on which the Synod upheld him. Augustine allows that Paul did receive all the gifts of grace catalogued in 1 Cor 12:28, even providing evidence for each from the letters and Acts to document this shared point. Nevertheless, he disputes that even this impressive list should be considered the full measure of perfection in virtue, given that "there are other graces in addition to these which are not mentioned here" [*sed sunt et aliae gratiae, quae hic commemoratae non sunt*]. Surely, he argues, "however greatly the Apostle Paul excelled others as a member of Christ's body" [*quamuis esset apostolus Paulus multum excellens membrum Christi corporis*] he still did not surpass the head of the body, Christ, who was human in both soul and body. And, furthermore, Paul did not receive the graces he was given by God because of his moral worth, but by God's free bestowal.

are talking about yourself [*Dic mihi, sancte Apostole, de te ipso, ubi nemo dubitat quia de te ipso loqueris*].[40]

Augustine claims the ultimate authority for his Pauline portrait – the apostle him-self – whom he conjures up, places in the witness box,[41] and asks to speak on behalf of Augustine's portrayal of him. The art of true portraiture as here depicted is situated between the extremes defined by the epideictic rhetoric Chrysostom so thoroughly practiced – blame and praise. Augustine claims to be motivated by neither, but seeks the simple truth from the author's own words. As a rhetorician Augustine realizes that his most persuasive evidence will come from Pauline pas-sages in which the *ego* who speaks is incontestably Paul (unlike the disputed passage that is his lection, Romans 7), so that is where he turns to solicit the indisputable apostolic testimony. He first carefully selects Phil 3:13–14, to demonstrate that Paul was not yet perfected like the angels.[42] But because adversaries could read the imperfection described there in relation, not to moral purity, but to his as yet unattained immortality, Augustine asks his subject, Paul (who is now acting as ekphrasist for himself), for another snapshot to prove his ethical limitations: "Tell us, holy apostle, about some other clearer place, where you are not seeking immortal-ity, but where you are confessing infirmity" [*Dic nobis, sancte Apostole, alium aliquem manifestiorem locum, non ubi quaeris immortalitatem, sed ubi confiteris infirmitatem*].[43] The obvious next stop in the gallery of the Pauline epistles is 2 Corinthians, with its extensive discussions of Paul's weakness. Augustine selects two passages, 2 Cor 4:7 and 12:7, to support his portrait of Paul as a man who struggled with the desires of the flesh. For him the *coup de grâce* is less Paul's thorn in the flesh than his *need for* such a thorn to hold in check his innate urge to be prideful.[44] With this image in hand Augustine taunts his rival portraitist:

---

[40]   *serm.* 154.4 [PL 38.834; trans. Hill, *Sermons III/5*, 70].

[41]   The rhetoric of this sermonic passage matches that in *gest. Pel.* 14.36 [text Vrba–Zycha, CSEL 42.92; trans. Holmes, NPNF 5.199–200, with my adaptations]: "Let us say to him, 'Holy Apostle Paul, the monk Pelagius declares that you were worthy to receive all the graces of your apostolate. What do you say about this?' 'I am not worthy,' he says, 'to be called an apostle' (1 Cor 15:9) Shall I then, under pretence of honoring Paul, dare to believe Pelagius on Paul instead of Paul himself? I will not do it, for if I do so I shall confer more onus on myself than honor on him'" [*dicamus ei: sancte Paule apostole, Pelagius monachus dignum te dicit fuisse, qui acciperes omnes gratias apostolatus tui; tu ipse quid dicis? non sum, inquit, dignus uocari apostolus. itane, ut honorem deferam Paulo, Pelagio magis de Paulo credere audebo quam Paulo? non faciam; me namque potius onerabo quam illum honorabo, si fecero*]. We note again Augustine's claim to be taking the high moral ground by his refusal to praise Paul gratuitously.

[42]   See the neat figurative expression of this same Pauline portrait contained in Phil 3 in *pecc. mer.* 2.13.20: "Although he was already a perfect traveller, he had not yet attained the perfect end of his journey" [*quamuis iam esset perfectus uiator, etsi nondum erat ipsius itineris perfectione peruentor*] [text CSEL 60, ed. Karl Vrba and Joseph Zycha (Leipzig: Freytag, 1913) 93; trans. Peter Holmes, NPNF 5.53].

[43]   *serm.* 154.5 (PL 38.835; trans. Hill, *Sermons III/5*, 71].

[44]   In this Augustine provides an anticipatory rebuttal to those who would explain Paul's confession of weakness in 2 Corinthians as a reference only to bodily, but not spiritual infirmity.

So now then, now say that there was as much justice in him as there is in the holy angels [*Jam ergo modo dic quia tanta in illo erat justitia, quanta est in Angelis sanctis*]. Or perhaps a holy angel in heaven, in order not to grow proud, receives as a goad a messenger of Satan, to be knocked about [*An forte et angelus sanctus in coelo, ne extollatur, accipit stimulum angelum satanae, a quo colaphizetur*]? Far be it from us to suspect such a thing about the holy angels [*Absit hoc de sanctis Angelis suspicari*]. We are human, we acknowledge that the holy apostles were human [*Homines sumus, Apostolos sanctos homines agnoscamus*]; chosen vessels, certainly, but still fragile; still wanderers abroad in this flesh, not yet triumphantly victorious in the heavenly home country [*vasa electa, sed adhuc fragilia; adhuc in hac carne peregrinantes, nondum in coelesti patria triumphantes*].[45]

Augustine's portrait of Paul in his anti-Pelagian writings (which he claims is an exact replica of the apostle's own), of which *Sermo* 154 provides a representative example, is of a man in valiant struggle against the concupiscence of the flesh. Although he refused to consent to that lust, Paul was not freed from the need continually to do battle against it. And despite the fact that Augustine vehemently denies that Paul gave in to these lusts and could therefore be regarded as a negative *exemplum*,[46] this Paul is still not an "archetype of virtue" so much as an archetype of the fraught human moral condition. Augustine claims neutrality in his approach to Paul – seeking neither to insult nor unduly praise him. Chrysostom, of course, deliberately sought out precisely what Augustine claimed to eschew – praises to Paul – which he expressed with a personal ardor for Paul not brought to similar literary expression in Augustine. The Antiochene's portrayal of the apostle in many ways epitomizes one phalanx of Augustine's enemies, both in dimension and in the image of Paul as having lived the angelic *politeia* on earth. Yet John would agree with Augustine's insistence on Paul's carnality and real life in the flesh, even as he would adamantly refuse any suggestion that it was for him a hindrance to virtue. But for both bishops Pauline portraiture was the arena of combat over anthropological speculation on the nature of human existence and free will. Furthermore, as was the case with Chrysostom, no less for Augustine did the anti-portraits against which he was contending – whether Manichean or Pelagian – fundamentally shape his own resulting images of Paul. Especially in the Pelagian controversy, the person of Paul – as moral exemplar or image of the human moral dilemma – played a most pronounced role,[47] with John (whom we might with a

---

[45] *serm.* 154.6 [PL 38.835–36; trans. Hill, *Sermons III/5*, 71].

[46] See *serm.* 154.10: "The doing here, you see, is the lusting, it isn't the consenting to the lust; in case anyone should now look to the apostle to get himself an example of sinning, and should himself set a bad example" [*Ipsum enim agere concupiscere est, non concupiscentiae consentire: ne aliquis jam in Apostolo peccandi sibi quaerat exemplum, et det malum exemplum*] [PL 38.837; trans. Hill, *Sermons III/5*, 74].

[47] John Ferguson recognized the general role of moral examplars in the Pelagian controversy ("some portion of the dispute turned upon whether in fact sinlessness is imputed to patriarchs, prophets and saints of scripture" [*Pelagius* (Cambridge: Heffer & Sons, 1956) 165], but did not highlight Paul in particular. We should note that Paul's conspicuous place for Augustine was no less true of Pelagius; see the observation of Alexander Souter about Pelagius' commentary on

dose of anachronism term a "semi-Pelagian")[48] and Augustine on opposite sides.[49] That controversy provides a clear instance of the centrality of personal portraits – particularly of Paul – in debates about ideas (such as on sin, freedom and divine grace) in the late fourth and early fifth century. In both Augustine's and Chrysostom's oratory it is telling that Paul stands ready to provide live testimony when called upon, often by a direct summons from a reader who presents himself as on intimate speaking terms with the apostle. The process of author-centered hermeneutics was at work in both bishops, but it took different forms. Each experienced Paul differently, even as each lived into Paul's reflective life in disparate ways. But they share the fact that in both cases they sketched their own selves even as they portrayed their apostolic author.[50]

From even this brief comparison we can conclude that Chrysostom and his great contemporary Augustine, the two most influential Pauline interpreters in East and West, respectively, both engaged in "biographic" exegesis of Paul, but the distinct lives, temperaments, contexts, textual selection,[51] and literary genres created a dif-

---

the Pauline epistles: "No subject occurs with more persistence than the influence of example on conduct. The author is never weary of referring especially to the force of the Apostle's good example in the lives of his converts" (Pelagius' Expositions of Thirteen Epistles of St. Paul, Vol. I, Introduction [Cambridge: Cambridge University Press, 1922] 69). Souter's judgment was confirmed in general more recently by B. R. Rees, Pelagius: A Reluctant Heretic (Suffolk: Boydell, 1988) 76: "the main authority for his views [Pelagius], like Augustine, found in Paul." But more research could fruitfully be done on the role and techniques of constrution of Paul's person in both the theological reflections and literary expressions of the Pelagian debates.

[48] With Schaff, Saint Chrysostom, 46: "We may say that in tendency and spirit he was a catholic Semi-Pelagian or Synergist before Semi-Pelagianism was brought into a system." It is important to remember in this connection that John Cassian was ordained by Chrysostom, and originally came to the West on a mission to Pope Innocent on John's behalf. In this regard we should perhaps mention the cryptic and enigmatic notice about "Pelagius the monk," in a letter from Chrysostom's last year (ep. Olymp. 17.4f [SC 13.386]: "I suffered much pain concerning Pelagius the monk" [σφόδρα ἤλγησα ὑπὲρ Πελαγίου τοῦ μονάζοντος]). But the authenticity of the reference, let alone its meaning, is uncertain (see Malingrey's caution: "il est difficile de savoir si Jean a pu, dès 407, être au courant dans son exil de débats qui ne deviendraient officiels qu'en 411, au concile de Carthage; plus difficile encore de savoir, au cas où il les aurait connus, quelle attitude pouvait être celle de Jean en face d'un courant dont l'origine ascétique avait a priori ses faveurs et qui était encore très récent. On a trop vite tiré de cette allusion obscurale la preuve que Jean avait condamné le pélagianisme, alors qu'on sait par ailleurs que des pélagiens se réclamaient de lui" [SC 13.388–89]).

[49] But we must correct the picture of head-to-head combat by remembering that Chrysostom did not have the later Augustine to contend with. The position he more often had to refute was one occasioned by his own rhetoric of extremes: a despair and lassitude about imitating Paul because of his massive superiority and unique spiritual endowments. One wonders how, if he had been faced directly with the Augustinian alternative, Chrysostom's Pauline portraits would have been reshaped or reconfigured in response.

[50] Fredriksen Landes, Augustine on Romans, xii: "Augustine's early commentaries on Romans provide us with an oblique self-portrait, for it is here that we find articulated the silent half of that debate between Old and New Self that so informs his brilliant, melancholy response to Simplicianus, and whose portrait Augustine presents to us in the Confessions."

[51] Further study should investigate the relative predominance of different letters, such as

ferent kind of film on which the Pauline images were etched. Setting Augustine alongside Chrysostom in this way allows us to see by contrast the extraordinary level of the Antiochene's exuberance and hyperbolic praise for Paul that leads him well beyond what might be theologically defensible in his quest for a lofty Christian vision of the humanly possible. The advantage of placing Chrysostom alongside Augustine is that it in turn brings into relief the extent to which the North African's theological work evolved from and was expressed in terms of an encounter, not only with Paul's words and ideas, but also with the *person* of the apostle to the Gentiles.

Pauline Portraiture in the Late Twentieth Century[52]

Vigorously author-centered interpretations of Paul are not confined to the late fourth and early fifth centuries, despite that period's markedly intense interest in the apostle.[53] Contemporary portraits of Paul,[54] for instance, are also painted in relation to possible, and actual, anti-portraits. Even when not stated overtly, schol- ars today, as much as Chrysostom in the fourth century, battle Pauline portraits they consider distortions of the man, his message, and their own theological, ecclesial and social commitments. While the anti-types may not be Nero, or Plato, or Julian, the most influential counter-portraits of Paul in the last thirty years have been those of Augustine and Luther, harmonized into a single image: Paul the agonized Jew who sought to find a gracious God by means other than his own Jewish legalistic ethical perfectionism. Modern scholars such as E. P. Sanders and Krister Stendahl have sought to peel off the Lutheran overlay on the Pauline portrait and "restore the original" that lay behind, in his own native and distinct

---

Romans, and, particularly, the Pastorals, in Augustine and Chrysostom's portraiture, as well as the complex place of Acts in these composite portraits.

[52] I shall concentrate here on American scholarship, to control the scope of this study, and also because many of the strands of contemporary Pauline research in the last few decades were launched and continue to be well represented here, as well as for the obvious reason that it is the immediate context of my own scholarship. (I include a few non-Americans where they are part of those same conversations.) I am well aware that my choices are far from exhaustive, and that one most significant comparison – actual preaching on Paul in churches today – goes unanalyzed here, although it would provide a certainly logical and surely fruitful point of comparison with Chrysostom's homilies. My purpose in the context of this argument is to establish and explore connections with academic Pauline scholarship (where I feel I am best positioned to make useful comparisons, and where I think those will prove valuable), but I would be delighted to see others take this study in that direction.

[53] Brown, *Augustine of Hippo*, 151: "The last decades of the fourth century in the Latin church, could well be called 'the generation of S. Paul.'" This was no less true in the Greek East at the same time.

[54] Ben Witherington III, *The Paul Quest: The Renewed Search for the Jew of Tarsus* (Downers Grove: InterVarsity Press, 1998) provides an overview of the major movements in recent schol- arship on "the historical Paul," though one can read over the top of these "historical portraits" to see the acts of scholarly production at work in the array of research he surveys.

form.[55] That "original" has been restored by the cleaning and repainting of master artists who have done their homework, as all restorers must, in the history and conventions of the period. His anti-Semitism (the modern virus) and individualism scrubbed away, the Paul of Sanders and Stendahl has had new contours drawn in with the aid of the Dead Sea Scrolls and less biased pictures of first-century Judaism seen "in its own light" and not in the refracted counterpose of an imagined, pristine and reformative infant Christianity. These Pauline portraits are intentionally drawn with an eye on a studio model, a reconstructed mannequin of a "normal" first-century Jew. For Sanders this illuminates the extent to which Paul ultimately diverges from the normative into a distinctive religious system, a portrait which must hang in a new gallery.

The Paul of James D.G. Dunn is based upon the portrait refashioned by Sanders, but insists on its rightful place in the Judaica museum.[56] This version of the apostle is at home among the "old masters" of first century "covenantal Judaism,"[57] but is displayed in a discrete wing of the Judaica museum set aside for an artistic movement that challenges the establishment, in an architectural addition *meant* to be an integral part of the existing edifice (though the plumbing and electrical systems, as is so often the case, sadly never did fully coordinate). All these portraits are situated in a museum haunted by a face that doesn't deserve a picture, but nonetheless dominates the scene and the viewing experience totally: Adolf Hitler. His image – either the Chaplinesque clowning Hitler, the goosestep and salute inspiring orator, or the Auschwitz-designing madman – explains the prevailing tendencies of fresh Pauline portraits in the second half of this century to cast Paul in deliberate anti-type to Hitler and his genocidal anti-Judaism with which Christianity, with Paul as its precursor, might be deemed in collusion. The "new perspective"[58]

---

[55] Krister Stendahl, "The Apostle Paul and the Introspective Conscience of the West," *HTR* 56 (1963) 199–215, reprinted in *idem, Paul Among Jews and Gentiles and Other Essays* (Philadelphia: Fortress, 1976) 78–96; E.P. Sanders, *Paul and Palestinian Judaism: A Comparison of Patterns of Religion* (Philadelphia: Fortress, 1977); *idem, Paul, the Law, and the Jewish People* (Philadelphia: Fortress, 1983).

[56] Among Dunn's many publications on Paul, see especially the essays in *Jesus, Paul and the Law, The Theology of Paul's Letter to the Galatians* (Cambridge: Cambridge University Press, 1993); and *The Theology of Paul the Apostle* (Grand Rapids: Eerdmans, 1998).

[57] Portraits of Paul emphasizing his Jewishness of course have a long history (see the brief summary in Sanders, *Paul and Palestinian Judaism*, 1–12). The most important recent academic reconstructions of Paul by Jewish portraitists have accented his ultimate divergence from Judaism: Alan F. Segal, *Paul the Convert: The Apostolate and Apostasy of Saul the Pharisee* (New Haven/London: Yale University Press, 1990), who organizes his study around three "portraits": Paul the Jew, Paul the Convert, and Paul the Apostle, and Daniel Boyarin, *A Radical Jew: Paul and the Politics of Identity* (Berkeley: University of California Press, 1994), who largely sides with Dunn (see pp. 51–56). And then, of course, there is the revival of the old (melo)dramatic picture of Paul as not really a Jew, but a scheming proselyte, by Hyam Maccoby, *The Mythmaker: Paul and the Invention of Christianity* (San Francisco: Harper & Row, 1986).

[58] The phrase was coined by Dunn (James D.G. Dunn, "The New Perspective on Paul," *BJRL* 65 [1983] 95–122, repr. with an additional note in *idem, Jesus, Paul and the Law*, 183–214).

(an interestingly artistic term in itself) on Paul that has emerged in these last three decades, painted particularly in colors from Rom 9–11, is of a solitary religious genius with Jewish facial features who stands against Hitler, raging and sometimes weeping at the heinous uses to which his "false" evil anti-Judaistic portrait has been put.

There are still other wings in the gallery of contemporary Pauline scholarship. The Paul of Hans Dieter Betz and Abraham J. Malherbe[59] has been painted with a new but old set of colors – the brilliant hues so loved by the Greeks who painted their statues to bring majestic and redolent life to inert but lovingly and expertly sculpted smooth stone. The museum of Betz and Malherbe contains many rooms filled with faces familiar to classicists – Socrates, Plato, Aristotle, Cicero, Musonius Rufus, Epictetus, Seneca, Quintilian, Plutarch, Lucian – in whose company Paul is comfortably established, not as their superior (as in Chrysostom's version of the *Antike und Christentum* debate),[60] but as their equal, an intellectual who thought through the theological and philosophical issues of his day in well-reasoned, persuasive prose to audiences who may or may not have been up to the level of the dialogue. In the seasoned hands of these scholars Paul stands tall, as though in the first century gallery at the lovely Ny Carlsberg Glyptotek museum in Copenhagen, eye to eye in his rightful place among the great thinkers of antiquity, now willing to continue the liberal dialogue extending to the present about the meaning of beauty, truth, justice, freedom, and the divine. The direct anti-portrait to the work of these scholars would perhaps be the surreal or cubist picture of the confused Paul painted by Heikki Räisänen,[61] though Betz and Malherbe also dispute portraits of Paul in which the apostolic retinue is summed up with the single emblem of an Old Testament scroll, with few traces of a Hellenistic identity.[62]

---

[59] The works of both scholars are far too extensive to list here. Among Hans Dieter Betz's voluminous works setting Paul within his Greco-Roman context, see *Der Apostel Paulus*; *Plutarch's Theological Writings and Early Christian Literature* (SCHNT 3; Leiden: Brill, 1975); *Plutarch's Ethical Writings and Early Christian Literature* (SCHNT 4; Leiden: Brill, 1978); *Galatians: A Commentary on Paul's Letter to the Churches in Galatia* (Hermeneia; Philadelphia: Fortress, 1979); *2 Corinthians 8 and 9: A Commentary on Two Administrative Letters of the Apostle Paul* (Hermeneia; Philadelphia: Fortress, 1985); *Paulinische Studien. Gesammelte Aufsätze III* (Tübingen: J.C.B. Mohr [Paul Siebeck] 1994), and a huge host of articles. Important works by Abraham Malherbe on Paul's Hellenism include *Paul and the Thessalonians: the Philosophical Tradition of Pastoral Care* (Philadelphia: Fortress, 1987); *Paul and the Popular Philosophers* (Minneapolis: Fortress, 1989); "Determinism and Free Will in Paul: The Argument of 1 Corinthians 8 and 9," *Paul in his Hellenistic Context*, ed. Troels Engberg-Pedersen (Minneapolis: Fortress, 1995) 231–55 (a volume which effectively represents this approach to Paul).

[60] For the modern research quest bearing this name, see Hans Dieter Betz, "Antike und Christentum," *RGG*⁴ 1 (1998) 542–46; and on its role throughout the history of New Testament interpretation: *idem*, "Antiquity and Christianity," *JBL* 117 (1998) 3–22, reprinted in his *Antike und Christentum: Gesammelte Aufsätze IV* (Tübingen: J.C.B. Mohr [Paul Siebeck] 1998) 267–90.

[61] *Paul and the Law* (Philadelphia: Fortress, 1986).

[62] Any hint of Hellenism in Paul was explicitly denied earlier in the century by Albert Schweitzer, *Paul and His Interpreters: A Critical History* (trans. W. Montgomery; London: Adam &

Wayne Meeks and his students, and others, have painted Paul in the everyday colors of an ancient traveller and denizen of bustling urban scenes in the first century of the Roman imperium.[63] Their portraits are not solitary head and shoulders paintings, or even full-body individual sculptures, but group montages of Paul set into the context of the Christian communities he founded in the urban landscape of Greece and Asia Minor. Consciously opposed to the types of portraits that set Paul alone in an otherwise empty frame, or on a pedestal, Meeks and others have not focused in their artistry so much on the face of Paul as on the details of his environment, engaging in a lively, earthy, imaginative impressionism that creates plausible and palpable social scenarios from the too-few and too-random pieces of evidence left behind of urban realities. Their Paul is a workaday man, portrayed in his social locations and among his companions, associates and acquaintances, a man at home in the urban scene of the Greek east, a realistic, inventive community organizer of the Christ cult.

The anti-portrait against which another group of contemporary scholars raise their exegetical brushes is the unworldly, apolitical, or downright oppressive Paul, a vision of a man so interested in the heavenly realm he proclaimed that he was either disinterested in or myopically unattuned to social injustice on earth. Most graphically representative of this line of interpretation is Neil Elliott, who sought to "liberate" Paul from the false portrait that has endured in the history of inter-pretation down to the present as "the agent of oppression," an image that has been perniciously propagated by those in power to secure their own gain at the expense of the poor and marginalized.[64] His portrait of the apostle is particularly vivid, and ironically (though unintentionally) echoes some of Chrysostom's images – "Paul

---

Charles Black, 1912), in favor of a single, thick coat of Jewish apocalyptic eschatological paint. While no one today would go quite that far, the Pauls of Sanders and Dunn, in their stress on Paul's Jewish identity, are painted in rather different colors than the more Greco-Roman images of Betz and Malherbe (as was the work of Sanders' teacher, W. D. Davies, *Paul and Rabbinic Judaism: Some Rabbinic Elements in Pauline Theology* [3rd ed.; London: S.P.C.K., 1970]).

[63] The classic book remains Wayne A. Meeks, *The First Urban Christians; The Social World of the Apostle Paul* (New Haven: Yale University Press, 1983). Also important has been the work of Abraham J. Malherbe, Meeks' colleague, in this arena (*Social Aspects of Early Christianity* [2nd, enlarged ed.; Philadelphia: Fortress, 1983]). Under their teaching, social-historical reconstruction of the Pauline churches was a hallmark of the work of a whole generation of Yale students: Hock, *Social Context of Paul's Ministry*; Stanley K. Stowers, *The Diatribe and Paul's Letter to the Romans* (SBLDS 57; Chico: Scholars Press, 1981); idem, "Social Status, Public Speaking and Private Teaching: the Circumstances of Paul's Preaching Activity," *NovT* 26 (1984) 59–79; Alan C. Mitchell, "Rich and Poor in the Courts of Corinth: Litigiousness and Status in 1 Corinthians 6.1–11," *NTS* 39 (1993) 562–86; Martin, *Slavery as Salvation*; idem, *The Corinthian Body* (New Haven: Yale University Press, 1995). But investigations into the social history of early Christianity have not been limited to these; see also, e.g., Gerd Theissen, *The Social Setting of Pauline Christianity: Essays on Corinth* (trans. John H. Schütz; Philadelphia: Fortress, 1982), and J. Paul Sampley, *Pauline Partnership in Christ: Christian Community and Commitment in Light of Roman Law* (Philadelphia: Fortress, 1980).

[64] Neil Elliott, *Liberating Paul: The Justice of God and the Politics of the Apostle* (Maryknoll, NY: Orbis, 1994). Elliott cites several specific moments where this picture of Paul was invoked for evil – South Carolina in 1709, the Massachusetts Bay Colony in 1637, Chełmno, Poland in 1941–45,

is in chains today, a slave of Death"[65] – especially in the way in which he scripts Paul as alive and active in the present. Elliott identifies three jigsaw pieces that make up this nefarious picture of Paul maligned and enslaved to a counterfeit identity: 1. the subordinationist Paul of the pseudepigraphical letters; 2. Paul the "social conservative"; and, 3. "Paul as a theological genius, propounding his own rather idiosyncratic doctrine of salvation in competition with other religions, especially Judaism."[66] Elliott's main method in constructing his own portrait of Paul as champion of the oppressed is to disallow the use of certain graphic materials in portraits of "the real Paul," such as all non-canonical letters and passages deemed (by his reckoning) ungenuine. Oddly enough, this Paul of liberation is the most selective and least flexible portrait of recent years, in that it is based upon a positive reading of a very small number of passages (with Gal 3:28 at the center), and a dismissing treatment of much of the remainder in light of those. In contrast, Antoinette Wire sees Paul as hardly a consistent social liberal; so she deliberately removes him from center stage and puts in his place the Corinthian women prophets whom she reconstructs from bits and pieces of the apostle's own (not usually complimentary) rhetoric about them.[67] This is portraiture as historical about-face.

The portrait of Paul that emerges from the recent cultural anthropological analysis of Bruce Malina and Jerome Neyrey seeks to unmask the way in which most portraits of Paul have been too much mere reflections of their authors. Hence it, too, is formulated against an anti-portrait. The counterfeit they seek to expose is any modernizing image of the apostle that paints him with the attributes charateristic of Western culture: individualism, psychological introspection, and personality development. Their replacement, which they take to be a more "fair and responsible" picture than current models based upon "ethnocentric and anachronistic projections," is intended to be a strange and alien picture for their viewing public of late twentieth century North Americans, for it represents a man who comes from a time and place so disparate from the present context that in viewing his true portrait one should experience "culture shock."[68] Yet their final portrait of Paul is strikingly bland and featureless, since they assume him to be "a quintessential first-century Mediterranean,"[69] by which they mean he exhibits a very stereotypical template of group-embedded human characteristics based upon contemporary cross-cultural models. The result is that their Paul is curiously the most modern of all the portraits, given that its starting point is a current analysis and critique of Western culture, as enshrined now in some sociological theories. Paint-

---

and Guatemala in 1982 – but he attributes this misleading portrait much more universally to "the theological tradition of the last fifteen centuries" (*Liberating Paul*, 22).

[65] Ibid., 21.

[66] Ibid., 21–22.

[67] *Corinthian Women Prophets*, on which see my review essay in *RelSRev* 19 (1993) 308–11.

[68] Malina-Neyrey, *Portraits of Paul*, quotations from pages 12, 13, and 1, respectively.

[69] Ibid., 11.

ing with the broad brush of synchronic sociological theory about modal personalities and collectivist cultures, ironically in the final analysis Malina and Neyrey are
not really able to render much of a likeness of Paul, except in clumsy profile
outline,[70] due to their uncompromising assumption that he was, basically, *not* a
distinct individual.[71]

Chrysostom and the Task of Pauline Interpretation

With late antique and contemporary Pauline portraits before our eyes,[72] we can
appreciate fully the extent to which Pauline interpretation is fundamentally an
artistic exercise in conjuring up and depicting a dead man from his ghostly images
in the ancient text, as projected on a background composed from a selection of
existing sources. All these portraits are based upon a new configuration of the
surviving evidence, set into a particular, chosen, framework.[73] The images they
produce, ekphrastic monuments to real persons in the past with (necessarily) freshly
imagined faces, and verisimilitudinous lines scripted from a single, one-sided report about them, become the *dramatis personae* in the docudrama that is exegesis.
This way of describing the exegetical task does not repudiate the historical goals of
contemporary scholars in their efforts to reconstruct Paul, but instead gives proper
attention to the centrality of imagination in historiography. Yet students of Paul
have long nervously realized that Albert Schweitzer's dictum about historical Jesus
research may apply to them, as well:

> But it was not only each epoch that found its reflection in Jesus; each individual created Him
> in accordance with his own character. There is no historical task which so reveals a man's
> true self as the writing of a Life of Jesus. No vital force comes into the figure unless a man
> breathes into it all the hate or all the love of which he is capable. The stronger the love, or
> the stronger the hate, the more life-like is the figure which is produced.[74]

If we replace Jesus in this quotation with Paul, it is strikingly evident that Schweitzer
has formulated a version of Chrysostom's own hermeneutical claim about the role

---

[70] "... we must admit that we know nothing of his character, personality, idiosyncrasies, likes
and dislikes, and other vast dimensions of his life" (ibid., 217).

[71] I have critiqued their ways of dismissing any evidence of individualism in Paul's letters in
my review in *JR* 78 (1998) 611–13.

[72] I have deliberately refrained from including my own portrait of Paul in the above catalogue
because I do not wish to exceed the parameters of this study; but my writings on Paul are
naturally no less rooted in a portrait of the author than those of my colleagues described above,
and I think reflect an admixture of several of those models.

[73] Hence aspects of such "panegyrical practices," although they normally take place behind
the scenes of contemporary exegesis, are nonetheless not "utterly foreign and currently unthinkable," as Young (*Biblical Exegesis*, 116, quoted in chap. 7, p. 386, put it). But full-blown overt
encomia to Paul are surely not *au courant* in contemporary scholarship.

[74] Albert Schweitzer, *The Quest of the Historical Jesus: A Critical Study of Its Progress from Reimarus
to Wrede* (New York: Macmillan, 1968, original 1906) 4.

of love – and hate – in portraying, and therefore understanding, his apostolic author. The vividness of depiction, as Schweitzer has it, depends upon the level of emotional engagement with the biographical subject, a dictum further confirmed by Chrysostom's oeuvre. Yet Chrysostom's portraiture also illustrates quite effectively that the relationship between author and reader is more complex than Schweitzer's initial "mirror reflection" *topos* might suggest. The process of engagement with the author, Paul, that each Pauline interpreter lives out in his or her lifetime of reading the letters is far more dynamic and intertwined than this suggests, and the fact that it is a relationship that is being formed over time means that there is not just empty space between reader and author (allowing the same image to be refracted without interruption), but a living continual conversation containing misunderstandings, rephrasings, reappraisals, and on-going association with a voice that speaks, whether one comes to love it, hate it, or simply lose interest in it. We see this afresh in the way Chrysostom (and Augustine) addresses Paul in the second person, queries him directly about his meaning, and provides him with new platforms from which to speak. By his example Chrysostom foregrounds a crucial hermeneutical issue – the disposition of the reader for the author, Paul – that goes almost completely unaddressed in contemporary scholarship. It is not only portraits of the author Paul that affect readings – for good or for bad, richness or shallowness – but also the quality of relationship that a reader has with him, as grounded and expressed in those portraits, that plays an inestimably influential role in the interpretive task.

Chrysostom's "love hermeneutics" codifies his claim to understand his author because of an intense ardor for him. Just as friends share all things in common, John claims access to the confidential secrets of his companion. Chrysostom's writings brilliantly evoke the power of love in exegesis and encomium, and they may properly stir contemporary readers to evaluate the quality and level of engagement they have with their author. Nonetheless, however much this romantic sensibility may charm, love hermeneutics cannot be the sole standard of interpretation for Pauline or any other texts, for several reasons. One is that the claim to love the author is a slippery one, given that, as we have so often insisted, to some degree that beloved is one's own construct, so love for the author can be an expression of self-love that, if not tinged with self-criticism, might render interpretation simply an exercise in reaffirmation of the self under a new guise – an exegetical narcissism. Second, love for the author may blind a reader to instances where one should responsibly break the mimetic cycle, rather than endlessly replicate its ethically or theologically flawed perspective. This danger is most graphically illustrated, for instance, in John's virulent anti-Judaizing, on the claim that Paul was not just his model in villification, but his collaborator (see p. 233, n. 147). Third, while Chrysostom wants to claim that love is prerequisite for understanding, in the contemporary context (as in John's) the Pauline letters are not the sole province of anyone, but are public documents available to a range of readers who approach them and their author from a wide variety of perspectives and demeanors.

Chrysostom's love hermeneutics was itself both an expression of his genuine experience in reading and a quite direct bid for authority over alternative readings. Again Schweitzer's insight comes home to roost, for many of Chrysostom's portraits of Paul have been occasioned and indelibly formed by the anti-portraits – some written in hate – against which he fights. Hence portraits of Paul, written in love and in hate, rub off one another in the art-critical horizons of academy, church and world. But the example of John's love hermeneutics also provides us with a fresh way to map the tenor and demeanor of different works of scholarship. While the claim to love the author cannot guarantee the accuracy or adequacy of interpretation, it does offer contemporary Pauline scholarship a new way of looking at its own enterprise – as the record of ongoing conversation between human beings who do not encounter one another in some neutral, depersonalized way. Each Pauline interpreter – whether motivated by love, curiosity, cautious enthusiasm, suspicion, scepticism, or downright hatred – is answerable to the question of why he or she bothers with him in the first place.

But Pauline portraiture and exegesis, either for Chrysostom or for contemporary scholars, is not merely an exercise in projective fantasy about an imaginary figure. Chrysostom the Antiochene, for whom the historical reality of Paul of Tarsus mattered greatly, demonstrates that historiography and imagination need not cancel each other out, especially when the writer is self-conscious about what she or he is doing and for what audience. As students of antiquity have long known, the best historical writing is done by scholars whose imaginations allow them to move from the collection and interpretation of sources to form in their minds realistic and vivid pictures of a world gone by. But that is not the last step of the process, for the portrait gained through that process must, by means of creative adaptation of some existing literary conventions, be displayed in the public arena for delectation and ongoing, living revision. Hence the rhetorical task of the ekphrasist applies no less to contemporary Pauline interpreters than to John. Chrysostom's engagement with Paul in the form of epideictic discourse is a palpable reminder that all exegetical art is packaged in some form, and thereby sets up a relationship with its own audience, within some established expectations and recognizable persuasive strategies. Chrysostom's live pulpit oratory is a different "exegetical product" from most contemporary Pauline scholarship, but many of the same dynamics of rhetorical presentation of the subject and his meaning are shared by the two. Contemporary academic writers on Paul first must seek, no less than John did, to entice their audiences into listening to Paul and attending to his person and ideas, even before they proffer particular interpretations. And these audiences are lured by other media and insistent voices every bit as tempting as the theatre and racetrack of the Antiochenes with which John aggressively competed.

Chrysostom's writings on Paul further demonstrate how Pauline portraitists carry out their work in relation to the vision of the social order held by their community, either in a reinforcing, a critical or a noncommittal way. The role of biblical interpretation in social and ecclesial movements is of course currently a widely contested topic,[75] one that is still largely being managed at the moment by a tacit segregation of tasks and audiences of biblical scholarship among the academy, the church and the "popular press," with often the same people playing different roles on different days of the week. Chrysostom's hermeneutical example speaks to this situation in some interesting ways. At first glance it appears that contemporary academic Pauline scholarship does not engage in what Chrysostom does – exhortations to imitate the Pauline portraits it produces, due to the fact that its predominant genres (commentaries, monographs, journal articles, book reviews) are not recognizably exhortatory forms. But others have argued that, because of Paul's own rhetoric of μίμησις, even if the scholar does not issue the call to imitate the portrait he or she has produced of Paul, the canonical Paul does it anyway. At present the blurry line of demarcation between "ideologically neutral" scholarship and writings self-consciously seeking to mold church or society in a Pauline image is challenged by books such as Elliott's *Liberating Paul*, who promotes his Paul, an image defended on the basis of exegetical and historical arguments, as the basis for liberation praxis on the ground.[76] This leads one to wonder if the genres of commentary and homiletics, completely intermingled in Chrysostom's corpus, *are* utterly distinct in contemporary academic biblical scholarship. Surely, at the very least, all modern scholars of Paul attempt, as did Chrysostom, to persuade their audiences of the importance and relevance of Paul and his ideas for present life. But of course Chrysostom meant to do more than that. Chrysostom's example – the quest to transform late antique society by means of a portrait of Paul the urban ascetic ethical archetype – offers a vision of the exegetical task that will strike some contemporary readers as a dizzyingly hopeful specter of the power of Christian discourse to transform the world, and others as a frightening portent of Christian compulsion to conformity inimical to an age of religious pluralism.[77] What Chrysostom particularly contributes to this (most necessary) current debate is the fact that his studio is open, his portraits are explicitly placed on display. In him we can see behind the Wizard of Oz's curtain to the machine that generates the larger-than-life image of the reconstituted author. In his epideictic art we have the manual on which the machine is built; in his homilies we have the vehicle of production; in his images we can see the imaginative quality of exegetical practice brought to light, as well as its world-creating capacities – for good and for evil.

---

[75] A clarion call to social engagement in biblical scholarship was issued by Elisabeth Schüssler Fiorenza in her presidential address to the Society of Biblical Literature in 1987 ("The Ethics of Biblical Interpretation: Decentering Biblical Scholarship," *JBL* 107 [1988] 3–17), a program she has carried out in abundant scholarship since. Over ten years later the guild remains divided on the question, in many places unaffected by her critique, in others transformed by it.

[76] See my review in *CBQ* 58 (1996) 546–47.

[77] See the concerns expressed by Castelli, *Imitating Paul*, especially 119–36.

Ultimately what is at stake in Pauline portraiture is Pauline authority.[78] Each portrait produced is either laudatory or derogatory, a basis for allegiance or for excoriation of the man and his writings. Although contemporary scholars, even Christian ones, no longer celebrate Paul as the bearer of the triumph of Christianity over its enemies as Chrysostom did, nonetheless Paul is still treated as a metonym for the Christian tradition when it comes to the hotly contested issues of the present – treatment of slaves, women, homosexuals – where what *Paul* thought about each of these topics is considered tantamount to *what the church teaches*.[79] But these authority claims are – or should be – far more complex. Just like Chrysostom, contemporary Pauline scholars inherit in the figure of Paul one whose relationship to the transcendent is ambiguous: often laying claim to continual inspiration, but also freely admitting the limitations of divine assistance in his life, and, even the conferral of divine chastisement. The humanness of Paul expressed in the latter is perhaps what makes him enduringly fascinating for modern readers, even as it was what rendered him so valuable for Chrysostom's catechetical and exhortatory program. But the same Paul of extreme and common human frailty had always at other times to be upheld as a conduit of divine wisdom, grace and power, a dynamic scholars continue to replicate, even as they have learned it from the apostle himself. Even in, or perhaps exactly in, that human weakness, it is argued, Paul's great wisdom and theological brilliance is manifest. As Chrysostom played Paul's sufferings and miracles, lack of education and rhetorical prowess, ordinariness and uniqueness off against one another, contemporary scholars also must imagine their Paul somewhere between these poles. There is a Paul for everyone to be had, or rather carefully constructed here. And each Paul governs certain types of readings of his letters: as rhetorical *tours de force*, as philosophical charters for Christian communities, as oracular pronouncements from one recently back from the third heaven, as ethical enchiridia. But the relationship between persona and authority remains debatable. Is Paul's authority to be found in the sublimity or uniqueness of his thought, the bravery he evinced in the face of

---

[78] See, e.g., the vehement reactions to Heikki Räisänen's image of Paul as inconsistent in *Paul and the Law*, such as C.E.B. Cranfield, "Giving a Dog a Bad Name: A Note on H. Räisänen's *Paul and the Law*," *JSNT* 38 (1990) 77–85.

[79] The literature on each of these three topics is legion. On slavery see Martin, *Slavery as Salvation*; Allen Dwight Callahan, "Paul's Epistle to Philemon: Toward an Alternative *Argumentum*," *HTR* 86 (1993) 357–76; *idem*, "John Chrysostom on Philemon: A Response to Margaret M. Mitchell," *HTR* 88 (1995) 149–56; J. Albert Harrill, *The Manumission of Slaves and Early Christianity* (HUT 32; Tübingen: J.C.B. Mohr [Paul Siebeck], 1995). Paul's treatment of women has rightly brought a torrent of literature, a start on which may be had from the bibliographical appendices in Wire, *Corinthian Women Prophets*, and Anne Jensen, *God's Self-confident Daughters: Early Christianity and the Liberation of Women*, trans. O.C. Dean (Louisville: Westminster/John Knox, 1996). For an entrée into the considerable research into Paul and homosexuality, see now Bernadette Brooten, *Love Between Women: Early Christian Responses to Female Homoeroticism* (Chicago: University of Chicago Press, 1996), and Jeffrey S. Siker, *Homosexuality in the Church: Both Sides of the Debate* (Louisville: Westminster/John Knox, 1994).

untold sufferings, his ascetic prowess, the magnificence of his miracles, or the grandeur of his eventual success? Such judgments are of course reached (or, *de facto*, inherited) by each generation, each religious or other community, though the role of Pauline portraits in the enterprise goes largely unappreciated. All these elements were operative (though tensively) in Chrysostom's Pauline portraits, along with the authority of a recognizably distinct voice and personality that enticed his reader into continuing dialogue.

The Death and Resurrection of the Author

Along with the contributions they make to studies of Christian society and rhetoric in the late fourth century, and to Pauline scholarship down the ages, Chrysostom's portraits of Paul are suggestive resources for the study of hermeneutics generally. In his encomiastic portraits of Paul, I have argued, Chrysostom sought to create "a meaningful relation between the living and the dead."[80] Chrysostom's epithets, encomia and *ekphraseis* of Paul self-consciously sought to effect this nec-romantic intention. Chrysostom himself testified that Paul's own words had that power for him – to raise the specter of the apostolic author, like a φάντασμα, before his very eyes. By this hermeneutical sensibility, and especially the explicit language in which he describes what he intends to do, Chrysostom's is a valuable voice to add to contemporary debates about the relationship between reader, text and author in the circle of interpretation. Roland Barthes' 1968 essay, "La mort de l'auteur"[81] was one pivotal moment amongst New Critical, post-structuralist, deconstructionist and other hermeneutical waves of the past few decades that privileged either the text or the reader over the author as the central locus or entryway to interpretation.[82] These trends have had an impact on biblical scholarship as well, with ahistorical modes of interpretation and reader-response criticism gaining ground in some circles, and historical research largely continuing, though with its historicist wings tacitly clipped. The result is a contemporary methodological scene that can best be described as eclectic and fragmented. Yet even in the midst

---

[80] To borrow the phrase Momigliano applied to the task of the biographer (*Development of Greek Biography*, 104). The applicability of the phrase to encomia proper is justified by Momigliano's argument that the roots of encomium and biography were inseparably intertwined from the fourth-century B.C.E. onwards (ibid., 43–64, 102).

[81] This essay is most easily available in its English translation, "The Death of the Author," by Stephen Heath, *Image, Music, Text: Roland Barthes, Essays Selected and Translated* (New York: Hill and Wang, 1977) 142–48, as also in Seán Burke, *Authorship: From Plato to the Postmodern* (Edinburgh: Edinburgh University Press, 1995) 125–30 (I cite the former pagination).

[82] Barthes famously declared that "the birth of the reader must be at the cost of the death of the author" ("Death of the Author," 148) a sentiment rather at odds with Chrysostom's perspective, in which reading makes the author come alive.

of this (unresolved) ferment, as the survey of Pauline scholarship just conducted shows, the author, Paul, has been alive and well in Pauline studies.

Chrysostom's vivid and creative portraits of Paul, I suggest, constitute a valuable resource for contemporary hermeneutical studies still chewing on many of the issues raised in "the death of the author" debates.[83] In particular, he shows that there is a large space between "biographical positivism"[84] and authorial negation, a spectrum of possible forms of engagement with the author that are less susceptible, perhaps, to the simplistic caricatures of author-centered hermeneutics that led to the declarations of its demise. John himself, though unwavering in his commitment to the historical figure of Paul, nonetheless saw it as his duty to reconstitute and recompose his author time and time again. His Paul was not dead, but alive, both in the spoken words of his letters and in the oratorical resurrections Chrysostom the orator scripted for him.[85] Chrysostom's discourse on Paul participates, in some fascinating ways, in all of the major hermeneutical issues at stake in the late twentieth-century debates about the author which were largely generated by the study of lyric poetry: is a text "a mirror" of the world that the author merely positions, or is it "a lamp" that emanates from and discloses his or her inner life?[86] What is the difference between a critic and an author? What is the relationship between "traditional" and original composition in constructs of "authorship"? How are public and private aspects of the creative process associated with one another? What is the connection between an historical intention (however expressed) and later possible meanings or significances? How have divine inspiration and creative agency been thought to be connected? What are the political implications of authorship and readership? Are author, text and reader "subject" or "object" in relation to one another? How are the dynamics of absence and presence, death and life, at work in texts and reading? What varying models of "authority" does "authorship" invoke? How are literary criticism and theology parallel and intersecting concerns?[87] Chrysostom is so interesting for hermeneutical

---

[83] A most useful survey and critique of this literature may be found in Seán Burke, *The Death and Return of the Author: Criticism and Subjectivity in Barthes, Foucault and Derrida* (Edinburgh: Edinburgh University Press, 1992), and his anthology, *Authorship: From Plato to the Postmodern.*

[84] To use the locution of Burke, *Death and Return*, 14.

[85] Clark makes the exact same connection, but to stress the multiple voices in the text: "Far from proclaiming 'the death of the author,' the Fathers believed that I Corinthians 7 bespoke a plurality of authors, very much 'alive'" (*Reading Renunciation*, 262).

[86] I am citing the famous distinction of M.H. Abrams (*The Mirror and the Lamp: Romantic Theory and the Critical Tradition* [Oxford: Oxford University Press, 1988]). The mirror image of course derives from Plato (*Resp.* 10.595A-608B). Abrams argues that, although there are glimpses in antiquity that literature evokes the inner life of its author (such as Ps-Longinus, *Subl.* 9.2: "sublimity is the true ring of a noble mind" [ὕψος μεγαλοφροσύνης ἀπήχημα], and also in the role of the ἦθος and πάθος of a rhetor in a discourse), it was only in the nineteenth-century German and English Romantics that these timid observations became a literary theory – that rather than a mirror a text is an expression of its author's emotions and personality, a window into his or her soul (Abrams, *The Mirror and the Lamp*, 71–74, 226–62).

[87] For example, it is often remarked that the death of the author and the death of God go

theory precisely because his interpretations of Paul challenge many of the dichoto-
mies that have ruled the debate. He presents a phenomenon that may confound
some of the critical maps: a pre-Romantic with a heightened "Romantic"
sensibility in his engagement with the author.[88] As a figure who breathed the
cultural air o f late antiquity that was imbued with these questions, Chrysostom fills
in the apparent historical gap in critical reflections on the role of the author in the
interpretive task,[89] and undermines arguments that "the author" is a distinctly
modern concept.[90]

To cite just a few examples of how John of Antioch's Pauline portraiture illustrates "the disruptive enigmas of authorship,"[91] we should first note that Chrysostom functions complexly as both reader and author in his Pauline portraiture,
which makes him a dual subject for the exploration of authorial hermeneutics.
Furthermore, John's exalted view of his author, Paul, did not carry along with it a
univocal or uniform picture of his author or his intentions (as high authorial
hermeneutics are supposed to do), but instead proclaimed a much more fluid,
multi-valent inventor, even as he finessed the authority claims by refusing to pit
Paul and his own expressiveness against Christ, who John clearly thought inspired
his utterances. John found ways, by his artistry, to articulate and embody a complex
relationship between his sacred text and its author, and between the private and
public acts of reading and interpretation, that might be usefully brought into the
discussion. Not only an analogue to the "resurrection of the author" in current

---

hand in hand, or that anti-authorial criticism bears analogies to negative theology (see Barthes,
"Death of the Author," 146–47; Burke, *Death and Return*, 22–27).

[88] I share Clark's insistence that patristic authors be brought into these discussions ("Some
contemporary literary critics imagine that such theoretical insights are applicable only to the
poetry and prose written since the late nineteenth century" [*Reading Renunciation*, 372]), and
would want also to argue for the necessary *mutuality* of that conversation (i.e., not only do
modern and postmodern literary critics illuminate patristic texts, but patristic authors are important resources for those hermeneutical studies, as well).

[89] For example, Burke's anthology leapfrogs from Plato to the Middle Ages. His piece on the
Middle Ages (A.J. Minnis, "The Significance of the Medieval Theory of Authorship" in *Authorship*, 23–30), makes claims for significant innovations in the thirteenth century that were already
at work in sophisticated ways almost a millennium earlier (e.g., "But in the thirteenth century, a
new type of exegesis emerged, in which the focus had shifted from the divine *auctor* to the human
auctor of Scripture" [p. 27]).

[90] "The author is a modern figure, a product of our society insofar as, emerging from the
Middle Ages with English empiricism, French rationalism and the personal faith of the Reformation, it discovered the prestige of the individual, of, as it is more nobly put, the 'human person'"
(Barthes, "Death of the Author," 142–43). Burke (*Authorship*, 7) offers as counter-evidence to this
view Minnis' argument (see previous note) for an earlier emergence of the author ("Minnis
provides compelling evidence against the assumption that the author is a relatively modern
category of thought and locates its emergence in the thirteenth-century shift from an allegorical
to a literal interpretation of the Bible"), but this still gives too much away. The ancient material
such as John's homilies can be brought forward to contravene such sweeping claims as these.

[91] The phrase is Burke's (*Authorship*, x).

literary theory from the cemetery to which s/he has been philosophically or aesthetically relegated in the last four decades, Chrysostom's interpretation of Paul in its vigorously author-centered way illustrates that, at least for epistolary texts, a separation of the author from his writings is simply impossible. And, if this is the case in this instance, it constitutes a valuable counter-example that should be addressed by any universalizing statements from the study of lyric poetry that the author is irrelevant to literary criticism at large. Moreover, the explicitly rhetorical purpose and techniques of Chrysostom's hermeneutical praxis raise important questions about the rhetoric of scholarly discourse about literature in general, as ways are sought to publicize more widely for the benefit of others the initially private experience of encounter with text and author in the act of reading. Perhaps most fascinating is the way in which John employs the artistic *topoi* himself hermeneutically, in calling on his audience to be the "authors" of their own lives, in imitation of the literarily and oratorically constructed living archetype, Paul.

Final Images

In the words of Paul's letters, those documents containing the image of his soul, Chrysostom said he heard the voice of a dear friend. The act of reading Paul's letters drew him into a lifelong relationship with the still-living author who met him on the page. But while John's interpretations of Paul begin with an intense interpersonal encounter, they do not remain there. He did not summon Paul from the dead for a private seance, but for public expositions and introductions of his beloved saint to a wider Christian audience who might join their love circle. Graphic portraiture is an inherently public art; verbal portraiture likewise belongs not to private study, but to communal reception. The venue of Chrysostom's Pauline interpretation was not simply the writer's desk, but the orator's pulpit. His Pauline images were composed, most importantly, for the edification and delight of his congregational audiences. Because of its inherently synesthetic dimension, this hermeneutical foundation of Chrysostom's Pauline interpretation itself has been most powerfully expressed in the history of iconographical representations of Chrysostom and Paul. We began our investigation in chapter 2 with the dramatic scene of Paul's nocturnal visits to inspire his foremost interpreter, Chrysostom, as based on the legend preserved by George of Alexandria. That image had been set in the standard author-portrait type, with John in his monastic cell, seated at his slanted writing desk composing one of his homilies on Paul's epistles. But the traditional scene of scribal activity was adapted in this case[92] to portray the

---

[92] Inspiration of the author by a Muse or a figure symbolizing Wisdom is not uncommon in author portraits, either among "pagans" or Christians (see, for instance, the author portrait of the evangelist Mark in the *Rossano Gospels*, fol. 121ʳ, from the sixth-seventh century, and the early sixth-century *Vienna Dioscurides*, fol. 5ᵛ, which has a portrait of the medicinal writer Dioscurides

legendary tale that the dead author, Paul, who had been present in the room both in the text of his letters and in a pictorial icon on the wall, had come to life and stood peering over Chrysostom's shoulder, whispering exegetical advice into his ear. In the doorway can be spied the shadowy figure of Chrysostom's secretary, Proklos, the requisite witness of this extraordinary sign of John's complete accuracy and reliability as the definitive interpreter of the apostle's writings. This embellished image became the standard inspired author portrait of John with Paul throughout the Middle Ages and beyond.[93] In fact it became so familiar that its basic contours could be recognizably enshrined into a single outsized initial Kappa in a manuscript of the *Liturgy of Saint John Chrysostom*, or a medieval *Menologion*.[94]

But despite its familiarity, canny iconographers recognized the missing dimensions in this picture, for it portrays Chrysostom's exegetical art as far too private an affair. Consequently, in later depictions the still-familiar scene of John inspired by his beloved Paul experiences yet another transformation [see Plate 4]: the slanted writing tablet becomes a lectern, the monastic cell a church sanctuary, the sole witness now a host of priests and suppliants. And, most striking of all, the scroll of Chrysostom's homilies now cascades off the front of the pulpit, turning from parchment into a fountain of living water from which a host of clergy and the faithful drink.[95] Some kneel and eagerly lap up the sweet water as it pours forth. Proklos is still in the scene but, since it is no longer a private experience in need of an authenticating witness, he has become a suppliant. And, lest the exclusive attention on Paul overwhelm or lead to theological compromise, the artist has also added a direct Christ-infusion into Chrysostom,[96] the "fount of wisdom" who, with Paul's inspiration, paints his "imperial portraits" in his Pauline homilies,[97] by which the souls of the faithful may come to know Paul, emulate him, and be satisfied.

In a full-scale version of this scene painted in a church in Macedonia in the fourteenth century [see Plate 5, and Appendix 2, no. 10], the traditional image has

---

and an artist inspired by Ἐπίνοια, "Thought" [K. Weitzmann, *Late Antique and Early Christian Book Illumination* (New York: Braziller, 1977), pls. 33 and 17, respectively; see also Weitzmann's comment on the artistic tradition on p. 65]). That this form underlies the scene of Paul inspiring Chrysostom was argued by Sirarpie Der Nersessian, "A Psalter and New Testament Manuscript at Dumbarton Oaks," *Dumbarton Oaks Papers* 19 (1965) 153–83, 178, and Christopher Walter, *Art and Ritual of the Byzantine Church* (London: Variorum, 1982) 102–103.

[93] See Appendix 2.

[94] See Appendix 2, nos. 5 and 6, and Plate 6.

[95] The wonderful image I am here describing is *Milan, Ambrosian A 172 Sup.*, fol. 263ᵛ (for bibliographic details see Appendix 2, no. 9).

[96] Christ is depicted in a heavenly arched box in the upper right hand corner, and from his right hand an illumining spray is directed to John's writing hand. The same function, in abbreviated form, is performed by the tiny disembodied divine inspiring hand in *Jerusalem Σταύρου 109* (see Appendix 2, no. 5).

[97] The very first words of the *Argumentum* to the homily series on Romans are being written by John on the scroll at his desk-become-pulpit (quoted above in chap. 2, p. 37).

become even more complex, mirroring the interpretive task it seeks to capture. Chrysostom sits at his desk with a codex resting upon his knee, in which he is intently writing. Upon the desk, proceeding surreally from the mouth of a snake, is a lectern or copy-stand, upon which a scroll is draped. John receives an instantaneous, double-dose of inspiration for his interpretive efforts: Paul hovers over his shoulder, whispering into his left ear, while a personified wisdom figure suspended from heaven touches his head. Directly from Chrysostom's desk (not the scroll, interestingly) comes a profuse torrent of water, from which a collection of ecclesiastical figures – priests, monks, choristers – draw draughts of water to drink. This is a fine example of what becomes an iconographic type of its own – John Chrysostom as the source of wisdom. What is perhaps most compelling in this extraordinary scene is the message on the scroll John offers to the ecclesiastical assembly gathered at his stream for sustenance. It is the opening words of a Chrysostomic homily[98] on Psalm 50: "Artists imitate nature by their craft …." John's literary message, directed both to the assembly who dip in their jugs to catch a draught from the torrent of his wisdom and to all who view the wall painting, is at once about the art of portraiture and the art of life. It is an interpretive principle quite familiar from our study of John's portraits of Paul:

Artists imitate nature by their craft; and mixing their colors they paint images of visible bodies and make people and animals and trees and wars and battles … Thus also the prophets are artists of virtue and vice. For they paint with speech the sinner, the just, and repentant, the standing, the falling, the raised up, the shaken.[99]

---

[98] The homily is actually spurious, but the fourteenth-century artist would not have known that (hom. in Ps. 50 2.1 [55.565]).

[99] Οἱ ζωγράφοι μιμοῦνται τῇ τέχνῃ τὴν φύσιν, καὶ κεραννύντες τὰ χρώματα, γράφουσι τὰς εἰκόνας τῶν ὁρωμένων σωμάτων, καὶ ποιοῦσιν ἀνθρώπους, καὶ ἄλογα, καὶ δένδρα, καὶ πολέμους, καὶ μάχας … Οὕτω δὴ καὶ οἱ προφῆται ζωγράφοι τινές εἰσιν ἀρετῆς καὶ κακίας. Γράφουσι γὰρ καὶ οὗτοι τῷ λόγῳ τὸν ἁμαρτωλὸν, τὸν δίκαιον, τὸν μετανοοῦντα, τὸν ἑστῶτα, τὸν πίπτοντα, τὸν ἐγειρόμενον, τὸν σαλευόμενον. Having only seen photographs of this wall painting, I have relied upon the transcription of Svetozar Radojčić, "Die Entstehung der Malerei der paläologischen Renaissance," *Jahrbuch der österreichischen byzantinischen Gesellschaft* 7 (1958) 105–23, 116: ΟΙ ΖΩΓΡΑΦΟΙ ΜΙΜΟΥΤΕ ΤΗΝ ΤΕΧΝΙΤΗΝ ΦΥΣΙΝ ΚΑΙ ΚΕΡΑΝΥΝΤΕ. But Radojčić's translation ("O Maler, ahmt die künstlerisch schaffende Natur nach und mildert sie durch Mischung!"), which is also the basis of his proposal that the scene is directed to artists in particular, is not accurate, because he did not recognize that this was a quotation of an existing homily. The text can be identified as hom. in Ps. 50 2.1 [55.565], which begins: Οἱ ζωγράφοι μιμοῦνται τῇ τέχνῃ τὴν φύσιν, καὶ κεραννύντες. As such the scroll quotation contains a declarative sentence about the role of art and discourse, not a vocative exhortation to artists themselves. Hence Radojčić's original interpretation falls afoul both of the Greek syntax and of the identification of the white-hatted figures as choristers, not painters (as Xyngopoulos, "Fount of Wisdom," 10–11, argued in the case of a different image). A. Müsseler's entry, "Johannes Chrysostomus," in the standard *Lexikon der christlichen Ikonographie*, ed. W. Braunfels (Freiburg: Herder, 1974) 7.93–101, 97, replicates Radojčić's problematic interpretation (the earlier report on the full site, by M.N.L. Okunev, did not seek to identify the quotation ["Lesnovo," *L'art byzantin chez les slaves: les balkans* (pt. 1; Orient et byzance 4; Paris: Geunther, 1930) 222–63, 236–37]; nor does Walter, *Art and Ritual*, 114). In a later work (*Lesnovo* [L'ancien art yougoslave; Belgrade: Izdavaćki Zavod, 1971]

Scripture and art, this depiction of John declares, share the same function – the accurate depiction, through the proper "mix" of colors, of the virtuous life, that which is to be imitated. And Paul is the muse who inspires this holy hermeneutic. Thus John's hermeneutical process, from private encounter with the author to public reinstantiation of him, comes to its culmination in a precise corollary to his recipe for the ethical life which is its predominant message – the proper "mix" of colors (i.e., virtues) exemplified by the saints, Paul outstanding among them. The late medieval artist who painted this scene recognized well that "Johannes sei selbst Maler gewesen."[100]

The Byzantine iconographical tradition that preserved and thus packaged Chrysostom for us was responsible, not only for maintaining the artistic types and tropes that conveyed such sublime truths, but also for educating a viewing public in how to receive the images thus produced. One such author was John Euchaïtes, an eleventh-century poet who composed *ekphraseis* of iconographical types in the elegant form of iambic verse. His epigram on the portrait-type of Paul inspiring Chrysostom brings us to the end of our inquiry into Pauline hermeneutics à la Chrysostom:

> Be silent, spectator, and stay a short while,
> lest you disturb the great conversation,
> and deprive the world of words inspired.
> For now Paul comes, coursing on the air,
> bringing them from the third heaven.
> The wonder of the world, the golden mouth,
> moves his hand with Scriptural assistance.
> Emulate, then, the man you see before the doors.[101]
> Marvel with him, and wait with patience.

> Σίγα, θεατά, καὶ βραχὺν μεῖνον χρόνον,
> Μή πως ταράξῃς τὴν καλὴν συνουσίαν,
> Καὶ ζημιώσῃς κόσμον ἐνθέους λόγους.
> Ἐξ οὐρανοῦ γὰρ ἄρτι τούτους τοῦ τρίτου
> Ἥκει κομίζων Παῦλος αἰθεροδρόμος.
> Κινεῖ δὲ χεῖρα πρὸς γραφῆς ὑπουργίαν
> Οἰκουμένης τὸ θαῦμα, τὸ χρυσοῦν στόμα.
> Ζήλου, τὸ λοιπόν, ὃν πρὸ τῶν θυρῶν βλέπεις,
> Τούτῳ τε συνθαύμαζε, καὶ συγκαρτέρει.[102]

---

xi) Radojčič's translation is improved: "Les peintres imitent la nature qui crée en artiste et la délaient," but the scroll saying is still wrongly regarded as John's "conseils aux peintres."

[100] Müsseler, "Johannes Chrysostomus," 97, who argues that there was a later artistic tradition to this effect. The humanist Erasmus was subsequently to describe Chrysostom as a painter (see chap. 4, n. 41). The present study would suggest that perhaps John's own claim to be "painting imperial portraits" (*hom. in Ac.* 30.4 [60.227–28], quoted in chap. 2, n. 82) might be at least partially responsible for this.

[101] Proklos, Chrysostom's secretary, the witness to these continual nightly scenes of conversation.

[102] John Euchaïtes, *in magnum festorum tabulas* 13 [120.1134–35].

Appendix 1

English Translation of *de laudibus sancti Pauli* 1–7

A Prefatory Note to the Translation

What follows is my translation of John Chrysostom's seven homilies *de laudibus sancti Pauli*, representing the exegetical decisions and rhetorical analyses which have been the basis of the arguments in this book pertaining to these orations. I have included this translation so that these works and my argument may be more accessible to a wider readership, and in particular to provide the reader of this book an opportunity to analyze the texts for herself or himself if the Greek text is inaccessible.

I have sought to render Chrysostom's nicely cadenced rhetorical Attic prose with a priority on retaining, as far as possible, the grammatical structure of the original, so that those who follow me can understand how I have unpacked the syntax. But this value has often come into conflict with an equally strong desire informing this translation: to replicate some of the oral nature of these texts. I have sought a mean here between these two values, as best I could.

Among the many other challenges facing a translator of these orations, I would like to single out just a few specific points. One is the rendering of terms, especially favored words, such as προθυμία and προαίρεσις. Both are technical terms of Chrysostom's moralizing; προθυμία refers to "the eager will to act" in an ethical manner. Because this paraphrase is far too cumbersome, I have also used "the will to act" and "willingness." This becomes even more complicated by a second favored term, προαίρεσις, which is literally "free choice," "free will," or "the exercise of free will." In this case, too, sometimes context requires the shorter locution, "will," which therefore overlaps at times with προθυμία. Indeed, Chrysostom himself often knowingly uses the two in tandem. I hope my renderings are consistent enough that the reader can discern which Greek term lies behind these English equivalents (notes supplying lexical data in the relevant analyses in the body of the book will also assist in this) and, perhaps more importantly, that readers will be able to infuse the short-hand term, "will," when they see it, with the element of fervency that is characteristic of προθυμία and that of volition that adheres to προαίρεσις.

Another difficulty in terms of smooth English style is Chrysostom's predilection for beginning independent clauses with causal conjunctions and particles. These often mark significant logical connections in the text, but at other times they are more exclamatory or decorative. The differentiation between the two of necessity has relied upon my judgment of the argumentative context in each case. If I had rendered γάρ as "for" in every one of its two hundred and sixty-five instances in these seven speeches, the English would have been unbearable, and the logic no more decipherable. The reader will find a number of paraphrases to mark causal connections between clauses (although the limitation in English of terms which can mark causality but begin independent clauses has doubled the challenge). The same is true of the adversative conjuctions ἀλλά and δέ. A last stylistic matter concerns Chrysostom's frequent use of correlative clauses of various types. These are very common to Attic prose generally, but especially so in epideictic rhetoric because of its fondness for comparison. But they also get tedious in English after a while ("as much in this case ... so much more so in the other"), so I have in places altered my translation of this construction for the sake of fluidity. On the other hand, I have largely left the repetitious nature of many of the arguments, given that it is a feature of Chrysostom's style, and since I have taken as my charge the translation, but not rewriting, of his speeches!

It is customary style in epideictic comparisons (as elsewhere in these compositions) to limit the use of proper names for both the honoree and any persons brought in for contrast, in favor of the demonstrative pronouns οὗτος and ἐκεῖνος. For the sake of clarity in the translation, however, I have chosen sometimes to employ the appropriate proper names.

Within the translation I use brackets to mark my own clarifying statements; parentheses demarcate John's own side comments. All the Old Testament Scripture references (which are placed in parentheses), for both quotations and deliberate allusions, are to the Septuagint, John's Bible.

This translation is based upon Auguste Piédagnel's critical edition in *Sources chrétienne*, vol. 300. The numbers in brackets reflect the pagination of that volume.

Homily 1

1.1 [112]. One would not be mistaken in calling Paul's soul a meadow of virtues and a spiritual paradise, for he flowered forth in grace so abundantly that he gave proof that the philosophy of his soul was worthy of that grace. For when he became a vessel of election (Acts 9:15) and cleansed himself so thoroughly, the gift of the spirit was plentifully poured into him. And from this source he in turn gave birth to marvelous rivers for us, not like the *[114]* fountain of paradise which generated just four rivers, but many more, flowing out every single day, not irrigating the land, but elevating the souls of people to bear the fruit of virtue. What speech is sufficient to tell of his virtuous deeds? Or what sort of tongue will be able to achieve proper praises for him? For when one soul brings together all the virtues in humanity, and all of them to the highest degree – not only the human virtues, but even those of the angels – how shall we successfully render the magnitude of the praises? Yet for this reason we shall not keep silent, but indeed because of it especially we shall speak. For this is the greatest form of encomium, when the magnitude of the virtuous deeds overwhelmingly wins out over the skill of the speech; and our defeat is more magnificent to us than countless trophies.

1.2 [114]. Now, then, what would make a good starting point for our praises? Where else than from this very initial point – demonstrating that he possessed the virtues of all people at once? For if prophets or patriarchs or just ones or apostles or martyrs displayed some noble quality, he possessed all these things together to a superlative degree that none of them attained, whatever the particular virtue of each.

1.3 [116]. Consider this. Abel offered a sacrifice (Gen 4:4), and for that he was extolled. But if you bring forward for comparison Paul's sacrifice, it is shown to be as superior to Abel's as heaven is to the earth. Now what kind of sacrifice do you wish me to speak of? For there was not just one, because he sacrificed himself every single day, and, indeed, he rendered a still double offering in that, on the one hand, he died every single day (1 Cor 15:31), and on the other, he carried around the dying in his body (2 Cor 4:10). For he continually met with dangers, and was slaughtering himself by his free choice, and put to death his fleshly nature in such a way that he was affected not less than the slaughtered sacrificial victims, but, indeed, much more. For he did not offer a cow or sheep, but it was himself he slaughtered,

twice over, every single day. That is why he so boldly said: "For I am already poured
out as a drink-offering" (2 Tim 4:6), calling his own blood a libation.

1.4 [116]. Yet he was not satisfied with these sacrifices, but when he had conse-
crated himself thoroughly, he offered the whole world, both land and sea, Greek
and barbarian, and in general all the land upon which the sun casts its gaze. Becoming just like a winged creature, he traversed all this land, not simply journeying
through, but pulling up the thorns of sins, and sowing the word of piety, driving out
deception, and bringing in *[118]* the truth, making angels from human beings – or,
rather, transforming human beings from demons into angels. Therefore when after
his many toils and these numerous trophies he was about to depart, in order to
console his disciples he said: "Even if I am poured out as the sacrifice and offering
of your faith, I rejoice and join in rejoicing with all of you. So also you rejoice and
join me in rejoicing" (Phil 2:17–18). What could be the equal of this sacrifice,
which he slew after drawing the sword of the spirit, which he offered on the altar
above the heavens? So Abel was murdered when treacherously attacked by Cain,
and for this has been the more renowned? But I have enumerated for you the
thousands of deaths [of Paul], as many as the days this blessed man lived preaching
the gospel. However, if you wish to learn about how the slaughter of each pro-
ceeded, to the point of the plot involved, Abel fell at the hands of his brother, who
had previously neither been harmed nor benefitted [by him]; but Paul was killed
by the very people whom he was hastening to rescue from countless evils, and for
whose sake he was suffering all that he suffered.

1.5 [118]. But Noah was just, perfect in his generation (Gen 6:9), and the only one
of all who was like that? Yet Paul, too, was the only one of his caliber among all
people. Noah saved only himself with his children; but Paul, when a much more
terrible flood seized the world *[120]*, snatched not just two or three or five relatives,
but the whole world from the midst of the waves when it was about to be drowned
in the sea. He did this not by fastening planks together and making an ark, but by
composing letters to serve as planks. The ark of Paul's letters was not such a type as
to be carried about in a single place, but it reached the very ends of the world, and
from that time until now he brings all people into this ark. For, having prepared his
ark in proportion to the multitude of those to be saved, welcoming people who
were less intelligent than animals, he made them contenders with the powers above,
and with his ark proved victorious over Noah's. For Noah's ark took on board a
raven and sent it out again as a raven (Gen 8:6–7); it received a wolf, yet did not alter
its beastly nature. However, Paul wasn't like this, but, taking on board wolves, he
made them sheep, and taking on hawks and jackdaws, he completely transformed
them into doves, and, casting out all the irrationality and beastliness that belongs to
human nature, in its stead he introduced the gentleness of the spirit. And this ark
remains sailing until now, and has not broken apart. For not even the storm of

wickedness was strong enough to loosen its planks, but instead, sailing above the storm, it put an end to the tempest. And with good reason! For these planks have been glued, not with asphalt and pitch, but with the holy spirit.

1.6 [120]. But everyone marvels at Abraham because when he heard, "Come out from your land and from your kin" (Gen 12:1), he left homeland and house and friends and relatives *[122],* and all he had was the command of God. And we, too, admire him for this. But what could be Paul's equal? He did not leave homeland and house and relatives, but the world itself for Jesus' sake, or rather, heaven itself, and even the heaven above heaven he disdained, and sought only one thing, the love of Jesus. Listen to him showing this and saying, "Neither things present, nor things to come, nor height, nor depth shall be able to separate us from the love of God" (Rom 8:38–39). Did Abraham throw himself into dangers to snatch his nephew away from the barbarians (Gen 14:12–16)? Well, Paul snatched away, not his nephew nor three or five cities, but the whole world, not from barbarians, but from the very hand of the demons, enduring countless dangers every single day, and acquiring a great measure of security for others by his own deaths. But then there is the chief of good deeds and the height of philosophy – the sacrificing of his son. Still, even here we shall find that the primacy belongs to Paul, for he sacrificed not a son, but himself, time and time again, as I have said before.

1.7 [122]. Now, for what might one marvel at Isaac? Well, many other things, but especially his forebearance, because, when digging wells and being driven from his own territory, he did not proceed against his enemies (Gen 26:15–33). Instead, he endured even seeing his wells reburied, and always moved on to another place, not going out to meet his aggressors, but standing out of the way and everywhere withdrawing from his own possessions until he might satisfy their unjust desire *[124].* But Paul, seeing not wells but his own body buried with stones, did not merely withdraw as Isaac did, but contended by going in and leading the people who were hurling stones at him into heaven. For as much as this well was reburied, so much more did it burst out, and spewed forth many rivers for endurance.

1.8 [124]. Well, does Scripture marvel at Jacob, Isaac's son, for his constancy? But what sort of steely soul could demonstrate Paul's endurance? For he served, not two periods of seven years (Gen 29:15–30), but his whole life for the bride of Christ (2 Cor 11:2–3). He was not only burned up by the heat of the day and the frost of the night, but he endured countless blizzards of trials, at one time being whipped (2 Cor 11:24–25; cf. Acts 22:24–25), at another having his body pelted with stones (2 Cor 11:25; Acts 14:19), by turns fighting with beasts (1 Cor 15:32), and sparring with the sea (2 Cor 11:25–26; Acts 27), in perpetual hunger day and night (2 Cor 11:27) and cold (2 Cor 11:27). Everywhere he was leaping over the *[126]* trenches and snatching the sheep out of the throat of the devil.

1.9 [126]. But Joseph was chaste, was he not (Gen 39:7–20)? However, I fear it might be laughable to praise Paul for this virtue, the man who crucified himself to the world, and regarded not only the attractive features of human bodies, but all things, as we do dust and ashes. He was as unmoved by them as a corpse encountering another corpse. So precisely did he lull to sleep the surges of nature, that he never, ever, experienced a single human passion.

1.10 [126]. Are all people amazed at Job? And with good reason. For he was a great athlete, and *[128]* fit for comparison with Paul himself, due to his endurance, his purity of life, his testimony of God, the severity of his battle, and the marvelous victory that ensued from it. However, Paul fought like this continually, not for many months, but many years; not dissolving clods of dirt with his pus (Job 7:5) and sitting on a dunghill (Job 2:8), but continually falling into the spiritual "mouth of the lion" (2 Tim 4:17). Wrestling with countless trials and temptations, he was more solid than any rock. It was not by three or four friends that he was reproached, spit upon, and reviled, either, but by all the disbelieving false brethren.

1.11 [128]. But was Job's hospitality and care for those in need great? We will not dispute that, either. Well, we shall find that his charity falls as far short of Paul as a body differs from a soul. For the actions Job displayed for those maimed in body, Paul performed for those mutilated in soul, setting straight all those who were lame and crippled in reasoning, and clothing the naked and shameless with the cloak of philosophy. Yet even with respect to bodily concerns Paul surpassed Job, to the degree that it is so much better to help those in need when living with them *[130]* in poverty and famine than it is to do so from one's surplus of goods. While the one man's house was opened to everyone who approached it, the other's very soul was expanded for the whole world, and received entire peoples. Therefore he said, "You are not confined in us, but you are confined in your compassion" (2 Cor 6:12). The one, since he had countless herds of sheep and cows, was generous in regard to those in need; but the other, though he owned nothing more than his own body, from that very source supplied those in need, and cried out saying: "These hands served for my needs and those who were with me" (Acts 20:34). By the labor of his body he acquired revenue for the hungry and famished.

1.12 [130]. But did the worms and the wounds produce terrible and unendurable pains for Job (Job 2:9; 7:5)? Even I agree that they did. But if you compare with them the whippings Paul received during so many years, and the perpetual famine, and the nakedness, and the chains, and the prison, and the dangers, and the plots (those arising from his own people, those from outsiders, those from tyrants, those from all the world), and to these things you add the even more bitter torments – I mean, the pains he experienced over those who were stumbling, the care for all his churches, the fire he endured on behalf of those who were scandalized (2 Cor

11:23–29) – you will see how *[132]* the soul that bore these things was more solid than a rock, and won out over iron and steel. And, in fact, the very things Job suffered in his body, Paul suffered in his soul, and the despondency he felt over each person who was scandalized ate away at his soul more cruelly than any worm. This caused him to shed continual fountains of tears, not only during the days, but also the nights (Acts 20:32). He was more keenly torn apart by this pain for each of them than any woman in the throes of labor pains. Hence he said: "My children, for whom I am in labor pains again" (Gal 4:19).

1.13 [132]. At whom might one be amazed after Job? Surely Moses. But Paul surpassed him, too, by a wide margin. For while he possessed other great virtues, also, the chief deed and highest achievement of that holy soul was that he chose to be left out of the book of God for the sake of the salvation of the Jews (Ex 32:32). But whereas Moses chose to die along with the others, Paul chose, not to join with them in death, but for the others to be saved while he was deprived of the boundless glory (Rom 9:3). The one sparred with Pharaoh, the other with the devil, day after day. The one fought on behalf of one nation, the other on behalf of the whole world. And he was dripping, not with sweat, but in place of sweat had blood flowing from every pore, and set straight, not just the civilized world, but also the uninhabited territory; not just Greece, but the barbarian land, as well.

1.14 [134]. Now one could bring in Joshua, and Samuel, and the other prophets, but so we don't make this speech too long, let's move on to the most illustrious of them; for when Paul is seen to be better than these, then no dispute will remain about the others. Who then are the most illustrious? Who else after those we have mentioned, except David, and Elijah and John (the Baptist)? Of these last two, one was the forerunner of the first coming of the Lord, and the other of his second appearance – that is why they share the same title [i.e., "forerunner"] with one another. Then what quality should we choose about David? His humility (2 Kgdms 12:13; Ps 50) and love for God. Who more than David possessed these things, but, still, who isn't inferior to Paul's soul when it comes to performing both of these virtuous deeds? What was so marvelous about Elijah? Is it that he shut up the heavens and brought about a famine (3 Kgdms 17:7–16; 18:1–6), and called down fire (3 Kgdms 18:36–39; 4 Kgdms 1:9–14)? No, I don't think it is for any of these things, but because he was zealous for the Lord, and more vehement than fire. But if you would look at Paul's zeal, you will see that it exceeds Elijah's as much as Elijah outshone the other prophets. What could possibly be equal to those words which he spoke in zeal on behalf of the glory of Lord: "I would wish to be anathema for the sake of my brethren *[136]*, my kin according to the flesh" (Rom 9:3)? Therefore, when heaven and crowns and prizes were set before him, he put it off and delayed, saying, "To remain in the flesh is more necessary for your sakes" (Phil 1:24). For this reason, too, he did not consider the visible creation, nor the spiritual, to be a sufficient object by which to manifest his love and zeal, but he sought another creation, one not even in existence (Rom 8:39), so as to demonstrate what he wished and desired. Now, as for John, did he eat locusts and wild honey (Mk 1:6 and pars.)? But Paul spent his time in the midst of the world just as John did in the desert, though he did not feed on locusts and wild honey, but set an even more frugal table than this, not even having enough food for his daily needs on account of his zeal for the gospel proclamation. But, did John exhibit great boldness toward Herod (Mk 6:17–20 and pars.)? Sure, but Paul stopped up the mouths of thousands of men like Herod, not one or two or three, and, indeed, ones much more cruel than that tyrant.

1.15 [136]. Finally, it remains only to compare him with the angels. So, leaving the earth behind, let's go up to the vaults of the heavens! But let no one accuse our discourse of audacity for this *[138]*. Since, if Scripture called both John and the priests "angel" (Mk 1:2 and pars.; Mal 2:7), then why is it a cause for wonder if we compare the man who is more excellent than all with those celestial powers? What, then, is their greatness? That they obey God with complete precision, which is what David said in admiring them: "Mighty in strength, doing his word" (Ps 102:20). Because nothing about the angels is a match for their obedience, even if they are infinitely incorporeal. For this especially is what makes the angels blessed – that they obey God's commands, that they never transgress. But, indeed, one can see this standard kept with precision also by Paul. For Paul carried out not only God's word, but obeyed both the commands and things beyond the commands, as he shows when he says: "What then is my reward? That by preaching without pay I might set forth the gospel of Christ" (1 Cor 9:18). For what else does the prophet [David] marvel at the angels? "The one who makes his angels winds," he says, "and his ministers a fiery flame" (Ps 103:4). But one can see this, too, in the case of Paul. For he ran through the whole world just as though he were wind and fire, and purified the earth. But hasn't he yet reached heaven? Well, what is truly marvelous is that he was such as this while on the earth, and he vied with the incorporeal powers when clad in a mortal body.

1.16 [140]. Of what magnitude of blame would we not be worthy if, when one man has achieved at once all the virtues in himself, we are not zealous to imitate him in even a tiny way? Therefore, having set these things in our mind, let us free ourselves from this accusation, and let us strive to reach his zeal, so that we might be able to attain the same goods, by the grace and beneficence of our Lord Jesus Christ, to whom be the glory and the power, now and always, forever and ever. Amen.

Homily 2

2.1 [142]. What a human being is, and how great is the noble birthright of our nature, and what degree of virtue this creature is capable of showing – these things were demonstrated more by Paul than all others. And he now stands, as he has from when he first came, with a splendid voice defending the Lord our creator against all those who condemn the way we were fashioned. He exhorts people to virtue, stops up the shameful mouths of the blasphemers, and demonstrates that the gap between angels and humans is not so great, if *[144]* we would wish to be attentive to ourselves. For Paul did not obtain another nature, nor share a different soul, nor inhabit another world, but, having been reared on the same earth, and land, and laws, and customs, he exceeded all human beings who have existed from the time there have been human beings. Now where are those who say, "virtue is difficult, and vice is easy?" For Paul contradicts them when he says, "the present ease of affliction superabundantly effects an eternal weight of glory" (2 Cor 4:17). And if such afflictions as he speaks of are easy, how much more so are the pleasures which come from our own nature.

2.2 [144]. Now what is marvelous about Paul is not only that, in his abundant will to act, he did not experience the sufferings the pursuit of virtue brings, but that he did not even pursue it for the sake of a reward. For we do not endure the sweaty exertions required for virtue even when rewards are set before us; but he, even without prizes, embraced virtue and loved it. He leapt with complete ease over the things supposed to be an obstacle to it, and did not offer as an excuse either weakness of body, or the crisis of circumstances, or the tyranny of nature, or anything else. Although he had been entrusted with a greater object of care than all the generals and kings on the earth, nonetheless he flourished in virtue every single day. And when the dangers to him grew more intense, he acquired fresh will to act, as what he said shows: "forgetting the things behind, and reaching out for the things ahead" (Phil 3:13). When death was expected he invited others to share in this pleasure, saying: "Rejoice and join me in rejoicing" (Phil 2:18) *[146].* When dangers and abuses and all dishonor were at hand, again he leapt for joy, and wrote in his letter to the Corinthians: "Therefore I am contented in weaknesses, in abuses, in persecutions" (2 Cor 12:10).

2.3 [146]. He called these trials "weapons of righteousness" (2 Cor 6:7) to show that out of them the greatest things come to fruition, and that from all directions he was unconquered by his enemies. Everywhere when whipped, insulted, reviled, as though marching in triumphal processions and raising up continual trophies everywhere on earth, he took such pride in it, and acknowledged his gratitude to God, saying, "Thanks be to God who always leads us in triumph" (2 Cor 2:14). He used to pursue the discredit and insult suffered for the gospel more than we do honor; death more than we do life; poverty more than we do wealth; sufferings more than others do relief – and not simply more, but so much more! – and being grieved more than others seek rejoicing, and praying for his enemies more than others pray against them. Paul overturned the order of things, or, rather, it is we who have overturned it, whereas he was the one who kept to the order just as God had legislated it. For all the latter actions [i.e., Paul's] are in accord with nature, whereas the former [i.e., "ours"] are the opposite *[148].* What is the proof of this? Paul, as a human being, ran after these afflictions more than he did those pleasures.

2.4 [148]. For Paul there was only one thing that was fearful and to be avoided – offending God, and nothing else – just as there was no other thing to be desired than to please God. I am not speaking of "nothing" in reference to things here present, either, but even of things to come (Rom 8:38). Don't speak to me of cities and nations and kings and legions and weapons and possessions and provinces and power, for he did not consider these things equal to a cobweb. But lay out instead the things in the heavens, and then you will see his ardent love for Christ. For Paul did not marvel at the dignity of angels or archangels nor any other such thing, in like proportion to his love for Christ. For he had the greatest possession of all in himself – the love of Christ. With this love he considered himself more blessed than all people; apart from it he prayed not even to belong to the dominions and the powers and the principalities (Rom 8:38–39; cf. Col 1:16). With this love he wished more to be among the most lowly of the punished than, apart from it, among the elite and honored.

2.5 [148]. For Paul there was only one form of punishment, to fail to gain this love. This would be Gehenna for him, this would be chastisement, this would be *[150]* evils uncountable, just as also what was enjoyment was to obtain this love. This is life, this is creation, this an angel, this present things, this things to come, this a kingdom, this a promise, this the goods beyond counting. He considered no other perishable earthly reality either grievesome or pleasant. But he was as disdainful of all visible things as of a rotting plant. To him tyrannies and peoples breathing wrath seemed to be gnats. And death, chastisement and punishment were children's playthings to him – except, that is, anytime he endured them for Christ's sake. Then he would embrace them, and so pride himself in his chain as not even Nero did when crowned with the diadem. He inhabited the prison as though heaven itself, and accepted wounds and whippings with more pleasure than those who snatch up contest prizes. He loved the sufferings no less than the prizes, considering the sufferings to be a prize. That is why he even called them "a grace" (Phil 1:29).

2.6 [150]. Consider this. There was a prize – "to die and be with Christ"; but "to remain in the flesh" – this was the competitive struggle (Phil 1:23–24). Nevertheless, Paul chose the latter over the former, and said it was more necessary for him. To be anathema from Christ (Rom 9:3) was a struggle and painful toil – indeed well above struggle and *[152]* toil. Because to be with Christ was a prize. But he chose the one over the other for the sake of Christ. But likewise one might say that all these tribulations endured for Christ's sake were pleasure for Paul. And I, too, say that all the things which cause despondency in us produced great pleasure in him. And why am I speaking of dangers and the other hardships? For Paul was in constant despondency, as he said, "who is weak and I am not weak; who is made to stumble and I do not burn?" (2 Cor 11:29). Besides, one could say that even despondency is pleasurable. For many of those who have lost children, if they give way to lament receive consolation from it, but if prevented, grieve painfully. In the same way, then, Paul, by crying night and day (Acts 20:31) received continual consolation. No one so mourned over his or her own wicked deeds as he did over those of others. For what kind of state do you suppose he should be in when Jews remain unsaved, given that he prayed to be deprived of the heavenly glory so that they might be saved (Rom 9:3)? From this it is clear that their not being saved was much more terrible, for if it were not more terrible, then Paul would not have uttered that prayer. For he chose the easier option, as it were, the one having more consolation. But this was not simply a matter of what he wished, as he even cried out, "because I have grief and pain in my heart" (Rom 9:2).

2.7 [154]. So, then, this man who grieved every single day (so to speak), for the inhabitants of the world, for all in common (both nations and cities), and for each one individually, to what could one possibly compare him? To what sort of iron? To what sort of steel? What might one call that soul? Golden, or steely? For it was more solid than any steel, and more precious than gold and precious stones. It will outdo the former material in malleability, and the latter in costliness. To what then might one compare it? To none of the things which exist; but if gold could become steel, and steel gold, then perhaps in some way his soul would attain its likeness from their combination. But why must I compare it with steel and gold? Place the whole world opposite his soul, and then you will see Paul's soul outweighing it in the balance. If Paul said of those who distinguished themselves in sheepskins and caves in a small part of the world that the world is not worthy of them (Heb 11:37–38), how much more should we say of him that he was worthy of all? Indeed, if the world is not worthy of him, what is worthy? Perhaps heaven? But even this is too small. For if Paul himself *[156]* preferred the love of the Lord to the things in heaven (Rom 8:38–39), how much more will the Lord, who exceeds Paul in goodness as much as goodness surpasses evil, prefer him to countless heavens? For the Lord does not love us in the same way as we love him, but so very much more that it cannot be expressed in words.

2.8 [156]. Now consider what lofty experiences the Lord deemed Paul worthy of, even before the coming resurrection. He snatched him up into paradise, led him into the third heaven, made him a partner in the kind of secrets that no one bearing human nature is lawfully allowed to speak (2 Cor 12:2–4). And with good reason. For while walking on the earth he continually did everything as though he were going about with angels. Although bound up with a mortal body he exhibited the purity of the angels, and even when subject to such great constraints, he made it his fervent ambition to appear in no way inferior to the powers above. For he ran around the world like a bird, and like an incorporeal being disdained sufferings and dangers. He had contempt for earthly things as though he had already attained heaven; he was as continually vigilant as if he were dwelling with the incorporeal powers themselves. Indeed, quite often angels are given charge of different nations, but not a single one of them so managed the nation with which he was entrusted as Paul did the whole world. Now, don't say to me, "Paul was not the one managing these things," for I myself acknowledge this, as well. But just because *[158]* he was not himself the one accomplishing all these things, that doesn't mean Paul should be excluded from the praises these acts deserve, because he had prepared himself in such a way as to be worthy of this abundant grace. Michael was given charge of the nation of the Jews (Dan 10:21; 12:1), but Paul of earth and sea, both civilized and uninhabited territories.

2.9 [158]. Now I am not saying these things to insult the angels (perish the thought!), but to prove that it is possible for one who is a human being to be with the angels and to stand near them. And why were the angels not given charge of the things Paul was? So that you might have no defense for slacking off, nor be able to take refuge in the difference between human and angelic nature for your state of ethical torpor. And besides, the marvel becomes even greater. For how is it not marvelous and incredible that a word which leapt forth from a tongue of clay sent death fleeing, destroyed sin, set straight an incapacitated nature, and made the earth into heaven? Therefore I admire the power of God and for these things I marvel at Paul's will to act, since he received so great a share of grace, due to the fact that he had prepared himself so well.

2.10 [158]. And I urge you not only to marvel at, but also to imitate this archetype of virtue. For in this way *[160]* we shall be able to share in the same crowns as he.

But if you are amazed when you hear that if you perform the same virtuous deeds you will attain the same goods, listen to him saying it: "I have fought the good fight, I have completed the race, I have kept the faith. Finally, the crown of righteousness is reserved for me, which the Lord, the just judge, will give to me on that day. And not only to me, but also to all those who have loved his appearing" (2 Tim 4:7–8). Do you see how he calls all to the same common destiny? Therefore, since the same things lie in store for all, then let us all be zealous to become worthy of these promised goods. And let us look not only at the height and volume of Paul's virtuous deeds, but also at the intensity of the will to act by which he gained such great grace. Let us look also at the kinship of nature which we have with him, for he shared in all the same things with us. And in this way the most difficult actions will seem to us easy and light. Then after toiling for such a short period of time we shall continually wear that undecaying and immortal crown, by the grace and beneficence of our Lord Jesus Christ, to whom be the glory and the power, now and always, and forever and ever. Amen.

Homily 3

3.1 [162]. The blessed Paul, when demonstrating the power of the human will to act, and the fact that we are able to fly to heaven itself, by-passed the angels and archangels and the other powers as examples. Instead, one time he used an appeal to himself alone when commanding them to become imitators of Christ, saying, "Be imitators of me, just as also I am of Christ" (1 Cor 11:1). And at another time, without mentioning himself, he makes them ascend to the example of God himself, saying, "therefore, be imitators of God, as beloved children" (Eph 5:1). Next, in order to show that nothing brings about this imitation so well as living for the common good and looking to the advantage of each, he adds: "Walk in love" (Eph 5:2). For the same reason, after saying "be imitators of me" (1 Cor 11:1), immediately he discusses love (1 Cor 13), thus demonstrating that this is the virtue that makes one especially near to God. The *[164]* other virtues are inferior to it, and all revolve around human beings – for example, the conflict with desire, the war regarding the belly, the battle against avarice, the fight against anger. But loving is something common to us and to God. This is why Christ said, "Pray for those who abuse you, so that you might be like your Father in heaven" (Mt 5:44–45).

3.2 [164]. Therefore, knowing that this is the chief of the virtues, Paul demonstrated it with great precision. For example, no one so loved enemies, no one so benefitted those plotting against him, no one suffered so many things on behalf of those who had grieved him. For he did not look upon the things he was suffering at their hands, but considered the nature they had in common, and to the degree that they became more savage, all the more did he pity their insane behavior. Just as a father is disposed toward a child gripped by brain fever (for the more the sick child abuses himself and violently struggles, the more the father has pity on him and sheds tears on his behalf) so also Paul, discerning the illness of those who were bringing these afflictions on him (because of the abundance of demons they had), was roused to greater solicitation.

3.3 [166]. For instance, hear how gently, how compassionately he speaks to us about them, the very people who whipped him five times, who stoned him, who bound him, who thirsted for his blood, and desired him to be torn apart every single day. "For I testify about them," he says, "that they have zeal for God, but not according to knowledge" (Rom 10:2). And again, when holding back those who were attacking them [i.e., the Jews] he said:"Don't be haughty, but fearful. For if God did not spare the natural branches, neither will he spare you" (Rom 11:20–21). Since Paul saw the Lord's judgment coming out against them, he did what was in his power to do. He cried continually over them, he was in pain, he prevented those who wished to rush out against them, and he made it his fervent ambition to find, from the possible options, at least a shadow of an excuse for them. And since he was not able to persuade them by argument on account of their unyielding and hard nature, he continually took recourse to prayers, saying:"Brothers, my wish and my prayer to God is for salvation on their behalf" (Rom 10:1). He extended to them even favorable hopes, saying, "the gracious gifts and call of God are irrevocable" (Rom 11:29), so that they might not give up completely and perish. All these actions were those of a man full of concern and ardently inflamed on their behalf, as when he says:"the deliverer will come from Zion, and he will banish impieties from Jacob" (Rom 11:26; Is 59:20). And he was very much cut to the heart and bitterly vexed at seeing them perishing. Therefore he used to conceive of many consolations *[168]* for himself for this pain, at one time saying, "the deliverer will come from Zion, and he will banish impieties from Jacob," and at another, "thus also they disbelieved, so that by your mercy they, too, might be shown mercy" (Rom 11:31).

3.4 [168]. Jeremiah does this, too, arguing with force and contending to find some excuse for those who have sinned, once saying:"If our sins weigh against us, act for your own sake" (Jer 14:7), and then again, "the way of a man does not belong to him, nor will someone go out walking and straighten out his path as he goes" (Jer 10:23), and again somewhere else:"Remember that we are dust" (Ps 102:14). For it is customary for those who make an appeal on behalf of sinners, even if they do not have any reasonable argument, to conceive of at least some shadow of an excuse. Even though it is not held to be accurate, nor is it able to draw credibility, nevertheless the excuse gives consolation to those grieving over the perishing. Hence, let us not examine such excuses too precisely, either, but let's take up these statements in the recognition that they belong to a soul in pain who seeks to say something on behalf of those who have sinned.

3.5 [170]. And was Paul like this only to Jews, but not to outsiders? No! He was more gentle than all, toward both his own people and strangers. Accordingly, listen to what he says to Timothy:"a servant of the Lord should not fight, but be gentle to all, skilled in teaching, forbearing, instructing with meekness those set against him, that perhaps God might grant them repentance for knowledge of the truth, and they might sober up from the snare of the devil, where they have been held captive by him to do his will" (2 Tim 2:24–26). Do you wish to see Paul and observe how he spoke to those who had sinned? Listen to what he said when writing to the Corinthians:"I fear lest when I come I might not find you to be as

I wish" (2 Cor 12:20), and a little bit later, "Lest again my God might humble me when I come to you, and I shall mourn over many who have previously sinned and not repented for the licentiousness and impurity that they practiced" (2 Cor 12:21). Even writing to the Galatians he said, "My children, for whom I am in labor pains again, until Christ might be formed in you" (Gal 4:19). And listen to him speaking about [the Corinthian] who had committed the sexual sin, how Paul was pained no less than he, and appealed, saying, "reaffirm love for him" (2 Cor 2:8). And at the time when he cut the man off from the community (1 Cor 5), he did it with many tears. "For," he says, "from much affliction and distress of the heart I wrote to you, not so that you might be grieved, but that you might know the love which I have [172] abundantly for you" (2 Cor 2:4). And again, "I became to the Jews as a Jew, to those under the law as though under the law, to the weak as though weak; I have been all things to the whole lot of them, so that I might save some wholly" (1 Cor 9:20–22). And elsewhere again, "so that I might present every person as perfect in Christ Jesus" (Col 1:28).

3.6 [172]. Do you see the soul that passed over the whole earth? For he expected he could present every human being, and, for his part, he did present them all. For as though he himself had begotten the entire world, thus was he troubled, thus did he run about, thus was he zealous to lead all into the kingdom. He did so by healing, encouraging, promising, praying, supplicating, frightening the demons, driving off the corrupted, through his personal visits, through his letters, through his words, through his deeds, through his disciples, through his own self, picking up the fallen, strengthening those who were standing, raising those lying in the dirt, healing the downtrodden, goading on the slackers, casting threats at his enemies, keeping a sharp eye on his adversaries. Like some noble general, he himself carried baggage, he himself was the armor carrier, himself the shield bearer, himself the man on the flank, himself being all things for the camp.

3.7 [174]. And it was not only in spiritual matters, but also in material ones that he demonstrated great forethought, great zeal. For instance, listen to how he wrote to a whole people about a single woman, saying, "I recommend to you Phoebe, our sister, who is a deacon of the church in Cenchreae, so that you might receive her in the Lord worthily of the saints, and furnish her with whatever she might need from you" (Rom 16:1–2). And again, "Recognize the house of Stephanas … so that you be subjected to the authority of such as these" (1 Cor 16:15–16). And again, "recognize such men" (1 Cor 16:18). Giving assistance in these matters is the distinguishing feature of the tender love the saints exhibited. Thus also Elisha rendered service to the woman who gave him hospitality, not only in spiritual things, but he was zealous to compensate her in material goods, also. That is why he said, "Do you have any message for the king, or for the ruler?" (4 Kgdms 4:13).

3.8 [174]. Why are you surprised if Paul was furnishing letters of recommendation, whereas even when summoning people to come to him he did not consider it beneath his dignity to exert care for their travelling provisions and to set it down *[176]* in a letter? For when he wrote to Titus he said: "Be zealous to send Zenas the lawyer and Apollos on their way fitly equipped, so that they might lack nothing" (Tit 3:13). And if he exerted such zeal in recommending those whom he sent out on a journey, how much more so would he do everything possible if he saw people anywhere in danger. For example, see how he wrote a letter to Philemon, exercising such great zeal on behalf of Onesimus. See how intelligently, how carefully, he writes! Now the man who did not beg off from composing an entire epistle for a single household slave – and at that one who had run away, and absconded with many of his master's belongings – just imagine how grand he was when it came to others. For he considered only one thing to be worthy of shame: overlooking anything necessary for salvation. This is why he was always on the move, and didn't hesitate to expend anything on behalf of those being saved, neither words, nor money, nor body. Surely the man who repeatedly gave himself over to death would all the more not spare his possessions if such were present. And why do I say, "if such were present?" For indeed it is possible to prove that he did not spare even things that were not present. Now don't think this is a riddle, but listen again to him writing to the Corinthians: "with greatest pleasure I shall spend, and I shall be expended on behalf of your souls" (2 Cor 12:15). And as he said in his speech to the Ephesians, "You yourselves know that *[178]* these hands served for my needs and those of the people with me" (Acts 20:34).

3.9 [178]. Paul was so great in love, the chief of the virtues, that he was more fervently ardent than any flame. And just as iron when it lands in fire becomes completely fire, so also Paul, ignited with the fire of love, has become completely love. As though a common father of the whole world, thus he served as a representative of the very human beings he had begotten. But, however, he outdid all fathers in caring for both bodily and spiritual needs, giving everything – money and words and body and soul – on behalf of those he loved. For this reason he called it the fullness of the law (Rom 13:10), the bond of perfection (Col 3:14), the mother of all good things, and the beginning and end of virtue. Hence he also says, "the goal of the promise [sic] is love from a pure heart and a good conscience" (1 Tim 1:5); and again, "For 'you shall not commit adultery,' 'you shall not murder,' and any other commandment is summed up in 'you shall love your neighbor as yourself'" (Rom 13:9).

3.10 [178]. Therefore, since love is the beginning and end and sum total of the virtues, let us zealously imitate Paul in this, because it was from love that he became such as he was. Now don't speak to me of the dead he raised (Acts 20:7–12), nor the lepers he cleansed (Acts 19:11–12) *[180].* God will not demand any of these things from you. Acquire the love of Paul and you will have a completed crown. Who says these things? The very foster-father of love himself, this man who placed love above signs and marvels and countless other things. Since Paul succeeded in love so surpassingly, for this reason he knows precisely its power. He became such as he was from this; nothing made him so worthy as the power of love. Hence he said, "Be zealous for the greater spiritual gifts; and I am showing you a still more superlative way" (1 Cor 12:31), meaning that love is the most excellent and easiest way. So now, let us also continually walk the walk of love, so that we might see Paul – or, rather, Paul's master – and attain the undefiled crowns, by the grace and beneficence of our Lord Jesus Christ, to whom be the glory and the power, now and always, and forever and ever. Amen.

Homily 4

4.1 [182]. The blessed Paul, the one who brought us together today, and illuminated the world, this man was blinded at the time of his call (Acts 9:8–19). But his
blinding has become the enlightenment of the world! For since he saw badly, God
rightly blinded him, so that he might see again usefully. In that one stroke God both
provided Paul a proof of his own power, and prefigured his future in suffering. In
this way God taught him the manner in which the gospel was to be preached: that
it was necessary for Paul to cast off all that was his own, shut his eyes and follow him
everywhere. Hence Paul himself, to disclose this very message, declared: "if anyone
among you thinks he is wise, let him become foolish, so that·he might become
wise" (1 Cor 3:18). In fact, it is not possible to see again rightly if one has not
formerly been well blinded *[184]*, cast off the reasonings that were troubling him,
and turned completely to the faith.

4.2 [184]. But let no one on hearing these things think that this call was a matter
of compulsion, for he was able to return again to the way from which he had come.
Indeed many, after seeing other, greater marvels, turned back again, both in the
New and in the Old Testament – for example, Judas, Nebuchadnezzar, Elymas the
magician, Simon, Ananias and Sapphira, the entire Jewish people. But not Paul. He,
after gazing upon the undefiled light, intensified his course and flew toward
heaven. And if you want to know the reason he was blinded, listen to him saying,
"For you have heard about my behavior then in Judaism, that I was persecuting the
church to the highest degree and trying to lay it waste, and I was advancing in
Judaism above many of the peers in my race, being as I was exceedingly zealous for
my ancestral traditions" (Gal 1:13–14). Since, therefore, Paul was so severe and
unapproachable, he stood in need of a bit that was even more severe, lest, led by the
strength of his will, he might misunderstand what was said. That is why, forestalling
Paul's mania, God first calms the waves of his ferocious wrath by blinding, and then
speaks to him. In this way he demonstrates *[186]* the unapproachability of his
wisdom, and the superiority of his knowledge. God did this so that Paul might
learn who it was he was fighting against – a God whom he could not withstand,
not only in punishments, but even in kindesses. For darkness did not blind Paul, but
the superabundance of light cast him into darkness.

4.3 [186]. But one might say, "Well why in the world didn't this happen at the beginning?" Don't seek an answer to this, nor be so meddlesomely curious about it, but leave the suitable time to the incomprehensibility of God's providence. For even Paul himself does this, saying, "But when God, who set me apart from my mother's womb and called me through his grace, thought it well to reveal his son in me" (Gal 1:15–16). Now indeed when Paul says this, then don't you be any more curious about it. Because that moment, that very moment, was the advantageous one, when stumbling blocks had been thrown from his path. Then from this let us learn that no one ever, not even those who preceded him, nor Paul himself, found Christ on his own, but Christ revealed himself. Hence he said, "You did not choose me, but *[188]* I chose you" (Jn 15:16). Yet why was it that when Paul saw the dead raised by Jesus' name he did not believe? For although he saw a lame man walking (Acts 3:1–10), demons running away (Acts 5:16; 8:7), and paralytics strengthened (Acts 8:7) (for no one who was so curious about the apostles could have been ignorant of these things), Paul bore no fruit from it? Even when Stephen was stoned, and he was present and saw his face, "like the face of an angel" (Acts 6:15), he gained no benefit from that, either. But how could he have gained any benefit from it – because he had not yet been called.

4.4 [188]. Now when you hear these things, don't think that the call was compulsory. God does not compel, but allows people to be masters of their own choices even after the call. For he revealed himself to Jews when it was useful, but they did not wish to receive it, on account of their love for human glory (cf. Jn 12:43). Now what if one of the unbelievers should say, "how do we know that God called Paul from heaven and he was persuaded? Why didn't he call, me, too?" You will say to him: "Do you believe this? Tell me completely, man! Very well, if you do believe, then this is a sufficient sign for you. But if you do not believe that God called from heaven, then how is it you say, 'why didn't he call me, too?' On the other hand, if *[190]* you believe that he called, then this is a sufficient sign for you. So, then, believe, for God calls you from heaven, if you have a right-minded soul. But if you are senseless and twisted, then not even a voice borne to you from above will suffice for salvation."

4.5 [190]. How often did the Jews hear a voice borne from heaven, and they did not believe? How many signs did they see, in both the New and in the Old Testament, and they were not improved? But in the Old Testament, the Jews, after seeing countless wonders, made the golden calf (Ex 32:4), whereas the prostitute of Jericho, who had seen none of these things, showed a marvelous faith in the matter of the spies (Josh 2:1–24). And in the land of the promise, although miracles were taking place, they remained more unperceiving than stones, whereas the Ninevites by just looking at Jonah believed and repented, and drove off the divine wrath (Jonah 3:1–10). And in the New Testament, during the very appearance of Christ, the thief, when seeing him crucified, was reverent toward him (Lk 23:39–43), whereas [the Jews], after seeing him raise the dead, bound and crucified him.

4.6 [190]. But what about incidents nearer to us? Did not fire from the temple, leaping out from the foundations in Jerusalem, attack the *[192]* builders, and thus turn them away from that lawless undertaking? Yet nevertheless, they were not changed, nor did they lay aside their obtuseness. How many other marvels have happened after that one, and from them they have not benefitted at all. For example, there is the thunderbolt that fell down upon the roof of the temple of Apollo. It was the oracle of this very demon who had compelled the then-reigning emperor [Julian] to move the body of the martyr [St. Babylas] that was lying nearby, saying it could not speak as long as it saw the martyr's casket lying nearby (for it was situated in the neighborhood). Again, after this happened, the same emperor's uncle, after desecrating the holy vessels, became worm-eaten and expired (cf. Acts 12:23). And the treasurer of the imperial assets, on account of another lawless act committed by him against the church, split open in the middle and died (cf. Acts 1:18). And, again, the streams in our territory, which are superior *[194]* to rivers in their flow, all at once retreated and fell off when the emperor was polluting the district with sacrifices and libations, although this had never happened to them before. And what might one say about the famine over the whole world that coincided with the emperor in the cities it befell, or the death of the emperor himself in the land of Persia, the trick that occurred before his death, the battalion intercepted in the midst of the barbarians as though with some dragnet or fishing seines, or the marvelous and incredible journey back from there? For when the impious emperor piteously fell, and another, a pious man, succeeded him, all these horrible things immediately came undone. The soliders who had been taken in the midst of the nets and had no way out at all, from any direction, when God finally assented, were set free from the barbarians and returned with complete safety *[196]*. Who would not find these incidents a sufficient inducement to piety?

4.7 [196]. But what about present events, are they not even more marvelous than these? Is not the cross preached, and the world runs toward it? Is not death proclaimed to be a matter of reproach, and all leap to it? Yet, were not countless men crucified? Were not two thieves impaled on crosses with Christ himself? Was it not the case that not many were wise? Not many were powerful (cf. 1 Cor 1:26)? And whose name so triumphed at that time? But why should I speak of the wise and powerful, for were there not glorious emperors? Who has so prevailed over the whole world in a short time? Now don't mention to me the various and assorted heresies, for they all preach the same Christ, even if all do not do it soundly. They all worship that man who was crucified in Palestine under Pontius

Pilate. Don't these events seem to be a clearer proof of his power than that voice borne from heaven? Why did no emperor prevail in the way Christ has triumphed, even when there were countless *[198]* obstacles? For indeed kings battled against it, tyrants drew themselves up for war, and whole peoples rose up against it, but our cause nevertheless was not diminished by these hindrances, but indeed was becoming even more magnificent. From where then, tell me, does such a great power come?

4.8 [198]. "He was a magician," someone says. Well, then, he was the only magician that turned out like this. Surely you have heard that among the Persians and the Indians there have been many magicians, and there are still some even now. But not even their name is known anywhere. "But what about the man from Tyana?" someone says. "That man was a cheat and a charlatan and he was renowned." Where, and when? In a tiny part of the world, and for a short time, then he was quickly snuffed out and perished, leaving behind neither a church nor a people, nor any other such thing. And why do I mention the magicians and charlatans whose lives have been snuffed out? From what power did all the cults of the gods cease, both the Dodona and the *[200]* Claros, and all these wicked workshops fall silent and be muzzled?

4.9 [200]. From what power, then, is it that demons shiver with fear, not only at the man who was crucified, but even at the bones of those slain on his behalf? Why is it that even at hearing the word "cross" they leap away? Surely this deserves derision. For is the cross magnificent and distinguished? No, on the contrary, it is shameful and reproachable, for it belongs to one condemned. Death is the worst of evils, accursed to Jews and abominable to Greeks. From where then comes the demons' great fear of it? Is it not, then, from the power of the one who was crucified? For if they feared the cross in itself, this especially would be unworthy of divine beings. After all, many people were crucified, both before and after Christ, and two along with him. What would happen, then, if someone should say, "in the name of the thief who was crucified," or some other such guy, or another? Will the demon flee? Certainly not, but it will even laugh! But if you add, "Jesus, the Nazarene," they flee as though from a fire. What then could you say? From where did Christ triumph? Was it because *[202]* he was a swindler? But his commands are not of that type, and besides, there have been many swindlers. Because he was a magician? But his doctrines do not bear witness to this. And there has always been a great load of magicians. Because he was a wise man? But there have often been many wise men. Who, then, ever triumphed like this? No one, ever, nor was anyone even the tiniest bit close.

4.10 [202]. From all this it is clear that it was not because he was a magician, nor because he was a swindler, but because he was a reformer of these things, and a divine and unconquerable power – that is why he prevailed over all – and into this tentmaker Christ breathed such a large measure of power, to which the facts themselves testify. Because a man standing in the marketplace, having a trade in skins, became so powerful that he led the entire human race – Romans, Persians, Indians, Scythians, Ethiopians, Sauromatians, Parthians, Medes and Saracenes – singly to the truth; and in less than thirty years at that! From where was it, then, tell me, that the man who hung about the market, and stood in a workshop, and took in hand a knife, himself came to teach and practice such a great philosophy, and persuaded the others, even nations, both cities and countryside *[204]*, despite the fact that he did not demonstrate the power of eloquence, but, to the utter contrary, was unlearned, to the lowest degree of poor learning? As evidence, hear him saying with no shame, "even if I am unskilled in word, I am not in knowledge" (2 Cor 11:6). Nor had he acquired much money, for he himself even says: "until this very hour we hunger and thirst and are buffeted" (1 Cor 4:11). But why should I speak of money, when he often did not even have enough food to meet his basic needs, nor have a garment in which to dress himself? He was not illustrious on account of his vocation, either, as his disciple shows when he says, "he remained with Aquila and Priscilla because they shared the same trade; for they were tentmakers by trade" (Acts 18:3). Neither was he distinguished by great ancestors. For how could he be, having such a trade? Nor was he distinguished by his native country, nor his people. But nevertheless, when he came into *[206]* the public eye, and simply appeared, he threw everything pertaining to his adversaries into confusion, he encompassed all things, and, like a fire falling into stubble and grass, he thus incinerated the demonic powers and changed everything into whatever he wished.

4.11 [206]. And not only is it marvelous that he, being as he was, had such great powers, but also that the majority of those he was instructing were poor, unskilled, uneducated, living in famine, undistinguished folk born of undistinguished stock. Paul himself proclaimed these facts and was not ashamed to mention their poverty, or, rather, even to beg on their behalf. For, he says, "I am going to Jerusalem doing a service for the saints" (Rom 15:25). And again, "on every first day of the week let each of you set aside a measure of your own goods so that there are not collections only when I come" (1 Cor 16:2). And he even commended the fact that the majority of them were from among the unskilled when he wrote to the Corinthians: "Look at your calling, that not many are wise according to the flesh" (1 Cor 1:26). And that they were from undistinguished stock is clear when he says, "not many are of noble birth" (1 Cor 1:26). And they were not only not of noble birth, but were of very low status. For, he says, "God chose the weak things of the world, even things that are nothing, so that he might abolish the things that are something" (1 Cor 1:28). But perhaps though he was unskilled and uneducated, he was in some way a persuasive *[208]* speaker? Not even this, as he himself again proves when he says, "And I came to you, not proclaiming to you the testimony with preeminence of eloquence or wisdom. For I had decided not to know nothing among you except Jesus Christ, and him crucified. And my word and my gospel proclamation were not in persuasive words of wisdom" (1 Cor 2:1–2, 4).

4.12 [208]. But perhaps the message he preached was sufficient to draw disciples? Yet listen to what he says about it: "Since Jews ask for signs and Greeks seek wisdom, but we preach Christ crucified, a stumbling block to Jews and foolishness to Greeks" (1 Cor 1:22). But did he have the benefit of a secure arena to preach in? He couldn't even stop to take a breath because of the dangers then present! For, he says, "I was in weakness and in fear and in great trembling before you" (1 Cor 2:3). And this was the case not only for Paul himself, but his disciples, too, continually suffered the same things, as he says: "Remember the former days, in which, after you were enlightened, you endured a great contest of sufferings *[210]*, sometimes held up for shame with reproaches and afflictions, at other times being partners with those who were suffering in this way. For you even welcomed the seizing of your belongings with joy" (Heb 10:32–34). Again when writing to the Thessalonians he says, "For you yourselves suffered the same things at the hands of your own compatriots as also they did from the Jews, who killed the Lord and their own prophets and persecuted us, and do not please God, but oppose all human beings" (1 Thess 2:14–15). Once again in writing to the Corinthians he says, "The sufferings of Christ abound in you, and, just as you are partners in the sufferings, thus also in the comfort" (2 Cor 1:5, 7). And to the Galatians: "you suffered so many things in vain, if indeed it was in vain" (Gal 3:4).

4.13 [210]. Therefore, when the one preaching is unskilled and poor and undistinguished, and the message preached not alluring, but even scandalous, and the ones hearing it poor and weak and nobodies, and the dangers continuous and unremitting for both teachers and disciples, and the one being proclaimed a victim of crucifixion, what caused it to conquer? Is it not clear that it was some divine and ineffable power? I suppose it is clear to every one. And one can perceive this from a consideration of the opponents, as well. For when you see the opposite qualities to these coming together – wealth, noble birth, greatness of fatherland *[212]*, forcefulness of rhetoric, security, wide-spread cultic service to the gods, and religious novelties routinely snuffed out in an instant – but nonetheless you see these Christians with the opposite background prevailing, what is the cause of this? Tell me! For the same thing happened as if, although the emperor was not able to conquer the barbarians with battalions and weapons and a marshalled army, some poor, naked, and solitary man who did not even have a javelin in his hand nor a garment to wear should come in and accomplish what the others were not strong enough to do with weaponry and armaments.

4.14 [212]. So don't be lacking in sense, but every single day cast your vote and worship the power of the one who was crucified. For if you saw someone making military preparations against cities, building trenches, moving siege machines up to the walls, forging weapons, enlisting soldiers, in possession of an endless supply of money, but not able to seize one city, whereas another man attacks with a naked body, and, using his hands alone, overruns not one and two and twenty cities, but countless numbers throughout the whole world, and takes the men and all others captive, you would not say that this was done by a human power! This is clearly the case even now. For this is why God allowed the thieves to be crucified along with him, and for some deceivers to appear before he did, so that from this comparison the superiority of the truth might be proven even to the most imperceptive of people, and that you might learn that Christ was not one of those, but the difference between him and them is huge and boundless. For nothing *[214]* was powerful enough to obscure his glory, not sharing the same sufferings, nor coinciding in time. For if it were the cross that the demons feared, and not the power of the man who was crucified, then this pair of thieves (Mk 15:27 and pars.) would stop up the mouths of those who say such things. But if it were the difficulty of the times that accomplished everything, then the followers of Theudas and Judas (Acts 5:36–37) furnish a rebuttal, given that they tried the same things as we, with even many other signs, and were killed. As I have said, this is why God allowed these things – to demonstrate his deeds by their superiority. Consequently he allowed false prophets to appear at the time of the prophets, and false apostles at the time of the apostles, so that you might learn that he cannot leave any of his deeds in obscurity.

4.15 [214]. Shall I tell you from another direction about the marvelous and incredible power of the gospel message, and prove to you that Paul was raised up and increased even by those who battled against him? Once some people, fighting against this man, Paul, were preaching this dogma in Rome. Because they wished to provoke Nero, who was fighting with Paul, they took upon themselves the task of preaching the gospel *[216]* so that when the word was kindled and more disciples were made, the wrath of the tyrant would rage hotter, and the beast would become more fierce. Paul himself says this when he wrote to the Philippians, "I want you to know, brothers and sisters, that my circumstances have come out even more for the advancement of the gospel, so that the majority of the brethren, having become exceedingly confident by my chains, dare more fearlessly to speak the word. For some preach Christ on account of jealousy and strife, but others on account of goodwill. Some do it from contention, not uprightly, but supposing they will add more affliction to my chains. But others preach out of love, knowing that I am destined for a defense of the gospel. For what is the point? Only that by every means, whether in pretense or in truth, Christ is proclaimed (Phil 1:12, 14–18). Do you see how many were preaching from contention? But nevertheless, he was triumphing through the deeds of his opponents.

4.16 [216]. Now along with these there were other hindrances. For the old laws were not only no help, but they opposed and fought him. There was also the wickedness and ignorance of the slanderers who said, "they have Christ as their king." They did not know about that awe-inspiring and boundless kingdom above, but *[218]* brought the slanderous accusation against the Christians that they were establishing a tyrannical state in the world. All in public and each one privately fought against them: in public, by saying that the commonwealth is being done away with and the laws are being overthrown; in private, that each house is being torn apart and destroyed. For, indeed, at that time a father did battle against his child, and a son denied his father, and wives their husbands, husbands their wives, daughters their mothers (Mt 10:35–36; Lk 12:53), relatives their relatives, friends their friends. This was a variable and many-sorted war, creeping into the houses, tearing relatives apart, shaking up senates, upsetting law-courts, as the ancestral customs and feasts were destroyed, and the cultic service of demons, which was more coveted by the ancient lawgivers than all other concerns, was overthrown. In addition, the suspicion of tyranny caused them to be persecuted from all directions. And one could not say that these things happened [just] among the Greeks, whereas it was silent among the Jews, but they, too, went even more harshly on the attack. For they used to charge him with the destruction of their commonwealth. As it says, "he does not stop speaking *[220]* words of blasphemy against this holy place and the Law" (Acts 6:13 [sic]; cf. 21:28).

4.17 [220]. But, nevertheless, when the fire was being kindled from all directions, from the houses, from the cities, from the fields, from the desert, from the Greeks, from the Jews, from the rulers, from the subjects, from the relatives, from the land, from the sea, from the emperors, and they were all provoking one another to savagery and attacking more harshly than any beast, this blessed man, leaping into furnaces of such magnitude, standing in the midst of wolves, and pelted from all directions, not only was not overwhelmed, but even led them all to the truth. And let me tell of other, worse battles than these: the war over the false apostles, and, what grieved him most of all, the struggle over the weak among his own people (2 Cor 11:29), given that many believers were being corrupted. However, he was sufficient to overcome even this. From whence and from what sort of power? "Our weapons," he says, "are not fleshly, but powerful for God's sake, for the destruction of fortresses, as we destroy reasonings and every lofty thing raised up against the knowledge of God" (2 Cor 10:4–5). On account of this he was changing and refashioning everything, all at once.

4.18 [220]. And just as when a fire has been kindled, as the thorns become partly consumed by it they yield and give way to the flame *[222]*, and clear the fields, thus also when Paul's tongue spoke and attacked everything more violently than fire, everything yielded and gave way to it – demonic cults, feasts, festivals, ancestral customs, corrupt laws, popular anger, tyrannical threats, plots from his own people, and the malefactions of false apostles. Here is still another comparison: you know how when the sun rises darkness is driven off, beasts keep hidden and lurk in their dens, thieves run away, murderers take refuge in caves, pirates keep away, grave robbers retire, and adulterers, thieves and burglars, seeing that they are about to be put to shame by the sun's illuminating rays, go off somewhere far away and hide themselves. Everything – both land and sea – becomes translucent and radiant, when the sun's rays shine from above upon it all: the oceans, the mountains, the fields, the cities. Well, in the same way, once the gospel had appeared and Paul was scattering its seed everywhere, deception was driven off, and the truth returned. But the smell of burnt offerings, the smoke, cymbals and drums, drunken bouts and orgies, sexual offences, adulteries, and all the other things that are not good to mention (namely, the rites performed in the temples of the idols) were coming to a halt and being spent, melted away as wax is by fire, consumed as chaff by a flame. But the radiant flame of the truth was ascending, beaming and lofty, to heaven itself, raised up by those hindering it, and increased by those obstructing it. No danger was able to hold back its *[224]* momentum and ungovernable force, not the tyranny of ancient habit, nor the power of ancestral customs and laws, nor the fact that the laws of Christian teaching strain belief, nor any other of the things mentioned.

4.19 [224]. In order to learn what a great thing this is, threaten the Greeks – I'm not saying with dangers and deaths and famines, either, but with a small monetary loss – and you will see them change heart instantly. However, this is not the case with us; but when all our people are being massacred and slaughtered, and every-where embattled with various types of combat, our cause has been blossoming all the more. And why should I speak of present day Greeks, those cheap and despi-cable people? Let's bring forward the marvelous Greeks of the past, the ones who were renowned for philosophy – Plato, Diagoras, the Clazomenaean [Anaxagoras] and many other such types – and then you will see the power of the gospel proclamation. For after Socrates' hemlock, some of his disciples went off to Megara, afraid lest they might suffer the same *[226]*, while others were deprived of their native land and freedom, and won over no convert, except one woman. The man from Citium [Zeno], having left his republic behind in writing, thus came to his end. Although at that time there was nothing to impede them, no danger, no lack of training, but indeed they were proficient speakers, and they were rich in posses-sions, and had the fortune to belong to a universally celebrated native land, none-theless, they had no power at all. Such is the case with deception that even when no one troubles it, it falls in ruins; such with the truth that, even when many battle against it, it is promoted.

4.20 [226]. The truth of these matters itself proclaims the twin principle I just enunciated, and there is no need of speeches, nor words, because the world has given voice to it from all directions – cities, fields, land, sea, inhabited and uninhabited territory, mountain ridges. He did not even leave the desert bereft of his benefactions, but filled it especially with the good things he came to bring us from heaven, through Paul's tongue, through the grace put into him. For since he provided a will to action worthy of the gift, grace shined forth profusely, and the mass of achievements we have mentioned here was successfully accomplished through his tongue.

4.21 [228]. Since, therefore, God so honored our race as to consider one man worthy to be the cause of such a proliferation of virtuous deeds, let us emulate him, let us imitate him, let us be zealous to be like him ourselves, and not consider this impossible. For what I have repeatedly said, I shall not stop saying: that the same body was in him as is in us, the same rearing, and the same soul. But his exercise of free will was tremendous, and his will to act magnificent – and this is what made him such as he was. Therefore let no one despair, let no one grow weary. For if you put it in your minds to do so, there is nothing to hinder you from receiving the same grace. For God does not show partiality (Acts 10:34; Rom 2:11). And it was he who formed Paul and he who created you; just as he is Paul's Lord, so also is he yours; just as he proclaimed Paul, thus also he wishes to crown you. Therefore let us submit ourselves and purify ourselves, so that, having received the grace which is so abundant, we might attain the same goods, by the grace and beneficence of our Lord Jesus Christ, to whom be the glory and the power, now and always, forever and ever. Amen.

Homily 5

5.1 [230]. Where now are those who accuse death, and say that this passible and corruptible body is for them an impediment to virtue? Let them listen to Paul's virtuous acts and cease from this wicked slander. For what harm has death caused the human race? What impediment has corruptibility caused to virtue? Consider Paul, and you will see that our being mortal brings us the greatest benefits. For if he were not mortal, then he would not have been able to say, or, rather, would not have been able to demonstrate what he said through his deeds, that, "every single day I die, by the boast about you which I have in Christ Jesus" (1 Cor 15:31). For everywhere we just need a soul and the desire to act, and there will be nothing to hinder our being placed in the front ranks. Was not this man, Paul, mortal? Was he not unskilled? Was he not poor and earning his *[232]* bread from daily labor? Did he not have a body endowed with all the constraints of nature? Then what prevented him from becoming such a man as he was? Nothing. Therefore let no one be disheartened to be poor, let no one be displeased to be unskilled, nor suffer pain for being among the lowest ranks, but only those who have a weakened soul and an enfeebled mind. For this alone is a hindrance to virtue – wickness of soul and weakness of purpose – and apart from this there is no other obstacle. And this is made clear by the example of this blessed man who has now brought us together. For just as these circumstances did him no harm, so also their opposites – rhetorical skill, abundant riches, renowned ancestry, fine reputation, being in a position of power – none of these benefitted the outsiders in the least.

5.2 [232]. Why should I speak of human beings? Indeed, should I confine my speech to the earth when it is possible to speak of the powers above, the dominions, the authorities, and the rulers of this dark age (Eph 6:12)? For how did their possessing so lofty a nature benefit them? Are not all the powers coming to be judged by Paul and those in his likeness? "Don't you know," he says, "that we shall judge angels, much less matters of daily life" (1 Cor 6:3)? Therefore let us not suffer pain for any other reason than wickedness alone, nor rejoice and be made glad for any other reason than virtue alone. If we are zealous for virtue, there is nothing to hinder us from becoming like Paul.

5.3 [234]. For he did not become such as he was from grace alone, but also from his own fervent will. And this is why it was from grace, since it was also from his will. He had both sets of qualities abundantly, the things of God breathed into him, and those he possessed from his own free will. Do you wish to learn about "the things of God"? Demons were frightened by his garments (Acts 19:12). But I don't marvel at this (nor because illnesses fled from Peter's shadow [Acts 5:15]), but I marvel because, before he received divine grace, from the very starting gate and beginnings, he appeared doing such amazing things as the following: without possessing this power, nor having received the laying on of hands, he was so inflamed with zeal for Christ that he roused the entire Jewish populace against himself (Acts 9:19–23). And, seeing that he was in such grave dangers and that the city was blockaded, he was lowered down the wall through a window (Acts 9:25; 2 Cor 11:31–33). Yet after he was lowered down he did not fall into timidity, nor into cowardice and fright, but from the experience he received a greater will to act *[236]*. Paul gave way to the dangers on account of the divine plan, but he gave way to no one when it came to the teaching. Snatching up the cross again, he followed its path (Mk 8:34 and pars.), although he still had close at hand the example of what had happened to Stephen, and he saw Jews breathing murder (Acts 9:1) against him more than the others, and how they desired to taste of his very flesh. Therefore, he neither fell into dangers precipitantly, nor when he fled them did he become in turn more weak. He loved the present life exceedingly because of the gain to be had from it, and just as exceedingly he disdained it, because of the philosophical perspective he gained from this disdain, or [perhaps] because he was in a hurry to go off to Jesus (Phil 1:23).

5.4 [236]. As I always say about him, and never shall stop saying, no one falling into contradictory actions has practiced both so accurately. For example, no one so desired the present life as he, not even those with a passionate love for their lives; no one so disdained it, not even those dying the worst death. This is how pure of desire Paul was: he was not devoted to a single thing in the present life, but always determined his own desire by the will of God *[238]*. At one time he said living was more necessary than communion and conversation with Christ (Phil 1:24), but at another that it was so grievous and burdensome that he groaned and hastened to leave it (2 Cor 5:4; Phil 1:23). He desired only those things that would bring him godly gain, even if they happened to be contradictory to what he had done before. For he was a variable and many-sorted man, not acting hypocritically, of course (God forbid!), but becoming all things that were required for the needs of the gospel and the salvation of humanity. And in doing this he was imitating his own Lord.

5.5 [238]. For God also appeared, even as a human being, when it was necessary for him to appear that way, and in fire once long ago when the time required it.

One time he appeared in the form of a foot-soldier and army man, at another in the image of an old man, now in a cool breeze, then as a traveler, now in the form of a human being, nor did he even beg off from dying. But when I say, "this was necessary," let no one think it was a logical necessity, for it was only so because of his love for humanity. And sometimes God sits on the throne, and other times on the *[240]* Cherubim. He has done all these things with a view to his underlying providential designs. Hence he said through the prophet:"I have multiplied visions, and have been given likenesses by the hands of the prophets" (Hos 12:11).

5.6 [240]. Therefore Paul should not be condemned if, in imitation of his own Lord, at one time he was as a Jew, and at another as one not under the Law; now was keeping the Law, then despising it; at one time was cleaving to the present life, at another condemning it; now was demanding money, then rejecting what was offered; sometimes he was sacrificing and shaving his head, and other times anathematizing those who did such things; once he circumcized, at another time he cast out circumcision. For the deeds were contradictory, but the mind and intention from which they arose were very much in agreement and united with one another. *[242]* He continually sought one thing – the salvation of those hearing his words and seeing his actions. That is why at one time he exalts the Law and at another destroys it. For not only in what he did, but also in what he said, he was variable and many-sorted. However, he did not change his mind, nor become someone else, but he remained the very man that he was, and made use of each of the courses of action I mentioned for the present need. Therefore, don't reproach him for these things, but for them all the more proclaim his praises and crown him.

5.7 [242]. Take the case of a physician. When you see him at one time cauterizing, at another feeding, now using an iron implement, then giving a medicinal remedy, once withholding food and drink, and another time providing the sick their fill of these things, sometimes completely covering up a person with a fever, and at other times ordering him to drink a full cup of cold water, you do not condemn his variability, nor his constant changing. But instead you praise his craft especially when you see that it introduces with confidence treatments which seem contradictory and harmful to us, and guarantees that they are safe. For this is a man who is an expert craftsman. If we accept a physician who does these contradictory things, how much more *[244]* should we proclaim the praises of Paul's soul, which in the same way attends to the sick? For those who are sick in their souls have no less need of concoction and treatment than those who are ill in the body. Indeed, if you should approach them with straightforwardly consistent measures, all the efforts for their salvation will be undone.

5.8 [244]. If human beings do these things, why is it a surprise that God, who is able to do everything, has adopted this principle of healing, and doesn't always deal with us in a straightforward fashion? Since God wished us to be virtuous willingly, and not by compulsion and force, he had need of this approach; not because it was impossible for him (banish the thought!), but because of our weakness. For he is able merely by nodding, or, rather, only wanting it, to make everything just as he wishes. But we, having at one time become our own masters, refuse to obey him in everything. But if he were to draw us along unwillingly, then he would destroy precisely what he gave us – the freedom of control, I mean. Hence, so that this might not happen, God had need of many forms of approach. I have not said these things to you frivolously, but to show the variability and cleverness of the blessed Paul. Therefore, when you see him fleeing dangers *[246]*, marvel the same as when you see him rushing forward to meet them. For just as the latter is proof of bravery, the former is of wisdom. When you see him telling his magnificent exploits, marvel the same as when you see him speaking modestly. For just as the latter shows humility, the former indicates magnanimity of soul. When you see him boasting, marvel the same as when you see him refusing praise. For the latter shows an uninflated character, and the former compassion and love for others. This is because he was doing all these things to administer the salvation of the many.

5.9 [246]. Hence he said, "if we are out of our minds, it is for God; if we are right-minded, it is for you" (2 Cor 5:13). No one else had such compelling reasons for madness, nor was anyone else so pure of boastfulness. Consider this: "Knowledge puffs up" (1 Cor 8:1). We would all say this with him. Yet he had knowledge of a caliber not found in any of the human beings ever born, but nevertheless he did not exalt himself, but spoke modestly even about this. Thus he says, "we know in part, and we prophesy in part" (1 Cor 13:9), and again, "Brothers, I do not yet consider myself to have apprehended it" (Phil 3:13), and, "if any think they know something, not yet do they know anything" (1 Cor 8:2). Or another example: fasting puffs up. This *[248]* is made clear by the Pharisee who says, "I fast twice a week" (Lk 18:12). But Paul, not merely fasting, but even starving, called himself a "miscarriage" (1 Cor 15:8).

5.10 [248]. Why should I speak of fasting and knowledge, when he had so many and such continual moments of converse with God as were shared by none of the prophets or apostles, and nevertheless he used to humble himself for them? Now don't tell me that these experiences were written down [in the letters]. For he hid the majority of them, and didn't tell all, so that he not confer great glory on himself; nor did he keep silent about them all, so as not to open the mouths of the false apostles. For that man did nothing frivolously, but did all in conjunction with a just and reasonable cause. And he pursed contradictory actions with such great wisdom that he has attained the same praises from all directions. Such is my point: it is a great good not to boast about oneself. But the person who does it when the moment requires is more to be praised for speaking than for having remained silent. And if he had not done this, then he would be more worthy of blame than those who offer praise for others, but at the wrong time. For if he had not boasted, then he would have lost and abandoned everything, and advanced the cause of his enemies. Thus he knew how to employ it always in the right circumstance, and how to do this forbidden thing with a right purpose – to confer such benefits that he earns no less esteem for it than he would receive for following what is pre-scribed. Indeed, Paul was more esteemed in the moment of boasting *[250]* than anyone else would be when hiding his good deeds; for no one has done such good deeds in concealing his actions as Paul has done in proclaiming his.

5.11 [250]. And what is still more marvelous is the fact that, not only did he speak out, but he stopped precisely at the point of present need. For he did not employ the practice of boasting immoderately, under the pretext that the circumstance gave him license to do so, but he knew how far one should go. And even this did not satisfy him, but, lest he corrupt the others and make them praise themselves frivolously, he calls himself a fool (2 Cor 12:11). After all, he did this when the need called for it, but the others, seeing him do it, would likely take up the practice by his example, yet do it frivolously and in vain. This is what happens in the case of doctors, as well, for often the physician applies a medicine in a timely fashion, and someone else, by applying it at the wrong time, causes injury and obscures the potency of the medicine.

5.12 [250]. Therefore, lest this happen here too, observe how he corrects himself in advance when he is about to boast, not once or twice, but repeatedly shrinks away from doing it. For, he says, "I wish you would put up with a little foolishness from me" (2 Cor 11:1), and again, "What I speak I do not speak according to the Lord, but as though in foolishness. In whatever respect someone dares to speak in foolishness, I dare, too" (2 Cor 11:17, 21). And even though he had expressed such strong hesitation, he was not satisfied even at that, but when about to embark on encomia again, he hides himself, saying, "I know *[252]* a man," and again, "On behalf of such a man I shall boast, but on behalf of myself I shall not boast." And after all these statements, he says, "I have been a fool, you compelled me" (2 Cor 12:2, 5, 11). Who, therefore, is so foolish and extremely stupid as not to flee from the practice of superfluous boasting, and engage in it only when a timely circum-stance rendered it necessary? How could one not flee it when one sees that saint, even when a severe necessity befell him, hesitate and shrink away from boasting like a horse coming to a precipice and rearing back continually, even though he was destined to administer such important matters?

5.13 [252]. Do you wish me to offer another such proof of his behavior? This is what is marvelous: that he was not satisfied with his own conscience, but also taught us how we should pursue each of these strategies. Not only was he defending himself by taking recourse to the necessity of the times, but he was also teaching the others, so that when the time befell them, they would neither flee from the practice entirely, nor again pursue it at the wrong moment. Indeed through the comments he made it is almost as if he were saying: "It is a great evil to tell something great and marvelous about oneself." And this is the height of craziness *[254]*, beloved, to adorn oneself with encomia when there is no need, as though there were some compelling need. This is not "speaking according to the Lord" (2 Cor 11:17), but instead is a proof of madness, and it nullifies the entire reward of our deeds, after much exertion and labors. For Paul told everyone all these things, and more besides that he begged off from telling, when necessity befell him. But, even more than this, not even when necessity befell him did he continually pour out all his virtuous deeds in public, but he hid the most and the best of them. For, he said, "I shall go on to visions and revelations of the Lord. I fear lest someone might consider me to be above what they see or hear from me" (2 Cor 12:1, 6). He spoke these things to teach us all that not even when there is a necessity should we bring out into the public eye all the good deeds we are conscious of in ourselves, but only what will be useful for the listeners.

5.14 [254]. This was the case also with Samuel. There is nothing unreasonable about bringing to mind that saint, since his encomia serve our benefit, too. That man boasted once, too, and told of his own virtuous deeds. But which ones? Those that were of advantage to his hearers. For he did not prolong his speech with talk of his moderation, or humility, or refusal to bear grudges, but what did he speak about? About what the king at the time [Saul] especially had need to learn – justice and keeping one's hands clean of bribes (1 Kgdms 12:1–5) *[256]*. Also David, when he engaged in boasting, boasted of the things that could set his hearer on the right path. For he did not mention any other virtuous deed [when begging Saul to let him contend with Goliath], but brought forward publicly his defeat of the bear and the lion, and nothing else (1 Kgdms 17:34–37). For to draw out his speech further would have been the act of a vainglorious man and foolish braggadocio, whereas to say the very things which would be necessary for the present need is the part of one who loves humanity and looks to the advantage of the many. Which is precisely what Paul did. For the slanders being brought against him were that he was not a proven apostle, nor did he have any power. Consequently, because of those charges it was a necessity that he go into the matters which especially would prove his dignified position.

5.15 [256]. Do you see how many means he employed to instruct his hearer not to boast frivolously? First, by showing that he did this from necessity. Second, by calling himself a fool, and repeatedly begging off from engaging in it. Third, by not telling everything, but hiding his greater deeds – and this was when there *was* a necessity. Fourth, by assuming another persona and saying "I know a man" (2 Cor 12:2). Fifth, by not publicizing every other virtue, but only that portion for which the present time had special need.

5.16 [256]. But it was not only in boasting that he was like this, but also in insulting. Although it had been forbidden to insult a brother (Mt 5:22), Paul used this practice, too, in such a fitting manner that he is more esteemed for it than are those who speak in praise *[258]*. Notice how for this reason he calls the Galatians stupid, not once, but twice (Gal 3:1,3) and Cretans lazy bellies and wicked beasts (Tit 1:12), and is awarded praise for it. For he gave us a limit and a standard, so that we might not employ too much solicitation with those who are neglectful of God, but practice a more startling form of speech. The proper measure of all things resides in him. Indeed, for this reason Paul is highly esteemed in everything he does and says, in both insulting and praising, abandoning and soliciting, exalting himself and speaking modestly, boasting and lowering himself. And why should you be surprised if insult and reviling receive esteem, when murder and deceit and guile were esteemed in both the Old and the New Testaments?

5.17 [258]. Therefore, now that we have studied all these things accurately, let us marvel at Paul, let us glorify God, and let us deal with him in such a way that also we ourselves might attain the eternal goods, by the grace and beneficence of our Lord Jesus Christ, to whom be the glory and the power, now and always, and forever and ever. Amen.

Homily 6

6.1 [260]. Would you like it, beloved, if today we left behind Paul's great and admirable deeds and instead brought before you the things which some people think provide "a wrestling hold" against him? For we shall see that even these things make him no less illustrious and great than the deeds we usually praise. What, then, is it that provides a wrestling hold? "Well," one says, "he once appeared to be afraid of blows, for he sure looked that way when they held out the straps (Acts 22:25). And not only then, but also once again another time, in the incident of the purple seller, when he gave objections to those who wished to lead him out from the prison (Acts 16:35–40). By these acts he was doing nothing other than securing *[262]* his own safety and insurance against quickly falling into the same difficulties again." Well, now, what should we say against this? That nothing shows him so great and marvelous as these things just mentioned. For instance, although he had a soul of a type that was neither daring nor full of reckless pride, and a body that yielded to blows and trembled before whips, he had disdain for nothing less than all the incorporeal powers which are thought to be so frightening, when the occasion required it. Therefore, when you see him drawn out and frightened, remember those words with which he transcended the heavens, and vied with the angels, saying: "what will separate us from the love of God? Affliction, or misery, or persecution, or famine, or danger, or sword?" (Rom 8:35). Remember those words in which he said all such things are nothing: "for the present ease of our affliction superabundantly effects an eternal weight of glory for us, as we do not look upon the visible things, but upon the invisible" (2 Cor 4:17–18). Add to these things the daily afflictions, the deaths every single day (1 Cor 15:31). Considering all these trials, marvel at Paul, and no longer despair in yourself.

6.2 [264]. The apparent weakness of Paul's nature is itself the greatest proof of his virtue, because, despite the fact that he was not set free from the natural constraints of the many, he was such as he was. Since the extreme number of dangers he faced might provide most people with this false impression, and equally make them suspect that Paul was higher than all human creatures, he was such a man as he was. This is why God allowed him to suffer, so that you might learn that, although one of the many where nature is concerned, with respect to the will to act he was not only above the many, but even one of the angels. This is because, endowed with such a soul and such a body he continually endured countless deaths, and despised the things of the present, the things to come. Hence he uttered those magnificent and to most people incredible words: "I would wish to be anathema from Christ on behalf of my brethren, my kin according to the flesh" (Rom 9:3).

6.3 [264]. For it is possible, if we would only wish it, to win in every contest against nature – if we use the power of our will. None of the things Christ commanded is impossible for human beings. For if we would contribute as large a share of willingness as we have *[266]*, then God would weigh in the balance heavily for us, and thus we shall all become unassailable to all the terrors attacking us. What is truly blameworthy is not fearing blows, but enduring something unworthy of piety because of that fear; hence for the man who remains uncaptured in battle to have been afraid of blows proves him more admirable than the man who did not fear. Indeed, in that case what particularly shines through is his free will, since, while fearing blows is a matter of nature, enduring nothing unseemly on account of that fear is due to the free will correcting the weakness of nature, and proving victorious over that weakness. Neither is being grieved a cause for blame, but saying or doing something not pleasing to God because of grief. Now, if I were saying that Paul were not a human being, then rightly would you bring up to me his deficiencies of nature in an attempt to refute my argument by reference to his nature. But if I am saying – indeed, strongly maintaining – that, on the one hand, he was human and in no way superior to us in regard to nature, but, on the other, that he became better in regard to the exercise of his will, then you are bringing these negative images before me in vain. Or, rather it isn't in vain, but on Paul's very behalf, for by your objections you prove how great he was, given that with such a nature he possessed things that exceed that nature. Not only do you exalt him, but once again you stop up the mouths of those who have lost heart, by not allowing them to take recourse in the superiority of nature as an excuse, but pushing them to the zeal that comes from the proper exercise of free will.

6.4 [268]. "But," he says, "didn't he sometimes fear death, too?" Well, this, too comes from nature. Nevertheless Paul himself, the man who [you say] feared death, also said: "for we, those who are in the tent, groan, weighted down" (2 Cor 5:4); and again, "we ourselves groan inwardly" (Rom 8:23). Do you see how he introduces the power that comes from free will as a counterbalance to natural weakness? Even many martyrs when they were about to be led to their deaths often became pallid and filled with fear and anguish. But this is the very reason that they are especially marvelous, that, although they feared death, they did not flee death, on account of Jesus. Thus also Paul, though fearing death, doesn't beg off even from Gehenna on account of Jesus his beloved; and though trembling at his demise, he desires to pass away (Phil 1:23). And Paul was not the only one who was like this, but the chief of the disciples [Peter], too, although he repeatedly said

[270] he was ready to give his life (Mk 14:31 and pars.; Jn 13:37), had an intense fear of death. Hear what Christ said when speaking to him about this: "when you become old you will extend your hands, and another will tie you with a belt and lead you where you do not wish" (Jn 21:18), thereby describing the deficiency of nature, not of the will.

6.5 [270]. Nature shows her effects even against our will, and it is not possible to prevail over those deficiences, not even when one is vehemently disposed and zealous to do so. However, we do not in the least suffer damage for this, but are all the more to be marveled at, since what sort of blame is there in fearing death? Rather, what sort of praise isn't due to the man who, even as he fears death, endures nothing servile because of the fear? For there is no blame in having a nature with a deficiency, but in being enslaved to those deficiencies. How great and wonderful is the one who corrects the insult arising from nature by the bravery of his will! And *[272]* by this he also shows how great the power of will is, and muzzles those who say, "Why have we not been created good by nature?" What is the difference if this is by nature or by will? To what degree does the latter surpass the former? To the degree that the course of free will brings crowns and an illustrious acclaim.

6.6 [272]. But is what belongs to nature steadfast? Oh, but if you wish to possess a noble will, that is a thing much more solid than what comes of nature. Or do you not see that when the bodies of the martyrs are sliced up by swords, while nature gives way to the sword, the will neither submits to it nor is refuted by it? Now, tell me, didn't you see in Abraham's case (Gen 22:1–18) a will that prevailed over nature when he was commanded to sacrifice his son, and a will manifestly more powerful than nature? Or didn't you see the same thing happen in the case of the three Hebrew children (Dan 3:8–30)? Or haven't you heard the maxim the pagans tell: "from force of habit free will becomes second nature." Yet for my part, I would say it is even "first" nature, just as the arguments I have previously made have demonstrated. Do you see that, if the will is noble and roused to action, it is possible to possess the firmness that comes from nature, too? And, if one chooses and wishes to be good, rather than doing so under compulsion, that one can reap for oneself the fruit of more abundant praise?

6.7 [274]. This especially is virtue, as when he says, "I beat my body black and blue and enslave it" (1 Cor 9:27). I praise him most of all when I see that he performed his virtuous acts not without considerable tiring effort, so that his ease might not be a basis of indolence for those who come along later. And when again he says, "I have been crucified to the world" (Gal 6:14), I crown his will. For it is possible, yes, it is possible, to imitate the force of nature with the precise exercise of free will. If we bring this man, the very portrait statue of virtue, forward for inspection, we shall find that he strove to bring the virtues that were his by free will to the same level of solidity as nature.

6.8 [274]. For when beaten he suffered pain, but he disdained no less the incorporeal powers that do not suffer pain themselves, as one can hear in his words, which cause him to be thought by some as not even sharing our nature. For when he says, "The world has been crucified to me, and I to the world" (Gal 6:14), and again, "no longer do I live, but Christ lives in me" (Gal 2:20), what else can one say except that he had departed from his very body? And what *[276]* does it mean when he says, "a thorn in the flesh was given to me, a messenger of Satan" (2 Cor 12:7)? This statement is nothing other than a demonstration that his pain reached even to his body. With the abundance of his free will he drove the pain off from himself and pushed it away (even though it tried to pass inside him). What does it mean when he says many other things more marvelous than these, and rejoices when whipped, and boasts in his chains? What else could one say than what I have already, that in stating, "I beat my body black and blue and enslave it, and fear lest, having preached to others, I might myself fail to pass the test" (1 Cor 9:27), Paul demonstrates the weakness of his nature, and through these other statements I quoted he shows the nobility of his will?

6.9 [278]. And this is why both sets of things are in place, so that because of those great virtues you might not consider him to be of another nature and lose heart, nor because of these tiny matters condemn that holy soul, but even from the latter to lead yourself to good hopes by casting out despair. For this reason he sets forth again what belongs to the grace of God with great abundance, or, rather, not with abundance, but with gratitude, that you might not consider anything to be his own accomplishment. And he also mentions the things which are due to his will, lest you, by tossing all the credit God's way, should pass your life in slumber and snoring. You will find the measure and standard for all things residing with precision in Paul.

6.10 [278]. "But," he says, "he once cursed the coppersmith, Alexander" (1 Tim 1:20). Why was this? Well, it was not due to anger, but to distress on behalf of the truth. Yet the pain he suffered was not for his own sake, but because Alexander stood in opposition to the gospel proclamation. "For he strongly opposed," Paul said, "not me, but our words" (2 Tim 4:15). Consequently, the curse not only proved Paul's burning love for the truth, but also provided his disciples with consolation, since he said these things because likely all were scandalized when the people giving abuse to the word were not suffering in the least. But, what about the fact that *[280]* Paul sometimes prayed against other people, saying, "if it is just for God to repay with affliction those who are afflicting us" (2 Thess 1:6)? In saying this he was not desiring to inflict punishment on them (God forbid!) but was zealous for the abused to receive consolation. That is why he added, "and rest to the very ones who are being afflicted" (2 Thess 1:7). And when he himself suffers something unpleasant, hear how philosophically he takes it, and how he treats his opponents in return: "reviled, we bless; persecuted, we tolerate it; blasphemed, we offer comfort" (1 Cor 4:12–13). But if you would say that the things he said or did for the others were born of anger, then it is timely for you also to mention how Paul from anger had blinded and insulted Elymas (Acts 13:9–11), and how Peter from anger killed Ananias and Sapphira (Acts 5:1–11). But no one is so stupid and silly as to say such things. Indeed, we find Paul both saying and doing many other things which appear to be coarse, and these things are what demonstrate especially his gentleness. For example, when he hands the sexual malefactor in Corinth over to Satan, he does it from much love and an affectionate heart, as he shows from his second epistle (2 Cor 2:1–11). And when he threatens Jews and says *[282]*, "the wrath has come upon them at last" (1 Thess 2:16), he did not do so because he was full of anger – for indeed you hear him continually praying on their behalf (Rom 10:1) – but wishing to frighten them and bring them to a more sound frame of mind.

6.11 [282]. "But," he says, "he insulted the priest, declaring, 'God is going to smite you, you whitewashed wall'" (Acts 23:3). Now, I know that some people in defense of this say that Paul spoke it by way of prophecy, and I do not condemn those who say it, for indeed this happened, and the priest thus died. On the other hand, if some enemy with a sharper eye contests this, and, taking a more inquisitive look into it, rejoins, "well, if it were prophecy, then why would Paul defend himself saying, 'I did not know that he was the high priest?'" (Acts 23:5), then we would reply that Paul said this in order to instruct and admonish the others to be kindly disposed toward the leaders, just as Christ himself did. For after saying countless things (both speakable and unspeakable) about the scribes and the Pharisees, Jesus declared: "the scribes and the Pharisees sit upon the seat of Moses; therefore, do everything that they tell you to do" (Mt 23:2–3). In the same way here, too, Paul in a single breath both preserved the dignity of the high priesthood, and prophesied what was going to take place.

6.12 [284]. Furthermore, although he did cut off John (Acts 15:37–39), the act was a worthy expression of the foresight he possessed for the gospel. For it is necessary that the person who takes this ministry in hand not be at all sluggish, nor faint-hearted, but brave and vigorous. He must not undertake this excellent occupation unless he were likely in turn to give his life over countless times to death and dangers, just as Christ himself said: "if someone wishes to come after me, let him deny himself, let him take up his cross, and let him follow me" (Mk 8:34 and pars.). The man who is not disposed in this way betrays many others, and does more good if he keeps quiet and remains concerned with himself than if he comes forward into the public eye and receives a burden that exceeds his ability, because in the process he destroys both himself and those entrusted to his care. How is it not absurd if someone who knows nothing about how to pilot a ship or how to battle the waves, even when thousands of people try to force him, chooses not to sit at the rudder, whereas the man who comes to the preaching ministry advances to it simply and haphazardly, and thoughtlessly receives a matter of importance that can cause countless deaths? For neither a pilot, nor the man who fights the beasts, nor the one who chooses the part of the gladiator, nor anyone else *[286]* needs to have a soul so prepared for various forms of death and slaughter as the man who takes up the preaching ministry. This is because the dangers are greater, the antagonists more terrible, and this act of being slaughtered is not for ordinary gains. For the prize in store is heaven, and the punishment for sinners Gehenna, the destruction and salvation of the soul. Not only must the one who takes up the preaching ministry be so prepared, but also the faithful generally, for all are exhorted to take up the cross and follow. Yet, if all, then how much moreso the teachers and pastors, among whom John (who is also called Mark) was once numbered? Therefore he was justly cut off, given that after stationing himself in the front of the line of battle he comported himself extremely unbravely. Hence Paul removed him so that his sluggishness would not hinder the course of their forces.

6.13 [288]. Now, if Luke says, "there was provocation between them" (Acts 15:39), don't consider this a cause for blame. Being provoked to anger is not terrible, but becoming so irrationally and for no just reason, is. As Scripture says, "unjust anger will not be held guiltless" (Sir 1:22) – that is, not simply anger, but *unjust* anger. And again Christ says: "the one who is angry with his brother *in vain*" (Mt 5:22), not simply "is angry." And the prophet says, "be angry, and do not sin" (Ps 4:5). For, if one should not employ the emotion, not even when the occasion calls for it, then it has been placed in us in vain and without reason. But it is not in vain. The creator implanted this passion in us for the correction of sinners, so that it might rouse the elements of sluggishness and resignation in the soul, awaken the sleeping and the slackened. He placed the vigorous emotion of anger in our mind in the same way we add steel to iron, so that we might employ it suitably. For this reason Paul, too, frequently employed this emotion, and, though more loving than those who spoke gently, was provoked to anger, because everything he did was for the sake of the gospel, in coordination with what suited the occasion. For gentleness is not *[290]* a virtue in general, but is when the moment requires it; likewise, if this were not the case, then gentleness would become sluggishness, and anger rash overconfidence.

6.14 [290]. But I have not said all these things in order to defend Paul, for he has no need of our voice. His praise is not from human beings, but from God. But, as I said before, the reason for this discourse is so that we might instruct the hearers to employ all things suitably. For in this way we shall be able to derive profit from all directions, and with great ease sail into the waveless harbor, and attain the undefiled crowns, of which may we all be found worthy, by the grace and beneficence of our Lord Jesus Christ, to whom be the glory and the power, now and always, and forever and ever. Amen.

Homily 7

7.1 *[292]*. When those who bear the imperial standards enter into the cities, with a trumpet sounding before them and many soliders leading the way, the whole populace customarily runs out at once, both to hear the sound and to see the standard carried aloft and the bravery of its bearer. Therefore, since today Paul, too, makes an entrance, not into a city, but into the world, let us all run out together. For he also bears a standard, not of the king here below, but the cross of the Christ above, and his advance troops are not human, but angels. He does so both for the honor *[294]* of what is borne, and for the security of the one carrying it. For if angels are given as guardians by the Lord of all creation to the people who manage just their own lives and do nothing for the common good – as also Jacob said, "the angel has protected me since my youth" (Gen 48:15–16) – then how much more do the powers above accompany those who have had the world put in their hands, and bear such a great weight of gifts? Now those whom the outsiders deem worthy of this honorable post wear fine garments and an ornamental gold necklace, and are magnificently arrayed all over. But Paul, on the contrary, wearing a chain instead of gold, carries the cross. He is persecuted; he is whipped and famished.

7.2 *[294]*. But do not be sad at this, beloved. For indeed the latter's raiment was far superior and more magnificent than the former's – and he was a friend of God! That is why he did not grow weary in the bearing. For the truly amazing thing is that with bonds and whippings he was more magnificent than those who possess the purple robe and the diadem. Now, that *[296]* he was more magnificent – my words are no boast – his own garments show. For if you put thousands of diadems and many purple robes upon a man sick with fever, you will not be able to reduce the flame of the fever even a little bit. But Paul's handkerchiefs (Acts 19:12), when placed on the bodies of the sick, set every illness to flight, and for good reason. For if thieves, upon seeing the imperial standard, do not dare to enter, but run away without a backward glance, how much more do illnesses and demons flee when they see the standard Paul bears. And he bore it, not so that he might carry it alone, but so that he might make all people to be such as himself, and might teach them to carry it. That is why he said: "Be imitators of me, just as you have us as an example" (Phil 3:17), and again, "What you heard and saw in me, do these things" (Phil 4:9). And yet again, "It was granted to us, not only to believe in him, but also to suffer on his behalf" (Phil 1:29). For whereas the dignified positions of the present life appear greater when they devolve upon a single person only, it is the opposite with spiritual ones. With those, the position of honor shines especially when one has many companions in the preeminent post, and when the one *[298]* who shares it is not a lone individual, but has many enjoying the same dignities. Hence you see that all are standard-bearers, and each one bears Christ's name before nations and kings. But Paul carried it even before Gehenna and eternal chastisement (Rom 9:3), though he didn't command this, because those [he was speaking to] were not able to bear it.

7.3 [298]. Do you see what great virtue our nature is capable of? How nothing is more honorable than a human being, even if he or she remains mortal? For what could you tell me is greater than this man, Paul? What is his equal? Of how many angels and archangels is the man who said this thing [Rom 9:3] not worthy? For the one who in a finite and mortal body gave up everything that he owned for Christ, and, more than that, things he didn't own – for he gave up even the things present and things to come, and height and depth and another creation (Rom 8:38–39) – if this man had been in a bodiless nature, what would he not have said? What would he not have done? For I admire the angels, too, for the reason that they were deemed worthy of such great honor, not due to the fact that they happened to be bodiless. Since, even the devil was bodiless and invisible, but nevertheless he was more miserable than all because he offended the God who had created him. Consequently we say that human beings are miserable, not when we see that they are clothed in flesh *[300]*, but when we see them not using that flesh properly. Since also Paul was clothed in flesh. From what source, therefore, was he such as he was? Both from his own nature and from God; and this is the reason it was from God, since it was from his own nature. For God does not show partiality (Acts 10:34; cf. Rom 2:11). Now if you say, "How is it possible to imitate such people?" listen to what he says: "Be imitators of me, as also I am of Christ" (1 Cor 11:1). Paul has become the imitator of Christ, and you cannot even imitate the fellow slave? He emulated the Lord, and you cannot even emulate the man who was a slave like yourself? What sort of excuse will you have?

7.4 [300]. "And how did he imitate him?" someone says. Well, look at how this was the case from the outset and from his very beginnings as a Christian. Because *[302]* he came up from the divine waters of baptism with such great fire that he did not even wait for a teacher. He did not wait for Peter, nor did he go to James, nor to anyone else (Gal 1:17), but, raised up by his eager will to act, he so ignited the city [of Damascus] that a terrible war was kindled against him. Even when he was a Jew he used to do things beyond his station, binding, leading, confiscating property (cf. Acts 9:1–2). This is just like Moses who, although no one had appointed him, prevented the barbarians' injustice against his compatriots. These actions are proof of a noble soul and a free intent, not a soul that would tolerate the endurance of evil acts from others in silence just because no one had appointed him to rectify it. But by later appointing Moses, God demonstrated that he had justly hastened to the leadership, which is what God has done also in the case of Paul. For God showed that Paul had done well by engaging in the word and teaching at that moment, and quickly led him to the dignified status of the company of teachers.

7.5 [304]. Now if they had been hastening to do these things for the sake of honor and preeminence, then they would with reason be accused of playing court to them. But since they loved dangers, and were drawn to forms of death so that they might save all the others, who is so miserable as to bring an accusation against such willingness? For that they did these things because they were passionate for the salvation of the lost, even God's resolve shows, as does the destruction of those who were incited by this passion, but for an evil intent. In the past others, too, hastened to rule and preeminence, but all died – some were burned up (Judg 9:49), some were swallowed up in an earthquake (Num 16:31–32). This was because they did not do it for the sake of leadership, but on account of love for preeminence. Also King Uzziah hastened to act (in burning incense in the temple), but he became a leper (2 Chr 26:16–21). And Simon, too, acted in haste, but he was condemned, and met with the worst dangers (Acts 8:18–24). Paul acted in haste as well, yet he was crowned, not with priesthood and honor, but with service and labors and dangers. And because it was from great zeal and will to act *[306]* that he hastened out, therefore his praise is proclaimed and [it is clear that] he was magnificent from the beginning.

7.6 [306]. For just as the appointed leader, if he does not discharge his task properly, is worthy of a greater punishment, so even if one is not appointed but manages the job suitably (and I am not speaking of the duties of the priesthood, but those of the oversight of the many), he is worthy of all reward. That is why Paul, this man more fervent than fire, could not wait quietly for a single day, but at once rose up from the holy font of the baptismal waters, kindled a great flame in himself, and was not even conscious of dangers – not the ridicule and shame from Jews, not being held in disbelief by them, nor any other of such things. But, receiving another pair of eyes, the eyes of love, and another mind, he rushed in with great force like a raging torrent, dragging along all the viewpoints of the Jews, and demonstrating through the Scriptures that Jesus is the Christ (Acts 9:22). Although he did not yet have many spiritual gifts of grace, nor was he yet found worthy of such a great endowment of the spirit, nonetheless he was immediately inflamed, and performed all his deeds with a death-dealing soul. He did everything as though defending himself for the time that had passed, and, throwing himself into the part of the battle most filled with dangers and fears, he engaged himself in his toil.

7.7 [308]. Despite the fact that he was so daring and impetuous and breathing fire, yet again he was obedient and docile toward those who gave him instructions, so that the abundant force of his ardent will did not bring him into conflict with them. For when they approached him at the time that he was boiling and raging, and said that he should go off to Tarsus and Caesarea, he did not contradict them (Acts 9:30). They said it was necessary for him to be lowered through the wall, and he put up with it (Acts 9:23–25; 2 Cor 11:32–33). They advised him to be shaved, and he did not oppose them (Acts 21:23–25). They said not to enter into the theater, and he yielded to them (Acts 19:29–30). Thus he held a common advantage with the other believers – for peace, for concord – and everywhere he preserved himself for the proclamation of the gospel.

7.8 [308]. Consequently, when you hear that he sent his nephew to the chiliarch (Acts 23:16–18), wishing to extrapolate himself from the dangers, and when he calls upon Caesar (Acts 25:10–11) and *[310]* hastens to Rome, don't think these words betray cowardice. For the man who groaned because he remained in this life (Rom 8:23; 2 Cor 5:4), how would he not choose to be with Christ (Phil 1:22)? And the one who had contempt for the heavens and disdained the angels on account of Christ (Rom 8:38–39), how could he be desirous of present realities? Then why was he doing this? So that he might continue to proclaim the gospel, and depart this life with many others who had received their crowns. For he was afraid lest he might depart from here a man poor and impoverished when it came to the salvation of the many. This is the reason he said: "to remain in the flesh is more necessary for your sakes" (Phil 1:24).

7.9 [310]. Consequently [he called upon Caesar], because he saw that the tribunal was going to impose a positive verdict in his case (as Agrippa said to Festus, "this man could have been released, if he had not called upon Caesar" [Acts 26:32]). Then, bound and led away with innumerable other prisoners who had done innumerable terrible things, he was not ashamed to share the bonds with them, but he even looked out for all his sailing companions (although he was fully confident on his own behalf, and knew that he was safe). And so, he was conducted in bonds over so vast a sea, and went rejoicing, as though sent forth to take a most important official assignment. And, indeed, it was no small task that was awaiting him – setting straight the city of Rome. Nevertheless, he did not *[312]* treat those in the boat with contempt, but he brought them to order by telling them the vision that had appeared to him, from which they learned that all those who were sailing with Paul were going to be saved on his account (Acts 27:22–25). And he was doing this, not to exalt himself, but to render them docile to himself. This is why God allowed the sea to be raised up in a storm, so that through all circumstances, both in disobedience and obedience, Paul's grace might be demonstrated. For when he advised them not to put out to sea (Acts 27:9–11, 21) and they disobeyed, a hazard of the worst proportions ensued. Yet he was not burdensome, but again he looked out for them as a father would for his children, and did everything so that not one would be lost. And when he set foot in Rome, even there, how gently did he speak! How freely did he stop the mouths of the unconvinced (Acts 28:25–31)? Nor did he stop there, but he even ran off from Rome to Spain (Rom 15:24).

7.10 [312]. Paul was even more confident when faced with dangers, and from them he became even more daring – not only he himself, but also his disciples because of him. For just as they would surely have slackened up if they had seen him giving in and becoming more timid, so also when they saw him becoming more brave and when insulted going even more on the attack *[314]*, they preached the gospel with great boldness. Showing this he said: "as the majority of the brothers, having gained confidence from my bonds, dared all the more to speak the word without fear" (Phil 1:14). Because, when the general is noble, not only when slaying or killing, but even when wounded, he makes those commanded by him more confident, even more so when he is wounded than when wounding others. For when they see their general damp with blood and carrying about his wounded body, and not even thus giving way to his enemies, but standing nobly, shaking his spear, attacking his enemies, and not giving in to his miseries, they, too, draw themselves up for battle with a more ardent will to act. And this is precisely what happened in Paul's case. For upon seeing him bound and yet preaching in prison, scourged and yet subduing the scourgers, they received a greater share of boldness. To show this, he did not simply say, "having gained confidence," but adds: "daring all the more to speak the word without fear" (Phil 1:14). That is to say, "the brothers were more boldy outspoken now than when I had been freed." Then he himself received greater will to act. For indeed at that time he was incited *[316]* against his enemies, and the circumstances of persecution were for him the circumstances of greater boldness and the basis for greater confidence.

7.11 [316]. Once when Paul was shut up in prison, he shined forth to such a degree that the walls shook, the doors opened wide, and the jailer switched over to Paul's own cause (Acts 16:23–34). And his judge [Agrippa] was almost won over, such that even he said, "you are almost persuading me to become a Christian!" (Acts 26:28). Again he was stoned, and, going into the city that was assailing him [Lystra, Derbe], he transformed them (Acts 14:19–28). At one time Jews, and at another Athenians summoned him for an impending trial (Acts 18:12; 22:30–23:9; 17:18–34), and the judges became disciples, the opponents subjects. Just as fire spreads more when it sets upon different materials, and receives an increase from the flammable matter lying underneath, so also Paul's tongue converted to his own cause the people with whom it came into contact. Those who were fighting against him, taken captive by his *[318]* words, swiftly became fuel for this spiritual fire. And through [opponents] the gospel was raised up again, and advanced continually toward others. That is why he said, "I have been bound, but the word of God has not been bound" (2 Tim 2:9). They set him to flight as an act of persecution, but the result was the apostolate of teachers. His enemies were doing the very things his friends and associates would have done. They would not allow him to be fixed in one place, but through their plots and their exiles they circulated this physician everywhere, so all heard the words his tongue spoke. They bound him again, and incited him all the more. They drove out his disciples, and thereby sent a teacher to those who did not have one. They led him before a greater tribunal, and brought benefit to an even greater city.

7.12 [318]. That is why the Jews, embittered over the apostles, said: "What shall we do with these men" (Acts 4:16)? They said, "through the things we intend against them we are actually promoting their growth." They handed Paul over to the jailer so that he might securely restrain him, but he was more securely bound by Paul. They sent him with other prisoners so that he might not escape, but those prisoners he instructed in the gospel. They sent him by sea passage so that they might involuntarily provide for a quick end to the journey, and the [320] shipwreck which resulted became a platform for him to teach his shipboard companions. They continually threatened him with countless punishments so that the gospel message might be extinguished, but it was raised up all the more. This is just like what happened in the case of the Lord [Jesus], when the Jews said, "Let's kill him, lest the Romans come and destroy our city and our nation" (Jn 11:48), but the opposite resulted. For it was because they killed him that the Romans destroyed both their nation and their city. The things they thought were hindrances became acts of assistance to the gospel. Likewise, when Paul was preaching the gospel, the things his foes brought against him to eradicate the word were the very factors that made it increase, and elevated it to an indescribable height.

7.13 [320]. Therefore, for all these things let us give thanks to our ingenious God, let us pronounce a blessing on Paul, that man through whom these things took place, and let us pray that we too might attain the same good things, by the grace and beneficence of our Lord Jesus Christ, through whom and with whom be glory to the Father, together with the Holy Spirit, forever and ever. Amen.

Appendix 2

Artistic Images of John Chrysostom and Paul

This appendix provides a list of the images of Chrysostom and Paul known to me, including all those drawn upon in the course of this study. Most are from manuscript illuminations of various types,[1] but there are also a few wall paintings from churchs, and one icon. I have arranged them in the following three groups: "The Inspired Author Portrait," "John Chrysostom, the Source of Wisdom," and "Other Intimate Portraits of the Pair." There is overlap among these categories, but they serve to show the main types that are found, and suggest something of the various developments that took place in these iconographical traditions. For each image I have included salient bibliographies for those who wish to pursue this fascinating subject further; these are not exhaustive, but are as representative and up-to-date as possible. After these treatments I have included a brief list of the major literary sources pertinent to graphic images of Chrysostom and Paul.

A few scholars have devoted careful attention to images of Chrysostom in Byzantine art, among which those with the apostle Paul have a special place. The following major authorities, Christopher Walter in particular, have both helped me to locate the extant images and greatly influenced my overall interpretations of them:

André Grabar, *L'art de la fin de l'antiquité et du moyen age* (3 vols.; Paris: Collège de France, 1968).
Sirarpie Der Nersessian, "A Psalter and New Testament Manuscript at Dumbarton Oaks," *Dumbarton Oaks Papers* 19 (1965) 153–83, 178–79.
Anna Marava-Chatzinicolaou and Christina Toufexi-Paschou, *Catalogue of the Illuminated Byzantine Manuscripts of the National Library of Greece, vol. III: Homilies of the Church Fathers and Menologia, 9th–12th century* (Athens: Academy of Athens Centre of Byzantine and Post-Byzantine Art, 1997).
A. Müsseler, "Johannes Chrysostomus," *Lexikon der christlichen Ikonographie*, ed. W. Braunfels (Freiburg: Herder, 1974) 7.93–101.
Christopher Walter, "Biographical Scenes of the Three Hierarchs," *Revue des études byzantines* 36 (1978) 233–60, 250–59.

---

[1] Walter, "Biographical Scenes," 250, notes that manuscripts of Chrysostom's homilies were not nearly as lavishly illustrated as those of Gregory of Nazianzus, for example. In fact, only thirteen illuminated manuscripts of John's homilies are known (Walter provides a list on that page; see also Marava-Chatzinicolaou and Toufexi-Paschou's similar observation: "It is a surprising fact that there are very few illuminated manuscripts of Chrysostom's homilies, even if important 9th c. codices with fine illustrations do survive" [*Catalogue, Vol. III*, 49]).

Christopher Walter, *Art and Ritual of the Byzantine Church* (London: Variorum, 1982), esp. 102–103, 111–15.

A. Xyngopoulos, "ΑΓΙΟΣ ΙΩΑΝΝΗΣ Ο ΧΡΥΣΟΣΤΟΜΟΣ, 'ΠΗΓΗ ΤΗΣ ΣΟΦΙΑΣ'" ("St. John Chrysostom, Fount of Wisdom"), *Archaiologike Ephemeris* 81–83 (1942–44) 1–36.

The Inspired Author Portrait

In this category are images based on the legend first recorded by Chrysostom's biographer, George of Alexandria, in the 7th century.[2] The tale tells of how Chrysostom, when seated at his writing desk in his monastic cell hard at work on his homilies on the Pauline epistles (where he could glance for inspiration at a portrait of the apostle which hung on the wall, and direct his exegetical queries and praises to him), was visited by his author, who sprang to life in the night and leaned over his shoulder whispering exegetical suggestions into his ear.[3] Chrysostom's secretary, Proklos, peering in through the doorway, saw the mysterious visitor three nights in a row, and ultimately recognized that it was Paul by his likeness to the picture on the wall. "This picture of Saint Paul inspiring John Chrysostom, based upon the antique type of a Muse inspiring a poet which was used in the Rossano Gospels for the Evangelists, became his iconographical type,"[4] at the very least by the 11th century, when it is featured among the set iconographical scenes depicted by John Euchaïtes (on which, see below, p. 499). The ubiquity of this iconographical type of Paul dictating exegetical truths to John can also be seen in its appearance in manuscripts of diverse genres,[5] as the following catalogue will demonstrate.[6]

---

[2] *vita Joh. Chrys.* 27. See chap. 2, pp. 35–36.

[3] By analogy to this scene, *Coislin.* 66, fol. 4, introduces Chrysostom's *hom. in Mt.* with a picture of Chrysostom inspired by a portrait of the evangelist Matthew on his wall (see Walter, "Biographical Scenes," 256–57). But for a rather different depiction of Chrysostom and Matthew, see n. 35 below.

[4] Walter, *Art and Ritual*, 103 (he notes that "it is the only scene used to illustrate the Metaphrastic Life of John Chrysostom"). Although this legend is well known, the remarkable parallel in Libanios, *Ep.* 143 (quoted above in chap. 2, n. 7), which may have had a direct influence on the tale, or at least represent a *topos* common in and around Antioch, does not appear to have been brought into this connection before.

[5] Walter, "Biographical Scenes," 252.

[6] Variations on this scene combined with the "fount of wisdom" motif will be examined in the next category.

1. *Vatican Cod. gr. 766,* fol. 2ᵛ [Plate 1]

This image, itself of uncertain date,[7] was bound into the beginning of an 11th century manuscript of Pseudo-Oecumenius' *Commentarius in epistulas Pauli*. It is generally considered the best known example of the standard type just described ("the fullest, and, perhaps, the finest representation of this incident"),[8] for its clarity of expression and fullness of detail. All the elements of the legend are here accounted for: the icon of Paul on the wall, John in author pose inscribing his homilies, Paul in close contact with him, standing over John's shoulder whispering into his right ear, Proklos' skirt and foot in the doorway. Elaborate ecclesiastical architecture frames the scene on both sides. One of the most striking things about this image is how very similar the faces of John and Paul are.[9]

Literature: Walter, "Biographical Scenes," 252; *idem, Art and Ritual,* 103; Der Nersessian, "Psalter," 177–78; Xyngopoulos, "Fount of Wisdom," 15–16, and fig. 4; J. R. Martin, *The Illustration of the Heavenly Ladder of John Climacus* (Princeton: Princeton University Press, 1954) 23, and pl. 299.

2. *Athen. graec. suppl. 2535,* fol. 221ᵛ

11th–12th century manscript of the *Menologion*, or saints' lives, of Symeon Metaphrastes. This portrait, along with another solo image of John in the traditional pose of a hierarch, faces the *Vita* of John Chrysostom, who is listed by his feast day of November 13 (his traditional birthday). The other five miniatures originally belonging to this manuscript have been cut out. This is a much simpler image than the previous one, without border or architectural detail. But it is distinctly of this type, with Paul over John's shoulder, and Proklos peering in the doorway (there is no icon of Paul on the wall, however).

Literature: Marava-Chatzinicolaou and Toufexi-Paschou, *Catalogue, Vol. III*, 189–93, and fig. 290; Walter, *Art and Ritual*, 49, and fig. 23.

---

[7] The Vatican cataloguers list the miniature as 14th century, though without giving any corroborating evidence (R. Devreesse, *et al., Codices Vaticani Graeci III* [Vatican: Biblioteca Apostolica Vaticana, 1950] 281), but Walter ("Biographical Scenes," 252), upon consultation with Prof. Hugo Buchthal, saw no reason to date the image later than the 11th century. However, in Walter's book, published four years later (*Art and Ritual*, 103), he states that the miniature is from the 11th century, but the manuscript the 14th (perhaps in the interval he learned that the Vatican catalogue mistakenly switched the two dates?).

[8] Walter, "Biographical Scenes," 252.

[9] "However, in scenes of Saint Paul inspiring him, the artist sometimes introduces a close resemblance in his portrait to that of the apostle of whose writings John Chrysostom was the most authorized interpreter" (Walter, *Art and Ritual*, 107).

3. *Athen. 7,* fol. 2

12th century Psalter and Odes manuscript. This miniature accompanies the begin-ning of Chrysostom's homilies on the Psalms, analogously drawing upon the legend about the Pauline epistles.[10] The image follows precisely the same form as no. 1, though with less architectural detail. Proklos peeks out from a curtain in the door-way, but here his whole head is visible. "The painter depicts every detail of the narration. Paul, bald and with a wide beard, dictates to Chrysostom, who writes down what he hears. The composition of the group of the two saints with their haloes united, and opposite them Proklos with his awed expression, illustrates the content of the narration in a simple, unaffected manner. The animated expressions on the faces of the saints with their delicate brown features are exceptional."[11]

Literature: Marava-Chatzinicolaou and Toufexi-Paschou, *Catalogue, Vol. III*, 190–92; Der Nersessian, "Psalter," 179; Xyngopoulos, "Fount of Wisdom," 16–17 and fig. 5. The earlier catalogue of Paul Buberl, *Die Miniaturenhandschriften der Nationalbibliothek in Athen* (Kai-serliche Akademie der Wissenschaften in Wien, philosophisch-historische Klasse, Denk-schriften 60,2; Vienna: Hölder, 1917) 14 [pl. 40], did not identify either John or Paul, calling it merely "Schreibender Heiliger."[12] Also Buberl's designation of the folio number, which has been followed by others, should be corrected; it is folio 2, not 3.[13]

4. *Sinai Cod. 500,* fol. 175[r]

Menologion, circa 1063. For his feast day, November 13, Chrysostom is depicted in a simple scene bent over a codex resting on his lap (there is no copy stand), with his feet on a footstool. Paul is huddled intimately behind him, speaking words of exegetical inspiration. There is no portrait on the wall. Captions tell the two identities, and introduce "the Life of John Chrysostom."

Literature: Kurt Weitzmann and George Galavaris, *The Monastery of Saint Catherine at Mount Sinai: The Illuminated Greek Manuscripts, Volume One: From the Ninth to the Twelfth Century* (Princeton: Princeton University Press, 1990) 73–77.

5. *Jerusalem Σταύρου 109*

11th century manuscript of the *Liturgy of John Chrysostom*. The initial K from the invocation of the *Ektene*, the prayer right after the gospel,[14] has been ingeniously

---

[10] Xyngopoulos, "Fount of Wisdom," 17, n. 2.

[11] Marava-Chatzinicolaou and Toufexi-Paschou, *Catalogue, Vol. III*, 192.

[12] For other misidentifications of this illustration, see Xyngopoulos, "Fount of Wisdom," 16, n. 2; 17, n. 3.

[13] This according to a letter from Catherine Kordouli, Keeper of Manuscripts at the National Library of Greece, June 14, 1999.

[14] The prayer reads: Κύριε ὁ θεὸς ἡμῶν τὴν ἐκτενὴν ταύτην ἱκεσίαν πρόσδεξαι ("Lord our God, receive this, our extended supplication").

formed from the bodies of Paul and John in their poses of muse and author. Paul stands upright, as the vertical line of the kappa, with the profile of Chrysostom bent over his writing desk forming the angled legs of the letter. A divine hand of inspiration is also added to the scene, visually completing the kappa, and providing further theological endorsement for this inspirational activity.

Literature: A. Grabar, "Un rouleau liturgique constantinopolitain et ses peintures," *Dumbarton Oaks Papers* 8 (1954) 173, fig. 5; Der Nersessian, "Psalter," 179; Walter, "Biographical Scenes," 253; *idem, Art and Ritual*, 103.

6. *British Library Add. 36636,* fol. 179^r [Plate 6]

Medieval Menologion, volume 3: saints from November 2–13 (ending in the middle of the treatment of Chrysostom). As with Jerusalem Σταύρου 109, an historiated K is formed from John bending over his writing and Paul upright speaking over his shoulder. Forming the upper right angle of the K is not a divine hand, but Paul's own arm and hand, gesturing in emphasis, or pointing the way toward heaven. Captions in Greek identify the pair, and the scene is set against an architectual motif of an ecclesiastical edifice.

Literature: Nancy Patterson Ševčenko, *Illustrated Manuscripts of the Metaphrastian Menologion* (Chicago Visual Library Text-Fiche series 54; Chicago/London: University of Chicago Press, 1990) 125–128 (further bibliography on p. 128), and plate 3F9 (on microfiche).

7. *Hamilton Psalter, Berlin, Staatliche Museen Kupferstichkabinett 78.A.9,* fol. 109

In this early 14th century Psalter, the scene of John inspired by Paul illustrates Ps 48:4 [τὸ στόμα μου λαλήσει σοφίαν], in place of the more customary scene of John as a Pauline type in preaching to the nations.[15]

Literature: Walter, *Art and Ritual*, 103; Christine Havice, "The Hamilton Psalter in Berlin, Kupferstichkabinett 78.A.9," Ph.D. dissertation, Pennsylvania State University, 1978, 225–26 and 407 (also fig. 78, in a non-circulating second volume of plates, so I have not seen a copy of this image).

8. Wall Painting in the Monastery of Hilandar

This fresco in the exonarthex of the church (catholicon) of the monastery of Hilandar on Mt. Athos was originally painted in the early 14th century, but restored in 1804. There is debate about how much the restoration has altered the

---

[15] Walter, *Art and Ritual*, 58, 101: "the artist has presented John Chrysostom as the successor of Saint Paul as apostle of the Gentiles" (see also p. 103). On the unusual placement of the image here, see also Havice, "Hamilton Psalter," 225–26 (and her general note on p. 224: "Hamilton's iconography is often chaotic at best").

original form of the painting, which now consists of three scenes involving John. On the far right John is seated in a chair with Paul leaning over his back murmuring into his left ear (there is no icon of Paul on the wall in this scene). Behind them to the left is a double wooden door that is half-opened by Proklos who views their encounter. The next scene is Chrysostom standing at a lectern in devotional reading (the codex is open to Ps 118:26), held in place by a suspension apparatus commonly used by ascetics to keep them from falling asleep. In the third scene the saint is prostrate in prayer, offering his writings to the deity (with an icon of Mary as Theotokos standing on the wall this time).[16] Interpretation of this scene has been influenced by a similar episodic miniature of Chrysostom dating from around the same time, which does not include Paul.[17]

Literature: Gabriel Millet, *Monuments de l'Athos* (Paris: Leroux, 1927) vol. 1, pl. 79 no. 3; Xyngopoulos, "Fount of Wisdom," 18–21; *idem*, "Restitution et interprétation d'une fresque de Chilandar," *Hilandarski Zbornik* 2 (1971) 93–98; Walter, "Biographical Scenes," 258–59.

John Chrysostom, the Source of Wisdom

These images, as Xyngopoulos and Walter in particular have argued, are a development of the inspired author portrait to incorporate another tradition of the reception of Chrysostom's writings as the delivery of divinely inspired wisdom in the form of a bountiful spring of water.[18] Although that theme is also present in images of John without Paul, here I shall list only pictures where the two motifs are combined,[19] and Paul is present.

9. *Milan, Ambrosian A 172, Sup.*, fol. 263ᵛ [Plate 4]

12th century manuscript of Chrysostom's homilies on the Pauline Epistles. The oldest image of this type, it combines the authorial inspiration portrait with the

---

[16] Xyngopoulos, "Fount of Wisdom," 20, conjectured that this was originally an icon of Paul, before the recasting and repainting of the image in 1804.

[17] Walter, "Biographical Scenes," 258–59 disputes Xyngopoulos' suggestion that the Hilandar wall painting has been adapted from an original series of biographical events to fit the singular model of the Psalter Athos, *Vatoped 761*, fol. 232, of John as a man of prayer. Oddly, in that manuscript, while Paul is not shown inspiring John, still Proklos stands vestigially as a witness.

[18] This tradition has rich literary sources to draw upon (see Walter, *Art and Ritual*, 113–14).

[19] Walter, *Art and Ritual*, 113–14, provides examples of the theme independent of Paul, as in *Athen. 211*, fol. 84ᵛ, an important manuscript treated below. In that exquisite color image, "In the upper left-hand corner a man with a strange head-covering and a cape blowing in the wind tips over an amphora in whose neck a head is drawn with water pouring from its mouth which forms streams. Two men hasten to quench their thirst at the mellifluous spring of teaching. This face must be that of Chrysostom, and the man tipping the amphora personifies river" (Marava-Chatzinicolaou and Toufexi-Paschou, *Catalogue, Vol. III*, 34). Xyngopoulos notes the later history

"fount of wisdom" theme.[20] Within the codex this illumination is located in the first homily on Ephesians, and includes a line about baptism taken from the discourse at its top.[21] The text Chrysostom is penning on the scroll is the first line of the *Argumentum* to his homilies on Romans.[22] The visual transformation from author-portrait to fount of wisdom was neatly accomplished by the retention of the slanted writing surface, a desk turned into a pulpit. The scroll, as it flows over the top of the pulpit, becomes a gushing stream of water from which a host of clergy and the faithful eagerly drink. Proklos is still in the scene, but now as a suppliant rather than a witness to a private event. Christ has been added to the earlier set scene; from on high in the upper right hand corner he sends his own spray of illumination down onto John's writing hand.

Literature: Maria Luisa Gengaro, Francesca Leoni, Gemma Villa, *Codici decorati e miniati dell' Ambrosiana, ebraici e greci* (Fontes Ambrosiani 33A; Milan: Ceschina, 1960) 152, pl. LIII; Xyngopoulos, "Fount of Wisdom," 23–26, and fig. 7; Walter, "Biographical Scenes," 253; *idem, Art and Ritual,* 112–13, and fig. 24.

10. Fresco in the Church of the Archangel, Lesnovo [Plate 5]

The painting, which can be dated to 1349, is situated in a Byzantino-Serbian monastery in Lesnovo, in eastern Macedonia, between the town of Kratovo and the village of Zletovo, on the Western slopes of Mt. Osogovo.[23] The portrait of Chrysostom as the source of wisdom is located over an arch on the east side of the narthex, as part of a quartet of doctors of the church including Basil, Athanasius and Gregory of Nazianzus, who frame four arches which unite at the cupola. All four hierarchs are depicted in teaching scenes with an effluence of water, but only John is inspired from behind, by Paul, according to the standard scene representing the nocturnal inspiration legend. The title over Chrysostom's scene reads: Učitelistvo stago Joan Zlatoustago" ("Enseignement de saint Jean Chrysostom" [Okunev, "Lesnovo," 237]). Below it, John sits composing at his desk, with Paul leaning over his shoulder whispering in his ear, at the same moment as a celestial wisdom figure

of the form in representations of the three hierarchs, in which John is frequently associated with a fountain of wisdom ("Fount of Wisdom," 29–36).

[20] Xyngopoulos, "Fount of Wisdom," 28.

[21] "We have corrupted the baptism, and we groan that we be able to take it up again. Through the beloved [Eph 1:6], he says ..." [διαφθείραμεν τὸ βάπτισμα, καὶ στενάξωμεν, ἵνα δυνηθῶμεν αὐτὸ πάλιν ἀναλαβεῖν. Διὰ τοῦ ἠγαπημένου], φησίν (*hom. in Eph.* 1.3 [62.14]). There is an irregularity in the text of the manuscript at this point, according to Walter: "the earlier part of the text of this homily is written on the preceding folios but breaks off at the very point where he is writing of baptism. On the following folio, 264, there begins John Chrysostom's *Commentary* on the Galatians" (*Art and Ritual,* 113).

[22] "Continually when I hear the letters of the blessed Paul read ..." [Συνεχῶς ἀκούων ἀναγινωσκομένων τῶν Ἐπιστολῶν τοῦ μακαρίου Παύλου] (*hom. in Rom.* Arg. [60.391]).

[23] Now a remote place, in the Middle Ages it was rich and populous (Okunev, "Lesnovo," 223).

touches John's head. From the desk itself comes a torrent of water, into which priests, monks and choristers dip jugs to garner a drink. The text on the scroll upon the copy stand is the incipit to a spurious work attributed to Chrysostom, *hom. in Ps. 50* 2.1 [55.565], although this has not been previously noted in scholarship on the painting.[24]

Literature: M.N.L. Okunev, "Lesnovo," *L'art byzantin chez les slaves: les balkans* (pt. 1; Orient et byzance 4; Paris: Guenther, 1930) 222–63, 236–37 (description of the image), 262 (diagram of the church); Svetozar Radojčič, "Die Entstehung der Malerei der paläologischen Renaissance," *Jahrbuch der österreichischen byzantinischen Gesellschaft* 7 (1958) 105–23, 116; *idem, Lesnovo*, x–xi; A. Müsseler, "Johannes Chrysostomus," *Lexikon der christlichen Ikonographie*, ed. W. Braunfels (Freiburg: Herder, 1974) 7.93–101, 97; Walter, *Art and Ritual*, 114, and fig. 25; full color image of the entire cupola in Ivan M. Djordjevic, *Zidno slikarstvo srpske vlastele u doba Nemanjica* ("Wall-Paintings of the Serbian Nobility of the Nemanide Era") (Belgrade: Filozofski fakultet, 1994) pl. 16; and black and white photographs of three of the four in pl. 60–62 (Chrysostom is pl. 62).

11. Icon in the Collection of Dionysios Loberdos, Athens

This icon on a thin canvas is set within a border formed by portraits of saints of the church shown from the waist up. The image proper is set into a rectangle in the center of that border, and portrays John in a chair with Paul (identified by a caption in Greek) leaning over his shoulder, whispering into his ear. Simultaneously a divine bolt of illumination springs from the bottom of a heavenly orb set in the top of the scene directly into John's head. Water pours forth from the codex on the pulpit and a small representative crowd of choristers and others ready their vessels to capture John's powerful elixir. Proklos stands, as usual, in the doorway.

Literature: Xyngopoulos, "Fount of Wisdom," 1–36, and fig. 1 (detail) and pl. 1 (full image).

12. Wall Painting in the Monastery of St. Nikolaos Ntilios

This monastery wall painting from 1543 is a later type of the same combinatory image, with Paul inspiring John, from whose scroll flows water that is being drunk by priests and monks. Proklos pulls back a curtain in the doorway to stand as a witness. The title of the scene is "the beginning of Paul's speaking with mortals."[25]

Literature: Xyngopoulos, "Fount of Wisdom," 28–29, and fig. 9 (artist's sketch of the scene).

---

[24] For a full discussion of the image, and difficulties in its prior interpretation, see pp. 437–39 above, including a transcription and translation of the text on the scroll.

[25] Translating the transcription of Xyngopoulos, "Fount of Wisdom," 29: ΑΡΚΗ (ΑΡΧΗ;) ΤΟΥ ΠΑΥΛΟΥ ΦΘΕΓΓΕΘ(ΑΙ) ΣΥΝ ΤΟΙΣ ΑΝ(ΘΡΩΠ)ΟΙΣ.

Other Intimate Portraits of the Pair

Athen. 211, two illuminations from which are listed below, is the earliest extant illustrated collection of Chrysostom's homilies; hence it is of inestimable importance for the history of iconography of Chrysostom and Paul. Although this earliest set of manuscript illuminations of John does not contain the inspired author portrait-type of Chrysostom and Paul, it does have other remarkable scenes of the two intimately linked, which demonstrate that the close relationship between John and his beloved Paul was not solely connected to the legend told by George of Alexandria.[26] Indeed, the legend itself may be an attempt to put in narrative form what was already so well appreciated by readers of Chrysostom's oeuvre: that John claimed a special relationship with the apostle that was the basis for his superior interpretation of his writings. Scholars have argued that this manuscript is a graphic counterpart to many of the oratorical and literary traditions then current about Chrysostom (including his inspiration by Paul), most notably that of Leo VI, called "the Philosopher" (866–912), who composed an encomium to Chrysostom, and included his own version of Proklos' night vision.[27] This early manuscript is a rare glimpse at the iconographical possibilities afforded by the famous relationship between Paul and Chrysostom before the narrative scene of the nocturnal visitation became the fixed standard.[28]

13. *Athen. 211,* fol. 96 [Plate 3]

9–10th century manuscript of some of Chrysostom's homilies on Paul. This is a headpiece for a homily with the title, "Concerning Compunction and Tears, and on St. Paul" [Περὶ κατανύξεως καὶ δακρύων καὶ εἰς τὸν ἅγιον Παῦλον], a work not among the genuinely accepted writings, and still not accurately identified.[29] The illustration is a border ribbon in white, green and carmine with frequent decorative knots, which defines the rectangle within which the homily title is set.

---

[26] With Walter, "Biographical Scenes," 253: "The association of John Chrysostom with Saint Paul exists independently of George of Alexandria's anecdote."

[27] Marava-Chatzinicolaou and Toufexi-Paschou, *Catalogue, Vol. III*, 49: "In searching for the person who inspired our codex, who was clearly an admirer of Chrysostom, it seemed that some connection with the Hierarch's great encomiast, Leo the Wise, might be proposed. Many of the utterances found in the lengthy Discourse dedicated by Leo to Chrysostom have their counterpart in the miniatures of codex 211." For reference to Leo VI's *Or. 18, laudatio S. Joannis Chrysostomi*, see below in this Appendix, p. 499.

[28] "The miniatures in our codex were never imitated in other later manuscripts. They were mannered, sophistical and classicizing, and had no place among the dogmatic, set themes that came into use after the standardization of orthodox iconography which had already begun in the 9th century" (Marava-Chatzinicolaou and Toufexi-Paschou, *Catalogue, Vol. III*, 50).

[29] Marava-Chatzinicolaou and Toufexi-Paschou, *Catalogue, Vol. III*, 52, n. 65 refer us to the Migne catalogue 64.1377, but there is nothing on that page that corresponds. The title does not appear anywhere in the full corpus of writings contained in the *TLG*.

Set into the swooping line of this frame are two medallion portraits, Paul on top and John on the bottom (as is clear from Paul's characteristicly pointed beard, and John's *omophorion* with a cross stitched into it).

Literature: Marava-Chatzinicolaou and Toufexi-Paschou, *Catalogue, Vol. III*, 36–37, and fig. 22; André Grabar, *L'art de la fin de l'antiquité et du moyen age* (3 vols.; Paris: Collège de France, 1968) 1.809–10, and pl. 192a; Susan Pinto Madigan, "Athens 211 and the Illustrated Homilies of John Chrysostom," Ph.D. dissertation, University of Chicago, 1984.

14. *Athen. 211*, fol. 172 [Plate 2]

The same manuscript as no. 13. Another headpiece to a homily, this time with the title, "An Ascetical Discourse on Repentance, Self-control, and Virginity" [Περὶ μετανοίας καὶ ἐγκρατείας καὶ παρθενίας λόγος ἀσκητικός]. The homily is actually not by Chrysostom, but by a sixth-century patriarch of Constantinople, John IV, known as *Jejunator*, "the Faster,"[30] but the artist clearly thought it genuine. The headpiece is formed by a ribbon motif similar to the preceding (strikingly colored in white, green, and carmine), though with a simpler set of lines, in which a rectangle encloses the words of the title, and the border forms an open rectangle on the bottom, which is balanced by an arch at the top. In the cramped space of this arch the miniaturist has created an intimate scene, with Paul on the left and John on the right (as captions indicate), both heads bent over a single codex that spans the space between them. They are linked by hands on the book,[31] as they are by the halos that meet above it, their eyes looking down at the book, but not far from each other's gaze. Paul's hand is slightly raised, apparently in benediction.[32] The most recent editors of the manuscript have envisioned Paul here in an authoritarian pose, instructing Chrysostom, or even dictating to him,[33] but one should not overlook

---

[30] The work is CPG 7555 [PG 88.1937–77]. The homily begins with a very Chrysostomic-sounding praise of Paul as an entrée into the themes of the ascetic life: "The blessed Paul, who was the teacher of the Gentiles and of the church, the one who forgot the things behind him and stretched out for the things ahead (Phil 3:13), the one clad in a corruptible body and rivaling the incorporeal powers ..." [ὁ μακάριος Παῦλος, ὁ τῶν ἐθνῶν διδάσκαλος καὶ τῆς Ἐκκλησίας γενόμενος, ὁ τῶν ὄπισθεν ἐπιλανθανόμενος, καὶ τοῖς ἔμπροσθεν ἐπεκτεινόμενος, ὁ σῶμα φθαρτὸν περικείμενος, καὶ ταῖς ἀσωμάτοις δυνάμεσιν ἁμιλλώμενος] [88.1937].

[31] Marava-Chatzinicolaou and Toufexi-Paschou, *Catalogue, Vol. III*, 42, assume this is a Gospel book, but it could more likely be a collection of Paul's letters, or the lectionary in which Chrysostom often encountered them.

[32] Grabar, *L'art de la fin de l'antiquité*, 2.812, 836; Walter, "Biographical Scenes," 252.

[33] "These two outstanding personalities are remarkable for their intensely spiritual expressions at the moment when the word of God is being transmitted to the great Christian Hierarch" (Marava-Chatzinicolaou and Toufexi-Paschou, *Catalogue, Vol. III*, 42). They later questionably appropriate to this image the dynamics of the very different inspiration scene from the legend, when they describe the miniature as "the apostle Paul dictat[ing] the Homilies to Chrysostom" (p. 50). In this interpretation they are likely following Grabar, *L'art de le fin de l'antiquité*, 2.836: "Cette scène représente l'apparition de saint Paul à Jean Chrysostome que nous décrivent les anciens biographes du grand théologien. Ils nous montrent, en effet, Jean Chrysostome plongé,

the striking intimacy of the scene, in which the two men are depicted in the same proportion and pose, eye to eye over the book.[34] This is strikingly different from the inspired author portraits, or other scenes depicting authors and interpreters.[35]

Literature: Marava-Chatzinicolaou and Toufexi-Paschou, *Catalogue, Vol. III*, 42, and fig. 29; Grabar, *L'art de la fin de l'antiquité*, 2.812, 836–37, and pl. 3.193b; Walter, "Biographical Scenes," 253.

15. Fresco in the Church of Hagia Sophia, Ochrid, Macedonia

This 11th century church painting, situated between images of Jacob's ladder and the Liturgy of St. Basil the Great, has been the subject of diverse interpretations. What can be clearly discerned is a figure lying on a bed, surrounded by other holy figures (the supine one as well as those who are standing have a nimbus), and fed a scroll by a divine being of some sort. Cvetan Grozdanov has identified the painting as a death-bed scene of John Chrysostom, to whom the figure of "Divine Wisdom" feeds a scroll of the Pauline epistles. Paul himself (typically bearded and bald) is the most prominent of the apostles at the foot of John's bed.

Literature: Cvetan Grozdanov, "L'image de l'apparition de la sagesse divine à saint Jean Chrysostome dans l'église de sainte sophie à Ochrid" [French precis of Serbian article], *Recueil des travaux de l'institut d'études byzantines* 19 (1980) 147–155, 154–55 (French summary), with plates and a diagram of the fresco.

---

un jour, dans la lecture des oeuvres de saint Paul et demandant à Dieu de l'instruire, pour lui permettre de saisir le vrai sens des épîtres. Ses prières sont bientôt exaucées ..." [i.e., by the vision of Paul]. However, this image is quite different from the legend, and can be interpreted on its own terms. What we do *not* have in this scene is dictation, but instead a vision of textual encounter between two reading partners (no one is writing!). And Paul is not here represented in the pose of a muse, but a textual companion.

[34] Closer to this interpretation is Walter, "Biographical Scenes," 253: "John holds a book half-open, while Paul blesses him ... Since the scene differs from other examples where Paul is certainly inspiring John, it seems more plausible to see here rather Paul approving John's commentaries on his *Epistles*." However, the miniaturist is not just depicting Paul's seal of approval on these homilies; he has caught the very image of *how* the homilies were inspired – in devotional reading in which John met his author face-to-face (as I have argued above, chap. 2, p. 68).

[35] Compare, e.g., the formality in the scene of the evangelist Matthew extending the codex of his gospel to Chrysostom, who stands stiffly across from him, in *Sinai, Cod. 364*, fol. 2ᵛ (Weitzmann-Galavaris, *Monastery of Saint Catherine*, color plate XIV).

Literary Sources Pertaining to the Iconography of Chrysostom and Paul

George of Alexandria, 7th century biographer of Chrysostom. His *vita Joh. Chrys.* 27 is the earliest attested version of the legend of Paul's nocturnal visits to assist Chrysostom in writing homilies on his epistles.[36]

Leo VI, the Philosopher, byzantine Emperor who lived 866–912. *Or.* 18 is his *laudatio S. Joannis Chrysostomi* [PG 107.228-92]. In §15 he includes a version of the story of Proklos' testimony to John's inspiring visitor, Paul [107.256–57].

Symeon Metaphrastes, compiler-biographer of the 10th century. In his *Menologion* he included a life of Chrysostom among other saints either in the month of January, as January 27 is the feast of the translation of his relics (*vita sancti Joannis Chrysostomi* 23 [PG 114.1045–1209]), or, more often, in November, for the thirteenth of that month was his feast day in the East (commemorating his birthdate). Symeon's version of the legend of Paul inspiring Chrysostom is in §22–23 [114.1104–1108].

John Euchaïtes, 11th century metropolitan of Euchaïta, in Hellespont, who is also called "Mauropous." His work, *in magnas festorum tabulas per modum expositionis* (the Greek title is εἰς πίνακας μεγάλους τῶν ἑορτῶν ὡς ἐν τύπῳ ἐκφράσεως), features poetic *ekphraseis* of iconographical types in iambic verse. §13 takes as its subject the representation of the story of Paul inspiring Chrysostom, in poetic stance offering instruction to the spectator about how to react to the vision which an artist will set before him or her in an icon (PG 120.1134–35).[37] §14 continues with an instruction to the one who wishes to paint "the fiery tongue" of Chrysostom himself [120.1135].

---

[36] For bibliographic data, see chap. 2, n. 6.
[37] The text and my translation are given in chap. 8, p. 439.

Plates

Plates

Plate 1
Vatican Cod. gr. 766, fol. 2ᵛ.

Plate 2
Athen. 211, fol. 172.

Plate 3
Athen. 211, fol. 96.

Plate 4
Milan, Ambrosian A 172, Sup., fol. 263ᵛ.

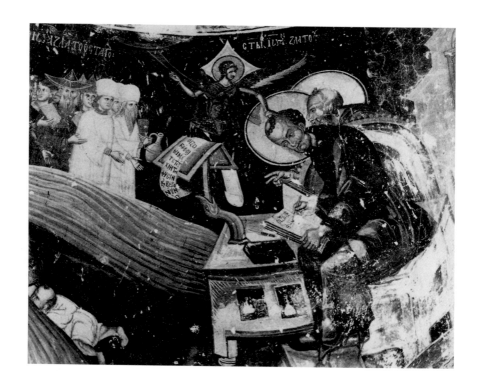

Plate 5
Fresco in the Church of the Archangel, Lesnovo, Macedonia.

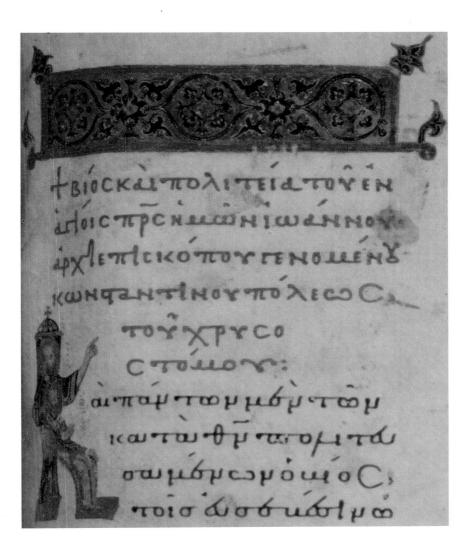

Plate 6
British Library Add. Ms. 36636, fol. 179ʳ.

Bibliography

Reference Works

Altaner, Berthold and Alfred Stuiber. *Patrologie: Leben, Schriften und Lehre der Kirchenväter.* 7th ed. Freiburg/Basel/Vienna: Herder, 1966.

Balz, H. and G. Schneider, eds. *Exegetisches Wörterbuch zum Neuen Testament.* 3 vols. Stuttgart: Kohlhammer, 1980–83.

Bauer, W. *A Greek-English Lexicon of the New Testament and Other Early Christian Literature.* Trans. and rev. W. F. Arndt, F. W. Gingrich and F. W. Danker. 2nd ed. Chicago: University of Chicago Press, 1979.

Berkowitz, Luci and Karl A. Squitier. *Canon of Greek Authors and Works.* 3rd ed. New York: Oxford Universtiy Press, 1990.

Betz, Hans Dieter, *et al.*, eds. *Religion in Geschichte und Gegenwart: Handwörterbuch für Theologie und Religionswissenschaft.* 4th edition. Tübingen: J. C. B. Mohr [Paul Siebeck], 1998–. 3rd edition, ed. K. von Galling. Tübingen: J. C. B. Mohr [Paul Siebeck], 1957–62.

Blass, F. and A. Debrunner. *A Greek Grammar of the New Testament and Other Early Christian Literature.* Trans. and rev. R. W. Funk. Chicago: University of Chicago Press, 1961.

Cross, F. L. and Elizabeth A. Livingstone, eds. *The Oxford Dictionary of the Christian Church.* 3rd ed. Oxford: Oxford University Press, 1997.

di Berardino, Angelo, ed. *Encyclopedia of the Early Church.* Trans. Adrian Walford. New York: Oxford University Press, 1992.

—. ed. *Patrology.* 4 vols. Trans. P. Solari. Westminster, MD: Christian Classics, Inc., 1986.

Ferguson, Everett, ed. *Encyclopedia of Early Christianity.* 2nd ed. New York: Garland, 1990.

Geerard, M., and F. Glorie, eds. *Clavis patrum graecorum.* Corpus Christianorum. 5 vols. Turnhout: Brepols, 1974–1987.

Glare, P. G. W. *Oxford Latin Dictionary.* Oxford: Clarendon, 1982.

Hornblower, Simon and Antony Spawforth. *The Oxford Classical Dictionary.* 3rd ed. Oxford: Oxford University Press, 1996.

Klauser, T., E. Dassmann, *et al.*, eds. *Reallexikon für Antike und Christentum.* Vol. 1–. Stuttgart: Hiersemann, 1950–.

Lampe, G. W. H. *A Patristic Greek Lexicon.* Oxford: Clarendon, 1961.

Liddell, H. G. and R. Scott. *A Greek-English Lexicon.* Rev. H. S. Jones and R. McKenzie. 9th ed. Oxford: Clarendon, 1940.

Murray, J. A. H., H. Bradley, *et al.*, eds. *The Oxford English Dictionary.* 2nd ed. Prepared by J. A. Simpson and E. S. C. Weiner. 20 vols. Oxford: Clarendon, 1989.

Quasten, Johannes. *Patrology.* 3 vols. Westminster, MD: Newman, 1960.

Smyth, Herbert W. *Greek Grammar.* Cambridge, MA: Harvard University Press, 1920. Repr. 1980.

Sophocles, E. A. *Greek Lexicon of the Roman and Byzantine Periods.* Hildesheim: Olms, 1983.

Wissowa, G., W. Kroll, et al., eds. *Paulys Realencyclopädie der classischen Altertumswissenschaft.* Vols. I–XXIV, IA.1–X.A, Supp. I–XV. Stuttgart: Metzler; Munich: Druckenmüller, 1894–1978.

Ancient Sources: Texts, Editions, Translations

Aelii Aristidis Smyrnaei quae supersunt omnia. Ed. B. Keil. 2 vols. Berlin: Weidmann, 1898. Repr. 1958.

Aristotle. Trans. H. P. Cooke, H. Tredennick, et al. 23 vols. LCL. Cambridge: Harvard University Press, 1938–60.

[Aristotle]. *Rhetorica ad Alexandrum.* Trans. H. Rackham. LCL. Vol. with *Aristotle. Problems II.* Cambridge: Harvard University Press, 1937.

Augustine. *Contra duas epistolas Pelagianorum.* Ed. K. Vrba and J. Zycha. CSEL 60. Leipzig: Freytag, 1913.

–. *Contra Faustum Manichaeum.* Ed. J. Zycha. CSEL 26/6, pt. 1. Leipzig: Freytag, 1891.

–. *De gestis Pelagii.* Ed. K. Vrba and J. Zycha. CSEL 42. Leipzig: Freytag, 1902.

–. *De peccatorum meritis et remissione.* Ed. K. Vrba and J. Zycha. CSEL 60. Leipzig: Freytag, 1913.

–. *Tractatus in Johannis evangelium.* Ed. D. R. Willems. CCSL 36. Turnbout: Brepols, 1954.

–. *Sancti Augustani Confessionum libri XIII.* Ed. Lucas Verheijen. CCSL 27. Turnhout: Brepols, 1981.

–. *The Nicene and Post Nicene Fathers.* First Series. Vols. 1–7. Ed. Philip Schaff. 1889. Repr. Grand Rapids, MI: Eerdmans, 1971, 1994.

–. *Confessions.* Trans. Henry Chadwick. Oxford: Oxford University Press, 1991.

The Works of Saint Augustine, A Translation for the 21st Century. Sermons III/3 (51–94) on the New Testament. Ed. John E. Rotelle. Trans. Edmund Hill. Brooklyn: New City Press, 1991.

–. *Sermons III/5 (148–183) on the New Testamtent.* Ed. John E. Rotelle. Trans. Edmund Hill. Brooklyn: New City Press, 1992.

Cicero. Trans. G. L. Hendrickson, H. M. Hubbell, et al. 28 vols. LCL. Cambridge: Harvard University Press, 1912–72.

[Cicero]. *Rhetorica ad Herennium.* Trans. H. Caplan. LCL. Cambridge: Harvard University Press, 1954.

Clement. *Stromata.* Ed. Otto von Stählin. 2 vols. GCS 15 and 17. Berlin: Akadamie-Verlag, 1939, 1909.

Die Pseudoklementinen I. Ed. Bernhard Rehm and Georg Strecker. GCS. Berlin: Akademie-Verlag, 1992.

Demetrius. *On Style.* Trans. Doreen C. Innes. In Aristotle vol. 23, *The Poetics.* LCL. Cambridge: Harvard University Press, 1995.

Demosthenes. Trans. J. H. Vince, C. A. Vince, et al. 7 vols. LCL. Cambridge: Harvard University Press, 1930–49.

Dio Chrysostom. Trans. J. W. Cohoon and H. L. Crosby. 5 vols. LCL. Cambridge: Harvard University Press, 1932–51.

Dionysius of Halicarnassus. *Critical Essays.* Trans. S. Usher. 2 vols. LCL. Cambridge: Harvard University Press, 1974–85.

Epictetus. Trans. W. A. Oldfather. 2 vols. LCL. Cambridge: Harvard University Press, 1925–28.

Eusebius. *Ecclesiastical History.* Trans. K. Lake and J. E. L. Oulton. 2 vols. LCL. New York: Putnam's Sons; Cambridge: Harvard University Press, 1926–32.

Eusebius Werke. Ed. Friedhelm Winkelmann. GCS 1/1. Berlin: Akadamie-Verlag, 1975.

Gregorii Nyssenii. Opera, VIII, pars I: opera ascetica. Ed. Werner Jaeger, et al. Leiden: Brill, 1952.

–. *Opera, X, pars I: sermones pars II.* Ed. G. Heil, et al. Leiden: Brill, 1990.

Harnack, Adolf. *Kritik des Neuen Testaments von einem griechischen Philosophen des 3. Jahrhunderts (Die im Apocriticus des Macarius Magnes enthaltene Streitschrift).* TU 37/4. Leipzig: Pries, 1911.

Hermogenes. Opera. Ed. H. Rabe. Rhetores Graeci. 6 vols. BT. Leipzig: Teubner, 1894.

"[Hermogenes] *On Stases:* A Translation with an Introduction and Notes." Ed. and trans. R. Nadeau. *SM* 31 (1964) 361–424.

Homer. *Iliad.* Trans. A. T. Murray. Revised by William F. Wyatt. 2 vols. 2nd ed. LCL. Cambridge: Harvard University Press, 1999.

–. *Odyssey.* Trans. A. T. Murray. Revised by George F. Dimock. 2 vols. 2nd ed. LCL. Cambridge: Harvard University Press, 1995.

Isocrates. Trans. G. Norlin and L. Van Hook. 3 vols. LCL. Cambridge: Harvard University Press, 1928–45.

John Chrysostom. *Patrologia graeca.* Ed. J.-P. Migne. Vols. 47–64. Paris, 1858–60.

Jean Chrysostome. *À Theodore.* Ed. Jean Dumortier. SC 117. Paris: Éditions du Cerf, 1966.

–. *À une jeune veuve.* Ed. Bernard Grillet. SC 138. Paris: Éditions du Cerf, 1968.

–. *Commentaire sur Isaïe.* Ed. Jean Dumortier and Arthur Lifooghe. SC 304. Paris: Éditions du Cerf, 1983.

–. *Commentaire sur Job.* Ed. Henri Sorlin and Louis Neyrand. SC 346, 348. Paris: Éditions du Cerf, 1988.

–. *Discours sur Babylas.* Ed. Margaret A. Schatkin, Cécile Blanc, Bernard Grillet and Jean-Noël Guinot. SC 362. Paris: Éditions du Cerf, 1990.

–. *Homélies sur Ozias.* Ed. Jean Dumortier. SC 277. Paris: Éditions du Cerf, 1981.

–. *Huit catéchèses baptismales inédites.* Ed. Antoine Wegner. SC 50. Paris: Éditions du Cerf, 1970.

–. *Lettre d'exil à Olympias et à tous les fidèles.* Ed. Anne-Marie Malingrey. SC 103. Paris: Éditions du Cerf, 1964.

–. *Lettres à Olympias.* Ed. Anne-Marie Malingrey. SC 13 bis. Paris: Éditions du Cerf, 1968.

–. *Panégyriques de S. Paul.* Ed. Auguste Piédagnel. SC 300. Paris: Éditions du Cerf, 1982.

–. *Sur l'incomprehensibilité de Dieu.* Ed. Anne-Marie Malingrey and Robert Flacelière. SC 28. Paris: Éditions du Cerf, 1970.

–. *Sur la providence de Dieu.* Ed. Anne-Marie Malingrey. SC 79. Paris: Éditions du Cerf, 1961.

–. *Sur la sacerdoce: dialogue et homélie.* Ed. Anne-Marie Malingrey. SC 272. Paris: Éditions du Cerf, 1980.

–. *Sur la vaine gloire et l'éducation des enfants.* SC 188. Paris: Éditions du Cerf, 1972.

–. *La virginité.* Ed. Herbert Musurillo and Bernard Grillet. SC 125. Paris: Éditions du Cerf, 1966.

Field, Frederick, ed. *Sancti patris nostri Joannis Chrysostomi, Interpretatio omnium epistolarum paulinarum.* 7 vols. Bibliotheca Patrum. Oxford: J. H. Parker, 1849–62.

Savile, H., ed. *Chrysostomi opera omnia.* 8 vols. Eton: Norton, 1610–12.

John Chrysostom. *The Nicene and Post-Nicene Fathers.* First Series. Vols. 9–14. Ed. Philip Schaff. 1889. Repr. Grand Rapids, MI: Eerdmans, 1969, 1975.

Christo, George Gus. *St. John Chrysostom, On Repentance and Almsgiving.* FC 96. Washington: Catholic University of America Press, 1998.

Haidacher, Sebastian, ed. "Drei unedierte Chrysostomus-Texte einer Baseler Handschrift." *ZKT* 31 (1907) 141–71.

Halton, Thomas. *In Praise of Saint Paul by John Chrysostom.* Washington: Catholic University of America Press, 1963.

Harkins, Paul W. *Saint John Chrysostom, Discourses against Judaizing Christians.* FC 68. Washington: Catholic University of America Press, 1979.

Hill, Robert C. *St. John Chrysostom. Commentary on the Psalms.* Vol. 1. Brookline, MA: Holy Cross Orthodox Press, 1998.

–. *St. John Chrysostom. Homilies in Genesis.* FC 74, 82 and 87. Washington: Catholic University of America Press, 1986–1992.

Hunter, David G. *A Comparison between a King and a Monk, Against the Opponents of the Monastic Life.* Studies in the Bible and Early Christianity 13. Lewiston: Mellen, 1988.

Schatkin, Margaret A. and Paul W. Harkins. *John Chrysostom, Apologist.* FC 73. Washington: Catholic University of America Press, 1985.

Shore, Sally Rieger. *John Chrysostom, On Virginity, Against the Opponents of the Monastic Life.* Studies in Women and Religion 9. New York: Mellen, 1983.

Julian. The Works of the Emperor Julian. Trans. Wilmer Cave Wright. 3 vols. LCL. London: William Heinemann, 1913. Repr. 1949, 1954.

Libanii Opera. Ed. Richard Foerster. 12 vols. Leipzig: Teubner, 1903–1923. Repr. Hildesheim: Olms, 1963.

Libanius. Trans. A. F. Norman. 2 vols. LCL. Cambridge: Harvard University Press, 1969–1977.

Lipsius, Richard Adelbert, ed. *Acta Apostolorum Apocryphorum.* Hildesheim: Olms, 1891. Repr. 1959.

"Longinus" On the Sublime. Trans. W. H. Fyfe. LCL. In Aristotle vol. 23, *The Poetics.* Cambridge: Harvard University Press, 1927.

Lucian. Trans. A. M. Harmon, K. Kilburn and M. D. Macleod. 8 vols. LCL. New York: Macmillan; Cambridge: Harvard University Press, 1913–1967.

Menander Rhetor. Ed. and trans. D. A. Russell and N. G. Wilson. Oxford: Clarendon, 1981.

Origène. *Contre Celse.* Ed. M. Borret. SC 132, 136, 147, 150. Paris: Cerf, 1967–69.

–. *Fragmenta ex commentariis in I Cor.* Ed. C. Jenkins. "Origen on 1 Corinthians." *JTS* 9 (1907–8) 231–247; 353–72; 500–14; *JTS* 10 (1908–09) 29–51. Supplemented by C. H. Turner. "Notes on the Texts of Origen's Commentary on 1 Corinthians." *JTS* 10 (1908–9) 270–76.

Palladios. *Dialogue sur la vie de Jean Chrysostome.* Ed. Anne-Marie Malingrey and Philippe Leclerq. SC 341, 342. Paris: Éditions du Cerf, 1988.

Philo. Trans. F. H. Colson, G. H. Whitaker, *et al.* 12 vols. LCL. Cambridge: Harvard University Press, 1929–53.

Philostratus: Imagines. Callistratus: Descriptiones. Trans. Arthur Fairbanks. LCL. Cambridge: Harvard University Press, 1931; repr. 1960.

Plato. Trans. H. N. Fowler, W. R. M. Lamb, *et al.* 12 vols. LCL. Cambridge: Harvard University Press, 1914–1935.

Pliny. Letters, and Panegyricus. Trans. B. Radice. 2 vols. LCL. Cambridge: Harvard University Press, 1916–38.

Plutarch's Lives. Trans. B. Perrin. 11 vols. LCL. Cambridge: Harvard University Press, 1914–26.

Plutarch's Moralia. Trans. Frank C. Babbitt, W. Helmbold, *et al.* 15 vols. LCL. Cambridge: Harvard University Press, 1927–69.

Plutarque. Oeuvres Morales. Ed. Robert Klaerr and Yvonne Vernière. Vol. 7, part 2. Paris: Société d'Édition "Les Belles Lettres," 1974.

Procopius. Trans. H. B. Dewing. 7 vols. LCL. Cambridge: Harvard University Press, 1914–40.

Quintilian. Trans. H. E. Butler. 4 vols. LCL. New York: Putnam's Sons, 1921–22.

Schneemelcher, Wilhelm. *New Testament Apocrypha.* Trans. and ed. R. McL. Wilson. 2 vols. Rev. ed. Louisville: Westminster/John Knox, 1991.

Seneca. *Ad Lucilium Epistulae Morales.* Trans. R. M. Gummere. 3 vols. LCL. New York: Putnam's Sons; Cambridge: Harvard University Press, 1918–25. Rev. ed. 1943, 1953.

Septuaginta. Ed. A. Rahlfs. Stuttgart: Deutsche Bibelgesellschaft, 1935.

Spengel, L. *Rhetores Graeci.* 3 vols. Leipzig: Teubner, 1853–56.

Staab, K. *Pauluskommentare aus der griechischen Kirche.* NTAbh 15. Münster: Aschendorff, 1933.

Stoicorum veterum fragmenta. Ed. H. F. A. von Arnim. 4 vols. Leipzig: Teubner, 1905–24.

Suetonius. Trans. J. C. Rolfe. 2 vols. LCL. Cambridge: Harvard University Press, 1914.

Swete, H. B., ed. *Theodori episcopi Mopsuesteni in epistolas b. Pauli commentarii.* 2 vols. Cambridge: Cambridge University Press, 1880–82.

Syriani in Hermogenem commentaria. Ed. H. Rabe. 2 vols. Rhetores Graeci 16. Leipzig: Teubner, 1892–93.

Thucydides. Trans. C. F. Smith. 4 vols. LCL. Cambridge: Harvard University Press, 1919–23.

Usener, Hermann and Ludwig Radermacher, eds. *Dionysii Halicarnasei quae exstant.* BT. Stuttgart: Teubner, 1965.

Walz, Christian, ed. *Rhetores Graeci.* 9 vols. Stuttgart/Tübingen: Cotta, 1832–36.

Weichert, Valentin, ed. *Demetrii et Libanii qui feruntur ΤΥΠΟΙ ΕΠΙΣΤΟΛΙΚΟΙ et ΕΠΙΣΤΟ-ΛΙΜΑΙΟΙ ΧΑΡΑΚΤΗΡΕΣ.* BT. Leipzig: Teubner, 1910.

Xenophon. Trans. C. L. Brownson, O. J. Todd, *et al.* 7 vols. LCL. Cambridge: Harvard University Press, 1918–25.

Secondary Literature Cited

Abrams, M. H. *The Mirror and the Lamp: Romantic Theory and the Critical Tradition.* Oxford: Oxford University Press, 1988.

Aldama, J. A. de. *Repertorium pseudochrysostomicum.* Documents, études et répertoires publiés par l'Institut de recherche et d'histoire des textes 10. Paris: Centre national de la recherche scientifique, 1965.

Aleith, Eva. *Paulusverständnis in der alten Kirche.* BZNW 18. Berlin: Töpelmann, 1937.

Allen, Pauline. "John Chrysostom's Homilies on I and II Thessalonians: The Preacher and his Audience." *Studia Patristica* 31. Ed. Elizabeth A. Livingstone. Louvain: Peeters, 1997. 3–21.

Altaner, Berthold and Alfred Stuiber. *Patrologie: Leben, Schriften und Lehre der Kirchenväter.* 7th ed. Freiburg/Basel/Vienna: Herder, 1966.

Ameringer, Thomas E. *The Stylistic Influence of the Second Sophistic On the Panegyrical Sermons of St. John Chrysostom: A Study in Greek Rhetoric.* Ph.D. diss., Catholic University of America, 1921.

Anderson, R. Dean. *Ancient Rhetorical Theory and Paul.* Contributions to Biblical Exegesis and Theology 17. Kampen: Kok Pharos, 1996.

Babcock, W. S., ed. *Paul and the Legacies of Paul*. Dallas: Southern Methodist University, 1990.

Bailly, Jean-Christophe. *L'apostrophe muette: essai sur les portraits du Fayoum*. Paris: Éditions Hazan, 1997.

Barclay, John M. G. *Jews in the Mediterranean Diaspora from Alexander to Trajan, 323 BCE–117 CE)*. Edinburgh: T & T Clark, 1996.

Barnard, L. W. *The Graeco-Roman and Oriental Background of the Iconoclastic Controversy*. Byzantina Neerlandica 5. Leiden: Brill, 1974.

Barrett, C. K. *Paul: An Introduction to His Thought*. Louisville: Westminster/John Knox, 1994.

Bassler, Jouette M., ed. *Pauline Theology, Volume I: Thessalonians, Philippians, Galatians, Philemon*. Philadelphia: Fortress, 1991.

–. *1 Timothy, 2 Timothy, Titus*. Abingdon New Testament Commentaries. Nashville: Abingdon, 1996.

Baur, C. *John Chrysostom and His Time*. 2 vols. Trans. M. Gonzaga. Westminster, MD: Newman, 1959.

–. *Jean Chrysostome et ses oeuvres dans l'histoire littéraire*. Université de Louvain Recueil de Travaux 18. Louvain: Bureaux du Recueil/Paris: Fontemoing, 1907.

Becker, Jürgen. *Paul, Apostle to the Gentiles*. Trans. O. C. Dean, Jr. Louisville: Westminster/John Knox, 1993.

Belting, Hans. *Likeness and Presence. A History of the Image before the Era of Art*. Trans. Edmund Jephcott. Chicago and London: University of Chicago Press, 1994.

Benz, Ernst. "Das Paulus-Verständnis in der morgenländischen und abendländischen Kirche." *ZRGG* 3 (1951) 289–309.

Betz, Hans Dieter. *2 Corinthians 8 and 9: A Commentary on Two Administrative Letters of the Apostle Paul*. Hermeneia. Philadelphia: Fortress, 1985.

–. "Antike und Christentum." *RGG*[4] 1 (1998) 542–46.

–. "Antiquity and Christianity." *JBL* 117 (1998) 3–22. Repr. in *Antike und Christentum: Gesammelte Aufsätze IV*. Tübingen: J. C. B. Mohr [Paul Siebeck] 1998. 267–90.

–. *Der Apostel Paulus und die sokratische Tradition: Eine exegetische Untersuchung zu seiner "Apologie" in 2 Korinther 10–13*. BHT 45. Tübingen: J. C. B. Mohr [Paul Siebeck], 1972.

–. *Galatians: A Commentary on Paul's Letter to the Churches in Galatia*. Hermeneia. Philadelphia: Fortress, 1979.

–. "*de laude ipsius.*" *Plutarch's Ethical Writings and Early Christian Literature*. Ed. Hans Dieter Betz. SCHNT 4. Leiden: Brill, 1978. 367–93.

–. "Paul's 'Second Presence' in Colossians." *Texts and Contexts: Biblical Texts in Their Textual and Situational Contexts. Essays in Honor of Lars Hartman*. Ed. Tord Fornberg and David Hellholm. Oslo: Scandinavian University Press, 1995. 507–18.

–. *Paulinische Studien: Gesammelte Aufsätze III*. Tübingen: J. C. B. Mohr [Paul Siebeck] 1994.

–. *Plutarch's Ethical Writings and Early Christian Literature*. SCHNT 4. Leiden: Brill, 1978.

–. *Plutarch's Theological Writings and Early Christian Literature*. SCHNT 3. Leiden: Brill, 1975.

–. "The Portrait of Jesus in the Sermon on the Mount." *Currents in Theology and Mission* 25 (1998) 165–75.

–. "The Problem of Rhetoric and Theology according to the Apostle Paul." *L'Apôtre Paul: personnalité, style et conception du ministère*. Ed. A. Vanhoye. BETL 73 (1986) 16–48, reprinted in *Paulinische Studien: Gesammelte Aufsätze III*. Tübingen: J. C. B. Mohr [Paul Siebeck] 1994. 126–62.

Bezdeki, Joannes. "Chrysostom." *Ephemeris Dacoromana* 1 (1923) 291–337.

Boer, M. C. de. "Images of Paul in the Post-Apostolic Period." *CBQ* 43 (1980) 359–80.

Bonsdorff, Max von. "Zur Predigttätigkeit des Johannes Chrysostomus: Biographisch-chronologische Studien über seine Homilienserien zu neutestamentlichen Büchern." Diss., Universität Helsingfors, Helsinki, 1922.

Bouwsma, William J. *John Calvin. A Sixteenth-century Portrait.* New York/Oxford: Oxford University Press, 1988.

Bovon, François. "Paul comme document et Paul comme monument." *Chretiens en conflit: l'Epitre de Paul aux Galates, Dossier pour l'animation biblique.* Ed. J. Allaz, et al. Essais bibliques 13. Paris: Labor et fides, 1987. 54–65.

Boyarin, Daniel. *A Radical Jew: Paul and the Politics of Identity.* Berkeley: University of California Press, 1994.

Brändle, R. "Johannes Chrysostomus I." *RAC* 18 (1998) 426–503.

Broger, Anne. *Das Epitheton bei Sappho und Alkaios: eine sprachwissenschaftliche Untersuchung.* Innsbrucker Beiträge zur Sprachwissenschaft 88. Innsbruck: Institüt für Sprachwissenschaft der Universität Innsbruck, 1996.

Brooten, Bernadette. "'Junia ... Outstanding among the Apostles' (Romans 16:7)." *Women Priests: a Catholic Commentary on the Vatican Declaration.* Ed. L. Swidler. New York: Paulist, 1977. 141–44.

—. *Love Between Women: Early Christian Responses to Female Homoeroticism.* Chicago: University of Chicago Press, 1996.

Brown, Peter. *Augustine of Hippo: A Biography.* Berkeley: University of California Press, 1967.

—. *Power and Persuasion in Late Antiquity: Towards a Christian Empire.* Madison: University of Wisconsin Press, 1992.

—. *The Body and Society: Men, Women and Sexual Renunciation in Early Christianity.* Lectures on the History of Religions, n. s. 13. New York: Columbia University Press, 1988.

—. *The Cult of the Saints: Its Rise and Function in Latin Christianity.* Haskell Lectures on the History of Religions, n. s. 2. Chicago: University of Chicago Press, 1981.

Bryson, Norman. "Philostratus and the Imaginary Museum." *Art and Text in Ancient Greek Culture.* Ed. Simon Goldhill and Robin Osborne. Cambridge Studies in New Art History and Criticism. Cambridge: Cambridge University Press, 1994. 255–83.

Buberl, Paul. *Die Miniaturenhandschriften der Nationalbibliothek in Athen.* Kaiserliche Akademie der Wissenschaften in Wien. Philosophisch-historische Klasse, Denkschriften 60,2. Vienna: Hölder, 1917.

Burgess, Theodore C. *Epideictic Literature.* The University of Chicago Studies in Classical Philology. Chicago: University of Chicago Press, 1902.

Burke, Seán. *Authorship: From Plato to the Postmodern.* Edinburgh: Edinburgh University Press, 1995.

—. *The Death and Return of the Author: Criticism and Subjectivity in Barthes, Foucault and Derrida.* Edinburgh; Edinburgh University Press, 1992.

Burkert, Walter. *Greek Religion.* Trans. J. Raffan. Cambridge, MA: Harvard University Press, 1985.

Callahan, Allen Dwight. "John Chrysostom on Philemon: A Response to Margaret M. Mitchell." *HTR* 88 (1995) 149–56.

—. "Paul's Epistle to Philemon: Toward an Alternative *Argumentum*." *HTR* 86 (1993) 357–76.

Calvin, John. "Praefatio in Chrysosotomi homilias." *Corpus reformatorum: Ioannis Calvini opera quae supersunt omnia.* Vol. 37. Ed. G. Baum, E. Cunitz, et al. Braunschweig: Schwetschke, 1870. 831–38. Trans. by John H. McIndoe in *Hartford Quarterly* 5 (1965) 19–26.

Cameron, Averil. *Christianity and the Rhetoric of Empire: the Development of Christian Discourse*. Sather Classical Lectures 55. Berkeley: University of California Press, 1991.

—. "Eusebius' *Vita Constantini* and the Construction of Constantine." *Portraits: Biographical Representation in the Greek and Latin Literature of the Roman Empire*. Ed. M. J. Edwards and Simon Swain. Oxford: Clarendon, 1997. 145–74.

Castagno, Adele Monaci. "Paideia classica esercizio pastorale ne IV secolo: il concetto di 'synesis' nell'opera di Giovanni Crisostomo." *Rivista di storia e letteratura religiosa* 26 (1990) 429–59.

Castelli, Elizabeth A. *Imitating Paul. A Discourse of Power*. Literary Currents in Biblical Interpretation. Louisville: Westminster/John Knox, 1991.

Chase, F. H. *Chrysostom. A Study in the History of Biblical Interpretation*. Cambridge: Deighton, Bell & Co., 1887.

Chidester, David. *Word and Light: Seeing, Hearing, and Religious Discourse*. Urbana: University of Illinois Press, 1992.

Clark, Elizabeth A. "Introduction." *John Chrysostom—On Virginity, and Against Remarriage*. Trans. Sally Rieger Shore. Studies in Women and Religion 9. New York: Mellen, 1983.

—. *Jerome, Chrysostom, and Friends: Essays and Translations*. Studies in Women and Religion 2. New York: Mellen, 1983.

—. *Reading Renunciation: Asceticism and Scripture in Early Christianity*. Princeton: Princeton University Press, 1999.

Coggan, Donald. *Paul. Portrait of a Revolutionary*. London: Hodder & Stoughton, 1984.

Coleman-Norton, P. R. "Saint John Chrysostom and the Greek Philosophers." *CP* 25 (1930) 305–17.

Colledge, Malcolm A. R. *The Art of Palmyra*. London: Thames & Hudson, Ltd., 1976.

Collins, Raymond F. "The Image of Paul in the Pastorals." *LTP* 31 (1975) 147–73.

Compton, Michael Bruce. "Introducing the Acts of the Apostles: a Study of John Chrysostom's *On the Beginning of Acts*." Ph.D. diss., University of Virginia, 1996.

Cox, Patricia. *Biography in Late Antiquity: The Quest for the Holy Man*. The Transformation of the Classical Heritage 5. Berkeley: University of California Press, 1983.

Cranfield, C. E. B. "Giving a Dog a Bad Name: a Note on H. Räisänen's *Paul and the Law*." *JSNT* 38 (1990) 77–85.

Crosby, Michael and William M. Calder III. "Libanius, *On the Silence of Socrates*: A First Translation and an Interpretation." *GRBS* 3 (1960) 185–202.

Danker, Frederick. "Paul's Debt to *De Corona* of Demosthenes: A Study of Rhetorical Techniques in Second Corinthians." *Persuasive Artistry: Studies in New Testament Rhetoric in Honor of George Kennedy*. Ed. Duane F. Watson. JSNTSup 50. Sheffield: Sheffield Academic Press, 1991. 262–80.

Dassmann, Ernst. "Archaeological Traces of Early Christian Veneration." *Paul and the Legacies of Paul*. Ed. William S. Babcock. Dallas: Southern Methodist University, 1990. 281–306.

—. *Paulus in frühchristlicher Frömmigkeit und Kunst*. Rheinisch-Westfälische Akademie der Wissenschaften. Vorträge G256. Opladen: Westdeutscher Verlag, 1982.

—. "Zum Paulusverständnis in der östlichen Kirche." *JAC* 29 (1986) 27–39, 33–38.

—. *Der Stachel im Fleisch. Paulus in der frühchristlichen Literatur bis Irenäus*. Münster: Aschendorff, 1979.

Dautzenberg, Gerhard. "Glossolalie." *RAC* 11 (1981) 225–46.

Davies, W. D. *Paul and Rabbinic Judaism: Some Rabbinic Elements in Pauline Theology*. 3rd ed. London: S. P. C. K., 1970.

Dee, J. H. *The Epithetic Phrases for the Homeric Gods* (Epitheta deorum apud Homerum): *a Repertory of the Descriptive Expressions for the Divinities of the* Iliad *and the* Odyssey. Albert Bates Lord Studies in Oral Tradition 14. New York: Garland, 1994.

DeHamel, Christopher. *A History of Illuminated Manuscripts.* Boston: Grodine, 1986.

Delehaye, Hippolyte. *Les passions des martyrs et les genres littéraires.* Studia hagiographica 13b. 2nd ed. Brussels: Société des Bollandistes, 1966.

Der Nersessian, Sirarpie. "A Psalter and New Testament Manuscript at Dumbarton Oaks." *Dumbarton Oaks Papers* 19 (1965) 153–83.

Devreesse, R., *et al. Codices Vaticani Graeci III.* Vatican: Biblioteca Apostolica Vaticana, 1950.

Di S. Maria, Melchiorre. "S. Paolo nella prospettiva di S. Giovanni Crisostomo." *Studiorum paulinorum congressus internationalis catholicus 1961.* AnBib 18. Rome: Pontifical Biblical Institute, 1963.

Djordjevic, Ivan M. *Zidno slikarstvo srpske vlastele u doba Nemanjica* ("Wall-Paintings of the Serbian Nobility of the Nemanide Era"). Belgrade: Filozofski fakultet, 1994.

Dobschütz, Ernst von. *Der Apostel Paulus II. Seine Stellung in der Kunst* (Halle: Waisenhaus, 1928).

Downey, Glanville. "Ekphrasis." *RAC* 5 (1959) 921–44.

–. *A History of Antioch in Syria from Seleucus to the Arab Conquest.* Princeton: Princeton University Press, 1961.

Doxiadis, Euphrosune. "From *Eikon* to Icon: Continuity in Technique." *Portraits and Masks: Burial Customs in Roman Egypt.* Ed. M. L. Bierbrier. London: British Museum Press, 1997. 78–80.

Dumortier, Jean. "L'auteur présumé du corpus asceticum des S. Jean Chrysostome." *JTS* n. s. 6 (1955) 99–102.

–. "La culture profane de S. Jean Chrysostome." *MscRel* 10 (1953) 53–62.

Dunn, James D. G. *Jesus, Paul, and the Law: Studies in Mark and Galatians.* Louisville: Westminster/John Knox, 1990.

–. "New Perspectives on Paul." *BJRL* 65 (1983) 95–122. Repr. in *idem. Jesus, Paul, and the Law.* 183–214.

–. "Once More, ΠΙΣΤΙΣ ΧΡΙΣΤΟΥ." *SBLSP* 1991. Ed. Eugene H. Lovering, Jr. Atlanta: Scholars Press, 1991. 730–44.

–. "Paul: Apostate or Apostle of Israel?" *ZNW* 89 (1998) 256–71.

–. *The Theology of Paul the Apostle.* Grand Rapids: Eerdmans, 1998.

–. *The Theology of Paul's Letter to the Galatians.* Cambridge: Cambridge University Press, 1993.

Edwards, M. J. "Epilogue." *Portraits: Biographical Representation in the Greek and Latin Literature of the Roman Empire.* Ed. M. J. Edwards and Simon Swain. Oxford: Clarendon, 1997. 227–34.

Edwards, M. J. and Simon Swain, eds. *Portraits: Biographical Representation in the Greek and Latin Literature of the Roman Empire.* Oxford: Clarendon, 1997.

Eleen, Luba. *The Illustration of the Pauline Epistles of the Twelfth and Thirteenth Centuries.* Oxford: Clarendon, 1982.

Elliger, Walter. *Die Stellung der alten Christen zu den Bildern in den ersten vier Jahrhunderten (nach den Angaben der zeitgenössischen kirchlichen Schriftsteller).* Studien über christliche Denkmäler. Vol. 20. Ed. J. Ficker. Leipzig: Dieterich, 1930.

Elliott, Neil. *Liberating Paul: The Justice of God and the Politics of the Apostle.* Maryknoll, NY: Orbis, 1994.

Elsner, Jás. *Art and the Roman Viewer: The Transformation of Art from the Pagan World to Christianity.* Cambridge: Cambridge University Press, 1995.

Fabricius, Cajus. *Zu den Jugendschriften des Johannes Chrysostomos: Untersuchungen zum Klassizismus des vierten Jahrhunderts.* Lund: Gleerup, 1962.

Fairweather, Janet. "The Epistle to the Galatians and Classical Rhetoric." *TynBul* 45 (1994) 1–38, 213–44.

Ferguson, John. *Pelagius.* Cambridge: Heffer & Sons, 1956.

Finney, Paul Corby. *The Invisible God: The Earliest Christians on Art.* New York/Oxford: Oxford University Press, 1994.

Fiorenza, Elisabeth Schüssler. "The Ethics of Biblical Interpretation: Decentering Biblical Scholarship." *JBL* 107 (1988) 3–17.

Fitzgerald, John T. "Virtue/Vice Lists." *ABD* 6.857–59.

Florus, Drepanius. *Expositio epistolarum b. Pauli apostoli, ex diversis opusculis sancti Augustini a venerabili Beda presbytero excerpta, et in unum corpus collecta.* Paris: Georgius Iosse, 1649.

Forbes, Christopher. "Comparison, Self-Praise and Irony: Paul's Boasting and the Conventions of Hellenistic Rhetoric." *NTS* 32 (1986) 1–30.

Fredriksen, Paula. "Augustine's Early Interpretation of Paul." Ph.D. diss., Princeton University, 1979.

—. "Beyond the body/soul dichotomy: Augustine on Paul against the Manichees and the Pelagians." *Recherches Augustiniennes* 23 (1988) 87–114.

Froehlich, Karlfried. "Which Paul? Observations on the Image of the Apostle in the History of Biblical Exegesis." *New Perspectives on Historical Theology. Essays in Memory of John Meyendorf.* Ed. B. Nassif. Grand Rapids, MI: Eerdmans, 1996. 279–99.

Furnish, Victor Paul. *II Corinthians.* AB 32A. Garden City, NY: Doubleday, 1984.

—. "Fellow Workers in God's Service." *JBL* 80 (1961) 364–70.

—. "Paul the ΜΑΡΤΥΣ." *Witness and Existence: Essays in Honor of Schubert M. Ogden.* Ed. Philip E. Devenish and George L. Goodwin. Chicago: University of Chicago Press, 1989. 73–88.

Ganoczy, A. and K. Müller. *Calvins handschriftliche Annotationen zu Chrysostomus: ein Beitrag zur Hermeneutik Calvins.* Veröffentlichungen des Instituts für Europäische Geschichte Mainz 102. Wiesbaden: Steiner, 1982.

Garrett, Duane A. *An Analysis of the Hermeneutics of John Chrysostom's Commentary on Isaiah 1–8 with an English Translation.* Studies in the Bible and Early Christianity 12. Lewiston: Mellen, 1992.

Gasparro, Giulia Sfameni. "Asceticism and Anthropology: *Enkrateia* and 'Double Creation' in Early Christianity." *Asceticism.* Ed. Vincent L. Wimbush and Richard Valantasis. New York/Oxford: Oxford University Press, 1995. 127–46.

Gengaro, Maria Luisa, Francesca Leoni, Gemma Villa. *Codici decorati e miniati dell' Ambrosiana, ebraici e greci.* Fontes Ambrosiani 33A. Milan: Ceschina, 1960.

Geoffroy-Scheiter, B. *Fayum Portraits.* Trans. Emily Lane. London: Thames and Hudson, 1998.

Gibbon, Edward. *The History of the Decline and Fall of the Roman Empire.* 7 vols. Ed. J. B. Bury. London: Methuen & Co., 1909.

Glad, Clarence E. *Paul and Philodemus: Adaptability in Epicurean and Early Christian Psychagogy.* NovTSup 81. Leiden: Brill, 1995.

Gleason, Maud W. *Making Men: Sophists and Self-Presentation in Ancient Rome.* Princeton: Princeton University Press, 1995

Gnilka, Joachim. *Der Philipperbrief.* HTKNT 10/3. Freiburg/Basel/Vienna: Herders, 1968.

Godin, A. *Érasme. Lecteur d'Origène.* Geneva: Droz, 1982.

Goggin, Sister Thomas Aquinas. *Saint John Chrysostom. Commentary on Saint John the Apostle and Evangelist.* FC 33 and 41. New York: Fathers of the Church, Inc. 1957–1960.

Gondos, L. "Epitheton." *Historisches Wörterbuch der Rhetorik.* Ed. G. Ueding. Vol. 2, ed. G. Kalivoda *et al.* Tübingen: Niemeyer, 1994. 1314–16.

Goodall, Blake. *The Homilies of St. John Chrysostom on the Letters of St. Paul to Titus and Philemon.* Berkeley: University of California Press, 1979.

Gorday, P. "Paul in Eusebius and Other Early Christian Literature." *Eusebius, Christianity, and Judaism.* Ed. H. W. Attridge and G. Hata. Studia Post-Biblica 42. Leiden: Brill, 1992. 139–65.

–. *Principles of Patristic Exegesis: Romans 9–11 in Origen, John Chrysostom, and Augusine.* New York: Mellen, 1983.

Gordon, Barry. "The Problem of Scarcity and the Christian Fathers: John Chrysostom and Some Contemporaries." *Studia Patristica* 22. Ed. Elizabeth A. Livingstone. Louvain: Peeters, 1989. 108–20.

Grabar, André. *L'art de la fin de l' antiquité et du moyen age.* 3 vols. Paris: Collège de France, 1968.

–. *Christian Iconography. A Study of its Origins.* Bollingen Series 35/10. Princeton: Princeton University Press, 1968

–. *L'empereur dans l'art byzantin: recherches sur l'art officiel de l'empire d'orient.* London: Variorum Reprints, 1971.

–. "Un rouleau liturgique constantinopolitain et ses peintures." *Dumbarton Oaks Papers* 8 (1954) 173.

Grant, Robert M. *Augustus to Constantine. The Rise and Triumph of Christianity in the Roman World.* San Francisco: Harper & Row, 1970.

–. "The Description of Paul in the Acts of Paul and Thecla." *VC* 36 (1982) 1–4.

–. *Heresy and Criticism: The Search for Authenticity in Early Christian Literature.* Louisville: Westminster/John Knox, 1993.

Greeley, Dolores, R. S. M. "St. John Chrysostom, Prophet of Social Justice." *Studia Patristica* 17/3. Ed. Elizabeth A. Livingstone. Oxford/New York: Pergamon, 1982. 1163–68.

Greer, R. *The Captain of Our Salvation: A Study in the Patristic Exegesis of Hebrews.* BGBE 15. Tübingen: J. C. B. Mohr [Paul Siebeck], 1973.

Grozdanov, Cvetan. "L'image de l'apparition de la sagesse divine à saint Jean Chrysostome dans l'église de sainte sophie à Ochrid" (French precis of Serbian article). *Recueil des travaux de l'institut d'études byzantines* 19 (1980) 147–55.

Guillaumin, Marie-Louise. "Bible et liturgie dans la prédication de Jean Chrysostome." *Jean Chrysostome et Augustin.* Ed. Charles Kannengiesser. Théologie historique 35. Paris: Éditions Beauchesne, 1975. 161–174.

Hadot, Pierre. "Preface." In *Philostrate: la galerie de tableaux.* Trans. Auguste Bougot. Rev. and annotated by François Lissarrague. Paris: Les Belles Lettres, 1991. vii–xxii.

Halkin, F. *Douze récits byzantines sur Saint Jean Chrysostome.* Subsidia hagiographica 60. Brussels: Société des Bollandistes, 1977.

Harnack, Adolf. *Kritik des Neuen Testaments von einem griechischen Philosophen des 3. Jahrhunderts (Die im Apocriticus des Macarius Magnes enthaltene Streitschrift).* TU 37/4. Leipzig: Pries, 1911.

Harpham, Geoffrey Galt. "Asceticism and the Compensations of Art." *Asceticism.* Ed. Vincent L. Wimbush and Richard Valantasis. New York/Oxford: Oxford University Press, 1995. 357–368.

–. *The Ascetic Imperative in Culture and Criticism.* Chicago: University of Chicago Press, 1987.

Harrill, J. Albert. *The Manumission of Slaves and Early Christianity.* HUT 32. Tübingen: J. C. B. Mohr [Paul Siebeck], 1995.

Harrison,Verna E. F."Word as Icon in Greek Patristic Theology." *Sobornost* 10 (1988) 38–49.

Harrisville, R. A. "ΠΙΣΤΙΣ ΧΡΙΣΤΟΥ: Witness of the Fathers." *NovT* 36 (1994) 233–41.

Harvey, A. E. *Renewal Through Suffering: A Study of 2 Corinthians.* Studies of the New Testament and its World. Edinburgh: T & T Clark, 1996.

Havice, Christine. "The Hamilton Psalter in Berlin, Kupferstichkabinett 78.A:9." Ph.D. diss., Pennsylvania State University, 1978.

Hay, D. M., ed. *Pauline Theology, Volume II: 1 and 2 Corinthians.* Philadelphia: Fortress, 1993.

Hays, Richard B. *Echoes of Scripture in the Letters of Paul.* New Haven: Yale University Press, 1989.

–. *The Faith of Jesus Christ: An Investigation of the Narrative Substructure of Galatians 3:1–4:11.* SBLDS 56. Chico, CA: Scholars Press, 1983.

–. "ΠΙΣΤΙΣ and Pauline Christology: What Is at Stake?" *SBLSP* 1991. Ed. Eugene H. Lovering, Jr. Atlanta: Scholars Press, 1991. 714–29.

Heath, Stephen. *Image, Music, Text: Roland Barthes, Essays Selected and Translated.* New York: Hill and Wang, 1977.

Heffernan, James A. W. "Ekphrasis and Representation." *New Literary History* 22 (1991) 297–316.

Hengel, Martin. *The Pre-Christian Paul.* Trans. John Bowden. Philidephia: Trinity Press International, 1991.

Hill, Robert C. "Akribeia: A Principle of Chrysostom's Exegesis." *Colloquium* 14 (1981) 32–36.

–. "Chrysostom's terminology for the inspired Word." *EstBib* 41 (1983) 367–73.

Hock, Ronald F. *The Social Context of Paul's Ministry: Tentmaking and Apostleship.* Philadelphia: Fortress, 1980.

Hoffmann-Aleith, Eva. "Das Paulusverständnis des Johannes Chrysostomus." *ZNW* 38 (1939) 181–88.

Hubbell, Harry M. "Chrysostom and Rhetoric." *CP* 19 (1924) 261–76.

Hunter, David G. *A Comparison between a King and a Monk, Against the Opponents of the Monastic Life.* Studies in the Bible and Early Christianity 13. Lewiston: Mellen, 1988.

–. "Libanius and John Chrysostom: New Thoughts on an Old Problem." *Studia Patristica* 22. Ed. Elizabeth A. Livingstone. Louvain: Peeters, 1989. 129–35.

Irmscher, Johannes and Georg Strecker. "The Pseudo-Clementines." *NTApoc* 2.483–541.

James, Liz and Ruth Webb. "'To Understand Ultimate Things and Enter Secret Places': Ekphrasis and Art in Byzantium." *Art History* 14 (1991) 1–17.

Jensen, Anne. *God's Self-confident Daughters: Early Christianity and the Liberation of Women.* Trans. O. C. Dean. Louisville: Westminster/John Knox, 1996.

Johnson, E. E. and D. M. Hay, eds. *Pauline Theology, Volume III: Romans.* Philadelphia: Fortress, 1995.

Johnson, Luke Timothy. *The Acts of the Apostles.* Sacra Pagina 5. Collegeville, MN: Glazier, 1992.

–. "Romans 3:21–26 and the Faith of Jesus." *CBQ* 44 (1982) 77–90.

Judge, E. A. "Paul's Boasting in Relation to Contemporary Professional Practice." *AusBR* 16 (1968) 37–50.

Kannengiesser, Charles. "Biblical Interpretation in the Early Church." *Historical Handbook of Major Biblical Interpreters.* Ed. Donald K. McKim. Downers Grove, IL: InterVarsity Press, 1998. 1–16.

–. "The Future of Patristics." *TS* 52 (1991) 128–139.

–, ed. *Jean Chrysostome et Augustin.* Théologie Historique 35. Paris: Éditions Beauchesne, 1975.

Kaster, Robert A. *Guardians of Language: the Grammarian and Society in Late Antiquity.* Berkeley: University of California Press, 1988.

Kelly, J. N. D. *Golden Mouth: The Story of John Chrysostom, Ascetic, Preacher, Bishop.* Ithaca, NY: Cornell University Press, 1995.

Kennedy, George A. *Greek Rhetoric Under Christian Emperors.* Princeton: Princeton University Press, 1983.

Kern, Philip H. *Rhetoric and Galatians: Assessing an Approach to Paul's Epistle.* SNTSMS 101. Cambridge: Cambridge University Press, 1998.

Kertsch, Manfred. *Exempla Chrysostomica: Zu Exegese, Stil und Bildersprache bei Johannes Chrysostomos.* Grazer Theologische Studien 18. Graz: Institut für Ökumenische Theologie und Patrologie an der Universität Graz, 1995.

Klaerr, Robert and Yvonne Vernière. *Plutarque, Oeuvres Morales.* Vol. 7, part 2. Paris: Société d'Édition "Les Belles Lettres," 1974.

Knox, John. *Chapters in a Life of Paul.* Rev. ed. Macon, GA: Mercer University Press, 1987.

Koskenniemi, H. *Studien zur Idee und Phraseologie des griechischen Briefes bis 400 n. Chr.* Suomalaisen Tiedeakatemian Toimituksia, series B, Annales Academiae Scientiarum Fennicae 102, 2. Helsinki: Suomalainen Tiedeakatemia, 1956.

Krueger, Derek. "Hagiography as an Ascetic Practice in the Early Christian East." *JR* 79 (1999) 216–232.

Krupp, Robert A. *St. John Chrysostom: A Scripture Index.* Lanham: University Press of America, 1984.

Lamberton, Robert. *Homer the Theologian: Neoplatonist Allegorical Reading and the Growth of the Epic Tradition.* Berkeley: University of California Press, 1986.

Landes, Paula Fredriksen. *Augustine on Romans.* SBLTT 23. Chico, CA: Scholars Press, 1982.

Lechner, M. "Paulus." *Lexikon der christlichen Ikonographie.* Ed. W. Braunfels. Freiburg: Herder, 1974. 8.133–34.

Lentz, John C. *Luke's Portrait of Paul.* SNTSMS 77. Cambridge: Cambridge University Press, 1993.

Leroux, Jean-Marie. "Monachisme et communauté chrétienne d'après Saint Jean Chrysostom." *Théologie de la vie monastique.* Théologie 49. Paris: Aubier, 1961. 143–90.

Leyerle, Blake. "John Chrysostom on Almsgiving and the Use of Money." *HTR* 87 (1994) 29–47.

Liebeschuetz, J. H. W. G. *Barbarians and Bishops: Army, Church, and State in the Age of Arcadius and Chrysostom.* Oxford: Clarendon, 1990.

Lietzmann, Hans. "Johannes Chrysostomos." *PW* 9/2 (1916) 1811–1828.

Lindemann, A. *Paulus im ältesten Christentum. Das Bild des Apostels und die Rezeption der paulinischen Theologie in der frühchristlichen Literatur bis Marcion.* BHT 58. Tübingen: J. C. B. Mohr [Paul Siebeck], 1979.

Lipsius, Richard Adelbert. *Die apokryphen Apostelgeschichten und Apostellegenden: Ein Beitrag zur altchristlichen Literaturgeschichte.* Braunschweig: Schwetschke, 1887.

Litfin, Duane. *St. Paul's Theology of Proclamation: 1 Corinthians 1–4 and Greco-Roman Rhetoric.* SNTSMS 79. Cambridge: Cambridge University Press, 1994.

Luedemann, Gerd. *Opposition to Paul in Jewish Christianity.* Trans. M. Eugene Boring. Minneapolis: Fortress, 1989.

Maccoby, Hyam. *The Mythmaker: Paul and the Invention of Christianity.* San Francisco: Harper & Row, 1986.

MacDonald, D. R. *The Legend and the Apostle. The Battle for Paul in Story and Canon.* Philadelphia: Westminster, 1983.

Madigan, Susan Pinto. "Athens 211 and the Illustrated Homilies of John Chrysostom." Ph.D. diss., University of Chicago, 1984.

Maguire, Henry. *Art and Eloquence in Byzantium*. Princeton: Princeton University Press, 1981.

—. *The Icons of Their Bodies: Saints and Their Images in Byzantium*. Princeton: Princeton University Press, 1996.

Malherbe, Abraham J. *Ancient Epistolary Theorists*. SBLSBS 19. Atlanta: Scholars Press, 1988.

—. "Antisthenes and Odysseus, and Paul at War." *HTR* 76 (1983) 143–73.

—. "Determinism and Free Will in Paul: The Argument of 1 Corinthians 8 and 9." *Paul in his Hellenistic Context*. Ed. Troels Engberg-Pedersen. Minneapolis: Fortress, 1995. 231–55.

—. *Paul and the Popular Philosophers*. Minneapolis: Fortress, 1989.

—. *Paul and the Thessalonians: the Philosophic Tradition of Pastoral Care*. Philadelphia: Fortress, 1987.

—. "A Physical Description of Paul." *Christians Among Jews and Gentiles. Essays in Honor of Krister Stendahl on His Sixty-fifth Birthday*. Ed. G. W. E. Nickelsburg and G. W. MacRae. Philadelphia: Fortress, 1986. 170–175.

—. *Social Aspects of Early Christianity*. 2nd ed. Philadelphia: Fortress, 1983.

Malina, Bruce J. and Jerome Neyrey. *Portraits of Paul: an Archaeology of Ancient Personality*. Louisville: Westminster/John Knox, 1996.

Mango, Cyril. *The Art of the Byzantine Empire 312–1453*. Medieval Academy Reprints for Teaching. Toronto: University of Toronto Press, 1986.

Mara, M. G. "Paul III. Commentaries on the Pauline Epistles." *EEC* 2.658–59.

Marava-Chatzinicolaou, Anna and Christina Toufexi-Paschou. *Catalogue of the Illuminated Byzantine Manuscripts of the National Library of Greece. Vol. III: Homilies of the Church Fathers and Menologia, 9th–12th century*. Athens: Academy of Athens Centre of Byzantine and Post-Byzantine Art, 1997.

Marrou, H. I. *A History of Education in Antiquity*. Trans. George Lamb. New York: Sheed and Ward, 1956.

Martin, Dale B. *Slavery as Salvation: The Metaphor of Slavery in Pauline Christianity*. New Haven: Yale University Press, 1990.

—. *The Corinthian Body*. New Haven: Yale University Press, 1995.

Martin, J. R. *The Illustration of the Heavenly Ladder of John Climacus*. Princeton: Princeton University Press, 1954.

Martin, Seán Charles. *Pauli Testamentum: 2 Timothy and the Last Words of Moses*. Tesi Gregoriana. Serie Teologia 18. Rome: Pontifical Gregorian University, 1997.

Martyn, J. Louis. *Galatians*. AB 33A. New York: Doubleday, 1997.

Maur, Ivo auf der. *Mönchtum und Glaubensverkündigung in den Schriften des hl. Johannes Chrysostomus*. Paradosis 14. Freiburg: Universitätsverlag Freiburg Schweiz, 1959.

Mayer, Wendy. "John Chrysostom and his Audiences: Distinguishing Different Congregations at Antioch and Constantinople." *Studia Patristica* 31. Ed. Elizabeth A. Livingstone. Louvain: Peeters, 1997. 70–75.

Mazzoleni, D. "Portrait." *EEC* 2.705.

Meeks, Wayne A. *The First Urban Christians: The Social World of the Apostle Paul*. New Haven: Yale University Press, 1983.

Merzagora, Augusta. "Giovanni Crisostomo commentatore di S. Paolo." *"Didaskaleion." Studi di letteratura e storia cristiana antica* n. s. 9. Ed. Paolo Ubaldi. Torino: Società editrice internazionale (1931) 1–73. Repr. Amsterdam: John Benjamins N. V., 1969. 1–73.

–. "Giovanni Crisostomo commentatore di S. Paolo: Osservazioni su l'esegesi filosofica (I)." *Studi dedicati alla memoria di Paolo Ubaldi.* Pubblicazioni della università cattolica del sacro cuore 16. Serie quinta: scienze storiche. Milan: Società editrice "vita e pensiero," 1937. 205–46.

Meyer, Louis. "Liberté et moralisme chrétien dans la doctrine spirituelle de saint Jean Chrysostome." *RSR* 23 (1933) 283–305.

Miles, Margaret R. "Image." *Critical Terms for Religious Studies.* Ed. Mark C. Taylor. Chicago: University of Chicago Press, 1998. 160–72.

Miller, Patricia Cox. "Dreaming the Body: An Aesthetics of Asceticism." *Asceticism.* Ed. Vincent L. Wimbush and Richard Valantasis. New York/Oxford: Oxford University Press, 1995. 281–300.

Millet, Gabriel. *Monuments de l'Athos.* Paris: Leroux, 1927.

Mitchell, Alan. C. "Rich and Poor in the Courts of Corinth: Litigiousness and Status in I Corinthians 6.1–11." *NTS* 39 (1993) 562–86.

Mitchell, Margaret M. "'The Archetypal Image': John Chrysostom's Portraits of Paul." *JR* 75 (1995) 15–43.

–. "Brief I. Form und Gattung." *RGG*[4] 1 (1998) 1757–60.

–. "Chrysostom, John." *Historical Handbook of Major Biblical Interpreters.* Ed. Donald K. McKim. Downers Grove, IL: InterVarsity Press, 1998. 28–34.

–. "John Chrysostom on Philemon: A Second Look." *HTR* 88 (1995) 135–88.

–. "John Chrysostom." *The Encyclopedia of Monasticism* (forthcoming).

–. *Paul and the Rhetoric of Reconciliation: An Exegetical Investigation of the Language and Composition of 1 Corinthians.* HUT 28. Tübingen: J. C. B. Mohr [Paul Siebeck], 1991. Repr. Louisville: Westminster/John Knox, 1993.

–. "Pauline Accommodation and 'Condescension' [συγκατάβασις]: 1 Cor 9:19–23 and the History of Influence" (forthcoming).

–. "Reading Rhetoric with Ancient Exegetes: John Chrysostom on Galatians" (forthcoming).

–. Review of *The Corinthian Women Prophets,* by A. C. Wire. In *RelSRev* 19 (1993) 308–11.

–. Review of *Golden Mouth: The Story of John Chrysostom-Ascetic, Preacher, Bishop,* by J. N. D. Kelly. In *Church History* 66 (1997) 85–87.

–. Review of *Liberating Paul: The Justice of God and the Politics of the Apostle,* by Neil Elliott. In *CBQ* 58 (1996) 546–47.

–. Review of *Portraits of Paul: An Archaeology of Ancient Personality,* by Bruce J. Malina and Jerome Neyrey. In *JR* 78 (1998) 611–13.

–. "Silver Chamber Pots and Other Goods Which are Not Good: John Chrysostom's Discourse on Wealth and Possessions" (forthcoming).

–. "'A Variable and Many-sorted Man': John Chrysostom's Treatment of Pauline Inconsistency." *JECS* 6 (1998) 93–111.

Momigliano, Arnaldo. *The Development of Greek Biography.* Expanded ed. Cambridge: Harvard University Press, 1993.

Murphy-O'Conner, Jerome. *Paul: A Critical Life.* Oxford: Clarendon, 1996.

Murray, Sister Charles. "Art and the Early Church." *JTS* 28 (1977) 303–45.

Müsseler, A. "Johannes Chrysostomus." *Lexikon der christlichen Ikonographie.* Ed. W. Braunfels. Freiburg: Herder, 1974. 7.93–101.

Naegele, Anton "Johannes Chrysostomos und sein Verhältnis zum Hellenismus." *Byzantinische Zeitschrift* 13 (1904) 73–113.

Nelson, Robert S. "To Say and to See." *Visuality Before and Beyond the Renaissance.* Ed. *idem.* Cambridge: Cambridge University Press (forthcoming).

Norden, Eduard. *Die antike Kunstprosa vom VI Jahrhundert v. Chr. bis in die Zeit der Renaissance.* 2 vols. Leipzig/Berlin: Teubner 1918.

Nowak, Edward. *Le chrétien devant la souffrance: étude sur la pensée de Jean Chrysostome.* Théologie historique 19. Paris: Éditions Beauchesne, 1972.

Okunev, M. N. L. "Lesnovo." *L'art byzantin chez les slaves: les balkans.* Orient et byzance 4, pt. 1. Paris: Guenther, 1930. 222–63.

Oliver, J. H. "The Ruling Power." *TAPA* 43 (1953) 871–1003.

Ollrog, Wolf-Henning. *Paulus und seine Mitarbeiter: Untersuchungen zu Theorie und Praxis der paulinischen Mission.* WMANT 50. Neukirchen-Vluyn, 1979.

Otero, Aurelio de Santos. "Later Acts of the Apostles." *NTApoc* 2.426–482.

Pagels, E. *The Gnostic Paul. Gnostic Exegesis of the Pauline Letters.* Philadelphia: Trinity Press International, 1975.

Penna, Angelo *et al.* "Paolo, apostolo." *Bibliotheca sanctorum.* Rome: Pontifica Università Lateranense, 1968.

Pervo, Richard I. *Luke's Story of Paul.* Minneapolis: Fortress, 1990.

Petersen, Norman R. *Rediscovering Paul: Philemon and the Sociology of Paul's Narrative World.* Philadelphia: Fortress, 1985.

Petit, Paul. *Les étudiants de Libanius.* Paris: Nouvelles Éditions Latines, 1957.

Pfitzner, V. C. *Paul and the Agon Motif. Traditional Athletic Imagery in the Pauline Literature.* NovTSup 16. Leiden: Brill, 1967.

Plassmann, Otto. *Das Almosen bei Johannes Chrysostomus.* Münster: Aschendorff, 1961.

Pohlenz, Max. "Philosophische Nachklänge in altchristlichen Predigten." *ZWT* 48 (1905) 72–95.

Praz, Mario. *Mnemosyne: the Parallel between Literature and the Visual Arts.* A. W. Mellon Lectures in the Fine Arts 1967. Bollingen Series 35/16. Princeton: Princeton University Press, 1970.

Pricoco, S. "Gennadius of Marseille." *EEC* 1.342.

Puech, Aimé. *Un réformateur de la société chrétienne au IV siècle. St. Jean Chrysostome et les moeurs de son temps.* Paris: Hachette, 1891.

Quasten, Johannes. *Patrology.* 3 vols. Westminster, MD: Newman, 1960.

Quinn, Jerome D. "Timothy and Titus, Epistles to." *ABD* 6.662.

Rabil, Albert. *Erasmus and the New Testament.* San Antonio: Trinity University Press, 1972. Repr. Lanham: University Press of America, 1993.

Radermacher, L. "Studien zur Geschichte der griechischen Rhetorik, II: Plutarchs Schrift *de se ipso citra invidiam laudando." Rheinisches Museum für Philologie* n. s. 52 (1897) 419–24.

Radojčič, Svetozar. "Die Entstehung der Malerei der paläologischen Renaissance." *Jahrbuch der österreichischen byzantinischen Gesellschaft* 7 (1958) 105–123.

–. *Lesnovo.* L'ancien art yougoslave. Belgrade: Izdavački Zavod, 1971

Räisänen, Heikki. *Paul and the Law.* Philadelphia: Fortress, 1986.

Rees, B. R. *Pelagius: A Reluctant Heretic.* Suffolk: Boydell, 1988.

Rensberger, D. "As the Apostle Teaches: The Development of the Use of Paul's Letters in Second Century Christianity." Ph.D. diss., Yale University, 1981.

Richardson, N. J. *The Homeric Hymn to Demeter.* Oxford: Clarendon, 1974.

Richter, Gisela M. A. "Greek Portraits: A Study of Their Development." *Latomus* 20 (1955) 12.

Ritter, Adolf Martin. "Between 'Theocracy' and 'Simple Life': Dio Chrysostom, John Chrysostom and the Problem of Humanizing Society." *Studia Patristica* 22. Ed. Elizabeth A. Livingstone. Louvain: Peeters, 1989. 170–80.

—. "John Chrysostom as an Interpreter of Pauline Social Ethics." *Paul and the Legacies of Paul.* Ed. W. S. Babcock. Dallas: Southern Methodist University Press, 1990. 183–99. '

Rose, H. J. "Epithets, Divine." *OCD*³ (1996) 401–402.

Rosenblatt, Marie Eloise. *Paul the Accused: His Portrait in the Acts of the Apostles.* Collegeville, MN: Liturgical Press, 1995.

Roth, Catherine P. *St. John Chrysostom, On Wealth and Poverty.* Crestwood, NY: St. Vladimir's Seminary Press, 1984.

Rougé, J. "Néron à la fin du IVᵉ siècle." *Latomus* 37 (1978) 79–87.

Rummel, Erika. *Erasmus' Annotations on the New Testament.* Toronto: University of Toronto Press, 1986.

Russell, D. A. *Criticism in Antiquity.* Berkeley/Los Angeles: University of California Press, 1981.

Sadurska, Anna and Adnan Bounni. *Les sculptures funéraires de palmyre.* Rivista di archeologia, supplementi 13. Rome: Bretschneider, 1994.

Sale, William M. "The Trojans, Statistics, and Milman Parry." *GRBS* 30 (1989) 341–410.

Sampley, J. Paul. "Paul, His Opponents in 2 Corinthians 10–13, and the Rhetorical Handbooks." *The Social World of Formative Christianity and Judaism.* Ed. Jacob Neusner, et al. Philadelphia: Fortress, 1988. 162–77.

—. *Pauline Partnership in Christ: Christian Community and Commitment in Light of Roman Law.* Philadelphia: Fortress, 1980

Sanders, E. P. *Paul and Palestinian Judaism. A Comparison of Patterns of Religion.* Philadelphia: Fortress, 1977.

—. *Paul, the Law, and the Jewish People.* Philadelphia: Fortress, 1983.

Schaff, Philip. "Prolegomena: The Life and Work of St. John Chrysostom." NPNF 9.3–23.

—. *Saint Chrysostom and Saint Augustine.* New York: Whittaker, 1891.

Schatkin, Margaret A. and Paul W. Harkins. *Saint John Chrysostom, Apologist.* FC 73. Washington: Catholic University of America Press, 1985.

Schäublin, Christoph. *Untersuchungen zu Methode und Herkunft der antiochenischen Exegese.* Theophania 23. Köln/Bonn: Peter Hanstein, 1974.

Schelkle, K.-H. *Paulus, Lehrer der Väter: Die altkirchliche Auslegung von Römer 1–11.* 2ⁿᵈ ed. Düsseldorf: Patmos, 1959.

Schleiermacher, F. D. E. *Hermeneutik.* Ed. Heinz Kimmerle. Heidelberg: Winter, 1959.

Schmithals, Walter. *Gnosticism in Corinth.* Trans. J. E. Steely. Nashville: Abingdon, 1971.

Schweitzer, Albert. *Paul and His Interpreters: A Critical History.* Trans. W. Montgomery. London: Adam & Charles Black, 1912.

—. *The Quest of the Historical Jesus: A Critical Study of Its Progress from Reimarus to Wrede.* New York: Macmillan, 1968. Original 1906.

Segal, Alan F. *Paul the Convert: The Apostolate and the Apostasy of Saul the Pharisee.* New Haven/London: Yale University Press, 1990.

Shore, Sally Rieger. *John Chrysostom, On Virginity, Against the Opponents of the Monastic Life.* Studies in Women and Religion 9. New York: Mellen, 1983.

Sider, Robert D. "Literary Artifice and the Figure of Paul in the Writings of Tertullian." *Paul and the Legacies of Paul.* Ed. W. S. Babcock. Dallas: Southern Methodist University Press, 1990.

—. Review of *Christianity and the Rhetoric of Empire,* by Averil Cameron. In *CHR* 78 (1992) 435–436.

—. "'Searching the Scriptures': John Chrysostom in the New Testament Scholarship of Erasmus." *Within the Perfection of Christ. Essays on Peace and the Nature of the Church in honor of Martin H. Schrag.* Ed. T. L. Brensunger and E. M. Sider. Nappanee, IN: Evangel Press, 1990. 83–105.

Siker, Jeffrey S. *Homosexuality in the Church: Both Sides of the Debate.* Louisville: Westminster/John Knox, 1994.

Simonetti, Manlio. *Biblical Interpretation in the Early Church: An Introduction to Patristic Exegesis.* Trans. John A. Hughes. Edinburgh: T & T Clark, 1994.

—. "Sulla struttura dei panegirici di S. Giovanni Crisostomo." *Rendiconti istituto Lombardo di scienze e lettere* (series 3/17) 86 (1953) 159–80.

Singer, Charles S. *The Renaissance in Rome.* Bloomington, IN: University of Indiana Press, 1985.

Smalley, B. *The Study of the Bible in the Middle Ages.* 2nd ed. Oxford: Blackwell, 1952.

Souter, Alexander. *Pelagius' Expositions of Thirteen Epistles of St. Paul, Vol.I, Introduction.* Cambridge: Cambridge University Press, 1922.

Staab, K. *Pauluskommentare aus der griechischen Kirche.* NTAbh 15. Münster: Aschendorff, 1933.

Staats, Reinhart. "Chrysostomus über die Rhetorik des Apostels Paulus: Makarianische Kontexte zu '*de sacerdotio* IV, 5–6.'" *VC* 46 (1992) 225–40.

Stanford, W. B. *The Ulysses Theme: A Study in the Adaptability of a Traditional Hero.* 2nd ed. Oxford: Blackwell, 1963.

Steinmetz, David C. "Calvin and the Patristic Exegesis of Paul." *The Bible and the Sixteenth Century.* Ed. *idem.* Durham: Duke University Press, 1990. 100–18.

Stendahl, Krister. "The Apostle Paul and the Introspective Conscience of the West." *HTR* 56 (1963) 199–215. Repr. in *Paul Among Jews and Gentiles and Other Essays.* Philadelphia: Fortress, 1976. 78–96.

Stötzel, Arnold. *Kirche als "neue Gesellschaft": Die humanisierende Wirkung des Christentums nach Johannes Chrysostomus.* Münsterische Beiträge zur Theologie 51. Münster: Aschendorff, 1984.

Stowers, Stanley K. *The Diatribe and Paul's Letter to the Romans.* SBLDS 57. Chico, CA: Scholars Press, 1981.

—. *A Rereading of Romans: Justice, Jews, and Gentiles.* New Haven: Yale University Press, 1994.

—. "Romans 7.7–25 as a Speech-in-Character (προσωποποιία)." *Paul in His Hellenistic Context.* Ed. Troels Engberg-Pedersen. Minneapolis: Fortress, 1995. 180–202.

—. "Social Status, Public Speaking and Private Teaching: the Circumstances of Paul's Preaching Activity." *NovT* 26 (1984) 59–79.

Strecker, Georg. *Das Judenchristentum in den Pseudoklementinen.* 2nd ed. Berlin: Akademie-Verlag, 1981.

Strong, Donald. *Roman Art.* Rev. ed. London: Penguin, 1982.

Ševčenko, Nancy Patterson. *Illustrated Manuscripts of the Metaphrastian Menologion.* Chicago Visual Library Text-Fiche series 54. Chicago/London: University of Chicago Press, 1990.

Swain, Simon. "Biography and Biographic in the Literature of the Roman Empire." *Portraits: Biographical Representation in Greek and Latin Literature of the Roman Empire.* Ed. M. J. Edwards and Simon Swain. Oxford: Clarendon, 1997. 1–37.

Tajra, Harry W. *The Martyrdom of St. Paul: Historical and Judicial Context, Traditions, and Legends.* WUNT 2/67. Tübingen: J. C. B. Mohr [Paul Siebeck], 1994.

Talbert, Charles H. *Reading Acts: A Literary and Theological Commentary on the Acts of the Apostles.* New York: Crossroad, 1997.

Tanner, R. G. "Chrysostom's Exegesis of Romans." *Studia Patristica* 17/3. Ed. Elizabeth A. Livingstone. Louvain: Peeters, 1982. 1185–97.

Tappert, T. G. *Luther's Works*. Vol. 54. Philadelphia: Fortress, 1967.

Theissen, Gerd. *The Social Setting of Pauline Christianity: Essays on Corinth*. Trans. John H. Schütz. Philadelphia: Fortress, 1982.

Thielman, Frank. *From Plight to Solution: A Jewish Framework for Understanding Paul's View of the Law in Galatians and Romans*. NovTSup 61. Leiden: Brill, 1989.

Thiselton, Anthony C. *New Horizons in Hermeneutics: The Theory and Practice of Transforming Biblical Reading*. Grand Rapids, MI: Zondervan, 1992.

Thompson, David L. *Mummy Portraits in the J. Paul Getty Museum*. Malibu: J. Paul Getty Museum, 1976.

Trakatellis, Metr. Demetrius. "Being Transformed: Chrysostom's Exegesis of the Epistle to the Romans." *GOTR* 36 (1991) 1–24.

Unnik, W. C. van. *Tarsus or Jerusalem: The City of Paul's Youth*. London: Epworth, 1962.

Valantasis, Richard. "A Theory of the Social Function of Asceticism." *Asceticism*. Ed. Vincent L. Wimbush and Richard Valantasis. New York/Oxford: Oxford University Press, 1995. 544–52.

Vandenberghe, B. H. *John of the Golden Mouth*. Westminster, MD: Newman, 1958.

—. *Saint Jean Chrysostome et la parole de Dieu*. Paris: Éditions du Cerf, 1961.

Vivante, Paolo. *The Epithets in Homer: A Study in Poetic Values*. New Haven: Yale University Press, 1982

Volkmann, Richard. *Die Rhetorik der Griechen und Römer in systematischer Übersicht*. Repr. ed. Hildesheim: Georg Olms, 1987.

Vouaux, Léon. *Les actes de Paul et ses lettres apocryphes*. Paris: Letouzey et Ané, 1913.

Walchenbach, J. R. "John Calvin as Biblical Commentator: An Investigation into Calvin's Use of John Chrysostom as an Exegetical Tutor." Ph.D. diss., University of Pittsburgh, 1974.

Wallace-Hadrill, D. S. *Christian Antioch: A Study of Early Christian Thought*. Cambridge: Cambridge University Press, 1982.

Walter, Christopher. *Art and Ritual of the Byzantine Church*. Birmingham Byzantine Series 1. London: Variorum, 1982.

—. "Biographical Scenes of the Three Hierarchs." *Revue des études byzantines* 36 (1978) 233–60.

Weir, Irene. *The Greek Painter's Art*. Boston: Ginn, 1905.

Weitzmann, Kurt. *Late Antique and Early Christian Book Illumination*. New York: Braziller, 1977.

Weitzmann, Kurt and George Galavaris. *The Monastery of Saint Catherine at Mount Sinai: The Illuminated Greek Manuscripts, Volume One: From the Ninth to the Twelfth Century*. Princeton: Princeton University Press, 1990.

Wilamowitz-Moellendorff, Ulrich von. "Die griechische Literatur des Altertums." *Die Kultur der Gegenwart*. Ed. Paul Hinneberg. 3rd ed. Berlin: Teubner, 1924. 1/8.

Wiles, Maurice. *The Divine Apostle: The Interpretation of St. Paul's Epistles in the Early Church*. Cambridge: Cambridge University Press, 1967.

Wilken, Robert L. *John Chrysostom and the Jews: Rhetoric and Reality in the Late 4th Century*. The Transformation of the Classical Heritage 4. Berkeley: University of California Press, 1983.

—. Review of *Thinking Biblically: Exegetical and Hermeneutical Studies*, by André Lacocque and Paul Ricoeur. In *First Things* 93 (1999) 68–71.

Wilson, A. N. *Paul: The Mind of the Apostle*. London/New York: W. W. Norton, 1997.

Wimbush, Vincent L. *Paul the Worldly Ascetic: Response to the World and Self-Understanding according to 1 Corinthians 7*. Macon, GA: Mercer University Press, 1987.

Windisch, Hans. *Der zweite Korintherbrief.* KEK. 9th ed. Ed. G. Strecker. Göttingen: Vandenhoeck & Ruprecht, 1970.

Wire, Antoinette Clark. *The Corinthian Women Prophets: A Reconstruction through Paul's Rhetoric.* Minneapolis: Fortress, 1990.

Witherington, Ben III. *The Paul Quest: The Renewed Search for the Jew of Tarsus.* Downers Grove, IL: InterVarsity Press, 1998.

Wolter, Michael. *Die Pastoralbriefe als Paulustradition.* FRLANT 146. Göttingen: Vandenhoeck & Ruprecht, 1988.

Xyngopoulos, A. "ΑΓΙΟΣ ΙΩΑΝΝΗΣ Ο ΧΡΥΣΟΣΤΟΜΟΣ, 'ΠΗΓΗ ΤΗΣ ΣΟΦΙΑΣ'" ("St. John Chrysostom, Fount of Wisdom"). *Archaiologike Ephemeris* 81–83 (1942–44) 1–36.

–. "Restitution et interprétation d' une fresque de Chilandar." *Hilandarski Zbornik* 2 (1971) 93–98.

Young, Frances M. *Biblical Exegesis and the Formation of Christian Culture.* Cambridge: Cambridge University Press, 1997.

–. *From Nicea to Chalcedon: A Guide to the Literature and its Background.* London: SCM, 1983.

–. "John Chrysostom in I and II Corinthians." *Studia Patristica* 18/1. Ed. Elizabeth A. Livingstone. Louvain: Peeters, 1986. 349–52.

–. "The Rhetorical Schools and Their Influence on Patristic Exegesis." *The Making of Orthodoxy: Essays in Honour of Henry Chadwick.* Ed. Rowan Williams. Cambridge: Cambridge University Press, 1989. 182–199.

Zese, Theodore N. "ΑΠΟΣΤΟΛΟΣ ΠΑΥΛΟΣ ΚΑΙ ΙΩΑΝΝΗΣ ΧΡΥΣΟΣΤΟΜΟΣ" ("The Apostle Paul and John Chrysostom"). *Kleronomia* 14 (1982) 313–23.

Passages Cited

Old Testament / LXX

New Testament

11:28	148, 304, 362
11:29	222, 304, 450, 465
11:31–33	332, 469
11:32–33	266, 485
12	176, 177, 247, 284, 350 n. 728
12:1	302, 348 n. 718, 473
12:1–10	348 n. 720
12:2	343, 347, 350 n. 729, 472, 474
12:2–3	349 n. 724
12:2–4	157 n. 119, 451
12:2–5	301, 350
12:4	317
12:5	350 n. 729, 472
12:6	349 n. 722, 473
12:6b	299 n. 470, 348 n. 718
12:7	299, 304, 305, 420, 478
12:10	448
12:11	166 n. 174, 344 n. 698, 345, 347, 349 n. 722, 350 n. 729, 472
12:12	291, 292, 304 n. 490, 380 n. 877
12:13	166 n. 174
12:15	456
12:20	128, 161 n. 149, 455
12:21	161 n. 149, 455
13:3	77, 77 n. 44, 113 n. 83, 124 n. 132, 296, 396
13:3–4	380 n. 877
13:7	321 n. 581
13:9	321 n. 581
13:10	357 n. 767
Gal	18 n. 69, 335 n. 650, 412 n. 12
1–2	120 n. 112
1:10	85 n. 115
1:13	320
1:13–14	458
1:14	86 n. 134, 109, 241
1:14–15	237 n. 174
1:15	237
1:15–16	459
1:17	265, 483
1:18	131 n. 162
1:22–23	260
2	45 n. 54, 288
2:2	84 n. 114
2:10	318, 360
2:19	130, 306 n. 498
2:19–20	133 n. 173

2:20	113 n. 83, 128, 130, 319, 478
3:1	352, 415 n. 23, 474
3:3	352, 474
3:4	219 n. 83, 463
3:5	291, 380 n. 877
3:27	130
3:28	427
4:10	233 n. 147
4:11	128
4:12	51, 233 n. 147
4:19	127, 148, 161 n. 149, 362 n. 799, 446, 455
4:20	83 n. 102
4:26	234
5:2	77
5:11	84 n. 114, 328
6:11	128
6:14	306 n. 498, 311, 319 n. 573, 477, 478
6:17	113 n. 83, 123, 130
Eph	251 n. 239, 392 n. 45
1:6	494 n. 21
2:19	234
2:21	130
3:1	85 n. 116, 91 n. 161, 165
3:1–7	165
3:7	165
3:8	164 n. 166, 349
3:10	79 n. 60
3:12	313 n. 537
4:1	39 n. 24, 85 n. 116, 91 n. 161, 178 n. 237, 179
4:25	249 n. 227
5:1	105, 159 n. 133, 453
5:1–2	159
5:2	160, 453
6:12	131, 291 n. 434, 468
6:17	143
6:18	321 n. 581
6:19	313 n. 537
Phil	409
1:1	85 n. 115
1:9	321 n. 581
1:12	464
1:12–18	221
1:14	178 n. 237, 268, 486
1:14–18	464
1:20	313 n. 537
1:21–26	122, 267, 311, 321, 333 n. 637, 334, 371

Early Christian Literature

ep. Innoc. 1–2	4 n.18
ep. Olymp.	4 n.18, 42 n.36
8.5	312 n.530
8.6	291 n.434
8.7	312 n.530
8.11	312 n.530
8.11d	305 n.497, 315
8.12	87 n.140
8.13c	49 n.68
8.46	291 n.434
10.3	90 n.158
13.3	32 n.110
17.3	305, 372 n.847
17.4f.	422 n.48
Eutrop.	3 n.11
2.8	399 n.80
2.13–14	291 n.433
2.14	77 n.47, 80 n.64, 86, 86 n.135, 246 n.212, 248 n.219, 271, 278 n.374
exp. in Job	
1.21	186 n.274
1.23	186 n.274
9.3	139 n.22
exp. in Ps.	
5	84 n.110
109.6	90 n.156, 395 n.55
110.4	75 n.26, 78–79, 84, 84 n.114, 85, 85 n.122, 86 n.132, 87, 235, 302 n.480
111.2	80 n.64, 275 n.360, 291 n.433
115.5	236
fem. reg.	4 n.12
6	292 n.434
7	79 n.56
fr. in Jer.	
1:5	237 n.171
31:29	50 n.75
fr. Job	3 n.10
2:9	362 n.801
fragmenta in 1 Jo.	3 n.10
fragmenta in Jac.	3 n.10

fragmenta in Petr.	3 n.10
grat.	
2	70 n.4, 77 n.44
4	91
hom. div.	
1.4	90 n.158, 91, 91 n.159
hom. in 1 Cor.	245 n.204, 387 n.21
3.3	82 n.83
3.4	243–244, 275 n.359
4.5	274 n.355
6.1	82, 292 n.436, 295 n.449
6.2	202 n.9
7.2	48–49
7.3	86 n.134, 241 n.193, 249 n.224, 296 n.456
8.3	349 n.727
11.1	317 n.557
11.4	57 n.110
12.1	350 n.728
12.2	50 n.73, 362 n.799
13	XVI, 104–121, 125 n.136, 129 n.159
13.1	108–109
13.2	104, 313 n.537
13.3	51 n.79, 51 n.80, 51 n.83, 52–54, 78 n.50, 105, 106, 106 n.52, 107–108, 110, 111, 113, 114, 117 n.98, 198 n.321, 390 n.34
13.3–4	104–118, 386 n.17
13.4	114–117
15.5	235, 237 n.167
15.6	235 n.155
19.2	361 n.793
21.2	361 n.793
22.2	79, 84 n.114
22.3	336 n.656
22.4	40 n.28, 251 n.241, 252
23.2	80 n.68
25.3–4	142 n.41
25.4	137 n.10
34.5	358 n.775
35.4	358 n.773, 358 n.778
35.5	44 n.44, 60 n.126, 98 n.18, 164 n.166, 345 n.699
36.3	32 n.110
36.6	196 n.315
38.4	339 n.672, 349 n.724
38.5	253 n.249

30.4	40 n.30, 51 n.82, 92, 439 n.100
31.1	40 n.26
31.3	82, 84 n.109
32.2	86 n.134, 241 n.193
37.1	129 n.156, 294 n.447
37.2	129 n.156, 294 n.446
39.2	248 n.221
40.1	56
40.4	60 n.129
43.1	37 n.17
43.2	98 n.19, 129 n.156, 282
43.3	232 n.146
44.1	165 n.170, 165 n.171, 339 n.669, 348 n.716
44.2	36 n.12
45.2	248 n.222, 318
46.3	365 n.816, 366 n.824, 367 n.825
47.1	36 n.12, 227 n.124, 231, 232, 241, 254 n.253, 280 n.380
47.3	372
48.1	237, 237 n.168
49.1	236, 300 n.474
50.3	151 n.84, 165 n.169
52.4	40 n.26, 78 n.53, 280 n.380
53.1	297 n.459
53.2	297 n.459
53.3	297 n.461, 297 n.463
53.4	83 n.101, 297 n.462, 414 n.20
54.1	129 n.156, 293 n.444
54.4	37 n.17
55	368–369
55.2	129 n.156, 294, 368 n.835
55.3	40 n.26, 79, 79 n.62, 80 n.65, 82, 83, 84, 84 n.105, 87 n.142, 151 n.84, 260 n.284, 261 n.285, 297–298, 313, 367 n.827, 367 n.828, 369, 369 n.836, 369 n.837, 407 n.121
hom. in Ac. 9:1	2 n.8
1–4	259
1.3	38 n.21, 39 n.24, 69 n.2, 80 n.64, 239 n.179, 254 n.258, 258, 259 n.275
1.4	73 n.22, 90 n.155, 251 n.232, 252 n.245
1.5	251 n.238, 395, 395 n.56
1.6	250, 251 n.233, 254 n.256, 254 n.257, 256 n.266
2.2	259 n.280, 260 n.281, 260 n.282
2.3	259 n.276
3.3	259 n.279
3.4	76, 252 n.248, 253–257, 260 n.283
3.5	213 n.58
4.3	71, 74 n.26, 77, 84, 84 n.105, 85 n.122, 86 n.132, 302 n.480, 303 n.487
4.5	362 n.799
hom. in Ac. princ.	2–3 n.8
1.3	57 n.112
2.4	87 n.142
2.6	67 n.150, 90, 395 n.54
3.3	356 n.765
3.4	292 n.438, 295 n.451, 295 n.453, 356 n.766
4.4	84, 328 n.612
hom. in Col.	
1.1	46 n.58, 49, 82 n.90, 83 n.99
7.5	42 n.35
10.1	391 n.40
10.3	75 n.29, 79 n.58, 81, 83 n.97, 235 n.158, 313 n.537
10.4	80 n.68, 274 n.357, 275 n.357, 282 n.389
11.3	79, 79 n.59, 87
12	186–190
12.2	186–187
12.3	129 n.157, 187–188
12.4	189, 189 n.288
hom. in Eph.	
Arg.	392 n.45
1.2	78 n.55
1.3	494 n.21
3.1	321 n.581
3.2	245 n.204
5.4	78 n.55
6.2	75 n.28, 86 n.134, 241 n.193
6.3	165 n.173, 166 n.176, 293 n.441, 293 n.442

Other Greek and Latin Texts

Modern Authors

Iconography